Readings in
MONEY, NATIONAL INCOME,
AND STABILIZATION POLICY

The Irwin Series in Economics

Consulting Editor Lloyd G. Reynolds *Yale University*

Readings in
MONEY, NATIONAL INCOME, AND STABILIZATION POLICY

Edited by

RONALD L. TEIGEN
Professor of Economics
University of Michigan

Fourth Edition   1978

RICHARD D. IRWIN, INC.   Homewood, Illinois   60430
Irwin-Dorsey Limited   Georgetown, Ontario   L7G 4B3

ISBN 0-256-02031-0
Library of Congress Catalog Card No. 78–52944

Printed in the United States of America

2 3 4 5 6 7 8 9 0 K 5 4 3 2 1 0 9

PREFACE

This new edition of *Readings in Money, National Income, and Stabilization Policy* reflects the same approach and viewpoint and is organized in the same way as the edition it supplants. However, many of the readings in the previous edition have been replaced with new, up-to-date material. Chapter 6, on international finance, is entirely new, and the chapter introduction has been expanded considerably in order to link the readings in the chapter to the general theoretical framework which is laid out in the introduction to Chapter 1. There also are substantial changes in the content of the other chapters, especially in the material on inflation and unemployment (Chapter 1, Section B) and on fiscal policy (Chapter 4). Overall, well over half of the readings in this fourth edition are new.

This fourth edition, like its predecessors, has been designed for supplementary use in courses in monetary economics, national income analysis, business cycles, and stabilization policy. Its contents reflect the editor's belief that in such courses a structural framework should be developed which enables the student to understand the mechanisms and linkages through which both monetary and fiscal policy produce their effects on income, employment, the price level, the rate of growth, and so on. To that end, these readings were selected to supplement the available textbooks on such topics as the relationship between monetary changes and changes in output, employment, and income; and the ways in which monetary and fiscal policy are related in their joint capacity as instruments of stabilization policy. Relatively few pages are devoted to material on the institutional details of the money and capital markets, the mechanics of treasury operations, and similar topics. Such subjects are well covered in most textbooks, and a good deal of supplementary reading material of this type can be obtained free of charge from the Federal Reserve System and other sources.

Thus, most of the book is devoted to aspects of monetary and fiscal policy in the context of the theory of income determination. The selection of readings reflects the editor's "view of the world"—a view which is accepted, by and large, by a great many economists, though not all. Variations from and alternatives to this point of view appear in many of the readings; however, most were selected to serve as "building blocks" for the development of the particular approach used, which is set forth in the rather extensive introductory material that precedes each of the chapters. These introductory sections also serve to relate the readings within each chapter to one another. The general viewpoint presented is consistent with the post-Keynesian posture of modern macroeconomics. In terms of stabilization policy, the readings are selected to show that the goal of full employment with reasonable price stability can best be pursued through the active use of flexible fiscal policy, supplemented by the use of monetary policy to achieve the desired balance between consumption and investment. Under a flexible exchange rate system of the kind now evolving, the authorities have considerable latitude to use the stabilization instruments in pursuit of domestic policy goals; but it is recognized that both fiscal and monetary instruments should occasionally be used to offset the effects on the domestic economy of impulses originating abroad.

In addition to the criteria mentioned above, the readings are selected to be comprehensible to typical advanced undergraduate students, and to be interesting to such students. Readability at this level was a major criterion in the choice of material, and the introductions to each chapter should be a substantial help to the student in the development and integration of ideas.

The first three editions of this book bore the name of my former colleague and friend Warren L. Smith, who died in 1972 during preparation of the third edition. It was thought inappropriate to continue to list Warren Smith as co-editor of this new edition. But though his name no longer appears on the cover, the book continues to reflect strongly the influence of his wisdom, judgment, and broad experience.

The preparation of this edition has been made possible by the help and cooperation of a number of people. Thanks are due to the authors and original publishers of the selections in this book for permission to use them, with special appreciation to Robert S. Holbrook and Henry C. Wallich for allowing the use of original material that has not been published elsewhere. The preparation of the manuscript was greatly facilitated by the help of Phyllis Romo.

April 1978   RONALD L. TEIGEN

CONTENTS

Good

Chapter 7
Coordination of Economic Policy **446**

Chapter

1

THE THEORY OF INCOME
DETERMINATION

The readings in this chapter are divided into two parts. Those in the first part
deal with the determination of aggregate income, employment, and prices and
the propagation of income changes, with special reference to the way in which
fiscal and monetary policies may influence aggregate demand. The readings in
the second part deal with the question of the inflationary process, its measurement and costs, and its relationship to employment.

A. Monetary and Fiscal Policies and Aggregate Demand

It is important for the student beginning the study of national income and
money and banking to develop an integrated framework which can be used effectively to analyze the problems and issues that arise. It is best to get this
framework at the start so that the relevant institutional material can be fitted
into it as study progresses. It is our hope that the material presented in this introduction, together with the readings contained in this section, will help the student to develop such a framework of analysis.

Economic reality is exceedingly complex, involving the outputs and prices
of thousands of goods and services, the wages of thousands of different kinds of
labor, and so on. The economist who tried to deal with all of the vast multitude
of variables and relationships involved would soon become hopelessly bogged
down. The only way to make headway, therefore, is to work with "models"
which abstract from most of the detail and focus on the important variables
related to the issue at hand. Of course, the model to be used depends on the
kind of problem being dealt with. The models we shall develop have proved
to be useful in analyzing the forces determining many of the major variables
relating to the economy as a whole: the level of national income and employ-

ment, the general level of prices, and so forth. While we shall attempt to keep the models relatively simple, we feel that they represent the major economic relationships sufficiently well to enable the student who has a thorough grasp of them to comprehend and analyze many important issues of economic policy. It should be pointed out that there has been much statistical testing of models which, while more detailed and complex than those presented here, are of essentially the same character; and the statistical testing suggests that they explain the behavior of the economy quite well. Indeed, the results of some of the statistical studies are presented in readings included in this book.

We shall begin with the simplest kind of Keynesian static multiplier model of income determination with which the student is almost surely familiar from his other reading. Then we shall proceed to introduce fiscal and monetary elements in a way which, we hope, will help the student to understand questions of economic policy. We shall use an algebraic and arithmetic approach for the most part; however, the algebra does not extend beyond that covered in a course that would be taken in high school, or at the most in the first year of college. We shall also stick to linear relationships—that is, relationships that appear as straight lines when plotted graphically. Linear relationships are often reasonably good approximations to reality; moreover, the gain in simplicity of presentation is great.

Throughout the present discussion, no attention is paid to changes in the price level; in effect, we shall be assuming that prices (and wages) are unchanged and that changes in the money values of variables are paralleled by changes in their real values. However, the analysis is broadened in the first reading in this section—the paper by Robert S. Holbrook—which treats prices and wages as variables which are determined by the interplay of economic forces as are income, employment, and so on.

The presentation in this introduction is divided into two major parts. The first deals with static analysis—that is, it is merely designed to tell what will ultimately happen to the variables when some change is introduced into the model, without making any effort to describe the time paths followed by the variables in the process of adjustment. The second part introduces some quite elementary dynamics.

1. STATIC ANALYSIS

Model I: The Simple Keynesian Multiplier

This model is represented by the following three algebraic equations:

$$C = C_o + cY \qquad \text{(consumption function)} \qquad (1.1)$$
$$I = I_o \qquad \text{(investment relationship)} \qquad (1.2)$$
$$Y = C + I \qquad \text{(equilibrium condition)} \qquad (1.3)$$

Here C is consumption expenditure planned by households, I is investment expenditure planned by firms, and Y is gross national product (GNP). The subscript o indicates that the variable is not explained within the model but is determined by outside forces. In this model C_o stands for the amount of consumption which is unrelated to income, and c is the marginal propensity to consume (MPC), assumed to be a positive fraction between zero and unity in value. By substituting the expressions for C and I given by equations (1.1) and (1.2) into equation (1.3), we obtain the following:

$$Y = cY + C_o + I_o. \tag{1.4}$$

When this is solved for Y, the following result is obtained:

$$Y = \frac{1}{1-c}(C_o + I_o). \tag{1.5}$$

If there is a change in C_o or I_o, income and consumption will also change. Suppose that investment spending rises to a new level, $I_o + \Delta I_o$, and remains there. Then we will find that income will also change by some amount, ΔY, so that the new level of income may be expressed as follows:

$$Y + \Delta Y = \frac{1}{1-c}(C_o + I_o) + \frac{1}{1-c}\Delta I_o. \tag{1.6}$$

Subtraction of (1.5) from (1.6) results in the following expression for the change of income (from the former equilibrium position to the new equilibrium) due to the change in investment spending:

$$\Delta Y = \frac{1}{1-c}\Delta I_o. \tag{1.7}$$

Since ΔI_o is multiplied by the term $1/(1-c)$ to obtain the income change, ΔY, this term is called the "multiplier." This is the standard textbook "formula" expressed in the statement, "the multiplier equals $1/(1 - MPC)$." The student should not, however, view it as a formula to be memorized but rather as a relationship which summarizes a complex pattern of economic behavior, a pattern to be thought through and understood. It is particularly important to realize that the multiplier expression changes as the details of the model change, and that in the real world the multiplier process cannot be summarized in as simple a formula as that shown above. We shall now make the model, and the multiplier expression, somewhat more realistic.

Model II: The Introduction of Fiscal Policy

One of the most serious shortcomings of the simple model just discussed is that no allowance is made for the activities of government. To correct this defect we shall introduce government expenditures and taxation. For simplicity, we shall assume that all taxes are levied on households and that consumption depends on *disposable* income—that is, income after taxes. The new model is expressed in the following equations:

$$
\begin{array}{lll}
C = C_o + cY_d & 0 < c < 1 & \tag{2.1} \\
Y_d = Y - T & & \tag{2.2} \\
T = T^* + xY & 0 < x < 1 & \tag{2.3} \\
I = I_o & & \tag{2.4} \\
G = G^* & & \tag{2.5} \\
Y = C + I + G & & \tag{2.6}
\end{array}
$$

In this and following models, as was the case above, the subscript o identifies variables which are determined by forces outside of the model and which cannot be controlled by the government for policy purposes. We now introduce a second category of variables determined outside of the model: those which are manipulable by the authorities. Such variables are sometimes called "policy instruments" and will be denoted by an asterisk (*) throughout the remainder of this discussion. In Model II, government spending for goods and services (G^*) and that part of tax collections which is unrelated to income (T^*) are policy instruments. The equation $G = G^*$ states that the entire amount of government spending is determined outside of the model, while the equation describing tax collections, equation (2.3), indicates that only a part of total collections is under the direct control of the fiscal authorities. T is total collections, and it is composed of T^*, the level set by the authorities, plus xY, the part related to the level of income. The coefficient x is the marginal propensity of the public to pay taxes out of GNP.[1] Finally, Y_d is disposable income (i.e., household income after taxes); and c is the marginal propensity to consume out of disposable income.

Upon substitution of equation (2.2) and (2.3) into (2.1), the following equation is obtained:

$$C = C_o - cT^* + c(1 - x)Y. \tag{2.7}$$

Then, equations (2.4), (2.5), and (2.7) can be substituted into equation (2.6) to obtain

$$Y = C_o - cT^* + c(1 - x)Y + I_o + G^*. \tag{2.8}$$

Solving this equation explicitly for Y, we obtain

$$Y = \frac{1}{1 - c(1 - x)} [C_o - cT^* + I_o + G^*]. \tag{2.9}$$

Suppose now that government purchases of goods and services are increased from G^* to $G^* + \Delta G^*$. The new equilibrium income will be given by

$$Y + \Delta Y = \frac{1}{1 - c(1 - x)} [C_o - cT^* + I_o + G^* + \Delta G^*]. \tag{2.10}$$

Subtracting (2.9) from (2.10) and dividing through by ΔG^*, we obtain the multiplier applicable to government purchases:

$$\frac{\Delta Y}{\Delta G^*} = \frac{1}{1 - c(1 - x)} . \tag{2.11}$$

Multipliers could also be computed for independent changes in investment (ΔI_o), in the level of consumption (ΔC_o), or in the level of taxes (ΔT^*). The first two of these multipliers would be the same as that for a change in government purchases while the multiplier for a change in taxes would be

$$\frac{\Delta Y}{\Delta T^*} = \frac{-c}{1 - c(1 - x)} .$$

This last multiplier is negative, because an increase in taxes would lower disposable income, reduce consumption, and lead to a decline in income.

There is a final technical point which should be noted. So far, all of the multipliers we have discussed have summarized the effects on GNP of a change in one of the variables determined by forces outside the model. The multiplier concept is more general than this, however, and it is possible to derive a multiplier expression which summarizes the effect of a shift in any of these variables on any variable determined within the model. Thus, for example, the effects

---

[1] Strictly speaking x as well as T^* should be regarded as a policy instrument, since changes in tax legislation could (and, in practice, usually would) change the slope as well as the level of the tax function. In the interest of simplicity, however, we are confining our analysis to changes in the level of taxes (T^*).

on total tax collections (ΔT) of a shift in the level of the consumption function (ΔC_o) can easily be derived. From the tax function (2.3) we note that

$$\frac{\Delta T}{\Delta C_o} = x\, \frac{\Delta Y}{\Delta C_o}.$$

Using the approach employed in deriving the multiplier $\dfrac{\Delta Y}{\Delta G^*}$ above, we find that

$$\frac{\Delta Y}{\Delta C_o} = \frac{1}{1 - c(1 - x)}.$$

It follows directly that

$$\frac{\Delta T}{\Delta C_o} = \frac{x}{1 - c(1 - x)}.$$

As a general rule, it is possible to derive multipliers showing the effects on any of the variables determined by the model (the variables Y, Y_d, T, C, I, and G in this case) of a change in any of the variables which are set by outside forces (C_o, I_o, T^*, and G^* here).

A numerical example may be helpful at this point. Suppose the marginal propensity to consume out of disposable income is 75 percent ($c = .75$) while the tax system is such that taxes tend to increase by 20 percent of any rise in GNP ($x = .2$). Suppose further that $C_o = 110$, $T^* = -80$, $I_o = 300$, and $G^* = 330$ (amounts expressed in billions of dollars). In this case the equations (2.1) to (2.6) become:

$C = 110 + 3(420) = 1370$

$C = 110 + \frac{3}{4}(.8y + 80) = 110 + .6y + 60$

$Y_d = 1680$

$T = 320$

$\begin{aligned} C &= 110 + .75Y_d \\ Y_d &= Y - T \\ T &= -80 + .2Y \\ I &= 300 \\ G &= 330 \\ Y &= C + I + G \end{aligned}$

$Y_d = Y + 80 - .2Y \rightarrow Y_d = .8y + 80$

$Y = 800 + .6y$

$.4y = 800$

$y = 2,000$

The multiplier relating changes in GNP to changes in government purchases (or investment, or autonomous changes in consumption) is

$$\frac{\Delta Y}{\Delta G^*} = \frac{1}{1 - c(1 - x)} = \frac{1}{1 - .75(1 - .2)} = 2.5,$$

and equilibrium, calculated from (2.9), is

$$Y = 2.5[800], \text{ or}$$
$$Y = \$2,000 \text{ billion.}$$

The values of all the variables, which can easily be calculated from the above equations, are given in the first ("original equilibrium") column of Table 1. Two additional variables, not referred to earlier, are shown in the table: private saving and the government deficit. Private saving is simply the difference between disposable income and consumption and amounts to $310 billion. The government deficit (expenditures minus taxes) is $10 billion. It may be noted that private saving ($310 billion) plus the government surplus (−$10 billion) is equal to investment ($300 billion). This is the equivalent of the well-known proposition that "saving must equal investment" for an economy containing a government sector but no foreign sector.

1680
1370
310

Now suppose government purchases of goods and services increase by $20 billion to a new annual level of $350 billion, and remain there. Since the multiplier for government purchases is 2.5, income will rise by $50 billion to a new equilibrium value of $2,050 billion. The new values of all variables are shown in the second ("new equilibrium") column of Table 1, and the changes from the original position are shown in the last column.

The new equilibrium will not, of course, be reached immediately. The movement of GNP and its components to the new level involves a complex and time-consuming set of economic adjustments. The chain starts when the increased government purchases stimulate production and employment, which adds directly to GNP. Incomes are raised; a portion of the additional income, 20 percent in this case, is paid over the government in taxes; of the remaining 80 percent, 25 percent is saved, and the other 75 percent—which amounts to 60 percent (75 percent of 80 percent) of the rise in GNP—is spent on consumption, thereby stimulating further production and employment in industries producing consumer goods. The process continues through repeated "rounds" of spending and responding until GNP has been raised by $50 billion (the multi-

Table 1: Numerical Example of Multiplier for Government Expenditures in Model II (in $ billions)

	Original Equilibrium	New Equilibrium*	Change
Gross national product (Y)...................	$2,000	$2,050	+$50
Consumption (C)........................	1,370	1,400	+ 30
Investment (I)............................	300	300	0
Government purchases (G)...............	330	350	+ 20
Taxes (T).................................	320	330	+ 10
Disposable income (Y_d)....................	1,680	1,720	+ 40
Private saving ($Y_d - C$).....................	310	320	+ 10
Government deficit ($G - T$)................	10	20	+ 10

* After an increase of $20 billion in the rate of government purchases.

plier of 2.5 times the initial increase of $20 billion in government purchases). The time lags and the speed with which the adjustment to the new level of GNP can be expected to take place are discussed below.

A reduction in the level of taxation—that is, a change in T^*—would also raise GNP. In this case, if $c = .75$ and $x = .2$, we have, as indicated earlier,

$$\frac{\Delta Y}{\Delta T^*} = \frac{-c}{1 - c(1 - x)} = \frac{-.75}{1 - .75(1 - .2)} = -1.875.$$

Thus a cut in taxes of $20 billion ($\Delta T^* = -20$) would raise GNP by $37.5 billion. The multiplier applicable to a tax cut is smaller in absolute value (1.875) than that applicable to an increase in government purchases (2.5). The reason is that the entire increase in government purchases is a direct increase in GNP, while a portion of the tax cut is saved, and only the part that is spent on consumption (75 percent in this case) adds to GNP. It is suggested that the student work out a table similar to Table 1 above to illustrate the effects on income and the other variables determined within the model of a tax cut of $20 billion.

Model II illustrates in a simple way the rationale for the use of fiscal policy—changes in government expenditures and taxes—to regulate aggregate demand for goods and services in the interest of full employment and price stability. This subject is taken up in considerable detail in Chapter 4. The model used in this illustration is substantially oversimplified. In practice, for example, not all taxes are levied on households—there are direct and indirect taxes on business as well—and some saving is done by businesses as well as by households. Despite the added complexities, however, the multiplier of 2.5 for government purchases that we used above is fairly realistic. Estimates obtained by sophisticated statistical techniques applied to much more complicated models have fairly consistently turned out to be in this neighborhood.

Model III: The Introduction of Money and Interest

The student will no doubt have noticed that we have not yet mentioned money or interest rates. It is now time to remedy this deficiency in our analysis. The essence of the problem can be handled quite well and without greatly complicating the presentation by adding additional variables and equations to Model II. The resulting Model III, which takes account of money and interest, includes the following equations, five of which (the first three and the fifth and sixth) are exactly the same as those of Model II.

$$C = C_o + cY_d \tag{3.1}$$
$$Y_d = Y - T \tag{3.2}$$
$$T = T^* + xY \tag{3.3}$$
$$I = I_o - vr \tag{3.4}$$
$$G = G^* \tag{3.5}$$
$$Y = C + I + G \tag{3.6}$$
$$M_d = M_o + kY - mr \tag{3.7}$$
$$M_s = M^* \tag{3.8}$$
$$M_d = M_s \tag{3.9}$$

Here, r is the interest rate (there is assumed to be only one interest rate). v is the slope of the investment function with respect to the interest rate, or, in Keynesian terminology, the slope of the marginal efficiency of capital (or investment) schedule. v is assumed to be greater than zero, but it carries a negative sign in the investment function—i.e., the lower the interest rate the more investment. M_d is the quantity (stock) of money (demand deposits and currency) demanded by the public and is assumed to be related positively to income and negatively to the interest rate. k is the number of dollars by which the public will desire to increase its money holdings per dollar increase in GNP (i.e., the slope of the money demand function with respect to income). k is, of course, positive—i.e., the higher the level of income the more money the public will want to hold (at a given interest rate). m is the slope of the demand for money function with respect to the interest rate. m is assumed greater than zero, but it carries a negative sign in the money demand function—i.e., the lower the interest rate, the more money the public will want to hold (at a given income). M_o is the amount of money demanded without regard to income or the rate of interest; its level is determined by forces outside of the model. M_s is the supply of money; it is equal to a constant, M^*, which can be changed at will by the monetary authorities (e.g., the Federal Reserve System) through actions such as open market operations, changes in the discount rate, or changes in the reserve requirements of the banks.

Model III is changed from Model II by introducing the interest rate into the investment equation (3.4) and by introducing three new equations, (3.7), (3.8), and (3.9), to represent the "monetary sector" of the economy. Equation (3.9) is an equilibrium condition which says that the demand for money must be equal to the supply of money in order for an equilibrium to exist.

Substituting (3.2) and (3.3) into (3.1), we obtain

$$C = C_o - cT^* + c(1 - x)Y. \tag{3.10}$$

Then, substituting (3.4), (3.5), and (3.10) into (3.6), we obtain

$$Y = C_o - cT^* + c(1 - x)Y + I_o - vr + G^*, \tag{3.11}$$

or, solving explicitly for r in terms of Y,

IS curve

$$r = \frac{C_o - cT^* + I_o + G^*}{v} - \frac{1 - c(1 - x)}{v} Y. \tag{3.12}$$

Next, substituting (3.7) and (3.8) into (3.9), we obtain

$$M^* = M_o + kY - mr, \tag{3.13}$$

or, solving explicitly for r in terms of Y,

$$r = \frac{M_o - M^*}{m} + \frac{k}{m} Y. \tag{3.14}$$

Equation (3.12) is the *IS* curve discussed in the Holbrook article in this chapter (reading 1). It is derived from equations (3.1) to (3.6) in the above model

Chart 1:   Determination of Income and Interest Rate by *IS* and *LM* Curves

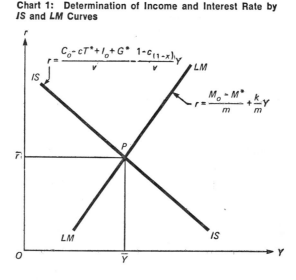

and represents the various combinations of income and the interest rate that will equilibrate the market for goods and services—that is, will result in aggregate demand $(C + I + G)$ being equal to total output (Y). The slope of the line $(\Delta r/\Delta Y)$ is $-[1 - c(1 - x)]/v$. Since c and x are both less than unity, $1 - c(1 - x)$ is necessarily positive, as is v. Consequently, the slope of the *IS* curve is negative—that is, it slopes downward to the right. The commonsense economic explanation is that a reduced rate of interest will lead to more investment, which, through the multiplier, will raise income; thus, a fall in the rate of interest will be associated with a higher level of income. The *IS* curve is shown as a downward-sloping line in Chart 1.

Equation (3.14) is the *LM* curve, also discussed in the Holbrook article. It is derived from equations (3.7) and (3.9) and represents the various combinations of Y and r that will result in equilibrium in the money market—i.e., equality of demand for and supply of money—with the given stock of money, M^*. The slope of the *LM* curve $(\Delta r/\Delta Y)$ is k/m. Since k and m are both positive numbers, the slope must be positive. It is useful to think of money holdings as consisting of two parts: transactions balances required for the conduct of current economic activity by households and firms and asset balances held as a part of wealth portfolios. The demand for transactions balances may then be regarded as related positively to income, and the demand for asset balances as being related negatively to the interest rate. (The demand for money is discussed at some length in Ronald L. Teigen's paper in this chapter.[2]) Then, moving along the LM curve, a rise in income will increase the transactions demand for money, thereby leaving a smaller portion of the fixed supply (M^*) of money available to satisfy the asset demand and causing the interest rate to rise as asset holders attempt to restore portfolio equilibrium by selling bonds. The LM curve is shown as an upward-sloping curve in Chart 1.

Equilibrium for the entire economy—including both the market for goods and services and the money market—occurs at the point of intersection of the IS and LM curves. This is point P in Chart 1, and the equilibrium values of GNP and the interest rate are $\bar{Y}$ and $\bar{r}$.[3]

The equilibrium level of GNP can be derived explicitly by eliminating r between equations (3.12) and (3.14). When this is done, we have

$$\frac{C_o - cT^* + I_o + G^*}{v} - \frac{1 - c(1 - x)}{v}\,Y = \frac{M_o - M^*}{m} + \frac{k}{m}\,Y,$$

or, solving explicitly for Y,

$$Y = \frac{1}{1 - c(1 - x) + \dfrac{vk}{m}}\left[C_o - cT^* + I_o + G^* - \frac{v}{m}\,(M_o - M^*)\right]. \quad (3.15)$$

This model contains three policy instruments which the authorities can adjust in order to control aggregate demand: the fiscal authorities can change government expenditures (G^*) or the tax level (T^*), while the monetary authorities can adjust the stock of money (M^*). Multipliers which show the leverage of each of these instruments in changing GNP can be calculated quite easily. For example, the multiplier for government expenditures ($\Delta Y/\Delta G^*$) can be derived as follows: suppose the level of government purchases of goods and services is increased from G^* to $G^* + \Delta G^*$. The new level of GNP is given by

$$Y + \Delta Y = \frac{1}{1 - c(1 - x) + \dfrac{vk}{m}}\left[C_o - cT^* + I_o + G^* + \Delta G^* - \frac{v}{m}\,(M_o - M^*)\right]$$

$$(3.16)$$

Subtracting (3.15) from (3.16) and dividing through by ΔG^*, we have

$$\frac{\Delta Y}{\Delta G^*} = \frac{1}{1 - c(1 - x) + \dfrac{vk}{m}} \quad (3.17)$$

---

[2] It should be noted that, as explained in Teigen's paper, some economists believe that the demand for money is almost entirely a transactions demand but that the transactions demand is dependent on both income and the interest rate. This leads to essentially the same conclusions about the functioning of money in the economy that are reached if the demand consists of a transactions component dependent on income and an asset component dependent on the interest rate.

[3] For an extension of this analysis to the determination of equilibrium income, interest rate, and other variables for an economy with a foreign sector and balance of payments, see the introduction to Chapter 6.

By a similar procedure, the multipliers for changes in taxes and in the stock of money can be derived:

$$\frac{\Delta Y}{\Delta T^*} = \frac{-c}{1 - c(1 - x) + \frac{vk\,]}{m}} \qquad (3.18)$$

$$\frac{\Delta Y}{\Delta M^*} = \frac{1}{[1 - c(1 - x)]\dfrac{m}{v} + k} \qquad (3.19)$$

Comparing the multiplier for government purchases (3.17) with that developed in Model II above (2.11), we find that the difference consists in the presence of the additional term vk/m in the denominator of (3.17). Since v, m, and k are all positive, the term vk/m is positive. It increases the denominator of (3.17) and therefore reduces the size of the multiplier. This term arises from the existence of monetary forces in Model III which were not included in Model II. In deriving expression (3.17) for the multiplier effects of a change in government purchases in Model III, it was assumed that the stock of money, M^*, was held constant. An increase in government purchases increases GNP, and the rise in GNP increases the demand for money for transactions purposes. With a constant stock of money, the needed transactions balances must be obtained from asset balances, and this necessitates a rise in the interest rate. This rise in the interest rate, in turn, reduces investment expenditure, thereby cancelling out a portion of the effect of the initial increase in government purchases and cutting down the size of the multiplier.

The relationships can perhaps best be understood by means of a numerical illustration. Suppose, as in the example used to illustrate Model II, that $c = .75$, $t = .2$, $C_o = 110$, $T^* = -80$, and $G^* = 330$. In addition, in this case let us suppose that the interest slope of the investment equation (3.4) is -4 (i.e., $v = 4$); the constant term of the investment equation, I_o, is 320; the income slope of the money demand equation (3.7), k, is .25; the interest slope of the money demand equation is -10 (i.e., $m = 10$); and the constant term of this equation, M_o, is 20. Finally, suppose the stock of money, M^*, is 470. In this case, the equations (3.1) to (3.9) become:

$$C = 110 + .75Y_d$$
$$Y_d = Y - T$$
$$T = -80 + .2Y$$
$$I = 320 - 4r$$
$$G = 330$$
$$Y = C + I + G$$
$$M_d = 20 + .25Y - 10r$$
$$M_s = 470$$
$$M_d = M_s$$

The multiplier for a change in government purchases (or for autonomous changes in consumption or investment) is

$$\frac{\Delta Y}{\Delta G^*} = \frac{1}{1 - c(1 - x) + \dfrac{vk}{m}} = \frac{1}{1 - .75(1 - .2) + \dfrac{4(.25)}{10}} = 2,$$

and equilibrium income, calculated from (3.15), is:

$$Y = 2[1,000]$$
$$Y = \$2,000 \text{ billion.}$$

The values of all variables are given in the first column of Table 2.

Now let us suppose that government expenditures increase by $20 billion from the original rate of $330 billion to a new annual rate of $350 billion, and remain there. Since, as we have seen, the multiplier is 2, this will raise GNP by $40 billion. The new equilibrium values of all variables are shown in the second column of Table 2. The main difference between the results shown here and those produced by an increase of $20 billion in government expenditures in Model II (see Table 1) is that in this case the rise in GNP increases the demand for money and drives up the interest rate from 5 to 6 percent, and this, in turn, reduces investment by $4 billion. That is why the multiplier is only 2 instead of 2.5 as in Model II.

Our illustration can also be presented in terms of *IS* and *LM* curves. In the

Table 2: Numerical Example of Multiplier for Government Expenditures in Model III (in $ billions)

	Original Equilibrium	New Equilibrium*	Change
Gross national product (Y)	$2,000	$2,040	+$40
Consumption (C)	1,370	1,394	+ 24
Investment (I)	300	296	− 4
Government purchases (G)	330	350	+ 20
Taxes (T)	320	328	+ 8
Disposable income (Y − T)	1,680	1,712	+ 32
Saving (Y_d − C)	310	318	+ 8
Government deficit (G − T)	10	22	+ 12
Interest rate (r)	5%	6%	+ 1%

*After an increase of $20 billion in the rate of government purchases.

original situation (before the increase in government expenditures), substitution into equation (3.12) yields the following numerical *IS* curve:

$$r = 205 - .1Y.$$

Similarly, the *LM* curve, obtained by substitution into (3.14) is

$$r = -45 + .025Y.$$

These two curves have been plotted in Chart 2 as the lines IS_1 and *LM*. The intersection (point *P*) yields the equilibrium values of $2,000 billion for GNP and 5 percent for the interest rate.

An increase of $20 billion in government spending shifts the *IS* curve to the right, and its equation becomes

$$r = 210 - .1Y.$$

This is plotted as line IS_2 in Chart 2. Its intersection with the new *LM* curve (point *Q*) yields the equilibrium values of $2,040 billion for GNP and 6 percent for the interest rate.

As can be seen from Chart 2, if the interest rate had not risen when government expenditures were increased, the equilibrium point would have moved from *P* to *R* and *GNP* would have risen by $50 billion for a multiplier of 2.5—the same as the multiplier in Model II. But due to the tightening of credit in the face of a fixed money supply, the equilibrium point moves to *Q* rather

Chart 2: Numerical Illustration of IS and LM Curves

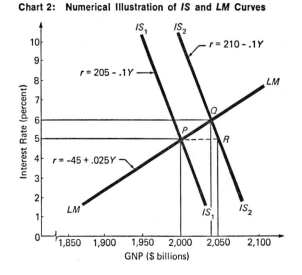

than R, GNP rises by $40 billion instead of $50 billion, and the interest rate rises from 5 to 6 percent. Thus, the operation of the "monetary effect" cuts the multiplier by 20 percent below what it would have been in the absence of the effect.

It will be useful to consider also the effects produced by an increase in the money stock. Suppose the stock is increased by $20 billion as a result, let us say, of open market purchases of U.S. government securities by the Federal Reserve System. The multiplier applicable to an increase in the money stock, according to (3.19) above, is

$$\frac{\Delta Y}{\Delta M^*} = \frac{1}{[1 - c(1 - x)]\dfrac{m}{v} + k} \, .$$

Using the values of our illustration, this becomes:

$$\frac{\Delta Y}{\Delta M^*} = \frac{1}{[1 - .75(1 - .2)]\dfrac{10}{4} + .25} = \frac{1}{1.25}$$

$$\frac{\Delta Y}{\Delta M^*} = .8$$

Thus, an increase of $20 billion in the money stock will increase GNP by $16 billion. The effects on all the variables in the system are shown in the second column of Table 3. For purposes of comparison, the original values are again shown in the first column. The increase in the money stock produces its effects by lowering the interest rate from 5 percent to 3.4 percent, thereby stimulating investment; the rise in investment spending stimulates production and income, setting off a multiplier effect which raises consumption. It is interesting to note that the increase in income leads to a rise in tax collections which reduces the government deficit.

According to our analysis of Model III, it is possible to change aggregate demand and GNP by fiscal policy measures—changes in government expenditures or in taxes—or by monetary policy—changes in the monetary stock. (It is suggested that the student work out another table similar to Tables 2 and

3 summarizing the effects of a $20 billion tax cut and compare the results with those produced by the other measures.) And, of course, the three types of measures could be combined in various ways to produce a desired effect on GNP. (Another suggested exercise for the student: calculate the size of the increase in the money stock that would be needed to accompany an increase in government expenditures in order to hold the interest rate at 5 percent and achieve a multiplier effect of 2.5.) Choice of the proper combination in given circumstances would depend on various considerations—the relative speeds with which they produce their results, their effects on goals other than the level of GNP, such as the rate of long-term growth, the nation's balance-of-payments position, and so on. Many of these considerations are discussed in readings in this book, especially in Chapters 4, 5, and 7. In particular, the introduction to Chapter 7 contains an extensive discussion of the relationship between multiple policy goals and the instruments of policy. The discussion is based on a linear model which is almost identical to Model III; thus a thorough understand-

Table 3: Numerical Example of Multiplier for an Increase in the Money Stock in Model III (in $ billions)

	Original Equilibrium	New Equilibrium*	Change
Gross national product (Y)	$2,000	$2,016	+$16
Consumption (C)	1,370	1,379.6	+ 9.6
Investment (I)	300	306.4	+ 6.4
Government purchases (G)	330	330.0	0
Taxes (T)	320	323.2	+ 3.2
Disposable income ($Y - T$)	1,680	1,692.8	+ 12.8
Saving ($Y_d - C$)	310	313.2	+ 3.2
Government deficit ($G - T$)	10	6.8	− 3.2
Money stock (M)	470	490.0	+ 20.0
Interest rate (r)	5%	3.4%	− 1.6%

* After an increase of $20 billion in the money stock.

ing of the material in the present section will be particularly useful to the student in studying the material in Chapter 7.

Model III provides a useful starting point for a discussion of some of the major doctrinal controversies that have plagued the subject of money, particularly those having to do with the relative efficacy of monetary policy and fiscal policy. This discussion is extended considerably in the two papers by Thomas Mayer and Ronald L. Teigen, respectively, which are found at the end of this part of Chapter 1 (readings 3 and 4). The policy controversies which we wish to examine here can conveniently be summarized as the opposing views of two schools of thought. The *Classical quantity theorists* (or "monetarists," as quantity theorists have come to be known) may be said to believe that fiscal policy can have no significant and lasting effect on real output or employment, while monetary policy is viewed by members of this school of thought as being very potent in terms of its effects on these variables. The terms "Classical" and "monetarist" will be used more or less interchangeably in what follows. At the other end of the spectrum are some of the *extreme versions of Keynesianism,* which view monetary policy as impotent and fiscal policy as being extremely effective. To see the basis for these views in terms of the analysis we have used so far, it will be useful to bring together once again the multipliers for changes in government expenditures and for changes in the money stock (assuming, as we have up to now, that the entire money stock is under the direct control of the monetary authorities—a qualification which we later will relax). These multipliers are:

$$\frac{\Delta Y}{\Delta G^*} = \frac{1}{1 - c(1 - x) + \dfrac{vk}{m}} \qquad (3.17)$$

$$\frac{\Delta Y}{\Delta M^*} = \frac{1}{[1 - c(1 - x)]\dfrac{m}{v} + k} \qquad (3.19)$$

At the beginning of this discussion, it should be emphasized that these multipliers describe very simple economies and in particular that, in these economies, prices and wages remain unchanged as income changes in response to policy or for any other reason. That is, these economies have significant amounts of unemployed resources, so that increasing demand is reflected in rising employment rather than price inflation. Such chronic underemployment is ascribable to a rigidity or inflexibility in the system—in this case, wage rates which are not free to respond to the relationship between the supply of and demand for labor. If the price of unemployed productive factors—i.e., the wage rate —were free to move as unemployed labor competed for work with those employed, presumably a wage could be found at which all of the workers who desired work could get it; however, if the wage rate is fixed by law or restricted in movement by some other arrangement, those out of work who want jobs may not be able to find them. Wage inflexibility and other rigidities which hinder the achievement of full employment undoubtedly are present in the real world, and it is therefore appropriate to conduct our analysis using a model which recognizes that they exist. The student should, however, be aware that theoretical analysis is sometimes also carried out using macroeconomic models which do not reflect these impediments to full employment; in effect, such models assert that full employment rather than underemployment is the normal state of affairs. If prices and wages are flexible and determined in competitive markets so that there exists more or less continuous full employment, it is apparent that the results of the application of monetary and fiscal policy will be different from the results in an economy which is chronically underemployed. One important dimension of the Keynesian-monetarist controversy over policy is the assumptions which each side makes about the functioning of labor markets, with Keynesians typically assuming money wage rigidity, and monetarists taking wage flexibility as the norm. This aspect is emphasized in the paper on monetarist economics by Ronald L. Teigen in this chapter (reading 4); and the monetarist conclusions on the relative effectiveness of monetary versus fiscal impulses could be ascribed to their assumptions about such markets.

It is also worth observing at the outset that conclusions regarding the effectiveness of policy based on models of the simple types presented here are likely to be somewhat sensitive to the degree of detail included. Innumerable marginal details about the world are, of course, omitted because they would greatly increase the algebraic complexity of the analysis without adding anything of substance to the conclusions. There is, however, an important detail which has been overlooked in most discussions about policy but which will have an important effect on the results of the analysis, especially when the models used include a demand-for-money function with zero interest sensitivity. This is the question of the interest sensitivity of the supply of money. Its implications for the controversy over policy which has been focused on the significance of the *demand* for money will be examined below.

With these thoughts in mind, let us turn to the Classical view as summarized earlier. In one version which we shall consider, the treatment of the demand for money differs substantially from the approach taken in Keynesian analysis. The Classical economists generally postulated that money balances were held only to finance the transactions of households and business and that the quantity of money demanded therefore depended only on transactions or income. Since money yielded no return, the possibility that the demand for money might also depend on the interest rate was not considered by most of them. This is the version of the Classical model mentioned in the preceding paragraph, in which the interest sensitivity of the demand for money balances, m, is assumed to be zero, and (3.7) reduces to:

$$M_d = kY. \tag{3.20}$$

This is the so-called quantity theory of money equation.[4] A model containing a demand-for-money function with an interest sensitivity of zero is generally viewed as belonging to the Classical approach (in a world in which wages are inflexible, monetarist policy conclusions depend on this assumption and exogenous control of the money supply by the monetary authority).[5] While assuming the interest elasticity of the demand for money to be zero may not seem to represent a major change in the model, this difference actually is crucial in terms of assessing the relative usefulness of monetary and fiscal policy in a chronically underemployed economy in which the supply of money is under the direct control of the central bank.[6]

It will be convenient to discuss monetary policy and fiscal policy in such

---

[4] The quantity theory can be expressed in two ways. The form given above, $M = kY$, is often called the "Cambridge equation" because it reflected the thinking of a group of economists in Cambridge University. The other version is $MV = Py$, where V stands for the income velocity of money, P is the price level, and y is real income ($Y = Py$). This version is often called the "Fisher equation," after the late Professor Irving Fisher of Yale. The quantity theory assumption is that the demand for money is not related to the rate of interest; if it were, the behavioral assumption that velocity is constant, which is crucial to this theory, is lost. Given the assumption that the demand for money is a pure transactions demand, $MV = Y$ is equivalent to $M = kY$; i.e., $k = 1/V$.

[5] This statement is subject to further qualifications. First, if prices and wages are assumed to be flexible, the Classical or monetarist conclusions about the effectiveness of monetary and fiscal policy hold even if the demand for money is interest sensitive—fiscal policy cannot change real income or employment, but merely shifts the mix between government and private spending, while changes in the money stock merely result in proportional changes in money wages and prices. This is the sort of model many monetarists now are using, as is shown in Teigen's paper on monetarism in this chapter (reading 4). Second, the Keynesian conclusions—namely, that both monetary policy and fiscal policy can change income and employment—hold for an underemployed economy even if the interest sensitivity of the demand for money is zero, as long as the interest sensitivity of the *supply* of money is not zero. This point is discussed later in this introduction, as well as in Teigen's paper in this chapter (reading 2) on the demand for and supply of money.

[6] The coefficient m represents the change in the demand for money as an asset corresponding to a unit change in the interest rate; that is, $\Delta M = -m\Delta r$, or $\Delta M/\Delta r = -m$. The *elasticity* of demand for money with respect to the interest rate ($\eta_{M^D \cdot r}$) is the *percentage* change in the demand for money divided by the *percentage* change in the interest rate. Thus:

$$\eta_{M^D \cdot r} = \frac{\Delta M/M}{\Delta r/r} = \frac{\Delta M/\Delta r}{M/r} = -\frac{m}{M/r}.$$

Since m appears in the numerator of this expression, when m takes the extreme values of zero or infinity, the elasticity also is zero or infinity.

an economy for the extreme cases in which the interest elasticity of the demand for money is zero in value, and in which it is infinitely large. In the version of the Classical case in which m, and hence this elasticity, is zero, it is seen from (3.17) that vk/m becomes infinitely large, and the fiscal policy or expenditure multiplier $\Delta Y/\Delta G^*$ becomes zero. In such a world, therefore, fiscal policy is ineffective; for example, an increase in government spending with no change in the money stock would necessarily raise the interest rate enough to depress private investment as much as government spending had increased, thereby merely reallocating resources from the private to the public sector but having no net effect on aggregate demand, output, or employment. From (3.19), however, it is apparent that the monetary policy multiplier, $\Delta Y/\Delta M^*$, reaches its maximum possible value, $1/k$, when m is zero. (Note: In the above numerical example, the money stock multiplier becomes 4 if $m = 0$—in contrast to the value of .8 that we calculated.) As m rises in value from zero, the term $[1 - c(1 - x)]m/v$ increases, reducing the value of this multiplier. The result that $\Delta Y/\Delta M^* = 1/k$, or that $\Delta M^* = k\Delta Y$, follows directly from the quantity theory equation, $M = kY$. On this basis, therefore, the typical Classical policy prescription for changing the level of money income is to use only monetary policy. While pamphleteers and popular writers had advocated government spending as a means of dealing with unemployment for many years, it is not surprising that this approach was not accepted by respectable professional economists until Keynes introduced the interest rate as a determinant of the demand for money in his *The General Theory of Employment, Interest and Money* in 1936. Nor is it surprising that modern monetarists, such as Milton Friedman, attach little or no importance to fiscal policy as a means of influencing aggregate demand (although, as we shall see below, members of this school of thought—particularly Friedman—have recently attempted to argue that fiscal policy is impotent while recognizing that the demand for money is interest sensitive).

The conclusion that aggregate income changes in direct proportion to the money stock if m is zero (assuming also, as above, that the supply of money does not respond to interest rate changes) is based on the usual comparative static equilibrium analysis, and does not take the dynamics of the system into account. Friedman agrees with the spirit of the Classical approach, but goes further and argues that monetary policy is not only powerful but erratic: while changes in the money stock have a strong leverage on income, the behavioral lags are variable and undependable so that, in some cases, the effect on income may be rapid, while in others it may be very slow.[7] This leads to his recommendations that discretionary monetary policy be abandoned and a "rule" providing for a constant percentage growth in the money stock be substituted for it, a proposal which has been debated with increasing intensity recently.[8] Friedman's views concerning lags are hotly disputed by many monetary economists.

In other writings, Friedman has contended that his views regarding monetary and fiscal policy do not depend critically on the absence of a significant interest elasticity of demand for money. Indeed, he has expressed the view that the

---

[7] The empirical evidence on which this conclusion is based is presented in Milton Friedman, "The Supply of Money and Changes in Prices and Output," in *The Relationship of Prices to Economic Stability and Growth,* Compendium of Papers Submitted by Panelists Appearing before the Joint Economic Committee (Washington, D.C., 1958), pp. 249–50.

[8] Chapter 5 contains readings which are concerned with this debate, and it is also taken up in Thomas Mayer's paper on monetarism in Chapter 1 (reading 3).

demand for money should, in principle, be responsive to interest rate changes. In his own empirical work, he does not find evidence in support of a significant degree of interest sensitivity.[9] But, in this respect, his results differ from those of most other investigators, as he has recognized.[10] Some of the evidence from studies which find significant interest sensitivity is summarized in Teigen's paper on the demand for and supply of money in this chapter. We have seen that if rigidity of money wage rates creates impediments to the automatic achievement of full employment, *both* monetary and fiscal policy will be capable of changing real income and employment unless the interest elasticity of demand for money is zero. However, as Friedman has pointed out, the situation is different if money wages are flexible.[11] Accordingly, it is useful to examine the effects of monetary and fiscal policy under these conditions.

As is shown in the paper by Holbrook in this chapter (reading 1), if money wages are flexible—that is, if they decline readily when the number of persons willing to work at the going wage rate exceeds the number of jobs available—the economy will normally tend automatically toward full employment regardless of the monetary and fiscal policies being followed. That is, real output and employment will be determined by the volume of real resources available and their productivity. The Classical quantity theory of money will hold in its extreme form: an increase in the stock of money will cause an equal proportional change in prices and in money income but will leave real income and employment unchanged. This will be true without regard to the magnitude of the interest elasticity of demand for money.[12] Fiscal policy will likewise not affect real income or employment. If government expenditures are increased without a corresponding increase in taxes, the government will have to borrow in the capital market to finance the resulting deficit. The additional government borrowing will necessarily raise interest rates enough to cause real private investment to decline as much as real government expenditures increase. The result will be a transfer of real resources from the private to the public sector of the economy, but total income and employment will be unaffected. Thus, as Friedman points out, fiscal policy will be incapable of affecting income and employment under a regime of flexible wages, whether or not the demand for money is sensitive to interest rates.

It should be noted, however, that even if wages are flexible, the effects of fiscal policy do depend to some degree on whether the demand for money is sensitive to interest rates. If the demand for real money balances depends only on real income and not on interest rates, the price level and therefore the level of money income is determined by the stock of money alone. In this case, a change in fiscal policy will leave the price level and money income unchanged. If, however, the demand for money is sensitive to interest rates, the outcome will be different. An increase in government expenditures not ac-

---

[9] See Milton Friedman, "The Demand for Money: Some Theoretical and Empirical Results," *Journal of Political Economy*, vol. 67 (August 1959), pp. 327–51. In order to get this result, Friedman uses a special definition of income.

[10] See Milton Friedman, "Interest Rates and the Demand for Money," *Journal of Law and Economics*, vol. 9 (October 1966), pp. 71–85.

[11] Ibid. See also his paper, "A Theoretical Framework for Monetary Analysis," *Journal of Political Economy*, vol. 78 (March/April 1970), pp. 193–238.

[12] Provided the interest elasticity is not infinitely large—if this is the case, the Classical mechanism which makes the economy tend automatically toward full employment may break down. (In this discussion, we are neglecting the so-called "Pigou effect.")

companied by an increase in taxes will, as explained earlier, cause interest rates to rise. If the demand for money is sensitive to interest rates, the rise in interest rates will cause a reduction in the amount of real money balances people want to hold (remember that real income is unchanged because it is determined by the amounts of real resources available and their productivity). With the nominal stock of money unchanged (by assumption), the price level will have to rise enough to bring the real value of cash balances into alignment with the reduced demand for such balances.[13] Thus, fiscal policy will, in this case, affect the price level and money income. To summarize: If wages are flexible, fiscal policy will be incapable of affecting real income and employment, whether or not the demand for money is elastic to interest rates; however, even with flexible wages, fiscal policy will have effects on the price level and money income unless the interest elasticity of demand for money is zero.

Assuming that the demand for money is sensitive to interest rates, as the bulk of the empirical evidence indicates, the above discussion raises an important question. Which of the following alternative assumptions is the more realistic: (a) wages are fully flexible so that monetary and fiscal policy are incapable of changing employment and real income, having effects only on the price level and money income; or (b) wages are rigid (or at least sticky), thereby giving monetary and fiscal policy an important leverage over employment and real income? It seems clear that in a world of imperfect markets, less than full mobility of resources, trade unions, minimum wage laws, and the like, the rigid-wage assumption is by far the more reasonable one to adopt. Accordingly, we shall continue to assume rigid wages during the remainder of this introduction, deferring the bulk of our discussion of wages and prices until the second part of this chapter.

There is still another dimension to the controversy over the role of interest rates in relation to monetary and fiscal policy—a dimension which has received less attention than it deserves. We refer here to the responsiveness of the money *supply* to changes in the interest rate through the operation of the banking system. Up to this point in our discussion, for simplicity, we have treated the stock of money, M^*, as a variable that is under the direct control of the monetary authorities. Strictly speaking, this is not correct. In the United States, the Federal Reserve System implements monetary policy primarily by buying and selling U.S. government securities in the open market, by changing the reserve requirements of member commercial banks, and by varying the discount rate at which member banks may borrow from the System. Thus, it is these variables rather

---

[13] This can be seen by examining the LM curve for a model similar to those presented above except that prices are now assumed to be free to change. The equation of the LM curve is derived by equating the demand for real money balances (which is assumed to depend on real income (Y/P) and the rate of interest) with the real value of the nominal money stock (M^*/P). Thus we have

$$\frac{M^*}{P} = M_o + k\frac{Y}{P} - mr.$$

If real income (Y/P) is fixed at the full-employment level and M^* is given, an increase in government expenditures which causes the interest rate to rise will reduce the demand for real money balances (the right-hand side of the equation). In order to maintain equilibrium in the money market, the supply of real money balances will have to be reduced also, and with M^* fixed this reduction can only be brought about by a rise in P. If P rises, Y must rise in the same proportion if Y/P is to remain constant. Thus, fiscal policy affects money income and prices. However, if $m = 0$ so that the interest rate does not affect the demand for money, none of these adjustments is necessary, and fiscal policy leaves money income and prices unaffected.

than the money stock itself that are properly regarded as being under the control of the authorities. Since the amount of reserves obtained by borrowing from the Federal Reserve as well as the amount of reserves held in excess of legal requirements seem to be affected by interest rates available in the market relative to the discount rate charged by the Federal Reserve, the money supply is determined jointly by the actions taken by the authorities and the responses of the banks and the public. One of the results is that the supply of money as well as the demand for money is sensitive to interest rates. The implications for monetary and fiscal policy of this more sophisticated approach to the supply of money are discussed thoroughly in the first paper by Teigen. We can bring our introductory discussion to completion by examining the results of substituting a very simple money supply equation for equation (3.8). Let us suppose that the monetary authorities are able to vary only the reserve base (R°) and that the commercial banks extend more loans and hence increase the amount of demand deposits in response to increases in the interest rate, and vice versa. Instead of (3.8), Model III now contains the following money supply equation:

$$M_s = aR^* + jr \qquad a > 0, j > 0. \tag{3.21}$$

We may now derive multiplier expressions summarizing the effects of fiscal policy and monetary policy in exactly the same way as before. Instead of the expressions given by (3.17) and (3.19), we now obtain:

$$\frac{\Delta Y}{\Delta G^*} = \frac{1}{1 - c(1 - x) + \dfrac{vk}{m + j}} \tag{3.22}$$

$$\frac{\Delta Y}{\Delta R^*} = \frac{a}{[1 - c(1 - x)]\dfrac{m + j}{v} + k} \tag{3.23}$$

In both of these expressions, we note that the interest sensitivity of the *supply* of money (j) is combined additively with the interest sensitivity of the demand for money (m). Thus even if the latter were zero, as most of the Classical economists have assumed, fiscal policy remains effective as long as the interest sensitivity of the supply of money is not zero. In the same way, the larger is the interest elasticity of the money supply, the less potent is monetary policy, given the value of the interest sensitivity of demand. It appears, then, that the crucial question relating to policy for an economy in which there are impediments to full employment is not whether the *demand* for money is interest sensitive, but whether either the demand *or* supply of money exhibit interest sensitivity. Only if *both* sensitivities are zero do the extreme Classical conclusions hold.

The Classical position represents one extreme view of the size of the interest elasticity of the demand for money (as we have noted, both the Classical and the Keynesian schools have disregarded the interest elasticity of the money supply). The other polar view is that the interest elasticity of demand is infinitely large; this is the "extreme Keynesian" assumption, and is sometimes referred to as the "liquidity trap" case. If m were infinitely large, the expenditure multiplier (3.17) becomes $1/[1 - c(1 - x)]$. The monetary sector has no inhibiting effect on the expenditure multiplier at all, and fiscal policy reaches maximum effectiveness. However, the monetary policy multiplier (3.19) becomes zero. Monetary policy is completely ineffective because changes in the money stock have no effect on the interest rate and hence on expenditures. The "liquidity trap" means that increases in the money stock are simply absorbed into idle balances, since it is universally expected that the interest rate will rise and bond prices fall. If the possibility of interest-induced changes in the money supply is recognized, a glance at equations (3.22) and (3.23) indicates that an infinitely large interest elasticity of supply will yield similar results—if j is infinitely large, (3.22) becomes $1/[1 - c(1 - x)]$, its largest possible value, while the multiplier summarizing the effects on income of changes in bank reserves, (3.23), becomes zero. Such a result might occur in a period of deep depression when interest rates were very low and seemed almost certain to rise in the near future. At such times the banks, fearing a fall in security prices, might be very reluctant to buy securities, and they might be extremely fearful of making additional loans at the prevailing very low interest rates in view of the high risks of default. Under these conditions, any increase in bank reserves, resulting, let us say, from open market operations, might merely cause the banks to add a corresponding amount to their excess reserves without leading to any increase in the money supply.

It is almost certain that neither the Classical nor the extreme Keynesian assumptions accurately characterize our economy under normal conditions. The evidence appears overwhelming that both the demand for and the supply of money possess some degree of interest elasticity but that neither of these elasticities is infinitely great.[14] With one further qualification in the case of monetary policy—that the sensitivity of investment to the interest rate is not zero—it may be seen from (3.22) and (3.23) that in this case both fiscal policy and monetary policy are capable of influencing income. Most recent studies have verified that investment (especially in new houses and in plant and equipment) responds to changes in the rate of interest. In a system with nonzero but finite interest elasticities of demand for and/or supply of money, and a nonzero interest elasticity of demand for investment, the efficacy of monetary policy, as well as fiscal policy, depends on the structure of *both the real sector (i.e., the markets for goods and services) and the monetary sector.* In fact, both the expenditure multiplier and the monetary policy multiplier expressions contain the same terms: the marginal propensities to consume and to add to money balances with respect to income; the responsiveness of investment, the demand for money, and the supply of money to the rate of interest; and the marginal response of tax payments to income.[15] From (3.22) and (3.23) it is easy to determine the conditions that are conducive to the effectiveness of monetary policy and of fiscal policy, respectively. It should not be concluded from the discussion of the polar cases above that all of the conditions which are favorable to fiscal policy are unfavorable to monetary policy, or vice versa. In fact, there are a number of conditions that are conducive to the effectiveness of both kinds of policy. Both multipliers will be larger:

---

[14] It should be noted that Keynes himself felt that this would be the normal situation and that both fiscal and monetary policy would therefore be capable of influencing aggregate demand. He regarded the "liquidity trap" situation as one that might occur only in times of deep depression, such as the 1930s. It is totally wrong to regard the liquidity trap case as the essence of Keynes' analysis.

[15] In addition, the monetary policy multiplier, (3.23), has in its numerator the sensitivity of the money supply to changes in the reserve base (a). If the money supply does not respond to changes in the reserve base, then monetary policy as expressed through open market operations can have no effect on the interest rate, investment, and income. As Teigen's article shows, the structure of the monetary system is such that this sensitivity is not zero. As a matter of fact the coefficient a turns out to be the standard credit expansion multiplier, as Teigen demonstrates.

1.   The larger the marginal propensity to consume with respect to disposable income (c), and the lower the marginal response of tax payments to income (x). This is true because these coefficients determine the size of induced expenditure and income changes set off by an initial change in government expenditures or tax collections produced by fiscal policy, or by an initial change in private investment resulting from a change in interest rates produced by monetary policy.

2.   The smaller is the responsiveness of the demand for money to changes in income (k). For a given increase in income, for instance, the interest rate will rise less and induced investment spending will fall less, the less cash is drawn into transactions balances to accommodate the rising level of income.

The two multipliers are affected differently by variations in the interest sensitivity of investment and of the demand for and supply of money $(v, m,$ and $j)$. Fiscal policy is more effective, and monetary policy less effective:

1.   The lower the interest sensitivity of investment expenditure (v). That is, the lower this sensitivity, the less will such expenditure be reduced by rising interest rates which accompany rising expenditure and income brought about by an increase in government expenditures or a reduction in taxes. On the other hand, the lower this sensitivity, the less effect will a given change in the money stock and the resulting interest rate change have on investment spending.

2.   The greater the interest sensitivities of the demand for money (m) and the supply of money (j). The greater these sensitivities, the less will expenditure be reduced by rising interest rates accompanying rising expenditure and income caused by expansionary fiscal measures; but, on the other hand, the less effect will a given monetary change have on the interest rates and hence on spending.

In summary, monetary policy is more effective when the interest sensitivities of the demand for and supply of money are low, so that changes in the money stock or reserve base have greater effects on the rate of interest, and when the interest sensitivity of investment expenditure is large, so that changes in the interest rate have larger effects on spending. Fiscal policy is more effective when the interest sensitivity of the demand for and supply of money is large, so that an increase in transactions requirements for money and the resulting reduction in money balances left to satisfy asset requirements does not affect the interest rate very much and also, to some extent, induces the banks to create new money balances, and when the interest sensitivity of investment expenditure is low, so that rising interest rates do not deter very much investment expenditure.

The conclusions of this discussion of the factors influencing the effectiveness of monetary and fiscal policy—as measured by the size of the multipliers $\Delta Y/\Delta G^*$ and $\Delta Y/\Delta R^*$—are summarized in Table 4.

The student will benefit, as he or she studies this book, from trying to see how the materials fit into the framework developed above, and how some of the readings suggest important extensions to this simple framework. As has already been noted, for example, some of the material in Chapter 5 is concerned with the size of v, the interest sensitivity of investment decisions. At the same time, other papers in Chapters 1 and 5 take the point of view that the "monetary transmission mechanism," or link between the monetary and real sectors of the economy, is much broader than the interest rate-investment relationship as expressed in the size of v. The monetarists have taken this position, and

Table 4

Increase in:	Effect on:	
	$\dfrac{\Delta Y}{\Delta R^*} = \dfrac{a}{[1 - c(1-x)]\dfrac{m+j}{v} + k}$	$\dfrac{\Delta Y}{\Delta G^*} = \dfrac{1}{1 - c(1-x) + \dfrac{vk}{m+j}}$
c.................	increase	increase
x.................	decrease	decrease
m.................	decrease	increase
j.................	decrease	increase
v.................	increase	decrease
k.................	decrease	decrease

in fact, they claim it as one of the identifying characteristics of monetarism. But Warren L. Smith's article in Chapter 5, "A Neo-Keynesian View of Monetary Policy," (reading 23) identifies three broad channels through which monetary influences can affect real variables; his list includes the general portfolio-adjustment process named by the monetarists. Thus, it appears that both sides have in common a more general view of the transmission mechanism than is represented in the somewhat elementary models discussed here. To take another example, the discussion of the working of banks and financial intermediaries in Chapter 2 and of the "slippages" in the financial system in Chapter 5 are significant primarily because they bear on the size of *m* and *j*, the interest sensitivities of the demand for and supply of money.

2. SOME RUDIMENTARY DYNAMICS

(a) The Dynamics of the Multiplier

Changes in aggregate demand, whether produced by autonomous shifts in private spending or by changes in fiscal and monetary policy, are not reflected immediately in changes in production and income. There are three major lags in the process of income generation: (1) the lag between the receipt of income and the expenditure of that portion of it that the recipient decides to spend; (2) the lag between changes in expenditure and related changes in production and income; (3) the lag between the earning of income and its receipt. These lags have been called the *expenditure lag*, the *output lag*, and the *earnings lag*, respectively. While the lags are essentially additive, it appears that the expenditure and earnings lags are relatively short and that the output lag is by far the longest and most important.[16] It arises because of the relationships between sales, inventories, and output. For example, an increase in sales of consumer goods will commonly lead to a reduction in retail inventories in the first instance. After a delay, which will depend on the practices of the industry, on marketing channels, and on the general business situation, retailers will increase their orders to restore depleted inventories, and these increased orders will in due course cause manufacturers to increase production and employment. Thus, significant changes in output usually occur only after a delay, which may be considerable.

Elementary expositions of the dynamics of income change commonly employ

---

[16] Lloyd A. Metzler, "Three Lags in the Circular Flow of Income," in *Income, Employment, and Public Policy: Essays in Honor of Alvin H. Hansen* (New York: W. W. Norton & Co., Inc., 1948), pp. 11–32.

an expenditure lag, assuming, for example, that consumption adjusts to income with a lag of one period. However, in view of the fact that the output lag appears to be the most important, we shall build our exposition around that lag. This seems more realistic, although the algebraic results are very similar with an expenditure lag.

Model IIA: A Dynamic Version of Model II

To begin our discussion of the dynamic multiplier—that is, the process through which the system adjusts from one equilibrium position to another when some component of spending changes—we will use a version of Model II, modified by dating all of the variables in such a way that this period's output (and hence current income) depends only on spending during the previous period. After we have become familiar with the adjustment process using this simple model, we shall turn to a version of Model III, in which the monetary sector plays a role. The dynamic version of Model II is as follows:

$$C_t = C_o + cY_d \tag{2a.1}$$
$$Y_{d_t} = Y_t - T_t \tag{2a.2}$$
$$T_t = T^* + xY_t \tag{2a.3}$$
$$I_t = I_o \tag{2a.4}$$
$$G_t = G^* \tag{2a.5}$$
$$Y_t = C_{t-1} + I_{t-1} + G_{t-1} \tag{2a.6}$$

Here the subscript t designates the value of the indicated variable in the current period, the subscript $t-1$ refers to the previous period, and so on. In equilibrium, the value of each variable is unchanged from period to period. Accordingly, all time subscripts can be dropped, and the solution of this model is the same as the solution of Model II. However, the interpretation of equation (2a.6) is now different—it is no longer an "equilibrium condition" (although equilibrium values of the variables can be obtained by assuming that equilibrium exists [that is, that $C_t = C_{t-1}$; $I_t = I_{t-1}$; and $G_t = G_{t-1}$], and substituting these values into the equation). Rather, (2a.6) is a statement of the rule that firms are assumed to follow in deciding how much to produce. It says that they produce in a particular period an amount equal to their sales in the previous period; that is, output is adjusted to sales with a lag of one period. Thus, equation (2a.6) implies that an increase in spending in the current period has no effect on current production and national income; rather, inventories are drawn down to fill the new orders, and production responds during the following period. Other rules could have been specified, of course, but this one is simple and at the same time realistic enough to be useful.

In Model IIA, the length of each "period" need not correspond to any particular unit of calendar time, such as a month or year, but is determined by the behavioral lag between a change in spending and the change in production which it induces. In reality, it is a "distributed lag"; that is, the change in production does not occur entirely in one period but is spread out over a number of periods. For example, the production adjustment may begin slowly, rise to a peak, and then gradually taper off. Here we treat the production response to a given change in sales as occurring in one discrete unit time period. In tracing the path followed by income in response to a spending change, we will also assume that the marginal propensity to consume out of disposable income (c) and the marginal propensity to pay taxes out of GNP (x) do not change in value over time.

We will consider the effects of two types of spending changes, using changes in government purchases of goods and services as an example—although, of course, similar effects would be produced by shifts in consumer spending, investment spending, or tax collections. In Case 1, we will suppose that government purchases rise from G^* to $G^* + \Delta G^*$ *during one period only*, and then revert to the original level, G^*, and remain there. In Case 2, we start from the same equilibrium and suppose that government purchases rise to $G^* + \Delta G^*$ and *remain at the new level indefinitely*. In each case, we will trace the path of income from the original equilibrium level to the new equilibrium position. While we will consider the effects of an increase in spending, the same analysis will apply in reverse for a spending decrease.

Case 1: One-Shot Injection. Starting from an equilibrium position, suppose that, in the first period under consideration, government purchases of goods and services rise from the original level, G^*, to a new level, $G^* + \Delta G^*$—that is, government purchases change by ΔG^*. In the second period, government purchases revert to their former level, G^*, and remain there in all future periods. Because production is determined only by the previous period's spending, income—that is, the total value of current production—does not change in period 1; rather, inventories are drawn down so that the investment actually realized by firms for the period is $I_o - \Delta G^*$, not I_o as planned (that is, inventory investment falls by the same amount that spending by government increases). Since income does not change, there is no change in tax collections, disposable income, or consumption expenditure.

In period 2, firms continue to produce the (as yet unchanged) amounts of output corresponding to spending by households and by firms themselves for investment purposes, and also produce the total amount bought by government in period 1, $G^* + \Delta G.^{*17}$ Therefore income rises by ΔG^* in period 2, and corresponding to this income increase, current tax collections rise by $x\Delta G^*$. Disposable income in period 2 changes by the amount of the change in income, ΔG^*, less the change in tax collections, $x\Delta G^*$, or by $(1 - x)\Delta G^*$, and so consumption spending in the amount of $c(1 - x)\Delta G^*$ is induced in period 2, drawing down inventories by this amount.[18] In period 3, firms produce an amount equal to their sales in period 2, which exceed the level prevailing in the initial equilibrium by $c(1 - x)\Delta G^*$. Thus income in period 3 is greater than its initial equilibrium level by this amount; however, it is lower than income in period 2, due to an increase in household savings of $(1 - c)(1 - x)\Delta G^*$ in period 2. The increment of income $c(1 - x)\Delta G^*$ in period 3 induces consumption spending of $c(1 - x)[c(1 - x)\Delta G^*]$, or $c^2(1 - x)^2\Delta G^*$, etc. In general, the initial increase in spending produces an increment of induced production (and hence income) in each succeeding period, beginning with the period following the spending change; each increment is smaller than the one preceding it, since a part of each is drained off by the government in taxes and another part is saved by households, until finally these increments approach zero in value and equilibrium is restored *at the original level of income.*

---

[17] Note that in this model, production in each period is equal to *planned* spending by all sectors in the previous period. Thus the inventory change that occurred in period 1 is disregarded in period 2.

[18] Since firms are producing the incremental amount bought by government in period 1, there is actually a net inventory accumulation of $\Delta G^* - c(1 - x)\Delta G^*$, or $[1 - c(1 - x)]\Delta G^*$, during the period.

It may help to illustrate the nature of this process if an example is employed, using the same numerical assumptions as in Model II. That is, suppose we have

$$C_t = 110 + .75Yd_t$$
$$Y_{d_t} = Y_t - T_t$$
$$T_t = -80 + .2Y_t$$
$$I_t = 300$$
$$G_t = 330$$
$$Y_t = C_{t-1} + I_{t-1} + G_{t-1}$$

The equilibrium values of the variables in this model are shown in the column labeled "original equilibrium" of Table 5. In period 1, government purchases of goods and services rise by $20 billion to $350 billion; they revert to $330 billion in period 2 and remain there in all succeeding periods. The paths followed by income and other variables are shown in columns numbered 1, 2, 3,

Table 5: The Dynamics of a "One-Shot" Spending Injection (in $ billions)

	Original Equilibrium	Time Period (t) 1	2	3	4		New Equilibrium
Y	$2,000	$2,000	$2,020	$2,012.0	$2,007.20	...	$2,000
C	1,370	1,370	1,382	1,377.2	1,374.32	...	1,370
I	300	300	300	300.0	300.00	...	300
G	330	350	330	330.0	330.00	...	330
T	320	320	324	322.4	321.44	...	320
Y_d	1,680	1,680	1,696	1,689.6	1,685.76	...	1,680
S	310	310	314	312.4	311.44	...	310
ΔY_t†	—	0	20	12.0	7.20	...	0

† ΔY_t refers to the difference between income in the tth period and the original equilibrium value.

and 4, where the column numbers correspond to the time periods. As can be seen, income rises to a peak of $2,020 billion during period 2, and then declines until it ultimately reaches the former equilibrium level of $2,000 billion as shown in the final ("new equilibrium") column. In the row labeled ΔY_t, the change in income in each period measured from the original equilibrium level is shown. The general expression for ΔY_t is shown in the following tabulation:

	Time Period (t) 1	2	3	4	n	New Equilibrium
ΔY_t	0	ΔG^*	$c(1-x)\Delta G^*$	$[c(1-x)]^2\Delta G^* \ldots$	$[c(1-x)]^{n-2}\Delta G^* \ldots$	0

Since c and x are positive fractions between zero and unity in value, $c(1-x)$ is also such a fraction, and $[c(1-x)]^m$ declines steadily in value as m increases. Since the new equilibrium position is not reached until an infinite amount of time has passed, the term $[c(1-x)]^m$ goes to zero, and the new equilibrium is therefore the same as the original equilibrium that existed before the "one-shot" increase in government purchases. The explanation is that, since government spending fell back to its original level in the second period of our example, and remained there, the equilibrium solution of the system is unchanged. However, the one-period spurt in spending initiated a dynamic process of adjustment which takes an infinite number of periods to complete. In each of these periods, income will be greater than equilibrium income, although it will be approaching the equilibrium value as time passes.

Case 2: Continuing Injection.   Now let us consider the dynamics of the case in which government purchases change and remain at the new level; that is, the case in which there is a change in the equilibrium level of government purchases. Let this change be represented by ΔG^* as previously (remember that shifts in consumption or private investment will have the same effect). As before, income will change by ΔG^* in period 2 as producers respond to the change in government spending in period 1. During period 2, there will be another injection of government spending greater than the old equilibrium by ΔG^*; at the same time, households will be induced to spend $c(1 - x)\Delta G^*$, which in turn will induce that much production in period 3, and so on. In each period after the second, income will differ from the initial equilibrium level by the sum of a new component of production for the government sector equal to the previous period's increased spending (compared to the former equilibrium level of government spending) and one or more components which

Table 6:   The Dynamics of a Continuing Spending Injection (in $ billions)

	Original Equilibrium	Time Period (t)					New Equilibrium
		1	2	3	4		
Y	$2,000	$2,000	$2,020	$2,032.0	$2,039.20	...	$2,050
C	1,370⎞	1,370⎞	1,382⎞	1,389.2⎞	1,393.52	...	1,400
I	300⎬	300⎬	300⎬	300.0⎬	300.00	...	300
G	330⎠	350⎠	350⎠	350.0⎠	350.00	...	350
T	320	320	324	326.4	327.84	...	330
Y_d	1,680	1,680	1,696	1,705.6	1,711.36	...	1,720
S	310	310	314	316.4	317.84	...	320
ΔY_t†	—	0	20	32.0	39.20	...	50
$\dfrac{\Delta Y_t}{\Delta G^*}$	—	0	1	1.6	1.96	...	2.50

† ΔY_t refers to the difference between income in the *t*th period and the original equilibrium value.

correspond to induced spending by the household sector in the previous period. The income changes for several such periods are written out in Table 6 using the numerical version of Model IIA.

To find the amount by which income has changed at the end of any period as a result of the change of government spending, all of the increments of induced production (and hence income) in that period which arise from this spending change must be added to the production which corresponds to the previous period's "new" additional government spending. For example, in period 3, income is $32 billion higher than its initial equilibrium level. This is due to the fact that, in period 2, government spending on goods and services was $20 billion higher than its initial level, inducing that much new production for the government sector in period 3; in addition, $12 billion of goods was produced in period 3 in response to the induced rise in consumption spending of $12 billion in period 2.

Model IIIA: A Dynamic Version of Model III

Now let us examine the effects on the process of income change of a shift in spending in a model containing a monetary sector. For this purpose we shall use a dynamic version of Model III. Since the adjustment of a household's or firm's cash balance is a simple matter and presumably takes less time to accomplish than either changes in spending plans or production decisions, we shall assume that there are no lags in the monetary sector. As was the case in Model IIA, therefore, the only lag in the system will be an output lag. The dynamic version of Model IIIA is as follows:

$$C_t = C_o + cY_{d_t} \tag{3a.1}$$
$$Y_{d_t} = Y_t - T_t \tag{3a.2}$$
$$T_t = T^* + xY_t \tag{3a.3}$$
$$I_t = I_o - vr_t \tag{3a.4}$$
$$G_t = G^* \tag{3a.5}$$
$$Y_t = C_{t-1} + I_{t-1} + G_{t-1} \tag{3a.6}$$
$$M_{d_t} = M_o + kY_t - mr_t \tag{3a.7}$$
$$M_{s_t} = M^* \tag{3a.8}$$
$$M_{d_t} = M_{s_t} \tag{3a.9}$$

In this discussion, we will consider only the "continuing injection" version of the process of income change, as it is the typical multiplier case. Starting from equilibrium, let there be an increase in government spending of ΔG^* in period 1. According to Model IIIA, in which income in any period responds only to spending in the previous period, this spending change will have no effect on income until period 2. In that period, producers will increase their output, and therefore income, by ΔG^*. As a consequence, changes in spending by both households and firms are induced in this period. The change in household spending can easily be deduced from the first three equations of our model. An income increase of ΔG^* causes an increase in disposable income of $(1 - x)\Delta G^*$, leading to a rise in consumption spending of $c(1 - x)\Delta G^*$ in the same period. To isolate the effects of a change in income on the spending decisions of firms, the investment equation (3a.4) must be examined together with the equations describing the monetary sector—(3a.7), (3a.8), and (3a.9). First, by differencing equation (3a.4), we note that

$$\Delta I_t = -v\Delta r_t, \tag{3a.10}$$

or that rising interest rates cause business firms to reduce investment, and vice versa. The effects of rising income on the rate of interest can be found from the monetary equations. Combining (3a.7), (3a.8), and (3a.9) produces the following *LM* equation:

$$M^* = M_o + kY_t - mr_t. \tag{3a.11}$$

If we write this equation in differenced form, remembering that the money supply, M^*, is assumed to remain constant, we get:

$$0 = k\Delta Y_t - m\Delta r_t; \tag{3a.12}$$

or, solving this equation for Δr_t in terms of ΔY_t, we find

$$\Delta r_t = \frac{k}{m} \Delta Y_t. \tag{3a.13}$$

Substituting this result into (3a.10) yields

$$\Delta I_t = -\frac{vk}{m} \Delta Y_t, \tag{3a.14}$$

the general expression for the change in planned investment spending which is induced by a change in income, ΔY_t. Since the income change in period 2 is ΔG^*, the induced change in investment spending in that period is

$$-\frac{vk}{m}\,\Delta G^*.$$

Thus the *total* change in induced spending in period t will be

$$\left[c(1-x)-\frac{vk}{m}\right]\Delta Y_t,$$

and in period 2 it will be

$$\left[c(1-x)-\frac{vk}{m}\right]\Delta G^*.$$

In addition, the autonomous spending increase of ΔG^* is assumed to continue.

Thus the total income change in period 3, which is the sum of induced and autonomous spending changes in period 2 in our model, is

$$\left[c(1-x)-\frac{vk}{m}\right]\Delta G^* + \Delta G^*.$$

This in turn will induce further new spending in period 3, according to the rule given above, of

$$\left[c(1-x)-\frac{vk}{m}\right]\left[c(1-x)-\frac{vk}{m}\right]\Delta G^*,$$

or

$$\left[c(1-x)-\frac{vk}{m}\right]^2\Delta G^*,$$

which, when added to the autonomous spending component ΔG^* will generate further income change in period 4, and so forth.

It may be useful to illustrate this process with a numerical example, using a model which yields the same equilibrium values for income and their other common endogenous variables as the numerical version of Model IIA, but which contains a monetary sector whose parameters have the same values as those of Model III, as follows:

$$C_t = 110 + .75Y_{d_t}$$
$$Y_{d_t} = Y_t - T_t$$
$$T_t = -80 + .2Y_t$$
$$I_t = 320 - 4r_t$$
$$G_t = 330$$
$$Y_t = C_{t-1} + I_{t-1} + G_{t-1}$$
$$M_{d_t} = 20 + .25Y_t - 10r_t$$
$$M_{s_t} = 470$$
$$M_{d_t} = M_{s_t}$$

Changes in income and several other variables which result from a continuing injection of $20 billion of new government spending initiated in period 1 are written out in Table 7.

Again we find the total amount of income change for any period due to a change in government spending by adding all of the increments of induced production (or income) in that period to the production corresponding to the previous period's "new" government spending. In the present example, for in-

Table 7: The Dynamics of a Continuing Spending Injection in a Model with a Monetary Sector (in $ billions)

	Original Equilibrium	Time Period (t)				New Equilibrium
		1	2	3	4	
Y	$2,000	$2,000	$2,020	$2,030	$2,035.0	...	$2,040
C	1,370	1,370	1,382	1,388	1,391.0	...	1,394
I	300	300	298	297	296.5	...	296
G	330	350	350	350	350.0	...	350
T	320	320	324	326	327.0	...	328
Y_d	1,680	1,680	1,696	1,704	1,708.0	...	1,712
S	310	310	314	316	317.0	...	318
M	470	470	470	470	470.0	...	470
r	5%	5%	5.5%	5.75%	5.875%	...	6%
ΔY_t†	—	0	20	30	35.0	...	40
$\dfrac{\Delta Y_t}{\Delta G^*}$	—	0	1	1.5	1.75	...	2.0

† ΔY_t refers to the difference between income in the tth period and the original equilibrium value.

stance, income in period 3 is $30 billion higher than its original equilibrium level. This change is due to three causes: First, government spending on goods and services in period 2 was $20 billion higher than its initial level, inducing that much new production for the government sector in period 3; second, $12 billion of goods was produced in period 3 in response to the induced rise in consumption spending of $12 billion in period 2; finally, $2 billion *less* of investment goods was produced in period 3 than initially because spending by firms declined by that amount in period 2 due to a rise in the rate of interest from 5 percent to 5.5 percent. It is possible to calculate multipliers for each successive time period. This is done by dividing the rise in income for that period by the increase in the level of government purchases that caused the rise. These multipliers are shown in the $\Delta Y_t/\Delta G^*$ rows of Tables 6 and 7: thus, in Table 7, the multiplier is 1.00 after two periods, 1.50 after three periods, and so on. It should be noted that the multipliers shown in Table 7 for each period are somewhat smaller than their counterparts in Table 6, except for the first two periods; this is due to restraining influence of the monetary sector on the expansion process in Model IIIA, a phenomenon which is not present in Model IIA. The multipliers calculated in this way, of course, eventually equal the static multipliers appropriate to the underlying model (2.00 in the case of Model IIIA, for example).

This concept of the multiplier differs from the *static equilibrium multipliers* expressed in equation (2.11) or equation (3.17). The multiplier expressions in those equations give the change in *equilibrium* income which would result from a sustained change in the level of government purchases in each case. The multiplier values shown in Tables 6 and 7—and also in Table 8 below—on the other hand, represent a dynamic or disequilibrium view of the multiplier. Rather than allowing the system to reestablish equilibrium, we have chosen to relate the amount by which income differs from its original equilibrium value at the end of any arbitrarily selected number of periods to the original spending change. Each of the expressions in the row labeled $\Delta Y_t/\Delta G^*$ in Tables 6 and 7 —or Table 8—is a multiplier. Since the multiplier process has not been allowed to work itself out completely, however, any such multiplier is sometimes called a "truncated" multiplier. When the dynamic process is fully worked out and equilibrium income is reestablished, the change in equilibrium income will be

Table 8: Changes in Income and Corresponding Values of the Truncated Dynamic Multipliers for Models IIA† and IIIA, Based on a Continuing Expenditure Change of ΔG^*

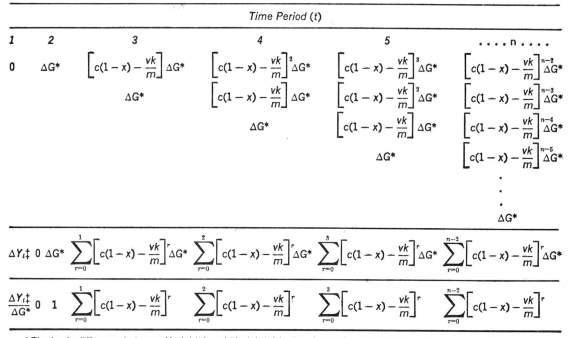

† The basic difference between Model IIA and Model IIIA is that, in the former, the interest sensitivity of the demand for investment, v, is zero; thus there is no link between the monetary sector and the rest of the model, and the monetary sector cannot affect expenditure decisions and hence is omitted. In this table, the expressions as written are based on Model IIIA, but if v, the interest sensitivity of investment demand, is set equal to zero, the expressions will reflect the properties of Model IIA.

‡ In this table, for convenience, we employ the standard notation for the sum of a series of terms having a variable in common. To take a simple example, suppose we wished to write the sum $Z_1 + Z_2 + Z_3 + Z_4 + Z_5$ in an abbreviated way. It is conventional to write this as $\sum_{r=1}^{5} Z_r$. This is read: "The summation of Z_r, with r taking on values from one to five." The symbol Σ is the *summation sign* and is the Greek letter sigma. In this expression, the subscript r provides a convenient way of handling the "length" of this sum—i.e., the fact that it includes all Z's from Z_1 to Z_5. In the expression

$$\sum_{r=0}^{n-2}\left[c(1-x)-\frac{vk}{m}\right]^r,$$

r is used to represent a variable exponent; that is, this expression represents the sum

$$\left[c(1-x)-\frac{vk}{m}\right]^0 + \left[c(1-x)-\frac{vk}{m}\right] + \cdots + \left[c(1-x)-\frac{vk}{m}\right]^{n-3} + \left[c(1-x)-\frac{vk}{m}\right]^{n-2}$$

or, since any number raised to the zero power is unity,

$$1 + \left[c(1-x)-\frac{vk}{m}\right] + \cdots + \left[c(1-x)-\frac{vk}{m}\right]^{n-3} + \left[c(1-x)-\frac{vk}{m}\right]^{n-2}.$$

that predicted by the comparable static multiplier equation. (This would be equation (3.17). But notice that, if we assume $v = 0$, which is the essential difference between Model IIA and Model IIIA, then the comparable static multiplier equation will be (2.11).) Thus the truncated multiplier approaches the static equilibrium multiplier in value over time. Both of these versions of the multiplier are consistent with the general definition of the multiplier as being the ratio of the change in income to the spending change which induced it.

The general expressions for the induced increase in income above the initial equilibrium level in any period. ΔY_t, and for the truncated multiplier for any period, $\Delta Y_t/\Delta G^*$, are developed in Table 8. In using this table, it is important to understand that the ΔY_t for any period is found by adding all of the items in the column corresponding to that period—that is, by adding *vertically* down a column. To find the value of the multiplier in the new equilibrium, we must evaluate a sum such as is found in the lower right-hand corner of Table 8, except that we must allow an infinite amount of time to pass. That, is, we consider the value of the sum:

$$\frac{\Delta Y}{\Delta G^*} = \lim_{t \to \infty} \sum_{r=0}^{t-2} \left[c(1-x) - \frac{vk}{m} \right]^r.$$

This sum is found in the following way:

a. Consider the partial sum

$$\frac{\Delta Y_t}{\Delta G^*} = 1 + \left[c(1-x) - \frac{vk}{m} \right] + \left[c(1-x) - \frac{vk}{m} \right]^2 + \cdots + \left[c(1-x) - \frac{vk}{m} \right]^{t-2}.$$

b. Multiply both sides of this expression by the term $-\left[c(1-x) - \frac{vk}{m} \right]$:

$$-\left[c(1-x) - \frac{vk}{m} \right] \frac{\Delta Y_t}{\Delta G^*} = -\left[c(1-x) - \frac{vk}{m} \right] - \left[c(1-x) - \frac{vk}{m} \right]^2 - \cdots$$
$$-\left[c(1-x) - \frac{vk}{m} \right]^{t-2} - \left[c(1-x) - \frac{vk}{m} \right]^{t-1}.$$

c. Add these two equations (note that all the terms on the right-hand side cancel out except the first term of (a) and the last term of (b)):

$$\frac{\Delta Y_t}{\Delta G^*} - \left[c(1-x) - \frac{vk}{m} \right] \frac{\Delta Y_t}{\Delta G^*} = 1 - \left[c(1-x) - \frac{vk}{m} \right]^{t-1}.$$

d. Factor $\Delta Y_t/\Delta G^*$ out of the left-hand side of this equation, and multiply both sides by $1/\left[1 - c(1-x) + \frac{vk}{m} \right]$:

$$\frac{\Delta Y_t}{\Delta G^*} = \frac{1}{1 - c(1-x) + \frac{vk}{m}} \left\{ 1 - \left[c(1-x) - \frac{vk}{m} \right]^{t-1} \right\}.$$

(Note: this is the general expression for the truncated multiplier.)

e. Let t approach infinity; then $\left[c(1-x) - \frac{vk}{m} \right]^{t-1}$ approaches zero,

$1 - \left[c(1-x) - \frac{vk}{m} \right]^{t-1}$ approaches unity, and $\Delta Y_t/\Delta G^*$ approaches the static equilibrium value $\Delta Y/\Delta G^*$. Thus, we obtain:

$$\frac{\Delta Y}{\Delta G^*} = \frac{1}{1 - c(1-x) + \frac{vk}{m}}.$$

We have shown that the truncated multiplier approaches the static equilibrium multiplier as the number of periods which have passed since the initial injection of spending becomes very large, just as was demonstrated for the specific numerical examples in Table 6 and 7. In the present case, also, the truncated multiplier is zero for the first period and unity in the second period; after that its value rises steadily until it approaches the limiting value represented by the static equilibrium multiplier.

   If the potential impact of a change in government spending on income is being studied, interest is focused on the resulting income level within a year, or some other relatively short period of time; it is not very useful to know what the new equilibrium level of income will be, since that level will not occur until an infinite amount of time has passed. Thus, the speed with which the multiplier process works is a matter of great practical significance, and this speed, measured in terms of calendar time, can be said to depend on two factors:

1. The number of unit time periods required to achieve some specified portion of the total ultimate effect; and
2. The length of a unit time period expressed in weeks or months.

The first of these factors, the number of time periods required, depends upon all of the marginal propensities and sensitivities in the multiplier expression—the marginal propensity to consume out of disposable income (c), the marginal propensity to pay taxes out of GNP (x), the marginal sensitivity of investment spending to the rate of interest (v), the marginal sensitivity of the demand for money balances to income (k), and the marginal sensitivity of the demand for money balances to the rate of interest (m). (If the model contained a supply-of-money relationship, instead of treating the money supply as fixed by the government, the number of periods required would also depend on the marginal sensitivity of the supply of money balances to the interest rate (j).) The nature of this dependence is illustrated in Table 9 by a number of numerical examples involving various values of the marginal propensity to consume and the marginal propensity to pay taxes. We are omitting the monetary sector in this illustration (assuming, in effect, that $v = 0$) as a means of keeping the presentation relatively simple, so that the calculations in Table 9 are based on Model IIA. The table is divided into four main sections, one each for marginal propensities to consume of 90 percent, 80 percent, 70 percent, and 60 percent. For each value of the marginal propensity to consume, multiplier calculations are presented for marginal propensities to pay taxes of 20 percent, 30 percent, and 40 percent. The values of the static equilibrium multiplier, as shown in column 2, decline as the marginal propensity to consume declines and as the marginal propensity to pay taxes increases. The same is true of the truncated multiplier calculated after five periods, as shown in column 3. It is interesting to note, however, that large multipliers work *relatively* more slowly than do smaller multipliers. Thus, while larger static multipliers (column 2) are associated with larger multipliers after five periods (column 3), the *percentage* of the total multiplier effect that is achieved at the end of five periods is smaller for large than for small multipliers, as is shown in column 4. Column 5 brings out this same tendency in a different way: it shows that the number of time periods needed to achieve 90 percent of the total static multiplier effect is larger for large than for small multipliers.

The second factor determining the speed of the multiplier is the length of a unit analytic time period, expressed in months or quarters. In terms of our model, for instance, it is the amount of calendar time between time t and time $t - 1$, or between $t + 1$ and t. The unit period used in this analysis is defined as the time which elapses between a spending impulse and the ensuing change in output or income. Thus our simple production rule, as expressed in equations (2a.6) or (3a.6) above, states that after a spending shift of any kind occurs, one analytic period passes before output is affected. The question is, what are the determinants of the calendar length of this period?

The most important factors include (1) the length of time required for sellers

Table 9: The Speed of the Multiplier for Various Combinations of the Marginal Propensity to Consume out of Disposable Income (c) and the Marginal Propensity to Collect Taxes Out of Total Income (x), Based on Model IIA†

	1	2	3	4	5
					Number of Periods Needed to
			Value of	Percent of Total	Achieve at
	Marginal		Truncated	Income Change	Least 90%
	Propensity	Static	Multiplier	Achieved by End	of Total
	to Collect	Multiplier	at End of	of Fifth Period	Income
	Taxes Out of Income (x)	Value	Fifth Period‡	(3) ÷ (2) × 100	Change§
c = .9					
	.2	3.57	2.61	73.1%	9
	.3	2.70	2.27	84.1	6
	.4	2.17	1.99	91.7	5
c = .8					
	.2	2.78	2.31	83.1	7
	.3	2.27	2.05	90.3	5
	.4	1.92	1.82	94.7	5
c = .7					
	.2	2.27	2.05	90.3	5
	.3	1.96	1.85	94.4	5
	.4	1.72	1.67	97.1	4
c = .6					
	.2	1.92	1.82	94.8	5
	.3	1.72	1.67	97.1	4
	.4	1.56	1.53	98.3	4

† In this table, the speed of the multiplier is measured in terms only of the number of periods needed to achieve 90 percent of the total change in income, and the change in income achieved by the end of the fifth period. The period referred to is the period required to adjust production to sales.

‡ This value is computed from the formula

$$\frac{\Delta Y}{\Delta G^*} = \frac{1}{1 - c(1-x)} \{1 - [c(1-x)]^{t-1}\}$$

when $t = 5$. This is the general expression for the truncated multiplier for model IIA.

§ This value is calculated through the use of an expression for the ratio $\frac{\Delta Y_t}{\Delta Y}$, which can be found from the general expressions for the truncated multiplier and the static multiplier given on p. 32 (assuming $v = 0$) as follows:

$$\frac{\Delta Y_t}{\Delta Y} = \frac{\Delta Y_t/\Delta G^*}{\Delta Y/\Delta G^*} = \frac{\{1 - [c(1-x)]^{t-1}\}/[1 - c(1-x)]}{1/[1 - c(1-x)]}.$$
$$= 1 - [c(1-x)]^{t-1}.$$

To find the number of periods needed to achieve 90 percent of the total change in income, set $\frac{\Delta Y_t}{\Delta Y}$ equal to 0.9 and solve for t:

$$0.9 = 1 - [c(1-x)]^{t-1}.$$

so

$$[c(1-x)]^{t-1} = 0.1.$$

Using logarithms, we have $(t-1)\log[c(1-x)] = \log 0.1;$

$$t \log[c(1-x)] = \log 0.1 + \log[c(1-x)]$$

and

$$t = \frac{\log 0.1 + \log[c(1-x)]}{\log[c(1-x)]}.$$

to perceive that sales have changed significantly and consequently to decide to place new orders; (2) the time needed to prepare and transmit orders; and (3) the time required to change the rate of production in response to a change in the order rate. These factors, in turn, are affected by further considerations such as the sizes of the stocks of sellers' finished-goods inventories and producers' raw-materials inventories, the availability of labor and of machine capacity, and so on.[19] Thus, the multiplier time period is best viewed as a composite of these individual lags.

There has been little or no significant empirical research on the length of the multiplier time period, but it may be possible to indicate at least in a crude way the probable dimensions of the speed of the multiplier. It does not seem unreasonable to assume that the factors mentioned above result in a unit multiplier period of one quarter of a year. If we take the marginal propensity to consume (c) to be 90 percent and the marginal propensity to pay taxes (x) to be 40 percent, values which are fairly realistic, the static multiplier is 2.17, and the multiplier applicable after five periods, or 15 months, is 1.99. Thus, according to this estimate, a sustained increase of $10 billion in the annual rate of government purchases should raise GNP, expressed at annual rates, by about $20 billion after five quarters or 15 months.

Attention should perhaps be called explicitly to four important assumptions underlying this discussion. First, as we have already pointed out, no allowance is made in the model used to analyze the speed of the multiplier for the restraining effect of the monetary sector. We have assumed that this effect is inoperative; that is, we suppose that the real and monetary sectors of the model are unrelated, or, alternatively, that the Federal Reserve supplies enough bank reserves to enable the money supply to meet the rising demand for money associated with increasing GNP without any increase in interest rates. If these assumptions are erroneous, the expansion will produce a "feedback" effect which will push up interest rates. This will reduce the size of the static multiplier, as we already know. Using the analysis on which Table 9 is based, we can also infer the effects on the speed of the multiplier of changes in the size of the various monetary sensitivities. The larger the interest sensitivities of the demand for money and the supply of money, the larger the static multiplier but the slower the multiplier process (in the sense represented by the calculations in Table 9). In other words, increases in m and j have the same effect on multiplier speed as increases in c. On the other hand, increases in the interest sensitivity of investment, v, or in the income sensitivity of the demand for money, k, have similar effects on the speed of the multiplier. The larger is either of these, the smaller the static multiplier value, but the more rapid the multiplier process.

The second assumption we have made is that there are sufficient unutilized resources to enable the expansion to take place without any appreciable effect on the price level. This assumption was emphasized earlier, in our comparison of Neoclassical and Keynesian views on monetary and fiscal policy, but it deserves repeating here. The situation will be different if the economy is operating close to full employment so that an increase in government spending will have its main effect on prices and only a moderate impact on output and employment. Third, no allowance is made for the possibility—indeed, probability—that businessmen will attempt to maintain or build up their inventories in the course of the expansion. If this were allowed for, it would undoubtedly raise the multipliers somewhat above the levels indicated.[20] Fourth, no consideration is

---

[19] For a thorough discussion of the factors determining the multiplier time period, see Gardner Ackley, "The Multiplier Time Period: Money, Inventories, and Flexibility," *American Economic Review*, 61 (June 1951), pp. 350–68.

[20] Actually the introduction of inventory investment complicates the analysis considerably. Since in full equilibrium inventories would presumably have reached the level in relation to sales that businessmen desired, there would, under these conditions, be no further addi-

given—either in this example or elsewhere in our discussion—to the possibility that an expansion of the multiplier type may induce an increase in private investment. This is, however, a likely possibility because the expanded sales will increase business profits and because the expanded production will increase the extent of utilization of existing plant and equipment. If such an increase in investment does occur, it is likely to add another important dimension to the expansion—in effect, raising the multiplier well above the levels we have been discussing. However, we have not attempted to include this possibility because, while the response of consumption to income changes is reasonably predictable, the investment response is a good deal less dependable, less well understood, and more likely to depend in a major way on the circumstances in which the expansion occurs.[21]

Some quantitative estimates of the size of the multiplier can be obtained from econometric models of the U.S. economy. One such model has been constructed and progressively refined by the Research Seminar in Quantitative Economics at The University of Michigan. This model is quite detailed, containing several dozen behavioral equations; however, it is basically similar to Model II, having equations to describe the behavior of households, firms, and the government sector. The coefficients are estimated statistically on the basis of past behavior of the variables. Typical values for the government spending and tax multipliers yielded by this model, based on recent estimates of its coefficients, are as follows:[22]

	Increase of $1 Billion in:	
	Government Purchases of Goods and Services	Federal Income Tax Collections
Effect on GNP after one year.....................	$1.9 billion	−$1.0 billion

This model, like all such econometric models of the economy, is dynamic in nature: that is, a change in (say) government purchases will set off a sequence of adjustments. However, it is important to note that the time unit used in such models is not an analytical multiplier time period but is rather some arbitrary unit of calendar time, usually a quarter or a year. The reason for this, of course, is that empirical observations on the variables are not available for such an essentially unmeasurable and irregular period as the multiplier time

tions to inventories. For this reason, inventory investment would have no effect on the static equilibrium multiplier. However, it would greatly affect the time path of movement from one equilibrium position to another; indeed, inventory investment may introduce a self-generating cycle in economic activity. In any case it would increase the effective truncated multipliers for the early stages of the expansion. See Lloyd A. Metzler, "The Nature and Stability of Inventory Cycles," *Review of Economic Statistics*, vol. 23 (August 1941), pp. 113–29.

[21] For a discussion of the multiplier effects of tax reduction, including probable effects on investment, see the *Annual Report of the Council of Economic Advisers*, January 1963, pp. 45–51.

[22] A discussion of the basic principles underlying the derivation of models such as this is found in Daniel B. Suits, "Forecasting and Analysis with an Econometric Model," *American Economic Review*, vol. 52 (March 1962), pp. 104–32. The model from which the above multiplier values were obtained is discussed in Saul H. Hymans and Harold T. Shapiro, "The Structure and Properties of the Michigan Quarterly Econometric Model of the U.S. Economy," *International Economic Review*, vol. 15 (October 1974), pp. 632–53.

period. The model referred to above is based on quarterly observations on the variables, and the multipliers in the above table relate to the estimated effects in the first year.

(b) Lags Associated with Adjustments in Monetary and Fiscal Policy

In addition to the lags involved in the working of the multiplier discussed above, there are further lags related to adjustments in monetary and fiscal policy that need to be considered. These lags are presented schematically in the following diagram, which relates specifically to monetary policy.

The process is assumed to start with a change in the economic situation which calls for some adjustment in monetary policy. For example, there might be a slowdown in the expansion of GNP and a rise in unemployment which calls for a shift toward a more expansionary Federal Reserve policy. The time when this occurs is indicated by the caption "action needed," at the left-hand end of the time scale.

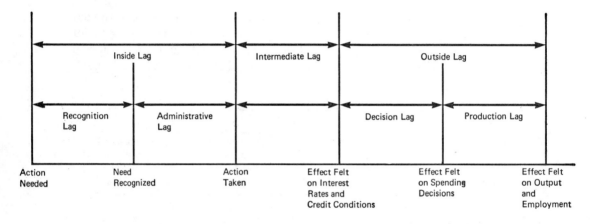

Three main elements in the lag in monetary policy adjustments can be distinguished:

1. The *inside lag.* This is the lag within the Federal Reserve System between the time action is needed and the time the action is actually taken. This lag can be broken into two subdivisions: (*a*) the *recognition lag* between the time action is needed and the time the need is recognized by the Federal Reserve authorities, and (*b*) the *administrative lag* between the time the need for action is recognized and the time the action (such as open market purchases of U.S. government securities) is actually taken. The length of the recognition lag presumably depends on the efficiency of the Federal Reserve in collecting and interpreting data relating to economic conditions. As a result of the organizational independence and flexibility of the Federal Reserve System, the administrative lag is presumably very short. These matters are discussed in several of the selections in Chapters 3 and 5.

2. The *intermediate lag.* This is the lag between the time the Federal Reserve takes action and the time the action produces a sufficient effect on interest rates (and other credit terms) to influence spending decisions significantly. The length of this lag depends on the behavior of commercial banks and other financial institutions and the functioning of financial markets—matters which are discussed in the selections in Chapters 2 and 5.

3. The *outside lag.* This is the lag between the change in interest rates (and credit conditions) and the initial impact on production and employment. This lag can be subdivided into two parts: (*a*) the *decision lag* between the change in interest rates and the change in spending decisions, and (*b*) the *production lag* between changes in spending decisions and the related initial changes in production and employment. It should be noted that the production lag referred to here is in principle the same lag between changes in sales and changes in production that formed the basis for our earlier discussion of the multiplier time period. However, in this case, we are not discussing the full cumulative multiplier effects but merely the "first round" effects of the change in policy. After the effects discussed here had occurred, the multiplier process would take over and produce further effects not here taken into account. The selection by Hamburger in Chapter 5 (reading 25) discusses the lags in monetary policy and summarizes some of the available empirical evidence on the combined lengths of the intermediate and outside lags. The effects of monetary policy impulses fall mainly on investment in new housing and other consumer durables and on business investment in plant, equipment, and inventories. Because of this multiplicity of channels and also because any given investment project may involve some time to plan, produce, and put in place, the total effect on output of a policy shift typically is distributed over a considerable period and most of the studies reviewed by Hamburger display such a "distributed lag" response. As the paper shows, there is some controversy concerning measurement of the lags in monetary policy, and the findings summarized should be taken as suggestive rather than in any sense conclusive.

For fiscal policy, the recognition lag is likely to be about the same as for monetary policy, since there is no reason to suppose that the economic intelligence apparatus of the authorities responsible for fiscal policy is either more or less efficient than that of the monetary authorities. However, the administrative lag for fiscal policy is likely to be much longer than that for monetary policy. This is especially true for tax adjustments, which ordinarily require a long (and uncertain) process of executive recommendation and legislative action. Changes in government expenditures may also require legislative action; however, even if all that is involved is a speedup of expenditures on projects that have already been approved by Congress, substantial time is likely to be needed to prepare plans and activate projects. All in all, the inside lag is likely to be much longer for fiscal than for monetary policy. On the other hand, the intermediate lag—which, in the case of fiscal policy, is the lag between the time when action is taken and the time when income or spending is affected—is likely to be much shorter for fiscal than for monetary policy. The decision lag also may be short—indeed, there is no such lag for changes in government purchases of goods and services. Since the production lag is in principle no different for fiscal than for monetary policy—although it may depend on the kind of expenditures that are involved—the outside lag is likely to be shorter for fiscal policy. To summarize:

Inside lag.........................longer for fiscal policy
Intermediate lag....................shorter for fiscal policy
Outside lag..........................shorter for fiscal policy

Because of the much greater length of the administrative component of the inside lag, the overall lag for fiscal policy may frequently be longer than for monetary policy. Note, however, that the long administrative lag is not inherent in fiscal policy, but is capable of being shortened greatly by changes in administrative arrangements. If this could be done—for example, by giving the President some authority to make countercyclical adjustments in tax rates, as is mentioned in Reading 18 (Chapter 4) by Blinder and Solow entitled "Lags and Uncertainties in Fiscal Policy"—fiscal policy might become more quick-acting than monetary policy. These authors also summarize the empirical evidence on the intermediate and outside lags of fiscal policy available from several econometric models, and they provide an interesting analysis of the effects of the income tax surcharge imposed in 1968.

1. THE INTEREST RATE, THE PRICE LEVEL, AND AGGREGATE OUTPUT

Robert S. Holbrook*

I. INTRODUCTION

Discussions of short-run income determination usually make use of the well-known *IS–LM* curve analysis,[1] in which real income and the rate of interest occupy the center of the stage. The price level, if it is allowed to vary at all, seldom appears explicitly, and does most of its work behind the scenes. In the typical presentation the price level is unaffected by variations in aggregate demand, so long as some arbitrary "full-employment" level is not exceeded. Once this full-employment level has been attained, however, further increases in demand result only in rising prices, without any increase in output. The price level is thus a sort of *deus ex machina* which is called upon when necessary, but does not play an active role throughout the analysis.

This paper uses a modified version of the usual technique and brings the price level directly into the analysis from the beginning. The

* Robert S. Holbrook is Professor of Economics, University of Michigan.

The author wishes to express his appreciation to Professors W. L. Smith, R. L. Teigen, and B. Munk, and to Harvey Rosen, for their suggestions and encouragement. The author regretfully accepts full responsibility for those errors and ambiguities which remain.

[1] This analysis was first developed by J. R. Hicks, in "Mr. Keynes and the 'Classics': A Suggested Interpretation," *Econometrica*, vol. 5 (April 1937), pp. 147–59. It is now very widely used as an expositional device in macroeconomic textbooks, e.g., M. J. Bailey, *National Income and the Price Level* (New York: McGraw-Hill, 1962), pp. 19–83; G. Ackley, *Macroeconomic Theory* (New York: Macmillan, 1961), pp. 369–87; and T. F. Dernburg and D. M. McDougall, *Macroeconomics* (New York: McGraw-Hill, 1968), pp. 161–75.

relationships between the price level and aggregate demand and supply will be illustrated through the derivation of aggregate demand and supply curves. These curves will then be used to examine the implications of several alternative assumptions about the nature of the underlying economic relationships.

Section II presents a quick review of the standard model of aggregate demand without a supply constraint and with fixed prices. Its purpose is primarily to familiarize the reader with the notation and techniques which are used later in the more complex analysis. In Section III the price level is permitted to vary, and an aggregate demand curve is derived. Sections IV and V introduce aggregate supply curves under the assumptions of flexible and rigid money wages, respectively, and examine the policy implications of these alternatives. Section VI concludes the body of the paper, and is followed by an appendix which presents an exact solution for some multipliers which are only described in Section V.

II. DEMAND WHEN PRICES ARE CONSTANT

Since the emphasis here is on the development of an expositional method, the model will be kept as simple as possible and almost all equations will be linear. It is assumed that the reader is familiar with the theory underlying the typical model of aggregate demand, and each equation will not be discussed in detail here. For such a discussion the reader is referred to any good macroeconomics text.[2]

[2] See, for example, those cited in note 1.

The initial version of the model assumes a fixed price level, and can be written as follows:

$$C = C_o + cY_d \qquad (1)$$
(consumption function)

$$I = I_o - vr \qquad (2)$$
(investment function)

$$Y_d = Y - T \qquad (3)$$
(definition of disposable income)

$$T = T^* + xY \qquad (4)$$
(tax function)

$$G = G^* \qquad (5)$$
(government expenditures)

$$Y = C + I + G \qquad (6)$$
(equilibrium condition)

$$M_d = s + kY - ur \qquad (7)$$
(demand for money)

$$M_s = M^* \qquad (8)$$
(supply of money)

$$M_s = M_d \qquad (9)$$
(equilibrium condition)

The symbols are defined as follows, all in real terms:

C = consumption expenditures
I = investment expenditures
Y_d = disposable income
Y = national income (or GNP)
T = taxes
G = government expenditures on goods and services
M_d = the amount of money demanded
M_s = the amount of money supplied
r = the rate of interest.

An asterisk beside a variable (i.e., M^*, T^*, and G^*) implies that it is a policy tool whose value is exogenously determined.[3] The first six equations can be solved for Y in terms of r to obtain the equation for the IS curve:

$$Y = \frac{C_o + I_o + G^* - cT^*}{1 - c(1-x)} - \frac{v}{1 - c(1-x)} r, \qquad (10)$$

while the solution to the final three equations yield the LM curve,

$$r = \frac{s - M^*}{u} + \frac{k}{u} Y. \qquad (11)$$

These curves are plotted in Figure 1. Their point of intersection (r', Y') simultaneously satisfies the equilibrium condition in each market, and thus

---

[3] To be perfectly correct, the coefficient of income in the tax function should also have an asterisk, since it is also policy-determined. This asterisk is omitted only to avoid unnecessary multiplication of symbols.

Figure 1

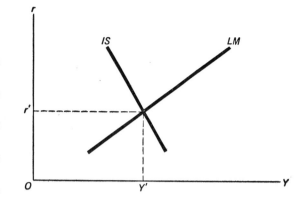

represents a solution for the entire system of nine equations.

These equilibrium values can also be obtained by substituting the value for r in (11) into (10). This yields

$$Y' = \frac{C_o + I_o + G^* - cT^* + \dfrac{v}{u}(M^* - s)}{1 - c(1 - x) + \dfrac{vk}{u}} \qquad (12)$$

and a value for r' could be obtained by substituting Y' from (12) in place of Y in (11).

Before introducing the price level explicitly, it is useful to examine the implications for this simple preliminary model of various restrictions on the equations. In this way the reader will become more familiar with the relationships between the equations and the diagrams and will gain facility in moving from one to the other. This facility will prove useful during discussions of the more complex versions of the model later in the paper. Let the interest elasticity of investment be zero, by setting v in (2) equal to zero. This implies that the second term on the right-hand side of (10) is zero, and Y no longer depends on the rate of interest. Given the value for Y, the quantity of money then determines the rate of interest (in [11]), but has no effect on aggregate demand. In this case, the IS curve in Figure 1 becomes vertical, and (12) reduces to

$$Y' = \frac{C_o + I_o + G^* - cT^*}{1 - c(1 - x)}.$$

Another possibility is that the demand for money is not responsive to the interest rate, i.e., that $u = 0$ in (7). Multiply both numerator and denominator of (12) by u before setting it equal to zero; the result is

$$Y' = \frac{M^* - s}{k} \qquad (13)$$

Table 1:   Income Multipliers under Alternative Assumptions (fixed prices)

Restrictions on the Model	$\dfrac{\Delta Y}{\Delta G^*}$	$\dfrac{\Delta Y}{\Delta M^*}$
A. None	$\dfrac{1}{1 - c(1 - x) + \dfrac{vk}{u}}$	$\dfrac{1}{\dfrac{u}{v}[1 - c(1 - x)] + k}$
B. Interest elasticity of investment = 0 ($v = 0$)	$\dfrac{1}{1 - c(1 - x)}$	0
C. Interest elasticity of demand for money = 0 ($u = 0$)	0	$\dfrac{1}{k}$
D. Liquidity trap ($r = r_0$)	$\dfrac{1}{1 - c(1 - x)}$	0

and Y is now determined by the money stock. The presence of s in the numerator of (13) allows for some desired minimum (or asset) balances which are unresponsive to the rate of interest. If s and u are both zero, (13) reduces to the pure quantity theory result. In either case, the LM curve in Figure 1 becomes vertical.

A third possibility is that the LM curve is horizontal, the liquidity trap situation. In this case (7), (8), and (9) can be replaced with the single equation,

$$r = r_{0}. \tag{14}$$

In this case, (10) determines Y', and the money stock plays no role.

A convenient way to characterize the results of these changes in the underlying assumptions is to examine the effect of each change on the various policy multipliers. Table 1 shows the multipliers for government expenditures and the money supply under the alternative assumptions just discussed. With the aid of the table, the policy implications of the assumptions should be quite clear. Fiscal policy (changes in G^* or T^*) has its greatest impact in cases B and D, while monetary policy is impotent. Precisely the opposite conclusion follows in case C.

Although s and u do not figure in the equation of the LM curve when it is horizontal, (14), it will be useful to examine what happens to them as the curve becomes more nearly horizontal. The typical curvilinear liquidity preference curve is shown in Figure 2 as GBH, where M_a is the asset demand for real money balances, as distinguished from the transactions demand (assumed to equal kY).[4] The line ABC is tangent to GBH at B, and serves as an approximation to

[4] For a discussion of the demand for money and its separation into asset and transactions demands, see, for example, Dernburg and McDougall, *Macroeconomics*, pp. 136–47.

Figure 2

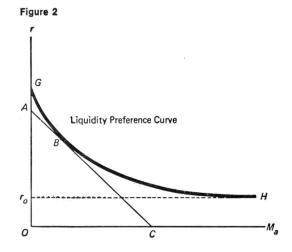

the true relationship between r and M_a in that neighborhood.

This tangent is the curve represented by the equation

$$M_a = s - ur. \tag{15}$$

Clearly, s is the value of M_a when r is zero, and is equal to the distance OC. Similarly, $-u$ is the reciprocal of the slope of the curve in the vicinity of B, and is equal to minus the ratio of OC to OA. As B moves farther to the right along the liquidity preference curve, OA becomes progressively smaller and OC larger, and both s and u become very large.[5]

Figure 3 depicts the values of s and u which

[5] As the curve approaches the horizontal, it can be shown that the ratio of s to u approaches r_0, and making this substitution in (12) while letting u become very large will result in a return to (10), with r_0 in place of r. The reader may already have noted that (15) is reversed from the normal "slope-intercept" form, as are many other equations in this paper and the economic literature, generally.

Figure 3

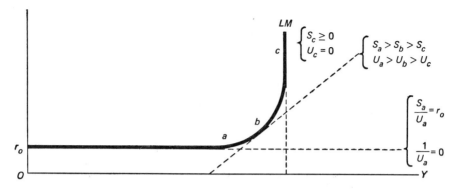

obtain for each of several segments of the *LM* curve, on the assumption that there is some minimum interest rate, r_o (which may be zero), and that the liquidity preference curve becomes progressively steeper at higher rates of interest. These relationships will be useful in the next section, where the slope of the *LM* curve becomes of crucial importance.

$$T = \frac{t^*}{p} + xY. \qquad (18)$$

After making the substitutions of (16) for (8) and (18) for (4), the *IS* and *LM* curves can again be obtained. The solution for the *LM* curve is presented in a slightly different format than before, for the sake of convenience in the discussion of Figure 5, below.

$$Y = \frac{C_o + I_o + G^*}{1 - c(1 - x)} - \frac{ct^*}{1 - c(1 - x)}\left(\frac{1}{p}\right) - \frac{v}{1 - c(1 - x)}r \quad (IS\ curve) \quad (19)$$

$$Y = \frac{m^*}{k}\left(\frac{1}{p}\right) - \frac{s}{k} + \frac{u}{k}r \qquad\qquad (LM\ curve) \quad (20)$$

III. DEMAND WHEN PRICES ARE VARIABLE

In this section a change in the price level is assumed to affect aggregate demand in two ways. The first is through an accompanying change in the real money stock. Let the monetary authorities control only the nominal stock of money and replace (8) with

$$M_s = \frac{m^*}{p}, \qquad (16)$$

where p is the price level.[6] The second effect of the price level is in the tax equation, (4). Assume that the tax law is written in nominal terms, such that nominal tax revenue is a certain number of dollars (t^*) plus a fixed fraction of nominal income. This can be written as

$$pT = t^* + xpY \qquad (17)$$

or

---

[6] "Nominal" refers to the "current dollar" or "money" value, as opposed to the "constant dollar" or "real" value. The nominal value of a variable can be deflated to its real value by dividing by the price level.

A change in the price level can be seen to affect the positions of the two curves, but not their slopes. A rise in the price level shifts the *LM* curve to the left and is equivalent to a reduction in M^* as described in Section II. The effect of a price change on the *IS* curve depends on the sign of t^*. Assume that the average tax rate, $\frac{T}{Y}$, increases with income, which implies that t^* must be negative (for a linear tax function).[7] On this assumption, the *IS* curve also moves to the left as prices rise, since tax revenue at a given real income level will be larger, with no offsetting expenditure increase.

These equations for the *IS* and *LM* curves can be combined as before to obtain solutions for Y and r, but this time they are each functions of the price level. The solution for Y is:

---

[7] The average tax rate is

$$\frac{T}{Y} = \frac{\frac{t^*}{p} + xY}{Y} = \frac{t^*}{pY} + x.$$

Since x and p are both positive, if T/Y is to be an increasing function of Y, t^* must be negative.

$$Y = \cfrac{C_o + I_o + G^* - \cfrac{vs}{u}}{1 - c(1-x) + \cfrac{vk}{u}}$$

$$+ \cfrac{\cfrac{vm^*}{u} - ct^*}{1 - c(1-x) + \cfrac{vk}{u}} \left(\frac{1}{p}\right). \quad (21)$$

Inspection of (21) reveals that it is a rectangular hyperbola, which approaches the Y axis as p approaches zero, as shown in Figure 4. As p becomes larger the second term on the right-hand side of (21) approaches zero, and Y becomes equal to the first term alone. This curve is seriously deficient, however, in that it is applicable only for a fixed pair of values for s and u. As the price level varies, the LM curve shifts; as it shifts, its slope at the intersection with the IS curve changes; and as its slope changes, the values of s and u are changing. The effect of these changes on the shape of the curve in Figure 4 must be examined before it will be possible to construct a curve which accurately reflects the effect on aggregate demand of a change in the price level.[8]

The procedure to be used is a combination of an analytical and graphical approach. Figure 5 shows a series of IS and LM curves drawn for different price levels and based on (19) and (20). So that these curves will be evenly spaced, the interval chosen (say J) is fixed in terms of the reciprocal of the price level

$$\left(\text{i.e., } \frac{1}{p_1} - \frac{1}{p_2} = \frac{1}{p_2} - \frac{1}{p_3} = \frac{1}{p_i} - \frac{1}{p_{i+1}} = J\right).$$

---

[8] It is likely that most, if not all, of the relationships described in (1) through (9) are really nonlinear, and a full exposition would have to examine the implications of all these nonlinearities. This paper is concerned primarily with the implications of a nonlinear liquidity preference curve, as it is this issue which tends to dominate elementary discussions of the determinants of aggregate demand.

The IS curve for a price level equal to p_i is shifted to the right of the IS curve for p_{i+1} by an amount equal to $\dfrac{Jct^*}{1 - c(1-x)}$. Similarly, the LM curve for price level p_i is shifted to the right of the LM curve for p_{i+1} by an amount equal to $\dfrac{Jm^*}{k}$.[9]

It is useful to examine the nature of the solution in the two limiting cases for the LM curve. When the LM curve is vertical (s and u both equal to zero), (21) can be reduced to[10]

$$Y = \frac{m^*}{k}\left(\frac{1}{p}\right). \quad (22)$$

For any price level above p_9, (22) describes the relation between output and the price level, and this is illustrated in Figure 6 by the hyperbola ABE (only the solid portion AB above p_9 is operative).[11]

At the other extreme, when the LM curve is horizontal at r_o, (21) becomes

$$Y = \frac{C_o + I_o + G^* - vr'}{1 - c(1-x)}$$

$$- \frac{ct^*}{1 - c(1-x)}\left(\frac{1}{p}\right). \quad (23)$$

This is another hyperbola, with its vertical asymptote offset to the right from the p axis by an amount equal to the first term. The important question which must be answered is whether this hyperbola is above or below ABE when the price level is such that the economy is the liquidity trap. Figure 5 shows that the level of income actually realized when the economy first reaches the liquidity trap (Y_2) is considerably less than that which would have occurred if the LM curve had been vertical throughout.[12] Thus, the hyper-

---

[9] The diagram is based on the assumption that

$$\frac{m_o}{k} > \frac{-ct^*}{1 - c(1-x)}.$$

It seems reasonable to suppose that this would be true for an actual economy, but the reader may be interested in examining the implications of the alternative assumption.

[10] This solution can be obtained by multiplying both the numerator and denominator by u, before setting u equal to zero.

[11] The curves in Figure 6 are not drawn to the same scale as those in Figure 5, but are exaggerated in the interest of clarity.

[12] The relevant curve at this point is LM_{p2}. The argument is essentially that LM_{p2} becomes vertical at some point considerably to the right of Y_2. Thus, if the LM curves did not slope down and to the left, but were entirely vertical (as assumed in deriving ABE), the level of income would be greater than Y_2 when the price level was p_2.

Figure 4

Figure 5

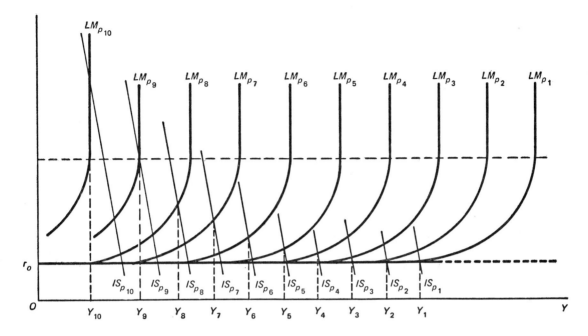

bola generated by (23) will be below the one generated by (22) at any price level below that at which we enter the liquidity trap region of the LM curve.[13] This hyperbola is drawn in Figure 6 as FCD, and the relevant portion is the segment labeled CD.

The two segments AB and CD have been constructed, and the only problem which remains is

to construct the missing link (BC). This intermediate segment is composed of a continuous series of points, each of which lies on a hyperbola whose equation (21) depends on the values of u and s at that point. It is possible to work through the problem analytically, but the solution is more easily obtained through another examination of Figure 5.

Start at the right end of Figure 5, in the liquidity trap situation, and let prices rise. The IS and LM curves shift to the left, the interest rate begins to rise, and income will be less than

[13] This will actually be true for somewhat higher price levels as well, and the point of intersection could easily be calculated.

Figure 6

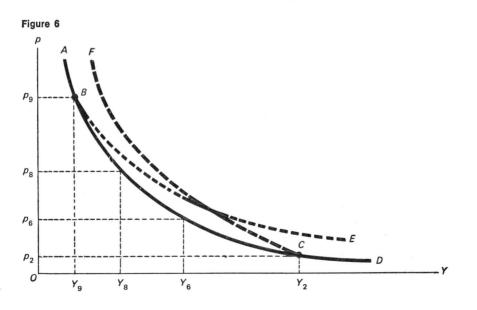

it would have been had the interest rate remained at r_o.[14] Thus, as the price level rises, the economy traces out a path below and to the left of FCD.

Now start at the left end of Figure 5, where the intersection is in the vertical portion of the LM curve, and let prices fall. The IS and LM curves move to the right, the interest rate begins to fall, but the asset demand for money becomes greater than zero and prevents the rate from falling as far as it would in the absence of such an asset demand.[15] Thus, again, income will be less than it would have been had the LM curve remained vertical, and the economy traces out a path below and to the left of ABE as prices fall below p_9. Eventually these paths meet, completing the segment BC which lies to the left of the two curves generated earlier. The entire curve ABCD will be called the "aggregate demand curve."[16]

It is useful to examine the effects of fiscal and monetary policy on the aggregate demand curve just derived. An increase in government expenditure shifts the IS curve to the right by an amount determined by the multiplier, and it could be expected that the aggregate demand curve will

respond in a similar fashion. By examining (21) and (23), it can be seen that a larger value for G^* will indeed result in a larger value for Y (given a value for the price level). Above point B, however, where (22) is the controlling equation (and the LM curve in Figure 5 is vertical) a change in G^* has no impact on demand (which is determined entirely by the real money stock). The result is a shift only in the BCD portion of the curve, as illustrated in part A of Figure 7.

The effect of an increase in the nominal money stock (m^*) with a fixed price level is to shift the LM curve to the right. Equations (21) and (22) imply that the ABC segment of the demand curve is also shifted to the right. In the liquidity trap case, however, when (23) holds, the nominal money stock is of no consequence. Thus the CD segment is unaffected by monetary policy, as is shown in part B of Figure 7. It seems highly probable that the economy is normally operating in the range BC of the aggregate demand curve —the range within which the interest elasticity of demand for money is neither zero nor infinitely large and both fiscal and monetary policy are therefore effective.

It is of no value to compute multipliers at this stage, because if the price level is assumed to be constant, the result is the same as that presented earlier in Table 1. But there is as yet no way to predict how the price level will react to policy changes, since the aggregate demand curve only provides us with a set of equally acceptable combinations of price and income. These pairs of values all satisfy the set of equations which are summarized in (21), when s and u are allowed to vary in accordance with the assumed curvature of the LM curve. By itself, however, the aggregate demand curve does not convey any information about the particular level of income at which the economy will achieve equilibrium.

---

[14] Figure 5 shows that when the price level rises from p_2 to p_3 the LM curve shifts far enough to the left so that the IS curve (which also shifts to the left) intersects it at an interest rate higher than r_o. If the LM curve had not begun to slope upward, the IS curve would have intersected it at r_o, and income would have been slightly larger than Y_3.

[15] For example, when the price level falls from p_9 to p_8, both curves shift to the right, but their intersection is to the left of the vertical portion of LM_{p8}.

[16] There are several macroeconomic texts which make use of versions of this aggregate demand curve in a somewhat different fashion from that used here [e.g., K. C. Kogiku, *An Introduction to Macroeconomic Models* (New York: McGraw-Hill, 1968), and J. Lindauer, *Macroeconomics* (New York: John Wiley, 1968)].

Figure 7

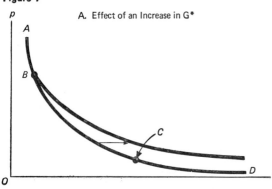

A. Effect of an Increase in G^*

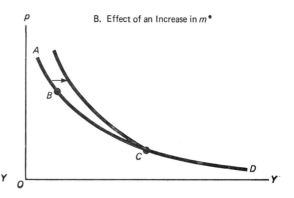

B. Effect of an Increase in m^*

IV. DEMAND AND SUPPLY WHEN WAGES ARE FLEXIBLE

The "aggregate supply curve" provides a second relationship between output (i.e., income) and the price level, and can be combined with the aggregate demand curve to establish a single pair of values which will satisfy both relationships simultaneously. Let the capital stock be fixed, while labor, the only variable factor of production, is subject to diminishing returns and is paid the value of its marginal product. This latter assumption insures that the demand function for labor is equal to the slope (or the first derivative) of the production function. These assumptions can be represented by the following two equations:

$$Y = eN - \tfrac{1}{2}fN^2$$

(production function)   (24)

$$\frac{w}{p} = e - fN_d; \text{ or } N_d = \frac{e}{f} - \frac{1}{f}\left(\frac{w}{p}\right)$$

(demand for labor)   (25)

The new variables introduced here are N, the number of workers employed; N_d, the number of workers demanded (assumed to be equal to N); and w, the money wage. These curves are depicted in Figure 8 where the real wage which employers are willing to pay (w/p) at a given level of employment is equal to the slope of the production function at that level of employment.

The more interesting element of the labor market (at least in Keynesian income theory) is the supply function; this paper examines the implications of two assumptions about the nature of the supply of labor. One assumption, typically associated with the classical model, is that the supply of labor is an increasing function of the real wage.[17] This assumption is sometimes characterized as one of "flexible wages," since wages are assumed to rise or fall as necessary to bring about an equilibrium in the labor market. The labor supply function for this case is:

$$N_s = g + h\frac{w}{p} \quad \text{(flexible wages)}. \quad (26)$$

and the equilibrium condition is represented by:

$$N_d = N_s \quad \text{(equilibrium condition)}. \quad (27)$$

The more interesting assumption about the supply of labor is that workers will supply any amount of labor demanded up to some limit at

---

[17] Most of the analysis does not require that it be an increasing function; it could be vertical or even "backward bending" so long as it is steeper than the labor demand curve at their intersection.

Figure 8

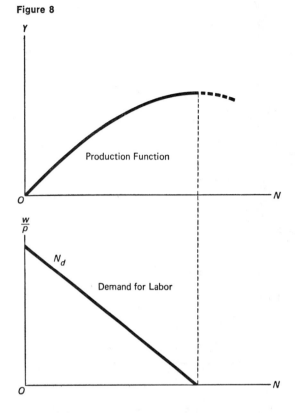

the existing money wage, but will not offer any labor at a lower money wage. This situation will be characterized as one in which "money wages are rigid downward." This section presents the case of flexible wages and derives an aggregate supply curve under that assumption, leaving the rigid wage case to Section V.

By substituting (25) and (26) into (27), an equilibrium value of the real wage, $\left(\dfrac{w}{p}\right)$, can be obtained. In a similar fashion one can solve for equilibrium quantities of labor employed (N'), and of output (Y'). These relationships are shown graphically in Figure 9.[18]

Figure 10 depicts the aggregate supply curve for the case of flexible wages superimposed on the aggregate demand curve derived earlier. The supply curve is simply a vertical line at $Y = Y'$, since in this case output is entirely determined in Figure 9, and is independent of the price level. The intersection of the demand and supply

---

[18] It is possible to solve explicitly for these equilibrium values, but they are merely complicated functions of the coefficients of the model. The only interesting fact is that the equilibrium level of output is fixed so that the supply curve is vertical.

Figure 9

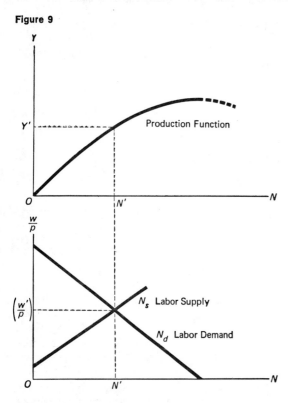

Figure 10

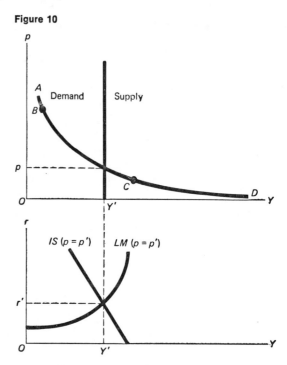

curves determines the price level (p'), and given the price level, one can solve for the rate of interest (r'). Either the IS curve (19) or the LM curve (20) can be used for this purpose, since the method of constructing the demand curve from which the price level was determined will insure that the IS and LM curves intersect at r' and Y'.

One clear implication of Figure 10 is that neither fiscal nor monetary policy can have any impact on output, and the multipliers of the sort illustrated in Table 1 are all zero. The effects of policy on the price level can be examined, however, with the aid of the earlier results and Figure 10.

Figure 7 showed that an increase in government expenditures will shift the aggregate demand curve to the right so long as the demand for money has an interest elasticity different from zero at that point. Thus, if the supply curve intersects the demand curve below B, expansionary fiscal policy will raise the price level, but if the intersection is above B there will be no effect on prices.[19]

An increase in the money supply will raise prices if the intersection is to the left of point C on the aggregate demand curve (i.e., if it is not in the liquidity trap region), and will have no effect if it is to the right of C. The rise in the price level will shift the IS curve to the left somewhat, and the new equilibrium will be reached with a slightly lower interest rate than before. It should be noted that the assumptions of this model give monetary policy a role in the determination of the rate of interest even in the case where prices and wages are flexible. The source of this influence is the nominal tax function; if taxes were fixed in real terms (or were zero) the IS curve would be unaffected by price changes and would fix the interest rate once the level of output was determined.[20] On the assumptions of this paper, the rate of interest is neither a strictly real nor a strictly monetary phenomenon but is determined jointly by both real and monetary forces.[21]

---

the rise in prices. This price rise increases tax revenue (through the nominal tax function), and both consumption and investment are reduced.

[20] It is the independence of the IS curve from monetary influences that frees the interest rate from monetary influences; the interest elasticity of the demand for money (so long as it is not zero) has no effect on this result.

[21] W. L. Smith ["A Graphical Exposition of the Complete Keynesian System," *Southern Economic Journal*, vol. 23 (October 1956), pp. 115–25] has

---

[19] Above point B the entire adjustment is made through a shift in the IS curve which raises the interest rate so as to reduce investment by precisely the amount of the increase in government spending. Below B, however, the LM curve also shifts, due to

Freeing the IS curve from monetary influence also yields the pure quantity theory result that changes in the money supply will bring about proportional changes in the price level. A simple means of observing this is to let t° be zero in (21), and fix Y at its full-employment level. Clearly, to maintain the resulting relationship,

arises when the demand for labor falls short of the maximum amount supplied. In that case it is assumed that the money wage (w) does not fall, although workers who are willing to work at the current money wage (w_o) cannot find employment. Equation (28) characterizes these relationships explicitly.

$$\begin{cases} \text{A.} \quad w = w_o \ \ \text{if} \ \ \left[\frac{e}{f} - \frac{1}{f}\left(\frac{w_o}{p}\right)\right] < \left[g + h\left(\frac{w_o}{p}\right)\right] \\ \text{B.} \quad N_s = g + h\left(\frac{w}{p}\right) \text{otherwise} \end{cases} \quad \begin{array}{c} \text{(money wages} \\ \text{rigid downward)} \end{array} \quad (28)$$

changes in m° would have to be accompanied by equal proportional changes in p. If t° is less than zero, the required change in p is somewhat less than proportional to the change in m°, since part of the effect is reflected in a change in r.

There are a number of other questions which could be explored with the use of the model as thus far presented, but the really interesting problems arise when wages are not flexible downward, and these are examined in the next section.

V. DEMAND AND SUPPLY WHEN WAGES ARE RIGID

In this section the initial assumptions about the demand for labor as expressed in (25) are retained, but the assumption about the supply of labor is modified. Assume that the maximum quantity of labor which will be supplied is an increasing function of the real wage, and that when demand exceeds the maximum supplied at a given real wage, real wages must be raised in order to obtain more labor. This is all entirely comparable to the case of flexible wages discussed in the previous section. The distinction

Case A holds if there is unemployed labor (supply exceeds demand), while case B holds if demand is equal to or greater than supply.

These assumptions are depicted graphically in Figure 11. Part B relates the real wage to the price level, given that the money wage is fixed at $w = w_o$,[22] while the curve labelled N_d in part A is the labor demand curve as before, and the dotted curve N_s indicates the maximum amount of labor which will be supplied at each real wage. If the price level is p_f, the level of employment would be OD, and this will be termed "full employment," since everyone who wants to work at that real wage is employed. If the price level were to fall to p_1, however, this would raise the real wage to $\dfrac{w_o}{p_1}$, and only OC labor would be demanded, while amount supplied would rise to OE.[23] The crucial assumption here is that the existence of unemployed labor will not affect the money wage (in particular it will not lower it), so that unless the labor demand curve can be shifted or the price level lowered, there is no way to bring about full employment. The situation when the price level is p_1 is often called an underemployment equilibrium since, despite the existence of excess supply in the labor market, there are no apparent forces generated by this excess supply which would tend to eliminate it.

demonstrated the same result by assuming a "real balance" or "Pigou" effect on consumption. It is argued that as the price level falls, the value of consumers' cash balances (and certain other assets) will rise, resulting in an increase in their wealth. This is assumed to have an expansionary effect on consumption expenditures, and the net effect is essentially equivalent to the one obtained in this paper through the use of the nominal tax function. For an exhaustive discussion of the Pigou effect and its ramifications, see D. Patinkin, "Price Flexibility and Full Employment," *American Economic Review*, vol. 37 (September 1948), pp. 543–64, reprinted with slight modifications in F. A. Lutz and L. W. Mints, eds., *Readings in Monetary Theory* (Homewood, Ill.: Richard D. Irwin, Inc., 1951), pp. 252–83.

[22] The equation of this curve $(w/p)\ (p) = w_o$, is that of a rectangular hyperbola.

[23] A vertical labor supply curve could be used here, which would reduce the excess supply at the lower price level, but would not eliminate it. It could also be assumed that labor supply will respond to higher money wages irrespective of the price level. This latter assumption is much more difficult to justify than the one in the text, however. Given the nature of wage contracts and the usual inability of the unemployed worker to bargain for a lower wage, the assumption used here is probably the most reasonable at this level of abstraction.

Figure 11

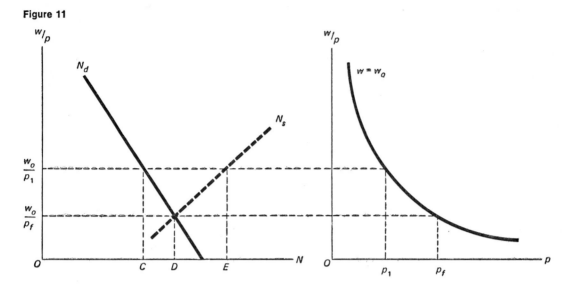

The effect of this assumption about the nature of the labor market on the shape of the aggregate supply curve can now be examined. Even under the new assumptions in (28), if the excess supply of labor is zero or negative, the classical results hold as in (26). Therefore at any price level above p_f the supply curve will be vertical as before. The new assumption only affects its shape below p_f, and that part of the curve will be examined more closely.

Substitute w_o for w in (25), solve for N and substitute that value into (24), to obtain

$$Y = \frac{1}{2f}\left[e^2 - \left(\frac{w_o}{p}\right)^2\right]. \qquad (29)$$

This is an increasing function of the price level (p), with a positive intercept on the vertical axis and a vertical asymptote at $Y = \frac{e^2}{2f}$. The upward sloping part of the aggregate supply curve in Figure 12 corresponds to the situation when output is less than the full-employment level, and the vertical portion, described in the preceding paragraph, corresponds to the situation when the

Figure 12

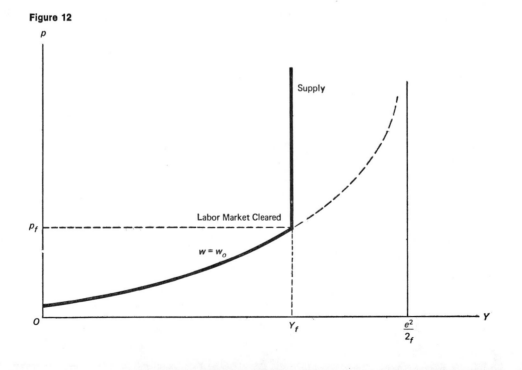

Figure 13

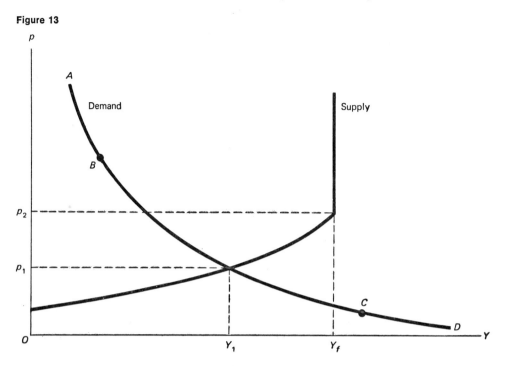

economy is at full employment. If demand is below Y_f, the sloping part of the curve is operative, but if demand equals Y_f it is the vertical part of the curve which is operative.[24]

---

[24] A simplification which is frequently made is to assume that the marginal product of labor is constant until capacity output is reached, at which point marginal productivity falls to zero or below. In this case, the labor demand curve is horizontal at less than capacity output, so that the real wage is fixed at that level, as shown in Figure A, below. If money wages are flexible, the shape of the labor demand curve has no effect on the aggregate supply curve, which will be vertical, as before. If money wages are rigid downward, however, both nominal and real wages are fixed, implying that the price level is also fully determined. The aggregate supply curve will thus be horizontal at that price level to the left of full-employment output and vertical at full-employment output, with a right angle at the junction, as in Figure B. In this case, monetary and fiscal policy can be used to move the economy to full employment output (Y_f) without any effect on the price level, while once full employment has been reached, no further expansion of output is possible, and any increase in demand results only in a rise in prices. Under the as-

An aggregate demand curve can now be superimposed on the new aggregate supply curve, to obtain a final solution for equilibrium price level and output, as in Figure 13. If $ABCD$ is the current demand curve then Y_1 is current output and p_1 the current price level. Either fiscal or monetary policy can be used to move the economy to full employment, Y_f, but either will be accompanied by a rise in the price level to p_2.

In the appendix the analytic solution is obtained, together with the multipliers for the several alternative cases. The advantage of the device illustrated in Figure 13, however, is that once it has been constructed, the answers to many theoretical questions as well as the results of most policy changes can be derived merely from observation, without working through the algebra and/or calculus necessary to produce an

---

sumptions in this paper, each increment in output comes at a higher and higher cost in terms of rising prices, and as demand expands the economy moves gradually from output expansion to price inflation.

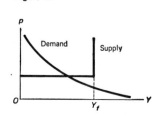

Figure A

Figure B

exact answer. An examination of some of these topics follows.

There is some confusion about the nature of the crucial assumption in a Keynesian model which leads to the possibility of an equilibrium at less than full employment. In particular, the question is raised as to whether it is the rigidity of money wages or the interest elasticity of the demand for money (or perhaps the liquidity trap) which makes this possible. In the version of the model used here, the culprit is clearly the behavior of labor supply, since the aggregate demand curve shows that demand can be increased without limit by a falling price level. As should be very evident by now, it is the assumption about the nominal tax function which insures this result. If this assumption had not been made, falling prices would not have had an impact on the IS curve, demand would have been at a maximum when the interest rate was at its minimum (liquidity trap) level, and further price declines would have had no impact on demand.[25] If the maximum level of aggregate demand were less than full-employment output and prices and wages were flexible, the economy would not achieve full employment, but neither would it achieve an equilibrium, since wages and prices would fall without limit, responding to the excess supply in the labor market. Thus, even when the position of the IS curve is unaffected by changes in the price level, the achievement of an unemployment *equilibrium* depends ultimately on the downward rigidity of wages.

Return now to the practical problem of monetary and fiscal policies designed to bring about full employment in the face of rigid wages. The effect of fiscal policy on the aggregate demand curve differs according to whether the economy is above or below point B in Figure 13, where points A, B, C, and D have the same meaning as in Figure 10. Thus if the supply curve intersects the demand curve in the AB region, fiscal policy will affect the level of investment through changes in the interest rate but will have no impact on aggregate output. Monetary policy would have to be used to move the economy toward

full employment in that case, and it would accomplish this by increasing the money available for transactions purposes, lowering the interest rate, and increasing investment and consumption. As output rises, however, prices also rise, which will act to reduce the real money stock and to increase taxes, and damp the expansion somewhat below what it would have been had prices been stable.

At the other extreme, if the supply curve intersects the demand curve in the CD region, monetary policy will have no impact, and only fiscal policy can be effective. Fiscal policy can increase the level of aggregate demand through the multiplier mechanism, but again the rising price level will act to increase tax revenue and keep the expansion below what it would have been if prices had remained constant.

If the curves intersect in the BC range of the demand curve, both fiscal and monetary policy can be effective in moving the economy toward full employment. In either case, however, the rising supply curve (reflecting the diminishing marginal product of labor) will cause the increase in output to be accompanied by an increase in the price level, and the expansive impact of either policy is somewhat dampened.

The rising price level which accompanies the rightward shift of the demand curve along the upward-sloping supply curve naturally brings to mind the problem of inflation. Within this framework, a price rise could be defined as resulting from "demand pull" if it is the result of a shift in the demand curve, and "cost push" if it is the result of a shift in the supply curve. A cost-push situation could arise, for example, as the result of an increase in the money wage to a higher level. This will not affect the vertical portion of the supply curve, but the sloping part will shift upward. Such cost-push inflation would be accompanied by a decline in total output and employment unless the demand curve were simultaneously shifted to the right through monetary or fiscal policy.

In this model, increasing output results in rising prices, but the process stops once the new equilibrium is reached. Inflation is usually defined as a continuing rise in the price level, however, and this would require a continuous movement in one curve or the other. One way in which continuing price increases could occur in this model would be if the policy makers are unwilling (or politically unable) to allow unemployment to rise above a certain level, U_1, while labor forces are strong enough to gain

---

[25] In the absence of the tax effect, other mechanisms could have been assumed through which falling prices would act to shift the IS curve to the right. The Pigou effect is one such mechanism, and another would be some sort of money illusion. The nominal tax function has been relied upon here because it seems most realistic and is not subject to the many objections which are raised regarding the validity of the alternate mechanisms.

Figure 14

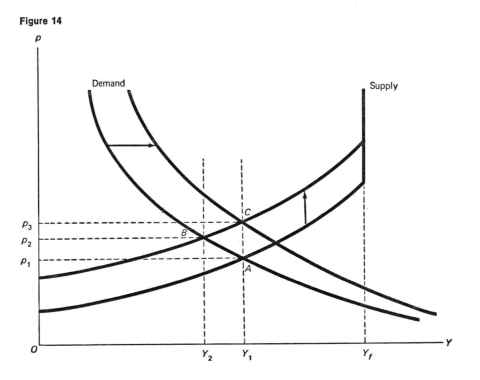

money wage increases as long as unemployment stays below U_2, and U_2 is above U_1. This can be represented in terms of aggregate demand and supply curves if the unemployment rates are translated into corresponding output levels, Y_1 and Y_2. The result is shown in Figure 14, where it is assumed that fiscal or monetary policy will be used in order to maintain demand at a level no lower than Y_1, while money wage increases will be sought and obtained as long as output is above Y_2. From an initial position at point A, wages increase, the supply curve rises, and the economy moves toward point B. This is politically untenable, by assumption, and the demand curve is shifted to the right toward point C. The process can continue indefinitely as long as Y_1 is to the right of Y_2, and the result is continuing inflation.[26]

The model assumes that price changes caused by shifts in the aggregate demand curve are reversible so long as the two curves intersect in the sloping portion of the supply curve (i.e., if the demand curve shifts and then returns to its former position the price level will also return to its former level). If the demand curve shifts so far to the right that it intersects the vertical part of the supply curve, however, the price level will no longer return to its earlier position as demand subsides. Travel upward along the vertical part of the supply curve implies that money wages are being bid up, so when demand begins to decline and the money wage remains at its new level, the economy moves to the left along a new sloping supply curve corresponding to the highest level of money wages attained. This process is illustrated in Figure 15, where it is assumed that the demand curve is initially at D_1 and then shifts to D_2. Output rises from Y_1 to Y_2, while the price level rises to p_2. Once full employment is reached at $w = w_1$, money wages are bid up to w_2. When demand subsequently falls back to D_1, money wages remain at w_2, and the new equilibrium level of income and prices is Y_3 and p_3 respectively, rather than Y_1 and p_1.[27]

---

[26] The inflation in this case is seen as resulting in part from market power on the supply side of the labor market. This is the only type of market power built into the system, since output is viewed as being produced under purely competitive conditions. If monopolistic elements in industry had been included, the cost-push forces could have arisen through administered price increases just as well as through wage increases.

---

[27] It is assumed in this discussion that money wages do not rise until absolutely full employment is reached. This could be modified by letting money wages begin to rise before the economy reaches full employment (due to bottlenecks, improvements in the bargaining position of unions, etc.). Depending on the precise nature of these alternative assumptions,

Figure 15

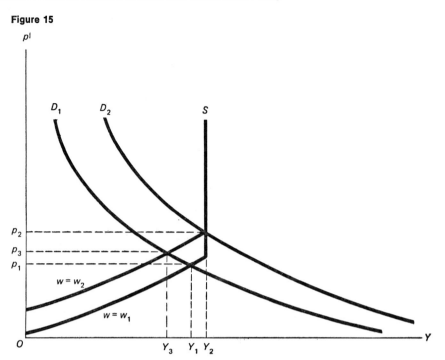

One final use to which this structure will be put is to examine the implication of an escalator clause in the wage contract for all workers. Taking the extreme case, suppose that all workers have their money wage tied directly to the price index, so that the real wage is fixed, rather than the money wage. This fixed real wage dictates a certain level of employment and output, and the supply curve becomes vertical at that output level. This level could, by chance, coincide with full employment, but it may also fall short. Any attempt to increase output by increasing demand will result in increasing prices and wages but no change in output. If, through bargaining, by law, or some other device one or more groups in this economy are able to raise their money wage relative to the price level, the supply curve will shift to the left, output will fall and prices will rise. This assumes that these higher wages, once achieved, are again protected by an escalator clause. The only means of raising output under such a system (besides lowering the real wage) is to raise the marginal product of labor by changing the nature of the production function. Neither fiscal nor monetary policy is effective, since the problem lies solely on the supply side.

---

the supply curve may become much steeper as it approaches full-employment output, or may even shift upward continuously, requiring a constantly *increasing* level of demand (and *rising* prices) to maintain a given *level* of output and employment.

VI. CONCLUSION

This paper has developed a framework for the analysis of a complete Keynesian (or classical) model which can provide immediate answers to most questions about the effect on the system of various policy decisions or of changes in the underlying assumptions. Several problems of analysis have been examined, and this framework has been used in their solution. Other problems could have been analyzed, including those of growth and technological change and the implications of price and wage controls, but these have been left for the interested reader.

The model used here is an extremely elementary one, utilizing the simplest equations throughout, and including only the minimum of complications. Other assumptions could be introduced in the area of business saving, imports, an interest-elastic money supply, etc. One area in particular which could benefit from more elaboration is investment. Such additions or modifications, however, would in most cases have little impact on the general shape of the aggregate demand and supply curves that have been developed here. Introduction of major new nonlinearities could change the character of the curves somewhat, but again, their general shape and behavior would still be unlikely to be greatly affected.

It cannot be overemphasized, however, that this paper has only described a device which may make it easier for the student to come to grips with many problems in macroeconomic analysis. The ability to make successful use of this device requires an understanding of the basic model which lies hidden beneath the supply and demand curves and depends ultimately on an understanding of the behavior of individuals, firms, and governments as they react to various economic stimuli.

$$\frac{dY}{dG^*} = \frac{1 + \left(\frac{vm^*}{u} - ct^*\right)\left(\frac{1}{w_o}\right)(e^2 - 2fY)^{-1/2}(-2fY)\left(\frac{1}{2}\right)\left(\frac{dY}{dG^*}\right)}{1 - c(1 - x) + \frac{vk}{u}}$$

$$= \frac{1}{\left[1 - c(1 - x) + \frac{vk}{u}\right] + \frac{f\left(\frac{vm^*}{u} - ct^*\right)}{w_o(e^2 - 2fY)^{1/2}}} \tag{A.3}$$

APPENDIX

Derivation of Multipliers in the Complete System for the Case of Fixed Money Wages

The equations needed are reproduced below. Equation (21) is the demand curve, while (29)

is the equation of that part of the supply curve which is relevant when the economy is at less than full employment.

$$Y = \frac{C_o + I_o + G^* - \frac{vs}{u}}{1 - c(1 - x) + \frac{vk}{u}}$$

$$+ \frac{\frac{vm^*}{u} - ct^*}{1 - c(1 - x) + \frac{vk}{u}}\left(\frac{1}{p}\right) \tag{21}$$

$$Y = \frac{1}{2f}\left[e^2 - \left(\frac{w_o}{p}\right)^2\right] \tag{29}$$

Solve (29) for $\frac{1}{p}$ as in (A.1), and insert that solution into (21), yielding (A.2).

$$\frac{1}{p} = \frac{1}{w_o}(e^2 - 2fY)^{1/2} \tag{A.1}$$

The simplest method for deriving multipliers from (A.2) is to differentiate Y with respect to the policy variables G^* and m^*. Those readers who are not familiar with this technique can proceed directly to Table A, where the multipliers are displayed. Since p is only an index of prices, it can be defined as equal to unity without loss of generality.

Differentiating Y with respect to G^* yields

but from (29) one can obtain

$$(e^2 - 2fY)^{1/2} = \frac{w_o}{p} = w_o, \tag{A.4}$$

and substituting this in (A.3), the final result is:

$$\frac{dY}{dG^*} = \frac{1}{\left(1 - c(1 - x) + \frac{vk}{u}\right) + \frac{f}{w_o^2}\left(\frac{vm^*}{u} - ct^*\right)}. \tag{A.5}$$

This is smaller than the multiplier illustrated in Table 1, since the second expression in the denominator of (A.5) is positive. The economic explanation, of course, is that increasing output lowers the marginal product of labor and raises the price of output. This rise in prices increases real taxes and decreases the real money supply, and both of these effects act to reduce demand below what it would have been had prices been stable.[28] This multiplier expression is presented in Table A, along with its value in various special circumstances.

The multiplier for monetary policy can be obtained in a similar fashion. Differentiating

---

[28] If the marginal product of labor had been constant, f would have been zero, and the second expression in the denominator would have been eliminated, the same result as before.

$$Y = \frac{C_o + I_o + G^* - \frac{vs}{u} + \left(\frac{vm^*}{u} - ct^*\right)(e^2 - 2fY)^{1/2}\left(\frac{1}{w_o}\right)}{1 - c(1 - x) + \frac{vk}{u}} \tag{A.2}$$

Table A: Income Multipliers under Alternative Assumptions (fixed nominal wages)

Restrictions on the Model	$\dfrac{dY}{dG^*}$	$\dfrac{dY}{dm^*}$
A. None	$\dfrac{1}{\left[1 - c(1-x) + \dfrac{vk}{u}\right] + \dfrac{f}{w_o^2}\left(\dfrac{vm^*}{u} - ct^*\right)}$	$\dfrac{1}{\left[\dfrac{u}{v}(1 - c[1-x]) + k\right] + \dfrac{f}{w_o^2}\left(m^* - \dfrac{uct^*}{v}\right)}$
B. Interest elasticity of investment = 0 $(v = 0)$	$\dfrac{1}{[1 - c(1-x)] - \dfrac{fct^*}{w_o^2}}$	0
C. Interest elasticity of demand for money = 0 $(u = 0)$	0	$\dfrac{1}{k + \dfrac{fm^*}{w_o^2}}$
D. Liquidity trap $(r = r_0)$ $\left(\text{or } \dfrac{1}{u} = 0\right)$	$\dfrac{1}{1 - c(1-x) - \dfrac{fct^*}{w_o^2}}$	0

(A.2) and making substitution as before, one obtains:

$$\frac{dY}{dm^*} = \frac{\dfrac{v}{u}(e^2 - 2fY)^{1/2}\left(\dfrac{1}{w_o}\right) + \left(\dfrac{vm^*}{u} - ct^*\right)(e^2 - 2fY)^{-1/2}\left(\dfrac{1}{w_o}\right)(-2f)\left(\dfrac{1}{2}\right)\left(\dfrac{dY}{dm^*}\right)}{1 - c(1-x) + \dfrac{vk}{u}}$$

$$= \frac{1}{\left[\dfrac{u}{v}(1 - c[1-x] + k)\right] + \dfrac{f}{w_o^2}\left(m^* - \dfrac{uct^*}{v}\right)} \tag{A.6}$$

It can be observed that this differs from the similar multiplier in Table 1 by the addition of a second term in the denominator, which plays essentially the same role it played in (A.5). This multiplier, as well as its value under special assumptions, is displayed in Table A. Similar multipliers for the price level, the interest rate, or any other endogenous variable can easily be obtained through the same general procedure.

2. THE DEMAND FOR AND SUPPLY OF MONEY

*Ronald L. Teigen**

The monetary relationships found in current macroeconomic models, particularly the demand-for-money function, are the result of a long process of theoretical development and empirical investigation. To the extent that such models are used as a guide for policy decisions, accurate knowledge concerning the proper form and arguments of these functions, and their elasticities, is crucial for the correct choice of economic policy instruments. Yet there is substantial disagreement among monetary economists concerning such basic issues as whether or not interest rates play a role in determining the demand for money. This disagreement reflects the fact that substantially different theories concerning the

* The author is indebted to Professor Warren L. Smith for his valuable comments.

role of money in the macroeconomic system have developed somewhat independently. It is the purpose of this paper to trace the development of these differing views, which may be categorized as Classical and Neoclassical on the one hand, and Keynesian and post-Keynesian on the other; to discuss briefly but critically the relevant empirical studies supporting them; and to demonstrate the implications for policy of a proper understanding of the behavioral relationships involved.

Section I summarizes the development of the theory of the demand for money from the Classics to the present; in Section II, the theory of the supply of money is discussed. Some empirical information on demand and supply elasticities is used to evaluate policy multipliers in Section III, and Section IV contains some concluding comments. A linear version of a macroeconomic model which includes a monetary sector is given in the Appendix. Fiscal and monetary policy multipliers are derived from this model and reference to the model and to these multiplier expressions will clarify many of the points discussed below.

I. THE DEMAND FOR MONEY

A. The Classical View

No attempt will be made to discuss the work of the many writers in the Classical tradition who considered the role of money and the reasons for holding it, as the subject has received extensive coverage elsewhere.[1] The Classical approach is summed up in the famous "quantity theory of money." This venerable[2] hypothesis reflects the Classical view that, since money has no inherent utility, the only rational motive for holding cash balances is to facilitate transactions. According to the Classics, money not needed for transacting should be converted into income-yielding assets, such as bonds. The Classical view of the demand

for money is conveniently summarized by Patinkin as follows:

In its cash balance version . . . neoclassical theory assumed that, for their convenience, individuals wish to hold a certain proportion, K, of the real volume of their planned transactions, T, in the form of real money balances. The demand for these balances thus equals KT. Correspondingly, the demand for nominal money balances is KPT, where P is the price level of the commodities transacted. The equating of this demand to the supply of money, M, then produced the famous Cambridge equation, $M = KPT$. In the transactions version—associated primarily with the names of Newcomb and Fisher—the velocity of circulation, V, replaced its reciprocal, K, to produce the equally famous equation of exchange, $MV = PT$. These equations were the paradegrounds on which neoclassical economists then put the classical quantity theory of money through its paces.[3]

This view of the role of money implies that the economic process is not accurately represented by static-equilibrium analysis, but is essentially dynamic—that is, it occurs through time. Under the comparative static theory of exchange, all market transactions in effect occur instantaneously. No one who emerged from the market-clearing procedure holding cash balances could be considered to be in equilibrium, since money, which is only useful for transacting, could have been exchanged for goods in the market and a higher level of utility could have been reached. Another way of stating it is that no transactions balances would be required under static assumptions, which imply that receipts of income and requirements for payment are in effect perfectly synchronized. In fact, however, income receipts and payment obligations do not arise simultaneously; rather, they occur at different points in time.

Modern analysts point out that the time dimension—or disparity between receipts and payments—is a necessary condition for the holding of transactions balances, but that it is not sufficient to explain their existence. If the institutional structure is such that currently idle transactions balances can be converted into income-yielding assets with practically perfect liquidity (such as savings deposits), why will not all such balances be exchanged immediately upon receipt for these assets, to be held until needed; at which time they can be reconverted into money? Some of the later writers in the Classical tradition recognized that, under static assumptions, no one would wish to hold cash balances and therefore the velocity of circulation (defined as the ratio

[1] See Don Patinkin, *Money, Interest, and Prices*, 2d ed. (New York: Harper & Row, 1965), chap. VIII and notes A–J for an exhaustive discussion of the Classical position, as well as for references to the important Classical works. In addition, there is a useful discussion of the views of a number of late Classical and early Keynesian writers in J. S. Gilbert, "The Demand for Money: The Development of an Economic Concept," *Journal of Political Economy*, 61 (April 1953), pp. 144–59.

[2] The quantity theory in crude form is said to be found in writings as early as the sixteenth century. See A. C. L. Day and S. T. Beza, *Money and Income* (New York: Oxford University Press, 1960), p. 277.

[3] Patinkin, *op. cit.*, p. 163.

of the money value of income, *Y*, or the money value of transactions, *T*, to the stock of money) would tend to approach infinity; they ascribed the fact that velocity is finite to the existence of uncertainty with respect to future transactions needs. This motive for holding money is termed the "precautionary motive" and is based on the notion that unforeseen contingencies—or opportunities—may arise which require immediate cash outlay and which may lead to further expense and inconvenience (in the case of a misfortune), or the loss of an unexpected purchasing opportunity, if adequate purchasing power is not available.[4] Like transactions demand, the demand for money to satisfy the precautionary motive was usually taken to be a function of the level of transactions.[5] Since perfectly liquid, income-yielding assets can satisfy the precautionary motive, if they are available, this motive does not furnish a satisfactory explanation for the existence of transactions balances. In an important modern approach to the demand for money, it has been shown that money balances will be held for transactions purposes if the cost of converting these balances into and out of income-yielding assets exceeds the return from holding these assets. This view will be discussed below.[6]

Summing up the general Classical view, the demand for money varies with the level of transactions. In the framework of a macroeconomic model, it is more convenient to refer to income than to transactions, and since the level of transactions is closely related to the level of income, the quantity theory may be expressed as

$$M = kY \qquad 0 < k < 1$$

or

$$M = kPQ$$

where *M* represents the nominal money stock, *P* is the price level, *Q* is a measure of the volume of physical output (GNP at constant prices, for example) and *Y* is the money value in current dollars of national income or product (such as GNP measured in current dollars).

The parameter *k*, the fraction of money income held as cash balances, is determined by institutional factors such as payment and transactions patterns and procedures (that is, *k* would tend to be larger the less often wage and salary payments are received; it would be smaller if most expenditures are made immediately after the receipt of income, rather than being spread out over time; and it would also be smaller the greater the degree of vertical integration in business firms). It is assumed to be stable over time, implying that the income velocity of money, Y/M, is constant.[7] The Classics assumed that the interest elasticity of the demand for money is zero, but one of the major Keynesian contributions is the demonstration that there are circumstances, depending on the rate of interest, in which it is rational to hold money balances as

---

[4] The precautionary motive has been discussed by a number of authors. See, for instance, Frank H. Knight, *Risk, Uncertainty and Profit* (London School of Economics and Political Science Reprints, 1948), pp. 76 ff., and Albert G. Hart and Peter B. Kenen, *Money, Debt, and Economic Activity*, 3d ed. (Englewood Cliffs, N.J.: Prentice-Hall, Inc., 1961), pp. 237–39 and 257–59.

[5] This approach was taken by Keynes, who classified the motives for holding money balances as (1) the transactions motive; (2) the precautionary motive; (3) the speculative motive. See J. M. Keynes, *The General Theory of Employment, Interest, and Money* (New York: Harcourt, Brace and Company, 1936), pp. 170–72.

[6] Some hints at a more extensive view of the demand for money can be found in the Classical literature. Wicksell seemed to acknowledge that money may act as a store of value over time, but he is careful to say that ". . . the object in view is nearly always that of procuring something else for it at a future time. In other words, it is the exchange value which it is desired to preserve; it is money as a future medium of exchange which is hoarded." [Knut Wicksell, *Money* (Volume II of *Lectures in Political Economy*, ed. Lionel Robbins, 2 vols., London: Routledge and Kegan Paul, Ltd., 1935), p. 8]. Thus Wicksell apparently is referring to the precautionary motive for holding money. Alfred Marshall once wrote, ". . . let us suppose that the inhabitants of a country . . . find it just worth their while to keep by them on the average ready purchasing power to the extent of a tenth part of their annual income, together with a fiftieth part of their property; then the aggregate

value of the currency of the country will tend to be equal to the sum of these amounts." [Alfred Marshall, *Money, Credit, and Commerce* (London: Macmillan and Company, Ltd., 1923), p. 33]. Rather than suggesting that there is a demand for money as a means of holding wealth as well as a transactions demand, Marshall appears to be extending the transactions concept to recognize that transactions may not only be related to income, but also may be affected by wealth (or property, to use his term). See Section I.D.3 below for a discussion of a modern version of this view.

[7] Without this requirement, the quantity equation becomes simply a definition of velocity, or its reciprocal. Only *M*, *P*, and *Q* can be observed: *k* (or *V*, in the "equation of exchange" version, $MV = PQ$) is measured, or defined, by substituting values for *M*, *P*, and *Q* into the equation. If we add the proposition that "velocity is a constant" or, equivalently, that "people desire to hold a constant fraction of their income in the form of money balances," the quantity equation becomes a testable hypothesis instead of a definition of velocity. Note that $k = 1/V$.

part of asset portfolios as well as for transactions purposes. If the demand for money is related to the rate of interest, as well as to income, velocity is no longer constant. Suppose, for example, that an interest rate term is added to the quantity equation:[8]

$$M = kY - mr \qquad m > 0$$

where r is the rate of interest. From the definition of velocity, we have

$$V = \frac{Y}{M} = \frac{Y}{kY - mr}.$$

Since the demand for money must equal the given stock of money, the expression $(kY - mr)$ must be constant. Thus the interest rate and income must change in the same direction. If Y rises, r must rise sufficiently so that the value of $(kY - mr)$ does not change; when Y rises, however, velocity rises, so velocity varies directly with the rate of interest and with income.

As a result of the assumption that income velocity is constant, the quantity theory implies that the income elasticity of the demand for money is unity.[9] This is easily demonstrated using the definition of elasticity:

$$\eta_{M \cdot Y} = \frac{\Delta M}{\Delta Y} \cdot \frac{Y}{M}.$$

If $M = kY$, $\Delta M = k\Delta Y$ and $\Delta M/\Delta Y = k$. Therefore

$$\eta_{M \cdot Y} = k \frac{Y}{M} = k \frac{Y}{kY} = 1.$$

These properties—constant velocity (or unitary income elasticity) and zero interest elasticity—are hallmarks of the pure quantity theory of the demand for money. In addition, in the Classical model, real output and employment are determined independently of the monetary sector, and it was assumed for reasons not taken up in this paper that the system always tended to be at full employment.[10] Consequently, real income or output could not be affected by economic policy. Monetary policy—changes in the stock of money by the monetary authority—simply tended to change the level of prices and money wages proportionately, leaving real wages, employment, and output unchanged. That is, the monetary policy multiplier, $\Delta Y/\Delta M$, had the value $1/k$ in the Classical model and affected money income through changes in prices only; the allocation of resources was unaffected. Fiscal policy—changes in taxing and spending—had no effect on output or prices. The expenditure multiplier, $\Delta Y/\Delta G$, had a value of zero: government expenditure was simply a means of diverting resources from the private sector to the public sector or vice versa [see equation (A.14) in the appendix; this multiplier is zero when $\eta_{L \cdot r}$, the interest elasticity of demand for money, is zero as the Classics assumed].

During the days of Marshall and Wicksell, the lack of national income data made empirical testing of the quantity theory very difficult. As will be shown below, our present information indicates that income velocity is definitely not constant (although it may be more or less constant over short periods of time), the demand for money is responsive to changes in the interest rate, and the income elasticity of the demand for money is probably less than unity (although there is substantial disagreement on this point). Thus the quantity theory as stated above appears to be inadequate. Under the leadership of Milton Friedman, another modern school of thought has developed whose goal is to "restate" the quantity theory in such a way that it is consistent with our knowledge of the world. Friedman's work is discussed in Section I.D. 2 below.

B. The Early Keynesian View

Keynes found the Classical transactions approach to the demand for money to be incomplete because it overlooked the possibility that people may choose to hold money *as an asset* instead of other liquid assets—particularly bonds—when their prices are expected to fall. The price of money, by definition, is fixed; however, the price of bonds in terms of money is not fixed, and Keynes pointed out that the decline in capital value of a bond corresponding to even a rather small increase in the rate of interest could

---

[8] The inverse relationship between the demand for money and the rate of interest is due to the assumption that higher-than-average observed values of r generate expectations that r will fall and that bond prices will rise; this leads to a smaller demand for money. See Section I.B. for a more extensive discussion.

[9] While the constant velocity assumption of the quantity theory implies a unitary income elasticity of money demand, a unitary income elasticity does not imply constant velocity. This can be seen by studying the work of Christ, Latané, and others discussed below.

[10] For a thorough discussion of the properties of the Classical model, see Gardner Ackley, *Macroeconomic Theory* (New York: The Macmillan Company, 1961), Part Two.

more than offset the coupon payment. If such a fall in the price of bonds were expected, it would not be irrational behavior to convert one's bonds into money, even though money is "sterile" in the sense that it pays no return or yields no utility. To account for such behavior, Keynes added an additional category—the speculative, or asset demand for money—to transactions demand and precautionary demand.[11] It should be emphasized that Keynes' theory of the demand for money was based on the assumption that liquid assets could be held in two, and only two, ways: riskless money and risky bonds (the risk arising only from the possibility of changes in capital value, since all bonds were assumed to be identical nonmaturing government bonds, called consols, which were free of risk of default). Under these circumstances, asset holders will rationally choose to hold their financial wealth as money when bond prices appear to be abnormally high, and therefore seem likely, on balance, to fall (i.e., wealth will be held as cash balances when interest rates appear to be unusually low), and as bonds in the opposite circumstances. Therefore, the demand for money as a means of holding financial wealth—the asset demand for money—varies inversely with the rate of interest.[12] This conclusion, of course, depends on the hypothesis that a higher-than-average observed value of the interest rate leads to the conclusion that the rate is likely to fall in the future, and vice versa. Such expectations are said to be "inelastic."

For simplicity, Keynes expressed the demand for money of an individual as the sum of a transactions demand (which included a precautionary component) and an asset demand as follows:

$$M_i = M_1(Y_i) + M_2(r), \frac{\Delta M_i}{\Delta Y_i} > 0, \frac{\Delta M_i}{\Delta r} < 0.$$

Here M_i is the ith individual's total demand for money, M_1 is the transactions demand component, assumed to be a positive function of the individual's income, and M_2 is the relationship expressing the individual's choice between money and bonds (the asset demand function), with the demand for money as an asset supposed to be inversely related to the rate of interest. With

respect to this component of demand, Keynes suggested that there may exist a floor below which the interest rate could not be driven. That is, there may exist some very low (but nonzero) value of the interest rate such that everyone would prefer to hold liquid wealth as cash balances whenever this rate of interest was reached, since it would unanimously be expected that the interest rate would rise in the future. The interest elasticity of the demand for money would be infinite at that level of interest rates. This situation has been labelled the "liquidity trap," since new injections of money would simply be absorbed into idle balances, without any effect on the rate of interest, rather than being converted into bonds and causing bond prices to rise (and the interest rate to fall). Graphically, the asset demand for money, as well as the total demand, increases as the interest rate falls and then becomes horizontal at the interest rate floor (if such a floor exists). The curves representing both the asset demand and total demand have sometimes been described as having an "inverse J" shape, and the derivation of the total demand for money balances is illustrated in Figure 1.

Although Keynes' formulation was intended only to approximate the behavior of an individual, it formed the basis for some early macroeconomic studies, chiefly those by Brown, Tobin, Khusro, and Kisselgoff.[13] Since these studies have been quite widely quoted as presenting substantial empirical evidence in support of the asset demand hypothesis, the methodology used and the validity of the results will be discussed briefly.

These writers attempted to demonstrate empirically that the "inverse J" asset demand function exists, and Keynes' additive demand function provided the basis for a simple approach to the problem. The studies are based on the common

---

[11] Keynes, pp. 195–200.

[12] This inverse relationship is of course due to the fact that the rate of interest varies inversely with the market value of bonds. In these discussions, all bonds are assumed to be government consols—bonds with no maturity date and no default risk. Their present discounted value or market price reduces to the simple expression $PDV = R/r$, where R is the coupon payment and r is the market interest rate.

[13] The studies to which reference is made are A. J. Brown, "The Liquidity-Preference Schedules of the London Clearing Banks," *Oxford Economic Papers*, No. 1 (October 1938), pp. 49–82; A. J. Brown, "Interest, Prices, and the Demand Schedule for Idle Money," *Oxford Economic Papers*, no. 2 (May 1939), pp. 46–69; James Tobin, "Liquidity Preference and Monetary Policy," *Review of Economic Statistics*, vol. 29 (February 1947), pp. 124–31, reprinted in American Economic Association, Arthur Smithies and J. Keith Butters, eds., *Readings in Fiscal Policy* (Homewood, Ill.: Richard D. Irwin, Inc., 1955), pp. 233–47; A. M. Khusro, "Investigation of Liquidity Preference," *Yorkshire Bulletin of Economic and Social Research*, vol. 4 (January 1952), pp. 1–20; Avram Kisselgoff, "Liquidity Preference of Large Manufacturing Corporations," *Econometrica*, vol. 23 (October 1945), pp. 334–44.

Figure 1: The Demand for Money Balances

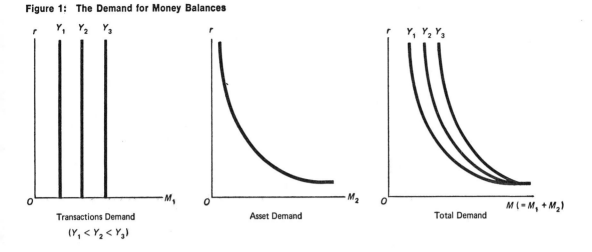

Transactions Demand

$(Y_1 < Y_2 < Y_3)$

Asset Demand

Total Demand

assumption that the asset demand for money was zero during some year in which the level of economic activity was extraordinarily high (usually 1929). The entire money stock for that year is assumed to have been needed to finance the flow of income, and the ratio of money stock to income for the year is used as an estimate of the proportion of income required for transactions balances for each year included in the study, on the assumption that this "transactions requirement factor" does not change from year to year. These estimates of transactions balances are then subtracted from the total money stock in each year, and the residuals are assumed to measure asset balances, which then are plotted against the interest rate. The studies generally covered the interwar period, and they appeared to show that idle balances, calculated as described, were not only inversely related to the interest rate but they followed the "inverse J" pattern which Keynes suggested.

It is doubtful whether these results constitute meaningful evidence on the nature of the asset demand for money. The assumptions on which the calculations of asset balances are based—that the ratio of transactions balances to income was constant over the entire period studied, and that asset balances were zero in years of high levels of economic activity—are open to serious question. Even if this procedure yielded accurate estimates of asset balances, however, there is a more basic problem.

The liquidity preference function is a demand curve, representing the demand for cash balances as a function of price, measured by the rate of interest. As in any market, the quantity observed at a given time, as well as the corresponding price, represents a point on the demand curve

and supply curve—that is, a point of supply-demand *intersection,* or an equilibrium quantity and price. Both the demand and supply curves tend to *shift* over time, either systematically in response to variables other than price, or randomly. When such shifting occurs, the observed supply-demand intersections tell us very little directly about the nature of either the supply curve or the demand curve. This is illustrated in Figure 2, where three such observations are shown. In this case, both the supply curve and the demand curve are drawn to be relatively inelastic, and they are both shifting steadily outward; the locus of points which is observed, however, appears rather elastic. Since supply is shifting relatively more extensively than demand, the curve traced by their intersections is downward sloping. It is tempting to interpret this curve to be a relatively elastic demand curve. As can be seen from an inspection of Figure 2, however, the curve itself tells us nothing about the properties of the true demand curve, which we cannot observe directly.

This general analysis is directly applicable to the analysis of the supply of and demand for asset balances, taking the rate of interest to be the price of holding these balances (since the supply of asset balances is a residual, it may be taken to be inelastic with respect to the rate of interest for purposes of discussion). It is clear from Figure 2 that the intersections will only "trace" the true demand curve if that curve is perfectly stable over time while supply is shifting. Such a situation is pictured in Figure 3. In the studies of Tobin and others, however, it seems almost certain that both the demand and supply curves were shifting in such a way as to generate a set of points somewhat similar to

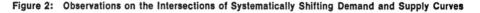

Figure 2:   Observations on the Intersections of Systematically Shifting Demand and Supply Curves

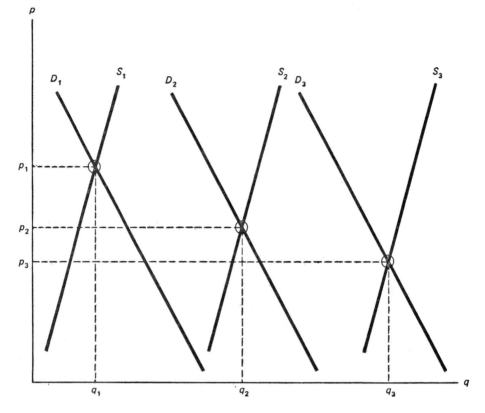

those in Figure 2. Over the interwar years—the period covered by most of these studies—the money stock increased considerably more rapidly than money income, so that the supply of asset balances probably increased. With respect to the demand for asset balances, these studies neglect the possibility that these balances may be related to wealth, and national wealth increased substantially during these years.[14] It appears, in conclusion, that the curves which Tobin and others believed to be aggregate asset-demand relationships actually provide no evidence as to the

nature of the aggregate asset demand for money.[15]

_____

[14] From June 1922, until June 1941, for example, the stock of money rose 127 percent (from $21.4 billion to $48.6 billion) while GNP in current dollars rose 47 percent (from $85.9 billion to $126.4 billion). National wealth, as measured by Goldsmith's data on net worth, rose from $328 billion in 1924 to $467 billion in 1929, a rise of 42 percent; fell to $302 billion by 1932; and then rose to $403 billion in 1941 for an overall increase of 23 percent. Source: Goldsmith et al., *A Study of Saving in the United States* (Princeton, N.J.: Princeton University Press, 1956), Table N-1 for the GNP data, and the *Federal Reserve Bulletin*, various issues, for the data on the money stock. See section I.D.3 below for a discussion of the role of wealth in the determination of the demand for money.

_____

[15] This view is supported by our knowledge of monetary conditions during the interwar period. The curves derived by Tobin and Khusro exhibit a general downward movement during the 1920s and a flattening out at a low interest rate during the 1930s. The speculative pressures characteristic of the 1920s probably caused the demand for liquid balances to decline during that period (Tobin assumes it reached zero in 1929). At the same time, reserves and the money stock were increasing, largely through extensive member-bank borrowing from the Federal Reserve System. The combination of a rightward shift in the supply schedule and a shift of demand to the left could result in the approximately vertical locus of intersection points which are observed for the 1920s. During the 1930s, the high level of liquidity in the banking system in the form of excess reserves would suggest a disequilibrium situation in which commercial banks stood ready to lend to creditworthy applicants at an interest rate somewhat higher than that which would eliminate excess reserves. That is, the money supply function appears to have been perfectly elastic at an "institutional minimum" rate of interest (it might be mentioned that this situation can be termed a "liquidity trap" on the supply side of the market). As the demand for money increased, a fairly level locus of intersection points would be observed. This is the general pattern found by Tobin and Khusro.

Figure 3:   Observations on Demand-Supply Intersections When Only the Supply Curve is Shifting

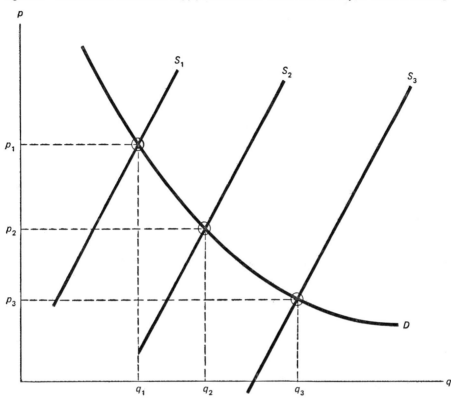

C. Some Refinements

A number of economists have attempted to reformulate the simple Keynesian demand for money function in such a way as to make empirical testing more meaningful. Two somewhat different approaches have been followed. One group of investigators has introduced other variables besides income and the rate of interest into the demand relationship, and thereby has lessened the problem of secular shifting mentioned above. Among studies of this type are those by Stedry and by Bronfenbrenner and Mayer.[16] Both of these studies follow Tobin in separating the money stock into transaction and asset components (in addition, Bronfenbrenner and Mayer attempt to explain total balances) and both introduce wealth as an additional explanatory variable for asset balances (although Stedry takes the ratio of transactions to wealth to be constant—a questionable assumption—in his empirical work, and uses transactions to represent the influence of wealth on the demand for liquid balances). Another approach has been used by several investigators who avoid the problems associated with attempts to classify the money stock according to transactions and asset uses by attempting to explain the total demand for money. The procedure used is typically to relate income velocity (or its reciprocal) to some function of the rate of interest. Studies of this type are those by Kalecki, Behrman, Latané, and Christ.[17] While these studies are not as vulnerable to criticism as is the work of Tobin, Khusro, and others mentioned above, they con-

---

[16] Andrew C. Stedry, "A Note on Interest Rates and the Demand for Money," *Review of Economics and Statistics*, vol. 41 (August 1959), pp. 303–307; Martin Bronfenbrenner and Thomas Mayer, "Liquidity Functions in the American Economy," *Econometrica*, vol. 28 (October 1960), pp. 810–34.

[17] M. Kalecki, "The Short Term Rate of Interest and the Velocity of Cash Circulation," *Review of Economic Statistics*, vol. 23 (May 1941), pp. 97–99; J. N. Behrman, "The Short-Term Interest Rate and the Velocity of Circulation," *Econometrica*, vol. 16 (April 1948), pp. 185–90; Henry A. Latané, "Cash Balances and the Interest Rate—A Pragmatic Approach," *Review of Economics and Statistics*, vol. 36 (September 1954), pp. 456–60; Henry A. Latané, "Income Velocity and Interest Rates: A Pragmatic Approach," *Review of Economics and Statistics*, vol. 42 (November 1960), pp. 445–49; Carl F. Christ, "Interest Rates and 'Portfolio Selection' Among Liquid Assets in the U.S.," in Christ et al., *Measurement in Economics* (Stanford, Calif.: Stanford University Press, 1963), pp. 201–18.

tain a common, and serious, flaw: they treat either the interest rate or the money stock (usually the former) as given, and fail to recognize that causality runs both from the rate of interest to the stock of money, and vice versa; that is, that the rate of interest and the stock of money are determined jointly by the intersection of a demand schedule and a supply schedule for money. Due to the neglect of this "simultaneity," the estimates of the coefficients of the demand function which are reported in these studies are "biased" and result in biased estimates of the respective demand elasticities. (Loosely speaking, the statistical estimate of a coefficient or elasticity is said to be biased if, on the average, its estimated value differs from the true value.) It is important to be aware of such biases in elasticity estimates because, as will be seen, policy decisions may be based on such estimates. This particular type is called "simultaneous equations bias."[18]

---

[18] As explained above, real-world observations on quantities and prices usually do not correspond either to a supply curve or a demand curve as such; rather, they are intersections of supply and demand curves, both of which are probably shifting systematically and/or randomly in response to outside forces. If this is the case, then single-equation statistical estimates of these curves, which essentially involve the fitting of a line to the observed data, actually result in curves which are neither true demand curves nor true supply curves. The usual estimation procedure (least squares linear regression) is to fit a line through the set of observations which minimizes the sum of the squared deviations of the observations on the dependent variable from the line. The illustration below demonstrates the source and nature of "simultaneous equations bias." Here both demand and supply curves are shifting randomly between D and D' and between S and S' respectively; furthermore, the supply curve is shifting more extensively than the demand curve. Therefore all of the observed intersections tend to lie in the trapezoid $ABCE$. If a "least-squares" line is fitted through these observations, such that the sum of the squared deviations of observed quantities from the line (measured horizontally) is minimized, it will pass through points A and C, and its slope will not be the slope of the demand curve—that is, the estimate of the slope is biased.

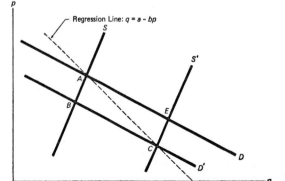

In spite of their shortcomings, these studies are significant because of the uniform support which they give to the existence of a relationship between money balances, on the one hand, and income *and* the rate of interest, on the other. Some of the results are summarized in Table 1. While the studies represented in this table covered somewhat different periods of time and employed rather widely-differing formulations (as shown in Column 6), in each study the statistically-estimated coefficient carried the expected sign (except for the national wealth term in Bronfenbrenner and Mayer's total balances equation) and, although not shown, each coefficient (except for the same Bronfenbrenner-Mayer term) was highly significant statistically. That is, we may assume with a very high degree of confidence that the true value of each of these coefficients (with the exception mentioned) is not zero. In most of the studies, the income elasticity of the demand for money is constrained to be unity by the approach adopted—the same income elasticity as is displayed by the Classical model.[19] It is quite noteworthy that each study discloses a substantial interest elasticity of demand for money (Table 1, Column 3) under these circumstances. In other words, the studies show that there is strong evidence supporting an interest-elastic demand function *given* the Classical assumption of a unitary income elasticity. However, the estimates are biased and suggest that further work must be done to obtain unbiased estimates for use as a basis for policy decisions.

---

[19] In any of the studies attempting to explain velocity (Latané, Christ, and Stedry), an income elasticity of unity is implied. Consider a general expression for the reciprocal of velocity where we follow the investigators mentioned in using M/Y as the dependent variable (in this derivation, the elasticity $\eta_{M \cdot Y}$ is to be considered a partial elasticity; that is, in differencing the equation $M = Y \cdot f(r)$, it is assumed that $\Delta f(r) = 0$):

$$M/Y = f(r) \quad \text{or} \quad M = Y \cdot f(r).$$

Since

$$\eta_{M \cdot Y} = \frac{\Delta M / \Delta Y}{M/Y},$$

we have

$$\Delta M = f(r) \Delta Y$$

or

$$\Delta M / \Delta Y = f(r),$$

and

$$\eta_{M \cdot Y} = \frac{f(r)}{f(r)} = 1.$$

Table 1: A Comparison of Several Demand-for-Money Studies

(1) Study	(2) Period Covered	(3) Interest Elasticity of Demand for Money	(4) Income Elasticity of Demand for Money	(5) R^2 (Fraction of Variance of Dependent Variable Explained by Equation)	(6) Regression Equation
Latané (1954)	1919–52	− .70	1.00	.76	$M = .8\dfrac{Y}{r_l} + .1Y$
Latané (1960)	1909–58	− .89	1.00	n.a.	$M = \dfrac{Y}{.77r_l + .38}$
Stedry (data from non-financial transactions)	1919–55	− .62	1.00*	.72	$\log M = -1.44 - .62 \log r_s + \log T$
Bronfenbrenner-Mayer:					
Idle balances	1919–56	−1.16	3.67†	.90	$\log M = 9.16 - 1.16 \log r_s + 3.67 \log NW$
Total balances	1919–56	− .33	1.23	.91	$\log M = .38 - .33 \log r_s - .42 \log NW + 1.23 \log Y$
Christ	1892–1959	− .58	1.00	.76	$M = \dfrac{.72Y}{r_l} + .13Y$

Here M is the money stock, Y is GNP (in the Bronfenbrenner-Mayer study, it is GNP less government purchases of goods and services), r is the interest rate (r_l is the long-term rate, and r_s is the short-term rate), T is debits to commercial bank demand deposits, and NW is real national wealth (Goldsmith series).

n.a. = not available.

* Stedry substitutes transactions for income in his work, so this figure is a "transactions elasticity."

† This equation uses national wealth but omits income; hence, this elasticity refers to national wealth.

Source: Henry A. Latané, "Income Velocity and Interest Rates: A Pragmatic Approach," *Review of Economics and Statistics*, vol. 42 (November 1960), pp. 445–49; Andrew C. Stedry, "A Note on Interest Rates and the Demand for Money," *Review of Economics and Statistics*, vol. 41 (August 1959), pp. 303–307; Martin Bronfenbrenner and Thomas Mayer, "Liquidity Functions in the American Economy," *Econometrica*, vol. 28 (October 1960), pp. 810–34; Carl F. Christ, "Interest Rates and 'Portfolio Selection' among Liquid Assets in the U.S.," in Christ et al., *Measurement in Economics* (Stanford, Calif.: Stanford University Press, 1963), pp. 201–18.

D. Some Modern Approaches to the Demand for Money

1. Interest-Elastic Transactions Demand.

Except for Friedman and some of his followers, most investigators have concluded that the available empirical evidence supports the hypothesis that the demand for money is related to income (or perhaps wealth) and the rate of interest. At the same time, the early Keynesian notion that this demand consists of a transactions component, based on income, and an asset component, based on the rate of interest, has lost favor as a testable empirical hypothesis. It is recognized that the assumptions which underlie it—that asset holders may choose only between money and bonds, all of which are assumed to be identical as to maturity and risk—are substantially at variance with the real world, even though the hypothesis is logically consistent, given those assumptions. Therefore an important aspect of modern work on the demand for money concerns the nature of this demand in an economy where liquid assets of many varieties, some almost identical with money, are readily available. In such a world, the type of choice which Keynes described as the demand for money as an asset really involves the choice between holding liquid assets whose

yield is high but for which the risk of capital loss is great and liquid assets whose yield and risk are both low. If an asset or spectrum of assets not including money can be found which satisfies the asset holder's desires for yield and safety, the simple Keynesian asset-demand hypothesis is no longer relevant to the holding of money balances, but rather determines the prices of the liquid assets or the structure of interest rates.[20] Savings deposits constitute one such as-

[20] An extensive body of theoretical and empirical literature on the term structure of interest rates has grown up during the past several years. For example, see F. A. Lutz, "The Structure of Interest Rates," *Quarterly Journal of Economics*, vol. 55 (November 1940), pp. 36–63, reprinted in American Economic Association, W. Fellner and B. Haley, eds., *Readings in the Theory of Income Distribution* (Philadelphia: The Blakiston Company, 1951), pp. 499–529; John M. Culbertson, "The Term Structure of Interest Rates," *Quarterly Journal of Economics*, vol. 71 (November 1957), pp. 485–517; David Meiselman, *The Term Structure of Interest Rates* (Englewood Cliffs, N.J.: Prentice-Hall, Inc., 1962); Arthur M. Okun, "Monetary Policy, Debt Management and Interest Rates: A Quantitative Reappraisal," in *Stabilization Policies: A Series of Research Studies Prepared for the Commission on Money and Credit* (Englewood Cliffs, N.J.: Prentice-Hall, Inc., 1963), pp. 331–80.

set; they are in fact perfectly liquid (i.e. they can be converted into money without delay at their face value) and they yield a positive return. Treasury bills which are close to maturity, while not completely free of risk of capital loss, formally speaking, are riskless as a practical matter, and also yield a return. Such assets dominate money as a means of holding wealth (though not as a means of payment). If the Keynesian asset demand for money becomes a means of determining the structure of interest rates—that is, the relative prices of these nonmonetary liquid assets—then any interest elasticity of the demand for money which exists must be due to the interest-responsiveness of transactions demand.

The possibility that the demand for transactions balances might be interest elastic was mentioned by Hansen in 1949; however, a systematic theory of the relationship between transactions balances and the rate of interest was first worked out by William J. Baumol and by James Tobin.[21] Their hypotheses, which are quite similar, recognize that there is an opportunity cost for holding transactions balances idle: it is the rate of return on time deposits or securities. Assuming that the transactions for which balances are held are spread out evenly over the period between income receipts so that the average transactions balance which is held over the period is not trivially small, it may be profitable to invest part of the inflow of income until it is needed for transacting, at which time the asset purchased may be reconverted into cash. Whether or not such activity is profitable depends, of course, on the rate of interest available on liquid assets compared with the costs of buying and selling securities.[22] As the return rises relative to cost, the in-

ducement to economize on transactions balances in this way becomes greater, and the average money balance corresponding to a given income level falls. Thus it is concluded that transactions balances are directly related to income and inversely related to the rate of interest. However, the relationship between average money balances and income tends to be nonproportional (the implied income elasticity is less than unity). The demand for money under this hypothesis is said to exhibit "economies of scale" in that the higher is the initial level of income, the smaller is the increase in money balances needed to finance a given income increase.[23]

As yet, very little empirical work has been done using the Baumol-Tobin hypothesis directly. It is an important hypothesis, however, for it recognizes that the Keynesian liquidity-preference theory does not reflect the real world accurately, and at the same time, it provides an alternative rationale for the interest elasticity of the demand for money. And a nonzero interest elasticity of demand for money is an important condition for the effective operation of both fiscal and monetary policy.

2. The Neoclassical Approach. Although it is now generally accepted that the interest elasticity of the demand for money is not zero, the

---

[21] Alvin H. Hansen, *Monetary Theory and Fiscal Policy* (New York: McGraw-Hill Book Company, 1949), pp. 66–67; William J. Baumol, "The Transactions Demand for Cash: An Inventory Theoretic Approach," *Quarterly Journal of Economics*, vol. 66 (November 1952), pp. 545–56; James Tobin, "The Interest-Elasticity of Transactions Demand for Cash," *Review of Economics and Statistics*, vol. 38 (August 1956), pp. 241–47.

[22] For example, suppose the recipient of $1,000 knew that this income would not be needed for transacting for a period of one month from receipt. If there were a fixed charge of $1.00 per transaction into and out of, say, Treasury bills, and in addition there were a variable charge of $.50 per $1,000 of securities transacted, then it will cost a total of $3.00 to buy a bill and sell it again at the end of the month. If the rate of return on the bill were 4 percent per year, the holder will earn $3.33 by holding for a month, for a net gain of $.33. At a rate of return of 3 percent, however, the holder will earn $2.50; this will not cover the cost of transacting, and he will

prefer to hold money. At a rate of return of 3.6 percent per year, the return for holding the bill one month will be exactly $3.00, and the income recipient will be indifferent between holding the bill and holding money. (Note: for simplicity, this example assumes that bills are the only liquid asset available as an alternative to holding money.)

[23] An interesting aspect of this approach is that the management of money balances is analogous to the management of inventories of physical goods. Baumol's article demonstrates explicitly how inventory-management principles can be applied to transactions balances, and he derives an expression for the optimal level of transactions balances relative to the interest rate and income in which these balances are shown to vary proportionately with the square root of income and in inverse proportion to the square root of the rate of interest. This finding implies that the income elasticity of the demand for money balances should be 0.5, and that the interest elasticity should be −0.5. The "square root rule" for inventory management has been known and used for some time in the management of inventories of physical goods. The square root relationship as applied to the management of money balances depends on certain simplifying assumptions which are unlikely to be fulfilled in the real world, and thus empirical results which yield elasticities slightly different than those noted above should not necessarily be interpreted as providing strong evidence against the hypothesis. For example, findings of income elasticities between 0.5 and unity could be viewed as being consistent with it.

work of one group of investigators continues to be based upon the quantity theory. The chief spokesman for the "modern quantity theorists" is Milton Friedman. Friedman and his followers view the relationship between income and money balances as the most stable macroeconomic relationship, and thus the one on which policy decisions should be based.[24] While the reformulated quantity theory used by Friedman includes several rates of interest in principle, he concludes that no such interest elasticity of money demand can be shown to exist empirically. However, the demand for money is shown to be quite responsive to changes in income (income is defined in a special way, as explained below); the income elasticity is 1.8—substantially greater than unity, rather than being less than unity as the Baumol-Tobin hypothesis would suggest.[25]

Friedman achieves a high income elasticity, and concludes that the interest elasticity is zero, through the use of some statistical techniques and certain definitions which are not commonly used by other investigators. First he chooses to define the money stock as consisting of currency outside banks plus *all* deposits—demand deposits and time deposits—in commercial banks, instead of employing the usual definition, based on money's unique function as a means of payment, of currency outside banks plus *demand* deposits in commercial banks.[26] Friedman justifies this usage by arguing that time deposits are such close substitutes for money that less error is introduced by including them as money than by omitting them.

If this argument is followed to its logical conclusion, of course, savings in other financial intermediaries—savings and loan shares, mutual savings bank deposits, etc.—should also be included. In any case, including commercial bank time deposits "stacks the cards" against the possibility of finding any significant interest elasticity of demand for money (as defined). As was pointed out in the discussion of the Baumol-Tobin hypothesis, variations in the interest rate relative to the cost of shifting into and out of other liquid assets (such as time deposits or short-term securities) are felt by some to be the source of the interest elasticity of money demand. Lumping time deposits together with the money stock obscures movements between them based on changes in the interest rate. Therefore, it is not surprising that an interest rate response cannot be found.[27]

In addition to using an unorthodox definition of the money stock, Friedman's definition of income differs from that usually employed in these studies. Instead of relating money stocks to GNP or some similar national-accounts concept of income, he uses aggregate "permanent income," defined as the sum over all households of the amounts each could consume while keeping its wealth intact. Less rigorously, it stands for the sum over all households of their expected average earnings. In practice, since "permanent income" cannot be observed directly, it is approximated by using a weighted average of present and all past values of disposable income, with weights declining exponentially for incomes further and further into the past. Under this hypothesis, real per capita money balances, m, are related to per capita permanent income, y_p, as follows:

$$m_t = \beta y_{p_t}^{\alpha},$$

or, in logarithmic form,

$$\log m_t = \log \beta + \alpha(\log y_{p_t}),$$

[24] Milton Friedman and David Meiselman, "The Relative Stability of Monetary Velocity and the Investment Multiplier in the United States, 1897–1958," in *Stabilization Policies: A Series of Research Studies Prepared for the Commission on Money and Credit* (Englewood Cliffs, N.J.: Prentice-Hall, Inc., 1963), pp. 165–268. For a general outline of the modern quantity theory, see Milton Friedman, "The Quantity Theory of Money—A Restatement," in M. Friedman, ed., *Studies in the Quantity Theory of Money* (Chicago: University of Chicago Press, 1956), pp. 3–21. Friedman's empirical conclusions concerning the interest elasticity of the demand for money are reported in Milton Friedman, "The Demand for Money: Some Theoretical and Empirical Results," *Journal of Political Economy*, vol. 67 (August 1959), pp. 327–51.

[25] These results, and the reasoning which is summarized in these paragraphs, are discussed in Friedman, "The Demand for Money . . . ," *op. cit.*

[26] More precisely, the usual definition of the money stock is currency outside banks plus "demand deposits adjusted"—total demand deposits less U.S. government deposits, interbank deposits, and checks in process of collection. Friedman's definition includes currency outside banks plus demand deposits adjusted plus time deposits in commercial banks.

[27] The results are biased against interest rate effects in another way. Friedman first regresses money balances on income (both defined in his particular way, as described). Thus, all variations in his money stock which correspond to changes in income are "explained." Then the residual variance—that which is unexplained in this regression—is regressed on the interest rate, and no significant relationship is found. This conclusion is biased against the interest rate, however, because there is a rather close relationship between interest rates and income. The closer is the relationship, the greater the variation in money balances ascribable jointly to income and the rate of interest which is explained by income alone. Only if there were no relationship at all between income and the rate of interest would the Friedman approach constitute an unbiased test.

where α represents the elasticity of demand for real money balances with respect to permanent income. Based on annual data for the United States from 1869–1957, Friedman estimates the income elasticity, α, to be 1.8. He employs this formulation to explain what he considers to be an apparently contradictory set of "facts": that the observed income velocity of money (defined, for example, as the ratio of gross national product to the money stock) rises during relatively high levels of economic activity and falls during recessions—i.e., it exhibits procyclical movements— but over the very long run, income velocity appears to be falling. It should be stated here that these "facts" are not altogether clear—while income velocity did fall from 1929 until 1946, it has been rising quite steadily since then, and most observers fail to discern a secular downtrend in it. In any case, if Friedman's facts were accurate, his finding of a permanent income elasticity of money demand substantially greater than unity—a sign that money balances are considered to be a "luxury" by households—reconciles the apparent paradox which these facts disclose. Observed velocity, based on standard definitions of income, rises and falls cyclically because observed income rises and falls relative to measured permanent income (since permanent income is measured by an average of incomes in the recent past, it tends to fluctuate much less than observed income). In the long run, however, permanent income is the meaningful concept (according to Friedman) and money balances rise faster than income, thus causing a secular decline in velocity. His distinction between observed and permanent income also results in his relatively high income elasticity of demand for money. Since his operational definition of permanent income is a weighted average of past incomes and hence is relatively more stable over time than observed income (but related positively to it), movements of the money stock are greater relative to movements of permanent income than to movements of observed income.

Friedman's findings are important, not only because they are the result of ingenious work and are presented persuasively, but because of their implications for the relative importance of monetary and fiscal policy. If the interest elasticity of the demand for money is zero (assuming the money stock is given), fiscal policy can have no effect on the level of income. Increases in government spending merely divert resources from the private sector to the government sector, with total demand unchanged. On the other hand,

monetary policy reaches maximum effectiveness. Other writings of Friedman reflect this view of the relative power of monetary and fiscal policy; on the basis of this conclusion and other evidence he has adduced, Friedman concludes that monetary policy affects income very strongly but with an undependable lag. Therefore he recommends that discretionary monetary policy should be abandoned because it results in considerable instability, and a "rule" should be substituted under which the money stock would be made to grow by a fixed percentage each year.[28]

3. *The Role of Wealth.*   In the above discussion, reference has been made to the use by some investigators of wealth as a variable in the demand-for-money function. The precise way in which changes in wealth affect the demand for money and for other assets is a subject of considerable current discussion, and at least three viewpoints—not necessarily inconsistent with one another—can be distinguished.

First, Bronfenbrenner and Mayer, Stedry, and others have attempted to show empirically that there exists a relationship between wealth and the demand for *idle balances*. The theoretical rationale for this view has been developed by Tobin in response to the particularly unsatisfactory early Keynesian theory of the asset demand for money. Under that theory, as noted above, wealthholders are governed by their expectations about future bond prices in deciding whether to hold their financial assets as money or as bonds (the only two financial assets assumed to be available). The theory is objectionable not only because such a two-asset world is completely unrealistic, but also because each wealthholder responds to his expectations (which are assumed to be held with certainty) by holding his entire portfolio either as bonds or as money—never as a mixture of the two. In the aggregate, under this theory, a smooth, downward-sloping function relating the demand for idle balances to the interest rate appears to exist only because different individual wealthholders presumably have

---

[28] Milton Friedman, "The Supply of Money and Changes in Prices and Output," in *The Relationship of Prices to Economic Stability and Growth*, Compendium of Papers Submitted by Panelists appearing before the Joint Economic Committee (Washington, D.C., 1958), pp. 249–50. For a critique of these findings, see John Kareken and Robert Solow, "Lags in Monetary Policy," in *Stabilization Policies: A Series of Research Studies Prepared for the Commission on Money and Credit* (Englewood Cliffs, N.J.: Prentice-Hall, Inc., 1963), pp. 14–25.

different expectations about future bond prices (or interest rates).

By introducing risk into this analysis, Tobin was able to show that individual economic units, behaving rationally, might hold *both* money and securities in their portfolios simultaneously.[29] In this analysis, it is assumed that the possible return (including capital gain or loss) from holding a bond for a certain length of time can be represented by a frequency distribution whose characteristics can be summarized by the average or expected value of returns and the variance or dispersion of possible returns. For the typical investor, who prefers higher to lower yields but dislikes risk, indifference curves between yield and risk may be drawn such that, as risk increases by constant amounts, he must be compensated by greater and greater increments of yield in order to maintain the same utility level. At the same time, an "opportunity locus" can be constructed specifying all of the yield-risk combinations available to him as he varies the composition of his portfolio from all money, at the one extreme, to all bonds, at the other. As the proportion of bonds in the total portfolio increases, both the yield and the variance (risk) of the portfolio rise. In the usual case, the individual risk-averting investor will maximize utility by holding a diversified portfolio, rather than holding all money or all bonds as the early Keynesian analysis suggested.

In the Tobin analysis, changes in the yield on securities, other things equal, change the position of the opportunity locus and induce the wealthholder to vary the composition of his portfolio.[30] Changes in wealth, however, should have no effect on an individual's desired portfolio composition unless there is reason to believe that such changes alter the shape of the indifference curves or change the opportunity locus (as might happen, for example, if the wealth-holder's portfolio were so large that his market transactions

had a noticeable effect on the price of securities). If these possibilities are disregarded, the Tobin theory suggests that changes in wealth change the demand for money in the same direction, and that, at least at the microeconomic level, the elasticity of the demand for money with respect to wealth is unity.

Tobin's analysis is an obvious improvement over the early Keynesian theory of the asset demand, particularly in that it introduces risk into the problem and allows for the holding of diversified portfolios. However, it is based on the same two-asset world as the earlier theory, and therefore on the assumption that money is not dominated by other assets as a means of holding wealth. If such assets exist—and savings deposits and Treasury bills close to maturity are obvious possibilities—then the Tobin theory has nothing to do with the demand for money as usually defined, but rather explains choices between nonmonetary financial assets of differing degrees of riskiness (including at least one such asset with zero risk but with nonzero yield).

Even if money as a means of holding wealth is inferior in every way to savings deposits or Treasury bills, it is possible to advance an alternative argument supporting wealth as an explanatory variable in the demand for money balances. The argument is that asset portfolios at any point in time would usually be observed to contain money balances, which are the temporary manifestation of uncompleted shifts between other assets. That is, they would constitute transactions balances in wealth portfolios, and the size of such balances would probably be related positively to total wealth.

If an asset demand for money exists, then, we would expect it to be determined by wealth and interest rates. If transactions demand were determined by income and interest rates (and perhaps also by wealth), the total demand for money would be a function of income, interest rates, and wealth. Because income and wealth are closely correlated, it is difficult to separate their influences in empirical studies, as is demonstrated by the work of Stedry and of Bronfenbrenner and Mayer. For this reason, the empirical evidence in support of this view is weak.

The third, and most general, view of the role of wealth stems from the notion that the demand for money is part of the overall problem of the demand for financial and physical assets; money is viewed as one of the very many ways of holding assets in general. The choice among these assets is presumably "constrained" by some

[29] James Tobin, "Liquidity Preference as Behavior Toward Risk," *Review of Economic Studies,* vol. 25 (February 1958), pp. 65–86.

[30] At the microeconomic level, this theory is consistent with either a negative or positive interest elasticity of the asset demand for money. The direction of the relationship depends on the shape of the individual's indifference curves, and it is not difficult to construct a case in which the elasticity is positive. The reason for the ambiguity is of course that a yield change results in both an income effect and a substitution effect. A positive interest elasticity would indicate that the former is greater in absolute value than the later (and of course opposite in sign).

measure of wealth in the same way that consumption choices are said to be constrained by income.[31] This approach is not necessarily antithetical to those discussed above; in fact, the Tobin approach can be thought of as a special case of the third view. It should be noted that the problem of dominance arises here as well as in the Tobin analysis. However, this third view, which is meant to encompass the transactions, precautionary, and speculative motives for money holding, leads to a demand-for-money function which omits income and includes only wealth and yields on the other assets as explanatory variables. Friedman's use of permanent income as a determinant of the demand for money balances identifies his work with this view. Brunner and Meltzer have reported the results of extensive tests of demand-for-money functions using wealth instead of income.[32] However, the role of wealth remains one of the major unsettled questions in monetary theory.

4. Joint Estimation of Monetary Elasticities. A recent development in the study of behavioral relationships in the monetary sector has been the estimation of elasticities which are relatively free of "simultaneous equations bias." As noted above, this bias arises when two or more variables are actually determined jointly by the interaction of a set of relationships (in the manner that the price and quantity traded of a good are jointly determined by the interaction of a supply function and a demand function, for example), but when the coefficients are estimated statistically using only one equation. In the demand-supply system mentioned, for example, the estimates would be biased if quantity were regressed on price in order to obtain a price elasticity of demand; such an estimate assumes that market price is not determined by the model and that causation runs from price to quantity rather than recognizing the two-way nature of causality.

A logical way to eliminate the simultaneous equations bias to which the demand coefficients (and elasticities) are subject in the studies noted is to demonstrate that a supply function for money exists, and then to estimate the coefficients of the demand-for-money function and the money supply function jointly, thus taking account of the interdependence of the functions.[33] Relatively little theoretical or empirical work has been done on the money supply relationship. However, there is good *a priori* reason to suspect that such a function exists due to the response of the commercial banking sector to changes in the profitability of making loans. One of the earliest pieces of empirical evidence on this point was reported in a study by Polak and White.[34] They found that the ratio of net free reserves of member banks (excess reserves less borrowings from the Federal Reserve banks) to demand deposits fell when the short-term interest rate rose, and vice versa. Net free reserves are sterile assets, but they provide a cushion of liquidity against unexpected reserve losses. The Polak-White assumption is that banks desire to hold net free reserves equal to some fraction of deposits in order to provide such a cushion, but that free reserves are "economized" when the return from loans rises, in order to supply more loans and deposits. Polak and White demonstrated empirically that the rate of interest was inversely related to the ratio of free reserves to demand deposits (that is, that banks respond to the interest rate in supplying deposits), but they did not use their supply hypothesis for the purpose of obtaining demand or supply elasticity estimates free of simultaneous equations bias.

Some work on demand and supply functions for money has also been done by Brunner and Meltzer, and they have reported joint estimates

---

[31] The Tobin liquidity-preference analysis previously is also based on utility maximization subject to a constraint. In Tobin's model, however, the constraint is the total size of the financial portfolio; in the most general view, the constraint is total wealth (financial and physical).

[32] Friedman, "The Demand for Money . . . ," *op. cit.;* Karl Brunner and Allan H. Meltzer, "Predicting Velocity: Implications for Theory and Policy," *Journal of Finance,* vol. 18 (May 1963), pp. 319–43; Allan H. Meltzer, "The Demand for Money: The Evidence from the Time Series," *Journal of Political Economy,* vol. 71 (June 1963), pp. 219–46; Allan H. Meltzer, "A Little More Evidence from the Time Series," *Journal of Political Economy,* vol. 72 (October 1964), pp. 504–8; Karl Brunner and Allan H. Meltzer, "Some Further Investigations of Demand and Supply Functions for Money," *Journal of Finance,* vol. 19 (May 1964), pp. 240–83.

[33] Space limitations prohibit a discussion of the techniques involved in the joint estimation of these coefficients. However, statistical procedures are available which make allowance for the interaction of the behavioral functions of a model and which yield joint estimates of the coefficients. It should be emphasized that estimates of coefficients may be biased even though the simultaneous equations problem is taken into account. If the model is incorrectly specified, it is subject to "specification bias."

[34] J. J. Polak and W. H. White, "The Effect of Income Expansion on the Quantity of Money," *International Monetary Fund Staff Papers,* vol. 4 (August 1955), pp. 398–433.

as well as single-equation estimates of the demand and supply coefficients, using various

bank reserves.[36] The following table lists the most important factors which affect reserves:

Sources	Uses
P = Federal Reserve portfolio of U.S. government securities	$R^{r(d)}$ = Required reserves for member bank demand deposits
B = Borrowings from the Federal Reserve System by member banks	$R^{r(t)}$ = Required reserves for member bank time deposits
A = All other sources less all other uses	R^e = Member bank excess reserves
	N = Currency held by the nonbank public

linear and nonlinear functional forms. Limitations of space preclude a discussion of their work here.[35] In general, the notion that the supply of money is determined by the economic system rather than being set by the monetary authority is relatively new, and work on determining the form of and variables in the supply function is only beginning.

II. THE SUPPLY OF MONEY

In this section, a theory of the supply of money will be developed which is somewhat similar to the approach suggested by Polak and White. The hypothesis is based on the notion that commercial banks act in a profit-maximizing way in response to changes in the return from lending relative to the cost. Both the return and the cost are represented by short-term interest rates: in principle, the return is the yield on loans, and the cost is measured by the cost of acquiring the reserves necessary to support the new loans. When it becomes more profitable to make loans, banks are assumed to be willing to supply more deposits and to increase the money stock. However, member banks are constrained in supplying deposits by the reserve requirements imposed by the Federal Reserve System, and if excess reserves are scarce, member banks will tend to increase their borrowings. Therefore this hypothesis states that member banks will tend to increase their borrowings and decrease their excess reserves when the return from lending rises relative to the cost of making loans. This analysis is developed within the framework provided by a very simple version of a standard consolidation of Federal Reserve System and Treasury accounts, showing the sources and uses of member

Since the left-hand side of this table must equal the right-hand side, we may write

$$P + B + A = R^{r(d)} + R^{r(t)} + R^e + N \quad (1)$$

and by rearranging terms, we find that

$$(P + A) = [R^{r(d)} + R^{r(t)} + (R^e - B)] + N. \quad (2)$$

The term $(P + A)$ includes the Federal Reserve System's holdings of U.S. government securities plus all of the other factors affecting reserves which are not explicitly mentioned.[37] These latter factors are watched carefully by the Federal Reserve System; in fact, the System makes daily forecasts of them. Unless the expected changes in these variables happen to coincide to some extent with planned changes in bank reserves de-

---

[36] The tabulation known as the "Sources and Uses of Member Bank Reserves," of which the above table is a very simple example, is a basic tool for the analysis of changes in the reserve base. A good discussion of its derivation and contents may be found in William J. Frazer, Jr., and William P. Yohe, *The Analytics and Institutions of Money and Banking* (Princeton, N.J.: D. Van Nostrand Company, Inc., 1966), chaps. 9–10. In brief, the "Sources and Uses" table as of a given date is derived by combining the consolidated balance sheet of the twelve Federal Reserve banks with the Treasury's statement of monetary assets and liabilities as of that date, canceling some offsetting items, consolidating other items, and rearranging the resulting entries. Sources and uses tables appear in several publications, most notably the *Federal Reserve Bulletin,* published monthly by the Board of Governors of the Federal Reserve System. It appears each month in that publication under the title "Member Bank Reserves, Federal Reserve Bank Credit, and Related Items."

[37] These factors include the monetary gold stock, Treasury currency (i.e., assets held by the Treasury to support its silver certificate and coin liabilities), Federal Reserve float, Treasury cash (the Treasury's monetary net worth, defined as the difference between its monetary assets and monetary liabilities), the U.S. Treasury general account, foreign and other deposits held at the Federal Reserve banks, and other Federal Reserve accounts.

---

[35] See, for example, Karl Brunner, "A Schema for the Supply Theory of Money," *International Economic Review,* vol. 2 (January 1962), pp. 79–109; Karl Brunner and Allan H. Meltzer, "Some Further Investigations . . . ," *op. cit.*

sired for policy reasons, the Federal Reserve will use open market operations to offset them and they may be viewed as being under the close control of the System.[38] Thus it is clear that the sum of the portfolio plus all of the items in the "other sources and uses" category is under the System's control as long as a policy of offsetting these items is followed. Likewise, it is clear that any change in this sum represents a policy decision by the System. Therefore the sum $(P + A)$ may be viewed as representing the Federal Reserve System's discretionary open market operations instrument, and for convenience we will use the definition

$$R^* = P + A.$$

On the other side of equation (2) we find total reserves (consisting of required reserves plus excess reserves) less member bank borrowing from the Federal Reserve, plus the stock of currency held by the nonbank public. Assuming that changes in the items which comprise the "all other sources and uses" category are offset by defensive open market operations in the manner outlined above, it is clear that all member bank reserves arise either through borrowing or from open market operations. Thus the terms in parentheses on the right-hand side of equation (2) above sum up to total reserves less borrowed reserves, or unborrowed reserves (those originating in discretionary open market operations). It follows that the Federal Reserve System, through discretionary open market operations, is able to control the sum of unborrowed reserves plus currency but cannot exercise direct control over either one separately. In fact, a given open market transaction will usually result in a fairly substantial change in currency holdings by the public. By deriving our money supply hypothesis within the structure of the sources-and-uses identity, however, these currency flows will be taken into account.

As noted above, the money supply hypothesis will be based on the proposition that given the cost of borrowing, rising loan rates induce banks to increase their borrowings from the Federal Reserve and to reduce excess reserves; by the same token, increases in the cost of borrowing, other things equal, induce banks to reduce their borrowing and to increase their cushion of excess

reserves. The difference between excess reserves and borrowing is known as "free reserves," and we will summarize the behavior described above by supposing that free reserves (R^f) fall when market rates of interest rise, but rise when the Federal Reserve discount rate rises, other things equal. Thus we can rewrite equation (2) as follows:

$$R^* = R^f(r, r_d) + R^{r(d)} + R^{r(t)} + N,$$
$$\frac{\Delta R^f}{\Delta r} < 0, \frac{\Delta R^f}{\Delta r_d} > 0, \tag{3}$$

where r is a short-term market rate of interest and r_d is the Federal Reserve discount rate. In order to convert this into a full-fledged money supply equation, we must introduce another definition and further behavioral assumptions.

The money supply is defined as consisting of demand deposits at commercial banks (except U.S. government deposits) plus currency in circulation outside banks. Thus we may write

$$M = D' + D'' + N, \tag{4}$$

where D' are demand deposits in member banks, D'' are demand deposits in nonmember banks, and N is defined in the same way as above. For simplicity, we will assume that the currency stock, nonmember bank demand deposits, and time deposits are all proportional to the money stock:

$$D'' = hM \quad 0 < h < 1 \tag{5}$$
$$N = nM \quad 0 < n < 1 \tag{6}$$
$$T = sM \quad 0 < s \tag{7}$$

From these assumptions and equation (4), it follows that $D' = (1 - h - n)M$. Next, we convert the required reserve terms in equation (3) into the corresponding deposit totals, where

g = reserve requirements on member bank demand deposits
$$0 < g < 1$$
t = reserve requirements on member bank time deposits[39]
$$0 < t < 1$$

so that $R^{r(d)} = gD'$ and $R^{r(t)} = tT$. It now follows that

$$R^* - R^f(r, r_d) - tsM - nM = g(1 - h - n)M$$

and therefore that (8)

$$M = \frac{1}{g(1 - h - n) + n + ts} [R^* - R^f(r, r^d)].$$

[38] Such open market operations are called "defensive" (as opposed to "dynamic" open market operations, which are those that are used in pursuit of policy goals). See Robert V. Roosa, *Federal Reserve Operations in the Money and Government Securities Markets* (New York: Federal Reserve Bank of New York, 1956), pp. 64–79.

[39] For simplicity, we are disregarding the fact that reserve requirements differ for different member bank categories and for different time deposit classes.

In words, this equation states that the supply of money is a multiple of the difference between the policy-controlled reserve base, R^*, and free reserves. The factor of proportionality relating the money supply to this difference is determined by the reserve ratio for demand deposits in member banks and the reserve ratio for time deposits in member banks (both of which are controlled by the Federal Reserve System), the ratio of nonmember bank demand deposits to the money stock, the currency ratio, and the ratio of time deposits to the money stock. While R^* is determined entirely by monetary policy, under our assumptions, the level of free reserves depends both on market forces, as expressed in the market rate of interest, and on policy decisions of the Federal Reserve System, as expressed through movements in the discount rate. We expect the supply of money to vary positively with R^*. Since free reserves vary inversely with market interest rates but directly with the discount rate, the relationship of the supply of money to these variables is just the opposite: the supply increases with increases in market interest rates but falls when the discount rate is increased, other things equal. Finally, the supply of money will respond inversely to changes in reserve requirements (g and t); when these increase, the supply of money falls, and vice versa.

Having become familiar with the procedure for deriving a supply function for money, we may now broaden the analysis somewhat in the interest of greater realism. We have assumed above that the demand for currency and the demand for time deposits were both proportional to the demand for money balances; however, recent studies seem to indicate that demand behavior in both cases is somewhat more subtle than this. It is usually found that the demand for both of these assets (as well as for money balances) is a function of the short-term market rate of interest (i.e., the rate on Treasury bills) and the rate on time deposits as well as income.[40] Thus we may replace equations (6) and (7) with the following:

We would expect the demand for both currency and time deposits to fall as market rates rise. Time deposit demand would increase with an increase in the rate on these deposits, r_t, while the demand for currency would presumably decline in those circumstances. For purposes of this illustration, we will assume that both time deposits and currency are superior goods; that is, that the demand for each is positively related to income.

Now we may see how these changes affect our supply-of-money hypothesis. On the basis of equations (4), (5), and (10), the definition of the money stock can now be written as follows:

$$M = D' + hM + N(r,r_t,Y). \quad (12)$$

As a consequence, D' may be expressed in the following way:

$$D' = M(1-h) - N(r,r_t,Y). \quad (13)$$

Now we again convert the reserve terms in equation (3) into the corresponding deposit totals on the basis of the respective reserve requirements, and then substitute equations (11) and (13) for time and demand deposits. This yields

$$R^* - R^f(r,r_d) - tT(r,r_t,Y) - N(r,r_t,Y) = g(1-h)M - gN(r,r_t,Y). \quad (14)$$

Solving equation (14) for M, the supply of money, we find:

$$M = \frac{1}{g(1-h)}[R^* - R^f(r,r_d) - tT(r,r_t,Y)] - \frac{(1-g)}{g(1-h)}[N(r,r_t,Y)]. \quad (15)$$

This formulation shows how changes in market yields, rates on time deposits, and income all affect the supply of money (it should be noted that these variables all have quite separate and simultaneous effects on the *demand* for money). Holding other things constant, increases in income will reduce the supply of money because holdings by the nonbank public of time deposits and currency will increase. In the first case, increases in time deposits absorb reserves which

$$N = N(r,r_t,Y) \quad \frac{\Delta N}{\Delta r}<0, \quad \frac{\Delta N}{\Delta r_t}<0, \quad \frac{\Delta N}{\Delta Y}>0 \quad (10)$$

$$T = T(r,r_t,Y) \quad \frac{\Delta T}{\Delta r}<0, \quad \frac{\Delta T}{\Delta r_t}>0, \quad \frac{\Delta T}{\Delta Y}>0 \quad (11)$$

[40] Some investigators find that only one of these rates—the Treasury bill rate—affects the demand for currency, while others find that both yields are important. For the purpose of this demonstration, we shall include both.

could be used to support an expansion of demand deposits. In the second, an increase in currency in itself constitutes an increase in the supply of money; however, it also represents an equivalent drain of reserves from the banking system and will therefore generate a multiple contraction of demand deposits. The net result will be a contraction of the money stock. Increases in market interest rates will decrease free reserve holdings of banks, the demand for time deposits, and the demand for currency; all of these effects will expand the money stock (in the case of currency, the argument is the reverse of that used above: currency will flow into the banking system, providing the base for a multiple expansion of deposits). Increases in the yield on time deposits will have a depressing effect on the supply of money through direct effects on time deposit demand; however, according to the hypothesis, there will be a simultaneous reduction in the demand for currency. The net effect depends on the relative size of the two elasticities of demand and the relative size of the terms $t/g(1-h)$ and $(1-g)/g(1-h)$.

In this section we have attempted to demonstrate that the supply of money is responsive both to market forces, as expressed in interest rates such as the yield on Treasury bills or similar market instruments or the rate on time deposits, and to policy instruments of the Federal Reserve System. This demonstration was based on certain behavioral assumptions having to do with the supposed response of free reserves, the demand for time deposits, and the demand for currency to various interest rates and income. It remains to demonstrate that these assumptions are supported by empirical evidence. A discussion of some recent evidence, and its implications for policy, is the subject of the next section.

III.   JOINT ESTIMATION OF SUPPLY AND DEMAND ELASTICITIES

A.   Empirical Results

Several empirical supply-of-money hypotheses have been developed along the lines described above and have been tested on postwar data. The coefficients of these supply functions were estimated within a structure in all of the studies to be discussed in this section. That is, other hypotheses describing behavior in both the financial and real sectors were developed, and the coefficients of all of these functions were estimated simultaneously in such a way that the problem of simultaneous equations bias, described in footnote 18 above, is overcome. The elasticity estimates for several of the monetary equations based on these coefficients are reported in Table 2.

These estimates are noteworthy in several respects. First, the interest elasticities of the demand for currency and demand deposits appear to be considerably smaller than was indicated by the single-equation studies summarized in Table 1. Most of those studies reported interest elasticities of demand of -0.6 to -0.9, whereas the values shown above are much smaller, generally lying below -0.2. De Leeuw finds slightly larger elasticities, but his formulation includes the yield on private securities rather than the bill rate; since the former is a longer-term rate than the latter, it fluctuates less and is bound to display a larger elasticity. However, it should be noted that several of the earlier studies used the short rate and obtained interest elasticities of the demand for money of from -0.6 to as high as -1.16 (Bronfenbrenner and Mayer). While part of this difference could be due to differences in the period covered, restriction of the income elasticity to be unity, etc., much of it must be due to disregard of the supply relationship. Second, these studies generally tended to find that elasticities which are based on coefficients estimated within a structure, both on the supply and demand sides, are somewhat larger than their biased counterparts. This is particularly true of the supply elasticities. Third, the estimates of the income elasticity of the demand for currency and demand deposits lie within a range between about 0.6 and 1.1. This may be interpreted as weak evidence in support of the Baumol-Tobin hypothesis, but it should be noted that the results really do not permit us to discriminate sharply between alternative hypotheses in this respect.[41] Finally, the rather low interest elasticities together with the high degrees of explanation achieved (as measured by R^2) suggest that the Keynesian "liquidity trap," the notion that the demand for money tends to become infinitely elastic at low rates of interest, does not exist. It might be mentioned in this context that some estimates of supply and demand functions have also been made using prewar data, and the interest elasticity of demand found in that study, -0.19, was of the same order of magnitude as those reported above.[42] This result provides no support for belief that a liquidity trap existed during that period. In fact, we have experienced low interest rates in both the prewar and postwar

---

[41] See footnote 23 on p. 64 above for a brief discussion of the elasticities implied by this hypothesis.

[42] See Ronald L. Teigen, "Demand and Supply Functions for Money in the United States: Some Structural Estimates," *Econometrica*, vol. 32 (October 1964), pp. 476–509, for a discussion of these results.

Table 2: Estimates of Long-Run Structural Elasticities of the Demand for Currency, Demand Deposits, and Time Deposits, and of the Supply of Money

| | Demand for | | | | | | | | | Supply of Money | |
| | Currency | | | Demand Deposits | | | Time Deposits | | | | |
Elasticity with Respect to → Study and Period Covered (all studies are quarterly)	r	r_t	Y	r	r_t	Y	r	r_t	Y	r	r_d
de Leeuw[1] (1948–62)	−.36*	−.14	n.a.	−.35*	−.17	n.a.	−.37	.68	n.a.	.25	−.35
Goldfeld[2] (1950III–1962II)	−.07	−.14	.64	−.11	−.18	.80	−1.62†	.37	.65	.22	−.08
Teigen[3] (1953–64)	n.a.	n.a.	n.a.	−.10	−.43	1.11	−2.82†	3.76	2.09	.14‡	−.10‡

n.a. = not available.

Note: In the above tabulation, the variables are defined as follows, unless otherwise noted:

r = rate on three-month Treasury bills.

r_t = rate on time deposits. (In the Goldfeld and de Leeuw studies, an annual series reported by the Federal Deposit Insurance Corporation is used; it is interpolated to yield quarterly data in a way described in the de Leeuw study. In the Teigen paper, this rate is a weighted average of commercial bank time deposit rates, the rate on savings and loan shares, and the rate on mutual savings bank deposits.)

Y = gross national product at current prices.

* Yield on private securities. It should be noted that at least part of the difference in results reported by de Leeuw compared to those in the other studies is based on this difference in specification.

† Yield on long-term U.S. government bonds. It should be noted that at least part of the difference in results reported by Goldfeld compared to those in the other studies is based on this difference in specification.

‡ Supply of demand deposits.

[1] Frank de Leeuw, "A Model of Financial Behavior," in James S. Duesenberry, Gary Fromm, Lawrence R. Klein, and Edwin Kuh, eds., The Brookings Quarterly Econometric Model of the United States (Chicago: Rand McNally & Co., 1965), chap. 13.

[2] Stephen M. Goldfeld, Commercial Bank Behavior and Economic Activity (Amsterdam: North-Holland Publishing Company, 1966).

[3] Ronald L. Teigen, "An Aggregated Quarterly Model of the U.S. Monetary Sector, 1953–1964" in Karl Brunner, ed., Targets and Indicators of Monetary Policy (San Francisco: Chandler Publishing Co., 1969), chap. IX.

periods, and these studies should have disclosed liquidity traps had they existed.

B. Policy Implications

The treatment of the supply of money as a behavioral relationship and the joint estimation of the monetary elasticities are innovations which are of some significance for both monetary and fiscal policy decisions. With respect to fiscal policy, the expression for the static multiplier applicable to a change in government purchases of goods and services, $\Delta Y/\Delta G$, will be altered because the elasticity of the supply of money with respect to the rate of interest is now included. The way in which this term enters may be seen by comparing the expenditure multiplier expressions based on a model with a given money stock and a model including a money supply relationship, respectively. The derivation of these multipliers is given in the Appendix.[43]

[43] In these multiplier expressions, the terms are defined as follows:

$\eta_{I \cdot r}$ = the elasticity of investment expenditure with respect to the rate of interest

$\eta_{L \cdot Y}$ = the elasticity of demand for money with respect to income

1. Multiplier for government purchases with given money stock:

$$\frac{\Delta Y}{\Delta G} = \frac{1}{1 - c(1 - x) + \dfrac{\dfrac{I}{Y}\,\eta_{I \cdot r}\eta_{L \cdot Y}}{\eta_{L \cdot r}}} \quad (16)$$

2. Multiplier for government purchases with a money supply relationship:

$$\frac{\Delta Y}{\Delta G} = \frac{1}{1 - c(1 - x) + \dfrac{\dfrac{I}{Y}\,\eta_{I \cdot r}\eta_{L \cdot Y}}{\eta_{L \cdot r} - \eta_{r \cdot M}}} \quad (17)$$

From (16) and (17), it can be seen that the introduction of the money supply elasticity, $\eta_{M \cdot r}$, tends to increase the size of the multiplier for given values of the other terms in the expression

$\eta_{L \cdot r}$ = the elasticity of demand for money with respect to the rate of interest

$\eta_{M \cdot r}$ = the elasticity of supply of money with respect to the rate of interest

c = the marginal propensity to consume out of disposable income

x = the marginal propensity to collect taxes out of total income

I = investment expenditures

Y = gross national product

—that is, for given values of the terms in (16), the introduction of $\eta_{M\cdot r}$ into (17) will make its value larger than the value of (16). As is true of the interest elasticity of demand, the larger the value of the supply elasticity, the larger the expenditure multiplier value. These two elasticities have different signs, and since they appear in (17) as a difference, increases in their respective absolute values increase the multiplier value, and decreases reduce it. It is easy to see why a positive supply elasticity with respect to the rate of interest increases the size of this multiplier. Increasing government expenditures raise the transactions demand for money, thereby increasing interest rates and deterring private investment spending to some extent; and interest rates will rise more the less money is available to finance the expansion in income. But if the supply of money responds positively to interest rate increases, the interest rate increase itself is restrained and total spending and income rise by larger amounts.

Introducing a supply function for money not only alters the multiplier for government purchases; it also permits the derivation of other interesting multipliers, particularly those related to monetary policy. If the money stock is taken as given, the only monetary policy multiplier which can be derived is $\Delta Y/\Delta M$. However, the evidence quoted above suggests that the Federal Reserve System does not determine the money stock unilaterally. On the basis of the simple supply function described in Section II of this paper (see equation (9) above), multipliers related to the instruments of monetary control actually at the disposal of the System—open market operations and changes in the discount rate—can be derived instead of the multiplier $\Delta Y/\Delta M$. The derivation of the multiplier on income for open market operations—$\Delta Y/\Delta R^\circ$—and the multiplier on income for discount rate changes—$\Delta Y/\Delta r_d$—is given in the Appendix. The expressions that result are:

Both the open market multiplier, $\Delta Y/\Delta R^\circ$, and the discount rate multiplier, $\Delta Y/\Delta r_d$, are smaller in value the larger the interest elasticity of supply. This follows from the fact that the rising interest rates which accompany attempts by the monetary authorities to restrict credit induce bankers to economize on reserves, increase borrowing, and expand loans and deposits, thus offsetting the attempt at restriction to some extent.

Finally, treatment of the money supply as a behavioral relationship enables us to derive an expression for the credit expansion multiplier, $\Delta M/\Delta R^\circ$. This expresses the degree to which the money stock will change for a given amount of open market operations. As shown in the Appendix, the following expression is obtained:

$$\frac{\Delta M}{\Delta R^*} = \frac{1}{g(1 - h - n) + n + ts} \left[\frac{1}{1 - \dfrac{\eta_{M\cdot r}}{\eta_{L\cdot r}}} \right].$$

(20)

It should be noted that this expression represents the "impact multiplier" for open market operations—that is, it expresses the degree to which the money stock will change disregarding the effects on the stock of money of changes in income which are induced by open market operations. This multiplier concept is used because it is more similar in spirit to the usual textbook credit expansion multiplier with which it is compared below than is the full multiplier (including the effects of income feedbacks).

Numerical values for these multipliers may be obtained by substituting values for the various elasticities and propensities involved and by using values which approximate reality for the other variables. Following are the values that will be used to evaluate multiplier expressions derived from a model containing a money supply function:

$$\frac{\Delta Y}{\Delta R^*} = \left[\frac{1}{g(1 - h - n) + n + ts} \right] \frac{\dfrac{I}{M}\,\eta_{I\cdot r}}{[1 - c(1 - x)][\eta_{L\cdot r} - \eta_{M\cdot r}] + \dfrac{I}{Y}\,\eta_{I\cdot r}\eta_{L\cdot Y}}$$

(18)

$$\frac{\Delta Y}{\Delta r_d} = \frac{\dfrac{I}{r_d}\,\eta_{I\cdot r}\eta_{M\cdot r}}{[1 - c(1 - x)][\eta_{L\cdot r} - \eta_{M\cdot r}] + \dfrac{I}{Y}\,\eta_{I\cdot r}\eta_{L\cdot Y}}$$

(19)

$$M = \$350 \text{ billion} \quad \eta_{L \cdot Y} = 0.8 \qquad c = 0.75$$
$$Y = \$1{,}760 \text{ billion} \quad \eta_{L \cdot r} = -0.15 \qquad x = 0.2$$
$$I = \$280 \text{ billion} \quad \eta_{M \cdot r} = 0.20 \qquad h = 0.2$$
$$r = 5.25 \text{ percent} \quad \eta_{M \cdot r_d} = -0.20 \qquad n = 0.25$$
$$r_d = 5.25 \text{ percent} \quad \eta_{I \cdot r} = -0.15 \qquad g = 0.13$$
$$t = 0.04$$
$$s = 1.3$$

The values used for h, n, g, t, s, the money stock, investment expenditures, income, the short-term rate of interest, and the discount rate are approximately equal to those observed as of mid-1977. The values of the elasticities of the demand for and supply of money are consistent with those given in Table 2 and are based on the short-term interest rate.[44] The value shown for the interest elasticity of investment expenditure is based on the recent work of Kareken and Solow.[45] They find that this elasticity, based on the long-term interest rate, is −0.4. Since the model from which the multipliers are derived contains only one rate of interest, it is necessary to convert this elasticity into an elasticity with respect to the short-term rate. The result is the value of −0.15 given above.[46]

[44] The value used for the elasticity of the supply of money with respect to the interest rate, 0.2, is slightly smaller than those given in Table 2. This smaller value was chosen because the studies referred to in Table 2 were conducted on the basis of money supply relationships which responded to interest rate changes through time deposits and currency as well as free reserves—i.e., these studies used money supply functions similar to equation (15), while the multipliers derived in this paper are based on a simpler money supply relationship [equation (3)], in which only the interest sensitivity of free reserves influences the money supply; time deposits and currency holdings are assumed to be proportional to total money holdings. Such a function formed the basis for the results reported in Teigen, op. cit., and the interest elasticity of the supply of money was found to be 0.2 in that study.

[45] John Kareken and Robert M. Solow, "Lags in Monetary Policy," in *Stabilization Policies: A Series of Research Studies Prepared for the Commission on Money and Credit* (Englewood Cliffs, N.J.: Prentice-Hall, Inc., 1963).

[46] This adjustment was made by noting that $\eta_{I \cdot r_s} = \eta_{I \cdot r_l} \eta_{r_l \cdot r_s}$. To determine the response of the short-term interest rate, r_s, to changes in the long-term rate, r_l, the expectations hypothesis concerning the relationship between short and long rates was employed. Under this hypothesis, the long rate is an average of short rates. Consequently, the long rate was regressed on the short rate, using quarterly data for the postwar period. The short rate used was the Treasury bill rate on new issues, and the long rate was the corporate Aaa bond yield; all of the data

Let us first consider the value of the government purchases multiplier. Using the expressions given in equations (16) and (17) we have:

$$\frac{\Delta Y}{\Delta G} = \cfrac{1}{1 - .75(1 - .2) + \cfrac{\dfrac{280}{1{,}760}(-.4)(1)}{(-.6)}}$$
$$= 1.98,$$

based on a given money stock. [Note: Since equation (16) is derived from a model in which the stock of money is assumed to be determined by the monetary authorities, it is appropriate to substitute values for the monetary demand elasticities which were found in single-equation studies. This has been done above; the values used for $\eta_{L \cdot r}$ and $\eta_{L \cdot Y}$ are −0.6 and 1, respectively, and are from the Christ study cited in Table 1. Since Christ used the long-term interest rate in his demand-for-money function, the value of the interest elasticity of investment expenditure is also based on the long rate.] Alternatively, we have:

$$\frac{\Delta Y}{\Delta G} = \cfrac{1}{1 - .75(1 - .2) + \cfrac{\dfrac{280}{1{,}760}(-.15)(.8)}{-.15 - .2}}$$
$$= 2.20,$$

based on an interest-responsive money supply. The introduction of the interest elasticity of money supply, and the changes in the other elasticities, have increased the value of the expenditure multiplier from the previous estimate of 1.98 to 2.20 (for the sake of comparison, we note that if the other elasticity values had remained un-

were smoothed using a four-quarter moving average. Based on a simple regression of the long rate on the short rate, the value of the elasticity $\eta_{r_l \cdot r_s}$ was found to be 0.44. When a time trend was added to the regression to attempt to account for other variables which might influence the relationship, a value of 0.17 was found for this elasticity. As a compromise, a value of 0.38 was used. Thus the value of −0.15 assigned to $\eta_{I \cdot r}$ above results from the multiplication of the elasticity based on the long rate of −0.4 found by Kareken and Solow by this factor of 0.38.

changed, the inclusion of an interest elasticity of money supply of 0.2 would have resulted in a multiplier value of 2.8). Thus an increase of government expenditure on goods and services of $1 billion is expected to increase equilibrium gross national product by $2.20 billion (note that a zero interest elasticity of investment demand or demand for money with respect to income, or an infinite demand or supply elasticity with respect to the interest rate, makes the second term in the denominator disappear, and the resulting "pure expenditure multiplier" reaches its maximum value of 2.5).

Using equation (18), the value of the multiplier relating open market operations to income changes can be calculated:

That is, the equilibrium money stock will increase by about $1.15 for each dollar of open market purchases of securities by the Federal Reserve System and will decrease by the same amount for each dollar of open market sales.

This value may seem unduly low on the basis of commonly held views concerning the size of this multiplier. A typical method of calculating its value is to assume that, at the outset, the commercial banking system is completely loaned up, with both excess reserves and borrowings equal to zero. Then, for every dollar of the money stock, there must exist $[g(1 - h - n) + n + ts]$ dollars of reserves in the private sector (including currency in circulation), and therefore:

$$\frac{\Delta Y}{\Delta R^*} = \left[\frac{1}{.13(1 - .2 - .25) + .25 + (.04)(1.3)} \right]$$

$$\left\{ \frac{\frac{280}{350}(-.15)}{[1 - .75(1 - .2)][-.15 - .2] + \frac{280}{1,760}(-.15)(.8)} \right\} = 2.01.$$

According to this estimate, open market purchases of $1 billion by the Federal Reserve System will increase equilibrium income by about $2 billion, and sales of $1 billion will decrease equilibrium income by the same amount.

The value of the discount rate multiplier is as follows:

$$\frac{M}{R^*} = \frac{1}{g(1 - h - n) + n + ts}$$

or

$$M = \frac{1}{g(1 - h - n) + n + ts} R^*. \quad (21)$$

$$\frac{\Delta Y}{\Delta r_d} = \frac{\frac{280}{5.25}(-.15)(-.2)}{[1 - .75(1 - .2)][-.15 - .2] + \frac{280}{1,760}(-.15)(.8)} = -10.05$$

Thus an increase (decrease) of one point in the discount rate will reduce (increase) equilibrium gross national product by $10 billion, according to this estimate.

Finally, equation (20) enables us to calculate a value for the credit expansion multiplier:

If open market purchases of amount ΔR^* are carried out by the monetary authorities, banks are assumed to expand their loans and deposits until a new equilibrium is reached in which excess reserves and borrowings are both again zero. That is:

$$\frac{\Delta M}{\Delta R^*} = \left[\frac{1}{.13(1 - .2 - .25) + .25 + (.04)(1.3)} \right] \left[\frac{1}{1 - \frac{.2}{-.15}} \right] = 1.15$$

$$(M + \Delta M) = \left[\frac{1}{g(1 - h - n) + n + ts}\right](R^* + \Delta R^*) \qquad (22)$$

and

$$\Delta M = \left[\frac{1}{g(1 - h - n) + n + ts}\right]\Delta R^* \qquad (23)$$

or

$$\frac{\Delta M}{\Delta R^*} = \left[\frac{1}{.13(1 - .2 - .25) + .25 + (.04)(1.3)}\right] = 2.67$$

This approach overlooks the response of member bank borrowing to interest rate changes which result from open market operations; such a response is the basis for the money supply function derived above. If the interest elasticity of the supply of money is zero, as is assumed in the approach summarized by equation (23)—that is, if there is no supply response on the part of the commercial banks—the value of the credit expansion multiplier based on the model used in this paper [equation (20)] corresponds to the value shown for equation (23). This can be seen by examining equation (20), which for convenience is reproduced as equation (24):

$$\frac{\Delta M}{\Delta R^*} = \frac{1}{g(1 - h - n) + n + ts}\left[\frac{1}{1 - \dfrac{\eta_{M \cdot r}}{\eta_{L \cdot r}}}\right]. \qquad (24)$$

If $\eta_{M \cdot r} = 0$, this expression is the same as equation (23). Therefore this equation (and the approach which it summarizes) is a special case of the general credit expansion multiplier given in equation (24).

IV. CONCLUSIONS

This paper has been an attempt to trace the main strands of the development of the theory of the demand for and supply of money from the Classical writers to the present and to summarize the available empirical evidence. The study of these behavioral relationships is important for decisions concerning the use of both fiscal and monetary policy. While some economists still hold to the view that the demand for money is determined only by income, and while it is quite common to assume the stock of money to be determined only by the monetary authorities without reference to the commercial banking system, it now appears that both of these views are incorrect. The weight of evidence supporting the

hypothesis that the demand for money is interest responsive seems almost overwhelming. And recent work on the supply of money indicates strongly that the neglect of commercial banks' supply response to interest rate changes cannot be justified, although the exact nature of this response is not yet fully understood.

If either the demand for money or the supply of money is interest responsive, both fiscal and monetary policy are effective in stimulating income (assuming that some category of spending responds to interest rate changes). The relative effectiveness of monetary policy, compared to fiscal policy, depends on the size of the interest elasticity of demand for and supply of money, the income elasticity of the demand for money, and other elasticities and propensities. Accurate knowledge concerning the size of these elasticities and propensities is therefore necessary for the proper use of policy. While all of the estimates presented above are subject to various biases, a substantial amount of research effort is now being devoted to the relationships discussed, and it is to be hoped that eventually these biases will be minimal and our knowledge of policy processes correspondingly improved.

APPENDIX

Model 1

This is a linear version of a standard liquidity preference model with a given money stock. Since it is to be used for the derivation of various multipliers, it will be convenient to write it in first difference form:

Real Sector

$$\Delta C = c\Delta Y_d \qquad\qquad 0 < c < 1 \quad (A.1)$$
$$\Delta Y_d = \Delta Y - \Delta T \qquad\qquad\qquad (A.2)$$
$$\Delta T = x\Delta Y \qquad\qquad 0 < x < 1 \quad (A.3)$$
$$\Delta I = -v\Delta r \qquad\qquad v > 0 \quad (A.4)$$
$$\Delta Y = \Delta C + \Delta I + \Delta G \qquad\qquad (A.5)$$

Monetary Sector

$$\Delta M^D = k\Delta Y - m\Delta r$$
$$0 < k < 1, \quad m > 0 \quad \text{(A.6)}$$
$$\Delta M^S = \Delta M^D = \Delta M \quad \text{(A.7)}$$

C = consumption expenditure
Y_d = disposable income
T = tax collections
Y = gross national product
I = investment expenditure
G = government expenditures on goods and services
M^D = demand for money balances
M^S = supply of money

To derive the income multiplier applicable to a change in government expenditures, we solve the model by substituting into equations (A.5) and (A.7), and then solving the resulting pair of equations jointly. That is, from equations (A.1) through (A.5), we have

$$\Delta Y = c\Delta Y_d - v\Delta r + \Delta G$$
$$= c(\Delta Y - x\Delta Y) - v\Delta r + \Delta G \quad \text{(A.8)}$$
$$= c\Delta Y - cx\Delta Y - v\Delta r + \Delta G.$$

From (A.6) and (A.7):

$$\Delta M = k\Delta Y - m\Delta r; \quad \text{(A.9)}$$
$$\Delta r = \frac{k}{m}\Delta Y - \frac{1}{m}\Delta M. \quad \text{(A.10)}$$

Substituting (A.10) into (A.8) and solving for ΔY:

$$\Delta Y = c\Delta Y - cx\Delta Y - \frac{vk}{m}\Delta Y + \frac{v}{m}\Delta M + \Delta G; \quad \text{(A.11)}$$

$$\Delta Y = \frac{1}{1 - c(1 - x) + \frac{vk}{m}}\Delta G$$
$$+ \frac{\frac{v}{m}}{1 - c(1 - x) + \frac{vk}{m}}\Delta M. \quad \text{(A.12)}$$

The government expenditure multiplier, $\Delta Y/\Delta G$, is derived by assuming that government expenditures change by the amount ΔG while the money supply is held constant ($\Delta M = O$). Then:

$$\Delta Y = \frac{1}{1 - c(1 - x) + \frac{vk}{m}}\Delta G$$

or

$$\frac{\Delta Y}{\Delta G} = \frac{1}{1 - c(1 - x) + \frac{vk}{m}}. \quad \text{(A.13)}$$

[Note that the same procedure can be used to find the effects of a change of ΔM in the given money stock when government expenditures are held constant. Then

$$\Delta Y = \frac{\frac{v}{m}}{1 - c(1 - x) + \frac{vk}{m}}\Delta M$$

or

$$\frac{\Delta Y}{\Delta M} = \frac{\frac{v}{m}}{1 - c(1 - x) + \frac{vk}{m}}$$

so

$$\frac{\Delta Y}{\Delta M} = \frac{1}{\frac{m[1 - c(1 - x)]}{v} + k}\Bigg].$$

In this expression for the government expenditure multiplier (as well as for the monetary policy multiplier), the "real" effects of changes in government spending (or changes in the money stock) are conveniently separated from the "monetary" effects. The denominator contains a sum consisting of a term containing the "real" parameters c (the marginal propensity to consume out of disposable income) and x (the marginal propensity to collect taxes out of total income). The "monetary" terms are the marginal propensity to hold money balances with respect to total income, k, and the interest rate coefficients of the demand-for-money and investment functions (m and v, respectively). It is common to express these monetary terms as elasticities; for example, in the case of the interest rate coefficient in the investment function, we know that the interest elasticity of the demand for investment is:

$$\eta_{I \cdot r} = \frac{\frac{\Delta I}{\Delta r}}{\frac{I}{r}}.$$

From (A.4), we have

$$\frac{\Delta I}{\Delta r} = -v.$$

Therefore

$$\eta_{I \cdot r} = \frac{-v}{\frac{I}{r}}, \quad \text{or} \quad v = -\eta_{I \cdot r}\frac{I}{r}.$$

Proceeding in this way for the terms k and m, and substituting the resulting expressions into (A.13), we get

$$\frac{\Delta Y}{\Delta G} = \frac{1}{1 - c(1 - x) + \frac{\frac{I}{Y}\eta_{I \cdot r}\eta_{L \cdot Y}}{\eta_{L \cdot r}}} .$$

[Note: in (A.14), the elasticities $\eta_{L \cdot Y}$ and $\eta_{L \cdot r}$ are the elasticities of the demand-for-money relationship with respect to total income and the rate of interest, respectively. The "L" in these expressions refer to "liquidity preference" or the demand for money. In the next section we will amend the model to include a supply-of-money relationship; supply elasticities will use the symbol "M" to stand for the money supply function.]

Model 2

This model is identical to Model 1 except that it includes a supply-of-money function rather than assuming that the stock of money is determined unilaterally by the monetary authority. The supply function to be used is based on equation (9) in the text:

$$\Delta M^S = z\Delta R^* - z\Delta R^f(r, r_d), \quad (A.15)$$

where r is the short-term interest rate, r_d is the Federal Reserve discount rate, and where

$$z = \frac{1}{g(1 - h - n) + n + ts} .$$

In order to use this equation in our model, we will assume for the sake of simplicity that free reserves are a linear function of the market rate of interest and the discount rate, and that they vary inversely with the former and directly with the latter. That is, we will assume

$$\Delta R^f = -b\Delta r + d\Delta r_d \quad b, d > 0 \quad (A.16)$$

so that

$$\Delta M^S = z\Delta R^* + zb\Delta r - zd\Delta r_d. \quad (A.17)$$

To derive multiplier expressions for the model including this supply relationship, the expressions for ΔM^D and ΔM^S are equated and the resulting expression is solved jointly with (A.8) for ΔY as before:

$$k\Delta Y - m\Delta r = z\Delta R^* + zb\Delta r - zd\Delta r_d. \quad (A.18)$$

This gives

$$\Delta r = \frac{k}{(m + zb)}\Delta Y - \frac{z}{(m + zb)}\Delta R^* + \frac{zd}{(m + zb)}\Delta r_d. \quad (A.19)$$

Substituting (A.19) into (A.8):

$$\Delta Y = c(1 - x)\Delta Y - \frac{vk}{(m + zb)}\Delta Y + \frac{vz}{(m + zb)}\Delta R^* - \frac{vzd}{(m + zb)}\Delta r_d + \Delta G; \quad (A.20)$$

$$\Delta Y = \frac{zv}{[1 - c(1 - x)](m + zb) + vk}\Delta R^* - \frac{zvd}{[1 - c(1 - x)](m + zb) + vk}\Delta r_d + \frac{1}{[1 - c(1 - x)] + \frac{vk}{m + zb}}\Delta G . \quad (A.21)$$

1. The Expenditure Multiplier. Now the government expenditure multiplier can be found by assuming that a change in expenditures occurs with no change either in unborrowed reserves or in the discount rate (i.e., $\Delta R^* = 0$ and $\Delta r_d = 0$) and we have

$$\frac{\Delta Y}{\Delta G} = \frac{1}{[1 - c(1 - x)] + \frac{vk}{m + zb}} \quad (A.22)$$

or, in terms of elasticities,

$$\frac{\Delta Y}{\Delta G} = \frac{1}{1 - c(1 - x) + \frac{\frac{I}{Y}\eta_{I \cdot r}\eta_{L \cdot Y}}{\eta_{L \cdot r} - \eta_{M \cdot r}}} \quad (A.23)$$

Thus the elasticity of the supply of money with respect to the interest rate enters additively in the denominator of the second denominator term. Since it is opposite in sign to the demand elasticity with respect to the interest rate, its inclusion tends to make the expenditure multiplier larger in value.

2. Monetary Multipliers on Income. Equation (A.21) contains two explicit terms which represent instruments of monetary policy—ΔR^* and Δr_d (the variable representing reserve requirement changes is hidden in the parameter z: reserve requirements are not treated as an important instrument of discretionary monetary policy in this analysis, although it would not be difficult to calculate multipliers with respect to reserve requirement changes). Open market operations are represented by ΔR^*, while Δr_d stands for changes in the discount rate.

A. Open Market Policy. To find the multiplier expressing the effects of open market operations on income, we assume $\Delta r_d = \Delta G = 0$ in equation (A.21), and find that:

$$\frac{\Delta Y}{\Delta R^*} = \left[\frac{1}{g(1 - h - n) + n + ts}\right]\frac{v}{[1 - c(1 - x)](m + zb) + vk}, \quad (A.24)$$

or, in terms of elasticities,

$$\frac{\Delta Y}{\Delta R^*} = \left[\frac{1}{g(1 - h - n) + n + ts}\right]\frac{\frac{I}{M}\eta_{I\cdot r}}{[1 - c(1 - x)][\eta_{L\cdot r} - \eta_{M\cdot r}] + \frac{I}{Y}\eta_{I\cdot r}\eta_{L\cdot Y}}. \quad (A.25)$$

B. Discount Rate Policy. The multiplier summarizing the effects on income of a change in the discount rate is derived by assuming $\Delta R^* = \Delta G = 0$ in equation (A.21), which yields:

$$\frac{\Delta Y}{\Delta r_d} = \left[\frac{1}{g(1 - h - n) + n + ts}\right]\frac{-vd}{[1 - c(1 - x)](m + zb) + vk}. \quad (A.26)$$

Converting this expression to elasticities, we have:

$$\frac{\Delta Y}{\Delta r_d} = \frac{\frac{I}{r_d}\eta_{I\cdot r}\eta_{M\cdot r_d}}{[1 - c(1 - x)](\eta_{L\cdot r} - \eta_{M\cdot r}) + \frac{I}{Y}\eta_{I\cdot r}\eta_{L\cdot Y}} \quad (A.27)$$

3. The Credit Expansion Multiplier. The credit expansion multiplier, $\Delta M/\Delta R^*$, expresses the relationship between open market operations and changes in the money stock. It can be derived by using equations (A.6) and (A.17). Dividing these two equations by ΔR^*, we have:

$$\frac{\Delta M^D}{\Delta R^*} = k\frac{\Delta Y}{\Delta R^*} - m\frac{\Delta r}{\Delta R^*} \quad (A.28)$$

$$\frac{\Delta M^S}{\Delta R^*} = z\frac{\Delta R^*}{\Delta R^*} + zb\frac{\Delta r}{\Delta R^*} - zd\frac{\Delta r_d}{\Delta R^*}. \quad (A.29)$$

Rearranging terms, and assuming that changes in R^* are unrelated to discount rate changes (i.e., $\Delta r_d/\Delta R^* = 0$), we have:

$$\frac{\Delta M^D}{\Delta R^*} + m\frac{\Delta r}{\Delta R^*} = k\frac{\Delta Y}{\Delta R^*} \quad (A.30)$$

$$\frac{\Delta M^S}{\Delta R^*} - zb\frac{\Delta r}{\Delta R^*} = z. \quad (A.31)$$

Now we assume that $\Delta M^D = \Delta M^S$; this yields two equations in the two unknowns

$$\frac{\Delta M}{\Delta R^*} \quad \text{and} \quad \frac{\Delta r}{\Delta R^*}.$$

Solving for $\frac{\Delta M}{\Delta R^*}$, we have:

$$\frac{\Delta M}{\Delta R^*} = z\frac{\left(m + kb\frac{\Delta Y}{\Delta R^*}\right)}{(m + zb)}. \quad (A.32)$$

This expression for the effects on the money stock of changes in the Federal Reserve System's portfolio includes the term $(kb)\,\Delta Y/\Delta R^*$, which reflects the "feedback" effects on the money stock of changes in income generated by the reserve change. It is generally acknowledged that the lag between a monetary change and the income change which it generates is quite long. Since the credit expansion multiplier derived here will be compared with textbook-type credit expansion multipliers (such as the reciprocal of the reserve requirement), which approach quite closely their equilibrium values after a relatively short period of time and do not take account of these income feedbacks, the "impact" version of equation (A.32) in which $\Delta Y/\Delta R^*$ is taken to be zero must be used in order to make a meaningful comparison. For $\Delta Y/\Delta R^* = 0$, we have

$$\frac{\Delta M}{\Delta R^*} = z\frac{m}{m + zb}. \quad (A.33)$$

This multiplier measures the effect on the money stock of changes in the Federal Reserve portfolio disregarding the effects of induced income changes. In terms of elasticities, it becomes:

$$\frac{\Delta M}{\Delta R^*} = \frac{1}{g(1 - h - n) + n + ts}\left[\frac{1}{1 - \frac{\eta_{M\cdot r}}{\eta_{L\cdot r}}}\right] \quad (A.34)$$

Since discussions of the effects of open market operations on money and credit are often carried on in terms of free reserves, it may be useful to express this multiplier in terms of the response of free reserves to interest rate changes, rather than in terms of the interest elasticity of the supply of money as we have above. To do so, we first reproduce equation (A.16):

$$\Delta R^f = -b\Delta r + d\Delta r_d \quad (A.35)$$

and note that, holding $\Delta r_d = 0$, this equation implies that

$$\frac{\Delta R^f}{\Delta r} = -b,$$

which further implies that

$$b = -\frac{R^f}{r}\, \eta_{R^f \cdot r}.$$

Using this result and equation (A.33), we find that the credit expansion multiplier may be expressed in the following way [which is equivalent to equation (A.34)]:

$$\frac{\Delta M}{\Delta R^*} = \frac{1}{g(1 - h - n) + n + ts + \dfrac{R^f}{M}\left(\dfrac{\eta_{R^f \cdot r}}{\eta_{L \cdot r}}\right)}.$$

$$(A.36)$$

---

3. SOME REFLECTIONS ON THE CURRENT STATE OF THE MONETARIST DEBATE*

Thomas Mayer†

In this paper I will attempt to present a brief survey of *some* of the issues that separate monetarists from Keynesians. They are: the effect of changes in the money stock on income, the monetarist transmission process, the stability of the private sector, the choice of a monetary policy target, and the stable money growth rate rule.[1] A major theme running through this survey is that on several of these issues we really do not know very much. This does not mean that all the work that has been done on these topics was unsuccessful. We have learned a great deal in recent years. In many ways, while not resolving the questions, we have refined our arguments substantially and have reached agreement on at least some points.

MONEY AND INCOME

On the question of whether changes in the money stock affect income substantially economists have made very significant progress; progress that consists not merely of a refinement of the arguments, but rather of approaching a consensus. The advice economists can give the central bank

* An earlier version of this paper appeared in *Zeitschrift für Nationalökonomie*, Vol. 38 (No. 2, 1978). Reprinted by permission of the publisher and the author. Thomas Mayer is Professor of Economics, University of California at Davis.

† The author is indebted for helpful comments to Thomas Cargill, Helmut Frisch, Steven Sheffrin and Ronald Teigen, who are, of course, not responsible for any remaining errors.

[1] For a discussion of the interrelation of these propositions and their role in monetarism, see Thomas Mayer (1978).

on this issue is a great deal more useful now than it was, say, 20 years ago.

The monetarist answer is, of course, that changes in the money stock have a major impact on income. But how major? In other words, how extreme are the monetarists? Let us look first at Friedman's famous introductory essay in his *Studies in the Quantity Theory of Money*. Friedman (1956, p. 3) described the quantity theory as

a theoretical approach that insisted that money does matter—that any interpretation of short-term movements in economic activity is likely to be seriously at fault if it neglects monetary changes and repercussions, and leaves unexplained why people are willing to hold the particular nominal quantity of money in existence.

In this moderate version the quantity theory is surely acceptable to most modern Keynesians. More recently, Friedman (1970, p. 319) wrote, ". . . changes in the supply of money have accounted for more than half the variance of money income for reasonably long periods and for changes measured over intervals of a year or more. But they certainly have not done so for all periods and all intervals." This, too, may be acceptable to many Keynesians. However, Friedman puts much less emphasis on the interest elasticity of demand for money than do Keynesians, and also much less emphasis on the impact of shocks in the real sector. As a result, in his analysis, changes in the supply of money play a much bigger role in determining income than they do in the Keynesian analysis.

Turning to the Brunner-Meltzer wing of monetarism, they too do not believe that all changes in nominal income are the result of changes in the quantity of money. In their model velocity is a function of the interest rate.[2] Since variables such as fiscal policy can affect the interest rate, income can change without the quantity of money being changed. And in the St. Louis approach, the correlation between changes in the money stock and income is low enough so that there is room for other variables to affect income. All in all, it is a caricature to say that monetarism asserts that practically all variation in income is due to changes in the money growth rate. Certainly the leading monetarists do not believe that only money matters.

In deciding how much money matters it is important to pay attention to the time period that is being considered. No reasonable monetarist believes that monthly movements of money and income show a close correlation, while many—probably most—Keynesians would agree that if the money growth rate rises by, say, 2 percent over two decades, this would increase the growth rate of money income by 2 percent. For example, the essentially Keynesian MPS econometric model of the United States economy generates long-run monetarist results. As Franco Modigliani (1977b, p. 20) has put it, ". . . monetarism is the non-monetarist world in which lags disappear."

This raises the question of what Keynesians believe about the effect of monetary changes on income. Axel Leijonhufvud (1968) has rightly challenged the previously widespread view that Keynes believed money to be unimportant.[3] In this he is supported by Keynes' biographer, Sir Roy Harrod, who wrote (1970, p. 621):

Keynes thought the quantity of the money supply of the greatest importance, and the whole *Treatise* is impregnated with discussions of its influence. . . . There is nothing in the *General Theory* to suggest that Keynes was repudiating all that finely wrought work of his about money in the *Treatise*.

In their study of Keynes' views on monetary policy D. E. Moggridge and S. Howson (1974, p. 245) wrote:

Keynes always believed that monetary policy was an important weapon of economic policy. . . . During the period . . . , say November 1931 and . . . March 1933 monetary measures came to occupy their characteristic later role, when they were subordinate

to other measures in the short term but of considerable long-term importance.

Don Patinkin (1976, p. 137) concluded in his study of Keynes' monetary thought:

I would conjecture that the difference between Keynes' policy views in the *Treatise* and in the *General Theory* stems less from the theoretical differences between these two books than from the experience of five additional years of unprecedented depression in England, during which the long-term rate of interest had continued unavailingly to decline.

Admittedly, however, there is one way in which Keynes reduced the accepted degree of emphasis on money. Money now was only one of several variables that determined money income, and by no means necessarily the major one. But this was not such a big change. As Patinkin (1969) has pointed out, fluctuations in velocity were given a high degree of prominence by the old (pre-Friedman) Chicago School. The same was true for the Cambridge School. In 1887 Alfred Marshall testified before the Gold and Silver Commission that:

I accept the common doctrine that prices generally rise, other things being equal, in proportion to the volume of metals which are used as currency. I think that changes in the other things which are taken as equal are very often, perhaps generally, more important than the changes in the volume of precious metals.[4]

But in the early days of the Keynesian revolution many Keynesians argued that the quantity of money was unimportant. For example, Alvin Hansen (1957, p. 50) wrote:

I think we should do well to eliminate, once and for all, the phrase "velocity of circulation" from our vocabulary. Instead, we should simply speak of the ratio of money to aggregate spending. The phrase "velocity of circulation" is, I feel, unfortunate because those who employ it tend to make an independent entity out of it and imbue it with a soul. This little manikin is placed on the stage, and the audience is led to believe that it is endowed with the power of making decisions directing and controlling the flow of aggregate spending. In fact it is nothing of the sort. It is a mere residual. We should get on much better if we substituted the word "ratio." The

---

[2] The Brunner and Meltzer estimate of the interest elasticity of demand for money is similar in magnitude to many estimates by Keynesians.

[3] Overall he makes a plausible case even though some of his citations from the *General Theory* also lend themselves to alternative readings.

[4] (Marshall, 1926, p. 34). When Marshall was asked, ". . . then I gather that your expression all other things being equal, covers so much ground, is so extensive a qualification of your general rule that prices depend on the quantity of the currency, that you would agree that there might be a sensible increase or diminution of the quantity of currency without a sensible increase or diminution necessarily following in prices?" His reply was: "yes." (p. 40.)

little manikin would then be forced back into ob-
livion, where it properly belongs.

This is, of course, very much the view expressed
two years later by the Radcliffe Report in
England (United Kingdom, Committee on the
Workings of the Monetary System, 1959).

But modern Keynesians, at least those within
the mainstream, now ascribe a very important
role to money. For example, Franco Modigliani
(1977a, p. 1) wrote recently: "Milton Friedman
was once quoted as saying, 'We are all Keynesians
now,' and I am quite prepared to reciprocate that
'we are all monetarists'—if by monetarism is
meant assigning to the stock of money a major
role in determining output and prices." Admittedly, other Keynesians, such as James Tobin,
may not be willing to classify themselves as
monetarists even in this way (cf. Tobin, 1972).

But this coming together of Keynesians and
monetarists does not mean that they agree completely about the relative importance of money.
There is still a substantial difference of degree.
And this leads to a major difference in research
strategy. While Keynesians believe that it is useful to try to predict changes in the determinants
of investment, monetarists believe that analyzing
the behavior of this variable is not an efficient
way of explaining fluctuations in income. Moreover, the Chicago School, unlike Brunner and
Meltzer, also ascribes only a small role to fiscal
policy.

Parenthetically, it is worth noting that one
should beware not to center the debate on the
question of whether or not fiscal policy is important, as many monetarists have followed David
Fand (1970) in doing. Although the role of fiscal
policy was the main bone of contention in the
famous debate originated by Friedman and
Meiselman and Andersen-Jordan, it is only one of
several disagreements about the determinants of
income fluctuations. The role of changes in the
marginal efficiency of investment is just as significant. In recent years the importance of this variable has been stressed by Paul Davidson (1972)
and Hyman Minsky (1975), among others.[5] The
fact that the strength of fiscal policy is not the
essence of the Keynesian-monetarist dispute about
income determination can be seen from the fact
that it is certainly possible for Keynesian, rather
than monetarist, theory to be valid, and yet for
fiscal policy to be completely powerless. *If* the

public takes full account of the interest payments that result from a deficit, and *if* it values
the income of future generations rationally, then
a tax cut or expenditure increase will not be effective (see Robert Barro, 1974). And Paul
David and John Scadding (1974), among others,
claim, rightly or wrongly, to have found empirical
evidence for such behavior. Hence, the question
of the importance of fiscal policy is no longer a
straightforward issue that distinguishes Keynesians from monetarists.

All in all, although Keynesians and monetarists still disagree about the relative importance
of changes in the quantity of money, the gap
between them has shrunk very substantially,
largely as a result of the Keynesians adopting a
more monetarist position. In this way, monetarists
have so far been victorious. But it is quite possible that ultimately it will seem as though the
Keynesians have won. This is because Keynesians have moved to occupy the strategic middle
ground, having been flexible enough to incorporate a major role for money in the Keynesian
schema, thus leaving to monetarists the role of
defending a more extreme position. The ultimate
verdict on the debate *may* well be the victory of
a moderate monetarism dressed in Keynesian
clothes.

Whether or not a stronger monetarist position
will ultimately be accepted depends in part on
whether the monetarists will succeed in solving
the problem of the empirical definition of money.
Here monetarists are in disagreement. While
Friedman uses M_2, Brunner and Meltzer use M_1.
Hence monetarist predictions of income can vary
substantially among themselves. And as long as
monetarists disagree among themselves it is hard
to convince the Federal Reserve to act in accordance with monetarist advice. If M_1 is growing at a relatively rapid rate, and M_2 at a relatively slow rate, what should the Fed do? In the
period 1970I–1975II the coefficient of determination between the quarterly growth rates of M_1
and M_2 was only 0.58, and for half-yearly growth
rates it was only a little higher (0.62). And even
if, as monetarists have sometimes asserted, this
divergence is due in good part to the regulation
of deposit interest rates, we must deal with the
world as it actually is, and that includes the
existence of these regulations.

The future success of monetarist theory will
also depend upon the type of monetary policy
being followed. Ironically, if we follow monetarist policy recommendations, and adopt a stable
money growth rate, then monetarist theory will
become less relevant and useful, because with a

---

[5] For an interesting discussion of the relative importance of changes in the marginal efficiency of
capital and in fiscal policy in different versions of
Keynesianism, see Coddington (1976).

stable money growth rate, the remaining fluctuations in nominal income will not be explicable by fluctuations in the money stock. An erratic monetary policy, on the other hand, will increase the explanatory power of monetarist theory. A similar thing is, of course, true for discretionary policy too. If a policy is perfectly timed and of just the right strength it will eliminate all fluctuations in income. Anyone looking at the data will then see fluctuations in monetary policy accompanied by no fluctuations in income, and will conclude that monetary policy has no effect at all on income. (Ando, Brown, Solow and Kareken, 1963)

THE MONETARIST TRANSMISSION PROCESS

One of the strongest criticisms of monetarism is that it relies on essentially unexplained correlations between money and income. Keynesians frequently accuse monetarists of relying on a black box, and argue that the true explanation of the correlation between money and income is that changes in income induce changes in the money stock (see Teigen, 1972, p. 21). How justified is this criticism?

To start with the Chicago School, Friedman provides few details about the transmission process. In his essay with Anna J. Schwartz (Friedman and Schwartz, 1963) we are given a tentative sketch of a transmission process that consists primarily of a description of how an increase in the supply of money generates portfolio shifts. As Arthur Okun (1963) has remarked, this description is very similar to the Keynesian one. (See also Teigen, 1972, pp. 17–21). Friedman and Schwartz then add a sketch of the ways in which an increase in the money growth rate can generate overshooting, and hence fluctuations, a topic to which Friedman returns in his *A Theoretical Framework for Monetary Analysis* (1971, pp. 55–61) without telling us very much about the basic transmission mechanism.

How serious is this omission? Friedman has argued that the transmission process is so complicated that any attempt to describe it in detail is foolhardy. If he is right, and money does affect income through a vast number of channels, on some of which we lack data, then silence is indeed the best policy.

Second, in a very general sense, we already have an explanation of the transmission process in microeconomics. Let us ask the following elementary question: Suppose we have a world with two goods, apples and nuts? If we now increase the public's endowment of apples, the price of apples in terms of nuts falls. And if we take away some of the endowment of apples while the producers of nuts are unwilling to reduce the price of nuts in terms of apples, then there is excess capacity in the nuts industry and unemployment results. If we now call apples "money" and nuts "goods," then elementary microeconomics provides a transmission process that can generate inflation and unemployment. While this example is trite it does answer the extreme argument sometimes made that monetarist theory has *no* transmission process.

Thus monetarism does not require a black box. But, all the same, one *would* like to know more about its transmission process. In part this is because more detail would allow us to test monetarist theory better since we would then have more points at which it could be falsified (cf. Popper, 1961). If we would know more about the transmission process we could probably decide better to what extent causation runs from money to income rather than from income to money. Moreover, it would help to answer what is a highly important policy question in the United States, the extent to which a restrictive monetary policy discriminates against certain industries.

But it is worth noting that the large Keynesian econometric models can also be faulted for having an unclear transmission process. They are so complex that one cannot grasp all that goes on in them, and sometimes one cannot see why certain results emerge in simulation exercises.

Let us look now at the Brunner-Meltzer approach (see, for example, Brunner and Meltzer, 1976). Here the story is completely different. They provide a transmission process that is so detailed and complex that it is indeed hard to retain it all. Admittedly, their transmission mechanism has been criticized as not really being monetarist. This is so because their theoretical model consists of a framework that could, in principle, generate Keynesian results, just as well as monetarist ones. It all depends on the values of the parameters. Dornbusch (1976, pp. 123–24) sets the following conditions for a model to be called monetarist: (1) equilibrium must be determined by stocks and not by flows; (2) it must use a broader transmission process than "the interest rate;" and (3) the model must exhibit stability. He then shows that the Brunner-Meltzer model is not necessarily stable, and that it can be reformulated in terms of "the interest rate." In addition, it does not require that the money stock play a crucial role.

The issues raised by Dornbusch are not simple ones. He is right that the formal model of Brunner and Meltzer does not require nominal income to be dominated by the quantity of money. Nothing prevents fiscal policy from playing a bigger role. But Brunner and Meltzer add to their formal model a set of specific assumptions about the signs and magnitudes of various coefficients, and with these in place, it generates monetarist results. One can, of course, argue that since these assumptions are not part of the formal model per se, the model itself is not monetarist. But this argument is unconvincing. Every reasonable model can generate both monetarist and Keynesian conclusions. It requires the addition of empirical assumptions before it can tell us something about the real world. Brunner and Meltzer's introduction into the model of particular empirical hypotheses about the coefficients is the normal way we proceed.

But Brunner and Meltzer's approach does differ from the standard procedure in one important way. Usually the empirical assumptions about the coefficients are justified by an appeal to inherent plausibility, or to previous empirical studies of the values of these coefficients. This is much less the case in Brunner and Meltzer's work. Instead they tend to approach the problem from another direction. They rely on outside evidence, such as time series correlation, to demonstrate that variations of the money stock dominate nominal income changes, and they then use this result to infer the signs and values of the coefficients in their model. But this procedure seems acceptable.

All in all, while the analysis of the transmission process is not the strongest aspect of monetarism, it is not so weak that it seriously damages the monetarist approach.

THE STABILITY OF THE PRIVATE SECTOR

Monetarists believe that the private sector is inherently stable. Recently this issue came to the forefront of the debate when Franco Modigliani (1977a, p. 1) stated in his presidential address before the American Economic Association that the "real issue of disagreement" between monetarists and Keynesians is the desirability of a monetary growth rate rule. This issue is, of course, intimately related to the stability of the private sector. This is so, not only because with a stable private economy government stabilization policy is less necessary, but also because if we assume that the private sector is highly stable, then the government must necessarily be destabilizing in

order to account for the degree of instability we actually experience.[6] In addition, the issue of stability is linked to the much broader issues of the extent to which one wants to rely on market forces. Many—though certainly not all—Keynesians, even if they would grant that the private sector equilibrates quickly enough, object to the nature of this equilibrium. For example, they would prefer to end a recession by increasing government expenditures because they would like to raise the proportion of government expenditures in GNP.

But, unfortunately, we know very little about the stability of the private sector. That the private sector is not stable was a central message of Keynes' *General Theory*. He treated the marginal efficiency of investment as highly unstable, dominated by "animal spirits." But his evidence for this consisted only of seemingly plausible assertions, such as his description of the stock market as an institution in which people try to predict what majority opinion will be, rather than as an institution that focuses on the fundamental underlying values of assets.[7]

In subsequent neo-Keynesian theory the proposition that the private sector is unstable was justified by reference to the interaction of the multiplier and accelerator. As Samuelson showed, certain values for the multiplier and accelerator coefficients result in an explosive system. And Hicks (1950) argued that such explosive values were plausible when taken in combination with floors and ceilings to income fluctuations.

But this approach is questionable. First, as the life-cycle and permanent income theories of the consumption function demonstrate, consumption depends on more than the income of a single year, though there is evidence (Mayer, 1972) that the current year's income does have a very substantial weight. Insofar as consumption depends on more than a single year's income, the danger of explosive behavior is reduced. More-

---

[6] The proposition that the private sector is stable requires a decision on how much fluctuation is consistent with calling it stable. I will use as a dividing line between stability and instability the degree of instability shown by the total economy; that is, by the private and public sectors combined.

[7] Yet, in another context, Keynes (1936) had anticipated the efficient markets theory. In his discussion (p. 142) of the effects of price expectations on interest rates, Keynes argued that inflationary expectations cannot raise the interest rate, because if prices are expected to rise the market will raise prices right away, so that market prices already take account of the available information.

over, we now know that consumption depends on nonhuman wealth as well as on income. And this too is stabilizing, in part because the introduction of wealth into the consumption function lowers the marginal propensity to consume. Furthermore, if income rises, interest rates rise, and the resulting fall in the market value of wealth lowers consumption.

The accelerator, too, appears less destabilizing now that Eisner (1967) has shown that investment responds, not to short run, but to longer run, changes in sales. Hence, neither traditional a priori arguments nor casual empiricism have succeeded in showing that the private sector is unstable, and the validity of this very basic Keynesian proposition remains to be resolved by detailed empirical investigation.

One possibility is to use an econometric model to simulate the performance of the economy over some period without the stabilization policy that was actually used, and to see if the simulated performance of the economy is more stable than the actual one. But the answer one obtains depends on the particular model one employs. The MPS model shows that in the absence of stabilization policy we would have experienced more instability (Modigliani, 1977a, p. 12) so that, on this definition of stability, the private sector is unstable. But the DRI model shows just the opposite (Eckstein, 1973).[8]

Another possible approach is to investigate whether the postwar economy, in which we did use stabilization policy, is stabler than the pre-1930 economy, when we relied for stability entirely on the private sector. Franco Modigliani (1977a, p. 13) has argued that the fact that the business cycle is now less severe than before 1930 suggests that stabilization policy has succeeded in offsetting some of the inherent instability of the private sector. But this is unconvincing, because prior to 1930 we experienced greater fluctuations in the money growth rate than we did in the postwar period. Monetarists argue only that, given a stable money growth rate, the private sector will be stable—not that it will be stable if the money supply varies a great deal due to monetary policy or to bank failures.

A third approach is to compare various coun-

tries, and to see whether countries with relatively stable money growth rates have relatively stable economies. Starleaf and Floyd (1972) found this to be the case. But as Franco Modigliani (1977a, p. 13) pointed out, this test founders on the problem that correlation may not indicate causation. Countries subject to strong exogenous shocks are likely to have as a result both a high degree of instability and also a highly variable money growth rate. (Cf. Teigen, 1975, pp. 155–56).

Victor Argy (1971) has suggested another solution: he compared for several countries the variance of nominal income and the variance of velocity, but unfortunately his results were far from clear-cut. Moreover, he had to make the strong assumption that with a stable money growth rate, velocity would have been the same as it actually was.

Martin Bronfenbrenner (1961a and b) and Franco Modigliani (1964) approached the problem in a different way. They first calculated the money growth rate required for stability, and then looked to see whether the actual money growth rate or a hypothetical stable money growth rate was closer to this optimal rate. This could show whether monetary policy was stabilizing, and (if one assumes that fiscal policy was neutral) whether the private sector is stable. But unfortunately the answer one obtains by this method depends upon what one assumes about the lag in the effects of monetary policy (Attiyeh, 1965; Mayer, 1967). More recently, McPheters and Redman (1975) resolved this problem by experimenting with a wide variety of assumptions about the length of the lag. They found that actual policy was destabilizing in their first period, 1961I–1969IV, but in the period 1967I–1971I the results depend upon the measure of the output gap and the lag assumptions used. For one of the two output gap measures used, all the lag assumptions showed discretionary policy performing better than the fixed rule.

What lesson can we derive from all of this work? None of it allows us to say with any degree of certainty whether stabilization policy is actually stabilizing. But perhaps there is something we can surmise. Let us assume that the private sector is highly unstable. In this case it is plausible that despite all the weaknesses of the above tests, they would still have succeeded in giving at least a presumption that such instability exists. And the converse holds if the private sector is, in fact, extremely stable. One does not need good ears to hear a very loud noise. This suggests that the private sector is probably neither very stable nor highly unstable, but has

---

[8] Besides, rational expectations theory suggests that in the absence of stabilization policy the parameters of the private sector behavioral relationships would be different. Unfortunately, we do not know whether they would differ in a way that would contribute to, or detract from, stability. In part, this depends on whether the private sector believes that current policy is successful in limiting fluctuations.

very roughly the same degree of stability as the private plus government sectors combined.

MONEY OR INTEREST RATES AS THE MONETARY POLICY TARGET

One of the most important problems of monetary policy is whether the central bank should use the money stock or the interest rate as its intermediate target. Sometimes a money stock target tells us that the central bank should be more expansionary while an interest rate target suggests a more restrictive policy, or vice versa. Hence, choice of the wrong target variable can make monetary policy destabilizing. But, unfortunately, despite the strong position many economists have taken on this issue, we are really very far from possessing a sure answer.

In part the problem arises from the difficulty of measuring either the money stock or interest rates. With respect to the money stock, one difficulty is that the preliminary estimates of it—and what the Fed has available to act on are only the preliminary estimates—are highly unreliable. Poole and Lieberman (1972, pp. 320–34) found that for the period 1961–70 the coefficient of determination between the preliminary and final estimates of the seasonally adjusted quarterly money growth rate of M_1 was only 0.68. (However, the preliminary estimates have perhaps improved somewhat since then.) The problem is due in part to faulty seasonal adjustments. Second, there is the problem of whether to use M_1 or M_2. In the period 1971I–1975IV, the coefficient of determination between their half-yearly growth rates was only 0.62.

On the other hand, interest rates also present serious measurement problems. First, how can we combine the interest rates for securities with different maturities into a single measure of "the interest rate"? Second, as Friedman has emphasized, we have no data at all for many important imputed rates. And third, how can we infer the expected real rate from the measured nominal rates?

For which variable is the measurement problem worse? Since the errors in deriving the expected real interest rate from the published array of nominal interest rates cannot be quantified, and since the error resulting from the need to specify money as either M_1, M_2 or $M_?$ cannot be quantified either, there is no way this question can be answered definitely. But it seems plausible that at times when the inflation rate is high relative to the real rate, or when there is much uncertainty about the inflation rate, it is the interest rate that has the more severe measurement problem. For example, at present, the U.S. inflation rate for the next year is widely expected to be at least 5 to 6 percent. If one therefore subtracts 5 percent from the 8 percent yield on a hypothetical one year security one gets an anticipated real rate of 3 percent, but if one subtracts 6 percent instead, one obtains an expected real rate of only 2 percent. This is a one third difference. If, for the sake of the example, one quite arbitrarily sets the real interest elasticity of income at 0.1, then, ignoring other effects of inflation, assuming that the expected inflation rate is 5 percent instead of 6 percent results in a 3 percent error in predicting income. Moreover, what price expectations for the next twenty years should one assume in approximating the expected real rate on a new twenty year bond?

But measurability is only part of the problem. As Poole (1970) has shown, the correct selection of a target variable also depends on the source of the destabilizing shock. All that the central bank can see from its data is that interest rates are rising, but it does not know whether this is due to an increase in the Cambridge k or to a rise in the incentives to spend. If the central bank wants to keep income constant, then when the demand for money per dollar of income rises, it should increase the money stock enough to keep the interest rate stable (i.e., it should have an interest rate target). But if the rise in interest rates is due to a rise in the incentives to spend, it should keep the money stock constant (i.e., use a money stock target), and let the increase in interest rates choke off some of the expenditures. But how does the central bank know which of these two cases it is facing? Even on the question of which of them is on the average the more likely, only guesses are available.

Fortunately, there is a way out. Control theory suggests that in many cases in which we are uncertain regarding which of two actions to choose, the best strategy is to do a bit of each (Kareken, 1972). This seems to suggest that if interest rates rise we should increase the money stock to some extent, but not enough to bring interest rates all the way back down again. But upon reflection it turns out that keeping the money growth rate constant is already a compromise (cf. Poole 1970; Leroy and Lindsey, 1976). If we were certain that the rise in interest rates is the result of an undesired rise in expenditures, we would not just want to keep these rates constant; we would instead want to raise them. Hence, keeping the money stock constant—that is, using a money stock target—seems consonant at least with some versions of control theory. But this does not fully solve the problem, because we have no assurance that the particular compromise inherent in a money growth rate target is the correct one. Suppose, for example, that in one economy most of the interest rate changes are due to changes in the Cambridge k, while in another economy most are due to fluctuations in expenditures. Surely, we would not want to suggest the same policy for both economies. But this is what the rule of keeping the money growth rate constant as interest rates rise amounts to. Hence, we still need knowledge about the sources of interest rate changes.[9]

Moreover, the selection of a target variable involves another very important consideration. It is hardly realistic to expect a government agency to follow the advice of outside economists to the letter. Hence, there is something to be said for advocating that it adopt that policy that is least likely to be distorted in its actual application.[10] Traditionally, the Federal Reserve has had a bias in favor of interest rate stability, a bias at least partially explicable by the pressures which Congress and the financial community bring to bear on it. And as James Meigs and William Wolman (1971, p. 24) have remarked:

institutions—including the job market—tend to select as central bankers those with a talent for a particular kind of role playing: the appearance—and perhaps also the fact—of a taste for stability. Those individuals who rise in central banks are people who can impress other people that they can keep their heads no matter what—and no matter whether it is true or not.

Insofar as the Federal Reserve does have a bias in favor of keeping interest rates stable, an interest rate target is dangerous because the Fed is tempted to select as the target value, not the interest rate that is most likely to bring income to its target level, but an interest rate that is close to the currently prevailing rate. It is probably fairly easy for the Federal Reserve to slip from having an interest rate target in the sense of the

previously discussed Poole model, to having an interest rate target in the sense of keeping the interest rate stable.

In this connection it is worth noting that some Federal Reserve economists (Corrigan, 1973; Pierce and Thompson, 1972) have shown that within the confines of both the MPS model and the St. Louis model modest departures of the money growth from its target has only relatively minor effects on GNP.[11] This has been used to argue that it is not worthwhile to allow sharp fluctuations in the Federal Funds rate to try to keep the money growth rate always at its target. (Cf. Corrigan, 1973, pp. 97–98.) But this argument does not justify using the interest rate as an *intermediate* target in the Poole sense. In this approach the interest rate is not used as an *intermediate* target of monetary policy at all; instead the interest rate, or rather its stability, is treated as an ultimate target on a par with the income target.

To summarize this discussion: First, we face serious measurement problems with respect to both the money stock and the interest rate. Given the current uncertainty about the future inflation rate, this problem is probably worse for the interest rate. Second, we do not know the relative predictability of the Cambridge k and of expenditure incentives. However, if both are equally unstable and unpredictable, this gives an advantage to the money stock target. Third, there is the question of which target rule a central bank is more likely to observe without letting itself be distracted by the wish to stabilize interest rates. Here, too, we have little information, but a money stock rule is likely to be superior. This suggests the following conclusions: (1) despite the ingenious and insightful work that has been done on this issue, there is still much uncertainty about which target variable a central bank should choose; and (2) that the limited information that is available suggests that the money growth rate is more likely to be the better target variable.

THE STABLE MONEY GROWTH RATE RULE

It is worth noting right at the outset that the case for a stable money growth rate rule does not

---

[9] Furthermore, as yet uncompleted work by John Pippinger suggests that this whole approach of Poole's applies only within the confines of a Keynesian model, and only to positions of equilibrium.

[10] In designing a policy, economists usually concern themselves with its feasibility only to the extent of considering its political acceptability, the availability of data, and sometimes administrative costs. But given past experience with government programs, there is much to be said for also considering the preconceptions of, and the outside pressures on, the government agency that is supposed to administer the policy.

[11] But note that even a half percent of GNP is a lot of income, and that it is therefore far from clear that a half percent departure of GNP from its target for six months is a lesser evil than the distortions that sharply fluctuating short term rates create in the financial sector of the economy. Moreover, Poole (1976) has shown that it is very doubtful that the Fed can actually stabilize interest rates by letting the money growth rate depart temporarily from its target.

rely on the assertion that this rule would eliminate all fluctuations in income, but merely that
it would reduce these fluctuations. Essentially it
is an assertion that the central bank adds to the
fluctuations inherent in the economy due to a
lack of technical knowledge of lags, etc., as well
as to an attempt to serve other goals, such as interest rate stabilization or exchange rate stability.

Monetarists believe that the Federal Reserve
is distracted from its income target by concern
with interest rates, etc., and hence frequently
takes actions that destabilize income. The Federal
Reserve could, of course, respond that these other
goals are important too, and that being able to
pay attention to them is a great advantage that
discretionary policy has over a monetary growth
rate rule. But this argument is far from convincing since it frequently happens that these other
goals that seem so important at the moment subsequently turn out to have been much less important. Would we really have been worse off if
we had not tried to save the Bretton Woods system, and it would have collapsed a few years
earlier? And similarly, interest rate stabilization is
much less likely to work in the long run than in
the short run.

The second major monetarist argument for a
stable money growth rate is that the lags of monetary policy are long and variable. It is the variability of the lags rather than their length that is the
much more serious problem because if the lags
are long but stable, and hence predictable, we
could estimate the mean lag, and then base our
current policy on a forecast of income far into
the future. But if the lag is sometimes long, and
sometimes short, then knowledge of the mean
lag, which is all that our traditional econometric
techniques provide, is insufficient. Friedman and
Schwartz (1963) concluded from a comparison
of the turning points in the money growth rate
and in business cycles that the lags are highly
variable. But this is not convincing because, as
Tobin (1970) and Brainard and Tobin (1968)
have shown, a comparison of turning points does
not provide conclusive evidence about which one
is the causal variable. And if such a comparison
does not tell us even the causal relation of the
two variables, it can hardly be used to measure
the lag between the change in the money stock
and its effect on income.

Until recently there existed no acceptable
method of measuring the variability of the lags.
But recently Thomas Cargill and Robert Meyer
(1978) and E. J. Tanner (1977) have approached the problem by using the new technique of variable-coefficient regression. Both

studies found that the lag of monetary policy is
highly unstable.

Another way to approach the problem of a
monetary rule versus discretionary policy is to
ask whether the private sector is stable. But, as
discussed above, the various empirical tests do
not provide reliable information on this. And
even if they did show that, in the past, discretionary policy has been destabilizing, it does not
follow that it will be in the future. In recent
years the Federal Reserve has learned a great
deal.

In any case, the traditional debate about a
monetary rule has to a considerable extent been
outdated by the development of "semi-rules" and
control theory. Cooper (1974), starting from the
basic paper of Phillips (1956), has investigated
the efficacy of rules whereby the Federal Reserve
has a reaction function based on the level of income, on the integral of the shortfall of income
from its target, and on the rate of change of income. He found in simulations using both the
MPS and St. Louis models that there exist reaction function rules that are an improvement over
a fixed growth rate rule. And Fisher and Cooper
(1973), using linear difference equation models,
have shown that even with highly variable lags
there exist feedback rules that to some extent
stabilize the economy. Furthermore, Benishay
(1972) has shown that, counterintuitively, in a
model with first order serial correlation in economic activity, variability of lags *increases* the
stabilizing power of policy. But there is the problem that if the Fed changes its behavior and
adopts such feedback rules, the private sector responds by changing its behavior too. Hence one
cannot determine how a policy would work by
using simulations of models whose coefficients
were derived from the behavior of the economy
under the old policy rules (Lucas, 1976).

Second, there is the problem that political
pressures may prevent the central bank from
adopting sophisticated feedback rules, and may
force it to adopt much cruder policies, such as
attempting to hold down interest rates. As Friedman has suggested, the case for a monetary rule
is as much political as it is economic. It may well
be the case that a constant growth rate rule, in
the form of a monetary constitution, is the best
politically feasible policy.

All in all, it appears that the available evidence
on the relative efficacy of discretionary monetary
policy, and a fixed monetary growth rate rule, is
insufficient to allow one to make a strong case for
either one, particularly as much of the case for a
monetary growth rate rule centers on the political

difficulties of operating a rational discretionary policy. And it is very hard to say what will be politically feasible in the future.[12]

CONCLUSION

This paper has surveyed the status of five monetarist propositions. On one of them, the role of money in income changes, there has been a substantial coming together of Keynesians and monetarists, though the gap between them is still major. On the second, the transmission process, the standard Keynesian criticism of monetarism as a "black box" does not seem compelling, though this, of course, does not necessarily imply that the monetarist transmission process is superior to the Keynesian one. Concerning the third issue, the stability of the private sector, neither side is able to make a halfway convincing case; we just do not know the answer. The fourth issue, the use of a money stock target versus an interest rate target, is also an issue about which we know little, though the case for using a money stock target does seem the stronger. Finally, there is the dispute about a monetary growth rate rule. Here, too, the available evidence is far from convincing.

REFERENCES

Andersen, Leonall, and Jerry Jordan (1968), "Monetary and Fiscal Actions: A Test of Their Relative Importance in Economic Stabilization," Federal Reserve Bank of St. Louis Review, November, pp. 11–24.

Ando, Albert, E. C. Brown, R. Solow, and J. Kareken (1963), "Lags in Fiscal and Monetary Policy," in Commission on Money and Credit. New York: Prentice Hall.

Argy, Victor (1971), "Rules, Discretion in Monetary Management, and Short Term Stability," Journal of Money, Credit, and Banking 3, February, pp. 102–22.

Attiyeh, Richard (1965), "Rules vs. Discretion: A Comment," Journal of Political Economy 73, April, pp. 170–72.

---

[12] One justification for continuing with discretionary policy is that this allows us to learn more about monetary policy. But this justification is subject to two major qualifications. One is that we could continue to study monetary policy even if we used a monetary rule, though, admittedly, we could not try out different policies, and such a shift in policy would probably reduce professional interest in monetary policy results from the inadequacy of available statistical techniques, and improvement in these techniques is independent of the monetary policy followed.

Barro, Robert (1974), "Are Government Bonds Net Wealth?" Journal of Political Economy 82, November/December, pp. 1095–1117.

Benishay, Haskel (1972), "A Framework for the Evaluation of Short-Term Fiscal and Monetary Policy," Journal of Money, Credit, and Banking 4, November, pp. 779–810.

Brainard, William, and James Tobin (1968), "Pitfalls in Financial Model Building," American Economic Review 58, May, pp. 99–122.

Bronfenbrenner, Martin (1961a), "Statistical Tests of Rival Monetary Rules," Journal of Political Economy 69, February, pp. 1–14.

——— (1961b), "Statistical Tests of Rival Monetary Rules: Quarterly Data Supplement," Journal of Political Economy 69, December, pp. 621–25.

Brunner, Karl, and Allan Meltzer (1976), "An Aggregative Theory for a Closed Economy," in Jerome Stein, ed., Monetarism. Amsterdam: North-Holland Publishing Co.

Cargill, Thomas, and Robert Meyer (forthcoming, 1978), "The Time Variation of the Response of Income to Monetary and Fiscal Policy," Review of Economics and Statistics.

Coddington, Alan (1976), "Keynesian Economics: The Search for First Principles," Journal of Economic Literature 14, December, pp. 1258–73.

Cooper, Phillip (1974), Development of the Monetary Sector, Prediction and Policy Analysis in the FRB-MIT Model. Lexington, Mass.: Lexington Books.

Corrigan, Gerald (1973), "Income Stabilization and Short-Run Variability in Money," Federal Reserve Bank of New York Monthly Review 55, April, pp. 87–93.

David, Paul, and John Scadding (1974), "Private Savings, Ultrarationality, Aggregation, and 'Denison's Law,'" Journal of Political Economy 82, March/April, Pt. 1, pp. 225–50.

Davidson, Paul (1972), "A Keynesian View of Friedman's Theoretical Framework for Monetary Analysis," Journal of Political Economy 80, September/October, pp. 864–82.

Dornbusch, Rudiger (1976), "Comments," in Jerome Stein, ed., Monetarism. Amsterdam: North-Holland Publishing Co.

Eckstein, Otto (1973), "Instability of the Private and Public Sectors," Swedish Journal of Economics 75, March, pp. 19–26.

Eisner, Robert (1967), "A Permanent Income Theory for Investment," American Economic Review 57, June, pp. 363–90.

Fand, David (1970), "Monetarism and Fiscalism," Banca Nazionale del Lavoro Quarterly Review, September, pp. 276–307.

Fisher, Stanley, and J. Phillip Cooper (1973), "Stabilization Policy and Lags," Journal of Political Economy 81, July–August, pp. 847–77.

Friedman, Milton (1956), "The Quantity Theory of Money: A Restatement," in Milton Friedman, *Studies in the Quantity Theory of Money*, Chicago: University of Chicago Press.

———— (1969), *The Optimum Quantity of Money and Other Essays*. Chicago: University of Chicago Press.

———— (1970), "Comment on Tobin," *Quarterly Journal of Economics* 84, May, pp. 318–27.

———— (1971), *A Theoretical Framework for Monetary Analysis*, New York National Bureau of Economic Research.

———— and Anna Schwartz (1963), "Money and Business Cycles," *Review of Economics and Statistics* 45, February, pt. 2, pp. 32–64.

Hansen, Alvin (1957), *The American Economy*. New York: McGraw-Hill.

Harrod, Sir Roy (1970), "Reassessment of Keynes' Views on Money," *Journal of Political Economy* 78, July/August, pt. 1, pp. 617–25.

Hicks, Sir John (1950), *The Trade Cycle*. Oxford: Oxford University Press.

Kareken, John (1972), "Discussion," in Federal Reserve Bank of Boston, *Controlling Monetary Aggregates II: The Implementation*. Boston, Mass.: Federal Reserve Bank of Boston.

Keynes, Lord John Maynard (1936), *The General Theory of Employment, Interest and Money*. London: Macmillan.

Leijonhufvud, Axel (1968), *On Keynesian Economics and the Economics of Keynes*. New York: Oxford University Press.

Leroy, Stephen, and David Lindsey (1976), "Determining the Monetary Instrument," Board of Governors, Federal Reserve System, unpublished manuscript.

Lucas, Robert (1976), "Econometric Policy Evaluation: A Critique," in *The Phillips Curve and the Labor Market*. Amsterdam: North-Holland Publishing Co., *Carnegie-Rochester Conference Series on Public Policy*, 1, pp. 19–46.

Marshall, Alfred (1926), *Official Papers*. London: Macmillan.

Mayer, Thomas (1967), "The Lag in the Effect of Monetary Policy: Some Criticisms," *Western Economic Journal* 5, September, pp. 324–42.

———— (1972), *Permanent Income, Wealth and Consumption*. Berkeley: University of California Press.

———— (1978), *The Structure of Monetarism*. New York: W. W. Norton.

McPheters, Lee, and Milton Redman (1975), "Rule, Semirule and Discretion during Two Decades of Monetary Policy," *Quarterly Review of Economics and Business* 15, Spring, pp. 53–64.

Meigs, James, and William Wolman (1971), "Central Banks and the Money Supply," Federal Reserve Bank of St. Louis *Review* 53, August, pp. 18–30.

Minsky, Hyman (1975), *John Maynard Keynes*. New York: Columbia University Press.

Modigliani, Franco (1964), "Some Empirical Tests of Monetary Management and of Rules vs. Discretion," *Journal of Political Economy* 72, June, pp. 211–45.

———— (1977a), "The Monetarist Controversy, or Should We Forsake Stabilization Policies?" *American Economic Review* 67, March, pp. 1–19.

———— (1977b), "The Monetarist Controversy," Federal Reserve Bank of San Francisco *Economic Review*, Supplement, Spring.

Moggridge, D. E., and S. Howson (1974), "Keynes on Monetary Policy 1910–1946," *Oxford Economic Papers* 26, pp. 226–47.

Okun, Arthur (1963), "Comment," *Review of Economics and Statistics* 45, February, pt. 2, pp. 72–77.

Patinkin, Don (1969), "Chicago Tradition, the Quantity Theory, and Friedman," *Journal of Money, Credit, and Banking* 1, February, pp. 46–70.

———— (1976), *Keynes' Monetary Thought*. Durham, N.C.: Duke University Press.

Phillips, A. W. (1956), "Some Notes on the Estimation of Time-Forms of Reactions in Interdependent Dynamic Systems," *Economica* 23, May, pp. 99–113.

Pierce, James, and Thomas Thomson (1972), "Controlling the Stock of Money," in Federal Reserve Bank of Boston, *Controlling Monetary Aggregates II: The Implementation*, Boston: Federal Reserve Bank of Boston.

Poole, William (1970), "Optimal Choice of Monetary Policy Instruments in a Simple Stochastic Macro Model," *Quarterly Journal of Economics* 84, May, pp. 197–216.

———— (1976), "Benefits and Costs of Stable Money Growth," in *Institutional Arrangements and the Inflation Problem*. Amsterdam: North-Holland Publishing Co., *Carnegie-Rochester Conference Series on Public Policy* 3, pp. 15–50.

———— and Charles Lieberman (1972), "Improving Monetary Control," *Brookings Papers on Economic Activity*, no. 2, pp. 293–335.

Popper, Karl (1959), *The Logic of Scientific Discovery*. New York: Science Editions.

Starleaf, Dennis, and Richard Floyd (1972), "Some Evidence with Respect to the Efficacy of Friedman's Monetary Policy Proposals," *Journal of Money, Credit, and Banking* 4, August, pp. 713–22.

Tanner, Ernest (1977), "Are the Lags in the Effects of Monetary Policy Variable?" unpublished manuscript.

Teigen, Ronald (1972), "A Critical Look at Monetarist Economics," Federal Reserve Bank of St. Louis *Review* 54, January, pp. 10–25.

———— (1975) "Monetary and Fiscal Influences on Economic Activity: Evidence from Denmark, Finland and Norway," *Swedish Journal of Economics* 77, pp. 149–64.

Tobin, James (1970), "Money and Income: Post Hoc Ergo Propter Hoc?" *Quarterly Journal of Economics,* May, pp. 301–17.

———— (1972), Friedman's Theoretical Framework," *Journal of Political Economy* 80, September/December, pp. 852–63.

United Kingdom, Committee on the Workings of the Monetary System (1959), *Report* (Radcliffe Report), London: HM Stationery Office.

4. A CRITICAL LOOK AT MONETARIST ECONOMICS*

Ronald L. Teigen

Until just a few years ago, the viewpoint which lately has come to be known as "monetarist" was not taken very seriously by anyone except a few dedicated disciples. Its central postulate—that changes in the level of aggregate money income were due essentially to prior money stock changes—was viewed as a totally inadequate oversimplification, especially since the proponents of this approach failed to provide an adequately detailed explanation of the theoretical structure upon which this tenet was based.[1] The empirical evidence presented in support of this "quantity theory" viewpoint was subjected to criticism so severe that the evidence has never been taken very seriously.[2]

However, recent years have witnessed something of a turnaround. The conventional wisdom as embodied in modern Keynesian theory has been cast into doubt, while monetarist thinking has increased greatly in popularity, to the point where its proponents, and even some of its critics, speak of a "monetarist revolution."[3] The reasons for this rather sudden change are no doubt related in part to the apparent inconsistency of the Keynesian analysis (or at least an elementary version of it) with economic events in the United States during the late 1960s,[4] in some degree

---

* From Federal Reserve Bank of St. Louis *Review,* January 1972, pp. 10–25. Reprinted by permission of the Federal Reserve Bank of St. Louis.

[1] In particular, Milton Friedman's well-known article, "The Quantity Theory of Money—A Restatement," in M. Friedman, ed., *Studies in the Quantity Theory of Money* (Chicago: University of Chicago Press, 1956), pp. 3–21, which has been cited as the basis for much monetarist work, has been shown by Don Patinkin to be a sophisticated version of Keynes' liquidity preference theory rather than the up-to-date statement of an alleged Chicago oral tradition that monetarists take it to be. See Don Patinkin, "The Chicago Tradition, the Quantity Theory, and Friedman," *Journal of Money, Credit and Banking* (February 1969), pp. 46–70.

[2] I am referring chiefly to the controversy triggered by the work of Milton Friedman and his associates in the late 1950s and early 1960s, especially Friedman's evidence on lags observed between changes in the rate of change of the money stock and changes in GNP, as presented in his paper, "The Supply of Money and Changes in Prices and Output," Joint Economic Committee, U.S. Congress, 1958, and elsewhere, and in the Milton Friedman and David Meiselman paper on, "The Relative Stability of Monetary Velocity and the Investment Multiplier in the United States, 1897–1958," in Commission on Money and Credit, *Stabilization Policies* (Englewood Cliffs, N.J.: Prentice-Hall, Inc., 1963). The regression

results reported in the latter paper were severely criticized by Donald Hester in the November 1964 *Review of Economics and Statistics* and by Albert Ando-Franco Modigliani and Michael DePrano-Thomas Mayer in the September 1965 *American Economic Review.* The lead-lag observations discussed in the former paper were criticized by John M. Culbertson in the December 1960 *Journal of Political Economy,* and by James Tobin in the May 1970 *Quarterly Journal of Economics.*

[3] See Karl Brunner, "The 'Monetarist Revolution' in Monetary Theory," *Weltwirtschaftliches Archiv* (No. 1, 1970), pp. 1–30, and Harry G. Johnson, "The Keynesian Revolution and the Monetarist Counter-Revolution," *American Economic Review,* Papers and Proceedings (May 1971), pp. 1–14.

[4] The apparent failure of the income tax surcharge of June 1968 to reduce aggregate demand rapidly has been interpreted by some to be evidence of the failure of the "new" economics. However, it is not at all clear that the surtax was ineffective. In a recently-published study by Arthur Okun, evidence is provided that, at least in some categories of spending (nondurable goods and services in particular), the surcharge seems to have reduced demand substantially. But in other categories (especially demand for new automobiles) no reduction is apparent. See Arthur M. Okun, "The Personal Tax Surcharge and Consumer Demand, 1968–70," *Brookings Papers on Economic Activity* (No. 1, 1971), pp. 167–204. More generally, the notion that demand should have been observed to fall after the surtax was imposed is based on simplistic and partial analysis. When the surtax is analyzed within the context of a complete model

to monetarist criticism of Keynesian analysis (mostly directed at a *very* elementary version of it), and in part to other causes, including substantial development by the monetarists of their own theoretical position, as well as the appearance of new and more convincing empirical findings.[5]

While the increase in popularity of monetarism has been rapid, and the rate of growth of the monetarist literature impressive, a critical literature has also appeared, charging that monetarist theory has turned out largely to consist of old concepts clothed in new names, and that the empirical evidence purportedly supporting the monetarist position is biased and undependable.[6] The purpose of the present paper is to attempt to summarize in a general way the main features of the present monetarist theoretical stance, and to examine the monetarist view of modern

(in which government spending is taken into account), and one which incorporates the sophisticated theories of consumption behavior recently developed—the "permanent income" hypothesis of Milton Friedman or the "life-cycle" hypothesis of Albert Ando and Franco Modigliani—there appear a number of considerations which suggest that no substantial diminution of total demand could be anticipated. This point of view is argued persuasively by Robert Eisner in his paper, "Fiscal and Monetary Policy Reconsidered," *American Economic Review* (December 1969), pp. 897–905. Eisner reasons that rising Government expenditure had been expanding demand rapidly at the time when the surtax was enacted; furthermore, under the Friedman and Ando-Modigliani theories, which postulate that it is some long-run measure of income or wealth rather than current-period income which determines a household's living standard, a temporary tax change (such as the 1968 surcharge) would be expected to have only minor effects on spending because it does not change long-run expected income significantly. See Milton Friedman, *A Theory of the Consumption Function* (Princeton, N.J.: Princeton University Press, 1957), and Albert Ando and Franco Modigliani, "The 'Life-Cycle' Hypothesis of Saving: Aggregate Implications and Tests," *American Economic Review* (March 1963), pp. 55–84.

[5] Harry Johnson, "The Keynesian Revolution and the Monetarist Counter-Revolution," suggests that the successful monetarist upsurge may also be due to the factors related to the conversion of the "Keynesian revolution" of the 1930s into the economic orthodoxy of the 1960s.

[6] Ibid., for a general discussion of monetarist theory and its relationship to Keynesian orthodoxy. There have been published a large number of papers critical of the recent monetarist empirical studies; references to some are given in footnote 2, and a summary of the criticism of more recent monetarist empirical work is contained in Ronald L. Teigen, "The Keynesian-Monetarist Debate in the U.S.; A Summary and Evaluation," *Statsøkonomisk Tidsskrift* (January 1970), pp. 1–27.

Keynesianism. Since much of the debate bears directly on the stabilization policy process and the relative usefulness of different instruments of policy, particular attention will be given to the nature of the transmission mechanism under the two approaches. The empirical evidence will not be discussed in a systematic way in this paper, although reference will be made to it, where appropriate, in the discussion of the theories. In conducting this comparison, I shall attempt to identify issues between the two camps which are real, and those which seem to be false.

THE STRUCTURE OF MONETARIST THOUGHT

Although the roots of modern monetarist thought extend far back in time (the writings of classical economists are often cited, Irving Fisher being particularly popular), it is only lately that detailed expositions of this theory have begun to appear. In this paper, no systematic discussion of the entire literature will be undertaken. Instead, important summary statements which recently have become available in articles by Andersen, Brunner, Fand, Friedman, and others will be taken to be representative of present-day monetarist thought.[7]

[7] Some of the important articles include Leonall C. Andersen, "A Monetarist View of Demand Management: The United States Experience," Federal Reserve Bank of St. Louis *Review* (September 1971), pp. 1–11; Leonall C. Andersen and Keith M. Carlson, "A Monetarist Model for Economic Stabilization," Federal Reserve Bank of St. Louis *Review* (April 1970), pp. 7–25; Leonall C. Andersen and Jerry L. Jordan, "Monetary and Fiscal Actions: A Test of Their Relative Importance in Economic Stabilization," Federal Reserve Bank of St. Louis *Review* (November 1968), pp. 11–24; Karl Brunner, "The Role of Money and Monetary Policy," Federal Reserve Bank of St. Louis *Review* (July 1968), pp. 9–24; idem, "The 'Monetarist Revolution' in Monetary Theory;" idem, "A Survey of Selected Issues in Monetary Theory," *Schweizerische Zeitschrift für Volkswirtschaft und Statistik* (No. 1, 1971), pp. 1–146; idem, The "Monetarist View of Keynesian Ideas," *Lloyds Bank Review* (October 1971), pp. 35–49; David I. Fand, "Keynesian Monetary Theories, Stabilization Policy, and the Recent Inflation," *Journal of Money, Credit, and Banking* (August 1969), pp. 556–87; idem, "Monetarism and Fiscalism," *Banca Nazionale del Lavoro Quarterly Review* (September, 1970), pp. 275–89; idem, "A Monetarist Model of the Monetary Process," *Journal of Finance* (May 1970), pp. 275–89; Milton Friedman, "A Theoretical Framework for Monetary Analysis," *Journal of Political Economy* (March/April 1970), pp. 193–238; idem, "A Monetary Theory of National Income," *Journal of Political Economy* (March/April 1971), pp. 323–37.

Models, Assertions, and Themes

As a useful starting point in establishing a general framework for the discussion to follow, we may refer to recent articles by Brunner and Friedman containing inclusive statements of the monetarist position.[8] Friedman provides an explicit statement of the static-equilibrium structure which he views as being consistent with both the monetarist and Keynesian schools of thought. The theme he stresses—that it is the particular features of or assumptions about particular characteristics of the general analytic structure, rather than the fundamental nature of the structure itself, which differentiate monetarists and Keynesians—also appears in the writings of Brunner and others. In summary form, the model set out by Friedman is as follows:

$$\frac{Y}{p} = C\left(\frac{Y}{p}, r\right) + I(r) \qquad (1)$$

$$M_0 = p \cdot L\left(\frac{Y}{p}, r\right) \qquad (2)$$

$$Y = py \qquad (3)$$

where Y is money income, p is the general price level, r is the rate of interest, M_0 is the nominal exogenously-set money stock,[9] y is real income or output, and C, I, and L stand for the consumption, investment, and demand-for-money functions, respectively.

Equation (1) is of course the familiar IS curve, from which can be obtained all combinations of real income and the interest rate which will make the flow of planned spending equal to available output, and hence will result in equilibrium in the market for goods and services. Equation (2) is the LM curve, which yields all combinations of real income, the interest rate, and the price level which will equate the demand for real balances with the real value of the nominal money stock. Equation (3) is a definition relating nominal income and real income or output through the price level. There are of course other markets which could be considered, but which are not explicitly accounted for in equations (1) or (2); in particular, the bond and labor markets are not made explicit. Friedman argues that the assumptions made by the two camps in order to accommodate these markets

and simultaneously close the system of equations constitute a fundamental point of difference between monetarists and Keynesians. As written in equations (1)–(3), the model posited by Friedman contains four endogenous variables—Y, p, r, and y—and therefore is underdetermined. Monetarism is said by Friedman to include with the above equations a vast number of additional relationships; specifically, a whole Walrasian system of demand equations, supply equations, equilibrium conditions, etc., which in and of themselves determine y, the level of real output. The inclusion of a Walrasian system of course implies that the equilibrium position of the model is one of full employment. (There is no such implication for the short-run dynamics of the system, however.) With real output predetermined from the standpoint of equations (1)–(3), equation (1) can be solved for the equilibrium value of the interest rate, and (2) yields the equilibrium price level. Elementary manipulation of this system gives the result that only the price level (and the money wage rate, which is not made explicit in equations (1)–(3)) will change in response to a money stock change; the equilibrium value of the interest rate is not shifted, and therefore is said to be determined only by "real" variables.[10] In other words, this version of the model displays the well known "classical dichotomy."

According to Friedman, the Keynesian approach utilizes a much different and less satisfactory procedure by assuming that the *price level,* rather than real income, is determined outside of the postulated structure (Friedman refers to ". . . a *deus ex machina* with no underpinning in economic theory.").[11] By taking the price level to be exogenous with respect to this structure, the number of variables again is reduced to three (Y, y, and r in this case). However, the system no longer is dichotomized, and all of the variables now are determined jointly rather than recursively. In particular, the static equilibrium levels of both real income and the interest rate can now be changed by both money stock and expenditure changes.[12]

[8] Friedman, "A Theoretical Framework," and Brunner, "The 'Monetarist Revolution'."

[9] In one version of Friedman's statement, the money supply is made a function of the interest rate rather than being assumed to be exogenous. However, this makes no essential difference to the present discussion, as Friedman points out.

[10] This statement is not accurate if the system contains a government sector which issues money-fixed claims against itself, and if real wealth is an argument in the expenditure functions, and/or if the government establishes a tax-expenditure system based on nominal variables.

[11] Friedman, "A Theoretical Framework," p. 222.

[12] In a more recent article, Friedman has proposed another means of closing this system of equations, which he labels a "third way" to distinguish it from the two procedures outlined in the body of the present paper. He views this approach as intermediate

It would be a mistake to conclude from the foregoing discussion that monetarists view themselves as differing from Keynesians only in terms of the assumptions utilized to provide a unique equilibrium solution to the static *IS-LM* model. There are several other typically monetarist assumptions about the static and dynamic dimensions of this system. Recently, Karl Brunner has introduced four propositions which he asserts are "defining characteristics of the monetarist position." There are: (1) the transmission mechanism for monetary impulses involves a very general kind of portfolio adjustment process ultimately affecting the relationship between the market price of physical assets and their production cost, rather than only the relationship between borrowing costs and the internal rates of return on potential acquisitions of new physical capital, as is asserted to be the mechanism characteristic of modern Keynesian analysis; (2) most of the destabilizing shocks experienced by the system arise from decisions of the government with respect to tax, expenditure, and monetary policy, rather than from the instability of private investment or of some other aspect of private-sector behavior, as the Keynesian view is said to assume. A related belief is that the demand-for-money function is very stable, while the policy-determined supply of money balances is unstable; (3) monetary impulses are the dominant factor in explaining changes in the pace of economic activity, in con-

trast to the Keynesian position which assertedly takes real impulses as primary; (4) in analyzing the determinants of change in the level of aggregate activity, detailed knowledge of "allocative detail" about the working of financial markets and institutions is of secondary importance and can be disregarded. This implies that the relationship between policy instruments and economic activity can be captured in a very small-scale model—perhaps even in one equation—while the Keynesian position is that knowledge of allocative detail (e.g., substitution relationships between various financial assets) is necessary for the proper understanding of policy processes, implying a need for complex structural models.[13]

The statements by Brunner and Friedman are attempts to sketch the fundamental structure of monetarism. As such, they do not emphasize or even identify explicitly some of the specific characteristic themes which permeate monetarist writing, including their own. Several such themes can be identified.

1. Great importance is attached to the demand-for-money function, and it is in fact the central behavioral relationship in the monetarist model.[14] Particular stress is laid on its stability, by which is meant not only that the variance of its error term is small, but much more importantly, that it contains very few arguments. Friedman has written that:

The quantity theorist accepts the empirical hypothesis that the demand for money is highly stable—more stable than functions such as the consumption function that are offered as alternative key relations. . . . . [T]he stability he expects is in the functional relation between the quantity of money demanded

---

in respect to its theoretical position vis-à-vis the others. However, since it reduces to a relationship between income and the past history of the money stock, as Friedman demonstrates, it seems clearly to fit in with the monetarist point of view. In this approach, it is assumed that the current market rate of interest and the expected market rate are kept equal by the actions of asset holders. The expected market rate, in turn, is set by the expected real rate plus the expected rate of price change (which by definition is the difference between the expected rate of change of nominal income and of real output). By assuming the expected real rate of interest, the expected rate of growth of real output, and the expected rate of growth of nominal income all to be determined outside the system, the market rate of interest is made into a variable determined outside the system also. Assuming further that the income elasticity of demand for money is unity, Friedman establishes a direct link between nominal income and the money stock (because under his assumptions, velocity becomes a predetermined variable); this, in turn, enables the "real" sector to be solved. One of the features of this procedure is that it provides an alternative to the assumption of full employment. However, it entails some disadvantages of its own, which are noted in the section of the present paper entitled "Stabilization Policy." See Friedman, "A Monetary Theory of Nominal Income."

[13] These "defining characteristics" are discussed at some length in Brunner, "The 'Monetarist Revolution'," Section II.

[14] Thus, for example, David Fand states, "The quantity theory, in its post-Keynesian reformulation, is a theory of the demand for money and a theory of money income," "Keynesian Monetary Theories," p. 561. Also, he writes, ". . . the modern quantity theory uses the money demand function to predict the level of money income and prices if output is given, or *changes* in money income if output varies with changes in [the money stock]," "Monetarism and Fiscalism," p. 228. Friedman has written, "The quantity theorist not only regards the demand function for money as stable; he also regards it as playing a vital role in determining variables that he regards as of great importance for the analysis of the economy as a whole, such as the level of money income or of prices. It is this that leads him to put greater emphasis on the demand for money than on, let us say, the demand for pins, even though the latter might be as stable as the former," "The Quantity Theory of Money—A Restatement," p. 16.

and the variables that determine it . . . [and] he must sharply limit, and be prepared to specify explicitly, the variables that it is empirically important to include in the function. For to expand the number of variables regarded as significant is to empty the hypothesis of its empirical content; there is indeed little if any difference between asserting that the demand for money is highly unstable and asserting that it is a perfectly stable function of an indefinitely large number of variables.[15]

2. A particular aspect of the demand for money emphasized by monetarists is that, in their analysis, the stable *demand* for money is concerned with real, not nominal, balances, while the authorities control the nominal *supply*, which tends to be quite variable relative to demand.[16] This state of affairs is usually contrasted with the Keynesian case, in which the demand for money is said to be a demand for nominal balances, either because it is (incorrectly) specified that way,[17] or because, as in Friedman's discussion summarized above, the price level is fixed so that real and nominal balances are the same. Monetarists use this distinction as part of a rationalization for their contention that their analysis implies a much broader concept of the transmission mechanism for monetary impulses than does the Keynesian model, being based on a very general portfolio adjustment process working through changes in a broad spectrum of asset yields and price level changes, in contrast to the narrow cost of credit channel which is implied by the Keynesian demand-for-money function. This point is developed further in the section entitled "The Transmission Mechanism for Monetary Impulses" below.

3. Further, monetarists believe the interest elasticity of demand for money balances to be quite low. Until recently, it was generally thought that they viewed this elasticity to be zero so

that the demand for money was linked directly to income as implied by the naive quantity theory. However, such a view has been rejected outright by Friedman and others;[18] if it ever was held, the accumulation of empirical evidence to the contrary has made it untenable now.[19]

Presently, monetarists take the reputedly different views held by themselves and Keynesians on the size of this elasticity as a basis for contrasting inferences about the expected behavior of velocity in response to a monetary shift. A substantial interest elasticity of demand for money, said to be the Keynesian position, is viewed as implying unstable velocity; Keynesians are viewed by monetarists as not being able to "depend" on the stability of velocity, for as the money stock rises and falls, offsetting velocity changes insulate the rest of the system to a great extent. On the other hand, while not believing velocity to be perfectly constant, monetarists take the position that ". . . although marginal and average velocity differ, the velocity function is sufficiently stable to provide a relation between changes in money and changes in money income."[20] In other words, some, but not much, short-run variation in velocity may be expected.[21] To some monetarists, the essential difference between the two positions is summed up in the demand for money-velocity nexus. Fand writes:

The post-Keynesian quantity and income theories thus differ sharply in their analysis of the money demand function. In the modern quantity theory it serves as a velocity function relating either money and money income or marginal *changes* in money and money income . . .; in the income theory, it serves as a liquidity preference theory of interest rates, or of *changes* in interest rates (if the price level is given and determined independently of the monetary sector).[22]

Although it has become fairly common practice to discuss the behavior of velocity in terms of

[15] Friedman, "The Quantity Theory of Money—A Restatement," p. 16.

[16] On this point Fand writes, "The sharp distinction drawn between the supply determined nominal money stock and the demand determined real stock—a key feature of monetarism—endows the authorities with effective control over the nominal money stock, while severely limiting the extent, and the circumstances, in which they may hope to influence the real value of this stock. If the former assumption extends their control over nominal variables, the latter assumption severely limits their influence and control on endogenous variables such as the real money stock." See "Monetarism and Fiscalism," pp. 280–81.

[17] This view is taken by David I. Fand in, "Some Issues in Monetary Economics," *Banca Nazionale del Lavoro Quarterly Review* (September 1969), pp. 228–9 and footnote 24, p. 229.

[18] Milton Friedman, "Interest Rates and the Demand for Money," *Journal of Law and Economics* (October 1966), pp. 71–86.

[19] Some of this evidence is summarized in David Laidler, *The Demand for Money: Theories and Evidence* (Scranton, Pa.: International Textbook Company, 1969).

[20] Fand, "Keynesian Monetary Theories," pp. 563–64.

[21] Monetarists do not necessarily expect velocity to change inversely with changes in the money stock. Friedman recently has written that ". . . the effect on [velocity] is empirically not to absorb the change in M, as Keynesian analysis implies, but often to reinforce it. . . .," "A Theoretical Framework," p. 217.

[22] See Fand, "Some Issues," p. 228.

the properties of the demand-for-money function, it is improper to do so because observed velocity depends on all of the behavior—real and monetary—in the macroeconomic system. This point will be discussed in greater detail below.

4. The final monetarist theme which I shall mention is concerned with the nature of the response of interest rates to a monetary shift. Monetarists distinguished three components in the observed movement of interest rates: a "liquidity" effect, which is the immediate response before income or other variables have changed, and thus is expected to be in the opposite direction of the monetary shift; an "income" effect, which is the induced reaction of interest rates to the change in income brought about by the monetary impulse, and hence is expected to be in the same direction as the money stock change; and a "price expectations" effect, which comes about because monetary changes cause lenders and borrowers to anticipate a changing price level and lead lenders to protect themselves against the expected depreciation in the value of their funds by charging higher rates. This last effect would cause market interest rates to change in the same direction as the monetary change.[23]

In looking back over this summary of monetarist thought, it becomes quite apparent that there is a good deal of truth to Friedman's contention that the differences between Keynesians and monetarists are essentially empirical rather than theoretical, having to do with the assumptions made about specific aspects of the commonly-accepted structure, the relative stability and importance in the analysis of different functional relationships, the sizes of various elasticities, etc.[24] There appears to be little disagreement between the two camps over the specification of Friedman's basic model.[25] And of Brunner's

four points, at least two are essentially empirical (points numbered (2) and (3) above), while one of the remaining two (point (1) above) makes a distinction between monetarist and Keynesian views of the transmission mechanism which I believe is false with respect to current post-Keynesian income-expenditure analysis. Only his last point—that it is appropriate to study the relationship between policy instruments and economic activity without depending on knowledge of "allocative detail"—appears to be one about which there are genuine differences at the theoretical (or perhaps more properly, the methodological) level. Finally, among the four monetarist themes mentioned above, the third one is clearly empirical in nature, and monetarists and Keynesians both in fact hold that this elasticity is nonzero but small in absolute value. In the next section, it is demonstrated that modern Keynesians take the price level to be endogenous, which suggests that the monetarist-Keynesian distinctions summarized above as the second theme are not valid. I shall try to show below that monetarist emphasis on the importance of the demand-for-money relationship (the first theme) is unwarranted, at least in so far as this relationship is viewed as the basis for predicting velocity. I shall also show that the two components of interest rate change in response to a monetary impulse identified in theme four as monetarist are either clearly present in or at least consistent with Keynesian analysis and assumption.

Monetarism, Keynesianism, and the Price Level

As already noted above, monetarists see one of the essential differences between the two sides to be the question of the determinants of the price level in comparative static equilibrium analysis. Keynesians are said to take prices to be fixed so that monetary shifts are reflected in output changes, while quantity theorists believe that monetary changes affect only the price level in this sort of analysis, with real output being determined by a separate subsector of the system.

---

[23] For a discussion of these distinctions, see e.g., William Gibson, "Interest Rates and Monetary Policy," *Journal of Political Economy* (May/June 1970), pp. 431–55.

[24] This position is expressed in several of Friedman's writings; for example, see Milton Friedman and David Meiselman, "The Relative Stability," p. 168, and Milton Friedman, "Post-War Trends in Monetary Theory and Policy," *National Banking Review* (September 1964), reprinted in M. Friedman, *The Optimum Quantity of Money and Other Essays* (London: Macmillan and Co., Ltd., 1969), p. 73.

[25] Not all monetarists view this particular model as an appropriate description on which to build an analysis, however. Brunner recently wrote, "It is useful to emphasize . . . that the logic of the monetarist analysis based on the relative price theory approach requires that attention be directed to the interaction between output market, credit market and Walrasian

money market. This requirement cannot be satisfied by the general framework used by Friedman. This framework is the standard *IS-LM* analysis offered in an essentially Keynesian spirit. And this very choice of basic framework actually creates the analytical problems clearly recognized by Friedman in his subsequent discussion. . . . Our analysis . . . established however that the standard *IS-LM* diagram is not a very useful device for the analysis of monetary processes." Karl Brunner, "A Survey of Selected Issues in Monetary Theory," p. 82.

There is no doubt whatsoever that many practitioners of the Keynesian viewpoint have assumed that prices could conveniently be taken as given for some problems—especially those associated with substantial unemployment—and that it has often been convenient for simplicity of exposition in undergraduate classroom exercises or for other purposes to make the assumption of rigid prices. It is quite dubious, however, that this assumption, or the liquidity trap assumption which also has been an important element in the monetarist view of Keynesianism, reflects the thinking of most Keynesian economists today.[26] Rather, the standard static "complete Keynesian system" is widely recognized to be one in which the general price level is one of the variables determined by the interaction of the system, and hence is free to move, but to be one in which there are imperfections in the labor market—most typically, a money wage rate which is inflexible downwards. In other words, rather than assuming that prices are fixed as a means of making the simple static model determinate, modern Keynesians introduce an aggregated labor market and production function into the analysis.[27] This could be viewed as the Keynesian equivalent of the "Walrasian system of equations" asserted by

Friedman to be the hallmark of the adherents to the modern quantity theory approach. It is of course much less satisfactory in that all labor market activity and all kinds of production are aggregated into perhaps as few as two equations (i.e., a reduced-form labor market equation and an aggregate production function) rather than having each market and each activity represented by specific equations. It is more satisfactory on two counts: first, the equations at least are explicitly specified, and second, these equations do not yield the full employment outcome, as is typically the case when depending on a Walrasian system.[28]

The essential difference in this regard between monetarists and Keynesians therefore would appear to be that the former view *all* prices (including wages) as flexible, while the latter consider all prices *except* the money wage rate to be flexible (money wages are viewed as inflexible, at least in a downward direction, due to such structural phenomena as minimum wage laws, union contracts, and the like). This distinction has significant implications for the analysis.

In the first place, the Keynesian treatment now cannot be said to be fundamentally less satisfactory than the monetarist one in terms of methodology, except perhaps on grounds having to do with problems of aggregation (Friedman, it will be recalled, used the pejorative term "deus ex machina" to describe what he understood to be the Keynesian approach). Rather, the difference now lies in the analytic usefulness of the assumptions themselves. Is it more appropriate to assume that wages and prices are flexible, or that money wages are sticky while prices can adjust? The answer to this question depends on the nature of the problem being studied in any particular case, and this suggests that an important difference between the two schools of thought may be that Keynesians are more concerned with short-run analysis (for instance, that related to countercyclical stabilization) while monetarist assumptions are more consistent with long-run analysis.

Second, dropping the rigid-price assumption tends to reduce the basis for the heavy emphasis placed by monetarists on the demand-for-money function and its properties. One place where such emphasis is evident is in the discussion of velocity. We turn next to an inquiry into the factors

---

[26] The liquidity trap is rejected by most economists today because little support for it has been found in the many empirical studies of the demand for money which have recently been made. For a summary of some of this evidence, see Ronald L. Teigen, "The Demand for and Supply of Money," supra, Table 2, page 92, or "The Importance of Money," *Bank of England Quarterly Bulletin* (June 1970), pp. 159–98.

[27] As evidence for the assertion that modern post-Keynesian static analysis in its most general form typically assumes the price level to be an endogenous variable, and that the system of equations usually is made determinate by introducing a supply subsector consisting of a labor market and aggregate production function, the following standard works are cited: Gardner Ackley, *Macroeconomic Theory* (New York: Macmillan, 1961), chap. IX; R. G. D. Allen, *Macro-Economic Theory* (London: Macmillan, 1967), chap. 7, esp. sections 7.6–7.8; Martin J. Bailey, *National Income and the Price Level*, 2nd. ed. (New York: McGraw-Hill, 1971), chap. 3, esp. section 2; Robert S. Holbrook, "The Interest Rate, the Price Level, and Aggregate Output," supra, pp. 38–60. Franco Modigliani, "The Monetary Mechanism and its Interaction with Real Phenomena," *Review of Economics and Statistics* (February 1963 Supplement); and Warren L. Smith, "A Graphical Exposition of the Complete Keynesian System," *Southern Economic Journal* (October 1956), reprinted in W. Smith and R. Teigen, eds., *Readings in Money, National Income, and Stabilization Policy*, 3d ed., as well as in several other standard collections of readings in macroeconomics.

[28] This discussion is not meant to imply that the simple static Keynesian system contains an adequate description of the processes which determine the price level. It states simply that the price level is an endogenous variable in the model.

affecting velocity, with particular emphasis on the relationship of velocity to the demand-for-money function.

The Demand-for-Money Function and Velocity

Monetarists, as we have already noted, tend to think of the demand-for-money function as a "stable velocity function" while holding that Keynesians view velocity as unstable, justifying this position by appeal to contrasting assumptions about the price level and the interest elasticity of demand for money (see e.g. the quotes from Fand and others above). The fact of the matter is that the behavior of velocity under the two approaches in response to a monetary shift depends basically on the assumptions made about the *labor market*, not about the demand for money or about prices, since, as we have seen, both approaches take prices as flexible and, if that is the case, the same general demand-for-money function $\left(\dfrac{M}{p} = L(y,r) \right)$ would be characteristic of both. This point can be demonstrated quite easily. First we note that the definition of velocity implies the following relationship:

$$E_{V \cdot M_0} = E_{y \cdot M_0} + E_{p \cdot M_0} - 1, \qquad (4)$$

where E stands for elasticities calculated on the basis of the interaction of the entire structure, so that (for instance) $E_{y \cdot M_0}$ represents the elasticity of real output with respect to changes in the nominal money stock when the response of the entire economic system to the money stock change is taken into account. To distinguish such "systemic" elasticities from "partial" elasticities—those calculated along one function only—the symbol η will be used to represent partial elasticities. Thus, for instance, $\eta_{L \cdot r}$ will stand for the interest elasticity of the demand for real balances, holding income and other variables constant.

Under the monetarist assumption of flexible wages and prices, real output is determined uniquely by Friedman's "Walrasian system" and, as he points out, is to be considered as predetermined from the standpoint of equations (1)–(3). This means that a monetary shift cannot change real output $\left(\text{i.e., the multiplier } \dfrac{dy}{dM_0} = 0 \right)$, so that $E_{y \cdot M_0}$, which is defined to be $\dfrac{M_0}{y} \dfrac{dy}{dM_0}$, is also zero. By differentiating equations (1)–(3) with respect to M_0 while holding y constant, it is easy to show that the elasticity $E_{p \cdot M_0}$, which is equal to $\dfrac{M_0}{p} \dfrac{dp}{dM_0}$,

has a value of unity. Inserting these results into (4) gives the quantity theory result that $E_{V \cdot M_0} = 0$, the "stable velocity" results referred to previously. It is important to note that no particular assumptions unique to the monetarist position were made about the demand for money *per se*; the assumption which yielded this result was that the demand for labor and the supply of labor both were functions of the real wage rate, and that the market was always cleared.

On the other hand, let us consider the Keynesian case, which we now define as one in which *money wages* are sticky (i.e., there exists money illusion in the supply of labor), but in which the price level is an endogenous variable. To analyze this case, we must add three equations to the basic model: an aggregate production function (equation (5) below); a labor market summary equation which states that the supply of labor services per unit time (N) is infinitely elastic over a wide range of employment at whatever money wage rate prevails, and that the demand for labor (N^D) is determined by the real wage (w) (equation (6)); and a definition which states that the real wage is the ratio of the money wage rate (W) and the price level (equation (7)). The bar over the money wage rate indicates that it is being held constant here.[29] This gives:

$$y = y(N) \qquad (5)$$
$$N = N^D(w) \qquad (6)$$
$$w = \frac{\overline{W}}{p}. \qquad (7)$$

By differentiating the system defined by equations (1)–(3) and (5)–(7) totally with respect to M_0, expressions for the systemic elasticities $E_{y \cdot M_0}$ and $E_{p \cdot M_0}$ can be found. They are as follows (see the appendix for their derivation):

$$E_{y \cdot M_0} = \cfrac{1}{\cfrac{\eta_{S \cdot y} \eta_{L \cdot r}}{\eta_{I \cdot r} - \eta_{S \cdot r}} + \eta_{L \cdot y} - \cfrac{1}{\eta_{y \cdot N} \eta_{N \cdot w}^{D}}} \qquad (8)$$

$$E_{p \cdot M_0} = -\cfrac{1}{\eta_{y \cdot N} \eta_{N \cdot w}^{D} \left[\cfrac{\eta_{S \cdot y} \eta_{L \cdot r}}{\eta_{I \cdot r} - \eta_{S \cdot r}} + \eta_{L \cdot y} \right] - 1}$$
$$(9)$$

---

[29] This is the simplest method of introducing a Keynesian-type assumption into the analysis; it is by no means the only possible way of doing so. The nature of and reasons for the existence of money illusion in the labor market is the subject of a considerable amount of literature. See, for example, Axel Leijonhufvud, *On Keynesian Economics and the Economics of Keynes* (London: Oxford University Press, 1968).

Here S stands for the savings function; otherwise all of the notation has already been defined. The usual slope assumptions are made, and on the basis of these assumptions, both of these systemic elasticities will be positive.[30] Whether velocity will rise, fall, or remain constant in the face of a monetary shift depends on the sizes of all of the partial elasticities and their relationships to one another as given by these expressions. The demand-for-money elasticities play a role, but are by no means the only relevant elasticities. In general, we would not expect the elasticity of velocity with respect to nominal money balances to be minus unity in value, as the "liquidity trap" assumption implies. It will approach that value if $\eta_{L\cdot r}$ or $\eta_{S\cdot y}$ are very large, or if the term $(\eta_{I\cdot r} - \eta_{S\cdot r})$ is very close to zero.[31]

To summarize, the main point of this exercise was to show that, using a common model with no special assumptions about the properties of the demand for money, it has been possible to derive "monetarist" and "Keynesian" results for the response of velocity to a monetary shift. It is improper to speak of the demand for money as a "velocity function," *especially* in the monetarist case where it is assumed that money wages are flexible so that the system equilibrates at full employment. In that case, the velocity elasticity will be zero no matter what the sizes of the demand-for money elasticities.

Eliminating the rigid-price assumption as a basic point of difference between the two schools reduces the basis for monetarist emphasis on the demand for money for other reasons besides its implications for velocity. It also is important for monetarist views on differences in the nature of the transmission mechanism for monetary policy. It is to this subject that we turn next.

The Transmission Mechanism for Monetary Impulses

One of the most characteristic themes of monetarism is the heavy emphasis which is placed

on differences between the quantities of money demanded and supplied as the prime factor motivating spending and, hence, changes in income and prices. Friedman and others have explained again and again how the authorities can change the nominal money stock, but how it is money holders who determine the velocity with which that stock is used, and ultimately who determine the stock of real balances through the effects of spending decisions on the price level. As Friedman puts it, "The key insight of the quantity-theory approach is that such a discrepancy [between the demand for and supply of money] will be manifested primarily in attempted spending, thence in the rate of change in nominal income."[32] In other words, when households and firms are holding more cash balances than are desired at current levels of income and interest rates, they convert these excess balances into other assets, both financial and physical; the market value of physical assets ultimately changes, making the production of new assets more attractive. The change in the general price level which occurs as a result of this process, and the change in output, both work toward a re-equating of the real value of the nominal money stock and the demand for real balances. Thus the monetarists clearly embrace a very general kind of portfolio adjustment view of the transmission mechanism in which the relevant portfolio contains financial and physical assets of all kinds.[33] It will be recalled that this is the first of Brunner's four "defining characteristics." At the same time, monetarists have been taking Keynesian analysis to task for focusing almost exclusively on interest rates representing the "cost of finance" as the channel through which monetary impulses are felt. The following quotation makes these distinctions very clear:

The Income-Expenditure theory of the Fiscalists adopts a particular transmission mechanism to analyze the effects of a change in the money stock (or its growth rate) on the real economy. It assumes that money changes will affect output or prices only through its effect on a set of conventional yields—on the market interest rate of a small group of financial assets, such as government or corporate bonds. A given change in the money stock will have a calculable effect on these interest rates . . . given by the liquidity preferences analysis, and the interest rate changes are then used to derive the change in invest-

[30] It is assumed that $\eta_{S\cdot r}$ is either positive or, if negative, that it is smaller in size than the absolute value of $\eta_{I\cdot r}$. A listing of all the slope assumptions is given in the appendix.

[31] Since the numerator of the expression for $\eta_{S\cdot y}$ is one minus the MPC, $\eta_{S\cdot y}$ is not expected to be large. As noted in footnote 26, belief in a very large interest elasticity of demand for money ($\eta_{L\cdot r}$) is not a characteristic Keynesian stance. Reference to the summaries of available empirical evidence mentioned in that footnote will show that this elasticity actually appears to be rather small (almost certainly less than unity in absolute value, and in many studies smaller in absolute value than 0.2).

[32] Friedman, "A Theoretical Framework," p. 225.

[33] A description of the classes of assets involved and the nature of their yields is given in Milton Friedman, "The Quantity Theory of Money—A Restatement."

ment spending, the induced effects on income and consumption, etc.

Monetarists, following the Quantity theory, do not accept this transmission mechanism and this liquidity preference theory of interest rates for several reasons: First, they suggest that an increase in money may directly affect expenditures, prices, and a wide variety of implicit yields on physical assets, and need not be restricted to a small set of conventional yields on financial assets. Second, they view the demand for money as determining the desired quantity of real balances, and not the level of interest rates. Third, and most fundamentally, they reject the notion that the authorities can change the stock of real balances—an endogenous variable—and thereby bring about a permanent change in interest rates. . . .

Monetarists reject the liquidity preference interest rate theory because it applies only as long as we can equate an increase in nominal money with a permanent increase in real balances. This suggests that the liquidity preference theory may be useful as a theory of the short run interest rate changes—the liquidity effect—associated with the impact effects of nominal money changes.[34]

Statements like this, and the quotation from Friedman in footnote 14 indicate that monetarists believe their view of the transmission mechanism to differ from the position they impute to the Keynesian camp most essentially in differences in assumptions about characteristics of the demand-for-money function. The interpretation of the interest rate term in this function plays a role; so does the question of price flexibility. As the preceding discussion and quotation indicate, monetarists think of their own view as an extremely general one. The interest rate term in their model really stands for a vector of yields on many assets, some of them financial yields determined in the money and capital markets, and some of them implicit yields on real assets. A monetary impulse sooner or later affects all of these yields, and hence adjusts the demand for real balances directly as well as indirectly through the effects of yield changes on income. At the same time, changes in the price level which result will adjust the real value of the nominal money supply. Therefore the adjustment process is seen as being summarized in the characteristics of the demand-for-real balances function and its relationship to the nominal money supply. Keynesians are said to include only a few market-determined yields on financial assets in their liquidity-preference function; furthermore, the price level is exogenously determined. Therefore the process of adjustment to a monetary impulse is supposedly seen by them in much

narrower terms—the entire process takes place through adjustment of the *demand* for money, and basically is said to focus on the cost of credit as reflected in market interest rates. Furthermore, the belief in a substantial interest elasticity of demand for money, often attributed to Keynesians, means that a monetary impulse will have a relatively small effect even on these rates.

These distinctions must be regarded as artificial. First, there is nothing inherent in the Keynesian system which is inconsistent with the introduction of a general portfolio adjustment transmission mechanism; and, indeed, there has been a substantial development in this direction in Keynesian thinking and practice during the last several years. On the theoretical side, the work of Tobin and others may be cited, while at the operational level, the developers of the Federal Reserve Board-MIT econometric model of the U.S. economy have attempted to incorporate such a mechanism into their model.[35] While all of the problems involved in this attempt have not yet been solved, work is continuing and improvements will be made. Second, as we have already shown, Keynesians take the price level to be endogenous, and thus recognize the same process of adjustment of the nominal money supply through price level changes as the monetarists.[36]

There remain certain problems with monetarist thought on two subjects related to the transmission mechanism. One is a misunderstanding, in my opinion, of the relationship between money and interest rates implied by Keynesian theory. The other has to do with the monetarist position on the money stock as a force driving income through the portfolio process mentioned above.

Liquidity Preference Theory, Money, and the Rate of Interest. Monetarists view themselves as holding a "monetary theory of the price level" under which monetary shifts are reflected (in

---

[34] Fand, "A Monetarist Model," pp. 280–81.

[35] For a non-monetarist example of the development of portfolio theory, see James Tobin, "An Essay on Principles of Debt Management," in Commission on Money and Credit, *Fiscal and Debt Management Policies* (Englewood Cliffs, N.J.: Prentice-Hall, Inc., 1963), pp. 143–218, esp. Part II. Features of the Federal Reserve Board-MIT model are discussed in Frank de Leeuw and Edward M. Gramlich, "The Channels of Monetary Policy," Federal Reserve *Bulletin* (June 1969), pp. 472–91.

[36] Semantic as well as real issues are involved in discussions of this subject. For example, Brunner labels anyone who subscribes to a portfolio adjustment view of the monetary transmission mechanism a "weak monetarist". See Karl Brunner, "The Role of Monetary Policy," Federal Reserve Bank of St. Louis *Review* (July 1968), pp. 9–24.

the longer run, at least) primarily in price level changes. They take the stance that Keynesians hold a "monetary theory of the interest rate." Under this phrase, at least two positions are subsumed. Some monetarists seem to think that Keynesians see the money supply together with the demand-for-money function (specified in nominal terms) as determining the level of interest rates. Others recognize that the interest rate in Keynesian analysis is determined jointly as one of the outcomes of an interacting system of relationships rather than just by one behavioral relationship (i.e., by some version of an *IS-LM* system like Friedman's summary model). Whichever view is held, however, it is asserted that Keynesian analysis leads to the conclusion that monetary shifts result in interest rate changes in the *opposite* direction, while monetarist analysis suggests that movement of *M* and *r* in the *same* direction will be observed.[37]

Neither version of the "monetary theory of the interest rate" is an accurate representation of Keynesian thought, for both imply that an expansionary monetary impulse (for example) can *only* result in a lower interest rate in the new equilibrium. In other words, it appears that of the two monetary effects on interest rates often mentioned by monetarists which are relevant for static analysis—the liquidity effect and the income effect—Keynesians are supposed to recognize only the liquidity effect, or more generally, are supposed to be basing their analysis on assumptions which can only result in an inverse relationship between monetary impulses and interest rate changes.

This is certainly not the case. When the entire structure is taken into account, rather than only

the liquidity preference function, the level of interest rates in the new equilibrium relative to the initial position is determined by a number of elasticities, most importantly those which are the determinants of the slope of the *IS* curve. If its slope is positive—which is the case if all of the propensities to spend with respect to total income sum to more than unity—then both income and interest rates will be higher in the new equilibrium than in the old.[38] This is such a well-known case as to require no further comment.

Of course, equilibrium positions are not observed in the real world; instead, the economy is always in transition, moving toward resting points, which themselves are repeatedly being disturbed. It may be inferred from some monetarist writings that it is the *observed* tendency of interest rates and money to move in the same direction which is thought to be inconsistent with Keynesianism, rather than the possibility that money and interest rates can move together in terms of comparative equilibrium points. In other words, the discussion may refer to the dynamics of the system, rather than the comparative statics. In this area, the monetarists have done us all a service by stressing the possible importance of price-expectation effects on interest rates, a phenomenon which typically has not been incorporated into dynamic Keynesian models. I will argue that observed parallel movements between money and interest rates are quite consistent with the basic *IS-LM* structure (no matter which way the *IS* curve slopes), given the reasonable and widely-accepted premise that the monetary sector adjusts much more rapidly than the real sector to external shocks. Under this premise, observed values of income and the rate of interest may be supposed, at least approximately, to be such that the *LM* equation is always satisfied during the process of adjustment from one equilibrium to another, while the *IS* equation is not. I will argue further that price-expectation effects are readily accommodated by this analysis.

The implications of these differing speeds of adjustment are illustrated on Figure 1, which happens to be drawn with a downward-sloping

[37] As an example of the first of these positions, the following quotation from a recent article by Fand is offered: "In the Keynesian theory the exogenously given quantity of money, together with the liquidity preference function, determines the interest rate." Fand, "Keynesian Monetary Theories," p. 564. The second is illustrated by a quotation from Zwick: "The alternative concepts of Keynes and Fisher concerning the adjustment of the economy to monetary changes are mirrored in their different notions concerning interest rate determination and the response of interest rates to monetary changes. The *IS-LM* framework suggests that, so long as the *IS* and *LM* schedules represent independent relations, a monetary expansion causes interest rates to fall because of the outward shift of the *LM* schedule. In the Fisherian model, a monetary increase raises the level of expenditures; the upward response of loan demand due to the increased expenditures causes interest rates to rise." Burton Zwick, "The Adjustment of the Economy to Monetary Changes," *Journal of Political Economy* (January/February 1971), p. 78.

[38] An upward-sloping *IS* curve cannot be obtained from Friedman's summary model, because only consumption spending is related to income in that model, and the notion that the MPC is less than unity is a fundamental postulate of macroeconomic analysis. However, the level of income might well appear in other expenditure functions, such as the investment relationship (where the rationalization would be that investment depends on profits, which in turn are a function of the level of income).

Figure 1: A Keynesian View of Money, Income, and Interest Rates

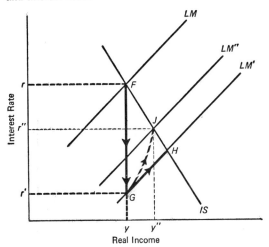

IS curve. Assume the system to be initially in equilibrium at point F, so that the equilibrium values of the interest rate and income levels are *r* and *y*. Now let there occur an expansion of the money supply, so that the LM curve shifts outward to a new position, LM'. According to the assumption made above concerning the relative speeds of adjustment of the monetary and real sectors, this shift will result first in a fall in the interest rate from its initial equilibrium level to a new level, *r'*. It should be noted that this is the "liquidity effect" which is recognized by monetarists as being present both in their own and in Keynesian thinking. It represents a movement along the liquidity preference function in response to a change in the money supply, holding income constant. Next, income will begin to respond, and income and the rate of interest both will rise along the segment GH of LM' to point H, the final equilibrium position. This movement, of course, reflects the "income effect." If rising income is accompanied by rising prices, there will also be an induced shift of the LM curve during the transition. For example, it might move to a position like LM" as shown. Alternatively, it could move to a position to the right of LM'.

Such LM shifts reflect the operation of two forces. First, rising prices reduce the real value of the new nominal money stock and "tighten the money market" after the initial expansionary pulse. This has the effect of moving the LM curve leftward. Second, rising prices may engender expectations of future price increases. If, as has been suggested, the demand for money depends on nominal interest rates while real expenditures are determined by real rates, then

the "price expectations effect" mentioned previously would cause a rightward LM shift, resulting in a lesser leftward overall shift in the LM curve than that brought about due only to the drop in the real value of the nominal money stock, or perhaps even a net rightward movement (in this discussion, the vertical axis is interpreted as measuring the real rate of interest). If these effects are present, the adjustment path followed from point G might be the dotted one instead of the solidly-drawn one, and the system would end up at a point like J instead of H, so that the new equilibrium income level would be *y"*, and the equilibrium real interest rate *r"*. Incidentally, if price-expectation effects are present, a value of *r"* for the real rate is quite consistent with a market rate above *r*.

We may conclude from this discussion that there is no reason to be surprised by the fact that during much of the time following an increase in the money supply, interest rates are observed to rise. A standard assumption about relative speeds of adjustment, much used by Keynesians, directly reflects both the "liquidity effect" and the "income effect" often discussed by monetarists, and is perfectly consistent with the presence of price expectation effects. Second, it is appropriate to point out that this entire discussion has been carried out in the context of a pure multiplier model. If accelerator effects are present, they may accentuate the pure multiplier effects of a monetary shift on interest rates, at least during parts of the adjustment period. Finally, there is the likelihood that in many cases in which interest rates and the money stock move together, the monetary authorities are reacting to shifts in spending. For instance, if total spending rises, interest rates will go up and the monetary authorities will often try to moderate the interest rate increase by expansionary open market operations, resulting in a rise in the money stock.

The Monetarist View of Money as a Force Driving Income. It is self-evident that monetarists typically have assigned great importance to changes in the money stock as the prime moving force behind income changes. For instance, one of Brunner's "defining characteristics of monetarism" is that ". . . the monetarist analysis assigns the monetary forces a dominant position among all the impulses working on the economic process."[39] And, of course, Friedman's investigations into the lead-lag relationship between changes in the rate of change of the money stock

---

[39] Brunner, "The 'Monetarist Revolution'," p. 7.

and changes in income are too well-known to require further comment.[40] At the same time, monetarist writings often seem to suggest that Keynesians view monetary policy as ineffective.

Keynesians view monetary policy as effective and useful, and to suggest the opposite is to raise false issues. But this does not mean that they necessarily consider changes in the money stock to have particular causal significance. Monetary policy is carried out through the traditional instruments—open market operations, discount rate changes, and variations in reserve requirements—and not by direct manipulation of the money stock. It is true that in simplified versions of the Keynesian model, monetary policy is represented by the money stock, which is assumed to be controlled by the authorities and which replaces the instruments named above. It is also possible that the authorities could control the nominal money stock to almost any desired degree of precision. But in the real world, or in the more sophisticated models of it, the nominal money stock is not exogenous, nor has it been controlled as an objective of policy by the central bank in the United States; it, or its components, are determined jointly by the central bank, the commercial banks, and the public, and it is basically a passive outcome of the interaction of the economic system, not a driving force.

The doubt the Keynesians feel concerning monetarist assertions about the potency of money stock changes reflects the fact that monetarist descriptions of the adjustment process themselves seem to give no particular reason for regarding money stock changes as causal. These descriptions typically run as follows, using an open market purchase of Treasury bills as an example:[41] At the outset, there is an exchange of assets between the central bank and a Government securities dealer, with the central bank giving the dealer its check drawn on itself in exchange for bills. This exchange results in the following: (1) a reduction in the yield on bills, with consequent disequilibrium among holders of securities; (2) an increase of bank reserves of an equivalent amount (disregarding drains into currency holdings, etc.); (3) an initial increase in the money supply of the same amount as the transaction; and (4) a decrease in bill holdings by the private sector, with a concomitant increase in the central bank's portfolio. In a process described in some detail by Friedman and Schwartz, the next step will involve action to readjust portfolios in response to yield and wealth changes; meanwhile, banks will be interested in expanding loans on the basis of their newly-acquired reserves (and incidentally in creating new deposits). Eventually the adjustment affects the yield on equities and therefore the market value of the existing stock of physical capital. The existing capital stock will rise in value, stimulating the production of new capital and thus causing income to rise. There may also be other effects, such as direct effects on spending of changes in wealth.

The question would seem to be whether it is the initial increase in the money stock, the full increase (including the new deposits generated as a consequence of loan decisions), the increase in bank reserves, the reduction in private bill holdings, the fall in yields, the increase in the central bank's portfolio, or some other factor which is responsible for the income change. Rather than arbitrarily selecting some one factor from this list, it would seem preferable to take the more general view that the initiating force was the disturbance of a portfolio equilibrium, effected in this case through open market operations. (Such a disturbance, with similar effects, could arise for other reasons: e.g., if there were a change in wealthholders' preferences for holding a particular security category at existing yields.) The change in the money stock is properly viewed as one of the several results (along with changes in income, interest rates, prices, etc.) of this disturbance. Such a position of course implies that monetary policy is effective, but does not assign the starring role in the drama to changes in the money stock.

STABILIZATION POLICY

Modern Keynesian static analysis, based on the complete Keynesian system with flexible prices and inflexible money wages, yields the result that both monetary and fiscal policy are able to effect changes in income, interest rates, prices, employment, and other variables. Monetarist analysis, however, takes the position that only monetary policy has significant effects on the pace of economic activity, at least in the short run. This suggests that the two schools of thought

[40] Milton Friedman, "The Supply of Money and Changes in Prices and Output," in *The Relationship of Prices to Economic Stability and Growth*, Compendium of Papers Submitted by Panelists Appearing Before the Joint Economic Committee, 85th Congress, 2nd sess., 1958, pp. 241–56.

[41] See, for instance, Milton Friedman and David Meiselman, "The Relative Stability," sec. VII, and Milton Friedman and Anna J. Schwartz, "Money and Business Cycles," *Review of Economics and Statistics* (February 1963 Supplement), esp. pp. 60–61.

disagree not in their views about monetary policy, but rather on the effectiveness of fiscal policy.

Until recently, monetarists were interpreted as basing their belief that fiscal policy is ineffective directly on the presumed existence of a stable demand-for-money function with zero interest elasticity, together with the assumption of an exogenously-set money stock. Such a demand-for-money function links money and income directly together, so that income cannot change unless the money stock changes. Shifts in government spending financed by bond issue, for instance, were said to result in interest rate changes of sufficient magnitude to reduce private spending to the degree required to keep total demand at a constant level.

However, given the many research studies which show otherwise, it has become impossible to maintain that the interest elasticity of the demand for money is zero. This development has had a considerable effect on the tone of monetarist discussions. Thus Fand, in discussing stabilization policy, refers to ". . . the *exceptional* case of a completely (interest) inelastic demand for money."[42] Furthermore, a relevant recent finding is that the *supply* of money is interest-elastic, and that this is sufficient to loosen the tight link between the money stock and income even if the interest elasticity of demand is zero.

Therefore monetarists have had to rationalize their dismissal of fiscal policy in other ways. Some have tried to find other means of solidifying the money-income link and of segregating the monetary sector from the remainder of the system by neutralizing the connection provided by the interest rate. One way of doing so is by considering the interest rate to be determined exogenously. This, in effect, is the procedure followed by Friedman in his paper entitled, "A Monetary Theory of National Income."[43] If interest rates do not respond to changes in real and financial variables, the rigid money-income connection is preserved. This may be considered the most extreme approach, because under it fiscal policy does not even affect the rate of interest and the division of output among the various sectors.

Another way is to make the standard quantity-theory assumption of flexible wages and prices, and hence full employment, while accepting the fact that the demand for and supply of money balances are interest-elastic. In such a world, fiscal policy cannot affect the levels of real variables like output or employment, which are entirely determined by the labor market and the production technology of the system—but then, neither can monetary policy.

Assumptions are not a matter of logic, assuming that they are internally consistent. In weighing these various approaches to the analysis of stabilization policy, the most important questions probably should be: Which of the alternative approaches is the most realistic and the most relevant for the real-world question of fiscal policy's effectiveness? Is it the case of flexible wages and prices, so that full employment is the rule and not the exception, and neither monetary policy nor fiscal policy can affect the level of real activity? Is it the case involving exogenously-determined interest rates, so that fiscal policy cannot even affect the division of output, let alone the level of activity? Or is it the case of flexible prices but a sticky wage level, in which case monetary and fiscal policy both are capable of affecting the level of real activity?

Brunner has taken a somewhat different approach to the analysis of fiscal policy than have most other monetarists. He asserts that fiscal policy is ineffective or perverse because the effects on asset values due to interest-rate changes of the cumulation or decumulation of claims against the Government held by the public, resulting from a fiscal policy deficit or surplus, outweigh the direct effects on the flow of output and income of new spending and taxing and of the changes in the stock of financial claims held by the private sector which result.[44] This position implies the view that the disturbance of portfolio equilibrium from *any* source (not only money stock changes) has powerful repercussions, and thus paradoxically tends to downgrade the importance of changes in the money stock. As far as is known, this position is not supported directly by empirical evidence.

SUMMARY

In this paper, I have attempted to sketch the main outlines of monetarist thought and to examine some aspects of the monetarist view of Keynesian analysis. In doing so, I have paid particular attention to the roles of the instruments of stabilization policy under the two views.

My examination of the monetarist-Keynesian debate has indicated that the version of Keynesianism which the monetarists use to establish a contrast for their own point of view is out of date and inadequate—a "vulgar" version of post-

---

[42] Fand, "Monetarism and Fiscalism," p. 289 (italics added).

[43] See the discussion of this approach in footnote 12.

---

[44] Karl Brunner, "The 'Monetarist Revolution'."

Keynesian thinking, to use Professor Johnson's term. When it is recognized that Keynesianism implies sticky wages and money illusion in the labor market rather than rigid prices, and that portfolio adjustment as the basis for the transmission of monetary impulses is not only consistent with the Keynesian approach but indeed is being built into Keynesian models, it is seen that there is very little if anything in monetarist theory which is new and different. Rather, the two approaches diverge in ways which basically are methodological and operational. The monetarists are willing to commit themselves to the use of very simple, very small (even one-equation) models for policy analysis; Keynesians typically are not. On this point, the monetarist stance seems to be a matter of faith rather than logic; the common theoretical basis on which both positions rest certainly implies the use of a structural approach.[45] There certainly are substantial differences in the kinds of operational assumptions that are made about particular dimensions of the theoretical structure, and these have implications of various kinds for policy. The typical Keynesian assumption of money wage inflexibility is consistent with a shorter-run analysis; it leads to the conclusion that both monetary policy and fiscal policy can affect the level of activity. The typical monetarist assumption of wage and price flexibility (i.e., of full employment) is more relevant for the analysis of secular changes.

This assumption essentially bypasses the whole question of short-run policy effects. For the long run, paradoxically, it suggests that fiscal policy is more important and interesting than monetary policy, for fiscal policy at least changes the rate of interest (unless the rate of interest is exogenously determined), and therefore the division of output, and presumably affects growth; whereas monetary policy affects only prices, money wages, and the like.[46] There appear to be some analytic confusions in many monetarist discussions. I have tried to show above that it is incorrect to view the demand-for-money function as a velocity relationship from either point of view. In the monetarist case, this is especially true because the stability of velocity in the face of monetary changes depends on assumptions about the labor market and is unrelated to the

characteristics of the demand-for-money relationship. It also appears that monetarist fascination with the money stock is unwarranted by monetarist logic, which seems to me to place great emphasis on portfolio disequilibrium as a potent driving force in the economy. It does not follow from this view, as a matter of logic, that observed changes in the money stock have any particular significance as a causative force.

On the positive side, monetarists have contributed to the development of macroeconomic thought by stressing that the links relied upon for years by most Keynesians to connect the real and monetary sectors overlook entirely the important substitution and wealth effects which are the concomitants of portfolio adjustment. They also have called our attention to the distinction, apparently first made by Irving Fisher many years ago, between market and real interest rates, and therefore to the potentially important role of price expectations in dynamic macroeconomics. These phenomena are extraordinarily difficult to capture in empirical models, but work is proceeding along these lines. It is to be hoped that during the next few years, they will be made standard features of Keynesian (that is, structural) theoretical and empirical models, and that dependable evidence will be gathered so that the *real* questions which divide us—chiefly, in my opinion, the question raised by Brunner and others concerning the need for large-scale structural models for aggregative analysis—can be answered satisfactorily.

APPENDIX

Following are the derivations which underlie equations (4), (8), and (9) in the text. They are based on equations (1)–(3) and (5)–(7), which are reproduced here for convenience:

$$y = C(y,r) + I(r) \qquad (1)$$

$$\frac{M_0}{p} = L(y,r) \qquad (2)$$

$$Y = py \qquad (3)$$

$$y = y(N) \qquad (5)$$

$$N = N^D(w) \qquad (6)$$

$$w = \frac{\overline{W}}{p} \qquad (7)$$

The following slope assumptions are used throughout: $O < C_y < 1$; $C_r < O$ or, if positive, $C_r < |I_r|$; $I_r < O$; $L_y > O$; $L_r < O$; $y_N > O$; $N^D_w < O$.

A. The Elasticity of Velocity

Equation (4) in the text is an expression for the elasticity of velocity with respect to a monetary shift, and is reproduced for convenience:

---

[45] Karl Brunner has written, "The monetarist disregards . . . the allocative detail of credit markets when examining patterns of allocation behavior. . . . Such detail is simply asserted . . . to be irrelevant for aggregative explanation." Ibid., p. 15.

[46] The reservations expressed in footnote 10 apply to this statement also.

$$E_{V \cdot M_0} = E_{y \cdot M_0} + E_{p \cdot M_0} - 1. \qquad (4)$$

It is derived by differentiating the expression for velocity $\left(V = \dfrac{Y}{M_0}\right)$ with respect to the money stock, and converting the result into elasticity form.

Thus we have:

$$\frac{dV}{dM_0} = \frac{1}{M_0}\frac{dY}{dM_0} - \frac{Y}{M_0^2}. \qquad (A.1)$$

From (3), we have

$$\frac{dY}{dM_0} = p\frac{dy}{dM_0} + y\frac{dp}{dM_0}. \qquad (A.2)$$

Substituting (A.2) into (A.1) and multiplying the resulting equation by $\dfrac{M_0}{V}$ yields

$$E_{V \cdot M_0} = E_{y \cdot M_0} + E_{p \cdot M_0} - 1, \qquad (A.3)$$

which is equation (4).

This result is derived only from definitions. Next we investigate the values of $E_{y \cdot M_0}$ and $E_{p \cdot M_0}$, and therefore of $E_{V \cdot M_0}$, which are implied by monetarist and Keynesian assumptions respectively.

B. The Monetarist Case

Monetarists assume that wages and prices are flexible so that real output, y, may be considered exogenous for the purpose of static analysis, and only equations (1) and (2) are relevant. Differentiating (1), which is the IS curve, yields:

$$C_y\frac{dy}{dM_0} + (C_r + I_r)\frac{dr}{dM_0} = \frac{dy}{dM_0}. \qquad (B.1)$$

However, if y is exogenous to this system, $\dfrac{dy}{dM_0} = 0$ so that we get:

$$(C_r + I_r)\frac{dr}{dM_0} = 0, \qquad (B.2)$$

which implies that $\dfrac{dr}{dM_0} = 0$.

Differentiating the LM curve (2) yields:

$$L_y\frac{dy}{dM_0} + L_r\frac{dr}{dM_0} = \frac{1}{p} - \frac{M_0}{p^2}\frac{dp}{dM_0}. \qquad (B.3)$$

Since we have found that, in this case,

$$\frac{dy}{dM_0} = \frac{dr}{dM_0} = 0,$$

(B.3) reduces to:

$$\frac{M_0}{p}\frac{dp}{dM_0} = E_{p \cdot M_0} = 1. \qquad (B.4)$$

Substituting these findings into (A.3), we find that $E_{V \cdot M_0} = 0$ using static analysis under monetarist assumptions.

C. The Keynesian Case

Keynesians take money wages to be inflexible while prices are an endogenous variable. This means that real income or output may no longer be considered exogenous; instead, it becomes endogenous, and equations (5)–(7) are added to the IS-LM system as represented by (1) and (2) in order to close the set of equations.

To derive expressions for the elasticities $E_{y \cdot M_0}$ and $E_{p \cdot M_0}$, we must again differentiate the system totally with respect to M_0, now treating y as a variable. In addition to equations (B.1) and (B.3), this differentiation yields

$$\frac{dy}{dM_0} = -y_N N_w^D \frac{\overline{W}}{p^2}\frac{dp}{dM_0} \qquad (C.1)$$

which is derived by differentiating equations (5)–(7) and substituting where possible.

It will be convenient to make some further substitutions. First, since the MPC with respect to income is one minus the MPS with respect to income, and since the MPC with respect to the interest rate is the negative of the MPS with respect to the interest rate, we make the substitutions $(1 - C_y) = S_y$ and $C_r = -S_r$, where S stands for the saving function (the model implies $S = S(y,r)$). Second, (C.1) can be used to eliminate the term involving $\dfrac{dp}{dM_0}$ in (B.3). Making these substitutions and collecting terms yields the following pair of equations in the two variables $\dfrac{dy}{dM_0}$ and $\dfrac{dr}{dM_0}$:

$$S_y\frac{dy}{dM_0} - (I_r - S_r)\frac{dr}{dM_0} = 0 \qquad (C.2)$$

$$\left(L_y - \frac{M_0}{\overline{W}y_N N_w^D}\right)\frac{dy}{dM_0} + L_r\frac{dr}{dM_0} = \frac{1}{p} \qquad (C.3)$$

Solving these equations for $\dfrac{dy}{dM_0}$ gives:

$$\frac{dy}{dM_0} = \frac{\dfrac{1}{p}}{\dfrac{S_y L_r}{I_r - S_r} + L_y - \dfrac{M_0}{\overline{W}y_N N_w^D}}. \qquad (C.4)$$

To convert this into elasticity form, two steps are needed:

a. each of the propensities (or partial derivatives) shown in the denominator may be converted into a partial elasticity by using the relationship between any two variables x and z given by the definition of a partial elasticity; i.e., if $z = f(x)$, then $\eta_{z \cdot x} = f_x \cdot \dfrac{x}{z}$ and thus $f_x = \dfrac{z}{x} \eta_{z \cdot x}$;

b. to find the systemic elasticity $E_{y \cdot M_0}$, both sides of (C.4) must be multiplied by $\dfrac{M_0}{y}$.

Carrying out these operations and cancelling terms where possible, we get

$$E_{y \cdot M_0} = \cfrac{1}{\dfrac{\eta_{S \cdot y}\eta_{L \cdot r}}{\eta_{I \cdot r} - \eta_{S \cdot r}} + \eta_{L \cdot y} - \dfrac{1}{\eta_{y \cdot N}\eta_N{}^D{}_{\cdot w}}} . \quad \text{(C.5)}$$

To find an expression for the systemic elasticity $E_{p \cdot M_0}$, equation (C.4) is substituted into (C.1) and a systemic expression for $\dfrac{dp}{dM_0}$ is derived.

When this expression is multiplied by $\dfrac{M_0}{p}$, the partial derivatives are converted to elasticities, and the necessary algebra is carried out, the following expression results:

$$E_{p \cdot M_0} = -\cfrac{1}{\eta_{y \cdot N}\eta_N{}^D{}_{\cdot w}\left[\dfrac{\eta_{S \cdot y}\eta_{L \cdot r}}{\eta_{I \cdot r} - \eta_{S \cdot r}} + \eta_{L \cdot y}\right] - 1} . \quad \text{(C.6)}$$

From (C.5) and (C.6), it can be seen that the behavior of velocity now depends on all of the partial elasticities in the system. First, if either $\eta_{y \cdot N}$ or $\eta_N{}^D{}_{\cdot w}$ are zero, output will not change in response to a real wage change brought about by a monetary shift, so that $E_{y \cdot M_0} = 0$ and $E_{p \cdot M_0} = 1$, resulting in stable velocity. Second, if either $\eta_{y \cdot N}$ or $\eta_N{}^D{}_{\cdot w}$ are extremely large, $E_{p \cdot M_0}$ approaches zero and the response of velocity to a monetary shift depends on a special case of equation (C.5) in which the last denominator term approaches zero. Whether $E_{V \cdot M_0}$ is positive or negative in this case depends on whether $E_{y \cdot M_0}$ is greater or smaller than unity. The condition for $E_{V \cdot M_0} < 0$ is that

$$|\eta_{I \cdot r} - \eta_{S \cdot r}| < \eta_{S \cdot y}(|\eta_{L \cdot r}|) + \eta_{L \cdot y}(|\eta_{I \cdot r} - \eta_{S \cdot r}|).$$

Thus the larger in value are $\eta_{S \cdot y}$, $\eta_{L \cdot y}$, and $|\eta_{L \cdot r}|$, the more likely it is that $E_{V \cdot M_0} < 0$. Finally, for nonzero but finite values of $\eta_{y \cdot N}$ and $\eta_N{}^D{}_{\cdot w}$, $E_{y \cdot M_0}$ and $E_{p \cdot M_0}$ will tend toward zero (and $E_{V \cdot M_0}$ toward -1) if $\eta_{S \cdot y}$ or $|\eta_{L \cdot r}|$ are very large, or if $(\eta_{I \cdot r} - \eta_{S \cdot r})$ is very close to zero in value. A large value for $\eta_{L \cdot y}$ would also give this result.

B. Inflation and Its Relation to Unemployment

During much of the period since the late 1940s, the United States has been experiencing a slow, general upward movement of prices, as measured by such price indexes as the Consumer Price Index (CPI), the Wholesale Price Index (WPI), and others. There have been periods—mostly notably that beginning in 1973, but also 1946–48, 1950–51, 1955–57, and in general the years since 1965—in which the rate of increase has accelerated; on the other hand, there have also been periods, such as 1958–64, when prices have been relatively stable, especially as measured by the WPI. However, the "cost of living" as measured by the CPI has been particularly prone to continuing increase, even in periods of substantial unemployment. This "stagflation" phenomenon has been particularly evident since 1973. For example, in May 1975 the seasonally-adjusted unemployment rate reached a postwar peak level of 9.0 percent; during that month the CPI was rising at an annual rate of 9.5 percent.

While even this recent outburst of inflation has been less than that experienced by some other countries, there is nevertheless widespread public concern over inflation's real and imagined consequences. Economists and economic policymakers are also concerned with the causes of inflation and the nature of the inflationary process, because inflation may entail real social costs, particularly with respect to the distribution of income and wealth.

According to the traditional view, inflation is attributable to excess demand for output at a given set of initial prices: "too many dollars chasing too few goods." Such "demand-pull" inflation could be prevented or halted without significant cost in unemployment by the simple expedient of adopting a sufficiently restrictive monetary and fiscal policy. Excessive growth of the money stock, especially growth resulting from government spending financed by printing money or by selling securities to the central bank, was often thought to be the prime cause, and the proper remedies appeared to be responsible government budgeting, avoidance of large deficits, and the financing of such deficits as do occur by selling bonds to the public rather than the banks. Some of the fallacies in the normative application of these policy prescriptions are discussed in the readings in Chapter 5. Our postwar experience has made them seem less than universally acceptable as ways of halting or avoiding inflation. While there have been times, especially during the periods of hostilities in Korea and Vietnam, when inflation has been fueled by heavy federal spending and budget deficits, there have also been extended periods when aggregate demand has been inadequate to keep unemployment at an acceptable level. Yet the price indexes—especially the CPI —have continued to creep upward, suggesting that the simple demand-pull theory does not satisfactorily explain all of our experience and that alternative explanations are needed.

A widely discussed alternative to the demand-pull theory of inflation has been the "cost-push" or "market power" hypothesis. According to this view there may be a continuing general rise in prices even though unemployment persists and aggregate demand is inadequate. This can happen because certain groups in the domestic economy, particularly strong labor unions and big business enterprises, are able to exercise monopoly power and thereby exert more or less continuous upward pressure on wages and prices.

The cost-push inflation hypothesis has led to a good deal of discussion and research, which has improved our understanding of the inflationary process by focusing attention on industry structure, market power, and so on—institutional considerations which are not taken into account in the demand-pull analysis. However, it is now apparent that any given inflationary experience may have both demand-pull and cost-push elements—increasing demand tightens particular labor markets, high profits and sales levels make producers reluctant to accept interruptions of production that strikes would bring, and declining unemployment among union members strengthens the position of unions in collective bargaining negotiations. It appears that the analytic distinction between demand and cost inflation is often not a useful device for categorizing particular inflationary experiences or for devising policies to deal with particular situations. Furthermore, the inflationary episode which began in 1973 demonstrated that external events—in that case, crop failures and the formation of the OPEC oil cartel—can cause the price indexes to begin to rise rapidly, quite apart from considerations of domestic aggregate demand or market power. For this reason it is probably more instructive to sort out the causes of inflation into those which affect aggregate demand (monetary or fiscal policy shifts, or changes in private spending decisions) and those which affect aggregate supply (market power, government regulations, cartels, crop failures, etc.). This is the categorization used in the paper by the Congressional Budget Office entitled "Inflation," which begins the second part of Chapter 1 (reading 5). The paper provides a very useful introduction to this topic. In addition to discussing the causes of inflation within the context of aggregate demand and supply, it reviews our recent experience, considers the role of expectations in causing inflation to persist, and presents some of the options currently being discussed for reducing the rate of price increase.

An assumption which is sometimes made in macroeconomic theory is that labor markets are perfectly competitive. Under this assumption, full employment is taken to mean the level of employment determined by the intersection of the demand for and supply of labor functions (see, for example, Robert S. Holbrook's discussion of the Keynesian system with flexible wages, contained in reading 1 in the first part of this chapter). However, once it is recognized that there are imperfections in the market process so that wages and prices may begin to rise in response to an increase in aggregate demand or to an exercise of market power while substantial unemployment continues to exist, the concept of full employment becomes imprecise. It becomes more natural to think of different levels of employment or unemployment, each associated with some level of demand for labor relative to its supply and thereby to some given rate of change of money wages and, ultimately, prices. The higher the level of employment, the more rapid the rate of wage and price increase over the usual range in which employment varies. In other words, there may be a range of price change-employment combinations among which society can choose, rather than there being one level of "full employment" determined by market forces.

Such a set of price change-employment combinations is known as a Phillips curve, named after A. W. Phillips, a British economist who first traced it out for the British economy. This curve shows that the rate of change of money wages (or prices) is inversely related to the level of unemployment, and rises more and more rapidly as unemployment declines. Further studies have shown that other economic variables, such as labor productivity, also play a role in the Phillips curve; and systematic changes in the composition of the labor force in recent years, involving increases in the fractions representing women and young people, seem to have been causing the Phillips curve to "shift" outward when the curve is plotted in the price change-unemployment rate space.

The paper by James Tobin (reading 6) surveys the development of the theory concerning Phillips curve relationships and deals extensively with a number of questions which bear on current controversies in this area. Much of this discussion is related to the fact that there exist today two opposing viewpoints concerning the Phillips curve and the underlying behavior and institutional structure which it represents. One side, which may be labeled post-Keynesian, holds that certain factors having to do with the adjustment of labor markets in response to external impulses, as well as institutional rigidities and market imperfections, result in the availability of lasting trade-offs at the aggregate level between unemployment and the rate of change of prices. While the precise trade-off available may vary with the stage of the business cycle in which the economy finds itself and may be less favorable in the longer run than in the immediate period, the important consideration is that, from the post-Keynesian viewpoint, a lasting trade-off exists. The Neoclassical stance (which has also come to be known as the "accelerationist" position) holds that trade-offs are at best only temporary. An expansion of aggregate demand, for instance, will bring with it rising prices, inducing producers to offer somewhat higher money wages in order to increase employment and output. While the new real wage actually may be lower, workers will be more immediately responsive to the increased money wage available for their services than to the fact that prices for goods are rising. Consequently, employment expands. But ultimately, workers will realize that rising prices have reduced the real value of their money wage increase. Employment and output will move back toward their initial levels, but prices and money wages now are higher than before. In the longer run, then, employment will return to the "natural" level determined by market forces. Under this view, stabilization policy manipulations can have no permanent effects on employment, although the rate of inflation may change. This process usually is discussed in terms of the *expected* inflation rate: demand expansion which causes the rates of wage and price increases to accelerate will induce workers to take jobs because their perception of what the inflation rate (and hence their real wage) will be has not adjusted to the new reality. When this adjustment in expectations occurs, employment will fall back to its original level.

In order to understand the arguments on each side, let us first set out the behavior summarized in the Phillips curve which both sides accept. In general, the Phillips curve is the outcome at the aggregate level of the behavior of many labor markets, each adjusting toward equilibrium, but each being disturbed again and again by autonomous shocks. These shocks generate excess demands or supplies in the individual markets. The rate of change of money wages is taken to be proportional to the excess demand for labor across these markets, which in turn is viewed as being inversely related to the unemployment rate. In summary, there arises out of this process an inverse relationship between the rate of change of money wages and the unemployment rate. The relationship is nonlinear because there is an irreducible minimum below which the unemployment rate cannot be driven by increases in demand, while it can increase more or less continuously with demand decreases. Obviously, the rate cannot go below zero; actually, the floor lies somewhat above zero because of the frictional unemployment involved in job changes, the rapid turnover of employees in low-paying, "dead-end" jobs, and other causes. An interesting implication of this nonlinearity in the wage change-unemployment relationship is that even if there exists overall "balance" in the demand for and supply of labor at a given wage, there will be more upward pressure on wages (and, eventually, on prices) in the individual labor markets exhibiting excess demand than there will be downward pressure from labor surplus markets. Thus, a rising wage and price level is perfectly consistent with aggregate labor market balance, and the net upward pressure will be greater, the wider is the difference in unemployment rates among labor markets.

From this background, Tobin examines the two points of view mentioned earlier. He notes that if there were indeed full long-run equilibrium in every segment of the labor market, the Neoclassical no-trade-off result would follow. However, because there are a great number of individual labor markets rather than one overall market, such equilibrium is never attained; instead, there is "unending sectoral flux" even when the whole set of markets taken together appears to be in balance (in the sense, e.g., of total vacancies equaling total unemployment). In this sense, we are never truly in the long run. And even if we were, Tobin points out that a long-run trade-off would be maintained if there were downward wage rigidities in some markets (not necessarily always the same markets).

This brings up the question of how the rigid-wage assumption sometimes made in static Keynesian models is to be interpreted. In the paper by Holbrook (reading 1), as well as in the Teigen paper on monetarism, static models of the Keynesian system are used which include aggregated labor market subsectors. Obviously a dynamic unemployment-wage change relationship does not fit comfortably into models of this kind. Instead, these models assume that the money wage rate is inflexible downward (or, in some versions of such models, that the supply of labor depends on the money wage rather than the real wage), and thereby produce the Keynesian result that monetary and fiscal policy impulses are able to cause permanent changes in employment, real wages, output, the interest rate, and so on. The use of this sort of assumption in static models has been criticized on grounds that it attributes "money illusion," or irrationality, to workers, who rationally should make labor-supply decisions based on the real wage only. According to Tobin, however, such assumptions can be interpreted in a way consistent with rational behavior. A worker's immediate concern is with the earned or prospective wage relative to the whole wage structure; therefore an attempt to, e.g., lower money wages in any given market will be resisted because it will be viewed as an attempt to reduce the position of workers in that market relative to other workers. However, given the demand for labor, the real wage must somehow be reduced if employment is to be increased. Since there is no rapid and easy way of adjusting the whole hierarchy of money wages downward, overall real wage reduction is achieved by a rising price level instead. The assumption of inflexible money wages found in static Keynesian models is a way of incorporating this dynamic labor market adjustment process.

As we have already noted, the Neoclassical economists, while agreeing with much of this description (though they typically reject the rigid-wage assumption), contend that the conventional Phillips curve is merely a transitory relationship.[1] In their view, both labor demand and supply behavior depend on the real wage. There is a so-called natural rate of unemployment consistent with stable prices (or perhaps with any one of several constant rates of change of prices), corresponding to that real wage rate at which the demand for and supply of labor are equal. Once workers realize that demand expansion which increases the money wage actually is reducing the real wage through price increases, they will demand and obtain higher money wages, and the real wage reduction below the equilibrium level can only be maintained by a further rise in prices. A lasting reduction in unemployment requires a continuously accelerating inflation, so that workers never learn to ask for a large enough wage increase to offset fully the current inflation (hence the term "accelerationist").

Tobin makes mention of a variation on this approach, known as "search theory." Workers and firms have incomplete information about wages, employment opportunities, and so forth elsewhere. There is therefore an inducement to spend time and effort getting such information, and there will typically be some "search unemployment" of an amount such that at the margin, the gains to be obtained from further information gathering and its associated costs are just balanced by the value of leisure. Under this view, an increase in demand which causes money wages to rise in a particular market will result in acceptance by searchers of jobs on the mistaken assumption that wage rates in other markets will remain constant, so that they have been fortunate enough to find jobs with higher relative real wages. Therefore employment will rise temporarily; but when it is noted that wages are also rising elsewhere, the searchers who accepted

---

[1] This view is expressed by Milton Friedman in "The Role of Monetary Policy," *American Economic Review*, vol. 58 (March 1968), pp. 1–17, reprinted in chapter 5 below. He has discussed it at greater length in his Nobel Lecture entitled "Inflation and Unemployment," *Journal of Political Economy*, vol. 85 (June 1977), pp. 451–72.

employment will realize their mistake, return to the pool of "search unemployment," and employment will fall again to its "natural" level.

The paper by Thomas M. Humphrey (reading 7) deals with aspects of the Phillips curve debate within the context of a rather general formal framework. This structure includes behavioral equations specifying the determinants of wage change, price change, and the formation of expectations regarding inflation. There is also a summary or "reduced form" equation (roughly equivalent to the solution of an *IS-LM* system, like equation (3.15) in the introduction to the first part of this chapter) expressing aggregate demand in terms of monetary and fiscal policy variables and other autonomous forces.[2]

Humphrey uses this structure effectively to sort out and discuss the various viewpoints mentioned above. By reference to his model, it is easy to see how the Phillips curve arises out of the interaction of wage- and price-setting decisions, and how expectations of inflation enter. It can be viewed as the outcome of a reduction of the wage and price equations, obtained by substituting Humphrey's equation (1) into the right-hand side of his equation (2), thus eliminating the current-period wage term. If the aggregate demand term, x, is replaced by the corresponding unemployment rate, we have a typical Phillips curve which incorporates the expected inflation rate and which is based on wage and price interaction. Humphrey then shows how the Phillips curve trade-off disappears when the expected and actual inflation rates are equal.

An important question for the Keynesian-accelerationist debate is therefore the nature of the expectations-formulation process, and it is a question which is discussed in some detail both by Humphrey and in the paper by Robert M. Solow (reading 8). A rather recent innovation in this area, discussed by Humphrey, is the development of the rational-expectations hypothesis. Under this view, individuals make use of all available information in forming their expectations about future inflation—including any systematic behavior on the part of the stabilization authorities. As Humphrey explains, discretionary policy would be powerless if the rational-expectations hypothesis were correct. However, the hypothesis depends on extremely strong assumptions about the availability and use of information, and does not seem to be consistent with much of our experience.

However expectations are formed, both Keynesians and monetarists now agree that an inflation expectations term should appear in the Phillips curve; but controversy continues over the size of the coefficient. In a perfectly rational world, and in the long run, this coefficient should be unity, as Solow demonstrates; but a number of empirical studies measure it to be considerably smaller. The question is an important one because, as indicated earlier, a coefficient of unity means there is no permanent trade-off, while a smaller coefficient indicates that a permanent trade-off can exist. Solow provides a very useful survey and thorough discussion of some of this evidence.

---

[2] The reader should not be misled by the notation. Humphrey's "L" subscript used on all explanatory variables means that *both* current-period and lagged values of those variables are operative, so that the four-equation structure is a fully interactive one.

5. INFLATION*

Congressional Budget Office

Broad agreement exists that inflation is harmful, and that it is likely to persist. This paper discusses these two comfortless judgments. To explain the first, it begins with a description of some characteristic effects of inflation. To explain the second—the persistence of inflation—it discusses the inflation process. The paper concludes with some anti-inflation policy options.

THE MEANING OF INFLATION

Inflation is often taken to mean a continuing rise in the *general* price level. A difficulty with this definition is that it glosses over a fundamental characteristic of inflation: Inflation changes relative prices.[1] That is, if a quart of milk costs twice as much as a loaf of bread before inflation, it is unlikely to cost exactly twice as much during or immediately after inflation. If a week's wages buy a television set before inflation, there is no assurance that they will do so afterwards.

In fact, inflation without changes in relative prices has never occurred; if it did, no one would mind very much. If pensions, wages, salaries, rent, profits, and the prices of all goods and services increased at the same rate, it would be a nuisance, but no one would be badly harmed.

Public concern with inflation is based in large part on its effects on the structure of relative prices and incomes. Some examples are given in Figure 1. The upper left graph compares the annual percent change in the Consumer Price Index (CPI) with the annual percent change in average hourly (nonfarm) labor compensation. Because output per worker grows over time, compensation tends to rise faster than prices. As may be seen in the figure, however, the margin of compensation over prices narrows during accelerating inflation. Indeed, in 1974 under the combined effects of inflation and recession, the CPI rose faster than compensation, and real earnings—the purchasing power of an hour's work—declined.

The behavior of the CPI and the prices of two specific types of goods, agricultural products and fuel, are compared in the upper right graph. Differences between the rate of change in the CPI and the rate of change in farm and fuel prices have tended to increase during periods of accelerating inflation. Moreover, while rising farm and fuel prices in 1972–73 and 1973–74, respectively, received much publicity, farm prices increased less than the overall CPI in 1967–68, 1970–71 and 1974–76. Similarly, fuel was becoming relatively cheaper during most of the period from 1958 through 1970.

The lower left graph depicts variations in the rates of change of crude and intermediate materials and finished goods prices. Price changes among these three broad categories appear most disparate during periods of increasing inflation. All three charts show the tendency for all prices to increase during inflation; but some prices increase much faster than others, with some prices leading the average and others following with a lag.

WHY RELATIVE PRICE CHANGES OCCUR DURING INFLATION

The relation between inflation and changes in relative prices is one in which causation seems to run both ways: changes in relative prices are caused by inflation and inflation is caused by increases in the absolute (and relative) prices of individual goods and services.

Inflation causes changes in relative prices because most individual prices are *not* changed either continuously or simultaneously. Over the past five calendar years, the annual rate of inflation in the United States, as measured by the CPI, has been 3.3, 6.2, 11.0, 9.1 and 5.8 percent. For relative prices to have remained unchanged, all prices would have had to rise continuously or in simultaneous steps at the same rate as the average. The facts are otherwise. Prices that change day-to-day or in lockstep with others are the exception; for example, open-market interest rates, prices of equity shares, and some wholesale commodity prices. The lower right hand graph of Figure 1 provides an example of one price that in recent years has responded quickly to changes in the rate of inflation—the three-month Treasury bill (interest) rate—and an example of one that

* From Congressional Budget Office, *Recovery with Inflation* (Washington: U.S. Government Printing Office, July 1977), pp. 27–42. Reprinted by permission of the Congressional Budget Office.

[1] D. R. Vining, Jr., and T. C. Elwertowski, "The Relationship between Relative Prices and the General Price Level," *American Economic Review* (September 1976), pp. 699–708.

Figure 1:   Inflation, Relative Prices, and Incomes

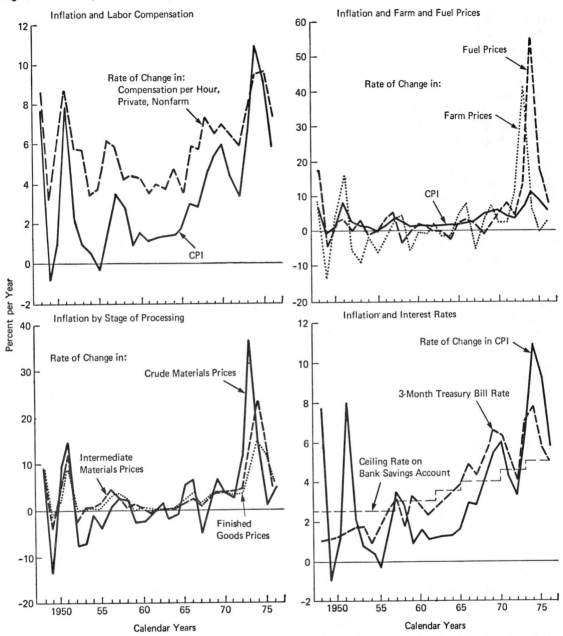

Sources: U.S. Department of Labor, Bureau of Labor Statistics for price and compensation data. Farm prices, fuel prices, and prices by stage of processing are components of the Wholesale Price Index. U.S. Treasury Department for Treasury bill rate. Federal Reserve Board for ceiling rate on bank savings accounts.

responds more slowly—the maximum interest rate paid on regular savings accounts at federally insured commercial banks. From 1965 to the present, the ceiling rate on savings accounts was changed only twice; over most of this period the rate of inflation exceeded the interest ceiling.

Another infrequently adjusted price is the

wage rate. Most wages are adjusted for inflation no more than once a year. Of the 10 million workers covered by major collective bargaining agreements (those covering more than 1,000 employees), fewer than 25 percent receive cost-of-living adjustments more frequently than once a year. In contrast, income tax rates rise automatically with current dollar income because of the progressive rate structure. Worse yet, some pensions and annuities are permanently fixed in dollar amount and thus decline in real value during inflation. In sum, because all prices do not increase at the same time or at the same rate, inflation changes relative prices and the distribution of real income.

An increase in an individual price also pushes up the general level of prices. The large absolute (and relative) increase in the price of energy is a commonly cited, recent example. Higher prices for petroleum and related increases in prices of electricity, natural gas, and coal contributed to a higher price level directly and indirectly by raising the cost of producing almost everything else. As was observed in late 1973 and 1974, the immediate effect of pervasively higher prices for goods and services accompanied by slowly changing wages and salaries was that consumer spending for some goods was reduced. Reductions in spending lower output and raise unemployment.[2] Monetary and fiscal policies may become more expansionary in response to higher unemployment rates. These policies may reduce unemployment, but they are also apt to perpetuate a high rate of inflation. Thus, individual price increases, through their effects on costs, unemployment, and government policy, can lead to inflation.

THE CAUSES OF INFLATION

Prices of individual goods and services are jointly determined by buyers and sellers. At each possible price, there is some quantity of the good that suppliers are willing to sell and that purchasers are willing to buy. The market price will tend toward that price at which desired sales are equal to desired purchases. Market prices are raised by developments that reduce the quantity offered for sale at any particular price (a fall in supply) or that increase the quantity buyers offer to purchase at any particular price (an increase in demand). When speaking of the entire economy, therefore, it is convenient to classify the causes of a higher general price level into those that increase aggregate demand and those that decrease aggregate supply.

Aggregate demand may be increased by an expansionary monetary policy, a tax cut, an in-

crease in government spending, a rise in the propensity to consume, an investment boom, or growing foreign demand for U.S. goods. Aggregate supply may be reduced by crop failures; the formation of cartels to restrict supply and raise price; restrictions on imports such as tariffs, quotas, and "orderly marketing agreements;" higher minimum wage laws; and government regulations and private agreements that interfere with an efficient use of resources.

Many of these factors were at work between the mid-1960s and the inflation surge of 1973–74. Monetary growth accelerated; government spending increased sharply during the Vietnam War; the tax incentives and sustained expansion of the early 1960s created a major investment boom. An expanding world economy coupled with U.S. devaluations stimulated exports and raised the price of imports, and crop failures were widespread in the early 1970s. Finally, world oil prices quadrupled in 1974. These factors were the major causes of the subsequent period of rapid inflation.

In assessing the recent high inflation, it is important to recognize a fundamental difference in inflation triggered by a fall in supply as distinct from one caused by an increase in aggregate demand. The difference is that with a fall in aggregate supply, such as might result from a crop failure or a reduced supply of energy, some real output is irretrievably lost. Economic policy cannot offset the direct, real effects of poor growing conditions or reduced supplies of natural resources, although policy can limit output reductions in sectors not directly affected by supply changes. Inflation triggered by increased demand, in contrast, will not initially reduce real output.

THE PERSISTENCE OF INFLATION

One basic reason for the persistence of inflation is that policymakers strive to achieve low unemployment as well as low inflation. When aggregate demand weakens and unemployment rises, economic policymakers may respond with more expansive policies. Similarly, efforts by policymakers to offset the unemployment effects associated with a fall in supply provide underpinning for continuing upward price pressures.

The response of economic policy to the unemployment effects of changes in aggregate demand and supply is not the only source of persistence in rising prices. Another very important one is the way consumers, labor, and business adapt to the expectation of inflation. In order to describe these adjustments, it is useful to distin-

---

[2] Higher energy prices also signal an increasing scarcity of energy and provide incentives for more resources to be used in the conservation and recovery of energy. The resulting shift of resources among uses may also contribute to higher transitional unemployment.

guish cases in which inflation occurs unexpectedly from those cases in which the inflation is anticipated. Consider first an economy with approximate price stability, in which the annual rate of price change varies only between 1 and 3 percent with an average of 2 percent. This was roughly the U.S. experience from the Korean War to the Vietnam War. Given the previous ten years' experience, it was reasonable to assume in 1965 that the inflation rate in the future would be about 2 percent. Reasonable, but wrong.

Because the inflation of the late 1960s and early 1970s was largely unanticipated, the implicit and explicit contracts of trade, finance, and employment were drawn without provision for inflation. As a result, inflation changed the relative price structure and thus led to large redistributions of income and wealth. Creditors generally suffered losses to debtors when debtors made repayment in dollars with reduced purchasing power. Workers whose wages did not keep pace with the average rate of change in prices saw their real incomes decline.[3] In general, those who had agreed to supply goods and services at specified prices on the assumption of a modest rise in prices were stuck with prices that were "too low" until those prices could be renegotiated.

The magnitude of losses resulting from the failure to foresee the inflation caused people to anticipate future inflation and to change their behavior accordingly. The length of long-term, fixed-price contracts tended to be shortened.[4] More time and effort were diverted from other uses to the attempt to forecast price changes and to profit from those forecasts. Catch-up wage settlements were made. Provisions for automatic cost-of-living adjustments were negotiated into many labor contracts. At the beginning of 1977, about 60 percent of the workers covered by major collective bargaining agreements were entitled to some cost-of-living escalation. In 1965, only 25 percent of these workers were entitled to such wage adjustments. Where permitted to do so by regulation, interest rates rose to include

a higher inflation premium. For example, the long-term, Aaa-rated corporate bond rate rose from 4.5 percent in 1965 to 8.8 percent in 1975. Household survey data show that changed expectations about the future course of prices were not confined to labor leaders, firms, and large investors. The Survey Research Center at the University of Michigan reported that respondents who expected the next year's inflation rate to exceed 4 percent increased from 27 percent in 1966 to 55 percent in 1975.

These changes in the anticipated rate of inflation and in people's behavior reduced, though they did not eliminate, the redistributional consequences of subsequent inflation. By reordering commercial agreements and financial plans on the expectation of inflation, however, they also provided inflation with a very strong momentum.

Once the expectation of inflation becomes incorporated into contracts, informal agreements, and plans, stopping that inflation becomes a very complex feat. Suppose, for example, that economic policymakers try to stop an anticipated inflation quickly through sharply restrictive monetary and fiscal policies. The first effect of these policies is to reduce total spending. But with many prices already scheduled to rise, the principal impact of the spending cutback will be to increase unemployment and to idle productive capacity. In time, these output effects will cause some downward revisions in actual and expected prices, if the demand weakness is considered to be more than just a temporary aberration. These price revisions, in turn, will tend to restore employment levels. Until inflationary expectations are revised downward, though, the major impact of the anti-inflation policy will be on real economic variables such as employment, production, and income.

An actual rate of inflation *below* the anticipated rate also has redistributional consequences similar in character but opposite in sign to those resulting from an actual rate *above* the anticipated rate. In this case, debtors lose and creditors gain. Buyers who have contracted to purchase goods at prices reflecting inflationary expectations lose and sellers gain.

Although the distinction between anticipated and unanticipated inflation is helpful in assessing inflation's effects and in appreciating how it acquires a momentum, all inflation is to some extent unanticipated. Not everyone will anticipate the actual rate correctly. Given wide variations in the actual inflation rate, such as that of the United States during the last five years, people will anticipate, with varying degrees of likeli-

[3] Some evidence suggests that inflation also changed the relative wage structure. See A. H. Packer and S. H. Park, "Distortions in Relative Wages and Shifts in the Phillips Curve," *Review of Economics and Statistics,* 55. 1 (February 1973), pp. 16–22.

[4] Benjamin Klein, "The Social Costs of Recent Inflation: The Mirage of Steady 'Anticipated' Inflation," *Institutional Arrangements and the Inflation Problem,* vol. 3 in the Carnegie-Rochester Conferences Supplement to the *Journal of Monetary Economics* (August 1976), pp. 185–212.

hood, a range of inflation rates. A large number of possible outcomes amounts to increased uncertainty. Such uncertainty is, in itself, undesirable and many people would pay something to avoid it. But awareness of a whole range of possible inflation rates also means that, as prices change, economic units will not be able to distinguish clearly a relative price change (for example, a change in the real value of what they have to sell) from a general inflation price change. People, therefore, experience greater difficulty in interpreting the meaning of price changes during inflation. As a result, the price mechanism becomes a less efficient communications system.

POLICY OPTIONS FOR REDUCING INFLATION

If policymakers wish to attempt to slow inflation, a wide variety of options is available. Most of these either reduce aggregate demand or increase aggregate supply. Four types of policies are considered here: a deflationary macroeconomic policy; wage-price controls or guidelines; ad hoc price reduction measures aimed at selected markets; and tax incentives designed to encourage price stability. These policies would have different effects on inflation, both with respect to timing and total impact. Most would prove costly in terms of other Congressional goals.

A Deflationary Fiscal or Monetary Policy

There is a sense in which it is correct to say that inflation continues only because economic policy permits it to do so. Monetary and fiscal policies exist that could arrest the rise in the price level. The cost of those policies in terms of unemployment and lost production would be great, however. Given the strength of inflationary expectations, even the goal of a modest reduction in the rate of inflation risks stalling the recovery, though the inflation-arresting effects of such a policy could be pronounced in the more distant future. The trade-off of current employment and output for future price stability could be avoided only if price expectations were to be revised down quickly in response to a deflationary policy and if the prices in contracts and agreements could be adjusted immediately in line with those new expectations.

Econometric analysis carried out by CBO suggests that a fiscal policy change equivalent to a $43 billion cut in federal government expenditures—about two percent of GNP—below a current policy projection starting in fiscal year of

Table 1: Estimated Effect of a Cut in Federal Government Spending to Reduce Inflation by 1 Percentage Point, Fiscal Years 1978, 1979, and 1980

	1978	1979	1980
Change in federal purchases (billions of dollars)..........	−43	−43	−43
Change in the inflation rate* (percentage points).........	−0.3	−0.8	−1.0
Change in real GNP (billions of 1972 dollars)......	−51	−61	−40
Change in the unemployment rate (percentage points).....	+1.2	+1.6	+1.2

Note: In all cases, "change" refers to the difference from a baseline projection without the spending reduction.

* Fourth quarter over fourth quarter change in the CPI.

1978 would be required to reduce the inflation rate by 1 percentage point in 1980. As shown in Table 1, such a policy is estimated to reduce real GNP (1972 dollars) by $51 billion in the first year and $61 billion (about 4 percent) in the second year. The negative effect on employment would be at its peak in the second year, when the average annual unemployment rate would be increased by 1.6 percentage points, or about a million and a half unemployed workers.

Incomes Policies or Wage-Price Controls

The importance of inflationary expectations in the perpetuation of inflation and the desire to reduce those expectations without paying a high price in terms of unemployment has often prompted the suggestion that wages and prices ought to be controlled more or less directly through so-called incomes policies.

The United States has had some experience with several forms of these: mandatory controls during the Korean War; guideposts and "jawboning" (attempting to affect prices by persuasion) during 1962–66; the New Economic Policy of 1971–74 which included periods of wage-price freeze as well as more flexible mandatory and voluntary controls; and the current activities of the Council on Wage and Price Stability whose principal instruments are persuasion and publicity.

Controls on prices and wages *seem* to be a direct and low-cost cure for inflation. During periods when such controls have been in effect, they appeared to have held down the rate of inflation somewhat. But, while the cost of a general deflationary monetary or fiscal policy is likely to be painfully apparent in the unemployment figures, the substantial costs of incomes policies are mostly hidden. The more restrictive the policy—

a complete freeze is an extreme example—the greater the likelihood it will succeed in temporarily holding down the measured rate of inflation, but the greater its costs.

A recent CBO study of incomes policies[5] reviewed U.S. experience and identified some of the difficulties associated with these programs. Fundamental among these has been the difficulty of establishing a ruling "principle behind the policy;" that is, a set of decision standards that are efficient and equitable while also effective and feasible. Such a set of standards may not exist. As a consequence, the policies seem to lead to inefficiencies and inequities and a breakdown of public support. The administrative cost of controls can also be substantial. In addition, these policies are often thought to create a depressing climate for business enterprise and investment.

Specific Market Interventions

There are two distinct, separable aspects of an anti-inflation strategy of intervention in particular markets. For one, it is suggested that the government intervene directly in some markets to hold down prices. For the other, the intent is to reduce and abolish government-mandated minimum prices.

The notion of a selective incomes policy is based on the idea that by directly retarding the rate of increase for those key goods and services that are going up in price most rapidly, inflation can be slowed. Rapid price increases in a particular sector are usually symptomatic of fundamental conditions peculiar to that industry. For example, a recent Council on Wage and Price Stability study of health care cost found ". . . that unique structural characteristics of the health care industry underlie its extraordinary inflationary behavior."[6] Specifically, ". . . the primary supplier of medical services, the physician, usually determines the level of services required by the consumer. . . . Moreover, medical services are largely paid for through a system of third-party payors, insurance companies and government health programs . . ." that weakens the incentives physicians, hospitals, and patients may have to hold down costs. "Any policies aimed at mitigating inflation in this sector must address these structural peculiarities."

---

[5] CBO Background Paper, *Incomes Policies in the United States: Historical Review and Some Issues* (May 1977).

[6] Council on Wage and Price Stability, *The Complex Puzzle of Rising Health Care Cost: Can the Private Sector Fit It Together?* (December 1976).

Even if some form of intervention—such as the proposed Hospital Cost Containment Act of 1977 which aims to restrict the growth of hospital revenues and capital expenditures—is adopted and proves effective in substantially cutting the rise in medical costs, the direct effect on inflation will be rather small. For example, if the 1976 rise in medical care costs had been cut by one fourth, the CPI would still have risen by 5.6 percent instead of the 5.8 percent actually realized.

A number of government policies, adopted for other reasons, are in force whose effects are to raise prices. Examples include minimum wage laws, agricultural and dairy price supports, restrictions on imports, the regulation of transportation rates, and environmental and health/safety regulations. Reduction or repeal of these measures over a period of time is sometimes suggested as a means of reducing the rate of increase in prices and lowering inflationary expectations. Repeal, of course, would cause some considerable losses to the beneficiaries of these policies and hence would encounter determined opposition.

All of these options for stopping inflation are costly: general deflation risks ending the recovery; wage and price controls can temporarily suppress inflation but at the cost of misallocating resources and creating inequities; selective controls aimed at particular sectors of the economy will eventually have to come to grips with the underlying reasons for rising prices in that sector; and many interests will defend the continuation of government price supports.

Tax-Based Incomes Policies and Related Proposals

In recent years there have been proposals to use tax incentives and other schemes to encourage more moderate price behavior. Like the incomes policies described above, these mechanisms are generally directed at decisions of individuals, with the goal of ensuring that wage rates, on average, do not rise much faster than labor productivity. Rather than overriding market forces, these newer proposals attempt to take advantage of market incentives by making moderate price and wage increases a matter of self-interest for firms and employees.

The best known of these proposals involves tax incentives to reward or penalize wage decisions that deviate from some established standard. A number of such tax proposals exist but only two specific examples are described below.

The first approach, aimed at employers, would tax employers who grant wage increases in excess of the standard.[7] It is assumed that the tax surcharge could not easily be passed on to consumers by way of higher prices because some competitors might not have incurred as large a surcharge. As a result of the tax, employers would become more resistant to wage demands.

A more recent proposal uses tax incentives to restrain employee wage demands.[8] Under this proposal, payroll taxes would be reduced for employees in proportion to the degree of wage restraint exercised. If the average wage for a firm increased 1 percent less than some designated standard, then the payroll tax rate would be cut by, perhaps, a full percentage point for the employees of that firm. The tax cut would last for one year only, unless wage increases in the following year were again held below that year's standard.

Other innovative anti-inflation mechanisms would not employ tax incentives, but would rely instead on the federal distribution of marketable wage-increase permits, without which firms could not raise wages.[9] These permits would allow wage increases equal to 3 percent of the annual wage bill (the assumed productivity increase) and would be distributed to firms in accordance with their previous annual wage bill and collected from firms according to current wages paid. Because the permits could be traded, growing firms that need to attract more workers would seek additional permits while others, particularly declining firms, would seek to sell their unused permits. But the overall wage bill for the economy could not legally increase faster than the value of total permits issued.

All of these proposals would encounter numer-

ous administrative problems. How is the "standard" wage increase to be determined? How are catchup wage increases and long-term contract agreements to be handled? The tax proposals would have to be carefully designed to prevent the establishment of loopholes.

Moreover, these proposals implicitly assume that labor cost pressures are the principal cause of inflation—a conjectural notion at best. Attemps to broaden the proposals to include profits, interest, and rent would, however, greatly increase their administrative complexity.

Nevertheless, the advantage of proposals that provide incentives for more moderate price changes cannot be dismissed. This appears to be an area where further research, and perhaps some experimentation, could be useful. For now, these proposals must be regarded as uncertain because they are untried.

CONCLUSIONS

The best hope for controlling inflation at a reasonably low cost may be in a multifaceted approach of preventing excessive aggregate demand and accelerating the growth in aggregate supply. That is the approach of the Administration's anti-inflation program, as outlined by President Carter on April 15, 1977, which proposes to use various, mild forms of several options simultaneously. In his statement, the President called for a wide range of measures including fiscal discipline with a coordinated monetary policy; increased efforts by the Council on Wage and Price Stability; consultation between labor, business, and government; restraint on hospital costs; reform of government regulation; and tax incentives for increased investment.

None of these policies is likely to reduce the rate of inflation quickly. Yet, taken together and implemented over time they may take a contribution to a slow unwinding of inflation, which is probably the best that can be expected over the next few years.

---

[7] Sidney Weintraub and Henry Wallich, "A Tax Based Incomes Policy," *Journal of Economic Issues* (June 1971), pp. 1–19.

[8] Lawrence Seidman, "A Payroll Tax Credit To Restrain Inflation," *National Tax Journal*, 29.4 (December 1976), pp. 398–412.

[9] Professor Abba Lerner, Queens College, City University of New York, among others, has proposed a wage permit anti-inflation policy.

6. INFLATION AND UNEMPLOYMENT*

James Tobin

The world economy today is vastly different from the 1930s, when Seymour Harris, the chairman of this meeting, infected me with his boundless enthusiasm for economics and his steadfast confidence in its capacity for good works. Economics is very different, too. Both the science and its subject have changed, and for the better, since World War II. But there are some notable constants. Unemployment and inflation still preoccupy and perplex economists, statesmen, journalists, housewives, and everyone else. The connection between them is the principal domestic economic burden of presidents and prime ministers, and the major area of controversy and ignorance in macroeconomics. I have chosen to review economic thought on this topic on this occasion, partly because of its inevitable timeliness, partly because of a personal interest reaching back to my first published work in 1941.

I. THE MEANINGS OF FULL EMPLOYMENT

Today, as 30 and 40 years ago, economists debate how much unemployment is voluntary, how much involuntary; how much is a phenomenon of equilibrium, how much a symptom of disequilibrium; how much is compatible with competition, how much is to be blamed on monopolies, labor unions, and restrictive legislation; how much unemployment characterizes "full" employment.

Full employment—imagine macroeconomics deprived of the concept. But what is it? What is the proper employment goal of policies affecting aggregate demand? Zero unemployment in the monthly labor force survey? That outcome is so inconceivable outside of Switzerland that it is useless as a guide to policy. Any other numerical candidate, yes even 4 percent, is patently arbitrary without reference to basic criteria. Un-

employment equal to vacancies? Measurement problems aside, this definition has the same straightforward appeal as zero unemployment, which it simply corrects for friction.[1]

A concept of full employment more congenial to economic theory is labor market equilibrium, a volume of employment which is simultaneously the amount employers want to offer and the amount workers want to accept at prevailing wage rates and prices. Forty years ago theorists with confidence in markets could believe that full employment is whatever volume of employment the economy is moving toward, and that its achievement requires of the government nothing more than neutrality, and nothing less.

After Keynes challenged the Classical notion of labor market equilibrium and the complacent view of policy to which it led, full employment came to mean maximum aggregate supply, the point at which expansion of aggregate demand could not further increase employment and output.

Full employment was also regarded as the economy's inflation threshold. With a deflationary gap, demand less than full employment supply, prices would be declining or at worst constant. Expansion of aggregate demand short of full employment could cause at most a one-shot increase of prices. For continuing inflation, the textbooks told us, a necessary and sufficient condition was an inflationary gap, real aggregate demand in excess of feasible supply. The model was tailor-made for wartime inflation.

Postwar experience destroyed the identification of full employment with the economy's inflation threshold. The profession, the press, and the public discovered the "new inflation" of the 1950s, inflation without benefit of gap, labelled but scarcely illuminated by the term "cost-push." Subsequently the view of the world suggested by the Phillips curve merged demand-pull and cost-push inflation and blurred the distinction between them. This view contained no concept of full employment. In its place came the tradeoff, along which society supposedly can choose the least

* From *American Economic Review*, vol. 62 (March 1972), pp. 1–18. Reprinted by permission of the publisher and the author. James Tobin is Sterling Professor of Economics, Yale University.

Presidential address delivered at the Eighty-Fourth Annual Meeting of the American Economic Association, New Orleans, Louisiana, December 28, 1971.

[1] This concept is commonly attributed to W. H. Beveridge, but he was actually more ambitious and required a surplus of vacancies.

undesirable feasible combination of the evils of unemployment and inflation.

Many economists deny the existence of a durable Phillips tradeoff. Their numbers and influence are increasing. Some of them contend that there is only one rate of unemployment compatible with steady inflation, a "natural rate" consistent with any steady rate of change of prices, positive, zero, or negative. The natural rate is another full employment candidate, a policy target at least in the passive sense that monetary and fiscal policy makers are advised to eschew any numerical unemployment goal and to let the economy gravitate to this eqilibrium. So we have come full circle. Full employment is once again nothing but the equilibrium reached by labor markets unaided and undistorted by governmental fine tuning.

In discussing these issues, I shall make the following points. First, an observed amount of unemployment is not revealed to be voluntary simply by the fact that money wage rates are constant, or rising, or even accelerating. I shall recall and extend Keynes's definition of involuntary unemployment and his explanation why workers may accept price inflation as a method of reducing real wages while rejecting money wage cuts. The second point is related. Involuntary unemployment is a disequilibrium phenomenon; the behavior, the persistence, of excess supplies of labor depend on how and how fast markets adjust to shocks, and on how large and how frequent the shocks are. Higher prices or faster inflation can diminish involuntary, disequilibrium unemployment, even though voluntary, equilibrium labor supply is entirely free of money illusion.

Third, various criteria of full employment coincide in a theoretical full stationary equilibrium, but diverge in persistent disequilibrium. These are (1) the natural rate of unemployment, the rate compatible with zero or some other constant inflation rate, (2) zero involuntary unemployment, (3) the rate of unemployment needed for optimal job search and placement, and (4) unemployment equal to job vacancies. The first criterion dictates higher unemployment than any of the rest. Instead of commending the natural rate as a target of employment policy, the other three criteria suggests less unemployment and more inflation. Therefore, fourth, there are real gains from additional employment, which must be weighed in the social balance against the costs of inflation. I shall conclude with a few remarks on this choice, and on the possibilities of improving the terms of the tradeoff.

II. KEYNESIAN AND CLASSICAL INTERPRETATIONS OF UNEMPLOYMENT

To begin with the *General Theory* is not just the ritual piety economists of my generation owe. the book that shaped their minds. Keynes's treatment of labor market equilibrium and disequilibrium in his first chapter is remarkably relevant today.

Keynes attacked what he called the classical presumption that persistent unemployment is voluntary unemployment. The presumption he challenged is that in competitive labor markets actual employment and unemployment reveal workers' true preferences between work and alternative uses of time, the presumption that no one is fully or partially unemployed whose real wage per hour exceeds his marginal valuation of an hour of free time. Orthodox economists found the observed stickiness of money wages to be persuasive evidence that unemployment, even in the Great Depression, was voluntary. Keynes found decisive evidence against this inference in the willingness of workers to accept a larger volume of employment at a lower real wage resulting from an increase of prices.

Whenever unemployment could be reduced by expansion of aggregate demand, Keynes regarded it as involuntary. He expected expansion to raise prices and lower real wages, but this expectation is not crucial to his argument. Indeed, if it is possible to raise employment without reduction in the real wage, his case for calling the unemployment involuntary is strengthened.

But why is the money wage so stubborn if more labor is willingly available at the same or lower real wage? Consider first some answers Keynes did not give. He did not appeal to trade union monopolies or minimum wage laws. He was anxious, perhaps over-anxious, to meet his putative classical opponents on their home field, the competitive economy. He did not rely on any failure of workers to perceive what a rise in prices does to real wages. The unemployed take new jobs, the employed hold old ones, with eyes open. Otherwise the new situation would be transient.

Instead, Keynes emphasized the institutional fact that wages are bargained and set in the monetary unit of account. Money wage rates are, to use an unKeynesian term, "administered prices." That is, they are not set and reset in daily auctions but posted and fixed for finite periods of time. This observation led Keynes to his central explanation: Workers, individually and in groups, are more concerned with relative than absolute real wages. They may withdraw labor if their wages fall relatively to wages elsewhere, even though they would not withdraw any if real wages fall uniformly everywhere. Labor markets are decentralized, and there is no way money wages can fall in any one market without impairing the relative status of the workers there. A general rise in prices is a neutral and universal method of reducing real wages, the only method in a decentralized and uncontrolled economy. Inflation would not be needed, we may infer, if by government compulsion, economy-wide bargaining, or social compact, all money wage rates could be scaled down together.

Keynes apparently meant that relative wages are the arguments in labor supply functions. But Alchian (pp. 27–52 in Phelps et al.) and other theorists of search activity have offered a somewhat different interpretation, namely that workers whose money wages are reduced will quit their jobs to seek employment in other markets where they think, perhaps mistakenly, that wages remain high.

Keynes's explanation of money wage stickiness is plausible and realistic. But two related analytical issues have obscured the message. Can there be involuntary unemployment in an equilibrium, a proper, full-fledged neoclassical equilibrium? Does the labor supply behavior described by Keynes betray "money illusion"? Keynes gave a loud yes in answer to the first question, and this seems at first glance to compel an affirmative answer to the second.

An economic theorist can, of course, commit no greater crime than to assume money illusion. Comparative statics is a nonhistorical exercise, in which different price levels are to be viewed as alternative rather than sequential. Compare two situations that differ only in the scale of exogenous monetary variables; imagine, for example, that all such magnitudes are ten times as high in one situation as in the other. All equilibrium prices, including money wage rates, should differ in the same proportion, while all real magnitudes, including employment, should be the same in the two equilibria. To assume instead that workers' supply decisions vary with the price level is to say that they would behave differently if the unit of account were, and always had been, dimes instead of dollars. Surely Keynes should not be interpreted to attribute to anyone money illusion in this sense. He was not talking about so strict and static an equilibrium.

Axel Leijonhufvud's illuminating and perceptive interpretation of Keynes argues convincingly that, in chapter 1 as throughout the *General*

Theory, what Keynes calls equilibrium should be viewed as persistent disequilibrium, and what appears to be comparative statics is really shrewd and incisive, if awkward, dynamic analysis. Involuntary unemployment means that labor markets are not in equilibrium. The resistance of money wage rates to excess supply is a feature of the adjustment process rather than a symptom of irrationality.

The other side of Keynes's story is that in depressions money wage deflation, even if it occurred more speedily, or especially if it occurred more speedily, would be at best a weak equilibrator and quite possibly a source of more unemployment rather than less. In contemporary language, the perverse case would arise if a high and ever-increasing real rate of return on money inhibited real demand faster than the rising purchasing power of monetary stocks stimulated demand. To pursue this Keynesian theme further here would be a digression.

What relevance has this excursion into depression economics for contemporary problems of unemployment and wage inflation? The issues are remarkably similar, even though events and Phillips have shifted attention from levels to time rates of change of wages and prices. Phillips curve doctrine[2] is in an important sense the postwar analogue of Keynesian wage and employment theory, while natural rate doctrine is the contemporary version of the classical position Keynes was opposing.

Phillips curve doctrine implies that lower unemployment can be purchased at the cost of faster inflation. Let us adapt Keynes's test for involuntary unemployment to the dynamic terms of contemporary discussion of inflation, wages, and unemployment. Suppose that the current rate of unemployment continues. Associated with it is a path of real wages, rising at the rate of productivity growth. Consider an alternative future, with unemployment at first declining to a rate one percentage point lower and then remaining constant at the lower rate. Associated with the lower unemployment alternative will be a second path of real wages. Eventually this real wage path will show, at least to first approximation, the same rate of increase as the first one, the rate

---

[2] Phillips himself is not a prophet of the doctrine associated with his curve. His 1958 article was probably the most influential macroeconomic paper of the last quarter century. But Phillips simply presented some striking empirical findings, which others have replicated many times for many economies. He is not responsible for the theories and policy conclusions his findings stimulated.

of productivity growth. But the paths may differ because of the transitional effects of increasing the rate of employment. The growth of real wages will be retarded in the short run if additional employment lowers labor's marginal productivity. In any case, the test question is whether with full information about the two alternatives labor would accept the second one—whether, in other words, the additional employment would be willingly supplied along the second real wage path. If the answer is affirmative, then that one percentage point of unemployment is involuntary.

For Keynes's reasons, a negative answer cannot necessarily be inferred from failure of money wage rates to fall or even decelerate. Actual unemployment and the real wage path associated with it are not necessarily an equilibrium. Rigidities in the path of money wage rates can be explained by workers' preoccupation with relative wages and the absence of any central economy-wide mechanism for altering all money wages together.

According to the natural rate hypothesis, there is just one rate of unemployment compatible with steady wage and price inflation, and this is in the long run compatible with any constant rate of change of prices, positive, zero, or negative. Only at the natural rate of unemployment are workers content with current and prospective real wages, content to have their real wages rise at the rate of growth of productivity. Along the feasible path of real wages they would not wish to accept any larger volume of employment. Lower unemployment, therefore, can arise only from economy-wide excess demand for labor and must generate a gap between real wages desired and real wages earned. The gap evokes increases of money wages designed to raise real wages faster than productivity. But this intention is always frustrated, the gap is never closed, money wages and prices accelerate. By symmetrical argument, unemployment above the natural rate signifies excess supply in labor markets and ever accelerating deflation. Older classical economists regarded constancy of money wage rates as indicative of full employment equilibrium, at which the allocation of time between work and other pursuits is revealed as voluntary and optimal. Their successors make the same claims for the natural rate of unemployment, except that in the equilibrium money wages are not necessarily constant but growing at the rate of productivity gain plus the experienced and expected rate of inflation of prices.

III. IS ZERO-INFLATION UNEMPLOYMENT VOLUNTARY AND OPTIMAL?

There are, then, two conflicting interpretations of the welfare value of employment in excess of the level consistent with price stability. One is that additional employment does not produce enough to compensate workers for the value of other uses of their time. The fact that it generates inflation is taken as prima facie evidence of a welfare loss. The alternative view, which I shall argue, is that the responses of money wages and prices to changes in aggregate demand reflect mechanics of adjustment, institutional constraints, and relative wage patterns and reveal nothing in particular about individual or social valuations of unemployed time vis-à-vis the wages of employment.

On this rostrum four years ago, Milton Friedman identified the noninflationary natural rate of unemployment with "equilibrium in the structure of real wage rates" (p. 8). "The 'natural rate of unemployment,'" he said, ". . . is the level that would be ground out by the Walrasian system of general equilibrium equations, provided that there is embedded in them the actual structural characteristics of the labor and commodity markets, including market imperfections, stochastic variability in demands and supplies, the costs of getting information about job vacancies and labor availabilities, the costs of mobility, and so on." Presumably this Walrasian equilibrium also has the usual optimal properties; at any rate, Friedman advised the monetary authorities not to seek to improve upon it. But in fact we know little about the existence of a Walrasian equilibrium that allows for all the imperfections and frictions that explain why the natural rate is bigger than zero, and even less about the optimality of such an equilibrium if it exists.

In the new macroeconomics of labor markets and inflation, the principal activity whose marginal value sets the reservation price of employment is job search. It is not pure leisure, for in principle persons who choose that option are not reported as unemployed; however, there may be a leisure component in job seeking.

A crucial assumption of the theory is that search is significantly more efficient when the searcher is unemployed, but almost no evidence has been advanced on this point. Members of our own profession are adept at seeking and finding new jobs without first leaving their old ones or abandoning not-in-labor-force status. We do not know how many quits and new hires in manufacturing are similar transfers, but some of them must be; if all reported accessions were hires of unemployed workers, the mean duration of unemployment would be only about half what it is in fact. In surveys of job mobility among blue collar workers in 1946–47 (see Lloyd Reynolds, pp. 214–15, and Herbert Parnes, pp. 158–59), 25 percent of workers who quit had new jobs lined up in advance. Reynolds found that the main obstacle to mobility without unemployment was not lack of information or time, but simply "anti-pirating" collusion by employers.

A considerable amount of search activity by unemployed workers appears to be an unproductive consequence of dissatisfaction and frustration rather than a rational quest for improvement. This was the conclusion of Reynolds' survey twenty-five years ago, p. 215, and it has been reemphasized for the contemporary scene by Robert Hall, and by Peter Doeringer and Michael Piore for what they term the secondary labor force. Reynolds found that quitting a job to look for a new one while unemployed actually yielded a better job in only a third of the cases. Lining up a new job in advance was a more successful strategy: two-thirds of such changes turned out to be improvements. Today, according to the dual labor market hypothesis, the basic reason for frequent and long spells of unemployment in the secondary labor force is the shortage of good jobs.

In any event, the contention of some natural rate theorists is that unemployment beyond the natural rate takes time that would be better spent in search activity. Why do workers accept such employment? An answer to this question is a key element in a theory that generally presumes that actual behavior reveals true preferences. The answer given is that workers accept the additional employment only because they are victims of inflation illusion. One form of inflation illusion is overestimation of the real wages of jobs they now hold, if they are employed, or of jobs they find, if they are unemployed and searching. If they did not under-estimate price inflation, employed workers would more often quit to search, and unemployed workers would search longer.

The force of this argument seems to me diluted by the fact that price inflation illusion affects equally both sides of the job seeker's equation. He over-estimates the real value of an immediate job, but he also over-estimates the real values of jobs he might wait for. It is in the spirit of this theorizing to assume that money interest rates respond to the same correct or incorrect inflationary expectations. As a first approximation, inflation illusion has no substitution effect on the margin between working and waiting.

It does have an income effect, causing workers to exaggerate their real wealth. In which direction the income effect would work is not transparent. Does greater wealth, or the illusion of greater wealth, make people more choosy about jobs, more inclined to quit and to wait? Or less choosy, more inclined to stay in the job they have or to take the first one that comes along? I should have thought more selective rather than less. But natural rate theory must take the opposite view if it is to explain why under-estimation of price inflation bamboozles workers into holding or taking jobs that they do not really want.

Another form of alleged inflation illusion refers to wages rather than prices. Workers are myopic and do not perceive that wages elsewhere are, or soon will be, rising as fast as the money wage of the job they now hold or have just found. Consequently they under-estimate the advantages of quitting and searching. This explanation is convincing only to the extent that the payoff to search activity is determined by wage differentials. They payoff also depends on the probabilities of getting jobs at quoted wages, therefore on the balance between vacancies and job seekers. Workers know that perfectly well. Quit rates are an index of voluntary search activity. They do not diminish when unemployment is low and wage rates are rapidly rising. They increase, quite understandably. This fact contradicts the inflation illusion story, both versions. I conclude that it is not possible to regard fluctuations of unemployment on either side of the zero-inflation rate as mainly voluntary, albeit mistaken, extensions and contractions of search activity.

The new microeconomics of job search (see Edmund Phelps et al.), is nevertheless a valuable contribution to understanding of frictional unemployment. It provides reasons why some unemployment is voluntary, and why some unemployment is socially efficient.

Does the market produce the *optimal* amount of search unemployment? Is the natural rate optimal? I do not believe the new microeconomics has yet answered these questions.

An omniscient and beneficent economic dictator would not place every new job seeker immediately in any job at hand. Such a policy would create many mismatches, sacrificing efficiency in production or necessitating costly job-to-job shifts later on. The hypothetical planner would prefer to keep a queue of workers unemployed, so that he would have a larger choice of jobs to which to assign them. But he would not make the queue too long, because workers in the queue are not producing anything.

Of course he could shorten the queue of unemployed if he could dispose of more jobs and lengthen the queue of vacancies. With enough jobs of various kinds, he would never lack a vacancy for which any worker who happens to come along has comparative advantage. But because of limited capital stocks and interdependence among skills, jobs cannot be indefinitely multiplied without lowering their marginal productivity. Our wise and benevolent planner would not place people in jobs yielding less than the marginal value of leisure. Given this constraint on the number of jobs, he would always have to keep some workers waiting, and some jobs vacant. But he certainly would be inefficient if he had fewer jobs, filled and vacant, than this constraint. This is the common sense of Beveridge's rule—that vacancies should not be less than unemployment.

Is the natural rate a market solution of the hypothetical planner's operations research problem? According to search theory, an unemployed worker considers the probabilities that he can get a better job by searching longer and balances the expected discounted value of waiting against the loss of earnings. The employed worker makes a similar calculation when he considers quitting, also taking into account the once and for all costs of movement. These calculations are like those of the planner, but with an important difference. An individual does not internalize all the considerations the planner takes into account. The external effects are the familiar ones of congestion theory. A worker deciding to join a queue or to stay in one considers the probabilities of getting a job, but not the effects of his decision on the probabilities that others face. He lowers those probabilities for people in the queue he joins and raises them for persons waiting for the kind of job he vacates or turns down. Too many persons are unemployed waiting for good jobs, while less desirable ones go begging. However, external effects also occur in the decisions of employers whether to fill a vacancy with the applicant at hand or to wait for someone more qualified. It is not obvious, at least to me, whether the market is biased toward excessive or inadequate search. But it is doubtful that it produces the optimal amount.

Empirically the proposition that in the United States the zero-inflation rate of unemployment reflects voluntary and efficient job-seeking activity

strains credulity. If there were a natural rate of unemployment in the United States, what would it be? It is hard to say because virtually all econometric Phillips curves allow for a whole menu of steady inflation rates. But estimates constrained to produce a vertical long-run Phillips curve suggest a natural rate between 5 and 6 percent of the labor force.[3]

So let us consider some of the features of an overall employment rate of 5 to 6 percent. First, about 40 percent of accessions in manufacturing are rehires rather than new hires. Temporarily laid off by their employers, these workers had been awaiting recall and were scarcely engaged in voluntary search activity. Their unemployment is as much as deadweight loss as the disguised unemployment of redundant workers on payrolls. This number declines to 25–30 percent when unemployment is 4 percent or below. Likewise, a 5–6 percent unemployment rate means that voluntary quits amount only to about a third of separations, layoffs to two-thirds. The proportions are reversed at low unemployment rates.

Second, the unemployment statistic is not an exhaustive count of those with time and incentive to search. An additional 3 percent of the labor force are involuntarily confined to part-time work, and another ¾ of 1 percent are out of the labor force because they "could not find job" or "think no work available"—discouraged by market conditions rather than personal incapacities.

Third, with unemployment of 5–6 percent the number of reported vacancies is less than ½ of 1 percent. Vacancies appear to be understated relative to unemployment, but they rise to 1½ percent when the unemployment rate is below 4 percent. At 5–6 percent unemployment, the economy is clearly capable of generating many more jobs with marginal productivity high enough so that people prefer them to leisure. The capital stock is no limitation, since 5–6 percent unemployment has been associated with more than 20 percent excess capacity. Moreover, when more jobs are created by expansion of demand, with or without inflation, labor force participation increases; this would hardly occur if the additional jobs were low in quality and productivity. As the parable of the central employment planner indicates, there will be excessive waiting for jobs if the roster of jobs and the menu of vacancies are suboptimal.

In summary, labor markets characterized by

---

[3] See Lucas and Rapping, pp. 257–305, in Phelps et al.

5–6 percent unemployment do not display the symptoms one would expect if the unemployment were voluntary search activity. Even if it were voluntary, search activity on such a large scale would surely be socially wasteful. The only reason anyone might regard so high an unemployment rate as an equilibrium and social optimum is that lower rates cause accelerating inflation. But this is almost tautological. The inferences of equilibrium and optimality would be more convincing if they were corroborated by direct evidence.

IV. WHY IS THERE INFLATION WITHOUT AGGREGATE EXCESS DEMAND?

Zero-inflation unemployment is not wholly voluntary, not optimal, I might even say not natural. In other words, the economy has an inflationary bias: When labor markets provide as many jobs as there are willing workers, there is inflation, perhaps accelerating inflation. Why?

The Phillips curve has been an empirical finding in search of a theory, like Pirandello characters in search for an author. One rationalization might be termed a theory of stochastic macroequilibrium: stochastic, because random intersectoral shocks keep individual labor markets in diverse states of disequilibrium; macroequilibrium, because the perpetual flux of particular markets produces fairly definite aggregate outcomes of unemployment and wages. Stimulated by Phillips's 1958 findings, Richard Lipsey proposed a model of this kind in 1960, and it has since been elaborated by Archibald, pp. 212–23 and Holt, pp. 53–123 and 224–56 in Phelps et al., and others. I propose now to sketch a theory in the same spirit.

It is an essential feature of the theory that economy-wide relations among employment, wages, and prices are aggregations of diverse outcomes in heterogeneous markets. The myth of macroeconomics is that relations among aggregates are enlarged analogues of relations among corresponding variables for individual households, firms, industries, markets. The myth is a harmless and useful simplification in many contexts, but sometimes it misses the essence of the phenomenon.

Unemployment is, in this model as in Keynes reinterpreted, a disequilibrium phenomenon. Money wages do not adjust rapidly enough to clear all labor markets every day. Excess supplies in labor markets take the form of unemployment, and excess demands the form of unfilled vacancies. At any moment, markets vary widely in excess demand or supply, and the economy as a whole shows both vacancies and unemployment.

The overall balance of vacancies and unemployment is determined by aggregate demand, and is therefore in principle subject to control by overall monetary and fiscal policy. Higher aggregate demand means fewer excess supply markets and more excess demand markets, accordingly less unemployment and more vacancies.

In any particular labor market, the rate of increase of money wages is the sum of two components, an equilibrium component and a disequilibrium component. The first is the rate at which the wage would increase were the market in equilibrium, with neither vacancies nor unemployment. The other component is a function of excess demand and supply—a monotonic function, positive for positive excess demand, zero for zero excess demand, nonpositive for excess supply. I begin with the disequilibrium component.

Of course the disequilibrium components are relevant only if disequilibria persist. Why aren't they eliminated by the very adjustments they set in motion? Workers will move from excess supply markets to excess demand markets, and from low wage to high wage markets. Unless they overshoot, these movements are equilibrating. The theory therefore requires that new disequilibria are always arising. Aggregate demand may be stable, but beneath its stability is never-ending flux; new products, new processes, new tastes and fashions, new developments of land and natural resources, obsolescent industries and declining areas.

The overlap of vacancies and unemployment—say, the sum of the two for any given difference between them—is a measure of the heterogeneity or dispersion of individual markets. The amount of dispersion depends directly on the size of those shocks of demand and technology that keep markets in perpetual disequilibrium, and inversely on the responsive mobility of labor. The one increases, the other diminishes the frictional component of unemployment, that is, the number of unfilled vacancies coexisting with any given unemployment rate.

A central assumption of the theory is that the functions relating wage change to excess demand or supply are nonlinear, specifically that unemployment retards money wages less than vacancies accelerate them. Nonlinearity in the response of wages to excess demand has several important implications. First, it helps to explain the characteristic observed curvature of the Phillips curve. Each successive increment of unemployment has less effect in reducing the rate of inflation. Linear wage response, on the other hand, would mean a linear Phillips relation.

Second, given the overall state of aggregate demand, economy-wide vacancies less unemployment, wage inflation will be greater the larger the variance among markets in excess demand and supply. As a number of recent empirical studies, have confirmed (see George Perry and Charles Schultze), dispersion is inflationary. Of course, the rate of wage inflation will depend not only on the overall dispersion of excess demands and supplies across the markets but also on the particular markets where the excess supplies and demands happen to fall. An unlucky random drawing might put the excess demands in highly responsive markets and the excess supplies in especially unresponsive ones.

Third, the nonlinearity is an explanation of inflationary bias, in the following sense. Even when aggregate vacancies are at most equal to unemployment, the average disequilibrium component will be positive. Full employment in the sense of equality of vacancies and unemployment is not compatible with price stability. Zero inflation requires unemployment in excess of vacancies.

Criteria that coincide in full long-run equilibrium—zero inflation and zero aggregate excess demand—diverge in stochastic macroequilibrium. Full long-run equilibrium in all markets would show no unemployment, no vacancies, no unanticipated inflation. But with unending sectoral flux, zero excess demand spells inflation and zero inflation spells net excess supply, unemployment in excess of vacancies. In these circumstances neither criterion can be justified simply because it is a property of full long-run equilibrium. Both criteria automatically allow for frictional unemployment incident to the required movements of workers between markets; the no-inflation criterion requires enough additional unemployment to wipe out inflationary bias.

I turn now to the equilibrium component, the rate of wage increase in a market with neither excess demand nor excess supply. It is reasonable to suppose that the equilibrium component depends on the trend of wages of comparable labor elsewhere. A "competitive wage," one that reflects relevant trends fully, is what employers will offer if they wish to maintain their share of the volume of employment. This will happen where the rate of growth of marginal revenue product—the compound of productivity increase and price inflation—is the same as the trend in wages. But in some markets the equilibrium wage will be

rising faster, and in others slower, than the economy-wide wage trend.

A "natural rate" result follows if actual wage increases feed fully into the equilibrium components of future wage increases. There will be acceleration whenever the nonlinear disequilibrium effects are on average positive, and steady inflation, that is stochastically steady inflation, only at unemployment rates high enough to make the disequilibrium effects wash out. Phillips tradeoffs exist in the short run, and the time it takes for them to evaporate depends on the lengths of the lags with which today's actual wage gains become tomorrow's standards.

A rather minor modification may preserve Phillips tradeoffs in the long run. Suppose there is a floor on wage change in excess supply markets, independent of the amount of excess supply and of the past history of wages and prices. Suppose, for example, that wage change is never negative; it is either zero or what the response function says, whichever is algebraically larger. So long as there are markets where this floor is effective, there can be determinate rates of economy-wide wage inflation for various levels of aggregate demand. Markets at the floor do not increase their contributions to aggregate wage inflation when overall demand is raised. Nor is their contribution escalated to actual wage experience. But the frequency of such markets diminishes, it is true, both with overall demand and with inflation. The floor phenomenon can preserve a Phillips tradeoff within limits, but one that becomes ever more fragile and vanishes as greater demand pressure removes markets from contact with the zeo floor. The model implies a long-run Phillips curve that is very flat for high unemployment and becomes vertical at a critically low rate of unemployment.

These implications seem plausible and even realistic. It will be objected, however, that any permanent floor independent of general wage and price history and expectation must indicate money illusion. The answer is that the floor need not be permanent in any single market. It could give way to wage reduction when enough unemployment has persisted long enough. But with stochastic intersectoral shifts of demand, markets are always exchanging roles, and there can always be some markets, not always the same ones, at the floor.

This model avoids the empirically questionable implication of the usual natural rate hypothesis that unemployment rates only slightly higher than the critical rate will trigger ever-accelerating deflation. Phillips curves seem to be pretty flat at high rates of unemployment. During the great contraction of 1930–33, wage rates were slow to give way even in the face of massive unemployment and substantial deflation in consumer prices. Finally in 1932 and 1933 money wage rates fell more sharply, in response to prolonged unemployment, layoffs, shutdowns, and to threats and fears of more of the same.

I have gone through this example to make the point that irrationality, in the sense that meaningless differences in money values *permanently* affect individual behavior, is not logically necessary for the existence of a long-run Phillips tradeoff. In full long-run equilibrium in all markets, employment and unemployment would be independent of the levels and rates of change of money wage rates and prices. But this is not an equilibrium that the system ever approaches. The economy is in perpetual sectoral disequilibrium even when it has settled into a stochastic macroequilibrium.

I suppose that one might maintain that asymmetry in wage adjustment and temporary resistance to money wage decline reflect money illusion in some sense. Such an assertion would have to be based on an extension of the domain of well-defined rational behavior to cover responses to change, adjustment speeds, costs of information, costs of organizing and operating markets, and a host of other problems in dynamic theory. These theoretical extensions are in their infancy, although much work of interest and promise is being done. Meanwhile, I doubt that significant restrictions on disequilibrium adjustment mechanisms can be deduced from first principles.

Why are the wage and salary rates of employed workers so insensitive to the availability of potential replacements? One reason is that the employer makes some explicit or implicit commitments in putting a worker on the payroll in the first place. The employee expects that his wages and terms of employment will steadily improve, certainly never retrogress. He expects that the employer will pay him the rate prevailing for persons of comparable skill, occupation, experience, and seniority. He expects such commitments in return for his own investments in the job; arrangements for residence, transportation, and personal life involve set-up costs which will be wasted if the job turns sour. The market for labor services is not like a market for fresh produce where the entire current supply is auctioned daily. It is more like a rental housing market,

in which most existing tenancies are the continuations of long-term relationships governed by contracts or less formal understandings.

Employers and workers alike regard the wages of comparable labor elsewhere as a standard, but what determines those reference wages? There is not even an auction where workers and employers unbound by existing relationships and commitments meet and determine a market-clearing wage. If such markets existed, they would provide competitively determined guides for negotiated and administered wages, just as stock exchange prices are reference points for stock transactions elsewhere. In labor markets the reverse is closer to the truth. Wage rates for existing employees set the standards for new employees, too.

The equilibrium components of wage increases, it has been argued, depend on past wage increases throughout the economy. In those theoretical and econometric models of inflation where labor markets are aggregated into a single market, this relationship is expressed as an autoregressive equation of fixed structure: Current wage incease depends on past wage increases. The same description applies when past wage increases enter indirectly, mediated by price inflation and productivity change. The process of mutual interdependence of market wages is a good deal more complex and less mechanical than these aggregated models suggest.

Reference standards for wages differ from market to market. The equilibrium wage increase in each market will be some function of past wages in all markets, and perhaps of past prices too. But the function need not be the same in every market. Wages of workers contiguous in geography, industry, and skill will be heavily weighted. Image a wage pattern matrix of coefficients describing the dependence of the percentage equilibrium wage increase in each market on the past increases in all other markets. The coefficients in each row are non-negative and sum to one, but their distribution across markets and time lags will differ from row to row.

Consider the properties of such a system in the absence of disequilibrium inputs. First, the system has the "natural rate" property that its steady state is indeterminate. Any rate of wage increase that has been occurring in all markets for a long enough time will continue. Second, from irregular initial conditions the system will move toward one of these steady states, but which one depends on the specifics of the wage pattern matrix and the initial conditions. Contrary to some pessimistic warnings, there is no arithmetic compulsion that makes the whole system gravitate in the direction of its most inflationary sectors. The ultimate steady state inflation will be at most that of the market with the highest initial inflation rate, and at least that of the market with the lowest initial inflation rate. It need not be equal to the average inflation rate at the beginning, but may be either greater or smaller. Third, the adjustment paths are likely to contain cyclical components, damped or at most of constant amplitude, and during adjustments both individual and average wage movements may diverge substantially in both directions from their ultimate steady state value. Fourth, since wage decisions and negotiations occur infrequently, relative wage adjustments involve a lot of catching up and leap-frogging, and probably take a long time. I have sketched the formal properties of a disaggregated wage pattern system of this kind simply to stress again the vast simplification of the one-market myth.

A system in which only relative magnitudes matter has only a neutral equilibrium, from which it can be permanently displaced by random shocks. Even when a market is in equilibrium, it may outdo the recent wage increases in related markets. A shock of this kind, even though it is not repeated, raises permanently the steady state inflation rate. This is true cost-push—inflation generated neither by previous inflation nor by current excess demand. Shocks, of course, may be negative as well as positive. For example, upward pushes arising from adjustments in relative wage *levels* will be reversed when those adjustments are completed.

To the extent that one man's reference wages are another man's wages, there is something arbitrary and conventional, indeterminate and unstable, in the process of wage setting. In the same current market circumstances, the reference pattern might be 8 percent per year or 3 percent per year or zero, depending on the historical prelude. Market conditions, unemployment and vacancies and their distributions, shape history and alter reference patterns. But accidental circumstances affecting strategic wage settlements also cast a long shadow.

Price inflation, as previously observed, is a neutral method of making arbitrary money wage paths conform to the realities of productivity growth, neutral in preserving the structure of relative wages. If expansion of aggregate demand brings both more inflation and more employment, there need be no mystery why unemployed workers accept the new jobs, or why employed workers do not vacate theirs. They need not be victims of ignorance or inflation illusion. They genuinely want more work at feasible real wages, and they also want to maintain the relative status they regard as proper and just.

Guideposts could be in principle the functional equivalent of inflation, a neutral method of reconciling wage and productivity paths. The trick is to find a formula for mutual deescalation which does not offend conceptions of relative equity. No one has devised a way of controlling average wage rates without intervening in the competitive struggle over relative wages. Inflation lets this struggle proceed and blindly, impartially, impersonally, and nonpolitically scales down all its outcomes. There are worse methods of resolving group rivalries and social conflict.

V. THE ROLE OF MONOPOLY POWER

Probably the most popular explanation of the inflationary bias of the economy is concentration of economic power in large corporations and unions. These powerful monopolies and oligopolies, it is argued, are immune from competition in setting wages and prices. The unions raise wages above competitive rates, with little regard for the unemployed and underemployed workers knocking at the gates. Perhaps the unions are seeking a bigger share of the revenues of the monopolies and oligopolies with whom they bargain. But they don't really succeed in that objective, because the corporations simply pass the increased labor costs, along with mark-ups, on to their helpless customers. The remedy, it is argued, is either atomization of big business and big labor or strict public control of their prices and wages.

So simple a diagnosis is vitiated by confusion between levels and rates of change. Monopoly power is no doubt responsible for the relatively high prices and wages of some sectors. But can the exercise of monopoly power generate ever-rising price and wages? Monopolists have no reason to hold reserves of unexploited power. But if they did, or if events awarded them new power, their exploitation of it would raise their real prices and wages only temporarily.

Particular episodes of inflation may be associated with accretions of monopoly power, or with changes in the strategies and preferences of those who possess it. Among the reasons that wages and prices rose in the face of mass unemployment after 1933 were *NRA* codes and other early New Deal measures to suppress competition, and the growth of trade union membership and power under the protection of new federal legislation. Recently we have witnessed substantial gains in the powers of organized public employees. Unions elsewhere may not have gained power, but some of them apparently have changed their objectives in favor of wages at the expense of employment.

One reason for the popularity of the monopoly power diagnosis of inflation is the identification of administered prices and wages with concentrations of economic power. When price and wage increases are the outcomes of visible negotiations and decisions, it seems obvious that identifiable firms and unions have the power to affect the course of inflation. But the fact that monopolies, oligopolies, and large unions have discretion does not mean it is invariably to their advantage to use it to raise prices and wages. Nor are administered prices and wages found only in high concentration sectors. Very few prices and wages in a modern economy, even in the more competitive sectors, are determined in Walrasian auction markets.

No doubt there has been a secular increase in the prevalence of administered wages and prices, connected with the relative decline of agriculture and other sectors of self-employment. This development probably has contributed to the inflationary bias of the economy, by enlarging the number of labor markets where the response of money wages to excess supply is slower than their response to excess demand. The decline of agriculture as a sector of flexible prices and wages and as an elastic source of industrial labor is probably an important reason why the Phillips trade off problem is worse now than in the 1920s. Sluggishness of response to excess supply is a feature of administered prices, whatever the market structure, but it may be accentuated by concentration of power per se. For example, powerful unions, not actually forced by competition to moderate their wage demands, may for reasons of internal politics be slow to respond to unemployment in their ranks.

VI. SOME REFLECTIONS ON POLICY

If the makers of macroeconomic policy could be sure that the zero-inflation rate of unemployment is natural, voluntary, and optimal, their lives would be easy. Friedman told us that all macroeconomic policy needs to do, all it should try to do, is to make nominal national income grow steadily at the natural rate of growth of aggregate supply. This would sooner or later result in price stability. Steady price deflation would be even

better, he said, because it would eliminate the socially wasteful incentive to economize money holdings. In either case, unemployment will converge to its natural rate, and wages and prices will settle into steady trends. Under this policy, whatever unemployment the market produces is the correct result. No tradeoff, no choice, no agonizing decisions.

I have argued this evening that a substantial amount of the unemployment compatible with zero inflation is involuntary and nonoptimal. This is, in my opinion, true whether or not the inflations associated with lower rates of unemployment are steady or ever-accelerating. Neither macroeconomic policy makers, nor the elected officials and electorates to whom they are responsible, can avoid weighing the costs of unemployment against those of inflation. As Phelps has pointed out, this social choice has an intertemporal dimension. The social costs of involuntary unemployment are mostly obvious and immediate. The social costs of inflation come later.

What are they? Economists' answers have been remarkably vague, even though the prestige of the profession has reinforced the popular view that inflation leads ultimately to catastrophe. Here indeed is a case where abstract economic theory has a powerful hold on public opinion and policy. The prediction that at low unemployment rates inflation will accelerate toward ultimate disaster is a theoretical deduction with little empirical support. In fact the weight of econometric evidence has been against acceleration, let alone disaster. Yet the deduction has been convincing enough to persuade this country to give up billions of dollars of annual output and to impose sweeping legal controls on prices and wages. Seldom has a society made such large immediate and tangible sacrifices to avert an ill defined, uncertain, eventual evil.

According to economic theory, the ultimate social cost of anticipated inflation is the wasteful use of resources to economize holdings of currency and other noninterest-bearing means of payment. I suspect that intelligent laymen would be utterly astounded if they realized that *this* is the great evil economists are talking about. They have imagined a much more devastating cataclysm, with Vesuvius vengefully punishing the sinners below. Extra trips between savings banks and commercial banks? What an anticlimax!

With means of payment—currency plus demand deposits—equal currently to 20 percent of *GNP*, an extra percentage point of anticipated inflation embodied in nominal interest rates produces in principle a social cost of $\frac{2}{10}$ of 1 percent of *GNP* per year. This is an outside estimate. An unknown, but substantial, share of the stock of money belongs to holders who are not trying to economize cash balances and are not near any margin where they would be induced to spend resources for this purpose. These include hoarders of large denomination currency, about one-third of the total currency in public hands, for reasons of privacy, tax evasion, or illegal activity. They include tradesmen and consumers whose working balances turn over too rapidly or are too small to justify any effort to invest them in interest-bearing assets. They include corporations who, once they have been induced to undertake the fixed costs of a sharp-pencil money management department, are already minimizing their cash holdings. They include businessmen who are in fact being paid interest on demand deposits, although it takes the form of preferential access to credit and other bank services. But, in case anyone still regards the waste of resources in unnecessary transactions between money and interest-bearing financial assets as one of the major economic problems of the day, there is a simple and straightforward remedy, the payment of interest on demand deposits and possibly, with ingenuity, on currency too.

The ultimate disaster of inflation would be the breakdown of the monetary payments system, necessitating a currency reform. Such episodes have almost invariably resulted from real economic catastrophes—wars, defeats, revolutions, reparations—not from the mechanisms of wage-price push with which we are concerned. Acceleration is a scare word, conveying the image of a rush into hyperinflation as relentlessly deterministic and monotonic as the motion of falling bodies. Realistic attention to the disaggregated and stochastic nature of wage and price movements suggests that they will show diverse and irregular fluctuations around trends that are difficult to discern and extrapolate. The central trends, history suggests, can accelerate for a long, long time without generating hyper-inflations destructive of the payments mechanism.

Unanticipated inflation, it is contended, leads to mistaken estimates of relative prices and consequently to misallocations of resources. An example we have already discussed in the alleged misallocation of time by workers who over-estimate their real wages. The same error would lead to a general over-supply by sellers who contract for future deliveries without taking correct account of the increasing prices of the things they must buy in order to fulfill the contract. Unanticipated deflation would cause similar miscalculations and misallocations. Indeed, people can make these same mistakes about relative prices even when the price level is stable. The mistakes are more likely, or the more costly to avoid, the greater the inflationary trend. There are costs in setting and announcing new prices. In an inflationary environment price changes must be made more frequently—a new catalog twice a year instead of one, or some formula for automatic escalation of announced prices. Otherwise, within the interval between announcements unchanged, the average misalignment of relative prices will be larger the faster the inflation. The same problem would arise with rapid deflation.

Unanticipated inflation and deflation—and unanticipated changes in relative prices—are also sources of transfers of wealth. I will not review here the rich and growing empirical literature on this subject. Facile generalizations about the progressivity or equity of inflationary transfers are hazardous; certainly inflation does not merit the cliché that it is "the cruelest tax." Let us not forget that unemployment has distributional effects as well as dead-weight losses.

Some moralists take the view that the government has promised to maintain the purchasing power of its currency, but this promise is their inference rather than any pledge written on dollar bills or in the Constitution. Some believe so strongly in this implicit contract that they are willing to suspend actual contracts in the name of anti-inflation.

I have long contended that the government should make low-interest bonds of guaranteed purchasing power available for savers and pension funds who wish to avoid the risks of unforeseen inflation. The common objection to escalated bonds is that they would diminish the built-in stability of the system. The stability in question refers to the effects on aggregate real demand. The Pigou effect tells us that government bondholders whose wealth is diminished by inflation will spend less. This brake on old-fashioned gap inflation will be thrown away if the bonds are escalated. These considerations are only remotely related to the mechanisms of wage and price inflation we have been discussing. In the 1970s we know that the government can, if it wishes, control aggregate demand—at any rate, its ability to do so is only trivially affected by the presence or absence of Pigou effects on part of the government debt.

In considering the intertemporal tradeoff, we

have no license to assume that the natural rate of unemployment is independent of the history of actual unemployment. Students of human capital have been arguing convincingly that earning capacity, indeed transferable earning capacity, depends on experience as well as formal education. Labor markets soggy enough to maintain price stability may increase the number of would-be workers who lack the experience to fit them for jobs that become vacant.

Macroeconomic policies, monetary and fiscal, are incapable of realizing society's unemployment and inflation goals simultaneously. This dismal fact has long stimulated a search for third instruments to do the job: guideposts and incomes policies, on the one hand, labor market and manpower policies, on the other. Ten to fifteen years ago great hopes were held for both. The Commission on Money and Credit in 1961, pp. 39–40, hailed manpower policies as the new instrument that would overcome the unemployment-inflation dilemma. Such advice was taken seriously in Washington, and an unprecedented spurt in manpower programs took place in the 1960s. The Council of Economic Advisers set forth wage and price guideposts in 1961–62 in the hope of "talking down" the Phillips curve (pp. 185–90). It is discouraging to find that these efforts did not keep the problem of inflationary bias from becoming worse than ever.

So it is not with great confidence or optimism that one suggests measures to mitigate the trade-off. But some proposals follow naturally from the analysis, and some are desirable in themselves anyway.

First, guideposts do not wholly deserve the scorn that "toothless jawboning" often attracts. There is an arbitrary, imitative component in wage settlements, and maybe it can be influenced by national standards.

Second, it is important to create jobs for those unemployed and discouraged workers who have extremely low probability of meeting normal job specifications. Their unemployment does little to discipline wage increases, but reinforces their deprivation of human capital and their other disadvantages in job markets. The National Commission on Technology, Automation and Economic Progress pointed out in 1966 the need for public service jobs tailored to disadvantaged workers. They should not be "last resort" or make-work jobs, but regular permanent jobs capable of conveying useful experience and inducing reliable work habits. Assuming that the additional services produced by the employing institutions are of social utility, it may well be preferable to employ disadvantaged workers directly rather than to pump up aggregate demand until they reach the head of the queue.

Third, a number of measures could be taken to make markets more responsive to excess supplies. This is the kernel of truth in the market-power explanation of inflationary bias. In many cases, government regulations themselves support prices and wages against competition. Agricultural prices and construction wages are well-known examples. Some trade unions follow wage policies that take little or no account of the interests of less senior members and of potential members. Since unions operate with federal sanction and protection, perhaps some means can be found to insure that their memberships are open and that their policies are responsive to the unemployed as well as the employed.

As for macroeconomic policy, I have argued that it should aim for unemployment lower than the zero-inflation rate. How much lower? Low enough to equate unemployment and vacancies? We cannot say. In the nature of the case there is no simple formula—conceptual, much less statistical—for full employment. Society cannot escape very difficult political and intertemporal choices. We economists can illuminate these choices as we learn more about labor markets, mobility, and search, and more about the social and distributive costs of both unemployment and inflation. Thirty-five years after Keynes, welfare macroeconomics is still a relevant and challenging subject. I dare to believe it has a bright future.

REFERENCES

Beveridge, W. H. *Full Employment in a Free Society*, New York 1945.

Doeringer, P., and Piore, M. *Internal Labor Markets and Manpower Analysis*, Lexington, Mass. 1971.

Friedman, M. "The Role of Monetary Policy," *Amer. Econ. Rev.*, March 1968, 58, 1–17.

Hall, R. "Why is the Unemployment Rate so High at Full Employment?," *Brookings Papers on Economic Activity*, 3, 1970, 369–402.

Keynes, J. M. *The General Theory of Employment, Interest, and Money*, New York 1936.

Leijonhufvud, A. *On Keynesian Economics and the Economics of Keynes.* New York 1968.

Lipsey, R. G. "The Relation between Unemployment and the Rate of Change of Money Wage Rates in the United Kingdom, 1862–1957: A Further Analysis," *Economica*, February 1960, **27**, 1–31.

Parnes, H. S. *Research on Labor Mobility,* Social Science Research Council, Bull. 65, New York 1954.

Perry, G. L. "Changing Labor Markets and Inflation and Optimal Unemployment Over Time," *Economica,* August 1967, 34, 254–81.

Phelps, E. S. et al. *Micro-economic Foundations of Employment and Inflation Theory,* New York 1970.

Phillips, A. W. "The Relation between Unemployment and the Rate of Change of Money Wage Rates in the United Kingdom, 1861–1957," *Economica,* November 1958, 25, 283–99.

Reynolds, L. G. *The Structure of Labor Markets,* New York 1951.

Schultze, C. L. "Has the Phillips Curve Shifted? Some Additional Evidence," *Brookings Papers on Economic Activity,* 2, 1971, 452–67.

Tobin, J. "A Note on the Money Wage Problem," *Quart. J. Econ.,* May 1941, 55, 508–16.

Commission on Money and Credit, *Money and Credit: Their Influence on Jobs, Prices, and Growth,* Englewood Cliffs 1961.

Economic Report of the President 1962, Washington 1962.

U.S. National Commission on Technology, Automation and Economic Progress, *Technology and the American Economy,* Washington 1966.

7. SOME CURRENT CONTROVERSIES IN THE THEORY OF INFLATION*

Thomas M. Humphrey

The theory of inflation is currently in an unsettled state. Largely discredited by recent episodes of stagflation in which joblessness and prices rose simultaneously, the once-dominant concensus view of a stable Phillips curve trade-off between unemployment and inflation has given way to a host of competing explanations. Today a variety of issues relating to the causes, transmission, and control of inflation are being debated. A careful sorting-out of these issues and a clarification of the rival claims and distinctive features of competing schools of thought may prove useful.

The purpose of this article is threefold. First, it develops a general classificatory framework within which particular issues can be organized and examined. Second, it uses this framework to survey some of the main debates that are current in contemporary discussions of the problem of inflation. Third, it identifies four distinct theories that emerge from these debates, specifies their distinguishing characteristics, and comments on the plausibility and relevance of each theory.

THE FOUR-EQUATION FRAMEWORK

The basic framework employed in this article consists of four relationships of the type that ap-

pear in many aggregative models of the inflationary process. These relationships are derived from the underlying market demand and supply equations that constitute fairly complete general equilibrium models of the economy. The relationships include (1) a wage equation explaining how the rate of increase of nominal wages is determined; (2) a price equation specifying how the rate of price inflation is determined; (3) a price-expectations equation explaining how people formulate their expectations about the future rate of inflation; and (4) a demand-pressure equation that describes how the level of excess aggregate demand—measured in terms of either output (relative to normal capacity) or unemployment—is determined.

In its most general form, the basic classificatory framework can be written as follows.

1. Wage Equation:
$$w = w[p_L, p^e{}_L, x_L, z_L].$$
2. Price Equation:
$$p = p[w_L, p^e{}_L, x_L, z_L].$$
3. Price-Expectations Equation:
$$p^e = p^e[p_L, z_L].$$
4. Demand-Pressure Equation:
$$x = x[(m - p)_L, f_L, z_L].$$

Here w is the percentage rate of change of nominal wages; p is the percentage rate of change of prices, i.e., the inflation rate; p^e is the expected future rate of change of prices, i.e., the antici-

* From the Federal Reserve Bank of Richmond *Economic Review,* July/August 1976, pp. 8–19. Reprinted by permission of the Federal Reserve Bank of Richmond and the author. Thomas M. Humphrey is Research Officer, Federal Reserve Bank of Richmond.

pated rate of inflation; and x is the level of excess demand, no distinction being made between labor and product markets.[1] The variables m and $m - p$ are the percentage rates of change of the nominal and real (price-deflated) money stocks, respectively, and f is the fiscal policy variable represented by the size of the government's budgetary deficit. The variable z is the vector of cost-push forces including such factors as trade-union militancy, monopoly power, and the political commitment to the goal of full employment and the consequent removal of the fear of unemployment as a factor constraining wage demands. The subscript L represents time lags denoting that the dependent variables may be influenced by lagged as well as contemporaneous values of the independent variables.

In the above framework, the wage equation states that the rate of money wage increase is determined by the actual and anticipated rates of rise of the cost of living, the excess demand for labor, and cost-push forces. The price equation relates the rate at which businessmen increase their product prices to the rate of rise of wages, to the rate at which prices in general are expected to rise, to excess demand in the product market, and to cost-push forces. The price-expectations equation states that the anticipated future rate of inflation is generated from experienced actual rates of price inflation and perhaps other influences also. Finally, the demand-pressure equation expresses the level of excess aggregate demand as a function of the rate of growth of the real stock of money, the strength of fiscal policy, and the vector of cost-push forces. Taken together, these relations form a simple four-equation system which, given the values of the independent and predetermined (lagged) variables, can be solved for the values of the dependent variables w, p, p^e, and x. These latter variables, being determined within the system, are said to constitute the dependent or *endogenous* variables of the model. By contrast, the fiscal policy, money

growth, and cost-push variables are considered *exogenous*, i.e., determined outside the system.

The exogenous variables are treated as the proximate causes or sources of inflation. They correspond to three leading explanations of how inflation gets started, namely, the fiscalist, the monetarist, and the cost-push views. The first two views constitute alternative versions of the so-called demand-pull theory of inflation. Whereas the fiscalist version concentrates on over-expansionary government fiscal policy as the primary source of demand inflation, the monetarist version focuses on the causal role of money growth, arguing that fiscal policy at best exerts only a transitory impact on the rate of inflation. Monetarist theories also tend to omit the cost-push variable as a cause of inflation, although they do acknowledge that cost increases are a vital intermediate link in the transmission mechanism through which inflationary pressures are propagated through the economy. By contrast, cost-push theories stress the inflation-initiating— as distinct from the mere inflation-transmitting— role of the cost-push variable, asserting that it enters the inflationary process both directly to determine wage- and price-setting behavior and indirectly to influence the rate of monetary growth, which is allowed to adjust passively so as to validate the cost inflation generated by unions and firms.

The latter point raises the question of the type of policy regime assumed in the general framework. As formulated above, it assumes an exogenous policy regime, i.e., one in which the authorities conduct their policies to insure that the main line of causation flows from the policy variables directly to the dependent excess demand variable rather than vice versa. As discussed later in the article, however, the framework can be modified to accommodate the reverse-causation assumption of an endogenous policy regime in which the authorities allow the policy variables at least partially to respond to and be determined by changes in excess demand. Thus, with suitable adjustment, the model is capable of handling both types of policy regimes.

Finally, it should be noted that the model contains no equations representing the bond and/or equity markets. Thus it is incapable of explaining the transmission of inflationary pressures through the financial sector of the economy. Instead, it concentrates on the transmission of inflation through the money, labor, and product markets. This shortcoming notwithstanding, the framework is still sufficiently general to accommodate important components of many theories

---

[1] It is not necessary to specify separate excess demand variables for the product and labor markets since the two measures are assumed to be linearly related. Excess demand in the product market is measured by the gap between actual and potential (i.e., normal or standard) output. Excess demand in the labor market is measured by the difference between the actual and natural rates of unemployment, where the latter is the rate that, given the inevitable frictions, rigidities, and market imperfections existing in the economy, is just consistent with demand-supply equilibrium in the labor market. The linear relationship between the two measures permits them to be used interchangeably.

of inflation. Specific theories—or at least parts of specific theories—emerge from the general framework when one suppresses certain variables, emphasizes others, and perhaps drops one or more of the equations. In any case, the four equations may be taken as a basis for outlining the main controversies among current expositors of the phenomenon of inflation.

The Wage Equation

The chief controversy relating to the wage equation concerns the determinants of wage-setting behavior. At least four views can be distinguished, namely, (1) the naive Phillips curve hypothesis, (2) the expectations-augmented/excess-demand hypothesis, (3) the pure cost-push hypothesis, and (4) the eclectic view.

The Phillips curve hypothesis states that the rate of money wage increase depends on the excess demand for labor (i.e., $w = w(x)$ where x is measured or proxied by the inverse of the unemployment rate). This theory is incapable of explaining how rapid wage inflation could persist in the face of slack labor markets in which excess demand is zero or negative.

The expectations-augmented/excess-demand hypothesis introduces the price-expectations variable into the Phillips curve and states that the rate of wage increase is determined by excess demand in the labor market and by workers' and employers' anticipations of future price inflation (i.e., $w = w(x, p^e)$). The logic underlying this formulation is straightforward. Demand pressure x pushes up wages. The greater the pressure the faster will wages rise. Even if demand pressure were absent or negative, however, wages would still exhibit a tendency to rise because workers are primarily concerned with real wages—i.e., with the purchasing power of money wages—and therefore bargain for money wage increases sufficient to protect real wages from anticipated future increases in the cost of living (represented in the equation by p^e, or price expectations). Similarly, employers interested in maintaining their relative position in the labor market must offer wage increases sufficient to match those increases that rival employers are expected to offer. Otherwise they will lose employees, and their relative market share will fall. Thus even in a situation of zero excess demand, employers on the average will be raising wages by the amount they expect wages and prices in general to rise. Nominal wages will rise, but each employer's real wage offer relative to the market average wage will remain unchanged.

Opposed to the expectations/excess-demand hypothesis is the pure cost-push view. More influential in the United Kingdom than in the United States, this theory holds that the rate of wage increase is initiated and determined by the vector of cost-push forces independently of price expectations and the state of excess demand (i.e., $w = w(z)$). Cost-push pressures include such forces as (1) monopoly market power, (2) trade-union militancy, and (3) wage earners' frustration arising from unfulfilled expectations regarding growth of real income and relative income shares. Labor unrest, frustration, and militancy are seen as causes and not—as in the monetarist theory—as consequences of inflation.

The cost-push hypothesis is in the class of theories that attribute inflation to monopoly power, whether wielded by unions or corporations. These theories assert that large organizations, seeking to enlarge their relative shares in the national income, utilize the market power in their possession to push wages and prices upward, thus spearheading and causing new rounds of inflation.

The monopoly power hypothesis has been criticized predominantly, but not solely, by monetarists on both theoretical and empirical grounds. First, critics state that the market power argument is at odds with the orthodox theory of monopoly behavior. According to the orthodox view, a monopolist sets a relative price for his product that maximizes profits in real terms and maintains that real price by adjusting his nominal price to allow for inflation. The logical implication is that, given the degree of monopoly power, monopolists would have no incentive to raise prices other than to catch up or keep pace with general inflation.[2] With real prices already established at profit maximizing levels, any further upward adjustment would only *reduce* profits. On the other hand, if prices are currently being raised to exploit hitherto unexploited monopoly potential, the question naturally arises as to why those gains were foregone or sacrificed in the past. In either case, monetarists argue, rising real prices imply nonrational (i.e., non-profit maximizing)

---

[2] In support of this contention, critics of cost-push cite empirical studies showing that when big firms do raise their prices they are usually trying to catch up with general inflation. Such catch-up price increases should not be interpreted as inflation-generating price increases. Similarly, when unions raise wages, they are often just trying to catch up with past price increases or protect wages from expected future price increases. They are not necessarily trying to increase their relative income share, which is probably already at its maximum, given the degree of their market power.

behavior, contrary to the basic axiom of conventional economic theory. True, rising real prices *would* be consistent with profit maximizing behavior if the degree of monopoly power were increasing.[3] But there is little empirical evidence that monopoly power is on the rise.

Responding to this criticism, cost-push theorists state that the monopoly power of labor *is* rising, as evidenced by the spread of unionization to groups not previously organized, e.g., public (government) employees. Also cited are factors such as liberal unemployment benefits and welfare payments that have raised workers' capacity to hold out in long strikes. With regard to the question of rational maximizing behavior, some cost-push advocates maintain that the conventional analysis cannot be applied to unions because the latter, unlike the business firms of traditional theory, do not necessarily maximize income.

To the critics, however, this last point is totally irrelevant. Trade unions, they argue, do not have to be income maximizers for the conventional analysis to apply. It still holds as long as union leaders attempt to maximize *some* variable —e.g., union membership, hourly wage rates, or the wage bill of a select portion of the union membership. That is, it still holds as long as union behavior results in a determinate equilibrium real wage. What *is* relevant, the critics assert, is the distinction between relative prices and absolute prices, i.e., the general price level. Cost-push theory is alleged to display a fundamental confusion involving the use of relative price concepts to explain the behavior of the absolute price level.

According to the critics of cost-push, market power is not a legitimate explanation of general inflation. Monopoly power determines relative prices, not the general price level or its rate of change. To be sure, the *particular* price of a monopolized product will be higher relative to other prices than it would be if the specific industry were competitive. But except for a slight rise due to resource misallocation, the overall or general level of prices would probably remain sub-

stantially unchanged. Likewise specific wage rates obtained by monopolistic unions will be higher in comparison with other wages than would be the case if all labor markets were competitive. Again, however, the overall level of wages need not be affected. In both cases, monopoly power affects the *structure* of wages and prices but not their general *level*. The logic behind this conclusion is straightforward and goes as follows. When a monopolist raises his price he reduces his output and his employment of factor inputs, thereby releasing resources to increase output and lower prices elsewhere in the economy. Similarly, when a monopolistic labor union raises its wage, it causes a diminution of employment in its sector, thereby releasing labor to other sectors where the increased labor supply acts to lower wage rates. In either case, the rise in monopoly prices (or wages) is offset by a compensating reduction in competitive prices (or wages), leaving the average level unchanged. Monopoly power determines relative prices (and hence quantities sold or employed), not absolute prices as claimed by the cost-push hypothesis.

Cost-push theorists rebut this latter criticism by challenging the validity of its underlying assumptions of perfect resource mobility and perfect price flexibility. They correctly point out that if resources are relatively immobile and prices downwardly inflexible, particular price increases can cause generalized inflation, i.e., in this case absolute prices are not independent of relative prices. In a world of sticky prices, inflation could occur for two reasons. First, the general price index, constituting an average of all prices, will necessarily rise purely as a matter of arithmetic when a rise in one of its components is not offset by a fall in the others. Second and more important, rising relative prices may induce additional inflation via the policymakers' reaction to their impact on employment. With a constant level of aggregate expenditure and downwardly rigid prices, particular price increases will generate compensating reductions not in other prices but rather in output and employment. Given society's high employment objectives, the authorities may have no choice but to accommodate the specific price increases with expansionary policies when employment falls below its target level. Thus the political constraints imposed by the commitment to high employment may enter directly into the process by which particular cost increases are transformed into generalized inflationary pressures.

In some quarters this explanation has been dismissed on grounds that it has been falsified by

---

[3] The point here is that the mere existence of monopoly power is not enough to produce inflation. The monopoly power must be steadily *increasing*. Monopoly power results in resource misallocation, thus reducing real income and raising the price level relative to what it would be if perfect competition prevailed. But this is an argument for *high*, not *rising*, prices. To produce inflation, i.e., a condition of continually rising prices, monopoly power must be ever-increasing. An existing degree of monopoly power cannot generate a sustained inflation.

experience, which shows that high levels of un-employment, while much deplored, have never-theless been tolerated for long periods. But many analysts accept the explanation as valid, and the debate between the cost-push theorists and their critics continues. There is, however, an eclectic view of wage-setting behavior that lies between the extremes of the pure cost-push and excess-demand views and incorporates elements of both. According to this third view, wages are pulled up by excess demand, pushed up by cost-push forces, and rise in response to increases in the cost of living, actual and anticipated. In equation form this eclectic view can be expressed as $w = w(p, p^e, x, z)$.

The Price Equation

Regarding the price equation, four issues have dominated recent discussion. The first concerns the proper specification of the independent vari-ables in the equation. What are the dominant de-terminants of price-setting behavior? There is unanimous agreement that the rate of wage in-flation affects the rate of price increase. But there is much less agreement about whether ex-cess demand plays a direct role in price de-termination. Both the Phillips curve and expecta-tions-augmented/excess-demand theories contend that it does, while the cost-push hypothesis claims it does not.

This latter point, incidentally, explains why cost-push theorists advocate incomes policies and direct controls as anti-inflation weapons. For if the rate of inflation is determined not by excess demand but rather by cost-push forces operating through wages and profit markups, then it fol-lows that inflation will be immune to traditional restrictive demand-management policies. In such cases it may be necessary to employ incomes poli-cies to influence the underlying cost-push forces and to use controls to directly constrain rates of wage and price increase.

Aside from the cost-push view, the other main theory of price-setting behavior that denies ex-cess demand a direct price-determining role is the so-called normal-cost hypothesis. This theory states that prices are determined by applying fixed percentage markups to unit production costs at normal (standard) levels of capacity utiliza-tion, with the markups set to yield target rates of return on equity. This hypothesis focuses on the rate of wage increase that constitutes the dom-inant component of changes in unit costs upon which price changes depend. Note, however, that the normal-cost hypothesis is not incompatible

with the notion that prices respond, with a lag, to excess demand, since that variable can influ-ence prices indirectly through the labor markets. The price equation in this case can be expressed either as $p = p(w)$ or $p = p(x_L)$ where the time-lag L represents the time it takes for demand pressure to influence product prices through the channel of factor costs.

The second issue is whether a long-run infla-tion-output (or inflation-unemployment) trade-off exists, thereby permitting the authorities to peg the unemployment rate at any desired level with-out risking persistent acceleration of the rate of inflation. The standard Phillips curve hypothesis implied the affirmative. But the notion of a per-manent trade-off was severely challenged by the so-called accelerationist school. Using an expecta-tions-augmented/excess-demand version of the Phillips curve price equation, this school demon-strated that the trade-off is only temporary, that it depends upon people being fooled by unantici-pated inflation (i.e., the difference between actual and expected inflation $p - p^e$), and that it van-ishes in the long run when price expectations fully adjust to price experience and are completely incorporated in wage- and price-setting behavior. Accelerationists argued that inflation stimulates economic activity only if it is unanticipated. An unexpected inflation induces producers, who are pleasantly surprised to find their product prices rising faster and their real (price-deflated) costs rising slower than expected, to expand output and unemployment. But the stimulative effects eventually disappear when the inflation becomes fully anticipated. This conclusion can be ex-pressed symbolically by rearranging the accel-erationist price equation $p = ax + p^e$ to read $p - p^e = ax$, where the coefficient a expresses the numerical magnitude of the trade-off be-tween the variables on the left- and right-hand sides of the equation. So written, the equation states that the trade-off is between unanticipated inflation $p - p^e$ and output (as represented by real excess demand x) and that it vanishes when inflation is fully anticipated and adjusted for, i.e., when $p - p^e = $ zero.[4]

---

[4] The no-trade-off view implies that the price-expectations variable enters the price equation with a coefficient of unity. To show this let the price equa-tion be $p = ax + \Phi p^e$ where Φ is the coefficient at-tached to p^e. Long-run equilibrium is characterized by equality between actual and anticipated rates of inflation, reflecting the tendency of price expectations to be correctly formed in the long run. Setting $p^e = p$ in the equation as required for long-run equilibrium and solving for p yields the expression $p = [a/(1 - \Phi)]x$. If the coefficient Φ is a fraction,

A separate but closely related issue is whether even an indefinitely accelerating inflation is sufficient to provide a permanent stimulus to real activity. Some accelerationist models that deny the existence of a long-run trade-off between output and the rate of inflation itself nevertheless imply that, if price expectations are formed in a certain way, there will be a stable trade-off between output and the *rate of acceleration* of the inflation rate (Δp). In other words, while expectations would eventually adapt completely to any stable rate of inflation, thereby negating the trade-off, those expectations would consistently lag behind a constantly accelerating rate. A policy of inflating the price level at a faster and faster pace can thus permanently fool all the people all the time and peg the economy at any desired level of output and employment.[5] As other economists have pointed out, however, it is unlikely that such a policy could fool the people forever. Eventually they would anticipate the rate of acceleration itself and adapt to it. The policy makers would then have to go to still higher derivatives or orders of rates of price change $(\Delta^2 p, \Delta^3 p, \ldots \Delta^n p)$ to stimulate the economy, and these higher derivatives, too, would eventually come to be anticipated.

It should be stressed, however, that many analysts remain skeptical of arguments denying the existence of permanent trade-offs involving inflation and its derivatives. These skeptics point to the stringent assumptions underlying the no-trade-off view. Not only must price expectations

adjustment to fully-anticipated inflation is incomplete, and a stable long-run trade-off exists between p and x. But if the coefficient Φ is unity, implying complete adjustment to anticipated inflation, the bracketed term is undefined and the trade-off vanishes.

[5] An example will demonstrate. Let the price equation be $p = ax + p^e$ where the unit coefficient attached to p^e implies the absence of a long-run trade off between p and x. From this equation it follows that the relationship among the rates of change of the variables p, x and p^e is given by the expression $\dot{p} = a\dot{x} + \dot{p}^e$ where the dots indicate rates of change (time derivatives) of the variables. Now assume that people are continuously revising their price expectations by some fraction b of the forecasting error between actual and predicted rates of inflation $p - p^e$. This expectations-generating mechanism is written as $\dot{p}^e = b\ (p - p^e)$ where $\dot{p}^e$ is the rate of change of price expectations. Substituting this latter equation into the one immediately preceding it and simplifying yields $\dot{p} = a\dot{x} + abx$. Finally, if excess demand is unchanging so that $\dot{x} = $ zero—as would be the case if the authorities were pegging x at some desired level—this last equation reduces to $\dot{p} = abx$, showing a trade-off relation between the rate of change of the rate of inflation $\dot{p}$ and excess demand x.

be correct and unanimously held, but those anticipations must be completely incorporated in all contracts to preserve the equilibrium structure of relative prices and real incomes. Skeptics argue that even if the first condition were satisfied—a heroic assumption—the second probably would be violated. For one thing, certain passive income groups—e.g., rentiers and pensioners—may be powerless to act on their price forecasts. Other groups that possess the power to adjust their nominal incomes for fully anticipated inflation may choose not to do so. An example would be where workers are more concerned about their relative (comparative) wages vis-a-vis each other than about the absolute level of real wages. These workers would be willing to accept inflation-induced reductions in real wages as long as other wages were similarly affected and relative wage relationships remained unaltered. Whether such hypothetical situations of incomplete adjustment under conditions of rational behavior do in fact actually occur, however, is an open question, and the controversy over the existence of long-run trade-offs remains unresolved.

A fourth issue is concerned with the causes of price rigidity or, more precisely, with explaining why prices tend to respond so slowly to shifts in demand. Interest in this topic has been greatly stimulated by the recent experience with inflationary recession or stagflation in which prices continued to rise long after excess demand had disappeared.

The traditional or classical model of price dynamics is of no help in explaining why inflation persists despite slack markets and high unemployment. According to the traditional model, prices adjust swiftly in response to excess demand or supply so as to clear the market. Nor is the Phillips curve model that expresses the rate of price change as a function of excess demand useful in interpreting stagflation. This model predicts that the rate of price change is zero when excess demand is eliminated and that price *deflation* accompanies excess supply. Neither model is consistent with experience showing that positive rates of price change can coexist with zero or negative excess demand for protracted periods of time. Apparently, many markets lack the short-run excess-demand price-adjustment mechanisms postulated by the classical and Phillips curve theories. What accounts for the actual slow-working price mechanism and for the consequent persistence of inflation even in the face of slack demand and high unemployment? At least three explanations have been offered.

In the expectations-augmented/excess-demand

model, prices can continue to rise even when excess demand is zero or negative as long as inflationary expectations are sufficiently strong. Stagflation is explained in terms of sticky price anticipations. Specifically, the model states that price expectations are based on past price experience. And if that experience has been one of inflation, price anticipations can continue to mount, putting upward pressure on prices even when aggregate demand is falling. With price anticipations still adapting to the inflationary past, the response of actual inflation to a reduction in aggregate demand will be agonizingly slow.

A second explanation attributes sluggish price adjustment to the prevalence of long-term contractual arrangements that fix prices for substantial intervals of time. Such contractual rigidities are said to distinguish so-called customer markets from spot-auction markets where flexible prices operate to keep the market continuously cleared. In customer markets, high search costs (time, effort, inconvenience, etc.) of comparison shopping give buyers an incentive to continue trading with customary sellers whose offers have proven satisfactory in the past. The customers of course must believe that the terms of the offers will remain unchanged, otherwise it might pay them to desert regular suppliers and shop elsewhere. The sellers themselves have an incentive to maintain stable prices in order to retain their established clientele. Since higher prices would encourage customers to shop elsewhere, sellers avoid or delay changing prices in response to short-run shifts in demand.

In effect, sellers implicitly agree to maintain their price offers in return for buyers' implicit promises of continued patronage. The agreement remains implicit because of the high legal costs of negotiating and spelling out an explicit formal written contract. Like all unwritten agreements, however, these implicit contracts only work if both parties assent to certain rules of fair play. In the case of customer markets the typical standard of fair play involves setting prices on the basis of long-run unit costs. Buyers are willing to accept price increases induced by permanent shifts in unit costs. Sellers in turn agree to absorb temporary cost increases just as they agree to ignore short-run shifts in demand when setting their prices. Thus prices remain unresponsive to short-run shifts in demand and costs.

A third explanation of sluggish price adjustment stresses producer interdependence and the need for price coordination. This view states that in many industries there is much uncertainty concerning the market-clearing price. Given this uncertainty, firms endeavor to avoid the market disruption, confusion, and perhaps even outright price warfare that could result if each sought individually to determine the equilibrium price. In order the prevent such confusion from developing, firms seek ways to coordinate price changes. Such coordination, if successful, will assure that firms raise prices in unison and that price changes will not occur when demand shifts are thought to be temporary and reversible. The preferred method of facilitating coordination is to base price changes on changes in standard unit labor and material costs, which tend to be the same for all firms in the industry. This cost-based pricing behavior assures that prices will respond only to costs, not to demand—although demand pressure may of course affect prices indirectly through the factor markets. It also assures that price changes will be uniform throughout the industry thereby minimizing the risk of competitive price undercutting.

The Price-Expectations Equation

The preceding sections have concentrated on alternative views of wage- and price-setting behavior. As previously noted, many of these explanations stress the role of expectations of future price inflation as a key determinant of rates of actual wage and price increase. In view of the central importance attached to price expectations, it is not surprising that much recent attention has focused on the mechanism by which those expectations are generated and revised. Concerning the formation of expectations, at least three hypotheses have emerged.

The first sees price expectations as determined by essentially unexplainable psychological forces. This view interprets the anticipated rate of inflation as a volatile, unstable variable subject to sudden and frequent shifts due to changes in subjective noneconomic factors that cannot be systematically explained within the framework of a macroeconomic model.

The second hypothesis, in sharp contrast with the first, states that price expectations are systematically determined by objective economic data, namely, actual rates of inflation experienced in the past. Known as the *adaptive-expectations* or *error-learning* hypothesis, this theory postulates that individuals form expectations of future rates of inflation from a geometrically weighted average of experienced past rates of inflation and then periodically revise those expectations if actual inflation turns out to be different than expected. In econometric studies of the inflationary process the adaptive-expectations model constitutes the most prevalent explanation of how price expectations are generated.

Despite its widespread use, many economists are dissatisfied with the adaptive-expectations hypothesis. They think it is an unrealistic and inaccurate description of how price anticipations are formed. Expectations, they claim, are as likely to be generated from direct forecasts of the future as from mere projections of the past. Moreover, people probably base their anticipations at least as much on current information about a variety of developments—e.g., money stock growth rates, imminent changes in political administration—as on data pertaining solely to past price changes. In short, one would expect rational individuals to utilize *all* the relevant information to improve the accuracy of their price forecasts. Yet the adaptive-expectations hypothesis holds that people look at only a small subset of the relevant information—namely, past price changes—in forming expectations. This does not appear to be consistent with rational forecasting behavior.

Disenchantment with the adaptive-expectations model has stimulated a search for an alternative explanation of the expectations-generating mechanism. This search has culminated in the formulation of the so-called *rational-expectations* hypothesis, which constitutes the third view of expectations formation as mentioned above.

According to the rational-expectations hypothesis, individuals will tend to exploit *all* the pertinent information about the inflationary process when making their price forecasts. If true, this means that forecasting errors ultimately could arise only from random (unforeseen) shocks occurring to the economy. At first, of course, forecasting errors could also arise because individuals initially possess limited or incomplete information about the inflationary mechanism. But it is unlikely that this latter condition would persist. For if the public is truly rational, it will quickly learn from these inflationary surprises and incorporate the new information into its forecasting procedures, i.e., the sources of forecasting mistakes will be swiftly perceived and systematically eradicated. As knowledge of the inflationary process improves, forecasting models will be continually revised to produce more accurate predictions. Eventually all systematic (predictable) elements influencing the rate of inflation will become known and fully understood, and individuals' price expectations will constitute the most accurate (unbiased) forecast consistent with that knowledge.[6] As incorporated in monetarist models, the rational-expectations hypothesis implies that thereafter, except for unavoidable surprises due to purely random shocks, price expectations will always be correct and the economy will always be at its long-run steady-state equilibrium.[7]

Monetarist advocates of the strict rational-expectations view argue that it carries some radical implications for stabilization policy. Specifically it implies that systematic policy actions—e.g., those based on feedback control rules—cannot influence real variables even in the short run, since rational agents would already have anticipated and acted upon those policies. To have an impact on output and employment the authorities must be able to create a divergence between actual and expected inflation. This follows from the monetarist view that inflation influences real variables only when it is unanticipated. The authorities must be able to alter the actual rate of inflation without simultaneously causing an identical change in the expected future rate. This may be impossible if the public can predict policy actions. Systematic policy actions are of course predictable policy actions. Stable policy response functions can be estimated and incorporated into the information used by forecasters. Rational agents, that is, can use past observations on the behavior of the authorities to predict future policy moves. Then, on the basis of these predictions, agents can correct for the policies beforehand by making appropriate adjustments to all nominal wages and prices. Consequently, when

---

[6] Specifically, the rational expectations hypothesis states that when expectations are formed rationally, the anticipated rate of inflation formed at the end of the preceding period p^e_{-1} is an unbiased predictor of the actual rate of inflation p, given all the information I_{-1} available at the end of the preceding period. That is, the expected value of p, given the information I_{-1}, is p^e_{-1}. In equation form, $p^e_{-1} = E(p|I_{-1})$ where E is the expectations operator. This latter formulation implies that the actual rate of inflation can differ from the expected rate only by a random forecasting error ϵ, i.e., $p - p^e_{-1} = p - E(p|I_{-1}) = \epsilon$. The forecasting error ϵ is of course statistically independent of all information known as of the end of the preceding period, since all statistical correlations between ϵ and I already would have been incorporated into the latter variable.

[7] In deterministic nonstochastic models of the type employed in this article, random shocks are ruled out. Therefore, in terms of the model, the rational-expectations hypothesis implies that the economy is perpetually in steady-state equilibrium.

stabilization actions do occur, they will have no impact on real variables since they will have been discounted and neutralized in advance. The only conceivable way that policy can have even a short-run influence on real variables is for it to be completely unexpected, i.e., the policymakers must act in an unpredictable random fashion. But random behavior hardly seems a proper basis for public policy.

Monetarist proponents of rational expectations use reasoning similar to the above to deny the effectiveness of discretionary stabilization policy. But advocates of countercyclical discretionary policy argue that such extreme conclusions are unwarranted. They point out that the strict rational-expectations hypothesis, despite its seemingly powerful logic, does not stand up well against the facts. According to this group, policy actions have pronounced and protracted short-run effects on real variables, the economy is rarely at or even near its long-run steady-state equilibrium path, forecasting remains an extremely hazardous and surprise-ridden business, and the rate of inflation responds sluggishly to restrictive policy. Something must be wrong with the strict rational-expectations view.

To critics, this view suffers from two main flaws. First, in common with all monetarist models, the rational-expectations hypothesis implies that transitory output effects can only arise from expectational errors, i.e., discrepancies between actual and expected rates of price change. In a rational nonstochastic world such errors never occur since expectations are always correct. Second, the rational-expectations hypothesis implies perfect price flexibility. This follows from expected prices, i.e., the current rate of inflation always adjusts completely and instantaneously to changes in the expected rate, so that steady-state equilibrium always prevails.

Both implications, critics hold, strain credulity. Far from being perfectly flexible, prices are actually sticky and respond slowly—as indicated by the persistence of stubborn inflation. Moreover, the long price-adjustment lags and the corresponding protracted output and employment effects observed in practice cannot be explained solely in terms of expectational surprises. Price setters just do not take that long to react to purely expectational errors. Long price delays and the associated quantity effects can only arise from contractual and institutional rigidities that prevent economic agents from adjusting to inflation even when it is correctly anticipated. Critics argue that once such contractual rigidities are taken into account, the strict version of the rational-expectations hypothesis ceases to hold. Instead, the forecasting procedure best suited to such cases may well be one that approximates the adaptive-expectations model.[8]

The Demand-Pressure Equation

The demand-pressure equation completes the model of the inflationary process. It does so by specifying the proximate determinants of the excess demand variable that interacts with other variables in the wage and price equations to determine the rate of inflation. Debates pertaining to the demand-pressure equation center on two issues.

The first issue involves the question of the relative importance of the three main independent variables in the equation: the rate of money stock growth, fiscal policy, and cost-push forces. Of these three variables, which exercises the major influence on demand pressure? Not surprisingly, the answer often depends upon whether the analyst is a nonmonetarist, a monetarist, or an advocate of the cost-push view. Moreover, within the monetarist camp the answer may differ depending upon whether one is an adaptive-expectations monetarist or a rational-expectations monetarist.

Many nonmonetarists would state that fiscal and monetary policy variables are of equal importance. Other nonmonetarists, while agreeing that monetary policy is important, would nevertheless rank it behind fiscal policy. Monetarists, on the other hand, would concentrate almost exclusively on the money growth variable and treat the fiscal variable as having negligible importance. True, they might grudgingly admit that fiscal policy could have a temporary impact on excess demand. But they would emphasize that any fiscal effects would be short-lived before vanishing altogether.

Although monetarists are unanimous in deemphasizing the impact of fiscal policy, they tend to differ on the question of the influence of monetary growth on excess demand. Members of the adaptive-expectations branch believe that changes

[8] The strict rational-expectations hypothesis departs from reality in still another way. It assumes that all relevant information is freely available so that forecasting accuracy can be perfected at zero marginal cost. In actuality, however, the cost of acquiring and processing additional information may be quite high relative to benefits—think of the cost of computer time. Confronted with high information costs, economically rational agents might well forego the pure rational-expectations approach in favor of cruder but less costly forecasting techniques, e.g., the adaptive-expectations model.

in the rate of monetary growth can generate temporary changes in real excess demand as long as expectations are unfulfilled. On the other hand, monetarists of the rational-expectations branch deny that monetary growth can influence real excess demand even temporarily. If expectations are formed rationally, the economy is always—except for random disturbances—at its steady-state equilibrium. And if steady-state equilibrium always prevails, it follows that shifts in the rate of monetary growth influence only nominal variables (e.g., the rate of inflation) but not real variables like excess demand. With expectations adjusting completely and instantaneously to actual outcomes, inflationary surprises are absent, and rational agents are never fooled into producing excess (i.e., greater than equilibrium) output.

While monetarists may disagree about the influence of monetary growth on real excess demand, they do agree that cost-push factors should not enter the demand-pressure equation. On this point they are in direct opposition to cost-push theorists, who hold that such forces play a major role in the determination of excess demand. The latter group argues that not only does the cost-push variable directly enter the demand-pressure equation with a negative sign, but that it also affects excess demand indirectly through the rate of inflation. With monetary growth held constant, cost-push pressure on prices will act to reduce real purchasing power, thereby causing real spending to fall. Thus, assuming constant monetary growth, the operation of cost-push forces causes excess demand to become negative and unemployment to rise.

It is evident from the preceding discussion that cost-push theorists also believe that the monetary growth variable plays an important role in the determination of excess demand. In fact, this belief constitutes the basis for their advocacy of accommodative monetary policy. Passive monetary growth is necessary to offset or counteract the contractionary influence of cost-push forces. On the other hand, an activist anti-inflationary monetary policy is definitely harmful. Not only is it incapable of controlling cost inflation, but it also intensifies the unemployment problem generated by cost-push forces. Cost inflation should be restrained by direct controls, not by demand-management policies.

A second debate concerns the process by which two of the determinants of excess demand —namely the monetary and fiscal variables— themselves are determined. On this latter question two issues are especially relevant. First, should the policy instruments be viewed as determined outside or inside the system? Second, are the policy instruments independent of each other?

Regarding the former issue, there are two views. One asserts that the policy instruments should be treated as exogenous variables whose magnitudes are fixed outside the model of the inflationary process. Advocates of this view believe that the main line of causation or channel of influence runs from the policy instruments to excess demand and prices rather than vice versa. The policy instruments can be treated not as dependent or accommodative variables responding to prior changes in demand but rather as the active independent variables that precede and cause shifts in demand. The alternative view is that the policy instruments should be treated as endogenous variables determined within the system by the policymakers' responses to changes in economic conditions. Advocates of this view see causation as running at least partially from aggregate demand and inflation to the policy variables. They argue that models of the inflationary process should contain additional equations—so-called policy reaction functions—describing how the authorities change the settings of the monetary and fiscal instruments in response to fluctuations in aggregate demand and the rate of inflation. An example of such a policy response function would be where the authorities pursue a target level of excess demand, seeking monetary growth and budgetary deficits consistent with the attainment of the target. In this case the target level of excess demand would enter the system as a datum to determine the values of the monetary and fiscal instruments, and the policy regime would be described by the equations $m = m(x)$ and $f = f(x)$.

In addition to the exogeneity-endogeneity issue, there is also the question of the independence of the policy instruments. Are the monetary and fiscal variables truly independent of each other or do they move together? This question is central to the debate over the causes of inflation. For if the instruments are in fact interrelated so that fiscal deficits are accompanied by accelerating monetary growth, it is virtually impossible to identify which is the unique source of inflation. Monetarists and nonmonetarists can cite the same evidence to support their respective views.

Many analysts believe that the policy instruments are not independent but instead are interrelated through the so-called government budget constraint. This constraint states the mathematical identity between the government's budget deficit and the means of financing it. Specifically, the budget constraint states that the deficit

$G - T$—i.e., the gap between government expenditures G and taxes T—must be financed by an increase in government debt ΔD and/or by an increase in the monetary base ΔB consisting of currency and bank reserves created by the central bank. In short, a fiscal deficit $G - T$ must be financed by debt issuance ΔD and money creation ΔB as expressed by the budget constraint identity $G - T = \Delta D + \Delta B$.

In principle, budget deficits $G - T$ could be financed entirely by new debt issues ΔD, provided interest rates were allowed to rise to sufficiently high levels. In practice, however, concern with the potentially disrupting effects of sharply rising interest rates insures that this drastic route is rarely taken. Instead, fiscal deficits are usually accommodated at least partially by money stock growth. Thus, the variables $G - T$ and ΔB tend to move together, making it difficult to identify which, if either, is the unique cause of inflation.

SUMMARY AND CONCLUSIONS

This article has examined within a simple aggregative framework some of the major current controversies in the theory of inflation. On the basis of alternative positions taken in these debates, at least four distinct theories can be identified. They are summarized as follows.

1. Adaptive-Expectations Monetarism. This theory states that inflation is determined by excess aggregate demand and price expectations; that expectations are generated by past price history and hence by previous excess demand; that excess demand results from excessive monetary growth; and therefore that excessive monetary growth, past and present, is the root cause of inflation. Only monetary growth matters; cost-push factors are totally ignored, and fiscal stimuli are largely dismissed on the grounds that they have no lasting impact on inflation. Inflation-unemployment trade-offs are seen as existing in the short but not the long run. That is, changes in monetary growth, by causing divergences between actual and expected rates of inflation, can generate large and protracted transitory changes in excess demand and associated real variables. In the long run, however, expectations will be fulfilled, excess demand will be zero, and monetary growth will influence only the rate of inflation. Monetary growth cannot affect real variables in steady-state equilibrium.

2. Rational-Expectations Monetarism. This version of monetarism predicts that, in the absence of unpredictable random disturbances,

steady-state equilibrium always prevails. Monetary changes produce no surprises, no disappointed expectations, no transitory impacts on real variables. Trade-offs are impossible even in the short run. This theory is hard to square with such phenomena as stagflation, the apparent intractability of the inflation rate, and the short-run nonneutrality of money.

3. Pure Cost-Push Theory. More popular in Britain than in the U.S., this theory postulates that wage and price increases are determined solely by noneconomic, sociopolitical cost-push forces independent of general economic conditions. Inflation is explained by the introduction of the cost-push variable in the wage and price equations. All other determinants are dispensed with. Thus monetary growth is denied a direct inflation-determining role, its only function being to passively accommodate push-induced cost increases in order to maintain output and employment at high levels.

4. Orthodox Nonmonetarism. Included in this category are a variety of models that may differ with regard to such features as long-run inflation-unemployment trade-off properties, relative weight given to monetary vs. fiscal influences, and the like. Whatever their individual differences, however, nonmonetarist models as a class have the following distinguishing characteristic. They permit all three exogenous variables—monetary growth, fiscal policy, push factors—to influence excess demand and the rate of inflation. Moreover, orthodox nonmonetarism shares with adaptive-expectations monetarism the view that policy actions will affect output and employment first and prices only later, often with very long lags. But whereas monetarists attribute these phenomena solely to price surprises (disappointed expectations) and lags in the revision of expectations, nonmonetarists believe that institutional and contractual rigidities are also to blame.

Of these four theories, two appear untenable when judged against the criteria of plausibility, realism, and relevance. These two, of course, are rational-expectations monetarism and the pure cost-push view. The former, as previously stated, conflicts with the observed tendency for quantities to bear the burden of adjustment to monetary changes, while prices respond very slowly and with long lags. The cost-push theory, on the other hand, implies a degree of trade-union market power and full-employment-at-any-cost policy that has never existed in the United States.

This leaves only adaptive-expectations monetarism and orthodox nonmonetarism as serious contenders for the distinction of constituting the most plausible theory of inflation. Both are capable of accounting for the phenomenon of stagflation, for the intractability or resistance of inflation to anti-inflationary demand-management policies, and for the tendency of quantities rather than prices to adjust to shifts in demand. Of the two, the nonmonetarist view seems to be the more convincing since it explains sluggish price adjustment in terms of contractual and institutional, as well as expectational, rigidities. In any case, if and when a new consensus view of inflation finally emerges, it will probably contain elements of both the monetarist and nonmonetarist explanations.

REFERENCES

The concepts and issues discussed in the text are more fully developed in the following sources.

Cagan, Phillip. *The Hydra-Headed Monster: The Problem of Inflation in the United States,* Washington, D.C.: American Enterprise Institute for Public Policy Research, 1974. Perhaps the best and most judicious survey of the present state of knowledge regarding inflation. Stresses the need-for-coordination explanation of sluggish price adjustment and shows that cost-oriented price-setting practices are not inconsistent with demand-pull theories of inflation.

Friedman, Milton. "Comments." *Guidelines, Informal Controls and the Market Place.* Edited by G. P. Schultz and R. Z. Aliber. Chicago: University of Chicago Press, 1966, pp. 55–61. A leading monetarist's critique of monopoly power theories of inflation. Argues that such theories imply irrational nonprofit maximizing behavior.

Gordon, Robert J. "Recent Developments in the Theory of Inflation and Unemployment." Northwestern University Center for Mathematical Studies in Economics and Management Science Discussion Paper no. 199, December 1975. (Mimeographed.) Contains a critical evaluation of the rational-expectations hypothesis and its application to economic policy. Also discusses markup pricing models and contractual-rigidity theories of sluggish price behavior.

Gray, Malcolm, and Michael Parkin. "Discriminating Between Alternative Explanations of Inflation." University of Manchester Inflation Workshop Discussion Paper no. 7414, December 1974. (Mimeographed.) The source of the four-equation classificatory framework used in the text. Gray and Parkin employ the four-equation schema to distinguish among monetarist, Keynesian, and cost-push models of inflation. They also show how alternative theories of inflation can be treated as particular special cases of the general framework.

Haberler, Gottfried. "Thoughts on Inflation: The Basic Forces." *Business Economics,* 10 (January 1975), 12–18. Comments on the monetarist critique of cost-push theories. Argues that the monopoly power of trade unions has been increasing, thereby putting upward pressure on wages and prices.

Humphrey, Thomas M. "The Persistence of Inflation." *1975 Annual Report.* Richmond: Federal Reserve Bank of Richmond. Discusses factors contributing to sluggish price adjustment and describes the adaptive-expectations or error-learning mechanism used to explain the generation of inflationary anticipations.

Institute of Economic Affairs. *Inflation: Causes, Consequences, Cures; Discourses on the debate between the monetary and trade union interpretations.* London: The Institute of Economic Affairs, 1975. Entertaining and instructive debate between proponents and opponents of monopoly power theories of inflation. Peter Jay attempts to defend the monopoly power theory against the attacks of monetarists David Laidler and Milton Friedman. In the course of the debate all the relevant points, pro and con, are raised.

Johnson, Harry G. *Inflation and the Monetarist Controversy.* Amsterdam: North-Holland Publishing Company, 1972. Chapters 1 and 2 contain a relentless monetarist critique of cost-push theories. On page 12 Johnson argues that monopoly power explanations of inflation conflict with the conventional economic theory of profit maximizing behavior.

Laidler, David, and Michael Parkin. "Inflation: A Survey." *Economic Journal,* 85 (December 1975), 741–809. An exhaustive survey of the literature on wage- and price-setting behavior, the formation of price expectations, and the determinants of excess aggregate demand. Presents a general model similar to the classificatory framework used in the text and then develops a simple monetarist model as a particular special case of the general model.

Okun, Arthur M. "Inflation: Its Mechanics and Welfare Costs." *Brookings Papers on Economic Activity,* 6 (1975, no. 2), 351–90. The most complete version of the contractual-rigidity explanation of sticky wages and prices.

Parkin, Michael. "The Causes of Inflation: Recent Contributions and Current Controversies." *Current Economic Problems.* Edited by M. Parkin and A. R. Nobay. Cambridge: Cambridge University Press, 1975. Surveys the main debates regarding wage- and price-setting behavior, the generation of inflationary expectations, and the determinants of excess aggregate demand. Reports on empirical as well as theoretical findings.

Sargent, Thomas J., and Neil Wallace. "Rational Expectations and the Theory of Economic Policy." *Studies in Monetary Economics,* no. 2. Minneapolis: Federal Reserve Bank of Minneapolis, June 1975. A clear and concise nontechnical exposition of the rational-expectations hypothesis by two of its chief adherents.

Tobin, James. "The Wage-Price Mechanism: Overview of the Conference." *The Econometrics of Price Determination.* Conference sponsored by Board of Governors of the Federal Reserve System and Social Science Research Council. Washington, D.C., October 30–31, 1970. Presents a general inflation model similar to the classificatory framework used in the text. Shows how alternative theories can be treated as particular special cases of the general model. Describes the logic of the accelerationist approach and summarizes some controversies associated with the wage, price, and price-expectations equations.

Trevithick, James A., and Charles Mulvey. *The Economics of Inflation.* New York: John Wiley and Sons, 1975. An excellent textbook survey of the theory of inflation. The expectations-augmented/excess-demand hypothesis is explained with great clarity in Chapter 7. See also Chapter 5, which describes alternative versions of the wage and price equations and Chapter 6, which deals with the role of trade unions and collective bargaining in the inflationary process.

---

8. DOWN THE PHILLIPS CURVE WITH GUN AND CAMERA*

Robert M. Solow

Any time seems to be the right time for reflections on the Phillips curve. So long as the actuality or threat of inflation remains a current problem, and so long as no clearly better organizing device presents itself, economists will argue about the Phillips curve. I do not intend to provide a complete survey of recent ideas on this subject, but only to comment on a few issues of theory and fact. In particular, I have stayed away from those aspects of the problem that were thoroughly discussed in James Tobin's splendid Presidential Address to the American Economic Association [14].

BEGINNINGS

The idea of a relation between the level of output or employment on the one hand and the rate of change of the money wage rate or the price level on the other is hardly new. There is casual reference to it in the *General Theory,* and a somewhat less casual remark in Joan Robinson's early *Essays in the Theory of Employment.*[1] It is not a very deep or subtle idea, and economics did not begin with Keynes; so it would hardly be surprising if such casual observations could be found in even earlier literature. Still, it fits more comfortably into Keynesian and post-Keynesian modes of thought, because the earlier economics tended to divorce real and monetary phenomena and therefore almost had to regard the level of aggregate output and the rate of change of the value of money as essentially independent, except perhaps for ephemeral disequilibria.

In any case, those casual remarks do not earn many brownie points. Really systematic attention to the relation between real tightness in the economy and the rate of inflation dates only from Phillips's paper of 1958. (I think Paul Samuelson and I coined the term "Phillips Curve" in a paper we gave at the 1959 AEA convention [12]). The

---

Robert M. Solow is Institute Professor and Professor of Economics, Massachusetts Institute of Technology.

[1] ". . . In any given condition of the labor market there is a certain more or less definite level of employment at which money wages will rise, and a lower level of employment at which money wages fall. Between the two critical levels there will be a neutral range within which wages are constant. . . . When employment stands above the critical level, then, if conditions are such that a general rise in money wages sets up no reaction to reduce effective demand there will be a progressive rise in wages with a constant level of employment, for prices and profits will rise with money wages and all the circumstances which led to a first rise in wages will remain in force and lead to a second. But the existence of unemployed workers anxious to find jobs exercises a drag upon trade unions and the rise in money wages will be slight and gradual. An increase in employment, in this situation, will strengthen the trade union position and tend to speed up the rise in money wages, but so long as unemployment remains appreciable the upward movement can not become overwhelmingly powerful" [11, pp. 7–8].

date is significant. What was in everyone's mind at the time was the experience of 1955–58, the years that gave currency to the phrase "creeping inflation," though by now they begin to look like the good old days. The Phillips curve was one way of making sense of that episode. Compensation per man-hour rose at an annual rate of 5.5 to 6 percent between 1955 and 1957 when the unemployment rate averaged just a bit over 4 percent, while compensation per man-hour rose at an annual rate of about 4 percent between 1957 and 1959 when the unemployment rate averaged something over 6 percent. Correspondingly, the private nonfarm deflator inflated at an annual rate of 3.5 percent in the earlier two years and 1.5 to 2 percent in the later two years. Those were not very good years for productivity increase—if we could achieve that kind of wage behavior now, it would probably be accompanied by a somewhat slower rise of the price level. In any case, with that sort of immediate historical backdrop and no great show of econometrics, Samuelson and I hazarded the guess that it would take at least 5.5 percent unemployment to stabilize the price level, and that 4 percent unemployment would be accompanied by wage increases of 5 percent a year and price increases of 2.5 percent a year. For a while that looked reasonable. Maybe five years is a reasonable lifetime for an educated guess. George Perry soon did a really first-class analysis and confirmed the orders of magnitude [9].

It did not occur to me then that the Phillips curve (or perhaps Phillips surface would be better, to signal that more than the unemployment rate governs the rate of wage increase) needed any subtle theoretical justification. It seemed reasonable in a commonsense way that the change in the money wage, like the change in any other price, should respond to the demand-supply balance in the labor market. That is the content of the passage from Joan Robinson already quoted. It was fairly obvious that the aggregate unemployment rate was not an ideal measure of the excess demand for labor. In the first place, one would want something like the excess of unfilled vacancies over the number of unemployed. In the second place, the implications of any given difference between vacancies and unemployment must depend on the degree of imperfection of the labor market and on the degree of substitutability of one kind of labor for another; so even if comprehensive data on vacancies existed for the United States (as they did not and do not), one would still not have an unambiguous measure of excess demand for labor. In the third place, even

if we were to agree to summarize the state of the labor market by the unemployment rate, it is hard to say what particular unemployment rate "ought" to correspond to wage stability; indeed, since measured unemployment has a component coming from voluntary turnover, new entrants and reentrants to the labor market, and minimal frictions, and since this component could easily change from time to time, the correspondence between the unemployment rate and the demand-supply balance in the labor market might be subject to unpredictable shifts. In spite of these qualifications and others, the unemployment rate seemed like a fair barometer of the pressure of demand in the labor market. I considered it a defensible hypothesis that excess demand for labor should drive its price up; though of course that leaves entirely open the question of the mechanism that determines the equilibrium unemployment rate, if there is one.

Nevertheless, the Phillips curve came under theoretical attack right away. Anti-Keynesians did not like it, although, as I have said, there is little that is specifically Keynesian about it, either historically or analytically. I think the main reason for this alignment is the one I have already mentioned; once upon a time economists had believed that there was no durable (I will not insist on permanent) gearing between real things and monetary things. Keynes had disagreed and apparently carried the day. Now it was argued that there could be no durable gearing between real things and the rate of change of monetary things, and some of the arguments sounded very much like the earlier ones.

Money is a veil; or, to put it more technically, all of the real equations are homogeneous of degree zero in prices so only relative prices matter, and they and only they are what can be determined by the real equations of general equilibrium. (By the way, the real question is not so much whether that argument is true as whether it is relevant in calendar time. It is very important to realize this. Failure to realize it has triggered innumerable wasted words.) Twenty-five years and one derivative later, it is argued that the rate of change of money prices is a veil. Therefore only unexpected inflation can be geared to real things. Events in the real economy will be insulated completely from expected inflation by changes in nominal interest rates, escalation provisions in intertemporal contracts, and eventually by the development of money substitutes. Since any steady rate of wage and price inflation must come to be accurately anticipated if it continues sufficiently long, only accelerating inflation or deflation can have a permanent connection with the real economy. It follows that the Phillips curve is an illusion except for the short run. In the short run, with expectations given, any variation in the rate of inflation is unexpected and can therefore have real causes and real consequences. In the long run, however, the only steady rate of inflation is an accurately expected one; whether it is 1 percent a year or 10 percent a year can have nothing to do with the real economy, which will have compensated for it completely. In a word, the change in the price level is a veil. You might say, the rate of change of a veil is a veil (per unit time).

THE ROLE OF EXPECTATIONS

There is something deeply satisfying—not to say suspicious—about any proposition that seems to deduce important assertions about the real world from abstract principles. Let us look at this one more closely. With particular reference to the behavior of money wages, it seems to say something like this: start with any wage equation or Phillips surface that gives the percentage rate of growth of the money wage as a function of the unemployment rate, the rate of increase of productivity, and perhaps other real economic variables. Then mere economic rationality tells you that you must add the expected rate of price inflation to the right-hand side of the equation. Why? Well, try the following thought experiment. Suppose that the price level had been constant for a long time, long enough for everyone to believe with certainty that it would remain constant. Then suppose that a particular configuration of real variables were consistent with a money wage growing at 1 percent a year, say. So we have one point on the Phillips surface. Now suppose something happens to convince everyone, with certainty, that from now on the price level will rise at 2 percent a year. Then "surely" the very same configuration of real variables can be consistent only with a money wage increase of 3 percent a year—because wages growing at 3 percent and prices rising at 2 percent is "essentially" the same thing as wages rising at 1 percent and prices not rising at all. This is just an elaborate way of saying that the rate of change of nominal magnitudes is a veil; but at least now we know that this belief (a definition of economic rationality combined with the judgment that the world behaves rationally) boils down to the statement that the expected rate of inflation appears additively, with a coefficient of one, in the wage equation.

We can keep things simple by assuming that the ratio of price level to unit labor cost (the "mark-up") is itself either constant or a function of real economic variables like the rate of growth of output, or the pressure of demand on capacity. Then it will turn out that an equation for the rate of change of the general price level will also have the expected rate of change of the general price level on the right-hand side, appearing additively, with a coefficient of one.

This arrangement has an important consequence. Go back to the situation I described earlier, in which the price level is constant, and has been constant long enough for the expected rate of inflation to be zero. Suppose again that real configuration is such that the money wage is rising 1 percent a year, and that this is fully consistent with a stable price level because productivity is rising at 1 percent a year and unit labor costs are thus constant. Now let something happen to change the real configuration suddenly—a sustained rise in exports, say, that reduces the unemployment rate. For a while, expectations are sluggish, so the expected rate of inflation will remain at or near zero. Since that term on the right-hand side of the wage equation is constant, the lowered unemployment rate will be translated into a faster rise in money wages, and therefore into a rising price level. So far this looks like a Phillips-curve story.

But, of course, if prices continue to rise, the expected rate of inflation can hardly stay at zero. It will start to catch up on the actual rate of inflation. If the actual rate of inflation should level off at some maintained figure, then eventually the expected rate of inflation would become equal to the actual maintained rate. But then, because of the structure of the price equation, the actual rate of inflation on the left and the expected rate of inflation on the right would just cancel each other off, and it would all be exactly as it was when both were zero. That is to say, the only real configuration compatible with steady inflation of x percent a year is the same one that is compatible with steady inflation at any rate. (There may be a family of equivalent real configurations instead of just one, but in the literature it is customary to speak of just one real variable, the unemployment rate, and to speak of the "natural rate of unemployment.")

Alternatively one can say that to maintain the new lower unemployment rate forever, it will be necessary to preserve forever the initial difference between the actual and expected rates of inflation, and the only way to do this, apart from mass hypnosis, is to have accelerating inflation, just fast enough so that expectations lag behind actuality by a fixed amount. For this reason, believers in this argument and in the existence of a natural rate of unemployment are often labeled "accelerationists." If the argument is right, then indeed the downward-sloping Phillips curve is a short-run phenomenon that is necessarily shifting whenever the economy is observed to be on it. The only permanent long-run Phillips curve, compatible with correct expectations, is vertical at the natural rate of unemployment.

TESTS OF THE ACCELERATIONIST HYPOTHESIS

Even propositions that are self-evidently true ought to be tested occasionally. In this case we need only check that the expected rate of inflation enters the wage equation additively with a coefficient of one. There is, however, a small problem: nobody knows what the expected rate of inflation actually is.

The earliest attempts to measure Phillips surfaces usually introduced a lagged rate of price increase as an independent variable. The reasoning was not so sophisticated as what I have just sketched; the idea was simply that a recent history of rapid price increase would make workers pushful and employers yielding, other things equal. Nevertheless, one could imagine a lagged rate of price increase serving as a proxy for the expected rate of inflation, on the overly restrictive hypothesis of static expectations. That is hardly convincing, and we shall have to do better. But it must be recorded that whenever and wherever the lagged rate of price increase appears as an independent variable in a wage equation, it appears to have a coefficient of roughly one-half, more often slightly less. This is significantly less than the accelerationists' theoretical value of unity, both in the statistical and analytical sense. If there were static expectations, and if the true coefficient were really one-half, then the long-run Phillips curve would be twice as steep as the short-run curve, but that is a long way from being vertical. And the world would behave not quite rationally.

Of course, one ought to be able to do better than static expectations, and anyhow you cannot kill a theory with a fact. There have been a few recent attempts to get at this question with a more sophisticated apparatus, notably by the Saint Louis Federal Reserve Bank [1], by Robert J. Gordon [5,6], and by Otto Eckstein and Roger Brinner [4]. They have succeeded in getting that crucial coefficient much closer to unity. I want to discuss these attempts at some length,

for two reasons. The first is that the question itself is intrinsically interesting. The second reason is that these studies—and some other current research on the Phillips surface that I shall also mention—raise some difficult general questions about the relation of theory to practice in our econometric age.

The analysis by the Saint Louis Federal Reserve Bank comes very close to verifying the accelerationist hypothesis. Gordon rejects it, but he produces a steeper Phillips curve than most—and in some variants is unable to reject the strict accelerationist hypothesis. Although they are in other respects quite different, these two analyses are rather similar in the way they try to measure "the expected rate of inflation." A natural step beyond the assumption of static expectations is the notion of representing the expected rate of price increase. The mechanism of adaptive expectations represents the expected rate of inflation as an infinite weighted sum of past observed rates of price increase, with the weights decaying geometrically toward zero as one goes further back into the past. There are various generalizations of this idea. An alternative is to take only a finite weighted sum of past rates of increase, with the weights constrained only to change smoothly and to go to zero at the end. Both Gordon and the Saint Louis economists choose this latter option. They both end by measuring the expected rate of inflation through a very long distributed lag on past rates of inflation, with weights whose center of gravity lies rather far in the past. And they both draw their weights from regressions relating nominal interest rates on Treasury securities to past rates of price increase and other variables.

In Gordon's most recent paper his preferred series of weights comes from a regression on the Treasury bill rate: the mean lag of expected behind actual price increases is about five quarters; more significantly, the weight attributed to the actual price change twelve quarters ago is still about one-fifth the size of the weight attributed to the current rate of inflation. (When the same process is applied to the rate of interest on three-to-five-year Treasury bonds, the mean lag is more than six quarters, and the weight for twelve quarters back is still more than half the weight on current price changes.)

In the case of the Saint Louis economists, the weights for price expectations come from a regression to explain the corporate Aaa bond rate, and the lag is even longer. The center of gravity of the lag distribution comes nine quarters in the past, and, since the weights are symmetric, fully half of the explanation of the currently expected rate of inflation rests on observed price changes between nine and seventeen quarters in the past.

INDIRECT MEASUREMENT OF INFLATIONARY EXPECTATIONS

I do not intend to criticize the use of mechanical models per se to measure the effects of expectations. I might do so if I had a better alternative to suggest, but I know of none. But I do think there are some dubious aspects of this particular device.

The most important preliminary is to understand *why* these long lags seem to be needed to make wage equations work; that is a matter of fact, not theory. The problem is this: why did wages (and unit labor costs and prices) rise more moderately in 1968 and 1969 when the unemployment rate was 3.5 percent than in 1970 and 1971 when the unemployment rate was first 5 percent and then 6 percent for months at a time? This is hardly an idle question. If we knew the answer to it, we would know why those early guesses that 4 percent unemployment would be accompanied by price increases of 2.5 percent a year have now given way to the much more pessimistic guess that prolonged 4 percent unemployment would be accompanied by inflation of the price level at a 5 percent annual rate, or perhaps even at a perpetually accelerating rate. More topically, we would understand why Mr. Nixon, who came into office in 1969 to set the economy free, was engaged in wage and price control by 1971.

The accelerationist hypothesis, combined with long lags in the formation of price expectations, has an answer to the puzzle. That is why it works in regressions. It says: wages rose so moderately in 1968 and 1969 because the 1 percent and 2 percent price increases of 1965 and 1966 were still holding down the expected rate of inflation. In effect, the momentary Phillips curve was unsustainably flat because some of the inflation was unanticipated. Symmetrically, wages rose so rapidly in 1970 and 1971, despite the recession, because the rapid price increases of 1968 and 1969 were still holding up the expected rate of inflation; it will take a long time to break down the inflationary expectations just as it took a long time to build them up. (This sounds contradictory, but it is not: prices were rising substantially in 1968 and 1969, just less than the tightness of the economy might have suggested.) The accelerationist and near-accelerationist models ac-

count for the puzzle by having expectations lag substantially behind facts, and by attributing an important effect to expectations. This is important because anyone who would like to do without the accelerationist hypothesis will have to find another way to explain the critical facts. I will come to some alternatives later.

I am, in fact, suspicious of that long lag, and only partly because I have a sneaking feeling that long lags provide too much leeway for the econometrician. Given enough flexibility in lag structure, you can explain anything; and what can explain anything explains nothing. A more important a priori reason for suspecting the long lag is this. The logic of the models says that the expected rate of inflation needs to be in there because wage bargains and wage decisions are real decisions, and money-wage changes can be converted to real changes only through the implicit intervention of expectations about the future of the price level. But most wage decisions are decisions for a year or even less. Obviously the highly visible heavy-industry collective bargaining contracts are two-year and even three-year decisions, but they cover only a fraction of the labor force, most of which is not even organized. Now if you want to form expectations about the price level in the next year or two, it is doubtful that events three years ago contain much useful information. The very distant behavior of the price level is what really matters for the extrapolation relevant to the purchase of a life insurance policy, but not to the setting of a wage rate that can be changed again soon.

When you think about it, Gordon's regression on the bill rate is very difficult to understand. A Treasury bill is at most a 90-day commitment; what matters is mostly the behavior of the price level in the next 90 days, and I find it hard to believe that the behavior of the price level between seven quarters ago and eight quarters ago contains any useful information not contained in much more recent data. In this regard, it is interesting that a regression using the three-to-five-year bond rate estimates a considerably longer lag, which is consistent with the fact that what is wanted is a longer extrapolation. And the Saint Louis economists, who use a long-term rate, estimate the longest lags of all. It may be, however, that the whole maturity structure is too closely knit together to permit this kind of discrimination. I continue to think that the long-lag sluggish-expectations variables are inappropriate measures of anything but rather long-run expectations about the price level, and what is relevant for wage behavior is something more sensitive to what has happened to prices in the immediate past.

DIRECT MEASUREMENT OF INFLATIONARY EXPECTATIONS

One could see more clearly what is happening if there were some usable direct measures of price expectations. In fact, there are at least two such, but neither is quite appropriate in the circumstances. J. A. Livingston, formerly financial editor of the *Philadelphia Bulletin,* has for years collected expectations about the change in consumer prices from a panel of about fifty business economists. When Gordon substituted this series for his own estimates of the expected rate of inflation, the over-all fit deteriorated slightly but the coefficient of the "expected rate of inflation" was very small—small enough to reject the accelerationist hypothesis out of hand, small enough, even, to give a fairly flat Phillips curve. Of course, the smallness of the regression coefficient may simply reflect the fact that the Livingston series is a very noisy proxy for the expected rate of inflation. (This might be so even if the business economists were accurate; it is the expectations of workers and employers that we really need.)

The Survey of Consumer Finances of the Survey Research Center at Ann Arbor, Michigan, has long asked questions about the price expectations held by its sample of respondents. Mere inspection at the results, however, raises questions in my mind about the interpretation of such survey results. In the first place, one wonders about the 10 to 20 percent of the sample that expected (or said it expected) prices not to rise at all in the next year, and said this steadily through 1966–69. One wonders how they differed from the smaller group, some 4–8 percent of the total, who expect prices to rise by 10 percent a year during that same period. The largest subgroup, about a third of the sample, was that predicting a price rise of 1–2 percent a year; about a quarter, each time, predicted that prices would rise by 5 percent in the coming year. The dispersion of replies is consistently so great—and the attraction of round numbers like 5 or 10 percent so strong—that one despairs of tracing any single "expected rate of inflation." It is true, partly because of this wide dispersion, that a crude average of these expectations changes sluggishly; but that is not the same thing as saying that the average responds with a long lag.

The most devastating direct commentary on the long-expectations-lag hypothesis comes from the survey results for 1969 and 1970. The theory gets its explanatory power by saying that inflationary expectations were much stronger in 1970–71 than in 1968–69. But in fact, the survey results suggest no stronger or more widespread expectations of rising prices in 1970 than there were one or two years earlier. In one way, just the opposite happened. In each of the four quarterly surveys in 1970, between 25 percent and 30 percent of the sample said they expected faster price increases in the next twelve months than in the past twelve months. In the fourth quarter of 1969 the figure was about the same; but in the second and third quarters, 45 percent and 39 percent of the sample said they expected accelerating inflation. In the last quarter of 1969 and all quarters of 1970, 20 percent and 26 percent of the sample said, "Prices will not go up; not ascertained if will." In the second and third quarters of 1969 only 10 percent and 14 percent gave that answer. In other words, this direct evidence, for what it is worth, says that inflationary expectations were weakening, not strengthening, in 1970, when the theory requires just the opposite. The survey figures do not show the sort of steady build-up of inflationary expectations between 1966 and 1970 that the new-style accelerationist story needs.

These impressions are confirmed and extended by a more systematic analysis of the survey data by George de Menil and Surjit Bhalla [2]. They code the sample responses in a reasonable but complicated way that I need not specify here. The result is a quarterly series for the expected rate of inflation in the forthcoming year. This series controverts the accelerationist story in more or less the way I have just described. There is no drastic build-up of inflationary expectations from 1966 to 1970. In fact, the constructed series shows very little change in that period, apart from irregular fluctuations. One can perhaps see a slight rise from 1966, but it peaks in mid-1969; by early 1971 the expected rate of inflation is as low as it had been in the previous ten years.

When de Menil and Bhalla use their constructed series as an independent variable in Phillips-curve estimations, they find that it performs just about as well as the more-popular indirect measurements. But always it attracts a coefficient considerably smaller than one, in fact, near one-half.

This is perhaps the place to comment on the work of Eckstein and Brinner [4]. Their mechanism for capturing expectational effects is a bit different from the usual. It comes in two parts. The first is a conventional moving average of past-observed rates of inflation, but with a considerably shorter lag than that used by Gordon and Saint Louis. What the others accomplish through the long lag, Eckstein and Brinner do with a nonlinear threshold effect. They include a new variable whose value is defined to be the average annual rate of inflation in the past two years, provided that average exceeds 2.5 percent, and zero otherwise.

With this machinery Eckstein and Brinner conclude that the long-run Phillips curve is not wholly vertical, but that it essentially turns vertical at a critical lower rate of unemployment, estimated to be about 4 percent, perhaps a trifle higher.

I am suspicious of this mechanism, too, for a different reason. It seems to be too ad hoc, too much invented to explain precisely the 1968–71 episode. Indeed, de Menil and Bhalla report that the threshold variable is statistically insignificant if the sample period ends before 1969. It can legitimately be said that the threshold is only crossed after 1968, so that one would hardly expect the variable to cut any ice in the earlier period. But then, in effect, we have no test of significance at all for the full period: the threshold variable is a dummy variable introduced to explain the single episode from 1969 to 1971. The data have been mined; the confession has been extracted by torture, and the case will not stand up in court. This raises a general point to which I want to return at the end of this essay.

I am far from sold, then, on either leg of the accelerationist position. The long lag of price expectations behind reality is dubious at best. Nor am I ready to believe for practical purposes that the expected rate of inflation—if it is a permissible abstraction at all—enters the wage equation with a coefficient of unity as "economic rationality" requires. There is nothing in the Survey Research Center data to suggest that one ought to impute economic rationality to the respondents in this subtle matter.

As a theorist, I feel it would be prudent to hedge a little. For some purposes it is sensible and natural to assume that economic behavior is rational; for some purposes I would still assume that the expected rate of inflation enters the wage equation with a coefficient of one, at least in the very longest of runs, in the very stablest of conditions. In the very longest of runs under the very stablest of conditions, the Phillips curve may therefore be vertical. In the light of the evidence,

however, I think it is folly to suppose *as a matter of logic* that 20 or 30 or 50 years of data culled from the real world will permit you to see the Phillips curve becoming vertical. For any span of years meaningful for the formulation and execution of economic policy, it may still be right and necessary to imagine the economy as trading off real output for price stability.

I do not think one can dismiss the explanations of recent wage and price behavior based on expectations, but I have tried to say why I am still in the market for something better. George Perry, who was one of the earliest quantifiers of the Phillips surface, has recently produced an alternative explanation of great interest [10].

LABOR-MARKET EXPLANATIONS

Perry's basic insight is that the aggregate unemployment rate may be an ambiguous measure of pressure in the labor market when the composition of the labor force and of the group of unemployed is changing. For example, it is plausible that an unemployed part-time worker should exercise less downward pressure on the money wage than an unemployed full-time worker. If, then, at a *given* over-all unemployment rate there would now be relatively more unemployed part-timers and relatively fewer unemployed full-timers than there would have been ten years ago at the *same* over-all unemployment rate, there would now be less downward pressure on the money wage. Therefore, money wages would rise more rapidly now at any given unemployment rate than they would have done ten years ago, at that unemployment rate. In other words, the Phillips curve would have shifted upward. Perry argues that such a change has indeed taken place.

The age distribution of the population has changed in response to the high birth rates of the forties and fifties; in addition, the participation rate of women in the labor force has increased. So today's labor force is more heavily weighted with the young and the female than the labor force of a decade ago. Moreover, as anyone knows who has looked at the statistics, the labor-market experience of the young and the female has worsened relatively; even in recessions, unemployment falls more heavily on them, whereas the unemployment rate for adult males stays remarkably low. Perry quantifies this observation by making the plausible assumption that an unemployed body generates downward pressure on the wage level proportional to the amount of "unemployed labor" he or she represents. In turn, the amount of unemployed labor can be measured by the number of dollars of wages it represents. This allows both for differences in hours normally worked and for differences in wage rates as well: thus an unemployed person who normally worked 40 hours a week at $4.00 an hour represents $160.00 worth of unemployment a week, more than twice as much as an unemployed person who normally worked 30 hours a week at $2.50 an hour—though each counts for one in the monthly tally of unemployment. By using average-hours-worked and average-hourly-earnings for a breakdown of the unemployed by age and sex, Perry is able to construct a weighted unemployment rate to use as an independent variable in his wage equation.

In addition, if the Phillips curve is nonlinear, a given weighted unemployment rate will have different effects on wages according as it represents the average of widely different age-sex specific unemployment rates, or the common experience of nearly all groups. To catch this effect, Perry calculates a dispersion index for his breakdown of the labor force.

This idea—that dispersion of experience among separate labor markets combined with a nonlinear wage response can have important substantive effects on the location of the Phillips curve—goes back to Lipsey's [7] early commentary on Phillips. It has been developed further by Tobin [14]. If wages are more flexible upward than they are downward with respect to excess demand for labor, and if mobility between labor markets is less than perfect, then even if the labor market is in aggregate balance—with unemployment here being offset by an equal number of vacancies there—wages will rise on the average. Moreover, with the aggregate pressure of demand held constant, increased dispersion will increase the rate at which wages will rise, and decreased dispersion will reduce it. Lipsey had in mind regional, industrial, and occupational labor markets; Perry applies the same thought to age-sex categories. Now occupations and industries exhibit systematic differences in the demographic composition of employment, so Perry is not so far from Lipsey. There is one interesting difference, however: direct mobility is possible between regions, industries, and occupations, but not between age-sex groups (except with the slow passage of birthdays and occasional major surgery). Although changes in relative wages can substitute for direct mobility in narrowing the differences among age-sex-specific unemployment rates, it may be a slower process. If it is, then changes of the kind that Perry finds in the

age-sex make-up of the labor force and in the dispersion of unemployment rates by age-sex group can generate long-lasting shifts in the conventional Phillips curve.

As Laplace found that he could explain the universe without invoking God as a hypothesis, Perry finds that he can explain recent history without invoking expectations. He finds that a short-lagged single rate of past price increase does as much for his wage equation as Gordon's long-lagged weighted-average proxy for price expectations. He finds also that whichever lagged price-increase variable he introduces, it enters with a coefficient well away from unity, and in the customary neighborhood of four-tenths. And finally he finds that he can explain both the 1970 experience and the earlier period in a unified way. Perry's model says something straightforward, if true: it says that right now the labor market is as tight with a 5.5 percent unemployment rate as it used to be, ten or fifteen years ago, with a 4 percent unemployment rate. That is to say, nowadays when the conventional body-count unemployment rate is 5.5 percent, the situation differs in two ways from a time ten years ago with the same conventional unemployment rate. In the first place, relatively more of the unemployed bodies are young and female, and relatively fewer are adult males. Thus relatively more are low-wage part-timers, and relatively fewer are high-wage full-timers. Measured Perry's way, there is less unemployment now than there used to be with the same measured unemployment rate. In the second place, there is more dispersion in the unemployment rates of different age-sex groups, with adult males having unusually low unemployment rates and women and youth having unusually high unemployment rates. For both reasons, a 5.5 percent unemployment rate now represents more upward push on wage rates than it used to. In fact, as I mentioned, Perry estimates that 5 or 5.5 percent unemployment now produces a push on wages about as strong as 4 percent unemployment used to do. Another way to put it is that the Phillips curve has shifted upward, so that any measured unemployment rate in the moderate range generates a rate of wage-increase about 1.5 percent per year higher than it used to. The main shift appears to have happened about 1962–63.

It should be kept in mind that when Perry says that 5 percent unemployment now is like 4 percent unemployment ten years ago, that is a statement about implications for wage inflation. It does not say that 5 percent unemployment now is just as bad as 4 percent unemployment used to be, so that if 4 percent was a proper target then, 5 percent is a proper target now. That would follow if the only consequence of unemployment that mattered was its effect on money wages. But if you think that the unemployment of young, female, and black people is worse (or, for that matter, better) than the unemployment of adult white males, then you have to make the welfare judgment in those terms. The proper target for you depends on your weighting of the consequences of different amounts of unemployment for social peace, equity, real output, and inflation.

I must say that I find Perry's results rather impressive. I think some caution is in order, however, for a simple methodological reason. One must always be wary of econometric results about the causal importance of some variable that has so far always moved in one direction through time. We are really after reversible relations; and I will feel happier about Perry's results if we should ever have a reduction in dispersion or in the proportion of women and the young in the labor force, and if, when that happens, the Phillips curve crawls back down along Perry's regression equations. Until then, I guess I believe those equations tentatively, but I would be prepared to punt at a moment's notice.

Next I would like to mention some very recent experiments of Charles Schultze [13], because they make a logical bridge from Perry's work to another way of looking at the problem. Schultze begins by suggesting that the voluntary quit rate may be a better indicator of labor-market tightness than the unemployment rate itself, because the quit rate should also contain information about the availability of unfilled jobs, on which no direct observations are available. Schultze finds that the quit rate performs just about as well as the unemployment rate as an independent variable in wage equations like Perry's.

But the most interesting thing he finds is this: from 1952 to 1965 there is a fairly close relationship between the quarterly quit rate (in manufacturing) and the quarterly rate of general unemployment. From 1966 to 1970, however, that relation consistently underpredicts the quit rate by a substantial amount. In other words, the quit-rate/unemployment-rate curve seems to have shifted upward, perhaps permanently, in 1966, in such a way that the quit rate is now higher for any given unemployment rate than it was before. (It is only fair to remark that Schultze's equation, like Perry's, tends to over-predict the rate of wage inflation in 1969, though they both track well in 1970. One of the advantages of the Gordon expectations formulation is that it can handle both

1969 and 1970, because it doesn't depend on a one-way shift in the demographic composition of the labor force, or in dispersion, or in the behavior of voluntary quits.)

Now if Schultze is right that the quit rate is a better indicator of excess demand in the labor market than the unemployment rate, then a shift in the quit-rate/unemployment-rate relation is equivalent to a shift in the Phillips curve. It signals that a given measured unemployment rate is now associated with a tighter labor market than used to be the case, and therefore that wages will increase faster at any unemployment rate than they used to. Schultze estimates about the same sort of shift in the Phillips curve as Perry did—from 3 percent inflation at 4 percent unemployment to 4.5 percent inflation at 4 percent unemployment (and 3 percent inflation at 5 percent unemployment).

It remains to wonder what is at the bottom of the shift to higher quit rates. Schultze does not offer any explanation. It is not hard to imagine logical possibilities, but none of them is easily verified. The upward shift in voluntary quits could come about from an outward shift in the (Beveridge) curve relating unfilled vacancies to unemployment. This in turn could be symptomatic of any kind of worsening of "structural unemployment" broadly interpreted: a poorer match of skills supplied to skills demanded, lessened intermarket mobility of labor, more uneven development of demand in different industries or regions. It is certainly possible that events have at last caught up with the prophets of structural unemployment, that what in 1961 they were saying had happened in 1957 did at last happen in 1967! Alternatively, one might adopt a more "voluntaristic" explanation. Changes in attitudes toward work and wages provide a kind of all-purpose independent variable, much like changes in expectations. Here, as with the demographic explanation, I will feel better when the new approach succeeds in explaining a sequence of events other than the one that called attention to it in the first place.

TACTICS IN ECONOMETRIC RESEARCH

It is useful to remember what started all this. An econometric relationship went sour; wage equations that seemed to work for the period from the end of the Korean War to the late 1960s began to fail. Under such circumstances, what can an econometrician do?

One reaction is to rethink the underlying relation and perhaps conclude that it has been misspecified initially. That is what the expectations theorists have done.

A different tactical reaction is to ask if the original relationship, though fundamentally sound, may have shifted. Perry attributes such a systematic shift to a change in the demographic composition of labor force and employment, Schultze to a change in the relation between the quit rate and unemployment.

Another possible response for the econometrician is to stand pat and do the best he can with minor refinements and reestimations of the old model. This is more or less what the Fed-MIT-Penn Model has done, as reported by George de Menil and Jared Enzler [3]. The wage equation in that model is still a more-or-less standard Phillips surface. Unlike some others, it finds a significant effect of the rate of change of the unemployment rate. Its only other special feature is that it gets a slightly higher coefficient on the (lagged) price-change variable than some others, 0.6 instead of, say, 0.4, but still quite far enough from unity to be evidence against the accelerationist view.

Price change is represented in the wage equation by a simple rate of change of the consumption deflator, lagged six months. De Menil reports the following test of the accelerationist hypothesis. He adds to the equation, along with this price-change variable, a long-lagged geometric-weighted average of past rates of price change. When that is done, the short-lag measure of price change continues to enter positively and the long-lag measure picks up a significantly negative coefficient. Moreover, the negative coefficient is absolutely larger than the positive one, which would have the unacceptable implication that the faster prices are rising, so long as they are rising steadily, the slower nominal wages will be rising. De Menil concludes that the long-lag variable does not belong to the wage equation.

This equation was estimated from a sample period that includes 1968, so it is perhaps pointless to look at its performance in 1968 (actually, it underestimates the rate of change of compensation per man-hour). In 1969, which was approximately as tight a year as 1968, the model tends to overestimate the rate of wage inflation, and then in the first quarter of 1970 it slips over into underestimation. I have not seen any report on the model's behavior since then. But since in simulations it tends to transmit changes in unemployment into wages fairly promptly—with over half the ultimate inflationary effect coming within six months—it seems very likely that it must have underestimated substantially the rate at which wages were rising from the spring of 1970 until the summer of 1971.

I want to record for future reference one other fact about the Fed-MIT-Penn equation. De Menil reports that it quite substantially underestimates the rate of wage increase in 1956. That is important, if only because it was the 1956 episode that marked the beginning of talk about "creeping inflation" as a possibly endemic disease in our economy.

Now I come to the hard question and the point of it all: What is a reasonable man—with something more than mere skepticism and something less than blind faith in econometrics—what is he to believe? Here are some important facts that used to seem orderly, and now act up. Should one accept an amended Phillips surface—and if so, which amendment seems best—or should one retreat into skepticism pure and simple?

As a practical matter, I am prepared to reject simple skepticism. It is not that economists ought to resist saying that they do not know when in fact they do not know—that is mere honesty and should override anything else. But it seems to me mistaken to conclude from the breakdown of an established regularity that it was nonsense all along. One ought to try to improve the toolbox, and in the meantime to attach greater uncertainty to the best predictions one can make. To pretend utter ignorance, however, is just that—a pretense.

Is it possible that the whole Phillips business is mistaken, and that a better explanation of money wages will be found along some quite different train of thought? That is certainly conceivable, but I think it is methodologically wrong to concede more than that without some indication of what the alternative train of thought may be. It is not only a true fact, but a useful principle, that you cannot lick something with nothing. And I have yet to see something.

Suppose the sensible alternative right now is to try to improve on the Phillips family of wage equations: the ingenuity of econometricians is bound to produce several ways to do that. The risky thing about empirical macroeconomics is not that it is too hard to find relationships that fit but that it is too easy. I have just finished describing —and criticizing—several variations, any one of which you could live with, so far as the data are concerned. Which one should a reasonable man adopt? And how can a reasonable man deny that there is likely to be some truth in all of them?

One of the reasons this is a hard sort of decision to make is that we have no clear idea about how good an explanation we are entitled to. That may sound like a peculiar thing to say: are we not entitled to a complete explanation? I have no wish to get hung up on deep philosophical questions about whether human or social behavior is causally determinate. My point is a much more pragmatic one. For as far ahead as one can imagine, there will be unexplained noise in econometric relations, and not simply white noise of constant variance—there will be occasionally large deviations that can only be explained away after the event, if then. In that case, given that economic knowledge is based not on controlled experiment but on ex post facto observation of history's single experimental run, there is always danger of over-fitting, of explaining those inexplicable deviations by mining the data of the recent past. There is little harm in that unless the process produces new econometric relations that are more likely, not less likely, to go sour when that big deviation goes away.

That is why I was intrigued by the fact that the Fed-MIT-Penn equation underpredicted the bulge of wage increases in 1956 and then apparently settled down to do rather well for the next twelve or thirteen years. It is possible—though this is not my favorite guess—that 1970–71 will in the end turn out to be like 1956: a deviation that went away.

Another possibility—and this intrigues me more—is that 1970–71 will turn out to mark a permanent shift in wage behavior, not a transitory residual, and not something that can properly be accounted for by the exchange of one independent variable for a slightly different one. Schultze's observation that the relation of the voluntary quit rate to the unemployment rate shifted sometime around 1966 fits in with this line of thought. And so does a very important fact that I have not mentioned until now. Money wages have been behaving anomalously almost everywhere! It is not only in the United States that 1970 and 1971 appear to have climbed off the Phillips surface that explained earlier years. The outstanding other case is Great Britain, which has had several years of extraordinarily high unemployment (by their standards) and still faced a wage explosion of the order of 12 or 14 percent a year in 1970–71, which has not abated since. I am told that the London Business School econometric model is now treating the money wage as exogenous in its forecasting work, having abandoned its earlier wage equation. But the coincidence is far more widespread than that. The same thing has happened in Italy, in France, and in the Scandinavian countries, all of which had resorted to wage and price control a year before

President Nixon's decision of August 1971. It is fair to say that in the last few years there has been inflation in all major industrial countries, and only in some of them can tight demand have been the sole explanation. For an interesting survey, see the paper by Nordhaus [8].

Now it does not follow logically from the fact that wages have been rising unusually rapidly—given the other circumstances—in many or all industrial countries that the explanation has to be the same in all of them. But it is natural to ask of any explanation proposed for the United States whether it can generalize to other places.

One possibility is that everywhere workers—and employers—have learned to form expectations in real terms; and when their expectations for real wages are frustrated by rising prices, they try to make good the deficiency in later years. This notion is very closely related to the accelerationist hypothesis I discussed earlier. The difference is that this hypothetical upsurge of consciousness of real changes need not be related to any long-lag weighted-average representation of expected price changes; and, indeed, it need not have been effective at all in the years from 1950 to, say, 1969 or 1970. If there is anything to this idea at all, it raises two very interesting questions. The first is, Is it temporary or is it, as with Eve's apple, a permanent loss of innocence? The second question follows on: What becomes of the theory of income and employment, quite apart from the theory of inflation, if labor can and does after all "bargain for the real wage?"

Finally I want to suggest one other possible explanation that does pay some attention to the worldwide character of the thing it is trying to explain. One expects unemployment to exert downward pressure on the money wage in roughly the same way that one expects excess supply of any commodity to put downward pressure on its price. If excess supply is known or expected to be temporary and limited, it is likely to have less effect on prices than if it is half-expected to be prolonged and severe. The same is true in the labor market, on both sides of the labor contract. Organized and unorganized workers are more likely to continue to press for higher wages at some moderate unemployment rate if they are confident that the unemployment rate will soon fall, or will not rise. Employers are less likely to resist wage increases, or even to chance substantial layoffs, if they expect that markets will soon improve and experienced labor will become fairly hard to get.

It would be the most natural thing in the

world if such expectations should seize workers and employers in the main industrial countries of the world, for the simple reason that they are probably true. (Those words were written before the recession of 1974–75. Now the question is open again.) If this is any part of the explanation—and I am inclined to think it represents a good part although not all of the explanation—then we are seeing a permanent shift in the wage equation, and the 1950s and 1960s will not come this way again. The awful thing is that I do not see how we can possibly know until some years have passed.

That leaves me in an uncomfortable but not impossible position. We have a modest grip on wage behavior, but it is obviously imperfect and uncertain. There are several plausible competing candidates for an improved version, or at least a version more descriptive of current conditions. One or more of these might turn out to be what we need, but it will take careful observation to decide among them. In time, we may have an improved grip on wage behavior; although in time we may also have more surprises and have to go back to the old drawing board. I said this is an uncomfortable position to be in, but in a way it is no more uncomfortable than the position of any nonexperimental scientist, which indeed it closely resembles.

REFERENCES

1. L. C. Andersen and K. M. Carlson, "An Econometric Analysis of the Relation of Monetary Variables to the Behavior of Prices and Unemployment," in *The Econometrics of Price Determination*, ed. O. Eckstein (Washington, D.C.: Federal Reserve System, 1972).

2. G. de Menil and S. Bhalla, "Popular Price Expectations," unpublished paper, Princeton University, 1973.

3. ———— and J. Engler, "Prices and Wages in the FR-MIT-Penn Econometric Model," in Eckstein, ed., *The Econometrics of Price Determination*.

4. O. Eckstein and R. Brinner, *The Inflation Process in the United States*, 92d Cong., 2d sess., 1972.

5. R. J. Gordon, "Inflation in Recession and Recovery," *Brookings Papers on Economic Activity*, 1971, no. 1.

6. ————, "Wage-Price Controls on the Shifting Phillips Curve," *Brookings Papers on Economic Activity*, 1972, no. 2.

7. R. G. Lipsey, "The Relation between Unemployment and the Rate of Change of Money Wage Rates in the United Kingdom, 1862–1957: A Further Analysis," *Economica*, February 1960.

8. W. D. Nordhaus, "The Worldwide Wage Explosion," *Brookings Papers on Economic Activity*, 1972, no. 2.

9. G. L. Perry, *Unemployment, Money Wage Rates, and Inflation* (Cambridge: MIT Press, 1966).

10. ————, "Changing Labor Markets and Inflation," *Brookings Papers on Economic Activity*, 1970, no. 3.

11. J. Robinson, *Essays in the Theory of Employment* (New York: Macmillan, 1973).

12. P. A. Samuelson and R. Solow, "Analytical Aspects of Anti-Inflation Policy," *American Economic Review*, May 1960.

13. C. Schultze, "Note on Recent Wage Behavior," *Brookings Papers on Economic Activity*, 1971, no. 2.

14. J. Tobin, "Inflation and Unemployment," *American Economic Review*, March 1972.

Chapter

2

COMMERCIAL BANKING AND
FINANCIAL INTERMEDIARIES

The financial system of the United States is complex and highly developed. There are about 14,700 commercial banks—that is, banks which accept deposits subject to check. These banks range in size from the Bank of America in California, which has total deposits of more than $60 billion, down to about 2,500 banks having less than $5 million of deposits. Only 39 percent of the banks are members of the Federal Reserve System, but member banks hold about 73 percent of total deposits. Payment of interest on demand (checking) deposits is prohibited, but commercial banks also accept interest-bearing time and savings deposits. Thus, in addition to serving as administrators of the nation's payment system and the primary channel through which money—defined as demand deposits and currency—is injected into or withdrawn from the economy, commercial banks also form part of an elaborate system of savings institutions. In addition to commercial banks, these institutions include a network of savings and loan associations which provide savings facilities on a nationwide basis, mutual savings banks which operate in a few of the 50 states, credit unions, and life insurance companies. Private pension and retirement systems, which invest funds set aside for employee retirement benefits by business concerns and state and local government units, and mutual funds have become increasingly important participants in the capital market in recent years.

Major borrowers include households which borrow on installment credit contracts for the purchase of automobiles and other consumer durable goods and on longer term mortgages for the purchase of houses; state and local government units which finance the construction of schools, highways, and streets, water and sewer facilities, and the like through the issuance of bonds; and the federal government, which at times borrows substantial sums to cover budget deficits. Private business enterprises commonly use internally generated funds—retained profits and depreciation allowances—to finance much of their investment in inventories and plant and equipment, but they are also heavy borrowers through loans and bond issues, particularly at times when economic activity is brisk.

There is a considerable amount of specialization on the part of financial institutions. The investment activity of savings and loan associations is largely confined to the acquisition of mortgages for the financing of housing construction. Mutual savings banks are also heavy participants in the mortgage market in the states in which they are located, although not quite to the same degree as savings and loan associations. Life insurance companies are important both as mortgage lenders and as suppliers of long-term financing for business enterprises. While commercial banks also play an important role in the mortgage market, they, together with individual investors, provide the most important market for the securities of state and local government units. In addition, commercial banks are the chief source of consumer installment credit, lending directly to households and also supplying funds to a large number of sales finance companies of widely varying size which specialize in consumer financing. Finally, commercial banks serve as the main source of loans to business firms, particularly the vast multitude of smaller enterprises.

The extent of competition in financial markets in the United States varies considerably, depending upon the type and geographic location of the borrower. For large, well-known business enterprises, the alternative sources of funds available are numerous and the degree of competition is high. For the household desiring to borrow on an installment loan or a mortgage, the situation varies from one city or community to another, but there is frequently a considerable amount of competition involving commercial banks, savings and loan associations, local agents of life insurance companies, and sales finance companies. The smaller business enterprise, on the other hand, frequently is limited in its source of loan funds to commercial banks located in its immediate vicinity, and these local banking markets frequently are rather concentrated. The geographical area within which a particular commercial bank is permitted to operate varies greatly from one part of the country to another. In some states, notably California, commercial banks are allowed to establish branches throughout the state. In a few states, branch banking is completely prohibited, while, in the majority of states, branches are permitted but on less than a statewide basis.

Since Federal Reserve policy works, in the first instance, primarily by controlling the supply of cash reserves available to the commercial banks, the responses of the banks to changes in the amount of reserves available to them are clearly a very important part of the mechanism by which the effects of monetary policy are transmitted to the economy. The paper by Jack Beebe (reading 9) which begins the readings in this chapter discusses the ways in which banks have made the adjustments required by changes in reserve availability. Suppose, for example, that customers' loan demands are increasing at a time when the Federal Reserve, desiring to restrain inflationary pressure, is supplying no additional reserves to the banking system through open market operations. There are two kinds of adjustments banks can make to accommodate their customers' requirements for funds in such a situation: they can reduce other types of assets to obtain funds to lend, or they can attract additional funds by increasing their liabilities. Asset adjustments would include reduction of excess cash reserves and sales of U.S. government or other securities out of existing portfolios. Liability adjustments would include borrowing excess reserves from other banks through the federal funds market, borrowing from the Federal Reserve banks, selling new securities in the capital markets, taking measures to attract more deposits, and borrowing from abroad through the so-called Eurodollar market.

During the 1950s, banks usually made such adjustments primarily by selling U.S. government securities from their portfolios. More recently, however, as Beebe explains, the emphasis has shifted rather dramatically toward "liability management." When banks need to obtain additional funds for lending, they now are likely to attempt to attract them by offering higher interest rates on negotiable certificates of deposits (CDs). Alternatively, if the interest rate ceilings on such deposits under the Federal Reserve's Regulation Q prevent the banks from raising rates sufficiently to obtain CD funds, they may attempt to meet their needs by borrowing in the Eurodollar market or by other means (however, there is no Regulation Q ceiling on rates for very large, negotiable CDs). "Purchased" funds of this kind can also be used to offset variations in demand deposits, over which banks have much less control. However, as Beebe points out, this sort of liability management has implications for the composition of bank assets. In competing for new funds via interest rate variation, there is pressure on banks to shift their asset portfolios toward less liquid, higher-yielding assets. As this shift occurs, banks become more vulnerable to fluctuations in financial markets. Beebe examines the changes in the composition of commercial-bank assets and liabilities that have occurred in the post–World War II period, provides evidence of an increase in the risk exposure of banks, and concludes that these developments make it increasingly problematical for the monetary authorities to impose direct restrictions on liability management.

Most of the adjustments referred to above will serve to transmit the effects of monetary policy beyond the commercial banks to the capital markets and other financial institutions. For example, bank sales of U.S. government securities will depress the prices of these securities and raise their yields. Since CDs compete against short-term securities, increases in the interest rates offered on CDs will exert upward pressure on other short-term interest rates. As banks have to incur higher costs to obtain funds for lending, they will raise interest rates charged on loans and, in some instances, also tighten lending standards, thereby making funds less readily available to borrowers.

According to the traditional view which was almost universally accepted until recently, commercial banks possess the power to create money on the basis of cash reserves and in the process to expand credit in the form of loans and investments, while other financial institutions—so-called intermediaries such as savings banks and savings and loan associations—serve only to collect the savings of the public and channel them into investment. This view of the financial system was first challenged by John G. Gurley and Edward S. Shaw. A portion of one of their papers on financial intermediaries is reprinted here (reading 10). In their view banks are unique among financial institutions in their ability to create demand deposits, which are used as means of payment and therefore constitute the major portion of the money supply. But other institutions likewise have the unique ability to create the particular kinds of financial claims that are their specialty—such as savings and loan shares in the case of savings and loan associations—and they all share with banks the ability to expand credit in the form of loans and investments. A similar view is expressed in the article by James Tobin (reading 11).

Those who hold this view that so-called financial intermediaries other than commercial banks share with banks the ability to create credit are generally of the opinion that these institutions should be subjected to controls—such as reserve requirements—similar to those that are applied to banks. If they are not controlled, it is said that their credit expansion will tend to accelerate when the banks are being restrained by Federal Reserve policies, with the result that the effectiveness of monetary policy in controlling credit will be weakened.

In trying to decide which point of view to accept, the student should be aware of a number of important considerations. First, while it is true that financial intermediaries can create credit, the nature of the process is different from that of commercial banks. Aside from their ability to attract deposits from banks, which will be discussed below, intermediaries depend heavily on flows of savings for new funds. Income is created by production; some of it is saved, and part of the saving takes the form of deposits at intermediaries, making new loanable funds available (on the assumption that the saver's alternative is to hoard the funds as idle cash balances). The spending generated by this round of income creation (partly financed by intermediary loans) induces new production, income, and saving, some of which flows into intermediaries, and so on. The time period associated with a round of income generation and the associated expansion of loanable funds through intermediaries is at least several months in length. By contrast, when new funds flow into the commercial banking system, new loans are created, and the associated deposits typically are checked away, only to reappear in a few days at another bank which then is able to expand credit, and so on. The two cases are different because the commercial banks manage the payments system and can expand loans essentially as fast as funds can be transferred from bank to bank by check, whereas the financial intermediaries depend on the income-generation process and conscious acts of saving for their flows of funds.

When financial intermediaries are viewed strictly as collectors and processors of savings, the above implies that their credit-creating effects may be more of a long-run than a short-run phenomenon. In terms of trend effects, there is indeed no question but what the growth of financial intermediaries has resulted in more credit being available at better terms than would be the case if there were no intermediaries. The reasons for this are explained in detail in the readings by Gurley and Shaw and by Tobin.

In the shorter run, however, intermediaries may be able to increase the total amount of credit available in another way; namely, by collecting idle cash balances and putting them to work. In a period of accelerating economic activity accompanied by monetary restraint, for instance, the yields on market securities will begin to rise, enabling financial intermediaries to increase the interest rates they pay to depositors. This may induce some holders of idle checking deposits at commercial banks to exchange them for deposits in intermediaries. Financial intermediaries typically are not subject to legal reserve requirements, and usually hold only a small amount of reserves relative to deposits. Because of the difference in reserve requirements, the intermediary is able to make a new loan of an amount depending on the reserve ratio it customarily observes (if the intermediary holds no reserves, and if there are no cash drains, and so on, then the loan can be of an amount equal to the deposits it has attracted). What has happened, in effect, is that the intermediary has mobilized an idle cash balance and converted it into an active balance by raising the rate it pays on its deposits. The student may wonder whether the idle balance would not have been mobilized if the intermediary did not exist, or did not raise its rates, through purchase by the owner of the balance of one of the market securities whose yields have risen. The answer is: very likely not; the cashholder was induced to exchange his funds for the intermediary deposit partly because he considered that deposit to be a very close substitute for money, whereas securities he could have bought in the market, such as government or industrial bonds, are much less moneylike.

While there is no question that intermediaries are capable of causing such cyclical deposit shifts and increasing the supply of credit in the face of monetary restraint, there is not much evidence that they do so. The exception seems to have been commercial banks themselves, whose time and savings deposit operations essentially function as financial intermediaries. By aggressive sales of certificates of deposit in times of restraint, for example, commercial banks have been able to attract considerable amounts of funds from other intermediaries as well as mobilizing idle balances in the banking system itself. Because reserve requirements for commercial bank time deposits are of the same order of magnitude as the cash ratios observed by intermediaries, the effects of shifts from intermediary to bank time deposits will mainly be on the allocation rather than the total volume of credit. In particular, intermediaries channel large quantities of funds into new housing construction, while banks devote much of their resources to commercial loans. Largely as a consequence of such changes in credit allocation, the housing industry has often been starved for funds while the rest of the economy is expanding. Several innovations designed to remedy this situation are discussed in Warren L. Smith's paper on government intermediaries and residential mortgage markets in Chapter 5 (reading 26). At other times, commercial banks have sold off government security holdings when demands for credit were high. The resulting increases in market yields have at times been adequate to cause idle balance holders to exchange these balances for bonds; these deposits then in effect were channeled (through the medium of new loans) to those anxious to borrow in order to purchase goods and services.

One of the questions raised by Tobin is whether banks can create money, an interesting parallel to the question discussed above of whether intermediaries can supply new loanable funds. In considering Tobin's arguments, it should be noted that his analysis, as well as that of Gurley and Shaw, is essentially static in character, describing the ultimate equilibrium that will be reached after all adjustments have been completed. He points out that while an injection of reserves into the banking system may generate a deposit-expansion process of the kind described in money and banking texts, ultimately the new deposits will disappear unless assetholders can be persuaded to hold them. In other words, they are like any other asset (such as claims against financial intermediaries, for example) in that they will be held if their yield is attractive relative to other asset yields. Since banks are prohibited by law from paying interest on demand deposits, the yields on other assets must be lowered if there is to be a permanent increase in the money stock. In contrast to Tobin's focus on initial and final equilibrium positions, the typical discussion of bank deposit expansion attempts to explain, at least in a rough-and-ready way, the dynamic sequence of adjustments which will occur during the process of equilibration. If some of the time lags are relatively long, as seems likely, the dynamic sequence of events may be quite important, even though the ultimate equilibrium reached may be that described by Gurley and Shaw and by Tobin.

It should also be noted that in the last several years, interest rates on time deposits and savings and loan shares have risen substantially, and the investing public has become more sensitive and sophisticated in shifting funds among deposits, shares, and open-market securities in response to changes in the relative returns on these alternative forms of financial assets. As a consequence, shifts of funds among these uses have become more significant, and management of interest rate ceilings of the Regulation Q type has become increasingly important, especially in terms of its impact on homebuilding. As we have mentioned, homebuilding relies heavily on savings and loan associations and mutual savings banks for its financing through mortgage loans, and the availability of these loans, in turn, depends importantly on the ability of the savings banks to attract and retain deposits. Smith's paper in Chapter 5 on residential mortgage markets (reading 26) discusses in some detail the effects on homebuilding of these institutional arrangements.

9. A PERSPECTIVE ON LIABILITY MANAGEMENT AND BANK RISK*

Jack Beebe

Since World War II, U.S. commercial banks have experienced a dramatic shift in asset composition, from an aggregate portfolio consisting largely of reserves and U.S. Treasury securities to one consisting largely of loans to the private sector. Since 1960, banks have come to rely increasingly on purchased money-market funds —varying their purchases by adjusting the rates paid on these funds ("liability management")— while simultaneously allowing their capital cushions to decline. These developments have made banks more sensitive to financial-market fluctuations and have made their liquidity depend importantly on their ability to purchase funds.

This paper examines changes in bank assets and liabilities since World War II, relates these changes to a rise in bank exposure to real and financial-market fluctuations, and uses this historical perspective to draw relevant implications for regulatory policy. The relative decline of liquid risk-free assets, the increase in purchased short-term liabilities, the diminished capital cushions, and the increased sensitivity of bank equity prices to stock-market fluctuations all provide evidence of increased bank exposure to financial-market fluctuations. Because of the increased risk exposure and because of the increased bank reliance on purchased funds as a major source of liquidity, bank regulators must weigh carefully the potentially perverse effects that liability-management restrictions (such as rate ceilings) can have on the banking sector's liquidity and stability. Since 1973 regulators have not used constraints on liability-management instruments

as a means of tightening policy. The analysis of this paper supports this direction in policy because sudden regulatory constraints on purchased funds can cause a liquidity crisis within the U.S. commercial-banking industry. Furthermore, such constraints may not be a necessary part of monetary policy.

Increased exposure to financial-market risk does not necessarily imply that a bank's total risk has risen. If the economy, financial markets, and regulatory policy have become more stable (less risky), then total bank risk might have declined even in the face of increasing risk sensitivity. It is generally accepted that perceived total risk in the economy and in financial markets declined over much of the postwar period through the late 1960s, and then increased in the 1970s.[1] Until recently, bankers may not have perceived any significant increase in the total risk of their portfolios. But recent developments, particularly since 1973, may well have changed this perception.

[1] See Herbert Runyon, "Real World Risk and Financial Institutions," Federal Reserve Bank of San Francisco *Economic Review* (Winter 1977), pp. 5–11. Additional evidence from varied sources supports this view. The P/E ratio in the stock market rose considerably in the late 1950s and early 1960s, and ignoring fluctuations of short duration, did not fall dramatically until 1973. In addition, monthly variation in stock market (S&P 500) returns generally declined through the late 1960s and then rose during the 1970s. Studies cite a number of possible explanations for a postwar decline in the market's perception of risk. William Nordhaus, "The Falling Share of Profits," *Brookings Papers on Economic Activity* no. 1, (1975), pp. 198–304: Henry Wallich, "Framework for Financial Resiliency," Conference on Financial Crises, New York University, May 21, 1976: and Stuart I. Greenbaum, "Economic Instability and Commercial Banking," Hearings of the Senate Committee on Banking, Housing and Urban Affairs, 94th Congress (October 31 and December 1 and 8, 1975).

* From Federal Reserve Bank of San Francisco *Economic Review*, Winter 1977, pp. 12–24. Reprinted by permission of the Federal Reserve Bank of San Francisco and the author. Jack Beebe is Senior Economist, Federal Reserve Bank of San Francisco.

The first section of this paper discusses the theoretical linkages between assets and liabilities in the framework that considers the trade-off between expected return and risk. The second section examines postwar trends in bank assets and liabilities, along with trends in the sensitivity of bank equity prices to the stock market. The third section analyzes the impact of changes in the structure of bank assets and liabilities on the cyclical sensitivity of banks, while the final section presents the policy implications.

I. THEORETICAL LINKAGES BETWEEN BANK ASSETS AND LIABILITIES

Liability management and changes in bank-asset composition are necessarily related. However, the relationships are complex and are affected by factors external to banking—such as general economic activity, net credit demands, changing perceptions of and attitudes toward risk, and regulatory constraints. Despite these complications, portfolio theory as applied to financial institutions suggests certain broad relationships between asset and liability structures.

If commercial banks operate in competitive financial markets, then there are important implications for bank portfolios.[2] The spread (i.e., rate differential) between the rate earned on assets and the rate paid on liabilities must be a measure of the value of the service that banks provide. Several aspects of this service are directly relevant to the relationship between bank assets and liabilities. Among other functions, banks invest funds and make loans. In performing this function, banks gather information, forecast, and screen borrowers, and for this receive a positive spread. In addition, banks pool and at times absorb risk by placing deposit funds across a spectrum of types and maturities of loans and investments, and also absorb risk by maintaining a capital cushion. (Thus, there is risk diversification across instruments at a point in time, and risk diversification over time such as a business cycle.) To the extent that banks (or their stockholders) take on risk, there should be a compensating expected return.[3] The importance

of risk and the manifestation of risk diversification in bank portfolios are central to a study of changes in banking assets and liabilities.

Liability Management as a Source of Growth

Liability management has two principal motivations; it can be used both to control bank growth and to purchase liquidity. Both of these aspects imply theoretical relationships among liability management, bank assets, and bank risk.

Liability management is an effective means for a bank to control its rate of growth. Put simply, a bank can accelerate its growth if it is willing to pay more for purchased funds than other banks do. However, a distinction must be made between the growth of a single bank and the growth of the entire banking system. As banks seek to accelerate their rates of growth, they will have to borrow additional funds from outside the banking sector. These funds may come from either of two sources: (1) an expanding level of total financial activity in the economy, or (2) an increase in the banking sector's *share* of total financial activity. The latter aspect—"bank intermediation," or simply "intermediation"[4]—is the more relevant measure in the context of this paper, which focuses on the banking sector's share of total borrowing and lending in the U.S. economy.

An individual bank can increase its share of bank intermediation by raising its rate on purchased funds marginally above that of its competitors, but when other banks follow this strategy, the effect will be to raise the market rate for purchased funds (relative to open-market rates) and to increase bank intermediation. If banks try to ensure faster growth by bidding up the rate for purchased funds (relative to other rates), they will have to seek earning assets with higher expected returns, and thereby maintain a positive spread that compensates for transaction costs and risk. Thus, as banks increasingly use liability management to gain a larger *share* of

---

[2] Many commercial banks operate in markets that are not highly competitive, largely because of regulations that often restrict entry of new banks or prohibit branch banking. Measured by dollar volume, however, most transactions take place in competitive markets, as a result of the sheer dollar volume of transactions at large city banks and the system of correspondent banking.

[3] Financial theory suggests that (given diversified portfolios) the pertinent risk to be considered is market-related and not firm-specific, from the stand-

point of either bank portfolios or loan differentials. Small banks do not hold diversified loan portfolios, in part because loans are concentrated in the local geographical area—and their risk is thus partly firm-specific—but the most important problem for the commercial bank sector as a whole is market-related risk.

[4] The term "intermediation" is used throughout to mean the commercial banking sector's share of financial-market activity. Two closely related measures are used—one based on banks' share of total financial market flows (lending and borrowing) and one based on banks' share of stocks (total assets or liabilities) in the financial markets.

total financial market activity, they will pay relatively more for their purchased funds, and will face the increasingly difficult task of achieving a high enough spread to offset the cost involved. In a competitive market, this process will likely force banks to seek earning assets that entail higher risk and/or less liquidity.

Liability Management as a Source of Liquidity

Liability management not only enables a bank to control its growth rate, but also enables it to exert greater control over the variability of its total liabilities—for example, by increasing purchased funds to offset a loss of demand deposits. To the extent that a bank expects to reduce such variability through liability management, it will expect a commensurate reduction in the variability of total bank credit. Thus, it can extend credit that entails greater transaction costs, greater short-term price variation, and/or less liquidity —the type of credit that financial market theory tells us should provide a higher expected yield. Therefore, an increase in liabilities *for which banks can freely vary the deposit rate* (and thus the quantity obtained) should be associated with higher-yield bank credit. In this respect, liability management provides a substitute for holding reserves, U.S. Treasury securities, or other low-yield short-term liquid assets. That is, liquidity on the liability side of a bank's portfolio (through, say, day-to-day trading in certificates of deposit or Federal funds) is a substitute for liquidity on the asset side (through, say, day-to-day trading in Treasury securities).

Although purchased funds may substitute for liquid assets, the two sources of liquidity are not perfect substitutes. First, holding liquid assets to meet future liquidity needs will normally result in different returns and risk than will holding illiquid assets with the anticipation of purchasing liquidity when needed in the future. Consider two banks, one that holds liquid (low yield) assets against demand deposits on the presumption that these assets will provide for future liquidity needs, and another that holds illiquid (high yield) assets on the presumption that, if necessary, it will later purchase funds to meet a future run-off in demand deposits. The comparative profitability of the two strategies will depend upon the ensuing financial environment. If there is no run-off in demand deposits and no liquidity squeeze, the strategy of holding illiquid assets will prove profitable. However, if demand deposits run off and market rates simultaneously rise, the strategy of holding liquid assets may be more profitable.

Purchased funds and liquid assets are imperfect substitutes for another reason as well. Regulatory restrictions on liability management—such as Regulation Q ceilings on certificates of deposit or increased reserve requirements on Eurodollar purchases—may effectively limit these funds as a source of liquidity to the commercial-banking sector. To the extent that banks rely on purchased funds rather than liquid investments as the primary source of liquidity, such restrictions can lead to a severe liquidity squeeze, as in 1966 and 1969–70. Although similar restrictions have not been used in the last few years, bankers cannot be certain that they will not be employed in the future. A possibility of regulatory restrictions— assuming they cannot effectively be avoided— may render liability management a poor substitute for liquid assets.

Implications for Aggregate Bank Portfolios

Both motivations of liability management— growth and liquidity[5]—suggest that an increase in the use of liability management should be associated with an increase in asset risk and/or a decrease in asset liquidity. Thus, asset composition may change in several ways, such as a decrease in marketability, increase in market-related or total risk, or increase in time to maturity. However, there is no reason that such changes should be motivated solely by changes in liability management. In fact, major changes in *asset composition* became well established prior to the changes in *liability management*. Thus, the two trends should be viewed as interrelated changes in bank *portfolio management*.

II. POSTWAR SECULAR TRENDS IN ASSETS AND LIABILITIES

Over the 1946–60 span, bank liabilities increased rather slowly (Chart 1). The average annual growth rate, 3.7 percent per year, fell considerably below the 6.5-percent average increase in nominal GNP and the very rapid 10.5-percent growth rate for deposits at thrift institutions (savings and loan associations, mutual savings banks, and credit unions). Throughout this span, the commercial banking sector relied principally on traditional demand and time deposits as sources of funds. Neither source expanded rapidly—2.5 percent annually for de-

---

[5] This paper ignores a third reason for liability management: legal avoidance of reserve requirements. New instruments have normally been subject to reserve requirements only with some time lag.

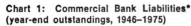

Chart 1: Commercial Bank Liabilities*
(year-end outstandings, 1946–1975)

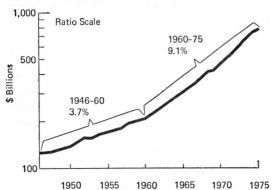

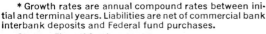

* Growth rates are annual compound rates between initial and terminal years. Liabilities are net of commercial bank
interbank deposits and Federal fund purchases.
Source: Flow-of-funds accounts.

Chart 2: Bank Intermediation-Stocks*
(year-end outstandings, 1946–1975)

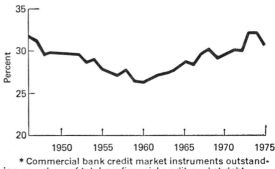

* Commercial bank credit market instruments outstanding as a share of total nonfinancial credit market debt.
Source: Flow-of-funds accounts.

mand deposits and 5.6 percent annually for time deposits. Banks normally held their rates on individual time accounts below both the Regulation Q ceiling and S&L deposit rates. In addition, many banks did not accept corporate time accounts.

Throughout the 1950s, most banks accepted slow growth either as sound banking practice or as something largely beyond their control. Monetary policy, regulatory constraints, and the memories of the turbulent 1930s all probably contributed to this conservative posture. However, as money-market rates rose in the 1950s, corporations began to shift their funds out of banks (particularly New York banks) and into money-market instruments. To compete effectively for corporate deposits and to acquire funds for lending, New York banks began in February 1961 to issue negotiable certificates of deposit (CD's), other city banks then followed, and security dealers began making a secondary market for these instruments.

Chart 1 shows the pronounced acceleration in the growth of bank liabilities after 1960. Over the 1960–75 span, bank liabilities increased at a 9.1 percent average rate (compared with average growth rates of 7.6 percent for nominal GNP and 10.1 percent for thrift-institution deposits). Banks arrested their earlier relative decline largely through the success of their innovations in liability management, such as large negotiable CD's, Federal funds transactions,[6] and borrowings from

[6] Banks had traded Federal funds among themselves in earlier years, but had purchased only insignificant amounts from outside the commercial banking sector until the mid-1960s.

foreign branches (Eurodollars). Other contributing factors included favorable monetary and regulatory policies, which until the late 1960s did little to inhibit the growth of purchased funds, and the reduction in the hitherto very rapid thrift-institution growth through the extension of Regulation Q to thrift-institution deposits in 1966.

Despite sharp declines during the 1966 and 1969 credit crunches and the 1970 recession, bank liabilities grew very rapidly from 1961 through mid-1974 as a whole. This period experienced relatively rapid economic growth and a strong rise in private—both consumer and business—spending and debt. But in addition, the banking sector's intermediary role increased significantly, reversing the earlier decline. As shown in Chart 2, bank intermediation declined from over 31 percent in 1946 to 26 percent in 1960, but then rose to 32 percent by the end of 1974 before declining somewhat again.

Secular Shifts in Bank-Asset Composition

The composition of bank assets has changed dramatically over the postwar span. Nonearning assets, vault cash and member-bank reserves, have risen at a sluggish pace, principally because (1) a slow increase in demand deposits has led to a net reduction in the effective required-reserve ratio and (2) more effective reserve management, motivated by rising interest rates, has reduced aggregate excess reserves. Thus, earning assets have risen from about 85 percent of bank assets in 1945–48 to about 90 percent in 1972–75.

Of greater consequence, however, has been the pronounced postwar shift in the composition of earning assets. Marketable U.S. Treasury securities declined from an average of 63 percent of aggregate bank credit outstanding in the 1945–48 period to an average of 10 percent in the 1972–75 period. Other governments—state, local and Federal agency—increased their share of bank credit outstanding from 5 to 19 percent over the same time span, and in particular, the loan share of the total jumped from 29 to 70 percent.

Banks entered the postwar era with what in retrospect can be considered abnormally high liquidity. At the end of 1945, U.S. Treasury securities constituted 73 percent of bank credit outstanding. Thus, banks were able to accommodate a substantial increase in loan demand by liquidating Treasuries, reducing their holdings from $91 billion in 1945 to $61 billion in 1960. Since 1960, the Treasury share of bank credit has continued to decline from 30 percent to only 10 percent in 1972–75. This period also marked the spread of liability management, and with minor exceptions (until late 1974) was characterized by heavy demand for private credit. In this environment banks were willing, if not anxious, to accommodate a rising market for bank loans by purchasing funds and simultaneously reducing their cushion of liquid secondary reserves (and capital accounts). Bankers may have been consciously taking additional risk with the expectation of greater reward. But in addition, in view of the apparent decline in perceived market risk in U.S. financial markets, bankers may not actually have been aware of any substantial rise in their total risk. In any case, bank asset structures became increasingly susceptible to financial-market fluctuations, despite the fact that liability management also provided (in theory) a buffer to offset asset illiquidity.

Contrasted to the declining share of U.S. Treasury securities was the growing postwar importance of Federal agency and state-local government issues. Treasury and agency issues may be considered substitutes for each other, but the latter carry some additional default risk and may be of longer maturity. Municipal securities may carry substantial default risk and vary widely in maturity. Thus, the shift in security holdings from U.S. Treasury to Federal agency and state-local government securities should be viewed as a shift away from liquid low-risk assets.[7]

Secular Trends in Liabilities and Capital Positioning

Postwar developments in liability management and capital structure are reflected in a change in the composition of aggregate bank liabilities, as shown in Table 2. (Large-bank data show more striking changes in liabilities, as they do for assets, but the emphasis here is on the total commercial-banking sector.) During the 1950s, bank liabilities consisted of equity capital and "traditional" sources of funds—net demand deposits, time deposits other than large CDs, and small amounts of Federal Reserve float and borrowing from Federal Reserve banks. Equity capital *increased* as a portion of total liabilities during the 1950s. But since 1960, purchased funds have risen from zero to 12 percent of the overall portfolio, while traditional sources of funds and capital (particularly equity capital) have declined as a share of the total.

Because of data limitations, Table 2 understates the growing importance of liability management. First, it includes among "traditional" sources the rapidly-growing category of time deposits other than large CDs, although the distinction between the time deposits and large CD categories has become increasingly fuzzy, particularly since Regulation Q ceilings no longer apply to some time-deposit categories. In addition, the table includes only part of the rapid increase of purchased funds transacted through holding companies, and excludes certain "off-balance sheet" items such as arbitrage transactions through agencies of foreign banks.

Despite data limitations, the figures in Table 2 show both a rapid increase in the importance of purchased funds and a decline in the equity (and total capital) base since 1960. When viewed as a source of liquidity, the increase in purchased funds from zero to 12 percent of the portfolio is very important. Likewise, when viewed in terms of leverage, the small decline in equity from 9.1 to 7.5 percent of total liabilities is also important. This change represents an increase in the leverage ratio (total liabilities/equity capital) from 11.0 to 13.3. If measured relative to "risky assets," leverage has of course shown an even greater increase. (Again, the change has been greater for large banks than for others.) Thus,

---

[7] There are additional reasons for the rapid increase in bank holdings of state-local government obligations. For one reason, there was probably much less perceived risk on municipal issues than there had been during the Depression of the 1930s. Banks bought such issues also because of their strong ties with local governments, or because of legal restric-

tions requiring the pledging of government issues against deposits. Finally, banks purchased municipals because they gained a comparative advantage from the tax-exempt status of such issues, although this factor is now declining in importance because other means are available of obtaining credits against taxable income.

Table 1:   Secular Changes in the Composition of Bank Credit Outstanding (percentage of total loans and investments, 1952–1975)

	Loans*					Investments			
	Total	C&I	Real Estate	To Indi-viduals	Other	Total	U.S. Treasury	S.&L. Gov't.	Other†
1952–55‡.............	46.3	18.8	11.7	9.7	6.2	53.6	42.6	7.6	2.6
1956–59................	54.6	22.1	13.7	11.6	7.2	45.4	34.2	8.4	2.1
1960–63................	59.1	21.0	14.6	13.2	10.2	40.9	28.6	10.0	1.8
1964–67................	65.4	23.6	16.3	14.8	10.8	34.5	19.2	13.0	2.4
1968–71................	67.3	25.2	16.6	15.1	10.4	32.7	13.9	15.3	3.5
1972–75................	70.0	24.8	18.0	15.0	12.3	30.0	9.8	14.9	5.4

* Equals "other loans" in *Federal Reserve Bulletin*, i.e., excludes Federal funds sold and securities purchased under agree-ments to resell.

† Consists mostly of securities issued by Federal agencies.

‡ Averages of semi-annual call data over each four-year period.

Source: *Federal Reserve Bulletin*, assets of all commercial banks.

between 1960 and late 1974, we have witnessed two striking secular trends—an increase in purchased funds and a decline in banks' capital cushion—along with the decline in asset marketability mentioned earlier.

Although the compositional shift from liquid assets to illiquid assets (Table 1) was well established prior to the advent of liability management (Table 2), the developments were closely related. On the asset side, rising interest rates, high private demand for bank loans, small Federal deficits, and a gradual waning of Depression fears led banks to reduce noninterest-bearing reserves and shift funds from liquid investments to (high yield) loans. On the liability side, rising interest rates (combined with Reg Q ceilings) and a favorable economic environment provided

the incentive for banks to move more aggressively into financial markets by purchasing more funds for bank lending. Furthermore, banks utilized purchased funds to provide some of the balance-sheet flexibility lost through the compositional shift in assets.

Stock Market Evidence of Bank Risk

These interrelated developments—the decline in asset liquidity, the growth of liability management, and the decline in bank capital—suggest that U.S. banks have become more exposed to risk, particularly the risk associated with general economic and financial conditions.

There is a way to test this proposition. Financial theory makes wide use of the "market model"

Table 2:   Secular Changes in the Composition of Commercial Bank Liabilities (percentages of total liabilties, 1952–1975)

	Traditional Sources			Purchased Funds				Capital			
	Total	Demand Dep., Net	Time, Excl. Large CDs	Total†	Large CDs‡	Federal Funds, Net§	Euro-dollars	Total	Equity	Debt	Misc.
1952–55	89.3	62.4	26.3	0.3	0.0	0.0	0.3	8.0	8.0	0.0	2.4
1956–59.......	88.0	57.7	29.5	0.1	0.0	−0.1	0.2	8.7	8.7	0.0	3.2
1960–63.......	85.5	51.0	33.6	2.3	1.9	0.0	0.4	9.1	9.1	0.0	3.2
1964–67.......	82.0	42.4	38.9	5.7	4.6	0.4	0.7	8.8	8.4	0.4	3.4
1968–71.......	79.0	37.2	41.0	7.3	4.8	1.0	1.4	8.5	8.0	0.5	5.2
1972–75.......	73.8	30.9	42.4	12.2	9.3	2.1	0.4	8.1	7.5	0.6	5.9

Note: Liabilities are net of interbank demand deposits and interbank Federal funds purchases.

* Includes borrowing from Federal Reserve banks and Federal Reserve float, not shown separately.

† Includes loans sold to holding companies, loans from foreign banking agencies, and time accounts at foreign banking agencies, not shown separately.

‡ Negotiable CDs over $100,000.

§ Consists of security RP's and float on commercial bank interbank loans.

Averages of year-end outstandings.

Sources: Flow of funds accounts for all items except equity capital which is from *Federal Reserve Bulletin*.

Table 3: Betas of Standard and Poor's Bank-Stock Indexes against the S&P 500

	9 NYC Banks			16 Banks Outside NYC		
	Beta	Std. Error of Beta	$\bar{R}^2$	Beta	Std. Error of Beta	$\bar{R}^2$
1947–49.......................	.39	.10	.31	.56	.16	.25
1950–52.......................	.36	.12	.18	.47	.13	.26
1953–55.......................	.37	.12	.19	.35	.12	.18
1956–58.......................	.37	.11	.22	.50	.10	.41
1959–61.......................	.63	.17	.28	.49	.12	.31
1962–64.......................	.98	.11	.69	1.06	.09	.81
1965–67.......................	.89	.23	.28	.74	.18	.32
1968–70.......................	1.11	.17	.53	1.09	.14	.63
1971–73.......................	.68	.19	.25	.78	.14	.47
1974–76*......................	1.09	.18	.52	1.22	.18	.59

Note. Based on rates of change in last-Wednesday-of-the-month prices after 1952 and monthly-average prices for preceding periods. The regression model is:

$$ln(P_{banks,\,t+1}/P_{banks,t}) = a + b\,ln(P_{500,\,t+1}/P_{500,t}) + e$$

* Data for 1976 are through August.

Source: Standard and Poor's price indexes for 9 NYC banks, 16 banks outside NYC and composite of 500 stocks.

and the concept of "beta."[8] Using the market model, returns of an individual security (or group of securities) are regressed against the returns in the overall stock market to determine the extent to which the individual security (or group of securities) is sensitive to overall stock-market fluctuations. (The model is shown in the notes to Table 3.) The stock market is represented by a broad index such as the Standard and Poor's Composite of 500 stocks (S&P 500). The resulting beta value is a measure of the sensitivity of the return of the individual security to the return in the market. For example, if a stock has a beta of 0.5 (perhaps a utility stock), we should expect on average for a 10-percent change in the level of the stock market to result in a 5-percent change in this stock's price. In contrast, if the beta is 1.5 (an airline stock), the same market return would result in a 15-percent change in the stock's price on average. (By definition the average stock's beta is 1.0.)

It is well known that the stock market is highly influenced by expectations regarding the general economic and financial environment. If banks are insulated from this environment, bank stocks should not be very sensitive to factors that affect the overall stock market and bank stocks should have a low beta. Estimated betas for Standard

and Poor's stock index of nine New York City and sixteen large banks outside New York City show that this was indeed the case for the postwar period through the 1950s (Table 3). However, since about 1960 these bank-stock indexes have become substantially more sensitive to fluctuations in the overall stock market (S&P 500). Since the stock market generally reflects anticipated business and financial conditions, these data suggest that common stocks of large banks have become more sensitive to the economic and financial climate in the past several decades.

The betas of these bank-stock indexes rose primarily between the late 1950s and early 1960s and have since fluctuated around the higher level. The R-squared values also rose during these intervals of rising beta, indicating a closer association between changes in these stock series and changes in the overall stock market and indicating that a greater percentage of their total price fluctuations is now market-related. The shift between the 1950s and 1960s occurred as large banks aggressively moved into the money markets to purchase funds, extended their loan commitments rapidly, and allowed their equity leverage to rise.

III. LIABILITY MANAGEMENT AND THE CYCLICAL STABILITY OF BANKING

An important question raised by the developments discussed above is whether the liquidity provided by liability-management (purchased)

---

[8] The market model and beta are described in recent textbooks on finance and investments. A short description is also contained in Franco Modigliani and Gerald Pogue, "An Introduction to Risk and Return," *Financial Analysts Journal*, March/April and May/June 1974.

Chart 3: Bank Intermediation-Flows (1952.1–1976.3)

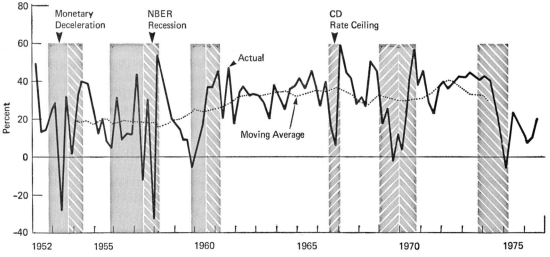

Note: Quarterly flows of commercial bank credit market instruments as a share of total funds raised by nonfinancial sectors including new equity issues.
    Sources: Actual data from flow-of-funds accounts. Dating of periods from Poole for periods of monetary deceleration. NBER for recessions, and Friedman for periods when CD rate exceeded ceiling rate.

funds can compensate for the decline in asset marketability experienced over the postwar period. If banks can stabilize the short-term variation in total liabilities (by varying the rate paid on purchased funds), then liability management can reduce the risk inherent in declining asset marketability. If purchased funds have actually served this function, then we should expect to see a reduction over time in the short-term variation of total bank liabilities, and therefore greater cyclical stability in bank credit. Is there any evidence that bank credit has become more cyclically stable?

Some evidence is provided by the pattern of bank intermediation—the share of total non-financial-sector borrowing provided in the form of commercial-bank credit (Chart 3). (The measure in Chart 3 is based on flows and is thus more sensitive to cyclical variation than is the measure based on stocks in Chart 2.) The movement of quarterly data reveals two important characteristics. First, there is a good deal of variability throughout the entire period. Analysis of the two underlying series that form the ratio shown in Chart 3 shows that both the flow of bank credit and the flow of total funds raised by nonfinancial sectors vary considerably and are highly correlated, but that the flow of bank credit is by far the more volatile series. Thus, the flow of bank credit is more sensitive to changes in economic and monetary conditions than is total borrowing in the economy, and larger relative

changes in the flow of bank credit are the principal cause of variations in the extent of intermediation.

The second characteristic is the shift in the pattern of quarterly deviations after 1961. Quarterly stability was practically nonexistent prior to that year. In contrast, the period since 1961 is marked by spans of relative stability interrupted by a few intervals of extreme instability. This change in the pattern of stability may be attributed in part to liability management, or it may be the result of changes in economic conditions and in monetary policy, including effects of Reg Q.

Because of the influence of monetary and economic conditions on bank intermediation, it is necessary to examine liability management and the stability of bank credit in a framework that recognizes broad changes in these external factors. Specifically, we may ask whether liability management has enabled the banking sector to stabilize the degree of bank intermediation during periods of "tight money." Although there is no commonly accepted method of defining tight money periods, two criteria provide a rough approximation: (1) a deceleration in the growth rate of money (M_1) preceding business cycle peaks,[9] and (2) the existence of binding ceiling

[9] William Poole, "The Relationship of Monetary Decelerations to Business Cycle Peaks," *Journal of Finance* (June 1975). The Poole study ended prior to the recent recession, so some judgment had to be made about this period. Although the NBER dates

rates on CDs, with secondary-market rates rising above the allowed ceiling rate on new CDs. According to these criteria, there have been six tight-money periods since 1952, separable into three different categories: (1) preliability management (i.e., prior to 1961), (2) liability management with constraints (the 1966:3–1966:4[10] and 1969:2–1969:4 periods), and (3) liability management without constraints (the 1973:4–1974.3 period). The latter distinction arises because, in the last several years, monetary policy makers have ceased using such constraints as ceilings on large CDs and high reserve requirements against Eurodollar deposits.[11]

During two of the three preliability-management periods of monetary restraint, disintermediation was substantial, while during the other it was modest—although highly variable within the period (Table 4 and Chart 3). Later, during the 1966 and 1969 periods, when liability management was constrained by effective Reg Q ceilings, disintermediation was severe despite attempts by banks to circumvent restrictions. In sharp contrast, during the one recent period of monetary restraint in which liability management was not constrained (1973:4–1974:3), bank intermediation was exceedingly high (38 percent, compared with the 1972–75 average of 32 percent). In this last period, bank intermediation did not decline significantly until the onslaught of the "inventory" recession in late 1974. Thus, there is strong evidence that *unconstrained* liability management can enable banks to maintain intermediation during periods of monetary deceleration.

This evidence can be supported by a more detailed examination of changes in major bank assets and liabilities (Table 5). In this analysis, bank credit is divided into loans and investments, and liabilities into traditional sources (net demand deposits, time deposits other than large CDs, borrowing from Federal Reserve banks, and

Table 4: Bank Intermediation—Flows	
Four-Year Averages	*Percentage*
Before liability management	
1952–55	20.0
1956–59	17.2
After liability management	
1960–63	30.8
1964–67	34.8
1968–71	30.2
1972–75	32.3
Periods of Monetary Deceleration and/or Binding CD Rate Ceilings	
Before liability management	
1952:4–1953:2	10.7
1955:4–1957:2	17.1
1959:4–1960:2	6.2
Liability management with constraints	
1966:3–1966:4	9.2
1969:2–1969:4	12.6
Liability management without constraints	
1973:4–1974:3	38.3

Data definitions and source: See Chart 3.

the recent business-cycle peak within the fourth quarter of 1973, the sharp "inventory recession" did not take effect until late 1974. This study concentrates on the inventory recession that occurred over the 1974:4–1975:1 period, because inventory purchases and short-term credit demands remained strong until this time. Uusing Poole's criterion and this recession dating, monetary deceleration "prior to a business-cycle peak" occurred over the 1973:4–1974:3 period.

[10] The period of effective CD ceilings in late 1966 coincided with a deceleration in the growth of money. However, since an NBER recession did not follow, the period did not meet Poole's criterion.

[11] For exact restrictions and dates of removal, see tables in any issue of the *Federal Reserve Bulletin*.

Federal Reserve float) and other liabilities (principally purchased funds and capital).

If purchased funds are to stabilize total bank credit in periods of monetary restraint, their growth rates should increase (or not decrease as much as those of traditional sources). Actually, "other liabilities" increased rapidly during the preliability management periods of monetary restraint, at a 3.3-percent average quarterly rate of increase. Although perplexing at first glance, this has a straightforward explanation, since the increase was almost entirely in equity capital (which includes retained earnings) and bank profits were high in these periods. Loan growth was not unduly restrained during these periods, because funds were available from other liabilities (particularly equity capital) and from net liquidation of investments.

In contrast, severe bank disintermediation occurred during the 1966 and 1969 periods of constrained liability management. For these periods on average, traditional sources grew slowly, 0.6 percent quarterly, compared with a 1.9-percent average for the 1961:1–1976:3 span. The growth rate of other liabilities (0.8 percent) was also low—especially low compared with a 4.6-percent average for 1961:1–1976:3. Consequently, during the 1966 and 1969 tight-money periods, controls on purchased funds reduced the increase in these funds far below normal, so that loan growth was severely restricted despite the liquidity provided by net sales of investments.

Table 5: Average Quarterly Rates of Change in Major Commercial Bank Assets and Liabilities*

Average Secular Rates

	Pre-Liability Mngt. 1952:1–1960:4	Post-Liability Mngt. 1961:1–1976:3
Bank credit	1.2%	2.2%
Loans	2.0	2.4
Investments	0.3	1.8
Liabilities	1.0	2.2
Traditional sources	0.9	1.9
Other Liabilities	3.0	4.6

Average Rates in Periods of Monetary Restraint

	Pre-Liab. Mngt. 1952:4–1953:2 1955:4–1957:2 1959:4–1960:2	Post-Liability Management	
		Constrained 1966:3–1966:4 1969:2–1969:4	Unconstrained 1973:4–1974:3
Bank Credit	0.6%	0.6%	2.6%
Loans	2.4	1.5	3.2
Investments	−1.2	−1.1	1.1
Liabilities	0.5	0.6	2.8
Traditional Sources	0.4	0.6	1.7
Other Liabilities	3.3	0.8	7.0

*Average percentage changes at quarterly rates in seasonally adjusted quarterly outstandings.
Definitions:
Total bank credit: Total bank credit (net of interbank deposits and Federal funds transactions).
Loans: Sum of mortgages, consumer credit, bank loans, n.e.c., and security credit.
Investments: Total bank credit minus loans as defined above.
Total liabilities: Total liabilities (net of interbank deposits and Federal funds purchases).
Traditional sources: Sum of net demand deposits, time deposits other than large negotiable CDs, borrowing from Federal Reserve banks, and Federal Reserve float.
Other liabilities: Total liabilities minus traditional sources as defined above.
Source: Flow of Funds Accounts.

The 1973:4–1974:3 period of monetary deceleration, in which Regulation Q ceilings were effectively removed, shows an entirely different pattern. Bank growth was rapid over this period. Other liabilities increased at a whopping 7.0-percent quarterly average rate, while loan growth averaged 3.2 percent quarterly. In addition, there seemed to be little need to liquidate investments to meet loan demand, since purchased funds fulfilled this function. (Of course, banks no longer had much flexibility for liquidating investments, since Treasury securities and other investments had already been reduced to only a small share of total bank assets.)

Recent Reversal in Liability Management

The rapid increase in purchased funds and expansion of bank loans to mid-1974 ultimately proved destabilizing to the bank sector, given the (unforeseen) recession in late 1974. But there is no reason that unconstrained liability management must always result in increased risk. The expansion following the inventory recession of 1974:4–1975:1 has been one in which earlier

trends in liability management have been reversed and bank portfolios have become less risky, as seen in the following table. (The figures may be compared with those in Table 5, top.)

	Quarterly Change (%) 1975:2–1976:3
Bank credit	1.4
Loans	0.5
Investments	3.3
Liabilities	1.4
Traditional sources	2.0
Other liabilities	−0.6

In contrast with the overall 1961–74 period, total bank credit and total liabilities have increased slowly. Loans have been nearly flat, but investments (especially marketable Treasury issues) have increased markedly. Deposits (excluding large CDs) have accelerated, while other liabilities have actually declined because of a marked drop in the amount of purchased funds.

Three questions immediately come to mind. Are we reverting back to a 1950-style pattern of bank portfolios and capital structures? Is the recent reversal attributable largely to forces external to banking (i.e., regulatory, economic or financial changes) or rather to a concerted effort on the part of bankers to reduce the risk exposure of their portfolios? Is the shift a precursor of future banking trends or is it merely transitory?

Answers to these questions extend beyond the boundaries of this paper, but some response is merited. First, despite the significance of these developments, casual analysis suggests that the recent conservative trend has not moved major liquidity and capital ratios back beyond where they were in the early 1970s. The second question has stirred considerable controversy,[12] but no final answers can be reached until we assess the relative importance of the factors—regulation, economic trends, and bank portfolio management —that have been instrumental in the recent reversal in trend. The same considerations will determine the answer to the third question—the permanency of this recent shift in bank behavior.

IV. CONCLUSIONS—POLICY IMPLICATIONS

This paper has attempted to show that the liquidity and stability of U.S. commercial banks have become more sensitive to economic and financial-market risk over the postwar span. This trend has resulted primarily from changes in bank portfolio management, on both the asset and liability sides.

The marked reduction in liquidity of bank assets over the postwar period has implications both for liability management and for monetary policy. Declining liquidity has been reflected in the shift in assets away from noninterest-bearing reserves and secondary reserves (U.S. Treasury securities). Although this trend has been partly offset by increased purchases of U.S. agency and state-local government securities, the most important development has been the sharp increase in loans to the private sector. Clearly, this compositional shift in assets has reduced asset marketability on balance.

Bank growth accelerated rapidly after the advent of liability management in 1961, and

subsequently (until late 1974) banks relied increasingly on purchased funds for both growth and liquidity. With purchased funds available, banks had an additional incentive to reduce asset liquidity. Banks—particularly large banks—presumably considered holding additional liquid assets to be a costly alternative to purchasing liquidity. Thus, the compositional shift in bank assets and the expansion of liability management can be seen to be closely interrelated.

Trends in bank asset and liability management cannot be appraised independently of the economic environment in which they occur. Bank portfolios are structured within a framework that depends largely upon expectations of risk and return. Although this paper has not examined postwar trends in total economic and financial risk, it is readily apparent that the banking sector's exposure (sensitivity) to such risk has risen. The relative decline of "risk free" assets (reserves and short-term Treasury issues), the relative decline of "interest insensitive" (traditional) deposits, the diminishing capital cushion of banks, and the rise of bank-stock betas all provide evidence of increased exposure to financial-market developments.

These considerations together have important implications for monetary policy. Stringent (that is, truly restrictive) limitations on purchased funds could create a severe liquidity squeeze within the U.S. commercial banking system. This is related to the fact that there is no large secondary market *outside the commercial bank sector* for loans as there is for securities. While there is a wide market for Treasury bills, most loans would be very difficult for a bank to sell in a liquidity squeeze. In this situation, the banking sector as a whole—and not simply individual large banks—has come to rely on liability management as its principal source of liquidity.

Given this fact, it is not surprising that banks devised ingenious instruments to circumvent CD ceilings during the 1966 and 1969 tight-money periods. Despite these efforts, bank disintermediation was heavy during those periods. Although it is difficult to assess the effects of liability-management curbs on total financial flows and total spending in the economy, the effect on the banking system was obviously disruptive.

Banks have purchased funds not only to stabilize the variance of bank credit during tight-money periods, but also to accelerate their growth during expansionary periods. In this respect, liability management has increased the banking sector's exposure to economic fluctua-

---

[12] See R. Alton Gilbert, "Bank Financing of the Recovery," Federal Reserve Bank of St. Louis *Review* (July 1976), pp. 2–9; Maury Harris, "The Weakness of Business Loans in the Current Recovery," Federal Reserve Bank of New York *Monthly Review* (August 1976), pp. 208–14; and Henry Kaufman, "New Conservatism Finds Roots in 'Vicious' Inflation, Helps Stretch Expansion," *The Money Manager* (August 9, 1976), p. 5.

tions. During the 1971–74 period, banks increasingly purchased funds to meet loan commitments, but in the process allowed their capital cushions and liquid investments to decline in relative terms. These measures presumably would have promised high returns in a stable economic environment, but they also served to make the banking system more vulnerable in the sharp recession at the end of 1974.

Policy-makers henceforth will be forced to weigh carefully any perverse effects on the commercial-banking system resulting from policies that attempt to restrict the flexibility of liability management. Actually, it is not clear that monetary policy needs to resort to such tactics, or even that restrictions of this type effectively curb economic spending. The 1973–74 tight-money period occurred without any resort to direct controls over liability management. This period of monetary deceleration may or may not have brought on the ensuing inventory recession, but the recession occurred without any prior curbs on liability management or severe disintermediation of bank funds.

10. FINANCIAL INTERMEDIARIES AND THE SAVING-INVESTMENT PROCESS*

John G. Gurley
and
Edward S. Shaw

It is fashionable these days to speak of the growing institutionalization of saving and investment. Rapid advances in recent years by pension funds, open-end investment companies, credit unions, and savings and loan associations, among others, have caught our eye. But the advance has been going on at least since the Civil War, and as Raymond Goldsmith has recently shown, it was quite pronounced during the first three decades of this century. It is with these three decades that our paper is primarily concerned. Our method of analyzing financial data, however, requires explanation since it is based on unconventional theory. Accordingly, the first portions of the paper are largely theoretical. After that, we get down to brass tacks.

DEFICITS, SECURITY ISSUES, AND GNP

It is easy to imagine a world in which there is a high level of saving and investment, but in which there is an unfavorable climate for financial intermediaries. At the extreme, each of the economy's spending units—whether of the household, business, or government variety—would have a balanced budget on income and product account. For each spending unit, current income would equal the sum of current and capital expenditures. There could still be saving and investment, but each spending unit's saving would be precisely matched by its investment in tangible assets. In a world of balanced budgets, security issues by spending units would be zero, or very close to zero.[1] The same would be true of the accumulation of financial assets. Consequently, this world would be a highly uncongenial one for financial intermediaries; the saving-investment process would grind away without them.

Financial intermediaries are likely to thrive best in a world of deficits and surpluses, in a world in which there is a significant division of labor between savers and investors. In the ideal world for financial intermediaries, all current and capital expenditures would be made by spending units that received no current income, and all current income would be received by spending units that spent nothing. One group of spending units would have a deficit equal to its expenditures, and the other group would have a surplus equal to its income. And, of course, the *ex post* deficit would necessarily be equal to the *ex post* surplus. In this setting, the deficit group would tend to issue securities equal to its deficit, and

* From the article of the same title, *Journal of Finance,* vol. 11 (May 1956), pp. 257–66. Reprinted by permission of the publisher and the authors. John G. Gurley is Professor of Economics, Stanford University. Edward S. Shaw is Professor of Economics (Emeritus), Stanford University.

[1] Securities might be issued by spending units to build up their financial assets or their holdings of existing real assets. However, in a world of balanced budgets, no spending unit would have a *net* accumulation of these assets, positive or negative.

the other group would tend to accumulate financial assets equal to its surplus. Security issues and financial-asset accumulations, therefore, would tend to approximate GNP or the aggregate of expenditures. No more congenial world than this could exist for financial intermediaries.

Unfortunately for these intermediaries, our own economy has been much closer to the first than to the second world. With some exceptions during the past half-century, the annual security issues of spending units over complete cycles have averaged somewhat below 10 percent of GNP in current prices. These issues include government securities, corporate and foreign bonds, common and preferred stock, farm and nonfarm mortgages, and consumer and other short-term debt. We shall call these primary security issues. Thus, at the turn of the century when GNP was around $20 billion, primary security issues ran a bit less than $2 billion per annum. In the late 1940s, with a GNP of approximately $250 billion, primary issues hovered around $20 billion per annum. Dividing the half-century into thirteen complete cycles, we find that the average annual ratio of primary issues to GNP was between 7 and 10 percent in nine of the cycles. The exceptional cases include World War I, when the ratio reached 20 percent, the 1930s, when the ratio fell to 3 or 4 percent, and World War II, when it climbed to 25 percent. However, if we consider longer phases, 1897–1914, 1915–32, and 1933–49, the ratio was between 9 and 10 percent in each phase. There is sufficient strength, then, in the link between borrowing and GNP to make the relationship useful for financial analysis. And while the ratio lies closer to zero than to 100 percent, still it is high enough to permit financial intermediation to be a substantial business.

THE ROLE OF FINANCIAL INTERMEDIARIES

What is the business of financial intermediaries? They lend at one stratum of interest rates and borrow at a lower stratum. They relieve the market of some primary securities and substitute others—indirect securities or financial assets—whose qualities command a higher price. This margin between yields on primary and indirect securities is the intermediaries' compensation for the special services they supply.

The financial institutions that fit these specifications are savings and loan associations, insurance companies, mutual savings banks, Postal Savings banks, investment companies, common trust funds, pension funds, government lending agencies, and others. In addition, we count the monetary system, including commercial banks, as one among many intermediaries. It is a vitally important intermediary, in view of its functions and its size. But its elevated rank among intermediaries does not alter the principle that the monetary system, like other intermediaries, transmits loanable funds by issues of indirect financial assets to surplus units and purchases of primary securities from deficit units. The indirect financial assets, deposits and currency that it issues or creates, are, like the indirect financial assets issued or created by other intermediaries, substitutes for primary securities in the portfolios of spending units. We shall return to this point in a few moments.

INTERNAL AND EXTERNAL FINANCE OF EXPENDITURES

In a world of balanced budgets, each spending unit's current and capital expenditures would be financed entirely from its current income. Thus, aggregate expenditures in the economy would be self-financed or internally financed. Internal finance would be equal to GNP.

In a world of deficits and surpluses, some expenditures would be financed externally. The extent of such financing is measured by the sum of the deficits (or surpluses) run by spending units. If at a GNP of $400 billion, the sum of all spending units' deficits is $40 billion, then 10 percent of GNP is financed externally and 90 percent is financed internally.

External finance may take two forms: direct finance and indirect finance. The distinction is based on the changes that occur in the financial accounts of surplus units' balance sheets. The finance is indirect if the surplus units acquire claims on financial intermediaries.[2] It is direct if surplus units acquire claims on debtors that are not financial intermediaries.[3]

---

[2] In our empirical work, we exclude from indirect finance some kinds of claims on intermediaries, such as accrued expenses or even stockholder equities, that are essentially like debt issues of nonfinancial spending units.

[3] It may help to illustrate these financing arrangements. Suppose that at a GNP of $400 billion the sum of all spending units' deficits is $40 billion. Suppose further that $40 billion of primary securities, such as corporate bonds and mortgages, are issued to cover the deficits. The primary securities may be sold directly to surplus spending units whose aggregate surplus will also be equal to $40 billion, looking at it *ex post*. In this case direct finance will take place, with surplus spenders acquiring various types of primary securities. Alternatively, if the primary securities are sold to financial intermediaries, surplus

While the proportion of GNP that is externally financed has not changed much over the past half-century, the proportion that is indirectly financed has risen and, of course, the proportion that is directly financed has fallen. In short, a growing share of primary issues has been sold to financial intermediaries.[4] But the relative gainers have been the nonmonetary intermediaries and the relative loser has been the monetary system. Now, if we look at these trends from the standpoint of surplus spenders, we have the following picture: the surplus units have accumulated financial assets in annual amounts that, over long periods, have been a fairly steady percentage of GNP. However, these accumulations have been relatively more and more in the form of indirect financial assets, and relatively less and less in the form of primary securities. Moreover, the accumulations of indirect financial assets have swung toward the non-monetary types and away from bank deposits and currency. Commercial banks and the monetary system have retrogressed relative to financial intermediaries generally.

A RECONSIDERATION OF BANKING THEORY

A traditional view of the monetary system is that it determines the supply of money: It determines its own size in terms of monetary debt and of the assets that are counterparts of this debt on the system's balance sheet. Other financial intermediaries transfer to investors any part of this money supply that may be deposited with them by savers. Their size is determined by the public's choice of saving media.

As we see it, on the contrary, the monetary system is in some significant degree competitive with other financial intermediaries. The growth of these intermediaries in terms of indirect debt and of primary security portfolios is alternative to monetary growth and inhibits it. Their issues of indirect debt displace money, and the primary

securities that they hold are in some large degree a loss of assets to the banks.

Bank deposits and currency are unique in one respect: they are means of payment, and holders of money balances have immediate access to the payments mechanism of the banking system. If money were in demand only for immediate spending or for holding in transactions balances, and if no other financial asset could be substituted as a means of payment or displace money in transactions balances, the monetary system would be a monopolistic supplier exempt from competition by other financial intermediaries.

But money is not in demand exclusively as a means of payment. It is in demand as a financial asset to hold. As a component of balances, money does encounter competition. Other financial assets can be accumulated preparatory to money payments, as a precaution against contingencies, or as an alternative to primary securities. For any level of money payments, various levels of money balances will do and, hence, various sizes of money supply and monetary system.

The more adequate the nonmonetary financial assets are as substitutes for money in transactions, precautionary, speculative, and—as we shall see—diversification balances, the smaller may be the money supply for any designated level of national income. For any level of income, the money supply is indeterminate until one knows the degree of substitutability between money created by banks and financial assets created by other intermediaries. How big the monetary system is depends in part on the intensity of competition from savings banks, life insurance companies, pension funds, and other intermediaries.

Financial competition may inhibit the growth of the monetary system in a number of ways. Given the level of national income, a gain in attractiveness of, say, savings and loan shares vis-à-vis money balances must result in an excess supply of money. The monetary authority may choose to remove this excess. Then bank reserves, earning assets, money issues, and profits are contracted. This implies that, at any level of income, the competition of nonmonetary intermediaries may displace money balances, shift primary securities from banks to their competitors, and reduce the monetary system's requirement for reserves. In a trend context, bank reserves cannot be permitted to grow as rapidly as otherwise they might, if nonmonetary intermediaries become more attractive channels for transmission of loanable funds.

Suppose that excess money balances, resulting from a shift in spending units' demand away

spenders will accumulate claims on these intermediaries, indirect financial assets instead of primary securities. In this event we say that the expenditures represented by the primary securities have been indirectly financed. If indirect finance occurs through commercial banks, surplus spenders accumulate bank deposits; if through savings and loan associations, they acquire savings, and loan shares; if through life insurance companies, policyholder equities; and so on.

[4] This growth has not been steady. Indeed, it is shown later that there was retrogression in intermediation from 1898 to 1921. The share of issues going to intermediaries rose in the 1920s, rose further in the 1930s, and remained high in the 1940s.

from money balances to alternative forms of indirect financial assets, are not destroyed by central bank action. They may be used to repay bank loans or to buy other securities from banks, the result being excess bank reserves. At the prevailing level of security prices, spending units have rejected money balances. But cannot banks force these balances out again, resuming control of the money supply? They can do so by accepting a reduced margin between the yield of primary securities they buy and the cost to them of deposits and currency they create. But this option is not peculiar to banks: other intermediaries can stimulate demand for their debt if they stand ready to accept a reduced markup on the securities they create and sell relative to the securities they buy. The banks can restore the money supply, but the cost is both a decline in their status relative to other financial intermediaries and a reduction in earnings.

The banks may choose to live with excess reserves rather than pay higher prices on primary securities or higher yields on their own debt issues. In this case, as in the previous two, a lower volume of reserves is needed to sustain a given level of national income. With their competitive situation improved, non-monetary intermediaries have stolen away from the banking system a share of responsibility for sustaining the flow of money payments. They hold a larger share of outstanding primary securities; they owe a larger share of indirect financial assets. They have reduced the size of the banking system at the given income level, both absolutely and relatively to their own size, and their gain is at the expense of bank profits.[5]

---

[5] We may mention a few additional issues in banking theory. As intermediaries, banks buy primary securities and issue, in payment for them, deposits and currency. As the payments mechanism, banks transfer title to means of payment on demand by customers. It has been pointed out before, especially by Henry Simons, that these two banking functions are at least incompatible. As managers of the payments mechanism, the banks cannot afford a shadow of insolvency. As intermediaries in a growing economy, the banks may rightly be tempted to wildcat. They must be solvent or the community will suffer; they must dare insolvency or the community will fail to realize its potentialities for growth.

All too often in American history energetic intermediation by banks has culminated in collapse of the payments mechanism. During some periods, especially cautious regard for solvency has resulted in collapse of bank intermediation. Each occasion that has demonstrated the incompatibility of the two principal banking functions has touched off a flood of financial reform. These reforms on balance have tended to emphasize bank solvency and the viability

A RECONSIDERATION OF INTEREST THEORY

It is clear from the foregoing remarks that this way of looking at financial intermediaries leads to a reconsideration of interest theory.

---

of the payments mechanism at the expense of bank participation in financial growth. They have by no means gone to the extreme that Simons proposed, of divorcing the two functions altogether, but they have tended in that direction rather than toward indorsement of wildcat banking. This bias in financial reform has improved the opportunities for nonmonetary intermediaries. The relative retrogression in banking seems to have resulted in part from regulatory suppression of the intermediary function.

Turning to another matter, it has seemed to be a distinctive, even magic, characteristic of the monetary system that it can create money, erecting a "multiple expansion" of debt in the form of deposits and currency on a limited base of reserves. Other financial institutions, conventional doctrine tells us, are denied this creative or multiplicative faculty. They are merely middlemen or brokers, not manufacturers of credit. Our own view is different. There is no denying, of course, that the monetary system creates debt in the special form of money: the monetary system can borrow by issue of instruments that are means of payment. There is no denying, either, that nonmonetary intermediaries cannot create this same form of debt. They would be monetary institutions if they could do so. It is granted, too, that nonmonetary intermediaries receive money and pay it out, precisely as all of us do: they use the payments mechanism.

However, each kind of non-monetary intermediary can borrow, go into debt, issue its own characteristic obligations—in short, it can create credit, though not in monetary form. Moreover, the nonmonetary intermediaries are less inhibited in their own style of credit creation than are the banks in creating money. Credit creation by nonmonetary intermediaries is restricted by various qualitative rules. Aside from these, the main factor that limits credit creation is the profit calculus. Credit creation by banks also is subject to the profit condition. But the monetary system is subject not only to this restraint and to a complex of qualitative rules. It is committed to a policy restraint, of avoiding excessive expansion or contraction of credit for the community's welfare, that is not imposed explicitly on nonmonetary intermediaries. It is also held in check by a system of reserve requirements. The legal reserve requirement on commercial banks is a "sharing ratio"; it apportions assets within the monetary system. The share of assets allocated to the commercial banks varies inversely with the reserve requirement. The proportion of the commercial banks' share to the share of the central bank and Treasury is the "multiple of expansion" for the commercial banking system. The "multiple of expansion" is a remarkable phenomenon not because of its inflationary implications but because it means that bank expansion is anchored, as other financial expansion is not, to a regulated base. If credit creation by banks is miraculous, creation of credit by other financial institutions is still more a cause for exclamation.

Yields on primary securities, the terms of borrowing available to deficit spenders, are influenced not only by the amount of primary securities in the monetary system—that is, by the supply of money—but also by the amount of these securities in nonmonetary intermediaries—that is, by the supply of indirect financial assets created by these intermediaries. Suppose that savings and loan shares become more attractive relative to bank deposits, resulting in an excess supply of money. Now, if we suppose that the monetary system chooses and manages to keep the money supply constant under these circumstances, the excess supply of money will cause yields on primary securities to fall. The activities of nonmonetary financial intermediaries, then, can affect primary yields. The same money supply and national income are compatible with various interest rate levels, depending upon the size of nonmonetary intermediaries and upon the degree to which their issues are competitive with money.[6]

The analysis is only a bit more complicated when we allow for issues of primary securities and the growth of income. Let us take these one at a time. At any income level, some spending units will have deficits and others surpluses. During the income period, the deficit spenders will tend to issue primary securities in an amount equal to their aggregate deficits. Now, if the surplus spenders are willing to absorb all of the issues at current yields on these securities, there will be no tightening effect on security markets. Surplus spenders will accumulate financial assets, all in the form of primary securities, and financial intermediaries will purchase none of the issues.

But this is an unlikely outcome. Ordinarily, surplus spenders can be expected to reject some portion of the primary securities emerging at any level of income and demand indirect financial assets instead, unless their preference for the latter is suppressed by a fall in prices of primary securities and a corresponding rise in interest rates charged to deficit spenders. This incremental demand for indirect financial assets is in part a demand for portfolio diversification. The diversification demand exists because there is generally no feasible mixture of primary securities that provides adequately such distinctive qualities of indirect securities as stability of price and yield or divisibility. The incremental demand for indirect assets, however, reflects not only a negative response, a partial rejection of primary securities, but also a positive response, an attraction to the many services attached to indirect assets, such as insurance and pension services and convenience of accumulation. Part of the demand is linked to the flow of primary security issues, but another part is linked more closely to the level of income.

For these reasons, then, ordinarily some portion of the primary issues must be sold to financial intermediaries if present yields on these securities are to be defended. Assuming for the moment that the monetary system is the only financial intermediary, the increase in the money supply must be equal to the portion of primary issues that spending units choose not to accumulate at current yields. If the monetary system purchases less than this, spending units will accumulate the residual supply at rising interest rates to deficit spenders. The emergence of security issues and a diversification demand for money based on these issues means that the money supply must rise at a given income level to maintain current yields on primary securities.

Still retaining the assumption that the monetary system is the only financial intermediary, we now permit income to grow. As money income gains, spending units demand additions to their active or transactions balances of means of payment. An upward trend in money payments calls for an upward trend in balances too. The income effect also applies to contingency or precautionary balances. If spending units are increasingly prosperous in the present, they feel able to afford stronger defenses against the hazards of the future.[7]

---

[6] We can reach the same conclusion by looking at the supply of and the demand for primary securities. The shift in demand to savings and loan shares reduces spending units' demand for bank deposits by, say, an equivalent amount. Consequently, the demand by spending units for primary securities is unchanged at current yields. Also, there is no change in this demand by the monetary system, since we have assumed the money supply constant. However, there is an increase in demand for primary securities by savings and loan associations. So, for the economy as a whole, there is an excess demand for primary securities at current yields, which is the counterpart of the excess supply of money.

Downward pressure on primary yields is exerted as long as the indirect debt of nonmonetary intermediaries is to some degree competitive with money and as long as the additional demand for primary securities by these intermediaries is roughly equivalent to their creation of indirect debt.

---

[7] For periods longer than the Keynesian short run, it is hardly safe to assume that transactions and contingency demands for additional money balances are proportional to increments in the level of money income. They may be elastic to interest rates on such primary securities as Treasury bills and brokers' loans. For any increment in money income, they may rise with real income. As a larger share of national income involves market transactions, as population moves from farms to cities, as a dollar

The combination of the income and diversification effects simply means that, when income is rising, a larger share of the issues must be purchased by the monetary system to prevent a rise in primary yields. The system must supply money for both diversification and transactions, including contingency, balances.

We may now introduce nonmonetary intermediaries. The growth of these intermediaries will ordinarily, to some extent, reduce the re-

quired growth of the monetary system. We have already presented the reasons for this, so it suffices to say that primary yields may be held steady under growth conditions even with a monetary system that is barely growing, provided other intermediaries take up the slack.

In summary, primary security issues depend on aggregate deficits, and the latter in turn are related to the income level. At any income level, the diversification effect of these issues means that financial intermediaries must grow to hold primary yields steady. If income is rising, too, there is an incremental demand for money and perhaps for other indirect assets for transactions and contingency balances, requiring additional intermediary growth. To the extent that the issues of nonmonetary intermediaries are competitive with money balances of whatever type, the required growth of the monetary system is reduced by the expansion of other intermediaries.

---

of income is generated with more or fewer dollars of intermediate payments, as credit practices change, as checks are collected more efficiently or as deposits cease to bear interest and bear service charges instead, one expects the marginal ratio of active balances to income to vary. And incremental demand for contingency balances must be sensitive not only to income, and perhaps to interest rates, but to the evolution of emergency credit facilities, to job security and social security, to an array of circumstances that is largely irrelevant in short-period analysis.

---

11. COMMERCIAL BANKS AS CREATORS OF "MONEY"*

James Tobin

I. THE OLD VIEW

Perhaps the greatest moment of triumph for the elementary economics teacher is his exposition of the multiple creation of bank credit and bank deposits. Before the admiring eyes of freshmen he puts to rout the practical banker who is so sure that he "lends only the money depositors entrust to him." The banker is shown to have a worm's-eye view, and his error stands as an introductory object lesson in the fallacy of composition. From the Olympian vantage of the teacher and the textbook it appears that the banker's dictum must be reversed: depositors entrust to bankers whatever amounts the bankers lend. To be sure, this is not true of a single bank; one bank's loan may wind up as another bank's deposit. But it is, as the arithmetic of successive rounds of deposit creation makes clear, true of the banking system as a whole. Whatever their other errors, a long line of financial heretics have been right in speaking of "fountain pen money"

* From Deane Carson, ed., *Banking and Monetary Studies* (Homewood, Ill.: Richard D. Irwin, Inc., 1963), pp. 408–19. Reprinted by permission of the publisher and the author. James Tobin is Sterling Professor of Economics, Yale University.

—money created by the stroke of the bank president's pen when he approves a loan and credits the proceeds to the borrower's checking account.

In this time-honored exposition two characteristics of commercial banks—both of which are alleged to differentiate them sharply from other financial intermediaries—are intertwined. One is that their liabilities—well, at least their demand deposit liabilities—serve as widely acceptable means of payment. Thus, they count, along with coin and currency in public circulation, as "money." The other is that the preferences of the public normally play no role in determining the total volume of deposits or the total quantity of money. For it is the beginning of wisdom in monetary economics to observe that money is like the "hot potato" of a children's game: one individual may pass it to another, but the group as a whole cannot get rid of it. If the economy and the supply of money are out of adjustment, it is the economy that must do the adjusting. This is as true, evidently, of money created by bankers' fountain pens as of money created by public printing presses. On the other hand, financial intermediaries other than banks do not create money, and the scale of their assets is limited by their liabilities, i.e., by the savings the public entrusts to them. They cannot count on receiving "deposits" to match every extension of their lending.

The commercial banks and only the commercial banks, in other words, possess the widow's cruse. And because they possess this key to unlimited expansion, they have to be restrained by reserve requirements. Once this is done, determination of the aggregate volume of bank deposits is just a matter of accounting and arithmetic: simply divide the available supply of bank reserves by the required reserve ratio.

The foregoing is admittedly a caricature, but I believe it is not a great exaggeration of the impressions conveyed by economics teaching concerning the roles of commercial banks and other financial institutions in the monetary system. In conveying this mélange of propositions, economics has replaced the naïve fallacy of composition of the banker with other half-truths perhaps equally misleading. These have their root in the mystique of "money"—the tradition of distinguishing sharply between those assets which are and those which are not "money," and accordingly between those institutions which emit "money" and those whose liabilities are not "money." The persistent strength of this tradition is remarkable given the uncertainty and controversy over where to draw the dividing line between money and other assets. Time was when only currency was regarded as money, and the use of bank deposits was regarded as a way of economizing currency and increasing the velocity of money. Today scholars and statisticians wonder and argue whether to count commercial bank time and savings deposits in the money supply. And if so, why not similar accounts in other institutions? Nevertheless, once the arbitrary line is drawn, assets on the money side of the line are assumed to possess to the full properties which assets on the other side completely lack. For example, an eminent monetary economist, more candid than many of his colleagues, admits that we don't really know what money is, but proceeds to argue that, whatever it is, its supply should grow regularly at a rate of the order of 3 to 4 percent per year.[1]

II. THE "NEW VIEW"

A more recent development in monetary economics tends to blur the sharp traditional distinctions between money and other assets and between

commercial banks and other financial intermediaries; to focus on demands for and supplies of the whole spectrum of assets rather than on the quantity and velocity of "money"; and to regard the structure of interest rates, asset yields, and credit availabilities rather than the quantity of money as the linkage between monetary and financial institutions and policies on the one hand and the real economy on the other.[2] In this essay I propose to look briefly at the implications of this "new view" for the theory of deposit creation, of which I have above described or caricatured the traditional version. One of the incidental advantages of this theoretical development is to effect something of a reconciliation between the economics teacher and the practical banker.

According to the "new view," the essential function of financial intermediaries, including commercial banks, is to satisfy simultaneously the portfolio preferences of two types of individuals or firms.[3] On one side are borrowers, who wish to expand their holdings of real assets—inventories, residential real estate, productive plant and equipment, etc.—beyond the limits of their own net worth. On the other side are lenders, who wish to hold part or all of their net worth in assets of stable money value with negligible risk of default. The assets of financial intermediaries are obligations of the borrowers—promissory notes, bonds, mortgages. The liabilities of financial intermediaries are the assets of the lenders—bank deposits, insurance policies, pension rights.

Financial intermediaries typically assume liabilities of smaller default risk and greater predictability of value than their assets. The principal kinds of institutions take on liabilities of greater liquidity too; thus, bank depositors can require payment on demand, while bank loans become due only on specified dates. The reasons that the intermediation of financial institutions can accomplish these transformations between

[1] E. S. Shaw, "Money Supply and Stable Economic Growth," in *United States Monetary Policy* (New York: American Assembly, 1958), pp. 49–71.

[2] For a review of this development and for references to its protagonists, see Harry Johnson's survey article, "Monetary Theory and Policy," *American Economic Review*, vol. 52 (June 1962), pp. 335–84. I will confine myself to mentioning the importance, in originating and contributing to the "new view," of John Gurley and E. S. Shaw (yes, the very same Shaw cited in the previous footnote, but presumably in a different incarnation). Their viewpoint is summarized in *Money in a Theory of Finance* (Washington, D.C.: The Brookings Institution, 1960).

[3] This paragraph and the three following are adapted with minor changes from the author's paper with William Brainard, "Financial Intermediaries and the Effectiveness of Monetary Controls," *American Economic Review*, vol. 53 (May 1963), pp. 384–86.

the nature of the obligation of the borrower and the nature of the asset of the ultimate lender are these: (1) administrative economy and expertise in negotiating, accounting, appraising, and collecting; (2) reduction of risk per dollar of lending by the pooling of independent risks, with respect both to loan default and to deposit withdrawal; (3) governmental guarantees of the liabilities of the institutions and other provisions (bank examination, investment regulations, supervision of insurance companies, last-resort lending) designed to assure the solvency and liquidity of the institutions.

For these reasons, intermediation permits borrowers who wish to expand their investments in real assets to be accommodated at lower rates and easier terms than if they had to borrow directly from the lenders. If the creditors of financial intermediaries had to hold instead the kinds of obligations that private borrowers are capable of providing, they would certainly insist on higher rates and stricter terms. Therefore, any autonomous increase—for example, improvements in the efficiency of financial institutions or the creation of new types of intermediaries—in the amount of financial intermediation in the economy can be expected to be, *ceteris paribus*, an expansionary influence. This is true whether the growth occurs in intermediaries with monetary liabilities—i.e., commercial banks—or in other intermediaries.

Financial institutions fall fairly easily into distinct categories, each industry or "intermediary" offering a differentiated product to its customers, both lenders and borrowers. From the point of view of lenders, the obligations of the various intermediaries are more or less close, but not perfect, substitutes. For example, savings deposits share most of the attributes of demand deposits; but they are not means of payment, and the institution has the right, seldom exercised, to require notice of withdrawal. Similarly there is differentiation in the kinds of credit offered borrowers. Each intermediary has its specialty—e.g., the commercial loan for banks, the real-estate mortgage for the savings and loan association. But the borrowers' market is not completely compartmentalized. The same credit instruments are handled by more than one intermediary, and many borrowers have flexibility in the type of debt they incur. Thus, there is some substitutability, in the demand for credit by borrowers, between the assets of the various intermediaries.[4]

---

[4] These features of the market structure of intermediaries, and their implications for the supposed uniqueness of banks, have been emphasized by Gurley

The special attention given commercial banks in economic analysis is usually justified by the observation that, alone among intermediaries, banks "create" means of payment. This rationale is on its face far from convincing. The means-of-payment characteristic of demand deposits is indeed a feature differentiating bank liabilities from those of other intermediaries. Insurance against death is equally a feature differentiating life insurance policies from the obligations of other intermediaries, including banks. It is not obvious that one kind of differentiation should be singled out for special analytical treatment. Like other differentia, the means-of-payment attribute has its price. Savings deposits, for example, are perfect substitutes for demand deposits in every respect except as a medium of exchange. This advantage of checking accounts does not give banks absolute immunity from the competition of savings banks; it is a limited advantage that can be, at least in some part for many depositors, overcome by differences in yield. It follows that the community's demand for bank deposits is not indefinite, even though demand deposits do serve as means of payment.

III. THE WIDOW'S CRUSE

Neither individually nor collectively do commercial banks possess a widow's cruse. Quite apart from legal reserve requirements, commercial banks are limited in scale by the same kinds of economic processes that determine the aggregate size of other intermediaries.

One often cited difference between commercial banks and other intermediaries must be quickly dismissed as superficial and irrelevant. This is the fact that a bank can make a loan by "writing up" its deposit liabilities, while a savings and loan association, for example, cannot satisfy a mortgage borrower by crediting him with a share account. The association must transfer means of payment to the borrower; its total liabilities do not rise along with its assets. True enough, but neither do the bank's, for more than a fleeting moment. Borrowers do not incur debt in order to hold idle deposits, any more than savings and loan shares. The borrower pays out the money, and there is of course no guarantee that any of it stays in the lending bank. Whether or not it stays in the banking system as a whole is an-

---

and Shaw, *op. cit.* An example of substitutability on the deposit side is analyzed by David and Charlotte Alhadeff, "The Struggle for Commercial Bank Savings," *Quarterly Journal of Economics,* vol. 72 (February 1958), pp. 1–22.

other question, about to be discussed. But the answer clearly does not depend on the way the loan was initially made. It depends on whether somewhere in the chain of transactions initiated by the borrower's outlays are found depositors who wish to hold new deposits equal in amount to the new loan. Similarly, the outcome for the savings and loan industry depends on whether in the chain of transactions initiated by the mortgage are found individuals who wish to acquire additional savings and loan shares.

The banking system can expand its assets either (*a*) by purchasing, or lending against existing assets; or (*b*) by lending to finance new private investment in inventories or capital goods, or buying government securities financing new public deficits. In case (*a*) no increase in private wealth occurs in conjunction with the banks' expansion. There is no new private saving and investment. In case (*b*), new private saving occurs, matching dollar for dollar the private investments or government deficits financed by the banking system. In neither case will there automatically be an increase in savers' demand for bank deposits equal to the expansion in bank assets.

In the second case, it is true, there is an increase in private wealth. But even if we assume a closed economy in order to abstract from leakages of capital abroad, the community will not ordinarily wish to put 100 percent of its new saving into bank deposits. Bank deposits are, after all, only about 15 percent of total private wealth in the United States; other things equal, savers cannot be expected greatly to exceed this proportion in allocating new saving. So, if *all* new saving is to take the form of bank deposits, other things cannot stay equal. Specifically, the yields and other advantages of the competing assets into which new saving would otherwise flow will have to fall enough so that savers prefer bank deposits.

This is *a fortiori* true in case (*a*) where there is no new saving and the generation of bank liabilities to match the assumed expansion of bank assets entails a reshuffling of existing portfolios in favor of bank deposits. In effect the banking system has to induce the public to swap loans and securities for bank deposits. This can happen only if the price is right.

Clearly, then, there is at any moment a natural economic limit to the scale of the commercial banking industry. Given the wealth and the asset preferences of the community, the demand for bank deposits can increase only if the yields of other assets fall. The fall in these yields is bound to restrict the profitable lending and investment opportunities available to the banks themselves.

Eventually the marginal returns on lending and investing, account taken of the risks and administrative costs involved, will not exceed the marginal cost to the banks of attracting and holding additional deposits. At this point the widow's cruse has run dry.

IV. BANKS AND OTHER INTERMEDIARIES COMPARED

In this respect the commercial banking industry is not qualitatively different from any other financial intermediary system. The same process limits the collective expansion of savings and loan associations, or savings banks, or life insurance companies. At some point the returns from additional loans or security holdings are not worth the cost of obtaining the funds from the public.

There are of course some differences. First, it may well be true that commercial banks benefit from a larger share of additions to private savings than other intermediaries. Second, according to modern American legal practice, commercial banks are subject to ceilings on the rates payable to their depositors—zero in the case of demand deposits. Unlike competing financial industries, commercial banks cannot seek funds by raising rates. They can and do offer other inducements to depositors, but these substitutes for interest are imperfect and uneven in their incidence. In these circumstances the major readjustment of the interest rate structure necessary to increase the relative demand for bank deposits is a decline in other rates. Note that neither of these differences has to do with the quality of bank deposits as "money."

In a world without reserve requirements the preferences of depositors, as well as those of borrowers, would be very relevant in determining the volume of bank deposits. The volume of assets and liabilities of every intermediary, both nonbanks and banks, would be determined in a competitive equilibrium, where the rate of interest charged borrowers by each kind of institution just balances at the margin the rate of interest paid its creditors. Suppose that such an equilibrium is disturbed by a shift in savers' preferences. At prevailing rates they decide to hold more savings accounts and other nonbank liabilities and less demand deposits. They transfer demand deposits to the credit of nonbank financial institutions, providing these intermediaries with the means to seek additional earning assets. These institutions, finding themselves able attract more funds from the public even with some reduction in the rates they pay, offer better terms to borrowers and bid up the prices of existing earning assets. Consequently commercial banks release some earning assets—they no longer yield enough to pay the going rate on the banks' deposit liabilities. Bank deposits decline with bank assets. In effect, the nonbank intermediaries favored by the shift in public preferences simply swap the deposits transferred to them for a corresponding quantity of bank assets.

V. FOUNTAIN PENS AND PRINTING PRESSES

Evidently the fountain pens of commercial bankers are essentially different from the printing presses of governments. Confusion results from concluding that because bank deposits are like currency in one respect—both serve as media of exchange—they are like currency in every respect. Unlike governments, bankers cannot create means of payment to finance their own purchases of goods and services. Bank-created "money" is a liability, which must be matched on the other side of the balance sheet. And banks, as businesses, must earn money from their middleman's role. Once created, printing press money cannot be extinguished, except by reversal of the budget policies which led to its birth. The community cannot get rid of its currency supply; the economy must adjust until it is willingly absorbed. The "hot potato" analogy truly applies. For bank-created money, however, there is an economic mechanism of extinction as well as creation, contraction as well as expansion. If bank deposits are excessive relative to public preferences, they will tend to decline; otherwise banks will lose income. The burden of adaptation is not placed entirely on the rest of the economy.

VI. THE ROLE OF RESERVE REQUIREMENTS

Without reserve requirements, expansion of credit and deposits by the commercial banking system would be limited by the availability of assets at yields sufficient to compensate banks for the costs of attracting and holding the corresponding deposits. In a régime of reserve requirements, the limit which they impose normally cuts the expansion short of this competitive equilibrium. When reserve requirements and deposit interest rate ceilings are effective, the marginal yield of bank loans and investments exceeds the marginal cost of deposits to the banking system. In these circumstances additional reserves make it possible and profitable for banks to acquire additional earning assets. The expansion process lowers interest rates generally—enough to induce the public to hold additional deposits but ordinarily not enough to wipe out the banks' margin between the value and cost of additional deposits.

It is the existence of this margin—not the monetary nature of bank liabilities—which makes it possible for the economics teacher to say that additional loans permitted by new reserves will generate their own deposits. The same proposition would be true of any other system of financial institutions subject to similar reserve constraints and similar interest rate ceilings. In this sense it is more accurate to attribute the special place of banks among intermediaries to the legal restrictions to which banks alone are subjected than to attribute these restrictions to the special character of bank liabilities.

But the textbook description of multiple expansion of credit and deposits on a given reserve base is misleading even for a régime of reserve requirements. There is more to the determination of the volume of bank deposits than the arithmetic of reserve supplies and reserve ratios. The redundant reserves of the thirties are a dramatic reminder that economic opportunities sometimes prevail over reserve calculations. But the significance of that experience is not correctly appreciated if it is regarded simply as an aberration from a normal state of affairs in which banks are fully "loaned up" and total deposits are tightly linked to the volume of reserves. The thirties exemplify in extreme form a phenomenon which is always in some degree present: the use to which commercial banks put the reserves made available to the system is an economic variable depending on lending opportunities and interest rates.

An individual bank is not constrained by any fixed quantum of reserves. It can obtain additional reserves to meet requirements by borrowing from the Federal Reserve, by buying "Federal Funds" from other banks, by selling or "running off" short-term securities. In short, reserves are available at the discount window and in the money market, at a price. This cost the bank must compare with available yields on loans and investments. If those yields are low relative to the cost of reserves, the bank will seek to avoid borrowing reserves and perhaps hold excess reserves instead. If those yields are high relative to the cost of borrowing reserves, the bank will shun excess reserves and borrow reserves occasionally or even regularly. For the banking system as a whole the Federal Reserve's quantitative controls determine the supply of unborrowed reserves. But the extent to which this supply is left unused, or supplemented by borrowing at the discount window, depends on the economic circumstances confronting the banks—on available lending opportunities and on the whole structure of interest rates from the Fed's discount rate through the rates on mortgages and long-term securities.

The range of variation in net free reserves in recent years has been from −5 percent to +5 percent of required reserves. This indicates a much looser linkage between reserves and deposits than is suggested by the textbook exposition of multiple expansion for a system which is always precisely and fully "loaned up." (It does not mean, however, that actual monetary authorities have any less control than textbook monetary authorities. Indeed the net free reserve position is one of their more useful instruments and barometers. Anyway, they are after bigger game than the quantity of "Money"!)

Two consequences of this analysis deserve special notice because of their relation to the issues raised earlier in this paper. First, an increase —of, say, a billion dollars—in the supply of unborrowed reserves will, in general, result in less than a billion-dollar increase in required reserves. Net free reserves will rise (algebraically) by some fraction of the billion dollars—a very large fraction in periods like the thirties, a much smaller one in tight money periods like those of the fifties. Loans and deposits will expand by less than their textbook multiples. The reason is simple. The open-market operations which bring about the increased supply of reserves tend to lower interest rates. So do the operations of the commercial banks in trying to invest their new reserves. The result is to diminish the incentives of banks to keep fully loaned up or to borrow reserves, and to make banks content to hold on the average higher excess reserves.

Second, depositor preferences do matter, even in a régime of fractional reserve banking. Suppose, for example, that the public decides to switch new or old savings from other assets and institutions into commercial banks. This switch makes earning assets available to banks at attractive yields—assets that otherwise would have been lodged either directly with the public or with the competing financial institutions previously favored with the public's savings. These improved opportunities for profitable lending and

investing will make the banks content to hold smaller net free reserves. Both their deposits and their assets will rise as a result of this shift in public preferences, even though the base of unborrowed reserves remains unchanged. Something of this kind has occurred in recent years when commercial banks have been permitted to raise the interest rates they offer for time and savings deposits.

VII. CONCLUDING REMARKS

The implications of the "new view" may be summarized as follows:

1.   The distinction between commercial banks and other financial intermediaries has been too sharply drawn. The differences are of degree, not of kind.

2.   In particular, the differences which do exist have little intrinsically to do with the monetary nature of bank liabilities.

3.   The differences are more importantly related to the special reserve requirements and interest rate ceilings to which banks are subject. Any other financial industry subject to the same kind of regulations would behave in much the same way.

4.   Commercial banks do not possess, either individually or collectively, a widow's cruse which guarantees that any expansion of assets will generate a corresponding expansion of deposit liabilities. Certainly this happy state of affairs would not exist in an unregulated competitive financial world. Marshall's scissors of supply and demand apply to the "output" of the banking industry, no less than to other financial and nonfinancial industries.

5.   Reserve requirements and interest ceilings give the widow's cruse myth somewhat greater plausibility. But even in these circumstances, the scale of bank deposits and assets is affected by depositor preferences and by the lending and investing opportunities available to banks.

I draw no policy morals from these observations. That is quite another story, to which analysis of the type presented here is only the preface. The reader will misunderstand my purpose if he jumps to attribute to me the conclusion that existing differences in the regulatory treatment of banks and competing intermediaries should be diminished, either by relaxing constraints on the one or by tightening controls on the other.

Chapter

3

THE FEDERAL RESERVE SYSTEM

The readings contained in this chapter are primarily concerned with the tools, mechanisms, and administration of monetary policy, as opposed to its effects. The separation between the material included here and that included in Chapter 5 is somewhat artificial. However, the purpose of the present chapter is to explain the major instruments available to the Federal Reserve for the conduct of monetary policy; to appraise the relative usefulness of these instruments; to explore certain issues pertaining to the guides to be used in carrying out monetary policy; and to consider the relation of the monetary authority to the rest of the government—the question of Federal Reserve "independence." In Chapter 5 we will examine the channels through which monetary forces affect economic activity and discuss the conduct of monetary policy in a somewhat broader perspective.

The three chief instruments of monetary policy in the United States are open market purchases and sales of U.S. government securities, changes in the discount rates charged to member banks when they borrow from the Federal Reserve banks, and changes in the legal reserve requirements applicable to deposits at member banks. In the first paper included in this chapter, by Warren L. Smith (reading 12), each of these instruments is discussed and appraised. The conclusion reached by the author is that the open market instrument is the most flexible, effective, and useful tool available to the Federal Reserve. The paper considers the appropriate ways of coordinating the use of other instruments—especially the discount rate—with open market operations.

In order to produce desired effects on aggregate demand for goods and services and thereby affect output, employment, and prices—its "ultimate" goals—the Federal Reserve appears to select certain "proximate" goals of a more directly monetary character, such as interest rates, the stock of money, and so on, as the immediate objects of its actions. A proximate goal that has at times commanded a good deal of attention is the level of "free reserves"—the difference between the excess reserves of member banks and their outstanding borrowings from the Federal Reserve. The volume of free reserves has at times been given a good deal of weight by the Federal Reserve itself as an indicator of monetary conditions—although probably not as much as the System's critics sometimes imply. However, in many outside commentaries—in the newspapers, for example—it is certainly true that excessive attention has been paid to free reserves in judging the posture of monetary policy.

Measures of the reserve position of member banks have long occupied a prominent position as indicators of credit conditions and as guides to policy in the thinking of Federal Reserve officials. Originally, in the 1920s, primary emphasis was placed on member bank borrowing; the argument was that since member banks were reluctant to be in debt to the Federal Reserve, open market sales of securities, by reducing the volume of unborrowed reserves, would force the banks to borrow, and as their borrowing increased they would tighten lending standards and raise interest rates on loans. According to this view, causation ran from borrowings to market interest rates. Later on, primarily as a result of the vast increase in excess reserves in the 1930s, the doctrine was reformulated, using free reserves instead of borrowings as a measure of the reserve position of member banks. Nevertheless, essentially the same reasoning continued to be applied: a decline in free reserves (stemming mainly from an increase in borrowings such as might be induced by open market sales) would cause interest rates to rise and credit to tighten. Thus a decline in free reserves was unambiguously a sign of tighter credit; and, conversely, an increase in free reserves was an indication of easier credit.

Recent theoretical and empirical work has cast serious doubt on this simplistic view of the role of free reserves. It now appears that instead of causation running from free reserves to interest rates, it is primarily the other way around. That is, as market interest rates rise, with the Federal Reserve discount rate remaining constant, banks have an incentive to borrow more from the Federal Reserve to take advantage of the favorable climate for lending and investing, thereby causing free reserves to decline. Although the response of the banks may be constrained by their reluctance to be in debt and by the Federal Reserve's opposition to excessive or continuous borrowing by member banks, it is nevertheless present. On the other hand, if the discount rate is raised, the increase in the cost of borrowing in relation to the returns available on loans and investments will cause the banks to reduce their borrowings, causing free reserves to increase.

It may be noted that it is this tendency for free reserves to decline as market interest rates rise and to increase as interest rates fall that underlies the interest-elasticity of the money supply, as explained in the paper by Ronald Teigen on the demand for and supply of money in Chapter 1 of this book (reading 2). This in turn makes the change in the money supply occurring in response to an open market purchase or sale of securities by the Federal Reserve smaller than it would otherwise be. The "money multiplier" presented in Teigen's paper (equation (20) on page 74) is

$$\frac{\Delta M}{\Delta R^*} = \frac{1}{g(1 - h - n) + n + ts} \left[\frac{1}{1 - \dfrac{\eta_{M \cdot r}}{\eta_{L \cdot r}}} \right].$$

Here ΔM is the change in the stock of money (demand deposits and currency), ΔR^* is the change in the Federal Reserve's portfolio of U.S. government securities, g is the reserve requirement for member bank demand deposits, h is the marginal ratio of nonmember bank demand deposits to the money stock, n is the marginal ratio of currency to the money stock, t is the reserve requirement for time deposits, s is the marginal ratio of time deposits to the money stock, $\eta_{M \cdot r}$ is the interest elasticity of the supply of money, and $\eta_{L \cdot r}$ is the interest elasticity of the demand for money. As shown in the appendix to Teigen's paper (equation (A.36), page 81), this can be converted to

$$\frac{\Delta M}{\Delta R^*} = \frac{1}{g(1 - h - n) + n + ts + \dfrac{R^f}{M}\left(\dfrac{\eta_{R^f \cdot r}}{\eta_{L \cdot r}}\right)},$$

where R^f is free reserves, and $\eta_{R^f \cdot r}$ is the interest elasticity of the banks' demand for free reserves. It is clear that an increase in the value of $\eta_{R^f \cdot r}$ will increase the denominator of this expression, thereby reducing $\Delta M / \Delta R^*$. If $\eta_{R^f \cdot r}$ is zero, the expression reduces to a multiplier of the standard type appearing in orthodox textbook discussions of credit expansion.

With free reserves sensitive to interest rates in the manner indicated, it is not correct to view changes in the level of free reserves as a dependable indicator of changes in monetary policy. For example, as pointed out in Smith's paper on the instruments of credit control, credit tightening brought about by open market sales will generally be associated with a fall in free reserves, but credit tightening caused by a rise in the discount rate will be associated with an increase in free reserves.

Furthermore, free reserves may be a seriously misleading indicator of monetary policy, especially in recession periods. If a decline in private demand for goods and services causes a decline in production, employment, and income, there is almost certain to be a fall in credit demand, which will cause interest rates to drop even if the Federal Reserve takes no positive action to expand credit. Such a fall in interest rates is a species of automatic monetary stabilizer, which will help somewhat in checking the decline in income and employment, although it can hardly reverse the decline and start the economy moving upward again. When market interest rates fall relative to the discount rate—which is usually not adjusted downward nearly as rapidly as market rates decline—banks will reduce their borrowings from the Federal Reserve, thus causing free reserves to increase. If observers take the rise in free reserves to be a sign that an actively easier monetary policy is being followed, they will be seriously misled. Indeed, since reduced borrowings cause total reserves and therefore the supply of money and credit to decline, monetary conditions will not ease as much as they would have if the decline in interest rates had not produced an increase in free reserves.

It may be noted that the same problem exists in connection with the use of interest rates as a guide to policy, since, as pointed out above, a decline in private demand will cause interest rates to fall. Unless they are careful, the authorities may take the decline in interest rates as an indication that monetary policy has actively become easier when all that has in fact occurred is a passive response of interest rates to a decline in private demand. This does not mean that interest rates are of no value as a guide to policy. Indeed, since as is shown in Chapter 5, there is considerable evidence that changes in interest rates and associated changes in credit availability are one of the important linkages through which the effects of monetary policy are transmitted to the all-important real sector of the economy, it is appropriate for the authorities to place considerable emphasis on interest rates as a guide to the conduct of policy.

At the same time, however, it is certainly desirable to pay some attention to the money supply, for several reasons. For one thing, the tendency of the banks to repay borrowings at the Federal Reserve as interest rates decline causes total reserves and the money supply to fall in the absence of Federal Reserve action when private demand decreases. Thus, if the Federal Reserve makes sure that the rate of growth of the money supply increases when a recession sets in, it has some assurance that it is acting positively to induce recovery. The fact that the money supply has fairly commonly declined—or at least its rate of growth has decelerated—during recession periods makes one wonder whether the Federal Reserve may not at times have been misled by excessive emphasis on free reserves or interest rates into believing it was following an actively easy monetary policy when it was not in fact doing so. Another reason for using the money stock as an intermediate target, which is particularly relevant for periods of significant price change, is that in such periods market interest rates have built into them an expected price change component. For example, if it is expected that prices will rise at a 4 percent rate per year, then the "real" equivalent of a 7 percent market yield on a security with a year to maturity is 3 percent. The logical interest rate target for the monetary authorities would be the "real" rate, since that is likely to be the one which affects spending decisions. However, expectations vary among individuals and firms, and it is difficult for the authorities to know what the "real" rate is.

Considerations such as these, as well as the influence of monetarism with its insistence on the importance of variations in the money stock, have led the Federal Reserve System to shift its emphasis over the past few years from almost exclusive reliance on indicators of money market conditions, such as free reserves and interest rates, to a method of operation which gives considerable importance to the growth rate of monetary aggregates, particularly over periods longer than a few weeks or months. The first shift in this direction occurred in 1966, when a "proviso clause" was inserted into the instructions to the open market trading desk, permitting deviation from the desired money-market conditions if bank credit appeared to be growing too fast or too slowly.

In mid-1970s, the Federal Reserve System's Open Market Committee began to concern itself with the rates at which the narrowly-defined money stock, or M_1, and the "bank credit proxy" were growing. In 1971, the Open Market Committee also began to monitor the growth of M_2, a somewhat broader money-stock measure, and growth targets for all of these aggregates were established; and in 1972, the growth of reserves available to support private deposits, or RPD, was added to the list.[1] It was hoped that RPD growth would become the most useful short-run guide for policy, and the Federal Reserve began to establish "tolerance ranges" for the RPD growth rate—the range of short-run values thought to be consistent with longer-run targets—covering the current and the succeeding

---

[1] Following are the definitions of the monetary aggregates referred to in this discussion: M_1 is demand deposits at commercial banks (except domestic interbank deposits and U.S. government deposits), less cash items in process of collection and Federal Reserve float. M_2 is M_1 plus savings and time deposits at commercial banks (except very large, negotiable certificates of deposit). M_3 is M_2 plus mutual savings bank deposits, savings and loan shares, and credit union shares. The bank credit proxy is total member bank deposits subject to reserve requirements, plus certain other items. Reserves available to support private deposits are total member bank reserves less reserves required for government and interbank deposits.

month. The Open Market Committee finally decided, early in 1976, to discontinue use of the RPD growth rate as a policy guide; but the practice of defining short-run tolerance ranges for other variables—both the growth rates of certain aggregates, and the federal funds rate—has continued to the present. The tolerance range for the federal funds rate defines the set of values which is thought to be consistent with the longer-run growth rate targets for the aggregates, and movements of the rate within this range are watched carefully as an indication of the demand for and supply of bank reserves.

In March 1975, Congress passed House Concurrent Resolution 133, which directed the Federal Reserve System to report its plans regarding rates of growth for monetary aggregates to Congress on a regular basis. This development led the System to begin to formulate its longer-run M_1, M_2, and M_3 targets in terms of growth-rate ranges, and such target ranges now are set and reported to Congress each quarter to cover the coming one-year period. An overall view of the procedures followed by the Federal Reserve in setting and attempting to realize these target ranges is provided in the paper by Richard G. Davis (reading 13). The next two papers examine the strengths and weaknesses of the present system, and discuss some alternatives. In his paper (reading 14), Henry C. Wallich discusses in some detail the properties of the different aggregates for which growth rate target ranges are defined, the use of short-run tolerance ranges along with the one-year target ranges, and the question of interest rates versus aggregates as a focus of policy. In the following paper (reading 15), William Poole deals mainly with the problem of "base drift" mentioned by Wallich. As Poole points out, the Federal Reserve's current practice of setting its target ranges anew each quarter based on newly-available data on the aggregates tends to foster irregularity in money growth rates—that is, it makes possible the kind of "stop-and-go" policy which attention to growth rates was intended to minimize— and also might inadvertently result in the current policy targets for a given quarter being inconsistent with the target set in some past quarter. He suggests defining the growth targets in such a way that the base essentially would be kept constant.

It is a way of life with policymakers to be operating with uncertainties of all kinds. Some of these are discussed in the papers by Davis, Wallich, and Poole: for example, they describe the difficulties for monetary growth rate targets caused by periodic data revisions and seasonal adjustment procedures. There are also uncertainties of a much more fundamental type facing the policymaker, such as those relating to the true structure of the system. If this structure were known, policymaking would be easy. Intermediate targets could be dispensed with, and policy could be brought directly to bear on target levels of income, employment, and so on. But since there is uncertainty about the exact linkages between the instruments of policy and the ultimate targets, intermediate targets are selected and pursued. Davis mentions the difficulties caused by slippages in the relationships between money and the economy over time, and in the paper by William Poole in Chapter 5 (reading 30), it is shown that the choice of an intermediate target should be influenced by the relative degree of uncertainty about the structures of the monetary and real sectors of the economy.

The findings of recent research to the effect that free reserve levels are sensitive to interest rates also suggest that perhaps monetary policy could be made more effective if a different approach to discount administration were employed. Relying on the reluctance theory of member bank borrowing, the System has not attempted to make the discount rate a "penalty rate"—that is, has not kept it consistently higher than the interest rates the banks could earn by investing borrowed funds. If the profit motive governs member bank borrowing at least partially, however, the discount window as presently managed may constitute a serious offset to open market policy. This question is discussed in Smith's article on the instruments of monetary control (reading 12), which also contains a comparison of open market operations, the discount rate, and reserve-requirement variation in terms of their relative usefulness in achieving policy goals and a discussion of their proper coordination.

12. THE INSTRUMENTS OF GENERAL MONETARY CONTROL*

Warren L. Smith

I. INTRODUCTION

At the present, the Federal Reserve System possesses three major instruments of general monetary control: the power to buy and sell securities in the open market; the power to fix discount rates and regulate other conditions of member bank borrowing; and the power to change within specified limits the reserve requirements of member banks. This paper deals with the relative usefulness of these three credit-control instruments and with problems of their proper coordination.[1]

II. THE PRIMACY OF OPEN MARKET OPERATIONS

Nearly all students of American monetary affairs would probably agree that open market operations constitute the primary weapon of monetary policy. The initiative with respect to such operations lies firmly in the hands of the Federal Reserve System, and the weapon possesses great flexibility with respect to both timing and magnitude. That is, operations can be used to produce large or small changes in credit conditions, and the direction of operations can be changed almost instantaneously.

In addition to their use to control credit in the interest of economic stability and growth, open market operations are carried on continuously for the purpose of offsetting the short-run effects on member bank reserves resulting from factors outside the control of the Federal Reserve—changes in float, currency in circulation, gold stock, Treasury and foreign deposits at the Reserve banks, and so on. These operations, which have been increasingly perfected in recent years, serve the important function of maintaining an even keel in the central money market. They also act as a kind of camouflage which frequently makes it rather difficult to discern and interpret the longer-run objectives of System policy as reflected in open market operations. Thus, since open market operations are generally going on continuously and are directed at the accomplishment of a rather complex variety of objectives, they are relatively free from the psychological overtones (sometimes called "announcement effects") that frequently accompany changes in discount rates or in reserve requirements. For reasons that will be explained below, I believe this absence of psychological implications is a rather important advantage of open market operations.

To the extent of its net purchases or sales of Government securities, the Federal Reserve changes not only the supply of bank reserves but the amount of interest-bearing Federal debt held by the public. In addition, by varying its purchases and sales in various maturity sectors of the market, it can influence the maturity composition of the publicly-held debt and, to some extent at least, the term-structure of interest rates. Thus, open market operations are a form of debt

* From *National Banking Review*, vol. 1 (September 1963), pp. 47–76. Reprinted by permission of the publisher. The late Warren L. Smith was Professor of Economics, University of Michigan.

[1] In addition to the three general credit-control instruments, the System has from time to time employed selective controls, including the regulation of consumer and real estate credit. At the present time, however, the only important selective control power that the System has is the authority to regulate margin requirements applicable to loans for purchasing and carrying securities. This paper makes no effort to deal with the uses of selective controls or their coordination with general controls.

management. They should be closely co-ordinated with the Treasury's debt management decisions concerning the maturities of securities to issue or retire in its cash borrowing, refunding, and debt retirement operations.

For a period of about, eight years beginning in March 1953, the Federal Open Market Committee, which is responsible for the conduct of System open market operations, adhered to the so-called "bills-only" policy, the key feature of which was that open market operations for the purpose of effectuating stabilizing monetary policy were confined to short-term securities, chiefly Treasury bills. Early in 1961, this policy was altered to a more flexible one which permitted operations in all maturity ranges of the U.S. Government securities market.[2] The primary reason for the 1961 change in policy was the emergence of a serious balance of payments deficit partly caused by substantial outflows of short-term capital to foreign money centers at a time when the domestic economy was suffering from substantial unemployment and underutilization of productive capacity.

Although System open market purchases of longer-term securities have actually been quite modest since early 1961, the greater flexibility of open market policy, together with associated shifts in the conduct of Treasury debt management activities, has undoubtedly helped to make it possible to maintain and even increase U.S. short-term interest rates in line with those abroad, thus preventing excessive outflows of short-term funds, while at the same time preventing increases in the long-term bond yields and mortgage interest rates which influence plant and equipment expenditures, capital outlays of State and local governments, and housing construction.[3]

Open market operations are firmly established as the fundamental weapon of monetary policy in the United States. Accordingly, the important questions concerning the proper coordination of monetary control instruments really have to do with the extent to which the other weapons—discount policy and reserve requirements policy—should be used to supplement (and perhaps in certain special circumstances to replace) upon market operations. Let us begin by considering discount policy.

III. THE ROLE OF DISCOUNT POLICY

For many years prior to the Treasury–Federal Reserve Accord of March 1951, the amount of member bank borrowing from the Reserve banks was negligible. Throughout the later 1930s, the volume of excess reserves was continuously so large that it was seldom necessary for member banks to borrow. And during World War II, the Federal Reserve kept the banks amply supplied with reserves through open market operations so that there was little occasion for borrowing. The atrophied state of the discount mechanism is indicated by the fact that, for the entire period 1934 to 1943, member bank borrowing averaged less than one-tenth of 1 percent of total member bank reserves.

Since the Accord, the volume of borrowing has increased, especially during periods of credit restraint when the reserves of member banks have been under pressure. The Federal Reserve has encouraged this revival of the discount mechanism and has attempted to restore the discount rate to the important role it is supposed to have played in monetary policy prior to the 1930s.[4] But while member bank borrowing has increased in magnitude since the Accord, it is still very much less important as a source of reserves than it was in the 1920s. From 1951 to 1959, borrow-

---

[2] The changes were made at the meetings of the Federal Open Market Committee on February 7 and March 28, 1961. See the Record of Policy Actions of the Federal Open Market Committee in the *Annual Report* of the Board of Governors of the Federal Reserve System covering the year 1961, pp. 39–43 and 54–55.

[3] In addition to open market operations and debt management, other policy actions have helped to "twist" the interest-rate structure; i.e., to raise short-term rates while exerting as much downward pressure as possible on long-term rates. The increase in interest-rate ceilings applicable to time deposits by the Federal Reserve and the FDIC at the beginning of 1962 enabled U.S. commercial banks to compete more effectively with foreign banks for deposits and also attracted an enlarged supply of funds into time deposits—funds which were largely channelled into mortgages and State and local government securities, thus bringing down yields on such securities. And

the reduction of reserve requirements on time deposits from 5 to 4 percent in October and November 1962, combined with action to sustain Treasury bill yields, undoubtedly also helped to some extent.

[4] In connection with the Accord itself, the Treasury and the Federal Reserve agreed upon the desirability of reviving the discount mechanism as a means for making adjustments in bank reserve positions. See the identical statements concerning the Accord by the Secretary of the Treasury and the Chairman of the Board of Governors in *Monetary Policy and Management of the Public Dept–Replies to Questions and Other Materials for the Use of the Subcommittee on General Credit Control and Debt Management* (Joint Committee on the Economic Report, 82nd Cong., 2nd sess.) (Washington, D.C.: U.S. Government Printing Office, 1952), Part I, pp. 74–76 and 349–51.

ing averaged 3.2 percent of total member bank reserves with average borrowings reaching peak levels of approximately 4½ percent of total reserves in the years 1957 and 1959, when monetary policy was relatively tight.[5] In contrast, during the period 1922 to 1929, borrowing averaged 30.0 percent of total reserves, with the ratio rising as high as 40 percent in 1923 and 1929.

A. The Discount Rate as a Cost Factor

It is possible to distinguish two main facets of Federal Reserve discount policy. In the first place, the discount rate represents the cost of borrowed reserves, and the rate is changed from time to time for the purpose of regulating member bank borrowing. Changes in the rate for this purpose should be co-ordinated as closely as possible with open market operations. In addition, however, the discount rate at times plays an independent role in monetary policy, serving as a signal to the economy of changes in Federal Reserve policy. Let us first consider the discount rate as a regulator of member bank borrowing.

1. Cost versus "Reluctance" as a Regulator of Borrowing. Due to the organization of the banking and financial system in the United States, it has not been feasible to establish the discount rate as a "penalty rate" in the sense in which this has been the case in Britain. There a penalty rate has been possible because the discount houses rather than the banks have customarily done the borrowing from the Bank of England. Since the discount houses have made a practice of carrying quite homogeneous portfolios of commercial bills and, in recent years, Treasury bills, it has been feasible to keep the Bank rate above the yield on such bills, so that when the discount houses are "forced into the bank" (as the phrase goes), they lose money on their borrowings. Traditionally, this penalty rate has served to keep borrowing from the Bank of England to a minimum and to make the interest rate structure highly sensitive to monetary action carried out through the co-ordinated use of open market operations and the discount rate.[6]

In the United States, member banks borrow directly from the Reserve banks, and since there are very many member banks operating in numerous local and regional, as well as national, credit markets and investing in a great variety of earning assets bearing a wide range of yields, it is not feasible to maintain a true penalty rate.[7]

Since the 1920s, it has come to be widely accepted doctrine that use of the System's discount facilities is restrained by a tradition against borrowing on the part of member banks.[8] As evidence in support of this view, which has come to be known as the "reluctance theory," it was pointed out that in the 1920s open market interest rates were more closely related to the amount of outstanding member bank borrowing than they were to the discount rate, suggesting that member banks did not like to be in debt and, when they were, tended to liquidate secondary reserve assets in order to repay their borrowings, thus forcing up open market interest rates.[9]

Although the purposes for which banks borrow —to maintain their reserve positions in the face of customer withdrawals or clearing drains and to meet temporary (e.g., seasonal) increases in their customers' demands for loans—are commonly so pressing as probably to be quite cost-inelastic, it does not follow that member bank borrowing is insensitive to the discount rate. Banks have a choice of obtaining additional funds by borrowing at the Federal Reserve or by liquidating secondary reserves or other investment securities. Given a certain "reluctance to borrow," the major factor influencing the choice

[5] Editor's note: From 1960 to 1969, borrowings averaged 1.8 percent of member bank reserves, and from 1970 to 1976, they averaged 2.4 percent. The percentage rose as high as 4.0 percent in 1969, 5.0 percent in 1973, and 5.6 percent in 1974. It fell to 0.6 percent in 1975, and 0.2 percent in 1976.

[6] For a good recent discussion, see R. S. Sayers, *Modern Banking*, 4th ed., (Oxford: Clarendon Press, 1958), pp. 104–14. As indicated by Sayers, both the indirect nature of the relation between the commercial banks and the Bank of England and the penal

Bank rate have become somewhat attenuated in recent years, as the Bank has developed the alternative practice of supplying funds to the discount houses and in some cases to the commercial banks themselves by purchasing Treasury bills at the market rate.

[7] In order to be a penalty rate with respect to a particular bank, the rate does not need to be higher than the expected return on all of the bank's earning assets. In fact, in a sense, it is a penalty rate if it is higher than the expected return on the lowest yielding assets in the bank's portfolio. However, the discount rate can be a penalty rate in this sense in relation to some banks and not others, due to differences in the composition of the banks' portfolios.

[8] This argument was advanced in W. W. Riefler, *Money Rates and Money Markets in the United States* (New York: Harper & Bros., 1930), esp. chap. ii. According to Riefler, the tradition against borrowing existed among commercial banks prior to the formation of the Federal Reserve System and was strengthened during the 1920s by the System's discouragement of borrowing for other than temporary purposes.

[9] Ibid., pp. 25–28; also W. R. Burgess, *The Reserve Banks and the Money Market,* rev. ed., (New York: Harper & Bros., 1946), pp. 219–21.

will presumably be the relevant cost of funds obtained by the various methods, and this depends chiefly on the relation between the discount rate and the yield on assets that the bank might liquidate. In principle, the relevant comparison is between the discount rate and the expected yield on the asset whose liquidation is being considered over the period of time for which the funds will be needed, taking account of any capital gains or losses that may be involved. For instance, if interest rates are expected to fall during the period, the relevant interest rate for comparison with the discount rate may be higher than the current interest rate on the asset. This factor will be more important the longer the maturity of the asset.[10]

Thus, there is little doubt that commercial banks are "reluctant" to borrow in the sense that borrowing is felt to involve a form of disutility. However, the banks' reluctance can be overcome provided that the profits to be obtained from borrowing (as compared with other means of obtaining reserves) are sufficiently attractive— that is, banks balance the disutility of borrowing against the utility of further profits.[11] Moreover, not all banks are equally reluctant to borrow:[12] this is evidenced by the fact that the Federal Reserve has found it necessary to discourage "continuous borrowing" and to bolster the banks' reluctance in its regulations covering discounts and advances.[13] In addition, the System keeps the borrowing practices of individual member banks under constant surveillance and in this way attempts to reinforce the banks' reluctance to

borrow. At the same time, the System apparently does not unequivocally refuse to lend to member banks, despite the fact that it has authority to do so under the Federal Reserve Act.[14]

2. Coordination of Open Market Operations and Discount Policy. It used to be said with reference to monetary policy in the 1920s that open market operations served the function of making the discount rate effective.[15] In order to implement a restrictive monetary policy, the Federal Reserve would sell Government securities in the open market; this would put pressure on member bank reserve positions and cause them to increase their borrowings. At this point the discount rate would be raised, and the increase in borrowings was supposed to help to insure that the discount rate increase would be transmitted through into an increase in other interest rates.[16]

In view of the primary role of open market operations under present conditions, it is better to look at the matter the other way around and to say that the discount rate can be used to support and strengthen the effectiveness of open market operations. Thus, when the System, for example, wishes to implement a restrictive policy during a period of inflation, it uses open market operations to keep down the supply of reserves in relation to the swelling demands for credit. As a result, interest rates rise and member banks, finding their reserve positions under increased pressure, tend to increase their borrowings from the Reserve banks. In order to discourage the creation of additional reserves through borrowing, the System can raise the discount rate in pace with the increase of other interest rates. Thus the discount rate can be used to supplement and strengthen open market operations. Conversely, when the System desires to ease credit

[10] See W. L. Smith, "The Discount Rate as a Credit-Control Weapon," *Journal of Political Economy,* vol. 66 (April 1958), pp. 171–77; Ralph Young, "Tools and Processes of Monetary Policy," in N. H. Jacoby, *United States Monetary Policy* (New York: The American Assembly, Columbia University, 1958), pp. 13–48, esp. pp. 26–27.

[11] For a systematic development of this point of view, together with some evidence to support it, see the interesting article by M. E. Polakoff, "Reluctance Elasticity, Least Cost, and Member-Bank Borrowing: A Suggested Integration," *Journal of Finance,* vol. 15 (March 1960), pp. 1–18.

[12] On this, see Lauchlin Currie, *The Supply and Control of Money in the United States* (Cambridge: Harvard University Press, 1935), chap. viii.

[13] See Regulation A of the Board of Governors regulating member bank borrowing as revised effective February 15, 1955 (*Federal Reserve Bulletin,* January 1955, pp. 8–14). The Foreword to the revised Regulation contains a statement of "General Principles" (pp. 8–9) which attempts to delineate in a general way the purposes for which member banks should and should not use the System's discount facilities.

[14] On the subtleties of nonprice rationing in the administration of the discount window, see C. R. Whittlesey, "Credit Policy at the Discount Window"; R. V. Roosa, "Credit Policy at the Discount Window: Comment"; and Whittlesey, "Reply," *Quarterly Journal of Economics,* vol. 73 (May 1959), pp. 207–16, and 333–38.

[15] Burgess, *op. cit., p.* 239.

[16] This is rather similar to the classical British practice of selling in the open market to reduce the cash reserves of the commercial banks. To replenish their cash reserves, the banks would call some of their loans to the discount houses. The discount houses, in turn, would be forced to borrow from the Bank of England at the (penalty) Bank rate, and as a result of the ensuing adjustments bill rates would be forced up. Thus, open market operations were said to have the function of "forcing the market into the Bank."

conditions, it provides additional reserves through open market operations, and in order to discourage member banks from using a portion of the new reserves to repay indebtedness at the Reserve banks, the discount rate can be lowered.[17]

A variant of this reasoning which stresses the reluctance of member banks rather than the discount rate has also been expressed by persons connected with the Federal Reserve System. According to this view, most member bank borrowing arises out of the fact that in a unit banking system such as ours with a very large number of banks, individual banks often find their reserve positions unexpectedly depleted as a result of unfavorable clearing balances associated with redistribution of reserves among the banks. Borrowing is a handy means of making temporary adjustments in reserve positions; if the depletion of a bank's reserve position lasts very long, the bank may later adjust by liquidating secondary reserves, using the proceeds to repay its borrowing at the Reserve bank.[18] The pressure on banks to make prompt adjustments in portfolios in order to repay borrowing depends on the level of the discount rate in relation to other interest rates.

At times when monetary policy is tight and the Federal Reserve is maintaining pressure on bank reserve positions in the interest of limiting excessive growth of bank credit, more banks will be managing their reserve positions closely, reserve deficiencies will occur more frequently, and member bank borrowing will increase.[19] Due to

the fact that the banks are reluctant to borrow, the increase in borrowing causes them to adopt more cautious lending policies and to reduce the availability of credit. However, since banks balance the disutility of borrowing against the utility of increased profits, it is necessary to make successive upward adjustments in the discount rate as interest rates rise due to the effects of the restrictive policy, in order to stiffen the banks' reluctance to remain in debt and to encourage them to contract their loans and investments.

It may be noted, however, that short-term open market interest rates are subject to a considerable amount of random variation in the short run and that, under present arrangements, the discount rate is only changed at irregular and rather infrequent intervals. For this reason, the differential between the discount rate and other interest rates varies rather erratically. This is apparent from Chart 1, which shows the movements of the discount rate and the yield on outstanding Treasury bills since 1953. As a result of the continuously shifting relation between the discount rate and other interest rates, the willingness of banks to borrow presumably undergoes considerable erratic variation.

3. *Does Borrowing Reinforce or Offset Open Market Operations?* There has been some discussion as to whether the increase in member bank borrowing that occurs during a period of credit restriction is a factor which intensifies the restrictive effects or a loophole which weakens the effectiveness of monetary policy.[20] It is almost certainly true that, as a result of the reluctance of member banks to borrow, banks tend to follow somewhat more restrictive and cautious policies as far as loans are concerned when they are in debt to the Reserve banks than when they are not in debt. However, the important thing to bear in mind is that if banks were constrained not to borrow when their reserve positions were impaired by a restrictive policy, they would have to adjust their reserve positions in some other way. This would ordinarily mean contraction of loans or investments.[21] Thus, in the absence of

[17] See the statement of the Chairman of the Board of Governors concerning the relation between the discount rate and open market operations in *United States Monetary Policy: Recent Thinking and Experience* (Hearings before the Subcommittee on Economic Stabilization of the Joint Committee on the Economic Report, 83rd Cong., 2d sess.) (Washington, D.C.: U.S. Government Printing Office, 1954), p. 11. A similar view is suggested in C. E. Walker, "Discount Policy in the Light of Recent Experience," *Journal of Finance*, vol. 12 (May 1957), pp. 223–37, esp. pp. 232–34.

[18] Roosa, *op. cit.*, p. 335.

[19] Ibid., p. 336. A similar argument is presented by Young, *op. cit.*, who says (p. 34): "As a policy of monetary restraint continues or is accentuated, there will be more frequent and more widespread reserve drains among member banks. This will lead an increasing number of banks to borrow temporarily at the discount window of the Reserve Banks in order to maintain their legal reserve positions. For each bank, the borrowing will be temporary, but the repayment by one bank draws reserves from other banks, which in turn will have need to borrow at a Reserve Bank. Thus, restrictive monetary action leads to a larger volume of member bank borrowings, as more banks find their reserve positions under pressure more often."

[20] Roosa seems to imply that it has an intensifying effect ("Credit Policy at the Discount Window," *op. cit.*). Whittlesey ("Credit Policy at the Discount Window," and "Reply" [to Roosa's comment], *op. cit.*) contends that it is an offset, although not, under present conditions, a very important one.

[21] Another possibility is that banks might make greater use of the Federal funds market to adjust their reserves. Although use of this market has increased in recent years, the number of participating banks is still rather small, and there are technical impediments to a substantial increase. (See *The Fed-*

Chart 1:   Federal Reserve Discount Rates and Market Yield on Treasury Bills, 1953–1962

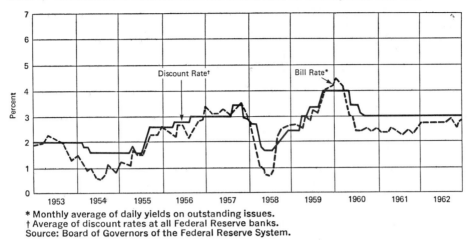

* Monthly average of daily yields on outstanding issues.
† Average of discount rates at all Federal Reserve banks.
Source: Board of Governors of the Federal Reserve System.

borrowing, the adjustment would itself *consist in* restricting credit. On the other hand, to the extent that borrowing occurs, restrictive effects are postponed and banks are merely put in such a position that they are somewhat more likely to restrict credit at some future time. Moreover, it should be noted that borrowing by one member bank for the purpose of adjusting its reserve position adds to the *aggregate* reserves of all member banks and thus indirectly takes some of the pressure off other banks. Adjustment of reserve positions through liquidations of securities, on the other hand, does not add to the reserves of the system of banks.[22]

Thus, it seems clear that the effect of increased member bank borrowing at a time when a restrictive policy is being applied is to offset rather than to reinforce the restrictive policy. The effect may not be very important in itself, since the induced increase in borrowing is not likely to be large enough to pose a serious problem for the authorities; it merely means that a somewhat more restrictive open market policy is required than would otherwise be necessary. However,

eral Funds Market [Washington, D.C.: Board of Governors of the Federal Reserve System, 1959]). Increased use of the Federal funds market during periods when credit is being restricted economizes the use of existing reserves, reduces excess reserves, and thereby constitutes an offset to the initial restrictive action (see H. P. Minsky, "Central Banking and Money Market Changes," *Quarterly Journal of Economics,* vol. 71 [May 1957], pp. 171–87). Thus, resort to the Federal funds market has effects similar to member bank borrowing (as explained below).

[22] Smith, "The Discount Rate as a Credit-Control Weapon," *op. cit.,* pp. 172–73; also P. A. Samuelson, "Recent American Monetary Controversy," *Three Banks Review,* March 1956, pp. 10–11.

there are a number of other offsetting reactions in the banking and financial system—such as shifts in the composition of bank portfolios from Government securities to loans, adjustments by financial intermediaries, and so on—and the addition of one more such reaction, even though not quantitatively very large, may not be wholly without significance.

Another point of view that has been expressed concerning the discount mechanism is that, while it has an offsetting effect, this effect is actually helpful to the monetary authorities, because it can be likened to a brake on an automobile. It is said that brakes, by making it possible to control the car more effectively, permit one to drive at a higher rate of speed than would otherwise be possible.[23] Similarly, the discount mechanism, although seeming to weaken monetary controls, actually strengthens them by making it possible to use other controls (chiefly open market operations) more vigorously. However, this is not a proper analogy. If the automobile simile is retained, the discount mechanism is more like a defective clutch than a brake, and few would argue that a slipping clutch makes it possible to drive at a higher rate of speed.[24] A brake is a discretionary weapon and not a device that

[23] P. A. Samuelson, "Reflections on Monetary Policy," *Review of Economics and Statistics,* vol. 42 (August 1960), p. 266.

[24] If the motor were too powerful for the car—e.g., if a Cadillac motor were mounted in a Volkswagen —I suppose a clutch that slipped might be helpful. But the proper analogy for the relation between monetary policy and the stability of the economy may well be just the reverse; i.e., monetary policy can be likened to a Volkswagen motor which has been assigned the task of operating a heavy Cadillac.

Chart 2:   Free Reserves of Member Banks*, 1953–1962

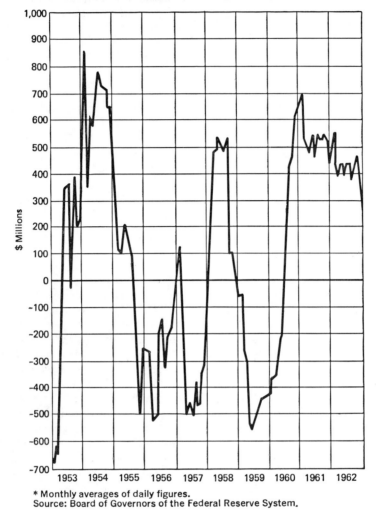

* Monthly averages of daily figures.
Source: Board of Governors of the Federal Reserve System.

automatically operates more intensively, the harder one pushes on the accelerator.

4. A Critique of the Concept of "Free Reserves."   A by-product of the revival of the discount mechanism since the Accord is the emphasis that has been placed on the level of "free reserves" as an immediate guide to System policy. "Free reserves," of course, are simply the difference between aggregate member bank excess reserves and aggregate member bank borrowings. It appears that, increasingly in the last few years, the System has been setting its proximate goals of monetary policy in terms of "target" levels of free reserves. As can be seen from Chart 2, free reserves have been positive (excess reserves greater than borrowings) during periods of credit ease, as in 1943–54, 1958, and 1960–63, while during periods of credit restriction, free reserves

have been negative (i.e., borrowings have been greater than excess reserves, or there have been "net borrowed reserves").[25] It has become commonplace to judge the objective and direction

[25] Editor's note: Borrowings have exceeded excess reserves most of the time from 1965 through 1974. Excess reserves have been greater than borrowing during 1975–1976. The reader should note that the distinction between country banks and reserve city banks regarding reserve requirements and reserve holdings, which was in effect when this paper was written, was done away with for most purposes in 1972 when the Board of Governors made all member banks of a similar size subject to the same reserve requirement, whether they were categorized as a country bank or a reserve city bank. As indicated in the note to Chart 3, the category "central reserve city bank" was abolished in 1962. See the editor's note in footnote 54 for a more detailed description of the 1972 reserve requirement reforms.

Chart 3: Excess Reserves of Member Banks by Reserve Requirement Classifications* 1953–1962

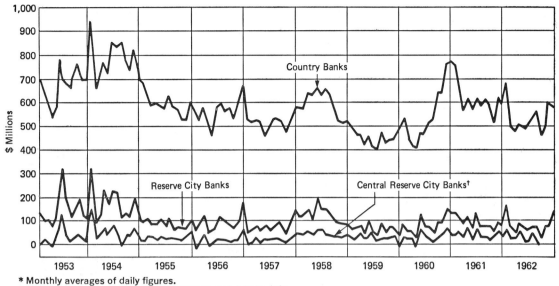

* Monthly averages of daily figures.
† Central Reserve City Classification terminated July 28, 1962.
Source: Board of Governors of the Federal Reserve System.

of monetary policy to a considerable extent by the changes that take place in free reserves.[26]

The first thing to notice about free reserves is that the two components that compose them—excess reserves and borrowings—are distributed quite differently among member banks. Excess reserves tend to be heavily concentrated in the hands of country banks, while most of the borrowing is ordinarily done by reserve city banks. (See Charts 3 and 4.) Country banks tend to hold fairly substantial amounts of excess reserves most of the time, and are able to absorb pressure by drawing down such excess reserves. Reserve city banks, on the other hand, manage their reserve positions more closely, hold relatively small amounts of excess reserves, and borrow more frequently from the Federal Reserve when they are placed under pressure. Of course, these behavior patterns do not coincide exactly with the arbitrary classifications of banks for reserve requirement purposes—some reserve city banks, for example, undoubtedly hold large excess reserve positions closely. Nevertheless, it is quite clear that there are substantial differences among banks with respect to holdings of excess reserves

and reliance on borrowing from the Federal Reserve. And there is no reason to suppose that an increase in borrowings on the part of one group of banks would be exactly offset, insofar as effects on credit conditions are concerned, by an equal increase in holdings of excess reserves by another group of banks. That is to say, for example, that $500 million of net borrowed reserves might have quite different implications depending upon whether it was the resultant of $1.5 billion of borrowings and $1 billion of excess reserves or the resultant of $700 million of borrowings and $200 million of excess reserves.

It should be noted, however, that in practice a very large proportion of the variation in free reserves is attributable to variation in borrowings.[27] The amount of excess reserves is negatively correlated with member bank borrowing; consequently, an increase (decrease) in free reserves is likely to be attributable partly to a decrease (increase) in borrowings and partly to an increase (decrease) in excess reserves. However, as a comparison of Charts 3 and 4 indicates, the variation in borrowings is much greater than the variation in excess reserves; in fact, the variance of borrowings accounts for about 62 percent of the variance of free reserves, whereas the variance of excess reserves accounts for only 7.7 percent, the remainder being attributable to the effects of the negative correlation that exists be-

[26] No matter what the shortcomings of free reserves as a guide to monetary policy, it is appropriate for those who are attempting to judge the character of System policy to pay close attention to this magnitude simply because the System does seem to use it as a guide.

[27] Young, *op. cit.*, p. 35.

Chart 4: Discounts and Advances of Member Banks by Reserve Requirement Classifications*, 1953–1962

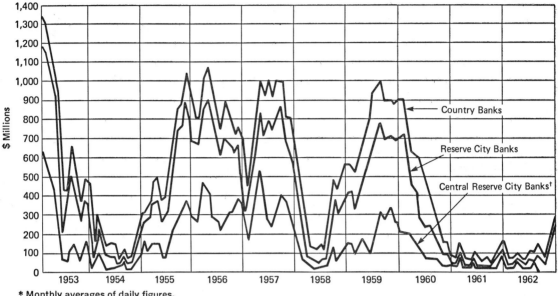

* Monthly averages of daily figures.
† Central Reserve City Classification terminated July 28, 1962.
Source: Board of Governors of the Federal Reserve System.

tween borrowings and excess reserves.[28] This suggests that the behavior of free reserves is largely explained by the behavior of borrowings and that excess reserves are not ordinarily a very important factor.

It was pointed out earlier that the amount of borrowing that member banks will want to do can be expected to depend, among other things, on the relation between the discount rate and other interest rates, which can for our present purposes be represented by the Treasury bill rate. Since borrowing is the main element in free reserves, this suggests that the amount of free reserves member banks will desire to hold will vary

---

[28] Free reserves (R) is given by

$$R = X - B,$$

where X = excess reserves and B = borrowings from Federal Reserve banks. The variance of R is given by

$$\sigma_r^2 = \sigma_x^2 + \sigma_b^2 - 2r_{xb}\sigma_x\sigma_b, \qquad (1)$$

where σ_x^2 = variance of excess reserves, σ_b^2 = variance of borrowings, and r_{xb} is the coefficient of correlation between excess reserves and borrowings. Based on monthly data (averages of daily figures) for the period January 1953, through March 1960, r_{xb} is −.697. Using expression (1) the variance of excess reserves accounts for 7.7 percent of the variance of free reserves, the variance of borrowings accounts for 61.8 percent, and the remaining 30.5 percent is accounted for by the tendency for borrowings to vary inversely with excess reserves (as reflected in the term $-2r_{xb}\sigma_x\sigma_b$).

inversely with the difference between the bill rate and the discount rate. As the bill rate rises relative to the discount rate, banks will tend to increase their borrowings and desired free reserves will fall; conversely, as the bill rate falls in relation to the discount rate, they will tend to repay existing indebtedness to the System, and desired free reserves will rise.[29]

Thus, during a period of credit restriction, as market interest rates rise with the discount rate lagging behind, desired free reserves will decline, and the banks will attempt to reduce actual free reserves. If the Federal Reserve attempts to hold free reserves constant, it will have to adjust its open market policy to increase total reserves, thereby weakening the overall restrictive effect of its policy. Conversely, when economic activity begins to level off in the late stages of an expansion, market interest rates may begin to fall. Under these circumstances, with a given or lagging discount rate, desired free reserves will increase, and if the Federal Reserve attempts to hold free reserves constant, it will have to tighten its open market policy, and the overall

---

[29] This is pointed out by Milton Friedman in *A Program for Monetary Stability* (New York: Fordham University Press, 1959), pp. 41–43. See also the excellent study by R. J. Meigs, *Free Reserves and the Money Supply* (Chicago: University of Chicago Press, 1962).

restrictive effect on monetary policy is likely to become stronger.[30]

This suggests that it is wrong to believe that a constant level of free reserves means a constant degree of credit tightness or ease. At the very least, it would be necessary to adjust the discount rate continuously to the changing level of market rates. Even if this were done, changes in other factors would mean that the effective degree of credit restriction could vary substantially while the level of free reserves was held constant.

Nor is an increase (decrease) in free reserves an unambiguous indication that credit has become easier (tighter). For example, if credit is tightened by raising the discount rate, the rise in the cost of borrowed reserves will cause the banks to reduce their borrowings, making offsetting adjustments in their reserve positions perhaps by selling Treasury bills. Total reserves will decline and interest rates will rise. But this tightening of credit will be accompanied by an increase in free reserves—indeed the increase in free reserves will be the means through which credit-tightening comes about.

On the other hand, if credit is tightened by open market sales of securities while the discount rate remains constant, the resulting rise in the bill rate (and other short-term open market interest rates) will make borrowing relatively more attractive as a means of obtaining reserves. The resulting increase in borrowing will reduce free reserves—thus, a tightening of credit will be associated with a decline in free reserves. But even in this case, the increased borrowing that is reflected in declining free reserves tends to increase total reserves and thereby to offset a portion of the restrictive effect of the initial open market sales.

"Free reserves" is an artificial construct, which has had the unfortunate effect of providing a spuriously exact guide to the monetary authorities—or at least has been so interpreted by persons outside the Federal Reserve System.[31] If the discount rate were regulated in such a way as to maintain a constant differential between it and the Treasury bill rate (a possibility that is discussed below), the amount of free reserves might perhaps become a somewhat better index of credit conditions than it is at present. Even in that case, however, it would commonly be a mistake to assume that a constant level of free reserves would necessarily mean a constant degree of credit tightness or ease. It would be better under most circumstances for the System to set its proximate goals in terms of interest rate behavior and growth of total reserves and to allow free reserves to seek the levels required to achieve these goals.

B. The Discount Rate as a Signal

Thus far, we have been considering changes in the discount rate as an adjunct to open market operations, the purpose of which is to serve as a partial governor of member bank indebtedness by regulating the cost of obtaining reserves by borrowing as compared with sales of secondary reserves.

To some extent, the discount rate also plays an independent role in monetary policy by serving as a signal of the intentions of the monetary authorities. Particularly at turning points in business conditions, a change in the discount rate is often the first clear indication of a basic alteration in monetary policy. Discount rate changes of this kind are said to have psychological effects or "announcement effects," which may influence business conditions by altering the expectations of businessmen and financial institutions.[32]

1. Difficulties of Interpreting Discount Rate Adjustments. It is commonly taken for granted that the announcement effects of discount rate changes are normally such as to strengthen the impact of monetary policy. However, those who advance the expectations argument have not explained in any detail the way in which the expectational effects are supposed to work. Actually, there are several different possible expectational effects, and in the case of each of them there is some uncertainty concerning even the direction (let alone the magnitude) of the effects.

One of the difficulties is that many changes in the discount rate are merely technical adjustments designed to restore or maintain an appropriate relationship between the discount rate and other rates of interest, as indicated above. Most of the periodic adjustments that are made during periods when interest rates are gradually rising or falling are of this nature. However, the interpretation placed on even these rather routine changes is sometimes unpredictable, because their

---

[30] Friedman, *op. cit.,* p. 42.

[31] The fact that the System officials are aware of the shortcomings of the free reserves concept is apparent from the criticisms directed at it by Ralph Young (*op. cit.,* pp. 35–36). Young points out one defect not referred to above—the fact that the amount of free reserves is subject to considerable day-to-day and week-to-week variations, due to unpredictable changes in factors outside the control of the Federal Reserve authorities.

[32] See, for example, Burgess, *op. cit.,* pp. 221–30.

timing may be affected by various considerations not directly related to stabilization policy. Sometimes, for example, discount rate adjustments may be accelerated in order to get the possible accompanying disruptive effects on the securities markets out of the way before an important Treasury debt management operation is scheduled. Or, on the other hand, action may be postponed until the repercussions of a forthcoming debt management operation are out of the way. Furthermore, the very fact that technical adjustments are sometimes interpreted by the public as having policy implications may affect System decisions concerning the timing of such adjustments. Such factors as these not only tend to make the interpretation of discount rate changes difficult, but are also partly responsible for the System's difficulties, referred to earlier, in adjusting the discount rate frequently enough to maintain a reasonably stable relation between that rate and other interest rates.[33]

Partly as a result of erratic timing and partly due to the fact that the business situation is usually fraught with some uncertainty, discount rate changes that are in fact meant to be merely routine adjustments are sometimes endowed with importance as "straws in the wind" regarding System policy by the press and by students of financial and economic affairs. And sometimes even a *failure* to change the discount rate so as to maintain "normal" interest rate relationships is taken as a sign of a change of System policy. Moreover, it is quite common for different commentators to place different interpretations on System action—or even lack of action—with respect to the discount rate.

The truth is that changes in the discount rate constitute the crudest kind of sign language.[34]

Why this Stone Age form of communication should be regarded as superior to ordinary English is really quite difficult to understand. And, in this particular case, the use of such crude signals is subject to a special disadvantage arising from the fact that the signal itself has an objective effect on the situation in addition to serving as a means of communication.' That is, changes in the discount rate combine action and communication, and there may be times when it is proper to act and not speak and other times when it is proper to speak and not act.

It is possible that some of the disadvantages of discretionary discount rate changes could be overcome, if the changes that were made were accompanied, at least under some circumstances, by statements explaining the reasons underlying the action. However, a change in the discount rate requires action by the boards of directors of the Federal Reserve banks and approval by the Board of Governors.[35] As a result, a very large number of persons are involved and the reasons for the action may vary among the different participants—some of whom may not thoroughly approve of the action—thus making it difficult to agree upon a generally acceptable accompanying statement.[36] This raises an interesting ques-

---

[33] As Friedman puts it (*op. cit.*, p. 40): "The discount rate is something that the Federal Reserve must continually change in order to keep the effect of its monetary policy unchanged. But changes in the rate are interpreted as if they meant changes in policy. Consequently, both the System and outsiders are led to misinterpret the System's actions and the System is led to follow policies different from those it intends to follow."

[34] Some writers seem to show no realization of the difficulties involved in this peculiar form of communication. For example, Walker (*op. cit.*, pp. 229–30) says: "Discount policy—particularly with respect to changes in the rate—is a simple and easily understandable technique for informing the market of the monetary authorities' views on the economic and credit situation. Open-market operations, which are used to cushion the effects of seasonal influences as well as for cyclical and growth purposes, may at times be confusing to some observers because the System may be supplying funds to the market . . .

when cyclical developments clearly dictate a restrictive monetary policy, or vice versa. The time-honored device of raising or lowering discount rates, however, can hardly be susceptible to misinterpretation by even the most uninformed observers."

[35] In this connection, see the interesting paper by H. C. Carr, "A Note on Regional Differences in Discount Rates," *Journal of Finance*, vol. 15 (March 1960), pp. 62–68, which uses differences in the timing of discount rate changes on the part of different Reserve banks as a means of classifying the banks as "leaders," "follow-the-leaders," "middle-of-the-roaders," and "dissenters." By studying rate increases and rate decreases separately, he also tries to discern differences in the banks' attitudes toward inflation and deflation.

[36] This is pointed out by Burgess (*op. cit.*), who says: "No reasons for the action are ordinarily given out at the time, partly because the decision represents the views of many people, who have perhaps acted for somewhat diverse reasons, so that it would be an extremely difficult task to phrase a statement which would fairly represent the views of all the directors of the Reserve Bank concerned and the Washington Board; and partly because it would be equally difficult to make any statement which did not either exaggerate or minimize the importance of the change. Such a statement is always subject to misinterpretation, as has been repeatedly illustrated." This statement was written a number of years ago, but it probably still reflects rather accurately the problem involved and the attitudes of those responsible for the administration of the discount rate.

tion: how can the general public and the business community help but be confused in their interpretations of a change in the discount rate when the persons who are responsible for making the change are not themselves entirely clear about the reasons for it?

2. Announcement Effects of Discount Rate Adjustments. In addition to the confusion resulting from the fact that some discount rate adjustments are meant to be signals of a change in monetary policy while others are not, there is a further question whether the resulting announcement effects, even when they are intended, will help to stabilize the economy. Announcement effects work through expectations, and the relationships involved are quite complex. It is possible to break down expectational reactions into reactions of lenders, reactions of borrowers, and reactions of spenders.[37]

a. Expectational Effects on Lenders and Borrowers. A discount rate change may cause shifts in lenders' supply curves of funds and/or in borrowers' demand curves, the nature of these shifts depending upon the kind of expectations prevailing among lenders and borrowers. If interest rate expectations are elastic, a rise (fall) in present interest rates creates expectations of an even larger proportionate rise (fall) in future interest rates, whereas, with inelastic expectations, a rise (fall) in present interest rates induces the expectation of a smaller proportionate rise (fall) in future interest rates.[38]

Let us take the case of a discount rate increase and suppose that initially it causes a rise in market interest rates. If lenders have elastic expectations, they may reduce their present commitments of funds in order to have more funds available

to invest later on, when interest rates are expected to be relatively more favorable. Conversely, if lenders have inelastic expectations, they may increase the amounts of funds they are willing to supply at the present time. Borrowers, on the other hand, may postpone their borrowing if they have inelastic expectations and accelerate it if they have elastic expectations. For a reduction in the discount rate, all of these reactions are reversed.

According to this view, the announcement effects of a discount rate adjustment will be clearly of a stabilizing nature if lenders have elastic expectations and borrowers have inelastic expectations, since in this case an increase in the discount rate will reduce both the demand for and the supply of funds, while a reduction in the discount rate will increase both demand and supply. On the other hand, if lenders have inelastic and borrowers elastic expectations, the effects will be clearly destabilizing, while if both groups have elastic or both have inelastic expectations, the outcome is uncertain and will depend on the relative strengths of the two reactions.[39]

Thus, in order to get favorable reactions on both sides of the market, it is necessary for lenders and borrowers to have the opposite kinds of expectations—a phenomenon that does not seem very likely. However, the significance of all of these considerations is considerably reduced due to the fact that, in practice, their main effects may be confined to producing changes in the interest rate structure. That is, a lender who has elastic interest rate expectations is not very likely to reduce the total supply of funds offered in the market; rather, he is likely to reduce his supply of funds in the longer-term sectors of the market, putting the funds into the short-term sector, while he awaits the expected rise in yields. Or, if he has inelastic expectations, he may shift funds from the short- to the long-term sector. Conversely, a borrower who has elastic expectations may not accelerate his total borrowings, but instead merely increase the proportion of his borrowing in the long-term market. Or, if he has inelastic expectations, he may shift a portion of his borrowings from the long- to the short-

---

[37] Our approach follows that adopted in dealing with the expectational effects of monetary policy in general by Assar Lindbeck in his study entitled *The "New" Theory of Credit Control in the United States,* Stockholm Economics Studies, Pamphlet Series No. 1 (Stockholm: Almquist & Wiksell, 1959), pp. 25–29, and 38–39. To a considerable extent, borrowers and spenders are the same people, of course, but it is useful to consider the two activities separately.

[38] We are using the Hicksian concept of the elasticity of expectations, defined as

$$N = \frac{r_2 - r_1^e}{r_1^e} \bigg/ \frac{r_2 - r_1}{r_1},$$

where r_1 and r_2 stand for the present interest rate before and after the change, r_1^e and r_2^e stand for the expected future interest rate before and after the change. Elastic expectations, as the term is used above, means $N > 1$, while inelastic expectations means $N < 1$. See J. R. Hicks, *Value and Capital* 2d ed. (Oxford: Clarendon Press, 1946), chap. xvi.

[39] In the case of an increase in the discount rate, if both lenders and borrowers have elastic expectations, lenders will reduce their offerings of funds while borrowers will increase their demands. If both have inelastic expectations, lenders will increase their supplies and borrowers will reduce their demands. In each of these cases, the outcome will depend upon the relative magnitudes of the respective shifts of demand and supply, as well as on the interest elasticities of demand and of supply.

term market.[40] With our present limited knowledge concerning the effects of changes in the structure of interest rates on the level of expenditures, it is impossible to judge the effects of such shifts in the supply and demand for funds between the long- and short-term markets. It does seem safe to conclude, however, that the effects would not be very important.

b. Expectational Effects on Spenders. A discount rate adjustment may affect not only interest rate expectations of lenders and borrowers but also the sales and price expectations of businessmen on which spending plans are based. However, it is not entirely clear what the nature of these effects would be or how they would affect economic stability. Taking the case of an increase in the discount rate, two situations (doubtless there are many variants of these) may be distinguished to illustrate the possibilities.

First, if inflationary expectations were already widespread and quite firmly established, if the possibility of restrictive anti-inflationary action by the Federal Reserve had not adequately been taken into account in the formation of these expectations, and if there was widespread confidence that monetary policy was capable of bringing inflation promptly and firmly under control, then a rise in the discount rate heralding the onset of a vigorously anti-inflationary monetary policy might have a bearish effect on sales and price expectations and thereby cause cutbacks and cancellations of expenditure plans. In

---

[40] If lenders have elastic and borrowers inelastic expectations, both demand and supply will tend to shift from the long- to the short-term market following a rise in the discount rate, and the shifts will tend to cancel each other out as far as their effects on the interest rate structure are concerned. It may be noted that the typical behavior of the interest rate structure is consistent with the hypothesis that both borrowers and lenders have inelastic expectations, since in this case (with a rise in the discount rate), demand would shift from the long- to the short-term market while supply would shift from the short- to the long-term market and these reactions would cause a rise in short-term interest rates relative to long-term rates. When rates are generally high, short-term rates actually do often tend to be higher than long-term rates. This is also consistent with the behavior postulated by the general expectational theory of the interest rate structure when expectations are inelastic, as set forth in Tibor Scitovsky, "A Study of Interest and Capital," *Economica*, vol. 7, n.s. (August 1940), pp. 293–317; see also F. A. Lutz, "The Structure of Interest Rates," *Quarterly Journal of Economics*, vol. 55 (November 1940), pp. 36–63, reprinted in W. Fellner and B. F. Haley, eds., *Readings in the Theory of Income Distribution,* (Homewood, Ill.: Richard D. Irwin, Inc., 1946), pp. 499–529.

this case, the announcement effects would be helpful to the authorities.

Second, if the outlook was somewhat uncertain but shifting in an inflationary direction, if observers were unaware of the Federal Reserve's concern about the situation and were waiting to see whether the System would act, and if—perhaps on the basis of past experience—it was felt that monetary policy (even though potentially effective) would take considerable time to be brought to bear effectively enough to check the inflation, then a rise in the discount rate might have a bullish effect by confirming the emerging view that the near-term outlook was inflationary. In this case the announcement effects would be destabilizing.

Similar alternative expectational reactions could be postulated in the case of a reduction in the discount rate for the purpose of stimulating business activity. Although it is difficult to generalize concerning such matters and the effects might differ considerably from one situation to another, the second of the possible patterns of reaction outlined above seems, in general, considerably more plausible than the first. That is, it seems likely that the announcement effects of discount rate changes on the expectations of businessmen may frequently be of such a nature as to weaken rather than strengthen the effectiveness of monetary policy. At the same time the actions of the Federal Reserve are only one of the factors—and ordinarily not a major one—on which business expectations are based, and it is therefore doubtful whether the announcement effects of discount rate changes are really very important one way or the other.

We may conclude that the "psychological" effects of discount rate changes on the domestic economy—like all expectational phenomena in economics—are highly uncertain and that the discount rate as a weapon of "psychological warfare" is of very dubious value to the Federal Reserve.

A change in the discount rate has traditionally been used as a "signal" by some countries in an entirely different connection. In time of balance of payments crisis, a sharp increase in the discount rate may be used to communicate to the rest of the world a country's determination to defend by whatever means may be necessary the external value of its currency. Britain has used discount rate changes for this purpose on occasion since World War II, and this was a major reason why Canada abandoned the "floating discount rate" system (discussed below) and raised the rate to 6 percent at the time of the

Canadian balance of payments crisis in June 1962. While a long tradition has perhaps made discount rate increases a reasonably effective means of international communication in some situations of this kind, there are surely other equally satisfactory means available; e.g., English, French, Latin, or Zulu.

C. Conclusions Concerning Present Discount Policy

The above analysis suggests that the discount rate as presently handled is not a very effective element in Federal Reserve policy. At times when a restrictive policy is applied, the induced increase in member bank borrowing constitutes a minor "leakage" in the controls, since it permits member banks to postpone contraction of their loans and investments and also adds to the total supply of member bank reserves. For the purpose of controlling the amount of borrowing, the Federal Reserve relies on adjustments in the discount rate, together with a tradition against borrowing that prevails among member banks and System surveillance of the borrowing practices of the banks. Due to the fact that open market interest rates fluctuate continuously while the discount rate is changed only at somewhat unpredictable discrete intervals, the relation between the discount rate and open market rates (which largely determines the incentive to borrow) behaves in a very erratic fashion. The System relies on "free reserves" as an immediate short-run guide for monetary policy; however, the restrictive effect of a given amount of free reserves varies with (among other things) the relation between the discount rate and the yields on assets—especially Treasury bills—that banks might alternatively liquidate to adjust their reserve positions.

Discretionary changes in the discount rate may at times have rather unpredictable effects on the business and financial situation, partly because it is often uncertain whether such changes are meant to be passive adjustments to keep the discount rate in line with other interest rates or whether they represent independent moves to tighten or ease credit. To the extent that changes in the discount rate do influence business conditions directly, they do so chiefly through psychological or "announcement" effects, the nature of which depends upon the kinds of expectations held by lenders, borrowers, and spenders. Although these announcement effects are quite complex and probably not of great importance in most cases, it seems likely that on occasion they may tend to increase economic instability.

D. Possible Reforms in Discount Policy

A number of students of monetary affairs have expressed discontent with the present discount policy of the Federal Reserve, although some of them have not made specific suggestions for a change.[41] However, at least three fairly specific proposals for reform have been suggested. Two of these would de-emphasize discount policy— one by getting rid of the discount mechanism entirely and the other by tying the discount rate to market interest rates and thereby eliminating discretionary changes in it. The third would move in the opposite direction by trying to reform the discount mechanism in such a way as to make the discount rate a much more powerful weapon of credit control. We shall discuss each of these proposals in turn.[42]

1. Abolition of the Discount Mechanism. The proposal has been advanced quite forcefully by Professor Milton Friedman that the discount mechanism should be abolished altogether.[43] Friedman argues that the legitimate function of the central bank is to control the stock of money and that the discount rate is an ineffective instrument for this purpose. Many of his arguments

---

[41] See, for example, E. C. Simmons, "A Note on the Revival of Federal Reserve Discount Policy," *Journal of Finance,* vol. 11 (December 1956), pp. 413–31.

[42] Editor's Note: In the mid-1960s, the Federal Reserve System itself made a thorough study of the discount mechanism. The conclusions and recommendations arising from the study were published in 1968, and research papers done in connection with the project were published by the Federal Reserve System in 1971 and 1972. The major innovation recommended was that each member bank should be granted a "basic borrowing privilege," or line of credit from the Federal Reserve, which would make it easier for the individual bank to handle short-term adjustment problems. The Federal Reserve has never acted on the report as a whole. The only change in its discounting procedures which has resulted was the authorization in 1973 of a "seasonal borrowing privilege" making a line of credit available to individual member banks (especially smaller banks) which experience regular seasonal reserve losses.

[43] Friedman, *A Program for Monetary Stability, op. cit.,* pp. 35–45; see also his testimony in *Employment, Growth and Price Levels* (Hearings before the Joint Economic Committee, Part 9A) (Washington, D.C.: U.S. Government Printing Office, 1959), pp. 3019–28. A. G. Hart also suggested the possibility of abolishing discounting a quarter of a century ago in connection with a discussion of the 100 percent reserve plan; see his "The 'Chicago' Plan of Banking Reform," *Review of Economic Studies,* vol. 2 (February 1935), pp. 104–16, reprinted in F. A. Lutz and L. W. Mints, eds., *Readings in Monetary Theory* (Homewood, Ill.: Richard D. Irwin, Inc., 1951), pp. 437–56.

are similar to the ones set forth above, and his analysis was cited at several points in our discussion.

One difficulty with the complete elimination of discounting is that the discount mechanism serves a useful function as a "safety valve" by which banks are able to make adjustments in their reserve positions and the Federal Reserve is able to come to the aid of the banking system—or individual banks—in case of a liquidity crisis. In order to provide a means for individual banks to make short-run adjustments in their reserve positions, Friedman proposes the establishment of a fixed "fine" to be assessed on reserve deficiencies; the fine to be set high enough to be above likely levels of market interest rates, in order to prevent the device from becoming an indirect form of borrowing from the Federal Reserve.[44] As far as liquidity crises are concerned, he contends that, due to the success of deposit insurance in practically eliminating bank failures, such crises are now scarcely conceivable and that the "lender of last resort" function of the Federal Reserve is now obsolete, so that we need not worry about its elimination. It may be noted that if the discount mechanism were eliminated, it would be possible to use the repurchase agreement technique as a means of providing emergency assistance to the banking system in times of crisis.[45]

2.   Tying the Discount Rate to the Treasury Bill Rate.   An alternative to the complete abolition of borrowing would be to change the discount rate at frequent intervals in such a way as to maintain an approximately constant relation between it and some open market interest rate, such as the Treasury bill rate. For example, each week as soon as the average rate of interest on Treasury bills at the Monday auction became known, the discount rate could be adjusted so as to preserve a constant differential between the two rates.[46]

Under this arrangement, the discount rate would no longer be a discretionary credit control weapon, and the unpredictable and often perverse announcement effects on the expectations of businessmen and financial institutions would be done away with. To the extent that the Federal Reserve wanted to influence expectations and felt that it could manage such effects so as to contribute to economic stability, it could implement these effects through the issuance of statements concerning its intentions, the economic outlook, and so on. While the present writer is rather dubious about the value of such activities, it is surely true that to the extent that they can contribute anything useful they can be handled better by verbal means than through reliance on such a crude signal as the discount rate.

The major question involved in the adoption of an arrangement for tying the discount rate to the bill rate would be the choice of the proper differential between the two. Obviously, the discount rate should be above the bill rate; beyond this the establishment of the differential is a matter of judgment. The larger the differential, the smaller would be (a) the average amount of borrowing and (b) the swings in borrowing that would occur as credit conditions changed. In view of the wide variations among individual banks with respect to both portfolio composition and expectations, the present writer feels that a fairly large differential of perhaps 1 percent would be desirable, in order to keep down the amount of borrowing, which, for reasons discussed earlier, represents a minor leakage in monetary controls. But there does not seem to be any analytical principle that provides a basis for selecting the proper differential. Doubtless the best procedure would be to experiment with various differentials, retaining each one long enough to observe its effectiveness.

Under this arrangement, in contrast to the complete elimination of discounting, the discount mechanism would continue to be available to serve as a means of making temporary adjustments in bank reserve positions and as a "safety valve" that could be used in times of crises. If

---

[44] Friedman, *A Program for Monetary Stability, op. cit.*, pp. 44–45.

[45] This possibility was mentioned by Hart in connection with his suggestion for the elimination of the discount mechanism (*op. cit.*, p. 110 in original, p. 447 in *Readings in Monetary Theory*).

[46] See Smith, "The Discount Rate as a Credit-Control Weapon," *op. cit.* Friedman (*A Program for Monetary Stability, op. cit.*, p. 45) refers to such an arrangement as an alternative (albeit a less desirable one in his opinion) to complete abolition of discounting. He points out, quite correctly, that if the differential between the discount rate and the bill rate were made large enough, the plan would be

equivalent to abolishing discounting. Professor J. M. Culbertson ("Timing Changes in Monetary Policy," *Journal of Finance,* vol. 14 [May 1959], pp. 145–60, esp. 157–58) concludes with respect to discount policy that the Federal Reserve "should subordinate the discount rate by making adjustments in it routinely in response to changes in market rates and should seek a less ambiguous vehicle for such communication with the public as may be useful."

this approach were adopted, it would probably be desirable to give up the efforts to rely on such an intangible and unreliable means of controlling discounting as the traditional "reluctance" of member banks and the so-called surveillance of the Federal Reserve, recognizing borrowing as a "right" rather than a "privilege" of member banks, and relying entirely on the discount rate (in relation to the bill rate) as a means of controlling it.[47]

A procedure of the kind discussed above was employed in Canada from November 1956, to June 1962. During this period, the Bank of Canada adjusted its lending rate each week so as to keep it ¼ of 1 percent above the average rate on Treasury bills at the most recent weekly auction. The reasons given for adpoting such an arrangement in 1956 were similar to those set forth above.[48] The policy was abandoned at the time of the Canadian balance of payment crisis in June 1962, when, as part of a program for dealing with the crisis, the discount rate was raised to 6 percent as a signal to the rest of the world of Canada's determination to defend the external value of the Canadian dollar.[49] The traditional discretionary discount rate policy has been employed in Canada since that time.

3. *Increasing the Effectiveness of the Discount Rate.* A proposal for reform of the discount mechanism very different from the two discussed above has recently been advanced by Professor James Tobin.[50] Instead of dismantling the discount mechanism entirely or abolishing discretionary changes in the discount rate, Tobin would greatly increase the importance of the rate

and turn it into a major weapon of credit control.

The Tobin proposal calls for two changes in present procedures:

1. The Federal Reserve would pay interest at the discount rate on member bank reserve balances in excess of requirements.
2. The prohibitions against payments of interest on demand deposits and the ceilings on the payment of interest on time and savings deposits would be repealed.

These changes would greatly increase the leverage of the discount rate by making it an important consideration for banks that are not in debt to the Federal Reserve as well as for those that are. The opportunity cost to a bank of increasing its loans and investments would be the return it could earn by holding excess reserves, and this cost would be firmly under the control of the Federal Reserve. Moreover, the interest rate offered by the banks to holders of idle deposits would presumably be linked rather closely to the rate paid on excess reserves, since the bank could always earn a return on its deposits at least equal to one minus its reserve requirement times the discount rate. Thus, if the Federal Reserve wished to tighten credit, it could raise the discount rate, and this would increase the opportunity cost of lending for all of the member banks (whether they were in debt or not) and would, therefore, make them willing to lend only at higher interest rates than previously, while at the same time causing the banks to raise interest rates on deposits, thereby increasing the attractiveness of bank deposits relative to other assets on the part of the public.[51] The

---

[47] In this connection, Friedman (*A Program for Monetary Stability, op. cit.*) says: "If rediscounting is retained, it should be a right, not a privilege, freely available to all member banks on specified terms." It appears that Friedman exaggerates the amount of discretion exercised by the System with respect to lending to individual banks, although the views expressed by System officials, concerning the "administration of the discount window"—such as Roosa's attempt ("Credit Policy at the Discount Window: Comment," *op. cit.*, pp. 333–34) to draw a distinction between saying "No," and refusing to say "Yes" —are so ambiguous that it is very difficult to judge the amount of discretion employed.

[48] See Bank of Canada, *Annual Report of the Governor to the Minister of Finance*, 1956, pp. 45–46.

[49] See Bank of Canada, *Annual Report of the Governor to the Minister of Finance*, 1962, pp. 3–4 and 72–73.

[50] James Tobin, "Towards Improving the Efficiency of the Monetary Mechanism," *Review of Economics and Statistics*, vol. 42 (August 1960), pp. 276–79.

[51] Allowing the banks to pay interest on deposits would have two related advantages. One is that it would probably reduce the propensity for the velocity of deposits to increase when a restrictive policy was applied, since the banks would be able to raise interest rates on deposits making them more attractive and weakening the tendency for rising interest rates on other claims to induce shifts of deposits into the hands of persons having a high propensity to spend. The other advantage is that it should reduce the amount of real resources devoted to the task of economizing the use of cash balances. Since the revival of flexible monetary policy, many large corporations, as well as state and local governments, have developed extensive facilities for handling short-term investments in order to minimize their holdings of sterile cash balances, and the amount of skilled personnel devoting its time to this kind of activity at present is certainly not trivial (see C. E. Silberman, "The Big Corporate Lenders," *Fortune*, August 1956, pp. 111–14, 162–70). Resources devoted to this purpose represent a form of economic waste, since the real cost of creating deposits is virtually zero so that

discount rate could be used independently to control credit, or it could be combined with open market operations. It is not clear, however, what principle should govern the division of responsibility between the two weapons.

The proposal is ingenious and would certainly be practical and capable of being put in operation without causing disruption. And it might have the incidental advantage that the payment of interest on excess reserves might encourage more banks to become members of the Federal Reserve System. What is not clear, however, is why a flexible monetary policy could be implemented more effectively by means of the discount rate under this proposal than is now possible by means of open market operations. It is true that the proposal would presumably permit the Federal Reserve to control the cost of bank credit very effectively, but this can already be done—in principle at least—by open market operations. In part, the problems of monetary policy seem to stem from the fact that the demand for bank credit is not very sensitive to changes in interest rates and other monetary variables, so that it has proved to be difficult to operate forcefully enough to produce prompt changes of the degree necessary for effective stabilization. Perhaps it would be possible to bring the forces of monetary policy to bear more rapidly by means of the Tobin proposal but this is by no means obvious. If the proposal merely provides another way of doing what is already possible, it hardly seems worthwhile.

The repeal of the existing restrictions relating to payment of interest on deposits is in no way dependent upon provision for the payment of interest on excess reserves, and there is much to be said for the repeal of these restrictions, even if the remainder of the Tobin proposal is not adopted.

4. Conclusions. Of the three proposals for reforming the discount mechanism, the present writer feels that the strongest case can be made for the procedure of changing the discount rate each week in such a way as to maintain a constant

spread between the discount rate and the Treasury bill rate. This would be a less drastic reform than the complete elimination of discounting, would eliminate the unpredictable effects of discretionary changes in the discount rate, would preserve the discount mechanism as a safety valve, and would eliminate the effects on credit conditions that now result from erratic variations in the relation between the discount rate and open market rates. The Tobin proposal for increasing the potency of the discount rate as a credit-control weapon is worthy of careful study, but it is not yet clear that the proposal would greatly strengthen the hand of the Federal Reserve.

If the present system of making discretionary adjustments in the discount rate at irregular intervals is retained, it would be desirable to reform the administration of the discount mechanism, perhaps by shifting the authority for making changes in the rate from the individual Reserve banks to the Federal Open Market Committee. The purpose of such a change would be to reduce the number of persons involved in decisions regarding the discount rate so that it would be easier to agree on the reasons for making changes. This would facilitate the issuance of explanatory statements at the time changes are made, in order to eliminate the confusion that often results due to the varying interpretations that are frequently placed on rate changes in the absence of explanations. It should then be feasible to make more frequent technical adjustments in the rate with less need to worry about the danger of disruptive effects on the credit situation, thereby permitting closer co-ordination of the discount rate with open market operations.

IV. THE ROLE OF VARIABLE RESERVE REQUIREMENTS[52]

Since the accord with the Treasury in March 1951, the Federal Reserve has made no systematic anticyclical use of changes in member bank reserve requirements. Reductions in the reserve requirement percentages applicable to demand deposits were made in the recessions of 1953–54 (reductions in July 1953, and June–August 1954) and 1957–58 (reductions in February–April 1958). In the recession of 1960–61, re-

---

there is no economic gain from exercising economy in their use. This is pointed out by Tobin and is emphasized even more strongly by Friedman (*A Program for Monetary Stability, op. cit.,* pp. 71–75). The two advantages (reducing destabilizing velocity changes and discouraging efforts to economize in the use of costless deposits) are related in the sense that the propensity to waste resources in economizing cash balances tends to increase during periods of credit restriction and rising interest rates, and this increased application of resources helps to permit a destabilizing rise in velocity.

[52] Much of the discussion in this section is based upon the author's study entitled "Reserve Requirements in the American Monetary System," in *Monetary Management,* prepared for the Commission on Money and Credit (Englewood Cliffs, N.J.: Prentice-Hall, Inc., 1963), pp. 175–315.

serves were released by permitting member banks to count vault cash as reserves—to a limited extent beginning in December 1959, and without limitation beginning in November 1960. And, finally, reserve requirements applicable to time deposits were reduced from 5 to 4 percent in October-November 1962, at a time when output was expanding but unemployment remained high.

Under present provisions, the Board of Governors can change requirements on demand deposits between 10 and 22 percent for reserve city banks and between 7 and 14 percent for country banks, while it can change requirements on time deposits between 3 and 6 percent; as this is written (July 1963) the requirements are 16½ percent and 12 percent for demand deposits at reserve city and country banks, respectively, and 4 percent for time deposits.[53] The Board may permit member banks to count all or part of their vault cash as required reserves; at the present time vault cash may be counted in full.[54]

A. Variable Reserve Requirements as a Credit Control Weapon

A change in reserve requirements alters both the amount of excess reserves available and the

---

[53] Under legislation passed in July, 1959, the "central reserve city" classification of member banks was eliminated effective July 28, 1962.

[54] Editor's note: Since this paper was written, there have been several significant changes in the definitions and procedures to be followed in the computation of required reserves. Among the most important of these are the change in 1968 from the use of current-week deposits to deposits held two weeks earlier as the basis for the calculation of current-week required reserves; and the change in late 1972 to reserve requirements based on a bank's size rather than its location. Under the new system, the marginal reserve ratio increases as net demand deposits rise. As of June 30, 1977, the reserve requirement scale applicable to net demand deposits in member banks was as follows:

Amount of Net Demand Deposits ($ millions)	Percent
0–2	7
2–10	9.5
10–100	11.75
100–400	12.75
Over 400	16.25

The reserve requirement for passbook savings deposits presently is 3 percent for all member banks. The requirement applicable to time deposits depends on the deposit's size and maturity. The legal limits within which the Board of Governors can change demand deposit requirements remain 10 to 22 percent for reserve city banks and 7 to 14 percent for other banks. For time deposits, the limits are 3 to 10 percent. For this purpose, any bank holding more than $400 million of net demand deposits is considered a reserve city bank.

credit expansion multiplier, which determines the amount of potential credit expansion per dollar of excess reserves. For relatively small changes in reserve requirements, the first of these effects is much more important than the second—with net demand deposits amounting to roughly $100 billion, a reduction of one percentage point in requirements releases approximately $1 billion of excess reserves.

However, changes in reserve requirements have harsh and rather indiscriminate effects, at least when the changes made amount to as much as ½ or 1 percentage point, as has been customary in recent years. This does not cause serious problems in the case of reductions in requirements, because, as explained below, excessive bank liquidity generated by such reductions can be—and in practice has been—sopped up by open market sales of securities. Increases in requirements, however, have troublesome side effects which are not quite so easily dealt with.

Increases in requirements affect all banks—or at least all the banks in a particular reserve requirement classification—including some banks that are plentifully supplied with liquid assets which permit them to make easy adjustments in their reserve positions, as well as banks whose liquidity positions are less comfortable. To the extent that banks are forced to carry out troublesome portfolio readjustments, they are able to see clearly that these adjustments were forced upon them by Federal Reserve action; whereas the adjustments resulting from open market operations are either voluntary or, to the extent that they are involuntary, appear to be the result of impersonal market forces. Thus, frequent reserve requirement increases are likely to cause resentment among member banks and, under present conditions, might even be a significant deterrent to membership in the Federal Reserve System. Moreover, while the initial effect of reserve requirement increases is felt by all the banks, it is likely that there will be substantial secondary effects which will be concentrated on banks in the larger money centers as interior banks draw down correspondent balances and sell Government securities in the central money market in order to restore their reserve positions.

B. Coordination of Reserve Requirement Changes and Open Market Operations

To some extent, it is possible to soften the unduly harsh impact of changes in reserve requirements by proper co-ordination with open market operations. The open market operations associated with the mid-1954 reductions in reserve requirements, which were designed to encourage continuing recovery from the recession of 1953–54, provide a good example of this coordination. The reserve requirement reductions that were made resulted in the injection of what the Federal Reserve authorities felt was an unduly large amount of excess reserves within a short period of time.[55] Accordingly the Federal Reserve sold securities in the open market at about the same time the reserve requirement reductions were made, in order to absorb a portion of the released reserves: then, over a period of several months, it purchased securities in order to feed reserves back into the economy at times when additional reserves appeared to be needed in the interest of orderly recovery.[56] Thus, a skillful blending of reserve requirement changes and open market operations produced a smooth and gradual adjustment.

Similar recent examples of the use of open market operations to soften the impact of reserve requirement increases during periods of inflation are not available, since the Federal Reserve has not made use of reserve requirement increases since the Accord.[57] The blending of open market

operations with reserve requirement adjustments would probably not result in quite such a smooth adjustment in this case, because the problem here is not only to prevent an unduly sharp impact on the total supply of money and credit, but to alleviate harsh impacts on individual banks. Since some banks which were squeezed especially hard might not possess securities of the maturities being purchased by the System, these banks might not be helped directly by open market operations.

If reserve requirement changes have important advantages as a means of controlling credit, the technical difficulties in making two-way adjustments could be greatly reduced by making smaller changes in the requirements than have been customary in the past and by smoothing the impact by means of open market operations. It has been suggested that more frequent and smaller changes be made, and there is no technical reason why this could not be done.[58] And if more frequent use of reserve requirement changes would clearly permit the Federal Reserve to conduct monetary policy more efficiently than would otherwise be possible, the fact that such adjustments might be somewhat unpopular with commercial bankers should not be taken too seriously. The real question is: What advantages do reserve requirement adjustments have in comparison with other credit-control weapons, especially open market operations? To this question we now turn.

C. Possible Usefulness of Reserve Requirement Changes

Under most circumstances, the effects of (for example) expanding credit by lowering reserve requirements will almost surely be different in detail from those produced by the same amount of expansion (measured in terms of the increase in income-generating expenditures) produced by open market purchases. That is, the spending units which will be induced to increase their

---

[55] In a succession of changes in June, July, and August 1954, demand deposit reserve requirements were reduced by 2 percentage points at central reserve city banks and 1 percentage point at reserve city and country banks, while time deposit reserve requirements were reduced by 1 percentage point at all classes of banks. These adjustments released about $1.5 billion of reserves.

[56] Between June and August 1954, the Federal Reserve reduced its holdings of Government securities (average of daily figures) by $1.0 billion, while the net effect of factors outside the control of the Federal Reserve was to reduce member bank reserves by another $200 million. Thus, total reserves declined by $1.2 billion, and required reserves fell by the same amount, leaving excess reserves unchanged. From August to December 1954, the Federal Reserve increased its portfolio of Government securities by $0.9 billion as it fed reserves back to the banking system to meet seasonal demands. (Calculations based on data from *Federal Reserve Bulletin*, February 1955, p. 149).

[57] During the immediate postwar inflation in 1948 while the Federal Reserve was "pegging" the market for Government securities, reserve requirement increases were used on several occasions in an effort to implement a policy of credit restraint. In this situation, however, member banks were plentifully supplied with Government securities, which were saleable at virtually fixed prices. Consequently, the banks tended merely to sell more securities than they otherwise would have sold, and these securities had to be purchased by the System to prevent securities prices from falling. Thus, banks were able to replenish their reserves readily, and there was little

effect on the cost or availability of credit. In this situation, open market purchases were, in effect, used to offset more or less permanently the effects of reserve equipment increases. Such operations did tend to reduce bank liquidity somewhat, since the banks were giving up liquid securities for less liquid required reserves; however, the operations were not on a sufficiently large scale to make this a significant factor.

[58] See C. R. Whittlesey, "Reserve Requirements and the Integration of Credit Policies," *Quarterly Journal of Economics*, vol. 58 (August 1944), pp. 553–70.

expenditures will be different in the two cases, as will the types of expenditures affected. Unfortunately, however, our knowledge of relative "incidence" of the two weapons is very poor, so that, while we may be sure that there are differences, there is very little that can be said about them. For this reason, we can scarcely even discuss intelligently the "mix" of the two that should be used to accomplish particular objectives. The best we can do is to indicate some rather general considerations which differentiate reserve requirement adjustments from open market operations and some special situations in which the reserve requirements weapon may be especially appropriate.

1. Neutrality. The Federal Reserve authorities in recent years have shown a strong antipathy toward selective credit controls and have taken the position that the central bank should confine its efforts to the control of the total supply of money and credit, leaving the task of allocating credit to market forces. This attitude has been reflected, for example, in the System's opposition to the establishment of consumer credit controls even on a stand-by basis. Although there are other considerations involved also, this philosophy seems to be one of the bases for the Federal Reserve's adherence to the "bills-only" policy between 1953 and 1961. During this period, the System carefully eschewed efforts to control the maturity structure of interest rates, leaving this to the determination of market forces.

If such a philosophy of "neutrality" were to be pushed to its logical conclusion, it would lead to reliance on reserve requirement adjustments as a means of monetary control. Even bills-only is not entirely neutral in its effects on the interest rate structure, since changes in the money stock produced by this method involve, as a by-product, changes in the stock of securities of a particular maturity (namely, Treasury bills) and have a special impact on short-term interest rates. Reserve requirement changes, on the other hand, have no direct effects on interest rates or on stocks of securities—all such effects are produced by the decisions and activities of borrowers and lenders (including commercial banks).

The "neutrality" argument for reliance on reserve requirement changes would carry weight only with those who accept the "neutrality" philosophy. Moreover, its implementation would require that all monetary adjustments be accomplished by reserve requirement changes. This would include the day-to-day operations of the Federal Reserve designed to counteract the effects of uncontrollable factors (float, currency

in circulation, etc.) affecting member bank reserves. These operations seem clearly to serve a useful, if not indispensable, function in keeping the money market on an even keel and are now quite efficiently carried out by means of open market operations. While it would undoubtedly be possible to make smaller and more frequent adjustments in reserve requirements than have been employed in the past, it would surely be wholly impracticable to employ reserve requirement changes on a day-to-day basis. For this, as well as other reasons, the "neutrality" argument for the use of reserve requirement adjustments appears to be purely academic and of no practical importance.

2. Announcement Effects. Like discount rate adjustments and unlike open market operations, changes in reserve requirements are overt actions of the Federal Reserve which are widely reported and commented upon in the press. As such, they are likely to have "announcement effects" through their influence on the expectations of businessmen and financial institutions. In fact, it seems quite likely that the reductions in reserve requirements that were made in 1953 and 1958 were motivated partly by a desire to convince the public that the System intended to take vigorous antirecession action.

The question of announcement effects was discussed at some length in connection with discount rate changes, and the conclusion of that discussion was that such effects are uncertain and unpredictable. This conclusion seems to apply also to reserve requirement changes. For example, it seems at least as plausible to suppose that a dramatic reduction in reserve requirements in the early stages of a recession will strengthen the feeling that business conditions are worsening, as to suppose that it will make people optimistic by showing that the Federal Reserve is actively on the job trying to maintain stability.

I believe the fact that reserve requirement changes tend to have announcement effects is a disadvantage rather than an advantage. The best way to produce announcement effects—if and when such effects seem likely to be desirable—is by means of carefully-worded public statements explaining the views or intentions of the authorities. Action and communication should, in general, be carefully separated rather than rigidly linked together.

3. Speed of Reactions. It has been argued that reserve requirements changes have more widely diffused effects than open market operations and therefore may affect economic conditions more promptly. The reasoning behind this argument is that open market operations are consummated in the central money market of the country in New York and therefore have their initial impact chiefly on the reserve positions of the money market banks. Effects are gradually diffused throughout the country, primarily by means of interregional flows of funds set in motion by the adjustments of these banks to the initial changes in their reserve positions—a process which takes some time to carry through. Reserve requirement changes, on the other hand, instantaneously affect the reserve positions of all banks and therefore produce more rapid effects on credit conditions outside the central money markets. Federal Reserve officials apparently accept this argument and think it is especially relevant with respect to antirecession policies, since Chairman Martin of the Board of Governors has used it to explain why the System used reserve requirement reductions as a means of attacking the recessions of 1953–54 and 1957–58.[59]

One study covering the period from mid-1951 to mid-1953, when the Federal Reserve relied on open market operations to tighen credit rather gently at first and then with increasing intensity, suggests that the effects were felt first in New York and that there were noticeable lags in their transmission to the rest of the country.[60] The free reserve position of central reserve city banks appears to have been affected earlier and more strongly than that of other banks, and New York City banks showed an earlier and more pronounced tendency to shift the composition of their portfolios from investments to loans than did banks outside New York City. The author of this study suggests more frequent use of changes in reserve requirements, in order to shorten the lags in the regional transmission of monetary policy.

While this study is somewhat suggestive, it is not clearly convincing, since the statistical series involved are so ragged in their behavior as to be difficult to interpret, and because one cannot be sure that such differences in regional reactions as were present were not due to factors unrelated to monetary policy. There are several reasons for doubting whether the difference in

the reaction speeds of the two weapons is great enough to be an important consideration. In the first place, as noted above, while the initial impact of reserve requirement changes is widely diffused, adjustments of interior banks via changes in correspondent balances and security transactions are likely to pass a disproportionate share of it back to the central money markets. Furthermore, to the extent that the initial effects of open market operations are more concentrated, the fact that central money market banks are very sensitive to changes in their reserve positions and prompt in reacting thereto would suggest that the transmission of effects to other parts of the economy is likely to get under way quickly and proceed rapidly. And finally, the other lags in monetary policy appear to be so long that it is doubtful whether such differences as do exist between the two weapons are of appreciable importance in the overall picture. In fact, one cannot even be sure that there is not frequently some advantage in open market operations, because commercial banks all over the country adjust their reserves through sales of securities (which largely clear through the central money market) so that purchases (for example) of securities may have some tendency to direct the flow of new reserves to the points where they are most needed, instead of scattering them indiscriminately over the map.[61]

4. National Emergencies. One circumstance in which the power to raise reserve requirements might be used to good purpose is in times of a war or major national defense emergency, which requires the expenditure of large amounts of borrowed funds by the Government during a period of full employment. Under such conditions, there is much to be said for the Treasury's

---

[59] See Martin's testimony in January 1960 *Economic Report of the President* (Hearings before the Joint Economic Committee, 86th Cong., 2d sess.) (Washington, D.C.: U.S. Government Printing Office, 1960), pp. 163–212

[60] I. O. Scott, Jr., "The Regional Impact of Monetary Policy," *Quarterly Journal of Economics*, vol. 69 (May 1955), pp. 269–84.

---

[61] Chairman Martin of the Board of Governors has stated his belief that an increase in reserve requirements would be the best way to offset the effects on member bank reserves of a substantial gold inflow, if circumstances required such offsetting (see his testimony in January 1960 *Economic Report of the President,* [Hearings before the Joint Economic Committee, *op. cit.*], p. 187). Perhaps this would be true in some circumstances, but the present writer is inclined to believe that open market sales of securities might often be the more appropriate weapon for this purpose, since the funds resulting from the sale of gold to the Treasury by foreign governments are often likely to find their way to the central money market, so that the way to offset the effects of these flows with the minimum impact on domestic business activity might be through the sale of Treasury bills, which would, in the main, withdraw funds from the central money market.

obtaining such funds as it needs but cannot raise through taxation or through borrowing from the nonbank public by selling securities directly to the Federal Reserve, with the System raising reserve requirements to immobilize the excess reserves that are created when the Treasury spends the money. This process would avoid the accumulation of excessive liquidity in the hands of the commercial banks and the accompanying threat of post-emergency inflation and would save the Treasury some interest costs. It would, of course, require that the Federal Reserve be given virtually unlimited power to raise reserve requirements.

5. *Conclusions.* The upshot of the above discussion is that there appear to be few if any circumstances in normal times when reserve requirement changes are clearly superior to open market operations as a means of controlling credit. Reserve requirement changes have "announcement effects" while open market operations do not, but these may frequently turn out to be a nuisance rather than an aid to the Federal Reserve and, to the extent that they are desirable, can be produced more effectively by other methods. Conceivably, reserve requirement changes may affect business conditions more promptly than open market operations; however, this is not certain, and in any case the advantage is unlikely to be great enough to be of much significance. In view of the superior administrative efficiency of the open market operations, together with the unpopularity among commercial bankers of frequent two-way adjustments of reserve requirements, there is much to be said for relying exclusively on open market operations under normal circumstances.[62]

---

[62] Another issue that has come up recently relating to the choice between open market operations and reserve requirement changes is the differing effects that these two weapons have on the Treasury's interest costs and on the profits of commercial banks. For example, the creation of a given amount of additional money by open market purchases will result in lower costs to the Treasury and lower profits to the banking system than would the creation of the same amount of money by lowering reserve requirements. (For an extensive discussion, see Smith, "Reserve Requirements in the American Monetary System," *op. cit.*, pp. 216–49). However, this matter is relevant chiefly in connection with long-term developments related to the choice between open market purchases and reserve requirement reductions as alternative means of providing reserves to support the secular growth of the money supply. It has little bearing on the relative merits of the two weapons as alternative means of producing two-way anti-cyclical changes in credit conditions.

V. CONCLUDING COMMENTS

As they are used at the present time, open market policy, discount policy, and reserve requirements policy are three instruments of monetary control with essentially a single purpose—the regulation of the total supply of money and bank credit. Open market policy is powerful, effective, and administratively flexible; it is unquestionably the key weapon of general monetary control. Discount policy, as reflected in changes in the discount rate, has a weak and to some extent even perverse effect on the total supply of money and credit and is, at the same time, a rather inept and confusing device for waging "psychological warfare" against economic instability via the public's expectations. Reserve requirements policy is a powerful weapon but too cumbersome for frequent use and not clearly capable of accomplishing anything under ordinary circumstances that cannot be done at least as well by means of open market operations.

Doubtless the three weapons have somewhat different economic effects; however, detailed knowledge of the impact of monetary changes is inadequate to permit a meaningful differentiation. Consequently, it is not possible to specify the circumstances in which one of these weapons rather than the others should be used. They are all designed to serve the same purposes—one effectively and the other two rather ineptly.

Accordingly, I would favor placing complete reliance on open market operations, under ordinary circumstances, as the means of conducting general monetary policy. The best way of handling the discount rate would probably be to tie it to the Treasury bill rate as explained earlier in this paper. Reserve requirements should probably be fixed at an appropriate level and kept there.[63] I would also favor the elimination of the present threefold classification of banks for reserve requirement purposes and the establishment of uniform reserve requirements for demand deposits at all banks, including nonmember banks. There does not appear to be any logical basis for differentiating among banks as far as reserve requirements are concerned, and uniform requirements would increase somewhat the precision of

---

[63] The question of what is the "appropriate" level of reserve requirements is beyond the scope of this paper and, in any case, is a matter of judgment. It is in connection with this question that the effects of reserve requirements on bank profits and Treasury interest costs referred to in footnote 62 become relevant.

open market policy as a means of controlling the total supply of money and bank credit.[64]

There may be circumstances under which the Federal Reserve should try to affect economic activity by influencing the public's expectations, although this is clearly a tricky and possibly even dangerous form of activity. To the extent that it is employed, it should be divorced from actions designed to control bank reserves and should take advantage of the subtleties of everyday language. One of the advantages of open market operations is that they are necessarily being carried out continuously and are largely devoid of so-called announcement effects.

One final question should perhaps be raised: Does not the situation of the last three years or so when monetary policy has had to be directed simultaneously at stimulation of the domestic economy and protection of the balance of payments against excessive outflows of short-term capital argue for the retention of all of the traditional credit control weapons, in order to maximize the flexibility of the monetary authorities? I do not believe so. It is true that, for example, by lowering reserve requirements and simultaneously selling enough Treasury bills to keep the bill rate from falling, the authorities could presumably stimulate the domestic economy to some extent without increasing outflows of short-term capital. But such a result could equally well be brought about by requisite purchases of longer-term securities combined with sales of bills. It is difficult to see that adjustments in reserve requirements and the discount rate give the authorities any ability to change the structure of interest rates and the total credit supply that could not equally well be accomplished by sufficiently flexible use of Federal Reserve open market and Treasury debt management operations.

[64] Smith "Reserve Requirements in the American Monetary System," *op. cit.*, pp. 175–99.

---

13. MONETARY OBJECTIVES AND MONETARY POLICY*

Richard G. Davis

Since the spring of 1975 the Federal Reserve has been announcing projected growth ranges for several measures of money and bank credit. The use of such monetary "targets" raises a wide range of issues in monetary economics, from the rather narrowly technical to the more broadly philosophical. Since the subject is vast and space is limited, I shall have to be content with a terse and selective summary of some of the main issues posed by the use of monetary targets. Specifically, I want to (1) describe the procedures for setting projected monetary growth ranges currently in use, (2) try to suggest some historical reasons for the evolution of these procedures, (3) describe the broad strategic considerations that enter into the setting of the monetary growth ranges, (4) discuss some general problems in determining just what numerical values should be chosen under given circumstances, and (5) discuss some problems in realizing projected growth ranges once they are set.

Under the current procedure, the Chairman of the Federal Reserve Board announces projected growth ranges for the coming four-quarter period in quarterly presentations to (alternately) the House and Senate banking committees. These presentations are made in response to a joint Concurrent Resolution of the House and Senate passed in March 1975.

At the outset I should perhaps note that the term "targets," often applied to these monetary growth ranges, actually has no particular official standing. Indeed in some respects the term is misleading since it may seem to imply that particular numerical values for the money supply, rather than the general health of the economy, is the "target" of policy. And it may seem to imply a degree of rigidity with regard to the pursuit of these money supply ranges that does not exist. Notwithstanding these difficulties, I will frequently use the term "target" for lack of a more convenient alternative.

The ranges themselves are defined in terms of

* From Federal Reserve Bank of New York *Quarterly Review* (Spring 1977), pp. 29–36. Reprinted by permission of the Federal Reserve Bank of New York and the author. Richard G. Davis is Senior Economic Advisor, Federal Reserve Bank of New York.

Chart 1: Money Supply Growth Rates

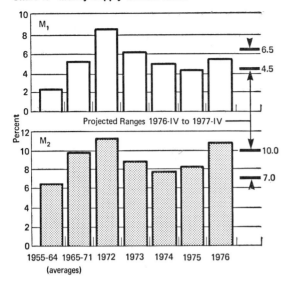

Projected Ranges 1976-IV to 1977-IV

M_1 — 6.5, 4.5

M_2 — 10.0, 7.0

1955-64 1965-71 1972 1973 1974 1975 1976
(averages)

Percent

rate ranges for M_1 and M_2 and compares them with actual growth rates over some recent past periods. While the targets are stated in growth rate terms, given the base period levels, these growth rates can of course also be translated directly into upper and lower limits on the dollar levels four quarters hence. A translation into dollar levels is sometimes useful as a means of following how the aggregates may be tracking relative to the targets. Chart 2 shows the growth path of M_1 over the four quarters of 1976 relative to the upper and lower limits implied by the target growth rates at the beginning of 1976.

HISTORICAL EVOLUTION

Quite apart from the immediate impetus to publicly announced monetary targets provided by the Congressional Concurrent Resolution, the present targeting procedure represents the product of a long evolution in thinking over the postwar period. When active countercyclical monetary policy first got under way in the postwar period, the Federal Reserve faced a new situation and new objectives for which the experience of earlier decades really offered little guidance. Clearly, one of the main objectives of policy was to provide countercyclical ballast. This meant "tightening" when expansion threatened to become unsustainably exuberant and "easing" when the economy became soft. At first, it was pretty much universal practice both inside and outside the Federal Reserve to calibrate policy in terms of money market conditions or the behavior of short-term interest rates. Policy was said to be "easing" or "easy" when short-term rates were falling or low and to be "tightening" or "tight" when rates were rising or high.

After some experience with this framework, however, it became evident that the behavior of interest rates was not always a good way to calibrate the impact of policy. The trouble was that, even in the short run, interest rate movements depend only in part on what the Federal Reserve does and much more on what the economy itself does by way of generating demands for money and credit. As a result, interest rates can give off misleading signals of policy's impact at crucial junctures in the business cycle, with the movements in rates reflecting the effect not of policy but of cyclical developments in the economy itself.

Perhaps the *locus classicus* of such situations occurred in early 1960 when the economy went into recession and interest rates fell even though bank reserves and the money supply continued to

upper and lower limits for growth rates in three definitions of the money supply (and one of bank credit) as measured from the most recent quarterly average levels to the prospective levels four quarters ahead. The current target period thus covers growth over a one-year period ending with the fourth quarter of 1977. The group of monetary measures that are targeted at the moment includes M_1 (currency plus demand deposits), M_2 (M_1 plus commercial bank time and savings deposits other than large negotiable CDs), and M_3 (M_2 plus deposits and shares at mutual savings banks and savings and loan associations). Chart 1 shows the current growth

Chart 2: M_1 Levels Relative to Projected One-Year Range

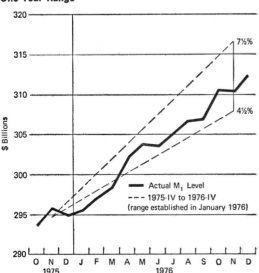

$ Billions

7½%

4½%

Actual M_1 Level
1975-IV to 1976-IV
(range established in January 1976)

O N D J F M A M J J A S O N D
1975   1976

contract until the middle of the year. The conjunction of a falling money supply and bank reserves along with falling interest rates made it quite clear that declining rates reflected weakening credit demands at a time when the economy was going into recession. Under such conditions, it didn't seem to make much sense to describe monetary policy as "easy" simply because interest rates were falling. The feeling spread in the 1960s that this kind of situation might not be at all rare and indeed might be a systematic feature of business-cycle behavior. As a result, wariness about identifying monetary "tightness" and "ease" with interest rate movements increased. At the same time, the advantages of identifying policy directly by the behavior of movements in the money supply and bank reserves seemed to become more apparent.

This trend in thinking was clearly also spurred by a roughly concurrent increase in the popularity of "monetarism"—a view that claims a dominant importance for the behavior of the money supply in determining a wide range of short and longer run economic developments. Nevertheless, there is little intrinsic connection between the question of what indexes to use in measuring and guiding monetary policy and the larger issues posted by monetarism about the behavior of the economy as a whole.

In any case, the accelerating rates of inflation we began to experience in the late 1960s undoubtedly further undermined confidence in the use of interest rates and increased the appeal of monetary aggregates as measures of policy. With the relatively high rates of inflation that emerged in the late 1960s, an old idea resurfaced, namely, that actual market rates of interest really consist of two parts: (1) a so-called real rate of interest which equals the market rate adjusted for any depreciation in the purchasing power of the principal over the life of the loan and (2) an inflationary component to compensate for this depreciation.

With high and variable rates of inflation, given market interest rates obviously will not have a constant meaning in terms of the real "tightness" or "ease" they imply about financial markets. Under these conditions the behavior of market rates becomes a rather elastic measuring rod. Moreover, even if the monetary authorities could in theory control at least some nominal interest rates by pegging the prices of some debt instruments, they have no control at all over the "real" interest rate, i.e., the nominal rate adjusted for inflation. Finally, the emergence of inflation over recent years as an absolutely first-

rank economic problem has tended to reemphasize the long-run strategic importance of monetary growth rates.

THE STRATEGY OF SETTING MONETARY TARGETS

To return to the current practices regarding monetary targets, it is easy, at least on one level, to describe how the numerical monetary target ranges are set. Procedurally, the result is the outcome of a vote by the Federal Open Market Committee (FOMC). In choosing among alternatives, the individual Committee members obviously vote for that set of target numbers they think is most likely to produce good results for the economy over the coming year *given the information at hand.* For each member, this decision depends upon two elements: (1) his preferences among possible outcomes for the economy and (2) his views about what outcomes are in fact likely to result from the choice of particular target ranges. The economics staffs at the Board of Governors of the Federal Reserve System and at the Reserve Banks try to provide some assistance on this latter aspect of the problem by trying to project the consequences for the economy of alternative target ranges. These projections may be made in a variety of ways, ranging from the use of econometric models to purely judgmental projections, with various combinations in between. Obviously, however, the various staff judgments will not always agree, will not always be right, and will not always be accepted by the Committee members.

Immediate circumstances aside, Chairman Arthur F. Burns and other senior Federal Reserve officials, including President Paul A. Volcker of the New York Reserve Bank, have frequently emphasized that the overall process of setting monetary aggregate targets has been influenced since its inception by a longer run strategy: This strategy is one of gradually bringing down growth rates in money to levels that in the long run may prove compatible with price stability.

The linkage suggested by this strategy between the longer run behavior of money and price stability, however, does not necessarily imply a "monetarist" view of inflation—certainly not in the sense of believing, as Milton Friedman has put it, that inflation is "always and everywhere a purely monetary phenomenon." The events of the past few years, it seems to me, should have made it clear that, in the short run, inflation can lead a life of its own quite independent of current or past monetary development. The 12 percent inflation of 1974, for example, was clearly traceable in a large part to special factors and cannot be explained by monetary growth alone.

But on a longer term basis, it doesn't take much massaging of the data to suggest a general if imperfect parallelism between monetary growth and inflation (Chart 3). Even over this longer run, there is a serious question under present day conditions as to whether the causality doesn't run as much from prices to money as from money to prices. Central banks and governments all over the world have often found themselves under intense pressure to validate price increases stemming from nonmonetary sources because the short-run alternatives have seemed to be pressures on interest rates and employment. Consequently, although in a narrow, purely economic view of the inflation problem, rapid monetary growth might be regarded as the "cause" of long-run inflation, a more comprehensive view of the entire process must put the blame on a multitude of political, social, and economic pressures. These pressures have given an inflationary bias to modern economies, one that has often been accommodated by monetary expansion simply because in the short run this has seemed to be the least undesirable among available alternatives.

Yet despite reservations about purely monetary theories of inflation, economists do generally agree that avoidance of excessive monetary growth is at least a necessary—though not necessarily a sufficient—condition for long-run price stability. Thus, it was evident by 1972 that a

Chart 3: Money and Price Changes in the Long Run (changes at annual rates, measured from 12 quarters earlier)

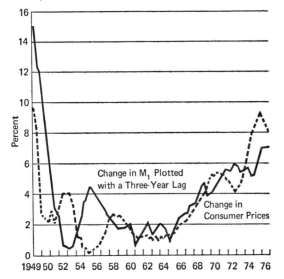

Chart 4: M₁ and M₂ Ranges for One Year Ahead

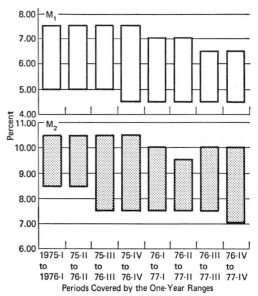

long-term strategy of gradually slowing monetary growth rates had become desirable. As Chart 1 shows, growth rates did in fact slow in 1973 and 1974 but, beginning in 1975, the pressing immediate problem of ensuring an adequate economic recovery became a factor. Nevertheless, the longer term objective of gradually lowering monetary growth rates has continued to be reaffirmed—most recently in February by Chairman Burns in his regular quarterly testimony to the Congress. As Chart 4 shows, all but one of the eight individual changes in monetary target ranges for M₁ and M₂ that have been made over the past two years have been in the direction of modest downward adjustments in the upper or lower ends of the ranges of one or more of the money supply measures.

The current targets are clearly still well above the levels that would be likely to prove consistent with long-run price stability. To be sure, no one can say with certainty just what these growth rates are, but the historical record seems to suggest rough estimates of about 1 to 2 percent for M₁ and about 3 to 4 percent for M₂.

Movements to such levels could not be made all at once, however. Inflation, once set in motion, tends to be extremely persistent under modern conditions, even after demand pressures have disappeared. Thus at least *some* inflation seems inevitable, no matter what monetary policy does, for a certain period ahead. If monetary growth rates do not take this fact into account, they risk being insufficient to finance adequate growth of real economic activity. This consideration provides a strong reason for setting monetary targets under these conditions above levels appropriate for long-run price stability, moving down to those levels as inflation recedes.

PROBLEMS IN SETTING TARGETS

A major problem in setting targets is that there can be slippages in the relationship between money and the economy over periods of time and in orders of magnitude substantial enough to be important to policymakers. To the extent that such slippages exist, determining target levels needed to achieve any given economic result will have to involve a significant amount of judgment. The existence of slippages means that appropriate target ranges simply cannot be mechanically deduced from past behavior —as would be implied, for example, by a literal and uncritical use of projections from an econometric model.

The relationship between the growth of money and the growth of GNP can deviate from past patterns, for example, if the public's desire to hold money balances under given conditions— the "demand for money function" in the parlance of economists—changes. No one thinks the demand for money under given conditions is absolutely stable, but there are substantial differences of opinion as to just how important shifts in money demand may be. We have recently had highly suggestive (to me) evidence that the demand for money can in fact deviate far enough from the norm to have quite significant policy implications. Thus, over the first year of the current economic expansion, the income velocity (turnover) of M_1 balances rose very rapidly, by almost 8 percent. It is normal for velocity to rise at above-trend rates the first year of economic expansion, but the 1975–76 rise was abnormally rapid even so—the rate of increase exceeded the average for the four preceding upturns by nearly 60 percent. What is most striking about this abnormally rapid rise in velocity is that it occurred despite some net downward drift in the yields on a wide range of financial instruments (including common stocks) that are alternatives to holding money. Economists assume that declines in such yields ought to *reduce* the incentive to economize on noninterest-bearing M_1 balances. Thus they would normally expect interest rate declines to *reduce* velocity or at least slow its growth, not to produce the unusually rapid increase that actually occurred.

That velocity did, nevertheless, increase so rapidly suggests a weakened desire to hold money balances under given conditions. And there have been some institutional developments recently that could explain a shift of funds out of M_1 balances. These developments—including the spreading use of NOW accounts and the opening-up of savings accounts to business, for example—could explain the apparent reduction in the demand for M_1 balances that the figures on velocity seem to imply. The point of all of this is simply that anyone looking ahead at the very beginning of the recovery and trying to guess an appropriate rate of M_1 expansion for the year ahead would have had a real problem. Relying on past statistical relationships alone would have led him to a serious overestimate of the M_1 growth needed to finance the rather vigorous 13 percent growth of nominal GNP that actually occurred.

A second technical problem that complicates setting aggregate targets has to do with the changing relationships among the various monetary measures that are targeted. Over the years, M_2 and M_3 have on average grown more rapidly than M_1 (Chart 5). Thus under normal circumstances we would expect the M_2 and M_3 target ranges to be above the corresponding M_1 ranges —as they have over the past two years. Complicating the problem, however, is the fact that the differentials between the growth rates of M_1 and the other two measures have at times varied sharply.

The explanation for these shifting relative

Chart 5: Long-Term Trends in Growth of M_1, M_2, and M_3 (changes at annual rates from 12 quarters earlier)

growth rates lies mainly in the sensitivity of the time and savings deposits included in M_2 and M_3 (but not in M_1) to competition from open market instruments, such as Treasury bills and commercial paper. This sensitivity in itself might cause no particular problem if interest rate differentials between time and savings deposits and open market instruments were roughly constant. But, in fact, these interest rate differentials show rather sizable changes. These changes, in turn, follow roughly the overall average level of interest rates as it varies with the business cycle. In part, the changes in interest rate differentials result from Regulation Q, which puts limits on deposit interest rates and thus may prevent them from following market rates up when the latter are rising. But Regulation Q is only part of the story. For various reasons, deposit rates tend to be slow to adjust to changes in competing market rates even when market rates are relatively low and the legal ceilings are not a consideration.

The result of the sluggish adjustment of bank deposit rates to rising open market rates is often a flow of funds out of interest-bearing deposits along with a corresponding slowdown in M_2 and M_3 growth relative to M_1. Conversely, when market rates are falling, funds tend to flow back into time and savings accounts, resulting in abnormally rapid M_2 and M_3 growth relative to M_1. These movements clearly can create some dilemmas in setting targets. Over the past year, for example, M_1 grew 5.5 percent, about the middle of the 4½ to 7½ percent target range set early in the year, while M_2 grew by about 10.9 percent, somewhat above the upper end of its 7½ to 10½ percent range. The unusually wide spread between M_1 and M_2 growth in 1976 undoubtedly did reflect in large part the unusual declines in open market interest rates during the year. These declines clearly encouraged massive flows of funds out of market instruments and into the various types of time and savings deposits.

What is the proper attitude to take toward the unusually rapid growth rates of M_2 and M_3 in these circumstances? One possibility is simply to make some allowances for the fact that interest rate relationships between deposits and market instruments are out of line with their long-run equilibria and adjust upward the target ranges for M_2 and M_3 relative to M_1. This in fact is what the FOMC did at its October meeting. (The change was subsequently modified in January as bank time and savings deposit rates seemed to be adjusting downward to a more normal relationship with market rates.)

PROBLEMS IN HITTING TARGETS

Not only are there difficult problems in setting targets, there are equally difficult problems in achieving them once set. The trouble starts from the fact that the Federal Reserve does not control the money supply directly. Its direct influence is limited to the volume of reserves supplied through its open market operations, the terms and conditions on which it permits banks to obtain reserves through the discount window, and the level at which it sets required reserve ratios. Obviously, these tools are very important influences on the level of the money supply. Indeed, over a sufficiently long time horizon, they may be essentially determining. Nevertheless, the short-run slippage can be—and often is—enormous.

Week-to-week and even month-to-month figures on the seasonally adjusted annual growth rates in any of the monetary measures represent little more than statistical "noise" (Chart 6). These short-run movements are often heavily influenced, if not dominated, simply by problems of seasonal adjustment. It is hard to overemphasize the influence that seasonal adjustment procedures alone, with their inevitable uncertainties, can have over short-run annual growth rates computed for the monetary aggregates. Last year, for example, the difference between seasonally adjusted and unadjusted monthly changes at annual rates in M_1 varied from 4.5 percentage points (in March) to as high as 38.4 percentage points (in February). Even on a quarterly average basis, seasonality is critical, with differences between adjusted and unadjusted annual rates of

Chart 6: Behavior of M_1: Narrow Money Supply (changes from previous month; annual rates, seasonally adjusted)

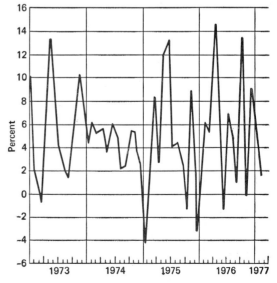

growth amounting to as much as 6.4 percentage points (in the fourth quarter). Obviously, uncertainties about the appropriate seasonal adjustment factors can translate into large uncertainties about annualized growth rates even over periods as long as a quarter.

Seasonality aside, other important short-run influences on monetary growth rates include flows between the public and the Treasury and shifts in the volume of trading on financial markets. These factors can have a substantial impact, at least temporarily, on the public's holdings of demand deposit balances. As a result, monetary growth rates tend to fluctuate sharply and erratically in the short run. To get a meaningful feel for how monetary growth rates are developing, it is really necessary to look at time horizons of six months or longer (Chart 7).

The erratic character of short-run monetary movements greatly complicates the task of deciding whether corrective actions are needed to achieve longer run targets. If no action is taken, there is a risk that the errors will cumulate and that temporary deviations will turn into long-run misses. If, however, action is taken prematurely to offset a random movement that would have corrected itself, the action will soon have to be reversed. In this case the end result may be unnecessary disturbances in reserve supplies and money market conditions.

There is, unfortunately, no really good way to detect when short-run deviations in monetary growth from longer run targets are truly temporary and when they reflect more fundamental

Chart 8:   Two-Month Tolerance Ranges in 1976

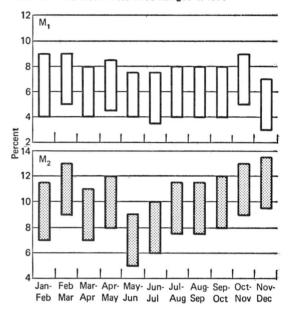

developments. Judgment, and the concomitant risk of error, is unavoidable in these situations. To avoid overreacting to short-term developments, the Federal Reserve has in practice tended to "tolerate" short-run swings in monetary growth rates over fairly wide ranges. The limits to such "toleration" have usually been expressed as upper and lower limits on two-month average growth rates—known, obviously enough, as "tolerance ranges." These ranges are set at levels that reflect the Open Market Committee's estimates of the various short-run influences that may be impinging on the monetary aggregates at any given time. As a result, the short-term tolerance ranges for any particular two-month period may differ significantly from the underlying one-year target ranges (Chart 8). Moreover, reflecting the highly unpredictable nature of short-term movements, the percentage point spreads embodied in the two-month tolerance ranges have normally been set wider than the spreads contained in the one-year target ranges.

The Federal Reserve is constantly looking for ways to improve its forecasts, and therefore its potential control, of short-run movements in the monetary aggregates. It is possible that over time, better data, changed institutional arrangements, more refined forecasting procedures, and improved tactical methods could lead to better short-run control. My own view, however, is that much of the problem of erratic short-run movements is likely to prove rather intractable. Some economists have suggested that improved short-

Chart 7:   Growth of M₁: Narrow Money Supply (annual rates, seasonally adjusted)

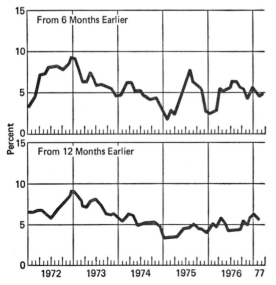

run control could be achieved by making forecasts of the (nonborrowed) reserve-deposit multiplier[1] over the month ahead, then simply supplying nonborrowed reserves in line with the desired level of deposits. While such a procedure may have some attractions, I have seen nothing to suggest that this technique would by itself significantly reduce the inherent difficulties of short-term monetary control.

To put the problem of short-term control in perspective, however, there seems to be little or no evidence that short-run fluctuations in monetary growth rates, even over periods of up to six months, have major impacts in the economy. Thus, it may be that the problem of short-run control is really not intolerably serious, however vexing it may be to those that have to try to deal with it.

CONCLUSION

Even this short review of monetary aggregate targets clearly indicates that there are many problems connected with them: problems in setting the targets, problems in hitting the targets, and indeed limits to what the approach can accomplish in improving the performance of the economy. In no sense has the use of monetary targets been able to turn what used to be called the "art" of central banking into a rigid mechanical process for controlling and monitoring the flow of money and credit. Judgment is required in determining at what levels the targets should be set and under what conditions and in what ways they should be changed. Judgment is also required in making the week-to-week and month-to-month decisions with regard to open market operations appropriate to achieving the targets. And, finally, judgment is required in deciding how to respond when monetary performance seems to be getting out of line with what had been expected and intended.

Nevertheless, despite all these caveats, the setting of monetary objectives covering fairly long time spans—however provisional and subject to change—seems to me one of the more constructive innovations in macroeconomic policymaking of recent years—not just in this country, but in others as well. It is a development, moreover, that seems especially useful in a period when high and variable rates of inflation have become one of our most serious problems.

---

[1] That is, the multiple that the total of banking system deposits is of total banking system nonborrowed reserves.

---

14. INNOVATIONS IN MONETARY POLICY*

Henry C. Wallich†

Central banks in numerous countries today have established money supply growth targets. The Reserve Bank of Australia, the Bank of Canada, the Bank of England, the Federal Reserve, the German Bundesbank, and the Swiss National Bank have adopted this approach in one form or another. While I believe that such targets can make valuable contributions under present in-

flationary conditions, I do not view them as wholly exogenous improvements in central bank technique. They are the consequence, rather, of high rates of inflation.

Historically, central banks have relied primarily on interest rates as their principal guide. In a severe inflation, however, interest rates cease to be a good guide. Nominal rates may rise very high, but they do not convey an accurate measure of the degree of restraint or stimulation implied. To the noneconomist, high nominal rates probably convey an impression of excessive restraint and so may generate political pressure against the anti-inflationary use of monetary policy. To the economist, nominal rates of inflation present the puzzle of translation into real rates. Short-term rates, which must be measured against actual more than expected inflation, often become negative. Long-term real rates must be derived from ex-

* A paper delivered at the meeting of the Southern Economic Association, Atlanta, Georgia, November 18, 1976. Reprinted by permission of the author. Henry C. Wallich is a Member of the Board of Governors of the Federal Reserve System.

† I am greatly indebted to David Lindsey and Ray Lombra for numerous valuable suggestions, and to Wayne Ayers for general assistance with the paper. Responsibility for errors, of course, remains my own. The views presented are my own, and do not necessarily represent those of my colleagues on the Federal Reserve Board.

pectations of inflation, which may differ among lenders as well as borrowers. Since the inflation premium is taxable to the lender and deductible to the borrower, after-tax real rates become largely indeterminate. For a wide range of taxable lenders and borrowers they probably have at times been negative in the United States.

The money supply and its rate of growth, on the other hand, are variables that intuitively relate to inflation. It is easy to see—and perhaps, therefore, more readily possible to convince the public and the legislature—that a 10 percent rate of growth of the money supply over considerable periods will tend to raise prices. Real balances can be computed on the basis of observed rather than expected inflation. But, in any event, real balances play a less important role than real interest rates, in an analysis that consists principally in relating the nominal money supply to nominal GNP and its price and volume components. Thus inflation gives a monetarist—or near-monetarist—tinge to nearly ·all ·monetary policy making. This is particularly so when, as has been the almost universal experience so far, inflation rates are highly variable and, therefore, hard to predict.

Sticking to a money supply target does not mean that the policymaker has necessarily changed his view of the transmission mechanism of monetary policy. In particular, it does not mean that he now subscribes to some sort of "direct" effect of money on the real sector. A money supply target is perfectly consistent with the belief that money works through interest rates and rates of return in a broad sense. For this very reason, under conditions of price stability, the policymaker may have thought it appropriate to work on interest rates directly instead of via the money supply. During inflation, however, he finds that the interest rates his policies produce will have a more predictable effect if he calibrates his action by the money supply and allows interest rates to take on such values as interaction between the money supply and the rest of the economy may determine. To recognize this principle, however, is only to posit a number of questions, both theoretical and statistical, that must be resolved for its application. Today I want to speak about some of these problems as they seem to have presented themselves in American experience.

DEFINITIONAL PROBLEMS

Debates about the proper definition of the monetary aggregates are as old as the effort to quantify these aggregates. I need merely list some currently important issues. M_1 is beset by problems such as the appropriate inclusion or exclusion of government deposits, of foreign deposits, and transit items. In addition, the demand for M_1 has recently been affected by institutional changes that have increased the moneyness of time and savings deposits, such as telephone transfers, NOW accounts, and savings deposits for business. These institutional changes as well as others may jointly have accounted for a reduction in the growth rate of M_1 of as much as two percentage points over the past year. Partly for this reason, the relationship of M_1 to income seems to have changed sufficiently to cause ordinary money demand equations to currently over-predict, in a simulation beginning in mid-1974, by something like $25 billion.

M_2, which has had a good record of stability in relation to income over the last ten years, nevertheless suffers from a variety of frailties. Savings deposits are increasingly serving as transactional balances. Thanks to Regulation Q, changes in market rates of interest lead to disintermediation and reintermediation. Furthermore, while large negotiable certificates of deposit are excluded for weekly reporting banks, they are not excluded for nonweekly reporters. Nonnegotiable large CDs are included for all banks, although banks freely switch one type to the other at the holder's request. Some $20–25 billion of large CDs, along with an increasing volume of consumer CDs with maturities of up to six years, now are included in M_2. Thus M_2 is spreading in two directions—becoming more monetary at one end and less so at the other.

Given the uncertainties attaching to both M_1 and M_2 and likewise to the higher M's, a possible remedy would be to give some weight to both instead of making a choice, and over time perhaps to vary these weights, as the Federal Reserve has done. It must be remembered, however, that such weighting systems in effect count M_1 twice, since it is contained in M_2.

Looking beyond M_1 and M_2, it becomes clear that some liabilities of nonbanks included in M_3 and even of nonfinancial institutions are sufficiently similar to some components of M_2 to make the drawing of a strict dividing line implausible. If one wishes to attribute a special quality to bank liabilities, one must consider also the advisability of paying special attention to bank credit as against nonbank credit. This would compel one to consider the asset side of bank balance sheets. It would raise the question, for instance, whether the fact that in the present expansion a large part of money creation has been against government securities rather than against business loans significantly reduces the expansionary power of the money supply thus created.

Finally, all aggregates are subject to the difficulties of seasonal adjustment. Monthly data would be difficult to interpret without adjustment. But different adjustment procedures, even though individually plausible, may give significantly different results in the short run. A study of 30 alternative M_1 adjustments, even after eliminating extremes, showed an average range for monthly adjustments of 4 percentage points in terms of annual growth rates. Annualized monthly rates of growth of the aggregates, therefore, must be treated with considerable reserve.[1]

So much for a small sampling of the conceptual, definitional, and statistical difficulties in establishing a money supply target. A few comments may be in order also with respect to the level at which the policy maker may want to set his target or targets, although this is more a question of objectives than of techniques.

STRATEGY OF TARGET SETTING

The money supply growth targets of all central banks today are far higher than is consistent with long-run price stability. In the absence of a trend in velocity, the growth of money over time would thus have to equal that of real GNP in order to maintain stable prices. Given a moderate upward trend in M_1 velocity, the noninflationary annual increase might be of an order not much above zero. It is perfectly obvious, then, that rates of money growth must be brought down over time if ending inflation is a goal of policy. The question is whether this should be done by a unidirectional reduction of the money supply targets, albeit perhaps a very slow one, or whether anticyclical considerations should be allowed, at times, to cause a reversal of this downward tendency. A steady downward path poses the risk of undesirable cyclical effects, such as a slowing of money growth in the face of a cyclical contraction. The alternative of upward and downward adjustments runs the risk that the intended long-term downward trend will, in fact, never materialize. It also reduces the credibility of the exercise and creates pro-inflationary

---

[1] Edward R. Fry, "Seasonal Adjustment of M_1," *Staff Economic Studies,* Board of Governors of the Federal Reserve System, 1976.

expectations. During a cyclical expansion, when an anticyclical stance requires restraint, this potential conflict, however, may lose relevance.

SPECIFICATION OF ONE-YEAR TARGETS

Once basic decisions have been made about rates of money growth, problems arise concerning the manner of specifying the targets. There is the choice between a single number and a range. A single number virtually guarantees a miss but by virtue of that fact also provides a reasonable excuse for missing. The uncompromising character of a single-number target, however, is also more apt to provoke controversy. A target range is easier to hit but, by the same token, a miss may be more severely criticized. At the same time, a range is likely to be less controversial because it is less specific.

Next, there is the phenomenon of "base drift" that is invited by periodic targets set in terms of growth rates as required by Concurrent Resolution 133, rather than absolute levels. Base drift occurs when the level attained after three months is not precisely on the midpoint growth path of the range but must nevertheless be used as the base for the next quarter's annual target range. Base drift could, of course, be corrected by adjusting the new growth ranges so as to bring the projected path back onto the old track with a lag of some months or quarters. This procedure, however, would lead to targets that change quarterly and might involve odd fractions, possibly confusing the public. Alternatively, the midpoint of the original growth path might be chosen for the location of the base of any new target range. It should be remembered, however, that base drift simply increases the flexibility already injected into the target procedure by the use of a range. It is to some extent an arbitrary decision whether to incorporate that flexibility in a wider range or in a less rigid determination of the base.

The degree of flexibility inherent in a target expressed as a range of growth rates increases with the passage of time as the upper and lower limits increasingly diverge in dollar terms. Thus, in the initial weeks after the setting of a target range the policymaker has less room for maneuver—or for error—than he has later on. This could be remedied by using the distance between the lower end and the upper limit achieved after six months or a year as the standard and allowing the policymaker the same degree of latitude early and late in the target period. Graphically, this would imply representing the target ranges by bands of constant widths instead of by cones.

Such a procedure, however, would probably allow excessive latitude during the early period following the setting of the target range. This matter is better dealt with by appropriate handling of the two-month targets that the Federal Reserve also employs. This topic, therefore, will be examined next.

SHORT-RUN TARGETS

Federal Reserve policy techniques—not, of course, its major objectives—are significantly influenced by the decentralized structure of the system. The Federal Open Market Committee (FOMC) meets monthly. In terms of travel time and competing demands upon the members' working time at their home base, this seems not an unreasonable frequency, although other arrangements obviously are possible. One month, therefore, is the natural interval for formulating and executing policy decisions. The Open Market Manager at the Federal Reserve Bank of New York, who is in the market every day, must be given instructions for this period. A centralized monetary authority would not be so constrained. It could conceivably make minor policy decisions from day to day, although it might not find that very convenient.

Given the instability of the aggregates over short periods of time, however, a month would be a very short period over which to confine the aggregates to a narrow range. Efforts to do so, aside from producing large jumps in the Federal funds rate, might well cause the Fed to over-react to preliminary indications of changes in the rate of growth that more complete figures could disavow. The money supply figures do not come into being fully known and accurate on a certain day. They evolve gradually from fragmentary reports. Reasonably hard data are available—and are published—eight days after the end of the statement week. A first revision appears 15 days after the statement week and further revisions follow quarterly as data on nonmember banks become available.

There are several options for dealing with the problem of short-run instability of the aggregates. One would be to set a very wide range for a monthly growth rate. A second would be to ignore short-term variations in the growth of the aggregates altogether. A third, which the System has chosen, is to average the growth of two successive months in order to get a little more stability into the growth rate. A further variant of this approach would be to lengthen this averaging period. The resulting greater stability of the averaged data would, of course, be purchased at the cost of reduced sensitivity to new data.

Further options are offered by the possibility to employ not only past but estimated data. The FOMC's present procedure, in fact, relies primarily upon estimated data. Of the two-months' averages which are employed for formulating short-term targets, only one week is reasonably firm and has been published. The rest of the two months is estimated, though some fragmentary data are available. It would be possible also to lengthen the averaging period forward by including more distant estimates, as well as backward, again trading stability for sensitivity. The longer the averaging period, the more closely must the aggregates be tied to the one-year targets in order to avoid the need for subsequent drastic readjustments. Here again, a problem of base drift presents itself.

Implicit in the various options cited is the question how quickly and strongly the Fed should react to new incoming data, at the risk that they may represent only "noise." By chasing the data, the Fed runs the risk of making false starts, of having to reverse frequently, of misleading the market and whipsawing it. By ignoring new data, it runs the risk of acting too late, of having to act more forcefully than if action had been timely, and perhaps of being pushed off track altogether. Optimal control theory tells us that all new information, in this case particularly the incoming aggregates, should be considered, but that it should be filtered to eliminate noise as far as possible. One possible way of approximating this principle would be to give a lower weight to newer and more uncertain data. Establishing the weights remains a problem however.

The question whether it is wise for the Fed to watch and follow the data closely is often coupled with the question whether it is wise for the market to watch and follow the Fed. It is obvious that, if Fed operations have an influence on the market, the market is bound to engage in Fed-watching. But the nature of the Fed's influence on the market depends very much on the choice of instrument used by the Fed—the Federal funds rate, as at present, or some reserve aggregate. This consideration leads to the much discussed issue of the funds rate versus a reserve aggregate as the policy instrument.

FEDERAL FUNDS RATE VERSUS NONBORROWED RESERVES

The Federal Reserve policy strategy is based in large part on the monetary aggregates, but its short-run tactical instrument is the Federal funds rate. Under the funds rate approach, the Federal Reserve estimates the level of short-term interest rates, including the funds rate, at which the public, given projections of income, will want to hold the amount of money the Federal Reserve intends to supply. Then reserves are supplied in an amount that will maintain that level of the funds rate, and that will cause the banks to generate the targeted amount of money.

Under a nonborrowed reserves (NBR) approach, the Federal Reserve might estimate, via a multiplier approach, the amount of required reserves that would be related to the aggregates it intends to supply. In such an approach it would then be necessary to estimate the amount of excess reserves and borrowed reserves that would prevail at the short-term interest rates, including the funds rate, consistent with the targeted money supply. In this way it would thus be possible to arrive at an estimate of the volume of nonborrowed reserves that must be supplied to reach the target.

The principle for choosing between interest rates and aggregates as means of stabilizing income developed by William Poole[2] can be applied also, with appropriate modifications, to the objective of stabilizing money or its rate of growth. Given fully known and stable relationships, the choice of an interest rate or aggregates instrument, of course, becomes immaterial. Either instrument fully determines the other. When there are shocks to one or the other of the variables, a simple criterion applies.

When the objective is to keep the money supply (or its growth rate) constant, the policymaker finds himself dealing with a money demand and a money supply function. The selection principle then is:

1. If the shock is to the money supply function, for instance by an increase in banks' demand for excess reserves, a constant interest rate will keep the money supply constant given a stable money demand function. An interest rate target, therefore, would be the appropriate one. The supply of reserves would have to be varied in order to accommodate the demand.

2. Alternatively, if the shock is to the money demand function, a reserve aggregates target will minimize the impact on the money supply. Keeping the money supply function constant by, for instance, keeping nonborrowed reserves constant,

would allow interest rates to rise as demand increases. This would dampen, although not entirely prevent, an increase in the money supply in response to the increase in demand.[3]

There is a good deal of empirical evidence to indicate that the precision of the two procedures is broadly the same. For a period of one month, the standard error is about 4.5 percentage points of the annual rate of growth of M_1, and 3 percentage points of the rate of growth of M_2.[4] Over a period of six months, the standard error for both procedures reduces to about one-half of a percentage point for M_1 and one-third of a percentage point for M_2. Thus, if we believe that short-run deviations from the aggregates targets are not important so long as longer run targets are hit, the issue of which of the two approaches is more precise loses much of its importance. If one believes, to be sure, that deviations even for relatively short periods have an impact upon the real sector and thus generate a feedback from the real sector upon the demand for money, greater attention to such short-run deviations would be necessary. In any event, however, the proposition that short-run deviations do not greatly matter does not imply that they can be ignored. They must be compensated for over the longer run. If no compensation for an overshoot or shortfall over one or two months is provided in the following months, the longer run result

---

[3] A more precise statement of this principle is that the relative stability of the money demand function must be compared with the reduced form money stock equation, relating the equilibrium money stock to a reserve aggregate and to income. The stability of the reduced form equation depends both on the instability of the money demand and the money supply function. Because movements in interest rates partially offset shocks to either of these, the stability of a reduced form equation combining both is greater than the average stability of both, assuming their errors are independent. When both supply and demand functions are equally stable, therefore, a reserves aggregate instrument is still preferable to an interest rate instrument.

[4] See James L. Pierce and Thomas D. Thompson, "Some Issues in Controlling the Stock of Money," *Controlling Monetary Aggregates II: The Implementation,* Federal Reserve Bank of Boston Conference Series, no. 9, September 1972; Richard J. Davis and Frederick C. Schadrack, "Forecasting the Monetary Aggregates with Reduced-Form Equations," *Monetary Aggregates and Monetary Policy,* Federal Reserve Bank of New York, 1974. Somewhat larger monthly errors over the more recent years 1974 and 1975 under either a Federal funds rate or reserve aggregate procedure have been estimated by William R. McDonough, "Effectiveness of Alternative Approaches to Monetary Control," Federal Reserve Bank of Dallas *Business Review,* August 1976.

---

[2] William Poole, "Optimal Choice of Monetary Policy Instruments in a Simple Stochastic Macro Model," *Quarterly Journal of Economics,* May 1970.

will be affected and must be expected to have its impact upon the real sector.

If all this is understood, it can fairly be said that the choice between the funds rate and the nonborrowed reserves procedure must rest, not on the degree of precision that can be attained in hitting the target, but on other aspects of these procedures.

The funds rate procedure offers an opportunity to limit the variability of the funds rate and other interest rates in the short run, since it automatically accommodates purely random and transitory shifts in the money demand schedule which should not, in any case, be transmitted to the real sector. For instance, it automatically provides a seasonal adjustment for the money supply. The funds rate procedure allows changes in rates to occur gradually and without frequent reversals. Avoidance of sharp interest rate instability means avoidance of the cost of such instability. Principally, these costs take the form of weakening the market mechanism by increasing the risks of dealing in and owning securities. Greater stability of interest rates reduces unpredictable flows into or out of thrift institutions triggered by Regulation Q ceilings. Transmission of these elements of instability to the real sector, to investment and savings decisions, in whatever degree they might occur, likewise is avoided if rates are more stable.

A second significant, albeit double-edged, gain from a more deliberate movement of the funds rate is the greater control that it provides over the entire rate structure. When the market knows that the monetary authorities use the funds rate to control the aggregates, it naturally will watch the aggregates closely for a tip-off on future movements of the funds rate. If, in addition, the market knows that the authorities try to avoid erratic movements in the funds rate, it will attribute policy significance to such movements. It then becomes logical for other short-term rates to move in response to changes in the aggregates that are expected to trigger a funds rate change. All short-term money market instruments are to some extent substitutes. Through term structure and expectation effects, longer rates may also be affected. Thus, by making the funds rate an important instrument of policy, the money authorities in effect are linking together the entire rate structure and are providing themselves with a lever to move that structure. The manner in which, in some European money markets of the past, the discount rate was linked by law or custom to other rates provides an analogy.

But this role of the funds rate, as noted, is two edged. The impact of a funds rate change upon market rates may at times be undesirable to the authorities, even though the funds rate movement may be necessary to control the aggregates. There is a possibility that the authorities might become reluctant to move the funds rate sufficiently fast and far, and if necessary to reverse earlier movements, when that should become necessary to prevent the aggregates from moving undesirably. Overshoots or shortfalls from the monetary targets could then develop. As an extreme case, the authorities might be tempted to regard the funds rate, not as an instrument to attain the aggregates, but as a policy objective in its own right. In that case, the shift from interest rates to monetary aggregates alluded to at the beginning of this paper would have been reversed.

These potential consequences of a funds rate approach would largely vanish if the authorities were prepared to move the funds rate frequently and sharply, without concern about reversals, false signals, and purely aiming at the closest possible control of the aggregates. In that event, the linkage between the funds rate and other market rates would weaken. If, for instance, the funds rate were expected to fluctuate randomly around some particular value over the next 90 days, Treasury bill rates presumably would take their cue from that expected average rather than from the day-to-day or week-to-week levels of the funds rate. This partial "uncoupling" of the rest of the rate structure from the funds rate would reduce its usefulness as a lever over other rates. It would also thereby reduce the sensitivity of the demand for money to funds rates movements which work via short-term interest rates. But it would make the funds rate more maneuverable for the purpose of hitting the aggregates targets.

Use of the nonborrowed reserves target would probably have precisely this effect of in some degree uncoupling the funds rate from the rest of the rate structure. Over short periods the funds rate probably would move around in an erratic way. Other rates would take their cue from some expected average of these movements rather than from any particular move or level. To the extent that this happened, the potential usefulness of the funds rate as a lever on other rates would disappear, which in some respects would be a loss. Moreover, since some degree of linkage no doubt would remain, there would be a cost, although much diminished, from this hypothetical instability of the funds rate. But reasonably close control of the aggregates over the longer run would be automatically more assured, and the danger of inadvertently slipping from an aggregates to an interest rate strategy would disappear. The market might lose its interest in Fed-watching, or at least would have to change its method of watching. An incidental potential benefit of a nonborrowed reserves target would be realized in case the Federal Reserve should ever decide to publish its policy decisions immediately, since announcement of the intended future behavior of nonborrowed reserves obviously would produce fewer complications than announcement of the intended future behavior of the funds rate.

A lesser potential although minor disadvantage of a nonborrowed reserves approach is that at times the money supply and interest rates may move in inconsistent directions—money and interest rates both moving up or down together. More serious perhaps the diminished link between the funds rate and the bill rate may make it more difficult to influence the demand for money which is guided, other things equal, by the bill rate. Unless the bill rate moves, holders of money balances have no portfolio motives to shift between balances and short-term instruments.

To summarize, there is not much that could be done under one regime that could not be done under the other. The aggregates could be effectively controlled, and the funds rate could be partly uncoupled from the rest of the interest rate structure by appropriate handling of the alternative instruments. It is with respect to the costs of such handling, and the risks involved in trying to avoid these costs, that the approaches differ.

---

15. INTERPRETING THE FED'S MONETARY TARGETS*

William Poole

House Concurrent Resolution .133, passed in March 1975, requires that

. . . the Board of Governors shall consult with Congress at semiannual hearings before the Commitee on Banking, Housing and Urban Affairs of the Senate and the Committee on Banking, Currency and Housing of the House of Representatives about the Board of Governors' and the Federal Open Market Committee's objectives and plans with respect to the ranges of growth or diminution of monetary and credit aggregates in the upcoming twelve months . . .[1]

The Federal Reserve has responded by setting targets for four different variables: M_1, M_2, M_3, and the bank-credit proxy.[2] (The proxy was later dropped from the list.) The first set of one-year targets covered the period from March 1975 to March 1976, while the second, third, and fourth sets were defined in terms of the growth of the quarterly average of the targeted variables from the second, third, and fourth quarters of 1975 to the corresponding quarters of 1976. The purpose of this report is to analyze initial experience with this targeting procedure.

The first and second sections outline the features and problems of the present targeting procedures, and the third examines the operational significance of the announced targets. An alternative method of expressing monetary targets is suggested next, and the final section offers a few comments on the possibility, suggested by some, of adding interest-rate targets to the present system.

In the discussion below, I have attempted to avoid all issues of the desirability of House Concurrent Resolution 133, as well as general issues of Federal Reserve independence. The relative merits of various monetary aggregates as policy targets will not be examined—the use of M_1 rather than M_2 or M_3 in the figures reflects expositional convenience only—and finally, except for a few comments in the last section, the advisability of monetary targets rather than interest-rate targets will not be discussed.

I do discuss issues concerning the comprehensibility of announced targets to the Congress and the general public. Whatever the political merits of House Concurrent Resolution 133, the mechanism should not be vulnerable to confusion caused by correctable defects in the way mone-

---

* From *Brookings Papers on Economic Activity* (No. 1, 1976), pp. 247–59. Copyright © 1976 by The Brookings Institution, Washington, D.C. Reprinted by permission of the publisher and the author. William Poole is Professor of Economics, Brown University.

[1] *Conduct of Monetary Policy*, Conference Report to Accompany H. Con. Res. 133, Rept. 94–91, 94:1 (Government Printing Office, 1975), p. 1.

[2] For definitions of these monetary aggregates, see table 1, note *c*.

Table 1: Growth Targets of Money and Credit Measures, and Actual Growth, Various Periods, March 1975–Fourth Quarter 1976 (percent change at annual rates)

Interval* and type of growth†	Monetary measure‡			
	M_1	M_2	M_3	Credit proxy
March 1975–March 1976				
Target.........................	5–7.5	8.5–10.5	10–12	6.5–9.5
Actual.........................	5.0	9.4	12.1	3.3
1975:2–1976:2				
Target.........................	5–7.5	8.5–10.5	10–12	6.5–9.5
Actual§.........................	4.4	9.0	11.6	3.2
1975:3–1976:3				
Target.........................	5–7.5	7.5–10.5	9–12	‖
Actual§.........................	3.2	8.3	10.6	—
1975:4–1976:4				
Target.........................	4.5–7.5	7.5–10.5	9–12	‖
Actual§.........................	3.8	9.8	11.3	—

* On *May 1, 1975*, the targets for March 1975 to March 1976 were announced; on *July 24, 1975*, for 1975:2 to 1976:2; on *November 4, 1975*, for 1975:3 to 1976:3; and on *February 3, 1976*, for 1975:4 to 1976:4.

† The actual growth rates are calculated from seasonally adjusted data.

‡ M_1 consists of demand deposits at commercial banks plus currency in circulation; M_2 is M_1 plus savings and time deposits at commercial banks other than large-denomination negotiable certificates of deposit; M_3 is M_2 plus deposits at mutual savings banks, savings and loan shares, and credit union shares; the credit proxy is total member-bank deposits subject to reserve requirements, plus Eurodollar borrowings, loans sold to bank-related institutions, and certain other nondeposit items.

§ Actual growth rate from base quarter to March 1976, the latest information available at time of this writing.

‖ Not targeted.

Sources: Targets, *Federal Reserve Bulletin*, vol. 61 (May 1975), p. 286; (August 1975), p. 495; (November 1975), p. 747, and vol. 62 (February 1976), p. 124. Actual, ibid. (April 1976), p. 12, and Board of Governors of the Federal Reserve System, Statistical Release H.6, May 6, 1976.

tary targets are expressed and explained by the Federal Reserve.

PRESENT MONETARY-TARGETING PROCEDURES

Table 1 summarizes the targets and experience to date with the quarterly procedure initiated in 1975. According to the preliminary data available for March 1976, the M_1 and M_2 targets for March 1976 were met, M_3 ran a whisker above its target range, and the credit proxy fell well below its range. The second, third, and fourth target announcements pertain to dates still in the future at the time of this writing; hence, for each of these periods, the entries in the table present the actual growth rates from the base quarters to March 1976, and may be viewed as "progress reports."

An examination of the table raises a question: Why was the first target range of M_1 met and yet, according to the progress reports, M_1 growth subsequently fell below the target ranges?

Figure 1 provides the answer to this question. In the figure each vertical bar shows the target range in the level of M_1, calculated by applying the target growth range to the base level shown at the apex of each cone-like figure, which in turn

is formed by connecting the ends of the bars to the base level.[3] Only the vertical bars themselves should be considered the targets, but a comparison of actual M_1 to the cones visualizes the progress reports. Since the money stock has not remained on the axes of the cones defined by earlier announcements, the base level underlying each new announcement—and therefore the target range for one year ahead in terms of the level of M_1—has to some extent been inconsistent with previously announced targets.

The Fed has defined targets for other aggregates in the same way as for M_1, and therefore the problem illustrated by Figure 1 is not confined to that aggregate. To date the inconsistencies have been smaller for M_2 and M_3 than for M_1, but they need not remain so in the future.

PROBLEMS WITH THE CURRENT PROCEDURES

The current targeting procedure has two defects, one major and the other minor. The major one is the probability of generating successive

---

[3] Since the second, third, and fourth announcements defined targets in terms of quarterly averages, the vertical bars have been placed at the middle months of the quarters for these targets.

Figure 1:   Federal Reserve's Target Ranges for M_1, Announced Quarterly in 1975 for One Year Ahead, and Actual M_1*

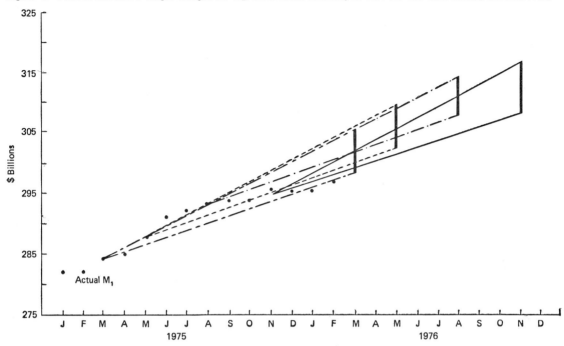

* M_1 is demand deposits at commercial banks plus currency in circulation. The cone-like figures define the policy targets as explained in the text. The heavy dots represent actual monthly M_1.
   Sources: Actual M_1, *Federal Reserve Bulletin*, vol. 62 (February 1976), p. A 12, and Board of Governors of the Federal Reserve System, Statistical Release H.6, May 6, 1976; targets, calculated from actual and target growth rates in Table 1.

targets that either are inconsistent or represent inadvertent departures from (more or less) steady growth paths desired by policymakers. This problem is illustrated by the apparently haphazard relationship of the successive cones in Figure 1. The minor defect is the potential for inconsistency among targets for multiple variables.

Inconsistencies in Base Levels

Defining monetary targets as the Fed has been doing is, I believe, unfortunate. Short-run fluctuations in the money stock may be desirable, or unavoidable, or both, but ought not to be automatically built into targets for one year ahead.

The economic arguments supporting this position can be explained readily. It is generally agreed that monetary fluctuations have effects on employment, prices, and so on that are distributed over time. If, for example, 6 percent growth in money is desirable, most economists will agree that 8 percent growth for one quarter followed by 4 percent growth the next will affect GNP and the other variables very much as would two quarters of steady 6 percent growth. If, however, an 8 percent quarter is followed by a string of 6 percent quarters, then, as the distributed-lag effects are worked out, the "extra" money growth

of the 8 percent quarter will have an influence on the economy. Many economists would expect this unreversed extra growth to lower unemployment temporarily and eventually to raise the price level permanently above what it otherwise would have been.[4]

Moreover, the economy's response to monetary fluctuations may depend in part on the views held in the private sector about the Fed's monetary strategy. If the public believes that short-run monetary fluctuations will be reversed, the impact of those fluctuations on the economy is likely

---

[4] Put more precisely, a reduced-form equation explaining unemployment by money growth would have a fairly long distributed lag with negative early lag coefficients, positive later ones, and either a zero sum of the coefficients (vertical long-run Phillips curve) or, possibly, a somewhat positive sum. Similarly, the reduced-form explanation of the inflation rate by the growth rate of the money stock has a distributed lag whose coefficients sum to one. Other things equal, a quarter with 2 percentage points of extra money growth that is not reversed in subsequent quarters will affect unemployment and prices over time as indicated in the example in the text. If the extra money growth is reversed, the effects on unemployment and prices will be limited to the *differences* between the distributed-lag coefficients for adjacent quarters; these differences will be small if the distributed-lag patterns are, as usually assumed, reasonably smooth.

to be small; if these fluctuations are not reversed, especially if they continue quarter after quarter in the same direction, the speed of the response of the private economy eventually will change as households and firms come to expect these continuations rather than reversals.

Monetary fluctuations arising from transitory financial-market disturbances and data and control errors are caused by factors that are by definition "temporary"—short-lived relative to the length of the distributed-lag effects of money on the economy. A "permanent" change in conditions —a change enduring relatively long compared with distributed-lag effects—may well call for a change in monetary targets. However, the present targeting procedure, by defining targets one year ahead in terms of growth rates on bases equal to actual levels of the money stock, implicitly treats *all* short-run monetary fluctuations on responses to permanent changes.

The quantitative importance of this issue for interpreting the Fed's monetary targets is most easily examined in the context of data revisions. These are readily observable and measurable, whereas control errors and the Fed's deliberate responses to temporary factors are not because the Fed's intentions are not. As an example, the first statement of one-year targets on May 1, 1975, included, among other data, the March 1975 level of M_1, reported to be $286.8 billion. As of this writing, however, M_1 for March 1975 —after a series of downward revisions reported in the issues of the *Federal Reserve Bulletin* for June and October 1975 and February 1976—is reported to be $284.1 billion, or 1.0 percent below the original estimate; a revision of this size is not trivial relative to a target growth range for M_1 that is 2.5 percentage points wide.

Revisions of this magnitude are by no means uncommon, and while the Fed has always emphasized data problems in the abstract, it has offered no guidance—in the quarterly hearings or elsewhere—on how such revisions should affect the interpretation of the targets. Because of all the technical detail involved, the Fed will find it particularly awkward to explain a situation in which data revisions alter estimates for adjacent base quarters in opposite directions, producing target levels for adjacent quarters that are highly inconsistent (in the sense relevant to economic policy).

Multiple Targets

The current practice of targeting three different variables raises relatively minor issues since the variables—M_1, M_2, and M_3—are highly correlated. However, any question about the accuracy of the Fed's aim can be answered unambiguously only when the target ranges for all three are hit or they are all missed. Moreover, should all three target ranges be missed, but some on the high side and others on the low, it might be argued that the Fed did not "really" miss its announced targets. Indeed, if the differential growth rates among the targeted variables are not what the Fed expected, it probably makes good sense for the policy makers to aim above some and below others.

The major problem with multiple targets, in my opinion, is that the greater the number, the greater the possibility that the targeting procedure will lose meaning. With only one target variable, the Fed would be under greater pressure either to hit that target or to provide persuasive reasons for missing. The convenience of the opportunity to hit by chance one of many targets invites indecision and delay in either hitting the primary target or marshaling evidence to justify the miss. Finally, with many targets, the Federal Reserve finds it much easier to discuss its policy publicly in terms of a mass of technical detail and to rationalize the addition or elimination of variables from the targeted set. The credit proxy, for example, was dropped as a target variable with no mention whatsoever in the November 4, 1975, announcement of targets.[5]

Significance of These Problems

The issues examined above are important for two reasons. House Concurrent Resolution 133 presumably was designed to increase congressional influence over monetary policy, in part by providing regular quarterly hearings for congressional comment on Federal Reserve plans. If that was the congressional intent, the present ambiguities in the definitions of the targets, which invite confusion and misunderstanding, surely do not further it. Second, the Federal Reserve has devised a targeting system under which targets

---

[5] An explanation of the reasons for dropping the credit proxy should have been provided. Immediately following the quotation at the beginning of this report, H. Con. Res. 133 says that "nothing in this resolution shall be interpreted to require that such ranges of growth or diminution be achieved if the Board of Governors and the Federal Open Market Committee determine that they cannot or should not be achieved because of changing conditions. The Board of Governors shall report to the Congress the reasons for any such determination during the next hearings held pursuant to this resolution."

for several variables will from time to time be inconsistent and, worse yet, targets for the same variable in successive quarters will from time to time be inconsistent if the successive targets are meant to hold simultaneously. That monetary targeting need not entail these problems is shown below, in my discussion of an alternative procedure.

OPERATIONAL SIGNIFICANCE OF THE ANNOUNCED TARGETS

In the four statements to date announcing targets, the Federal Reserve has adopted almost identical target growth rates, apparently reflecting the beliefs that unchanged money growth rates reflect unchanged policy and that no policy change has been needed. For example, the July statement contained this passage:

Economic prospects now are not materially different than the Federal Reserve anticipated 2 or 3 months ago, and we therefore as yet see no reason to alter the general course of monetary policy. Accordingly, the Federal Open Market Committee has reaffirmed its intent to seek the growth ranges announced earlier.[6]

But the Fed has also emphasized that short-run monetary control is very imprecise and that the one-year target growth rates do not necessarily imply comparable targets over shorter intervals. By reporting unchanged targets for growth rates —rather than levels—of the money stock, the Fed's announcements incorporate no provision for reversing abnormally high or low money growth over short periods and therefore are not in fact consistent with hitting the longer-run targets.

Since the Fed has emphasized that the targets for money growth are not to be interpreted as implying comparable targets over short periods, and since the procedure incorporates short-run monetary fluctuations into the target levels, the question is whether the Fed's open market operations will be designed to reverse short-run surges or shortfalls of money growth, or whether the new targets announced every quarter will in fact supersede previously announced targets. There is yet too little experience to suggest which course the Fed will choose. But in the particular case of the announcement on February 3, 1976, the market apparently accepted the latter interpreta-

tion of Fed response to the relatively slow M_1 growth in the second half of 1975—2.7 percent annual rate, June to December. Before February 3, the money markets had been expecting the Fed to push interest rates down; when the Fed reduced the minimum target growth rate for M_1 from 5 to 4.5 percent, money-market rates rose.

My prediction is that, for the most part, the Fed will tend to adjust the money stock to stay within the original target range. With three aggregates targeted, the target for one rather than its level might be adjusted—a quite sensible action since available evidence gives no strong reason for favoring one over another. But I find it difficult to believe that the Fed would risk a situation in which all of its target variables might fall significantly below (above) their originally projected and publicly announced target ranges at a time when the economy might in retrospect prove to have been weak (strong).

AN ALTERNATIVE METHOD OF EXPRESSING TARGETS FOR MONETARY AGGREGATES

The problems with the current procedures could be largely avoided by expressing the targets for M_1, M_2, and M_3 as illustrated for M_1 in Figure 2. In this figure, the most recently available official data on M_1 are plotted as a series of points.

The solid trend line starts at the actual 1975:1 average for M_1, with a growth rate of 6¼ percent, the midpoint of the original 5–7½ percent targets.[7] The 5–7½ percent targets were announced three times, and so the 6¼ percent trend line is simply extended out to 1976:3, still using the original 1975:1 base, rather than the *actual* money stock in the "new" base quarter.

The M_1 targets announced February 3, 1976, were 4½–7½ percent growth, with a midpoint of 6 percent. A vertical bar is drawn in the middle of 1976:3, the last quarter to which the 6¼ percent midpoint target applies. The new 6 percent midpoint target rate produces a path starting from a base level defined by the old target path for the money stock rather than by the actual 1975:4 average money stock. The 6 percent path, of course, gradually diverges from the old 6¼ percent path. Each time the 6 percent target is renewed, the 6 percent trend line will be ex-

[6] "Statement by Arthur F. Burns, Chairman, Board of Governors of the Federal Reserve System, before the Committee on Banking, Housing, and Urban Affairs, U.S. House of Representatives, July 24, 1975," in *Federal Reserve Bulletin,* vol. 61 (August 1975), p. 495.

[7] The careful eye may note that this trend line has a slight upward curvature since it was constructed by applying the money growth rate with quarterly compounding that is equal to 6¼ percent with annual compounding.

Figure 2:   Results Using Proposed Procedure for Reporting the Federal Reserve's Target Ranges for M₁, and Actual M₁, 1975–1976*

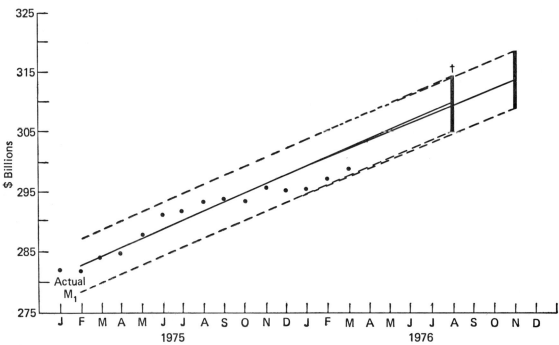

* M₁ is demand deposits at commercial banks plus currency in circulation. The parallel lines define the policy targets as explained in the text. The heavy dots represent actual monthly M₁.
† The 1975:1 target growth rate was renewed for the following two quarters, thus extending the period to 1976:3.
Sources: Actual, same as Figure 1; solid trend line, derived using a growth rate of 6¼ percent, the midpoint of the 5–7½ percent targets in table 1 (compounded quarterly), applied to the actual 1975:1 M₁ average, and a growth rate of 6 percent (the midpoint of the last target entry in Table 1), applied to a base level defined by the old path; band width, current trend level plus and minus 1½ percentage points. See text for further explanation.

tended and the vertical bar drawn three months further into the future.

The band defined by the dashed lines in the figure is a suggested reinterpretation of the target range. The present 4½–7½ percent range may be viewed as a level four quarters away equal to 1.06 times the current level, plus or minus 0.015 of that level. In Figure 2, the dashed bands are drawn 1½ percentage points above and below the target path represented by the solid line. The width of the band in November 1976 represents the same dollar spread (except for a very minor difference due to different base levels) as the width of the cone for November 1976 in Figure 1. The band width has been selected in this way in order that the suggested procedure correspond as closely as possible to the current procedure in the amount of leeway the Federal Reserve believes appropriate in selecting one-year targets for money growth.

Under the suggested procedure the Federal Reserve would present its targets for the growth of monetary aggregates not in terms of a range but in terms of one number defining the central growth trend and a second number defining band

limits as percentages of the level of the aggregate around the central growth trend.[8] By presenting charts such as Figure 2, the Fed would direct the public's attention to the level of the money stock within the band instead of actual rates for money growth over short periods of time. For example, as of this writing, the March 1976 level of M₁ would be viewed as being somewhat above the lower band rather than as having risen in the last six months at the relatively low rate of only 3.3 percent per year. This approach would also make it easy to provide a feel for data errors. Each observation of the money stock could be presented as a short bar representing the point estimate plus and minus the estimated standard error.

---

[8] The language of House Concurrent Resolution 133 seems to require disclosure of target growth rates based on actual base-period data for the money stock. These targets should be obtained by calculation from the actual base level to the ends of the target range one year ahead defined by the band in Figure 2. When base-period data are revised, the previously announced target growth rates would be revised by redoing the above calculation rather than automatically revising the target levels for one year ahead.

GENERAL COMMENTS ON INTEREST-RATE TARGETING

Although economists differ on the desirability of announced—and unannounced—monetary targets, they generally agree that it is technically feasible to hold a particular definition of the money stock within a band as defined in Figure 2. Disturbances may make it *undesirable* to hold a money-stock variable within such a band, but are unlikely to make it *impossible* to do so. Of course, it may not be possible to keep several different monetary variables within predetermined bands.

Interest-rate targeting is another matter. If interest-rate targets were announced—with or without accompanying monetary targets—missing them would be the rule rather than the exception unless the target bands were very wide. An attempt to hold a particular interest rate in a relatively narrow band when market pressures tend to push it outside is *cumulatively* destabilizing. Interest-rate pegging was abandoned after World War II not simply because it was undesirable but because it was infeasible. The market forces that destroyed the interest-peg policy did act slowly —surprisingly so, in my opinion—but they now operate much more rapidly. Under present conditions, an announced one-year target for interest rates would have to be abandoned every quarter, and in fact ordinarily would not last even through a quarter.

Short-run interest-rate targets for short-term securities could be announced and achieved most of the time, but would cause constant trouble. If publicly committed to an interest-rate range, the Federal Reserve would be blamed, much more than at present, for increases in interest rates, since they would reflect either failure to hold to announced targets or deliberate and announced changes in targets. Though confined to short-term securities, targets would nevertheless affect the long-term market, where capital losses from rate increases can be substantial.

If Fed policy is linked directly and immediately to the capital gains and losses experienced by bondholders, great pressure will be mobilized for political decisionmaking in these tax- and subsidy-like policy actions—a process involving public debate and the more or less formal approval of policy changes by elected public officials.

During this political decision-making process, market reactions anticipating interest-rate changes would make it more difficult to achieve targets, and political reactions after policy changes would make it more difficult to change future targets. On the other hand, it is feasible to determine money-stock targets through the political process. Changes in the money stock do not have unambiguous effects on the direction of interest-rate changes, and delay in changing the rate of money growth is not cumulatively destabilizing.

In summary, a precondition for announced policy targets—in the sense of targets for variables under the control of the policymakers rather than in the sense of goals for variables like employment or inflation—is that the targets be achievable. If announced monetary-policy targets are viewed as desirable for some combination of reasons involving the accountability of public officials and the provision of information to improve the functioning of private markets, those targets must involve monetary magnitudes rather than interest rates. If a formal procedure of announced targets for interest rates is introduced, the effects of the procedure are certain to be harmful and the system is likely to be short lived.

Chapter

4

FISCAL POLICY

The selections in the remainder of this book deal with the use of fiscal policy, monetary policy, and debt management policy to regulate aggregate demand in the interest of economic stability and growth. The context for the discussion in this and the next chapter is a closed economy—that is, although there may be occasional references to balance-of-payments problems, it is generally assumed that the policy makers are free to use the fiscal and monetary instruments to pursue domestic goals without being constrained by problems arising in the foreign sector. During almost the entire period since World War I up until about 1960, the U.S. balance-of-payments situation was such that we were able to use monetary and fiscal policy quite freely to control internal demand in the interest of domestic employment and price stability. At times—notably in the 1930s— we were strikingly unsuccessful in achieving satisfactory levels of employment, but our failure in this regard cannot in any sense be attributed to problems related to the balance of payments. However, during the 1960s and early 1970s, the situation changed markedly, and the balance of payments acted as a significant constraint on our freedom to use fiscal and monetary policy—especially the latter—to regulate internal demand. Under the fixed-exchange-rate system then in effect, the implications for the balance of payments of the domestic interest rate level was a continuing concern to the monetary authorities. But in 1973 the fixed-rate system broke down and was replaced by a system of "managed floating" under which the rates at which the major currencies exchange for each other are determined by market forces, with occasional intervention by the authorities. This system permits much more latitude to the stabilization authorities to use both policy instruments for domestic purposes. The balance of payments, its relationship to fiscal and monetary policy, and the changes that occurred in the international financial system in the early 1970s and their implications for policy are discussed in some detail in the selections included in Chapters 6 and 7 and in the chapter introductions.

This chapter is concerned with the proper use of fiscal policy. Fiscal policy is discussed before dealing with monetary policy and debt management (which are treated in the next chapter) because, in the United States at least, the major decisions about government expenditures and taxation are made in connection with the proposals concerning the annual federal budget, which are developed in the months preceding the beginning of the government's fiscal year on October 1. Thus, the decisions concerning the budget establish the overall economic framework within which Federal Reserve monetary policy must function. Furthermore, these decisions also determine the size of the publicly-held federal debt which the Treasury—and to some extent the Federal Reserve—must take the responsibility for managing.

It has increasingly come to be acknowledged that the potential of the economy for producing goods and services increases from year to year as a result of (1) growth of the labor force available for employment, (2) improvement in workers' skills as a result of improved education and training, (3) the accumulation of additional capital through investment and (4) invention and technological improvement which lead to the introduction of superior products and more efficient methods of production. At the same time, there is now quite general agreement that the federal government is able to influence the level of economic activity through the use of both its monetary policy and fiscal policy instruments, as explained in the introduction to Chapter 1. Prior to the 1930s, the main instrument used for this purpose was monetary policy, which, in the United States after the passage of the Federal Reserve Act in 1914, was the responsibility of the Federal Reserve System. Primarily as a result of the impact of Keynes' *General Theory*, which appeared in 1936, together with the work of a generation of scholars who followed up his insights, it is now recognized that by changing its expenditures in relation to its tax receipts, the federal government can exert a powerful effect on the flow of purchasing power, aggregate demand, and economic activity.

The prime responsibility of the stabilization authorities over any given time period is to match aggregate demand to the available productive capacity. Of course, the desired level of capacity utilization is not one in which literally every person and machine is employed. As a practical matter, such a level would be impossible to achieve in a dynamic economy; more importantly, any serious effort to drive the unemployment rate near to zero would result in an intolerable rate of inflation, given the institutional structure. Rather, the choice of an acceptable utilization rate represents a compromise between the costs of unemployment of a certain fraction of our resources, on the one hand, and of a particular rate of price change, on the other. Once such a target utilization rate has been chosen, it is possible to prepare estimates of "potential GNP" for each period under consideration, corresponding to the selected unemployment rate. This level of potential output represents the amount of output the economy is capable of supplying within a given period at the highest level of capacity utilization or employment of resources (both labor and capital) consistent with reasonably stable prices; it is thus a concept of aggregate potential *supply*. This level of potential output, which, of course, grows over time for the reasons mentioned above, becomes the aggregate demand target, and the task of stabilization policy is to ensure that aggregate demand is equal to potential output and that demand is growing at the same rate as potential supply.

This way of looking at the stabilization problem was first adopted by the Council of Economic Advisers in their 1962 Annual Report, when an unemployment rate of 4 percent formed the basis for estimates of potential GNP. It was assumed that other resources would be fully employed if that level of labor force utilization were achieved. Demographic and other changes in the composition and behavior of the labor force during the intervening years have led the Council of Economics Advisers and others to conclude that, based on available data, the appropriate full-employment unemployment rate as of this writing is at least 4.9 percent of the labor force, rather than 4 percent, and may even be higher on account of factors for which reliable information is less readily available. Other things equal, an increase in the estimated full-employment unemployment rate corresponds to a reduction in the estimated level of potential GNP. Furthermore, it is no longer assumed that full employment of the capital stock would necessarily accompany full employment of labor; a separate full-employment capacity utilization rate target for capital has been established, and is presently 86 percent as measured by the Department of Commerce index of capacity utilization.

The initial reading in the chapter, drawn from recent Annual Reports of the Council of Economic Advisers, discusses the concept of potential GNP as a policy target, its measurement, and factors affecting its growth (reading 16). Of particular concern in the latter context has been the measured slowdown in the growth of productivity, or output per labor hour, since the mid-1960s. Some of the causes of this slowdown, and the prospects for productivity change and potential output growth in future years, are examined in this reading.

In analyzing the economic effects of fiscal policy, one of the difficulties is that there is a two-way relation between the budget and GNP. To illustrate, if Congress passes legislation which results in increased expenditures on public works, this action taken by itself will stimulate production and employment and increase GNP while pushing the budget toward a deficit—thus, in this case, an *increase* in GNP is associated with an *increase* in the deficit. On the other hand, a decline in private spending brought about by some independent cause—such as a drop in private investment resulting from a deterioration of business expectations—will cause a decline in production, employment, and GNP. The fall in incomes will cause a drop in tax collections (with no change in tax legislation) and push the budget toward a deficit—that is, in this case, a *decrease* in GNP is associated with an *increase* in the deficit.

The first of these cases is an example of what is sometimes called *active* fiscal policy—involving legislative or administrative changes in government expenditure programs (or, alternatively, changes in tax *rates*) which may be employed for the deliberate purpose of influencing economic activity. The second case is an illustration of so-called *passive* fiscal policy—the government takes no deliberate action but taxes fall as a *result* of the decline in income (and some expenditures, such as those for unemployment compensation, may also rise), thus moving the budget toward a deficit. Such a passive change in fiscal policy will, of course, help to sustain the after-tax incomes of households and businesses whose pretax incomes have dropped, thus helping to limit the decline in business activity and employment. For this reason, passive fiscal policy is another name for the functioning of the so-called *automatic fiscal stabilizers*—the changes in expenditures and in tax revenues, for a given set of spending programs and tax rates, which occur in response to movements in the economy originating elsewhere.

The existence of this two-way relationship between the deficit and GNP creates difficulties in understanding fiscal policy and in interpreting the significance of observed changes in the government budget deficit or surplus. Various measures of fiscal influence have been developed to distinguish the active from the passive elements, the best known of which probably is the full-employment surplus (FES). Under this approach, different fiscal programs are "standardized" by calculating the surplus or deficit they would yield if the economy were operating at full employment, thereby correcting for the "passive" influence of varying income levels.

While the FES concept has been a very useful pedagogic and expository device for demonstrating that active and passive fiscal policy can yield quite different results, there remain a number of problems with its use as an analytic measure of active or discretionary policy. It is difficult to construct, and it rests on admittedly tenuous estimates of full-employment GNP, income shares at full employment, and so on. The FES will increase over time as full-employment income grows, without any change either in tax rates or in government spending, thereby signalling (incorrectly) a discretionary change towards restraint. Because the multiplier effects of a given increase of government expenditures on goods and services are greater than those of a tax reduction of the same magnitude, the effects of a given FES change will differ somewhat depending on whether the change is produced by an expenditure adjustment or a tax adjustment. And if the economy is operating very far below full employment, the effects of a given fiscal policy shift may differ considerably in size—and possibly even differ in direction—from what they would be if the economy actually were operating close to full employment.

These defects have led economists to search for other simpler and less ambiguous indicators of the thrust of active fiscal policy. There have been developments in two directions. The first is to weight the expenditure-change and tax-change elements of the budget measure appropriately to reflect the differences in multiplier effects mentioned above. The other is to use the current level of economic activity, rather than full employment, as the basis for calculating the effects on the budget of a discretionary fiscal policy change. Unlike the FES, which will change as capacity output rises, the budget indicator under the "standardized surplus" approach based on actual income will change only if (a) discretionary government spending changes, or (b) the tax rate structure is changed.

Both of these developments—different weights for spending and tax changes, and the use of actual rather than full-employment income—can of course be incorporated into one measure of fiscal impact: such a measure is the "weighted standardized surplus" discussed by Alan S. Blinder and Robert M. Solow in their paper, "Measuring Fiscal Influence" (reading 17). This paper also examines the FES and other measures of fiscal impact within the context of a model which is a version of Model II, the fiscal policy structure discussed in the introduction to Chapter 1 of this book.

Almost all professional economists would now reject the idea that the budget should be balanced each year. However, an alternative balanced budget rule has sometimes been suggested; namely, that the budget *as it would be if the economy were at full employment* should be kept in balance—that is, that the full-employment surplus should be kept equal to zero. In practice this would mean, for example, that any increase in government expenditures should be accompanied by a tax increase which would bring in enough revenue *under conditions of full employment* to cover the increased spending. This plan might be capable of producing a reasonably satisfactory degree of economic stability if it were accompanied by a vigorous and effective use of countercyclical monetary policy, and if the automatic stabilizers did their work. However, rigid ap-

plication of even such an attenuated budget balance rule would create difficulties. First, it would greatly reduce the government's flexibility in seeking to
achieve simultaneously a number of important goals—including not only full
employment but a satisfactory rate of long-term growth, allocation of the necessary quantity of national resources to defense and other government programs,
and so on. Second, if monetary policy is ineffective or constrained by other considerations, there is no assurance that even the goal of full employment (properly
defined to take account of behavior of the price level) can be achieved "on the
average" simultaneously with a balanced federal budget.

The general nature of the lags associated with policy adjustments was discussed in the introduction to Chapter 1. In the paper entitled "Lags and Uncertainties in Fiscal Policy: General Considerations, and the 1968–1970 Experience," (reading 18) Alan Blinder and Robert Solow provide a summary of the
evidence from several different econometric models of the economy on the "outside lag" of fiscal policy as measured by the period-by-period effect on GNP of
government spending changes. The reader should be aware that these period-by-
period GNP changes stimulated by a policy shift correspond to the "truncated
dynamic multipliers" for which analytic expressions are derived in Section A of
the introduction to Chapter 1 and displayed, for example, in Table 8 of that
introduction. Blinder and Solow also examine each of the main channels through
which fiscal instruments are believed to work, bringing out the disagreements
and uncertainties which exist as to the determinants of consumption, investment,
and so forth, and the ways in which fiscal changes affect these variables. These
uncertainties have important consequences for the vigor of policy response to a
given situation, the choice of instrument combinations, and so on. Their paper
concludes with a careful analysis of the effects of the 1968 tax surcharge. In
addition to being a model of technique, their evaluation casts serious doubt on
the widely-held view that fiscal policy was ineffective in this instance.

When federal expenditures exceed tax revenues, it is necessary to raise the
money in some fashion to cover the resulting deficit. This subject of "financing
the deficit" has had considerable discussion from time to time, and a number of
fallacies exist with respect to it. For instance, some discussions have implied
that a deficit is all right if it is needed to increase employment but that inflation
will result if the deficit is financed by borrowing from commercial banks, since
this will increase the money supply. Alternatively, it is sometimes said that a
tax reduction will have no effect on income if it is financed by borrowing from
the public, because the government will then be handing out money with one
hand and taking it away with the other. The Council of Economic Advisers staff
memorandum on "Financing a Federal Deficit" discusses the problem in its
several aspects; a careful reading of it should enable the student to see the
fallacies in the propositions referred to above. As the memorandum suggests, the
important question regarding the mode of financing for a spending increase or
tax decrease is not whether the resulting deficit should be financed by selling
bonds to the public or to the commercial banks, but rather is whether it should
be financed by issuing securities or money to the private sector. Both securities
and money are part of private-sector wealth, and this deficit-financing effect will
tend to shift the *IS* curve outward as long as the deficit exists (this is in addition
to the effects of the expenditure or tax change on the *IS* curve). This wealth
change will also affect the *LM* curve, increasing the demand for money balances.
If the financing of the deficit is done by bond issue, whether to banks or to

individuals, the increased demand for money is not matched by a money supply increase, and the *LM* curve shifts inward. The resulting rise in interest rates, which adds to the upward pressure on interest rates due to the spending change itself, is an important part of the "crowding out" phenomenon which has been given so much emphasis by the monetarists. However, contrary to the claims of some of them, there is no evidence that this interest rate increase totally cancels the direct expansionary effect on income of a spending increase or tax reduction in an underemployed economy. If, on the other hand, the deficit is financed by money issue, then the *LM* curve shifts outward, not inward, mitigating rather than augmenting the interest-rate rise due to the expenditure increase. In this case, we may say that the expansionary fiscal impulse has been accompanied by expansionary monetary policy.

While the above discussion has been based on the financial aspects of a change in the deficit due to an *expansionary* fiscal policy impulse, the reader should be aware that a change in the deficit or surplus brought about by *contractionary* policy also must be "financed"; that is, it also has a financial or wealth-related dimension, the reverse of the case described above. The reader should also understand that the financial effects in either situation can be substantial, because they continue period after period as long as the budget is out of balance, rather than occurring only during the period in which the initial impulse is felt. The way in which these financial effects of budget imbalance can be fitted into an *IS-LM* model of the type discussed in the introduction to Chapter 1 is shown in William L. Silber's paper, "Fiscal Policy in *IS-LM* Analysis: A Correction" (reading 20).

The size of the federal budget has increased rapidly since World War II, and the belief has increased that the budget has gotten out of control. In part, this has been ascribed to the inadequacy of the budget process used until recently, under which no committee in either House of Congress was responsible for assessing the size and composition of the budget as a whole, and its impact on the economy. In July 1974, legislation was passed which reformed the budget process in a number of dimensions. A very thorough discussion of the new procedures and institutions introduced as a part of the reform is provided in Joseph Scherer's paper, "New Directions for the Federal Budget?" (reading 21). This paper also examines trends in the budget, and shows that federal claims on output (purchases of goods and services) have *fallen* as a fraction of GNP during most of the postwar period. To the extent that the budget has increased in relationship to GNP, the cause has been the growth in transfer and grant programs.

Questions relating to the national debt—how fast it should grow (if at all), whether a debt such as we presently have in the United States is a threat to national solvency, who bears the "burden" of the public debt, and the nature of that burden—have received a great deal of attention in the press, in congressional addresses, and elsewhere. An unusual amount of irrationality and misunderstanding exists concerning these issues. A straightforward analysis of them is presented in Reading 22 entitled "Fiscal Policy and the National Debt," by David J. and Attiat F. Ott. A careful study of their paper should lead the reader to conclude that the important questions in this connection relate to such matters as the level of unemployment and the social productivity of government expenditures compared to private expenditures being displaced, not the size of the debt per se.

16. MEASURING AND REALIZING THE ECONOMY'S POTENTIAL*

Council of Economic Advisers

How much the Nation's economy can produce —its supply capability—depends on the quantity and quality of its productive resources, including manpower, plant and equipment, and natural resources. The economy's aggregate demand is the total of spending for final output by all groups —consumers, businesses, government, and foreign buyers. When aggregate demand matches supply capability, resources are fully utilized and production equals the economy's potential. If aggregate demand should fall short of supply capability, part of the output that the economy is capable of turning out would not be produced, and some resources would be wasted in idleness. On the other hand, excessive demand—too much spending in relation to potential output—would generate inflationary pressures on prices and costs.

The basic task of fiscal and monetary policies is to help ensure a match between demand and productive potential. These measures operate primarily by affecting the demand side of the balance. Government purchases of goods and services are directly a part of total demand; increases or decreases in such purchases change total spending in the same direction. In addition, other government expenditures indirectly influence total demand through their impact on private incomes. Social security benefits, for example, are "transfer payments" which add to the purchasing power of individuals, and thus encourage additional private spending, especially for consumer goods and services.

Taxes, on the other hand, reduce the ability and willingness of families and business firms to spend, by drawing purchasing power out of private hands. By raising (or lowering) tax rates, the Federal Government can hold down (or add to) the flow of private spending.

Monetary policies affect private spending primarily by changing the cost and availability of funds required to finance certain types of expenditures. If borrowing becomes expensive and difficult, expenditures for new homes, business machinery, and other things may be discouraged or postponed.

The economy's potential output is continually expanding as a result of the growth of the labor force and increases in productivity. Economic policy must therefore aim at a moving target—helping demand to grow in pace so that an appropriate balance with potential is maintained. If demand does not expand or if it grows only sluggishly, men and machines become unemployed.

THE CHOICE OF A TARGET

Economic potential or capacity is not an absolute technical ceiling on output. It allows for some margin of unused human and physical resources. Even in most extreme boom, there are always some people unemployed, some who could be attracted into the labor force, some who would be willing to "moonlight" or work overtime. Similarly, there are always some plants that could be operated more intensively or for longer hours. To operate the economy at its utmost technical capacity would require demands far in excess of supply in most markets, with resulting rampant inflation.

The relevant concept of capacity, therefore, must allow for some margin of idle resources. The choice of a specific margin involves an appraisal of the behavior of prices and costs in a high-employment economy. But this appraisal involves more than a technical evaluation. If potential output is to be viewed as a target for policy, the choice of the ideal level of utilization is a social judgment that requires a balancing of national goals of high employment and reasonable price stability.

Balances of this sort are never simple. Both unemployment and inflation involve social and individual costs. The severe economic burden borne by those who have no jobs is obvious. At the bottom of the 1957–58 recession, there were more than five million workers out of jobs; and during 1958 more than 14 million workers experienced one or more spells of unemployment. Still others were forced to accept part-time employment or were relegated to jobs beneath their capacity. Some, in resignation, abandoned the search for jobs. The loss of income was tremen-

---

* This reading was constructed using materials from *The Annual Report of the Council of Economic Advisers,* January 1969, pp. 61–64; and *The Annual Report of the Council of Economic Advisers,* January 1977, pp. 45–57. Reprinted by permission of the Council of Economic Advisers.

dous. The costs in frustration, despair, and bitterness cannot be measured.

Some of the costs of unemployment linger on because skills and supplies of labor are impaired. When over-all unemployment is excessive, employers have little incentive to provide job training programs for the unskilled or to upgrade workers to better paying jobs. Labor unions become increasingly concerned about job security of existing members and often take measures that limit the supply of available labor for the longer run.

Although the burden of a slack economy falls most heavily on the unemployed, the loss of production associated with underutilized resources imposes serious costs on nearly all groups. The incomes lost by the unemployed represent far less than half of the total shortfall of output and income. A slack economy sharply reduces the profits of large and small businesses and cuts government tax revenues. Moreover, part of the burden falls on future generations, because underutilization of capacity weakens investment incentives, slowing the rate of capital accumulation and limiting future productivity gains.

It is difficult to balance the costs of inflation against those of an absolute loss of output and employment, because they are quantitatively and qualitatively different. Inflation has highly arbitrary and inequitable effects on the distribution of income and wealth. It benefits debtors at the expense of creditors; it hurts persons, such as some pensioners, whose incomes and asset values are fixed in money terms, and benefits those whose incomes and asset values increase more than in proportion to the over-all rise in prices. Since the impact of inflation on the welfare of an individual depends on the way in which both his income and the value of his wealth respond to the change in prices, its effects on broad classes of the population cannot be easily characterized. But there are many persons, in nearly all walks of life, who experience significant losses as a result of inflation. In general, financially sophisticated persons, who foresee the consequences of rising prices, can take steps to protect themselves, while the less sophisticated may lose.

There is also a danger that inflation can set in motion speculative behavior that will cause further acceleration of price increases, with serious consequences for economic and social stability. There are even extreme examples in history of the breakdown of financial and economic systems as a result of galloping inflation.

Finally, inflation may have adverse consequences for our balance of payments. If prices rise more rapidly in the United States than in other countries, our competitive position in world markets can be seriously undermined.

PRODUCTIVITY GROWTH AND RESOURCE UTILIZATION

In designing economic policy to cope with cyclical fluctuations in economic activity, it is important not to overlook the longer-term issue of growth. In the past 25 years more than two-thirds of the increase in real national output has been generated by increases in average labor productivity, or output per labor-hour. Over the past decade, however, productivity growth has shown a marked decline, even after adjusting for cyclical effects. Since 1966 the trend rate of growth in measured output per labor-hour has decreased by about one third from the rate attained in the 1950s and early 1960s. If productivity gains continue to be small, real wages will continue to grow more slowly than in the 1950–65 period.

THE PRODUCTIVITY SHOWDOWN, 1966–1976

Productivity growth in the private sector averaged 3.3 percent per year between 1948 and 1966, almost 1 percentage point above the 1929–75 average. Between 1966 and 1973, however, the private productivity growth rate was only 2.1 percent per year, below the long-run trend. This slower advance may have contributed to increased inflationary pressures and may have led to lower growth in real wages.

As shown in Chart 1 the reduction in private

Chart 1: Productivity in the Private Business Economy

* Growth rate of 3.3 Percent per Year.
Source: Department of Labor.

productivity growth is striking. While part of this poor performance can be attributed to the recent recession, the falloff in productivity was evident even before 1974. Slower growth in capital per worker, a larger proportion of less experienced workers in the labor force, and the changing industrial composition of labor input have all contributed to this slowdown. Higher relative energy prices and slower technical progress may also have played a part. However, the reasons for the slowdown are not fully understood at this time because the decline in productivity growth appears to be larger than the sum of the estimated effects of these factors.

Growth of Capital and Labor

One important source of productivity growth is the increase in the amount of capital per hour of labor input. Between 1948 and 1966 capital per labor-hour in the private sector grew by about 3.1 percent per year; during the 1966–73 period this growth rate fell to 2.8 percent per year. Since 1973 the growth of capital per labor-hour has apparently fallen to 1.7 percent, after adjustment for cyclical factors. The decrease can be attributed to a faster rate of growth of labor input not matched by corresponding increases in the capital stock. The larger growth in the labor force since the mid-sixties has been a result of the postwar baby boom and of an increased percentage of women in the work force. Although the average growth rate of fixed nonresidential capital in 1966–73 was higher than the average growth rate for 1948–66, the effective growth rate of capacity may well have increased less because of higher obsolescence rates and increased expenditures on pollution abatement and safety equipment. While both types of investment contribute to our well-being they do not in general increase our capacity to produce measured output. Estimates of the contribution of increases in the capital-labor ratio to productivity growth are very sensitive to the measure of capital stock used; our analysis suggests that perhaps one-tenth to one-third of the productivity slowdown since 1966 can be explained by slower growth in effective capital per labor-hour.

Composition of the Labor Force

In the last decade the proportion of the labor force made up of teenagers and young adults has been rising. Workers in these groups tend to be less productive to the extent that they have less experience and training than other workers. Pro-ductivity is measured by output per labor-hour, and these labor-hours do not reflect differences in training and experience. Early retirement has also reduced the proportion of experienced workers. Thus lower productivity growth is a natural consequence of a fall in the average work experience of those in the labor force. Changes in the age-sex composition of the labor force can explain more than 0.1 percentage point (or about 10 percent) of the productivity growth differential between 1948–66 and 1966–73.

Median educational attainment in the labor force has also increased more slowly in the past decade than it did in the previous 10 years. In many age and sex categories of workers there has been a slight slowdown in the rate of increase in years of schooling. It is, however, unlikely that this small change had a significant effect on average productivity.

Employment Shifts between Sectors in the Economy

Changes in the industrial composition of employment have also been a factor in lowering average productivity growth. Before 1970 the shift of workers out of agriculture contributed to growth in productivity. Even though the rate of growth of productivity in agriculture was high, the average level of productivity was below the general average, and the movement of workers from agriculture to other sectors increased aggregate productivity. Since the late 1960s this shift out of agriculture has slowed, and productivity growth from this source has been much reduced. Almost one-third of the difference between the trend rate of private productivity growth in 1948–66 and 1966–73 can be attributed to the higher rate of reduction in agricultural employment in the earlier period.

A higher rate of increase in the number of workers in the low-productivity service sector has also been a factor in the slowdown in productivity growth. However, the effect of shifts in employment in the private nonfarm sector are much smaller than the effect of the movement of workers out of agriculture.

To some extent shifts in employment between sectors and changes in the amount of capital per labor-hour measure the same thing and thus represent double counting of changes in the capital-labor ratio. Low-productivity sectors may be less capital intensive, and therefore a shift in employment toward low-productivity sectors can be accompanied by a decrease in the growth of capital per worker. There are also independent effects, however, since capital per worker can change within each sector.

Other Factors Affecting Productivity

Productivity growth that is not caused by increases in capital per labor-hour or changes in the composition of the labor force is attributed to a catch-all residual category. Measurement errors of many kinds comprise part of the residual, but most of it is probably traceable to various forms of technical progress, such as improvements in the quality of capital and new techniques for combining inputs to increase production.

While allocation of resources to research and development should generate technical progress and increase residual productivity growth, the quantitative relation between productivity and research is not well documented. Even though a close causal relation between aggregate research and development expenditures and residual productivity growth cannot be proved, such expenditures and their share of total output give some indication of probable productivity growth in the future. Research and development expenditures, which grew rapidly from 1955 to 1969, have fallen in real terms since 1970. The share of research and development in GNP reached a peak of 3.0 percent in 1964 and fell to 2.3 percent in 1975.

Although changes in labor force composition and slower growth in fixed capital per worker have been a partial cause of the productivity slowdown in the last decade, much of it must be attributed to other factors. Significantly greater productivity may be generated by the technical improvements incorporated in new capital equipment, a consideration which would increase the impact of the slowdown in the growth of the capital-labor ratio. However, it seems unlikely that the effect of this "embodied" technical progress could explain most of the large difference in residual productivity growth before and after 1966.

Since the productivity slowdown coincides with the entrance into the labor market of those born during the post–World War II baby boom, the slowdown in productivity may be in part a consequence of the time required to adjust to changes in relative factor proportions. If so, productivity growth similar to that in 1966–76 may continue through 1980, since the labor force is projected to grow at relatively high rates until that time. After 1980 the growth rate of the working-age population will decline, and the labor force will expand more slowly unless the slower population growth is offset by increases in the proportion of the population in the labor force.

THE FULL-EMPLOYMENT UNEMPLOYMENT RATE

Assessing long-run trends in economic growth requires a standard to measure labor resource utilization. Although an explicit definition is difficult, the full-employment unemployment rate is generally understood to mean the lowest rate of unemployment attainable, under the existing institutional structure, that will not result in accelerated inflation. Given the inexact relation between changes in the rate of inflation and the rate of unemployment, estimates are necessarily imprecise, but in the early 1960s the Council of Economic Advisers selected 4 percent as an estimate of the full-employment unemployment rate in the economic circumstances existing at that time. This estimate referred to the overall measure of unemployment as a percentage of the civilian labor force and was based on an examination of economic conditions in the mid-1950s when the overall unemployment rate fluctuated around 4 percent. During the 20 years since then a number of relevant changes have occurred which give reason to believe that the full-employment unemployment rate equivalent to 4 percent in the mid-1950s has increased.

Since the mid-1950s a dramatic change in the composition of the labor force has apparently led to an increase in the movement of workers in and out of the labor force. High rates of labor force turnover generally increase measured unemployment, since first entry and reentry into the labor force generally involve a period of job search and are counted as unemployment in the labor force statistics. Hence for approximately the same tightness in the labor market, the measured unemployment rate will be higher if a larger proportion of job seekers are persons formerly outside the labor force.

Data on reasons for unemployment indicate that the high rates of labor force entry and reentry account for most of the higher unemployment rates among youths compared with adults, and that the unemployment rates for job losers and job leavers differ very little among demographic groups (Table 1). Youths are far more likely than adults to combine work in the labor market with some other activity such as schooling or work at home. Students move in and out of the labor force in search of part-time and full-time employment during the school recess, and

Table 1: Civilian Unemployment Rates by Age, Sex, and Reason for Unemployment, 1973 (percent)

Age and sex	All civilian workers*	Job losers and job leavers†
25 years and over:		
Men	2.5	2.0
Women	4.0	2.3
16–24 years:		
Men	9.9	4.9
Women	11.2	4.1

* Unemployment as percent of civilian labor force in group specified.
† Unemployment as percent of civilian labor force excluding new entrants and reentrants.
Sources: Department of Labor (Bureau of Labor Statistics) and Council of Economic Advisers.

during the school term many search for part-time employment. A rising proportion of youths in the labor force would therefore be associated with a rising proportion of new entrants and reentrants—and hence, other things being equal, with a rise in the unemployment rate. Since the mid-1950s teenagers and young adults have, in fact, constituted an increasing proportion of the labor force, from 15 percent in 1955 to 24 percent in 1976, because of the postwar baby boom that has increased the proportion of youths in the working-age population, and because of a rise in the labor force participation rate of students.

The difference between the overall unemployment rate and that for subgroups of the population has widened markedly since the mid-1950s, partly because of these changing labor force proportions (Table 2). The unemployment rates for adults, experienced workers, and the long-term unemployed in 1965 and 1973, were all roughly equal to the rates in 1956, a year in which the overall rate of unemployment approximated the full-employment estimate of 4 percent. Yet for the later years the overall unemployment rate was much higher, rising to 4.5 percent in 1965 and to 4.9 percent in 1973.

The apparent secular rise in the unemployment rate for young persons relative to adults suggests that the change in the composition of the labor force does not explain all of the shift between the overall unemployment rate and the rate for adults. Direct data are not available, but some of this change in the structure of unemployment rates may be due to increased movement in and out of the labor force by youths. Among youths there has been an increase in school enrollment rates since the mid-1950s and students are more likely than other youths to alternate between working or job seeking and attending school.

There also appears to have been an increase in the measured unemployment rate for adult women relative to adult men, but because of a change in the survey the data reported after 1967 are not strictly comparable with earlier years. Moreover how greatly this survey change has affected the difference in unemployment rates between adult men and adult women is uncertain. If there has been a rise in the actual unemployment rate of adult women relative to adult men, it may be due to an increase in labor force participation for married women. Many married women leave the labor force when a child is born and return intermittently for several years. A disproportionate increase in the component of the adult female labor force in which the labor force turnover is highest would thus tend to raise the unemployment rate of adult females relative to that of adult men. Because the estimates of these developments are still uncertain, however, it is difficult to assess their influence on the overall unemployment rate.

Other developments in the past 20 years may have tended to increase the full-employment unemployment rates of all demographic groups. For example, broader coverage of unemployment compensation is likely to raise the rate of unemployment associated with a particular degree of

Table 2: Civilian Unemployment Rates for Selected Groups, 1956, 1965, and 1973 (percent)

Group	1956	1965	1973
All civilian workers	4.1	4.5	4.9
Experienced wage and salary workers	4.4	4.3	4.5
Long-term unemployed workers*	.8	1.0	.9
Age groups:			
25–54 years	3.3	3.2	3.2
55 years and over	3.4	3.2	2.7
16–24 years	8.5	10.1	10.5

Note: Unemployment as a percent of civilian labor force in group specified, except as noted.
* Unemployed 15 weeks or longer as percent of total civilian labor force.
Source: Department of Labor, Bureau of Labor Statistics.

tightness in the labor market. The most recent extension of coverage, in 1975, placed an estimated 12 million wage and salary workers under the temporary special unemployment assistance program. As a result of 1976 legislation, coverage under the regular State programs is to be extended to about 9 million of these 12 million workers. Other circumstances suggest that the financial burden of unemployment has been lessened for many families: the rise in the proportion of families with two adult earners because of the growth in women's labor force participation; and an increase in other public transfer programs for the low-income unemployed. These factors have tended to weaken the tie between current consumption and current earnings, and they may have increased the extent of unemployment that is consistent with a full-employment economy.

Other changes may have had the opposite effect. These include the rising level of education, the relative increase in white-collar occupations, and more efficient job search because of improvements in transportation and communication. Because the reasons for differences in unemployment rates by education level are not well understood, it is not clear whether the rise in education by itself has been accompanied by a stable or a changing education-specific full-employment unemployment rate for given age and sex groups. The effects of improved labor market efficiency are also ambiguous since it is not clear whether greater efficiency in the search for jobs lessens the rate of unemployment at full employment.

There is no unique procedure for adjusting the full-employment unemployment rate for the changing demographic composition of the labor force and for the changing relationships in the unemployment rates of various demographic groups. Moreover any estimating procedure is subject to sampling variability. Using available data on labor force composition and unemployment rates, and adjusting for the increased proportion of young persons in the labor force and for the increase in their unemployment rate relative to adults, the Council of Economic Advisers has estimated that the full-employment unemployment rate equivalent to 4.0 percent in 1955 is now 4.9 percent. This estimate corresponds with the widening in the difference between the overall unemployment rate and the unemployment rate for adults observed in Table 2.

The effects of many of the other factors which are believed to influence the full-employment unemployment rate are much more difficult to quantify. Partly because of this difficulty there is considerable dispute about their relative importance, but it is likely that they have raised the full-employment unemployment rate even higher than the current estimate, perhaps closer to 5½ percent. The current benchmark estimates, however, incorporate only the effects for which the evidence is substantial. As further evidence becomes available—perhaps through more data on unemployed persons classified by reason for unemployment, or perhaps through observed changes in wages and prices as actual unemployment rates decline—the current estimate of the full-employment unemployment rate might be further refined.

It is important to bear in mind, however, that the full-employment unemployment rate will not remain constant. For example, as the population ages and youths represent a smaller percentage of the labor force, the full-employment unemploy rate will also tend to decline. The overall unemployment rate that represents full employment can be expected to change with time as demographic, social, and economic factors affect the rates at which workers move in and out of jobs, and in and out of the work force.

Potential GNP is a measure of the aggregate supply capability of the economy, or the amount of output that could be expected at full employment. More precisely, potential GNP is the output the economy could produce with the existing technology under assumed conditions of high but sustainable utilization of the factors of production —labor, capital, and natural resources. It does not represent the absolute maximum level of production that could be generated by wartime or other abnormal levels of aggregate demand, but rather that which could be expected from high utilization rates obtainable under more normal circumstances.

The significant slowdown in average productivity growth suggests that the rate of growth of potential output was lower in the past 10 years than has been previously estimated. The revision of the national income and product accounts also reduced the rate of growth of real GNP. Moreover the widespread shortages of physical capacity and the resulting inflationary pressures experienced in 1973 suggest that previous estimates of potential GNP are overstated. The Council has therefore reestimated potential GNP, taking into account the lowered rate of productivity growth, the factors contributing to this slowdown, and the increase in the full-employment unemployment rate. The new estimates of potential output are experimental in the sense that they are based on highly aggregated measures of labor, capital, and output; and they must therefore be considered interim revisions. A more definitive study would use disaggregated data on labor and capital inputs and more evidence on the education and experience of the work force.

Estimates of Potential GNP

The benchmark level of resource utilization implicit in the Council of Economic Advisers' previous estimates of potential output was an overall unemployment rate of 4 percent; it was assumed that full utilization of other resources, such as capital and land, would accompany 4 percent unemployment. The new estimates of potential attempt to include explicitly the contribution to output of fixed capital; hence a benchmark for capital utilization as well as for labor utilization must be set. Full employment of fixed capital is assumed to be attained when the manufacturing capacity utilization index calculated by the Department of Commerce reaches 86 percent. This is the capacity utilization rate attained in the first and second quarters of 1973. In 1969, another year of high employment, manufacturing capacity utilization was 85 percent; 86 percent is thus a relatively optimistic estimate of sustainable capacity utilization. The capacity utilization index that represents the same degree of resource utilization may change over time, since capital input is at least as heterogeneous as labor input. A higher proportion of old equipment in the capital stock would probably lower the capacity utilization benchmark. Inadequate data make estimation of such a variable benchmark very difficult, however, and it has not been attempted here.

The full-employment benchmark has been changed from a constant 4 percent unemployment rate to a rate that varies over time. The new labor utilization benchmark adjusts for the increase in the proportion of younger workers in the labor force since 1955, and for the observed increase in unemployment rates for younger workers relative to those for adults. As discussed earlier, these adjustments imply a rate that rises from 4.0 percent in 1955 to 4.9 percent in 1976. The definition of the new estimate of potential GNP in 1976 is, then, the output in 1972 dollars that the economy would produce if the Department of Commerce manufacturing capacity utilization rate were 86 percent and the unemployment rate 4.9 percent.

The new potential GNP estimates are com-

pared to the previous estimates in Table 3, and are shown graphically in Chart 2. The average annual growth rate of potential from 1962 to 1976 is now estimated to be 3.6 percent per year, a reduction from the former estimate of 3.9 percent per year; and the rate is projected to be about 3½ percent per year in the near future. The reduction in the growth of potential GNP results in an estimate that is $58 billion in 1972 dollars (or about 4 percent) lower in 1976 than that previous estimate of potential. Most of the reduction in the estimate of the growth of potential output is due to slower growth in labor productivity since 1966. In 1976, $30 to $40 billion of the estimated reduction in potential output can be attributed to this factor.

Some of the reduction in the growth rate of potential output can also be attributed to the recent benchmark revisions of the national income and product accounts, which incorporate new source data and estimating procedures. The revised real GNP estimates are evaluated in terms of 1972 rather than 1958 prices. The result of these changes has been to lower growth rates of real GNP.

The change in the unemployment benchmark lowers slightly our estimates of how the expanding labor force has increased potential GNP. Using a full-employment benchmark of 4.0 percent rather than 4.9 percent in 1976 would raise potential GNP by 0.3 percent to 1.1 percent, depending on how the reduction in unemployment is distributed over the labor force. Thus between $5 billion and $15 billion of the $58 billion reduction in potential for 1976 can be attributed to the change in the assumed unemployment rate at potential.

The downward revision in potential GNP results in a current growth rate for potential output that is about the same as the 3½ percent per year originally estimated by the Council of Economic Advisers for the period from 1952 to 1962. Increases in the labor force growth rate since that time have been offset by decreases in the rate of productivity growth, yielding a growth rate of potential output which is nearly constant. This downward revision does not appear to be sensitive to the particular method which we have used to estimate potential. Experiments with a number of alternative procedures give similar results and indicate that the new estimates are robust, given current information. For example, a calculation for the period from 1968 to 1973 which adds labor force growth of 2.0 percent to productivity growth of 1.8 percent and subtracts 0.3 percent

Table 3:   Potential and Actual Gross National Product, 1952–1976 (billions of 1972 dollars)

Year	Potential GNP		Actual GNP	GNP Gap	
	New	Old		New (new potential less actual)	Old (old potential less actual)
1952.................	584.9	592.2	598.5	−13.6	−6.3
1953.................	608.2	613.0	621.8	−13.6	−8.8
1954.................	629.7	634.4	613.7	16.0	20.7
1955.................	651.4	656.6	654.8	−3.4	1.8
1956.................	673.9	679.6	668.8	5.1	10.8
1957.................	697.2	703.4	680.9	16.3	22.5
1958.................	721.3	728.0	679.5	41.8	48.5
1959.................	746.2	753.5	720.4	25.8	33.1
1960.................	771.9	779.9	736.8	35.1	43.1
1961.................	798.6	807.1	755.3	43.3	51.8
1962.................	826.4	835.4	799.1	27.3	36.3
1963.................	857.1	865.9	830.7	26.4	35.2
1964.................	890.3	898.4	874.4	15.9	24.0
1965.................	925.0	932.1	925.9	−.9	6.2
1966.................	960.8	967.0	981.0	−20.2	−14.0
1967.................	996.3	1,003.3	1,007.7	−11.4	−4.4
1968.................	1,031.7	1,040.9	1,051.8	−20.1	−10.9
1969.................	1,068.3	1,081.6	1,078.8	−10.5	2.8
1970.................	1,106.2	1,124.9	1,075.3	30.9	49.6
1971.................	1,145.5	1,169.9	1,107.5	38.0	62.4
1972.................	1,186.1	1,216.7	1,171.1	15.0	45.6
1973.................	1,228.2	1,265.4	1,235.0	−6.8	30.4
1974.................	1,271.7	1,315.9	1,214.0	57.7	101.9
1975.................	1,316.9	1,368.6	1,191.7	125.2	176.9
1976.................	1,363.6	1,421.2	*1,265.0	*98.6	*156.2

Note. See text in this paper on "Productivity Growth and Resource Utilization" for differences between the old and new potential GNP.
   * Preliminary.
   Sources: Department of Commerce, Bureau of Economic Analysis (actual GNP) and Council of Economic Advisers (potential GNP).

for the decline in average hours worked per week, all at annual rates, yields a growth rate of potential output amounting to 3.5 percent yer year. More research would be useful, however, to further our understanding of the determinants of the economy's potential and the relation between the growth of potential and economic policy. The attempt made here to incorporate the effects of capital accumulation and labor force composition on economic growth is a step in this direction.

The decline in average hours worked is also a factor which contributes to a slower growth in potential output than might be expected from the high rate of growth in the labor force. Between 1966 and 1973 the tendency toward shorter workweeks accelerated somewhat. The slightly accelerated decline in the average workweek, added to the effect of the changing composition of the labor force, implies a growth rate of effective labor input (labor hours weighted by average hourly earnings) that is significantly lower than the growth rate of the labor force. For

example, from 1966 to 1973 the civilian labor force grew by 2.3 percent per year, while effective labor input grew by only 1.5 percent per year. Therefore, although the rapidly growing labor force implies a high rate of growth in potential output, reductions in the average workweek and changes in the age-sex composition of the labor force indicate that the increases are somewhat lower.

Productivity behavior since 1973 raises a further question about the current level of potential output. In the most recent downturn, the productivity decline started earlier and was much more severe than might have been expected from earlier recessions. The data indicate that part of this decrease may have been a permanent downward shift in the level of productivity. A conservative estimate of this shift lowers potential output to $1,330 billion in 1976. Thus the GNP gap may be about $30 billion lower than indicated.

There is reason to expect such a drop in productivity to accompany the OPEC oil em-

Chart 2: Gross National Product, Actual and Potential (seasonally adjusted annual rates)

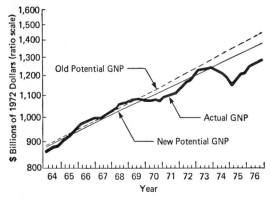

Note. See text in this paper on "Productivity Growth and Resource Utilization" for differences between the old and new potential GNP.

Sources: Department of Commerce and Council of Economic Advisers.

bargo and the subsequent quadrupling of crude oil prices. The new high energy prices should have made some capital equipment and some energy-intensive production processes inefficient, with a consequent loss in economic capacity. This loss would not be included in capital stock estimates, because the method normally used for estimating the aggregate capital stock depreciates new investment over a fixed period and does not adjust for short-term changes in obsolescence.

The statistical methods used to adjust for cyclical variations in productivity are necessarily based on the presumption that the variations in productivity over the business cycle are related in a stable way to measures of the cycle, such as the unemployment rate and capital utilization rates. Since the data indicate that the current slowdown may have produced an atypical reaction in productivity, it is possible that productivity will continue to increase and reach its former trend in the next 2 years. This possibility would imply private productivity growth rates for 1977 and 1978 well in excess of the 2 percent trend.

On the other hand, it has been nearly 2 years since the recession reached its trough, and there has been little evidence of cyclical productivity gains this late in previous recoveries. Because of this uncertainty regarding the permanence of the recent decline in productivity, estimates of potential output will be similarly uncertain. The estimates of potential GNP presented in Table 3 and Chart 2 do not include a shift in the level of productivity in 1973–74, but instead assume that the downward movement will be offset by an

equivalent upward movement as recovery continues. The performance of the economy over the next 2 years will indicate whether or not a further revision in the estimates of potential GNP is necessary.

POLICY IMPLICATIONS

Neither potential GNP nor the full-employment unemployment rate will be reached in 1977. However, both may set limits to growth in coming years which cannot be exceeded without risking accelerating inflation and renewed instability. For example, the uncertainty that surrounds the estimates of potential output implies that caution must be observed as potential GNP is approached. If the 1974–75 reduction in the level of productivity proves to be permanent, physical capacity constraints similar to those encountered in 1973 may appear well before an unemployment rate of 4.9 percent is reached. If so, they will seriously interfere with our full-employment goals.

As discussed previously, there are reasons to believe that the full-employment rate may be above the 4.9 percent benchmark we have used to estimate potential output. In any case, policy makers should realize that a 4 percent goal is not likely to be sustainable in the current economic environment; and because of the tentative nature of the full-employment rate estimates they should watch closely for signs of accelerating wage inflation when the overall rate of unemployment falls to about 5½ percent. The analysis suggests, for example, that the 4.9 percent unemployment rate in 1973 may have been partly responsible for the accelerating inflation in 1973–74, although this interpretation is clouded by other events such as the wage and price controls and the extraordinary increases in the prices of food and fuel. It also suggests that economic programs which aim to reduce unemployment in particularly depressed areas or among disadvantaged groups can be a useful supplement to policies which focus on the economy as a whole. Moreover it must be remembered that even with our revised estimates, the current output is far below potential, and unemployment is much above full-employment levels. Thus aggregate demand policies, such as the tax program proposed by the President, are still necessary to reduce unemployment and close the existing gap between potential and actual output.

The uncertainty about the lowest rate of unemployment that will not result in accelerating inflation also has important policy implications. Not too long ago economic policy makers were able to illustrate the difficulties of achieving both a stable price level and a full-employment economy by referring to the fairly close negative association between the unemployment rate and the inflation rate during the 1950s and early 1960s. While it was never thought to be exact, the relationship indicated the inevitable upward pressure of high utilization of labor and capital on prices and wages, and it was used to calculate the tradeoff between inflation and unemployment. According to this relationship, the cost of an excessively low unemployment rate was a higher, though not necessarily increasing, rate of inflation.

During the last 10 years, however, this relationship has shifted dramatically and the concept of a stable tradeoff has become untenable. Nevertheless it is difficult to deny the essential fact that excessive expansion and extremely low unemployment rates ultimately produce higher and perhaps accelerating inflation. Nor can one deny that a slack economy with low utilization of capital and labor resources is usually moderating influence on prices and wages. However, because of an economy-wide persistence in price and wage inflation, these excess demand and excess supply effects sometimes seem to work very slowly, with their influence spread over a long period.

In the long run the lower estimated growth rate of potential output, if projected into the future, implies a decrease in the "fiscal dividend" to be gained from full employment. Projection of the new potential GNP estimates through 1980 gives an output that is 4.8 percent lower than the previous estimate, a difference amounting to about $130 billion in current dollars. The estimate of Federal tax receipts in 1980 is thus more than $30 billion lower if output is assumed to be the new potential GNP rather than the old estimate. Lower total output implies lower tax revenues available for further tax cuts or for new or expanded Federal Government programs.

The challenge for the future will be to devise new policies to cope with the problems of economic growth and productivity. Increased productivity growth is necessary if the economy is to provide jobs without incurring declines in the growth of real income for the many new workers in the labor force. Microeconomic policies have been devised or are being considered to increase production and employment beyond levels attainable through the management of aggregate demand.

---

17. MEASURING FISCAL INFLUENCE*

Alan S. Blinder
and
Robert M. Solow

Since Keynes, a common, though by no means universal, presumption in the economics profession has held that the government budget can influence the aggregate level of income and employment.[1] If this view is correct, an attempt to quantify the impact seems a natural next step; that is, after classifying policy A as "expansive" and policy B as "contractionary," economists would like to be able to say that policy C is "more expansive" than policy A and to give some *quantitative* meaning to such a statement. Such a measure is required for at least two distinct purposes.

1. *Historical assessments of past policy.* Summary measures of the quantitative impact of fiscal policy were first used in the literature to analyze past fiscal policy.[2] As such, these measures can indicate when fiscal policy was expansionary (and how much), when it was contractionary (and how much), and when it was

* From "Analytical Foundations of Fiscal Policy," in Alan S. Blinder *et al.*, *The Economics of Public Finance* (Washington, D.C.: The Brookings Institution, 1974), pp. 3–115. Copyright © 1974 by The Brookings Institution, Washington, D.C. Reprinted by permission of the publisher and the authors. Alan S. Blinder is Associate Professor of Economics, Princeton University. Robert M. Solow is Institute Professor and Professor of Economics, Massachusetts Institute of Technology.

[1] The chief dissenters have been the monetarists.

[2] The pioneering paper was E. Cary Brown's "Fiscal Policy in the Thirties: A Reappraisal," *American Economic Review*, vol. 46 (December 1956), pp. 857–79. See also Wilfred Lewis, Jr., *Federal Budget Policy in the Postwar Recessions* (Washington, D.C.: Brookings Institution, 1972).

more or less neutral in its aggregative effects. Such investigations reveal whether the government has been a stabilizing or destabilizing force.

2. *Policy planning.* More important, measures of fiscal influence should enable the economist to prescribe the right dosage of fiscal stimulus (or restraint) when an insufficient (or excessive) level of private demand is forecast. The experience with the 1968 income tax surcharge suggests that it is still easier to talk about accurate prescription than to write one.[3]

None of this necessarily argues for a *single number* to be used as "the" measure of fiscal influence. Whenever one attempts to reduce a multidimensional concept—like the influence of the government on aggregate economic activity—to a single dimension, index number problems inevitably arise. Furthermore, examples abound of democratic (and even undemocratic!) countries in which the announcement of the government budget marks the beginning of a vigorous economic debate without a focus on a single number like the deficit.[4] A case can indeed be made for educating the public to a multi-budget concept just as the Council of Economic Advisers under Walter Heller educated it to the full employment surplus.[5]

However, the political realities of the day seem to dictate settling on a single index to measure the overall expansionary or contractionary effect of any proposed tax and expenditure program. If economists do not come up with one, the public or the Congress will probably invent its own, and the choice is unlikely to be the best. Instead, then, of trying to talk the layman out of seeking such a number, economists might do better to lead him to a "sensible" concept of the government deficit. Furthermore, economics is not—or at least should not be—silent on such questions as how much increase in the automobile excise tax rate it would take to cancel out the expansionary effects of defense spending. If economic models can reduce the various dimensions of the government budget to a single, common, denominator, why not use them? For these reasons, we believe that developing a single number to measure fiscal influence is a legitimate scholarly exercise.

Given the decision to embark on such a course, we are faced immediately with a choice between two distinct families of measures. A "budget" measure seeks only to supply a number summarizing the congeries of taxation and expenditure programs; it is mute on the effects of the program on the gross national product. The great virtue of such a measure, it is often said, is its independence of any particular model of the economy.[6] Its great vice is that for this very reason it may not be very informative, since it is the economy, not the budget, that is ultimately important. The ordinary budget deficit is probably the best illustration of both the virtue and the vice.

A "fiscal impact" measure is a single number indicating the effect of the total budget on the gross national product, or any other variable of interest. Basically, such a measure is derived from a suitable budget measure by applying to the latter some appropriate "multiplier." A fiscal impact measure, unlike a budget measure, will convey interesting information, but its dependence on a specific model of the economy is obvious. As a practical matter, the measure can be quite sensitive to the model employed (we demonstrate this below). After surveying some suggested measures of each kind, we shall argue that a specific measure of fiscal impact is to be preferred.

The Actual Budget Deficit

Those who learn their economics from the press and the speeches of high government officials could be forgiven for believing that the fiscal policy impact of a budget program is summed up entirely in the difference between revenues and expenditures—the government deficit or surplus. A deficit is supposed to be expansionary, and a surplus restrictive, because government spending "puts money into the income stream" and taxation removes it. Most students who take an elementary course in economics presumably learn that this is not so. The balanced-budget theorem shows that it is not really the deficit that matters. A dollar of government spending is more expansionary than a dollar of taxes is restrictive, so that a balanced increase in spending and taxes will increase the level of income.

---

[3] At this writing controversy still exists over what went wrong on that occasion.

[4] For an argument against the use of a single number, see the comments by Warren L. Smith in Wilfred Lewis, Jr. ed., *Budget Concepts for Economic Analysis* (Washington, D.C.: Brookings Institution, 1968), pp. 131–32.

[5] See, for example, *Economic Report of the President together with the Annual Report of the Council of Economic Advisers, January 1962,* pp. 78–82. Hereafter, this document will be referred to as the *Economic Report,* followed by the year.

[6] We shall argue below that this is not, in fact, entirely true.

Table 1: Actual and Full Employment Deficits, 1929–1939 (in billions of constant dollars)

Year	Actual Deficit	Full Employment Deficit	Weighted Full Employment Deficit
1929	1.3	1.3	2.2
1930	3.2	2.1	3.0
1931	6.5	4.9	5.7
1932	4.7	1.4	3.0
1933	3.4	−1.7	0.9
1934	4.9	−0.3	2.7
1935	4.4	0.1	2.9
1936	6.0	2.0	4.9
1937	0.6	−3.3	0.4
1938	4.3	−1.0	2.4
1939	4.8	0.3	4.6

Source: From or computed from data in E. Cary Brown, "Fiscal Policy in the 'Thirties: A Reappraisal," *American Economic Review,* vol. 46 (December 1956), Table 2, p. 873.

Furthermore, economists have long realized that even an appropriately weighted deficit is woefully inadequate as a measure of fiscal policy since it is endogenous to all but the simplest models of income determination. As soon as the dependence of tax receipts on the level of activity is acknowledged, it is clear that increases in GNP will *automatically* reduce the deficit (or raise the surplus) unless the government takes countervailing action. Thus depressed levels of national income will *cause* large deficits even when the government is "really" being very contractionary, and vice versa. This is the central point of E. Cary Brown's pioneering paper.[7] Brown replaced the ordinary budget deficit by the weighted deficit at full exployment and showed how this change drastically altered the assessment of fiscal policy in the 1930s. Table 1 compares the actual budgetary deficits with the full employment deficits calculated by Brown. The contrast is quite dramatic. Some of the large budgetary deficits that alarmed Hoover and Roosevelt were actually sizable surpluses in the full employment budget. What is more, fiscal policy became steadily more *restrictive* between 1931 and 1933.

Brown's work raises the basic conceptual problem that has been the unifying theme of subsequent work—separating the *discretionary* aspects of fiscal policy (changes in tax schedules and spending) from the *automatic* ones. Although, in a deeper sense, no neat separation is possible—allowing the automatic stabilizers to work unhindered is, after all, a discretionary choice—

[7] "Fiscal Policy in the 'Thirties'."

such a dichotomy is needed for both historical assessment and policy planning.

The Full Employment Surplus

The most obvious, and by now the most popular, way to separate discretionary from automatic fiscal actions is to focus on the full employment budget. If the budget would be in surplus at full employment, fiscal policy is termed restrictive; if the budget would be in deficit, it is termed expansionary. Although the idea was anticipated by Brown, and in fact goes back much further, the concept of the full employment surplus appears to have been articulated first in testimony before Congress by Charles L. Schultze and Herbert Stein.[8] According to Schultze:

Given existing tax rates, full employment in the economy would mean a level of income which would produce certain revenues. . . . Taken together with expenditure programs, these revenues would yield a given surplus. . . .

An attempt to budget for an overly large surplus at full employment will prevent the economy from reaching full employment. . . .

Thus the actual level of the budget surplus is not the best measure of the impact of fiscal policy on the economy.[9]

The focus on the full employment budget can trace its antecedents at least as far back as the work of Beardsley Ruml and the Committee for Economic Development around the time of the Second World War.[10] The CED recognized that low levels of output were bound to cause budgetary deficits, and that it would be folly to try to balance the budget by raising tax rates, as was done in Hoover's time. It recommended that tax rates be set, instead, so as to yield a balanced budget, or perhaps a small surplus, at full employment.

By 1962, the full employment surplus (FES) had been enshrined in the *Economic Report of the President;*[11] eventually it became one of the

[8] Charles L. Schultze, testimony in *Current Economic Situation and Short-Run Outlook,* Hearings before the Joint Economic Committee, 86 Cong. 2 sess. (1961), pp. 114–22; and Herbert Stein, testimony in *January 1961 Economic Report of the President and the Economic Situation and Outlook,* Hearings before the Joint Economic Committee, 87 Cong. 1 sess. (1961), pp. 209–18.

[9] Schultze, *Current Economic Situation,* p. 120.

[10] See Herbert Stein, *The Fiscal Revolution in America* (Chicago: University of Chicago Press, 1969), especially pp. 184–86.

[11] *Economic Report, 1962,* pp. 77–81.

Table 2: Impact of Automatic Built-In Fiscal Stabilizers and Discretionary Policies on Federal Budget Surplus or Deficit, Four Recession and Recovery Periods, 1948–1961 (in billions of current dollars)

	Surplus (+) or deficit (−)		
Period	Automatic Component	Discretionary Component	Total
Recession			
1948:4–1949:2......	−3.7	−4.0	−7.7
1953:2–1954:2......	−6.6	+8.2	+1.6
1957:3–1958:1......	−8.7	−2.0	−10.7
1960:2–1961:1......	−6.8	−3.2	−10.0
Recovery			
1949:2–1950:2......	+6.1	+6.1	+12.2
1954:2–1955:2......	+10.4	−1.5	+8.9
1958:1–1959:2......	+17.4	−8.8	+8.6
1961*.............	+10.8	−7.4	+3.4

* The last quarter for which data were available when the calculations were made was 1961:94 (see source); however, that is not considered the terminal quarter of recovery.
Source: Wilfred Lewis, Jr., *Federal Fiscal Policy in the Postwar Recessions* (Brookings Institution, 1962), Table 4, p. 16.

centerpieces of the New Economics under Presidents Kennedy and Johnson.

At about the same time that the CEA under Heller was introducing the FES as a policy planning tool, Wilfred Lewis, Jr., demonstrated its usefulness in historical studies of fiscal policy. Using a concept like the FES to separate the discretionary and automatic aspects of stabilization policy, Lewis concluded that "the built-in fiscal stabilizers have made a substantial contribution to the stability of the postwar economy," while deliberate discretionary policies "generally have been less helpful."[12] Table 2 summarizes Lewis's results for the four business cycles from 1948 to 1961. Reading it, one should note that it is usually *changes* in a measure of fiscal impact that convey useful information. The discretionary deficit during the recovery period 1958–59, for example, was not in and of itself perverse; without it, there might have been no recovery. The real issue is whether the discretionary component of fiscal policy has been moving in the right direction, given the current economic situation.

The role of the full employment surplus can be illustrated in the context of the following rock-bottom model of income determination:[13]

$$C = C(Y - T) \quad \text{(consumption function)},$$

where C is real consumer spending, Y is real GNP, and T is real tax receipts;

[12] Lewis, *Federal Fiscal Policy*, pp. 15, 17.

[13] For a mathematical version of the following, see the appendix.

$$Y = C + A + G \quad \text{(income identity)},$$

where A is real autonomous private expenditures and G is real government purchases;

$$T = T(Y, \tau) \quad \text{(tax function)},$$

where τ is a tax parameter (think of it as the tax rate), or a vector of such parameters. The income determination equation is

$$Y = C[Y - T(Y, \tau)] + A + G, \quad (1)$$

and the actual budget surplus is $T(Y, \tau) - G$, while the FES is $T(Y^*, \tau) - G$, where Y^* is real GNP at full employment. The ordinary surplus is obviously an inadequate measure of the influence of fiscal policy since the first term is endogenous; that is, it fails to distinguish between the influence of the budget on the economy and the influence of the economy on the budget. The FES avoids this pitfall by measuring tax revenues at full employment.[14]

But, like the ordinary surplus, the FES runs afoul of the balanced-budget theorem: changes in tax receipts simply do not carry as much bang for the buck as changes in government purchases. Since the FES fails to weight tax receipts by the marginal propensity to consume, it is impossible to associate a given change in the FES with a specific change in income; it depends on how the change is apportioned between taxes and spending. As pointed out by Brown, the weighted full employment surplus would be a better measure.

But another problem arises with the full employment surplus, whether weighted or unweighted, which did not afflict the ordinary budget surplus. Suppose the tax regulations (that is, the vector of parameters, τ) are altered when the economy is very far below full employment. The revenue yield of this change *at actual income levels* may well be very different from the hypothetical revenue yield *at full employment*. Even the sign may be different. Consider, for example, a small reduction in personal income tax rates coupled with a very large increase in corporate tax rates. At low levels of business activity, with corporate profits depressed, this change might generate a net loss of revenues, even though at high levels of employment larger tax collections might result. This ambiguity, of course, is merely a reflection of the innate difficulty of collapsing two parameters (G and τ) into one. There is simply no way to do this that is correct for *every* level of GNP. The weighted FES is a true measure of the impact of budgetary changes on a full

[14] We abstract here from growth, so Y^* is assumed unchanged. This restriction will be dropped shortly.

employment economy; but such information may be of limited interest if the unemployment rate is 6 percent.

Whatever the educational benefits of the FES —and they appear to have been considerable— sophisticated investigations of fiscal influence require a different measure.[15]

The Concept of Fiscal Drag

The chief selling point of the FES over the ordinary budget deficit is that the former indicates only *discretionary* changes while the latter includes the effects of the automatic stabilizers. However, in a growing economy, even this is not true. With unchanged tax laws, a growing economy will generate ever-increasing tax receipts at full employment (or, for that matter, at any other constant level of utilization). The more elastic the tax schedule with respect to aggregate income,[16] the more important these "automatic" increments to the FES will be. If private demand is expanding too rapidly, such an automatic increase in full employment revenues may be desirable, but in other circumstances it will not be. Instead, it will place what Heller has called a "fiscal drag" on the system. According to Heller:

> . . . in a growth context, the great revenue-raising power of our Federal tax system produces a built-in average increase of $7 to $8 billion a year in Federal revenues . . . Unless it is offset by such "fiscal dividends" as tax cuts or expansion of Federal programs, this automatic rise in revenues will become a "fiscal drag" siphoning too much of the economic substance out of the private economy and thereby choking expansion.[17]

The role of fiscal drag in our rock-bottom model is clear. Since the FES is defined as $T(Y^*, \tau) - G$, its value will change if τ, G, or Y^* changes. Movements in the FES attributable to the first two arguments are discretionary; the automatic change in the FES due to economic growth is fiscal drag, according to Heller's definition.[18]

An alternative to Heller's definition of fiscal drag may be a more useful tool, since it accounts for the fact that some automatic increase in the full employment surplus may be desirable if autonomous expenditures are rising.

Suppose, for the sake of the argument, that the time path of real government expenditures is set optimally according to allocational criteria, and not varied for stabilization purposes. Thus, both A and G can be taken as exogenous by the stabilization branch.[19] According to the model, if the economy is to expand along its full employment growth path, tax rates must be manipulated so as to maintain

$$Y^* = C[Y^* - T(Y^*, \tau)] + A + G.$$

As we show in the appendix, this equation can be used to obtain the *discretionary change in full employment taxes needed to maintain full employment*. It seems natural, then, to define *adjusted fiscal drag* as the difference between the automatic increase in full employment taxes (Heller's definition) and the total tax increase required to maintain full employment. We show in the appendix that the *size* and *sign* of the adjusted fiscal drag depend on the relative growth of private and public autonomous demand in relation to capacity, and on the relative sizes of the multiplier and the marginal propensity to consume. Specifically, the *sign* of the adjusted fiscal drag depends *only* on the relative *sizes* of the increase in capacity that would be required to meet the autonomous growth in demand relative to the actual increase in capacity. Its *size* depends also on the marginal propensity to consume. On this definition, if autonomous demand and supply expand equally, no drag is exerted and no tax cut is needed.

The preceding discussion of fiscal drag, like most of the literature on measuring fiscal influence, has ignored changes in the price level. This procedure is legitimate only if the price level in fact never changes, or a "classical dichotomy" exists so that the price level does not impinge upon any real variables. In the short run, however, with commitments made in money terms with imperfect foresight, one can hardly ignore the real consequences of a changing price level. In particular, Gramlich has pointed out that, owing to progressivity, the government's real tax receipts will depend on the level of prices, P, and that, since many expenditure programs are

---

[15] For a recent discussion of the pros and cons of the full employment surplus, see Arthur M. Okun and Nancy H. Teeters, "The Full Employment Surplus Revisited," *Brookings Papers on Economic Activity* (1:1970), pp. 77–110, and the discussion of the paper, pp. 111–16.

[16] This elasticity is the product of the elasticity of the tax base with respect to national income, and the elasticity of tax receipts with respect to the base.

[17] Walter W. Heller, *New Dimensions of Political Economy* (Cambridge, Mass.: Harvard University Press, 1966; W. W. Norton, 1967), p. 65.

[18] Ibid., p. 181, note 9. For a mathematical version of what follows, see the appendix.

[19] This terminological division of the government's functions comes, of course, from Musgrave, *Theory of Public Finance*.

fixed in *money* terms, real spending may exhibit a similar dependence.[20]

To see this, suppose the tax laws make nominal tax receipts a function of nominal income:

$$PT = f(PY, \tau), \qquad (2)$$

where τ is again a set of tax parameters, and where the elasticity of $f(\cdot)$ with respect to PY exceeds unity—that is, it is a progressive tax function. Now suppose the price level rises with real output fixed. Clearly, *real* tax receipts will rise because money income will rise in the same proportion as the price level, causing money tax receipts—by progressivity—to rise more than proportionately with P.[21] In other words, pure price inflation as well as real growth gives rise to fiscal drag. For example, based on Waldorf's estimate of 1½ for the income elasticity of the personal income tax, a 4 percent inflation will add 2 percent to *real* tax receipts.[22] If, in addition, the state fixes nominal expenditures, PG, rather than real expenditures, G, in its budget statement, this effect will be even more severe.

Given this possibility, there are four reasons why the full employment surplus might change. Alterations in tax parameters or in real government purchases lead to the discretionary changes in the FES that are of interest for stabilization policy. But a rise in either potential GNP or the price level will automatically raise the FES—that is, cause fiscal drag. The appendix demonstrates that we can define a new concept of adjusted fiscal drag that accounts for the automatic stabilizing effects of inflation, simply by subtracting from our previous measure of adjusted fiscal drag the product of the rate of inflation, the marginal propensity to tax, and money GNP.

The Weighted Full Employment Surplus

Of the several problems the FES concept presents as a measure of fiscal influence, the easiest to remedy is its failure to recognize the differential strengths of taxes versus government expenditures. This was, in fact, accomplished by Gramlich in his doctoral dissertation and a subsequent conference paper.[23] In the rock-bottom model, the amendment merely requires weighting tax receipts by the marginal propensity to consume. If W denotes the weighted FES, then

$$W = cT(Y^*, \tau) - G,$$

where c is the marginal propensity to consume.

This "innovation," as we have seen, was anticipated in Brown's paper. It was also anticipated, in a slightly different form, in Richard Musgrave's concept of "fiscal leverage."[24] The main difference is that Musgrave's measure reflects fiscal impact whereas Gramlich's weighted FES is a budget measure. Essentially, fiscal leverage is the "weighted budget":

$$FL = \sum_{i=1}^{N} m_i G_i - \sum_{j=1}^{M} \mu_j T_j,$$

where $G_1 \ldots, G_N$ are different types of expenditures, $T_1, \ldots, T_M$ are different types of tax receipts, and the m_i and μ_j are the appropriate multipliers suggested by some model. The leverage, FL, includes both discretionary and automatic changes in the budget. Musgrave notes that a purer measure of the change in fiscal policy would be obtained by calculating fiscal leverage at some fixed level of income.[25] With this done, and with full employment income used as the reference point, the result is the weighted full employment deficit multiplied by some appropriate multiplier. In the rock-bottom model with

---

[20] Edward M. Gramlich, "Measures of the Aggregate Demand Impact of the Federal Budget," in Lewis, ed., *Budget Concepts for Economic Analysis,* especially pp. 117–19.

[21] To be precise, by (2):

$$T = \left(\frac{1}{P}\right) f(PY, \tau),$$

so

$$\frac{dT}{dP} = -\frac{f}{P^2} + \left(\frac{1}{P}\right) f_1 Y,$$

so

$$\left(\frac{P}{T}\right)\left(\frac{dT}{dP}\right) = -1 + \left(\frac{PY}{f}\right) f_1,$$

which is positive if and only if the tax structure is progressive.

[22] See William H. Waldorf, "The Responsiveness of Federal Personal Income Taxes to Income Change," *Survey of Current Business,* vol. 47 (December 1967), pp. 32–45. Charles J. Goetz and Warren E. Weber have shown that these inflation effects were sufficient to counter the tax cuts of 1964–65 and 1970. See their "Intertemporal Changes in Real Federal Income Tax Dates, 1954–70," *National Tax Journal,* vol. 24 (March 1971), pp. 51–63.

[23] Edward M. Gramlich, "The Behavior and Adequacy of the United States Federal Budget, 1952–1964," *Yale Economic Essays,* vol. 6 (Spring 1966), pp. 99–159; and "Measures of the Aggregate Demand Impact."

[24] Richard A. Musgrave, "On Measuring Fiscal Performance," *Review of Economics and Statistics,* vol. 46 (May 1964), pp. 213–20.

[25] Ibid., p. 214.

only one G and one T, fiscal leverage at full employment would be

$$FL^* = m(G - cT^*),$$

where m is the ordinary multiplier, and T^* is full employment revenues. In fact, since multipliers are hard to know with any precision, Musgrave actually suggests dividing this measure by the multiplier.[26] If this is done, the result is precisely the weighted full employment deficit.

We do not find any reason to prefer a budget concept, like the weighted FES, to a fiscal impact measure, like fiscal leverage at full employment. The alleged virtue of budget measures is their independence of any particular model. This is true of the FES (apart from the need to estimate tax revenues at full employment). However, once weights are introduced, one is forced to use estimated expenditure coefficients from some econometric model. In fact, things are even more complicated. In addition to choosing a model, one must choose a time horizon, since impact multipliers differ from second-quarter multipliers and so on. And this problem arises whether interest centers on multipliers (as in a fiscal impact measure) or only on ratios of multipliers (as in a budget measure). The superiority of a budget measure is thus hard to argue since it makes only trivially less demand on the available knowledge of the economic structure.

Gramlich's work makes it abundantly clear that W, a budget measure, is indeed sensitive to the model chosen for its estimation. He compares time series for W, which he constructs using six different econometric models, with the unweighted FES as calculated by Keith Carlson.[27] The Okun model aside—it does not purport to be a full-fledged econometric model anyway[28]—all models generate weighted FES series (using long-run expenditure coefficients) that are radically different from the unweighted FES. Unfortunately, the models appear to be far from agreement among themselves. For example, for 1964:1, the estimates of W (in constant 1958 dollars) range from \$12.6 billion to \$31.0 billion.[29] These differences are not quite so large as

they look. Because all the multipliers are local, they apply only to small changes in exogenous variables. If only first differences of W, instead of levels, are estimated, the models agree much more closely; for 1964:1, estimated changes in the weighted FES range from \$1.1 billion to \$3.0 billion.[30] Secondly, if the focus is on first-quarter rather than steady-state weights, even the levels are not that far apart. Again for 1964:1, the range is from \$40.1 billion to \$50.5 billion.[31] If these two adjustments are combined —that is, first differences in W are calculated from first-quarter weights—it is difficult to find any divergences among the models as large as \$1 billion.[32] Of course, even that amount may be a nontrivial difference for some purposes.

The Weighted Standardized Surplus

Even the weighted full employment surplus fails to deal with one of the difficulties with the FES that we outlined earlier: if income is far from the full employment level, the FES (and also W) may be misleading. We show in the appendix that the correct measure of discretionary fiscal policy in our rock-bottom model is

$$\Delta F = \frac{\Delta G - c\,T_\tau\Delta\tau}{1 - c(1 - T_Y)}, \qquad (3)$$

where $T_\tau(Y, \tau)$, $T_Y(Y, \tau)$, and c are all evaluated *at the initial levels of* Y *and* τ.

The denominator of this expression is simply the reciprocal of the multiplier. We may call the numerator the change in the "weighted standardized surplus." It is computed by deducting from the change in government purchases of goods and services the product of the marginal propensity to consume and the change in tax receipts attributable to changes in the tax code. The measure generalizes in an obvious way to accommodate a model of arbitrary complexity. It is only necessary to multiply the change in each fiscal instrument by the ratio of its own multiplier to the basic expenditure multiplier, and sum the multiplied products. This has, in fact, been done in two recent studies. In a volume prepared for the Organisation for Economic Co-operation and Development, Bent Hansen constructs a conceptual framework similar to that developed here.[33] He uses equation (3) to measure the *dis-*

[26] Ibid., p. 216.

[27] K. Carlson, "Estimates of the High-Employment Budget: 1947–1967," Federal Reserve Bank of St. Louis, *Review*, vol. 49 (June 1967), pp. 6–14..

[28] This model is contained in Arthur M. Okun, "Measuring the Impact of the 1964 Tax Reduction," in Walter W. Heller, ed., *Perspectives on Economic Growth* (New York: Random House, 1968).

[29] Gramlich, "Measures of the Aggregate Demand Impact," table 2, p. 125.

[30] Ibid., table 3, p. 126.

[31] Ibid., table A2, p. 141.

[32] Ibid., table A3, p. 142.

[33] Bent Hansen, *Fiscal Policy in Seven Countries, 1955–1965* (Paris: Organisation for Economic Co-operation and Development, 1969).

cretionary effect of government stabilization policy, and the obvious measure,

$$\Delta Y - \Delta A/(1 - c),$$

for the *total* effect of government policy. Subtracting the former from the latter gives him a measure of the *automatic* stabilizing effect of the tax structure:

$$AUTO = \frac{cT_Y\Delta A}{1 - c(1 - T_Y)} = \frac{\Delta A}{1 - c}$$
$$- \frac{\Delta A}{1 - c(1 - T_Y)}.$$

For empirical purposes, the rock-bottom model is obviously too crude. Hansen uses instead a model that is only slightly more sophisticated in that it (a) allows for two kinds of taxes (direct and indirect), (b) includes an import equation, and (c) allows for two types of government expenditure (goods and labor services).

Given measures of the discretionary and automatic effects of government policies, Hansen can construct hypothetical growth paths for each country in the absence of (a) any discretionary action ($\Delta F = 0$) and (b) the automatic stabilizers ($AUTO = 0$). Having done this, he can measure the percentage of the business cycle that was eliminated by discretionary and automatic fiscal actions. His results are summarized in Table 3. Clearly, the United States has ironed out more cyclical fluctuation than any other country. However, this does not necessarily mean that it has had the best fiscal policy, since for most of the period it was stabilizing the economy at a relatively low level of resource utilization. Also, nearly two-thirds of the accomplishment was due to the automatic stabilizers. Only Germany and

Table 3: Percentage of Business Cycle Eliminated by Discretionary and by Automatic Stabilization Policies, Selected Countries, 1955–1965

Country	Eliminated by Discretionary Policy	Eliminated by Automatic Policy	Total Percentage Eliminated
Belgium..............	5	16	21
France*..............	−35	48	13
Germany*............	14	12	26
Italy†................	−17	32	15
Sweden..............	5	n.a.	n.a.
United Kingdom......	−10	−3	−13
United States........	17	32	49

n.a. Not available.
* 1958–65.
† 1956–65.
Source: Bent Hansen, *Fiscal Policy in Seven Countries, 1955–1965* (Paris: Organisation for Economic Co-operation and Development, 1969), Table 2.6, p. 69. The figures pertain to central governments only.

the United States can claim any sizable achievements in discretionary stabilization, and such policies were actually destabilizing in France, Italy, and the United Kingdom. In England, notorious for its "stop-go" economics, even the automatic and total effects were destabilizing.

How adequate is the raw budget deficit as a proxy for the total effect of fiscal policy? While Hansen finds that this assessment varies greatly from one country to the next, for the United States the budget deficit and the *total* (not discretionary) fiscal effect have a remarkably high correlation (0.991), with the constant relating them approximately equal to the multiplier! For no other country is the agreement this good.[34] One wonders if this might be a reflection of the fact that the United States was furthest from a full employment growth path.

In an article that makes many of the points made here, Oakland constructs a rough series of quarterly changes in the weighted standardized surplus (which he calls the weighted initial surplus) from 1947 to 1966, and compares them with changes in the FES.[35] The two series generally give similar *qualitative* pictures of the impact of discretionary fiscal policy, but the *quantitative* divergence is often quite sharp. Some of this is, no doubt, due to the weighting. But the fact that the discrepancies tend to be largest in times of recession suggests that the FES tends to overstate the effect of changes in taxes when the economy is far below full employment. Table 4 compares Gramlich's series on changes in the weighted full employment surplus (based on the MIT-FRB model) with Oakland's series on changes in the weighted standardized surplus. The two columns are obviously not identical. On the other hand, they are positively correlated; in fact, adding $2 billion to $2½ billion to each estimated change in the weighted standardized surplus yields a fairly close approximation to the corresponding estimate of the change in the weighted full employment surplus. It is just barely conceivable that this systematic difference reflects the conceptual difference between the two measures. (Progression should make full employment revenues rise more rapidly than revenues standardized

[34] Ibid., pp. 73–81.

[35] William H. Oakland, "Budgetary Measures of Fiscal Performance," *Southern Economic Journal*, vol. 35 (April 1969), pp. 347–58, especially table 1. See also Saul H. Hymans and J. Philip Wernette, "The Impact of the Federal Budget on Total Spending," *Business Economics*, vol. 5 (September 1970), pp. 29–34, where an *unweighted* standardized surplus on an annual basis is considered.

Table 4: Change in Weighted Full Employment Surplus and Weighted Standardized Surplus, Second Quarter 1963 to Fourth Quarter 1966 (in billions of dollars)

Year and Quarter	Change in Weighted Full Employment Surplus	Change in Standardized Weighted Surplus	Difference
1963:2...........	3.5	1.3	2.2
3...........	1.0	−1.8	2.8
4...........	−0.6	−1.0	0.4
1964:1...........	−3.0	−5.2	2.2
2...........	−5.1	−6.2	1.1
3...........	0.6	0.6	0
4...........	2.5	0.7	1.8
1965:1...........	0.7	−1.8	2.5
2...........	−0.6	−1.3	0.7
3...........	−5.9	−9.6	3.7
4...........	0.8	−1.1	1.9
1966:1...........	−0.4	1.1	1.5
2...........	1.1	−4.5	5.6
3...........	−2.3	−6.5	4.2
4...........	−3.0	−4.9	1.9

Sources: For column 1, Edward M. Gramlich, "Measures of the Aggregate Demand Impact of the Federal Budget," in Wilfred Lewis, Jr., ed., *Budget Concepts for Economic Analysis* (Brookings Institution, 1968), Table 3, p. 126; column 2, William H. Oakland, "Budgetary Measures of Fiscal Performance," *Southern Economic Journal,* vol. 35 (April 1969), Table 1, p. 356.

Table 5: Changes in Unweighted Standardized Surplus and Unweighted Full Employment Surplus, Fiscal Years 1962–1973 (in billions of dollars)

Fiscal Year	Unweighted Standardized Surplus		Unweighted Full Employment Surplus
	McCracken	Hymans-Wernette	
1962........	—	−8.7	−4.4
1963........	—	−5.2	+4.6
1964........	—	−8.6	−7.2
1965........	—	−4.4	−0.8
1966........	—	−17.9	−4.6
1967........	—	−16.9	−6.9
1968........	−24.7	−24.9	+4.6
1969........	+11.2	+8.1	+18.6
1970........	−12.4	−11.4*	−5.1
1971........	−22.2	−11.7†	−2.2
1972........	−33.4	—	−11.4
1973........	−10.7†	—	+0.2

* Estimate
† Projection
Sources: Column 1, Paul W. McCracken, "Moving Toward External and Internal Economic Balance" (paper presented to the Southwestern Economic Association Convention, San Antonio, Texas, March 31, 1972; processed), p. 4; column 2, Saul H. Hymans and J. Philip Wernette, "The Impact of the Federal Budget on Total Spending," *Business Economics,* vol. 5 (September 1970), Table 1, p. 31; column 3, 1962–71, Council of Economic Advisers, unpublished tabulations; 1972–73, from Nancy H. Teeters, "The 1973 Federal Budget" *Brookings Paper on Economic Activity* (1:1972), Table 3, p. 223.

at a level of income below full employment.) But some of the years recorded in the table were themselves not very far from full employment, so that the differences may reflect statistical technique, and not definition. The two largest discrepancies occur in the second and third quarters of 1966, which suggests that they may result from Gramlich's procedure for adjusting for changes in the price level.

A measure of fiscal influence that in our terminology would be described as the change in the *unweighted* standardized surplus has been advocated by McCracken and by Hymans and Wernette. McCracken's annual time series on "the sum of the increase in outlays and the revenue cost of any changes in tax rates"[36] is given in the first column of Table 5 below. Earlier, Hymans and Wernette had suggested using "the current increase in government expenditures (net of induced changes in stabilizer elements such as unemployment insurance payments) less the increase in tax revenues (measured at current income levels) resulting from any changes in the structure of the tax system."[37] Their time series is

given in the second column of the table; it corresponds closely to McCracken's. For purposes of comparison, the last column of the table exhibits changes in the full employment surplus; during years of approximately full employment, the difference between this series and the two others is fiscal drag.

Like the FES, the unweighted standardized surplus does not depend on any particular model of the economy. While this trait is doubtless a virtue, the balanced-budget theorem undermines any fiscal measure that fails to weight appropriately the various components of the budget— that is, changes in an unweighted measure cannot be associated unambiguously with changes in economic activity. Therefore, the best procedure for the government might be to publish separately the main components of the standardized surplus—changes in expenditures, and revenue yields of changes in tax statutes—so that external users could supply their own weights.

RECAPITULATION

This has been a long, and at times involved, discussion of a complex measurement problem, so a brief review of what has been said may be useful.

We started by cataloguing some well-known

[36] Paul W. McCracken, "Moving Toward External and Internal Economic Balance" (paper presented to the Southwestern Economic Association Convention, San Antonio, Texas, March 31, 1972; processed), p. 3.

[37] Hymans and Wernette, "Impact of the Federal Budget," pp. 31–32.

objections to the ordinary budget surplus as a measure of the impact of fiscal policy on economic activity. Its first drawback—its failure to distinguish discretionary from automatic changes in the budget—is partially alleviated by using the full employment surplus instead; but only partially, since part of the change in the full employment surplus is automatic in a growing economy ("fiscal drag").

A second drawback, common to both the ordinary surplus and the full employment surplus, is the failure to weight the various components of the budget appropriately. Proper weighting requires some explicit or implicit model of the economy to compute, say, a weighted full employment surplus.

But such a measure has one additional failing that did not plague the ordinary deficit: it applies to a hypothetical full employment situation rather than to the actual state of the economy. Some changes in tax laws may have a revenue yield at full employment that is very different from that at actual employment; and, if this is so, the ramifications for aggregate demand will be correspondingly different. The desire to obtain a measure that both separates discretionary from automatic changes in the budget and is relevant to the current state of the economy leads naturally to the standardized surplus: the difference between the revenue yield of discretionary changes in tax and transfer programs and the change in government purchases of goods and services.

Finally, applying the appropriate weights to each component of the budget, as supplied by some model of the economy, leads to the weighted standardized surplus, our preferred measure. This measure, if computed in real terms, automatically adjusts for the effect of inflation on tax revenues in a theoretically reasonable way.

One further point must be made. Scant attention has been paid in this discussion to the practical problems involved in constructing a weighted standardized surplus, or any other measure that depends crucially upon a specific model of the economy. There are many macro models—econometric and otherwise—each giving somewhat different multipliers. Which model shall we use? Further, multipliers always have a time dimension. Should we base our fiscal impact measure on first-quarter multipliers, fourth-quarter multipliers, or what? These important questions obviously cannot be given definitive answers; we raise them merely to underscore the difficulties. Until much more knowledge is accumulated, perhaps the best procedure is to develop a number of different measures by using several models and alternative time horizons.

APPENDIX: MATHEMATICAL DEVELOPMENT OF THE MODEL

The Full Employment Surplus

In the simple model embodied in equation (1) in the text,

$$Y = C[Y - T(Y, \tau)] + A + G,$$

the local multiplier equation is found by differentiating totally and solving for dY:

$$dY = \frac{dA}{1 - C'(1 - T_Y)} + \frac{dG - C'T_\tau(Y,\tau)d\tau}{1 - C'(1 - T_Y)}. \tag{A-1}$$

This is only a small generalization of the simple multiplier formula for linear models since C' is the marginal propensity to consume and T_Y is the marginal propensity to tax. The second term is the correct fiscal impact measure.

Letting

$$R \equiv T(Y, \tau) - G$$

denote the actual budget surplus, the naive measure of fiscal influence would be.

$$dR = T_Y dY + T_\tau d\tau - dG,$$

which is not a valid index of fiscal policy since the first term is endogenous. In any case, it is not possible to write dY as a function of dR.

The frequently suggested alternative is the change in the full employment surplus:

$$d(FES) = T_\tau(Y^*, \tau)d\tau - dG. \tag{A-2}$$

Comparing this with the last term in (A–1) points up both of the major weaknesses of the FES: it fails to weight the change in taxes by the marginal propensity to consume, and it computes the revenue yield of changes in tax statutes at *potential* GNP instead of at *actual* GNP. Put most succinctly, any changes in τ and G that satisfy

$$dG = C' \cdot T_\tau(Y, \tau)d\tau$$

will leave Y unchanged by (A–1), but will alter the FES by (A–2). Conversely, any combination of fiscal actions that satisfies

$$dG = T_\tau(Y^*, \tau)d\tau$$

will have no effect on the FES but normally will affect the GNP.

The Concept of Fiscal Drag

When we allow for the fact that Y^* grows automatically over time, the change in the FES becomes

$$d(FES) = T_\tau(Y^*, \tau)d\tau - dG + T_Y(Y^*, \tau)dY^*.$$

The first two terms duplicate equation (A–2), and the last is fiscal drag on Heller's definition.

As was stated in the text, an alternative definition of fiscal drag (adjusted fiscal drag) is obtained by first computing the discretionary change in full employment taxes needed to maintain full employment. Since τ would have to be constantly manipulated to satisfy

$$Y^* = C[Y^* - T(Y^*, \tau)] + A + G,$$

the total differentials must satisfy

$$dY^* = C'dY^* - C'T_Y dY^* - C'T_\tau d\tau + dA + dG.$$

The requisite discretionary change is obtained by solving this for $d\tau$:

$$T_\tau d\tau = -\frac{1 - C'(1 - T_Y)}{C'}dY^* + \frac{dA + dG}{C'}.$$

$$(A–3)$$

Adjusted fiscal drag is defined as the difference between Heller's definition, $T_Y dY^*$, and the total tax increase that would be needed to preserve full employment:

$$AFD \equiv T_Y dY^* - (T_\tau d\tau + T_Y dY^*),$$

where $T_\tau d\tau$ is as defined in (A–3). In brief, AFD is simply the negative of (A–3).

It is clear from (A–3), then, that AFD will be positive if and only if the increase in potential GNP, dY^*, exceeds the increase in capacity that is required to meet the autonomous growth of demand,

$$\frac{dA + dG}{1 - C'(1 - T_Y)}.$$

If these are equal—if aggregate demand and aggregate supply grow equally—there is no fiscal drag on this definition.

When the price level may vary, if we ignore the possibility mentioned in the text that nominal spending (PG) rather than real spending (G) is fixed by Congress, it is natural to compute the real full employment surplus as

$$FES = \frac{f(PY^*, \tau)}{P} - G,$$

where $PT = f(PT, \tau)$ is the tax function in nominal terms. Changes in the FES will therefore be

$$d(FES) = f_1 Y^*(dP/P) - (f/P)(dP/P) + f_1 dY^* + (f_2/P)d\tau - dG.$$

In this expression, only the last two terms represent discretionary changes in fiscal policy; the first three are the fiscal drags (by Heller's definition) attributable to inflation and real growth:

$$FD = (f_1 Y^* - T)(dP/P) + f_1 dY^*.$$

This shows that inflation contributes to fiscal drag if and only if $f_1 PY > PT$, that is, only if the tax function is progressive.

In a like manner, we can refine our concept of adjusted fiscal drag to account for the automatic stabilizing effect of inflation. We again wish to manipulate τ to maintain

$$Y^* = c[Y^* - (1/P)f(Y^* P, \tau)] + A + G;$$

that is,

$$dY^* = C'dY^* - (C'/P)f_1 Y^* dP - (C'/P)f_1 PdY^* + (C'/P^2)f - (C'/P)f_2 d\tau + dA + dG.$$

Or, solving for the required discretionary tax change in real terms:

$$AFD = -\frac{f_2 d\tau}{P} = \frac{1 - C'(1 - f_1)}{C'}dY^* + f_1 PY^* \frac{dP}{P} - \frac{dA + dG}{C'}.$$

The middle term—the product of the marginal propensity to tax, nominal GNP, and the rate of inflation—is the appropriate inflation adjustment mentioned in the text.

18.   LAGS AND UNCERTAINTIES IN FISCAL POLICY: GENERAL CONSIDERATIONS, AND THE 1968-1970 EXPERIENCE*

Alan S. Blinder
and
Robert M. Solow

LAGS AND UNCERTAINTIES: GENERAL CONSIDERATIONS

On any view, successful operation of discretionary fiscal policy requires some dependence on forecasting. Since the accuracy of economic forecasts deteriorates as the period of forecast lengthens, the length of the lag with which fiscal policy works is important information. In general, the longer the lag, the further ahead it is necessary to forecast, and the less likely it is that policy actions will achieve their desired objective.[1]

Traditionally, the total lag in fiscal and monetary policy has been broken down into three components: the recognition lag, the policy lag, and the outside lag.[2] The first consists of the time that elapses between the need for a policy action and the realization by the authorities that such an action is in fact necessary. It exists because economic data take time to collect, process, and analyze. Now that high-speed computers are in use

on a widespread basis, the recognition lag is probably short enough not to present a major problem. Nevertheless, it is not zero; perhaps one or two quarters will elapse between a change in the pace of macroeconomic activity and its perception. A more serious problem may be posed by inaccuracies in the preliminary national income accounts data.[3] Substantial errors in provisional estimates of gross national product and its components obviously can yield a badly distorted view of the pace of economic activity; the hazard this presents to policy makers should be clear enough.

The second lag is really not a matter of economics at all. In principle, once the need for a fiscal action is recognized, government purchases can be varied or withholding schedules altered within a matter of weeks. However, congressional action is required before many of the important fiscal instruments may be employed. The lengthy legislative battle over the Revenue and Expenditure Control Act of 1968 provides ample evidence that the policy lag may be very long indeed. Such historical episodes have given rise to frequent proposals to streamline fiscal decision making, say, by giving the President some discretion over tax rates, at least in the short run.[4] But to date the Congress has exhibited absolutely no inclination to relinquish any of its tax-levying authority; and this is pretty much a dead issue.

Empirical Evidence on Lags in Fiscal Policy

The bulk of economic research has naturally been directed at the one lag that is purely economic in nature—the outside lag, the period between the execution of a fiscal policy move and the time its effects on the economy are ultimately felt. The existence of a substantial outside lag has

* From "Analytical Foundations of Fiscal Policy," in Alan S. Blinder et al., *The Economics of Public Finance* (Washington, D.C.: The Brookings Institution, 1974), pp. 3–115. Copyright © 1974 by The Brookings Institution, Washington, D.C. Reprinted by permission of the publisher and the authors. Alan S. Blinder is Associate Professor of Economics, Princeton University. Robert M. Solow is Institute Professor and Professor of Economics, Massachusetts Institute of Technology.

[1] This statement is, perhaps, overstrong. It is now recognized that lags in economic behavior tend to be distributed lags. The first effects of a policy change may be felt very quickly, even though the ultimate effects may not be realized for some time. Thus, even if the average lag is rather long, a fairly myopic policy, playing on the immediate effects of each policy move, is in principle possible. In practice such a policy might require intolerably sharp swings in fiscal instruments to correct for the lagged impacts of previous actions. So some degree of forecasting accuracy will surely be imperative. On this last point see Robert S. Holbrook, "Optimal Economic Policy and the Problem of Instrument Instability," *American Economic Review*, vol. 62 (March 1972), pp. 57–65.

[2] See, for example, Albert Ando, E. Cary Brown, Robert M. Solow, and John Kareken, "Lags in Fiscal and Monetary Policy," in E. Cary Brown and others, *Stabilization Policies*, A Series of Research Studies prepared for the Commission on Money and Credit (Englewood Cliffs, N.J.: Prentice-Hall, 1963), pp. 1–163.

[3] For a quantitative assessment of this problem, suggesting that the errors are sizable, see Rosanne Cole, *Errors in Provisional Estimates of Gross National Product* (New York: Columbia University Press for the National Bureau of Economic Research, 1969).

[4] See for example, *Money and Credit: Their Influence on Jobs, Prices and Growth*, The Report of the Commission on Money and Credit (Englewood Cliffs, N.J.: Prentice-Hall, 1961), pp. 136–37.

often been used to build a case against discretionary fiscal or monetary policy (more on this later); and probably no empirical issue in macroeconomics now draws more dispute than the precise lag structures in the various key macroeconomic relations. Since fiscal policy actions reverberate through the economic structure in complex ways, most notions about policy lags nowadays come from experimenting with complete macroeconometric models. Typically, a model is run both with and without the policy move being analyzed, and the difference between the two solutions, quarter by quarter, is taken as an estimate of the size and timing of the effects of the policy. In the real world, mere discussion of a policy change can precipitate important effects—as when debate over increasing an excise tax generates anticipatory purchases—but no formal system of equations can be expected to account for such phenomena.[5] Moreover, the pervasive autocorrelation in most economic time series makes timing relationships notoriously difficult to pin down econometrically. But, despite these shortcomings, the models again offer the best evidence on lag structures to be had; so it is worth surveying briefly what they have to say.

The National Bureau of Economic Research–National Science Foundation seminars on comparison of econometric models provides a fruitful point of departure.[6] The main fiscal policy action analyzed by these models was a sustained increment in nominal government spending. The models also traced the effects of higher government spending and an increase in personal income taxes, each with an accommodating monetary response to stabilize short-term interest rates. But these are mixed fiscal-monetary policy experiments, and the time pattern of their effects tells very little about the response of the economy to pure fiscal policy.

Figure 1 shows the cumulative multipliers from several of the models. In each case, the graph indicates the total change in nominal GNP from a sustained $1 billion increment in nominal govern-

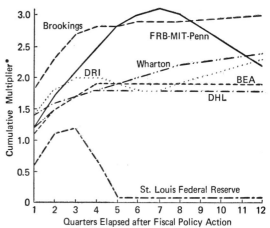

Figure 1: Quarterly Cumulative Impact of Sustained Increment in Nominal Nondefense Government Spending, Selected Econometric Models of the United States

* Cumulative multipliers = $\Delta GNP/\Delta G$ (current dollars), where G is government spending. The periods for which the multipliers are calculated generally cover a ten-year span. Some of the models use $1 billion increments, some $5 billion increments. Multipliers for quarters 9, 10, and 11 are not available, and have been interpolated linearly.
Source: Gary Fromm and Lawrence R. Klein, "A Comparison of Eleven Econometric Models of the United States, in American Economic Association," *Papers and Proceedings of the Eighty-fifth Annual Meeting, 1972 (American Economic Review,* vol. 63, May 1973), table 5, p. 391.

ment purchases. The reader is again reminded that the increment in real government expenditure is generally declining over time as a result of inflation, so these are not the government spending multipliers of pure theory.

Although the lag structures obviously differ, all the models save that of the St. Louis Federal Reserve clearly show a substantial short-run impact for fiscal policy. The Wharton model, for example, shows a four-quarter multiplier of 1.8, which builds to about 2.4 after three years. According to the FRB-MIT-Penn model, the multiplier actually peaks at about 3.1 after seven quarters, and has declined to just over 2 by the end of three years. In the Bureau of Economic Analysis (BEA) and Michigan (DHL-III) models, the four-quarter multipliers are identical to the twelve-quarter multipliers; and in the Brookings and Data Resources (DRI) models they are very close. In short, the models suggest that at least 75 percent, and probably much more, of the ultimate effect is felt within the first year after the initiation of the policy.[7] The St. Louis model is the iconoclast. Its computed multiplier peaks

---

[5] The FRB-MIT-Penn model deals with this problem by recording some changes in policy instruments —for example, the investment tax credit—before the fact. While this may be a useful way to keep an econometric model "on track," the procedure is rather ad hoc, to say the least.

[6] See Gary Fromm and Lawrence R. Klein, "A Comparison of Eleven Econometric Models of the United States," in American Economic Association, *Papers and Proceedings of the Eighty-fifth Annual Meeting, 1972 (American Economic Review,* vol. 53, May 1973), table 5, p. 391.

---

[7] The actual simulation results for several of the models show no tendency to converge to a steady-state multiplier. The decision to cut off consideration of the results after twelve quarters was an arbitrary one.

at just over unity in the second and third quarters after the policy change, and reaches its steady-state value of 0.1 by the fifth quarter.

While in our view the manner in which the multiplier experiments were conducted makes the nominal multipliers more meaningful, it is also possible to deflate both GNP and government expenditures in each quarter and compute the ratio of the cumulative increment in real GNP to the cumulative increment in real government spending (which is falling steadily due to inflation). Such computations, the results of which are displayed in Figure 2, give us something akin to—but hardly identical with—the real government expenditure multipliers of pure theory. The time paths turn out to be similar to those of Figure 1, except for a more pronounced tendency for the cumulative multipliers to decline in later quarters owing to the well-known contractionary effects of a rising price level.

These results generally confirm the few previously published simulation experiments with econometric models. For example, Fromm and Taubman, reporting extensively on simulations with the Brookings model using a variety of policy instruments, find a real government expenditure multiplier of 2.9 after ten quarters.[8] About two-thirds of the ultimate effect has already appeared after two quarters, and the first-quarter impact multiplier is 1.4.[9] De Leeuw and Gramlich find weaker, but also rather fast-acting, fiscal effects by simulating an early version of the FRB-MIT model. Their maximum real multiplier of 1.8 is reached after five quarters, but more than 90 percent of this is in hand by the second quarter after the policy change. After the fourth quarter, monetary side effects and inflation reduce the multiplier steadily to just 1.0 by the end of four years.[10] Simulations run by Evans using one version of the Wharton model imply that essentially all of the effects of an increase in government purchases are felt within the first quarter. His impact multiplier of 1.98 scarcely differs from the twelve-quarter multiplier of 2.07.[11] Finally, the

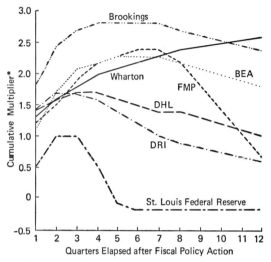

Figure 2: Quarterly Cumulative Impact of Sustained Increment in Real Nondefense Government Spending, Selected Econometric Models of the United States

Quarters Elapsed after Fiscal Policy Action

* See note *, Figure 1. Multipliers are calculated analogously, using data in 1958 dollars.
Source: Gary Fromm and Lawrence R. Klein, "A Comparison of Eleven Econometric Models of the United States," in American Economic Association, *Papers and Proceedings of the Eighty-Fifth Annual Meeting, 1972 (American Economic Review,* vol. 63, May 1973), table 5, p. 391.

Moroney-Mason model displays an impact multiplier of 1.2, a fourth-quarter multiplier of 2.1, and a steady-state multiplier of about 2.7 (all in current-price terms).[12]

These models seem to agree that a government able to see six to nine months ahead—not necessarily with complete accuracy, but well enough to know whether stimulus or restraint will be needed, and whether the dosage should be large or small—can make intelligent fiscal policy. Of course, it can also make mistakes, but that is hardly news.

Lags and the Workability of Discretionary Policy

The need for forecasting and the weakness of forecasts are sometimes made the basis of a pessimistic view of the practical possibility of a stabilizing fiscal policy. Norman Ture, for example, mentions three "basic premises" of what he calls the "new" view of fiscal policy:

1. In the absence of an active compensatory tax policy, the economy would be highly unstable

[8] Gary Fromm and Paul Taubman, *Policy Simulations with an Econometric Model* (Washington, D.C.: Brookings Institution, 1968).

[9] Ibid., table 2.5, p. 48.

[10] Frank de Leeuw and Edward M. Gramlich, "The Channels of Monetary Policy," *Federal Reserve Bulletin,* vol. 55 (June 1969), table 4, p. 489.

[11] Michael K. Evans, *Macroeconomic Activity: Theory, Forecasting, and Control; An Econometric Approach* (New York: Harper and Row, 1969), table 20.3, p. 567. Evans in fact computes a forty-quarter multiplier (essentially the steady-state outcome) of 1.93.

[12] J. R. Moroney and J. M. Mason, "The Dynamic Impacts of Autonomous Expenditures and the Monetary Base on Aggregate Income," *Journal of Money, Credit and Banking,* vol. 3 (November 1971), pp. 793–84.

and would experience intolerable swings in the rate of employment and periodic inflationary outbursts.

2. Potential deviations of the economy from the trend of steady, noninflationary growth can be detected sufficiently in advance of their actual occurrence to allow the offsetting, stabilizing tax changes to be made on a timely basis . . .

3. Moderate temporary changes in income taxes induce quick, significant, and systematic, hence predictable, responses in the spending of households and businesses.[13]

Ture proceeds to deny the truth of each of these "basic premises." Healthy skepticism, by definition, is a good thing. Surely some of the claims about the delicacy and deftness with which stabilizing fiscal policy can be managed have been excessive; the catch-phrase "fine tuning" suggests what we have in mind. But such claims do not usually appear in the professional literature. They are more often made in advocacy of specific fiscal policy actions, and can perhaps be excused on the ground that, in the American system of government, one must claim to be able to do everything in order to be permitted to do anything. Nevertheless, we conclude that the skepticism of Burns, Ture, and others is itself excessive. They make a case against fine tuning and interpret it as a case against discretionary fiscal policy altogether.

The first of Ture's "basic premises" reflects the view that the object of stabilization policy is to iron out a persistent and violent business cycle: "intolerable swings in the rate of employment." This view leads to the notion that the primary guide to policy needs is the direction of movement of the major economic indicators. In recent years this view has been generally replaced by another: that in the absence of an active stabilization policy the economy would sometimes exhibit a persistent tendency for slack—that is, for excess capacity and unemployment—and sometimes a persistent tendency for demand to outrun productive capacity. These "gaps" may be large or small, depending on the strength of private demand, the volume of government expenditures, and the revenue-raising capacity of the tax sys-

tem. There are some cumulative tendencies that make it harder to eliminate a gap the longer it has persisted, but one would hardly call the economy "highly unstable." The primary object of discretionary fiscal policy is to close such a gap when one appears, or at least to narrow it.

This view of fiscal policy does not of course reduce it to a merely qualitative or directional exercise. The size of a fiscal stimulus or restraint should be proportioned to the size of the existing or expected gap, so numerical estimates of the effects of policy moves, such as those discussed earlier, are still required. Furthermore, the need for forecasting remains, as Ture's second premise correctly suggests. It is necessary to know whether a gap will still exist when the effects of a policy move are actually felt. Nevertheless, two consequences follow from this view of the fiscal policy problem that considerably weaken the argument of Burns and Ture.

In the first place, if the fiscal policy problem is more like steering a wayward but moderately stable vehicle in the right direction, and less like walking a tightrope, then groping toward the target is a feasible policy and minor errors of judgment are not catastrophic.

In the second place, much of the evidence on the unreliability of forecasts is evidence of an inability to predict algebraic changes in time series, particularly the incidence of turning points. But, on our view of the problem, the main requirement is for an answer to the much simpler question: in the absence of any discretionary change in policy, will output and employment much exceed or fall much short of capacity so many quarters ahead?[14] No attempt has been made to test that ability systematically, so we cannot make any strong statement one way or the other. But since the task is easier than precise forecasting, the results of any such test would very likely be more optimistic than the results of Zarnowitz and others frequently cited as a source of pessimism.[15] The combination of the difficulty of forecasting and the intrinsic lag between the time the need for a policy move is recognized and the time its actual effects are felt, does undoubtedly make fine tuning a chancy and difficult, perhaps impossible, job. But it does not make impossible the achievement of substantial stabilization effects through discre-

[13] Norman B. Ture, "Priorities in Tax Policy for the Next Decade," Tax Foundation, *Tax Review*, vol. 29 (January 1968), pp. 1–2. Also see Ture, "The New Economics: Stabilizing Tax Policy," Selected Papers 25 (Chicago: University of Chicago, Graduate School of Business, 1967; processed). Similar ideas are expressed less directly by Arthur F. Burns at several points in his *The Business Cycle in a Changing World* (New York: Columbia University Press for the National Bureau of Economic Research, 1969), especially pp. 284–85, 290–95, 310–11.

[14] This is recognized by Ture, "New Economics," p. 9; but earlier (p. 5) he talks entirely in terms of cyclical turning points.

[15] Victor Zarnowitz, *An Appraisal of Short-Term Economic Forecasts*, Occasional Paper no. 104 (New York: Columbia University Press for the National Bureau of Economic Research, 1967), pp. 4–8.

tionary fiscal policy. At least that is our conclusion from both recent history and the recent literature on the determinants of private expenditures.

An important distinction must be made between fine tuning and what might be called "continuous adaptation." Reliance on fine tuning implies a great deal of optimism, a belief that stabilization policy can be pursued accurately enough to keep the economy always within a hair's breadth of full employment (or some other target). It presupposes the ability to forecast accurately both the course of private spending under present policy and the marginal effects of changes in policy. Even if one is not that optimistic, we still believe that it is better to make many small fiscal (and monetary) policy moves than a few large ones. For example, moving tax rates up and down by small amounts with each annual budget, in whatever direction seems appropriate in the light of current knowledge and forecasts, is better than waiting until growing excesses or deficiencies in aggregate demand call unmistakably for a major shift in the degree of fiscal stimulus. (Perhaps this system could be established best by giving the President some limited authority to alter tax rates.) The main reason for a policy of continuous adaptation is the nonlinearity of economic behavior: it is more than twice as hard to make a smooth correction in a boom or slump once it has gone twice as far. Moreover, the democratic process is likely to make big changes in fiscal policy the occasion for other changes in taxes and expenditures unrelated to economic stabilization. The outcome is likely to be unsatisfactory from both points of view. Finally, occasional big changes in tax rates and the volume of spending are more unsettling to private decision making than a steady stream of small changes, none big enough to disturb the private calculus.[16] Thus, except for responses to big exogenous shocks, the need for major reversals in fiscal policy ought to be read as a signal of past error.

Another point has to be made, though its detailed discussion does not belong here. Regardless of the economics of the problem, fiscal policy can be paralyzed by political events.[17] One could

certainly argue that this was the case between 1966 and 1970—that stabilizing fiscal policy fell victim to sharp differences of opinion within the Congress and within the country on quite different matters: the war in Vietnam, problems of race and poverty, even law and order. This possibility is sometimes made the basis of the argument that some discretionary power over tax rates ought to be lodged in the President. On balance, that is probably so. But it is naive to believe that a President could afford to act on purely technical grounds at a time of deep political division, or that at such a time Congress would be prepared to see much of its leverage taken away.

The Predictability of Fiscal Policy Effects

There has been, and there continues to be, gradual progress in understanding of the qualitative nature and quantitative dimensions of different fiscal policy instruments. Generally speaking, the instruments that are analyzed are changes in government purchases of goods and services, in the rules governing transfer payments, in the definitions of the base for various taxes, and in tax rates. The effects of primary importance are usually taken to be changes in the volume and composition of national output, the level of employment, and the rate of change of prices. Predicting the impact of any fiscal policy tool involves two conceptually distinct steps. Except in the case of government purchases, which are themselves a component of aggregate demand, the first step is generally to analyze the effects of any policy action on the proximate determinants of some component of private spending. For example, it is obviously vital to know how any proposed change in the personal income tax statutes will affect disposable income. The second step is to study the relations between each component of private demand and its proximate determinants. This second step is usually more difficult, as exemplified by the unending debate over the determinants of business fixed investment. But the first step may also involve some knotty problems; analyzing the incidence of the corporate income tax is perhaps the clearest example.

The ability to predict the consequences of fiscal policy actions thus depends primarily on progress in quantitative macroeconomics. Therefore, virtually every bit of new theoretical or empirical knowledge about the macroeconomy has some bearing on the nature and predictability of fiscal policy. As more precise econometric knowledge of the key functional relationships has ac-

[16] This is essentially the typical argument for the superiority of floating over fixed exchange rates.

[17] See the discussion by Joseph A. Pechman in "Fiscal Policy: Performance and Prospects" (paper prepared for delivery to the Midwest Economic Association, April 1968; processed). The point is also made by critics of fiscal policy.

cumulated, quantitative understanding of fiscal policy has been sharpened. And, with fairly reliable answers to some of the cruder questions firmly established, analytical and practical interest has turned to the much more subtle and tricky questions of the timing of responses to policy actions. Here the difficulties are enormous, and very little is settled.

An attempt to survey all the available quantitative knowledge on the determinants of the components of aggregate demand is obviously beyond the scope of this paper. Instead, we shall content ourselves with an abbreviated look at the main qualitative channels through which the key fiscal policy instruments are believed to work, with an emphasis on those areas where major uncertainties still exist.

Not much needs to be said about government spending. Federal outlays on goods and services are a direct contributor to aggregate demand on the "first round"; after that the multiplier process begins and the numerical value of the multiplier depends on all the important functional relationships in the model. We have already seen that the major econometric models differ somewhat on the exact value of the multiplier. But the significance of these differences should perhaps not be exaggerated; a fiscal policy planner will not often be led astray if he uses a multiplier of 2 in his back-of-the-envelope calculations. The main issues of econometric debate for the near future appear to be over timing. Which type of government purchase exhibits the fastest impact on aggregate spending? Which component of federal spending can be altered most expeditiously in accord with stabilization requirements?

For the most part, countercyclical variations in government transfer programs (to the extent that they are applied at all) are aimed at influencing consumer expenditures by altering disposable income. The macroeconomic theory of consumption is, perhaps, the area in which the widest consensus has evolved. Most economists nowadays subscribe to the notion that consumption is a fairly constant fraction of some concept of long-run income. In the "permanent income" variant, originated by Friedman,[18] long-run income is taken to be a distributed lag on past measured income. If this lag is assumed to have the geometric form, as it often is, the theory leads to predicting consumption as a linear function of current income and lagged consumption. In the

"life cycle" variant of Modigliani, Brumberg, and Ando,[19] consumption is deduced to be a linear function of current *labor* income (which serves as a proxy for lifetime labor income) and lagged net worth (which serves as a proxy for lifetime property income). The two theories generate essentially the same predictions, although any two empirical studies will differ over the precise timing. An increase (decrease) in transfer payments will at first have a relatively minor impact on consumption since the short-run marginal propensity to consume (MPC) is rather low; however, if the increase (decrease) is maintained, consumption spending will eventually rise (decline) by nearly as much as the change in disposable income since the long-run marginal propensity to consume is equal to the long-run average propensity to consume, which is almost unity. The main issue here is whether temporary and permanent variations in disposable income are treated differently by consumers. We will discuss this question in some detail in our analysis of the 1968 income tax surcharge below. One further econometric issue is whether the propensity to consume out of transfer payments differs from the propensity to consume ordinary income. Although the received doctrine on the subject is that they are not very different, some recent work by Taylor calls this conclusion into question.[20]

The economic issues surrounding the effectiveness of changes in the personal income tax as a stabilizing device are basically the same. Personal tax payments are losses of disposable income, which should affect consumer spending in the same way as any other decline in income. As indicated above, the main outlines of this channel of fiscal policy are well established and the remaining empirical questions are on fine points. For example, should we measure disposable income in the way the Commerce Department does—net of tax *payments*—or should we deduct taxes when the *liability* accrues? Two studies of the impact of the 1964 tax reduction il-

---

[18] Milton Friedman, *A Theory of the Consumption Function* (Princeton, N.J.: Princeton University Press for the National Bureau of Economic Research, 1957).

[19] See Franco Modigliani and Richard Brumberg, "Utility Analysis and the Consumption Function: An Interpretation of Cross-Section Data," in Kenneth K. Kurihara, ed., *Post Keynesian Economics* (New Brunswick, N.J.: Rutgers University Press, 1954); and Albert Ando and Franco Modigliani, " 'The Life Cycle' Hypothesis of Saving: Aggregate Implications and Tests," *American Economic Review*, vol. 53 (March 1963), pp. 55–84.

[20] Lester D. Taylor, "Saving out of Different Types of Income," *Brookings Papers on Economic Activity* (2:1971), pp. 383–407.

lustrate that the answer may influence our view of the speed with which fiscal policy works. They also illustrate the grave econometric problems involved in estimating timing relations.

Both Okun and Ando and Brown utilize a "permanent income" consumption function that predicts quarterly expenditures of consumers as a linear function of current disposable income and last quarter's consumption.[21] Okun estimates his consumption function in current-price terms, using the official concept of disposable income (which deducts tax payments), and finds a short-run MPC of 0.37, and an eventual long-run MPC of 0.95. By the fourth quarter after any tax cut, consumption is already up 82 cents for each $1 of reduced taxes. Ando and Brown work with taxes on a liability basis, but do their estimation in constant-dollar terms, so it is hard to make a clean comparison. Worse yet, they present two radically different consumption functions, one estimated by ordinary least squares and the other by a method due to Liviatan which is intended to eliminate the bias present in least squares regressions when the lagged dependent variable appears as an independent variable and the disturbances are serially correlated.[22] The least squares estimate resembles Okun's in the long run (their long-run MPC is 0.94), but implies a rather slower response of consumption to a tax cut—the short-run MPC is only 0.21, and the first-year effect is only 59 cents of additional consumption for each $1 of tax reduction. But the estimates based on the Liviatan procedure imply a much faster response. According to these estimates, which are a priori preferable on statistical grounds, a $1 tax reduction leads to 76 cents of increased consumption in the same quarter, and has had virtually its full effect (93 cents) after one year. Since discretionary changes in personal income tax liabilities can be made very quickly, this estimate is very optimistic about the speed with which fiscal policy can operate on aggregate consumer expenditure.

But how is one to choose between this optimistic estimate on the liability basis and the much more sluggish consumption functions pro-

duced by Ando and Brown on the liability basis and by Okun on the Commerce Department cash-payment basis? Even at this late date one hesitates to base high policy on refined matters of least squares bias. Ando and Brown find that their more fast-acting consumption function tracks the post-1964 behavior better than their other one; but this is merely another way of saying that consumers responded very quickly to the 1964 tax reduction. Presumably a much slower-acting consumption function would have done a superior job of tracking behavior after the 1968 tax surcharge. It appears, then, that empirical study of the consumption function—at least as to timing questions—is not yet exhausted.

Much more controversy surrounds the workings of the less direct instruments of fiscal policy, such as the corporation income tax and the investment tax credit. Agreement on the nature of these channels of fiscal policy obviously awaits some consensus on the determinants of business investment; and the empirical and theoretical divergences among economists in this area are only too well known.

While popularity is not the same as accuracy, some variant of the "neoclassical" theory of investment, pioneered by Jorgenson and several collaborators,[23] is certainly encountered most frequently in econometric work. On this view, the desired stock of real capital is a function of nominal output and the nominal user cost of capital. The latter is, very roughly, the product of the price of capital goods times the sum of the depreciation rate and a weighted average of the after-tax costs of debt and equity funds, suitably adjusted to account for the tax system. In Jorgenson's work, which employs a Cobb-Douglas production function, the desired capital stock is constrained to be homogeneous of degree one in output and degree minus one in user cost. Other, more general, specifications drop this restriction.[24] Net investment is assumed to be a distributed lag

[21] See Okun, "Measuring the Impact of the 1964 Tax Reduction," pp. 25–49; and Albert Ando and E. Cary Brown, "Personal Income Taxes and Consumption Following the 1964 Tax Reduction," in Albert Ando, E. Cary Brown, and Ann F. Friedlaender (eds.), Studies in Economic Stabilization (Washington, D.C.: Brookings Institution, 1968), pp. 117–37.

[22] Nissan Liviatan, "Consistent Estimation of Distributed Lags," International Economic Review, vol. 4 (January 1963), pp. 44–52.

[23] See Dale W. Jorgenson, "Capital Theory and Investment Behavior," in American Economic Association, Papers and Proceedings of the Seventy-fifth Annual Meeting, 1962 (American Economic Review, vol. 53, May 1963), pp. 247–59; Robert E. Hall and Dale W. Jorgenson, "Tax Policy and Investment Behavior," American Economic Review, vol. 57 (June 1967), pp. 391–414; and Jorgenson's summary of the literature, "Econometric Studies of Investment Behavior; A Survey," Journal of Economic Literature, vol. 9 (December 1971), pp. 1111–47.

[24] See, for example, Charles W. Bischoff, "The Effect of Alternative Lag Distributions," in Gary Fromm, ed., Tax Incentives and Capital Spending (Washington, D.C.: Brookings Institution, 1971), pp. 61–130.

function of changes in the desired capital stock and replacements are assumed proportional to the existing stock. A one-time change in the desired stock, therefore, sets in motion a train of investment responses. On this theory, changes in tax provisions (such as the rate of corporate profits tax or investment tax credit) have their initial impact on the prices of capital goods relative to other things. An increase in the rate of tax credit, for example, obviously enhances the profitability of fixed investment by lowering the user cost. Oddly enough, an increase in the corporation income tax rate has an ambiguous effect. It clearly reduces the flow of future returns from any capital investment, but it may simultaneously reduce the after-tax discount rate.[25] Other complex fiscal weapons, such as changes in depreciation regulations, can also be analyzed by studying their effects on the user cost of capital.

Of course, the determinants of business investment are not to be decided upon by a popularity poll of econometricians. Several investigators have found some measure of liquidity to be a useful explanatory variable. They argue, for example, that past profits serve as an indicator of future profitability; or that firms have rather rigid dividend requirements and will invest any earnings above these requirements.[26] The usefulness of a liquidity variable can even be rationalized along more or less neoclassical lines. Since floating a new issue of debt or equity involves nonnegligible transactions costs, internal financing (through earnings retention) is cheaper than external financing. Thus the user cost of capital will be lower the greater the proportion of total financing that is accounted for by internal funds. Liquidity theories of investment give the most scope to the corporate income tax as a fiscal policy tool, since it influences retained earnings immediately and directly. Such theories attach rather less importance to tools like the investment tax credit that play on relative price effects.

A third major school of thought sees investment expenditures as determined largely by the accelerator—that is, as being proportional to changes in output—at least in the long run. Eisner, one of the most influential proponents of this view, has advocated a permanent income theory of investment analogous to the permanent income theory of consumption.[27] In this model, the desired stock of capital is proportional to long-run expected sales, and the latter is a distributed lag on past actual sales. Note that, if the relative price of capital goods and rates of interest are roughly constant in the long run, the neoclassical model also has this implication. But the policy implications of these two views of investment differ radically. According to the accelerator theory, the best way to spur investment spending is to increase aggregate demand, presumably through higher government spending or lower personal taxes or both.

If the controversy over the proximate determinants of investment is substantial, the controversy over the precise timing of the investment response to fiscal policy is monumental. This is due not so much to weaknesses in the imaginations of the investigators as to the unsolved—and perhaps unsolvable—problems of estimating timing relationships. It seems clear from the literature, both theoretical and econometric, that the response must involve a distributed lag of some length and possibly some complexity. But, no matter how sophisticated the estimation technique, the hard fact remains that most economic time series look very much like lagged values of themselves.

One might have hoped that the succession of investment incentives in recent years would have produced what economists are always looking for—a "controlled experiment." After all, we have seen accelerated depreciation (1954), relaxed depreciation guidelines (1962), the investment tax credit (1962), repeal of the Long amendment, which had required firms to deduct the amount of the credit from the depreciation base (1964), reduction of the tax rate on corporate profits (1964), suspension of the investment tax credit (October 1966), and its later resumption (originally scheduled for December 1967, but actually occurring in March 1967). Perhaps it is an indication of the vanity of such hopes that no consensus has yet emerged on the quantitative effectiveness of such fiscal devices in controlling plant and equipment purchases.[28]

[25] See Robert E. Hall and Dale W. Jorgenson, "Application of the Theory of Optimum Capital Accumulation," in Fromm, *Tax Incentives and Capital Spending*, especially pp. 17–18.

[26] See, for example, Edwin Kuh, "Theory and Institutions in the Study of Investment Behavior," in American Economic Association, *Papers and Proceedings of the Seventy-fifth Annual Meeting, 1962* (*American Economic Review*, vol. 53, May 1963), pp. 260–68.

[27] See, for example, Robert Eisner, "Investment: Fact and Fancy," ibid., pp. 237–46; or his, "A Permanent Income Theory for Investment: Some Empirical Explorations," *American Economic Review*, vol. 57 (June 1967), pp. 363–90.

[28] The reader can get some of the flavor of the discussion in Fromm, *Tax Incentives and Capital Spending*, a symposium volume published by the

It is impossible to summarize the disagreements briefly. Here are just a few examples. Hall and Jorgenson estimate the aggregate volume of investment spending (in 1954 dollars) induced by all investment incentives from 1954 to 1963 inclusive to be $4.5 billion of equipment and $2.2 billion of structures. Coen, arguing that the elasticity of substitution between labor and capital is more like 0.2 or 0.4 than the 1.0 assumed by Hall and Jorgenson, claims that the figure ought to be $1.4 billion for equipment and $1.2 billion for structures (both in 1954 dollars). In addition, Coen has a rather different model of his own, but its estimates of the effects of investment incentives are not exactly comparable to those of Hall and Jorgenson.

Charles Bischoff has estimated some of these fiscal policy effects on equipment spending only, using a model related to that of Hall and Jorgenson but far from identical to it. Hall and Jorgenson estimate the effect of the 1964 cut in the corporate tax rate to have been a *reduction* of equipment purchases of $403 million in 1965 and $398 million in 1966 (both in 1965 prices). Bischoff attributes increases of $52 million and $166 million, respectively, in the two years. Hall and Jorgenson credit the repeal of the Long amendment with $1.3 billion, $1.4 billion, and $1.1 billion of equipment purchases (in 1965 prices) in 1964, 1965, and 1966. Bischoff finds a negligible stimulus in 1964, $940 million in 1965, and $2.04 billion in 1966. Hall and Jorgenson credit the 1962 depreciation guidelines with the stimulation of roughly a billion dollars of equipment purchases in each year from 1962 to 1966; the Bischoff figures show no effect in 1962, $52 million in 1963, and then $374 million, $561 million, and $613 million in the next years (1965) dollars).

In brief, fixed investment is today the subject of extensive research and considerable disagreement. As with consumption, most (but not all) of the debate is over the link between investment spending and its proximate determinants rather than the link between the latter and the fiscal policy tools. At least for the present, attempts to control the volume of investment by tax incentives ought to be regarded as cases of "multiplier uncertainty" (see the following paragraphs). There is every reason to believe that our understanding of the investment process will improve; and, as it does, so will the capacity of governments to discriminate more finely in allocating the burden of stabilization policy between investment and consumption. It seems likely, however, that the intrinsic irreducible variability, or "noise," is proportionately greater in investment than in consumption. This, of course, is what one would expect from an activity so closely attuned to expectations about future sales, future prices, and future profits. There may well be serious limits to the degree of fineness with which fiscal policy planners can deliberately act upon private investment.

Multiplier Uncertainty and Fiscal Activism

What are the theoretical implications for the conduct of discretionary policy of the uncertainty that attaches to many fiscal policy instruments, and to the course of the macroeconomy in general? Should policy makers simply ignore these uncertainties and proceed as if their best guesses were in fact certainties? Should they abandon all discretionary actions and rely instead on the inherent stability of the economic system, as modified by the automatic stabilizers? Or does the existence of uncertainty suggest modification of the decisions that would be taken under certainty, without going all the way to abandonment of discretionary policy?

To answer these questions, as Brainard has pointed out, we must distinguish carefully between two kinds of uncertainty—uncertainty about policy multipliers, and all other kinds of uncertainty.[29] This can best be illustrated by use of a simple "reduced form" model of the determination of GNP. Assume that GNP, the only target of policy, can be expressed as a linear function of k policy instruments, F_i; m exogenous variables that are beyond the control of the authorities, X_j; and a stochastic disturbance, u:

$$Y = a_1 F_1 + \cdots + a_k F_k + b_1 X_1 + \cdots + b_m X_m + u. \qquad (32)$$

The St. Louis Federal Reserve equation discussed above is a special case of this formulation, in which $k = 2$ and $m = 0$. The kinds of uncer-

Brookings Institution in 1971 (cited in note 24 above). See also, "Tax Policy and Investment Behavior: Comment," by Robert M. Coen; "Comment" on the same paper by Robert Eisner, and "Tax Policy and Investment Behavior: Reply and Further Results," by Robert E. Hall and Dale W. Jorgenson, all in *American Economic Review*, vol. 59 (June 1969), pp. 370–401; and "Further Comment," by Eisner in the same journal, vol. 60 (September 1970), pp. 746–52.

[29] William Brainard, "Uncertainty and Effectiveness of Policy," in American Economic Association, *Papers and Proceedings of the Seventy-ninth Annual Meeting, 1966* (*American Economic Review*, vol. 57, May 1967), pp. 411–25. The following paragraphs draw freely on this analysis.

tainty that *can* legitimately be ignored by policy makers, in the sense that they should simply form expectations of these uncertain variables and then proceed as if these expectations were certainties, include uncertainty over the values that the exogenous variables will assume in future periods (the Xs), imprecise knowledge of the coefficients of the exogenous variables (the bs), and lack of knowledge of the future values of the stochastic disturbance (u). Henri Theil and others have shown that, if these are the only types of uncertainty that plague the policy maker, he should formulate his policy *one period ahead* just as if he were living in a world of certainty where X, b, and u were all sure to take on their expected values.[30]

But Brainard has pointed out that things are not so simple when there is uncertainty surrounding the policy multipliers (the as). In fact (though this cannot be rigorously established for the many-instrument case), there is a general presumption that the greater the uncertainty over the multiplier, the more conservatively the policy instrument should be used. To see this in the case of a single policy instrument ($k = 1$), let us follow Brainard in assuming that the authorities attempt to minimize the expected squared deviation of Y from its target value, $(Y - Y^*)^2$, subject to equation (32) with k set equal to unity and the symbol X used as a shorthand notation for the random variable: $b_1 X_1 + \ldots + b_m X_m + u$. Thus, it is desired to minimize

$$E(Y - Y^*)^2 = E(aF + X - Y^*)^2.$$

Taking the first derivative with respect to the policy instrument, F, and setting the result equal to zero, yields the policy rule

$$F = \frac{\bar{a} Y^* - E(aX)}{E(a)},$$

which can be rewritten as

$$F = \frac{\bar{a}(Y^* - \bar{X}) - \text{cov}(a,X)}{(\bar{a})^2 + \sigma_a^2},$$

where $\text{cov}(a, X)$ is the covariance between the policy multiplier and X, and σ_a^2 is the variance of the policy multiplier. Note that only in the special case where a is known with certainty will the policy rule call for bringing the expected value of Y all the way to its target value: $F =$

$(Y^* - \bar{X})/\bar{a}$. If the covariance between a and X is negligible, the indicated fiscal policy is more conservative than this in the sense that the authorities attempt to close only part of the gap. In particular,

$$F = \frac{(Y^* - \bar{X})/\bar{a}}{1 + v^2}, \tag{33}$$

where v is the coefficient of variation of the policy multiplier. Clearly this implies a smaller policy response the greater the uncertainty over the multiplier. For example, if our econometric estimate of a (the marginal impact of F on GNP) is about 2.0 with a standard error of about 1.0, then v is ½, and the change in F should be about 20 percent *less* than the change that would fully close the gap in the certainty case. This is a relatively small allowance for a substantial degree of uncertainty. Of course, if a and X have a strong negative covariance, we can no longer be sure that fiscal policy should be more conservative in an uncertain world than in a certain world. The reason is that in such a case, if our estimate of the fiscal multiplier is too low, it is very likely that our estimate of X will simultaneously be too high, and vice versa. So errors in estimating the multiplier tend to compensate for errors in forecasting X.

In a multi-instrument context, things are more complicated because covariances among the various policy multipliers must also be considered. As a concrete example, suppose the greatest amount of uncertainty is over the interest elasticity of the demand for money. IS-LM reasoning says that if this elasticity turns out to be lower than expected, the multiplier for fiscal policy will be lower *and* the multiplier for monetary policy will be higher than expected. So less uncertainty will surround the impact of a fiscal-plus-monetary policy package than will surround either pure policy taken separately. Even when the covariance of two policy multipliers is positive, diversification will still normally yield gains.

The principal lesson from this analysis appears to be that in the presence of uncertainty over fiscal policy multipliers, it will generally be advisable to employ as many fiscal instruments as are available, and to employ most of them more conservatively than in a certain world. The present analysis is also relevant to our earlier discussion of the two views of the principal goal of stabilization policy: the "old view" (as exemplified by Ture and Burns) of lessening the severity of persistent business cycles, versus the "new view" of closing persistent gaps (positive or negative) between actual and potential output. In the

---

[30] See several of Theil's published works, such as *Economic Forecasts and Policy*, 2d ed. (Amsterdam: North-Holland, 1961), or *Optimal Decision Rules for Government and Industry* (Skokie, Ill.: Rand McNally, 1964). This conclusion also requires a quadratic welfare function.

old view, the divergence between the GNP level expected in the absence of discretionary policy (X) and the target level (Y^*) is small relative to the uncertainty over the fiscal multiplier, so equation (33) calls for only very mild policy responses. By contrast, the new view admits multiplier uncertainty, but holds that it is often rather small as compared with the gaps between actual and desired GNP. In such a case, equation (33) would call for an activist fiscal policy, though not necessarily for fine tuning (which we may characterize as small stabilization moves undertaken when X is not very far from Y^*).[31]

Fiscal Policy as an Anti-Inflationary Device

Most of our discussion thus far has focused on the effects of any fiscal policy move on aggregate demand and employment. But the twin goals of stabilization policy are usually taken to be the simultaneous avoidance of high levels of unemployment and high rates of inflation. Our rationale for paying such scant attention to inflation is as follows. The impact of fiscal policy on aggregate demand is relatively straightforward and immediate. A large body of received knowledge exists that can be brought to bear on the subject. But once we seek to determine how any increment in aggregate demand is apportioned between increases in real output and increases in prices, we must enter a second branch of macroeconomic theory—the theory of inflation. Here the state of the art is much less settled, and to attempt to summarize it would be both perilous and beyond the scope of this survey. We have made no such attempt, and will make none. Nevertheless, there are some simple remarks that can be made, but most commonly are not, about the effects of fiscal policy actions, especially tax increases, on aggregate supply.

The basic remark is so obvious that it is almost embarrassing that it does not appear in textbook expositions of the analytics of fiscal policy. It is simply this: Most taxes are, in the short or long run, incorporated into business costs, and therefore (at least partially) passed on to the consumers in the form of higher prices. Therefore, if the contractionary fiscal medicine administered to cure an inflation takes the form of higher taxes, it may well have the desired deflationary impact on aggregate demand, but also an unintended cost-push inflationary impact

on aggregate supply. The net result is, in many cases, unclear on purely theoretical grounds.[32]

In comparing these two opposing effects, an ambiguity arises that can be eliminated only by a more detailed model of the dynamics of inflation than we can take time to develop. An inflationary gap sets off a chain or process of *price increases;* whereas the passing on of a tax increase changes the *equilibrium price level.* If the inflationary process would go off to infinity, then any one-time, tax-induced increase in the price level is ultimately negligible. But if (say, in the absence of monetary accommodation) the inflation would eventually burn itself out and prices would converge to a new, and higher, level, then that new equilibrium will be higher than it would have been in the absence of a tax increase. If the Congress pays attention to the real value of the tax change, however, the true process is still more complicated. In that case a tax increase that contributes to higher prices might lead to further tax increases (to recoup the real revenue loss) which would then become part of the dynamic inflationary process.

The clearest example of an inflationary tax hike is probably an increase in excise taxes. Any such increase represents a decline in consumers' real income; but this is only one, if an important, impact. Unless demand for the product is completely inelastic, the primary effect is to redirect consumers' dollars away from the taxed good *by raising its price.* The inflationary tendency could hardly be more obvious. Further, to the extent that the unspent dollars flow into the markets for other consumer goods rather than into savings, their prices will be pushed upward as well.

A similar argument can be made with respect to the corporate income tax. This tax can be viewed as a selective excise tax on the use of capital, but not labor, as a factor of production. Unless there is no forward shifting at all, part of this tax will be paid by the consumers of the output of the corporate sector when they are confronted by higher prices. When this notion is combined with the uncertain effect of the corporation tax on investment spending, it begins to look like a very strange anti-inflation device indeed.

---

[31] For further discussion of these and related issues, see Arthur M. Okun, "Fiscal-Monetary Activism: Some Analytical Issues," *Brookings Papers on Economic Activity* (1:1972), pp. 123–63.

[32] This has been noticed by Thomas Wilson, who estimated that about half of the inflation in Canada over 1964–71 was directly attributable to tax increases of various sorts. See T. A. Wilson, "Taxes and Inflation," in Canadian Tax Foundation, *1972 Conference Report,* Proceedings of the Twenty-fourth Tax Conference (1973), pp. 174–84.

It has recently been recognized that an analogous argument applies to increases in the personal income tax as a tool to curb inflation.[33] This can be seen by examining the process of wage determination in a labor market. Let there be an aggregate demand function for labor:

$$N^d = N^d(w), \quad \frac{dN^d}{dw} < 0,$$

where w is the before-tax real wage and N^d is the quantity of labor demanded; and let there be an aggregate supply of labor function:

$$N^s = N^s[w(1 - \tau)], \quad \frac{dN^s}{d[w(1 - \tau)]} > 0,$$

where τ is the rate of income taxation.[34] From the market-clearing equation, $N^d(w) = N^s[w(1 - t)]$, it is easy to show that any increase in the income tax rate will push wages upward. In most reasonable macro models, such a wage push will lead, ceteris paribus, to a higher equilibrium price level. So an increase in the income tax will simultaneously reduce aggregate demand (by lowering the IS curve) and restrict aggregate supply (by inducing workers to demand a higher pretax wage). It will unambiguously lower output, but its effect on the price level is indeterminate a priori. For a typical model, it can be shown that the necessary and sufficient condition for a rise in the income tax rate, τ, to reduce the equilibrium price level is

$$m > \frac{\dfrac{\alpha}{1 - \tau}}{\dfrac{1 - \tau}{e_c} - \dfrac{1}{e_d}},$$

where m is the income tax multiplier, α is labor's share in national output, and e_s and e_d are, respectively, the supply and demand elasticities for labor.

The actual dynamics of the inflationary process are far more complicated than our approach indicates. The logical extension of the preceding analysis to a dynamic Phillips curve context calls for the inclusion of the rate of change of the personal tax rate as a determinant of the rate of change of money wages. R. J. Gordon has done approximately this in a recent Phillips curve study, and found that each 1 percent rise in the personal tax rate results in about a ⅛ percent rise in money wage rates in the short run. In the long run the effect is much greater since higher rates of change of money wages result in higher rates of inflation which in turn feed back (through expectations) into still faster rates of increase of money wages. Erik Lundberg pointed out long ago that if the tax system is progressive, and if prices respond rather fully to increased wage costs, it may take a very large wage increase to compensate for an autonomous price increase.[35]

We conclude then that tax raising may not be the best way to curb inflation. The same deflationary aggregate demand effect, without the accompanying inflationary aggregate supply effect, can always be achieved by expenditure reductions instead. For the sake of symmetry, we should also note that tight money as a cure for inflation runs into analogous objections. Restrictive monetary policies generally imply high interest rates, and interest payments are a significant component of costs to many firms.[36]

THE ECONOMICS OF FISCAL POLICY IN 1968–1970

The "New Economics"—a bad name for the general ideas we have been describing and espousing—became a household word after the success of the Revenue Act of 1964. "Success" in this context means that a major fiscal policy action, designed to move the economy to higher employment levels, was undertaken, and lo! employment expanded along just about the path that

[33] See the comments (to a paper by Eisner) by Bent Hansen and John H. Hotson, *American Economic Review*, vol. 61 (June 1971), pp. 444–51; and Robert Eisner, "What Went Wrong?" *Journal of Political Economy*, vol. 79 (May/June 1971), pp. 629–41. See also Alan S. Blinder, "Can Income Tax Increases be Inflationary? An Expository Note," *National Tax Journal*, vol. 26 (June 1973), pp. 295–301, upon which much of the following is based.

[34] This differs from the usual presentation of the full Keynesian model by ignoring any money illusion in the labor supply function. It is proven in ibid., Appendix, pp. 299–301, that this phenomenon is irrelevant for the question at hand; that is, the same results hold whether or not there is money illusion or wage rigidity in the labor market.

[35] Robert J. Gordon, "Inflation in Recession and Recovery," *Brookings Papers on Economic Activity* (1:1971), pp. 105–58. Gordon actually does something slightly different since his tax variable is not τ itself but rather $1/(1 - \tau)$, where τ is the average personal tax rate. A similar tax variable is used by Otto Eckstein and Roger Brinner, *The Inflation Process in the United States*, A Study Prepared for the Use of the Joint Economic Committee, 92 Cong. 2 sess. (1972); Erik Lundberg, *Business Cycles and Economic Policy* (tr., Harvard University Press, 1957).

[36] This problem may be of limited practical importance since only the interest rate on new debt, not that on existing contractual obligations, will be affected.

economists had predicted.[37] By contrast, the Revenue and Expenditure Control Act of 1968—essentially a 10 percent surcharge on personal and corporate income taxes and a proposed $6 billion cutback on expenditures—was intended to eliminate an inflationary gap and restrain a rising price level. It did not do so; at least, prices rose faster in 1969–70 than they did in 1968. The promises that accompanied this latter piece of legislation were not fulfilled, and this outcome has been widely interpreted outside the profession as a failure of the New Economics, which has now become just a bad name.

Inside the profession, the monetarists have argued that the experience of 1968–70 merely illustrates the importance of fiscal policy, and thus verifies their doctrine. Robert Eisner, surely no monetarist, has gone even further and argues that these events illustrate the impotence of *both* fiscal and monetary policy in relieving the inflationary pressure generated by the Vietnam war. This perhaps overstates his conclusion, since Eisner presumably believes that abandonment of the war and reduction of military (or civilian) expenditures would have been effective. It is only the tax side of fiscal policy that Eisner sees as ineffectual. His general point seems to be that an inflationary gap opened by excessive public spending can be closed only by reducing government spending, not by taxation or monetary policy.[38] If valid, this reasoning would seem to apply to inflation caused by an upward shift in any spending schedule—public or private, and therefore would cast severe doubt on the ability to manage the economy. Other economists have, at the very least, revised downward their estimates of the ability to fine tune the economy through stabilization policy. We cannot conclude this survey without offering an eclectic interpretation of the 1968–70 episode and its implications for the theory of fiscal policy.

There is an important preliminary point. The reasoning that prescribes a tax increase as an antidote for continuing inflation has two distinct steps. The first step claims that fiscal (or monetary) contraction will lead to a reduction in aggregate spending. The second step claims that the

fall in aggregate spending will relieve the inflationary pressure. The medicine will fail to work if either of these steps fails. Most of this survey, like most of the work on fiscal stabilization policy, has been concerned with the first step—the link from the government budget to aggregate demand. If it were found that the tax surcharge of 1968 changed aggregate demand in precisely the predicted amount, but nevertheless failed to curb inflation, then most of the analytical underpinnings of fiscal policy that we have been discussing would be completely vindicated. Much less is known about the second link—from aggregate demand to inflation. Aside from our brief comments on the inflationary-deflationary effect of the income tax in the preceding section, we have had little to say about this. Most of the recent work on the Phillips curve can be interpreted as an investigation of this important question. Research on inflation theory is proceeding rapidly and few areas of consensus have evolved; we make no attempt to survey the literature here.[39]

The Impact of Fiscal Policy

To assess the evidence generated by the 1968 experience, then, we must begin with a measure of the fiscal impact of the tax increase. As we pointed out above, the best measure would be the change in the weighted standardized surplus. In fact, no time series for a weighted standardized surplus over the 1968–70 period exists. But since the economy was very close to full employment in 1968 and 1969, a weighted full employment surplus (FES) is almost as good.[40] Unfortunately, we lack even this. As an imperfect substitute, we have computed a crude weighted FES based on FRB-MIT-Penn model weights as given by Gramlich.[41] This series is given in Table 1, where it is

---

[37] This episode is well documented by a leading participant, Walter Heller, in *New Dimensions of Political Economy* (Cambridge, Mass.: Harvard University Press, 1966; W. W. Norton, 1967), especially chap. 2.

[38] See his two articles, "Fiscal and Monetary Policy Reconsidered," *American Economic Review*, vol. 59 (December 1969), pp. 897–905, and "What Went Wrong?"

[39] Many of the interesting questions surrounding the step from curbing demand to curbing inflation are outlined in Eisner's stimulating paper, "What Went Wrong?"

[40] The unemployment rate averaged 3.6 percent in 1968 and 3.5 percent in 1969. The full employment surplus is conventionally calculated at 4 percent unemployment.

[41] As a reasonable compromise between first-quarter weights and steady-state weights, we employ the one-year weights, that is, the sum of the first four quarters. Gramlich's level of disaggregation is rather coarse; with government spending weighted as unity, he assigns weights of 0.657 to personal taxes and 0.135 to corporate taxes (based on the FRB-MIT-Penn model). See Edward Gramlich, "Reply," in Wilfred Lewis, Jr., ed., *Budget Concepts for Economic Analysis* (Washington, D.C.: Brookings Institution, 1968), p. 140.

Table 1: Quarterly Changes in Unweighted and Weighted Full Employment Surpluses, 1968–1970 (in $ billions)

Year and Quarter	Change in Unweighted Full Employment Surplus	Change in Weighted Full Employment Surplus
1968:2	−1.7	−3.1
3	6.3	2.3
4	2.4	0.7
1969:1	11.0	4.6
2	4.4	3.1
3	−2.9	−3.2
4	0.9	−1.0
1970:1	−0.9	−1.1
2	−8.2	−9.1

Source: Data for actual FES are from Nancy H. Teeters, "Budgetary Outlook at Mid-Year 1970," *Brookings Papers on Economic Activity* (2:1970), Table 1, p. 304. This source also provided the raw data from which the weighted full employment surplus was calculated; the weighting procedure is discussed in text note 41.

juxtaposed against the ordinary FES. The most salient point made by this table is that using an unweighted FES drastically overstates the swing in fiscal impact. The ordinary FES indicates a substantial movement toward restraint by any standard—from a $13.5 billion *deficit* in the full employment budget in 1968:2 to a $10.5 billion surplus in 1969:2.[42] When we apply weights— recall that the contraction came largely in the form of tax hikes—the swing toward restraint looks considerably smaller; it amounts to under $11 billion over the same four quarters.

In any case, according to theory the 1968 fiscal package should have contracted the level of economic activity—not necessarily in absolute terms but relative to what would have occurred without the revenue act. But by how much? As we have pointed out earlier, to give an answer to that question requires a complete model of the economy, and then the answer is subject to all the uncertainties of the model. Furthermore, even given an estimate of the expected impact on gross national product, one cannot check simply by seeing whether GNP fell by the expected amount. Instead, the estimated path of GNP has to be compared with still another estimate—the hypothetical path of GNP in the absence of the fiscal policy change. Even keeping score in this ball game is a difficult matter.

Nevertheless, one must conclude that the response of the economy to fiscal policy from the second half of 1968 until 1970 was less than had been anticipated. Arthur Okun, who was chair-

man of the Council of Economic Advisers when the surtax was enacted, has suggested by how much, in his view, the outcome fell short of official expectations:

It was hoped and expected that this legislative victory would usher in a period of gradual disinflation. . . . A real growth rate of about 2 percent between mid-1968 and mid-1969 was expected to push the unemployment rate up slightly above 4 percent from its 3½ percent level of the time. . . .

Actual developments did not follow the flight plan. The slowdown was not nearly so pronounced as had been anticipated. Still, economic activity did change pace. If GNP had advanced as rapidly in the five quarters after the enactment of the fiscal program as it had in the preceding two quarters, it would have been $965 billion rather than the $942 billion actually reached in the third quarter of 1969. The moderation in the growth rate of real output was more marked—from 6½ percent in the first half of 1968 to 3½ percent in the second half and 2½ percent in the first half of 1969.[43]

The Effect on Consumption

The 1968 *Economic Report* forecast that, with reasonably prompt enactment of the surcharge,[44] money GNP for 1968 would be about $846 billion. In fact it was about $20 billion higher.[45] Even recognizing that some political wishful thinking probably influenced the official forecast, this is a rather large discrepancy. The largest part of the underestimate of GNP was accounted for by consumption expenditures, which were underpredicted by $11 billion as the saving rate tumbled from 7.4 percent in 1967 to 6.7 percent in 1968. (The Council of Economic Advisers predicted slightly under 7.1 percent for 1968.) This is an important error in view of the fundamental role that the consumption function plays in eclectic Keynesian theory. While the Council's forecast for 1969 in the January 1969 *Economic Report* was much more accurate, it is interesting to note that virtually the entire GNP error is accounted

---

[42] A combination of tax reduction and expenditure increases resulted in an expansionary reversal in the first half of 1970.

[43] Arthur M. Okun, *The Political Economy of Prosperity* (Washington, D.C.: Brookings Institution, 1970), pp. 91–92.

[44] Although enactment was postponed until late June, the surcharge was made retroactive to April 1 for individuals and January 1 for corporations. Earlier enactment would no doubt have done better, but probably only slightly better.

[45] *Economic Report of the President together with the Annual Report of the Council of Economic Advisers, February 1970,* p. 177. Hereafter, this document will be referred to as the *Economic Report,* followed by the year.

for by a $6.7 billion underestimate of consumption spending.[46]

Some economists—in particular, Eisner[47]—have argued that temporary changes in income tax rates are likely to be weak or useless for stabilization purposes, because consumption spending is geared to permanent income or some other variant of long-run disposable income.[48] In this view, the 10 percent surcharge was foredoomed to failure.

The precise extent to which the marginal propensity to consume out of temporary increases in disposable income falls short of the marginal propensity to consume out of permanent changes is still a matter of econometric debate. The findings of Katona and Mueller suggest that transitory increases in income have a much smaller immediate effect on consumer spending than do sustainable increases. There is evidence, however, that many transitory windfalls are eventually either spent on major purchases or in compensation for transitory reductions in income, or frittered away. In any of these cases, they add to consumer spending.[49] It is not always clear that consumers can distinguish between permanent and temporary changes in disposable income. However, if the MPC out of temporary increases and decreases is very low, and if temporary changes in tax rates are perceived as such, the multiplier effects of such changes are bound to be negligible. Specifically, suppose the marginal propensity to consume out of temporary changes in disposable income is β, a small number, and that the MPC for permanent changes is c, a larger number. Then even a temporary tax change would give rise to some first-round change in consumption spending; and the rest of the multiplier chain would proceed according to the *permanent* MPC, because consumers could hardly be expected to realize the temporary nature of the secondary and tertiary changes in disposable income. It is easily seen

that the multiplier for a discretionary tax increase is[50]

$$(-\beta)/[1 - c(1 - \tau)],$$

where $1 - \tau$ is the fraction of a change in GNP that becomes a change in disposable income. Eisner suggests that β is about 0.1,[51] in which case the temporary tax multiplier would be only ¼ even if $c(1 - \tau)$, the permanent marginal propensity to consume with respect to GNP, were as high as 0.6. It is certainly reasonable to expect β to be less than c, but Eisner's figure of 0.1 seems unreasonably small, especially since a portion of consumer expenditures as measured in the national accounts (durables) is really part of saving rather than consumption.

Okun has investigated this question in the following way. The consumption equations (usually somewhat disaggregated) of four major econometric models are fed the actual data they need in order to grind out estimates of consumption spending from the third quarter of 1968 through the third quarter of 1970.[52] Each model then proceeds to generate a sequence of consumption forecasts on each of two polar assumptions: (a) that the reduction in disposable income on account of the surcharge is treated like any other change in disposable income ("full effect"); and (b) that it is ignored by consumers—that is, that the additional tax payments should be added back to get an appropriate measure of disposable income ("zero effect"). The two sequences of consumption forecasts for each model can then be compared to the real-world outcome, to see which of the extreme assumptions comes closer to the truth. It would perhaps make more sense to test some intermediate hypothesis like "half effect" or "three-quarters effect." Since most of the models contain only minor nonlinearities, the appropriate linear combinations of the zero-effect and full-effect results are fair approximations for this purpose. We do this in Table 2.

Okun's results are interesting, though not always easy to interpret. For nondurable goods and services, the full-effect predictions are perceptibly better than the zero-effect ones. For

[46] This is not to say that all other components of GNP were predicted accurately, but only that there were countervailing errors.

[47] See his two articles cited in notes 33 and 38 above. See also the comments on his 1969 article by Bent Hansen, John H. Hotson, Barbara Henneberry and James G. Witte, and Keith M. Carlson, and Eisner's reply in *American Economic Review*, vol. 61 (June 1971), pp. 444–61.

[48] It is possible to question whether taxpayers ever regard tax increases as temporary. But if they ever do, the 1968 surcharge was presumably such a case because it was so explicitly temporary.

[49] George Katona and Eva Mueller, *Consumer Response to Income Increases* (Washington, D.C.: Brookings Institution, 1968), especially pp. 105–6.

[50] One way is to observe that the multiplier chain per dollar of tax increase is

$$- \beta - c(1 - \tau)\beta - c^2(1 - \tau)^2\beta - \cdots.$$

[51] Eisner, "Fiscal and Monetary Policy Reconsidered," p. 900.

[52] Arthur M. Okun, "The Personal Tax Surcharge and Consumer Demand, 1968–70," *Brookings Papers on Economic Activity* (1:1971), pp. 167–211. Where lagged consumption is an argument in an equation, the equation's earlier forecast is fed back.

Table 2: Root Mean-Squared Errors in Predicting Total Consumption under Various Hypotheses, Four Models (in billions of 1958 dollars)

| | Model | | | |
Hypothesis	Data Resources	Michigan	Office of Business Economics	Wharton
Full effect	2.1	3.3	2.5	2.5
Half effect	1.5	2.8	1.5	3.4
Zero effect	2.2	3.3	1.8	4.7

Source: Computed for the period 1968:3 through 1970:3 from data in Arthur M. Okun, "The Personal Tax Surcharge and Consumer Demand," *Brookings Papers on Economic Activity* (1:1971), table 2, pp. 188–89.

durable goods except automobiles, there is little to choose between them, though three of the four models make the full-effect hypothesis marginally more accurate than the zero-effect one. For automobiles, zero effect is plainly closer to the mark. In fact even it underpredicts automobile purchases substantially: from the middle of 1968 to the end of 1969 auto purchases were unusually high not only relative to measured disposable income but also relative to disposable income *plus* the surcharge! Actually, this circumstance is not entirely favorable to the zero-effect hypothesis. If there was in fact a substantial exogenous—or at least unexplained—burst of demand for cars, then this, rather than the permanent income hypothesis, may explain the strength of consumption after the surcharge. In that case, the moral to be drawn would be not that fiscal policy is impotent, but simply that all stabilization policy is difficult when the strength of private demand shifts unpredictably.

However, this disaggregated interpretation of consumption behavior may not be the appropriate one for comparing the zero-effect and full-effect hypotheses. If there was indeed exogenous strength in automobile demand, consumers may have financed their purchases partly from saving and partly by diverting expenditures from other consumption goods. In that case, had it not been for the high volume of auto spending, other consumption spending would have been higher; this reasoning favors the zero-effect hypothesis. When total consumption expenditure, rather than the three components, is considered, the two hypotheses come out about equally well. This observation suggests a "half-effect" hypothesis as a compromise; and, indeed, it appears to be somewhat better for predicting total consumption than either of the polar extremes, as Table 2 reveals.

The 1968–70 history of consumer spending thus does not appear to provide conclusive evidence of the powerlessness of fiscal policy as a stabilization tool. One reason why consumption rose so strongly after the surcharge is that an upsurge of demand, especially for automobiles, probably was in the works anyway. It was not foreseen, and the restraint on disposable income was too weak to yield the desired result. Another reason is that *temporary* income tax changes should certainly be discounted somewhat to allow for permanent income effects. The size of this discount is not clear, but 50 percent seems a reasonable guess of the effectiveness of temporary across-the-board tax changes relative to permanent ones.[53] Eisner's guess that the MPC out of temporary fluctuations in disposable income is 0.1 seems to be wide of the mark.

The Effect on Investment

Consumption spending was not the only component of GNP to surprise the designers of fiscal policy in 1968. Inventory investment was seriously underestimated, presumably out of fear of the remaining overhang of inventories after the rapid accumulation in 1965–67, and perhaps also due to the general overestimate of the contractionary effect of the surcharge. Also, the strength of business fixed investment was substantially underestimated in 1969.[54] That plant and equipment spending is difficult to predict ac-

[53] For example, when Okun freely estimates (that is, without constraints and adjustments) the fraction of the income loss from the surcharge that was treated as permanent by consumers, his percentages for the four models are 53, 47, 34, and 133. The last percentage, which is wildly inconsistent with the others, is for the Wharton model, which has the odd property of actually *over*estimating consumption spending even assuming the surcharge had full effect. See "Personal Tax Surcharge," p. 190.

[54] The Council of Economic Advisers forecast an increase of about $7 billion or $8 billion in 1969; the expansion was actually $10.6 billion. For a discussion of some possible reasons for this, see Okun, *Political Economy of Prosperity*, pp. 94–95.

curately is hardly news. A fundamental question for countercyclical policy arises only if there is some reason to expect investment to move perversely against stabilization efforts.[55]

Eisner has proposed such a reason.[56] Suppose, as seems plausible, that investment spending is fundamentally guided by expected long-run profitability. Then an explicitly temporary increase in corporate income tax rates will affect the *timing* of investment much more than the *volume*. As Eisner notes, the installation of new plant and equipment carries with it many ancillary expenses that are immediately tax deductible, though closely associated with the act of investment. In addition, under favorable tax provisions, much of the depreciation can be taken in the first few years of the life of the project. Astute corporations may therefore respond to a temporary tax increase by advancing planned expenditures, so that the installation costs and depreciation can be charged against the higher tax rates, while the returns on the investment are not reaped until the lower tax rates are back in effect. This is, in principle, a possibility. Its importance depends on the magnitude of the ancillary expenses and early depreciation write-offs; they must be large enough to more than offset the reduction in the earliest part of the stream of after-tax quasi-rents. The most important item here is very likely to be the first year or so of depreciation allowances. For example, use of double-declining-balance accounting with a five-year lifetime can generate a first-year depreciation allowance of 40 percent of the purchase price. To write that off under a 10 percent surcharge "saves" 4 percent of the cost of the capital asset, which, if not tremendous, is surely not negligible. At the very least, this weakening of fiscal policy control over investment spending is a hidden cost of such devices as accelerated depreciation and artificially short depreciation lives.

The same arguments that weaken the case for the stabilization potential of temporary variations in the corporate income tax suggest that temporary variations in taxes and subsidies like the investment credit may be very useful. The timing effects of variations in the investment tax credit reinforce the policy—that is, a temporary suspension or reduction of the credit provides a powerful motive to postpone investment until the credit is restored. A similar line of reasoning sug-

gests that more attention might be paid to the possibility of temporary consumption taxes.[57] These would have strongly favorable timing effects,[58] though some care would have to be devoted to selecting the base if the tax were not to be highly regressive.

Errors in the Government Sector

Another source—unexpected and often overlooked—of the failure of the surcharge to live up to its advertising was the official underestimate of government purchases. The size of the surcharge was predicated on an increase in federal expenditures of $6 billion in 1968. In fact, even after Congress inserted an expenditure limitation in the act, federal spending rose $8.8 billion for the year. This may not have been so surprising; at the time, many observers believed the expenditure control provisions to be no more than window dressing. Perhaps more important was the substantial underestimate of the rise in state and local government purchases. The *Economic Report* forecast an increase of $8 billion to $9 billion; in fact, the rise was $11.3 billion.[59] For total government purchases, the underestimate in 1968 comes to about $5.6 billion. One way to appreciate the true order of magnitude of this error is to set it against the fact that the personal

---

[55] However, a serious practical question arises even if the response of investment is in the right direction but is very small.

[56] "Fiscal and Monetary Policy Reconsidered," p. 900, note 7.

[57] Although probably every teacher of macroeconomics has at one time or another discussed the use of temporary taxes that seek to exploit intertemporal substitution effects for stabilization purposes, there is remarkably little literature on the subject. A fleeting reference to *temporary* consumption taxes as a stabilizer appears in E. Cary Brown, "Analysis of Consumption Taxes in Terms of the Theory of Income Determination," *American Economic Review*, vol. 40 (March 1950), especially p. 76. James Tobin advocated the use of some such device, probably a variable tax credit on net investment, in his Janeway Lectures at Princeton University (forthcoming from Princeton University Press). William H. Branson discussed the likely effectiveness of a variety of temporary taxes and, based on the belief that businesses are more sensitive to the subtleties of intertemporal pricing than consumers, concluded that the best bet might be a temporary tax (subsidy) on some long-lived investment goods. See his "The Use of Variable Tax Rates for Stabilization Purposes," in Richard A. Musgrave, ed., *Broad-Based Taxes: New Options and Sources* (Baltimore, Md.: Johns Hopkins University Press for the Committee for Economic Development, 1973).

[58] Prior discussion of such taxes has a perverse timing effect. Thus, to be an effective stabilization tool, they would probably have to be discretionary within statutory limits.

[59] The *Economic Report* for each year, 1963–68, managed to underestimate the year's rise in state and local spending.

tax part of the surcharge was designed to raise $8 billion at the 1968 level of GNP. The underprediction of government purchases thus directly offsets 70 percent of the surcharge on personal income taxes. Further, if one applies appropriate multiplier weights, as in the calculation of a weighted budget surplus, the error on the spending side offsets even more of the income tax increase, and may even make the net fiscal impact expansionary.

Monetary Factors: The Theory Illustrated (Painfully)

Finally, we must say something about the monetary policy that preceded and accompanied the tax increase. The relevant question is not merely whether overall stabilization policy was well coordinated—which it was not—but whether the size of the fiscal dose adequately took into account the lagged effects of earlier monetary expansion. In our view, it did not. We suspect that, if the lagged and contemporaneous effects of monetary and fiscal policy were fully accounted for, the impact of fiscal-cum-monetary policy would be judged only mildly contractionary, or perhaps even expansionary, during most of the surcharge period.

The period of tight money associated with the "credit crunch" ended in January 1967. As an indication of what happened next, unborrowed reserves of member banks increased more than $1.7 billion in the second half of 1967, stayed level in the first half of 1968, and rose some $1.5 billion in the second half of 1968. The result was an expansion of the money supply (narrowly defined) at a 7.3 percent annual rate over the January 1967–January 1969 period, the fastest sustained rate of monetary growth for any period since 1946.[60]

To convert this history into an estimate of the impact of monetary policy on GNP requires a sequence of current and lagged money multipliers from an econometric model. We have done some rough computations using the money multipliers from the versions of the FRB-MIT and Brookings models that were published at that time.[61] The

two models give quantitatively different but qualitatively similar results. They both assert that the impact of monetary policy on GNP was expansionary from the middle of 1968 until the end of 1969, especially in the last quarter of 1968 and the first half of 1969. (These estimates include the cumulated lagged effects of earlier changes in unborrowed reserves.[62]) As for orders of magnitude, the FRB-MIT model suggests a contribution to GNP averaging about $16 billion in the last quarter of 1968 and the first half of 1969; the estimates from the Brookings model run about half that.[63]

These models also provide estimates of the deflationary effect of the personal income tax surcharge. Here too they differ. The Brookings model attributes to the surcharge a negative contribution to GNP of about $9 billion, at annual rates, in the fourth quarter of 1968 and the first half of 1969. The FRB-MIT model gives two answers, depending on the set of tax multipliers used: one version gives an average deflationary impact of just under $16 billion in those three quarters, while the other version puts it at about $5 billion.

Combining the monetary and fiscal impacts for each model produces the story outlined in Table 3. The three models give rather different assessments of countercyclical policy. According to the 1968 FRB-MIT model, monetary expansion was just about strong enough to counter the substantial influence of the surcharge and provide a mild stimulus to the economy during 1968:3–1969:1. Starting with 1969:2, contractionary policy began to take hold, becoming quite potent in the last half of 1969. The 1969 FRB-MIT model is less sanguine about the effectiveness of tax increases. As a result, it shows a strongly expansionary net impact of countercyclical policy for the first four quarters after the surtax. Only in 1969:3, according to this model, was any contraction felt; and even this was short-lived. The Brookings model ascribes less potency to *both* fiscal and monetary policy, but tells a story that

---

[60] The data on unborrowed reserves are from *Economic Report, 1969* and *1970*, pp. 289 and 241, respectively, and are not seasonally adjusted. The money stock data are from "Money Supply and Time Deposits, 1914–69," Federal Reserve Bank of St. Louis, *Review*, vol. 52 (March 1970), table II, p. 7, and are seasonally adjusted.

[61] For the FRB-MIT model, see two papers by Frank de Leeuw and Edward Gramlich, "The Federal Reserve-MIT Econometric Model," *Federal Re-*

serve Bulletin, vol. 54 (January 1968), pp. 11–40, and "The Channels of Monetary Policy." For the Brookings model, see Fromm and Taubman, *Policy Simulations.*

[62] For approximation purposes, we allowed lags only up to six quarters. Some models profess much longer lags than this.

[63] This should not necessarily be interpreted as evidence that the Fed was managing monetary policy incompetently. It has been argued that the monetary expansion was in response to the surcharge, which the Fed thought would pass the Congress much sooner than it did.

Table 3: Net Impact on Money GNP of Fiscal and Monetary Policies, Two Models, 1968–1969 (in $ billions)

Model	1968:3	1968:4	1969:1	1969:2	1969:3	1969:4
FRB-MIT 1968*....................	3.8	2.4	2.5	−4.3	−16.2	−13.7
FRB-MIT 1969†....................	7.8	10.9	13.1	8.6	−0.7	3.4
Brookings........................	−2.1	−3.4	−1.2	0.9	−8.1	−5.4

* Computed using tax multipliers of the 1968 version.
† Computed using tax multipliers of the 1969 version.
Source: FRB-MIT and Brookings econometric models.

is not qualitatively different from the 1968 FRB-MIT model. According to the Brookings multipliers, the surcharge was able to overwhelm the monetary expansion during 1968:3–1969:1, but only by a relatively small margin. Only in the last half of 1969 did it apply a significant brake to the economy.[64]

If the three models yield any consensus, it is this: The deflationary impact of the surcharge was either weaker, or only marginally stronger, than the inflationary influence of past monetary policy. The models agree that if any significant contractionary influence was felt, it was only in the latter half of 1969. It is somewhat encouraging (to the model builders at least!) to observe that these predictions come quite close to what most observers believe happened in the post-surtax period.

The Lessons of 1968

In summary, our reading of the 1968–69 episode does not suggest the need for any fundamental revision of the eclectic theory of income determination presented here, despite the disappointing results of the 1968 act. But the analysis does indicate that the size[65] of the deflationary dose was definitely inadequate to the need for at least four reasons:

1. There appears to have been an exogenous strengthening of consumer demand, especially for automobiles, roughly coincident with the enactment of the surtax. This development underscores the difficulty of fine tuning, but in no way casts doubt on the analytical underpinnings of fiscal policy with which this survey has been concerned.

2. The effectiveness of the personal and corporate income tax surcharges on consumption and

investment was insufficiently discounted for the explicitly temporary nature of the actions, a point that was apparently ignored in the pre-1968 literature.[66]

3. Both federal and state and local government expenditures on goods and services were seriously underestimated. If the published forecasts represent what those in government actually believed, then much (and perhaps all) of the deflationary impact of the tax increase was dissipated in canceling out the unexpected surge in government purchases.

4. There was a hangover of expansionary monetary policy dating back to the reversal of monetary policy after the credit crunch, and not reversed by any tightening in 1968. Fiscal restraint probably did not allow adequately for the need to offset the lagged effects of this monetary expansion. But this *reinforces* rather than *undermines* the received doctrine on monetary factors as we outlined it above.

In addition, one should perhaps give some weight to the difficulty of legislating very large tax increases at any time, but especially in a frenetic political climate such as prevailed in 1968. If this political difficulty is real, it operates against the success of deflationary stabilization policy. But it is a problem of politics and not economics, and in no way casts doubt on the analytical foundations of fiscal policy.

We conclude that the experience of 1968–69 should be sobering but not stunning. Fine tuning is difficult—perhaps even impossible—given our present state of knowledge. Any stabilization move so subtle as to seek to alter the unemployment rate by a single point or less runs the risk of being nullified by unpredictable (or at least unpredicted) shifts in the strength of private (or public) demand. This is cause for care in advertising, but not for paralysis.

---

[64] The preceding calculations were based on data taken from various *Economic Reports,* which have since been revised.

[65] The timing was also certainly off; but that has to be accounted one of the lesser disasters of the Vietnam War.

---

[66] But see Albert Ando and E. Cary Brown, "Personal Income Taxes and Consumption Following the 1964 Tax Reduction," in Ando and others, *Studies in Economic Stabilization,* especially p. 137.

19. FINANCING A FEDERAL DEFICIT*

Council of Economic Advisers Staff Memorandum

Discussions of deficit financing have long made a distinction between the inflationary impact of financing through credit expansion—i.e., selling securities to commercial banks—and the noninflationary impact of financing through "real saving"—i.e., selling securities to the non-bank public. It seems appropriate to review this distinction.

A Federal deficit can be financed: (1) by drawing down Treasury cash balances; (2) by selling securities to nonbank investors; (3) by selling securities to the commercial banks; or (4) by selling securities to the central monetary authority. Regardless of which of these methods is employed, a Federal deficit is accompanied by an equivalent dollar-for-dollar increase in the net financial assets of nonbank investors—an increase which would necessarily show up as saving in our statistical records.

If the deficit is financed by drawing down Treasury cash (deposit) balances, the result is to increase the public's money holdings by the amount of the deficit. (If the Treasury draws down its balances at Federal Reserve—as distinct from commercial—banks, member bank reserves are also increased, permitting a multiple expansion of private credit. However, since this secondary credit expansion increases the assets—in the form of deposits—and liabilities of the nonbank public by equal amounts, it does not affect the *net* financial assets of the nonbank public.)

If the deficit is financed by selling bonds to non-bank investors, the result, when the Treasury has spent the money collected from the sale of bonds, is that the public ends up with the same amount of money as originally but with more financial assets in the form of Government bonds. It is this method of deficit financing which has been traditionally labeled as good, sound, noninflationary debt management.

The third and fourth methods—selling securities to commercial banks and to the central monetary authority—tend to be lumped together and considered inflationary. It is these two methods which need to be more closely considered.

If the deficit is financed by selling securities to the commercial banks, the banks pay for the securities by creating demand deposits for the Treasury, which, when spent, add to the public's

money holdings. But this tells us little until we know where the commercial banks obtain the reserves needed to be held against these deposits.

If we suppose that the total amount of bank reserves is fixed, then the commercial banks can buy additional government securities in either of two ways. They might sell to the public an equivalent volume of other financial assets which they hold, reducing the public's money balances. In this case the results are exactly the same as the results of the second method: that is, the public holds the same amount of money but more of other financial assets than it did before by the exact amount of the deficit. Alternatively banks could reduce their lending to the nonbank sector, in which case the public's liabilities to the banks are reduced, which means an increase in the public's *net* financial assets.

On the other hand, the central bank might supply additional reserves in an amount exactly equal to the commercial bank purchases of new Federal debt. If it did this by open market purchases, it is clear that the effect would be virtually the same as if the new Federal securities had been purchased directly by the central bank, which is the fourth method listed above.

In this fourth case, it is clear that there could and would be a multiple expansion of credit. Private deposits would rise initially by the amount of the deficit itself. However, only a fraction of the added reserves would be needed to support the new deposits created in payment for the securities, and the remainder could finance an expansion of private credit. There would be a further rise of deposits resulting from the private credit expansion, but this would be matched by an equal expansion of private liabilities to the banks, with no added effect on *net* private assets.

Naturally there is a wide range of intermediate possibilities between the two extremes of providing no additional reserves and providing extra reserves in the amount of the deficit. For example, the central bank could create only enough additional reserves to support the new deposits created by the purchase of the securities. Or, the central bank could provide a somewhat larger or smaller amount of extra reserves.

Those who automatically look with disfavor on financing a deficit by sales of securities to commercial banks make no distinction among

---

* Reprinted by permission of the Council of Economic Advisers.

these various alternatives. They simply assume that all bank purchases of government securities are "inflationary." But the crucial question is not whether banks buy the bonds. It is rather what policy the central bank follows.

Each of the methods we have considered involves an increase in the public's total net holding of financial assets by an amount exactly equal to the amount of the deficit. In this sense they all involve financing a deficit through private "saving." But this is a purely definitional matter and is not very helpful in economic analysis. What we need to know is what the effect of the various methods is on the economy.

If the deficit is financed by selling bonds directly to the nonbank public, or if they are sold to the banks but no additional reserves are created, interest rates will rise, and this will have a restraining effect on private spending, which will partly offset the expansionary effect of the deficit itself. If, on the other hand, additional bank reserves are created which permit the bonds to be absorbed without any increase in interest rates, there will be no offset against the expansionary effect of the deficit. And, if more than this amount of reserves is created (as for example, by selling the bonds to the central bank or its equivalent), there will be an expansionary *monetary* effect to be added to the expansionary fiscal effect.

Thus we always have *two* effects to consider: the effect of the *fiscal* action (a reduction in taxes or an increase in expenditures) which produced the deficit—and which is always expansionary—and the effect of the method used to *finance* the deficit, which depends in significant measure on central bank policy, and which might be counter-expansionary (if no new reserves are created), neutral, or an addition to the expansionary effect of the deficit.

In determining which course the central bank should take with respect to commercial bank reserves, one must consider the economic setting in which the deficit occurs. If a Federal deficit occurs because total income, and thus Federal revenue, falls away in a recession, interest rates will tend to decline even if the quantity of reserves is held constant. But in these circumstances, it will usually be both appropriate and desirable that the central monetary authority pursue an actively expansionary policy—that is, providing additional reserves to the commercial banks so that interest rates fall even more than they would have with constant reserves. On the other hand, if the Federal deficit occurs because a national emergency requires large increases in

expenditures at a time when the economy is already at full employment, it is appropriate and desirable to counter the expansionary effect of the deficit itself by a tightening of monetary policy, which would mean no increase—or even a contraction—of reserves. In fact, the deficit should have been avoided in the first place.

On the other hand, a deficit arising from fiscal action to stimulate the economy to move from a position of under-utilization to full employment does not readily fit either of the above two cases. The increased expenditures or reduced tax rates—which produced the deficit—will cause incomes and business activity to rise. The rise in activity will produce a general increase in the demand for money and credit, which—unless bank reserves are increased—will tend to raise interest rates and restrict credit. Thus, if the deficit is financed under conditions of monetary restraint, its stimulating impact will be partly offset. Another way of putting this is that a larger tax cut or increase in expenditures will be needed to achieve a given target level of income and employment if the stimulative fiscal action is accompanied by restrictive monetary policy. Any rise in interest rates or reduction in credit availability that accompanies a tax cut, for example, will reduce private demands for houses, automobiles, plant and equipment and so on, thereby diluting the effect of the expansionary fiscal policy.

It is important to note, however, that even if the central bank supplied no extra reserves, so that the bonds (or an equivalent volume of bank-held securities) had to be sold to the nonbank public, the rise in interest rates that would occur could, at most, provide only a partial offset to the expansionary effect of the deficit. If a deficit is brought about, for example, by reducing taxes, the effect is to increase *disposable income* and (as pointed out earlier) the *net liquid assets* of consumers; these effects are present no matter how the deficit is financed—although, of course, the *composition* (as distinct from the size) of the increase in the stock of net liquid assets depends on the method of financing. It is not correct to argue that the expansionary effect of the tax reduction financed with no increase in bank reserves would be fully offset by the equal amount of security sales to the public. The idea that "the extra money you give consumers by tax reduction would be taken away by security sales" incorrectly identifies the effects of increases in *disposable income* and in *net liquid assets,* which clearly make consumers better off, with a *voluntary asset exchange,* in which security-buyers swap one form of asset (cash) for another (securities).

In the foregoing analysis, balance-of-payments effects have been ignored. In fact, in recent years, these effects have had an important influence on policy.

To the extent that international differences in short-term interest rates may influence the outflow of short-term funds, it may be necessary or desirable (depending on the state of the other items in the balance of payments) to hold domestic interest rates higher than would otherwise be desirable for reasons of domestic policy. A balance has to be struck between the stimulating domestic effects of an easier monetary policy and the necessity or desirability of stemming a loss of international reserves.

It should be noted, however, that it is primarily short-term interest rates that influence international capital flows, while long-term rates are more important as far as the domestic econ-omy is concerned. Consequently, when a deficit is needed to stimulate the domestic economy and the balance of payments situation calls for financing of the deficit in such a way as to raise interest rates, it is appropriate for the Treasury to emphasize short-term borrowing in order to maximize the benefits to the balance of payment and minimize the harm to the domestic economy.

In conclusion it should be recognized that the question of how to finance the deficit is really subordinate to the more general questions of (a) how expansionary should monetary and fiscal policy be in a given situation, and (b) what should be the appropriate "mix" of monetary and fiscal elements? Concentrating on deficits (or surpluses) per se is not the most useful approach to the problems of fiscal policy, nor is concentrating on the financing of deficits per se the most useful approach to the problems of monetary policy.

---

20. FISCAL POLICY IN *IS-LM* ANALYSIS: A CORRECTION*

William L. Silber

There are a number of articles in the literature which have stressed the importance of including the monetary aspects of fiscal policy in analyzing the effectiveness of stabilization policy; see, e.g., [1; 2; 4; 9, chap. 22; 10; 12]. Some of these studies (Christ, and Ott and Ott) have introduced a budget restraint on the government sector and then demonstrated that the total multiplier effect of increased expenditure by the government depends on whether the increased spending is financed by taxes, money creation, or bond sales. There are a few textbooks which have tried to integrate the monetary effect of fiscal policy into an *IS-LM* framework [7, 11]. These attempts are quite important for expository purposes. Unfortunately, the treatment has been correct in only one type of financing of a fiscal action, namely, when a deficit (surplus) is financed (dis-posed of) by changes in the money supply. The debt-financed deficit (or surplus with debt retirement) has not been treated as explicitly and where it has been discussed the analysis has been faulty. Our major concern here is to integrate properly the debt aspects of fiscal policy into *IS-LM* analysis.

We make a number of modifications so that this particular question can be analyzed within the simple (traditional) *IS-LM* framework. First, while the government's budget constraint is introduced in our model, an equilibrium condition is not imposed on the government sector. The budget constraint specifies that total government expenditure equals tax revenue plus the change in money supply plus the change in bond supply. In long-run equilibrium, all changes in stocks or flows are equal to zero so the budget constraint implies that all expenditures are financed by taxation. In our case we are taking the method of financing a government expenditure into the multiplier calculation, but we are not imposing the equilibrium condition on the government sector since we are interested in precisely the case where the deficit or surplus remains unaltered. In other words, our concern is with short-run equilibrium

* "Fiscal Policy in *IS-LM* Analysis: A Correction," by William L. Silber, is reprinted from the *Journal of Money, Credit, and Banking*, vol. 2 (November 1970), pp. 461–72. Copyright © by the Ohio State University Press. All rights reserved. Reprinted by permission of the publisher and the author. William L. Silber is Professor of Economics and Finance, Graduate School of Business Administration, New York University.

because as long as there is a deficit, there can be no long-run equilibrium. The article by Ott and Ott [10] examines the properties of a system in which the government's budget is also in equilibrium.

A second factor that is modified in our treatment relates to the simple assumption in *IS-LM* models that there is only one interest rate, i.e., the rate on the "composite" bond of the Keynesian model. In particular, we shall ignore Tobin's supply price of capital and how that is affected by an increased supply of government bonds.[1]

Traditional *IS-LM* analysis examines the total impact of an increase in government spending *G* by shifting the *IS* curve to the right, e.g., from IS_1 to IS_2 in Figure 1. In the basic Hicks-Keynes model, with exogenous taxes and a fixed money supply, the implicit assumption must be that bond sales are used to finance the deficit expenditure. One would expect that an increase in bond supply, *ceteris paribus,* would raise interest rates since the public must be induced to increase its holdings of bonds relative to money. If there was equilibrium at the old rate of interest, the increase in bond supply must raise the rate. It seems, however, that the movement from *A* to *B* in Figure 1 due to the rightward shift in the *IS* curve, and the rise in rates from r_1 to r_2, does not come about due to the increase in the stock of bonds outstanding. Rather, rates rise because as income rises there is an increase in transactions demand for money. Rates must go up, therefore, to reduce speculative demand in order to keep the fixed money supply equal to total money demand.

That the effect of bond supply is ignored becomes quite obvious if a number of particular examples are considered. First, as long as the increase in *G* is maintained (with fixed taxes as the experiment requires), there is a continuous deficit that must be financed by increases in bond supply. Hence, at point *B* in Figure 1, total government bonds outstanding is still increasing. The rate of interest (and income) cannot, therefore, remain unchanged at r_2 (and Y_2) while bond supply is still rising.[2]

A second example of the failure to take changes in bond supply into account in *IS-LM* analysis is as follows. Assume a one-period debt-financed government expenditure and then a re-

[1] For an explicit treatment of our question in Tobin's context, see [6, 13].

[2] At least two basic texts have suggested that the movement for r_1 to r_2 due to ΔG comes from the impact of increased bond supply. See [3, p. 169; 7, pp. 98–99].

Figure 1

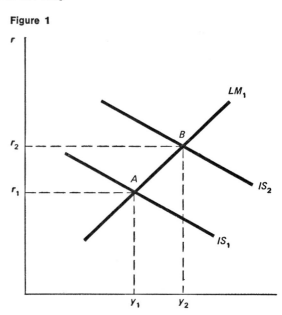

turn to the original level of *G*. Technically, the *IS* curve shifts to the right and then returns to its initial position. According to traditional *IS-LM* analysis, therefore, the old level of income and interest rate is still the equilibrium position. Yet there has been a once-and-for-all increase in government bonds held by the public. It seems unreasonable to say that an increase in bonds relative to money can be absorbed without a change in interest rates (or income). *Ceteris paribus,* there should be an increase in rates. Our objective is to incorporate the effects of changes in bond supply into the *IS-LM* model so that the inconsistencies just described can be eliminated.

In effect, the basic *IS-LM* analysis assumes that bond supply is fixed, just as the capital stock is fixed. Implicitly, the *IS-LM* analysis ignores the impact of a government deficit or surplus on the stock of bonds outstanding just as it ignores the impact of net investment on the stock of capital outstanding. In general terms, the *IS-LM* model seems to be eliminating the impact of flows (deficit, investment) on stocks (bonds outstanding, capital). This may be a reasonable simplification, and as long as such treatment is consistent it is acceptable. Once the financial side of a deficit is accounted for in the case of new money finance, however, the case of bond finance should be given symmetrical treatment. In particular, when a deficit is financed by money creation, the impact of the flow (deficit) on the stock (money supply) is incorporated in the *IS-LM* framework. In this case a rightward shift in the *LM* curve is included along with the rightward shift in the *IS* curve.[3] The impact of the deficit on the stock of a financial asset (money) is included in the *IS-LM* model. Hence, the impact of the deficit on the stock of another financial asset (bonds) must be given similar treatment. After all, the money market could be dropped from the *IS-LM* model just as easily as the bond market.

The *IS-LM* Model

The basic Hicks-Keynes *IS-LM* model can be represented algebraically as follows:

$Y = C + I + G$	(commodity-market equilibrium)	(1)
$C = a + b(Y - T) + \mu W$	(consumption function)	(2)
$I = d - er$	(investment function)	(3)
$G = \bar{G}$	(government spending)	(4)
$T = \bar{T}$	(tax function)	(5)
$M^d = hW + fY - qr$	(demand for money)	(6)
$M^s = \bar{M}$	(supply of money)	(7)
$M^d = M^s$	(money-market equilibrium)	(8)
$W = K + M + B$	(definition of wealth)	(9)
$G - T = \Delta M + \Delta B$	(government's budget constraint)	(10)

The notation that is used in equations (1) through (10) is as follows:

$Y = GNP$

r = interest rate

I = private investment

C = consumption

G = government spending

a = constant term in the consumption function

b = marginal propensity to consume

T = taxes

d = constant term in the investment function

e = interest sensitivity of investment

M^d = money demand

h = wealth sensitivity of money demand function

f = income sensitivity of M^d

q = interest sensitivity of M^d

M^s = money supply

W = wealth

K = physical capital

B = government bonds

A number of familiar basic assumptions are made. First, for simplicity all equations are as-

³ See [11, pp. 343–45; 12; 7, p. 100]. It is noted by Pesek and Saving that as long as the deficit is financed by new money creation no long-run equilibrium is possible since the *LM* Curve continues to shift to the right. This shall come up again later in the paper.

sumed to be linear. Second, prices are held constant. Third, there is no banking system, i.e., money is the liability of the government. Given this basic system, our objective is to examine the effect of an increase in G financed by an increase in the supply of government bonds. The increase in bond supply enters the model via a change in wealth. An increase in wealth raises the demand for money, i.e., $\partial M^d / \partial W = h$ from (6). It is clear that $0 < h < 1$ since first, an increase in wealth will not all be demanded in the form of money and second, if the increase in W comes about via an increase in M there will be an excess supply of money (as should be the case) only if $h < 1$.

Once wealth is included as an argument in the M^d equation it is clear that the increased government bonds brought about by the deficit causes a condition of excess demand in the money market (since money supply is unchanged). In other words, the increase in the demand for money when bond supply rises produces a leftward movement in the *LM* curve. This results from the increased demand for money at every combination of Y and r. With money supply fixed, the increase in M^d (due to the bond supply increase) means that either Y must fall or r must rise in order to restore the equilibrium condition $M^s = M^d$.

In Figure 2, for example, if we start out with LM_1 and IS_1, the long-run equilibrium is at point A assuming that government expenditure equals tax receipts, i.e., no government borrowing or new money creation. If G increases, this causes the IS curve to shift to the right, say, to IS_2. If the deficit is financed by new money creation, the LM curve shifts to the right, say, to LM_2 and "equilibrium" B is established. If the deficit is financed by bond sales to the public, the LM curve shifts to the left, say, to LM_3 and "equilibrium" C is established. Most previous discussions of the bond-finance case maintain that

Figure 2

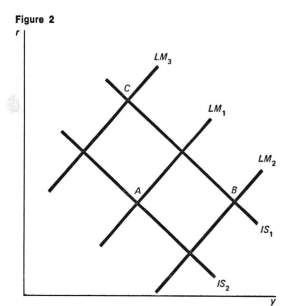

the *LM* curve remains fixed (see Footnote 2). This clearly cannot be the case when the effects of the deficit on the stocks of financial assets outstanding, both money or bonds, are treated symmetrically.

It must be noted, however, that neither "equilibrium" point *B* nor *C* is a long-run equilibrium. As long as there is a deficit, it will have to be financed by either increases in money or bonds, since we have assumed, as is customary in this case, that taxes are exogenous. In other words, as long as there is a deficit, wealth continues to rise. At the end of n budget periods, for example, wealth will have increased by $n(G - T)$, since in each budget period $(G - T)$ is financed by an equivalent ΔB, (or ΔM). If we start out with $G = T$ and then impose an increment ΔG, wealth rises by $n\Delta G$.[4] If there is complete money finance, then the *LM* curve continues to shift to the right. If there is complete bond finance (both interest and principal), the *LM* curve continues to shift to the left. In the case of money finance the continuous rightward shift in the *LM* curve produces ever increasing levels of income (either real income if there is less than full employment or money income and inflation when full employment is reached). In the case of bond finance, the leftward shift in the *LM* curve at first mitigates

the expansionary impact of ΔG and at some point produces a contractionary effect, that is the equilibrium point *C* eventually moves to the left of *A*.

Until now we have ignored the impact of wealth on consumption. From (2) we see that $\partial C/\partial W = \mu$. Hence, as long as wealth rises, the *IS* curve shifts to the right. This occurs both for increases in bonds or increases in money. In the case of money finance, the positive impact on *Y* of the rightward shift in the *LM* curve is reinforced by the continuous rightward shift in the *IS* curve. In the case of bond finance, the negative impact on *Y* of the leftward shift in the *LM* curve is counteracted by the rightward shift in the *IS* curve. In this case income might increase or decrease depending upon the shifts in the *IS* and *LM* curves and the slopes of the two curves.

Before exploring the shift and slope conditions explicitly, a number of points should be made. First, the second effect just discussed—the impact of the deficit on the *IS* curve—is known as the "Lerner effect."[5] Lerner argued that the impact of the accumulation of government debt due to a deficit was certain to bring GNP up to its full employment level via a direct wealth impact on consumption expenditures. As we can see from the analysis just concluded this ignores the contractionary portfolio impact of the increase in wealth in the form of bonds.

It is also important to note, once again, that in the basic *IS-LM* model the stock of physical capital is kept constant despite the fact that net investment varies. A relaxation of this assumption could conceivably alter our results. We have not done so here since once that assumption is relaxed, the basic framework of the Hicks-Keynes *IS-LM* analysis must be abandoned. Our objective is to put the treatment of the bond-financed government deficit on equal footing with the case of the money-financed government deficit in the *IS-LM* context. In other words, the impact of all financial flows (produced by government deficits) on financial stocks outstanding (money and government bonds) is incorporated in short-run *IS-LM* analysis, while the impact of the flows of physical assets (investment) on physical stocks (capital) is omitted from the *IS-LM* model. When we treat the investment-capital accumulation-wealth relationship explicitly we are in a growth context rather than in the short-run world of *IS-LM* analysis.

Given the broad outlines just described for the solution to the question of the impact of a debt-

---

[4] Since the budget constraint is $G - T = \Delta M + \Delta B$, it follows that $\Delta G - \Delta T = \Delta^2 M + \Delta^2 B$. In the case where $\Delta^2 B = 0 = \Delta T$, i.e., complete money finance, we obtain $\Delta G = \Delta^2 M$. After n deficit periods the change in wealth is $n(G-T)$. The incremental wealth associated with a larger deficit is $n\Delta G$. Or, where $G = T$ as an initial condition, the increment in wealth due to a ΔG is $n\Delta G$ after n budget periods. The exact same results follow for complete bond finance.

[5] See [8, p. 275].

financed government expenditure, we can now solve the *IS-LM* model algebraically and examine the formal expression for $\Delta Y/\Delta G$. We will then be able to isolate the precise conditions for expansionary and contractionary impacts on Y of a money and a debt financed government expenditure. Solving (1–5) and (6–8) produces the familiar expressions for the *IS* and *LM* curves, (11) and (12), respectively.

$$Y = \frac{a - b\overline{T} + \mu W + d + \overline{G}}{1 - b} - \frac{e}{1 - b} r; \quad (11)$$

$$r = \frac{hW - \overline{M}}{q} + \frac{f}{q} Y. \quad (12)$$

Solving (11) and (12) for Y produces

$$Y = \frac{a - b\overline{T} + d + \overline{G} + \mu W + (e/q)\overline{M} - (eh/q)W}{1 - b + \frac{ef}{q}}. \quad (13)$$

From (13) the expression for $\Delta Y/\Delta G$ (allowing for potential variation in W and M) is

$$\frac{\Delta Y}{\Delta G} = \frac{1 + \mu(\Delta W/\Delta G) + (e/q)(\Delta M/\Delta G) - (eh/q)(\Delta W/\Delta G)}{1 - b + \frac{ef}{q}}. \quad (14)$$

There are a number of possible cases from expression (14).

Case I. If we ignore the financing side of ΔG, then $\Delta W/\Delta G$ and $\Delta M/\Delta G$ are zero; and we have the familiar expression[6]

$$\Delta Y/\Delta G = \frac{1}{1 - b + \frac{ef}{q}}. \quad (15)$$

This is the equilibrium response in Y to a change in G. It is positive since the denominator of (15) is positive.

Case II. Suppose the budget is balanced $(G = T)$. Assume all ΔG is financed by money creation.[7] From the government's budget con-

---

[6] Some of the literature on macroeconomies suggests that (15) in our text is the complete multiplier for a *debt-financed* government expenditure, see [7, pp. 98–99].

[7] We are assuming here for simplicity (and throughout the analysis set forth below) that the initial conditions are $G = T$. This assumption provides for an initial equilibrium Y whereas, if G-T were some positive constant Y would be changing. In the latter situation our results apply to a case of imposing a larger deficit. See footnote 4 for an additional comment.

straint (10), the deficit $(G + \Delta G) - T$ is financed by ΔM. The ΔM will equal ΔG after one budget period, say a year. After n budget periods, however, $\Delta M = n\Delta G$, or $\Delta M/\Delta G = n$. Furthermore, from (9) we see that since K and B are constant, $\Delta W = \Delta M$. Hence $\Delta W/\Delta G = n$. Substituting the expressions for $\Delta M/\Delta G$ and $\Delta W/\Delta G$ into (14) produces an expression for $\Delta Y/\Delta G$ after n budget periods,

$$\left[\frac{\Delta Y}{\Delta G}\right]_n = \frac{1 + \mu n + (e/q)n - (eh/q)n}{1 - b + \frac{ef}{q}}$$

$$= \frac{1 + \mu n + (1 - h)(en/q)}{1 - b + \frac{ef}{q}}. \quad (16)$$

Since we showed above that $0 < h < 1$ the expression in (16) is positive and varies positively with n. In other words, Y expands continuously as long as there is a deficit. (Note that we are assuming throughout, for simplicity, that the multiplier process incorporated in the denominator of (14) and hence, (16) works itself out within each budget period.)

Case III. If all of ΔG is financed by ΔB then after n budget periods $\Delta B = n\Delta G$ and $\Delta W/\Delta G = n$. Since $\Delta M/\Delta G$ is now zero, expression (14) becomes:

$$\left[\frac{\Delta Y}{\Delta G}\right]_n = \frac{1 + \mu n - (eh/q)n}{1 - b + \frac{ef}{q}}. \quad (17)$$

After n budget periods the impact of ΔG on Y can be expansionary or contractionary. If the numerator of (17) is positive, $\Delta Y/\Delta G > 0$; if the numerator is negative, $\Delta Y/\Delta G < 0$. More formally:

$$\frac{\Delta Y}{\Delta G} \gtrless 0 \quad \text{as } 1 + \mu n - (eh/q)n \gtrless 0, \quad (18)$$

or,

$$\frac{\Delta Y}{\Delta G} \gtrless 0 \quad \text{as } 1 + \mu n \gtrless (eh/q)n. \quad (19)$$

Dividing through by n produces

$$\frac{\Delta Y}{\Delta G} \gtrless 0 \quad \text{as} \quad \frac{1}{n} + \mu \gtrless eh/q. \quad (20)$$

As n gets large the conditions reduce to

$$\frac{\Delta Y}{\Delta G} \gtrless 0 \quad \text{as} \quad \mu \gtrless eh/q. \quad (21)$$

From (2), $\mu = \Delta C / \Delta W$, from (3), $e = |\Delta I / \Delta r|$ and from (12), which is the LM curve, $h/q = \Delta r / \Delta W$. Therefore,

$$\frac{\Delta Y}{\Delta G} \gtrless 0 \quad \text{as} \quad \Delta C / \Delta W \gtrless |\Delta I / \Delta r| \, (\Delta r / \Delta W). \quad (22)$$

In other words, as n gets large $\Delta Y / \Delta G$ will be positive if the positive impact of increases in wealth on consumption spending is greater than the negative impact of wealth on investment spending (via the positive impact of wealth on the rate of interest). The value of $\Delta Y / \Delta G$ will be negative when the contractionary impact on investment is greater than the expansionary impact on consumption.

When n is small, i.e., only a few budget periods have elapsed since the initial ΔG, the impact on income is more likely to be positive since the direct spending impact on Y of ΔG becomes relatively more important. The direct spending impact of ΔG on Y is represented by unity on the left side of (18). When $n = 1$, for example, (18) reduces to

$$\frac{\Delta Y}{\Delta G} \gtrless 0 \quad \text{as} \quad 1 + \mu \gtrless (eh/q). \quad (23)$$

The left side of (23) is certainly larger than unity while the right side will be greater than unity only if e—which is $\Delta I / \Delta r$—is very much greater than $\Delta M^d / \Delta r$, which is q. If these two are equal then $\Delta Y / \Delta G > 0$ since $h < 1$.

Case IV. Combined increases in money and bonds is an alternative way of financing ΔG. Let p be the proportion of ΔG financed by bonds in each budget period. After n budget periods, therefore, $\Delta B = pn\Delta G$ and $\Delta M = (1 - p)n\Delta G$. Equation 14 then becomes

$$\left[\frac{\Delta Y}{\Delta G}\right]_n = \frac{1 + \mu n + (e/q)(1 - p)n - (eh/q)n}{1 - b + \dfrac{ef}{q}}. \quad (24)$$

From (24) we see

$$\frac{\Delta Y}{\Delta G} \gtrless 0 \quad \text{as} \quad 1 + \mu n + (e/q)(1 - p)n - (eh/q)n \gtrless 0, \quad (25)$$

or

$$\frac{\Delta Y}{\Delta G} \gtrless 0$$

$$\text{as} \quad \frac{1}{n} + \mu \gtrless (e/q)[h - (1 - p)]. \quad (26)$$

Note that when $p = 1$, (26) collapses into (19), the case of all bond finance. When $p = 0$, (24) collapses into (16), which is the case of all money finance.

One question that arises is what proportion of ΔG must come in the form of ΔM in order to negate the contractionary impact of bond finance on Y. If $(1 - p) = h$, and we ignore the wealth effect on consumption (i.e., $\mu = 0$), then (24) collapses into the elementary multiplier of the Keynesian system as shown in Case I above [see (15)]. In other words, the LM curve is fixed if $(1 - p) = h$. This occurs, quite simply, because the proportion of ΔG financed by ΔM, $(1 - p)$, equals the increased demand for money due to the increment in wealth (h). Note also that when $\mu > 0$ this case illustrates the simple Lerner argument regarding rightward movements in the IS curve (with a fixed LM curve) as long as the deficit persists.

CONCLUSION

It has been demonstrated that traditional IS-LM analysis has not treated the bond-finance and new money-finance cases of government deficits symmetrically. When proper treatment is given to the former case, we found that in the simple world of IS-LM analysis, government expenditure financed by selling bonds to the public can be contractionary. Even when GNP does go up due to ΔG, the increase that occurs is overstated in the traditional (but incomplete) IS-LM model of income determination. The failure to incorporate the monetary effects of *debt* finance into the LM function is the major source of confusion. While other studies have treated this question, it has never been formally incorporated into IS-LM models. This has led to incorrect conclusions regarding the multiplier effects of government spending.

We also noted that there is still a case in which it is possible to experiment with a fixed LM

curve. If the deficit is financed with a combined increase in money and debt the *LM* curve could remain constant. This will occur when the increase in the supply of *M* just compensates for the increase in the demand for *M* brought about by the simultaneous increase in bond supply. Thus, within the *IS-LM* framework it is still possible to examine fiscal policy with a fixed *LM* curve although that occurs in a situation of mixed money and bond finance rather than pure bond finance.

LITERATURE CITED

1. Christ, C. "A Short-Run Aggregate Demand Model of the Interdependence and Effects of Monetary and Fiscal Policies with Keynesian and Classical Interest Elasticities," *AER* (May 1967).
2. ———. "A Simple Macroeconomic Model with a Government Budget Restraint," *JPE* (January 1968).
3. Dernburg, T. and D. MacDougal. *Macroeconomics.* 3d ed., New York: McGraw-Hill, 1968.
4. Friedman, M. and W. Heller. "Monetary Policy Versus Fiscal Policy," New York: W. W. Norton & Co., 1969.
5. Haberler, G. *Prosperity and Depression.* New York: Atheneum, 1963.
6. Keare, D. H. and W. L. Silber. "Monetary Effect of Long-Term Debt Finance," *AER* (June 1965).
7. Kogiku, K. C. *An Introduction to Macroeconomic Models.* New York: McGraw-Hill, 1968.
8. Lerner, A. R. *The Economics of Employment.* New York: McGraw-Hill, 1951.
9. Musgrave, R. A. *The Theory of Public Finance.* New York: McGraw-Hill, 1959.
10. Ott, D. J. and A. Ott. "Budget Balance and Equilibrium Income," *Journal of Finance* (March 1965).
11. Pesek, B. and T. Saving. *The Foundations of Money and Banking.* New York: Macmillan, 1968.
12. Ritter, L. S. "Some Monetary Aspects of Multiplier Theory and Fiscal Policy," *Review of Economic Studies* (1955–56).
13. Tobin, J. "An Essay on Principles of Debt Management," in *Fiscal and Debt Management Policies,* Commission on Money and Credit. New York: Prentice-Hall, 1963.

21. NEW DIRECTIONS FOR THE FEDERAL BUDGET?*

Joseph Scherer

The Federal budget reflects much of the history of the nation. Changes both on the revenue side and the spending side highlight 200 years of conflicts and compromises about the economic, political, and social priorities of the country. Within the past half century, moreover, the Federal Government has become one of the major influences on the nation's life. Much of the time, the changes have been evolutionary and gradual. Sometimes, however, as during the depression of the thirties, a compass change is clearly evident. Is the nation now on the threshold of another significant budget shift?

The recent Presidential campaign indicated that both candidates favored a curb on the expansion of the Federal Government and an improvement in its effectiveness. These objectives seemed to reflect the sentiments of a substantial portion of the electorate. The Congress, for its part, has instituted new budget procedures to assert control over spending. Altogether, forces to hold down the size of the budget seem to be at work.

Despite these auguries, the prospects for significant restraints on spending are uncertain. Developments since World War II point the other way: Federal spending has increased more than twelvefold since fiscal 1947. Even after adjusting for inflation, Federal spending is almost three times higher than in 1947. Moreover, the current state of public opinion suggests that there is considerable ambiguity about how conflicting pressures on budget making will be reconciled. While

* From the Federal Reserve Bank of New York *Quarterly Review,* pp. 1–13. Reprinted by permission of the Federal Bank of New York and the author. Joseph Scherer is Economist, Federal Reserve Bank of New York.

the citizenry seems to favor less government, the national government is increasingly asked to tackle problems that used to be the responsibility of the private sector, or of state and local governments, or that had previously not been viewed as problems. The growth of the economy, which often helped to solve problems in the past, is a less certain solution today for two reasons. One is the question of whether satisfactory levels of economic growth can now be attained as easily as before. The other is the difficulty of making growth compatible with improved practices in regard to the environment.

Whenever the economy operates below capacity, there is bound to be pressure to use stimulative fiscal policy in order to promote greater economic activity and to reduce unemployment. However, spending measures and temporary tax cuts for countercyclical purposes tend to undercut the prospects for curtailing outlays and for permanent tax reductions. At present, the spending problem is accentuated because there are strong pressures to do more about newer concerns with respect to energy, pollution, and health. At the same time, some older concerns, such as the structural problems of high unemployment among teenagers, Vietnam veterans, and workers in urban areas as well as the pressure to relieve poverty, give little sign of abating.

The wish to reduce taxes clearly collides with the demand for new or expanded programs. It is not very likely that this conflict can be resolved by the new Congressional budget techniques and by proposed new procedures, such as sunset laws and zero-base budgeting. Sunset laws automatically terminate existing programs at specified dates; zero-base budgeting requires that spending for existing programs be justified each time an additional appropriation is under consideration. Techniques can only lead to efficient decision making after a consensus on priorities has been reached. Consensus is elusive because well-organized special interest groups can often mount heavy pressures to continue or to expand particular programs. What the new budget procedures *can* do is to pose for the Congress in unavoidable form the central question of economics: how to allocate scarce means—in this case government revenues—among alternative uses—in this case government outlays.

Budget Processes Old and New

As the size of the budget grew, a general dissatisfaction with the Congressional budget process became increasingly evident by the late sixties

and seemed to pick up momentum in the seventies when inflation accelerated. In 1969, a *New York Times* story carried the headline "Treasury Secretary Warns of Taxpayers Revolt." A recent Brookings Institution study reported that "Ten years ago, government was widely viewed as an instrument to solve problems; today government itself is widely viewed as the problem."[1] Solutions for the varied fiscal maladies were many, but there was one that cut across political, economic, and social differences—the Congress should get the budget under control. In hearings held on proposals for improving Congressional control over revenues and spending, support for such legislation was widespread and included members of the Congress, business leaders, university professors, and public interest groups. Congressman Al Ullman, chairman of the House Ways and Means Committee, testifying in 1973, said:

. . . the clear intent of the Constitution is that the Congress does have the power of the purse, that Congress does levy the tax and determine the expenditures. . . . Yet, under the procedures we follow today [1973] we have virtually handed all of this over to the Office of Management and Budget— something not intended by the Constitution.

At the same hearing, Roy L. Ash, the incumbent Director of the Office of Management and Budget (OMB), said:

Congressional actions that affect the budget are taken piecemeal and are uncoordinated for the most part.

Until the passage of the Congressional Budget and Impoundment Control Act on July 12, 1974, the budget process in the Congress was fragmented; indeed, there was virtually no satisfactory Congressional control over total Federal spending. In addition, the Congress had no committees charged with consolidating the various pieces of budget legislation into a meaningful whole as they entered the legislative hopper. Nor did it have a staff that could have provided it with such an overview. The new budget control act established a Budget Committee in the House and in the Senate to coordinate budget policy. It also established a Congressional Budget Office (CBO) to provide information and analysis comparable to that which the OMB provides the executive branch. The new structure operated on a preliminary, nonbinding basis during fiscal 1976. The new arrangements became mandatory beginning with the fiscal year 1977 that started on Oc-

---

[1] H. Owen and C. C. Schultze, eds., *Setting National Priorities, the Next Ten Years* (Washington, D.C.: Brookings Institution, 1976), page 7.

tober 1, 1976 and that will run through September 30, 1977.[2]

The 1974 budget act sets up a timetable for the Congressional budget process. This timetable is designed to insure that all appropriation bills for a new fiscal year are completed before a current fiscal year ends. In recent years, it was common for some appropriations to be passed after a new fiscal year had begun—occasionally as long as six months after. The act also requires the Congress to set an appropriate level of Federal receipts and outlays, determine budget priorities, and review any decisions by the President to impound any funds for programs already under way.

The new budget timetable is summarized in the accompanying box. In addition to setting new requirements, the act integrates previously existing executive and Congressional schedules. This integration should enable the Congress to exercise better control over spending and taxation and to assess the impact of the emerging budget on the economy. Under the new procedures, the President still submits his budget at approximately the same time in January as in the past; the present schedule specifies it be done by the fifteenth day after the Congress convenes. The actual budget process, of course, begins well before the President submits his budget, for that document represents the culmination of budget making within the executive branch. A new part of the whole budget process is the requirement laid down by the Congress that the President submit to it a "current services budget" much earlier—by November 10.

The Current Services Budget

The current services budget is meant to provide a bench mark or baseline against which any changes later proposed by the President or by the Congress can be measured. A current services budget is one that estimates Federal tax and spending programs on the assumption that they are continued without any change in policies. These estimates are presented for the current fiscal year and also for the fiscal year ahead. This budget must also take into account the effects of

expected changes in economic activity or of other trends. Examples of such changes are higher or lower levels of unemployment or inflation, variation in the number of social insurance beneficiaries, or variation in the number of recipients under programs that are mandated by existing legislation, such as those for veterans.

In the document submitted to the Congress last November, the Ford administration chose to submit four alternative current services budgets based on four alternative sets of economic assumptions or paths. These alternatives for calendar 1977 projected a gross national product (GNP) ranging from $1,874 billion to $1,905 billion, an unemployment rate ranging from 6.4 percent to 6.9 percent, and an increase in the GNP deflator (a measure of the general inflation rate) ranging from 5 percent to 6.5 percent. Total budget revenues under the four paths varied by almost $20 billion, but total spending varied by only about $6 billion. Under the new budget procedures, the Joint Economic Committee of the Congress (JEC) must evaluate whether the President's current services budget is reasonable. The range of estimates submitted for the fiscal 1977 and 1978 current services budgets was judged to be reasonable by the JEC.

The Standard Appropriation Process

Following the usual practice, President Ford presented a budget message in January accompanied by documents that gave a detailed and comprehensive view of Federal spending and receipts. It contained revisions for the current 1977 fiscal year and a proposed budget for the next year, fiscal 1978. The fiscal 1978 document also contained budget projections through fiscal 1982. The revenue and spending estimates for fiscal 1978 and subsequent years, of course, combined the continuance of existing programs, the phasing-out or elimination of other existing programs, and proposed programs for which new legislation would have to be enacted.

The standard procedure has been and continues to be that each new activity of the Federal Government—or the expansion of an old activity—must be authorized by a bill which has been passed by both houses of the Congress and has been signed by the President.[3] Such bills are con-

---

[2] Starting with the current fiscal year, fiscal years will run from October 1 through September 30 of the succeeding year. Fiscal years are identified by the year in which they end. From 1921 through fiscal 1976, the fiscal year of the Federal Government began on July 1 and ended on the following June 30. The shift from fiscal 1976 to the current fiscal year, 1977, left the July 1–September 30, 1976 quarter unattached to any fiscal year, and the period is officially known as "the transition quarter".

[3] Some bills, of course, are passed over a Presidential veto, and a few bills have become law without Presidential signature under the Constitutional provision that, if the President does not sign or veto a bill, it becomes law after ten days provided that the Congress is then in session.

Timetable for Budget Action

On or Before:	Action to Be Completed
November 10.....	President submits current services budget
Fifteen days after the Congress convenes.........	President submits official budget
March 15.........	Committees and joint committees submit reports to budget committees in House and Senate
April 1............	CBO submits report to budget committees
April 15...........	Budget committees report first concurrent resolution on the budget to their respective houses
May 15...........	Legislative committees report bills and resolutions authorizing new budget authority
May 15...........	Congress completes action on first concurrent resolution on the budget
Seventh day after Labor Day........	Congress completes action on bills and resolutions providing new budget authority and new spending authority
September 15.....	Congress completes action on second required concurrent resolution on the budget
September 25.....	If necessary, the Congress completes action on reconciliation bill or resolution, or both, implementing second required concurrent resolution
October 1.........	New fiscal year begins

sidered first by the appropriate legislative committee (in both the House of Representatives and the Senate) responsible for the subject the bill addresses. If necessary, the bill includes an *authorization* to appropriate up to a specified amount of money for the program. If the committees approve, the bill is brought to a vote before the full membership of each branch of the Congress. If the bills passed by the two houses differ in any respect, these differences must be resolved by a conference committee composed of members of the two houses. If there is an acceptable resolution, then identical bills are resubmitted for passage in each house and transmitted to the President for signature.

Actual authority to spend funds typically involves a further step—the passage of the *appropriation* bill, again by both houses of the Congress. (The stated amount on the appropriation bill may be no more, but may be less than, the amount in the authorization bill.) The appropriation bill must also be signed by the President. An appropriation specifically permits a Federal agency to order goods and services and to draw funds from the Treasury to pay for these goods and services as well as to meet payrolls up to some stated amount. Other spending may take the form of transfers of funds to state and local governments, to individuals, or to governments abroad and international agencies.[4]

Spending in any single fiscal year is always made up of a combination of spending from some appropriations carried over from previous years as well as from appropriations newly legislated. For example, the Ford administration's January budget document estimated that $129.2 billion would be spent in fiscal 1978 from the pool of previously authorized appropriations and that an additional $310.7 billion would come from new appropriations for new programs or to continue existing programs.

Since World War II, a practice has developed whereby the President may instruct the Bureau of the Budget (now the OMB) to hold spending for a particular activity below the amounts the Congress had appropriated. The Congress has increasingly viewed this practice as an infringement on its Constitutional prerogative to determine the appropriate amount of spending by the Federal Government, and the Congress has now passed legislation to assert its control. If a President wishes to withhold or postpone funding for an existing program, under the new Congressional control system he must send a special message to the Congress. The House and the Senate must approve such a rescission bill within 45 days if the rescission is to become effective. In contrast, if the President wishes to defer spending temporarily, Congressional approval is not required, but the deferral can be denied if one house passes a resolution against the proposal.

Steps to the First Concurrent Resolution

Under the new timetable for Congressional action on a proposed budget, the various committees with responsibilities for particular segments of budget legislation must report to the budget committee of their house by March 15. These reports give dollar estimates for the programs in their jurisdictions, for instance, social security, transportation, taxes. At the same time, the CBO and the budget staff in each of the

[4] For ongoing programs, many of which represent long-term national commitments, the appropriations process is somewhat different from the one described above. A prominent example is the funding of the social security programs.

houses are busy analyzing the President's proposals, drafting preliminary budget resolutions, and preparing reports that answer questions on the budget that are posed by various Congressional committees. By April 1, the CBO is required to present to each budget committee a report on alternative budget possibilities with respect to total revenues and expenditures and their major categories, as well as a discussion of national budget priorities. At the same time, each budget committee is preparing a similar budget package. By April 15, the budget committee in each house must submit its suggested first concurrent resolution on the budget for the next fiscal year. The committees, of course, take into account the material sent to them by the CBO on April 1.

After April 15, within the guidelines of the proposed first concurrent resolutions—they are really preliminary budgets—the contours of the Congressional budget begin to take on more specific form. Between April 15 and May 15, the first concurrent resolution must be debated and passed by both houses. Any differences between the two must be resolved in conference, and the final conference report must be passed by both houses before May 15. In addition, by May 15 the legislative committees in both houses are required to have reported out all programs requiring authorizations. The first concurrent resolution establishes the target for total receipts and outlays and for the deficit or surplus that the Congress aims to achieve. Moreover, the spending total must be broken down into 17 major categories.

Steps to the Second Concurrent Resolution

After May 15, all the Congressional committees continue to work on the proposals within their jurisdictions. They keep in mind the dollar limits set in the first concurrent resolution and aim to complete action on the necessary individual bills by the seventh day after Labor Day. During this period, a committee might seek to raise its tentative target, which would then create adjustment problems for the total budget. These problems can be resolved in a variety of ways, including the cutting of other spending programs or even by increasing revenues.

Action on the second concurrent resolution must be taken by September 15. This resolution sets final totals on the major categories of revenue and spending. Given the spending total and the revenue total, there should then exist a specific deficit or surplus that the Congress is deliberately

identifying as its goal for that budget. This is most noteworthy, since until last year there had been no requirement for such an explicit decision by the Congress. The second concurrent resolution changes the spending targets of the first resolution to spending ceilings and the revenue targets to revenue floors.

If the Congress cannot reach agreement by September 15, the legislation provides only a ten-day period for it to iron out its differences. However accomplished, joint agreement on a second concurrent resolution must be achieved no later than September 25. Consequently, when the coming fiscal year begins on October 1, the budget totals for that year are already set. There can still be changes made if the Congress decides that there is a need for new initiatives or for modifications of existing programs after the fiscal year begins. Such changes would require further concurrent resolutions.

Among the more important reforms of the budget act is a built-in antifilibuster device. To prevent delays by filibuster in the Congressional budget process, the reform legislation not only sets deadlines for each step, but also sets specific time limits for debate. In the case of the Senate, for example, the law states that "Debate in the Senate on any concurrent resolution on the budget . . . shall be limited to not more than 50 hours. . . ."

Experience with the New Process

The effectiveness of the new procedures was illustrated by the way the timetable operated to shape the budget for the current fiscal year. Last May, the first concurrent resolution for fiscal 1977 placed total expenditures at $413.3 billion, some $20 billion higher than the proposed spending total for fiscal 1977 in the budget President Ford presented in January 1976. The larger expenditures proposed by the Congress, according to an analysis by the staff of the House budget committee last spring, would have increased employment by about one million persons more than was implicit in the President's budget. The $413.3 billion total itself represented a compromise between differences that had existed earlier between the House and Senate over the size of the proposed jobs programs. The House had proposed higher outlays, including more spending on public works.

As with the first resolution, the proposed second concurrent resolutions passed by each house were not identical. But the differences this time were relatively minor and easily reconciled. A few weeks earlier, however, there had been considerable concern over the substantial divergences between the Senate and the House on the proposed tax legislation. The Senate wanted tax cuts much larger than the House did, not only for fiscal 1977 but also for succeeding years. Eventually, the reconciliation kept revenues, and therefore the deficit, close to the totals that had been set in the first resolution.

The disappointing course of the economy after passage of the second concurrent resolution last fall convinced President Carter by the time he took office that it was prudent to try to stimulate the economy further. He therefore proposed a $31 billion package of tax cuts and job creation programs, mostly for fiscal 1977 and 1978. Consequently, the Congress had to work on a third concurrent resolution incorporating these changes. Once again the versions passed by the House and the Senate differed, for the two bodies augmented President Carter's proposals by different amounts. Passage of the third concurrent resolution was achieved on March 3. It added $4.4 billion to spending and reduced expected revenues by $14.8 billion. The estimated deficit for fiscal 1977 was thereby raised to $69.8 billion, $19.3 billion above that of the second concurrent resolution, although the stimulus package itself had not been passed.

Assessment of the New Budget Controls

Any assessment of the new budget controls must take into account a loophole in the coverage of the budget. Some Governmental agencies, such as the Postal Service and some of the lending agencies, are not included in the budget. Outlays by these agencies were $7.2 billion in fiscal 1976, and the estimate for fiscal 1977 is $10.8 billion.[5]

If Congressional control over Federal Government activities is to be comprehensive, these off-budget organizations should be put into the budget. Under current arrangements, the financing of existing off-budget agencies is exempt from the provisions of the Congressional Budget and Impoundment Control Act of 1974, but there is no bar to prevent the Congress from putting them into the budget. Until the off-budget agencies are brought explicitly under budget control

procedures, a significant and perhaps widening gap in spending control will remain.[6]

When the new budget control system was adopted, it was viewed with considerable skepticism. Previous attempts to control spending had little impact. The spending ceilings in effect for a few years contained too many exceptions. The ceiling on outstanding Treasury debt that is still in existence has proved to be ineffective. More significantly perhaps, the new system interposed another layer within the existing Congressional structures. The new budget committees, with their responsibilities to set and to monitor binding ceilings on spending and to implement desired goals for revenues, encroach on the domains of existing committees. Political observers wondered whether these committees would allow their strongly entrenched powers to be eroded. After the first year of operation, however, the consensus was that the new system had been successfully launched. Continuing success, nevertheless, is far from a foregone conclusion. A tradition of solid achievement in Congressional budget control must be built to help safeguard the integrity of the new procedures. They should not become empty rituals.

Perspectives on the Budget

The bulk of spending under any new budget is based on legislative programs that have been in existence for years, even though in many cases new appropriations are required annually. Any new initiatives on spending and taxation are just the tip of the total budget iceberg. New initiatives, however, are likely to affect future budgets significantly. To understand any new budget, it is therefore helpful to review how it has evolved in size and in composition. Such a perspective can be gained by examining data from two related, though different views of the Federal Govern-

---

[5] These agencies finance some of their operations from funds obtained by borrowing, chiefly from the Federal Financing Bank (FFB), which in turn obtains its funds from the Treasury. Consequently, Treasury borrowing from the public is higher than the amount required to finance the recorded budget deficit.

[6] As defined in the budget document, "off-budget entities are federally owned and controlled, but their transactions have been excluded from the budget totals under provision of law". Some agencies are completely off-budget, such as the Pension Benefit Guaranty Corporation. Only a portion of the activities of some agencies are off-budget, such as the programs for the housing of the elderly and of the handicapped in the Department of Housing and Urban Development (HUD). Off-budget agencies must be differentiated from Government-sponsored agencies, such as the Federal Home Loan Banks (FHLB) and the Federal National Mortgage Association (FNMA), which are privately owned and operated and therefore completely excluded from the budget. These agencies borrow in the capital market by issuing their own debt instruments.

Chart 1: Federal Budget

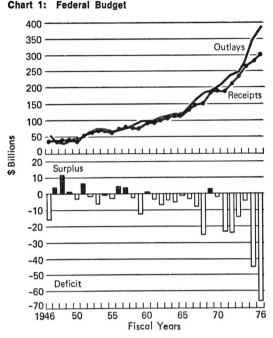

Source: The Budget of the United States Government, 1978.

ment—the view provided by the unified budget and the view provided by the Federal sector of the national income accounts (NIA).[7]

Taking the span of years since World War II, total unified budget Federal receipts and expenditures broadly trace a similar growth trend, although revenues move more erratically. After 1946, revenues typically fell short of spending; there have been only eight years of surpluses. For many years the deficits were generally small—under $5 billion (Chart 1). But beginning with fiscal 1971, deficits in the unified budget—with the exception of two years—were larger than $23 billion, and they reached a historic peak of $66.5 billion in the last fiscal year.

[7] For the purposes of this article, it proved most helpful to discuss Federal Government *spending* using the NIA categories and Federal Government *receipts* using the unified budget categories.

The unified budget is the official budget of the United States Government. The Federal sector in the NIA is a statistical estimate of Federal Government activities recalculated from budget data to provide a picture of the Federal Government consistent with the accounting system used to estimate total output of the economy—GNP. The estimate of total GNP is based on a comprehensive set of data—the NIA—made up of a number of subsectors, such as government, business, and consumers. While broadly similar, the unified budget of the Federal Government and the NIA Federal sector differ in agencies covered, in accounting techniques, and in the various descriptive categories into which programs are combined.

The cumulative deficit for the fiscal years 1947 to 1976 is more than $238 billion, which raised outstanding Federal debt on June 30, 1976 to $620 billion. A sizable portion of this debt, $150 billion, was held by the Government itself. Another sizable portion, $95 billion, was owned by the Federal Reserve System. Privately held net Federal debt has increased from $230 billion in calendar 1946 to $446 billion in 1975. The share of this debt in relation to all outstanding debt in the economy, nevertheless, has dropped from about 50 percent in the late forties to about 15 percent.[8]

Trends in Spending

It is convenient to look at Federal spending by the categories used in the NIA. Total NIA Federal spending has increased from $29.5 billion in fiscal 1947 to $373.0 billion in fiscal 1976. All of the broad categories of spending identified in the NIA have grown almost steadily. Much of this increase simply reflects the growth of population and the economy, as well as the effects of rising prices. In addition, however, Federal expenditures have been pushed ever higher by the adoption of newly developed programs plus the addition of new functions to previously existing programs.

Since World War II the Federal Government has grown larger not only in absolute terms but also in relation to other sectors of the economy. The typical test of relative size is to calculate how the Federal Government sector has grown by comparing it with the growth of GNP, the measure of total output of goods and services in the economy. On this basis, the Government sector has grown from 14 percent of GNP in fiscal 1947 to 23 percent in fiscal 1976. This growth has been somewhat erratic: a large upward thrust was associated with the Korean war, another not quite so large was associated with the Vietnam war, and a third was associated with the recent recession (Chart 2).

Outlays by Sector

Although they have exhibited very different patterns over the years, two components of Federal outlays, spending for goods and services and spending for transfer payments, account for the bulk of outlays. Federal purchases of goods and

[8] These debt data, compiled to cover in a consistent accounting framework all debt in the nation by major sector, are available only on a calendar-year basis. The latest data are for 1975.

Chart 2: Federal Government Expenditures as a Share of Gross National Product

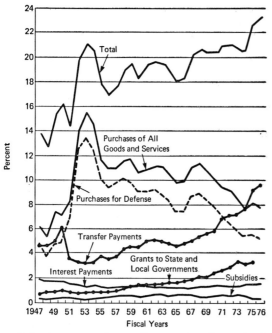

Federal government expenditures are based on national income accounts.

Sources: Economic Report of the President 1977; The Budget of the United States Government, 1978.

services increased from $13 billion in fiscal 1947 to $127.2 billion in fiscal 1976. Nevertheless, as a share of GNP these purchases are now only 2 percentage points higher than in 1947. They peaked at more than 15 percent during the Korean war and are currently down in the neighborhood of 8 percent. Defense spending is responsible for this relative decline and now accounts for about two thirds of all Federal purchases, compared with a peak of 87 percent during the Korean war.

Transfer payments, which consist of the various social insurance and the other general welfare and assistance programs, have expanded almost

continuously. These payments have increased from $10 billion in fiscal 1947 to $156.7 billion in fiscal 1976, a more than fifteenfold growth. As a percentage of GNP, they have about doubled— from less than 5 percent to almost 10 percent. By fiscal 1975, transfers exceeded total Federal purchases of goods and services and became the largest component among all the NIA Federal spending categories.

There has, of course, been substantial growth of other spending as well. The increase in Federal grants-in-aid to state and local governments, which include revenue-sharing payments, has been important. Grants to state and local governments have climbed from 0.7 percent of GNP in fiscal 1947 to 3.6 percent in fiscal 1976. They now provide more than 20 percent of state and local revenues. Interest payments on Federal debt have registered a sixfold rise in absolute dollar terms, and Federal subsidies have advanced eight fold from the end of fiscal 1946 through fiscal 1976. Still, both have remained relatively small in percentage terms, and together amount to only 2 percent of GNP.

Trends in Receipts

Despite frequent deficits, Federal receipts tended to increase at almost the same pace as spending until 1970. Most recently, due to the very deep 1973–75 recession, receipts have lagged behind spending by much wider margins than before. Consequently, deficits have widened substantially. Viewed over the long term, all categories of receipts in the unified budget have grown greatly, though some have risen faster than others. There were only temporary interruptions —due sometimes to slowdowns in economic activity, sometimes to changes in tax laws.

The individual income tax has been, and remains, the backbone of Federal Government revenues, accounting for about 45 percent of total receipts every year. Apart from the steady share

Table 1: Federal Budget Receipts: Distribution by Source (in percent)

Description	Fiscal 1946	Fiscal 1968	Fiscal 1972	Fiscal 1976
Individual income taxes..............	41.0	44.7	45.4	43.9
Corporation income taxes...........	31.1	18.7	15.4	13.8
Social insurance taxes and contributions......................	7.8	22.5	25.8	30.9
Excise taxes........................	16.9	9.2	7.4	5.7
Estate and gift taxes.................	1.7	2.0	2.6	1.7
Customs duties.....................	0.9	1.3	1.6	1.4
Miscellaneous receipts...............	0.5	1.6	1.7	2.7
Total receipts......................	100.0	100.0	100.0	100.0

Table 2:   Federal Government Budget Receipts by Source (in $ billions)

Description	Fiscal 1946	Fiscal 1968	Fiscal 1972	Fiscal 1976
Individual income taxes	16.1	68.7	94.7	131.6
Corporation income taxes	12.2	28.7	32.2	41.4
Social insurance taxes and contributions	3.1	34.6	53.9	92.7
Excise taxes	6.6	14.1	15.5	17.0
Estate and gift taxes	0.7	3.1	5.4	5.2
Customs duties	0.4	2.0	3.3	4.1
Miscellaneous receipts	0.2	2.5	3.6	8.0
Total receipts	39.3	153.7	208.6	300.0

Source: The Budget of the United States Government.

from the income tax, the composition of Federal revenues has changed markedly since 1946 (Table 1). Starting with a share of less than 8 percent of the total in 1946, employer taxes and individual contributions to social security and related programs now account for almost 31 percent. The jump reflects increases in contribution rates and the tax bases on which contributions are figured, broadened coverage, and the introduction of new types of coverage, such as for hospital bills and disability pay. In all, almost 75 percent of total Federal revenues is now collected from the individual income tax and the social insurance taxes. By contrast, the corporation income tax, which in 1946 constituted more than 31 percent of total revenues, has dropped to about 14 percent, even though its dollar contribution has been growing (Table 2). All other revenue sources now contribute only about 12 percent of the total, compared with 20 percent in 1946, because excise taxes have been reduced or eliminated.

The Government Sector in the Economy

There is no simple way to assess the impact of the Federal Government sector—or the budget—on the nation's economic system. Federal Government spending as a percentage of GNP provides only the roughest measure of the importance of the Government in the economy. From one point of view, saying that Federal Government spending amounts to 23 percent of GNP overstates its importance. The amount of the total output of goods and services that the Government purchases is down to about 8 percent of GNP. As Government purchases as a percentage of GNP have been declining, Government transfer payments to individuals and state and local governments have been rising relative to GNP. Since Federal Government transfer pay-

ments do not involve actual Federal purchases of goods and services, it has been said that their inclusion in an evaluation of the Federal sector leads to overstating the Federal Government's role. However, these transfers inevitably alter private spending. Had the Federal Government not received taxes from some people and transferred them to others, a different pattern and level of private spending would have prevailed.

Other budget practices suggest that the budget may well substantially understate the role played by the Federal Government in the economy and in the nation's noneconomic affairs. One understatement of the extent of Government influence results from the size of "tax expenditures." Tax expenditures—or tax subsidies—represent revenue losses arising from special provisions of the Internal Revenue Code (some of them are the "loopholes" about which there is a great deal of popular discussion). These special provisions make the tax liability of an individual or a business firm smaller than it otherwise would have been. Tax expenditures are simply another way by which public policy can attempt to promote particular types of economic activities or moderate undue tax burdens on persons or firms who are seen as facing special circumstances. Estimates of tax expenditures now must be included in the budget by law. The official estimate is that tax expenditures amounted to $95.4 billion in fiscal 1976.[9] Identification of the cost of specific tax expenditures should facilitate the evaluation of whether the benefits to the nation are worth the revenues lost.

Another form of Government influence which is often not recognized is the effect of the Government's credit programs. In fiscal 1976, direct

---

[9] Any estimates of tax expenditures are subject to a wide range of uncertainty because of the technical issues and ambiguities involved in calculating them.

loans outstanding had risen by $14.4 billion to $64.2 billion, and guaranteed or insured loans outstanding rose by $11.3 billion to $169.8 billion. Of course, loans that are guaranteed by the Government do not add to budget outlays unless borrowers default; consequently, these loans represent only a contingent, though large, liability of the Federal Government. In addition, about $10 billion of loans made by off-budget agencies also are excluded from budget spending totals, even though these disbursements increase the amount of Treasury borrowing.

Understatements about the budget also arise from accounting practices. The unified budget records certain kinds of receipts not as such, but as offsets to spending. This practice does not affect the size of the surplus or deficit, but it does lower the level of total receipts and total expenditures. Offsetting receipts from the public in fiscal 1976 amounted to $13.9 billion, thus reducing outlays from a gross level of $380.4 billion to $366.5 billion and reducing receipts to $300.0 billion, the figures that are cited in the total budget for fiscal 1976.

Finally, in recent years there has been a large increase in the number and in the scope of the regulatory functions of Government. They require relatively small numbers of governmental personnel and relatively small amounts of Federal spending. Nevertheless, these regulatory functions affect a wide range of activities. It sometimes seems as if more discontent with Government is generated from the regulatory and standard-setting functions than is generated from dissatisfaction with the levels of taxation or spending. While there are efforts to reduce Government regulation, reasons to introduce new ones seem constantly to arise—right now there is a good deal of pressure to introduce more regulations to protect consumers.

Questions of Budget Policy

Fundamental conflicts with respect to budget policy can be expected to continue for years to come. The charge that Government is too big is commonplace. At the same time there is a strong pressure to raise spending for defense and for health and social needs. There is a similar dichotomy about Government regulation. It is said to be stifling private competition, initiative, or prerogative, but recent calls to reduce regulation have met a mixed response from the industries involved.

Fiscal policy has become more controversial of late. For much of the postwar period, the fiscal prescription to combat a recession was simple: cut taxes and increase spending. In recent years, however, the persistence of inflation even during recessions has complicated the application of this standard policy prescription. Moreover, structural problems of the economy now seem to require policy measures to deal with specific concerns, such as teenage unemployment or the plight of the inner city. In brief, reliance on broad fiscal policy to solve national difficulties is being questioned. At the same time, the economy has seemingly become harder to manage. This is the context in which the principal budget issues that are likely to be concerning the President, the Congress, and the citizenry at large must be viewed.

1. Tax Policy. Federal Government taxes are a perennial center of controversy, with income taxes—individual and corporate—bearing the brunt of the criticism. Broadly viewed, there are three types of complaints: rates are too high, the tax structure is too complex, the structure is shot through with too many inequities. While almost everyone favors reform and rate reductions, there is difficulty in reaching a consensus on specific proposals. Nevertheless, the time for a fundamental reconstruction of the income tax seems to be coming. Former President Ford proposed some revisions in his January budget presentation, and the Carter administration announced that it will send to the Congress this fall recommendations covering both individual and corporate income taxes.

The basic problem underlying any attempted revision of the individual and corporate income taxes is the need to ensure that tax treatment of all forms of income is as uniform and equitable as possible. To do so properly requires a comprehensive approach, since piecemeal reform can give rise to new loopholes or to new forms of unequal treatment.

The merits of a tax reform are generally examined solely on the basis of tax considerations. Because government spending ultimately must be paid for by tax collections, a formidable constraint is placed on reforms that would reduce revenues in any major way. Another constraint is that broad-ranging changes in taxes and spending inevitably have important consequences on the overall operation of the economy. Finally, some tax arrangements are specifically designed to implement desired social policies. This results in tax complexity rather than simplicity, as well as favored treatment for selected categories of taxpayers. Consequently, the task of actually achieving the general objective of a simple and equitable income tax system has proved elusive—yet in a democracy this objective must continue to be pursued.

2. *Energy Shortages and Environmental Protection.* New complexities in budget making have arisen because of the increasing role that the Federal Government is playing in connection with energy and the protection of the environment. Legislation to cope with these issues will be a continuing concern of President Carter and his successors and of the Congress. Such legislation can be expected to be a combination of spending programs, tax changes, special incentives or subsidies, and new regulations. They are likely to have an enduring effect on the budget, and over the long run could materially affect the existing composition of spending and revenues. Even more important, they may well bring marked changes in the structure of the whole economy.

The nation's economy, both on the production and the consumption sides, developed on a foundation of cheap energy. The Organization of Petroleum Exporting Countries (OPEC) ended that era, and the resulting higher energy prices have been working their way into the entire price structure. Moreover, the persistent efforts by OPEC to maintain the price relationships between oil and other products that were set immediately after petroleum prices were quadrupled late in 1973, if successful, will tend to exert upward price pressures. Standard fiscal measures cannot deal adequately with inflation arising from such unusual developments.

The resolution of the nation's energy problems inevitably involves environmental considerations. Damage to the environment from all sources has already been responsible for the adoption of a variety of regulations. These clearly involve money costs. Yet lack of environment regulation can involve social costs that are not so easily perceived. It is now obvious that environmental pollution can no longer be treated with benign neglect. In fact, abuse of the environment itself has become a major contributing factor to price and supply pressures, as illustrated by the increasingly expensive search for clean water. There is little question that the present generation faces difficult decisions about how the bountiful natural heritage bequeathed to them should be handed on to their successors.

3. *Is Government Too Big?* With so many major problems facing the nation, will it continue its practice of shifting problems onto the lap of the Federal Government when all else fails? This results in Government taking on social and economic tasks that might more properly be taken care of by states and localities or by the private sector. Any such misdirection of efforts and resources cannot be fully corrected until the nation's priorities are more thoroughly reassessed and a new consensus forged.

Whatever is done about major priorities, there is at least a potential for better control over Federal spending. The budget control act and its procedures are already in place. And two proposals for further improvements are now being discussed: sunset legislation and zero-base budgeting (ZBB). A bill has already been introduced into the last Congress, the Government Economy and Spending Reform Act of 1976, which combines the sunset and ZBB concepts.

The sunset principle states that all programs must contain a specific and automatic termination date. After that date, it is necessary to reauthorize the program, presumably after searching reexamination. ZBB requires spending programs to be grouped according to objective and then arranged by priority in order to allocate available budget resources among them. Strict application of ZBB requires that spending for each program must be justified each time an appropriation for it is under consideration. A fully effective ZBB process should eliminate any need for the sunset principle. Given the relative newness of both concepts and the likelihood of the less than perfect implementation of any set of procedures, sunset laws are probably useful adjuncts to ZBB.

The sunset and ZBB procedures have been used in some state governments, and similar procedures have been in use by business. Stated as general principles, the goals are laudatory; implementation, however, runs the danger of greatly proliferating paper work. Expectations for each of these proposals should be tempered by government experience with cost-benefit analysis, a system that was adopted during the Johnson administration but one that was later abandoned in most Federal agencies because of very limited success.

Whatever techniques may be used to control Government spending, they cannot solve the basic dilemma of what the proper role and the proper size of the government sector should be in a free democratic society. The question of size does not merely involve the possibility of overwhelming the individual or his initiative. It may also bear on the problem of controlling inflation. There is a belief, held particularly widely in Europe, that big government itself can be a major contributor to inflation.

In the end, it is the citizenry that will have to come to grips with the issue of what tasks should be allocated to government and what tasks should be allocated to the private sector—business, families, foundations, or voluntary associations. To a substantial extent, the shift to the Government of duties that once were the responsibility of other organizations or the family stems from a perception that certain necessary tasks were not adequately being carried out. To prevent a further diminution of the responsibilities allotted to the private sector, as well as to recapture some that it has lost, will undoubtedly require new private initiatives and innovations. Simply railing at "big government" will not do the trick.

22. FISCAL POLICY AND THE NATIONAL DEBT*

David J. Ott
and
Attiat F. Ott

The federal government may incur budget deficits for two reasons: to stabilize the economy by increasing the level of total demand for goods and services in periods of unemployment and weak private demand; or because spending in periods of high employment exceeds tax receipts. In this latter case, the federal deficit is independent of the stabilization role usually associated with budget deficits.

A look at the federal budget trends reveals that over the last few years the federal government has been running increasing deficits. The outlook seems, at least for the short run, to be one of additional deficits. This means that the size of the national debt will continue to rise in the next few years with little assurance that a budget balance will be restored at full employment.

It is precisely this possibility that disturbs many critics of compensatory fiscal policy. In their view a growing budget deficit increases the size of government relative to the private sector, "crowds out" private investors by withdrawing from the capital market funds that would otherwise have been used to increase private capital formation, aggravates inflationary tendencies and threatens the nation's stability.[1] In addition, critics of budget deficits argue that increases in the national debt "impose a burden on future generations."

The "crowding out" argument was emphasized in statements by both the secretary of the treasury and the chairman of the Federal Reserve System. Chairman Arthur Burns testified that if the federal government were to run too large a deficit, "enormous strains . . . may be placed on money and capital markets. This means that interest rates may begin to shoot up, that many private borrowers may be crowded out of the market, that savings funds may once more be diverted from mortgage lenders, and that the stock market may turn weak again."[2]

Secretary William Simon, calling the 1976 budget deficits dangerous, stated that "excessive Federal demands on the capital markets would set in motion a vicious competition between the government and private borrowers for capital funds. Inevitably, mortgage borrowers . . . would be crowded out of the marketplace."[3] In contrast to these views was the statement of Arthur Okun, former chairman of the President's Council of Economic Advisers: "Of all the national economic problems facing us today, the one that is most exaggerated is that of financing the deficit. . . . We face a huge federal deficit because private saving is outrunning private investment by a wide margin. And that generates a superfluity of credit supplies relative to private credit demands which will absorb short-term Treasury securities very happily."[4]

---

* From David J. Ott and Attiat F. Ott, *Federal Budget Policy*, 3rd ed. (© 1965, 1969, 1977 The Brookings Institution, Washington, D.C.), chap. 7. Reprinted by permission of Attiat F. Ott and Brookings Institution. The late David J. Ott was Professor of Economics, Clark University. Attiat F. Ott is Professor of Economics, Clark University.

[1] See "Minority Views of James L. Buckley and James A. McClure," in *First Concurrent Resolution on the Budget—Fiscal Year 1976*, Report of the Senate Committee on the Budget, Report 94–77 (GPO, 1975), pp. 135–50.

[2] Chairman Arthur F. Burns's testimony on March 13, 1975, before the Senate Committee on the Budget, reprinted in ibid., p. 29.

[3] Testimony of William E. Simon in *The 1976 First Concurrent Resolution on the Budget*, Hearings before the Senate Committee on the Budget, 94:1 (GPO, 1975), vol. 2, pp. 1030–31.

[4] Arthur M. Okun, "What's Wrong with the U.S. Economy? Diagnosis and Prescription," *Quarterly Review of Economics and Business*, vol. 15 (Summer 1975), p. 30 (Brookings General Series Reprint 305).

In addition to the "crowding out" issue, both economists and policymakers have also voiced concern for future generations, as in a statement such as the following:

One of the greatest crimes of all . . . is one that is rarely considered by many Americans to be an offense at all. . . .

The full effects of this crime will not likely fall upon the generation that is committing it, but may call for reckoning far in the future, and, unless the present trend is reversed, each succeeding generation will pay more heavily for it. The offense is being compounded annually, and its long-range effects are cause for serious alarm. This is the crime: The generation that controls the economy of this nation today and those who have important government responsibility are callously and mercilessly burdening the livelihood and earnings of the generations that will follow us with a tremendous oppressive national debt.
. . . We are saddling our grandchildren . . . with the bills for our luxurious living. We have no moral right to do this.[5]

Others, however, argue that such a concern is unfounded; that the national debt imposes no burden since we "owe it to ourselves"; that "the real issue . . . [is] whether it is possible by internal borrowing to shift a real burden from the present generation, in the sense of the present economy as a whole, onto a future generation, in the sense of the future economy as a whole. What is important for economists is to teach . . . that the latter is impossible because a project that uses up resources needs the resources at the time that it uses them up, and not before or after."[6]

Thes conflicting views concerning the size of the federal budget deficits and the national debt raise the following questions: Who is right? Is there a real danger to the private economy from large and continued budget deficits? Is there a burden imposed by a national debt? Does the national debt lead to inflation and government bankruptcy? These questions are obviously crucial to the design of a fiscal program.

First, a definition of "national debt" is called for. Next is a brief summary of data relating the growth of the national debt to other economic magnitudes. The remainder of the chapter deals with the issues surrounding the national debt: (1) the burden of the debt in a deficit setting that has come about through attempts to alleviate

unemployment by use of increased expenditures or reduced taxes; (2) the burden of the debt in a full-employment setting; and (3) other issues connected with the debt, such as inflation and national solvency.[7]

DEFINITION OF THE NATIONAL DEBT

The federal debt consists of direct obligations or debts of the U.S. Treasury and obligations of federal government enterprises or agencies. In Table 1 the debt is broken down into "public issues"—that part of total debt held by private investors and the Federal Reserve System—and "special issues," that part held only by government agencies and trust funds. Of the issues sold to the public, some are "marketable"—that is, they are traded on securities markets—and some are "nonmarketable" and cannot be traded (for example, U.S. savings bonds). The latter may, however, be redeemed in cash or converted into another issue.

Distribution of the debt by types of holders as of June 1976 is shown in Table 2. Of the total, about 40 percent was held by government agencies, trust funds, and the Federal Reserve banks. Trust fund holdings are largely in the form of special issues, while those of the Federal Reserve are of the marketable type and are acquired through its open market operations. Of privately held debt, 26 percent was held by individuals, mostly in the form of savings bonds, another 26

Table 1: Federal Debt, by Type of Security, June 30, 1976

Type of Security	$ Billions
Interest-bearing public issues.............. .	489.5
Marketable............................	392.6
Treasury bills, certificates, and notes......	353.0
Treasury bonds...........................	39.6
Nonmarketable............................	94.6
U.S. savings bonds and notes............	70.1
Foreign*................................	21.5
Other†.................................	3.0
Convertible bonds...........................	2.3
Special issues...............................	129.8
Total gross federal debt‡.....................	620.4

* Certificates of indebtedness, notes, and bonds in the Treasury foreign series and foreign-currency-series issues.
† Depositary, retirement plan, state and local government, and Rural Electrification Administration bonds and Treasury deposit funds.
‡ Includes noninterest-bearing debt (of which $613 million on June 30, 1976, was not subject to statutory debt limitation).
Source: *Federal Reserve Bulletin*, vol. 62 (July 1976), p. A34.

---

[5] Senator John L. McClellan, "The Crime of National Insolvency," *Tax Review*, vol. 24 (January 1963), pp. 2–3.

[6] Abba P. Lerner, "The Burden of Debt," in James M. Ferguson, ed., *Public Debt and Future Generations* (University of North Carolina Press, 1964), p. 93.

[7] To simplify the discussion of the issues, it will be assumed that all federal debt is held by residents of the United States. This is not far from the truth: In 1976 about 89 percent of federal debt was held domestically.

Table 2: Ownership of Federal Debt, by Type of Holder, June 30, 1976 (par value)

Type of Holder	$ Billions
U.S. government agencies and trust funds....	149.6
Federal Reserve banks.......................	94.4
Private investors............................	376.4
Domestic...................................	306.5
Individuals...............................	96.4
Commercial and mutual savings banks....	96.9
State and local governments.............	39.5
Other......................................	73.7
Foreign and international....................	69.8
Total gross federal debt.....................	620.4

Source: *Federal Reserve Bulletin*, vol. 62 (December 1976), p. A34. Figures are rounded.

percent by commercial and mutual savings banks, 19 percent by foreign and international investors, and the remaining 29 percent by state and local governments and other private investors.

Almost all federal debt is issued by the Treasury Department. However, a few federal agencies are authorized to issue debt of their own, which is sold directly to the public or to other government agencies and funds. At the beginning of fiscal year 1977, the outstanding debt issued by these agencies was $11.7 billion.[8] As a result of the creation of the Federal Financing Bank, which buys new issues of agency debt and finances its purchases by borrowing from the Treasury, agency debt is expected to decline in the

[8] *The Budget of the United States Government, Fiscal Year 1978*, p. 208.

future. To prevent double counting, these holdings are excluded from gross federal debt.

The relationship between the budget deficit and the change in the size of the debt is shown in Table 3. As the table indicates, the unified budget deficit or surplus is the principal determinant of the change in the federal debt. However, the unified budget deficit or surplus, together with off-budget federal agencies' deficit or surplus, is a better indication of the change in the size of the debt held by the public.[9]

Statutory limitations have been placed on the amount of the federal debt (debt ceiling). The debt subject to the limit includes virtually all Treasury debt but excludes the major part of debt issued directly to the public by federal agencies (which is subject to special statutory limits). Although the ceiling on the amount of national debt outstanding has been imposed by Congress since 1917, it has almost always been adjusted upward to accommodate Treasury borrowing to finance government operations. The ceiling on the debt subject to limit was set at $700 billion through September 30, 1977, when it was scheduled to return to the permanent limit of $400 billion. Under the congressional budget act of 1974, a new procedure for determining the limit was instituted. Congress is to include in its concurrent

[9] Among off-budget federal entities are the rural electrification and telephone revolving fund, Rural Telephone Bank, housing for the elderly or handicapped fund, Pension Benefit Guaranty Corporation, and the Postal Service fund.

Table 3: Budget Financing and Change in Gross Federal Debt, Fiscal Year 1976

Description	$ Billions
Federal funds, deficit............................	68.9
Transactions with the public*...................	40.6
Transactions with trust funds..................	28.2
Minus: Trust funds, surplus.....................	2.4
Transactions with the public....................	−25.8
Transactions with federal funds................	28.2
Unified budget deficit...........................	66.5
Plus: Off-budget federal agencies, deficit........	7.2
Total deficit.....................................	73.7
Plus: Change in means of financing other than borrowing from the public†..........................	9.3
Total requirements for borrowing from the public..................	82.9
Plus: Reclassification of securities...............	0.5
Change in debt held by the public...............	83.4
Plus: Change in federal agency investments in federal debt.......	4.3
Change in gross federal debt....................	87.7

*Payments from federal funds to the general revenue sharing trust fund are treated as transactions with the public instead of transactions with a trust fund. The corresponding payments from the general revenue sharing trust fund are omitted.
†This includes change in cash and monetary assets, change in liabilities for checks outstanding, change in deposit fund balances, and seigniorage on coins.
Source: *The Budget of the United States Government, Fiscal Year 1978*, pp. 206, 210. Figures are rounded.

resolutions on the budget the appropriate level of the federal debt and the amount by which the debt subject to the limit should be increased. The first concurrent resolution on the budget adopted by Congress May 17, 1977, recommended a public debt for fiscal year 1977 of $708 billion. To permit the federal government to meet its obligations, the ceiling will have to be raised again as long as deficits are incurred.

Gross and Net Federal Debt

In discussing the federal debt, the concept of gross federal debt or national debt has been used. Gross federal debt includes the federal government borrowing from the public, government agencies' borrowings, and debt holdings of the Federal Reserve System. A more useful concept is that of the net federal debt held by the public. Net federal debt is defined as gross federal debt less the holdings of the Federal Reserve System and government investment accounts. This concept, rather than that of the gross federal debt, is the relevant one to use in analyzing the impact of the federal debt on the economy because it reflects the public's ability and willingness to absorb government securities in place of private securities. At the end of 1976, gross federal debt amounted to $654 billion while net federal debt was $410 billion, or about 60 percent of the gross debt. Table 4 shows the growth of gross and net federal debt for selected years during the period 1915–76.

The principal causes of the growth of the fed-

eral debt have been wars and depressions. During World War I the federal debt rose sharply from about $1 billion in 1915 to a level of almost $26 billion by the end of 1919. From there it decreased about $10 billion to $16 billion in 1930. The economic depression of the 1930s led to government deficit spending, and the federal debt increased by approximately $35 billion between 1930 and 1940. During World War II it grew tremendously, reaching $259 billion in December 1946. Since 1946 the debt has continued to grow, especially during years of recession. From 1965 to 1975, the gross federal debt increased almost 100 percent, a considerably larger increase than occurred from the mid-forties to the mid-sixties (it rose by only 37 percent from 1944 to 1964).

The fact that most of the growth of the debt occurred during major wars does not in itself mean that debt inevitably accompanies war. During recessions and periods of weak planned spending, expansionary fiscal policy is called for to promote economic recovery. Increasing government spending or cutting taxes, or both, produce federal deficits and an increase in the size of the federal debt. Over the period 1914–75, out of accumulated budget deficits of $447.4 billion, 60 percent was incurred during war years and about 21 percent during recession years.

Data on the Federal Debt

Looking at the growth of the gross or net federal debt in isolation reveals little except that it has grown tremendously over the years the U.S.

Table 4: Gross and Net Federal Debt, Selected Years, 1915–1976* ($ billions)

End of Calendar Year	Federal Debt		End of Calendar Year	Federal Debt	
	Gross	Net		Gross	Net
1915................	1.2	1.2	1950...............	256.7	199.9
1919................	25.8	25.3	1960...............	290.2	210.0
1930................	16.0	14.9	1966...............	329.3	219.2
1933................	23.8	21.4	1970...............	389.2	229.9
1940................	50.9	41.2	1971...............	424.1	247.9
1942................	112.5	94.1	1972...............	449.3	262.5
1943................	170.1	141.6	1973...............	469.9	261.7
1944................	232.1	191.7	1974†...............	492.7	271.0
1945................	278.7	227.4	1975†...............	576.6	349.4
1946................	259.1	208.3	1976†...............	653.5	409.5‡

* Gross federal debt is federal government borrowing from the public plus government agencies' borrowing plus debt holdings of the Federal Reserve System; net federal debt is federal government borrowing from the public.

† Beginning July 1974, excludes noninterest-bearing notes issued to the International Monetary Fund, to conform with presentations in the budget documents.

‡ Preliminary.

Sources: Raymond W. Goldsmith, *A Study of Saving in the United States,* vol. 1 (Princeton University Press, 1955), pp. 535, 985; Board of Governors of the Federal Reserve System, *Banking and Monetary Statistics* (FRB, 1943), p. 509; FRB, *Banking and Monetary Statistics, 1941–1970* (FRB, 1976), p. 882; *Economic Report of the President,* January 1976, p. 254; *Treasury Bulletin* (February 1977), pp. 21, 67. Net debt for 1930 and 1933 are averages of June data for the respective year and the following year, from FRB, *Banking and Monetary Statistics* (1943), p. 512.

government has been in existence. Gross federal debt rose from $1 billion in 1915 to $654 billion in 1976 and net federal debt rose to $410 billion during the period. But many other economic measures have risen spectacularly, in particular the volume of output and private debt. Likewise, federal net interest payments have grown immensely over the years, but so has our ability to carry them.

To get some perspective on the growth of federal debt, it is useful to make the comparisons shown in Figures 1 to 3. Figure 1 shows, for five-year intervals from 1900 to 1930 and annually thereafter, the net federal debt and the ratio of the net federal debt to GNP (in current dollars). The debt–GNP ratio was very low up to 1916, rose sharply during World War I, and then declined through the 1920s. In the 1930s it began another rise, which continued through World

Figure 2: Gross Federal and Nonfederal Debt, 1920–1975*

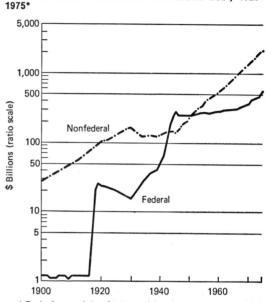

* End-of-year data. State and local government debt is not included in the nonfederal. Because the vertical axes are ratio scale, the steep lines show the rates of growth of federal and private debt.
    Sources: Federal debt, same as table 4; nonfederal debt, 1900 and 1912, Board of Governors of the Federal Reserve System; other nonfederal debt, appendix table A-9, D. J. Ott and A. F. Ott, *Federal Budget Policy*, 3d ed. (Washington: The Brookings Institution, 1977), pp. 160–161.

Figure 1: Net Federal Debt and Debt as a Percentage of Gross National Product, Five-Year Intervals, 1900–30, and Annually, 1931–1976

* Debt as of June 30 of each year.
† Debt as of June 30 of each year; GNP for the calendar year.
    Sources: Debt, 1900–1915, and GNP, 1900–1925, Raymond W. Goldsmith, *A Study of Saving in the United States*, vol. 1 (Princeton University Press, 1955), pp. 535, 985, and Goldsmith and others, *A Study of Saving in the United States*, vol. 3 (Princeton University Press, 1956), p. 427; debt, 1920–39, derived from Board of Governors of the Federal Reserve System, *Banking and Monetary Statistics* (FRB, 1943), pp. 509–10, 512; debt, 1940–66, FRB, *Banking and Monetary Statistics, 1941–1970* (FRB, 1976), pp. 882–83; debt, 1967–76, *Economic Report of the President, January 1977*, p. 275; GNP, 1930–76, U.S. Bureau of Economic Analysis, *The National Income and Product Accounts of the United States, 1929–74: Statistical Tables* (GPO, 1977), and *Survey of Current Business*, vol. 56 (July 1976) and vol. 57 (January 1977) issues.

War II. It has since fallen, and by the 1970s was back almost to the levels that prevailed in the middle 1920s—about 20 percent. In Figure 2 the growth of gross federal debt is compared with the growth of nonfederal debt since 1900. The figure shows clearly that gross federal debt grew faster than nonfederal debt during the periods 1917–19 and 1930–45, but that in the other fifty-seven years of the seventy-six-year period, nonfederal debt grew faster.[10]

Finally, Figure 3 shows net interest paid on the federal debt, both in dollars and as a percentage of GNP. Since 1900, interest paid on the federal debt has not reached 2.0 percent of GNP, a level almost reached just after World War II. The percentage fell to 1.2 in 1953 and hovered between 1.2 and 1.3 until the late 1960s, then rose again, reaching 1.6 percent in 1976. The growth of federal debt, then, though large in absolute terms, appears less awesome when it is related to the growth of output or of private debt.

_____

[10] Because the vertical axes in Figure 2 are calibrated according to a ratio scale, the slopes, or steepness of the lines, show the rates of growth of federal and private debt.

Figure 3: Net Interest Paid on Federal Debt at Five-Year Intervals, 1900–1930, and Annually, 1931–1976

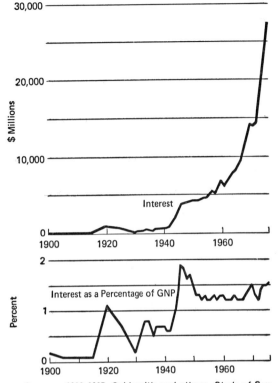

Sources: 1900–1925, Goldsmith and others, *Study of Saving*, vol. 3, pp. 427, 445; other years, U.S. Bureau of Economic Analysis, *National Income and Product Accounts of the United States, 1929–74*, and *Survey of Current Business*, July 1976 and January 1977 issues.

FEDERAL BORROWING AND THE "CROWDING OUT" EFFECT

Since 1901, the federal budget has been in a deficit position for 49 years out of 76. Budget deficits, especially in peacetime, have always been a source of alarm to those who represent the "conservative" view on fiscal matters. Defenders of deficit spending were in the past successful in persuading the nation of the wisdom of compensatory fiscal action: they dismissed as groundless the fear connected with large federal deficits during recessions or weak private demand. However, the relatively large size of the budget deficit for 1976, and of those projected for fiscal years 1977 and 1978, revived some of this fear. The "crowding out" effect of deficit spending is now a part of everyday journalistic language whenever the issue of federal deficit or public borrowing is discussed. What is "crowding out"? Crowding out is a term used to describe the adverse effect of government deficit on private investment.

To understand this issue as well as to gain an insight into the validity of some of the statements on "crowding out" made earlier in the chapter requires first an understanding of the relation between the deficit and the debt—the financing aspect of the federal deficit.

When the federal government runs a deficit it can finance it by one or more of the following means: drawing down Treasury cash balances; selling securities to the Federal Reserve System; selling securities to commercial banks; and selling securities to nonbank investors. Regardless of which of these methods is selected, a federal deficit leads to a dollar-for-dollar increase in the net financial assets of nonbank investors (or households).[11] Although all these methods of financing the debt affect private saving, the method chosen will have a different effect on the economy and thus on the effectiveness of the fiscal action for which the deficit was originally created.

There are two effects to consider: the effect of fiscal action producing the deficit, which is always expansionary; and the effect of the method of financing the deficit, which depends to a large extent on the action taken by the Federal Reserve System. An expansionary fiscal policy—an increase in government expenditures, a cut in taxes, or both—will increase the aggregate level of demand and output through the multiplier effect. However, the monetary aspect of the deficit—the financing method chosen—will also have an effect on the level of output, prices, and aggregate demand. A deficit policy that increases aggregate demand and output stimulates the demand for money balances. If the Federal Reserve System were not to accommodate fiscal actions by increasing the money supply (by buying government securities), the deficit would be financed by selling debt to the nonbanking public, such as insurance companies, other corporations, state and local governments, and individuals, or to commercial banks. Unless the Federal Reserve in-

---

[11] If the deficit is financed by drawing down Treasury cash balances, the public's money holding will increase by the amount of the deficit. Likewise, if it is financed by selling securities to commercial banks, the banks pay for the securities by creating demand deposits for the Treasury—deposits which, when spent by the government, add to the public's holdings of money and so on. For a detailed discussion on financing the federal deficit, see Council of Economic Advisers Staff Memorandum, "Financing a Federal Deficit," in Ronald L. Teigen, ed., *Readings in Money, National Income, and Stabilization Policy*, 4th ed. (Irwin, 1978), Reading 19 on pp. 277–279.

creases bank reserves, interest rates will rise and this will have a restraining effect on private spending, partly offsetting the expansionary effect of the deficit. The recent discussions of the "crowding out" of private spending by fiscal action are discussions of precisely this point. Unless the monetary authority is willing to monetize part of the debt, to add to commercial bank reserves, "crowding out" will occur and private spending will decline, thus offsetting part of the stimulus the deficit is supposed to create.

How serious is crowding out? And what is the impact of additional debt on the economy? The next two sections will attempt to answer these questions, first, in a setting where unemployment prevails, and second, in a full-employment setting.

The Burden of the Debt in an Unemployment Setting

Hostility to the size of the national debt as well as to its continued growth generally arises from the view that the debt will reduce private capital formation and impose a burden on future generations. To decide whether this view is justified, we will first consider a society where there is unemployment and where the government plans to run a deficit to finance additional expenditures or to cut taxes in order to restore output to a full-employment level. The issue then is, does government borrowing to finance a planned deficit create a burden for future generations?

In one sense at least, there is clearly no burden on later generations. A closed society cannot dispose of more goods and services than it currently produces; it cannot borrow tomorrow's output today. In a period of unemployment there is essentially no competition between the government and the private sector for resources. Goods and services acquired by the government at the time of the expenditure do not reduce the output available to consumers or private investors. Deficit financing to restore full employment leaves future generations better off to the extent that private investment is stimulated, inasmuch as in the absence of an expenditure increase or tax cut, the added investment would probably not take place and future generations would have a smaller stock of private capital and lower output. A further gain in future output (and thus a gain to future generations) results from government spending of an investment type—as, for example, for schools, bridges, and roads.

What about the interest payments on the debt

and the possible repayment of the principal that falls to the lot of future generations; are these not a burden? The answer is a qualified no. There is no aggregate burden on future generations that must make interest payments on the debt and perhaps repay the principal, for these are simply *transfers* of income (or wealth) among members of society. There may be "distributional effects" —wealth may be redistributed from taxpayers to bondholders to the extent that these are not the same individuals—but these do not necessarily leave the community in worse circumstances in the aggregate. However, the debt still imposes some burden on future generations because future taxes must be levied to service the debt. To illustrate this point, suppose that an individual exchanges his holdings of a government bond for a private bond with equal yield (discounting risk differential). At the time of the purchase the position of the individual would be the same. But what about future periods? With the public bond, the taxpayer is subjected to an "involuntary" levy in order to finance the interest payments on the debt, while no such levy would exist in the case of the private bond. This is the "real" cost of debt-financed public spending; public projects financed by debt creation do not explicitly yield revenues to meet interest payments. No real cost would exist, however, if it could be shown that the debt-financed expenditure augments private income sufficiently to offset the tax increase needed to service the debt.[12]

What about "crowding out" of private investors? In an unemployment setting, private demand (consumption and investment) is weak and therefore the demand for funds is likely to fall short of the money available for borrowers. Here Okun's comment cited at the beginning of this chapter would hold; when saving outruns investment demand, suppliers of credit are only too happy to accommodate public borrowing. This was the case in 1975 and 1976 when large federal deficits were accommodated without straining the capital market.

In short, to the extent that public borrowings do not displace private needs, deficit financing and increases in the national debt do not impose a burden on future generations. In fact, running deficits to promote full employment leaves future generations better off in increased real output and

[12] See James M. Buchanan and Richard E. Wagner, *Public Debt in a Democratic Society* (American Enterprise Institute for Public Policy Research, 1967).

investment. In this setting at least, intergenerational equity is not violated.[13]

The Burden of the Debt in a Full-Employment Setting

Now consider a society that is always at full employment regardless of what the government does or does not do about spending, taxes, and the like. Assume that the government plans to spend an additional $10 billion. Will it make any

___

[13] Franco Modigliani has come to a somewhat different conclusion on this question. He reasons that under certain conditions a deficit created to boost the economy from a depression or recession can leave future generations in circumstances worse than if no government action had been taken. Suppose recessions or depressions are temporary—that is, that the economy will recover eventually even if no government action is taken. Suppose further that consumers and firms together have a plan of desired capital accumulation. A recession then will reduce the present generation's capital below the desired level, since saving and investment are reduced as income falls. The reduction in capital below the desired level will force the members of the present generation to cut their consumption over their lifetimes (even after full employment is restored) to an extent equal to the loss in capital accumulation during the period of unemployment. In short, they will have to save more to accumulate the capital "lost" during the recession. The higher rate of capital formation after full employment is restored will tend, by the time the recession generation dies out, to build the stock of capital back to the level that could have been expected if there had been no temporary unemployment. On the other hand, if the government acts to combat the recession and creates new debt in doing so, the new debt to some extent will replace the "lost" capital in the net worth of investors. Thus the present generation will not seek to build the capital stock back to the planned level; it will be content with government bonds rather than physical capital. Later generations may thus have less private capital than if the government had not attacked the recession by running a deficit.

Of course, the crux of Modigliani's argument is his assumption that recessions are in fact temporary and that government debt is unproductive. If, however, budget deficits are financed by issuing money, and if asset holders receive a stream of real returns from holding money, or if money is a "factor of production," then even in Modigliani's argument, debt financing need not impose a burden, whether it occurs in a full-employment or unemployment setting. See his article, "Long-Run Implications of Alternative Fiscal Policies and the Burden of the National Debt," *Economic Journal*, vol. 71 (December 1961), pp. 731–55. For additional discussion of the burden of the debt from the point of view stressing the supply of capital, see Peter A. Diamond, "National Debt in a Neoclassical Growth Model," *American Economic Review*, vol. 55 (December 1965), esp. p. 1141.

difference if that expenditure is debt-financed or tax-financed?

Because there is full employment, goods and services acquired by the government must always be paid for by a reduction in the output available to the private sector at the time of the expenditure. So, whether tax-financed or debt-financed, the expenditure is immediate; it cannot possibly be paid for by future generations, and thus there is no burden on them in this sense.

As far as interest payments on the debt and possibly repayment of the principal are concerned, here, too, as in the unemployment setting, some burden will be imposed on future generations. However, while it is true that a closed, full-employment community cannot increase today's output by borrowing tomorrow's, the way in which today's output is used can affect the output of tomorrow, and debt financing has an impact on the use of today's output different from that of tax financing or the creation of money. It is through this impact that debt financing of expenditures may impose a significant burden on future generations.

If the economy is at full employment, then by definition the increase in government spending cannot increase total output. Prices will rise whether the increase in government spending is debt-financed, tax-financed, or financed through money creation.[14] But how is investment affected? Suppose an increase in government spending of $10 billion is debt-financed. Taxes on current private income, and therefore private disposable (after-tax) income, will be unchanged. If it is assumed that private consumption depends only on the level of disposable personal income, private consumption of goods will remain unchanged. Because private consumption outlays will be unaffected (and government expenditures will be increasing), the reduction in the private use of output must come out of private investment. Debt financing of an expenditure will thus result in a fall in private investment by the amount of the increase in government spending.[15]

How does this result compare with the result of tax financing a like amount? In the latter case,

___

[14] An increase in government spending has a larger multiplier effect than an equal increase in taxes. Thus, when taxes are raised to finance government spending, the net effect is expansionary and prices will rise.

[15] Under different assumptions, debt financing need not lead to a fall in private investment by an amount equal to the increase in government spending. To some extent it may reduce consumer spending rather than investment spending.

some part of the tax increase may come out of private personal income. Private consumption will decline as a result of the reduction in disposable personal income, but not by the total amount, since consumers in the aggregate reduce consumption by a fraction of a decrease in disposable personal income. The balance of the impact will fall on private investment. This means that both private consumption and investment will fall, with the total decline in both being just equal to the total increase in government spending. Furthermore, since individuals lack perfect foresight as to future tax policies, financing the deficits through taxation rather than debt issues would not distort individual choices through time; the cost of public expenditures through time cannot be shifted as may be the case when they are financed by issuing debt.

In periods of full employment, the result of money creation is similar to that of tax finance. At high levels of employment, any creation of additional purchasing power must be inflationary and cause the price level to increase. The results are equivalent to a tax on the holders of cash balances. To the extent that real cash balances affect consumption, inflation through money creation will spread the cost of financing the deficit among consumption activities as well as among investment activities.

A comparison of the three methods of financing government deficits during periods of full employment reveals that, although investment falls in both money-financed and tax-financed cases, it falls farther when the government deficit is debt-financed. Here lies the burden on future generations. The burden can be measured in terms of the loss of potential output that will result from the loss of potential private capital. That is, debt financing will reduce private investment more than tax financing the same amount, thereby leaving future generations with less capital equipment for production and restricting them to a lower level of private output than would obtain with tax financing.

A final point to consider is the relative productivity of government spending and private spending. If government expenditures are less productive than, or equally as productive as, private investment, the conclusions about the relative burden still hold. If, however, government investment is more productive, future generations will be better off by the reallocation of capital to the public sector, regardless of whether the expenditure is debt-financed, money-financed, or tax-financed; but they will be relatively less well off

with debt financing than with money creation or tax financing.[16]

In summary, deficit financing and increases in the national debt in a full-employment setting do not necessarily impose an absolute burden on future generations. If government expenditures are more productive than private investment, future generations will be better off with debt-financed expenditures than without such expenditures. However, it is also clear that, in this setting, future generations will benefit relatively more from such expenditures if they are financed by increasing taxes rather than by increasing the federal debt.

Deficits and Other Issues

The mere existence of a budget deficit is not a reliable measure of fiscal policy. A large deficit can result from an anti-inflationary fiscal policy if the government tightens up too much and induces a recession—or if expenditures drop in the private sector and the economy goes into a recession—and federal tax receipts fall as GNP declines. Large deficits occurred in the 1940s during a period of full employment and upward price pressures (which were to some extent suppressed by price and wage controls). On the other hand, during an earlier period, 1931–34, large deficits occurred during a period of severe unemployment and falling prices, and from 1972 to 1976, large deficits occurred with high inflation rates and rising unemployment. Thus there is no real basis for using the actual deficit or surplus to measure

---

[16] Some economists, notably E. J. Mishan, dispute the validity of the argument that a greater burden is imposed on future generations by borrowing than by taxing, even in a full-employment setting. Mishan argues that, since taxes reduce present consumption and borrowing reduces private capital for future generations, if one talks about a burden being imposed on future generations by borrowing, there is an equal obligation to consider the burden imposed on the present generation by taxing. Every decision society undertakes today affects future generations. Thus decisions to debt-finance government expenditures are no more of a burden on future generations than are decisions by individuals to consume rather than to invest. "After all, we could enormously increase provision for the future if we performed heroic feats of austerity during our lifetimes. Are we then not imposing a heavy burden on these future generations to the extent that we eschew these heroic feats of austerity and instead follow the path of our wonted self-indulgence?" "How To Make a Burden of the Public Debt," *Journal of Political Economy,* vol. 71 (December 1963), p. 540.

the inflationary or deflationary impact of federal fiscal action.

It is often implied that inflation is caused by increasing federal outlays, or that private and state and local government outlays are not inflationary but that federal government outlays are. It is said, too, that private or state and local government outlays are productive whereas federal government outlays are unproductive. GNP is said to be an inaccurate measure of a nation's output, because it includes in total output these unproductive government purchases of goods and services.

Such arguments show a faulty understanding of what determines a nation's output, the nature of output, and the causes of inflation or recession. If government purchases of goods and services are totally unproductive, society might just as well discontinue such outlays and use the resources thus freed in the private sector. It could eliminate expenditures on defense, courts, police, highways, and education, and use the resources to produce more cars, electric shavers, houses, and private planes. It should be obvious that federal (as well as state and local) government expenditures *are* productive in the sense that they satisfy certain social needs that are not met by the private market. These social needs are determined by elected representatives, who are generally (and in theory) responsible to the electorate.

It should be clear also that increases in private outlays for consumption and investment can at times be responsible for inflationary pressures, as they were in 1946–48, 1967–69, and 1973. Whenever excessive aggregate demand is at the root of inflation, the important thing is to bring about a reduction in spending—public and private—through the use of fiscal and monetary actions.

The Public Debt and National Bankruptcy

There is a great deal of emotion in people's attitudes toward the public debt. For example, statements are frequently made to the effect that, if the national debt reaches some particular level, the government's credit standing will be impaired and disaster will follow in the form of something casually referred to as "national bankruptcy." While it is difficult to evaluate these statements, it is not a new idea that there is a limit to the size of the national debt that can be carried without disaster. Individuals have long predicted that a debt of one-tenth, one-fifth, or one-half of the amount we now have would result in national

bankruptcy, and they have had to revise the limit upward when it was exceeded and ruin failed to follow.

How much can the federal government borrow? Is there a point beyond which borrowing would have to cease because people would refuse to lend? To answer these questions, one must understand the basis for the credit standing of governments, whether federal, state, or local. Governments have a power not shared by other borrowers; they can impose taxes with which to pay interest on their debt and repay the principal. As long as a government does not abuse its taxing power or extend its credits beyond its capacity to raise taxes, it will have the ability to borrow. It may have to pay high interest charges if its debt becomes large, but it can borrow as long as the public is willing to hold its debt instruments. And this is not all; central governments also have the power to coin and print money. They can always do this, instead of imposing taxes, to meet interest costs on their debts and to transfer resources from the private to the public sector. As a matter of fact, the securities of the U.S. Treasury are looked on by investors as a nearly riskless investment (from the standpoint of possible default on interest payments), despite the enormous increase in the debt in the last half-century.

This does not mean that there is no cause for concern about deficits and the growth of the debt. If the debt is growing because private demand is weak and the government is pursuing a policy of stimulating the economy with tax reductions (or expenditure increases), the deficit is not only harmless but a benefit to the health of the economy. If private spending is strong, however, and prices are rising, low tax rates and a deficit are poor policy indeed. In short, there are good deficits and bad deficits. Good deficits occur when fiscal policy is used to stimulate the economy or to cushion it against economic declines. Bad deficits occur when, in the face of strong private spending, government refuses to raise taxes or reduce expenditures to eliminate inflationary pressures.

The Psychological Effects

It has been held that, even though there may be no danger of burdening future generations, the stimulative effects of increasing the public debt to counteract recessions may be negated or partially offset by public hostility to debt increases. That is, irrational and unwarranted fear of such increases may reduce private spending (particularly investment), thereby offsetting the stimulative effect of the fiscal action producing the deficit. Businessmen may think to themselves, "With such fiscal irresponsibility in the White House, I will not commit my company to new capital outlays."

On the other hand, the announcement of stimulative federal fiscal actions may itself have quite the opposite effect. The stock market's reaction to tax cut suggestions in 1963, 1971, and 1975 and comments in the business press suggest that such positive fiscal action actually encourages business optimism and stimulates investment.

There is no clear answer as to which effect is likely to be dominant. It is hard to single out the effect on businessmen's expectations of any single action of an administration, including the actions of incurring a planned deficit. It is probably true that an administration's overall image has an important psychological influence on business investment decisions, but it is not clear what influence a deficit by itself has or how strong that influence may be.

SUMMARY

From the discussion in this chapter, it is clear that deficits may be economically defensible and even desirable under many conditions. They are undesirable, of course, when the economy is at full employment, when the state of resource allocation is the desired one, and when inflationary pressures exist. If deficits are incurred in an unemployment setting in order to restore full employment, they are all to the good. They tend to increase output and employment and impose no easily identifiable burden on future generations, provided that the use of the idle resources by government is as productive as their use by the private sector. Future interest payments and the repayment of principal are essentially financial transfers involving no aggregate burden. Arguments to the effect that increasing the federal debt will somehow lead to national ruin or bankruptcy have little foundation in fact. And while there may be adverse psychological effects from deficits, there may just as well be salutary ones.

Chapter

5

MONETARY POLICY

Monetary policy has been the subject of a good deal of controversy over the years, and views on its effectiveness have vacillated as circumstances have changed. Before the Federal Reserve System was established in 1913, there was little in the way of machinery by which the federal government could deliberately influence monetary and credit conditions. The money supply was primarily determined by the gold stock, which, in turn, was determined by gold production and the flows of international trade and payments.

In the 1920s fiscal policy was not yet recognized as a means of regulating aggregate demand, and monetary policy was the sole stabilization instrument. Fluctuations in economic activity were mild, and Federal Reserve policy was given considerable credit for the economy's good performance.

The reputation of monetary policy as a stabilization instrument declined drastically during the Great Depression of the 1930s, which ended only when the economy received a massive fiscal stimulus from heavy military spending associated with World War II. The wave of bank failures which culminated in the temporary shutdown of the whole banking system in March 1933 made bankers cautious, even though bank reserves had expanded due to gold inflows from politically unstable Europe. At the same time, borrowers who satisfied the banks' standards of creditworthiness were few and far between. Therefore excess reserves piled up and money and credit did not expand, leading many to conclude that monetary policy was ineffective. However, recent research on the experience in the 1930s indicates that the impotency of monetary policy in that period was somewhat exaggerated. First, it appears that a sharply contractionary monetary policy at the start of the decade was one of the factors responsible for the seriousness of the depression. Moreover, careful statistical studies of the behavior of money suggest that if a more expansionary policy had been followed later on, it might have helped to alleviate the depression.

During World War II and into the early postwar period, the Federal Reserve gave up its normal stabilization function and used all of its powers to assure the Treasury's ability to borrow at low and stable interest rates the huge quantities of funds needed to finance the war effort. But after the war, the Federal Reserve became increasingly restive at the restraints on its freedom to carry out its normal role in the task of economic stabilization. The bond-support policy finally was ended with the famous "Treasury-Federal Reserve Accord" of March 1951.

Since the Accord, monetary policy has been used with increasing vigor. Credit was tightened in late 1952 and early 1953 to check incipient inflation, and a vigorously expansionary monetary policy helped to induce a relatively prompt recovery from the 1953–54 recession. Serious inflationary tendencies appeared in the later stages of the 1954–57 expansion, and monetary policy was tightened from early 1955 onward. The ensuing recession of 1957–58 was sharp but short lived, and a marked easing of monetary policy which reduced interest rates sharply helped induce prompt recovery. However, the expansion that followed, lasting from the spring of 1958 to the spring of 1960, proved somewhat abortive, as the unemployment rate did not decline significantly below 5 percent.

By 1960, international capital movements had become much more sensitive to interest rate differentials among countries than before due to the increased degree of currency convertibility which had developed. Monetary policy therefore could not be used in the recession of 1960–61 as vigorously as in earlier recessionary periods. In the face of a large and worrisome U.S. balance-of-payments deficit, it was felt that a sharp decline in short-term interest rates such as had occurred in 1953–54 or in 1957–58 would induce such a large outflow of interest-sensitive capital as to threaten a serious international financial crisis. Consequently, the Federal Reserve was limited to actions which would not lower U.S. interest rates below their foreign counterparts.

A long period of economic expansion, lasting into 1969, began in early 1961. From 1961 until late 1965, there was little tendency for prices to rise. Fiscal policy played the major role in keeping the expansion going, with an especially important contribution being made by the tax reduction provided by the Revenue Act of 1964. Monetary policy accommodated the expansion with sufficient money and credit growth to meet the needs of expanding activity at interest rates competitive with those abroad.

In late 1965, with the economy near full employment, a sharp rise in defense spending related to the Vietnam conflict unaccompanied by a tax increase generated severe inflationary pressures. Accordingly, beginning at the end of 1965 monetary policy moved sharply toward restriction; and this, together with a temporary suspension of the 7 percent investment tax credit, helped slow the pace of expansion sharply by early 1967. However, the impact of monetary restriction in 1966 fell with special severity on residential construction and created severe strains in financial markets. After the economic slowdown of early 1967, monetary policy again became vigorously expansionary. In the fall of 1967, President Johnson recommended a 10 percent personal and corporate tax surcharge, but it was not enacted by Congress until nearly a year later, and took effect in July 1968. The Federal Reserve tightened monetary policy somewhat as a means of tempering inflationary pressures while the tax proposal was being debated in Congress, relaxed its policy of restraint when the tax bill passed in the expectation that inflationary tendencies would begin to moderate, and then began to move back to a restrictive posture in late 1968 when it appeared that the tax increase by itself might not be sufficient to check inflation.

The restraint imposed by monetary and fiscal policy in 1968–69 eventually took its toll, resulting in a marked decline in real output and an increase in unemployment in 1970, although the price indexes continued to climb. The slowdown in activity was accompanied by a certain amount of turmoil in financial markets, creating additional complications for the monetary authorities. The period was one of innovation and change in some aspects of monetary policy. While credit had been restricted sharply early in 1969, the impact on residential construction was noticeable but was somewhat softened by substantial support from various federal credit agencies to the mortgage market. These new arrangements are reviewed by Warren L. Smith in his paper, "The Role of Government Intermediaries in the Residential Mortgage Market" (reading 26).

In 1971, the economy responded to the stimulative monetary and fiscal policy climate which had characterized 1970 and began to recover from the 1969–70 recession. While both instruments of stabilization policy remained expansionary, the recovery was slow, with unemployment and inflation remaining at high levels. In addition to these difficulties, the country's balance-of-payments position deteriorated badly. On August 15, the President imposed a 90-day wage and price freeze which was to be followed by more flexible controls, in an attempt to break the inflationary mechanism, and also suspended dollar convertibility into gold. Subsequent attempts by trading countries to shore up the fixed-exchange-rate system were futile, and eventually it was abandoned, providing more freedom for stabilization policy to pursue domestic goals. The introduction to Chapter 6 contains a detailed discussion of the problems leading up to the abandonment of fixed exchange rates, and subsequent developments.

The recovery gained speed in 1972, with substantial increases in output and reductions in unemployment and the inflation rate. Both monetary and fiscal policy were quite expansionary, with money stock growth in the 9 percent range and with the federal budget on a full-employment basis moving sharply toward deficit at year's end. But while policy was becoming increasingly expansionary, the economy appeared to be approaching its productive capacity. An extra fillip was added to demand (and directly to upward price level movement) as the dollar was allowed to depreciate on the exchange markets. As a result of these developments, the rate of output growth declined, while price inflation accelerated in spite of the controls; these were subsequently terminatd in April 1974.

The late 1973–74 period witnessed the institution of the OPEC oil embargo as well as a sharp reversal in the stance of policy, and as a consequence the economy moved into its worst recession experience since the 1930s, this time accompanied by a high inflation rate which to an important degree had its roots in the policies pursued in 1972 and 1973. Real output fell during 1974 and the first quarter of 1975; yet the full-employment budget remained essentially balanced (the actual budget moved progressively into deficit due to the operation of the automatic stabilizers). In late March 1975, as the upturn was about to occur, the full-employment budget finally moved strongly into deficit with passage of the Tax Reduction Act. Some further expansionary pressure was provided early in 1977 when a "stimulus package" was enacted including additional personal income tax reduction, increased public service employment, acceleration of public works projects, and other features.

The stance of monetary policy during the recession and recovery has been a matter of some debate, partly because of changes in the Federal Reserve System's policy procedures. In the early 1970s, the System's Open Market Committee had shifted its attention from a fairly narrow range of intermediate targets—chiefly money market variables like free reserves and the federal funds rates—to a broader spectrum of monetary aggregates; and in recent years, target growth rate ranges have been defined each quarter over a one-year time horizon for M_1, M_2, and M_3.[1] A detailed discussion of current procedures and their development is found in Chapter 3. As explained there, the System also sets short-run (current and succeeding month) "tolerance ranges" for the growth of M_1 and M_2, and for the federal funds rate. Actual month-to-month growth rates of these aggregates have been quite erratic, and frequently have moved outside of the tolerance ranges since this practice was begun. As noted below, these frequent changes in monetary growth rates have caused some criticism of the Federal Reserve; but at least to some degree they reflect the fact that the money stock is endogenous and difficult to control from month to month, and responds to decisions by households, banks, and other business firms as well as the wishes of the monetary authority.

Presumably monetary growth rates measured with reference to the longer-run target ranges provide a better guide to the stance of monetary policy than do the erratically-moving short-run growth rates. However, even these longer-run growth rates are something of a puzzle: during much of the 1975–77 recovery period, M_1 grew at a rate which lay near the bottom of or below its target range, suggesting that policy was restrictive; while M_2 grew at a rate lying near the top of or above its range, suggesting that policy was expansionary. The failure of interest rates to rise during the recovery period also suggests monetary ease. However, the monetary base (currency in circulation plus member bank reserve balances), which is much more closely under the control of the Federal Reserve than is M_1 or M_2, grew more slowly after 1973 than it did in the 1972–73 period. Moreover, for some time the Federal Reserve has been lowering the upper and lower limits of the target ranges for the aggregates slowly but consistently. These moves, in the face of our most severe recession since the 1930s, suggest that the Federal Reserve, on the average, was not following an aggressively expansionary policy and apparently reflect the System's tendency to equate responsibility for monetary growth with responsibility for inflation.

Among the expenditure categories which were particularly weak during the recession were some that are usually identified as being especially susceptible to financial stringency: investment in residential housing, plant and equipment investment, and capital expenditures by state and local governments. It was widely believed that monetary policy should have been much more expansionary as a way of stimulating expenditures in these areas, but tight money probably was not the immediate cause of their decline. In spite of the rather slow rate of monetary growth since 1973, and the rapid rise during the recovery in income velocity, short-term interest rates have fallen since mid-1973, on the average, and long-term rates are approximately at their mid-1973 levels. As explained in Ronald L. Teigen's first article in Chapter 1, our knowledge of the macroeconomic system leads us to expect rising velocity to be accompanied by rising interest rates. Velocity has increased even more rapidly than usual during the upswing which began early in 1975, but interest rates have fallen. As yet there has been no convincing explanation why. The evidence suggests that there has been a downward shift in the demand for money, perhaps brought about by struc-

[1] M_1 includes the nonbank public's holdings of coins and paper money, plus checking accounts at commercial banks. M_2 is M_1 plus commercial bank savings and time deposits (except large negotiable certificates of deposit). M_3 is M_2 plus mutual savings bank deposits, savings and loan shares, and credit union shares.

tural changes in the deposit system such as the introduction of business passbook accounts, telephone transfers between savings and checking accounts, and so on.

Much has been learned about monetary policy in the past 25 years or so as a result of the accumulation of experience in using it, together with extensive research and study. Nevertheless, monetary policy continues to be the subject of controversy. In the late 1950s, there was much criticism of Federal Reserve monetary policy—and federal fiscal policy as well—for placing undue emphasis on price stability as a goal of policy when this goal could be achieved only at a high cost in terms of unemployment. This emphasis appears to continue, as mentioned earlier. The Federal Reserve has also been criticized for the frequent and sharp changes that have occurred in monetary policy in the past few years, on the grounds that such a "stop and go" policy, far from helping to stabilize the economy, has actually added to its instability. Others contend that these frequent changes in monetary policy have been necessitated by failure to take needed fiscal policy actions—or, as in the case of the 1968 tax surcharge, by excessive delay in taking such action. Because fiscal policy has not carried its share of the burden of economic stabilization, monetary policy has had to carry an undue share, thereby making necessary frequent monetary policy gyrations. In the shorter run, the frequent accelerations and decelerations in the growth of bank reserves, the money supply, and so on have reflected not only money stock endogeneity but also the Federal Reserve System's continuing concern with the need to accommodate shifts in the demand for liquidity and with orderly financial markets as well as with the steady growth of the monetary aggregates desired by those who oppose discretionary monetary policy and favor the adoption of some kind of "rule."

The first selection in this chapter (reading 23), by Warren L. Smith is concerned with the mechanisms through which monetary policy and fiscal policy affect income, employment, and prices from the point of view of neo-Keynesian analysis. Most of the ideas developed here are extensions of the analysis set forth earlier in this book—notably in the introduction to the first part of Chapter 1 and the papers by Holbrook and Teigen (on monetarism) which appear there. It was shown in these readings that if, as the Classical economists commonly assumed, wages and prices are flexible, an increase in the stock of money will cause an equal proportional increase in prices but will leave the equilibrium interest rate unchanged, and employment and output will remain at their full-employment levels. On the other hand, if money wages are inflexible downward, deficient aggregate demand can cause unemployment, and if interest rates fall to such a low level that opinion is virtually unanimous that they will rise in the near future—as was the case in the Great Depression of the 1930s—the demand for money may become almost infinitely elastic at current interest rates. Under such conditions, monetary policy may lose nearly all of its power to stimulate economic activity, and fiscal policy may have to be relied upon almost entirely to induce a return to high-employment conditions.

Under most circumstances in modern industrial economies, neither the extreme Classical nor the extreme Keynesian conditions are likely to prevail. Wages do not decline readily in response to moderate amounts of unemployment—this rigidity of wages gives monetary policy a significant amount of influence over real income and employment. Indeed, expansion stimulated by monetary policy is normally divided between an increase in employment and real output and an increase in the price level in proportions that depend on the existing volume of unutilized resources; the closer the economy is to full employment, the greater will be the increase in prices and the smaller will be the increase in output for a given expansionary impulse. Moreover, the demand for money is responsive to interest rates but not infinitely elastic, as the ultra-Keynesian position implies. The conditions just described constitute the environment of the neo-Keynesian approach described by Smith in his article, "A Neo-Keynesian View of Monetary Policy," (reading 23) in which both monetary and fiscal policy can affect aggregate demand, and changes in aggregate demand can affect both real output and the price level. The Smith paper is devoted largely to a detailed exposition of the various channels and mechanisms through which both kinds of policy affect output, employment, and so on, and the discussion is carried on with an eye toward the Keynesian-monetarist debate discussed by Teigen in Chapter 1. Smith points out that neo-Keynesians think of monetary policy as working through several different channels; in fact, the channels are the same ones as those seen by the monetarists. It is on the efficacy of fiscal policy that the two sides diverge. Smith examines carefully the effects of pure fiscal policy changes on both flows of income and stocks of wealth, and the further implications of these effects for spending decisions. He concludes that most of the available evidence indicates that fiscal policy is capable of having substantial effects on economic activity.

Up to this point, most of the discussion of stabilization policy has taken place within the framework of a static, deterministic model—that is, one in which the intertemporal aspects of decisions play no role, and in which there are no random elements nor any lack of knowledge concerning the structure of the system. Unfortunately, this is not the framework in which the policy maker operates. He must make decisions concerning targets to be pursued and the amount of policy action needed, even though these decisions must be made in a context of considerable uncertainty about the exact structure of the economic system. In his paper, "The Theory of Monetary Policy under Uncertainty" (reading 24), William Poole examines the implications of the presence of uncertainty for the choice of a monetary policy target. Poole's analysis is, of course, based on a number of simplifying assumptions—he takes income stabilization as the only ultimate policy goal, and assumes that the uncertainty concerns only the intercepts of the behavioral relationships in the structure, and not their slopes. Nonetheless, he demonstrates quite convincingly that the choice of policy targets should be influenced by the relative degree of uncertainty present concerning the structure of different subsectors of the economy, and not merely by opinions or evidence on the sizes of various elasticities in the structure.

Another important operational consideration is the short- and long-run effects of particular policy actions. It is widely agreed that the effects of a monetary impulse on real variables such as income and employment are spread out over time. Therefore an all-out attempt to achieve a desired target for income (for example) in the current period through the use of monetary policy will have repercussions on income and other variables in many following periods, possibly causing more serious instability later on. Furthermore, such an attempt might result in unacceptable effects on financial variables now or later. James L. Pierce discusses these problems in his paper "The Trade-Off between Short- and Long-Term Policy Goals" (reading 25) in this chapter, and illustrates some of them with simulations uisng a large econometric model of the U.S. economy.

The empirical work on the time lag in the functioning of monetary policy is examined more broadly by Michael J. Hamburger in his paper, "The Lag in the Effect of Monetary Policy: A Survey of Recent Literature" (reading 26). The length and dependability of the time lag between a monetary impulse and its effects on economic activity have long been matters of debate; and even the monetarists, who agree that monetary impulses are the dominant ones in this respect, differ sharply over the nature of the lags. Milton Friedman has argued that the monetary policy lags tend to be long and quite variable from one cyclical experience to the next, and his advocacy of a monetary rule is based partly on this undependability of timing. The St. Louis Federal Reserve Bank monetarists believe that the full effects of a monetary impulse occur dependably within a year, while still other monetarists believe that all effects are felt within the same quarter that the impulse occurs. Keynesians tend to take an intermediate position, believing that some effects are felt rapidly but that perhaps two or three years must pass before all the effects will have worked themselves out. These disputes are summarized and the evidence from simulations of several econometric models is presented by Hamburger. As his summary shows, the results are sensitive to the choice of the variable used to represent monetary policy. Monetarists tend to use the money stock to show that monetary policy has powerful effects on income. Nonmonetarists charge that while money may indeed affect GNP, GNP also affects money, and such current-period "feedback" is partly responsible for the measured effects. In other words, the question of money-stock endogeneity discussed by Teigen in his first paper in Chapter 1 (reading 2) is being raised here. As Hamburger notes, critics of monetarist procedures prefer to use some variable more likely to be autonomously determined, like unborrowed member bank reserve holdings, as a proxy for monetary policy.

Both Hamburger and Pierce refer to computer simulations using a large econometric model of the economy, and Hamburger also discusses results generated by "reduced form" models. These simulations provide estimates of the *total effects* on the economy of certain changes in monetary policy, including not only the initial impacts but also the secondary multiplier and accelerator effects. The large econometric model referred to as the FR-MIT model or FRB-MIT model was assembled by two teams of economists, one from the Board of Governors of the Federal Reserve System and the other associated with the Massachusetts Institute of Technology. The reduced form models essentially are the solutions of *IS-LM* systems like Model III in the introduction to Chapter 1 (although somewhat more detailed), and Hamburger's equation 1, for example, could be viewed as the first-differenced version of equation (3.15) on p. 9. The Andersen-Jordan or St. Louis Federal Reserve Bank equation, mentioned by Hamburger as well as by Blinder and Solow in their "Lags and Uncertainties" article in Chapter 4, (reading 18) also is of this type. (Note that Blinder and Solow also have presented simulation results on fiscal policy lags using the FRB-MIT model and some other large econometric models.)

Econometric studies like these do not always take full account of special institutional factors affecting the *availability* of financing for particular kinds of spending, and this may be especially true in the case of residential construction. The paper by Warren L. Smith (reading 27) on government intermediaries in the residential mortgage market discusses the several institutional and behavioral changes which have been made since the late 1960s by federal government agencies involved in this market. These changes are designed to strengthen the ties between the mortgage market and the capital market and to neutralize the role of changes in credit availability working through the usual channels in causing severe cyclical fluctuations in homebuilding. They were made in response particularly to the destructive effects of the "credit crunch" of 1966 on housing construction, as well as to the housing goals set in the Housing and Urban Development Act of 1968. The paper by the Congressional Budget Office entitled "Current Federal Residential Credit Programs" (reading 28) presents a fairly detailed summary of the current activities of several of the federal programs providing support for residential housing discussed by Smith.

In the next paper (reading 29), Milton Friedman presents an analysis of the objectives which, in his judgment, monetary policy can and cannot accomplish. He concludes with a recommendation that efforts to conduct a discretionary monetary policy to counteract fluctuations be abandoned. In his view, our knowledge of the magnitude and the speed of the responses of economic activity to changes in monetary policy is so poor that efforts to conduct a discretionary countercyclical policy are likely to add to instability rather than subtract from it. In place of efforts to carry out a discretionary policy, he proposes that the monetary authorities adopt a "monetary rule"—that is, a publicly stated policy of allowing the supply of money to grow at a steady rate year after year. He does not specify what exact growth rate he would prefer but indicates that a rate between 3 and 5 percent per year would probably be appropriate.[2] In his opinion, the adoption of such a rule would reduce uncertainty and would represent the greatest contribution the monetary authorities could make to economic stability given the present state of knowledge about the working of monetary forces.

Friedman states his opinions vigorously and authoritatively, but the student should be warned that several of the propositions he advances either have little relevance to recent discussions concerning monetary policy or would not be accepted by many other close students of monetary phenomena. As Friedman points out, there can be little doubt that the Federal Reserve would encounter great difficulties if it attempted to "peg" interest rates at very low levels which would create severe inflationary tendencies. But while there may be some political figures who would favor such a policy, it would command almost no support among economists. Some economists would favor the use of interest rates as guides in the conduct of monetary policy, but the interest rate targets would be based on forecasts of future economic conditions and would change frequently as the economic outlook changed. Such an approach would not involve the "pegging" of rates for extended periods of time. There can be little doubt that the Federal Reserve can control interest rates with sufficient precision to make such an approach feasible.

Friedman also believes that there is a so-called natural rate of unemployment and that unemployment can be reduced below this rate in the long run only at the cost of an accelerating inflation rate. The natural rate of unemployment can be achieved in conjunction with stable prices or alternatively with prices rising or falling at a variety of steady rates—that is, in Friedman's view, in the long run the Phillips curve is simply a vertical line drawn at the natural rate of unemployment. The reader will recall that this possibility was discussed in the introduction to Chapter 1 in conjunction with the papers by James Tobin, Thomas M. Humphrey, and Robert M. Solow (readings 6, 7, and 8). The issue

---

[2] It may be noted that Friedman commonly employs the M_2 definition of money, which includes time deposits in commercial banks as well as demand deposits and currency. It is this broader total that he suggests should grow at a rate of 3 to 5 percent per year. This would imply a somewhat slower growth of M_1.

involved here is a very complex one, but Friedman's conclusion is certainly viewed with great skepticism by many students of economic policy.

Another controversial aspect of Friedman's paper is his interpretation of recent monetary policy. He blames the spotty performance of the economy during 1965–68 and the inflationary pressures that developed during that period on an excessively unstable Federal Reserve monetary policy. Many other observers would, however, place the chief blame on the rapid increase in defense spending associated with the escalation of hostilities in Vietnam combined with the excessive delay in the enactment of a needed increase in taxes—that is, on the poor performance of fiscal policy. Indeed, some would contend that the Federal Reserve's adjustments in monetary policy helped significantly to moderate the destabilizing forces generated by sharp fluctuations in the federal budget.

The paper by Lyle E. Gramley (reading 30) presents the case against the adoption of a simple monetary rule of the kind proposed by Friedman and for continued efforts to conduct a discretionary monetary policy. As Gramley points out, it is not proper to conclude that merely because the economy's responses to monetary policy are not fully understood, a rule is necessarily preferable to a discretionary policy conducted on the basis of the best knowledge available. Gramley argued that discretion is better than a rule, and the editor of this volume is disposed to agree with him. But the issue is a complicated one which it is very difficult to settle conclusively, because we cannot replay history to see whether the economy would perform better or worse with a policy different from the one that was actually followed.

The last paper included in the chapter deals with debt management and its relation to monetary policy (reading 31). Debt management is a complex subject. Treasury cash borrowing and refunding operations—as well as the maturity composition of the Federal Reserve's purchases and sales of government securities in the course of its conduct of open market operations—affect the liquidity mix of the public's holdings of financial assets, as well as the maturity structure of interest rates. However, there is little solid evidence concerning the economic effects of such changes. We do not know, for example, how changes in liquidity or in the term structure of interest rates affect business investment decisions Nor do we even have clear scientific knowledge concerning the effects of debt management operations on the rate structure itself.

Given the unsatisfactory state of knowledge, it is not surprising that there are seriously conflicting views concerning debt management policy. A number of different possible approaches to policy are sketched out in the article by William D. Nordhaus and Henry C. Wallich. As the authors state, no generally accepted view on how the debt should be managed has emerged in the period since World War II. It is generally felt that debt management is a much less important matter for economic stabilization than either monetary or fiscal policy, and there are probably many alternative ways of managing the federal debt that are entirely consistent with effective use of the other policy instruments.

23. A NEO-KEYNESIAN VIEW OF MONETARY POLICY*

Warren L. Smith

Those of us who take an essentially Keynesian view in macroeconomics are often accused, somewhat unjustly, I believe, of minimizing the importance of monetary forces. That contention was probably true 20 years ago for a variety of historical and institutional reasons. But much water has passed over the dam since that time, and I believe it would now be difficult to find an example of the popular stereotype of the Keynesian economist who thinks fiscal policy is all-important and monetary policy is of no consequence. After all, in Keynesian analysis the power of monetary policy depends on the values of certain parameters, and if one is open-minded, he must be prepared to alter his views as empirical evidence accumulates. In some respects, this process has already proceeded quite far—some of the simulations performed with the FRB-MIT model, which is decidedly Keynesian in spirit, show monetary policy having very powerful effects indeed, albeit operating with somewhat disconcerting lags.

Thus, there is nothing inherent in the Keynesian view of the world that commits its adherents to the belief that monetary policy is weak. What is, it seems to me, distinctive about Keynesianism is the view that fiscal policy is capable of exerting very significant independent effects—that there are, broadly speaking, two instruments of stabilization policy, fiscal policy and monetary policy, and that the mix of the two is important. Indeed, I suppose most Keynesians would assign primacy to fiscal policy, although even this need not inevitably be the case. But in a certain fundamental sense, I believe the issue separating the Keynesians and the so-called Monetarist School relates more to fiscal than to monetary policy, since some Monetarists seem to deny that fiscal policy is capable of exerting any significant independent effects. In addition, the neo-Keynesian view seems to differ significantly from that of the Monetarists with respect to the role played by the stock of money in the process by which monetary policy affects the economy.

* From Federal Reserve Bank of Boston, *Controlling Monetary Aggregates*, Proceedings of the Monetary Conference held on Nantucket Island, June 8–10, 1969 (Boston, 1969), pp. 105–26. Reprinted by permission of the Federal Reserve Bank of Boston. The late Warren L. Smith was Professor of Economics, University of Michigan.

In this paper, I shall attempt to sketch what I would describe as a neo-Keynesian view of the process by which monetary and fiscal policy produce their effects on the economy and to evaluate some aspects of the recent controversy regarding stabilization policy in the context of this view. I shall then advance some suggestions concerning the conduct of monetary policy.

I. THE TRANSMISSION MECHANISM OF MONETARY POLICY

There appear to be several elements involved in the mechanism by which the effects of changes in monetary policy are transmitted to income, employment, and prices.

Portfolio Adjustments

The major advance in monetary theory in recent years has been the development of a systematic theory of portfolio adjustments involving financial and physical assets. This theory of portfolio adjustments fits very comfortably within a Keynesian framework and indeed greatly enriches Keynesian analysis and increases its explanatory power. The *General Theory*, itself, embodied a rudimentary theory of portfolio adjustments: the way in which the public divided its financial wealth between bonds and speculative cash balances depended on "the" rate of interest. The interest rate then affected investment expenditure, but Keynes failed to incorporate the stock of real capital into his analysis and relate it to the flow of investment spending. Indeed, many of the undoubted shortcomings of the *General Theory* stem from the failure to take account of capital accumulation.

The way in which monetary policy induces portfolio adjustments which will, in due course, affect income and employment may be described briefly as follows: A purchase of, say, Treasury bills by the Federal Reserve will directly lower the yield on bills and, by a process of arbitrage involving a chain of portfolio substitutions, will exert downward pressure on interest rates on financial assets generally. Moreover—and more important—the expansion of bank reserves will enable the banking system to expand its assets. If the discount rate is unchanged, the banks can be expected to use some portion of the addition to their reserves to strengthen their free reserve position by repaying borrowings at the Federal Reserve and perhaps by adding to their excess reserves. But the bulk of the addition to reserves will ordinarily be used to make loan accommodation available on more favorable terms, and to buy securities, thereby exerting a further downward effect on security yields.

With the expected yield on a unit of real capital initially unchanged, the decline in the yields on financial assets, and on the more favorable terms on which new debt can be issued, the balance sheets of households and businesses will be thrown out of equilibrium. The adjustment toward a new equilibrium will take the form of a sale of existing financial assets and the issuance of new debt to acquire real capital and claims thereto. This will raise the price of existing units of real capital—or equity claims against these units—relative to the (initially unchanged) cost of producing new units, thereby opening up a gap between desired and actual stocks of capital, a gap that will gradually be closed by the production of new capital goods. This stock adjustment approach is readily applicable, with some variations to suit the circumstances, to the demands for a wide variety of both business and consumer capital—including plant and equipment, inventories, residential construction, and consumer durable goods.

Wealth Effects

Since monetary policy operates entirely through voluntary transactions involving swaps of one financial asset for another, it does not add to wealth by creating assets to which there are no corresponding liabilities. Nevertheless, monetary policy does have wealth effects, which may be of considerable importance. An expansionary monetary policy lowers the capitalization rates employed in valuing expected income streams, thereby raising the market value of outstanding bonds as well as real wealth and equity claims thereto. In part, this strengthens the impact on economic activity of the portfolio adjustments, already referred to, by increasing the size of the net portfolios available for allocation. In addition, the increase in household wealth may significantly stimulate consumption. Indeed, in a recent version of the FRB-MIT model, the effect on consumption resulting from the induced change in the value of common stock equities held by households accounts for 35 to 45 percent of the initial impact of monetary policy in some simulations.

Credit Availability Effects

The portfolio and wealth effects appear to constitute the basic channels through which monetary policy has its initial impact on economic activity. In addition, however, the institutional arrangements for providing financing to certain sectors of the economy may be such as to give monetary policy a special leverage over the availability of credit to these sectors, thereby affecting their ability to spend. It is perhaps most illuminating to discuss changes in credit availability in the context of a restrictive monetary policy.

No doubt changes in credit availability affect many categories of expenditures to some degree. But the sector in which they are most clearly of major importance is homebuilding. Even in the absence of the rather unique institutional arrangements for its financing, housing demand might be significantly affected by monetary policy as changes in mortgage interest rates altered the desired housing stock. But as postwar experience has repeatedly shown, most dramatically in the "credit crunch" of 1966, changes in mortgage credit availability may greatly strengthen the impact of restrictive monetary policy on homebuilding and cause the effects to occur much more rapidly than the stock-adjustment mechanism would imply. There are three different ways in which mortagage credit availability may be affected by a restrictive monetary policy.

First, commercial banks may raise interest rates on consumer-type time deposits to attract funds to meet the demands of their customers. If savings and loan associations do not raise the rates paid to their depositors or raise them less than the banks raise their rates, households may rechannel their saving flows away from the savings and loan associations and toward the banks —or may even withdraw existing savings from savings and loan associations and shift them to banks. Even if, as has recently been the case, the Regulation Q ceilings are used to prevent the banks from attracting household saving away from savings and loan associations, a rise in short- and intermediate-term open-market interest rates may set in motion a process of "disintermediation," with savers channelling their funds away from fixed-value redeemable claims generally and directly into the securities markets. Either of these processes which cut down the flows of funds to savings and loan associations can have, of course, a powerful effect on housing activity. With frozen portfolios of older mortgages made at lower interest rates than currently prevail, these institutions may find it difficult to pay substantially higher interest rates to attract or hold funds even if the Home Loan Bank Board will allow them to.

Second, when commercial banks feel the effects of credit restraint, they normally reduce their mortgage lending in order to be able to accommodate the needs of their business borrowers.

Third, as interest rates rise, yields on corporate bonds typically rise relative to mortgage interest rates, and some institutional investors, such as life insurance companies, shift the composition of their investment flows away from mortgages and toward corporate bonds, which, in any case, have investment properties which make them more attractive than mortgages at equivalent yields. This tendency may be exacerbated by unrealistically low interest rate ceilings on FHA and VA mortgages and by State usury laws applicable to conventional mortgages.

The way in which mortgage credit availability impinges on homebuilding has changed with the passage of time. In the 1950s, when FHA and VA financing was more important than it has been recently and when the FHA and VA interest rate ceilings were more rigid than they are now, restrictive monetary policy affected housing mainly by diverting the flows of funds coming from investors having diversified portfolios away from mortgages and toward corporate securities. That is, the third effect listed above was the most important. In 1966, when homebuilding was drastically curtailed by monetary restraint, all of the effects were operating, but the first—the drain of funds away from savings and loan associations—was by far the most important. In 1968 and 1969, interest rates rose sufficiently to arouse concern about a repetition of the 1966 experience. But while housing seems to feel the effects of tight money, it proved to be much less vulnerable than was generally expected. There are several reasons for this, but the one most worthy of mention is the adoption by the Federal Reserve and the various Federal housing agencies of a number of measures designed to cushion or offset the effects of high interest rates on housing activity.

Secondary Effects

Working through portfolio effects, wealth effects, and credit availability effects, the initial impacts of monetary policy will generate additional income, and this will further increase the demand for consumer nondurable goods and services. It will also expand the demand for the services of durable goods, thereby giving a further boost to the desired stocks of these goods.

Thus, the familiar magnification of demand through multiplier and accelerator effects comes into play. It is often overlooked that the sharp reduction in the multiplier since the 1930s as a result of the greatly increased income-sensitivity of the tax-transfer system has presumably had important effects on the working of monetary as well as fiscal policy. Indeed, I would judge this increase in "built-in stability" through the fiscal system to be a major factor making monetary policy less potent today than in earlier times.

A further chain of secondary effects is set in motion as the rise in income increases demands for demand deposits and currency for transactions purposes, thereby reversing the initial decline in interest rates. This induced rise in interest rates will exert a dampening effect on the expansion by a partial reversal of the forces that initially triggered the rise in income. Whether or not this secondary effect will carry interest rates all the way back to their initial level (or higher) is an open question, concerning which I shall have some comments later on in this paper.

Effects on Real Output versus Prices

I think almost all economists of a Keynesian persuasion would accept the proposition that the way in which the effect of an increase in demand is divided between output response and price-level response depends on the way it impinges on productive capacity. Thus, expansion caused by monetary policy is generally no more or no less inflationary than expansion caused by fiscal policy (or, for that matter, by an autonomous increase in private demand). This statement needs to be qualified in a couple of minor respects. First, monetary expansion might be less inflationary than an equivalent amount of fiscal expansion over the longer run if it resulted in more investment, thereby causing labor productivity to increase more rapidly. Second, the impacts of monetary policy are distributed among sectors in a different way from those of fiscal policy; and, with less than perfect mobility of resources, the inflationary effect might depend to some degree on this distribution.

II. SOME CONTROVERSIAL ISSUES

I would now like to discuss several of the issues that seem to be at the heart of the recent controversy regarding monetary and fiscal policy.

The Effectiveness of Fiscal Policy

For the purpose of isolating the effects of fiscal policy from those of monetary policy, I believe a "pure" fiscal policy action should be defined as a change in government expenditures or a change in tax rates without any accompanying change in the instruments of monetary policy. Under our present institutional set-up, the instruments of monetary policy are open-market operations, changes in reserve requirements, and changes in the Federal Reserve discount rate. Open-market operations may be viewed as governing unborrowed reserves plus currency, with defensive operations offsetting undesired changes in this total that would result from erratic variations in float, gold stock, etc.

An increase in government purchases of goods and services, with tax rates constant, would affect the economy by three different routes. First, there would be a direct expansionary *income effect* resulting from the purchase of output by the government. Second, there would be an expansionary *wealth effect* as the private sector, experiencing an increment to its wealth entirely in the form of net claims against the government, increased its demand for real capital in an effort to diversify its portfolios.[1] These income and wealth effects would set off a multiplier-accelerator process of economic expansion. This expansion, in turn, would activate a partially offsetting monetary effect as the rise in income increased the demand for money. If the dial settings of the monetary instruments remained unchanged, this would drive up interest rates. The rise in interest rates would cause some reductions in those types of expenditures that were sensitive to interest rates through portfolio, wealth, and availability effects.

The wealth effect of fiscal policy may be quite powerful, particularly because it is cumulative— that is, it continues to operate until the budget has been brought back into balance, thereby shutting off the increase in net claims against the government. But, unfortunately, no effort that I know of has been made to incorporate it in an empirical model; consequently there is no way to formulate even a crude estimate of this importance.

If we neglect the wealth effect simply because we do not know how much weight to give it, we are left with the income effect and the offsetting monetary effect. The monetary effect will be greater (*a*) the greater the proportion of expenditures in GNP that are affected by interest

rates, (*b*) the greater (in absolute value) is the average interest elasticity of these expenditures, (*c*) the greater is the income elasticity of demand for money, (*d*) the smaller (in absolute value) is the interest elasticity of demand for money and (*e*) the smaller is the interest elasticity of the supply of money.[2]

Only if the interest elasticities of both the demand for and supply of money are zero will the monetary effect completely cancel out the income effect.[3] That is, there will be some leeway for fiscal policy to increase income if a rise in interest rates either induces economization in the use of demand deposits and currency or causes the supply of such monetary assets to expand (for example, by inducing banks to increase their borrowings at the Federal Reserve). Since the empirical evidence is overwhelming that both money demand and money supply possess some degree of interest elasticity, it seems clear that fiscal policy is capable of exerting an independent effect on income. This conclusion is heavily supported by evidence derived from large structural models of the U.S. economy. For example, while there is no unique multiplier for fiscal policy in the FRB-MIT model, a number of simulations with that model show fiscal policy to have very

---

[2] It is possible to derive a more elaborate version of the static Keynesian multiplier incorporating the monetary effect. The following is such a multiplier equation.

$$\frac{dY}{dG} = \frac{1}{1 - e + \dfrac{I}{Y}\dfrac{\eta_{Ir}\eta_{LY}}{\eta_{Lr} - \eta_{Mr}}}$$

Here Y is GNP; G is government purchases; e is the marginal propensity to spend out of GNP; I/Y is the proportion of GNP that is sensitive to interest rates; η_{Ir} (<0) is the average interest elasticity of interest-sensitive expenditures; η_{Lr} (<0) is the interest elasticity of demand for money; η_{Mr} (>0) is the interest elasticity of supply of money; and η_{LY} (>0) is the income elasticity of demand for money. The usual simple Keynesian multiplier without allowance for monetary effect is $1/(1-e)$. The monetary effect is incorporated in the third term (taking the form of a fraction) in the denominator of the equation above. Since this term is positive, its presence reduces the size of the multiplier. The statement in the text above regarding the factors determining the size of the monetary effect is based on this expression.

[3] In this case, the supply of money may be regarded as exogenously determined. If the demand for money depends only on income, income will have to change sufficiently to eliminate any discrepancies that arise between the demand for and supply of money. Thus, money controls income, and fiscal policy is incapable of affecting it. The reader will note that if both η_{Mr} and η_{Lr} are zero, the multiplier for fiscal policy given in footnote 2 above becomes zero.

---

[1] For an extensive theoretical treatment of the wealth effect, see James Tobin, "An Essay on the Principles of Debt Management," in *Fiscal and Debt Management Policies* (Englewood Cliffs, N.J.: Prentice-Hall, Inc., 1963), pp. 142–218.

substantial independent effects on economic activity.

It is often pointed out, especially by those who emphasize the role of money in the economy, that the effect produced by a stimulative fiscal action is dependent on the way in which the resulting deficit is financed. This is in a sense true, but this way of putting it is somewhat misleading. For example, it is sometimes stated that, in order to achieve the full Keynesian multiplier effect, the entire deficit must be financed by creating money—some statements even say high-powered money. What is necessary to achieve this result is to create enough money to satisfy the demand for money at the new higher level of income and the initial level of interest rates.

Ordinarily, the required increase in the supply of money will be only a fraction of the deficit, and the required increase in high-powered money will be an even smaller fraction. Moreover, there is a serious stock-flow problem. When income reaches its new equilibrium in a stable economy, the increased deficit (a flow) will be financed out of the excess of saving over investment generated by the rise in income. Additional demand deposits and currency are needed to meet the increased transaction demand at the higher income level, but this requires only a single increase in the money stock. In reality, there may be further complexities that require a modification of this principle—for example, if the demand for money depends on wealth as well as income or if the price level is determined by a Phillips Curve mechanism so that prices are not merely higher but are increasing more rapidly at higher levels of income.

Nevertheless, the principle is, I believe, basically correct. Rather than saying that the multiplier depends on how the deficit is financed, I think it is more accurate to say that it depends on the kind of monetary policy that accompanies the fiscal action. If monetary policy is such as to hold interest rates approximately constant, something analogous to the full Keynesian multiplier (with no monetary feedback) will be realized; if it allows interest rates to rise, the multiplier will be somewhat smaller; if it causes interest rates to fall, the multiplier will be somewhat greater.[4]

[4] If fiscal policy has a wealth effect working through changes in the public's holdings of net claims against the government, it seems quite likely that the magnitude of this effect will depend on the form taken by the change in net claims. For example, a change in public holdings of short-term debt may have a larger effect on aggregate demand than an equal change in holdings of long-term debt. To the

The Role of Money

Although I have used the term "money" in my discussion above, I am not sure the term is a very useful or meaningful one. Money (in the sense of means of payment) has two components, demand deposits and currency. Those two components are not, however, perfect substitutes—they are held, by and large, by different kinds of spending units; demand for them responds in different ways to different stimuli; and, because they are subject to markedly different reserve requirements, shifts between them alter the total amount of credit that can be supplied by the financial system. They are best regarded as two different financial assets and treated as such.

Moreover, there is no apparent reason why "money"—whether in the form of currency or demand deposits—is more or less important than any of the myriad other financial assets that exist. It is now generally agreed that the demands for demand deposits and currency depend on the yields available on alternative assets and on income or related measures (and possibly, but by no means certainly, on wealth). Thus, the quantities of currency and demand deposits held by the public are generally agreed to be endogenous variables determined in a general equilibrium setting along with the prices and quantities of other financial and real assets.

Nor is there any appreciable evidence that money—whether in the form of demand deposits or currency—affects peoples' spending on goods and services directly. Such empirical evidence as there is suggests that people change their expenditures on goods and services because (a) their income changes; (b) their wealth changes; (c) their portfolios are thrown out of equilibrium by changes in relative yields on real and financial assets by actions taken by the monetary or fiscal authorities; (d) credit availability changes for institutional reasons altering in one direction or the other their ability to finance expenditures they want to make; or (e) their propensities to spend or their preferences for different kinds

extent that this is the case, debt management policies which change the maturity composition of the public's holdings of government debt may have important economic effects. But there is no reason to focus special attention on the composition of increments to the debt resulting from deficits, since the increment to the debt in any year is only a tiny fraction of the total debt to be managed. In any case, as indicated earlier, we are entirely neglecting the wealth effect because in the present state of knowledge there is no way of forming a judgment concerning its importance.

of assets change for essentially exogenous reasons, such as changes in tastes, changes in technology, and so on. That changes in the stock of money per se would affect spending seems to me highly improbable.

Of course, if changes in stocks of demand deposits and currency—or the combination of the two—were tightly linked to those changes in yields, in wealth, and in credit availability through which monetary policy operates, changes in the stocks of these monetary assets might be highly useful measures of the thrust of policy even though they played no part in the causal nexus. But this, too, I think is unlikely. In a highly sophisticated financial system such as ours, in which new financial instruments and practices are constantly being introduced, it seems highly improbable that the demands for monetary assets are simple and stable functions of a few unchanging variables.

The many empirical studies of the demand for money that have been made in recent years have generally proved incapable of differentiating among alternative hypotheses. Consequently, one is free to choose among a variety of possible theories of the demand for money. The one that appeals to me is the hypothesis that money (i.e., demand deposits and currency) is dominated by time deposits and very short-dated securities, with the result that it is not a significant portion of permanent portfolios. This leaves the demand for monetary assets as an interest-elastic transactions demand along the lines postulated by Baumol and by Tobin.[5]

Such an explanation, however, makes sense only for relatively large business firms and wealthy individuals. It does not seem applicable to smaller units. Among such units, I suspect that the general rise in interest rates that has been going on for the past two decades has pushed these rates successively above the thresholds of awareness of different groups of people, causing them to abandon their careless habit of foregoing income by holding excessive cash balances. If I am right, this behavior is probably not readily reversible if interest rates should fall. It seems to me that there is still a substantial element of mystery about the demand for monetary assets—mystery that will probably be resolved, if at all, only on the basis of extensive study of the behavior of the cash-holdings of micro-units.

Relationship between Changes in Money and Changes in Income

None of the above should be taken to mean that there is no relation between changes in demand deposits and currency and changes in income. Indeed, I believe there are three such relationships, which are very difficult to disentangle.

First, an expansionary monetary policy that stimulated increased spending and income through portfolio effects, wealth effects, and credit availability effects would bring in its wake an increase in supplies of demand deposits and currency. This would be a sideshow rather than the main event, but it would nevertheless occur. But the size of the increase associated with a given stimulus might vary considerably from one situation to another.

Second, a rise in income caused by fiscal policy or by an autonomous shift of private demand, with the monetary dials unchanged, would react back on the money supply in three different ways.[6] (1) The rise in interest rates caused by the rise in income would cause the banks to increase their borrowings from the Federal Reserve and perhaps to economize on excess reserves. (2) The rise in market interest rates would cause investors to shift funds from time deposits and similar claims into securities if, as is likely, the interest rates on these claims did not rise fully in pace with market rates. This would cause the quantity of demand deposits to increase as investors withdrew funds from time accounts and paid them over to sellers of securities for deposit in demand accounts. (3) If banks and related institutions raised rates on time-deposit type claims, some holders of noninterest-bearing demand deposits would be included to shift funds to time accounts. To the extent that issuers of these claims held cash reserves against them, the amount of reserves available to support demand deposits would be reduced, requiring a contraction in these deposits. Effects (1) and (2) would cause the money supply to increase, while effect (3) would cause it to fall. It seems likely that (1) and (2) would outweigh (3), leading to an increase in the supply of monetary assets.

---

[5] See W. J. Baumol, "The Transactions Demand for Cash: An Inventory Theoretic Approach," *Quarterly Journal of Economics*, 66, November 1952, pp. 545–56; James Tobin, "The Interest Elasticity of the Transactions Demand for Cash," *Review of Economics and Statistics*, 38, August 1956, pp. 241–47.

[6] This discussion is based on an analysis developed in W. L. Smith, "Time Deposits, Free Reserves, and Monetary Policy," in Giulio Pontecorvo, R. P. Shay, and A. G. Hart, eds., *Issues in Banking and Monetary Analysis* (New York: Holt, Rinehart and Winston, Inc., 1967), pp. 79–113.

The probability of this outcome would be increased if the Federal Reserve was laggard in adjusting Regulation Q ceilings. Indeed, a rigid Regulation Q ceiling would completely immobilize effect (3) while maximizing the size of effect (2).

Third, under the rubric of "meeting the needs of trade" or "leaning against the wind," the Federal Reserve has, at times, adjusted the supply of reserves to accommodate, or partially accommodate, changes in the demand for money brought about by changes in income, thereby creating a third chain of causation running from income to money supply.

With perhaps three relations between money and income present at the same time—one running from money to income and two running from income to money—it is likely to be almost impossible to tell what is going on by direct observation. And, as Tobin has shown, in such a complex dynamic situation, it is almost impossible to infer anything conclusive about causation by studying the lags.[7]

Does Easy Money Cause Interest Rates to Rise?

One of the supposedly startling propositions that has been advanced recently is the notion that an easing of monetary policy—commonly measured in terms of the rate of increase in the money stock—will cause interest rates to rise and, conversely, that a tightening of monetary policy will cause interest rates to fall. To be sure, if the rate of growth of the money stock is accelerated, interest rates will decline at first. But before long, money income will begin to grow so rapidly that the resulting increase in the demand for money will, it is contended, pull interest rates back up above the level from which they originally started.

In the first place, this possibility has long been recognized in Keynesian economics. In a static Keynesian model it is possible for the IS curve to have a positive slope, with stability conditions requiring only that this slope be less than that of the LM curve. This could happen, for example, if income had a strong effect on investment.[8] In

such a situation, a shift to the right of the LM curve, which might be caused by an increase in the money stock, would cause the equilibrium interest rate to rise. A more realistic possibility is that the economy contains endogenous cycle-generators of the accelerator or stock-adjustment type, which cause income to respond so vigorously to a stimulative monetary policy that interest rates rise above their original level at an ensuing cyclical peak.

There is another chain of causation, working through the effects of inflation on nominal interest rates, which might cause a decline in real interest rates to be associated with a rise in nominal interest rates. This possibility has generally been neglected by Keynesians, but it is in no way inconsistent with Keynesian analysis. An expansionary monetary policy, which lowers nominal interest rates (and real interest rates) initially, will push the economy up the Phillips Curve, thus causing prices to rise more rapidly. As the increase in the actual rate of inflation generates a rise in the anticipated future rate of inflation, an inflation premium may get built into interest rates, causing nominal interest rates to rise. It seems possible that nominal interest rates could be pushed above their original level even though real interest rates remain below this level. This outcome would be more likely (a) the greater the expansionary effect of a given fall in the real rate of interest on real income, (b) the greater the decline in unemployment caused by a given increase in real income, (c) the greater the increase in the rate of inflation caused by a given decline in unemployment, and (d) the more sensitive the response of the anticipated rate of inflation to a change in the actual rate of inflation.[9] The prob-

---

be less than one plus a term measuring the size of the monetary feedback. (Even if the two propensities totaled less than unity, the IS curve could slope upward if a rise in interest rates caused total spending to rise. But this could occur only on the remote chance that the income effect dominated the substitution effect in saving behavior so powerfully that a rise in interest rates caused consumption to increase by more than it caused investment to decline.)

[9] Beginning with the equation $r = r' + p_e$, which expresses the relation between the nominal interest rate (r), the real interest rate (r') and the anticipated rate of inflation (p_e), the following expression can be rather easily derived.

$$\frac{dr}{dr'} = 1 + m \frac{dI}{dr'} \frac{du}{dY} \frac{dp}{du} \frac{dp_e}{dp}$$

Here m is the multiplier; dI/dr' is the response of interest-sensitive expenditures to a change in the real rate of interest; du/dY is the response of the unemployment rate to a change in real GNP; dp/du is the response of the rate of inflation to a change in the

---

[7] James Tobin, "Money and Income: Post Hoc Ergo Propter Hoc?" (mimeographed); also W. C. Brainard and James Tobin, "Pitfalls in Financial Model Building," *American Economic Review*, 58, May 1968, pp. 99–122.

[8] The actual condition required is that the sum of the marginal propensities to consume and invest must exceed one, but (as a condition for stability)

ability that nominal interest rates would be pushed above their initial level by this mechanism is very difficult to evaluate, however, primarily because we know very little about the extent to which, and the speed with which, an increase in the actual rate of inflation gets translated into an increase in the anticipated rate of inflation.

Thus, the notion that an expansionary monetary policy would ultimately cause nominal interest rates to rise above their initial level is in no way inconsistent with Keynesian views. Whether such a phenomenon actually occurs is a different matter. With fiscal policy changing and with the strength of private demand changing, it is not safe to conclude that, because an easing of monetary policy was followed at some later time by a rise of interest rates above their initial level, the easing of monetary policy *caused* the rise in interest rates. The best evidence I have seen is from simulations with the FRB-MIT model which show that an injection of bank reserves causes interest rates to fall sharply at first and then rise gradually but only part of the way back to their original level. But, of course, simulations starting from a different initial position might show different results. In all probability, the phenomenon in question occurs under some conditions but not under others.

III. SUGGESTIONS REGARDING POLICY

At the very beginning of this discussion of the conduct of monetary policy, let me make clear that I am not talking about the issue of rules versus discretion. That is a different subject, which I will discuss briefly at the conclusion of my paper. Assuming that the Federal Reserve will continue to conduct a discretionary policy, let us consider what is the best way to proceed with that task.

It seems to me that much of the recent literature on monetary policy has been obsessed with a search for a magic touchstone—some measure of the impact of monetary forces that can be used as the sole guide in the conduct of policy. Unfortunately, I don't believe there is such a

touchstone—the world is too complicated and we know too little about it for that. There is a second related obsession with the problem of characterizing monetary policy. Is it "tight" or "easy"? Is it "tighter" or "easier" today than it was, say, six months ago?

The first of these questions is clearly a matter of judgment and opinion. The second, comparative form of the question sounds more capable of a scientific answer, but in fact I think it is equally unanswerable. Does it mean, "Is monetary policy contributing more to aggregate demand today than it was six months ago?" If it does mean that—and I can think of no other interpretation—I wouldn't have the faintest idea how to go about answering it. The problem facing the Federal Reserve, however, is not how to characterize monetary policy but how to carry it out, and this puts things in a somewhat different light.

Since monetary policy affects economic activity with substantial lags, policy must clearly be based on forecasts of future economic conditions. While our knowledge has improved considerably, we still cannot be very sure about the lags, which undoubtedly depend upon underlying conditions. Moreover, the lags vary from sector to sector. It seems quite clear that monetary policy can affect homebuilding quite rapidly, at least under some conditions, if the dials of policy are adjusted in the right way. The lags in the effects on the other sectors appear to be considerably longer. Forecasting is also a difficult task, but there is no way to escape the need for it. Not the least of the difficulties of monetary policy, as has been demonstrated several times in the last three years or so, is the forecasting of fiscal policy.

While the ultimate goals of policy are high employment, price stability, the rate of growth of output, and so on, these cannot be used as immediate guides to policy, because it takes so long for policy measures to affect them. The authorities must choose as guides to policy some more immediate and more specifically monetary variables that appear to be related to the goals they are trying to achieve.

There are a number of monetary aggregates that the Federal Reserve can control with varying degrees of precision if it chooses to do so. It can obviously control its portfolio of securities exactly, and it can control unborrowed reserves plus currency outside member banks quite closely by employing defensive open-market operations to offset changes in uncontrollable factors affecting reserves, such as float, gold stock, Treasury deposits at Federal Reserve banks, etc. It can

unemployment rate (i.e., the slope of the Phillips Curve); and dp_e/dp is the response of the anticipated rate of inflation to a change in the actual rate of inflation. Since three of the components of the second term on the right-hand side of the equation (dI/dr', du/dY, and dp/du) take on negative values, the second term as a whole is negative. Whether a fall in the real rate of interest will cause the nominal rate of interest to rise or fall depends on whether the second term on the right is larger or smaller than unity.

probably control total reserves plus currency (the monetary base) fairly accurately either by using open-market operations to offset changes in member bank borrowing or by changing the administration of discount policy to reduce the fluctuations in borrowing. The stock of demand deposits and currency would be more difficult to control, but I suspect that its average value over a quarter's time could be controlled fairly satisfactorily.

Alternatively, policy could be directed at regulating interest rates, although some interest rates would be easier to control than others. The Treasury bill rate could be controlled with any desired degree of accuracy under present operating procedures, because the Federal Reserve deals directly in the Treasury bill market. By a shift in its operating procedures, the Federal Reserve could control the yield on some other maturity of Federal debt. I believe it could, instead, maintain fairly close control of a variety of alternative interest rates on private debt—such as the Aaa corporate bond yield—although it would have to influence such rates indirectly unless it were to deal in private debt.

The basic issue of monetary policy is: Should the Federal Reserve focus primarily on controlling some monetary aggregate or should it focus on controlling interest rates? I believe there is a very strong *prima facie* case for a policy that is oriented toward interest rates. The reason is that the portfolio effects, wealth effects, and credit availability effects through which the impacts of monetary policy are transmitted to the economy are better measured by changes in interest rates than by changes in monetary aggregates. The vast bulk of the empirical evidence supports this view, indicating that it is through interest rates that monetary policy affects expenditures on goods and services. Indeed, I know of no evidence that any monetary aggregate that the Federal Reserve could control has an effect on expenditures.

Of course, if there were tight and well understood linkages between some monetary aggregate—say, the stock of demand deposits and currency—and interest rates, it would matter little which the Federal Reserve attempted to control, because a money target would imply an interest rate target. There are indeed linkages between monetary aggregates and interest rates—these linkages are, in my judgment, sufficient to prevent the Federal Reserve from controlling both monetary aggregates and interest rates except to a very limited extent. But the linkages are not well understood and are subject to change as a result of financial innovations and changes in patterns of financial behavior. Consequently, it does make a difference whether the Federal Reserve selects a monetary aggregate or an interest rate as a guide to policy.

Advantages of Treasury Bill Rate as a Guide to Policy

My specific suggestion is that the Federal Reserve focus on the Treasury bill rate as its basic guide for monetary policy. There are several advantages in this approach. First, the Federal Reserve can, without any basic change in its operating procedures, control the Treasury bill rate with virtually any degree of accuracy it desires. Second, there are many occasions on which the bill rate must be a focus of attention anyway, because it is the key short-term rate affecting international capital flows. Third, the bill rate is closely related to market interest rates on those forms of short- and intermediate-term debt that compete with fixed-value redeemable claims and are therefore of critical importance for the availability of mortgage funds. Fourth, there is considerable evidence that the bill rate works through an expectational mechanism to affect those long-term rates that are important in determining the cost of capital to business firms, State and local governments, and home buyers. Moreover, the wealth effect of monetary policy works through capitalization rates that would be indirectly affected by a policy aimed in the first instance at the Treasury bill rate.

Of course, the bill rate target would have to be selected on the basis of a forecast of economic activity several quarters ahead, including a forecast of fiscal policy. One could, for example, use a model such as the FRB-MIT model to estimate a pattern of behavior of the bill rate that could be expected to achieve the desired performance of the economy over the next three or four quarters, given the anticipated fiscal policy. This target could then be adjusted on the basis of special factors or judgmental considerations. I would not propose to peg the bill rate exactly but to establish a range of, say, 20 basis points within which it would be permitted to fluctuate. The bill rate target would, of course, be reexamined at each meeting of the FOMC on the basis of the latest forecast of the economic outlook.

I would not, however, adhere dogmatically to such a "bills-only" policy. If long-term interest rates should fail to respond in the anticipated way to a change in the bill rate target, I would not hesitate to nudge them along by open-market operations in long-term Treasury securities. Nor would I entirely neglect monetary aggregates. I would want to supplement the bill rate target with some kind of quantitative guideline to prevent gross mistakes in policy. In the case of a non-growing economy, using the stock of demand deposits and currency as the quantitative guideline, the matter is relatively simple—one should be sure that this stock increases when the economy is below full employment and declines when it is above full employment. The problem here is one of distinguishing between automatic and discretionary elements of policy—similar to the problem in fiscal policy that gave rise to the full-employment surplus concept. When the economy is weak, for example, interest rates decline automatically even if the monetary authorities do nothing, and it is desirable to be sure that the authorities are reinforcing this tendency by discretionary measures rather than offsetting it as they sometimes appear to have done in the past.

The problem of developing a suitable monetary guideline is considerably more complicated in the case of a growing economy. My procedure would be to begin by estimating a "normal" rate of monetary growth. For example, if the target point on the Phillips Curve is 4 percent unemployment which is judged to be associated with 2 percent inflation, if the rate of growth of productive capacity under full employment conditions is estimated to be 4 percent per year, and if the income elasticity of demand for monetary assets is judged to be unity, the "normal" rate of monetary growth would be estimated at 6 percent per year. At any particular time, if the objective of policy was to restrain the economy, growth should be less than 6 percent; if the objective was to stimulate the economy, growth should be more than 6 percent.

There is a problem of deciding what aggregate to use as an index of monetary growth. Should it be the monetary base as calculated by the Federal Reserve Bank of St. Louis, the money supply, total bank credit, or some other aggregate? Unfortunately, the significance of a change in the rate of growth of any of the commonly used aggregates depends upon the public's preferences for different categories of financial assets, including currency, demand deposits, time deposits, and securities. Since these preferences appear to change for reasons that we do not yet fully understand, problems of interpretation are bound to arise. My quite tentative suggestion would be to use the monetary base as the index of monetary growth. But I would also monitor the behavior of the other aggregates closely. If

the selected bill rate target resulted in growth of the base inconsistent with the guideline for several weeks and if the behavior of the other aggregates seemed to support the conclusion that monetary growth was too slow or too fast, the whole situation, including the bill rate target, should be carefully reexamined.

Other Dimensions to Be Considered

I think an approach along the lines developed above would make sense in providing an overall rationale for monetary policy. But there are important dimensions that are omitted in the above discussion. It has long been my contention that those responsible for the conduct of monetary policy must pay close attention to its impacts on particular sectors of the economy, especially when a restrictive policy is being followed. An example of this dimension of monetary policy is the variety of measures that have been taken by the Federal Reserve and a number of other Federal Government agencies during the past year to cushion the impact of high interest rates on homebuilding.

The Federal Reserve has attempted to shield the savings and loan associations from bank competition by maintaining low ceiling rates on savings deposits and those forms of time deposits that compete most directly with savings and loan shares. The Federal Home Loan Bank Board has acted to encourage continued mortgage lending by savings and loan associations by reducing the liquidity requirement applicable to the associations and by making advances available to them. In addition, the Home Loan Banks have attempted to manage their own borrowings in the capital market in such a way as to minimize the possible impact on deposit flows. The Federal National Mortgage Association increased its mortgage holdings by $1.6 billion in 1968, and increased the scope and flexibility of its stabilizing activities in the mortgage market by introducing a new program of weekly auctions of mortgage commitments, beginning in May 1968. The ceiling rate applicable to FHA and VA mortgages was raised from 6 percent to 6¾ percent in May and was raised further to 7½ percent in January 1969. Finally, in its general conduct of monetary policy, the Federal Reserve has kept its eye on the flows of funds to savings and loan associations with a view to avoiding, if possible, a rise in short- and intermediate-term interest rates sufficient to set off a "disintermediation crises" of the type that occurred in 1966.

The impact of monetary policy on the economy

would, I believe, have been substantially different in 1968, and thus far in 1969, in the absence of these precautionary actions by the Federal Reserve and by the various agencies with responsibilities in the housing field. In all probability, we would long since have experienced a sharp decline in housing starts and residential construction expenditures similar to that which occurred in 1966. There are a number of reforms which might be adopted to increase the efficiency and flexibility of the mortgage market and to reduce the excessive impact that monetary policy now tends to have on homebuilding. Unless and until such reforms are implemented, however, I believe it is appropriate for the monetary authorities to concern themselves specifically with the effects of their policies on the housing sector. Indeed, I believe structural measures of the kind employed in 1968–69 should be thought of as part of monetary policy and should be applied as the situation seems to warrant on the basis of close cooperation between the Federal Reserve and the other agencies involved.

No matter how skillfully monetary policy is conducted, things are bound to go wrong from time to time. The underlying strength of private demand will sometimes prove to be stronger or weaker than was anticipated; fiscal policy will depart from its expected path; and the timing and magnitude of the economy's response to monetary actions will seldom be exactly as anticipated. I do not count myself among the group of economists who believe the business cycle is dead. If we seriously attempt to keep the economy moving along a selected high-employment growth path, resisting departures from that path in either direction, I believe we can still expect some economic fluctuations. The hope is that we can keep these fluctuations mild. But our success in that respect is much more critically dependent on improving the performance of fiscal policy than it is on changing the techniques of monetary management. Improved fiscal policy would relieve the Federal Reserve of its recent impossible task of offsetting the effects of profoundly destabilizing movements of the Federal budget. Even operating within the framework established by a reasonably well-designed fiscal policy, the Federal Reserve is bound to make occasional mistakes, but it should be able to make an effective contribution to economic stabilization and do so without the sharp gyrations in monetary variables that we have witnessed recently.

IV. RULES VERSUS AUTHORITIES

There is no reason, in principle, why one holding Keynesian views must necessarily favor discretion over a monetary rule. One could believe that our knowledge of the responses and the lags in the system is so poor that efforts to conduct a discretionary policy add to instability rather than subtract from it. I think discretion conducted on the basis of the best information available can do a better job than a rule, but I find the question a very complex one, and I do not see how anyone can be sure of the answer.

Before a rule involving steady growth of some aggregate such as the monetary base could be seriously considered, however, it seems to me there would have to be procedural or institutional changes in three areas.

First, there would have to be some assurance of better fiscal policy than we have had recently. Our problems of the last three years are primarily the result of inaction and inordinate delay in fiscal policy, and discretionary monetary policy has helped by either taking the place of needed fiscal restraint or supplementing it when it was too-long delayed.

Second, if monetary policy is to disregard interest rates entirely, I believe we need an overhaul of the arrangement for financing housing.

And, third, interest rates cannot be disregarded until the international monetary system has been reformed in some way to remove the balance-of-payments constraint on domestic interest rates.

Having said all of this, let me add that I believe the discussion of monetary rules is largely academic anyway. Even assuming that a rule were adopted, I feel certain that there would be overwhelming pressure to abandon it the first time it appeared that discretion would enable us to achieve a better performance—and that, I believe, would occur quite soon after the rule was adopted.

24. THE THEORY OF MONETARY POLICY UNDER UNCERTAINTY*

William Poole

INTRODUCTION

This study has been motivated by the recognition that the key to understanding policy problems is the analysis of uncertainty. Indeed, in the absence of uncertainty it might be said that there can be no *policy* problems, only *administrative* problems. It is surprising, therefore, that there has been so little systematic attention paid to uncertainty in the policy literature in spite of the fact that policy-makers have repeatedly emphasized the importance of the unknown.

In the past, the formal models used in the analysis of monetary policy problems have almost invariably assumed complete knowledge of the economic relationships in the model. Uncertainty is introduced into the analysis, if at all, only through informal consideration of how much difference it makes if the true relationships differ from those assumed by the policy-makers. In this study, on the other hand, uncertainty plays a key role in the formal model.

BASIC CONCEPTS

The theory of optimal policy under uncertainty has provided many insights into actual policy problems [1, 2, 3, 6]. While much of this theory is not accessible to the nonmathematical economist, it is possible to explain the basic ideas without resort to mathematics.

The obvious starting point is the observation that with our incomplete understanding of the economy and our inability to predict accurately the occurrence of disturbing factors such as strikes, wars, and foreign exchange crises, we cannot expect to hit policy goals exactly. Some periods of inflation or unemployment are unavoidable. The inevitable lack of precision in reaching policy goals is sometimes recognized by saying that the goals are "reasonably" stable prices and "reasonably" full employment.

While the observation above is trite, its impli-

cations are not. Two points are especially important. First, policy should aim at minimizing the average size of errors. Second, policy can be judged only by the average size of errors over a period of time and *not* by individual episodes. Because this second point is particularly subject to misunderstanding, it needs further amplification.

Since policy-makers operate in a world that is inherently uncertain, they must be judged by criteria appropriate to such a world. Consider the analogy of betting on the draw of a ball from an urn with nine black balls and one red ball. Anyone offered a $2 payoff for a $1 bet would surely bet on a black ball being drawn. If the draw produced the red ball, no one would accuse the bettor of a stupid bet. Similarly, the policy-maker must play the economic odds. The policy-maker should not be accused of failure if an inflation occurs as the result of an improbable and unforeseeable event.

Now consider the reverse situation from that considered in the previous paragraph. Suppose the bettor with the same odds as above bets on the red ball and wins. Some would claim that the bet was brilliant, but assuming that the draw was not rigged in any way, the bet, even though a winning one, must be judged foolish. It is foolish because, on the average, such a betting strategy will lead to substantially worse results than the opposite strategy. Betting on red will prove brilliant only one time out of 10, on the average. Similarly, a particular policy action may be a bad bet even though it works in a particular episode.

There is a well-known tendency for gamblers to try systems that according to the laws of probability cannot be successful over any length of time. Frequently, a gambler will adopt a foolish system as the result of an initial chance success such as betting on red in the above example. The same danger exists in economic policy. In fact, the danger is more acute because there appears to be a greater chance to "beat the system" by applying economic knowledge and intuition. There can be no doubt that it will become increasingly possible to improve on simple, naive policies through sophisticated analysis and forecasting and so in a sense "beat the system." But even with improved knowledge some uncertainty will always exist, and therefore so will the ten-

* From William Poole, "Rules-of-Thumb for Guiding Monetary Policy," in *Open Market Policies and Operating Procedures—Staff Studies* (Washington, D.C.: Board of Governors of the Federal Reserve System, 1971), pp. 135–89. Reprinted by permission of the Board of Governors of the Federal Reserve System and the author. William Poole is Professor of Economics, Brown University.

dency to attempt to perform better than the state of knowledge really permits.

Whatever the state of knowledge, there must be a clear understanding of how to cope with uncertainty, even though the degree of uncertainty may have been drastically reduced through the use of modern methods of analysis. The principal purpose of this section is to improve understanding of the importance of uncertainty for policy by examining a simple model in which the policy problem is treated as one of minimizing errors on the average. Particular emphasis is placed on whether controlling policy by adjusting the interest rate or by adjusting the money stock will lead to smaller errors on the average. The basic argument is designed to show that the answer to which policy variable—the interest rate or the money stock—minimizes average errors depends primarily on the relative stability of the expenditures and money demand functions rather than on the values of the parameters that determine whether monetary policy is in some sense more or less "powerful" than fiscal policy.

MONETARY POLICY UNDER UNCERTAINTY IN A KEYNESIAN MODEL[1]

The basic issues concerning the importance of uncertainty for monetary policy may be examined within the Hicksian IS-LM version of the Keynesian system. This elementary model has two sectors, an expenditure sector and a monetary sector, and it assumes that the price level is fixed in the short run.[2] Consumption, investment, and government expenditures functions are combined to produce the IS function in Figure 1, while the demand and supply of money functions are combined to produce the LM function. If monetary policy fixes the stock of money, then the resulting LM function is LM_1, while if policy fixes the interest rate at r_0 the resulting LM function is LM_2. It is assumed that incomes above "full employment income" are undesirable due to inflationary pressures while incomes below full employment income are undesirable due to unemployment.

If the positions of all the functions could be predicted with no errors, then to reach full employment income, Y_f, it would make no difference whether policy fixed the money stock or the interest rate. All that is necessary in either

[1] For the most part this section represents a verbal and graphical version of the mathematical argument on [3].

[2] Simple presentations of this model may be found in [4, pp. 275–82] and [5, pp. 327–32].

Figure 1

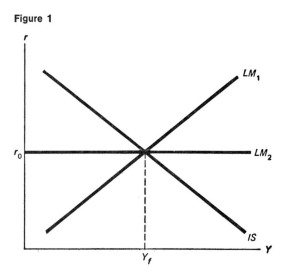

case is to set the money stock or the interest rate so that the resulting LM function will cut the IS function at the full employment level of income.

Significance of Disturbances. The positions of the functions are, unfortunately, never precisely known. Consider first uncertainty over the position of the IS function—which, of course, results from instability in the underlying consumption and investment functions—while retaining the unrealistic assumption that the position of the LM function is known. What is known about the IS function is that it will lie between the extremes of IS_1 and IS_2 in Figure 2. If the money stock is set at some fixed level, then it is known that the LM function will be LM_1, and accordingly income will be somewhere be-

Figure 2

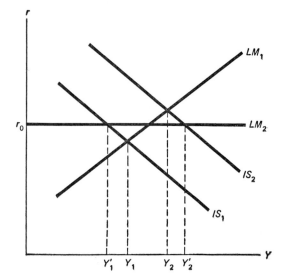

Figure 3

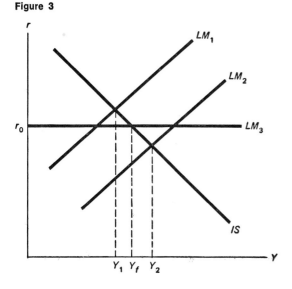

Figure 4

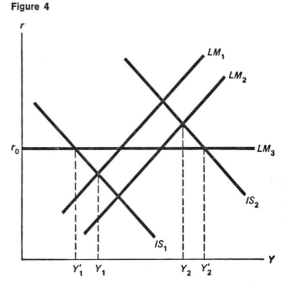

tween the extremes of Y_1 and Y_2. On the other hand, suppose policy-makers follow an interest rate policy and set the interest rate at r_0. In this case income will be somewhere between Y'_1, and Y'_2, a wider range than Y_1 to Y_2, and so the money stock policy is superior to the interest rate policy.[3] The money stock policy is superior because an unpredictable disturbance in the *IS* function will affect the interest rate, which in turn will produce spending changes that partly offset the initial disturbance.

The opposite polar case is illustrated in Figure 3. Here it is assumed that the position of the *IS* function is known with certainty, while unpredictable shifts in the demand for money cause unpredictable shifts in the *LM* function if a money stock policy is followed. With a money stock policy, income may end up anywhere between Y_1 and Y_2. But an interest rate policy can fix the *LM* function at LM_3 so that it cuts the *IS* function at the full employment level of income, Y_f. With an interest rate policy, unpredictable shifts in the demand for money are not permitted to affect the interest rate; instead, in the process of fixing the interest rate the policy-makers adjust the stock of money in response to the unpredictable shifts in the demand for money.

In practice, of course, it is necessary to cope with uncertainty in both the expenditure and monetary sectors. This situation is depicted in

Figure 4, where the unpredictable disturbances are larger in the expenditure sector, and in Figure 5 where the unpredictable disturbances are larger in the monetary sector.

The situation is even more complicated than shown in Figures 4 and 5 by virtue of the fact that the disturbances in the two sectors may not be independent. To illustrate this case, consider Figure 5 in which the interest rate policy is superior to the money stock policy if the disturbances are independent. Suppose that the disturbances were connected in such a way that disturbances on the LM_1 side of the average *LM* function were always accompanied by disturbances on the IS_2 side of the average *IS* function. This would mean that income would never go as low as Y_1, but rather only as low as the intersection of LM_1 and IS_2, an income not as low as Y'_1 under the interest rate policy. Similarly, the highest income would be given by the intersection of LM_2 and IS_1, an income not so high as Y'_2.[4]

Importance of Interest Elasticities and Other Parameters. So far the argument has concentrated entirely on the importance of the relative sizes of expenditure and monetary disturbances. But is it also important to consider the slopes

[3] In Figure 2 and the following diagrams, the outcomes from a money stock policy will be represented by unprimed *Y*s, while the outcomes from an interest rate policy will be represented by primed *Y*'s.

[4] The diagram could obviously have been drawn so that an interest rate policy would be superior to a money stock policy even though there were an inverse relationship between the shifts in the *IS* and *LM* functions. However, inverse shifts always reduce the margin of superiority of an interest rate policy, possibly to the point of making a money stock policy superior. Conversely, positively related shifts favor an interest rate policy.

Figure 5

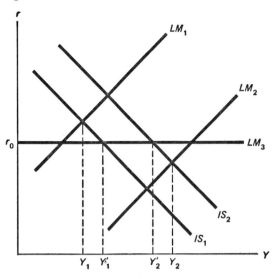

Figure 7

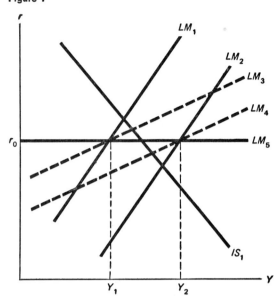

of the functions as determined by the interest elasticities of investment and of the demand for money, and by other parameters? Consider the pair of IS functions, IS_1 and IS_2, as opposed to the pair, IS_3 and IS_4, in Figure 6. Each pair represents the maximum and minimum positions of the IS function as a result of disturbances, but the pairs have different slopes. Each pair assumes the same maximum and minimum disturbances, as shown by the fact that the horizontal distance between IS_1 and IS_2 is the same as between IS_3 and IS_4. For convenience, but without loss of generality, the functions have been drawn so that under an interest rate policy represented by LM_2 both pairs of IS functions

Figure 6

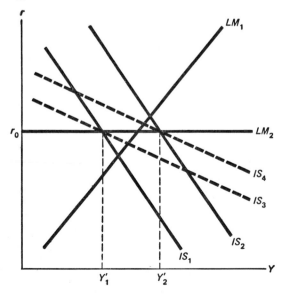

produce the same range of incomes. To keep the diagram from becoming too messy, only one LM function, LM_1, under a money stock policy has been drawn. Now consider disturbances that would shift LM_1 back and forth. From Figure 6 it is easy to see that *if* shifts in LM_1 would, given the pair IS_1 and IS_2, generate income fluctuations less than from Y_1' to Y_2'—which fluctuations would occur under an interest rate policy—*then* with the pair IS_3 and IS_4 income fluctuations would also be less than from Y_1' to Y_2'. A money stock policy would, therefore, be preferred regardless of which IS pair obtains.

The importance of the slope of the LM function is investigated in Figure 7 for the two LM pairs, LM_1 and LM_2, and LM_3 and LM_4. The functions have been drawn so that each pair represents different slopes but an identical range of disturbances. It is clear that if shifts in IS_1 are large enough, then a money stock policy will be preferred regardless of which pair of LM functions prevails.

The argument of the preceding two paragraphs can be made more precise by saying that if variability of the LM function is small enough relative to the IS function, than a money stock policy will be preferred to an interest rate policy regardless of the interest elasticities of the expenditures and money demand functions. How small is "small enough" depends on the income elasticity of the demand for money.[5] When the

<hr/>

[5] For the mathematical argument, see equation (14) in [3].

variability of *LM* relative to *IS* is not "small enough," then a money stock policy will be preferred for relatively high values of the ratio of the interest elasticity of the demand for money to the interest elasticity of expenditures; an interest rate policy will be preferred for relatively low values of this ratio.[6] The intuitive reason for this result is that monetary disturbances will have a larger impact on income the lower is the interest elasticity of money demand and the higher is the interest elasticity of expenditures.

The upshot of this analysis is that the crucial issue for deciding upon whether an interest rate or a money stock policy should be followed is the relative size of the disturbances in the expenditure and monetary sectors. Contrary to much recent discussion, the issue is not whether the interest elasticity of the demand for money is relatively low or whether fiscal policy is more or less "powerful" than monetary policy.

To avoid possible confusion, it should be emphasized that the above argument is in terms of the choice between a money stock policy and an interest rate policy. However, if a money stock policy is superior, then the steeper is the *LM* function, up to a point, the lower is the range of income fluctuation, as can be seen from Figure 7. It is also clear from Figure 6 that under an interest rate policy an error in setting the interest rate will lead to a larger error in hitting the income target if the *IS* function is relatively flat than if it is relatively steep. But these facts do not affect the choice between interest rate and money stock policies.

The "Combination" Monetary Policy. Up to this point the analysis has concentrated on the choice of either the interest rate or the money stock as the policy variable. But it is also possible to consider a "combination" policy that works through the money stock and the interest rate simultaneously. An understanding of the combination policy may be obtained by further consideration of the cases depicted in Figures 2 and 7.

In Figure 8 the disturbances, as in Figure 2, are entirely in the expenditure sector. As was seen in Figure 2, the result obtained by fixing the money stock so that LM_1 prevailed was superior to that obtained by fixing the interest rate so that LM_2 prevailed. But now suppose that instead of fixing the money stock, the money stock were reduced every time the interest rate went up and increased every time the interest

Figure 8

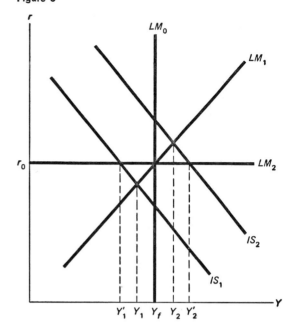

rate went down. This procedure would, of course, increase the amplitude of interest rate fluctuations.[7] But if the proper relationship between the money stock and the interest rate could be discovered, then the *LM* function could be made to look like LM_0 in Figure 8. The result would be that income would be pegged at Y_f. Disturbances in the *IS* function would produce changes in the interest rate, which in turn would produce spending changes sufficient to completely offset the effect on income of the initial disturbance.

The most complicated case of all to explain graphically is that in which it is desirable to increase the money stock as the interest rate rises and decrease it as the interest rate falls. In Figure 9 the leftmost position of the *LM* function as a result of disturbances is LM_1 when the money stock is fixed and is LM_2 when the combination policy of introducing a positive money–interest relationship is followed. The rightmost positions of the *LM* functions under these conditions are

[7] The increased fluctuations in interest rates must be carefully interpreted. In this model the *IS* function is assumed to fluctuate around a fixed-average position. However, in more complicated models involving changes in the average position of the *IS* function, perhaps through the operation of the investment accelerator, interest rate fluctuations may not be increased by the policy being discussed in the text. By increasing the stability of income over a period of time, the policy would increase the stability of the *IS* function in Figure 8 and thereby reduce interest rate fluctuations.

Figure 9

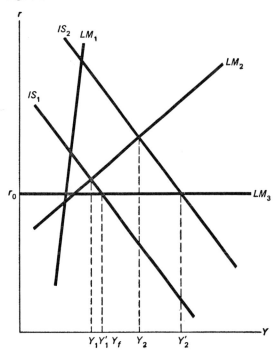

not shown in the diagram. When the interest rate is pegged, the LM function is LM_3. If either LM_1 or LM_2 prevails, the intersection with IS_1 produces the lowest income, which is below the Y_1' level obtained with LM_3. But in the case of LM_2, income at Y_1 is only a little lower than at Y_1', whereas when IS_2 prevails, LM_2 is better than LM_3 by the difference between Y_2 and Y_2'. Since the gap between Y_2 and Y_2' is larger than that between Y_1 and Y_1', it is on the average better to adopt LM_2 than LM_3 even though the extremes under LM_2 are a bit larger than under LM_3.

Extensions of Model. At this point a natural question is that of the extent to which the above analysis would hold in more complex models. Until more complicated models are constructed and analyzed mathematically, there is no way of being certain. But it is possible to make educated guesses on the effects of adding more goals and more policy instruments, and of relaxing the rigid price assumption.

Additional goals may be added to the model if they are specified in terms of "closer is better" rather than in terms of a fixed target that must be met. For example, it would not be mathematically difficult to add an interest rate goal to the model analyzed above, if deviations from a target interest rate were permitted but were treated as being increasingly harmful. On the other hand,

it is clear that if there were a fixed-interest target, then the only possible policy would be to peg the interest rate, and income stabilization would not be possible with monetary policy alone.

The addition of fiscal policy instruments affects the results in two major ways. First, the existence of income taxes and of government expenditures inversely related to income (for example, unemployment benefits) provides automatic stabilization. In terms of the model, automatic stabilizers make the IS function steeper than it otherwise would be, thus reducing the impact of monetary disturbances, and reduce the variance of expenditures disturbances in the reduced-form equation for income. This effect would be shown in Figure 6 by drawing IS_1 so that it cuts LM_2 to the right of Y_1' and drawing IS_2 so that it cuts LM_2 to the left of Y_2'.

The second major impact of adding fiscal policy instruments occurs if both income and the interest rate are goals. Horizontal shifts in the IS function that are induced by fiscal policy adjustments, when accompanied by a coordinated monetary policy, make it possible to come closer to a desired interest rate without any sacrifice in income stability. An obvious illustration is provided by the case in which the optimal monetary policy from the point of view of stabilizing income is to set the interest rate as in Figure 5. Fiscal policy can then shift the pair of IS functions, IS_1 and IS_2, to the right or left so that the expected value of income is at the full employment level.

If the interest rate is not a goal variable, then fiscal policy actions that shift the IS function without changing its slope do not improve income stabilization over what can be accomplished with monetary policy alone, provided the lags in the effects of monetary policy are no longer than those in the effects of fiscal policy. An exception would be a situation in which reaching full employment with monetary policy alone would require an unattainable interest rate, such as a negative one.

These comments on fiscal policy have been presented in order to clarify the relationship between fiscal and monetary policy. While monetary policy-makers may urge fiscal action, for the most part monetary policy must take the fiscal setting as given and adapt monetary policy to this setting. It must then be recognized that an interest rate goal can be pursued only at the cost of sacrificing somewhat the income goal.[8]

---

[8] An interest rate goal must be sharply distinguished from the use of the interest rate as a mone-

All of the analysis so far has taken place within a model in which the price level is fixed in the short run. This assumption may be relaxed by recognizing that increases in money income above the full employment level involve a mixture of real income gains and price inflation. Similarly, reductions in money income below the full employment level involve real income reductions and price deflation (or a slower rate of price inflation). The model used above can be reinterpreted entirely in terms of money income so that departures from what was called above the "full employment" level of income involve a mixture of real income and price changes. Stabilizing money income, then, involves a mixture of the two goals of stabilizing real output and of stabilizing the price level.

However, interpreted in this way the structure of the model is deficient because it fails to distinguish between real and nominal interest rates. Price level increases generate inflationary expectations, which in turn generate an outward shift in the IS function. The model may be patched up to some extent by assuming that price changes make up a constant fraction of the deviation of income from its full employment level and assuming further that the expected rate of inflation is a constant multiplied by the actual rate of inflation. Expenditures are then made to depend on the real rate of interest, the difference between

the nominal rate of interest and the expected rate of inflation. The result is to make the IS function, when drawn against the nominal interest rate, flatter and to increase the variance of disturbances to the IS function. These effects are more pronounced: (a) the larger is the interest sensitivity of expenditures; (b) the larger is the fraction of price changes in money income changes; and (c) the larger is the effect of price changes on price expectations. The conclusion is that since price flexibility in effect increases the variance of disturbances in the IS function, a money stock policy tends to be favored over an interest rate policy.

REFERENCES

1. Brainard, William. "Uncertainty and the Effectiveness of Policy." *American Economic Review: Papers and Proceedings of the 79th Annual Meeting of the American Economic Association,* vol. 57 (May 1967), pp. 411–25.
2. Holt, Charles C. "Linear Decision Rules for Economic Stabilization and Growth." *Quarterly Journal of Economics,* vol. 76 (February 1962), pp. 20–45.
3. Poole, William. "Optimal Choice of Monetary Policy Instruments in a Simple Stochastic Macro Model." *Quarterly Journal of Economics,* vol. 84 (May 1970), pp. 197–216.
4. Reynolds, Lloyd G. *Economics.* 3rd ed. Homewood, Ill.: Richard D. Irwin, Inc., 1969.
5. Samuelson, Paul A. *Economics.* 7th ed. New York: McGraw-Hill, 1967.
6. Theil, Henri. *Optimal Decision Rules for Government and Industry.* Amsterdam, Neth.: North-Holland Publishing Company, 1964.

tary policy instrument. By a goal variable is meant a variable that enters the policy utility function. Income and interest rate goals might be simultaneously pursued by setting the money stock as the policy instrument or by setting the interest rate as the policy instrument.

25. THE TRADE-OFF BETWEEN SHORT- AND LONG-TERM POLICY GOALS*

James L. Pierce†

INTRODUCTION

The existence of long lags in the response of the real sectors of the economy to changes in

* From *Open Market Policies and Operating Procedures—Staff Studies* (Washington, D.C.: Board of Governors of the Federal Reserve System, 1971), pp. 97–105. Reprinted by permission of the Board of Governors of the Federal Reserve System and the author. James L. Pierce is Professor of Economics, University of California at Berkeley.

monetary policy is well documented. These lags may require an horizon for monetary policy strategies that spans many calendar quarters. Even if long planning horizons are desirable, specific operating strategies still must be adopted for the actual short-run conduct of monetary policy. These, however, should be consistent with the

† The author would like to thank William Poole for his constructive comments on an earlier version of this paper.

long-term goals. If short-run considerations—such as stabilization of money market interest rate movements—cause modification of the operating strategy, the long-run goals in terms of income, employment, and the price level may suffer. This paper discusses some of the areas in which short- and long-term goals may conflict and attempts to evaluate the costs to the long-term targets of imposing short-run side conditions on policy actions.

SHORT-RUN VERSUS LONG-RUN GOALS

Available econometric evidence indicates that variations in monetary policy instruments can exert little influence on the nonfinancial sectors of the economy in the short run. Experiments with a recent version of the Federal Reserve–MIT model indicate that, other things equal, a $1 billion increase in the money stock in a given quarter will produce only a $0.3 billion increase in nominal gross national product in that quarter. Further, inspection of the coefficients for the relevant equations in the model suggests that even this small response is probably overstated. It is interesting to note that the long-run multiplier relation between money and nominal GNP is substantial. Other things equal, a $1 billion permanent rise in the money stock leads to a permanent increase in nominal GNP of approximately $3.2 billion.

Given the short-run multiplier, attempts to establish short-run (quarter by quarter) control over the economy may require variations in policy instruments that are unacceptably large. An example may clarify the issue. Assume that during a generally inflationary period, the decision is made to attempt to stop the inflation within a single quarter. To accomplish this end, a sharp rise in interest rates, and probably a substantial reduction in the levels of the monetary aggregates, would be required during the quarter. Even if this strategy were successful, a new problem would immediately develop. With the passage of time beyond the quarter, the economy would continue its deflationary adjustment— probably at an increased rate—in response to the monetary restriction. If an overresponse of the economy to the original policy restriction is to be avoided, policy must reverse itself immediately by sharply reducing interest rates and expanding the monetary aggregates. This easing of policy would require in turn a restrictive policy the next quarter. Thus, by never looking more than one quarter ahead, large short-term reversals

of policy would be required to stabilize the economy.

Whether this myopic strategy of trying to hit targets in the real sector on a quarter-by-quarter basis can be successful over the long run depends, among other things, upon the existing parameters of the system.[1] It is quite possible that pursuit of such a strategy would have no long-run future because ever larger changes in monetary policy instruments would be required to achieve stability in the real sector. Even if the strategy produced permanent economic stability, it could create extreme fluctuations in financial markets.

It is quite possible, however, that large fluctuations in financial variables would alter interest rate expectations enough to weaken greatly the efficacy of the myopic policy strategy. Rapid reversals of monetary policy may encourage investors to expect wide fluctuations in short-term interest rates. In this situation, efforts to reduce long-term rates would be thwarted by investor expectations of a rise in rates in the near future. Thus, the pursuit of the myopic policy strategy could be self-defeating.

There are two obvious ways to approach the problem posed by the small amount of short-term control over the economy. First, monetary policy could pursue the myopic rule of attempting to hit a target quarter by quarter but could subject the strategy to constraints imposed by financial conditions. Thus, a specific target value for employment or for the price level would be pursued provided the act of attempting to hit the target did not cause excessive fluctuations in interest rates. If interest rates moved more than was deemed desirable, policy instruments would be changed sufficiently to bring interest rates within the allowable range. The imposition of such constraints could greatly reduce the ability of monetary policy to achieve short-term goals.

The second approach would involve a lengthening of the policy-planning horizon. In this situation, policy would take a view longer than one quarter into the future. The aim would be to achieve the best path of, say, employment over some interval of time consistent with acceptable performance of financial markets. Extension of the horizon would allow problems of the real sector and of the financial sector to coexist on

---

[1] For a simple treatment of this problem, see E. Gramlich, "The Usefulness of Monetary and Fiscal Policy as Discretionary Stabilization Tools," presented at the Conference of University Professors sponsored by the American Bankers Association, September 1969.

a more equal basis. No immutable constraints would be placed on the system by money market conditions if the planning horizon could be extended. However, by giving up some short-term control over variables in the real sector, it should be possible to reduce fluctuations in financial variables to more manageable proportions.

Conceptually, it should be possible to determine the trade-off between (1) short-term control over employment and prices and (2) stability of the financial sector. In general, a lengthening of the policy-planning horizon to promote short-run stability in financial markets will come at the cost of reduced control over nonfinancial variables. Alternatively, a shortening of the planning horizon will come at the cost of increased short-run fluctuations in financial variables.

Lengthening the horizon for major policy goals raises some obvious problems. Because the long-term goals of employment and prices are relatively far in the future, it is easy to give them a back seat to the short-run stabilization problems often encountered in financial markets. The problem with this approach is that overattention to short-run problems may have important implications for the paths required to hit desired long-run targets. Further, if short-run constraints are continually imposed, it may be impossible to hit the long-run goals in the time specified. Under those circumstances it may be necessary to lengthen the horizon and to accept the ensuing costs of less desirable performance of the real sector.

The previous paragraph suggests that over the longer run the goals of price and output stability may not conflict with the goal of money market stability. Overzealous attempts to stabilize the money market in the short run may distort output and prices to the point that large changes in interest rates are required in the longer run to bring the economy under control. By allowing wider short-run fluctuations in money market conditions, it might be possible to avoid large swings in interest rates over the longer run.

The discussion suggests that, given a set of initial conditions in the economy, there is an optimal policy strategy available. The strategy determines simultaneously the length of the planning horizon, the paths of target variables such as employment and prices over the period, and the expected stability of financial markets. The determination of specific strategies is a problem in optimal control theory and is beyond the scope of this paper. Instead, the paper attempts to assess the trade-offs involved and illustrates problems that may arise from pursuing particular policy strategies.

SOME SIMULATION EXPERIMENTS

This section describes some simulation experiments that were conducted to illustrate the problems encountered when short-term and long-term goals conflict. The structure of a recent version of the FR–MIT model was used for the simulation exercises.[2]

The first experiment assumes a monetary policy that focuses on the rate of growth of the money stock provided the change in the Treasury bill rate over any quarter does not exceed some arbitrary value. An unconstrained growth in money is assumed to promote desired long-run behavior of the real sector. However, if the policy-determined money stock for a quarter led to a projected change in the bill rate over that quarter that exceeded the constraint value, then the money supply was changed sufficiently to bring the change in the bill rate back to its allowable range. In those situations in which monetary policy is attempting to offset either boom or recession, this constrained policy would lead to a performance of the economy that is inferior to one which is unconstrained.

If shifts in the demand for money are the source of wide interest rate fluctuations when policy is attempting to hit a money stock target, the situation is changed. Here, it would be appropriate to introduce interest rate constraints. Such constraints would automatically satisfy the demand for money after some point. Limiting interest rate movements in this case would promote long-run stability.[3] The results of the simulation experiments suggest, however, that one should have strong reasons for believing that shifts in money demand are causing wide quarter-to-quarter fluctuations in interest rates. If unexpected shifts in aggregate demand are the cause, long-run goals may suffer greatly.

To illustrate the problems that arise during

[2] Some of the simulation results reported here are drawn from an earlier paper on a related topic. See J. Pierce, "Some Rules for the Conduct of Monetary Policy," in *Controlling Monetary Aggregates* (Federal Reserve Bank of Boston, 1969).

[3] For a theoretical discussion of the desirability of interest rate versus money stock stabilization in a stochastic world, see W. Poole, "Optimal Choice of Monetary Policy Instruments in a Simple Stochastic Macro Model," *Quarterly Journal of Economics*, vol. 84 (May 1970), pp. 197–216.

periods of excess aggregate demand, various simulations of the FR–MIT model were run for the 1963–68 period. First, a control simulation was run that took all exogenous variables at their historical values but assumed that the money stock grew at a constant annual rate of 4.25 percent. This was the constant rate at which the initial money stock in 1962-IV had to grow to achieve its actual value in 1968-IV. Then additional simulation experiments were conducted by applying the same exogenous variables and the same 4.25 percent money growth rate to the model provided that the Treasury bill rate did not change during the quarter by more than a specified absolute amount. If the bill rate fell outside the allowable range, bank reserves and the money supply were changed sufficiently to bring the bill rate back to the nearest boundary of the range. All other exogenous variables were assumed to remain unchanged. Several absolute change values were attempted; results for absolute changes of 30 basis points and 10 basis points are reported.

The results indicate that the placement of sufficiently narrow bounds on the change in the bill rate can have a large impact on the simulated value of GNP. Figure 1 shows the differences between the simulated values of GNP for the steady rate of growth of money and those subject to maximum absolute changes in the bill rate of 30 and 10 basis points, respectively. In both cases, because interest rates could not rise in the later periods, there was a tendency to add to the existing excess demand conditions.

As indicated earlier, if interest rate fluctuations are caused by erratic shifts in the demand for money, then stabilization of interest rates may be a reasonable course of action. The simulation results suggest, however, that interest rate stabilization can be costly during periods of strong excess demand.

It is interesting to note that if stabilization of financial markets takes the form of constraining the rate of growth of the money stock, the problems encountered during periods of shifting aggregate demand are diminished. Assume that monetary policy attempts to hit an employment target by setting market interest rates at appropriate levels. Introducing a constraint on the allowable range of growth rates of the money stock in this situation can under some circumstances lead to improved performance of the economy. If it happens that the interest rate selected is not the correct one because aggregate demand is either stronger or weaker than expected, variations in the rate of growth of the money stock can provide important evidence of this condition. For example, if aggregate demand is stronger than expected, given the interest rate and the demand for money, the growth in the money stock will be greater than expected. If the acceleration in the growth rate of money is taken as a signal to raise the interest rate, the growth rate of money will fall and the excessive growth in aggregate demand will be reduced.

If the unexpected growth in the money stock is the result of a shift in the demand for money, then the monetary expansion should be accommodated. In this situation, interest rates should not rise. There is really no way to avoid making judgments concerning the causes of fluctuations in the money stock and in interest rates. If the source is unexpected strength or weakness in aggregate demand, one course of action is called for. If the source is erratic shifts in the demand for money, quite a different policy reaction is required. The purpose of the simulation experiments was not to "prove" that aggregate demand is always the cause of money market fluctuations. Rather, the purpose of the exercises was to illustrate the potential costs of pursuing a policy strategy that implicitly assumes that money market fluctuations are caused primarily by an erratic, unpredictable demand for money.

Simulation experiments with the model were conducted to measure the impact of constraints on the growth rate of money. The control simulation was one in which the interest rate was made to rise at a constant annual rate from a base period of 1963-I to achieve its actual value in 1968-I. In this simulation, the money stock is endogenous. Additional policy simulations were then conducted in which constraints on the growth rate of money were imposed on this interest rate policy. If the rate of growth of the en-

Figure 1: Effect on GNP of 4.25% Growth in Money Subject to Maximum Absolute Change in Bill Rate (deviations from straight 4.25% money-growth simulation)

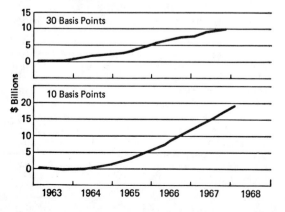

dogenous money stock fell outside the allowable range, the interest rate was changed sufficiently to bring the growth in money back to the nearest boundary of its allowable range.

Figure 2 shows the difference between the values of GNP from the control simulations and those for maximum ranges of 3 to 5 percent and of 3.5 to 4.5 percent in the annual growth rate of money. The results indicate that this combination of interest rate and money supply policies would have been beneficial over the period of simulation.

Further simulation experiments were conducted taking the conditions of the 1960–61 recession as the starting point for the policy exercises. The results were similar to those described above for periods of excess demand. Control simulations were conducted for the period 1960–III to 1968–I under the assumption of a constant rate of growth of the money stock. Given the actual history of the exogenous variables in the system and given the initial conditions, the time required to get initially to full employment was a decreasing function of the money growth rate. Particularly rapid growth rates, however, lead to substantial overshooting and can create chronic excess demand. Quite predictably, imposition of a constraint on policy in the form of maximum allowable quarterly changes in the Treasury bill rate made it more difficult to hit the full employment target. The interest rate constraint produced a slowing of the rate of expansion of output and employment from the recession base and lengthened the time necessary to hit a full employment target. The results also indicate that the degree of the slowdown of economic expansion resulting from the constraint depends upon how quickly the target level of employment is to be reached and how narrow is the allowable range of the quarterly change in interest rates.

It should be emphasized that a restriction on changes in interest rates is potentially less disruptive to the economy than is a restriction on the level of rates. Constraints on the maximum short-term change in interest rates can retard but not arrest desired adjustments of the economy. The existence of ceilings or floors on the level of interest rates may prevent the adjustments from ever occurring. Pegging the level of interest rates can lead to a total loss of control by policy over output, employment, and prices.

The recession results for a money supply constraint are also similar to those obtained for the excess demand case. A monetary policy that attempts to achieve its objectives through influencing money market conditions—interest rates—can

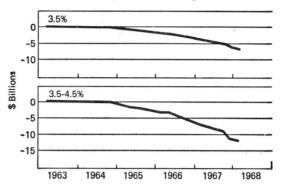

Figure 2: Effect on GNP of Constant Bill-Rate Growth Subject to Maximum Money-Growth Rates (deviations from straight bill-rate-growth simulation)

be enhanced in the recession case by imposing a constraint on the rate of growth of money. If the course of aggregate demand proves to be other than expected, variations in the interest rate promoted by the constraint imposed by an allowable range of growth in money rates will serve to push the rate of expansion in the desired direction.

CONCLUSIONS

The brief discussion in the preceding section suggests that high priority should be placed on coordinating short-run operating procedures with the longer-run goals of monetary policy. Failure to achieve such coordination can lead to a serious reduction in the ultimate effectiveness of monetary policy. Stabilizing short-term interest rate fluctuations can lead to destabilizing shocks to the real sectors of the economy.

Better information on the stability of the demand functions in the economy is sorely needed. The focus of policy on money market conditions may be badly misplaced if the money demand function is relatively stable and predictable through time. Certainly the hypothesis that the demand for money is erratic and unpredictable is not well documented. It is curious, therefore, that policy decisions should depend so strongly on money market conditions.

It might be argued that the central bank is obligated to stabilize the markets for debt instruments. An unfortunate paradox can result here. An overly zealous attempt to stabilize interest rates can so disturb the real sectors of the economy as to lead ultimately to extreme variations in market interest rates. The experience of the last few years appears to bear out this contention. It would appear that a monetary policy based almost exclusively on stabilizing short-run money market conditions is a luxury we can ill afford.

On a conceptual basis the appropriate course of action for policymaking appears to be clear. Given staff projections of the course of the economy over the coming year or so, the instruments of monetary policy should be set to promote the desired time paths of variables such as employment and prices over the period. In order to make such decisions meaningful, several policy alternatives should be presented showing alternative time paths for the target values in the real sector.

The policy alternatives should be compared both in terms of the expected values of such variables as output, employment, and prices, and in terms of the dispersion of these projections around their expected values. In assessing the variability of the projections, it is necessary to provide evidence as to the possible impacts on the projections of various shocks to the system. How sensitive are the projections to shifts in the demand for money or in the demand for investment goods? An analysis of the impact on the projections of alternative assumptions concerning the values of certain key exogenous variables such as Government spending is also crucial. Furthermore, it is quite likely that the sensitivity of the projections to shocks and alternative values of exogenous variables is not independent of the existing state of the economy. At times projections are quite insensitive to fairly large changes in the underlying specifications of the system, but at other times they are extremely sensitive to these specifications. It is essential, therefore, that evidence be provided concerning the likely dispersion of relevant variables around their projected values.

The fluctuations in interest rates and monetary aggregates implied by the various policy alternatives should also be projected. On the basis of all of this information, trade-offs between expected money market stability and the behavior of variables in the real sector can be assessed. The need for reliable econometric models and for seasoned judgment in these exercises is obvious. At this point, our ability to generate the required set of projections is quite limited. These limitations suggest that policy strategies should be fairly simple and straightforward. Elaborate policy strategies do not seem consistent with our ability to assess and trace through time the impact of policy acts on the economy.

Given a policy strategy over the coming year or so, how can the strategy be reduced to day-by-day operating procedures? Here, there is need for a document that presents projections of financial conditions to be expected over the near term. A blending of projections obtained from quarterly and monthly econometric models is sorely needed. Conceptually, such blends are difficult but possible. On the basis of these short-term projections and the basic policy strategy mentioned above, specific operating instructions can be formulated. Here, limitations on the ability to make short-term projections suggest that the operating procedures adopted should be fairly simple.

We now come to the central problem. How can we continue to link the basic policy strategy with operating procedures as the economic forecasts are modified and as monetary policy strays off course? As policy is currently conducted, there is no effective means of varying the basic strategy as new information comes in, and there is no way to relate changing conditions to actual operating procedures.

Ideally, we would like to generate new long-term forecasts each quarter and to map out new alternative policy strategies each quarter. Often, however, the new information that comes in leads to conflicting conclusions about changes in the future course of the economy. Further, econometric models and other procedures often do not predict with sufficient accuracy to allow useful quarter-by-quarter changes in implied operating strategy. The discussion of the original projections also suggests that the initial strategies may at times be very much in doubt.

A possible strategy under these conditions is to set quarterly operating instructions in terms of some combination of interest rates and money stock. A policy that sets an interest rate subject to constraints on the rate of growth of money is a very appealing candidate. By setting a range to the allowable growth of money, shifts in the money demand function are automatically accommodated up to the extreme points of the range. The width of the range should depend in part on estimates of likely quarterly fluctuations in the demand for money. In setting the range, however, it must be recalled that the wider the allowable range, the greater the potential loss in output and employment when variations in aggregate demand are the cause of money growth fluctuations. For this reason, a relatively narrow band, for example, 4 to 6 percent, seems desirable as a working principle.

Certainly, if there are persuasive arguments explaining why an unusual shift in money demand occurred in a particular quarter, then a growth rate of the money stock outside the range should be allowed. The point is, however, that relaxation of the constraints should be a rare event. In every case when such an action is being considered, the burden of proof should rest squarely on those who believe that an unexpected movement of money outside the range is caused by money demand and not by aggregate demand. Further, the longer the condition of unusually high or low money growth persists at existing interest rates the greater should be the presumption that the interest rate is inappropriate and should be changed.

These recommendations do not call for a drastic departure from current procedures; they call primarily for greater attention to be paid to the long-run objectives of economic stabilization policy. Such objectives are designed to put short-run stabilization of money market conditions in the context of possible costs to the economy in terms of income, employment, and prices.

Truly effective implementation of policy requires that operating strategies intended to achieve desired long-term goals be set forth explicitly. Such strategies must be followed under conditions of great uncertainty about the course of the exogenous variables in the system and about the performance of our models. In such a situation it would appear to be a mistake to focus attention primarily on the uncertainties of the money market. Monetary policy decisions must come to grips with the uncertainties we face with respect to aggregate demand. A policy strategy that relies as much as possible on projections but that also combines a setting of interest rates with allowable ranges on the money growth rate appears to be most appropriate for the near future.

---

26. THE LAG IN THE EFFECT OF MONETARY POLICY: A SURVEY OF RECENT LITERATURE*

Michael J. Hamburger†

During the last ten years the views of economists —both monetarists and nonmonetarists—on the lag in the effect of monetary policy on the economy have changed considerably. This article examines some of the recent evidence which has served as the basis for these changes.

Prior to 1960, quantitative estimates of the lag in the effect of monetary policy were rare. While there had always been disagreement on the effectiveness of monetary policy, a substantial number of economists seemed to accept the proposition that there was sufficient impact in the

reasonably short run for monetary policy to be used as a device for economic stabilization. Although this view did not go unquestioned—see, for example, Mayer [26] and Smith [29][1]—the main challenge to the conventional thinking came from Milton Friedman. He argued that monetary policy acts with so long and variable a lag that attempts to pursue a contracyclical monetary policy might aggravate, rather than ameliorate, economic fluctuations. In summarizing work done in collaboration with Anna Schwartz, he wrote [16]: "We have found that, on the average of 18 cycles, peaks in the rate of change in the stock of money tend to precede peaks in general business by about 16 months and troughs in the rate of change in the stock of money precede troughs in general business by about 12 months. . . . For individual cycles, the recorded lead has varied between 6 and 29 months at peaks and between 4 and 22 months at troughs."

Many economists were simply not prepared to believe Friedman's estimates of either the length or the variability of the lag. As Culbertson

* From Federal Reserve Bank of New York, *Monetary Aggregates and Monetary Policy* (New York, 1974), pp. 104–13. Reprinted by permission of the Federal Reserve Bank of New York and the author. Michael J. Hamburger is Adviser, Federal Reserve Bank of New York.

† The author wishes to acknowledge the helpful comments of Richard G. Davis, David H. Kopf, Robert G. Link, and other colleagues at the Federal Reserve Bank of New York. In addition, the excellent research assistance of Susan Skinner and Rona Stein is gratefully acknowledged. The views expressed in this paper are the author's alone and do not necessarily reflect those of the individuals noted above or the Federal Reserve Bank of New York.

[1] The numbers in brackets refer to the works cited at the end of this article.

[11] put it, "if we assume that government stabilization policies . . . act with so long and variable a lag, how do we set about explaining the surprising moderateness of the economic fluctuations that we have suffered in the past decade?" Culbertson's own conclusion was that "the broad record of experience support[s] the view that [contracyclical] monetary, debt-management, and fiscal adjustments can be counted on to have their predominant direct effects within three to six months, soon enough that if they are undertaken moderately early in a cyclical phase they will not be destabilizing."

Kareken and Solow [5] also appear to have been unwilling to accept Friedman's estimates. They summarized their results as follows: "Monetary policy works neither so slowly as Friedman thinks, nor as quickly and surely as the Federal Reserve itself seems to believe. . . . Though the *full* results of policy changes on the flow of expenditures may be a long time coming, nevertheless the chain of effects is spread out over a fairly wide interval. This means that *some* effect comes reasonably quickly, and that the effects build up over time so that some substantial stabilizing power results after a lapse of time of the order of six or nine months."

However, as Mayer [27] pointed out, this statement is inconsistent with the evidence presented by Kareken and Solow. They reported estimates of the complete lag in the effect of monetary policy on the flow of expenditures for only one component of gross national product (GNP), namely, inventory investment, and this lag is much longer than Friedman's lag. For another sector—producers' durable equipment—they provided data for only part of the lag, but even this is longer than Friedman's lag. Thus, Mayer noted that Kareken and Solow "should have criticized Friedman, not for overestimating, but for underestimating the lag."

More recently, it is the *monetarists* who have taken the view that the lag in the effect of monetary policy is relatively short, and the nonmonetarists who seem to be claiming longer lags. This showed up in the reaction to the St. Louis (Andersen and Jordan) equation [4]. According to this equation, the total response of GNP to changes in the money supply is completed within a year.

In his review of the Andersen and Jordan article, Davis [12] wrote "the most surprising thing about the world of the St. Louis equation is not so much the force, but rather the speed with which money begins to act on the economy." If the level of the money supply undergoes a $1 billion once-and-for-all rise in a given quarter, it will (according to the St. Louis equation) raise GNP by $1.6 billion in that quarter and by $6.6 billion during four quarters. In contrast, Davis found that in the Federal Reserve Board–Massachusetts Institute of Technology model—which was estimated by assuming nonborrowed reserves to be the basic monetary policy variable—a once-and-for-all increase in the money supply of $1 billion in a given quarter has almost no effect on GNP in that quarter and, even after four quarters, the level of GNP is only about $400 million higher than it otherwise would be. Thus, he concluded, "what is at stake in the case of the St. Louis equation is not merely a 'shade of difference' but a strikingly contrasting view of the world—at least relative to what is normally taken as the orthodox view roughly replicated and confirmed both in methods and in result by the Board-MIT model."[2]

The Federal Reserve Board-MIT model (henceforth called the FRB-MIT model) is not the only econometric model suggesting that monetary policy operates with a long distributed lag. Indeed, practically every *structural* model of the United States economy which has been addressed to this question has arrived at essentially the same answer.[3]

The most recent advocates of short lags are Arthur Laffer and R. David Ranson [25]. They have argued that: "Monetary policy, as represented by changes in the conventionally defined money supply [demand deposits plus currency], has an immediate and permanent impact on the level of GNP. For every dollar increase in the money supply, GNP will rise by about $4.00 or $5.00 in the current quarter, and not fall back [or rise any further] in the future. Alternatively, every 1 percent change in the money supply is associated with a 1 percent change in GNP."

This article reviews some of the recent professional literature on the lag in the effect of monetary policy, with the objective of examining the factors which account for differences in the results. Among the factors considered are: (1)

---

[2] The properties of the Federal Reserve-MIT model are discussed by de Leeuw and Gramlich [13, 14] and by Ando and Modigliani [6].

[3] See Hamburger [21] and Mayer [27]. For a recent discussion of why the lag should be long, see Davis [12], Gramlich [19], and Pierce [28]. The alternative view is presented by White [31], who also gives reasons for believing that the procedures used to estimate the parameters of large-scale econometric models, particularly the FRB-MIT model, may yield "greatly exaggerated" estimates of the length of the lag.

the type of statistical estimating model, i.e., structural versus reduced-form equations; (2) the specification of the monetary policy variable; and (3) the influence of the seasonal adjustment procedure. For the most part, the analysis is confined to the results obtained by others. New estimation is undertaken only in those instances where it is considered necessary to reconcile different sets of results.

STRUCTURAL VERSUS
REDUCED-FORM MODELS

We turn first to the question of whether it is more appropriate to use structural or reduced-form models to estimate the effects of stabilization policy on the economy. A structural model of the economy attempts to set forth in equation form what are considered to be the underlying or basic economic relationships in the economy. Although many mathematical and statistical complications may arise, such a set of equations can, in principle, be "reduced" (solved). In this way key economic variables, such as GNP, can be expressed directly as functions of policy variables and other forces exogenous to the economy. While the difference between a structural model and a reduced-form model is largely mathematical and does not necessarily involve different assumptions about the workings of the economy, a lively debate has developed over the advantages and disadvantages of these two approaches.

Users of structural models stress the importance of tracing the paths by which changes in monetary policy are assumed to influence the economy. Another advantage often claimed for the structural approach is that it permits one to incorporate a priori knowledge about the economy, for example, knowledge about identities, lags, the mathematical forms of relationships, and what variables should or should not be included in various equations (Gramlich [20]).

On the other hand, those who prefer the reduced-form approach contend that, if one is primarily interested in explaining the behavior of a few key variables, such as GNP, prices, and unemployment, it is unnecessary to estimate all the parameters of a large-scale model. In addition, it is argued that, if the economy is very complicated, it may be too difficult to study even with a very complicated model. Hence, it may be useful simply to examine the relationship between inputs such as monetary and fiscal policy and outputs such as GNP.

Considering the heat of the debate, it is surprising that very little evidence has been presented to support either position. The only studies of which I am aware come from two sources: simulations with the FRB-MIT model, reported by de Leeuw and Gramlich [13, 14], and the separate work of de Leeuw and Kalchbrenner [15]. The latter study reported the estimates of a reduced form equation for GNP, using monetary and fiscal policy variables similar to those in the FRB-MIT model. The form of the equation is:

Equation 1

$$\Delta Y_t = a + \sum_{i=0}^{7} b_i \Delta NBR_{t-i} + \sum_{i=0}^{7} c_i \Delta E_{t-i}$$
$$+ \sum_{i=0}^{7} d_i \Delta RA_{t-i} + u_t$$

where

ΔY = Quarterly change in GNP, current dollars.

ΔNBR = Quarterly change in nonborrowed reserves adjusted for reserve requirement changes.

ΔE = Quarterly change in high-employment expenditures of the Federal Government, current dollars.

ΔRA = Quarterly change in high-employment receipts of the Federal Government in current-period prices.

u = Random error term.

All variables are adjusted for seasonal variation, and the lag structures are estimated by using the Almon distributed lag technique.[4]

Chart I illustrates the lag distributions of the effect on GNP of nonborrowed reserves—the principal monetary variable used in the studies just mentioned. The chart shows the cumulative effects of a one dollar change in nonborrowed reserves on the level of GNP as illustrated by four experiments, the reduced-form equation of de Leeuw and Kalchbrenner and three versions of the FRB-MIT model. The heavy broken line traces the sum of the regression coefficients for the current and lagged values of nonborrowed reserves in the de Leeuw-Kalchbrenner equation (i.e., the sum of the b_i's). The other lines show the results obtained from simulations of the FRB-

---

[4] Use of the Almon [1] procedure has become quite popular in recent years as it imposes very little a priori restriction on the shape of the lag structure, requiring merely that it can be approximated by a polynomial. In the applications discussed in this article, it is generally assumed that a second- or a fourth-degree polynomial is sufficiently flexible to reproduce closely the true lag structure.

Chart 1: Cumulative Effects of a $1 Change in Nonborrowed Reserves on GNP

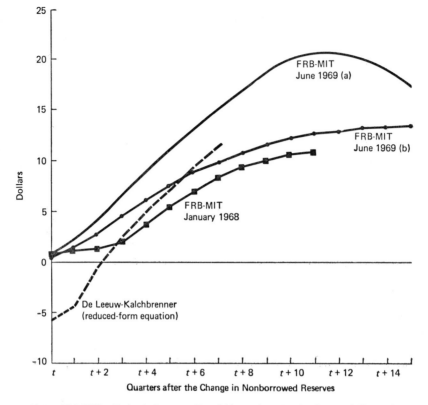

Note: FRB-MIT = Federal Reserve Board-Massachusetts Institute of Technology econometric model.

MIT model; FRB-MIT 1969(a) and FRB-MIT 1969(b) represent simulations of the 1969 version of the model, with two different sets of initial conditions.[5] FRB-MIT 1968 gives the simulation results for an earlier version of the model.

Although there are some large short-run differences in the simulation results, these three experiments suggest similar long-run effects of

nonborrowed reserves on income. Such a finding is not very surprising; what is significant, in view of the debate between those who prefer structural models and those who prefer reduced forms, is that after the first three or four quarters the de Leeuw-Kalchbrenner results lie well within the range of the simulation results.[6]

Thus, we find that when nonborrowed reserves

---

[5] For the FRB-MIT 1969(a) simulation, the values of all exogenous variables in the model, except nonborrowed reserves, are set equal to their actual values starting in the first quarter of 1964. For the FRB-MIT 1969(b) simulation, the starting values for these variables are their actual values in the second quarter of 1958. The obvious difference between these two sets of initial conditions is the difference in inflationary potential. The quarters during and after 1964 were ones of high resource utilization, and an expansion of reserves at such a time might be expected to stimulate price increases promptly. On the other hand, there was substantial excess capacity in 1958 and a change in reserves under such conditions would be expected to have a minimal short-run effect on prices. The difference in these price effects is significant since it is movements in *current*-dollar GNP which are being explained.

[6] De Leeuw and Kalchbrenner do not estimate lags longer than seven quarters. While it is conceivable that the curve representing their results could flatten out (or decline) after period t-7, the shape of the curve up to that point and the results obtained by others, such as those shown in Chart 2, make this possibility seem highly unlikely. The initial negative values for the de Leeuw-Kalchbrenner curve arise because of the large negative estimate of b_o in equation 1; the estimates for all other b's are positive. As de Leeuw and Kalchbrenner pointed out, it is difficult to provide an economic explanation for changes in nonborrowed reserves having a negative effect on GNP in the current quarter. It seems more reasonable, therefore, that the result reflects "reverse causation," running from GNP to nonborrowed reserves—that is, the Federal Reserve's attempt to pursue a contracyclical monetary policy. This point is discussed at greater length in Hamburger [22].

are chosen as the exogenous monetary policy variable, i.e., the variable used in *estimating* the parameters of the model, it makes very little difference whether the lag in the effect of policy is determined by a structural or a reduced-form model. There is, to be sure, no assurance that similar results would be obtained with other monetary variables or with other structural models (including more recent versions of the FRB-MIT model). In the present case, however, the use of reduced-form equations does not lead to estimates of the effects of monetary policy on the economy that differ from those obtained from a structural model. For the purposes of our analysis, this finding implies that the type of statistical model employed to estimate the lag in the effect of monetary policy may be less important than other factors in explaining the differences in the results that have been reported in the literature.

SPECIFICATION OF THE MONETARY POLICY VARIABLE

Another important difference among the various studies of the lag is the variable used to represent monetary policy. The aim of this section is not to contribute to the controversy about the most appropriate variable, but rather to summarize the arguments and spell out the implications of the choice for the estimate of the lag in the effect of policy.

In recent years, three of the most popular indicators of the thrust of monetary policy have been the money supply, the monetary base, and effective nonborrowed reserves.[7] Monetarists prefer the first two variables on the grounds that they provide the most appropriate measures of the impact of monetary policy on the economy. Critics of the monetarist approach contend that these variables are deficient because they reflect the effects of both policy and nonpolicy influences and hence do not provide reliable (i.e., statistically unbiased) measures of Federal Reserve actions. The variable most often suggested by these economists is effective nonborrowed re-

serves.[8] In reply, the monetarists have argued that, since the Federal Reserve has the power to offset the effects of all nonpolicy influences on the money supply (or the monetary base), it is the movements in the money variable and not the reasons for the movements which are important (Brunner [7] and Brunner and Meltzer [8]). However, this sidesteps the statistical question of whether the money supply or the monetary base qualify as exogenous variables to be included on the right-hand side of a reduced-form equation. (For a further discussion, see Gramlich [20] and Hamburger [22].)

Chart 2 presents the cumulative percentage distributions of the effects of various monetary variables on nominal GNP, as implied by the parameter estimates for equations similar to equation 1, that is, reduced-form equations relating quarterly changes in GNP to quarterly changes in monetary and fiscal policy variables. The monetary variables are effective nonborrowed reserves, the monetary base, the narrowly defined money supply (private holdings of currency and demand deposits), and total reserves. The latter is defined as effective nonborrowed reserves plus member bank borrowings from the Federal Reserve. It is also approximately equal to the monetary base less the currency holdings of nonmember banks and of the nonbank public. Once again, the lag structures for the monetary and fiscal policy variables are estimated using the Almon distributed lag technique. In all cases, with the possible exception of the monetary base, the lags chosen are those which maximize the $\bar{R}^2$ (coefficient of determination adjusted for degrees of freedom) of the equation. Percentage distributions are used to highlight the distribution of the effects over time as opposed to their dollar magnitudes.[9]

---

[7] Nonborrowed reserves adjusted for changes in reserve requirements. A similar adjustment is made in computing the monetary base, which is defined as total member bank reserves plus the currency holdings of nonmember banks and the nonbank public. The reserve figure included in the base is also adjusted to neutralize the effects of changes in the ratio of demand deposits to time deposits and changes in the distribution of deposits among banks subject to different reserve requirements.

[8] Among others, see de Leeuw and Kalchbrenner [15], Gramley [18], and Hendershott [23].

[9] The estimates shown in Chart 2 are derived from the equations reported by Corrigan [10] and by Andersen and Jordan [4]. Corrigan's results are used for the nonborrowed reserves, total reserves, and money supply curves (the nonborrowed reserves equation is not shown in his article but is available on request). He did not estimate an equation for the monetary base. The fiscal policies variables used in all three equations are the changes in the Government spending and tax components of the "initial stimulus" measure of fiscal policy. The monetary base curve is derived from the Andersen and Jordan results. The fiscal measures used in this study are the Government expenditure and receipt components of the high-employment budget. The criterion used by Andersen and Jordan to select their lag structures is described by Keran [24].

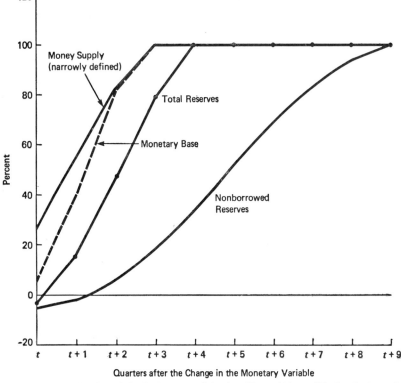

Chart 2: Cumulative Percentage Distributions of the Effects of Various Monetary Aggregates on GNP

Quarters after the Change in the Monetary Variable

Sources: Corrigan (10), Andersen and Jordan (4), and Keran (24). See footnote 9.

The results indicate that the choice of the exogenous monetary policy variable has a significant effect on the estimate of the lag in the effect of policy. If the money supply, the monetary base, or total reserves are taken as the monetary variable, the results suggest that the total response of GNP to a change in policy is completed within four or five quarters. On the other hand, those who consider nonborrowed reserves to be the appropriate variable would conclude that less than 40 percent of the effect occurs in five quarters and that the full effect is distributed over two and a half years.[10]

Thus, the evidence suggests that the relatively short lags that have been found by the monetarists in recent years depend more on their specification of the monetary policy variable than on the use of a reduced-form equation. Whether or not these estimates understate the true length of the lag, they seem roughly consistent with the prevailing view among economists in the early

1960s. They are, for example, essentially identical with Mayer's [26] results which suggested that most of the effect of a change in policy occurs within five quarters. As indicated above, wide acceptance of the proposition that monetary policy operates with a long lag—i.e., a substantial portion of the impact of a policy change does not take place until a year or more later— is of relatively recent vintage and appears to have been heavily influenced by the results of those who do not consider the money supply to be an appropriate measure of monetary policy impulses.

THE SEASONAL ADJUSTMENT PROBLEM

One of the most recent investigations of the effects of monetary and fiscal policy on the economy is that conducted by Laffer and Ranson for the Office of Management and Budget [25]. Perhaps the most striking finding of this study is that every change in the money supply has virtually all its effect on the level of GNP in the quarter in which it occurs. Or, to put this dif-

---

[10] A similar conclusion was reached by Andersen [2], who found even longer lags when nonborrowed reserves are used as the monetary policy variable.

ferently, there is little evidence of a lag in the effect of monetary policy. This finding which stands at odds with most other evidence, both theoretical and empirical, is attributed by Laffer and Ranson largely to their use of data that are *not* adjusted for seasonal variation.[11] They contend that the averaging (or smoothing) properties of most seasonal adjustment procedures tend to distort the timing of statistical relationships. Hence, specious lag structures may be introduced into the results.

As shown below, however, the results reported by Laffer and Ranson are much more dependent on their choice of time period (1948–69) than on the use of seasonally unadjusted data. For, if their nominal GNP equation is re-estimated for the period 1953–69 (the period employed in the current version of the St. Louis model [3] and in most other recent investigations), it makes very little difference whether one uses seasonally adjusted or unadjusted data. They both indicate that a significant portion of the effect of a change in money does not occur for at least two quarters.

The equation selected by Laffer and Ranson to explain the percentage change in nominal GNP is:[12]

Equation 2

$%\Delta G$ = Quarterly percentage change in Federal Government purchases of goods and services.

ΔSH = Quarterly change in a measure of industrial man-hours lost due to strikes.

$%\Delta S\&P$ = Quarterly percentage change in Standard and Poor's Composite Index of Common Stock Prices (the "S&P 500").

D_1 = Seasonal dummy variable for the first quarter.

D_2 = Seasonal dummy variable for the second quarter.

D_3 = Seasonal dummy variable for the third quarter.

All data used in the calculations are unadjusted for seasonal variation. The three dummy variables (D_1, D_2, and D_3) are introduced to allow for such variation and to permit estimation of the seasonal factors. In principle, joint estimation of the seasonal factors and the economic parameters of a model is preferable to the use of data generated by the standard type of seasonal adjustment procedure. However, in having only three dummy variables, Laffer and Ranson assume that the seasonal pattern in income is constant over

$$%\Delta Y = 3.21 + 1.10\%\Delta M_1 + .136\%\Delta G - .069\%\Delta G_{-1} - .039\%\Delta G_{-2} - .024\%\Delta G_{-3} - .046\Delta SH$$
$$\quad (4.9) \quad (5.5) \qquad (6.9) \qquad (3.3) \qquad\qquad (1.9) \qquad\qquad (1.2) \qquad\qquad (3.7)$$
$$\quad + .068\%\Delta S\&P_{-1} - 9.8\,D_1 + 2.5\,D_2 - 3.0 D_3$$
$$\qquad (2.2) \qquad\qquad (12.1) \quad (2.6) \quad (4.1)$$
$$R^2 = .958 \quad SE = 1.31 \quad \text{Interval: 1948-I to 1969-IV}$$

where

$%\Delta Y$ = Quarterly percentage change in nominal GNP.

$%\Delta M_i$ = Quarterly percentage change in M_1 (the narrowly defined money supply).

---

[11] Other studies which find very short lags in the effect of monetary policy are cited by Laffer and Ranson [25].

[12] The numbers in parentheses are t-statistics for the regression coefficients. SE is the standard error of estimate of the regression. A subscript preceded by a minus sign indicates that the variable is lagged that many quarters. In estimating their model, Laffer and Ranson use quarterly changes in the natural logarithms of the variables. This is roughly equivalent to using quarter-to-quarter percentage changes.

the entire sample period. If this assumption is not correct, it becomes a purely empirical question as to whether their procedure is any better or worse than the use of seasonally adjusted data.

Stock market prices are included in the equation on the assumption that the current market value of equities provides an efficient forecast of future income. The variable representing the percentage of man-hours lost due to strikes (SH) is included for institutional reasons.

Aside from these factors, the Laffer-Ranson equation is quite similar to the St. Louis equation. The most important difference is that the former contains only the current-quarter value of money. This implies that a change in the money supply has a once-and-for-all effect on the level of income. Equation 3 shows the results obtained when four lagged values of the percentage

Table 1: Regressions Explaining the Percentage Change in Gross National Product

Equation	Constant	$\%\Delta M_1$	$\%\Delta M_{1-1}$	$\%\Delta M_{1-2}$	$\%\Delta M_{1-3}$	$\%\Delta M_{1-4}$	$\%\Delta G$	$\%\Delta G_{-1}$	$\%\Delta G_{-2}$	$\%\Delta G_{-3}$	ΔSH	$\%\Delta S\&P_{-1}$	D_1	D_2	D_3	$\bar{R}^2$	SE
1948-I to 1969-IV																	
2	3.21 (4.9)	1.10 (5.5)					.136 (6.9)	−.069 (3.3)	−.039 (1.9)	−.024 (1.2)	−.046 (3.7)	.068 (2.2)	−9.8 (12.1)	2.5 (2.6)	−3.0 (4.1)	.958	1.31
3	3.36 (3.9)	1.03 (4.4)	−.41 (1.7)	.49 (2.1)	−.31 (1.3)	.30 (1.3)	.136 (7.1)	−.073 (3.7)	−.034 (1.7)	−.024 (1.3)	−.045 (3.6)	.095 (2.9)	−9.5 (7.6)	1.3 (0.9)	−2.9 (2.4)	.961	1.26
1948-I to 1952-IV																	
2a	5.05 (4.8)	.61 (1.6)					.125 (5.7)	−.119 (5.6)	−.022 (1.2)	−.015 (0.6)	−.050 (3.3)	.221 (3.2)	−11.0 (8.8)	−1.5 (0.8)	−2.7 (2.3)	.983	0.86
3a	2.38 (1.06)	1.11 (2.0)	−.29 (0.5)	−.18 (0.2)	−.24 (0.3)	.66 (1.4)	.121 (3.7)	−.122 (4.0)	−.024 (0.9)	−.030 (0.9)	−.036 (1.9)	.171 (2.0)	−7.2 (2.3)	3.7 (0.8)	1.0 (0.3)	.983	0.86
1953-I to 1969-IV																	
2b	4.16 (5.1)	.73 (3.1)					.143 (3.8)	−.008 (0.2)	−.042 (1.1)	−.048 (1.3)	−.002 (1.4)	.061 (1.8)	−11.2 (10.2)	1.8 (1.6)	4.2 (4.2)	.964	1.20
3b	5.18 (5.1)	.64 (2.4)	−.40 (1.3)	.88 (3.1)	−.07 (0.3)	−.05 (0.2)	.160 (4.4)	.002 (0.1)	−.044 (1.2)	−.068 (1.9)	−.026 (1.7)	.079 (2.1)	−11.6 (7.8)	−1.8 (1.0)	−5.2 (3.6)	.968	1.13

Note: Values of "t" statistics are indicated in parentheses. For explanation of the symbols other than those shown below, see equation 2 above.
$\bar{R}^2$ = Coefficient of determination (adjusted for degrees of freedom).
SE = Standard error of estimate of the regression.

Table 2:   Selected Regression Results for Equations Explaining the Percentage Change in Gross National Product

Equation	Time Period	Data	Regression Coefficients					$\bar{R}^2$
			$\%\Delta M_1$	$\%\Delta M_{1_{-1}}$	$\%\Delta M_{1_{-2}}$	$\%\Delta M_{1_{-3}}$	$\%\Delta M_{1_{-4}}$	SE
3.........	1948-I to 1969-IV	NSA	1.03	−.41	.49	−.31	.30	.961
			(4.4)	(1.7)	(2.1)	(1.3)	(1.3)	1.26
3b........	1953-I to 1969-IV	NSA	.64	−.40	.88	−.07	−.05	.968
			(2.4)	(1.3)	(3.1)	(0.3)	(0.2)	1.13
3b'.......	1953-I to 1969-IV	SA	.37	−.08	.53	.32	−.21	.541
			(1.8)	(0.3)	(1.9)	(1.2)	(1.1)	0.71

Note: Values of "t" statistics are indicated in parentheses. For explanation of the symbols other than those shown below, see equation 2 on page 345.
R^2 = Coefficient of determination (adjusted for degrees of freedom).
SE   = Standard error of estimate of the regression.
NSA   = Not seasonally adjusted.
SA   = Seasonally adjusted data are used for M_1, GNP, and G.

change in M_1 are included in the model. Only the coefficient of the money variables are shown below; the rest of the results for this equation as well as those for equation 2 are reproduced in the first portion of Table I.

Equation 3

$$\%\Delta Y = 3.36 + 1.03\%\Delta M_1 - .41\%\Delta M_{1_{-1}} + .49\%\Delta M_{1_{-2}} - .31\%\Delta M_{1_{-3}} + .30\%\Delta M_{1_{-4}} \ldots$$
$$(3.9)\quad(4.4)\qquad(1.7)\qquad\quad(2.1)\qquad\qquad(1.3)\qquad\qquad(1.3)$$
$$\bar{R}^{-2} = .961\quad\quad SE = 1.26\quad\quad \text{Interval: 1948-I to 1969-IV}$$

Following Laffer and Ranson, the coefficients of this equation are estimated without the use of the Almon distributed lag technique. Although some of the lagged money coefficients approach statistical significance, equation 3—like equation 2—implies that the current and long-run effects of money on income are, for all practical purposes, the same. An increase of 1 percent in M_1 is associated with a roughly 1 percent rise in income in the current quarter and a 1.1 percent rise in the long run.

To test the hypothesis, suggested above, that it is the time interval used by Laffer and Ranson which is largely responsible for this result, equations 2 and 3 were reestimated for the subperiods 1948-I to 1952-IV and 1953-I to 1969-IV. The results (see the two lower sections of Table I) show that: (a) the relationship between money and income in the 1948–52 period is not statistically significant (equations 2a and 3a) [13] and (b)

[13] The contribution of the five money variables to the explanatory power of equation 3a may be evaluated by using the statistical procedure known as the F-test. When this is done, we find that the relationship between money and income is not significant even at the .20 confidence level. It should also be noted that the poor showing of the money variables in the 1948–52 period cannot be attributed

there is a significant lag in the effect of money on income during the more recent period. Indeed, the largest single change in income as a result of a change in money during this period occurs after a lag of two quarters (equation 3b). [14]

Perhaps the most interesting feature of the results is the similarity between the "money coefficients" for the period 1953–69 (equation 3b) and those which have been obtained by other researchers using seasonally adjusted data for the same period. To demonstrate this, equation 3b was reestimated with seasonally adjusted data for M_1, GNP, and G. The coefficients for the current and lagged money variables for this equation (3b') and for equations 3 and 3b are

simply to the shortness of the period and hence the limited number of degrees of freedom. These conditions do not prevent us from finding statistically significant relationships for most of the other variables included in equations 2a and 3a.

[14] In fairness to Laffer and Ranson, it should be noted that even for equation 3b we are unable to reject the hypothesis (at the .05 confidence level) that the current-quarter money coefficient is less than 1.0. However, there appears to be no necessary reason why the current-quarter effect should be singled out for special consideration. Thus, equation 3b also implies that after six months the cumulative effect of money on income is not significantly different from zero.

The hypothesis that the same regression model fits the entire Laffer-Ranson sample period (1948–69) may be evaluated by means of a procedure developed by Chow [9]. Doing this, we find that the hypothesis may be rejected at the .01 confidence level, that is, the differences in the parameter estimates of equations 2a and 2b and equations 3a and 3b are statistically significant.

Chart 3: Cumulative Effects of a One Percent Change In Money on GNP

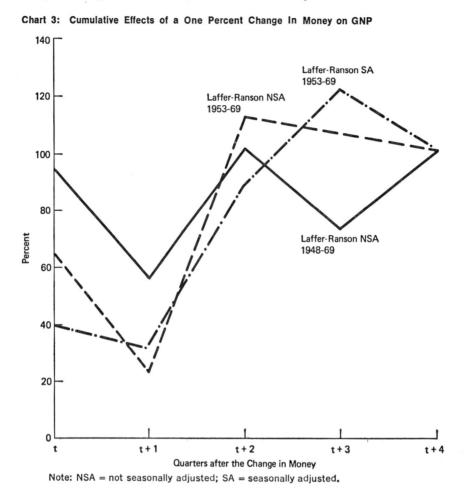

Note: NSA = not seasonally adjusted; SA = seasonally adjusted.

reported in Table 2. Once again the equations are estimated *without* the use of the Almon distributed lag technique. Chart 3 shows the cumulative percentage distribution of the effects of money on income as implied by these equations. It is clear from the chart that it is the time period chosen by Laffer and Ranson which is largely responsible for their controversial result rather than the use of seasonally unadjusted data. This shows up even more dramatically when the equations are estimated with the Almon procedure. When this is done, there is very little difference between the distributed lag implied by the Laffer-Ranson equations (using seasonally unadjusted data but fitted to the 1953–69 period) and that implied by the St. Louis equation [3], see Chart 4.[15] Thus, once the period through the

Korean war is eliminated from the analysis, it makes no difference at all whether the relationship between money and income is estimated with seasonally adjusted data or unadjusted data and dummy variables. Both procedures yield a relatively short, but nevertheless positive, lag in the effect of monetary policy.[16]

THE ALMON LAG TECHNIQUE

Finally, it seems worthwhile to say a few words about the use of the Almon technique and its effect on the estimates of the structure (or distribution) of the lag. As noted earlier, this procedure has become quite popular in recent

---

[15] For comparative purposes, the constraints imposed in estimating the Laffer-Ranson equations with the Almon procedure are the same as those used in the St. Louis equation, i.e., a fourth-degree polynomial with the $t + 1$ and $t - 5$ values of the money coefficients set equal to zero.

[16] An almost identical conclusion is reached in a paper by Johnson [23a]. Laffer and Ranson provide an alternative explanation of the difference between their own lag results—shown in equation 3—and the St. Louis results. However, there is no mention in their article that the time period employed to estimate their equations is considerably different from that used in the St. Louis model and most other recent studies.

Chart 4:   Cumulative Percentage Distribution of the Effects of Money on GNP

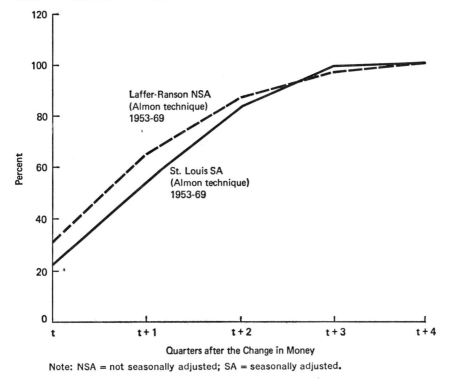

Note: NSA = not seasonally adjusted; SA = seasonally adjusted.

years. It tends to smooth out the pattern of the lag coefficients and makes them easier to rationalize. However, the extent of the differences in the estimates obtained for individual lag coefficients, with and without the use of the technique, provides some reason for concern.

For example, in his experiments with the St. Louis equation, Davis found that either 29 percent or 46 percent of the ultimate effect of money on income could be attributed to the current quarter. The lower number was obtained when the equation was estimated using the Almon technique, while the higher value occurred when the Almon constraint was not imposed on the equation. The explanatory power of the equation was essentially the same in both cases.[17] In the Laffer-Ranson model as well, substantially different estimates of the lag structure are consistent with about the same $\bar{R}^2$. In this model the estimates of the current-quarter effect of money on income are 31 percent with the Almon technique and 64 percent with unconstrained lags (compare the Laffer-Ranson NSA curves for the 1953–69 period in Charts 3 and 4). On the other hand, over the first six months it is the Almon

technique which yields a faster response of income to money, for both the Davis experiments and the Laffer-Ranson model, than is obtained with unconstrained lags.

The wide divergence in these estimates of the impact of monetary variables over short periods, depending on the nature of the estimating procedure employed, suggests that existing estimates of the underlying lag structure are not very precise. One reason for this may be that the pattern of the lag varies over time.[18] In any event, the uncertainties surrounding the structure (distribution) of the lag are not eliminated by the Almon technique. Thus, use of any existing estimates of the lag structure as a firm basis for short-run policy making would seem rather hazardous at this time.

CONCLUDING COMMENTS

One finding stands out from the results presented above, namely, that there is a lag in the

---

[17] See Davis [12]. The estimates of R^2 are .46 and .47, respectively. The period used to estimate the equation was 1952-I to 1968-II.

[18] Some support for this hypothesis is provided by the simulation results for the FRB-MIT model shown in Chart 1 as well as the results obtained by Warburton [30] and Friedman and Schwartz [17] in their analyses of the timing relations between the upswings and downswings in money and economic activity.

effect of monetary policy. Nevertheless, estimates of the length of the lag differ considerably. Of the three factors considered in this paper that might account for these differences, the most important is the specification of the appropriate monetary policy variable (or variables) in the construction of econometric models. Use of non-borrowed reserves as the exogenous monetary variable suggests that less than 40 percent of the impact of a monetary action occurs within five quarters and that the full effect is distributed over two and a half years. On the other hand, use of the money supply, the monetary base, or total reserves suggests that most of the effect occurs within four or five quarters. The latter estimate of the lag may appear to be relatively short. However, it does not seem to be grossly out of line with the view held by the majority of economists in the early 1960s.

The two other factors considered and found to be less important in explaining the differences in the estimates of the length of the lag are (1) the type of statistical estimating model (structural versus reduced-form equations) and (2) the seasonal adjustment procedure. In both of these instances, though, there is not enough evidence available to draw very firm conclusions; hence further work might prove fruitful.

Finally, more work is also needed to help refine estimates of the distribution of the lag. Existing estimates of the lag structure do not appear to be sufficiently precise to justify large or frequent short-run adjustments in the growth rates of monetary aggregates.

WORKS CITED

1. Almon, S. "The Distributed Lag between Capital Appropriations and Expenditures." *Econometrica* (January 1965), pp. 178–96.
2. Andersen, L. C. "An Evaluation of the Impacts of Monetary and Fiscal Policy on Economic Activity." In *1969 Proceedings of the Business and Economic Statistics Section* (Washington, D.C.: American Statistical Association, 1969), pp. 233–40.
3. Andersen, L. C., and Carlson, K. M. "A Monetarist Model for Economic Stabilization." *Review* (Federal Reserve Bank of St. Louis, April 1970), pp. 7–27 (especially p. 11).
4. Andersen, L. C., and Jordan, J. "Monetary and Fiscal Actions: A Test of Their Relative Importance in Economic Stabilization." *Review* (Federal Reserve Bank of St. Louis, November 1968), pp. 11–24.
5. Ando, A., Brown, E. C., Solow, R., and Kareken, J. "Lags in Fiscal and Monetary Policy." In Commission on Money and Credit, *Stabilization Policies* (Englewood Cliffs, N.J.: Prentice Hall, Inc., 1963), pp. 1–163 (especially p. 2).
6. Ando, A., and Modigliani, F. "Econometric Analysis of Stabilization Policies." *American Economic Review* (May 1968), pp. 296–314.
7. Brunner, K. "The Role of Money and Monetary Policy." *Review* (Federal Reserve Bank of St. Louis, July 1968), pp. 8–24.
8. Brunner, K., and Meltzer, A. H. "Money, Debt, and Economic Activity." *Journal of Political Economy* (September/October 1972), pp. 951–77.
9. Chow, G. "Tests of Equality between Two Sets of Coefficients in Two Linear Regressions." *Econometrica* (July 1960), pp. 591–605.
10. Corrigan, E. G. "The Measurement and Importance of Fiscal Policy Changes." *Monthly Review* (Federal Reserve Bank of New York, June 1970), pp. 133–45.
11. Culbertson, J. M. "Friedman on the Lag in Effect of Monetary Policy." *Journal of Political Economy* (December 1960), pp. 617–21 (especially p. 621).
12. Davis, R. G. "How Much Does Money Matter? A Look at Some Recent Evidence." *Monthly Review* (Federal Reserve Bank of New York, June 1969), pp. 119–31 (especially pp. 122–24).
13. de Leeuw, F., and Gramlich, E. M. "The Channels of Monetary Policy." *Federal Reserve Bulletin* (June 1969), pp. 472–91.
14. de Leeuw, F., and Gramlich, E. M. "The Federal Reserve–MIT Econometric Model." *Federal Reserve Bulletin* (January 1968), pp. 11–40.
15. de Leeuw, F., and Kalchbrenner, J. "Monetary and Fiscal Actions: A Test of Their Relative Importance in Economic Stabilization—Comment." *Review* (Federal Reserve Bank of St. Louis, April 1969), pp. 6–11.
16. Friedman, M. *A Program for Monetary Stability* (New York: Fordham University Press, 1960), especially p. 87.
17. Friedman, M., and Schwartz, A. J. *A Monetary History of the United States, 1867–1960* (Princeton: Princeton University Press, 1963).
18. Gramley, L. E. "Guidelines for Monetary Policy—The Case Against Simple Rules." A paper presented at the Financial Conference of the National Industrial Conference Board, New York, February 21, 1969. Reprinted in R. L. Teigen (ed.) *Readings in Money, National Income, and Stabilization Policy* (Homewood, Ill.: Richard D. Irwin, Inc., 1978), pp. 374–79.
19. Gramlich, E. M. "The Role of Money in Economic Activity: Complicated or Simple?" *Business Economics* (September 1969), pp. 21–26.
20. Gramlich, E. M. "The Usefulness of Monetary and Fiscal Policy as Discretionary Stabilization

Tools." *Journal of Money, Credit and Banking* (May 1971, Part 2), pp. 20, 506–32 (especially p. 514).

21. Hamburger, M. J. "The Impact of Monetary Variables: A Survey of Recent Econometric Literature." In *Essays in Domestic and International Finance* (New York: Federal Reserve Bank of New York, 1969), pp. 37–49.

22. Hamburger, M. J. "Indicators of Monetary Policy: The Arguments and the Evidence." *American Economic Review* (May 1970), pp. 32–39.

23. Hendershott, P. H. "A Quality Theory of Money." *Nebraska Journal of Economics and Business* (Autumn 1969), pp. 28–37.

23a. Johnson, D. D. "Properties of Alternative Seasonal Adjustment Techniques, A Comment on the OMB Model." *Journal of Business* (April 1973), pp. 284–303.

24. Keran, M. W. "Monetary and Fiscal Influences on Economic Activity—The Historical Evidence." *Review* (Federal Reserve Bank of St. Louis, November 1968), pp. 5–24 (especially p. 18, footnote 22).

25. Laffer, A. B., and Ranson, R. D. "A Formal Model of the Economy." *Journal of Business*

(July 1971), pp. 247–70 (especially pp. 257–59).

26. Mayer, T. "The Inflexibility of Monetary Policy." *Review of Economics and Statistics* (November 1958), pp. 358–74.

27. Mayer, T. "The Lag in Effect of Monetary Policy: Some Criticisms." *Western Economic Journal* (September 1967), pp. 324–42 (especially pp. 326 and 328).

28. Pierce, J. L. "Critique of 'A Formal Model of the Economy' by Arthur B. Laffer and R. David Ranson." In United States Congress, Joint Economic Committee, *The 1971 Economic Report of the President, Hearings*, Part I (February 1971), pp. 300–12.

29. Smith, W. L. "On the Effectiveness of Monetary Policy." *American Economic Review* (September 1956), pp. 588–606.

30. Warburton, C. "Variability of the Lag in the Effect of Monetary Policy, 1919–1965." *Western Economic Journal* (June 1971), pp. 115–33.

31. White, W. H. "The Timeliness of the Effects of Monetary Policy: The New Evidence from Econometric Models." *Banca Nazionale del Lavoro Quarterly Review* (September 1968), pp. 276–303.

27. THE ROLE OF GOVERNMENT INTERMEDIARIES IN THE RESIDENTIAL MORTGAGE MARKET*

Warren L. Smith

The most striking development in the residential mortgage market in recent years has been the massive support provided directly or indirectly by governmental or quasi-governmental agencies. Table I shows the net increases in residential mortgage debt and the portion accounted for by (*a*) net acquisitions of residential mortgages by the Federal Government (largely GNMA and its predecessor, the special assistance and management and liquidating functions of old FNMA) and by FNMA, and (*b*) the change in advances by the Federal Home Loan Banks to savings and loan associations. Over the four and one half year period from the beginning of 1966 to

mid-1970, Federal support, defined as the increase in mortgage holdings of the Federal Government and FNMA plus the increase in FHLB advances, amounted to 26.1 percent of the total increase in residential mortgage debt. In the latest year and a half—from the beginning of 1969 through the first half of 1970—Federal support amounted to 47.1 percent of the increase in mortgage debt. The recent volume of Federal support is much greater than was forthcoming in earlier years; from 1954 through 1965, Federal support averaged only 5.5 percent of the total increase in residential mortgage debt and in only two years did it exceed 10 percent.[1]

There can be no doubt that a portion of this exceptionally high level of Federal support for the mortgage market in the last few years can be attributed to a desire to offset a part of the

* From *Housing and Monetary Policy*, Proceedings of the Monetary Conference at Melvin Village, New Hampshire, October, 1970 (Boston, 1970), pp. 86–101. Reprinted by permission of the Federal Reserve Bank of Boston. The late Warren L. Smith was Professor of Economics, University of Michigan.

[1] These two years were 1957 (13.2 percent) and 1959 (18.0 percent).

Table 1: Net Increase in Residential Mortgage Debt and Portion Accounted for by Federal Support Activities, (amounts in billions of dollars)

	(1)	(2)	(3)	(4)	(5)	(6)
		Net Acquisitions by		Change in FHLB Advances		Ratio of Federal Support to Total Increase in
	Total Increase in Residential Mortgage			to Savings and Loan	Total Federal	Mortgage Debt [(5) ÷ (1)]
Year	Debt[a]	U.S. Government[c]	FNMA[c]	Associations	Support	percent
1966...............	$13.5	$0.9	$1.9	$0.9	$3.7	27.4
1967...............	16.1	0.9	1.1	−2.5	−0.5	—
1968...............	18.8	1.1	1.6	0.9	3.6	19.1
1969...............	20.0	0.8	3.9	4.0	8.7	43.5
1970[b]...............	15.5	0.7	5.5	2.6	8.7	56.1

[a] Includes the categories, "home mortgages" and "multifamily residential mortgages" as shown in the Federal Reserve flow of funds accounts.

[b] First six months, at seasonally adjusted annual rate.

[c] Prior to September 1968, data relating to the special assistance and management and liquidating functions of former FNMA are included under U.S. Government while secondary market operations are included under FNMA. Beginning with the division of former FNMA into GNMA and new FNMA in September 1968, GNMA is included under U.S. Government.

Editor's note: Following are data on residential mortgage debt and federal support activities for the period 1970–76, extending the data shown above. Note that the entries for 1970 are annual rates based on that year's first six months only. The 1970 data given below are for the entire year. Net acquisitions include residential mortgages backing securities issued by GNMA, the Federal Home Loan Mortgage Corporation, and the Farmers Home Administration, as well as other mortgage holdings of agencies. Only the categories, "home mortgages" and "multifamily residential mortgages" are included, except for the $1.7 billion shown as net U.S. government acquisitions in 1970. For this year alone, it was not possible to separate farm and commercial mortgage acquisitions from residential mortgage acquisitions using the published data. Therefore the $1.7 billion figure probably overstates U.S. government acquisitions for residential mortgages, but the error is believed to be small. The data for years following 1970 reflect only residential mortgage acquisitions.

| | | Net Acquisitions by | | Change in FHLB Advances | | Ratio of Federal |
| | Total Increase in Residential Mortgage | | | to Savings and Loan | Total Federal | Support to Total Increase in |
Year	Debt	U.S. Government	FNMA	Associations	Support	Mortgage Debt
1970...............	$21.3	$1.7	$4.5	$1.3	$7.5	35.2
1971...............	38.3	3.4	2.3	−2.7	3.0	7.8
1972...............	55.3	3.2	2.0	—	5.2	9.4
1973...............	56.8	3.6	4.4	7.2	15.2	26.8
1974...............	41.6	9.0	5.4	6.7	21.1	50.7
1975...............	40.7	13.6	2.2	−4.0	11.8	29.0
1976...............	65.5	14.8	1.1	−2.0	13.9	21.2

At the end of 1976, FNMA held $32.9 billion of residential mortgages, and had $3.4 billion of commitments outstanding. The Federal Home Loan Mortgage Corporation held $4.3 billion of residential mortgages and had $0.3 billion of commitments outstanding. Other government agencies (GNMA, the Farmers Home Administration, the Federal Housing and Veterans Administrations, and the Federal land banks), held $10.7 billion of residential mortgages at the end of 1976.

Source: *Flow of Funds Accounts, 1945–1968: Annual Total Flows and Year-End Assets and Liabilities*, March 1970; and *Flow of Funds, Seasonally Adjusted, 2nd Quarter, 1970* (preliminary, August 13, 1970).

disproportionate impact of restrictive monetary policy on the housing sector. At the same time, however, I believe a substantial part of it can be attributed to a change in the importance attached to housing among our national goals and to changes in the structure and functioning of the mortgage market, the full implications of which we have not yet seen. In this paper, I shall first attempt to sketch the structural changes in the mortgage market as they relate to the establishment of a greater role for governmental or quasi-governmental intermediaries, and, sec-

ond, to speculate on the functioning of the new system of housing finance toward which these developments are rapidly leading us.

STRUCTURAL CHANGES IN THE MORTGAGE MARKET

Perhaps the most basic change in our attitudes toward housing and the mortgage market can be attributed to the establishment of a quantitative 10-year housing goal, calling for the production of 26 million new or substantially rehabilitated housing units in the Housing and Urban Development Act of 1968. Since 1949, the United States has had a statutory national goal of "a decent home and a suitable living environment for every American family." However, it was not until the passage of the 1968 Act that this objective was translated into a definite quantitative target. While the 1968 Act did not establish a set of policy instruments to be used to achieve the target, it did require the preparation by the Secretary of Housing and Urban Development of annual reports on national housing goals, and two such reports have thus far been prepared. The existence of a statutory quantitative national goal and the requirement of annual reports indicating the actions being taken to achieve that goal have, I believe, served to energize the activities of the Federal Government relating to housing and have led to innovations that would probably not otherwise have taken place. Whether it is desirable to have a specific national target for homebuilding alone among the many desirable activities that compete for our limited national resources is an issue on which I shall not comment.

In the wake of the Housing Act of 1968, a number of institutional and behavioral changes relating to the Federal Government's role in the mortgage market have already occurred, and a number of further innovations are in prospect.

First, the 1968 Act itself provided for an important reorganization of FNMA. FNMA was divided into two parts: A reorganized FNMA, which was constituted as a Government-sponsored private corporation to take over the responsibility for secondary market operations; and GNMA, which was established as an institution to be operated and financed by the Federal Government to continue the special assistance and management and liquidating functions of old FNMA. In May 1968, prior to the reorganization and in anticipation of it, FNMA changed its method of conducting secondary market operations by substituting the so-called free-market system of making commitments to buy mortgages on the basis of weekly auctions for the previous system based primarily on outright purchases at posted prices.

These changes in the structure and operations of FNMA have permitted a substantial increase in the scope and effectiveness of FNMA's operations. The "free-market" system has enabled the organization to focus its support at the important commitment stage where it does the most good in sustaining residential construction. It has also permitted FNMA to determine the volume of the support it will provide while letting the mar-

ket determine prices. The shift of FNMA to private auspices has taken its operations out of the Federal budget, thereby removing the budget constraint and enabling it to expand the scale of its operations substantially. FNMA's portfolio of mortgages has increased from $6.5 billion in May, 1968, when the free-market system went into operation to $14.1 billion in July, 1970; and its outstanding commitments have increased from $0.5 billion to $4.7 billion over the same period.

GNMA has played an important role in the financing of the various Federal programs for providing housing to low- and moderate-income families, receiving important assistance from FNMA in carrying out this task.[2] In addition, the 1968 Act authorized GNMA, acting as an agent of the Federal Government, to guarantee principal and interest payments on securities issued by private institutions and backed by pools of FHA-insured or VA-guaranteed mortgages. Operations under this program have already begun and give promise of becoming more important in the years ahead.

No doubt as a result in large part of the commitment to a numerical national housing goal contained in the Housing and Urban Development Act of 1968, the Federal Home Loan Bank System has recently come to be much less dominated by its regulatory responsibilities and more concerned about supporting homebuilding through the medium of expanding its advances to member savings and loan associations. During the 10 months from March 1969 through January 1970, when restrictive monetary policy was imposing a severe constraint on net inflows of deposits to savings and loan associations, the Home Loan Bank

[2] Since GNMA's operations fall within the Federal Budget, its lending activities add to the Federal deficit. In order to minimize the budgetary impact of the financing of Federal housing programs, a cooperative arrangement (referred to as the "Tandem Plan") has been worked out between GNMA and FNMA. The procedure works as follows: In the financing of multi-family projects of nonprofit sponsors which provide either rent supplements or interest subsidies for lower-income families, GNMA issues commitments to buy mortgages at par, while FNMA undertakes to buy them at a special price which is equal to the market price plus an adjustment for the fact that the costs of servicing these mortgages are lower than for single-family home mortgages. When the time comes for the financing to be carried out, if FNMA's special price has reached par, FNMA purchases the mortgages. If, however, FNMA's special price is below par, GNMA buys the mortgages at par and resells them to FNMA at the special price. Thus, GNMA's net cash outlay, which is a charge against the Federal budget, is limited to the difference between par and FNMA's special price.

System increased its outstanding advances by $4.5 billion. This expansion of advances, together with a reduction of $2.4 billion in holdings of liquid assets in part permitted by liberalization of FHLB requirements, enabled savings and loan associations to increase their holdings of mortgages by $7.3 billion despite an increase of only $0.6 billion in their deposit liabilities. When deposit inflows to associations began to pick up in the spring of 1970, the Federal Home Loan Bank System undertook a new program involving preferentially low interest rates on advances designed to encourage associations to postpone repayment of advances and instead to use the renewed inflows of deposits to expand mortgage loans. This program was undertaken in anticipation of the passage of the Emergency Home Finance Act of 1970, Title I of which authorized the appropriation of funds to subsidize a program of low-cost advances by the Home Loan Bank System. The Act was signed into law by President Nixon on July 24 of this year.

NEW SYSTEM OF HOUSING FINANCE

The Emergency Home Finance Act of 1970 contains two additional provisions, either or both of which may prove to be of major importance in the future development of the mortgage market. First, Title II authorizes FNMA for the first time to conduct secondary market operations in conventional mortgages. Second, Title III establishes a Federal Home Loan Mortgage Corporation (FHLMC), which is, in effect, a subsidiary of the Federal Home Loan Bank System; this new Corporation is also authorized to conduct secondary market operations in conventional mortgages, financing its operations by the sale of its own securities. The Corporation is also empowered to buy and sell FHA-insured and VA-guaranteed mortgages.

The developments I have been describing constitute the building blocks of a new—and, I believe, substantially improved—system of housing finance in the United States which can be expected to come to maturity in the next decade or so. The essence of the new system lies in the development of a number of bridges connecting the mortgage market with the open securities markets. It is possible to sort out eight links of this kind which already exist or may develop under the new system.

1. The Home Loan Banks may make advances to savings and loan associations, enabling these institutions to expand their holdings of mortgages in excess of their inflows of deposits.

These advances are financed by sales of securities in the open market by the Federal Home Loan Bank System. This link has existed and has been used to a limited extent for many years; its use has been expanded substantially in the last two or three years as a result of the aggressive attitude of the Federal Home Loan Bank Board. However, it seems likely that its use in the future as in the past will be largely confined to the offsetting of the effects of declines in inflows of deposits during periods of restrictive monetary policy. Any effort to expand the volume of advances secularly as a means of channeling additional funds into housing is likely to be unsuccessful, because of the traditional tendency of many savings and loan associations to eschew continuous indebtedness to the Home Loan Banks.

2. FNMA has the power to purchase FHA-insured and VA-guaranteed mortgages, financing these purchases by selling its own securities in the open market. As indicated above, it currently chooses to exercise this power largely through the "free-market" system of auctioning mortgage commitments, although it also purchases a much smaller quantity of mortgages to finance federally assisted housing, either directly or through GNMA. This link between the bond and mortgage markets has also existed for many years, but the scale on which it can be used has been vastly expanded since the Housing and Urban Development Act of 1968 changed the status of FNMA to a private corporation, thereby freeing it from a severe Federal budget constraint.

3. Instead of selling its own securities to finance its acquisitions of FHA-insured and VA-guaranteed mortgages, FNMA may issue mortgage-backed securities against pools of these mortgages, obtaining from GNMA guarantees of payment of principal and interest on the securities. This method of financing has already been used by FNMA, which currently has $1 billion of such mortgage-backed bonds outstanding. As yet, it is too early to tell whether it will prove to be less expensive for FNMA to finance its operations by issuing its own debt or by issuing mortgage-backed securities. FNMA securities are not guaranteed by the United States but are general obligations of, and are guaranteed only by, FNMA. However, FNMA has a high financial rating and has the power, in emergencies, to borrow directly from the U.S. Treasury to the extent of $2.25 billion. Thus, it is not clear that the GNMA guarantee is capable of making mortgage-backed securities more attractive to investors than FNMA's own securities. Under some circumstances, however, there may be an advan-

tage in the use of mortgage-backed securities, since these securities do not count against the debt limit of FNMA, which has currently been set by the Secretary of Housing and Urban Development at 20 times the sum of FNMA's capital and surplus.

4. GNMA may acquire mortgages in pursuance of its special assistance function, financing these purchases by selling its own notes to the U.S. Treasury, which obtains the necessary funds by borrowing from the public through the issuance of direct Treasury debt.

5. GNMA is prepared to guarantee mortgage-backed securities of the "pass-through" type—i.e., on which principal and interest are transmitted to the investor as collected—to be issued by mortgage lenders on the basis of pools of FHA-insured and VA-guaranteed mortgages. Indeed, an amount somewhat in excess of $50 million of these securities has already been issued. The securities are sold on a negotiated basis to private investors in a manner somewhat similar to the private placement of corporate securities. Pass-through securities can be issued by, for example, mortgage companies on the basis of relatively small pools of mortgages (minimum $2 million) and are intended to tap new sources of mortgage funds, such as private pension and trust funds and state-and-local government pension funds.

6. Under Title II of the Emergency Home Finance Act of 1970, FNMA may purchase conventional mortgages from private holders, financing its purchases by sale of its own securities in the market. The legislation includes safeguards designed to insure the maintenance of the quality of conventional mortgages included in FNMA's portfolio and to assure that the funds disbursed by FNMA in purchasing conventional mortgages will go to lenders who are currently participating in mortgage lending activities.

7. The FHLMC created under Title III of the Emergency Home Finance Act of 1970 is specifically authorized to purchase, or make commitments to purchase, conventional mortgages from savings and loan associations or from other financial institutions (e.g., commercial banks) whose deposits or accounts are insured by an agency of the United States. It seems clear that the main activity envisaged for the Corporation is the purchase of conventional mortgages from savings and loan associations with these purchases being financed by issues of the Corporation's own debt. The Corporation provides, in effect, an alternative channel, in addition to the traditional advances mechanism, by which the Federal Home Loan Bank System can provide additional funds to savings and loan associations for mortgage lending, tapping the open securities markets to finance the operation. This new channel has an important advantage over advances by the Home Loan Banks as a means of adding permanently to the funds available for mortgage lending, because advances add to the liabilities of the savings and loan associations, which must, in principle at least, ultimately be repaid, whereas sales of mortgages to FHLMC do not increase such liabilities. The distinction here is somewhat akin to that between "owned reserves" and "borrowed reserves" in international finance.

8. FHLMC is also authorized to purchase FHA-insured and VA-guaranteed mortgages and to use these mortgages as a basis for issues of mortgage-backed securities with a GNMA guarantee. This provides an additional channel by which FHLMC can tap the bond market to obtain funds to be injected into the mortgage market, presumably in the main through savings and loan associations.

There are other possible channels through which the bond market might be tapped to obtain funds for mortgage lending. For example, under the provisions of the Housing and Urban development Act of 1968 which established the mortgage-backed securities program, it would be possible, say, for a group of savings and loan associations to establish a pool of FHA-insured and VA-guaranteed mortgages, against which it would issue mortgage-backed bonds (as distinct from the pass-through type of mortgage-backed securities) with a GNMA guarantee. However, all issues of mortgage-backed securities must have the approval of the Treasury, and it seems likely that the Treasury will want to avoid a great proliferation of small issues of these securities which would not be conducive to the development of an effective market for them. Thus, for the moment, it appears that the issuance of mortgage-backed bonds is likely to be carried out largely by FNMA as one means of financing its portfolio of mortgages. Whether it will even be important here depends upon whether experience demonstrates that FNMA can raise funds more cheaply by issuing mortgage-backed bonds than by issuing its own securities. FHLMC may also issue mortgage-backed bonds with a GNMA guarantee; indeed, as this is being written the Corporation is in the process of accumulating a pool of FHA-insured and VA-guaranteed mortgages in preparation for its first issue of such bonds. However, it seems likely that the Corporation will ultimately focus mainly on what appears to be its primary function, namely, providing support for the conventional mortgage market, financing itself chiefly by issuing its own securities.

Although thus far its extent has been quite limited, it is possible that the pass-through type of mortgage-backed security with a GNMA guarantee has the greatest promise for attracting new sources of funds, such as pension and trust funds, into the mortgage market on a significant scale. The reason is that it permits securities to be designed individually on a negotiated basis to meet to the maximum possible extent the preferences of these institutions.

Assuming that the secondary market facility for conventional mortgages under the auspices of FHLMC proves workable and develops on a substantial scale, I would expect the use of Federal Home Loan Bank advances to recede to its old function of meeting temporary liquidity needs of savings and loan associations resulting primarily from deposit withdrawals. Indeed, it might be desirable to "fund" a portion of the advances now outstanding through purchases of mortgages by FHLMC with the associations using the proceeds to repay advances. This approach seems preferable to the cumbersome procedure provided for in Title I of the Emergency Home Finance Act of 1970 of giving a Federal subsidy to the Federal Home Loan Bank Board to enable the Home Loan Banks to lower the interest rates on these advances as a means of persuading the savings and loan associations not to repay them.

IMPLICATIONS OF THE EMERGING SYSTEM OF MORTGAGE FINANCE

By exploiting the linkages between the bond market and the mortgage market that are described above, I believe the financing of housing in the United States can be improved in some very important ways. The most far-reaching changes are likely to occur in the response of housing and the mortgage market to changes in credit conditions brought about by monetary policy.

There can be little doubt that restrictive monetary policy has a disproportionate—indeed, discriminatory—effect on homebuilding under the present institutional set-up. In part, the response of residential construction to changes in monetary conditions reflects the fact that the desired stock of housing depends upon mortgage interest rates. To the extent that housing demand responds disproportionately to changes in monetary policy on this account, there is nothing about the result that

can be described as "discriminatory" toward housing. But it seems quite clear that during the postwar period, only a part—and at times probably a relatively small part—of the response of homebuilding to restrictive monetary policy can be attributed to the demand-restraining effects of high mortgage interest rates. Two other major sets of forces appear to be involved.

1. When credit tightens and market interest rates rise, commercial banks have an incentive to raise interest rates on savings deposits to attract or hold funds which they need to meet the burgeoning credit demands of their customers. If banks are permitted to raise savings deposit rates, they will pull funds away from savings and loan associations. Even if Regulation Q ceilings are used to hold down rates on back savings deposits, as has recently been the case, the rise in open-market interest rates may induce savers to channel their savings flows away from savings and loan associations and toward direct investment in securities. Since savings and loan associations are heavily specialized in mortgage financing, such a process of "disintermediation" may drastically reduce the availability of mortgage funds. And since savings and loan associations engage heavily in the practice of "borrowing short and lending long," they often have such a large portfolio of old mortgages made at an earlier time when interest rates were lower, that they are slow to benefit from rising interest rates, making it difficult for them to raise rates on their deposits to keep them in line with market rates, even if the regulatory authorities will permit them to do so.

2. The existence of ceilings on mortgage interest rates under state usury laws—and, on occasion, of unrealistically low ceiling interest rates applicable to FHA-insured and VA-guaranteed mortgages—has at times kept mortgage interest rates from rising fully in pace with yields on competitive investments, such as corporate bonds, thereby causing investors who hold diversified portfolios, such as life insurance companies and mutual savings banks, to shift the direction of their investments away from mortgages and toward the bond market.

It seems clear that as a result of these forces, mortgage interest rates have not served to clear the mortgage market during periods of monetary restraint. Credit rationing has played an important part in matching demand and supply, with the result that some potential home buyers who would have been willing to pay the current interest rate for mortgages have been unable to obtain credit.

A great improvement in the functioning of our financial system would be accomplished if we could find a way to move from the present cumbersome and inefficient system of mortgage finance to a system in which mortgage interest rates moved in such a way as to clear the market. Under such a system all potential mortgage borrowers who were willing to pay the going interest rate would be able to find accommodation, and the elements of arbitrary rationing of mortgage funds that now exist would be eliminated.

A MARKET CLEARING ARRANGEMENT FOR THE MORTGAGE MARKET

The development of links between the bond market and the mortgage market of the kind described earlier in this paper provides, I believe, a mechanism which will make it possible to move toward a market clearing arrangement in the mortgage market. However, so many new institutional devices have been introduced into the mortgage market that it seems necessary to develop some kind of plan according to which they can be combined into a coherent system. Let me suggest one way of fitting together the pieces of the jigsaw puzzle.

First, every effort should be made to move toward a system in which mortgage interest rates are fully flexible. Title VI of the Emergency Home Finance Act extends through January 1, 1972, the provisions enacted in May 1968, which give the Secretary of Housing and Urban Development the power to set the maximum interest rates on government-supported mortgages at any level he deems necessary to meet market conditions. As I understand it, the intention is to use the authority provided under this legislation to put into effect on a trial basis the dual market system for FHA and VA mortgages that was recommended by the Commission on Mortgage Interest Rates.[3] This system should provide sufficient flexibility to enable the market to work effectively, and hopefully it may prove to be a transitory arrangement in the process of moving toward complete elimination of the rate ceilings. It is also necessary to continue the efforts to achieve liberalization of the usury laws applicable to mortgage interest rates in many states.

Second, I would like to see a vigorous development of secondary market operations in conventional mortgages by the new FHLMC. There

are many problems involved in getting such a program under way—problems that arise mainly because conventional mortgages are not homogeneous with respect to risk and other investment properties. Assuming these problems can be solved, I would like to see the operations of the Corporation develop along the following lines. FHLMC would establish a schedule of purchase prices for mortgages having different maturities and bearing different interest rates. The yields corresponding to these purchase prices would bear a stable and consistent relationship to the current borrowing costs of the Corporation. The schedule of purchase prices would be changed frequently—perhaps once a month—as borrowing costs changed. The Corporation would stand ready to buy such mortgages as were offered to it by savings and loan associations at this schedule of prices.

Under such a system, potential mortgage borrowers should always be able to obtain accommodation, provided they were willing to pay the prevailing interest rate. Suppose restrictive monetary policy caused "disintermediation" with the result that inflows of funds to savings and loan associations were curtailed. In such circumstances, savings and loan associations could set interest rates on new mortgage loans which were above the interest rates at which FHLMC would buy existing mortgages by an amount sufficient to cover the costs associated with sales of such mortgages to FHLMC. The associations could then make new loans at these rates, selling mortgages out of their existing portfolios to obtain the funds.[4] If there was excess demand at the existing schedule of rates, FHLMC would experience an increase in its holdings of mortgages which it would have to finance by selling more of its own securities. As the volume of its outstanding debt increased, its cost of borrowing would rise, pushing up interest rates on mortgages until the excess demand for mortgages was eliminated and the market was in equilibrium. The adjustments to a marked increase in the demand for living space and an associated increase in the demand for mortgage credit with no change in the underlying credit situation would

---

[3] *Report of the Commission on Mortgage Interest Rates to the President of the United States and to the Congress* (Washington: U.S. Government Printing Office, August 1969), pp. 63–73.

[4] It might appear that a problem could arise due to the reluctance of savings and loan associations to take capital losses on sales of old mortgages. However, this could easily be avoided by selling only recent originated mortgages to FHLMC. Indeed, the Emergency Home Finance Act of 1970 imposes strict limitations on the authority of FHLMC to purchase conventional mortgages which were originated more than one year prior to the date of purchase.

bring a similar set of adjustments into operation.

It would be possible to make the operations of the system symmetrical by having FHLMC sell mortgages out of its portfolio when market conditions warranted, using the proceeds to repay a portion of its debt. This could be accomplished by having it post a schedule of selling prices for mortgages that was somewhat higher than its schedule of buying prices. The yields corresponding to the selling prices might be somewhat lower than the current borrowing costs of the Corporation. Under such an arrangement, if housing demand should slacken at a time when inflows of deposits to savings and loan associations were large, instead of mortgage interest rates falling enough to insure that the entire inflow of funds to savings institutions found lodgment in the mortgage market, a different sequence of events would occur. As soon as mortgage interest rates fell enough relative to other capital market rates to be slightly below the yields corresponding to the posted selling prices of the Corporation, savings and loan associations would begin to buy old mortgages from the Corporation rather than new ones in the market. This would put FHLMC in possession of funds which it could use to retire a portion of its debt. This would serve to inject funds into the capital market generally, bringing down the general level of interest rates, rather than concentrating the downward pressure entirely on the mortgage market.

It should be recognized, however, that there are asymmetries in the system that make it less important to have FHLMC sell mortgages when interest rates decline than to buy them when interest rates rise. During periods of relatively low interest rates, the mortgage market clears under the present system. Moreover, if mortgage demand declines and interest rates fall, there is presumably some incentive for savings and loan associations to lower the interest rates on their deposits. Such a decline in deposit rates might divert funds away from savings and loan associations and help to cause a general decline in interest rates throughout the capital market. However, interest rates on deposits are notoriously sticky in a downward direction; consequently, there might be some benefit to housing over a full cycle of rising and falling interest rates if FHLMC operated asymmetrically, buying mortgages during periods of rising interest rates but not selling them during periods of falling rates. Under such a method of operation, the portfolio of FHLMC would (a) grow during periods when the private market experienced excess demand

for mortgage funds because housing demand was strong relative to the volume of funds becoming available through private channels, and (b) remain constant under conditions in which the private market would clear without assistance.

Third, I would favor a continuation of the present FNMA system of weekly auctions of commitments to buy FHA and VA mortgages. This program has proved to be helpful not only in providing builders with a dependable basis for forward planning but also as a means of pumping a great deal of money into the mortgage market. I would expect, however, that the FNMA auctions would become a less important source of mortgage funds under a system in which interest rates moved consistently to clear the market. Under the FNMA auctions up to now, a very high proportion of the commitments have actually been taken up before the commitment period expired. To a considerable extent this is undoubtedly related to the fact that in periods when market interest rates are relatively high—as has been the case throughout the period since the auction technique was put into operation—the mortgage market has not cleared. That is, mortgage credit has not been available to many borrowers even if they were willing to pay the going interest rate. Under such conditions, many of the participants have undoubtedly used the auctions as a way of protecting themselves against lack of availability of mortgage funds, and auctions have helped to fill the credit availability gap.

Under a market clearing system in which borrowers could be assured of being able to obtain mortgage credit at a price, I would expect participation in the auctions to decline because borrowers would need to protect themselves only against the possibility of adverse movements of interest rates and not against the prospect of lack of availability of funds. Moreover, I would not expect as high a proportion of the commitments to be taken up as has been the case up to now. In some cases, interest rates would prove to be higher than the borrower anticipated and he would take up the commitment, but quite frequently rates should prove to be lower than he expected and it would be advantageous for him to borrow elsewhere.

I must confess that the FNMA auctions have some rather arbitrary aspects that do not really appeal to me. FNMA must decide each week the quantity of funds it is to make available. This involves an essentially subjective judgment about the amount of funds the market "needs." Second, not infrequently FNMA apparently finds that if it were to allot the full amount of commitments it initially announced as being available, it would be forced to accept offers it judges to involve "unreasonably" high prices. In such cases, the amount of funds actually allotted is cut back below that initially announced as being available. I would be happier if some way of conducting FNMA operations could be devised that was determined to a greater extent by objective market criteria and involved fewer subjective and, to my mind, essentially arbitrary decisions. It may be that in an environment in which interest rates moved to clear the mortgage market a different mode of operation involving less emphasis on quantities of funds supplied and more emphasis on mortgage interest rates as a guide to FNMA operations would be desirable.

Fourth, I believe it would be desirable to try to extend the use of the "pass-through" type of mortgage-backed securities with a GNMA guarantee. This program has not amounted to much yet in terms of volume, but it strikes me as the one element among the new instruments of mortgage finance that might be capable of attracting a significant amount of pension and trust fund money.

I view the arrangements I am suggesting primarily as a means of enabling housing to compete more effectively for its fair share of the funds available for investment in the face of the changing vicissitudes of the capital market. I do not think of these arrangements as a way of contributing—except possibly to a minor extent—to the process of mobilizing the vast increase in mortgage credit that will be needed over the next decade to meet the housing goals set forth in the Housing and Urban Development Act of 1968. The necessary funds to meet these goals will only be forthcoming if we rearrange our

fiscal and monetary policies in such a way as to achieve the necessary flows of funds through the capital market. The establishment of an arrangement under which interest rates would move to clear the mortgage market would merely mean that homebuilding would be able to obtain the share of total credit flows to which it was entitled. To the extent that it might be necessary to use restrictive monetary policy from time to time to curtail aggregate demand, the impact on homebuilding would reflect, as it should, the response of home buyers to high costs of financing. It would no longer be either appropriate or desirable to engage in frantic actions designed to cushion the impact of credit conditions on housing.

It should be noted, however, that it would be quite proper for the Federal Government to act to offset the effects of restrictive credit conditions on subsidized housing programs designed to assist low- and moderate-income families. The way to accomplish this would be to increase the subsidy payments to the extent necessary to offset the higher interest costs involved in financing such programs.

Finally, it should be recognized that the establishment of an arrangement under which interest rates moved to clear the mortgage market would almost certainly reduce the potency of monetary policy as an instrument of economic stabilization. Under the present system, the largest and fastest impact of monetary policy is on residential construction, and this impact is to a considerable extent attributable to changes in mortgage credit availability. If the availability effects on housing were eliminated, monetary policy would, I am convinced, be significantly weakened. It would take larger monetary policy actions and larger swings in interest rates to produce a given effect, and the lags of response would become longer.

---

28. CURRENT FEDERAL RESIDENTIAL CREDIT PROGRAMS*

Congressional Budget Office

Federal residential housing finance programs can be classified broadly under six credit policies. The major policy categories, the method of credit assistance, the initial beneficiary, and the way in

which the programs affect the budget are briefly described below.

1. Interest Rate Subsidies

Government National Mortgage Association (GNMA) Tandem Plans, the Farmers' Home Administration (FmHA) Interest Credit, and

* From "Housing Finance: Federal Programs and Issues," Staff Working Paper, Congressional Budget Office, 1976, pp. 11–20. Reprinted by permission of the Congressional Budget Office.

HUD's Section 235 Homeownership Programs provide below-market-interest rate loans. Basically three methods apply: the government either pays part of the interest on private loans, makes the direct loans bearing interest rate subsidies, or (under the so-called "Tandem Plan") commits to purchase private lenders' below market interest mortgages at prices providing a slightly higher than market return. When the government buys them, it ultimately intends to sell at a price that usually represents a loss, because the *selling price* on the mortgages purchased at below market interest rates must reflect the current market rate of interest. Interest rate subsidies on GNMA programs are typically 1½ percentage points (below market rates) for single-family units, and are expected to average 2 percentage points for multi-family housing. FmHA interest credit loans typically carry a subsidy of 6 percentage points. Section 235 subsidies vary with the market interest rate, currently subsidizing the difference between market rates and an income-related rate as low as 5 percent on single-family home mortgages.

The major objective of the GNMA programs is to mitigate cycles in housing construction. When interest rates are cyclically high and housing construction is declining, GNMA makes commitments to provide funds at below-market-interest rates in order to induce additional construction. According to cyclical patterns in the housing industry, GNMA-financed construction should have some effect on housing during tight money periods. However, it appears that most GNMA-financed construction would have taken place in the absence of the program. Many Tandem loans went to high-income borrowers, who might well have bought new homes without assistance; other Tandem money was used to fulfill lending commitments already previously agreed to by private lenders. Treasury borrowing to finance the GNMA program attracted some funds that would otherwise have gone into mortgages through private lending.[1]

However, it is important to distinguish between conventional mortgages and mortgages on properties that are also receiving lower-income subsidies (under sections 235 and 236 in the past, and Section 8 in the future). GNMA pro-grams may be much more necessary in the latter cases than in the former, because primary lenders have not been willing to make loans on subsidized housing if they must then hold them.

The budget impact of these programs is complex. The impact on outlays over the long run is roughly equal to the value of the interest rate subsidy—i.e., the difference between the face value of the mortgages that GNMA buys and the market value of the same mortgages when GNMA sells them. In any particular fiscal year, however, the major determinants of outlays are GNMA portfolio management decisions: outlays will be high if GNMA mortgage purchases exceed mortgage sales; will be low or even highly negative if sales equal or exceed purchases. Outlays also include, of course, operating expenses of various types. In terms of budget authority, new permanent authority plus revolving authority carried over from previous years are required in amounts equal to the total portfolio of mortgages and commitments carried by GNMA, plus operating expenses. Sales of mortgages from the portfolio thus restore budget authority which is then available for additional purchases. GNMA currently has cumulative mortgage purchase authority of $20.5 billion, of which about $12.2 billion is unused (i.e., neither used for mortgages owned nor committed to future purchases, and includes $2 billion appropriated but not released by the Secretary, HUD), as of May 31, 1976.

The Section 235 program, as reconstituted in January 1976, differs from GNMA and FmHA interest subsidies. Under Section 235, HUD subsidizes mortgage interest payments by homeowners. HUD payments of part of lower-income homeowner's mortgage interest are such that the effective interest rate to the homeowner is as low as 5 percent, and his total payments do not exceed 20 percent of his (adjusted) income. Thus the subsidy may continue over the life of the mortgage.

The objectives of the 235 program are to assist lower-income families to become homeowners, and to increase construction of new housing for such families. Under the original 235 program abandonments of properties and defaults were high, in part due to program abuses and very low down-payment requirements. The reconstituted program aims at reducing these problems, in part by increased down-payment requirements and in part by increased minimum interest rates and income standards—both aiming the program at higher income people.

For fiscal year 1976, $42.5 million was re-

---

[1] See George M. von Furstenberg, "The Economics of the $16 Billion Tandem Mortgages Committed in the Current Housing Slump," unpublished paper; and Ronald Utt, "A Study of the Impact of the Government National Mortgage Association's Tandem Plan on Housing Productions," December 11, 1974 (revised December 1975).

served,[2] to subsidize an estimated 50,000 units, at an average maximum subsidy of $850 per year. The income range of participating families is expected to be $9,000 to $11,000 per year, and the average mortgage amount is expected to be $23,000. Ninety percent of the units are to be newly constructed, and 10 percent substantially rehabilitated.

The FmHA programs, in contrast to GNMA and the 235 program, are basically aimed at providing adequate housing in rural areas—not in countering construction cycles. The program does appear to expand rural credit provision although the number of beneficiaries is limited.

2. Direct Loans

The federal government makes loans directly to those specific kinds of borrowers who are unable to find mortgage credit elsewhere. Direct lending was a preferred approach during the 1950s, a period of frequent budget surpluses. The shift away from direct loans to "tandem plans" (discussed earlier) occurred primarily to avoid increases in the budget deficit. Existing direct loan programs include:

a. Section 502 Homeownership Loans made from the Rural Housing Insurance Fund under the Farmers' Home Administration to low-and-moderate homebuyers in rural areas. Loans are financed by the sales of guaranteed FmHA notes (e.g., Certificates of Beneficial Ownership) to the public or to the Federal Financing Bank (FFB), an off-budget agency. Recently the FFB has been the only purchaser. The FFB charges one-eighth to one-half percent higher than the interest rate charged by FmHA on the direct loans, depending on FFB costs of borrowing from Treasury.

Budget outlays vary considerably from year to year, because of variations in defaults and foreclosures and the timing of loans and financing. Outlays also represent net interest expense (difference between interest rate charged by FmHA and the interest paid by FmHA to its public and private creditors) and operating expenses. In fiscal year 1975, operating losses in this program were $175 million, on $9.5 billion of loans outstanding. Nearly $167 million of total

operating losses occurred from interest credit and default expenses within the 502 Homeownership program. For example, the 1975 biannual review of interest credit borrowers shows that each 502 borrower receives an interest subsidy of approximately $684 per year on an average loan amount of $18,800. Median family incomes of 502 loan recipients are around $7,300 to $8,740.

b. VA Direct Loans are made to veterans from the Direct Loan Revolving Fund for new purchases, construction and improvement and for farm purchases.[3] As of fiscal year 1975, the net cumulative value of direct loans outstanding totalled nearly $68 billion. Proportionately, the number and value of annually approved loans have decreased substantially in the last decade; only 2,665 loans were closed in fiscal year 1975. The average loan was $18,344, bearing a 9 percent interest rate on a 25-year life. Generally, net income is realized by VA, since their borrowing costs from Treasury are lower than their direct loan interest rates.

c. Section 312 Rehabilitation Loans are available through HUD for substantially rehabilitated properties in areas specifically defined "uninsurable, high-risk, and in serious decline." The maximum loan is $12,000 per dwelling unit for residential structures. Loan priority is given to low- and moderate-income families subject to discretionary approval by HUD field offices. Private lending institutions service the loans for which HUD pays the fees. The interest rate is also subsidized, HUD paying the difference between the market rate and 3 percent. The net value of cumulative rehabilitation loans outstanding totalled $215.6 million in fiscal year 1975.

d. Some other smaller loan programs directly provide subsidized mortgages: e.g., elderly and handicapped citizens ($508.5 million); and physical disaster loans ($1.3 billion), administered by the Small Business Administration.[4]

3. Insurance and Guarantees

Currently, the government provides numerous insurance and guarantee programs. The primary objective is to increase the availability of mortgage credit, possibly on more liberal terms. An insurance or guarantee eliminates almost all risk of default, generally covering up to 90 percent of any losses. The insurance or guarantee may

---

[2] Total amount available and obligated is $264 million pursuant to court order. Official accounting books carry this amount; however only $42.5 million is reserved for units approved within fiscal year 1976. As of May 3, fiscal year 1976, HUD had approved 12,017 home loans representing slightly over $10.2 million.

[3] Farm purchases include residences on farms. No separate budget accounting distinguishes home types within Subfunction 704, Direct Loan Revolving Fund.

[4] These represent cumulative loans made as of fiscal year 1975.

come at two different points in the lending process: mortgage payments by the homeowner to the lender may be insured or guaranteed by a federal agency (as is done by FHA), or the agency may guarantee privately-issued securities backed by home mortgages (as in the GNMA mortgage-backed securities program). Federally insured lending has declined as a share of all mortgage lending, giving way to private insurance, but remains important in at least three specific submarkets: (1) a portion of the conventional market not privately insured, including lower-income families; (2) the multifamily market in which FHA remains the major insurance force; and (3) primary market lenders that originate loans for their own portfolios and require insurance in order to market or improve the "sales-value" of mortgage backed securities issued by them and guaranteed principally by the Government National Mortgage Association or the Federal Home Loan Mortgage Corporation. Federal insurance programs are numerous and only the major ones are described here.[5]

a. The Federal Housing Administration (FHA) has 40 major insurance programs administered through four subaccounts under the Federal Housing Insurance Fund. Paid-in premium fees are the principal income source and until recently, FHA insurance operations yielded net income.

Sizeable budget outlays ($1.1 billion in fiscal year 1975), have resulted from increasing defaults. In general, the traditional FHA insurance programs (203 and 207) still yield net incomes. But the high default rates, particularly in subsidized Section 235, 236, and 221(d) (3) programs, have caused net losses in General and Special Risk Funds. As of fiscal year 1975, the cumulative number of FHA insurance contracts outstanding totalled 6.1 million with $87 billion of insured mortgage balances.

b. The Veterans Administration (VA) guarantees mortgage loans taken out by eligible veterans. No charge is made to the borrower for the guarantee. Premiums paid by lenders provide revenues to cover the operating expenses of the VA Loan Guaranty Revolving Fund. Unlike the FHA fund, no appropriations have been required. At the end of fiscal year 1975, VA loans guaranteed numbered 3.8 million with mortgage balances of $27.9 billion, based on a 50 percent mortgage guaranty.

c. Under the GNMA mortgage-backed se-

curities program, GNMA guarantees securities issued by private lending institutions and backed by mortgages insured or guaranteed by FHA, VA, or FmHA. $5.9 billion worth of such securities were sold in fiscal year 1975, and a total of $17.7 billion worth was outstanding at the end of that year. GNMA estimates that almost $10 billion more will be sold in 1976. However, the long-run future of the program is limited by the decline in the number of new mortgages now being insured or guaranteed by FHA, VA, or FmHA. The program has been somewhat successful in attracting additional funds into the mortgage market—for example, roughly one-third of the securities are purchased by pension funds, which would probably not otherwise invest as much in mortgages. However, a large number of securities are held by primary mortgage lenders themselves; to this extent the program does not increase funds available for housing but merely adds the GNMA guarantee to the FHA, VA, or FmHA insurance or guarantee on mortgages held by mortgage lending institutions.

FmHA Certificates of Beneficial Ownership perform a similar function, except that here the underlying mortgages are originated and held by FmHA itself, rather than by private lenders.

d. The Federal Home Loan Mortgage Corporation (FHLMC; called "Freddy Mac") guarantees securities issued by S&Ls that are members of the Federal Home Loan Bank System. The securities are backed principally by government insured or guaranteed mortgages (i.e., FHA/VA).

4. Secondary Market Support

Purchases of mortgages from primary lenders and subsequent resale or other refinancing of large blocks of these mortgages by federal and federally sponsored credit agencies have expanded greatly in the last ten years. The original purpose of this kind of activity, as performed by the old FNMA during the 1930s, was to induce lenders to write the then revolutionary low down payment, long-term, federally insured mortgages. FNMA's willingness to purchase these mortgages made them more easily converted into cash (i.e., liquid) and thus more attractive. More recently, the expanded level of activities by FNMA (now a private federally sponsored corporation), GNMA, and FHLMC and FHLBB, has two main objectives: The first, similar to the original concept of FNMA, is to induce primary mortgage lenders to continue making mortgage loans, especially on higher risk housing designed for federally subsidized lower-income occupants. The other purpose

---

[5] Detailed descriptions are contained in the President's *Annual Housing Goals Report* to the Congress.

is to offset cyclical declines in private mortgage credit supplied to residential borrowers.

On the evidence, federal secondary market operations do channel loanable funds into residential mortgages, primarily through thrift institutions, and do provide countercyclical assistance. However, some or all of these funds may have found their way to residential mortgages even without the federal activity; whether the *net* effect of floating federal securities to raise loanable funds that are redirected into thrifts significantly increases the supply of mortgage credit is simply not known.

Analyses of one-shot FNMA mortgage purchases and FHLBB advances to S&Ls, using computer-based simulation models, do show some of the hoped-for effects: short-term decreases in home mortgage interest rates and then increases to slightly below the rates in effect prior to the simulated credit assistance. Overall, however, the effects of secondary lending by federal and federally sponsored credit agencies are still questions. Analysis of the agencies' performance is generally confined to FNMA's traditional countercyclical support of government-underwritten mortgage lending and the equally traditional functions of the FHLBB system in supplying advances to supplement savings inflows and loan repayments to S&Ls to meet FHLBB regulated liquidity requirements. GNMA, FmHA, and FHLMC activities are generally ignored because their operations are relatively new or insufficient data exists. On balance, secondary lending has been countercyclical since 1965 and a mixed pattern of procyclical and countercyclical performance by federal and federally sponsored credit agencies in the pre-1965 period.[6]

Since the early 70s, federal and federally sponsored credit agencies residential mortgage purchases have increased dramatically. At the end of calendar year 1974, federal and federally sponsored credit agencies held $65 billion worth of residential mortgages or nearly 13 percent of total residential mortgage debt outstanding in comparison to $4 billion held in calendar year 1955, or less than 4 percent of the total. Gross acquisitions by federal and federally sponsored credit agencies have fluctuated annually from

$7.9 billion in calendar year 1970 to $14.9 billion in calendar year 1974, while net acquisitions ranged from $6.2 billion to $12.0 billion during the same period.[7] These numbers can be compared to total net acquisitions of $81.6 billion worth of residential mortgages in calendar year 1974.

5. Tax Expenditures

Tax expenditures are, particularly in terms of dollar value, a very important part of federal housing policy. Some of these expenditures are directed specifically toward mortgage credit.

Federal income tax deductions of mortgage interest on owner-occupied homes lowers homeowners' actual borrowing cost significantly, at an expected cost to the Treasury of $4.7 billion in 1976.[8] Other housing-credit-directed tax expenditures include deductions for construction-period interest paid by builders and excess bad debt reserve deductions (larger than expected actual losses) for mutual savings banks and S&Ls.

These tax subsidies represent relatively uncontrollable federal expenditures, determined by the level of activity of private individuals and institutions eligible for the deductions.

As an example, in 1969 the tax allowance for excess bad debt reserves allowed deductions of up to 60 percent of taxable income as additions to reserves. The allowable percentage of income is being reduced by law and will be reduced to 40 percent by 1979.[9] Estimated revenue losses are $570 million in fiscal year 1977. The tax expenditure may have little effect on the amount of investment thrifts hold in residential mortgages, since their choice of investments is already restricted by regulation. Another aspect of the provision is its cyclical nature: The savings to S&Ls are lowest when money is tightest.

---

[6] For detailed analysis of federal and federally sponsored credit agencies performance see Leo Grebler, "Broadening the Sources of Funds for Residential Mortgages," Federal Reserve Staff Study, *Ways to Moderate Fluctuations in Housing Construction,*" published December 1972, and George M. von Furstenberg, "The Economics of the $16 Billion Tandem Mortgages Committed in the Current Housing Slump."

---

[7] Net acquisitions equal gross acquisitions less sales. In essence, it measures the net effect of transactions in both primary and secondary mortgage markets. For detailed technical definitions and statistics for mortgage lending see, Arnold H. Diamond "The Supply of Mortgage Credit, 1970–1974," U.S. Department of Housing and Urban Development, October 1975, pp. 311–15.

[8] See *Tax Expenditures,* Committee on the Budget, United States Senate, March 1976.

[9] To use the maximum, S&Ls are required to keep 82 percent and mutual savings banks 72 percent of their assets in residential mortgages and certain liquid assets. Allowable bad debt asset percent *less* than the maximum 82 percent and 72 percent of assets, down to 60 percent after which the special reserve provision no longer applies.

6   Regulation of Mortgage Lending Institutions

A number of regulations regarding the behavior of major mortgage lending institutions have significant impacts on housing finance. As indicated in the previous chapter the important regulations are:

Ceilings on Deposit Interest Rates. The Federal Home Loan Bank Board and the Federal Reserve Board respectively limit the interest thrift institutions and commercial banks can pay on time and savings deposits and certificates of deposits, maintaining a higher rate for thrifts than for commercial banks.[10] These limits affect the ability of the lenders to compete for savings with which to make loans particularly in tight money periods.

Limitations on Investments by Thrift Institutions. Thrift institutions are prohibited from making many kinds of loans (such as consumer, construction, commercial paper, and corporate bond investments) and are limited to mortgage lending and certain liquid assets.[11]

Limitations on Services by Thrifts. Thrift institutions are prohibited from offering checking accounts or other forms of payment on demand to potential depositors, as well as from making many types of loans customers might desire.[12] These prohibitions limit the ability of thrifts to compete with commercial banks for deposits with which to invest in mortgages (al-

though thrifts clearly enjoy other compensating advantages) and thus may reduce long-term mortgage credit supply.

Ceilings on FHA-Insured and VA-Guaranteed Loan Interest Rates. The HUD Secretary establishes maximum interest rates lenders can charge for FHA-insured and VA-guaranteed loans and adjusts them periodically. Charges of points (essentially prepayment of additional interest) are not regulated, however, and lenders typically use them to compensate for difference between conventional mortgage rates and federal ceilings.

State Usury Laws. Maximum permitted interest rates are regulated by some states for mortgage (and other) lending, and some of the states also limit maximum charges of points. In high interest periods such as the most recent credit cycle, these limitations have become operative in a number of states where ceilings stood at 8 percent, 9 percent, and 10 percent levels. States do legislate increases in ceiling rates, often after market rates have risen significantly above the ceiling and caused serious declines in lending.

Discrimination in Lending. Discrimination against individuals in mortgage lending is prohibited by federal law. The Home Mortgage Disclosure Act of 1975 requires lending institutions to indicate the breakdown of mortgage loans they make by census tract, which will provide information on whether discriminatory lending policies are being practiced against whole areas. A suit has been filed against federal agencies regulating lending for nonenforcement of antidiscrimination provisions, but has not yet come to trial.

These activities have no major direct impact on the federal budget.

---

[10] Current maximum passbook rates are 5 percent for commercial banks and 5¼ for thrifts.

[11] Tax provisions give thrifts incentive to select to put most of their funds in mortgage lending rather than the other permitted assets.

[12] Some states presently have temporary permission from the FHLBB to offer NOW accounts.

29. THE ROLE OF MONETARY POLICY*

Milton Friedman†

There is wide agreement about the major goals of economic policy: high employment, stable prices, and rapid growth. There is less agreement that these goals are mutually compatible or, among those who regard them as incompatible, about the terms at which they can and should be substituted for one another. There is least agreement about the role that various instruments of policy can and should play in achieving the several goals.

My topic for tonight is the role of one such instrument—monetary policy. What can it contribute? And how should it be conducted to contribute the most? Opinion on these questions has fluctuated widely. In the first flush of enthusiasm about the newly created Federal Reserve System, many observers attributed the relative stability of the 1920s to the System's capacity for fine tuning—to apply an apt modern term. It came to be widely believed that a new era had arrived in which business cycles had been rendered obsolete by advances in monetary technology. This opinion was shared by economist and layman alike, though, of course, there were some dissonant voices. The Great Contraction destroyed this naive attitude. Opinion swung to the other extreme. Monetary policy was a string. You could pull on it to stop inflation but you could not push on it to halt recession. You could lead a horse to water but you could not make him drink. Such theory by aphorism was soon replaced by Keynes' rigorous and sophisticated analysis.

Keynes offered simultaneously an explanation for the presumed impotence of monetary policy to stem the depression, a nonmonetary interpretation of the depression, and an alternative to

monetary policy for meeting the depression and his offering was avidly accepted. If liquidity preference is absolute or nearly so—as Keynes believed likely in times of heavy unemployment—interest rates cannot be lowered by monetary measures. If investment and consumption are little affected by interest rates—as Hansen and many of Keynes' other American disciples came to believe—lower interest rates, even if they could be achieved, would do little good. Monetary policy is twice damned. The contraction, set in train, on this view, by a collapse of investment or by a shortage of investment opportunities or by stubborn thriftiness, could not, it was argued, have been stopped by monetary measures. But there was available an alternative—fiscal policy. Government spending could make up for insufficient private investment. Tax reductions could undermine stubborn thriftiness.

The wide acceptance of these views in the economics profession meant that for some two decades monetary policy was believed by all but a few reactionary souls to have been rendered obsolete by new economic knowledge. Money did not matter. Its only role was the minor one of keeping interest rates low, in order to hold down interest payments in the government budget, contribute to the "euthanasia of the rentier," and maybe, stimulate investment a bit to assist government spending in maintaining a high level of aggregate demand.

These views produced a widespread adoption of cheap money policies after the war. And they received a rude shock when these policies failed in country after country, when central bank after central bank was forced to give up the pretense that it could indefinitely keep "the" rate of interest at a low level. In this country, the public denouement came with the Federal Reserve-Treasury Accord in 1951, although the policy of pegging government bond prices was not formally abandoned until 1953. Inflation, stimulated by cheap money policies, not the widely heralded postwar depression, turned out to be the order of the day. The result was the beginning of a revival of belief in the potency of monetary policy.

This revival was strongly fostered among economists by the theoretical developments initiated by Haberler but named for Pigou that pointed out a channel—namely, changes in wealth—

* From *American Economic Review*, vol. 58 (March 1968), pp. 1–17. Reprinted by permission of the publisher and the author. Milton Friedman is Paul Snowden Russell Distinguished Service Professor Emeritus of Economics, University of Chicago, and Senior Research Fellow, Hoover Institution (Stanford University).

Presidential address delivered at the Eightieth Annual Meeting of the American Economic Association, Washington, D.C., December 29, 1967.

† I am indebted for helpful criticisms of earlier drafts to Armen Alchian, Gary Becker, Martin Bronfenbrenner, Arthur F. Burns, Phillip Cagan, David D. Friedman, Lawrence Harris, Harry G. Johnson, Homer Jones, Jerry Jordan, David Meiselman, Allan H. Meltzer, Theodore W. Schultz, Anna J. Schwartz, Herbert Stein, George J. Stigler, and James Tobin.

whereby changes in the real quantity of money can affect aggregate demand even if they do not alter interest rates. These theoretical developments did not undermine Keynes' argument against the potency of orthodox monetary measures when liquidity preference is absolute since under such circumstances the usual monetary operations involve simply substituting money for other assets without changing total wealth. But they did show how changes in the quantity of money produced in other ways could affect total spending even under such circumstances. And, more fundamentally, they did undermine Keynes' key theoretical proposition, namely, that even in a world of flexible prices, a position of equilibrium at full employment might not exist. Henceforth, unemployment had again to be explained by rigidities or imperfections, not as the natural outcome of a fully operative market process.

The revival of belief in the potency of monetary policy was fostered also by a reevaluation of the role money played from 1929 to 1933. Keynes and most other economists of the time believed that the Great Contraction in the United States occurred despite aggressive expansionary policies by the monetary authorities—that they did their best but their best was not good enough.[1] Recent studies have demonstrated that the facts are precisely the reverse: the U.S. monetary authorities followed highly deflationary policies. The quantity of money in the United States fell by one-third in the course of the contraction. And it fell not because there were no willing borrowers—not because the horse would not drink. It fell because the Federal Reserve System forced or permitted a sharp reduction in the monetary base, because it failed to exercise the responsibilities assigned to it in the Federal Reserve Act to provide liquidity to the banking system. The Great Contraction is tragic testimony to the power of monetary policy—not, as Keynes and so many of his contemporaries believed, evidence of its impotence.

In the United States the revival of belief in the potency of monetary policy was strengthened also by increasing disillusionment with fiscal policy, not so much with its potential to affect aggregate demand as with the practical and political feasibility of so using it. Expenditures turned out to respond sluggishly and with long lags to attempts to adjust them to the course of economic

activity, so emphasis shifted to taxes. But here political factors entered with a vengeance to prevent prompt adjustment to presumed need, as has been so graphically illustrated in the months since I wrote the first draft of this talk. "Fine tuning" is a marvelously evocative phrase in this electronic age, but it has little resemblance to what is possible in practice—not, I might add, an unmixed evil.

It is hard to realize how radical has been the change in professional opinion on the role of money. Hardly an economist today accepts views that were the common coin some two decades ago. Let me cite a few examples.

In a talk published in 1945, E. A. Goldenweiser, then Director of the Research Division of the Federal Reserve Board, described the primary objective of monetary policy as being to "maintain the value of Government bonds. . . . This country" he wrote, "will have to adjust to a 2½ percent interest rate as the return on safe, long-time money, because the time has come when returns on pioneering capital can no longer be unlimited as they were in the past" [4, p. 117].

In a book on *Financing American Prosperity*, edited by Paul Homan and Fritz Machlup and published in 1945, Alvin Hansen devotes nine pages of text to the "savings-investment problem" without finding any need to use the words "interest rate" or any close facsimile thereto [5, pp. 218–27]. In his contribution to this volume, Fritz Machlup wrote, "Questions regarding the rate of interest, in particular regarding its variation or its stability, may not be among the most vital problems of the postwar economy, but they are certainly among the perplexing ones" [5, p. 466]. In his contribution, John H. Williams—not only professor at Harvard but also a long-time adviser to the New York Federal Reserve Bank—wrote, "I can see no prospect of revival of a general monetary control in the postwar period" [5, p. 383].

Another of the volumes dealing with postwar policy that appeared at this time, *Planning and Paying for Full Employment*, was edited by Abba P. Lerner and Frank D. Graham [6] and had contributors of all shades of professional opinion—from Henry Simons and Frank Graham to Abba Lerner and Hans Neisser. Yet Albert Halasi, in his excellent summary of the papers, was able to say, "Our contributors do not discuss the question of money supply. . . . The contributors make no special mention of credit policy to remedy actual depressions. . . . Inflation . . . might be fought more effectively by raising inter-

---

[1] In [2], I have argued that Henry Simons shared this view with Keynes, and that it accounts for the policy changes that he recommended.

est rates. . . . But . . . other anti-inflationary measures . . . are preferable" [6, pp. 23–24]. A *Survey of Contemporary Economics*, edited by Howard Ellis and published in 1948, was an "official" attempt to codify the state of economic thought of the time. In his contribution, Arthur Smithies wrote, "In the field of compensatory action, I believe fiscal policy must shoulder most of the load. Its chief rival, monetary policy, seems to be disqualified on institutional grounds. This country appears to be committed to something like the present low level of interest rates on a a long-term basis" [1, p. 208].

These quotations suggest the flavor of professional thought some two decades ago. If you wish to go further in this humbling inquiry, I recommend that you compare the sections on money—when you can find them—in the Principles texts of the early postwar years with the lengthy sections in the current crop even, or especially, when the early and recent Principles are different editions of the same work.

The pendulum has swung far since then, if not all the way to the position of the late 1920s, at least much closer to that position than to the position of 1945. There are of course many differences between then and now, less in the potency attributed to monetary policy than in the roles assigned to it and the criteria by which the profession believes monetary policy should be guided. Then, the chief roles assigned monetary policy were to promote price stability and to preserve the gold standard; the chief criteria of monetary policy were the state of the "money market," the extent of "speculation" and the movement of gold. Today, primacy is assigned to the promotion of full employment, with the prevention of inflation in a continuing but definitely secondary objective. And there is major disagreement about criteria of policy, varying from emphasis on money market conditions, interest rates, and the quantity of money to the belief that the state of employment itself should be the proximate criterion of policy.

I stress nonetheless the similarity between the views that prevailed in the late 'twenties and those that prevail today because I fear that, now as then, the pendulum may well have swung too far, that, now as then, we are in danger of assigning to monetary policy a larger role than it can perform, in danger of asking it to accomplish tasks that it cannot achieve, and, as a result, in danger of preventing it from making the contribution that it is capable of making.

Unaccustomed as I am to denigrating the importance of money, I therefore shall, as my first

task, stress what monetary policy cannot do. I shall then try to outline what it can do and how it can best make its contribution, in the present state of our knowledge—or ignorance.

I. WHAT MONETARY POLICY CANNOT DO

From the infinite world of negation, I have selected two limitations of monetary policy to discuss: (1) It cannot peg interest rates for more than very limited periods; (2) It cannot peg the rate of unemployment for more than very limited periods. I select these because the contrary has been or is widely believed, because they correspond to the two main unattainable tasks that are at all likely to be assigned to monetary policy, and because essentially the same theoretical analysis covers both.

Pegging of Interest Rates

History has already persuaded many of you about the first limitation. As noted earlier, the failure of cheap money policies was a major source of the reaction against simple-minded Keynesianism. In the United States, this reaction involved widespread recognition that the wartime and postwar pegging of bond prices was a mistake, that the abandonment of this policy was a desirable and inevitable step, and that it had none of the disturbing and disastrous consequences that were so freely predicted at the time.

The limitation derives from a much misunderstood feature of the relation between money and interest rates. Let the Fed set out to keep interest rates down. How will it try to do so? By buying securities. This raises their prices and lowers their yields. In the process, it also increases the quantity of reserves available to banks, hence the amount of bank credit, and, ultimately the total quantity of money. That is why central bankers in particular, and the financial community more broadly, generally believe that an increase in the quantity of money tends to lower interest rates. Academic economists accept the same conclusion, but for different reasons. They see, in their mind's eye, a negatively sloping liquidity preference schedule. How can people be induced to hold a larger quantity of money? Only by bidding down interest rates.

Both are right, up to a point. The *initial* impact of increasing the quantity of money at a faster rate than it has been increasing is to make interest rates lower for a time than they would otherwise have been. But this is only the beginning of the process, not the end. The more rapid rate of monetary growth will stimulate spending, both through the impact on investment of lower market interest rates and through the impact on other spending and thereby relative prices of higher cash balances than are desired. But one man's spending is another man's income. Rising income will raise the liquidity preference schedule and the demand for loans; it may also raise prices, which would reduce the real quantity of money. These three effects will reverse the initial downward pressure on interest rates fairly promptly, say, in something less than a year. Together they will tend, after a somewhat longer interval, say, a year or two, to return interest rates to the level they would otherwise have had. Indeed, given the tendency for the economy to overreact, they are highly likely to raise interest rates temporarily beyond that level, setting in motion a cyclical adjustment process.

A fourth effect, when and if it becomes operative, will go even farther, and definitely mean that a higher rate of monetary expansion will correspond to a higher, not lower, level of interest rates than would otherwise have prevailed. Let the higher rate of monetary growth produce rising prices, and let the public come to expect that prices will continue to rise. Borrowers will then be willing to pay and lenders will then demand higher interest rates—as Irving Fisher pointed out decades ago. This price expectation effect is slow to develop and also slow to disappear. Fisher estimated that it took several decades for a full adjustment and more recent work is consistent with his estimates.

These subsequent effects explain why every attempt to keep interest rates at a low level has forced the monetary authority to engage in successively larger and larger open market purchases. They explain why, historically, high and rising nominal interest rates have been associated with rapid growth in the quantity of money, as in Brazil or Chile or in the United States in recent years, and why low and falling interest rates have been associated with slow growth in the quantity of money, as in Switzerland now or in the United States from 1929 to 1933. As an empirical matter, low interest rates are a sign that monetary policy *has been* tight—in the sense that the quantity of money has grown slowly; high interest rates are a sign that monetary policy *has been* easy—in the sense that the quantity of money has grown rapidly. The broadest facts of experience run in precisely the opposite direction from that which the financial community and academic economists have all generally taken for granted.

Paradoxically, the monetary authority could assure low nominal rates of interest—but to do so it would have to start out in what seems like the opposite direction, by engaging in a deflationary monetary policy. Similarly, it could assure high nominal interest rates by engaging in an inflationary policy and accepting a temporary movement in interest rates in the opposite direction.

These considerations not only explain why monetary policy cannot peg interest rates; they also explain why interest rates are such a misleading indicator of whether monetary policy is "tight" or "easy." For that, it is far better to look at the rate of change of the quantity of money.[2]

Employment as a Criterion of Policy

The second limitation I wish to discuss goes more against the grain of current thinking. Monetary growth, it is widely held, will tend to stimulate employment; monetary contraction, to retard employment. Why, then, cannot the monetary authority adopt a target for employment or unemployment—say, 3 percent unemployment; be tight when unemployment is less than the target; be easy when unemployment is higher than the target; and in this way peg unemployment at, say, 3 percent? The reason it cannot is precisely the same as for interest rates—the difference between the immediate and the delayed consequences of such a policy.

Thanks to Wicksell, we are all acquainted with a concept of a "natural" rate of interest and the possibility of a discrepancy between the "natural" and the "market" rate. The preceding analysis of interest rates can be translated fairly directly into Wicksellian terms. The monetary authority can make the market rate less than the natural rate only by inflation. It can make the market rate higher than the natural rate only by deflation. We have added only one wrinkle to Wicksell— the Irving Fisher distinction between the nominal and the real rate of interest. Let the monetary authority keep the nominal market rate for a time below the natural rate by inflation. That in turn will raise the nominal natural rate itself, once anticipations of inflation become widespread, thus requiring still more rapid inflation

---

[2] This is partly an empirical not theoretical judgment. In principle, "tightness" or "ease" depends on the rate of change of the quantity of money supplied compared to the rate of change of the quantity demanded excluding effects on demand from monetary policy itself. However, empirically demand is highly stable, if we exclude the effect of monetary policy, so it is generally sufficient to look at supply alone.

to hold down the market rate. Similarly, because of the Fisher effect, it will require not merely deflation but more and more rapid deflation to hold the market rate above the initial "natural" rate.

This analysis has its close counterpart in the employment market. At any moment of time, there is some level of unemployment which has the property that it is consistent with equilibrium in the structure of *real* wage rates. At that level of unemployment, real wage rates are tending on the average to rise at a "normal" secular rate, i.e., at a rate that can be indefinitely maintained so long as capital formation, technological improvements, etc., remain on their long-run trends. A lower level of unemployment is an indication that there is an excess demand for labor that will produce upward pressure on real wage rates. A higher level of unemployment is an indication that there is an excess supply of labor that will produce downward pressure on real wage rates. The "natural rate of unemployment," in other words, is the level that would be ground out by the Walrasian system of general equilibrium equations, provided there is imbedded in them the actual structural characteristics of the labor and commodity markets, including market imperfections, stochastic variability in demands and supplies, the cost of gathering information about job vacancies and labor availabilities, the costs of mobility, and so on.[3]

You will recognize the close similarity between this statement and the celebrated Phillips Curve. The similarity is not coincidental. Phillips' analysis of the relation between unemployment and wage change is deservedly celebrated as an important and original contribution. But, unfortunately, it contains a basic defect—the failure to distinguish between *nominal* wages and *real* wages—just as Wicksell's analysis failed to distinguish between *nominal* interest rates and *real* interest rates. Implicitly, Phillips wrote his article for a world in which everyone anticipated that nominal prices would be stable and in which that anticipation remained unshaken and immutable whatever happened to actual prices and wages. Suppose, by contrast, that everyone anticipates that prices will rise at a rate of more than 75 percent a year—as, for example, Brazilians

did a few years ago. Then wages must rise at that rate simply to keep real wages unchanged. An excess supply of labor will be reflected in a less rapid rise in nominal wages than in anticipated prices,[4] not in an absolute decline in wages. When Brazil embarked on a policy to bring down the rate of price rise, and succeeded in bringing the price rise down to about 45 percent a year, there was a sharp initial rise in unemployment because under the influence of earlier anticipations, wages kept rising at a pace that was higher than the new rate of price rise, though lower than earlier. This is the result experienced, and to be expected, of all attempts to reduce the rate of inflation below that widely anticipated.[5]

To avoid misunderstanding, let me emphasize that by using the term "natural" rate of unemployment, I do not mean to suggest that it is immutable and unchangeable. On the contrary, many of the market characteristics that determine its level are man-made and policy-made. In the United States, for example, legal minimum wage rates, the Walsh-Healy and Davis-Bacon Acts, and the strength of labor unions all make the natural rate of unemployment higher than it would otherwise be. Improvements in employment exchanges, in availability of information about job vacancies and labor supply, and so on, would tend to lower the natural rate of unemployment. I use the term "natural" for the same reason Wicksell did—to try to separate the real forces from monetary forces.

---

[3] It is perhaps worth noting that this "natural" rate need not correspond to equality between the number unemployed and the number of job vacancies. For any given structure of the labor market, there will be some equilibrium relation between these two magnitudes, but there is no reason why it should be one of equality.

---

[4] Strictly speaking, the rise in nominal wages will be less rapid than the rise in anticipated nominal wages to make allowance for any secular changes in real wages.

[5] Stated in terms of the rate of change of nominal wages, the Phillips Curve can be expected to be reasonably stable and well defined for any period for which the *average* rate of change of prices, and hence the anticipated rate, has been relatively stable. For such periods, nominal wages and "real" wages move together. Curves computed for different periods or different countries for each of which this condition has been satisfied will differ in level, the level of the curve depending on what the average rate of price change was. The higher the average rate of price change, the higher will tend to be the level of the curve. For periods or countries for which the rate of change of prices varies considerably, the Phillips Curve will not be well defined. My impression is that these statements accord reasonably well with the experience of the economists who have explored empirical Phillips Curves.

Restate Phillips' analysis in terms of the rate of change of real wages—and even more precisely, anticipated real wages—and it all falls into place. That is why students of empirical Phillips Curves have found that it helps to include the rate of change of the price level as an independent variable.

Let us assume that the monetary authority tries to peg the "market" rate of unemployment at a level below the "natural" rate. For definiteness, suppose that it takes 3 percent as the target rate and that the "natural" rate is higher than 3 percent. Suppose also that we start out at a time when prices have been stable and when unemployment is higher than 3 percent. Accordingly, the authority increases the rate of monetary growth. This will be expansionary. By making nominal cash balances higher than people desire, it will tend initially to lower interest rates and in this and other ways to stimulate spending. Income and spending will start to rise.

To begin with, much or most of the rise in income will take the form of an increase in output and employment rather than in prices. People have been expecting prices to be stable, and prices and wages have been set for some time in the future on that basis. It takes time for people to adjust to a new state of demand. Producers will tend to react to the initial expansion in aggregate demand by increasing output, employees by working longer hours, and the unemployed, by taking jobs now offered at former nominal wages. This much is pretty standard doctrine.

But it describes only the initial effects. Because selling prices of products typically respond to an unanticipated rise in nominal demand faster than prices of factors of production, real wages received have gone down—though real wages anticipated by employees went up, since employees implicitly evaluated the wages offered at the earlier price level. Indeed, the simultaneous fall *ex post* in real wages to employers and rise *ex ante* in real wages to employees is what enabled employment to increase. But the decline *ex post* in real wages will soon come to affect anticipations. Employees will start to reckon on rising prices of the things they buy and to demand higher nominal wages for the future. "Market" unemployment is below the "natural" level. There is an excess demand for labor so real wages will tend to rise toward their initial level.

Even though the higher rate of monetary growth continues, the rise in real wages will reverse the decline in unemployment, and then lead to a rise, which will tend to return unemployment to its former level. In order to keep unemployment at its target level of 3 percent, the monetary authority would have to raise monetary growth still more. As in the interest rate case, the "market" rate can be kept below the "natural" rate only by inflation. And, as in the interest rate case, too, only by accelerating infla-

tion. Conversely, let the monetary authority choose a target rate of unemployment that is above the natural rate, and they will be led to produce a deflation, and an accelerating deflation at that.

What if the monetary authority chose the "natural" rate—either of interest or unemployment—as its target? One problem is that it cannot know what the "natural" rate is. Unfortunately, we have as yet devised no method to estimate accurately and readily the natural rate of either interest or unemployment. And the "natural" rate will itself change from time to time. But the basic problem is that even if the monetary authority knew the "natural" rate, and attempted to peg the market rate at that level, it would not be led to a determinate policy. The "market" rates will vary from the natural rate for all sorts of reasons other than monetary policy. If the monetary authority responds to these variations, it will set in train longer term effects that will make any monetary growth path it follows ultimately consistent with the rule of policy. The actual course of monetary growth will be analogous to a random walk, buffeted this way and that by the forces that produce temporary departures of the market rate from the natural rate.

To state this conclusion differently, there is always a temporary trade-off between inflation and unemployment; there is no permanent trade-off. The temporary trade-off comes not from inflation per se, but from unanticipated inflation, which generally means, from a rising rate of inflation. The widespread belief that there is a permanent trade-off is a sophisticated version of the confusion between "high" and "rising" that we all recognize in simpler forms. A rising rate of inflation may reduce unemployment, a high rate will not.

But how long, you will say, is "temporary"? For interest rates, we have some systematic evidence on how long each of the several effects takes to work itself out. For unemployment, we do not. I can at most venture a personal judgment, based on some examination of the historical evidence, that the initial effects of a higher and unanticipated rate of inflation last for something like two to five years; that this initial effect then begins to be reversed; and that a full adjustment to the new rate of inflation takes about as long for employment as for interest rates, say, a couple of decades. For both interest rates and employment, let me add a qualification. These estimates are for changes in the rate of inflation of the order of magnitude that has been experienced in the United States. For much more sizable changes, such as those experienced in South American countries, the whole adjustment process is greatly speeded up.

To state the general conclusion still differently, the monetary authority controls nominal quantities—directly, the quantity of its own liabilities. In principle, it can use this control to peg a nominal quantity—an exchange rate, the price level, the nominal level of national income, the quantity of money by one or another definition—or to peg the rate of change in a nominal quantity—the rate of inflation or deflation, the rate of growth or decline in nominal national income, the rate of growth of the quantity of money. It cannot use its control over nominal quantities to peg a real quantity—the real rate of interest, the rate of unemployment, the level of real national income, the real quantity of money, the rate of growth of real national income, or the rate of growth of the real quantity of money.

II. WHAT MONETARY POLICY CAN DO

Monetary policy cannot peg these real magnitudes at predetermined levels. But monetary policy can and does have important effects on these real magnitudes. The one is in no way inconsistent with the other.

My own studies of monetary history have made me extremely sympathetic to the oft-quoted, much reviled, and as widely misunderstood, comment by John Stuart Mill. "There cannot . . . ," he wrote, "be intrinsically a more insignificant thing, in the economy of society, than money; except in the character of a contrivance for sparing time and labour. It is a machine for doing quickly and commodiously, what would be done, though less quickly and commodiously, without it: and like many other kinds of machinery, it only exerts a distinct and independent influence of its own when it gets out of order" [7, p. 488].

True, money is only a machine, but it is an extraordinarily efficient machine. Without it, we could not have begun to attain the astounding growth in output and level of living we have experienced in the past two centuries—any more than we could have done so without those other marvelous machines that dot our countryside and enable us, for the most part, simply to do more efficiently what could be done without them at much greater cost in labor.

But money has one feature that these other machines do not share. Because it is so pervasive, when it gets out of order, it throws a monkey wrench into the operation of all the other machines. The Great Contraction is the most dramatic example but not the only one. Every other major contraction in this country has been either produced by monetary disorder or greatly exacerbated by monetary disorder. Every major inflation has been produced by monetary expansion—mostly to meet the overriding demands of war which have forced the creation of money to supplement explicit taxation.

The first and most important lesson that history teaches about what monetary policy can do—and it is a lesson of the most profound importance—is that monetary policy can prevent money itself from being a major source of economic disturbance. This sounds like a negative proposition: avoid major mistakes. In part it is. The Great Contraction might not have occurred at all, and if it had, it would have been far less severe, if the monetary authority had avoided mistakes, or if the monetary arrangements had been those of an earlier time when there was no central authority with the power to make the kinds of mistakes that the Federal Reserve System made. The past few years, to come closer to home, would have been steadier and more productive of economic well-being if the Federal Reserve had avoided drastic and erratic changes of direction, first expanding the money supply at an unduly rapid pace, then, in early 1966, stepping on the brake too hard, then, at the end of 1966, reversing itself and resuming expansion until at least November, 1967, at a more rapid pace than can be maintained without appreciable inflation.

Even if the proposition that monetary policy can prevent money itself from being a major source of economic disturbance were a wholly negative proposition, it would be none the less important for that. As it happens, however, it is not a wholly negative proposition. The monetary machine has gotten out of order even when there has been no central authority with anything like the power now possessed by the Fed. In the United States, the 1907 episode and earlier banking panics are examples of how the monetary machine can get out of order largely on its own. There is therefore a positive and important task for the monetary authority—to suggest improvements in the machine that will reduce the chances that it will get out of order, and to use its own powers so as to keep the machine in good working order.

A second thing monetary policy can do is provide a stable background for the economy—keep the machine well oiled, to continue Mill's analogy. Accomplishing the first task will contribute to this objective, but there is more to it than that. Our economic system will work best when producers and consumers, employers and employees, can proceed with full confidence that the average level of prices will behave in a known way in the future—preferably that it will be highly stable. Under any conceivable institutional arrangements, and certainly under those that now prevail in the United States, there is only a limited amount of flexibility in prices and wages. We need to conserve this flexibility to achieve changes in relative prices and wages that are required to adjust to dynamic changes in tastes and technology. We should not dissipate it simply to achieve changes in the absolute level of prices that serve no economic function.

In an earlier era, the gold standard was relied on to provide confidence in future monetary stability. In its heyday it served that function reasonably well. It clearly no longer does, since there is scarce a country in the world that is prepared to let the gold standard reign unchecked—and there are persuasive reasons why countries should not do so. The monetary authority could operate as a surrogate for the gold standard, if it pegged exchange rates and did so exclusively by altering the quantity of money in response to balance of payment flows without "sterilizing" surpluses or deficits and without resorting to open or concealed exchange control or to changes in tariffs and quotas. But again, though many central bankers talk this way, few are in fact willing to follow this course—and again there are persuasive reasons why they should not do so. Such a policy would submit each country to the vagaries not of an impersonal and automatic gold standard but of the policies—deliberate or accidental—of other monetary authorities.

In today's world, if monetary policy is to provide a stable background for the economy it must do so by deliberately employing its powers to that end. I shall come later to how it can do so.

Finally, monetary policy can contribute to offsetting major disturbances in the economic system arising from other sources. If there is an independent secular exhilaration—as the postwar expansion was described by the proponents of secular stagnation—monetary policy can in principle help to hold it in check by a slower rate of monetary growth than would otherwise be desirable. If, as now, an explosive federal budget threatens unprecedented deficits, monetary policy can hold any inflationary dangers in check by a slower rate of monetary growth than would otherwise be desirable. This will temporarily mean higher interest rates than would otherwise prevail—to

enable the government to borrow the sums needed to finance the deficit—but by preventing the speeding up of inflation, it may well mean both lower prices and lower nominal interest rates for the long pull. If the end of a substantial war offers the country an opportunity to shift resources from wartime to peacetime production, monetary policy can ease the transition by a higher rate of monetary growth than would otherwise be desirable—though experience is not very encouraging that it can do so without going too far.

I have put this point last, and stated it in qualified terms—as referring to major disturbances—because I believe that the potentiality of monetary policy in offsetting other forces making for instability is far more limited than is commonly believed. We simply do not know enough to be able to recognize minor disturbances when they occur or to be able to predict either what their effects will be with any precision or what monetary policy is required to offset their effects. We do not know enough to be able to achieve stated objectives by delicate, or even fairly coarse, changes in the mix of monetary and fiscal policy. In this area particularly the best is likely to be the enemy of the good. Experience suggests that the path of wisdom is to use monetary policy explicitly to offset other disturbances only when they offer a "clear and present danger."

III. HOW SHOULD MONETARY POLICY BE CONDUCTED?

How should monetary policy be conducted to make the contribution to our goals that it is capable of making? This is clearly not the occasion for presenting a detailed "Program for Monetary Stability"—to use the title of a book in which I tried to do so [3]. I shall restrict myself here to two major requirements for monetary policy that follow fairly directly from the preceding discussion.

The first requirement is that the monetary authority should guide itself by magnitudes that it can control, not by ones that it cannot control. If, as the authority has often done, it takes interest rates or the current unemployment percentage as the immediate criterion of policy, it will be like a space vehicle that has taken a fix on the wrong star. No matter how sensitive and sophisticated its guiding apparatus, the space vehicle will go astray. And so will the monetary authority. Of the various alternative magnitudes that it can control, the most appealing guides for policy are exchange rates, the price level as defined by some index, and the quantity of a monetary total—currency plus adjusted demand deposits, or this total plus commercial bank time deposits, or a still broader total.

For the United States in particular, exchange rates are an undesirable guide. It might be worth requiring the bulk of the economy to adjust to the tiny percentage consisting of foreign trade if that would guarantee freedom from monetary irresponsibility—as it might under a real gold standard. But it is hardly worth doing so simply to adapt to the average of whatever policies monetary authorities in the rest of the world adopt. Far better to let the market, through floating exchange rates, adjust to world conditions the 5 percent or so of our resources devoted to international trade while reserving monetary policy to promote the effective use of the 95 percent.

Of the three guides listed, the price level is clearly the most important in its own right. Other things the same, it would be much the best of the alternatives—as so many distinguished economists have urged in the past. But other things are not the same. The link between the policy actions of the monetary authority and the price level, while unquestionably present, is more indirect than the link between the policy actions of the authority and any of the several monetary totals. Moreover, monetary action takes a longer time to affect the price level than to affect the monetary totals and both the time lag and the magnitude of effect vary with circumstances. As a result, we cannot predict at all accurately just what effect a particular monetary action will have on the price level and, equally important, just when it will have that effect. Attempting to control directly the price level is therefore likely to make monetary policy itself a source of economic disturbance because of false stops and starts. Perhaps, as our understanding of monetary phenomena advances, the situation will change. But at the present stage of our understanding, the long way around seems the surer way to our objective. Accordingly, I believe that a monetary total is the best currently available immediate guide or criterion for monetary policy—and I believe that it matters much less which particular total is chosen than that one be chosen.

A second requirement for monetary policy is that the monetary authority avoid sharp swings in policy. In the past, monetary authorities have on occasion moved in the wrong direction—as in the episode of the Great Contraction that I have stressed. More frequently, they have moved in the right direction, albeit often too late, but

have erred by moving too far. Too late and too much has been the general practice. For example, in early 1966, it was the right policy for the Federal Reserve to move in a less expansionary direction—though it should have done so at least a year earlier. But when it moved, it went too far, producing the sharpest change in the rate of monetary growth of the post-war era. Again, having gone too far, it was the right policy for the Fed to reverse course at the end of 1966. But again it went too far, not only restoring but exceeding the earlier excessive rate of monetary growth. And this episode is no exception. Time and again this has been the course followed—as in 1919 and 1920, in 1937 and 1938, in 1953 and 1954, in 1959 and 1960.

The reason for the propensity to overreact seems clear: the failure of monetary authorities to allow for the delay between their actions and the subsequent effects on the economy. They tend to determine their actions by today's conditions —but their actions will affect the economy only six or nine or twelve or fifteen months later. Hence they feel impelled to step on the brake, or the accelerator, as the case may be, too hard.

My own prescription is still that the monetary authority go all the way in avoiding such swings by adopting publicly the policy of achieving a steady rate of growth in a specified monetary total. The precise rate of growth, like the precise monetary total, is less important that the adoption of some stated and known rate. I myself have argued for a rate that would on the average achieve rough stability in the level of prices of final products, which I have estimated would call for something like a 3 to 5 percent per year rate of growth in currency plus all commercial bank deposits or a slightly lower rate of growth in currency plus demand deposits only.[6] But it would be better to have a fixed rate that would on the average produce moderate inflation or moderate deflation, provided it was steady, than to suffer the wide and erratic perturbations we have experienced.

Short of the adoption of such a publicly stated policy of a steady rate of monetary growth, it would constitute a major improvement if the monetary authority followed the self-denying ordinance of avoiding wide swings. It is a matter of record that periods of relative stability in the

---

[6] In an as yet unpublished article on "The Optimum Quantity of Money," I conclude that a still lower rate of growth, something like 2 percent for the broader definition, might be better yet in order to eliminate or reduce the difference between private and total costs of adding to real balances.

rate of monetary growth have also been periods of relative stability in economic activity, both in the United States and other countries. Periods of wide swings in the rate of monetary growth have also been periods of wide swings in economic activity.

By setting itself a steady course and keeping to it, the monetary authority could make a major contribution to promoting economic stability. By making that course one of steady but moderate growth in the quantity of money, it would make a major contribution to avoidance of either inflation or deflation of prices. Other forces would still affect the economy, require change and adjustment, and disturb the even tenor of our ways. But steady monetary growth would provide a monetary climate favorable to the effective operation of those basic forces of enterprise, ingenuity, invention, hard work, and thrift that are the true springs of economic growth. That is the most that we can ask from monetary policy at our

present stage of knowledge. But that much—and it is a great deal—is clearly within our reach.

REFERENCES

1. Ellis, H. S. ed. *A Survey of Contemporary Economics.* Philadelphia 1948.
2. Friedman, Milton. "The Monetary Theory and Policy of Henry Simons," *Jour. Law and Econ.,* October 1967, *10,* 1–13.
3. ———, *A Program for Monetary Stability.* New York 1959.
4. Goldenweiser, E. A. "Postwar Problems and Policies," *Fed. Res. Bull.,* February 1945, *31,* 112–21.
5. Homan, P. T. and Machlup, Fritz, ed. *Financing American Prosperity.* New York 1945.
6. Lerner, A. P. and Graham, F. D., ed. *Planning and Paying for Full Employment.* Princeton 1946.
7. Mill, J. S. *Principles of Political Economy,* Bk. III, Ashley, ed. New York 1929.

30. GUIDELINES FOR MONETARY POLICY—THE CASE AGAINST SIMPLE RULES*

Lyle E. Gramley†

There are several things that seem worthwhile mentioning by way of a prelude to the substance of my remarks. First, I do not regard it as my function to defend, explain, or otherwise comment on the course of monetary policy during the past several years. My comments will be confined to the more general question of running monetary policy by simple rules, and what the empirical evidence seems to say about the issue. Second, of necessity, I must take the Federal Reserve off the hook for what I have to say. I could scarcely present a Federal Reserve consensus in any brief period without grossly misrepresenting someone's position, since there is at least as much diversity of view within the Federal Reserve as elsewhere on the appropriate

* A paper delivered at the Financial Conference of the National Industrial Conference Board, New York, February 21, 1969. Reprinted by permission of the author. Lyle E. Gramley is a Member of the Council of Economic Advisers.

† The views expressed in this paper are the responsibility of the author alone and are not necessarily shared by the Board of Governors or by the author's staff colleagues.

guidelines for monetary policy. You might already have guessed that from reading the November 1968 *Review* of a certain Midwestern Reserve Bank, whose brand of monetary policy is known around the Board as Brand X.

Third, I do not intend to present a personal point of view on how a central bank should run its affairs. My function is to present sympathetically the case against simple rules in monetary management—and in particular the case against rules defined in terms of growth rates of the money stock, or related monetary aggregates. In this role, I find myself in something of a quandary. Among my friends outside the Board, I seem to have developed a reputation, such as it is, for being an anti-quantity theory man, perhaps even a violent one. At the Board, on the other hand, I am not infrequently accused of having dangerous leanings in the opposite direction, since I have a habit of insisting that a Yo-Yo is not the appropriate physical analogy for monetary policy.

Fourth, since my subsequent remarks about simple rules and quantity theories will be rather critical, it seems appropriate to emphasize at the outset that the fields of monetary economics and stabilization policy, in my judgment, owe an enormous debt to Professor Friedman for insisting that the role of money as a determinant of national income be given more careful consideration than it was from the period of roughly 1935 to 1965. Apart from a few lonely souls such as Milton Friedman, monetary economists argued for about three decades that central banking was largely wasted motion and sneered at those with contrary ideas. Professor Friedman fought for more careful attention to monetary variables when the going was the roughest—and he deserves our commendation.

The danger now is that the pendulum has swung too far in the other direction. Recognition of nonmonetary factors as a potential disequilibrating influence in the economy is in grave danger of being overlooked. An increasing proportion of economists, financial writers, and others appears to be reaching the conclusion that nonmonetary factors can be safely disregarded as important potential sources of economic turbulence, and that fiscal policy is the wet noodle among our economic stabilization tools.

The case for discretionary monetary management starts from the premise that money matters, and matters a great deal. But other things can and do matter too—specifically, fiscal policy and changing propensities to spend in the private sector. The case also hinges on the assumption that we have learned enough about the sources and the nature of economic fluctuations to do something useful about them, and that the prospects for learning more remain bright.

Let me begin the defense of this case by discussing a grubby statistical problem. Technical arguments may be a little boring, but this one cannot be avoided if the evidence supporting the case for steady growth of the money stock is to be evaluated properly.

As you are well aware, one of the principal supports for the monetarist position is the empirical evidence of a relatively stable relation between money and income, or between changes in these variables—evidence of the kind represented by Professor Friedman's extensive studies or by the Andersen-Jordan paper in the November 1968 issue of the Federal Reserve Bank of St. Louis Review.[1] In the latter study, changes in GNP from 1952 through mid-1968 are regressed on variables taken as proxies for monetary and

fiscal actions, with the monetary variables alternately defined as changes in the money stock or in the monetary base, i.e., currency plus total bank reserves. In the Andersen-Jordan regressions, fiscal variables turn out not to bear a statistically significant relation to changes in nominal income. The results, therefore, cast serious doubts about the role of fiscal policy as a stabilizing instrument and by implication on the significance of *all* nonmonetary factors as determinants of nominal income. Meanwhile, monetary variables come booming through as important determinants of GNP.

The problem with this study, and with others of its kind that I am familiar with, is that they are potentially biased, in a statistical sense, towards overemphasis of monetary factors as determinants of income. I use the word "potentially" advisedly since it is hard to prove one way or another, even though the nature of the argument is straight-forward. The argument runs as follows.

If the central bank sits on its hands and does nothing, a rise in GNP resulting from (say) an expansive fiscal policy tends to increase the money stock, mainly because it induces banks to borrow more from the central bank and to reduce excess reserves, but partly also because the induced rise in interest rates reduces demand for time deposits, and thus permits an increase in demand deposits and the money stock. The money stock is not independent, in a statistical sense, of current changes in GNP. Consequently, a regression of GNP on the money stock combines the effects of GNP on money with those of money on GNP. Regressions of GNP on money would not, therefore, yield statistically unbiased estimates of the effects of monetary policy on the economy. Rather similar arguments hold if the monetary variable used is the monetary base.

On the other hand, if the Federal Reserve has not sat on its hands, but has behaved the way monetarists often claim, the potential bias in the historical data is much larger. Professor Friedman, for example, has argued that the Federal Reserve's inept performance in monetary management (as he sees it) results heavily from the fact that too often it leans against the trend of the credit markets—moderating upward pressure on interest rates during economic expansion, and cushioning the downward rate adjustments that occur in recessions. As a result, he argues, the money stock tends to accelerate or decelerate at just about the time it should be doing the opposite.

If you believe that story, it follows that regressions of GNP on the money stock, with or without

---

[1] L. C. Andersen and J. L. Jordan, "Monetary and Fiscal Actions: A Test of Their Relative Importance in Economic Stabilization," Federal Reserve Bank of St. Louis *Review,* November 1968, pp. 11–24.

other variables to represent fiscal policy, are biased even more towards overestimating the effects of monetary factors as economic determinants. Indeed, a close correlation between money and GNP could occur in those circumstances even if monetary policy had no effect at all on national income.

This problem of statistical bias is an old and familiar story—and monetarists as well as their critics are quite well aware of it. The question at issue, of course, is whether it is a serious enough problem to really worry about. I suggest that it is.

Consider for a moment the implications of concluding that fiscal policy has no discernible effect on money income, apart from its effects on the money stock. This is the conclusion you would reach, presumably, if you accepted as reliable, and statistically unbiased, the evidence set forth in the St. Louis Bank article mentioned earlier, in which fiscal variables were found not to bear a statistically significant relation to money income. The properties of an economic system in which fiscal policy acts the way it does in the Andersen-Jordan model have been discussed in the economic literature for 100 years or more and are reasonably well understood. It is widely known that fiscal policy would have no effect on money income, apart from induced changes in the money stock, if and only if the demand for money were completely interest inelastic. And if that were true, changes in private spending propensities *also* would have no effect on money income, except through their impact on the demand for, or the supply of, money. Indeed, in such a world, the behavior of the money stock would completely determine the course of money income if the demand function for money were stable.

The demand function for money has probably been estimated statistically as many times as, and perhaps more than, any single behavioral equation commonly used in economics. While the nature of the public's demand for money is not understood to anyone's full satisfaction, the empirical evidence accumulated over the past 10 to 15 years—of which a significant part comes from the monetarist camp itself—points overwhelmingly to the conclusion that the public's desired holdings of money balances are interest sensitive. And this is true whether money is defined narrowly to exclude time deposits of commercial banks or broadly to include them.

In view of this, it seems to me, Andersen and Jordan should not have concluded that their regressions had satisfactorily sorted out the relative roles of monetary and fiscal policy as determinants of GNP. Rather, they should have concluded that something was rather badly wrong with their method.

As I noted, this bias problem is an old familiar one; nevertheless, precious little has been done about it until just recently. I commend for your reading, in this respect, a "Comment" on the Andersen-Jordan study by two staff members at the Board (Frank de Leeuw and John Kalchbrenner).[2] De Leeuw and Kalchbrenner find that different results emerge from the Andersen-Jordan equations if the monetary and fiscal variables are redefined in such a way as to reduce the degree of statistical influence running from GNP to the policy variables. Most importantly, the monetary policy variable is redefined as the monetary base less the public's holdings of currency and member bank borrowings. With this definition, monetary factors decline in importance, and fiscal variables turn out to have significant effects on GNP after all. Also, the relative potency of monetary and fiscal policies resulting from use of the Andersen-Jordan equations, as modified by de Leeuw and Kalchbrenner, turn out to be in the same ball park as those emerging from the larger and more elaborate FRB-MIT model developed by the Board staff working jointly with Professors Ando and Modigliani. Since the structure of the FRB-MIT model differs markedly from the Andersen-Jordan single-equation models, the coincidence of results would seem to be more than accidental.

Let me move now to the next point, which is that, even taken at face value, regressions relating GNP to the money stock (or relating changes in these variables) over the long sweep of history generally are quite consistent with the view that nonmonetary factors play a significant role in determining national income. In elaborating this contention, it seems appropriate to concentrate particularly on the empirical work of Professor Friedman, the leading advocate of the monetarist view.

An article of his published in *The Journal of Law and Economics* a couple of years ago discussed a simple regression equation relating annual changes in M_2—that is, the money stock defined to include time deposits—and GNP. Friedman defines money this way for pragmatic

---

[2] Frank de Leeuw and John Kalchbrenner, "Monetary and Fiscal Actions: A Test of Their Relative Importance in Economic Stabilization—Comment," *Federal Reserve Bank of St. Louis Review*, April 1969, pp. 6–11; see also L. C. Andersen and J. L. Jordan, "Reply," same issue of the *Review*, pp. 12–16.

reasons—M_2 is more closely related to GNP, over the long run, than M_1. What I have to say about the flexibility of the M_2–GNP relation thus applies in spades to the relation between M_1 and GNP.

Friedman's equation, based on data from 1870 to 1963, shows a correlation between annual changes in M_2 and GNP of .70.[3] This means that half of the annual changes in nominal income are explained by contemporaneous changes in M_2, and the other half are not. The significance of that degree of accuracy can be illustrated by considering what Friedman's equation says about changes in nominal income during recent years.

From 1962 onward, the equation predicts better than in earlier years. Given knowledge of the annual percentage change in M_2 and the previous year's income, it predicts levels of nominal income for the years 1962–66 with an accuracy of about 1¼ percent. This is worth about $11 billion in GNP, given the present size of the economy, an error that is not negligible when we are talking about average annual levels. Indeed, I suspect a prediction that GNP in 1969 will hit an annual average of $921 billion (the CEA forecast) plus or minus $11 billion would strike almost everyone in this room as unusually imprecise. But in the preceding 10 years—that is from 1952 to 1961—the predictions from Friedman's equation are far worse. The mean absolute error over the 10-year period is roughly 3¼ percent, or about $28 billion in terms of today's GNP. What would you do with a 1969 GNP forecast of $921 billion, plus or minus $28 billion?

A 3¼ percent average prediction error produces a strange picture of short-term economic developments during the 1950s. Annual percentage changes in current income predicted by Friedman's equation are about equal for the three years 1953–55, though you will remember that income growth turned negative in the recession year 1954 and rose sharply in 1955. His equation also predicts an acceleration of income growth in the recession year 1958 and a slight reduction in the boom year 1959. And if its description of short-term economic changes leaves something to be desired, its longer term predictions are even more astonishing. The predicted growth of nominal income over the ten years 1952–61 as a whole is only a bit over one half as large as the actual growth that took place.

If these results surprise you, they shouldn't,

since there has always been a good deal of variability in the M_2–GNP relation. The facts are there to read in Professor Friedman's *Monetary History of the United States*. Annual variations of 3 percent or more in the income velocity of M_2 are the rule, not the exception. They occur in two thirds of the some 90-odd years covered by the study. Even if the first 12 years of this period of history are thrown out on grounds of unreliable data, as Friedman suggests, and if the years of the Great Depression and the two World Wars are also discarded, for reasons that are not so clear, annual velocity changes of 3 percent or more still occur in more than one half of the remaining years.

As I read the historical evidence, therefore, one of the two main pillars on which the monetarist position rests is a bit shaky. The second one strikes me as even less stable. It is the contention that the money stock should grow at a constant rate because, to quote Professor Friedman, ". . . we simply do not know enough, we are not smart enough, we have not analyzed sufficiently and understood sufficiently the operation of the world so [that] we know how to use monetary policy as a balance wheel."[4] Consequently, he argues, we ought to convert monetary policy from a factor that he contends has been positively destabilizing to one that is neutral.

The argument has intuitive appeal, but not much more. If we do not know how to use monetary instruments to offset the disequilibrating effects of nonmonetary factors, then we do not know enough to accentuate these effects either—or to judge whether the central bank has done so.

To strike an analogy, Friedman's argument is that the central bank is like a person lost near the edge of a forest, with insufficient evidence as to the shortest way out.

Friedman advises the wanderer to stay put, since otherwise he may wander deeper into the woods. He may, but then again he also may wander out. Friedman's advice is sound if the wanderer can be reasonably sure that a rescue party is on the way. But if there is no rescue party, the poor lost soul might just as well start walking—he might just stumble onto some tracks that lead him home.

The point I am making is perhaps obvious, but I did not originate it. The credit goes to Professors Lovell and Prescott, who deal with the question at considerable length, and in a

---

[3] Milton Friedman, "Interest Rates and the Demand for Money," *The Journal of Law and Economics,* vol. 9, October 1966, p. 78.

[4] "The Federal Reserve System after Fifty Years," House Banking and Currency Committee, 88th Congress, vol. 2, *Hearings,* 1156.

theoretical fashion, in a recent article.[5] They conclude that in the absence of knowledge about the strength and timing of monetary changes, it cannot be demonstrated that a policy rule specifying a constant growth rate of the money stock is superior, in terms of smoothing out income fluctuations, to a rule specifying that interest rates be stabilized. Also, one cannot demonstrate the superiority of either rule over any specific set of policies pursued by the central bank.

Rational conduct of monetary policy—whether by the pursuit of rigid rules or by allowing central banks substantial discretion in deciding the course of monetary affairs—cannot be specified if we assume complete lack of knowledge. Our understanding of how the economic system works is imperfect, and we must recognize that an optimal policy strategy has to take uncertainty into account. But we must begin with what we know, and build on it. The Lovell-Prescott approach is an excellent example of one direction of fruitful inquiry.

Perhaps I am a hopeless optimist on this score, but I think we have learned a great deal in the past 10 years or so about the use of stabilization policy—and particularly monetary instruments. The most hopeful sign, in this regard, is the fact that we are gradually whittling away the wide diversity that once existed as to the effects of monetary policy on the economy. A consensus has developed that monetary policy is vitally important to economic performance, and the estimates of the money multipliers seem to be converging. Our understanding of the paths of transmission has increased greatly, and here, too, people from opposing camps find they have more in common than they thought. Professors Tobin and Friedman speak much the same language when they are talking about the processes of monetary policy. And the Board's staff, working together with Professors Ando and Modigliani, has developed a model in which the wealth effects of monetary policy, working through the markets for equities, bear directly on consumer spending in a way that would warm even Milton Friedman's heart. This is a far cry from the simple-minded Keynesianism of the 1930s and early 1940s or the equally naive quantity theories expounded at that time.

Lags, of course, there are, but they are not hopelessly long. I understand Professor Friedman's current view is that the average lag is something like six months between changes in the growth rate of money and changes in the growth rate of GNP. Our own empirical work at the Board suggests the average lag may be slightly longer, but we, too, find that significant economic effects can be obtained within the space of half a year by manipulating the instruments of monetary policy. We are making progress, also, in understanding why the lags are variable, and how to estimate the lengths of lags in economic systems in which this variation occurs.

Above all, we are learning how immensely complex the economic and financial world really is. Money, however we define it, is not unique, in any meaningful sense of that word. Demand deposits substitute for CD's, for other classes of commercial bank time and savings accounts, for claims on nonbank intermediaries, and for market securities.

This does not mean, of course, that the central bank can ignore the money stock and concentrate on (say) interest rates. The behavior of the money stock contains useful information for measuring and interpreting monetary policy, more information, I think we should acknowledge, than most economists other than the monetarists have recognized. Reducing the growth rate of bank demand deposits, and hence the narrowly defined money stock, *does* reduce the growth rate of GNP. But so also does a reduction in the growth rate of commercial bank time deposits, or a decline in the growth rate of savings and loan shares or mutual savings bank deposits. In fact, there is no reason in theory for regarding a dollar change in the growth rate of claims against nonbank intermediaries as any less significant, in terms of its effects on GNP, than a dollar change in M_2 or in M_1. We ignore fluctuations in commercial bank time deposits or in claims against nonbank intermediaries at our peril in a world in which all sectors of the financial market are becoming more closely related, and in which the processes of monetary policy are increasingly extending beyond the boundaries of the narrowly defined money stock.

Surely, Professor Friedman would not deny, in principle, that we ought to try to take into account these more complex aspects of the effects of central bank policies on economic activity in the formulation of monetary policy. What is needed is an analytic framework, a conceptual apparatus, to do this more systematically and with greater success than we have been able to in the past. That is precisely the goal of our research effort at the Board, and I am fully con-

[5] Michael C. Lovell and Edward Prescott, "Money, Multiplier Accelerator Interaction, and the Business Cycle," *Southern Economics Journal*, vol. 35, July 1968, pp. 60–72.

vinced that these efforts are paying off, in the sense that we have been already, are now, and will be in the future, getting informational inputs that are useful for improving monetary policy decisions.

We occasionally hear remarks that belittle the usefulness of large econometric models such as ours, on the grounds that such models are unstable, not robust, poor predictors, and so on. If, by those comments, it is meant that the art of building large mathematical models is still undeveloped and needs improvement, I fully agree. But if it means that such models are in a substantive sense inferior to the one-equation models produced by Professor Friedman or by Andersen and Jordan, I disagree wholeheartedly.

Finally, let me note that models of monetary policy variables and their effects on the economy,

whether they be one-equation models or more complex ones, never can be (and I would argue never should be) push-button devices that provide automatic, unqualified answers to policy questions—answers that human judgment cannot then refine further, or discard altogether if it seems appropriate. We send spaceships to the moon with human lives aboard mainly to permit on-the-spot reaction to developments that cannot always be anticipated and allowed for in advance. Changes in plans made in such a context must, obviously, take into account what we know, as well as what we don't know. Spacemen are not allowed to play God in the decision-making process, and central bankers should not have such freedom either. But reducing them to subhumans, grinding out a constant growth rate of money, is not justified by logic or by empirical fact.

31. ALTERNATIVES FOR DEBT MANAGEMENT*

William D. Nordhaus
and
Henry C. Wallich

Public debt management, in the sense of manipulation of a given stock, has been a policy problem at least since World War II. During this time, dissatisfaction with the handling of the debt has surfaced sporadically. A feeling that the average maturity of the debt should be longer than it was has been pervasive. But no generally accepted philosophy of the public debt management has emerged.

Various objectives have been urged for debt management. An anticyclical impact seems an obvious possibility. A balance of payments-oriented debt policy, seeking to lower long- and raise short-term rates, was tried in the form of Operation Twist. Cost minimization regardless of anticyclical considerations has been proposed. Most of the time a policy of tailoring to the needs of the market ("sell what they will buy,"

* From Federal Reserve Bank of Boston, *Issues in Federal Debt Management,* Proceedings of a Conference at Melvin Village, New Hampshire, June 1973 (Boston, 1973), pp. 9–25. Reprinted by permission of the Federal Reserve Bank of Boston and the authors. William D. Nordhaus is a Member of the Council of Economic Advisers. Henry C. Wallich is a Member of the Board of Governors of the Federal Reserve System.

a not too distant relative of cost minimization) has been followed.

A variety of theoretical approaches has been given a workout on debt-management problems. The effect of wealth on consumption—contrasting the economist's belief that the public debt is private wealth with the banker's view that the debt is a burden—has been one of them. The theory of portfolio choice has been another. Alternative views concerning the relative weight of money and of liquid assets in the determination of aggregate demand have found application. The theory of the term structure of interest rates has attracted possibly the largest amount of theoretical attention.

While uncertainty about the proper objectives of debt management has been constant, other aspects of the situation have changed. Table 1 shows alternate measures of the impact of the debt. The volume of the debt, in relation to both GNP and the total volume of public and private debt, has contracted drastically since 1950. Public debt instruments became a relative rarity in many institutional and personal portfolios. In this sense, one might say that, while the problem was not solved, in good part it went away. Interest rates rose, however, so that without accounting

Table 1: Alternative Measures of Impact of Federal Debt Held by Public

	(1) Net Federal Debt	(2) GNP	(3) Net Federal Debt as Percent of Total Public and Private Debt	Net Federal Interest Payments as Percent of GNP	
				(4) Not Accounting for Inflation	(5) Accounting for Inflation
1946.........	$229.5	110.1%	57.9%	2.0%	
1950..........	218.1	76.8	44.9	1.6	−3.1%
1955..........	232.5	58.4	34.9	1.2	−0.3
1960..........	243.3	48.3	27.8	1.4	0.1
1965..........	275.3	40.2	22.1	1.3	0.7
1971..........	365.7	34.8	18.3	1.3	−0.2

Sources: Column (1) Total Federal Government and agency debt, end of year (*Economic Report of the President*, (*ERP*) 1973, Table C-62), billions of dollars.
Column (2) Equals Col. (1) divided by Gross National Product (*ERP*, 1973, Table C-1).
Column (3) Equals Col. (1) divided by total public and private debt (*ERP*, Table C-62).
Column (4) Net interest payments (*ERP*, 1973, Table C-66 and 1958, Table B-62) divided by Gross National Product.
Column (5) Accounting for inflation involves multiplying an estimate of the "real" interest rate times column (2). The real interest rate is derived as the difference between the actual rate (derived from columns (2) and (4)) and the average rate of change of the GNP deflator over the past 5 years for first four rates and 6 years for 1971 (*ERP*, 1973, Table C-4).

for inflation the net interest burden remained almost constant as a fraction of GNP. We have also shown the "real" interest burden in column 5 of Table 1, a measure accounting for the presence of inflation. By this measure, real interest payments were negative in early years, and have remained quite low except for the early 1960s.

A final shift in emphasis has occurred as the Federal Reserve moved toward a new theory of monetary policy, in which the monetary aggregates play a relatively smaller role. Monetary policy aimed at a money supply target was seen to be more vulnerable to the consequences of even keeling during financing periods. On the other hand, failure to even keel poses a greater threat to the success of financings under a money-supply than under an interest-rate target.

Debt management has traditionally focused on the role of the Treasury in determining the structure of the Federal Debt. There is an implicit separation of functions between the Treasury and the Federal Reserve under which the Treasury determines the gross distribution of government liabilities of different maturities while the Fed determines the net distribution. No matter what securities the Treasury chooses to issue, the Fed could, through its open-market operations and regulatory policies, ensure private investors would hold a portfolio of government securities of the Fed's choosing. The responsibility of the Treasury then would be limited to two objectives: to keep the Fed supplied with a sufficient bundle of maturities with which to

operate, and in its financing operations to keep out of the way of the Fed. This separation of functions has never been explicitly followed in the United States. The Fed does not, by maturity-switching open-market operations, sterilize the impact of Treasury actions, or even the consequences of the passage of time, upon the maturity structure of publicly held securities. Its preference for dealing in bills and for thus limiting monetary policy to changes in the monetary base, instead of changes in monetary base and asset structure, favors this policy of self-limitation. Close cooperation between Treasury and the Fed, and some regard by the Treasury for the cyclical implications of its debt actions, can serve as a substitute for an explicit "separation of functions" under which the Treasury would determine only the gross and the Fed the net (publicly held) maturity structure of the debt.

We shall shortly ask whether the maturity structure of the Federal debt makes any difference. If it does, there are almost certainly advantages in centralizing monetary policy in a single authority. The obvious place is the Fed. In case of inadequate coordination, or of conflict of views, as has occurred, decentralization of policy can be costly or even destabilizing.[1] The British

---

[1] For a formal analysis of the effects of centralization or decentralization of policy on the outcomes, see R. N. Cooper, "Macroeconomic Policy Adjustments in Interdependent Economies," *Quarterly Journal of Economics*, February 1969. For an analysis of the benefits of risk diversification by employing simultaneously several policy instruments the effects

system of debt management features some of the techniques here described. Its concomitant in the British framework—far-reaching control by the Treasury over central bank policies—is a possible but certainly not necessary consequence of the technical "separation of functions."

We do not, however, propose any change in existing Treasury-Federal Reserve procedures. We proceed instead on the assumption that the Treasury does determine not only the maturity structure of the gross debt, but in large measure also that of the net debt. If maturity structure matters, then debt management is interwoven with monetary policy and the Treasury has a responsibility in the areas both of anticyclical and structural (long-term) monetary policy.

On the question whether maturity structure matters, the theory of debt management is today confronted with relatively recent empirical findings concerning the effect of that structure, as it relates to government securities, upon the term structure of interest rates. There is considerable evidence that it is very difficult to change the term structure of rates. As Modigliani and Sutch conclude:

Our findings . . . suggest that the responsiveness of the rate structure to variations in the age composition of the national debt outstanding was at best weak, even in a period in which the national debt was large, both in absolute and relative size . . . On the basis of a rather extensive battery of tests based on a variety of measures of age composition, we have been able to uncover persistent and fairly convincing evidence that at least variations in the supply of debt in the intermediate range, especially in the one-to-five-year range, tended to produce moderate variations in the spread for intermediate maturities, that is, maturities in the corresponding age class. On the other hand, we have been unable to uncover solid or even suggestive evidence that the age composition of the supply affects significantly longer rates as measured by the average long-term rate or the twelve-year rate.[2]

The rationale for the ineffectiveness of debt structure in affecting rate structure usually is stated in terms of the "expectations hypothesis." The pure expectations hypothesis about riskless rates can be formulated as follows:

A.   The term structure of interest rates is determined solely by expectations of future rates.

There is considerable evidence that the pure expectations hypothesis is not correct, but that a weaker hypothesis—which we shall call "approximate term structure invariance"—is valid:

B.   There are systematic deviations of the term structure from that predicted by the pure expectations hypothesis, with long rates generally above short rates. The rate structure, however, is almost invariant with respect to changes in the composition of government debt.

A number of studies of the effect of the composition of government debt on the term structure of interest rates point to these conclusions and are summarized in Table 2. The most impressive point about these results is that there is very little effect of change in the maturity structure on interest rates. The studies are not unanimous in their estimate of the impact of changes on the *direction* of effect. The *size* of the effect varies by a factor of almost three between the findings of Okun and those of Scott. The one fairly consistent finding is that the effect is very limited, as indicated by the hypothesis of approximate term structure invariance. A subjectively weighted average estimate from Table 2 might be that a 1 percent shift from shorts to longs would change the rate differential by 5 basis points. This means that to twist the rate structure by 1 full percentage point would currently require a maturity switching operation of $50 billion.

Findings of a failure of the term structure of interest rates to react to the maturity structure of the public debt have been puzzling to market practitioners because they so often observe the rate impact of large issues. The difference in observations between practitioners and econometricians seems to be that between a very short-run impact effect and a permanent stock effect. Even though a large issue may depress the market for comparable maturities temporarily, the effect may disappear within a few days or weeks, so that little trace is left on the quarterly or even monthly data usually employed in econometric studies.[3]

---

of which are not known with certainty, see William Brainard, "Uncertainty and the Effectiveness of Policy," *American Economic Review, Papers and Proceedings,* May 1967.

[2] Modigliani and Sutch, "Debt Management and the Term Structure of Interest Rates: An Empirical Analysis of Recent Experience," *Journal of Political Economy,* 1967, pp. 587–89.

[3] Okun reports no flow effect for periods of one quarter, Okun, *op. cit.,* p. 161. Hamburger and Silber, *op. cit.,* present a regression showing a distributed lag on the Treasury bill rate for monthly data, but the effect does not show any rate of change (or flow) effect (p. 263). In fact, their monthly equation shows a distributed lag with all coefficients having the same sign; a rate of change effect implies that

Table 2:   Estimates of Moving 1 Percent of Federal Debt from 1-Year to 20-Year Bonds

	Basis Points		
	Change in Short-Term Interest Rate	Change in Long-Term Interest Rate	Change in Spread between Long- and Short-Term Interest Rates
Okun[1]	−2.20	0.83	3.03
Scott[2]	−12.77	−4.79	7.98
	(2.81)*	(1.44)	(2.07)
Modigliani and Sutch[3]	—		−.912
Hamburger and Silber[4]	0.0		(.798)

Note: Let D be total interest-bearing Federal debt. The table shows the estimated effect of an open market operation which simultaneously sells D/100 in bonds with maturity greater than 20 years and buys D/100 in bonds with maturity less than 1 year. The effect of a 1 percent increase in 20-year bonds and a 1 percent decrease in 1-year bonds will be to raise the average maturity of the total debt by .19 years. Scott and Modigliani and Sutch estimate the effects on interest rates of a 1 year increase in the average maturity of the debt. Their estimates have been multiplied by .19 in order to obtain the figures in this table.
   * The standard errors are given in parentheses when the sources present them.
   [1] Arthur M. Okun, "Monetary Policy, Debt Management and Interest Rates: A Quantitative Proposal," pp. 142–188 in *Financial Markets and Economic Activity.* Edited by Donald Hester and James Tobin, New Haven, Yale University Press, 1967. Okun's sample period was 1946-I to 1959-III. The value of net interest-bearing debt for 1953-I was $119 billion. A 1 percent shift on average represents a switch of $1.2 billion. We have used Okun's equation (8) presented in Tables 1 and 4.
   [2] Robert Haney Scott, "Liquidity and the Term Structure of Interest Rates," *Quarterly Journal of Economics,* 79 (February 1965), pp. 135–45.
   [3] Modigliani and Sutch, "Debt Management and the Term Structure of Interest Rates: An Empirical Analysis of Recent Experience," *Journal of Political Economy,* 1967, pp. 569–89.
   [4] Michael J. Hamburger and William L. Silber, "Debt Management and Interest Rates: A Re-examination of the Evidence," *The Manchester School,* December 1971, pp. 261–66. The sample period is 1961-I to 1966-II, during which the average debt was $202 billion. A 1 percent shift from bills to 20-year bonds therefore represents a switch of $2 billion. We have presented their preferred equation, equation (2).

In the short run the impact effect may be largely obliterated by portfolio adjustments of lenders. In the long run, any remaining effects may be removed by adjustments of borrowers in the maturity of their liabilities.

In addition to changes in the term structure of rates, i.e., principally the short-long spread, manipulation of the maturity structure of the public debt may affect the level of rates, quite possibly without altering the structure. Again, the empirical results cited in Table 2 cast doubt on whether there is any durable effect of composition of the debt on the *level* of rates. In principle, a reduction in maturity increases liquidity. An increase in the liquidity of assets reduces the demand for money, causing the existing money supply to become excessive at the existing level of interest rates. A shortening of the public debt therefore might have the same effect on interest rates as an increase in the money supply.

This effect, too, could be neutralized by countervailing shifts in the maturity structure of private debt. Some lenders, as well as borrowers, prefer long-term to short-term debt, and may move into maturity areas vacated by the Treasury. It should be pointed out that the effect of changes in the maturity of private claims and li-

abilities on the liquidity of lenders and borrowers, respectively, is very unlikely to be symmetrical, i.e., unlikely to be mutually neutralizing. Treasury action could be neutralized likewise, of course, by action of the central bank, especially if the latter uses interest rates rather than the money supply as its principal policy guide.

OBJECTIVES OF DEBT MANAGEMENT

The major issues of debt management revolve around whether debt management should be oriented primarily toward cyclical or structural objectives and, to the extent that structural objectives predominate, what these should be. Historically, anticyclical debt management has received a fair amount of academic support, pointing to an anticyclical lengthening and shortening of the debt. Experience has demonstrated that such a policy is not easy to carry out: the policy involves selling large amounts of long-term debt during periods of expansion and rising rates, a period when such sales are difficult by the Treasury's traditional techniques of selling bonds. As noted above, the Fed does not automatically sterilize Treasury operations. This indicates that the Treasury should continue to have cyclical objectives in mind. Nor should the anticyclical objective be abandoned to the extent where the Treasury, having financed short dur-

current and lagged coefficients have opposite signs. Perhaps there is a flow effect for a week, a day, a second, a nanosecond . . .

ing a long expansion, would feel free to engage in massive refunding during an ensuing recession. Avoidance of debt operations that gratuitously conflict with monetary policy objectives could be viewed as in line with the principle of "keeping out of the way of the Fed." We shall examine this as one of the possible "structural" objectives, to which we now turn.

1. Adequate Money Supply

In the early postwar days, when the public debt was large relative to private debt and when private short-term instruments were not plentiful, a debt structure conducive to providing and maintaining an adequate money supply and adequate liquidity had attraction. This would have meant: (a) enough medium-term securities which banks could hold without undue risk but also without experiencing excessive liquidity, to make the money supply adequate; (b) enough short-term debt to meet bank and nonbank demand for highly liquid instruments; and (c) all the rest of the debt in savings bonds or long-term marketable bonds. This criterion has little meaning at a time when the money supply is overwhelmingly based on private debt and when the investments that banks buy typically are tax exempt.

2. Maximum Protection Against the Political Risks of Short-Term Debt

The traditional central bank view is that short-term public debt is dangerous. Political pressure can compel central banks to monetize such debt in order to forestall a rise in interest costs on an important part of total debt. American experience shows that political pressures to monetize long-term debt can be even stronger—see the rate-structure pegging episode of the late 1940s.

3. Minimum Cost to the Treasury

This would probably mean a debt in all short-term securities, unless the consequent increase in this type of paper should cause short-term rates to rise above long-term rates. It would not mean a debt all in interest-free currency, since the Federal Reserve would have to compensate such excess creation of bank reserves and thereby give up assets whose income otherwise would go to the Treasury. An "all shorts" public debt posture has many uncomfortable aspects and risks beyond the traditional danger of excessive monetization by the central bank.

At a more theoretical level, the concept of "debt monetization" carries a somewhat different, although currently not operational, connotation. In line with the view that payment of interest on demand deposits would lead to larger holdings of money and hence to greater liquidity and greater welfare without an increase in inflationary pressure, it should be noted that such a policy would move toward "monetization" of the debt by narrowing the rate spread between bonds and money and so making money more like bonds. Likewise, it has been argued that under certain conditions the true cost of public expenditures can be measured better by the interest cost of borrowing they require than by their capital cost, while for certain redistributive measures more "bang for a buck" can be attained if the buck is borrowed at a low interest rate.

4. Optimal Public Debt from the Viewpoint of the Private Sector: Public Debt as Financial Intermediation

The negative implications of concentration on short-term debt lose some of their sting when it is remembered that the choice is not simply whether the Treasury should finance short or long. To a certain extent the choice is whether the Treasury (i.e., the public sector) should finance long and the private sector short, or vice versa. If it is granted that the supply of long-term funds is not infinitely elastic, then long-term government financing either cuts off some private financing or drives it into the short-term area. Quite aside from the Treasury's possible desire to keep down interest costs by financing short, the private sector has an interest in keeping the public debt relatively short-term. We shall give a few instances of this interest of the private sector in a short-term public debt, and then present a more formal argument to make the same basic point and arrive at a more general statement about optimal debt management in terms of public debt as financial intermediation.

In an economy in which the long-term rate normally is above the short, long-term money is the scarcer and more valuable article. Debtors, on balance, regard the disadvantages of short-term debt as weighty enough to justify paying a premium for long-term money. If the government can make do equally well with either kind of debt, it obviously ought to avoid borrowing the premium type and so contributing to its scarcity.

Private borrowers, furthermore, confront both market and credit risk. Market risk relates to the possibility that the market may be unfavorable at the time of borrowing or refunding, credit risk to the possibility that the borrower's credit standing may deteriorate. The Federal Government confronts only market risk. Both borrowers can spread their risks if they have a choice of borrowing both long and short. The Federal Government can broaden this option for the private borrower if it stays out of the long-term market and allows the private borrower a better chance to select the kind of maturity that his risk situation makes preferable.

For lenders, finally, short-term assets are advantageous as indicated by their normal willingness to accept a lower interest rate on liquid instruments. If the government, without incurring compensating costs, can create liquidity, it should do so.

One approach to the optimal debt structure is to consider the government debt as a form of changing the structure of total private holdings. Consider an economy where liquid wealth is held by households and capital is held by firms. An analysis of portfolios would indicate that households prefer short assets, while firms prefer long liabilities. We assume for simplicity that for a flat term structure individuals keep all assets in short securities and firms issue all liabilities long. Figure 1 shows the ratio of long assets to total assets of households as HH as a function of the rate differential; similarly the (negative) liabilities of firms are shown as FF. In terms of theory, we can say that short securities are the "preferred habitat" of households while long securities are the "preferred habitat" of firms. They must compromise, of course, and the outcome comes at λ^* with the long rate at a premium δ^* above the short rate.

We assume that risk differentials are sufficiently great so that speculators do not close the rate differential δ^*, but that these risks are not social risks. If this is the case the government can make both households and firms better off by engaging in "intermediation," e.g., issuing short debt and buying an equal amount of long debt. This process should proceed until the term structure is flat. If the government is a debtor, this argues for issuing only short debt until the term structure is flat. Assuming HH and FF are homogeneous in total wealth, issuance of short debt amounts to changing the supply function from FF to $F'F'$ in Figure 2.[4]

This policy lowers interest-rate differentials from δ_0 to δ_1 and lowers the fraction of debt in long

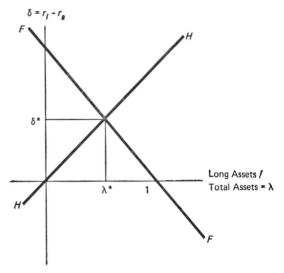

Figure 1: Market Supply (FF) and Demand (HH) Functions for Long-Term Assets

securities from λ_0 to λ_1. Why is it that in this scheme there might be a small effect of debt composition on the rate differential? Either the HH line, or else the FF line, is very flat. In the former case, the government succeeds in changing the composition of private debt, but the rate effect is small; in the second case, firms undo public debt management with their own debt policy.

It is easily seen that simply issuing short securities will not erase the yield differential if the HH line goes through the origin. To erase the differential the government can buy long debt, say in secondary mortgage markets. In this case, the HH curve moves to the right as to $H'H'$ in Figure 2B. The policy shown in Figure 2B actually performs a sufficient amount of buying long and selling short so that the term structure is completely flat. There will be a unique combination of such short sales and long purchases which will (a) provide a flat yield curve and (b) assure that the entire net debt is held. We will call this policy the *debt management technique which flattens the term structure of interest rates,* or the flattening policy.

It is easy to see that the monetary authorities have enough instruments to flatten the term structure. In the general case there are n demand and supply functions for the n assets, each function being homogeneous in the n rates of interest. There are n instruments since government debt has n maturities. Under normal conditions the targets can all be met, subject to the proviso that full achievement of such an objective may

---

[4] At a point δ in Figure 2 the FF curve shifts to the left by the fraction $\mu = D^f/(D^f + D^g)$, where D^f and D^g are total liabilities of firms and government, respectively.

Figure 2A: Outcome When Government Issues Short Debt Only

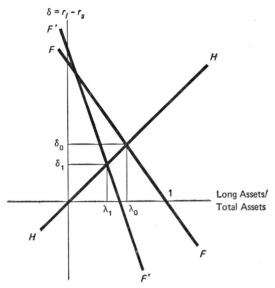

Figure 2B: Outcome When Government Issues Short Debt and Buys Private Long Debt

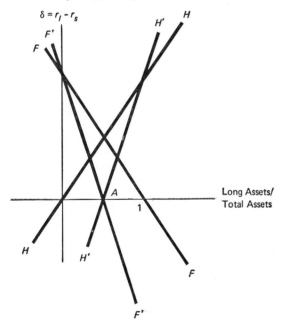

involve the Treasury in substantial short-term borrowing and long-term lending.

What is the rationale for a policy of flattening the rate structure? The basic reason is that over the long run a rate structure which is anything but flat reflects the presence of inefficiencies. Just as money will not be held as an asset without transactions costs, so the observed stable ascending rate structure seems to us to be consistent with a pattern of preferred habitats and risk

aversion as shown in Figure 1. By flattening the rate structure the government finances the debt in such a way as to remove the inefficiencies associated with risks.

It should be noted that the flattening of the rate structure does not necessarily increase the welfare of all participants. The short-term borrower and the long-term lender who have below average aversion to risk or who were operating in their preferred maturity range lose the risk premium from which they were benefiting in their respective ways. But on balance the reduction of a private risk that is not also a social one is bound to raise aggregate welfare. It is true also that there are private intermediaries, one of whose functions it is to convert short-term into long-term money, making a profit by "riding the yield curve." This activity is itself not a riskless one, however, as the recent experience of the thrift institutions has shown, and in any event has on average not been carried to the point of producing a flat term structure. There is room, therefore, for some structural influence emanating from the public debt in the direction of a flatter yield structure. Financial intermediation, involving lending as well as borrowing, is part of the current activities of the public sector, but our analysis is concerned not with Federal lending agency operations and their possible expansion, but with the principles underlying the influence of debt management upon the term structure of interest rates.

How does a policy of debt management aiming to flatten out the yield structure relate to other policy objectives of debt management? It should be seen only as an absolute goal when no other goals are in competition with optimal debt management. It appears to us to be very similar to the objective of minimizing the cost of debt. On the other hand, it should be viewed as a *very long-run policy* and one around which stabilization objectives can move. Thus we would not view a policy of Twist such as that used in 1962 as inconsistent with this objective as long as Twist was clearly seen to be a cyclical policy and not as a substitute for expansionary domestic policies and a higher foreign exchange rate. Moreover, a policy of faster (or slower) growth could be achieved by a greater (or lesser) monetization of debt.

5. Providing Adequate Gross Debt for Cyclical Debt Management

We have presented a set of reasons, based on structural grounds, that favor a Federal debt financed largely with short-term interest bearing securities. Two major reservations need to be stated concerning such a policy. One is the familiar set of objections to governmental short-term financing: given that the Federal debt is almost certainly permanent, a heavy concentration on short-term issues appears "unsound" in the light of the canons of traditional private finance; it carries a heavier market risk than long-term debt because the stream of interest payments is more variable; it is vulnerable to political and other pressures that could lead to inflationary debt financing. We have stated earlier some considerations that reduce the weight of these objections.

The second reservation relates to the fact that a predominately short-term debt precludes the possibility of twisting the term structure of rates. The Fed cannot substitute short for long debt in the market if there is no public long debt in the market. We assume here that the present institutional framework will be preserved, which prevents the Fed from dealing in private securities in the open market. Many economists have argued that in certain conditions the yield curve should be twisted; in 1962, for example, a quarter-hearted attempt was made to lengthen the debt in order to promote investment while attracting short-term capital from abroad. Especially in a world without perfect markets, such situations (or even in mid-1974 the reverse!) may well arise again. A case can therefore be made for either: (1) having a sufficient quantity of gross long debt so that the monetary authorities can buy and sell long debt; or (2) changing the existing framework to allow the monetary authorities to operate in securities other than those of the Treasury.

One question involves the magnitudes of debt of different maturities necessary for the Fed to engage in meaningful monetary policy of this kind. The studies summarized in Table 2 place the change in the ratio of short debt to total debt required to twist the term structure by 100 basis points around 20 percent of marketable interest-bearing Federal debt, i.e. about $50 billion. This is roughly equal to the total of marketable Treasury securities outstanding with maturities exceeding five years.

Given the realities of the market, anticyclical operations in long-term securities of such orders of magnitude are not promising. Over the years, as total wealth rises, the Federal debt is likely to constitute a continuously diminishing proportion of it. The chances of a meaningful impact on the rate structure via open-market operations in long-

term debt will further diminish. It might be asked, therefore, whether the hope of achieving such effects should be allowed to dominate debt structure policy.

6. Minimum Interference with the Fed

"Keeping out of the way of the Fed" is another of the possible objectives of debt management. In other words, instead of seeking to achieve positive effects, the goal would be to avoid negative effects resulting from interference with monetary policy. This goal at one time would have loomed so large as to be impossible to achieve. Shortly after World War II, all thinking about monetary policy was dominated by concern over its effect on the debt. During the pegging period, cooperation between the Treasury and the Fed paralyzed monetary policy.

Today, three forms of interference are readily apparent. One is the constraint that at times has resulted from the need to finance large budget deficits in a rapidly expanding economy, when capital markets were already strained by private demands. This is basically a fiscal policy problem —the budget probably should not be in such heavy deficit at these times. When it is, the result almost certainly will be a heavy concentration on short-term debt. Large-scale long-term financing would drive up long-term rates excessively. Even a strict interpretation of the expectations theory would not deny this—heavy long-term financing would probably change expectations. Only short-term debt can be sold in sufficient volume without great rate increases—provided the Federal Reserve gives the banks the reserves with which to buy these issues, thereby improperly accelerating the growth of the money supply.

A second form of interference with monetary policy can result from a heavy volume of short-term debt outstanding from an earlier period. An effort to keep the monetary aggregates growing stably under conditions of expansion will raise short-term interest rates and make the interest cost of the debt very burdensome. It will also put upward pressure on rates charged by banks for short- and medium-term credit. The answer to this problem is that of orthodox debt management: avoid short-term debt by keeping the debt funded. The pros and cons of this advice are familiar. It does not appear that this form of interference with monetary policy should be decisive for the choice of debt management policies.

The practice of even-keeling the market during Treasury financings is a third form of interference. A variety of views seems to exist among market technicians about the variables and techniques involved in even-keeling, about the duration and rigor of individual episodes, and even about the need to protect Treasury financings by this form of market stabilization. We conclude that there is a significant possibility, which frequently materializes, that even-keeling may interfere with monetary policy particularly under a policy regime aiming at stable growth of the monetary aggregates.

Fortunately, techniques are available to offset the adverse effects of even-keeling upon monetary policy, assuming the practice cannot be dispensed with altogether. The orthodox counsel again would be to reduce the number of financings by lengthening the debt. But even-keeling could be eliminated altogether if (1) the debt were all in bills, assuming auctions to require no even-keel, or (2) all short and long financings were shifted to an auction basis, or (3) all issues were made sufficiently small, perhaps by reopening of old issues, to make their pricing and sale no more difficult than that of corporate issues. The Treasury already has experimented with (2), through a "Dutch Auction" of a bond, which will be reported on in another paper at this conference. Of these techniques, the Dutch Auction may well be the best, since it does not prejudice the form of Treasury issues as would the other two. It is evident, then, that the conclusions of this paper pointing in the direction of a predominately short-term debt can be made consistent with a debt policy whose principal objective is to keep out of the way of the Fed.

7. Purchasing-Power Bond

No discussion of debt management is complete that does not pay its respects to the merits of a purchasing-power bond. This time honored subject has been endowed with powerful actuality by our high rate of inflation. We shall ignore the familiar pros and cons debated in the past—the need to give the small saver a positive real interest rate, the danger of seeming to "throw in the towel" in the fight against inflation, and so forth, and only note briefly two points that appear to have been neglected in the debate.

In a risk-averse market, investors will be prepared to pay a premium for the elimination of the inflation risk. Thus, the rate at which such a bond could be sold might turn out to be lower than the real rate. The latter has been variously computed as falling in the range of 3–4 percent. It might be worthwhile finding out whether this is so, perhaps by having a government agency, rather than the Treasury, put out such an experimental issue.

Second, the Treasury would be deceiving itself if it were to ignore the fact that it is already putting out securities that are near substitutes for purchasing-power securities. The coupons of all issues currently sold obviously contain an inflation premium. This however, is an inefficient and costly method of inflation-proofing a security. The premium contained in the coupon is taxable. Hence it must be high enough to attract, as marginal investors, taxable buyers for whom the post-tax premium still constitutes adequate protection. For tax-exempt buyers, that premium is excessive. The situation is the reverse of that prevailing in the market for tax-exempts, where middle-bracket buyers have to be attracted to sell enough bonds, giving high-bracket buyers an unnecessarily high return. A purchasing-power bond, providing for a tax-exempt inflation adjustment, would avoid this extra cost.

We have no expectation that the Treasury will issue a purchasing-power bond, any more than that it will hereafter voluntarily finance all of its debt short-term. But it may be useful to the Treasury to have to rethink from time to time the reasons why it will not.

Chapter

6

INTERNATIONAL FINANCE

The selections included in this book up to this point have been concerned with the use of monetary and fiscal policy in an environment from which problems of international trade and the balance of international payments have been excluded. In other words, in the jargon of the economist, we have been discussing a "closed economy."

In reality, of course, the U.S. economy is closely linked to the rest of the world. In 1976, for example, our exports of goods and services amounted to $163 billion, while our imports came to $156 billion. Although each of these totals amounted to less than 10 percent of U.S. GNP, imported consumer goods are a significant element in our high standard of living, while both imported raw materials (especially petroleum) and export markets for our products are of major importance to some of our industries. Moreover, since most of our trading partners are less self-sufficient and more dependent on foreign trade than we are, our trade is even more important to the rest of the world than it is to us. In addition to our trade relations, our financial markets are closely linked to the financial markets of other countries through a complex network of international borrowing and lending activities.

As a result of these trade and financial ties, our prosperity is affected by economic developments occurring in other countries and by policies followed by other governments. And the converse is true, perhaps in even greater degree: Since trade with the United States is of major importance to many other countries, economic developments here and the policies we follow will often have a major impact on the prosperity of the rest of the world.

The way in which economic impulses are transmitted from one country to another and the nature of the resulting interdependence that exists among countries depends to a considerable extent on the structure of the international monetary system—that is, the complex web of rules and arrangements governing financial relations among countries. From early 1947 until the beginning of 1973, world trade was based on a financial system involving fixed exchange rates among currencies which had its origins in the Bretton Woods Conference of 1944, at which the International Monetary Fund (IMF) was established. This system bore some resemblance to the so-called gold exchange standard that was developed in the 1920s, under which participating countries held their reserves partly in gold and partly in national currencies—such as the dollar and sterling —which were themselves freely convertible into gold. The gold exchange standard proved to be unstable, and under pressures of the Great Depression in the early 1930s, it broke down completely as a result of the speculative movements of funds induced by fears of currency devaluation. The result was nearly a decade of international monetary chaos which helped to spread depression throughout the world and brought a drastic decline to world trade. The Bretton Woods system contained features designed to prevent a repetition of the international financial disaster of the 1930s, and the strength of the system was most clearly reflected in the vigorous growth and prosperity of the world economy and the rapid expansion of international trade that occurred during the quarter century or so of its life. But the system also contained problems which became more apparent with the passage of time, and these plus certain external events —notably the rapid expansion of aggregate demand in the U.S. economy during the 1960s—eventually led to its downfall when, in 1971, the United States suspended the convertibility of the dollar into gold in response to massive short-term capital outflows; and when, in February 1973, several European countries decided to let their currencies float jointly against the dollar (while maintaining fixed rates among themselves). Such changes were inconsistent with the Bretton Woods system, which was based on fixed exchange rates among all currencies and on dollar-gold convertibility.

The problems inherent in the fixed-rate system can be classified under these headings: adjustment, confidence, and liquidity. The *liquidity problem* arose because in a growing world economy with fixed exchange rates, there is need for a growing stock of international reserves to enable countries to finance balance-of-payment deficits while underlying corrective forces are working to eliminate deficits. For various reasons, there is no way to control the growth of gold and the currencies widely held as reserves so as to ensure that they will grow in pace with the world's needs for them. As a means of dealing with this problem, a new international reserve asset, the Special Drawing Right or SDR, was created, and a plan was formulated to provide for the growth of reserves in this form in the amounts deemed necessary to meet the requirements of the international economy. The First Amendment to the International Monetary Fund's Articles of Agreement established the Special Drawing Account in July 1969.

The *confidence problem* arose because of fear that a country experiencing a persistent balance-of-payments deficit would exhaust its supply of international monetary reserves and be forced to devalue its currency to eliminate its deficit. Holders of a currency about to be devalued could make large profits if they had the foresight to anticipate the devaluation and transfer their funds into another currency before it occurred. Waves of such speculative activity were the objective manifestation of the confidence problem, and these had the effect of further weakening an already shaky currency.

The *adjustment problem* arose because there were only a limited number of corrective actions that a country experiencing a balance-of-payments deficit could take. These actions could under some circumstances be either unpleasant for the country involved or undesirable from the standpoint of world economic efficiency. The same is true for actions required to deal with a balance-of-payments surplus. The inherent logic of the fixed-exchange-rate system called for deficit countries to moderate the growth of income and put downward pressure on prices, thus retarding imports and encouraging exports. Conversely, a surplus country was supposed to adopt expansionary policies. The trouble was that this prescription put pressure on countries to accept either more unemployment or more inflation than they desired for domestic reasons. Furthermore, it contained an asymmetry: While deficit countries were under increasing pressure to adjust as they lost reserves, surplus countries were under no such pressures as their reserves accumulated; and it was widely believed that the system imposed a deflationary bias on the trading world as a whole.

In addition to these problems, it was sometimes true that the fiscal and monetary policies appropriate for dealing with a country's balance-of-payments problems were inconsistent with those needed for the domestic situation. For instance, in the early 1960s, the U.S. economy experienced excessive unemployment (calling for expansionary policies), while its balance of payments displayed a chronic deficit (for which restrictive policies were needed). There was some scope for dealing with such inconsistencies when they occurred by using fiscal policy primarily to deal with the domestic situation and assigning monetary policy to the balance-of-payments problem. However, these changes in policy mix might interfere with other objectives: for example, an increase in interest rates designed to increase capital inflows and improve the balance of payments might conflict with the economic growth goal, which requires a high level of business investment in plant and equipment. High interest rates also affect different sectors of the domestic economy quite unevenly, and may cause serious problems for the housing industry and for state and local government capital expenditure projects. As a consequence, this remedy can be relied upon only to a very limited extent.

These problems were widely recognized and discussed, and various suggestions for reform were advanced during the 1950s and 1960s. The extreme solution, which had a considerable number of advocates among economists, was to allow exchange rates to fluctuate freely in response to changes in private demand and supply with no intervention by governments. In principle, this would completely eliminate the balance-of-payments problem, since exchange rates would adjust automatically in such a way as to keep payments in continuous equilibrium. However, many students of international financial problems doubted the wisdom of such an extreme solution, chiefly because they feared it would induce destabilizing speculation in foreign exchange, increase risks of international trade, and result in a diminution in trade. Consequently, alternative proposals were advanced which would allow more flexibility of exchange rates than existed under the Bretton Woods system without going all the way to completely flexible rates. One such proposal was to widen the band of values within which exchange rates were allowed to vary under the fixed-rate system, thus increasing somewhat the flexibility of the system and allowing a wider scope for market forces. Another set of proposals involved the gradual adjustment of parities through a "crawling peg" system. Under one variant of this scheme, the parity for a currency at any moment would be the average of actual values over some past period such as a year. Thus if the actual rate were persistently above or below its official parity, the parity itself would be adjusted automatically and systematically.

However, these discussions were overtaken by the force of events. The United

States had a balance-of-payments deficit in most years following World War II, but other countries at first were eager to obtain dollars, both to pay for needed imports and to restore their foreign exchange reserves. As a result, U.S. deficits initially created no problems for us. By 1958, however, the leading industrial countries had overcome the decline in their competitive positions caused by the war and were able to compete effectively in world markets. Having restored their dollar holdings to desired levels, they became less willing to accept and hold more dollars and more inclined to convert portions of the added dollars resulting from continuous U.S. deficits into gold, thus reducing our gold stock

Our problems were considerably complicated by domestic developments in the latter 1960s. The sharp increase in U.S. defense spending to support the escalation of the Vietnam conflict in late 1965 had direct and indirect effects on the U.S. balance of payments. The increase in military spending overseas added directly to the deficit, while rising incomes and prices caused imports to expand and our competitive position in export markets to be weakened. Consequently our merchandise trade balance fell from a surplus of almost $7 billion in 1964 to a $2.3 billion deficit in 1971. During this period, income from U.S. investments abroad rose, offsetting a portion of the trade surplus deterioration; and in the latter years of the 1960s, high domestic profits together with high interest rates caused by heavy credit market demands and a generally restrictive monetary policy attracted a large flow of foreign funds into U.S. financial assets. In addition, restrictions on U.S. capital outflows through banks and business firms operating overseas were tightened up. Consequently, the overall U.S. balance of payments showed modest surpluses in 1968 and 1969. But the situation changed drastically beginning in 1970. In addition to the trade-balance deterioration already mentioned, private long-term and (especially) short-term capital flowed out in massive amounts. These flows were partly a response to a substantial spread between European and U.S. interest rates in favor of Europe, but also reflected an increasing belief that the dollar was fundamentally weak relative to other currencies and that changes in the system were imminent.

These beliefs became reality on August 15, 1971, when the United States announced that the convertibility into gold of dollars held by foreign monetary authorities was suspended; and subsequently when the currencies of other industrial countries were briefly allowed to float upward relative to their previous parities (and to the dollar). In an attempt to salvage the system, exchange rate realignments were negotiated at the Smithsonian meetings in December 1971, but uncertainties about the viability of the new rate structure led to speculative capital movements and to pressures which finally resulted early in 1973 in the abandonment by most major industrial countries of attempts to maintain fixed rates. With other countries no longer willing to buy or sell their own currencies for dollars to maintain the rate structure, and with the United States no longer willing to convert foreign dollar holdings into gold, the Bretton Woods system ceased to exist.

In its place, a system of "managed floating" has arisen within which exchange rates are determined in foreign exchange markets by supply and demand forces, with these forces sometimes reflecting intervention by government financial authorities as well as private behavior. Quite a large number of countries continue to intervene to the degree necessary to maintain a fixed relationship, or "peg," between their currencies and those of some other country or countries, usually because of close trading relationships. But world trade and financial transactions now are dominated by countries whose currencies float, and fairly substantial exchange-rate changes for such currencies can and do occur through the market mechanism in response to trade flows and capital movements, to maintain balance in the balance of payments.

Meanwhile, efforts continued to produce a new international financial format to replace the Bretton Woods agreement. The IMF had already recognized the need for a more comprehensive reform of the system before the existing structure broke down in 1973, and it established a Committee on Reform of the International Monetary System and Related Issues (the Committee of Twenty) in July 1972 to begin work along these lines. In mid-1974 the Committee of Twenty issued its final report and an accompanying Outline of Reform, covering the longer run shape of the system and a program of immediate action on which the Committee was agreed. Immediate steps included the creation of an Interim Committee of the Board of Governors on the International Monetary System to oversee the operation of the system until the IMF Articles of Agreement could be amended to establish a Council of Governors for this task. Also recommended were the establishing of guidelines for the management of floating exchange rates, study of the role of gold in the new system, improvements of procedures for managing world liquidity, and others. Among the developments anticipated in the Committee's longer run assessment were establishment of more effective and symmetrical adjustment procedures for members in balance-of-payments disequilibrium, and an increasingly prominent role for SDRs as the reserve asset at the expense of gold and particular reserve currencies. A larger role for the Intenational Monetary Fund in international surveillance and management was also foreseen.

The Interim Committee set to work to produce draft amendments to the IMF charter covering these, and some other, issues. This effort culminated early in 1976 with the development of an extensive proposed Second Amendment to the IMF Articles of Agreement, which was agreed upon by the Interim Committee in its meeting at Jamaica in January and adopted by the IMF Board of Governors in April of that year. The amendment has been submitted to the IMF's members and becomes effective when three-fifths of them, representing 80 percent of the Fund's voting power, ratify it.

This amendment formalizes a number of important changes in the functioning of the IMF and the world monetary system. Each IMF member country may choose its own preferred exchange-rate arrangement (from a freely-floating rate to one pegged to some other currency, basket of currencies, etc.), provided that country undertakes to foster orderly economic and financial conditions and agrees not to prevent effective balance-of-payments adjustment. While reintroduction of a system of "stable but adjustable" par values is mentioned as a possibility, such a change would require a "high majority" of total voting power and could be vetoed by the United States, which holds 20 percent of the votes.

The role of gold in the international financial system is sharply reduced. Under the amendment, the "official price" of gold is abolished, the IMF will take no action in the market to influence the price of gold, and there are to be no obligations on members to use gold in transactions with the IMF. Furthermore, the function of gold as the unit of value of the SDR, and as the base for the par value of currencies, is eliminated. (This latter provision would appear to bar gold as the basis for a possible reconstituted fixed-rate system.) In short, the SDR replaces gold in the IMF's operations. As a consequence, the Fund decided to auction off a part of its present gold holdings.

The remaining articles of the Second Amendment broaden the use of the

SDR with the specific objective of securing its position as the international monetary system's chief asset, and deal with the mechanics and organization of the IMF. Overall, the amendments essentially ratify the de facto changes in the system that have occurred since 1971. There remain issues not dealt with in these articles: the adjustment problem and the question of control of world liquidity, both mentioned in the *Outline of Reform,* are examples. And the question of the direction in which exchange-rate arrangements will develop remains unsettled.

This latter question is the subject of the paper by Ethier and Bloomfield which opens the chapter (reading 32). They argue that managed floating, rather than free floating or a fixed-rate type of system, is likely to be the norm for a considerable period of time, and therefore that agreement among participants on rules of conduct will be needed to prevent interventions which might be detrimental to the interests of some countries or the international community as a whole. Ethier and Bloomfield advocate introduction of a "reference rate" system, under which there would be a "reference exchange rate" defined for each currency. This reference rate structure, in their words, ". . . would constitute, in effect, a statement by the central banks of their collective view regarding the equilibrium structure of exchange rates." But rather than *requiring* central banks to intervene to *maintain* this rate structure, the proposal *prohibits* them from intervening to force exchange rates *away from* their reference values (once the rate moves outside of a band around the reference rate). This system would be consistent with freely-floating rates (intervention is never required) or with pegging, and could even be combined with a "crawling reference rate" mechanism to adjust the reference rate structure, if automatic adjustment of the structure were thought to be desirable.

Of course, this is only one of several directions that evolution of the international financial system might take, and while it is the one preferred by Ethier and Bloomfield for reasons they indicate, their article is particularly useful because they also discuss other alternatives. Among these are rules regarding intervention which are based on reserve accumulation or decumulation, or rules which limit intervention to that which "leans against the wind" and counters movements in exchange rates, without use of a reference rate system.

While the world financial system has been evolving, so have ways of thinking about the interactions between the exchange rate, the balance of payments, and the level of economic activity. At the simplest level, it is possible to introduce a "foreign sector" of sorts into the most elementary models of income determination. For example, Model I or Model II in the introduction to Chapter 1 of this book could be modified by introducing two new equations, one dealing with the determination of exports and the other with imports, into the model and by changing the equilibrium condition to reflect these changes. Thus Model I (or Model II) would now include equations (6.1) and (6.2), and the former equilibrium condition $Y = C + I + G$ would be replaced by equation (6.3).

$$EX = EX_0 + te \qquad (6.1)$$

$$IM = IM_0 + bY - ie \qquad (6.2)$$

$$Y = C + I + G + EX - IM \qquad (6.3)$$

Here EX is gross exports of goods and services, expressed in dollars. IM is gross imports, also expressed in dollars. The exchange rate, e, is measured as the number of units of domestic currency per unit of foreign currency. A deprecia-

depreciation of the exchange rate (increase in e) is assumed to cause exports to rise and the value of imports, expressed in the domestic currency, to fall.[1] The new equilibrium condition essentially states that, in equilibrium, the dollar value of the amount of goods available to the economy ($Y + IM$) must equal the value of goods claimed from the economy ($C + I + G + EX$).

In such a model as this, with no financial sector, only the current account portion ($EX - IM$) of the whole balance of payments is represented.[2] As pointed out in the paper by Marina v.N. Whitman (reading 33), however, two longstanding approaches to balance-of-payments analysis have typically used only this simple structure, or parts of it. The so-called elasticities approach, in fact, focuses only on the trade-balance relationship—the difference between exports and imports—and on the effect of devaluation or of an income change on the trade balance without taking into account its interaction with the rest of the system. Defining $B = EX - IM$, where B is the trade balance in dollar terms; taking income to be constant; and given the assumption stated in footnote 1; it is clear that an exchange-rate devaluation (a rise in e) would move the trade balance toward surplus; while an increase in GNP, holding the exchange rate constant, would cause the trade balance to move toward deficit. In the "absorption" approach, the full structure is utilized so that income is determined within the system. Using the above definition of B together with the equilibrium condition (6.3), we can write $B = Y - (C + I + G)$, or, by substitution from the rest of the model,

$$B = [1 - c(1 - x)]Y - (C_0 + I_0 + G^* - cT^*)$$

in the case of the modified version of Model II. On this basis, it is easy to show that an increase in domestic spending or "absorption" via changes in one or more of the items grouped in parentheses—C_0, I_0, G^*, or T^*—will cause income to increase and the trade balance to deteriorate in this model, while an exchange rate depreciation will improve the trade balance.[3]

In the "elasticities approach," then, only the export and import relationships themselves are used, while the "absorption" analysis utilizes a self-contained income-determination mechanism (including the foreign sector); in either case, only the trade balance is being examined. A somewhat more complete model is needed for the "monetary approach" to the balance of payments, which takes into account the interaction of the full balance of payments—exports, imports,

---

[1] The inverse relationship shown between the dollar value of imports and the exchange rate implies that the elasticity of demand for physical imports with respect to the exchange rate must be greater than unity in absolute value. This elasticity value is assumed here and in the remainder of this discussion.

[2] Note that in the fixed-exchange-rate case, the equation $B = EX - IM$ plays no role in the simultaneous solution of the model. In adding equations (6.1) and (6.2) to Models I or II, we have also added only two new variables, EX and IM. In the flexible-exchange-rate case, however, e becomes a variable. For the system to be determinate, we then must incorporate one more equation. We use the version of the balance-of-payments equation which states that the balance of payments must be in balance; i.e., $EX - IM = 0$ or $EX = IM$.

[3] The reader may verify this by calculating the multipliers $\Delta B/\Delta E$, (where E, or exogenous expenditure, is defined as $C_0 + I_0 + G^*$), $\Delta B/\Delta T^*$, and $\Delta B/\Delta e$. The values of these multipliers will depend on the values of $\Delta Y/\Delta E$, $\Delta Y/\Delta T^*$, and $\Delta Y/\Delta e$, respectively. In doing these calculations, note that the introduction of a foreign sector into the model has reduced the value of the expenditure and tax multipliers on income, from $1/[1 - c(1 - x)]$ and $-c/[1 - c(1 - x)]$ to $1/[1 - c(1 - x) + b]$ and $-c/[1 - c(1 - x) + b]$ respectively. The reason is that part of the effects of an autonomous spending or tax change now "leak out" of the economy because of the effects on imports of the induced income change. This leakage is reflected in the presence of b, the marginal propensity to import with respect to an income change, in the denominators of the open-economy versions of these multipliers.

and international lending and borrowing or capital flows—with the domestic economy. Since capital flows among countries depend on interest-rate relationships, an amended version of Model III, the *IS–LM* model from the Introduction to Chapter 1, is the simplest structure which will serve our purpose since the market interest rate is determined jointly with the other variables in that model. Again we simply add equations (6.1) and (6.2) to Model III, and replace the equilibrium condition for the income-expenditure part of the model with equation (6.3). The demand-for- and supply-of-money equations, and the equilibrium condition for the monetary sector, are unaffected. We now use a broader definition of the balance of payments than earlier. The relevant balance-of-payments equations are:

$$BP = EX - IM - F \qquad (6.4)$$
$$F = F_0 - fr \qquad (6.5)$$

where (6.4) defines the balance of payments, *BP*, as the trade balance in dollar terms less net capital outflows to other countries (F). The latter depend inversely on the interest rate: When the domestic rate of interest falls, for example, net capital outflows increase as investable funds move abroad seeking higher return. In this case, as in the earlier one, equations (6.4) and (6.5) are not part of the simultaneous solution of the whole model when the exchange rate is fixed. Values for income and the interest rate determined in the solution of the *IS-LM* system (including the export and import equations) are inserted into (6.4) and (6.5) to calculate the level of capital flows and the surplus or deficit in the balance of payments. In particular, it should be noted that balance in the overall balance of payments (the condition that total payments *to* abroad equal total receipts *from* abroad, or that $BP = 0$) will not necessarily be achieved for given values of the parameters and autonomous variables.

In this fixed-rate case, however, the version of (6.4) in which $BP = 0$ can be combined with (6.5), (6.1), and (6.2) to produce another summary equation akin to the *IS* and *LM* curves derived in the Introduction to Chapter 1. This new curve represents all of the combinations of income and the interest rate which will balance the balance of payments (that is, keep $BP = 0$). It is precisely the *BP* line which William H. Branson discusses in his comment on Whitman's paper (reading 34). Based on the above model, the equation of the *BP* line is:

$$r = \frac{F_0 - EX_0 + IM_0 - (t + i)e}{f} + \frac{b}{f} Y. \qquad (6.6)$$

This relationship slopes upward when plotted in the *r,Y* quadrant: as income rises causing imports to increase and the trade balance to deteriorate, the interest rate must rise to induce an offsetting capital inflow (or lessening of an outflow) in order for overall balance to be maintained. An *IS-LM* model with a *BP* line (hereafter called an *IS-LM-BP* model) is plotted in Chart 1. Notice that the *LM* curve's position is unaffected by the introduction of a foreign sector, but that parameters from (6.1) and (6.2) show up in the *IS* equation. This equation is now as follows:

$$r = \frac{C_0 - cT^* + I_0 + G^* + EX_0 - IM_0 + (t + i)e}{v}$$
$$- \frac{[1 - c(1 - x) + b]}{v} Y \qquad (6.7)$$

Note that both its intercept and slope are changed by introducing a foreign sector

Chart 1: An *IS-LM* System with a Foreign Sector and Balance-of-Payments Balance

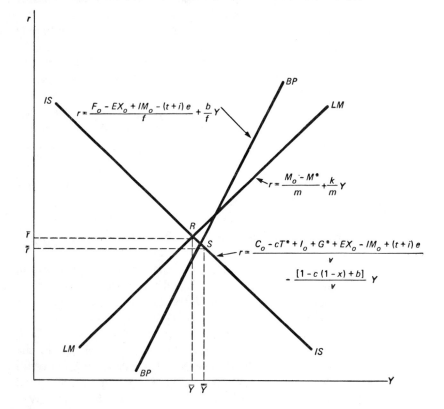

Models of this type provide the starting point for the Whitman-Branson discussion of the "monetary approach" to the analysis of a macroeconomic system via the interaction of the domestic economy and the foreign sector. As Branson points out, the "global monetarist" view with which Whitman begins her discussion can be viewed as an extreme case of the general *IS-LM-BP* view, and can perhaps best be understood by working toward it step by step from this general approach.

Consider first the model depicted in Chart 1 above, under a fixed exchange rate regime. In the situation shown, where the *BP* line fails to go through the *IS-LM* intersection, interaction of the *IS* and *LM* systems will put the economy at point $\bar{r}$, $\bar{Y}$, and the balance of payments will be in disequilibrium. The interest rate r, which with $\bar{Y}$ will produce "internal balance" by satisfying the *IS* and *LM* equations, is too high for balance in the balance of payments. Thus at point R there must be a balance-of-payments surplus (since at the lower interest rate needed to satisfy the *BP* equation, net capital outflow would be greater than at $\bar{r}$, given $\bar{Y}$).

This surplus means that the private sector will be selling foreign exchange to the Federal Reserve System in exchange for credits to commercial bank reserve accounts. In other words, the reserve base and the domestic money stock will increase unless the monetary authorities "sterilize" the payments surplus by appropriate open market sales of government securities. Likewise, if *BP* lies above R, bank reserves and domestic money stock will fall unless offsetting purchases are undertaken. Without sterilization, the imbalance will cause the *LM* ·curve to shift toward the *IS–BP* intersection at point S, changing the overall equilibrium of the system from $\bar{r}, \bar{Y}$ to $\bar{\bar{r}}, \bar{\bar{Y}}$ in the process. The system will be in full equilibrium, internal and external, when all three curves pass through point S.

According to both Whitman and Branson, the essence of the "monetary approach" to balance-of-payments analysis involves use of some type of macro-economic model which includes a monetary sector and which therefore can accommodate the full balance of payments—both current and capital accounts—together with recognition that the monetary effects of balance-of-payment imbalances will not necessarily be sterilized and that these monetary impulses which originate in the foreign sector can have consequences for the domestic economy. It is clear from Chart 1 and the expressions for the *IS, LM,* and *BP* curves that a possible alternative to sterilization might be the use of monetary and fiscal policy instruments together with an appropriate exchange-rate change to eliminate the imbalance and cause the curves to pass through any desired r, Y point. Another appealing option which this analysis suggests is to allow the exchange rate to move flexibly in response to market forces in such a way as to maintain continuous balance in the balance of payments. In this case, the *IS, LM,* and *BP* equations become a simultaneous system in the three unknowns, $Y, r,$ and $e,$ so that *BP, IS,* and *LM* will all pass through the same r, Y point. In effect, this means that the authorities are free to concentrate on domestic goals without being constrained by concern over balance-of-payment imbalance.

Although the simple *IS-LM-BP* model outlined above is useful for illustrating the "monetary approach" to balance-of-payments analysis, it has shortcomings which must be remedied to adapt it for serious policy analysis. In the first place, it focuses on only one asset—money—and on equilibrium between the demand for money and its supply. Secondly, wealth plays no role in the system. Many analysts are now working with elaborated "portfolio balance" versions of the basic *IS-LM-BP* system. In these models, demands for and supplies of other assets than money are made explicit. Wealth, defined as the sum or the values of all assets, appears in behavioral relationships in the *IS* sector, where e.g., consumption may respond to changes in wealth; and in the *LM* sector, where changes in the stock of some particular asset will change interest rates and cause a reallocation of wealth among its components. Finally, it is recognized in some of these models that the flows of assets that occur through the capital account of the balance of payments, as well as through the financing of imbalances in the government budget, constitute changes in wealth; and that such wealth changes will cause further adjustments in spending and in portfolio allocation as long as they continue. Models constructed along these lines, which focus on conditions necessary for equilibrium in the stocks of particular assets as well as the flows of expenditures, provide the basis for a much richer and more general analysis than our simple *IS-LM-BP* system. Both Branson and Whitman provide some discussion of their use in balance-of-payments analysis.

Up to now, we have been considering the development of this analysis along rather traditional lines. Early in her paper, Whitman states that recently a small group of economists "has stood traditional balance-of-payments analysis on its head" by applying to it a set of strong monetarist assumptions, some of them similar to those discussed in Chapter 1 in the context of a closed economy. While the "global monetarist view" is related to the more general monetary approach which we have been discussing, the incorporation of these monetarist assumptions modifies considerably the model we have been using.

First, global monetarists typically make the "small country" assumption: The economy in question is assumed to be small enough so that its actions can have no appreciable effect on the world interest rate or inflation rate. Any attempt to change the domestic interest rate or price level via policy initiatives would generate flows of financial assets or goods between the home country and the rest of the world which would continue until interest rate or price level discrepancies were eliminated. Since the interest rate is effectively fixed, the *LM* equation becomes a quantity theory relationship, making other behavioral equations—in particular, the *IS* system—superfluous for the determination of nominal income. It is further assumed that labor markets work effectively and that real output is set at its full-employment level without regard for the level of demand. That is, output is taken to be autonomously determined rather than being infinitely elastic with respect to aggregate demand as was implicitly assumed in our *IS-LM-BP* structure. With the price level, real output, and the interest rate all given, the demand for money balances also becomes a datum. If the supply of money differs from the demand for it, the system must contain a mechanism for adjusting the supply if equilibrium is to be attained. The balance of payments is such a mechanism: An excess supply of money, for instance, will cause spending to rise and will produce a payments deficit. Money will flow out until the supply of money again equals the autonomously-determined demand for it; at that point the balance-of-payments deficit will disappear. Thus domestic monetary policy is impotent under these assumptions—all it can do is to change the composition of the money stock between its domestic credit and international reserve components. Fiscal impulses are useless, too, for the same reasons as discussed in Chapter 1. And changes in the exchange rate can have only transitory balance-of-payments effects. An exchange-rate change will change the domestic price level because the "law of one price," $P = eP_f$, is assumed to hold (P and P_f are the domestic and foreign price levels, respectively). If the domestic price level P changes due to a change in e, given P_f, then the demand for money changes relative to the supply, and trade flows result which adjust the supply until it equals the new demand. At that time, the balance of payments will again be in balance.

Under "global monetarist" assumptions, the domestic inflation rate must equal the world rate as long as the exchange rate is fixed. This is a direct consequence of the "law of one price." By allowing the exchange rate to float, a country can determine its own inflation rate rather than being tied to the world rate. However, the global monetarists advocate fixed rather than flexible rates. As we have seen, flexibility has no permanent balance-of-payments effect under this view, and the increased risks and other costs associated with flexible rates are judged to outweigh their advantages.

These and other aspects of the "global monetarist" point of view on balance-of-payments analysis are discussed thoroughly in the Whitman and Branson papers. The reader should try to think of "global monetarism" as a special case of the general monetary approach to the balance of payments, and should remember that what really distinguishes the two views from each other are the underlying assumptions. The general monetary approach does not assume full employment, does not necessarily make the "small country" assumption nor assume that the "law of one price" is always satisfied, and allows for some scope for domestic policy. As was true of the discussion of monetarism in Chapter 1, it is probably fair to say that the "global monetarist" view is most relevant in a long-run context, while the more general monetary approach is useful in thinking about the shorter run.

While the meaning of "balance" in the balance of payments is easy enough to grasp within the framework of a simple model, it is less intuitive in the real world. Under the Bretton Woods regime, there grew up in the United States and elsewhere a number of different concepts of how balance was to be defined —the current-account balance, the liquidity balance, the balance on official reserve-transactions basis, and so forth. Each definition was based on a somewhat different notion as to which transactions in the overall account were autonomous and which transactions accommodated or financed the autonomous ones. As Marina Whitman's paper points out, this pattern of development was rooted in a Keynesian view that the fundamental focus of interest was on "real" (e.g., current-account) rather than financial transactions. A different set of definitions probably would have evolved if the prevailing view of the world during the past thirty years had been monetarist, with its central emphasis on financial behavior.

However, given our legacy from the past, the recent shift from fixed to floating rates also has consequences for the presentation of balance-of-payments statistics. The U.S. statistics are now presented in a revised format, based on recommendations of an Advisory Committee on the Presentation of Balance-of-Payments Statistics of the U.S. Office of Management and Budget. This new mode of presentation, issues for analysis and policy which it raises, and some questions regarding continuity with data generated under the previous system and comparability with other countries are discussed in the paper entitled "The Presentation of the Balance of Payments" by Robert M. Stern (reading 35).

32. MANAGING THE MANAGED FLOAT*

Wilfred Ethier
and
Arthur I. Bloomfield

The quadrupling of oil prices at the end of 1973, superimposed on an already accelerating worldwide inflation, a world commodity boom, recessionary tendencies in some leading industrial countries, and other uncertainties and unsettled conditions, made it inevitable that the widespread floating of exchange rates inaugurated in March 1973 would have to continue for an indefinite period. By the same token, it was clear that the plans under way for a comprehensive reform of the international monetary system based on "stable but adjustable par values" would have to be postponed.

The Committee of Twenty of the International Monetary Fund, which had been working on these plans for over a year, decided at its January

* Essays in International Finance, No. 112, October 1975. Copyright © 1975. Reprinted by permission of the International Finance Section of Princeton University and the authors. Wilfred Ethier and Arthur I. Bloomfield are, respectively, Associate Professor and Professor of Economics, University of Pennsylvania.

1974 meeting that reform would have to be a more evolutionary and step-by-step process and that attention should be focused on interim measures of a more immediately relevant but less comprehensive character. In its *Outline of Reform with Accompanying Annexes* (*IMF Survey*, June 17, 1974), approved by the IMF Board of Governors in September 1974, the Committee laid down the framework of a longer-run reform of the international monetary system, as well as a detailed program for immediate action. Included in the latter were guidelines it had drawn up for the management of floating exchange rates.

In a paper prepared in April 1974 (Ethier and Bloomfield, 1974), the authors of this essay investigated the general problem of managed floating, and in particular proposed a set of rules that we called the "Reference Rate Proposal." This essay will elaborate that discussion in the light of developments since that time, and will also briefly compare the Reference Rate Proposal with the guidelines of the Committee of Twenty and with those advanced by Mikesell and Goldstein in a recent *Essay* in this series.

THE MANAGED FLOAT TO DATE: SOME BACKGROUND

Since its inception in March 1973 during a period of economic and political turmoil throughout the world, the system of widespread floating has operated much more satisfactorily than many had expected. Despite substantial and perhaps at times exaggerated swings in exchange rates, foreign trade and investment do not appear, by and large, to have been seriously affected by the float. The business and banking community seems to have adjusted itself to the new regime without undue inconvenience; many of its leaders have in fact expressed their preference for the new system over the old (see, e.g., *The Economist*, Supplement, December 14, 1974, pp. 19, 29, 51). The spot and forward-exchange markets have generally functioned well, despite episodic aberrations, especially in the earlier part of the period. Exchange speculation has not proved predominantly destabilizing, as had been feared in some quarters. International monetary crises of the kind that plagued the Bretton Woods system have been avoided. To the extent that countries have allowed their currencies to float freely, they have acquired a greater degree of freedom to pursue macroeconomic policies aimed at domestic goals. The differential effects on individual industrial countries of the oil crisis, world inflation, and world recession have been cushioned. There has so far been comparatively little evidence of the aggressively competitive national behavior long regarded as a major threat posed by a floating-rate system.

The float has not, of course, been entirely free or unmanaged. Monetary authorities have intervened in the exchange market from time to time, and in some cases on a more continuing basis, in order to influence the movements and levels of exchange rates. The exchange-rate regime that has emerged has been a hybrid one. A number of continental European currencies combined in the "snake" scheme—the German mark, French franc, Dutch guilder, Belgian-Luxembourg francs, and Danish, Swedish, and Norwegian kroner—are floating jointly against the dollar and other outside currencies with occasional official intervention, while being kept by exchange operations within a narrow band vis-à-vis each other. Other leading currencies, including the U.S. and Canadian dollars, the pound sterling, the Swiss franc, the Japanese yen, and the Italian lira, have been

floating independently, although subject to greatly differing degrees of exchange intervention. The majority of the remaining currencies have been pegged to the dollar, sterling, or the French franc, but these pegs have been altered with varying degrees of frequency. Since the currencies to which they are pegged are floating, these currencies also fluctuate against outside currencies even when the pegs are not altered. A number of Middle Eastern currencies are tied to Special Drawing Rights (SDRs), which are themselves now valued as a "market basket" of sixteen major currencies.

Some supporters of floating rates argue that rates must be completely unmanaged if the full benefits of the system are to be realized. They oppose all official exchange operations to influence exchange rates. Even if this view is valid in principle, it is unrealistic to envisage a perfectly free float. Most central banks will continue to intervene in the exchange market to smooth out erratic swings in rates or to cope with emerging "disorderly" market conditions. They will be under strong pressure to intervene in order to offset or moderate market forces threatening to push their exchange rates to levels that interfere with the achievement of domestic economic goals. They may be tempted deliberately to depreciate their exchange rates or to keep them at unduly undervalued levels in order to gain competitive trade advantages in time of recession, or to maintain them at unduly overvalued levels or even deliberately to appreciate them in time of inflation. And, for a variety of reasons, some central banks may want their currencies to float jointly with others or be pegged to individual foreign currencies or a composite of currencies—all of which would require intervention. For these and other reasons, a perfectly unmanaged float would seem out of the question.

Since widespread floating will persist for a considerable period and the float will be managed in varying degrees by national authorities, internationally agreed rules of conduct are necessary to regulate the management of floating exchanges. In the absence of such rules or guidelines, individual countries could engage in official exchange operations that were detrimental to the interests, or inconsistent with the operations, of other countries. National or bloc conflicts of policy in exchange intervention could pose a serious threat to orderly trade and financial arrangements and to the interests of the international community at large. Moreover, rules regarding official exchange intervention by no means exhaust the kinds of rules that might be needed in a regime of wide-spread floating, as will be noted later. For example, exchange rates can be deliberately influenced not only by official exchange operations but also by capital controls, monetary policies, and trade or exchange restrictions.

As it happens, there appear to have been no major conflicts of policy in exchange-rate management since the inauguration of the float. To be sure, the exchange rates of the leading currencies have undergone substantial swings against each other—especially in the case of the dollar against continental European currencies—during the period since March 1973. And the central banks concerned have intervened from time to time, in some cases on a very substantial scale, to moderate these swings, to cope with large-scale, short-term capital movements induced by a variety of economic and political forces, and to support their currencies against strong downward or upward pressures. But far from working at cross-purposes, central banks have shown a high degree of cooperation in their exchange-market interventions. This has been true not only of interventions internal to the "snake" but also of relations between the Federal Reserve System and the leading continental European central banks. Official exchange operations in the latter case have often been closely coordinated. Thus, the Federal Reserve has sometimes intervened to support the dollar in periods of sharp decline against European currencies by selling those currencies (acquired through swap drawings on the central banks concerned), while the European central banks have simultaneously bought dollars in the exchange market. When the dollar has strengthened, the Federal Reserve has characteristically bought European currencies in the market, in large part in order to liquidate the earlier swap drawings, while European central banks have occasionally lent further support to their currencies by selling dollars at the same time.

Nor has there been as yet any clear evidence of deliberate exchange depreciation by any of the leading industrial countries in order to gain competitive trade advantages. During a period of worldwide inflation, this has not been entirely surprising. But even the existence of substantial unemployment in nearly all these countries during the past year—to say nothing of the unequal impact of the oil crisis on national balance-of-payments positions—has not induced competitive exchange depreciation. European central banks have at times resisted, by exchange intervention or other measures, what they regarded as excessively sharp appreciations, but there is little

evidence that any of them have thereby kept their exchange rates at unduly undervalued levels.

Indeed, if there has been any evidence so far of competitive exchange-rate policies, it has pointed rather in the opposite direction. Some of the major industrial countries, most notably Japan, the United Kingdom, and Italy, have sold foreign exchange on a large scale throughout much of the period to resist or moderate a depreciation of their currencies. A desire to reinforce domestic anti-inflationary policies (i.e., to export inflation) has undoubtedly played an important, though probably not dominant, role in these interventions. At various times in 1973 and 1974, moreover, the "snake" countries sold exchange on a significant scale to cushion a sharp decline of their currencies against the dollar. A desire to maintain orderly market conditions was probably more important in this case than anti-inflationary considerations. In any event, it is clear that the industrial countries have so far tended to lean against the wind more often when their currencies were under downward than upward pressure.

What emerges strongly from a survey of official exchange intervention since the float is that there have been no major national conflicts of policy resulting from aggressively competitive or predatory behavior in the management of the float. In somewhat broader perspective, this lack of conflict may be viewed as part of a general coincidence of national interests that has more or less characterized the international monetary scene since 1971. There seems to have been a broad consensus among the main industrial countries as to the "appropriate" levels of, and "acceptable" range of fluctuations in, their exchange rates against each other. For example, there was general agreement at the start of this period that the dollar was overvalued, and on two separate occasions it proved possible to reach multinational agreements on new structures of par values or central rates. During most of this period, economic activity in the major nations has been more closely in phase than at any other time since World War II, and price trends have been broadly similar. Finally, there has been a natural desire to avoid common crises in the face of the disintegration of the old system.

It would be a serious mistake to rely upon this unprecedented consensus for the indefinite future or, more specifically, over the period (of unknown length) of widespread managed floating, for the coincidence of interests upon which the consensus has rested is very fragile. Signs of its dissolution have already appeared. Large-scale unemployment and a cessation of growth have occurred in many countries, and governments vary in the relative importance they ascribe to anti-recession and anti-inflation measures. The oil crisis is having sharply different impacts on the balances of payments of individual countries. With the abatement of the commodity boom of 1973–74, agricultural issues are again becoming sources of potential conflict. Finally, the underlying uncertainty concerning basic economic interrelations in the world economy that led to widespread floating also mitigates against complacency regarding the continued absence of major conflicts in exchange-rate policy. International rules for the management of the float thus become increasingly important.

GENERAL PRINCIPLES REGARDING RULES

What kinds of rules should we have? How comprehensive and ambitious should the set of rules be, which specific areas should they cover, and what particular form should they take?

Consider the first of these questions, the very general one of how comprehensive the set of rules should be. Their scope could fall anywhere between the extremes of no rules at all and a complete, detailed specification of a new international monetary system. But the latter would require a degree of international agreement on the basic issues of reform that has not been forthcoming, and rules pertaining to a regime of managed floating are needed as soon as possible. Thus we deem it necessary to consider minimal reform programs. The rules should be general enough and nonrestrictive enough to be acceptable to most nations and enforceable without prior agreement on such basic, long-run issues as asset convertibility or the role of the dollar. They should also be flexible enough to encourage progress toward agreement on a longer run, permanent reform, and to be compatible not only with a broad range of such reforms but with interim arrangements between individual central banks. On the other hand, the rules must of course have enough teeth to offer some protection against the major dangers from managed floating.

The next question pertains to the scope of behavior to be covered. Rules appropriate to a system of extensive, managed, exchange-rate floating could conceivably encompass a large number of areas. These could include (1) permissible and nonpermissible (and/or mandatory and nonmandatory) official exchange intervention; (2) the medium of intervention and the methods to be used; (3) the coordination of

official intervention so that countries will not work at cross-purposes when engaged in permissible intervention; (4) the settlement of currency balances acquired through intervention; (5) the use of existing currency balances acquired through past intervention (e.g., the "dollar overhang"); and (6) the use of policies other than exchange intervention to affect exchange rates, such as capital controls, exchange restrictions, and monetary policies.

International agreement on (1) is most important, since it deals with a matter on which lack of agreement could have the most serious consequences. This is the area most directly relevant to the possibility of competitive exchange behavior or exchange-rate policy conflicts generally—the primary reason for rules.

Thus the rules must certainly address themselves to (1), but what about the other areas? Area (3), and to some extent (2), have to do with the general subject of central-bank cooperation. Such cooperation has been rather prominent and important thus far in the float, as it has been throughout the post-war period—in sharp contrast to the experience of the 1930s. Indeed, it is possible that the steady development of central-bank cooperation over a quarter-century will be regarded in the future as the single most significant by-product of the Bretton Woods system. But these areas must be left for the most part to the flexible, ad hoc responses of central banks to particular circumstances; they need not, and indeed cannot, be provided for in advance by specific rules.

In addition, prescriptions calling for central-bank cooperation or for prior consultation under specific circumstances cannot be relied upon to take the place of formal rules in other areas, notably (1), because such cooperation may be least reliable when the need is greatest—in the face of sharply divergent national interests. In such areas, there must be some formal code of behavior more concrete than a procedure of central-bank cooperation and consultation.

With regard to areas (4) and (5), we might also rely to some extent upon ad hoc arrangements between specific central banks. For example, there are the arrangements made by the "snake" countries for Italy's benefit in 1972, before that country dropped out of the scheme; another example is the 1973 agreement between the Federal Reserve and the Bundesbank to "split" the profits or losses resulting from coordinated exchange intervention. Nevertheless, a general agreement on specific rules would be necessary to deal with this area at all comprehensively, and this would obviously require at least a conditional accord on such contentious issues as asset convertibility. Thus areas (4) and (5) cannot really be dealt with in a minimal reform program, and the set of rules should not include, as an integral component, general rules dealing with the settlement of currency balances acquired through intervention, though arrangements between specific central banks can be expected from time to time. A central bank that unilaterally decided to buy foreign exchange would therefore have no assured means of disposing of the balances acquired except through subsequent (permissible) sales on the exchange market. The possibility of exchange losses consequent upon intervention would, of course, be one element in the bank's decision as to whether or not to intervene.

The rules should, nonetheless, at least be compatible with all methods of dealing with areas (4) and (5) that might eventually be agreed upon.[1] It would also be desirable for the rules to contain features that might aid in implementing such an agreement. We shall presently discuss our Reference Rate Proposal in this context.

Item (6) clearly constitutes an area for potential rules because of the marked interdependence between the exchange markets and other economic policies. For example, exchange-rate movements during the current float have been influenced in the great majority of countries by changes in controls over capital movements. These controls were tightened in the first half of 1973. Early in 1974, however, the United States lifted its controls over capital exports and many European countries relaxed their controls over capital imports—in both cases at least partly to check the rise in the dollar against the "snake" currencies. There was a renewed tightening of some European controls late in 1974 and in 1975. A number of countries have also periodically adjusted their monetary policies with an eye to influencing movements in their exchange rates. Trade policies have occasionally been altered with the same end in mind, the Italian import controls being a good example. Success in eliminating overt policy conflicts in the exchange markets might indeed simply shift the scene of such conflicts. But this is really a quite separate issue. It is clearly desirable to coordinate national economic policies and to remove conflicts to as great an extent as possible, regardless

of what is happening in the exchange markets or what rules have been adopted regarding intervention. Thus problems relating to capital controls, trade measures, monetary policies, etc., are beyond the scope of this essay, it being understood that cooperation in these areas is of great importance in its own right and that any set of rules should facilitate such cooperation as much as possible.

We are left, then, with area (1), the nature of the rules to be adopted regarding official exchange intervention. Three broad types of rules (not necessarily mutually exclusive) are possible here: (a) The rules could specify circumstances under which official intervention by a central bank was mandatory. The Bretton Woods system was of this type, as were most of the suggested reforms of that system, such as wider bands or the crawling peg; any rules of this type would have to be much more flexible to be considered now. (b) The rules could instead be of the opposite sort and specify circumstances under which certain types of intervention were prohibited. (c) Instead of pertaining directly to intervention, the rules could specify circumstances under which prior consultation or international cooperation of some sort would take place.

A scheme based upon rules of type (a) or (c) would, in our judgment, be impractical and/or inadequate. The latter, for example, is realistic only in the sense that such a rule is likely to be adopted by default, and the former is precluded by the very impossibility of establishing a fixed equilibrium exchange-rate structure that, we have argued, makes floating inevitable. Any sort of prespecified mandatory intervention, no matter how flexible, would potentially lead to the sort of crises that repeatedly occurred under, and ultimately toppled, the Bretton Woods system. We opt, therefore, for rules of type (b).

What kind of intervention should be prohibited? We wish to prevent competitive exchange-rate policies by central banks, but which concrete acts are of this kind? *Any* official intervention designed to influence the exchanges is by its very nature an attempt to interfere with market forces. But completely clean floating, as suggested earlier, is just not in the cards. We should like to rule out attempts to export inflation or unemployment through deliberately induced exchange-rate movements. But any exchange-rate movement, regardless of its cause, will to some extent influence domestic and foreign economic performance, and who is to judge what evil lurks in the hearts of central bankers? Not that motive need be all that important in any case; the atti-

---

[1] Some of the longer run possibilities in these areas are examined in the *Outline of Reform* of the Committee of Twenty.

tude and response of the rest of the world to one central bank's actions will clearly depend upon economic conditions in the rest of the world. Furthermore, our concern should not be only with official intervention to push exchange rates away from prevailing levels. Intervention to maintain palpably overvalued or undervalued exchange rates could equally be regarded as unneighborly behavior. The Bretton Woods system in the 1960s offers a number of clear examples of such behavior. It is simply not possible to give an operational definition of central-bank activity that constitutes "competitive exchange-rate behavior." Indeed, this is one more potent reason why we need a highly flexible set of rules. Our rules should be confined to attempting to prevent both those visible, overtly aggressive acts most likely to induce retaliation and the prolonged maintenance of outdated exchange rates.

To summarize, rules pertaining to the managed float should embody the following general principles: (1) They should constitute a minimal reform program, at once broadly acceptable and highly flexible, that avoids the unresolved long-run issues. (2) They should contain formal regulations regarding official exchange intervention and not rely solely on central-bank cooperation and consultation. (3) They should be designed to prevent the most egregious sort of central-bank conflict in the exchange market rather than any difficulty that could conceivably arise. (4) They should specify when intervention is *not* permissible, rather than when it is mandatory. (5) This specification should be in terms of concrete acts of intervention rather than in terms of the presumed motives for such acts. (6) They should be compatible with simultaneous efforts to foster central-bank cooperation and to deal with the possibility of conflicts arising from policies other than intervention that are designed to influence exchange rates. (7) They should not impede the evolution of a long-run reform of the international monetary system, whatever shape that might take.

THE REFERENCE RATE PROPOSAL

These general principles have been embodied in a specific program, the Reference Rate Proposal, to which we now turn.[2] The scheme requires that a "reference exchange rate" be established for the currency of each participating

---

[2] See Ethier and Bloomfield (1974), and, for a subsequent discussion of the idea, see also Williamson (1975).

nation. The following two rules constitute the proposal:

1. No central bank shall sell its own currency at a price below its reference rate by more than a certain fixed percentage (possibly zero) or buy its own currency at a price exceeding its reference rate by more than the fixed percentage. This is the sole restriction imposed upon central-bank intervention.
2. The structure of reference rates shall be revised at periodic prespecified intervals through some defined international procedure.

Rule 1 in essence turns the basic idea of a par value inside out: It gives a point of reference away from which the market exchange rate must not be deliberately forced by official intervention, as opposed to a pegged rate that the authorities must defend. It is important to emphasize that Rule 1 never *requires* any specific kind of market intervention. The authorities of each country would be completely free to allow a "clean" float for their exchange rate, either permanently or temporarily, and they would not need to obtain prior approval or give notice in order to enter into such "transitional floating." However, any central bank would also be free to attempt to maintain its exchange rate within some band of its reference rate. (Note that Rule 1 should be applied only to official intervention; it does not apply to exchange transactions that a central bank might passively execute on behalf of government agencies required to make payments abroad. Nor would it apply to purchases of foreign exchange by a central bank directly from state enterprises that had been encouraged to borrow abroad, as has happened in Great Britain and Italy in recent years.)

Under "normal" circumstances, one would expect to find exchange rates near their reference rates, with central banks intervening at their discretion to smooth out fluctuations, just as, under the Bretton Woods system, exchange rates in "normal" circumstances were well within the band limits at which intervention became mandatory. Not only would central banks tend, in varying degrees, to defend the reference rates, but the structure of such rates, formulated via Rule 2, would constitute, in effect, a statement by the central banks of their collective view regarding the equilibrium structure of exchange rates.

Under "abnormal" circumstances, central banks could allow greater deviations from reference rates in response to market pressures.

Clean floating or intervention to smooth out fluctuations or slow down movements away from reference rates would be permissible, but Rule 1 would prohibit attempts to induce or accelerate such movements. For example, if the rates established in February 1973 were to be regarded as reference rates, the subsequent central-bank behavior described above would have been compatible with the present proposal, whereas any attempts to accelerate the decline of the dollar in May–July of 1973, or in the early months of 1974, or in late 1974 and early 1975, would not have been compatible.

Rule 1 would also give the structure of reference rates a stability in abnormal circumstances quite the opposite of that imparted to par values by the Bretton Woods system. For example, it has often been observed that upward pressure on a pegged exchange rate presents traders with an opportunity for a "one-way gamble" that could cumulatively induce further inflows of funds. With Rule 1, such pressure would undoubtedly cause the authorities to allow the exchange rate to appreciate, with the rise above the reference rate perhaps being slowed by intervention. As the exchange rate was driven further above its reference rate, traders would realize that the central bank could sell but not buy the currency, adding an element of risk to further purchases by traders. The greater the appreciation of the exchange rate, the more it would have to fall before the central bank had the option of buying domestic currency. Traders would also know that any subsequent upward revision of the reference rate would not necessarily serve to guarantee their profits, as it would not imply the establishment or maintenance of a higher market exchange rate.

A central purpose of Rule 1 is to limit competitive exchange-rate behavior by central banks. No set of workable rules could comprehensively eliminate such behavior; even the Bretton Woods system was vulnerable in this respect. By not allowing central banks to force or accentuate departures of market rates from reference rates, we attempt merely to impose a very simple and workable rule that strikes at the most overtly aggressive sort of behavior.

The rule is defined in terms of explicit, central-bank *behavior* rather than in terms of presumed central-bank motivations; it is of the minimal-reform "thou shalt not" type that we concluded was necessary. It is thus intended to provide the great flexibility that would make the plan more acceptable politically and also to allow individual

central banks or groups of central banks unilaterally to adopt a variety of exchange regimes (clean floating, true pegged rates, group floating, wider banks, etc.), so long as they do not violate the rule. In addition, Rule 1 would facilitate the periodic revision of reference rates, that is, the implementation of Rule 2. For the lack of mandatory intervention implies that, by agreeing to a specific reference rate (which the authorities are under no obligation to defend), a nation will directly influence real economic variables only slightly, if at all, and will sacrifice relatively little national economic sovereignty. Furthermore, regular multilateral revisions of reference rates will be technically possible without inducing the exchange crises that must inevitably develop in a world of internationally mobile capital whenever the authorities are obligated to defend an exchange-rate structure that everyone knows is about to be revised.

In addition to limiting aggressive central-bank behavior of the kind noted, Rule 1 is thus intended to serve another purpose: It should facilitate the technical functioning of the exchange-rate system by greatly reducing the likelihood of crises, while still furnishing a point of reference for exchange rates. Rule 2 likewise has two functions. First, it provides for the periodic adjustment of reference rates so that reasonably realistic levels can be approached and maintained. The very uncertainty that makes floating inevitable would compel periodic adjustment in the structure of reference rates. But even without this uncertainty, such adjustment is necessary in order to minimize the possibility that countries will intervene to maintain overvalued or undervalued exchange rates. An unfortunate characteristic of the operation of the Bretton Woods system during the 1960s was the rigidity of the par values of several important currencies, notably the dollar, yen, and mark, in the face of changing circumstances. Second, Rule 2 is intended to be the means of injecting a formal international mechanism into the scheme. Such a mechanism can serve as a vehicle for international cooperation, as a lightning rod to draw away international conflicts and tensions from violations of Rule 1, and as a cornerstone for the possible future evolution of a reformed international monetary system.

The close interdependence between the two rules of our proposal should be emphasized. The degree to which Rule 1 attains its objectives clearly depends upon the success of Rule 2 in ensuring that the structure of reference rates is at all times reasonably "realistic." And the ease with which Rule 2 can be implemented depends upon Rule 1, for the following reasons: International agreement on a structure of reference rates can be more easily reached when little loss of economic sovereignty is involved, and international consultation on such matters need not trigger or accompany an exchange crisis.

This interdependence is reflected in the form of Rule 1, which allows for the possibility of a band around the reference rate within which intervention in either direction would be permissible. This band is related to the efficiency of the mechanism by which Rule 2 is applied. If the participating nations can agree to implement the rule in such a way as to adjust reference rates quickly and accurately, the band would serve little purpose and so would presumably be of narrow or even zero width. But if the agreed-upon mechanism leaves open the possibility that reference rates will remain at unrealistic levels for considerable periods, a rule prohibiting intervention to drive exchange rates away from these levels could make little economic sense. Rightly or wrongly, central banks might anticipate significant gains from such intervention. In any case, the existence of reference rates at unrealistic levels for lengthy periods would certainly weaken the commitment felt by the banks to Rule 1, jeopardizing the success of the plan even when the reference rates were, in fact, realistic. Thus a band within which intervention in both directions is allowed would be desirable and would reduce the likelihood of such episodes. The more effective the means of implementing Rule 2, the less necessary, and the narrower, would be the band in Rule 1.

IMPLEMENTATION OF THE PROPOSAL

We have argued that a system of managed floating should not rely for its smooth operation exclusively upon central-bank cooperation but should include some formal rules of behavior. This is not to say, of course, that such cooperation can be dispensed with; indeed, we regard it as essential. The many formal and informal arrangements among central banks should continue, and new ones would undoubtedly evolve with further experience. Perhaps, also, specific rules requiring such cooperation under certain circumstances could be formulated in connection with the proposal.

For example, it is conceivable that market intervention by one central bank, even if permissible under Rule 1, might run counter to the wishes of some other central bank. If France buys dollars to prevent the franc from appreciating, she is also preventing the dollar from depreciating, and this might not be desired by the U.S. authorities. There are a number of ways of dealing with such cases, which could arise under other exchange-rate systems as well. One possibility would be to prohibit or to limit unilateral intervention, but we doubt that rules of this sort would be either feasible or desirable. It may be possible to deal with these cases by requiring that Rule 1 apply simultaneously to all currencies involved in any intervention. That is, in the example referred to above, in order for France to be able to purchase dollars with francs it would be necessary not only for the franc to be above its reference rate, but also for the dollar to be below *its* reference rate (each in terms of a common standard or numeraire, discussed below). If the latter condition were not satisfied, the French authorities would have to find another intervention currency that was below its reference rate or else abstain from intervention altogether. But this sort of implementation of Rule 1 would be possible only if international agreement were reached on the issues of multicurrency intervention and perhaps reserve-asset settlement as well, and an important aspect of the Reference Rate Proposal is that it does not otherwise require such agreement. A third possibility would be to do nothing formally and thus allow the problem to be solved in a decentralized fashion by the action of individual central banks, presumably in accord with Rule 1. In this case, one would expect procedures of interbank cooperation and consultation to evolve and to be quite useful; a guideline calling on central banks to take into account the effects on other countries of their intervention policies, and perhaps also to notify them of their intentions, would be especially appropriate.

We noted earlier that policies other than exchange intervention can be used deliberately to influence exchange rates, and that success in eliminating policy conflicts in exchange markets might simply shift the scene of conflict elsewhere. As indicated, this is really a separate issue and beyond the scope of this essay. It is worth mentioning, however, that it may be possible to utilize the Reference Rate Proposal itself in a way that would deal to some degree with this problem. If Rule 2 is implemented by charging a specific international body (such as a standing committee of the IMF or its proposed Council of Governors) with revising the structure of reference rates at specific intervals, that body could also be instructed to take any such policy conflicts into account when setting the rates. For example, a country imposing "unjustified" restrictions on imports could find its reference rate lowered by such a committee as a result. Since reference rates need not be defended, this would be a substantive way of dealing with such conflicts without imposing serious economic sanctions. It would be important, however, to avoid hamstringing the operation of Rule 2 with disputes over whether specific national actions are justified or not. Thus the agency responsible for deciding such disputes should be distinct from the agency actually setting the reference rates.

The reference rates must of course be defined in terms of some standard. This is a point of very little importance for a minimal program, and could be decided upon at the commencement of the plan. For concreteness, we can think of the reference rates for the various currencies as being symmetrically defined in terms of SDRs, with the cross rate between each domestic currency and the central bank's chosen intervention currency as the rate thus relevant to Rule 1. We have deliberately worded the two rules in a symmetrical fashion, and the proposal no doubt would be more attractive if embedded in an international monetary system in which the various currencies play symmetrical roles. For example, Rule 1 could then be used, as discussed above, to deal with the problem of intervention at cross purposes; also see Williamson (1975) for an interesting further discussion along this line. We do regard it as important, however, that the Reference Rate Proposal be acceptable as a minimal reform program, independent of the degree of symmetry.

The precise mechanism for implementing Rule 2, and for the initial establishment of a reference-rate structure, is important but could also be decided upon at the commencement of the scheme. (The reference rates, of course, need not coincide with present par values or central rates.) A wide range of alternatives is possible. It could be agreed that each quarter (or at some other interval) the finance ministers or heads of central banks of some or all of the participating nations would renegotiate the structure of (some or all) reference rates. This would amount to holding periodic sessions like the negotiations of 1971, or alternatively like those of 1973, both of which successfully achieved agreement on new structures for the (far more binding) pegged exchange rates. Thus it would not be unrealistic to hope that such a procedure could be made workable. Alternatively, the revision of reference rates could be made by, or in conjunction with, an international institution such as the IMF or perhaps some agency created specifically for this purpose.

Various technical devices might be employed instead of, or in addition to, negotiation. For example, adjustment could be achieved through a system of "crawling reference rates," with the reference rates being revised by small amounts at frequent intervals in response to changes in objective indicators. To implement Rule 2 in this way would be to approach a gliding parity regime, as advocated by a number of economists for some years now, but from the side of floating exchange rates rather than pegged rates. The objective indicators that would trigger reference-rate changes would have to include both changes in reserves (to prevent extended support of an exchange rate that is clearly out of line) and market exchange rates (to prevent the reference rates of countries that seldom intervene from getting out of line). For example, a weighted average of past market exchange rates could be used to obtain a provisional value of the new reference rate, and this provisional value could then be adjusted upward or downward, as indicated by reserve changes, to obtain the actual value of the new reference rate. Of course, other technical devices could instead be used, and the relative importance of objective indicators and negotiation could be shifted. Different methods could also be used for different groups of countries. For example, the reference rates of certain "key" currencies could be determined by one of the methods discussed while the rates of other countries were then declared by the respective national authorities. Some such division of methods should be provided for in order to accommodate currency blocs, joint floating, or simply a failure to agree upon a single method.

We are somewhat skeptical about the possibility of wide, early agreement on any formal method for setting reference rates, and indeed we must grant the possibility that any provision involving the mandatory adjustment of reference rates might prove to be too much to achieve at the present time. Nevertheless, there should be a strong presumption that adjustments would be made in response to market forces. Adjustments would be indicated, for example, by pronounced deviations of market rates from reference rates; significant changes in the reserve levels of central banks undertaking intervention; and perhaps even other developments, such as a change in the price of oil that is expected to influence exchange markets in the period between successive regular revisions of reference rates. In any case, it will be easier to achieve progress toward the mandatory adjustment of reference rates than toward the mandatory adjustment of market rates, where so much more is at stake.

If all else fails, and if no agreement on an explicitly multilateral procedure can be reached, each central bank could unilaterally declare its own reference rate at periodic intervals. Consultation at least with its principal trading partners would then be in each central bank's own self-interest, and would be necessary to ensure that the N central banks do, in fact, establish a consistent set of N-1 exchange rates.

In a recent *Essay* in this series, Mikesell and Goldstein discuss proposed "alternative rules for official market intervention" in a floating-rate regime that could be applied to central-bank operations reflecting various hypothetical motivations. We prefer, and this preference is clearly reflected in the Reference Rate Proposal, a single rule or set of rules defined in terms of concrete operations rather than in terms of the possible motivations for those operations. Thus "alternative rules" appeal to us more as taxonomic devices than as useful operational guidelines. Nevertheless, it may be appropriate to inquire how the present proposal would be expected to work, or should be made to work, under the circumstances considered by Mikesell and Goldstein. We do this now, using their classification (but not their numbering) of circumstances that could prompt official exchange intervention.

1. *Neutral intervention to moderate exchange-rate fluctuations.* Under our proposal such intervention could be undertaken, at the option of the individual central bank, by supporting the exchange rate at its reference rate. There would be no direct limitations on the volume of intervention or on net reserve changes, as recommended by Mikesell and Goldstein; these would instead be taken into account in the revision of the reference rates via Rule 2.

2. *Intervention to offset the effects of political and economic "shocks," intervention to offset the effects of nonrecurring events having a serious but temporary impact on the payments balances, and extensive intervention to maintain rates consistent with long-run basic balance.* In practice, these three motives would prove difficult to distinguish from each other and also from the previous situation. In any case, they would presumably relate to the Reference Rate Proposal in the same way as (1).

3. *Intervention to offset cyclical movements in the trade balance.* Such intervention would be

possible, according to Rule 1, to the extent that a slump would otherwise cause a currency to appreciate above its reference rate and a boom would cause it to depreciate below. We do not think it either wise or practical to add a specific rule prohibiting such intervention, as Mikesell and Goldstein do. Reliance should instead be placed on Rule 2, which is specifically designed for such problems. Thus, if a prolonged slump induced upward pressure on a country's exchange rate, sooner or later its reference rate would be revised upward, thus preventing continued intervention to resist appreciation. The degree to which such intervention would be allowed would therefore be reflected in, and determined by the speed of adjustment embodied in the mechanism for implementing Rule 2. Also, if the mechanism included an international agency with at least some discretionary power, that agency could be specifically instructed to take cyclical factors into account in some special way, if this was deemed advisable.

4. *Intervention to adjust the volume or composition of official reserve assets.* Such intervention would violate Rule 1 if it tended to push exchange rates away from reference rates. The adjustment of official reserves through exchange-market operations would be possible under two distinct circumstances. First, it would be possible if the market exchange rates of the currencies involved happened to bear the appropriate relationships to their reference rates. For example, if the Bundesbank wished to sell some of its excess dollars for marks, it could do so when the mark happened to be below its reference rate. But the volume of such intervention would be severely limited both by the requirement that the exchange rate not be driven above the reference rate and by the eventual revision of the reference rate itself. Second, it would be possible if there were agreement to adjust the relevant reference rates. For example, if it were determined that Germany should dispose of a portion of her dollar reserves, the reference rate for the mark could be temporarily raised (and that for the dollar temporarily lowered), relative to what it would otherwise be, so as to permit the operation to take place. The effect of the proposal would then be to bring decisions involving a substantial adjustment of reserve assets within the well-defined international procedure used to implement Rule 2. This is as it should be.

5. *Intervention to maintain joint floats or pegged currencies.* As suggested earlier, these arrangements could be embodied in the implementation of Rule 2. Such intervention would not

violate Rule 1 if carried out in a way that was neutral with respect to third countries, i.e., that did not influence the exchange rates of the currencies in the joint float relative to other currencies.

ALTERNATIVES TO THE REFERENCE RATE PROPOSAL

There are, of course, other systems besides the Reference Rate Proposal that embody, in varying degrees, the general principles listed on page 404 above. We shall now compare some of these alternatives with the Reference Rate Proposal.

Reserve-Level Alternatives

There have been many suggestions for rules based in some way on reserve levels or on changes in these levels. Most of the alternative rules discussed by Mikesell and Goldstein are of this type. Reserve levels could easily be incorporated into our own proposal—for example, as indicators of how reference rates should be adjusted. Indeed, we would expect reserve levels to be used in this way, at least informally. But here we are more interested in the possibility of using reserve levels by themselves as a basis for differentiating between permissible and nonpermissible exchange intervention. For example, one could stipulate that target reserve levels rather than reference rates be set via Rule 2. There might then be many counterparts to Rule 1. Prohibiting central banks from accumulating reserves when their stocks were above target levels and from running down reserves when their stocks were below would rule out any intervention by a country once its reserve target was achieved and until it was revised. Indeed, the only scope for individual central-bank discretion regarding intervention would be in the speed with which actual reserves tracked the target levels. Such a restriction seems not only unrealistically severe but makes little economic sense. A band around the target reserve level would allow more discretion. In effect, it would impose a limit on the net amount of intervention within a period of time—the period between successive revisions of target levels. But such a rule could induce destabilizing speculation as traders observed reserves approaching their limit, and it would neither prohibit aggressive intervention within the band nor allow harmless intervention outside.

Still another possibility that avoids these difficulties and is closer in spirit to Rule 1 of the Reference Rate Proposal is the following rule: No central bank shall accumulate reserves when its stock of reserves exceeds the target level by more than a certain percentage *and* the price of its currency is not rising; no central bank shall decumulate reserves when its stock of reserves is below the target level by more than a certain percentage and the price of its currency is not falling. Such a rule is more cumbersome than Rule 1 because of its twofold nature and would therefore be harder to apply. It would be far more difficult to tell whether the rule was being violated or not. Who would know whether exchange rates were rising or falling when reserves were actually sold?

There is a significant objection to all reserve-level alternatives. In order to determine target reserve levels it is necessary to decide first what constitutes reserves, what the worldwide level of liquidity should be (and thus, by implication, the "average" amount of flexibility in the system), and how to adjust the target levels when exchange rates change (and thus, by implication, how to handle problems such as conversion guarantees). All of this is in *addition* to difficulties like those related to implementing the reserve-level counterpart of Rule 1 of the Reference Rate Proposal. Since the major reason for investigating a minimum reform proposal is that agreement on such issues seems remote, we regard this objection as very serious.

Finally, at a more basic level, the fundamental goal of any proposal is presumably to maintain an approximation to an equilibrium structure of exchange rates. There is, in truth, no such thing as an equilibrium structure of reserve levels. When reserve levels are used to define permissible intervention, they are really serving as proxies for exchange rates, and they need not be very exact proxies. Maintaining a specified set of reserve levels could, on occasion, induce undesirable changes in exchange rates, regardless of how speedily the targets were adjusted. Indirectly limiting exchange-rate behavior by limiting reserve-level behavior adds no desirable features to proposals that address exchange rates directly; it merely introduces another possible source of error.[3]

Leaning Against the Wind

A second class of alternative proposals would replace our suggested reference rates by the cur-

---

[3] For an extensive background discussion of objective indicators, including reserve levels, see Underwood (1973). Also Kenen (1975) examines alternative methods of adjusting exchange rates and concludes that reserve-level rules are the least efficient.

rent market rates. Again, a great many variants are possible. For example, recent proposals that central-bank intervention be limited to "leaning against the wind" fall into this class. As a prototype of these proposals, consider the following single rule: No central bank shall sell its own currency when its price is falling or buy its own currency when its price is rising. (This is the rule contained, with some qualifications, in Guideline 2 of the IMF *Outline of Reform.*)

The main difference between this proposal (which we shall refer to as Leaning Against the Wind) and our scheme is, of course, the absence of a structure of reference rates. Thus Leaning Against the Wind lacks both the point of reference in the exchange markets and the inherent vehicle for international cooperation that we regard as desirable features of our scheme. Of course, some may prefer to avoid such features.

There is a further technical difference between the two proposals. Under Leaning Against the Wind, a central bank could engineer a depreciation (or appreciation) by leaning more in one direction than the other whenever the opportunity arose. This could also happen under the Reference Rate Proposal. It follows simply from the lack of mandatory intervention. But, under Leaning Against the Wind, the new rate could then be defended, while under our rule it could not. For example, a central bank could "leak" a rumor of an impending trade deficit, easier money, etc., inducing a speculative sale of its currency on the exchanges. Under either scheme, the central bank would be allowed to refrain from intervention, permitting the exchange rate to depreciate until the (deliberately induced) speculative selling ceased. But, under Leaning Against the Wind, the central bank could then defend this new lower rate against any tendency to return to equilibrium and could justify such intervention. Under our plan, this would not be possible once the exchange rate fell below its reference rate.

Leaning Against the Wind could also be used as a justification for preventing adjustment to a new equilibrium exchange rate, as happened during the 1960s. This is also possible in the short run in our scheme and probably in any scheme other than pure floating. (One could conceivably argue that central banks should be allowed to lean only with the wind rather than against. Why should it always be desirable to resist market forces?) But Rule 2 of the Reference Rate Proposal provides a mechanism to deal with just this problem. By contrast, a resistance to basic market forces is inherent in the very idea of Leaning Against the Wind.

Finally, the Leaning Against the Wind proposal involves measuring central-bank behavior, not against a specific exchange-rate value, but rather against the way the exchange markets are changing. This would make violations of the rule much less obvious. The problem can be limited somewhat by a proper formulation of the Leaning Against the Wind rule, but it cannot be removed.

We should emphasize two points about the alternative discussed in this section. First, it is a prototype chosen for convenience to represent a number of possible variants. Second, although we have discussed the substantial differences between this alternative and the Reference Rate Proposal, the similarities are extensive, and it is our purpose to present the reader with alternative ways to implement the general principles we have advocated.

THE IMF GUIDELINES

Our earlier paper, "The Management of Floating Exchange Rates," was written in April 1974 before the release in June of that year of the *Outline of Reform* of the IMF Committee of Twenty, which included the "Guidelines for Countries Authorized to Adopt Floating Rates." We close this essay with a brief discussion of the Guidelines[4] in the light of the general principles underlying the Reference Rate Proposal (summarized on page 404 above).

The Guidelines are certainly meant to constitute only a minimal reform program and are thus consistent with our general principle (1). Indeed, they should perhaps not be regarded as a program at all:

They are termed guidelines rather than rules to indicate their tentative and experimental character. They should be adaptable to changing circumstances. No attempt is here made to indicate the precise procedures through which they would be implemented. These will be considered later, but they must essentially rest on an intensification of the confidential interchange between the member and the Fund (*IMF Survey,* June 17, 1974, p. 182).

The Guidelines are meant to be interim arrangements for the period of widespread floating while permanent reform is being worked out. They are also meant to become, or to develop into, rules for currencies allowed to float under the reformed

---

[4] The Guidelines are reprinted in the Appendix to Mikesell and Goldstein (1975).

system, which is expected to contain provisions authorizing such occurrences. Thus the Guidelines would satisfy our general principles (1) and (7). They would also satisfy our principle (6); indeed, Guidelines (5) and (6) concern themselves with interbank cooperation and conflict outside the exchange markets.

Guidelines (1), (2), and (3), which are directly addressed to central-bank exchange intervention, basically fulfill our principles (2), (3), and (5). They are formal rules, directed toward the most serious potential conflicts, and they are expressed for the most part in terms of the mechanics of intervention rather than the presumed motivation. They are perhaps not quite as specific as one might wish, but this is to be expected at the initiation of a "tentative and experimental" process, and the Guidelines are clearly intended to allow the evolution of more specific rules.

Our general principle (4), that the rules should specify when intervention is not permissible rather than when it is mandatory, is violated, however, and in two ways. Guideline (1) *requires* intervention (thereby ruling out the option of a clean float). The Guidelines are also meant to apply to currencies in authorized floats but do not mention the circumstances under which such floats will be authorized. This is no doubt due in part to the fact that floating has no legal basis at present. But the *Outline of Reform* clearly implies that, in the future, floating should require prior IMF approval. We prefer our principle (4) and therefore recommend that countries have the unconditional (at least *de facto*) option of floating, and that Guideline (1) be implemented in a permissive rather than mandatory fashion. (Mikesell and Goldstein also reach this conclusion.)

We conclude that, by and large, the IMF Guidelines accord well with our general principles regarding rules for a managed float. How do they specifically relate to the Reference Rate Proposal and some of its alternatives, discussed above, that also accord with these principles?

Guidelines (1) and (2) constitute an example of the kind of proposals we have classified as Leaning Against the Wind. Indeed, Guideline (2) contains basically the same rule we discussed in detail under that heading. Thus that discussion is directly pertinent to the IMF Guidelines.

Guideline (3), with its reference to a "target zone of rates" that a country might seek to establish with the Fund's permission, has a certain relationship to our Reference Rate Proposal. Indeed, the implementation of Guideline (3) could conceivably move the system toward something similar. This would require that "target zones" be established for all currencies, instead of merely being reserved as an option for those that are floating. It would also require a regular re-examination of the location of these target zones. The *Outline of Reform* implies that such target zones would be available only as a possible temporary tool for currencies in an authorized float, simultaneously with a system of par values.

We believe that our suggestions for implementing Guideline (3), together with the suggested substitution of permissible intervention for mandatory intervention, would significantly increase the value of the Guidelines both in dealing with the present managed float and in serving as a first step in the evolution of a new international monetary system. The *Outline of Reform* appears to envisage the future system as one comprised of "stable but adjustable par values," modified so as to accommodate occasional inevitable (but unwelcome) bouts of managed floating. Instead, we think it both preferable and more realistic to establish rules for a world in which extensive managed floating is the norm, and to allow these rules to evolve into a new system.

REFERENCES

Ethier, Wilfred, and Arthur I. Bloomfield, "The Management of Floating Exchange Rates," paper delivered at the Conference on World Monetary Disorder, sponsored by the Center for International Business and the School of Business and Management, Pepperdine University, held May 23–25, 1974, at Pepperdine University.

Kenen, Peter B., "Floats, Glides, and Indicators," *Journal of International Economics*, 5 (May 1975), pp. 107–51.

Mikesell, Raymond F., and Henry N. Goldstein, *Rules for a Floating-Rate Regime*, Essays in International Finance No. 109, Princeton, N.J., 1975.

Underwood, Trevor G., "Analysis of Proposals for Using Objective Indicators as a Guide to Exchange Rate Changes," *IMF Staff Papers*, 20 (March 1973), pp. 100–17.

Williamson, John, "The Future Exchange Rate Regime," *Quarterly Review of the Banca Nazionale del Lavoro* (June 1975), pp. 127–44.

33. GLOBAL MONETARISM AND THE MONETARY APPROACH TO THE BALANCE OF PAYMENTS*

Marina v.N. Whitman†

A decade or so ago, when the twin concerns about the balance of payments of the United States and the functioning of the international monetary system began to impinge on the consciousness of a public theretofore indifferent to such esoterica, the opinions of those who were already paying attention fell into a neat dichotomy. Government officials and "men of affairs," on the one hand, insisted that the continued health of international trade, investment, and the world economy required the maintenance of the Bretton Woods system of pegged exchange rates, under which changes in rates were made infrequently and as a last resort. Academic experts, on the other hand, were nearly unanimous in pressing the advantages of greater flexibility of exchange rates, with many urging that governments abstain altogether from intervention and allow exchange rates to be determined by the interplay of supply and demand in the marketplace, just like any other price.[1] The specter of competitive depreciation left over from the 1930s was replaced by concern about the rigidity of mechanisms for payments adjustment under the Bretton Woods system. Furthermore, the postwar wave of "elasticity pessimism" had given way to

"elasticity optimism" as new empirical studies, better specified and using more sophisticated statistical techniques than their predecessors, indicated that demand elasticities were indeed high enough to ensure exchange-market stability and thus the effectiveness of exchange-rate changes as an instrument of balance-of-payments adjustment.

A number of assumptions, explicit or implicit, underlay the economic analysis of payments adjustment in the fifties and sixties and the resulting implications for balance-of-payments policies. To begin with, although the problem was ostensibly to restore equilibrium, or reduce disequilibrium, in the balance of *payments*, Keynesian analysis, with its emphasis on the components of aggregate demand, focused on the balance of *trade* (net exports of goods and services), which is one of those components. Net exports were assumed to be a function of aggregate demand and of relative prices at home and abroad; in the face of downward rigidity of wages and prices in the domestic market, changes in the exchange rate were the most effective means of altering those relative prices—hence the stress on the elasticities of home demand for imports and of foreign demand for exports. Although some analysts explored the effect on the capital account of changes in the relative profitability of investing at home and abroad, the main body of analysis assumed that, whatever effects particular policies might have on the other accounts in the balance of payments, the impact on the goods and services account would be dominant.[2]

One implication of this approach is that, in a world of fixed exchange rates and Keynesian downward rigidity in wages and prices, the price-adjustment mechanism will not operate, at least in the deficit country, to restore payments equi-

* From *Brookings Papers on Economic Activity* (No. 3, 1975), pp. 491–536. Copyright © 1975 by The Brookings Institution, Washington, D.C. Reprinted by permission of the publisher and the author. Marina v.N. Whitman is Distinguished Public Service Professor of Economics, University of Pittsburgh.

† This paper was supported partially by financial assistance from the Departments of State, Treasury, and Labor under Contract No. 1722-520176. However, the views contained herein are solely the author's and do not necessarily represent the official position of the U.S. government.

I am grateful to Edmond Alphandery, Rudiger Dornbusch, Jacob A. Frenkel, Peter B. Kenen, Norman C. Miller, and to the discussants and members of the Brookings panel for their helpful suggestions.

[1] For two of the best-known academic briefs for flexible rates, see Milton Friedman, "The Case for Flexible Exchange Rates," in Richard E. Caves and Harry G. Johnson, eds., *Readings in International Economics* (Homewood, Ill.: Irwin, 1968), pp. 413–37, and Egon Sohmen, *Flexible Exchange Rates*, rev. ed. (University of Chicago Press, 1969). These essays were first published in 1953 and 1961, respectively.

[2] This is true in particular of the classic work by J. E. Meade, *The Theory of International Economic Policy*, vol. 1: *The Balance of Payments* (London: Oxford University Press, 1951). Surveying the literature in the late 1960s, Krueger noted that "there is no widely accepted theory incorporating both current and capital account items. The most thoroughly explored models in payments theory are those which consider only current account transactions and a means of payment." Anne O. Krueger, "Balance-of-Payments Theory," *Journal of Economic Literature*, vol. 7 (March 1969), p. 2.

librium automatically and painlessly after a disturbance; rather, the restoration or maintenance of such external equilibrium must be an explicit target of economic policy. In the absence of exchange-rate flexibility to alter relative prices, the most obvious mechanism for eliminating external imbalance is the Keynesian one: If exports are a function of foreign income (taken to be exogenously determined) and imports a function of domestic income, then a reduction of domestic income will lead to an improvement in the trade balance and thus in the balance of payments. Such a resolution of external payments problems is, however, likely to be unacceptable to governments committed to full employment as the primary domestic economic objective.[3] And so a vast literature, incorporating capital mobility, quickly arose, directed toward developing a combination of policy instruments that would enable governments to achieve simultaneously the targets of internal balance (full employment) and external balance (payments equilibrium).[4] But the proliferation of models of internal-external balance reinforced rather than weakened the conviction that governments would have greater success in achieving their domestic economic targets if they were able either to use exchange-rate changes as an additional policy tool (managed flexibility) or to exercise other policy instruments free of the balance-of-payments constraint imposed by pegged exchange rates (freely flexible rates). Furthermore, some argued, while, under fixed rates, changes in foreign income and expenditure would affect aggregate domestic income by altering the level of exports and thus the trade balance, freely flexible rates would insulate the domestic economy from foreign demand shifts and ensure that such disturbances would be bottled up where they originated, rather than spreading from one country to another via the Keynesian transmission belt.

Today, most major industrialized countries are no longer bound to pegged exchange rates. But a funny thing happened on the way to this flexible-rate nirvana. The post-Bretton Woods world of managed flexibility has produced surprises undreamed of in the analyses of the 1950s and 1960s; moreover, a small but influential group of international economists has stood traditional balance-of-payments analysis on its head. I have termed this group the "global monetarists"— "monetarists" because of their belief that macroeconomic phenomena can be analyzed best in terms of the relationship between the demand for and the supply of money, and "global" because of their conviction that, as a first approximation, the world consists, not of separable national economies, but of a single, integrated, closed economy.

From these two fundamental tenets arise a number of startling propositions. Put in their most extreme form they include the following: A change in the exchange rate will not systematically alter the relative prices of domestic and foreign goods and it will have only a transitory effect on the balance of payments. Any exercise of monetary policy to change the domestic component of the monetary base will, under fixed exchange rates, be offset by an equal and opposite change in the foreign component of that base. Thus, exchange-rate policy cannot permanently alter the balance of payments and monetary policy cannot lastingly affect the domestic economy, but a change in the exchange rate will have a direct impact on the domestic price level, and monetary policy will have a direct effect on the country's payments position (measured by the change in its reserves under a fixed-rate system, by the movement in its exchange rate under freely flexible rates, and by a combination of the two under managed flexibility). Not only are exchange-rate changes ineffective as an instrument of balance-of-payments policy for the long run, they are also unnecessary; indeed, there is no need to make external balance an explicit target of national economic policy, since an automatic adjustment mechanism can be counted on to restore such balance in the wake of an exogenous disturbance that moves a nation's balance of payments temporarily away from equilibrium. Finally, flexible exchange rates are not merely superfluous but positively detrimental to world economic welfare, because they eliminate the international pooling of risks and the efficiency ad-

---

[3] Furthermore, if the domestic economy is stable in isolation (that is, the marginal propensity to save exceeds zero), the Keynesian income-adjustment mechanism will fall short of an automatic full restoration of external equilibrium in the wake of a balance-of-payments disturbance, as long as the feedback effects of the resulting disequilibrium in the money market are either disregarded or assumed to be neutralized by policy actions.

[4] See Marina v.N. Whitman, *Policies for Internal and External Balance,* Special Papers in International Economics 9 (Princeton University, International Finance Section, 1970) for a survey of that literature. One practical application in the United States was "Operation Twist" of the early 1960s, which sought to attract capital inflows with high short-term interest rates while keeping long-term rates low to stimulate domestic expansion.

vantages of international money associated with fixed exchange rates.[5]

Far from being new, these propositions of the global monetarists represent a return to a tradition far older than the Keynesian approach they are challenging—to the price–specie-flow mechanism of David Hume, who argued that the international flows of reserves engendered by a payments imbalance would, through their effects on national money supplies and price levels and thus on the trade balance, automatically restore external balance.[6] Nonetheless, these views pose a direct challenge to the current orthodoxy, and they have revolutionary implications for balance-of-payments policy and even for balance-of-payments accounting.

THE SKELETON MODEL: A TRIPARTITE STRUCTURE

To assess these implications, and evaluate the relative merits of the Keynesian and the global-monetarist prescriptions for contemporary U.S. policy, requires first describing the analytical underpinnings of this new-old approach and ascertaining where it can, and cannot, be reconciled with current orthodoxy.[7] These tasks, in turn, call for an examination of the various, frequently intertwined, intellectual strands that together give the approach its distinctiveness. In order to anchor the discussion in a specific example, I have borrowed, with minor modifications, a stripped-down, one-commodity, two-country model which, while it cannot do justice to the richness and complexity either of the relevant literature in general or of its originator's work in particular, serves as a convenient aid to exposition:[8]

$$L = kP\bar{y} \tag{1}$$
$$L^* = k^*P^*\bar{y}^*$$

$$P = P^*e \tag{2}$$

$$M = \bar{D} + R \tag{3}$$
$$M^* = \bar{D}^* + R^*$$

$$\dot{M} = \dot{R} = H = B = -e\dot{H}^* = -e\dot{R}^* \tag{4}$$
$$= -e\dot{M}^*$$

$$Z = P\bar{y} - H \tag{5}$$
$$Z^* = P^*\bar{y}^* - H^*$$

$$H = \Pi(L - M) = H(P,M) \tag{6}$$
$$H^* = \Pi(L^* - M^*) = H^*(P^*,M^*),$$

where an asterisk indicates variables for the foreign country and a dot indicates rate of change, and

L = desired nominal money balances
k = desired ratio of nominal money balances to nominal income
$\bar{y}$ = real output (taken as exogenous)
P = money price of goods in terms of domestic currency
e = exchange rate (domestic currency price of foreign exchange)
M = nominal quantity of money
$\bar{D}$ = domestic component of the domestic money supply (taken as exogenous)
R = international component of the domestic money supply
B = trade-balance surplus, measured in domestic currency

[5] For a popular exposition of these views, see Jude Wanniski, "The Mundell-Laffer Hypothesis—A New View of the World Economy," *Public Interest*, no. 39 (Spring 1975), pp. 31–52. The economists referred to in the title are Robert Mundell and Arthur Laffer, two leading proponents of global monetarism. The modern incarnation of global monetarism was developed during the late 1950s and 1960s, primarily in a series of articles by Mundell, many of which are collected or further developed in two books by him: *International Economics* (New York: Macmillan, 1968) and *Monetary Theory: Inflation, Interest, and Growth in the World Economy* (Pacific Palisades, Calif.: Goodyear, 1971). Mundell's work in turn grew out of some earlier work by Polak: J. J. Polak, "Monetary Analysis of Income Formation and Payments Problems," *International Monetary Fund Staff Papers*, vol. 6 (November 1957), pp. 1–50, and J. J. Polak and Lorette Boissonneault, "Monetary Analysis of Income and Imports and Its Statistical Application," ibid., vol. 7 (April 1960), pp. 349–415.

[6] See Jacob A. Frenkel, "Adjustment Mechanisms and the Monetary Approach to the Balance of Payments: A Doctrinal Perspective," in E. Claassen and P. Salin, eds., *Recent Issues in International Monetary Economics* (Amsterdam: North-Holland, forthcoming, 1976).

[7] To make clear what is meant by "current orthodoxy," I quote from Johnson: "The quantity-theory counter-revolution . . . has been directed against the so-called income-expenditure school, by which is meant those economists in the Keynesian tradition who have concentrated their analysis and policy prescriptions on the income-expenditure side of the Keynesian general-equilibrium apparatus. (This focus has been the dominant impact of the Keynesian revolution on governmental and other practical thinking on economic forecasting and policy-making)." Harry G. Johnson, *Further Essays in Monetary Economics* (Harvard University Press, 1973), pp. 28–29.

[8] Rudiger Dornbusch, "Devaluation, Money, and Nontraded Goods," *American Economic Review*, vol. 63 (December 1973), pp. 871–80.

Z = desired nominal expenditure

H = flow demand for money (hoarding function)

Π = rate of adjustment of actual to desired money balances.

These equations define a simple macroeconomic general-equilibrium model, in contrast to both the conventional price-adjustment (elasticities) approach, which is clearly microeconomic and partial-equilibrium, and the income-adjustment approach which, although based on the Keynesian macroeconomic model, is not truly a general-equilibrium view in that it ignores the interactions between the goods market and the money market.[9] The global monetarists stress the importance of these interactions; more generally, they insist that, when one market is eliminated from a general-equilibrium model by Walras' law, the behavioral specifications for the included markets must not be such as to imply a specification for the excluded market that would appear unreasonable if it were made explicit.[10]

This model is also characteristic of the genre in that it specifies both the equilibrium characteristics of the long-run steady state, in equations 1 and 2, and the dynamic adjustment process by which the steady state is approached, in equations 4–6. In contrast with the "medium run" of conventional Keynesian analysis, which defines equilibrium in flow terms alone, in this approach full equilibrium involves the achievement of stock as well as flow equilibrium in all markets. Having thus resolved one of the inconsistencies of Keynesian analysis, however, this view retains and even intensifies another, in that it combines long-run full-equilibrium assumptions on the demand side with the essentially short-run assumptions of the stationary state on the output side.[11]

Finally, this two-country model describes a situation in which, under fixed exchange rates, the world is a closed, integrated economy, with a single money stock and price level, while each country is an open economy characterized by major leakages. Such an approach is internationalist, stressing the interactions among economies in an interdependent world and, by implication, the futility of attempting to analyze—or manage—a national economy in isolation. All this contrasts strongly with the traditional Keynesian focus on the national economy as the fundamental unit, in which "foreign repercussions" are second-order effects that can affect the magnitude but not the direction of the primary impact of disturbances or policies on a relatively "closed" economic unit.

In addition to reflecting some of the general characteristics of the global-monetarist approach, these equations make it possible to identify three strands of key assumptions that together distinguish this approach from the conventional Keynesian one, but that can be evaluated independently of one another.

The first equation embodies the neutrality assumption that is the linchpin of monetarism, whether in the context of a closed or an open economy.[12] In making the level of real income exogenous to the system, equation 1 assumes a classical world in which real output is constant (at the full-employment level)[13] and all prices,

---

[9] For an explanation of why these traditional modes of analysis are fundamentally Keynesian, see the section below on reconciliation of the various approaches.

[10] See Lance Girton and Don Roper, "A Monetary Model of Fixed and Flexible Exchange Rates Applied to the Postwar Canadian Experience," *American Economic Review* (forthcoming, 1976), and Harry G. Johnson, "The Monetary Theory of Balance-of-Payments Policies," in Jacob A. Frenkel and Harry G. Johnson, eds., *The Monetary Approach to the Balance of Payments* (London: Allen and Unwin; Toronto: University of Toronto Press, 1976).

[11] The equilibrium conditions for the stationary state can be converted into growth terms by recognizing that, under conditions of growth, money-market equilibrium requires, not a zero balance of payments, but rather a balance determined by the following conditions: (a) the rate of inflation must be

the same in both countries, and (b) in each country the growth of the real money stock must be equal to the increase in demand for real money balances occasioned by growth. For the equilibrium balance of payments these conditions together imply

$$B = \frac{M}{P}(g_P + g_y - g_D) = \frac{M^*}{P^*}(g_D{}^* - g_P - g_y{}^*),$$

where $g_i = (di/dt)/i$ for all variables. See Mundell, *Monetary Theory*, chap. 15, and for a similar formulation, Harry G. Johnson, "The Monetary Approach to Balance-of-Payments Theory," in Frenkel and Johnson, eds., *Monetary Approach*. All the long-run conclusions of the monetary approach derived from the stationary-state model can thus be translated into equilibrium growth terms without altering the qualitative results, except that in the latter case it is possible to obtain persistent flow-equilibrium deficits or surpluses on the basis of stock adjustments in the money market.

[12] For the argument that this proposition is the critical one in distinguishing monetarists from nonmonetarists, see Don Roper, "Two Ingredients of Monetarism in an International Setting," Seminar Paper 46 (Stockholm: Institute for International Economic Studies, April 1975; processed).

[13] Or, alternatively, at the level of Friedman's natural rate of unemployment.

including wages, are fully flexible. The one-to-one relationship between the supply of money and the aggregate price level implies an absence of money illusion and the long-run neutrality of money vis-à-vis real variables. The Cambridge form of equation 1 also assumes an interest-inelastic or "super-stable" demand-for-money function. This particular formulation embodies an additional implication: the impotence of fiscal policy to affect any aspect of the economy, including the price level.

The open-economy view that is the second leg of the global-monetarist stool is reflected in equation 2. This is the assumption of perfect commodity arbitrage, which ensures that, in the absence of barriers to trade, the "law of one price" must hold in integrated world commodity markets.[14] Although the assumption of this law at the microeconomic level of a single good is widely accepted, its elevation to a macroeconomic level distinguishes global monetarism from alternative approaches. In other words, an implicit assumption either of perfect substitutability, or of fixed relative commodity prices, enables the analysis to apply to a single-commodity world (which immediately translates the law into a "law of one price level," as here) or to a two-commodity world (where the distinction is between traded and nontraded goods). Such aggregation abstracts, in particular, from changes in the relative prices of exports and imports—that is, in a country's terms of trade. The terms of trade are a significant element of the elasticities approach because the implicit assumption it embodies—that the domestic-currency price of home goods is held constant either by perfectly elastic supply or by the government's stabilization policies—makes it possible to equate changes in the exchange rate with changes in the barter terms of trade, or at least to postulate a systematic relationship between the two. The global-monetarist approach, in contrast, makes an alternative assumption—that the nominal quantity of money is held constant under devaluation in the short run —which implies no such relationship. The absence of such a relationship justifies the level of commodity aggregation characteristic of global-monetarist models and their focus on exchange

rates to represent the relative prices of national *moneys* rather than of national *goods*.

The third leg of global monetarism, the automatic monetary mechanism for payments adjustment, often termed "the monetary approach" to the balance of payments,[15] itself has two parts. The first is the assertion that, when the central bank pegs the exchange rate, the national money supply becomes an endogenous, rather than a policy, variable. This view is reflected in equation 3, which (ignoring the base-money multiplier for simplicity) divides the money supply into domestic-credit and international-reserve components, and equation 4, which spells out the feedback from the balance of payments (a surplus or deficit being definitionally equivalent to a change in the country's stock of reserves) onto the national money stock.[16] It is in sharp contrast with the assumption, frequently implicit in conventional Keynesian analysis, that the monetary authorities sterilize the impact on the domestic money supply of international reserve flows arising from payments imbalance (and that the effects of such sterilization operations on the stock of private wealth can be ignored).

Equations 5 and 6 together embody the second part of the automatic adjustment mechanism of the monetary approach—the assertion (*a*) that the relationship between the demand for and the supply of money plays a key role in the functioning of all markets in the economy; and (*b*) that the demand for money is fundamentally a stock demand characteristic of asset markets rather than a flow demand appropriate to output (commodity) markets.[17] Specifically, equation 5 em-

---

[14] The counterpart of the "law of one price" in single-country models is the "small country" assumption, under which the domestic price level (and also the domestic rate of interest, in models that incorporate a bond market) is assumed to be exogenously determined, under fixed exchange rates, by the price level in the outside world.

[15] The incorporation of this view into the received wisdom of balance-of-payments theory is symbolized by the difference between the fourth edition of Charles P. Kindleberger's widely used text, *International Economics* (Homewood, Ill.: Irwin, 1968), which makes no mention of the monetary approach, and the fifth edition (Irwin, 1973), which devotes an entire chapter to it.

[16] Note that equation 4 assumes implicitly that the capital gains (losses) on international reserves, measured in domestic currency, arising from devaluation (revaluation) are sterilized by the central bank.

[17] This stock definition of equilibrium in asset markets has at least three major antecedents in the modern literature of international finance. The first is the "real-balance effect" described in the seminal article on the absorption approach by Sidney S. Alexander, "Effects of a Devaluation on a Trade Balance" (1952); the second is the distinction between stock and flow payments disequilibria made by Harry G. Johnson in his 1961 article, "Towards a General Theory of the Balance of Payments." Both of these papers are reprinted in Caves and Johnson,

Figure 1

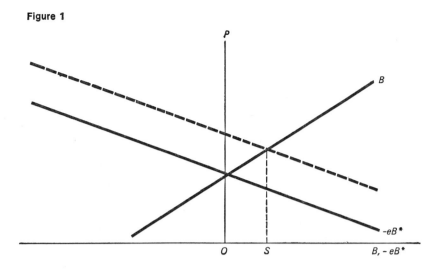

bodies a form of "real balance" effect that makes the desired level of expenditure a function of wealth as well as income. Here, this effect produces a flow demand for money which is represented in equation 6 as a function of the difference between the desired and actual stocks of money. Thus, although the underlying equilibrium in the money market is a stock equilibrium, it is not achieved instantaneously, and the flow demand for money (the hoarding function) arises from the gradual adjustment of actual money balances toward the desired stock. The existence of this partial-adjustment mechanism in the market for money balances drives a wedge between short-run and long-run equilibrium, and between the short-run impact and the long-run stationary-state effects of policy actions and other exogenous disturbances.

The very simplicity and rigidity of this particular model enable it to yield unambiguous analytical results and strong policy conclusions. Within its confines, the short-run effects of a one-shot change in the pegged exchange rate are clear: by raising the domestic price level (equation 2) and thus the demand for money balances (equation 1), a devaluation stimulates hoarding (equation 6) and brings about a clear-cut improvement in the payments balance (without, it

eds., *Readings in International Economics.* Finally, there are the open-economy portfolio-balance models, whose development began in the mid-1960s; for example, Ronald I. McKinnon and Wallace E. Oates, *The Implications of International Economic Integration for Monetary, Fiscal, and Exchange-Rate Policy,* Studies in International Finance 16 (Princeton University, International Finance Section, 1966).

should be noted, any terms-of-trade or relative-price effects) and a redistribution of the world money supply toward the devaluing country (equation 4). This is clear in the substitution from equations 1 and 4 into equation 6 to derive the two equations for B shown (for a situation of initial long-run equilibrium) in Figure 1. For the home country, $\bar{M} + (B/\Pi) = kP\bar{y}$, or $B = \Pi(kP\bar{y} - \bar{M})$. Thus, $(dB/dP) > 0$, giving the equation for B its positive slope in the diagram. For the foreign country, similarly,

$$B^* = \Pi^* \left(k^* \frac{P}{e} \bar{y}^* - \bar{M}^* \right)$$

But $B = -eB^*$, so $B = \Pi^* (-k^*P\bar{y}^* + e\bar{M}^*)$ and $(dB/dP) < 0$, giving the equation for $-eB^*$ its negative slope in the diagram. Furthermore,

$$\frac{dB}{de} = \Pi k\bar{y} \left(\frac{\Pi^*M^*}{\Pi k\bar{y} + \Pi^*k^*\bar{y}^*} \right) > 0,$$

so that devaluation causes an upward shift in $-eB^*$, producing a payments (trade) surplus equal to OS for the home country.

The effect on the balance of payments is only transitional, however; over time, as the world money stock is redistributed and $(L - M)$ approaches 0, S approaches 0 also, and $-eB^*$ moves gradually down toward its original position. In the long run, when full stock equilibrium is reached in the money market $(L = M)$, and hoarding is therefore equal to zero, the balance of payments is again zero as well. In the long run, furthermore, devaluation has no effect on any real economic variables, but simply raises the aggregate price level in proportion to the increase in the domestic money stock, which is the integral of the payments surplus over the transitional period (when $B = 0$, $P = (M/k\bar{y})$ and $(dP/dM) = 1$).[18] And, finally, because in the long run $R = L - D$, any change in the domestic component of the money supply (with the demand for money unchanged) is ultimately fully offset by an equal opposite change in the international-reserve component through the balance of payments.

CLOTHING THE SKELETON: SOME EXTENSIONS OF THE MODEL

The model just described was deliberately cut to its bare bones in order to reveal the essential structure underlying global monetarism. Many analysts have, of course, built on this skeleton by eliminating or severely modifying one or more of the three strands of global-monetarist assumptions while leaving the others intact. Some, for example, replace the classical full-employment assumption embodied in equation 1 with the Keynesian assumption of wage-price stickiness and underemployment, thus making real output endogenously variable and eliminating the proportionality between the nominal money stock and the price level. In so doing, they replace or supplement the Humean price–specie-flow mechanism that drives the model of the previous section with what Mundell has termed a Keynesian income–specie-flow mechanism.[19] This introduction of an elastic supply curve for output eliminates the neutrality assumption central to monetarism, but retains the automatic monetary mechanism of payments adjustment that makes payments imbalances transitory and inconsistent with stationary-state equilibrium.

A second class of extensions of this basic model involves broadening the spectrum of financial assets in the system to include bonds or other types of interest-bearing securities as well as money, thus reinserting the interest rate as an argument of certain behavioral relationships (for example, in equation 1 above) and reintroducing the portfolio-balance considerations pioneered in the open-economy context by McKinnon and

Oates.[20] In such models, the money-market stock-equilibrium condition of equation 1 is transformed into an asset-equilibrium condition that incorporates all financial assets.[21] Such models generally also introduce a "budget constraint" equation for the government sector, which acts as supplier of bonds to the private sector. This provision marks a contrast with the basic model utilized here which, although it may be used to analyze the impact of such policy-induced shocks as a devaluation or a one-shot change in the domestic component of the money supply, is essentially a model of the private sector. This extension of the model, furthermore, admits the existence of international capital flows and thus a distinction between the balance of trade and the balance of payments.

Relaxing the second strand of global monetarism, which I have termed the "law of one price level" and which is reflected in equation 2 above, means moving away from the high degree of aggregation employed in such a one-commodity model. Assuming the existence of nontraded goods, or of less-than-perfect substitutability between domestic and foreign goods (or assets), allows for the possibility of shifts in relative prices and restores some degree of independence to the domestic interest rate and price level.[22]

These extensions and refinements naturally introduce considerable ambiguity into the analytical conclusions that can be derived and qualify in one way or another the strong policy implications of the pure global-monetarist model. In

---

[18] It can easily be shown that the division of a devaluation between a rise in the home country's price level and a fall in the foreign country's price level is inversely proportional to the sizes of the two countries' initial money stocks. See Dornbusch, "Devaluation, Money, and Nontraded Goods," p. 874.

[19] Mundell, *International Economics*, p. 218.

[20] "Implications of International Economic Integration." Among more recent portfolio-balance models for an open economy are William H. Branson, "Macroeconomic Equilibrium with Portfolio Balance in Open Economies," Seminar Paper 22 (Stockholm: Institute for International Economic Studies, November 1972; processed); Rudiger Dornbusch, "A Portfolio Balance Model of the Open Economy," *Journal of Monetary Economics*, vol. 1 (January 1975), pp. 3–20; Jacob A. Frenkel and Carlos A. Rodriguez, "Portfolio Equilibrium and the Balance of Payments: A Monetary Approach," *American Economic Review*, vol. 65 (September 1975), pp. 674–88.

[21] The use of money balances rather than the total stock of financial assets as an argument of the expenditure function not only attributes special importance to money but also implicitly assumes a low (in the limit, zero) elasticity of substitution between money and other assets.

[22] For example, Branson, "Macroeconomic Equilibrium with Portfolio Balance"; Rudiger Dornbusch, "Capital Mobility and Portfolio Balance," in Robert Z. Aliber, ed., *The Political Economy of Monetary Reform* (London: Macmillan, forthcoming); and the second part of Dornbusch's "Devaluation, Money, and Nontraded Goods."

models allowing for shifts in relative prices between home and foreign or between traded and nontraded goods, for example, the short-run impact of a devaluation is no longer "neutral"; the alteration of relative prices affects real variables over the period of transition to a new stock equilibrium. More generally, in these more complicated models, the initial effect of various exogenous disturbances and the characteristics of the dynamic adjustment path toward long-run stock equilibrium are extremely sensitive to assumptions about the way in which expectations are formed,[23] which markets clear instantaneously and which approach equilibrium gradually, whether prices or quantities perform the clearing function, and the nature of the adjustment mechanism in markets that clear only with a lag.[24]

Despite the ambiguity produced by various modifications of the basic global-monetarist model, its long-run stationary-state implications necessarily remain robust to a wide variety of alternative specifications as long as the third strand of global monetarism, the monetary approach to the balance of payments, is retained. The essentials of the monetary approach, it will be recalled, are (1) the nonsterilization assumption, which links changes in the domestic money supply to disequilibria in the balance of payments as indicated in equations 3 and 4; and (2) the associated implication that the equilibrium values in the income-expenditure equation will be changing as long as the nominal quantity of money, M, is changing (as indicated by the dynamic adjustment process specified in equations 5 and 6), and that they cannot come to rest until the system is in full stock equilibrium.

The adjustment mechanism that characterizes the monetary approach to the balance of payments does not, however, require the incorporation of money directly into the expenditure function. In a model with interest-bearing assets, disequilibrium in the money market will feed back onto other markets, even if money is not an argu-

ment of the expenditure function, by causing changes in the rate of interest, which is traditionally an argument of both the expenditure and the money-demand functions. To put it in the familiar terminology of macroeconomics textbooks, shifts in the supply of or demand for money can affect aggregate demand either directly, by shifting the *IS* curve, or indirectly, by shifting the *LM* curve and thus the rate of interest. Therefore, unless the economy is assumed to be in a situation in which changes in the stock of money have no impact on income (either a Keynesian liquidity or marginal-efficiency trap), the automatic payments-adjustment mechanism, which is the linchpin of the monetary approach to the balance of payments, will still operate, whether the link between the money market and expenditures is direct or indirect.[25]

In sum, the kind of global-monetarist model that yields the policy implications outlined in the opening section of this paper involves much more than simply the monetary approach to the balance of payments.[26] The latter is "monetary" in the sense that it postulates a direct relationship between the balance of payments and the money supply and requires that the equation for stock equilibrium in the money market be included in the solution set for a model of an open economy. The strict global-monetarist view goes much further, however, implying either that monetary disturbances to the economy generally dominate nonmonetary ones or that the impact of any exogenous shock, whatever its nature and origin, can best be analyzed via the relationship between the demand for and the supply of money.

THE VARIOUS APPROACHES: A FORMAL RECONCILIATION

One way of exposing the analytical differences among the various approaches to balance-of-payments analysis is to make explicit the nature of the assumptions required to make them formally consistent with one another. Mundell outlines the

---

[23] Gordon argues that the nature of expectations formation, as well as the degree of short-run price flexibility, determines whether domestic stabilization policies can be effective in the short run. Robert J. Gordon, "Recent Developments in the Theory of Inflation and Unemployment," *Journal of Monetary Economics* (forthcoming, April 1976).

[24] For a detailed analysis of the differing implications of two specifications of the adjustment process in an otherwise identical model, see Polly Reynolds Allen and Peter B. Kenen, "Portfolio Adjustment in Open Economies: A Comparison of Alternative Specifications," *Weltwirtschaftliches Archiv* (forthcoming, March 1976).

[25] See Mundell, *International Economics*, chap. 15, and Carlos A. Rodriguez, "Money and Wealth in an Open Economy Income-Expenditure Model," in Frenkel and Johnson, eds., *Monetary Approach.*

[26] The two are often confused. In a strongly worded protest, Harry Johnson complains that "there has been a noticeable tendency to dismiss the new [monetary] approach as merely an international economics application of an eccentric and intellectually ludicrous point of view of a contemporary lunatic fringe referred to as 'monetarism.'" "The Monetary Approach to Balance-of-Payments Theory: A Diagrammatic Analysis," *Manchester School*, vol. 43 (September 1975), p. 221.

framework for such a reconciliation by characterizing three approaches to balance-of-payments analysis (at first abstracting, for simplicity's sake, from capital movements, so that the balance of trade and the balance of payments are identical; all aggregates are in nominal terms):

1. The elasticity approach takes the balance-of-payments equation, $B = X - M$ (where X and M are exports and imports, respectively), directly, differentiates it totally with respect to the exchange rate, translates the results into elasticities form, and thus establishes the "elasticity conditions" showing the effects of a change in the exchange rate on the balance of trade, "assuming that export and import prices adjust to equate the demand and supply of exports and imports."

2. The absorption approach takes, from national-income accounting, the relationship $B = Y - E$ (where Y is nominal income and E is domestic expenditure or absorption) and points out that a policy change, such as a devaluation, can improve the balance of trade only if it increases income by more than expenditures.

3. The monetary approach stresses that the balance of payments implies a change in the foreign-reserve holdings of the central bank, and that this change must equal the difference between the total increase in the domestic money supply and domestic credit creation; that is, $B = H - C$ (where H is hoarding or additional money stocks and C is domestic credit creation). The introduction of capital movements makes no difference to the validity of this approach.[27]

Mundell points out that the terms in each of the three approaches "can be defined so that they are all correct and assert identical propositions, even if capital movements are included." Taking all variables as ex post identities, he notes that "from national income accounting we have $Y \equiv E + B$; from banking accounts we have $H \equiv C + R$ [R is the increase in reserves]; and from the balance-of-payments accounts we have $R \equiv B - T$, where T represents net capital exports. It follows, then, that $R \equiv B - T \equiv Y - E - T \equiv H - C$."[28]

A simple equality among ex post or accounting identities is not very meaningful, however, and one must look behind these identities to see just how the variables are defined, and what implicit assumptions underlie these definitions, in order to produce the reconciliation just outlined. Furthermore, the discussion is complicated because

most of the comparison here have been cast in terms of the monetary approach on the one hand and the conventional or Keynesian approach on the other, and there are several significantly different variants of the latter despite the fundamental Keynesian spirit common to all of them.

The elasticities approach to balance-of-payments analysis is clearly Keynesian in the sense that only under Keynesian assumptions of unemployment and wage-price rigidity in domestic markets can it be assumed that "a devaluation would change the real prices of domestic goods relative to foreign goods in the foreign and domestic markets, thereby promoting substitutions in production and consumption," and that "any repercussions of these substitutions on the demand for domestic output could be assumed to be met by variations in output and employment."[29] However, these Keynesian assumptions alone are not sufficient to define the general-equilibrium implications of the partial-equilibrium elasticities approach. In particular, when the formal model underlying the elasticity conditions is spelled out, it generally makes the volume of exports and of imports (or, more precisely, foreign excess demand for export goods and domestic excess demand for import goods, respectively) each a function of its own money price, rather than of their relative prices and total real income (as in the barter model of pure trade theory) or of relative prices and the difference between actual and desired money stocks (as in a full general-equilibrium model). It turns out that the functional relationships implicit in the elasticities approach can be reconciled with those of general-equilibrium analysis, and thus with the monetary approach, under the followng assumptions: (1) in each country there is a nontraded commodity; (2) this commodity dominates the budgets of consumers; (3) the objective of stabilization policy (monetary or fiscal) in each country is to keep the money price of the nontraded good fixed; and (4) all cross-price elasticities between traded goods are zero.[30]

---

[27] Mundell, *International Economics*, pp. 150–51. The quote in point 1 is on p. 150.

[28] Ibid., p. 151.

[29] "Monetary Approach to Balance-of-Payments Theory." Note, incidentally, that it is not strictly necessary for relative *prices* of domestic and foreign goods to change in order to induce substitutions in production if the relative *costs* of *factors of production* change. Such changes are also ruled out by the usual Keynesian assumptions.

[30] Murray C. Kemp, *The Pure Theory of International Trade* (Englewood Cliffs, N.J.: Prentice-Hall, 1964), pp. 235–36, and Rudiger Dornbusch, "Exchange Rates and Fiscal Policy in a Popular Model of International Trade," *American Economic Review*, vol. 65 (December 1975), pp. 859–71.

The reconciliation of the monetary approach with the absorption approach is considerably less complicated, since "the monetary approach in its simplest form . . . can be considered as a pure absorption approach, in which the demand for money relative to its initial supply determines absorption [relative to income]."[31] Indeed, the father of the modern absorption approach himself noted that "the cash balance effect is perhaps the best known of the direct absorption effects."[32] One difference between the two approaches is that the monetary view focuses on the real-balance effect exclusively. A second is that the absorption approach incorporates by implication markets for commodities and money only, so that the difference between aggregate income and aggregate expenditure equals the balance of trade. The monetary approach, on the other hand, sometimes introduces a market for bonds, allowing disequilibrium in the money market to be reflected not only in the commodities market (and thus the balance of trade), but also in the market for bonds (and thus the capital account); hence, such a disequilibrium is reflected in the overall balance of payments (the trade account *plus* the capital account).[33]

It remains to note that the absorption approach is a variant—or, more accurately, a generalization—of Keynesian multiplier analysis. Both stem from the basic national-income accounting identity, $Y = C + I + X - M$ (omitting the government sector, $G - T$, for the sake of simplicity), where C is consumption and I is investment. Setting $C + I = E$ (expenditure or absorption) yields $Y - E = X - M = B$, the starting point for the absorption approach. The usual (linearized) multiplier analysis is a special case of the absorption approach in that it assumes (1) that changes in imports are a constant proportion, m, of changes in income; (2) that all changes in aggregate demand are met by changes in output at constant prices (either because supply is infinitely elastic below full employment or as a result of deliberate government policy[34]); and (3) that changes in saving are also a constant fraction, s, of changes in income. Taken together, these assumptions ensure, first, that a policy action—such as devaluation—designed to increase B will operate by increasing real output, Y; and, second, that multiplier effects on income will operate to reduce the impact effect of a devaluation on the balance of payments but will never, given a positive marginal propensity to save, eliminate or reverse it.[35]

Although the traditional Keynesian multiplier analysis takes a macroeconomic approach, as opposed to the basically microeconomic view of the elasticities approach, it implicitly assumes that the central bank prevents the continuous change in money balances implied by a persistent surplus or deficit in the balance of payments from feeding back onto the economy.[36] However, Prais has shown that the effects of changing money balances can be incorporated simply into the rigid-price multiplier framework, yielding an automatic income-adjustment mechanism for the elimination of a payments imbalance instead of the price-adjustment mechanism typically employed in monetary-approach models.[37] The results differ,

[31] Patrick Minford, "Substitution Effects, Speculation, and Exchange Rate Stability" (University of Manchester, 1975; processed), p. 143.

[32] Alexander, "Effects of a Devaluation," p. 367.

[33] Salop shows, in an ex post accounting framework, how one approach can be derived from the other, using Walras' law, introducing the market for bonds, and utilizing the budget constraints faced by the various sectors in the economy. Joanne Salop, "A Note on the Monetary Approach to the Balance of Payments," in Peter B. Clark, Dennis Logue, and Richard J. Sweeney, eds., *The Effects of Exchange Rate Adjustment* (U.S. Department of the Treasury, forthcoming, 1976).

[34] The latter assumption is made by Meade in *Theory of International Economic Policy*. Note that this approach also implies that the country is specialized in the production of its export good.

[35] It is possible also to combine the elasticity and multiplier approaches, taking the elasticity effect as impact effects, stemming from changes in the allocation of demand, which in turn generate multiplier effects. See, for example, Meade, chap. 15, and Johnson, "Monetary Theory of Balance-of-Payments Policies."

[36] This is not true of J. E. Meade, who included the money supply as well as the interest rate in his model. He then, however, assumed that monetary policy was either "Keynesian neutral" (maintained a constant rate of interest) or such as to ensure "internal balance." Either of these assumptions makes the money supply adapt passively to changes in the demand for it or to the policy requirements of internal balance, thus eliminating the influence of the money supply and the interest rate on the effect of a devaluation. See S. C. Tsiang, "The Role of Money in Trade-Balance Stability: Synthesis of the Elasticity and Absorption Approaches," in Caves and Johnson, eds., *Readings in International Economics*, pp. 391–92.

[37] S. J. Prais, "Some Mathematical Notes on the Quantity Theory of Money in an Open Economy," *International Monetary Fund Staff Papers*, vol. 8 (May 1961), pp. 212–26. A similar incorporation of monetary effects into the elasticities approach, via a simple arithmetic example, is given in Arnold Collery, *International Adjustment, Open Economies, and the Quantity Theory of Money*, Princeton Studies in

of course, from those of full global monetarism: Under its assumptions equilibrium will always be reached at the full-employment level, but the income-expenditure equilibrium and external balance achieved in the multiplier-plus-money approach would only accidentally be at full employment.

A number of authors who use the general-equilibrium monetary view to analyze policies affecting the balance of payments have expressed their models in a way that reveals the essential complementarity of the three approaches. As already noted, the monetary approach can be characterized as a kind of absorption approach in which the relation between desired and actual money stocks determines absorption relative to income. If a monetary model of the sort described earlier is expanded to incorporate two goods, and thus relative prices, it will, of course, reveal that the effects of monetary-induced changes in absorption on relative prices (and thus on the amount of reallocation required) depend on the magnitudes of the relevant elasticities.[38]

Many of the recent analytical refinements have emerged from this spelling out of the assumptions underlying alternative approaches, stimulated by the global-monetarist challenge and the responses to it. These improvements include the recognition that the partial-equilibrium assumptions underlying microeconomic analysis are inadequate to such fundamentally macroeconomic problems as devaluation—that, specifically, it is essential to make explicit the behavioral assumptions for all markets in a macroeconomic system, including the one eliminated from the solution set by Walras' law. They include, too, the now obvious but long-ignored point that exchange rates represent the relative prices of national *moneys,* which will correspond to the relative prices of national *goods,* or the terms of trade, only under very special assumptions. Since money is a financial asset, it follows logically that exchange rates should be determined (partly or wholly) in asset markets rather than entirely in product markets. Finally, there has emerged a new sensitivity to distinguishing between the

impact and long-run effects of particular disturbances, and to the importance that different specifications of the adjustment mechanism in particular markets may have in determining impact effects and the dynamic adjustment path to stationary-state equilibrium. Today these insights are so widely accepted as to be considered obvious, and they are incorporated into virtually every model analyzing the balance of payments, the exchange rate, or, indeed, the impact of a wide variety of policies in an open economy. As a result, it is frequently difficult to draw the line—to tell where the "soft monetarists" leave off and the "eclectic Keynesians" begin.[39]

Differing Implications for Policy

This blurring of distinctions and reconciliation of alternative approaches have taken place, however, at the level of formal models published in scholarly journals and read by a small group of specialists. At the level of policy making, and of public discussion conducted in the daily, weekly, and monthly media of news and opinion, the implications of global monetarism and of conventional Keynesian analysis are widely disparate. As a result of distillation and simplification, the nonspecialist sees the global-monetarist focus on long-run effects, on equilibrium analysis, on the stabilizing forces inherent in private-market behavior, and on price stability as crucially different in substance and policy implications, rather than merely in emphasis, from the Keynesian stress on the short and medium run, on disequilibrium analysis, on active government stabilization policy, and on full employment.

As noted at the beginning of this paper, perhaps the most startling implication of global monetarism is its direct challenge to the conventional view that monetary policy is (along with fiscal policy) a primary instrument for stabilizing the aggregate level of domestic economic activity, while the exchange rate is the major policy tool available for altering the balance of payments. In the eyes of the global monetarists, the endogeneity of the money supply in an open economy and the requirement for money-market equilibrium in stock rather than flow terms together imply that the pursuit of domestic objectives by altering the domestic component of the money supply will be frustrated by an offsetting change

International Finance 28 (Princeton University, International Finance Section, 1971), pp. 22–24.

[38] See Rudiger Dornbusch, "Alternative Price Stabilization Rules and the Effects of Exchange Rate Changes," *Manchester School,* vol. 43 (September 1975), pp. 275–92, and Alexander K. Swoboda, "Monetary Approaches to the Transmission and Generation of Worldwide Inflation" (paper presented at the Brookings Conference on Worldwide Inflation, Washington, D.C., November 1974; processed).

[39] The terminology is from Alan S. Blinder and Robert M. Solow, "Analytical Foundations of Fiscal Policy," in Blinder and others, *The Economics of Public Finance* (Brookings Institution, 1974), p. 58.

in the international component through reserve flows. Further, a shift in the exchange rate can affect the balance of payments only to the extent that it alters the demand for money relative to the supply, and at that only transitorily, over the period required for the restoration of money-market equilibrium. If one adds a third assumption—that perfect arbitrage exists across national boundaries in both commodity and capital markets—the processes just described will operate promptly, rather than over a relatively long term, thus depriving monetary policy of the ability to affect the domestic economy even in the short run.

In arguing that exchange-rate changes are both ineffective and unnecessary for the achievement of payments equilibrium, global monetarism turns its back on the father of modern monetarism, Milton Friedman, who was probably the earliest, best-known, and most persistent supporter of flexible exchange rates in the postwar period. The question at issue is whether the domestic money supply is best regarded under pegged rates as an endogenous or exogenous (policy) variable. Viewing the money supply as a variable under the control of the national monetary authority, even under pegged rates, Friedman supports exchange-rate flexibility as a means of eliminating payments imbalances that would otherwise arise from divergent national monetary policies (or random real disturbances) without interfering with freedom of international transactions and thus global efficiency.[40] The global monetarists, however, argue that the requirements for money-market equilibrium ensure the elimination of payments disequilibrium even under fixed exchange rates, and that such a regime is to be preferred on welfare grounds because it makes international risk-pooling possible and bestows the efficiency advantages associated with the existence of international money.[41]

Retaining the fundamental tenets of the monetary approach (the nonsterilization assumption

and the requirement of long-run stock equilibrium in the money market), but relaxing the assumptions of global monetarism by (a) permitting monetary changes to affect real variables in the short run and (b) assuming imperfect substitutability across national boundaries in either product or capital markets,[42] restores some short-run independence for domestic policy even under fixed exchange rates. But the long-run equilibrium results are the same: the assumptions of the monetary approach are sufficient to ensure the eventual restoration of proportionality between changes in the money stock and in the price level, and the worldwide convergence of national inflation rates.[43]

Under the assumptions of the monetary approach, devaluation obviously cannot be used to bring about a permanent alteration in a country's balance of payments. Unless all markets are assumed to adjust instantaneously, however, devaluation will cause a temporary improvement in the payments balance during the period of transition to the new equilibrium, and may thus retain its usefulness as a policy tool under certain circumstances. Specifically, it may be used either to achieve a one-shot increase in a country's stock of international reserves, or to finance a *temporary* budget deficit through money creation, without causing a temporary deterioration in the balance of payments.[44] Similarly, revaluation may be used to cause a temporary deterioration in a country's payments balance (and thus a decrease in its reserve stock) and a one-time reduction in its price level relative to that in the rest of the world.

Furthermore, whereas the monetary approach generally considers the effects of a devaluation

---

[40] Friedman, "Case for Flexible Exchange Rates," p. 414.

[41] Arthur B. Laffer, "Two Arguments for Fixed Rates," and Robert A. Mundell, "Uncommon Arguments for Common Currencies," in Harry G. Johnson and Alexander K. Swoboda, eds., *The Economics of Common Currencies* (Oxford: Allen and Unwin, 1973). Note that the risk-pooling argument is valid only "if it can be assumed that monetary policy errors and output variations are truly random and independent of the exchange rate regime chosen." Johnson, "Monetary Approach . . . A Diagrammatic Analysis," p. 229.

[42] An alternative assumption would be the existence of nontraded goods and assets. See Rudiger Dornbusch, "Real and Monetary Aspects of the Effects of Exchange Rate Changes," in Robert Z. Aliber, ed., *National Monetary Policies and the International Financial System* (University of Chicago Press, 1974).

[43] Branson points out that this convergence is also implied by a Keynesian trade-multiplier model that incorporates a price Phillips curve. William H. Branson, "Monetarist and Keynesian Models of the Transmission of Inflation," *American Economic Review,* vol. 65 (May 1975), pp. 115–19. Gordon notes, however, that the monetary approach adds new channels for international transmission of inflation to the traditional ones. Robert J. Gordon, "Recent Developments," p. 39.

[44] Dornbusch refers to this as the "capital levy aspect of a devaluation." See "Real and Monetary Aspects," p. 75.

on an economy that is initially in long-run equilibrium, exchange-rate changes are in fact generally undertaken from a position of short-run disequilibrium. In this context, an exchange-rate change may be justified as a faster way to eliminate disequilibrium than reliance on the monetary adjustment mechanism under fixed rates. The question arises, however, as to how a payments disequilibrium can occur in the first place; Johnson notes that "an appropriate rationale for introducing exchange-rate changes can be introduced by positing limitations on the scope for use of ordinary monetary policy." He adds, however, "that if the initial deficit or surplus that prompted the devaluation or revaluation under consideration was due to the inability of the monetary authority to pursue respectively a sufficiently contractionary or sufficiently expansionary monetary policy, the exchange rate change can only lead back transitorily to balance-of-payments equilibrium, and the deficit or surplus will recur (and be chronic) unless the relevant weakness of the power of conventional monetary policy is corrected."[45]

Implications for Accounting

The monetary approach to balance-of-payments analysis has unconventional implications also for the form and structure of balance-of-payments accounting—in particular, for the type of "balances" that have analytical significance. As has already been mentioned, the Keynesian approach focuses on the balance on goods and services, which corresponds to the "net exports" sector in the national income accounts. When the Keynesian approach is expanded to incorporate a flow theory of international capital movements, the corresponding accounting framework would logically include a balance on goods and services (the remaining item in the balance on current account, unilateral transfers, is something of an anomaly, which does not fit easily into any sectoral analytical framework), a balance on securities (the "capital account"), and a residual and offsetting reserve balance which includes the means of payment to finance the other two accounts. The optimal division among different balances can be debated endlessly, and the balances themselves endlessly proliferated, but the underlying principle is the same: there is a net balance that corresponds logically to each category of transactions for which there is a separate explanatory theory, and transactions that do not

fall into any of the explained categories belong "below the line," as accommodating items that finance the others.[46] Thus, Keynesians analyze the balance of payments from the "top down."

The monetary approach, in contrast, focuses primarily on the money market and regards the relationship between the (stock) demand for and supply of money as the critical determinant of the balance of payments. The appropriate analysis is thus from the "bottom up," focusing on changes in the balance on official-reserve transactions and frequently ignoring changes in the composition of the balance of payments among the nonmonetary items above the line. Specifically, whether a disequilibrium in the money market is eliminated through the current or the capital account is generally indeterminate,[47] so that such subbalances are not of major analytical significance. But international flows of reserves, far from being a mere residual, reflect the very disequilibrium in the money market that moves the whole system, since "it is primarily through their effects on the money supply that [international] transactions have any appreciable impact on aggregate economic activity."[48] In fact, any disturbance in international transactions that does not cause disequilibrium in the monetary account is not, in this view, a source of payments imbalance at all, since it must have been offset either by independent and coincidental changes or by induced changes elsewhere in the accounts.[49]

In a gold-standard world, without any reserve

[45] "Monetary   Approach . . . A   Diagrammatic Analysis," pp. 226–27.

[46] For an outstanding example of this approach to balance-of-payments analysis and forecasting, see Walter S. Salant and others, *The United States Balance of Payments in 1968* (Brookings Institution, 1963).

[47] For a "monetary approach" model that makes explicit the separate impact of disturbances on the current and the capital accounts, see Frenkel and Rodriguez, "Portfolio Equilibrium."

[48] Donald S. Kemp, "Balance-of-Payments Concepts—What Do They Really Mean?" Federal Reserve Bank of St. Louis, *Review*, vol. 57 (July 1975), p. 21.

The proponent of a Keynesian approach to payments adjustment argues, in contrast, for the exclusion of international transactions in short-term liquid assets from his aggregate balance-of-payments model because "gross reserve positions and the distribution of the stock of international short-term assets among nations have little effect upon international economic policy." See H. Peter Gray, *An Aggregate Theory of International Payments Adjustment* (New York: Macmillan, 1974), p. 36.

[49] William J. Fellner, " 'Monetary' versus 'Monetarist' Theories: Drawing the Distinction," in Clark and others, *Effects of Exchange Rate Adjustment*.

currencies, the balance that measures international flows of reserves, and hence the effect of international transactions on the domestic money supply, would correspond to the balance on official-reserve transactions, as measured in the U.S. balance-of-payments statistics. This would then be the crucial—indeed, the only meaningful —balance for the monetary approach, since it would represent both the pressures on the dollar from disequilibrium in the distribution of the world's money supply and the operation of the automatic adjustment mechanism to restore worldwide equilibrium in the money market. In a world of reserve currencies, however, a country such as the United States may, by making additional reserves available, affect the money supplies of other countries, without a corresponding impact on its own. Thus, the balance on official-reserve transactions of the United States includes not only transactions that alter some components of the monetary base (that is, changes in U.S. official holdings of gold and foreign currencies or in foreign deposits at Federal Reserve Banks), but also a variety of transactions that have no such impact (such as changes in holdings of special drawing rights, in the U.S. net position with the International Monetary Fund, or in holdings of U.S. interest-bearing assets by foreign official agencies). Yet the "balance on money account," or transactions affecting the monetary base, which the monetary approach regards as the only appropriate measure of net exchange pressure on a reserve currency under fixed exchange rates, is not among the numerous "balances" now calculated in the official U.S. balance-of-payments statistics.[50]

THE DUAL OF THE MONETARY APPROACH: THE ASSET APPROACH TO EXCHANGE-RATE DETERMINATION

All of the discussion so far has assumed a regime of fixed—or pegged—exchange rates. Only under such a regime do balance-of-payments disequilibrium and its adjustment become policy issues. But the analytical approach has its counterpart, or dual, in a world of freely flexible exchange rates: the asset-market approach to exchange-rate determination. The fundamental symmetry of the long-run stock-equilibrium implications of the two approaches can be seen in equations 1 through 6. These equations can be used to solve for an endogenous exchange rate

with only one modification: since the exchange rate now varies to maintain payments equilibrium throughout, reserve movements are always zero and the national money stock in each country becomes an exogenous variable under the control of its monetary authority. The long-run equilibrium exchange rate is then determined by the relationship between the price levels in the two countries (equation 2), each of which is in turn a function of the relationship between the desired and the actual stock of national money (equation 1).[51] (Note, incidentally, that a regime of flexible exchange rates implies two distinct national moneys, separated by the changing price relationship between them, and eliminates any meaningful concept of a world money stock.) Despite the long-run symmetry between the monetary approach under pegged rates and its flexible-rate analogue, the adjustment process is quite different in the two regimes. Under fixed exchange rates, *quantities* adjust gradually, in the form of reserve flows, to bring about equality between the actual stock of money and the desired level of real balances. Under flexible rates, with the nominal quantity of money fixed in each country, changes in the *valuation* of the stock through changes in the exchange rate bring about instantaneous full stock adjustment in the money market.[52]

Unfortunately, this stripped-down model is inadequate to generate some of the more interesting policy implications of the asset approach to exchange-rate analysis. Two extensions, in particular, are critical: One is the specification

---

[50] Kemp, in "Balance-of-Payments Concepts," p. 22, calculates such a balance for 1974.

[51] The exchange rate will also be determined by the requirements of asset-market equilibrium in the short run, even if limitations on commodity arbitrage are assumed to permit the emergence of temporary deviations from the purchasing-power-parity condition of equation 2. In this case, the condition for money-market equilibrium, $L = M$, must be rewritten (for the home country, and analogously for the foreign country) as

$$\frac{M}{w\bar{P} + (1-w)\bar{P}^*e} = k\bar{y},$$

where w is a weight, and M determines e directly. For a more detailed discussion of the monetary approach to exchange-rate determination in the short run versus the long run, see Rudiger Dornbusch, "The Theory of Flexible Exchange Rate Regimes and Macroeconomic Policy," *Scandinavian Journal of Economics* (formerly *Swedish Journal of Economics*) (forthcoming, 1976).

[52] Frenkel and Rodriguez, "Portfolio Equilibrium," and Pentti J. K. Kouri, "The Exchange Rate and the Balance of Payments in the Short Run and in the Long Run: A Monetary Approach," *Scandinavian Journal of Economics* (forthcoming, 1976).

of assumptions regarding the formation of expectations. Obviously, expectations play no role in the determination of the stationary-state equilibrium itself, since they must be static under that condition. But they will significantly influence the dynamic adjustment path in a model in which the exchange rate is determined by the stock-equilibrium conditions appropriate to asset markets rather than by the equality between flow supply and flow demand that characterizes commodity markets. The possible explanations of how expectations are formed are numberless, so that a wide variety of conclusions regarding the impact effect of exchange-market disturbances and the nature of the dynamic adjustment path can emerge within the general framework of the asset-market approach. It turns out, however, that several widely used simple models of expectations formation yield one common result: when there are adjustment lags, the impact effect of a disturbance on the exchange rate will exceed the long-run equilibrium effect; that is, the exchange rate will initially overshoot in response to a disturbance, and then retreat gradually toward its new long-run equilibrium value along the dynamic adjustment path.[53]

A second important extension of the model is the introduction of a second financial asset—bonds—and, with it, the rate of interest. Given this additional market, the long-run condition for stationary-state equilibrium in asset markets requires that the current-account balance be equal to zero, so that the total stock of wealth is unchanging, and that international flows of capital thus be zero as well.[54] This particular extension makes possible the analysis of the effects of fiscal as well as monetary policy. One implication of this extended model, for example, is the critical role played by international capital mobility in the relative efficacy of fiscal policy under different exchange-rate regimes. Applying the conventional IS-LM analysis to an open economy without capital mobility, one can easily demonstrate that fiscal policy has a greater impact on domestic economic activity under flexible than under fixed rates, because the exchange rate will always move so as to prevent any reduction in the domestic multiplier effect via leakage through

the trade balance. But the domestic impact of fiscal policy falls as capital mobility increases until, with fully integrated capital markets, fiscal policy becomes totally ineffective as a domestic stabilization tool. Any expansionary measure, such as increasing net government expenditures (with a given money supply), will put upward pressure on the rate of interest. The resulting inflow of capital will cause an appreciation of the currency, and the resulting deflationary impact on the trade balance will exactly offset the initial multiplier effect of fiscal policy on domestic income. With a given liquidity-preference schedule and an exogenously frozen interest rate, the requirements of money-market equilibrium will prevent any change in domestic income without a change in the money supply, and "global crowding out" will render fiscal policy useless.[55]

One of the arguments frequently advanced in favor of flexible exchange rates is that they enable countries to insulate themselves from monetary disturbances originating abroad, bottling up such disturbances in their country of origin. And, indeed, in the simple model of equations 1–6, this is the case. An increase in the foreign money supply, which under fixed rates would lead ultimately to increases in the domestic money supply and price level equal to those abroad, would, under flexible rates, be offset by an appreciation of the domestic currency in response to the incipient surplus arising from the foreign excess supply of money; and that appreciation would leave the domestic money supply, price level, and all domestic real variables unchanged.

Once interest rates and internationally mobile securities are introduced into the picture, however, the insulation provided by flexible exchange rates becomes incomplete. Now an increase in the foreign money supply will lower interest rates not only in the country where the disturbance originates but in the home country as well. With an unchanged domestic money stock, an upward-sloping LM curve requires that the lower interest rate be accompanied by a lower level of income if money-market equilibrium is to be maintained. Flexible exchange rates do not abolish interdependence in a world of capital mobility.[56] Indeed,

---

[53] See, for example, ibid.

[54] The portfolio-balance requirements could also be met in principle by what Mundell calls quasi-equilibrium, in which the government deficit (which pumps financial assets into the private sector) exactly equals the trade deficit (which drains such assets out of that sector). See Mundell, *International Economics*, p. 226.

[55] See Whitman, *Policies for Internal and External Balance*, pp. 20–21. The speed with which this "crowding out" occurs depends on how rapidly trade flows are assumed to adjust to changes in the exchange rate.

[56] Arnold Collery, "Macro-economics in an Open Economy under Purchasing-Power Parity," in Aliber, ed., *National Monetary Policies*, and Rudiger Dornbusch, "Flexible Exchange Rates, Capital Mobility

Cooper has pointed out that the impact of certain types of disturbances abroad may actually be aggravated rather than softened or eliminated by flexibility of exchange rates. As an example, he cites an exogenous shift in asset preferences that increases the foreign demand for domestic securities at a constant rate of interest. The result would be an appreciation of the domestic currency, leading to a current-account deficit, and a reduction of domestic aggregate demand and income (as well as, in a two-commodity model, a reallocation of resources away from tradable and toward non-tradable goods).[57] Thus, the insulation of countries from disturbances originating abroad provided by freely flexible exchange rates depends heavily on the type of disturbance assumed to dominate in the international arena.

In a world of rate flexibility, exchange-market disequilibrium is measured, not by any payments "balance," but rather by changes in the effective (that is, weighted) exchange rate of the dollar vis-à-vis other countries. But here, again, the asset-market approach views such changes as reflecting disequilibrium in the distribution of the world's stock of money (or financial assets in general), in contrast to the conventional Keynesian approach, which is more apt to analyze them in terms of flow disequilibrium in the goods or securities markets.[58] In a world of managed floating, market pressures on a currency are reflected both in the net international flow of reserves and in movements in the effective exchange rate, although no one has yet developed a single composite unit to measure empirically the total pressure reflected through both these channels.

Finally, the monetary approach implies a definition of "international policy coordination" in a world of managed floating somewhat different from that of conventional analysis. It is widely recognized that, in order to avoid inconsistency among exchange-rate targets under such a regime and a resulting disorder similar to the competitive depreciations of the 1930s, rules for intervention in the exchange markets are essential.[59] The mon-

etary approach stresses, however, that rules for intervention are fundamentally inadequate to the problem of inconsistent targets, since there is more than one means to pursue such targets. "A government can cause its currency to depreciate almost as well by having its central bank buy domestic bonds as by having it buy foreign currency."[60] On the other side, the recent history of managed floating is replete with instances of countries supporting their currencies indirectly, through foreign borrowing, rather than directly in the exchange markets. What is crucial is the relationship between the demand for and the supply of money, not whether the money is created by buying (or selling) domestic or foreign assets. Thus, true policy coordination to avoid inconsistent target setting requires, in the monetary approach, not rules governing intervention in the exchange markets, but rules guaranteeing the compatibility of national monetary policies, and fiscal policies to the extent that they are financed by money creation or affect the demand for money. International coordination as defined by the monetary approach is much more demanding, and much more restrictive of national economic sovereignty, than the limited rules for exchange-market intervention that are conventionally regarded as the means of avoiding inconsistent and thus destabilizing exchange-rate targets among nations.[61]

SOME EMPIRICAL ISSUES UNRESOLVED

In any attempt to evaluate the contribution of global monetarism and the monetary approach to the analysis of current policy issues, certain obvious empirical questions arise.

Law of One Price

For one thing, how realistic is the assumption of the "law of one price," or of a high degree of

and Macroeconomic Equilibrium," in Claassen and Salin, eds., *Recent Issues in International Monetary Economics.*

[57] Richard N. Cooper, "Monetary Theory and Policy in an Open Economy," *Scandinavian Journal of Economics* (forthcoming, 1976).

[58] For an empirical evaluation of the equilibrium dollar-mark exchange rate within the monetary framework, see *Citibank Money International,* vol. 3 (April 30, 1975).

[59] The question of rules for intervention was a major topic in the IMF's discussions of international monetary reform. See Committee on Reform of the

International Monetary System and Related Issues (Committee of Twenty), *International Monetary Reform: Documents of the Committee of Twenty* (International Monetary Fund, 1974), annex 4, sec. B.

[60] Michael Mussa, "The Exchange Rate, the Balance of Payments, and Monetary and Fiscal Policy under a Regime of Controlled Floating," *Scandinavian Journal of Economics* (forthcoming, 1976).

[61] Furthermore, a recent study concludes that "the systematic use of sterilization policies by two or more countries . . . may lead to explosive reserve flows and, therefore, to the breakdown of the system." Paul De Grauwe, "The Interaction of Monetary Policies in a Group of European Countries," *Journal of International Economics,* vol. 5 (August 1975), p. 225.

substitutability across national boundaries in both commodity and financial-asset markets?[62]

The assumption really takes two forms, depending on the length of run and the adjustment mechanism involved. The weaker form is that of the purchasing-power-parity concept, which asserts that, over long periods of time (decades, for example), changes in exchange rates tend to offset—or be offset by—changes in relative price levels. This concept has stood up well to empirical verification for long periods, although there is ample evidence of substantial short-run deviations.[63] The "law of one price" asserts substantially more, however, than a long-run tendency toward purchasing-power parity among countries. In particular, it asserts that high elasticities of substitution prevail among countries for most tradable goods and financial assets, and that, because world markets are highly integrated, a single price must prevail in all markets for goods and assets that are close substitutes for one another. This view implies that competitive forces will *quickly* and *directly* eliminate changes in relative prices stemming from exchange-rate changes by offsetting changes in domestic prices. Although recent studies indicate a very high degree of market integration and international substitutability for primary commodities, other investigations conclude that the close-substitutes hypothesis fails to hold for manufactured goods in general for the time periods examined and at the levels of aggregation employed; that is, "the relative dollar prices of industrial outputs do seem to change substantially and permanently [over

the six-year period 1968–73] when exchange rates change."[64] Estimates made in two recent studies imply that the United States can expect to retain for some time over half of a change in the effective exchange rate in the form of a relative price advantage for manufactured exports.[65] Similarly, there is empirical evidence that, despite increasing integration of financial markets, investors do not regard foreign and domestic long-term financial assets as perfect substitutes for one another.[66] For short-term money-market assets, in which international integration has proceeded the furthest, the evidence on the degree of independence retained by national interest rates is somewhat inconclusive.[67]

Sterilization

Another empirical question—one that is central not only to the strong conclusions of global monetarism but also to the weaker ones of the monetary approach—is whether governments can and do engage in a "deliberate nullification" of the impact of a payments imbalance on the domestic supply of money. By now, a considerable literature has arisen from empirical investigations of the extent to which various nations at various times have successfully "sterilized," or offset the effects of a payments imbalance on the domestic monetary base, and also of the extent to which the domestic impact of monetary policy is offset by international capital flows.[68] While these

---

[62] Although Frenkel has argued forcefully for "the irrelevance of commodity arbitrage" in the asset view of exchange-rate determination (and thus, by extension, in the monetary approach to balance-of-payments analysis), the fact remains that this assumption is common to many of the models of this genre. And it is certainly essential for the derivation of many of the strong policy implications of full-fledged global monetarism. See Jacob A. Frenkel, "A Monetary Approach to the Exchange Rate: Doctrinal Aspects and Empirical Evidence," *Scandinavian Journal of Economics* (forthcoming, 1976).

[63] On the first point, see Harry J. Gailliot, "Purchasing Power Parity as an Explanation of Long-Term Changes in Exchange Rates," *Journal of Money, Credit and Banking*, vol. 2 (August 1970), pp. 348–57, and Arthur B. Laffer, "The Phenomenon of Worldwide Inflation: A Study in International Market Integration," in David I. Meiselman and Arthur B. Laffer, eds., *The Phenomenon of Worldwide Inflation* (American Enterprise Institute, 1975), pp. 27–52. On the second point see, for example, Ronald I. McKinnon, "Floating Exchange Rates, 1973–74: The Emperor's New Clothes," *Journal of Monetary Economics* (supplement, forthcoming, 1976).

[64] Peter Isard, "The Price Effects of Exchange Rate Changes: Some Evidence from Industry Data for the United States, Germany, and Japan, 1968–73," in Clark and others, *Effects of Exchange Rate Adjustment.*

[65] J. R. Artus, "The Behavior of Manufactured Export Prices," and S. Y. Kwack, "The Effects of Foreign Inflation on Domestic Prices and the Relative Price Advantage of Exchange Rate Changes," in ibid.

[66] Herbert G. Grubel, "Internationally Diversified Portfolios: Welfare Gains and Capital Flows," *American Economic Review*, vol. 58, pt. 1 (December 1968), pp. 1299–1314.

[67] See, for example, Richard J. Herring and Richard C. Marston, "The Monetary Sector in an Open Economy: An Empirical Analysis for Canada and Germany," Working Paper 7-74 (University of Pennsylvania, Rodney L. White Center for Financial Research, 1974; processed), and Richard C. Marston, *American Monetary Policy and the Structure of the Eurodollar Market*, Princeton Studies in International Finance 34 (Princeton University, International Finance Section, 1974).

[68] See, for example, Victor Argy and Pentti J. K, Kouri, "Sterilization Policies and the Volatility in International Reserves," and Warren D. McClam, "Monetary Growth and the Euro-currency Market," in Aliber, ed., *National Monetary Policies;* Herring

studies indicate that at least some degree of sterilization has been or could be undertaken in the short run by the countries surveyed, they also suggest a wide range of experience, even among industrialized nations. Considerable evidence indicates that Japan, for example, has in recent years been able to sterilize most of the balance-of-payments impact on its monetary base; in Germany, conversely, the money supply has been much closer to being endogenously determined even in the short run. At least one instance of "perverse" behavior—that is, reinforcement rather than neutralization of the balance-of-payments impact on the monetary base—has been suggested by the data. Besides indicating wide variations in experience among countries, the studies conducted so far have all been subject to serious problems of simultaneity, revealing the need for much more work to develop better empirical tests of the general applicability of the monetary approach and its policy implications.

In contrast to this general uncertainty, the United States is clearly a special case, for which the money supply is primarily an exogenous variable, controlled by the monetary authorities, rather than the endogenous variable postulated by the monetary approach. This is partly a simple matter of size; as Swoboda has noted, the monetary approach implies that, under fixed exchange rates and with money multipliers assumed equal in all countries, open-market purchases of securities cause reserve losses that are inversely proportional to the country's relative economic size and thus expansions in the domestic money supply in direct proportion to that size.[69] To put it another way, even though the monetary approach implies that no country can alter its *share* of the world money stock through monetary policy, the sheer size of the U.S. share ensures its ability to alter the total magnitude of the world money stock and

thus the size of its own money supply. For an economy as large as the United States, monetary policy retains a domestic impact, even under fixed exchange rates in an integrated world economy.

In addition to this sort of indirect control that a large economy has over its own money supply, it can also exercise direct control to the extent that it can effectively sterilize the impact of the balance of payments on its domestic money supply.[70] Presumably, the capacity to sterilize is partly a function of a country's economic size, as well as of the size of its stock of international reserves. But the status of the United States as a reserve-currency country is probably even more important than its weight in the world economy in enabling it to neutralize the feedback from the balance of payments to the domestic money supply. As noted above, a measured deficit in the balance of payments of a reserve-currency country may be accompanied, not by any loss of primary reserve assets, but rather by an increase in certain kinds of liabilities to foreign monetary authorities. The creation of these liabilities will often result in partial or full automatic sterilization of the balance-of-payments impact on the U.S. money supply, without any deliberate action on the part of the U.S. monetary authorities.[71] Given both its size and its reserve-currency position, it is hardly surprising that the sterilization coefficients estimated for the United States in empirical studies have generally not differed significantly from unity. For the United States, the domestic money supply remains an exogenous policy variable even under fixed exchange rates and in the face of increasing international integration of markets.

Effective "deliberate nullification" in the case of the United States—and perhaps other countries, as their currencies are increasingly held as reserve assets—by no means negates all the policy implications of the monetary approach. Specifically, it does not disturb the postulated relationship between domestic monetary policy and the balance of payments, nor the channels by which domestic disturbances in the sterilizing country are transmitted to the rest of the world. It also introduces three important changes into the analysis: (1) It restores monetary policy as a

and Marston, "Monetary Sector in an Open Economy"; Pentti J. K. Kouri, "The Hypothesis of Offsetting Capital Flows: A Case Study of Germany," *Journal of Monetary Economics,* vol. 1 (January 1975), pp. 21–39; Norman C. Miller and Sherry S. Askin, "Domestic and International Monetary Policy," *Journal of Money, Credit and Banking* (forthcoming, 1976); and Niels Thygesen, "Monetary Policy, Capital Flows and Internal Stability: Some Experiences from Large Industrial Countries," *Swedish Journal of Economics,* vol. 75 (March, 1973), pp. 83–99, as well as other studies cited in the aforementioned.

[69] Relative economic size is measured in terms of the country's share of the world's money supply. See Alexander K. Swoboda, "Gold, Dollars, Eurodollars and the World Money Stock" (Geneva: Graduate Institute of International Studies, 1974; processed), p. 9.

[70] Swoboda notes that a successful sterilization policy in one country gives that country an effective weight of one in the determination of the world's money stock (ibid., p. 10). The same point is noted in Girton and Roper, "Monetary Model."

[71] Swoboda, "Gold, Dollars, Eurodollars," pp. 15–18.

policy variable operating on the domestic economy, under fixed as well as flexible exchange rates. (2) It destroys the symmetry whereby a given amount of domestic money creation has the same impact on the world money supply, regardless of the origin of the disturbance; asymmetries are introduced because low-powered money in a reserve-currency country becomes high-powered, or base, money in other countries. (3) It renders the monetary policy of all countries other than the reserve-currency country totally ineffective and ensures that they bear the full burden of the classical adjustment process.[72] In addition, in the case of a reserve-currency country, the a priori relationship between changes in the money supply and the balance of payments is negative, as opposed to the positive relationship that prevails in the case of non-reserve-currency countries, whose money supplies are indeed endogenous. Finally, note that no more than one country in the system can sterilize completely the impact of payments imbalances on its money supply without destabilizing the system as a whole.[73]

In addition to efforts to estimate sterilization coefficients, a few more comprehensive attempts have been made to test the monetary approach to the balance of payments, either alone or by comparing it with alternative approaches—for example, to the analysis of the balance-of-payments impact of devaluation.[74] Such tests are hampered by a number of technical difficulties, chief among them the fact that direct estimation of the balance-of-payments equation implied by the monetary approach involves the estimation of an accounting identity rather than a true behavioral relationship. Thus, only indirect tests of some of the implications of the monetary approach are legitimate, and these are inevitably arbitrary and subject to varying interpretations. Furthermore, no investigator has combined all the variables associated with the various approaches to devaluation in a single equation, as would be required for an appropriate comparison of their relative explanatory power. In any case, apart from these technical problems, the various efforts to test the monetary approach directly have proved inconclusive, with estimated coefficients turning out significant with the correct sign in some cases but not in others, and with the estimated magnitudes of the coefficients frequently differing significantly from their a priori values. At present, both supporters and critics of the monetary approach can find considerable ammunition in empirical results. As Blinder and Solow have noted with respect to the various empirical tests of the competing hypotheses of monetarism and Keynesianism in a closed-economy context, "The issue is simply not to be settled by comparing goodness of fit of one-equation models that are far too primitive to represent *any* theory adequately."[75]

Managed Flexibility

Finally, one must ask whether the monetary approach—or, indeed, any existing balance-of-payments theory—is applicable to the international monetary framework within which the world now operates. The monetary theory is well defined for a world on the gold standard or even for a world of pegged exchange rates in which parities are changed infrequently.[76] And it has an analogue—the asset approach to exchange-rate determination—for a world of freely flexible exchange rates without government intervention. But the rules by which the monetary authorities conduct themselves, and the implications of those rules for the behavioral properties of a world of managed flexibility, have yet to be explored. The

---

[72] For an analysis of the gold-exchange standard along these lines, see Jacques Rueff, *Balance of Payments* (Macmillan, 1967).

[73] See De Grauwe, "Interaction of Monetary Policies."

[74] Among such studies are B. B. Aghevli and M. S. Kahn, "The Monetary Approach to Balance of Payments Determination: An Empirical Test," in International Monetary Fund, *The Monetary Approach to the Balance of Payments: An Anthology* (forthcoming, 1976); B. Brittain and Sri Kumar, "Monetary Balance of Payments Theory: Implications and Tests," Working Paper (First National City Bank, 1974; processed); Thomas J. Courchene, "The Price-Specie-Flow Mechanism and the Gold-Exchange Standard," in Johnson and Swoboda, eds., *Economics of Common Currencies;* Hans Genberg, "An Empirical Comparison of Alternative Models of Currency Devaluation" (Geneva: Graduate Institute of International Studies, November 1974; processed); Wolfgang Kasper, "The Emergence of an Active Exchange-Rate Policy—Some Quantitative Lessons," in Kasper, ed., *International Monetary Experiments and Experiences,* Papers and Proceedings of the Symposium on International Monetary Problems, Port Stephens, Australia, August 1975 (Canberra, Australia: forthcoming, 1976); Pentti J. K. Kouri and Michael G. Porter, "International Capital Flows and Portfolio Equilibrium," *Journal of Political Economy,* vol. 82 (May/June 1974), pp. 443–67. See also the various empirical studies in Frenkel and Johnson, eds., *Monetary Approach.*

[75] Blinder and Solow, "Analytical Foundations," p. 65.

[76] It does not encompass, however, any of the expectational or other dynamic effects of frequent changes in exchange rates.

implicit assumption made by many analysts is that managed flexibility can be fully characterized as a situation "somewhere between" fixed and freely flexible rates, which can be formally incorporated by introducing a "combined" variable to represent pressure on the currency in the form either of reserve flows or of changes in the effective exchange rate. But certain anomalies in recent experience—such as the apparent failure of the worldwide demand for reserves to decline substantially with the greater flexibility of exchange rates—suggest that the behavioral characteristics of managed flexibility may be qualitatively different from those of a pegged-rate or freely flexible regime, rather than some simple average of the characteristics of the two limiting cases.

SOME FUNDAMENTAL ISSUES IN POLITICAL ECONOMY

Some significant issues in political economy arise in any attempt to evaluate the analytical contributions and policy relevance of the challenges to current orthodoxy that are the focus of this survey. In discussing the issues, two major distinctions between global monetarism and the monetary approach must be borne in mind. First, as an earlier section has emphasized, the monetary approach is only one of the three strands of assumptions that define global monetarism, along with the full-employment assumption and the "law of one price level" (or, in some models, the "small country" assumption). Second, whereas both global monetarism and the monetary approach tend to focus on the characteristics of the system in stationary-state equilibrium, adherents of the monetary approach generally recognize that such long-run tendencies are compatible with many specifications of impact effects and dynamic adjustment mechanisms; extreme global monetarism, on the other hand, tends to draw policy implications from the characteristics of long-run stock-equilibria, suggesting by implication that they are actually achieved rapidly enough to make the characteristics of the transition unimportant.

Indeed, this question—"How long is the long run?"—is critical to the applicability of stationary-state general-equilibrium analysis to policy issues. It is important for the positive economics of forecasting, because the more gradual is the approach to equilibrium, the more certain it is that disturbances and changes in behavioral parameters will impinge during that approach, deflecting the economy from its initial path to the new equilibrium, and the more difficult it becomes to estimate the ceteris paribus effect of a particular exogenous change. The question is significant for the normative economics of policy prescription as well, not simply because of the notoriously short time horizon of policymakers but, more fundamentally, because of the very real social costs that may be associated with disequilibrium states or with different adjustment mechanisms.

Thus, the factors that affect the speed of adjustment to equilibrium become important: the effectiveness of commodity arbitrage across international boundaries, the degree of capital mobility, the strength of real-balance effects, and the proportion of traded to nontraded goods in the economy. It makes no difference to the nature of the full-equilibrium state whether purchasing-power parity is thought to be established via perfect substitutability and international arbitrage, or is regarded as a monetary phenomenon independent of such arbitrage. But it does make a very substantial difference to the length of run implied for the adjustment process. To put the problem slightly differently, economists disagree relatively little about the long-run general-equilibrium characteristics of the economic system. But for the short run, when the system diverges either from some of the behavioral relations or from one or more equilibrium conditions, there is substantial disagreement about which relationships can be assumed to hold throughout and which not, about which markets can be assumed to be continuously in equilibrium and which not. And, the longer the "short run" is, the more important these divergences become in determining the policy implications of the competing approaches.

Closely related to the question of the length of run over which adjustment takes place is the question of whether the assumption of fundamental stability that underlies equilibrium analysis is valid. If the world is in fact subject to frequent disturbances and shifts in behavioral parameters, then the equilibrium model is not appropriate for policy analysis, nor is it obvious that a mode of analysis that always begins with equilibrium can yield meaningful answers for a system whose initial state is inevitably disequilibrium. Furthermore, a fundamental proposition of global monetarism (and, to a lesser extent of the monetary approach) is that strong self-corrective tendencies operate in the economic system. But disturbances may in fact be cumulative rather than self-correcting; Okun has argued that, in fact, "the [econometric] evidence of both Keynesian and monetarist models of economic activity suggests that we live in an economy of persistence, rather than self-correction."[77]

Implicit in the monetary approach to the balance of payments, which views it from the bottom up, focusing on changes in reserve stocks,[78] is the assumption that changes in the composition of the balance among the nonmonetary items "above the line" are irrelevant. By contrast, the Keynesian approach, which looks separately, from the top down, at the forces affecting each category of transactions grouped into a "balance," views the composition of the balance of payments as itself a relevant question for analysis and a legitimate concern of policy. The analytical and policy relevance of the composition of the balance of payments must be considered from two aspects. One is the *stability* of selected subbalances or categories of international transactions. In particular, the adjustment costs associated with reallocation of factors of production suggest that fluctuations in the goods-and-services account may well have a negative rather than a neutral impact on the economy even if offsetting changes in some other account prevent any net balance-of-payments effect. This view, certainly, is implicit in the persistent focus of Keynesian analysis on the goods-and-services account. The second aspect is whether different *levels* of particular subaccounts may have different welfare implications and therefore be a legitimate focus of analysis. Keynesians frequently argue, for example, that the persistence of unemployment and downward wage rigidity makes the goods-and-services account a legitimate instrument of full-employment policy. At a more sophisticated level, Williamson has recently used the tools of optimal-control theory to demonstrate that different combinations of current- and capital-account balances have different implications for international indebtedness and thus will trace out different growth paths of consumption. His analysis implies, furthermore, that only under very special assumptions will the dynamically optimal composition coincide with the composition that would be generated by a market-determined exchange rate.[79] Thus, it would appear that both the Keynesian and the monetary approaches can be faulted in their handling of balance-of-payments composition. Keynesian analysis overlooks the interdependence among the various accounts through failure to incorporate the stock-equilibrium conditions that bind them together. The monetary approach, on the other hand, tends to neglect the particular configuration of the current and capital accounts associated with the period of transition to stationary-state equilibrium, and thus to overlook the economic effects of different levels of indebtedness, which are the stock counterpart of different payment configurations, not only on the adjustment path, but also on the long-run equilibrium itself in anything other than the stationary state.

Indeed, once one acknowledges that the nature of the adjustment path may itself influence the level at which long-run equilibrium is ultimately achieved, it becomes clear that the concentration of the monetary approach on monetary aggregates and the *general* price level obscures some important questions. In particular, by generally assuming a one-to-one relationship between wages and prices, it tends to ignore the importance of short-run changes in this relationship (which are likely in the wake of a devaluation, for example), not only for the distribution of income, but also for the level of employment, the rate of investment, and the rate of economic growth.[80]

The various questions raised so far apply, although in differing degrees, not only to global monetarism but to the monetary approach as well.

[77] Arthur M. Okun, "Fiscal-Monetary Activism: Some Analytical Issues," *BPEA, 1:1972*, p. 147. More specifically, Meltzer argues that if the global-monetarist model (which he calls the Mundell model) is modified to incorporate fiscal policy, the fixed-exchange-rate system is likely to be unstable. See Allan H. Meltzer, "The Monetary Approach to Inflation and the Balance of Payments: Theoretical and Empirical Contributions at the Leuven Conference," in Michele Fratianni and Karel K. Tavernier, eds., supplement to the journal, *Kredit und Kapital*, published in West Germany (forthcoming, 1976).

[78] Harry Johnson argues that "the crucial distinction for the Yale School [of Keynesians] . . . is between the financial sector and the real sector (or between stock and flow analysis) rather than between the banking system and the rest of the economy (as various versions of the contemporary quantity theory would have it). . . ." *Further Essays in Monetary Economics*, p. 38.

[79] J. H. Williamson, "On the Normative Theory of Balance-of-Payments Adjustment," in G. Clayton and others, eds., *Monetary Theory and Monetary Policy in the 1970s*, Proceedings of the 1970 Sheffield Money Seminar (London: Oxford University Press, 1971), pp. 235–56. The problem of a nonoptimal composition of the balance of payments is also noted in Alexander K. Swoboda, "Monetary Policy under Fixed Exchange Rates: Effectiveness, the Speed of Adjustment, and Proper Use," *Economica*, n.s., vol. 40 (May 1973), pp. 136–54.

[80] For a monetary-approach model that allows the wage-price relationship to vary, see Dornbusch, "Real and Monetary Aspects," cited in note 42. Changes in this relationship are explicitly excluded by the assumptions of global monetarism, among which are the absence of money illusion and the neutrality of money vis-à-vis real variables.

Most of the heterodox policy implications cited at the beginning of this paper, however, are derived from the full set of global-monetarist assumptions, including the tendency to regard the conditions of stationary-state equilibrium as relevant for policy analysis. The monetary approach, taken alone, raises important questions about the efficacy of exchange-rate policy—or, at least, focuses on some constraints under which it operates—that were frequently ignored in Keynesian analysis. In particular, it makes clear that countries cannot persistently inflate at different rates without eventually forcing a change in the rate of exchange between their currencies, and that these changes, in turn, feed back onto the domestic price level in ways that are not fully reflected in either elasticities or multiplier analysis. But global monetarism denies the utility not only of national exchange-rate policies, but also of *any* form of macroeconomic stabilization policy, both because the level of real income is assumed to be exogenous and because the requirements of stock equilibrium deprive exogenous disturbances of anything beyond transitional effects on real economic variables. Yet, in the real world, economies do in fact remain for considerable periods in disequilibrium—in particular, with persistent unemployment—and both exogenous disturbances and stabilization policies have nontrivial effects. In a world where the stabilization of income and employment at high levels (or along a reasonable growth path) is a primary concern of policymakers, an analytical model that eliminates these concerns by assumption operates under a certain handicap.

The macroeconomic assumptions of global monetarism appear to rest, explicitly or implicitly, on the microeconomic foundations provided by the classical "pure," or barter, model of international specialization and exchange. One of the critical assumptions of this model is that reallocations of production along the aggregate production-possibilities curve take place without friction or cost. Yet, in fact, the reallocation of factors of production from one use to another imposes real costs; in particular, the real income lost as a result of the unemployment associated with the reallocation process, whether or not it is subsumed under the rubric of frictional unemployment, represents a permanent loss to the society. Thus, a valid aim of government policies is to minimize the losses associated with reallocation; or, more accurately, to maximize the benefits net of the losses associated with it.

The recognition of adjustment costs, and their minimization, as a legitimate target of economic policy, also suggests that the optimal adjustment

process may vary according to the disturbance that gives rise to it.[81] In particular, the changes in relative prices and associated factor reallocations that characterize the classical adjustment mechanism (under both fixed and flexible rates) may be essential to restore equilibrium in the face of a trend disturbance or one that takes the form of a one-time permanent shift. Such responses may entail unnecessary adjustment costs, however, in the case of self-reversing disturbances.[82] The postwar history of the "fundamental disequilibrium" criterion for exchange-rate change incorporated in the Articles of Agreement of the International Monetary Fund makes clear how difficult it is to distinguish ex ante among the classes of disturbance, and warns how great is the temptation to diagnose a disturbance as self-reversing in order to avoid the social and political pain of even necessary reallocations. But the search for a least-cost adjustment mechanism remains valid, and the distinctions among disturbances just outlined imply that the "quasi-adjustments" (or financing of imbalances) that governments frequently resort to as alternatives to the classical adjustment mechanism and its associated reallocations may indeed be, in the case of self-reversing disturbances (such as certain shifts in asset preferences), the least costly and therefore the most appropriate response. Global monetarism, which views all disturbances and all responses through their impact on the demand for and supply of money, inevitably ignores such distinctions, to which the traditional piecemeal Keynesian approach to balance-of-payments analysis and its policy implications has tended to be more (sometimes excessively) sensitive. More generally, global monetarism, with its emphasis on the automaticity of the adjustment process and its

---

[81] The question of the optimum *speed* of adjustment is also relevant, although the criteria are not well defined. Okun is concerned that the automatic price-adjustment mechanism (for example, under fixed rates) may be too slow: "According to the St. Louis model, price flexibility works very slowly to restore equilibrium, with a process of adjustment that lasts for many years" ("Fiscal-Monetary Activism," p. 150). While Gray also worries sometimes about the slowness of this adjustment process (*Aggregate Theory*, p. 4), at other points in his argument (ibid., chap. 5), he is concerned that the market adjustment mechanism may sometimes work too quickly (for example, under flexible rates). Friedman argues that "there seems no reason to expect the timing or pace of adjustment under the assumed conditions [freely flexible rates] to be systematically biased in one direction or the other from the optimum . . ." ("Case for Flexible Exchange Rates," p. 434).

[82] Gray, *Aggregate Theory,* chap. 5.

suppression of structural characteristics, is ill suited to the incorporation of divergences between private and social optima. In contrast, the traditional Keynesian framework views the achievement of equilibrium—both internal and external—as a specific objective of deliberate government policy, rather than as the automatic result of the operation of market forces.[83]

Finally, there is the question of whether the nation-state or the world is the best primary focus of analysis. The monetary approach has rightly called attention to certain long-run tendencies toward international integration which were not reflected in the Keynesian analyses of the fifties and sixties. Global monetarism goes much further, essentially denying any relevance to national boundaries. In other words, its assumption of perfect substitutability and perfect arbitrage across national boundaries in both commodity and asset markets essentially erases the distinction between "domestic" and "foreign" and implies that only the world (rather than the national) values of variables and parameters are relevant to behavioral relationships.[84]

As Cooper has noted, the efficiency implications of pure trade theory argue that, for private transactions, the artificial boundaries of the nation-state should have no significance; for private markets in both goods and factors of production, the optimum currency area is the world. The economic justification for nation-states, then, lies in the existence of public or collective goods and of differences in the consumption preferences for such goods among the citizens of different nations.[85] The greater the divergences among countries with respect to the transformation curve or the indifference map for public goods, the greater will be the welfare costs of international economic integration in the sphere of such goods that must be set off against the efficiency gains from integration of private markets.[86]

Indeed, one can read in the recent history of international economic relationships a growing tension between the rapid increase—and acknowledged benefits—of international market integration in the private sphere and the almost total absence of integration or even coordination of public policy across national boundaries, which reflects at least in part a recognition of the welfare costs of such integration where collective goods are concerned. It seems logical, then, that the global-monetarist approach, with its stress on the inherent efficiency and stability of the private sector and its view of government intervention as a source of exogenous shocks, should emphasize the openness of national economies and the importance of adjustment mechanisms dependent on market integration, and should rest its preference for fixed over flexible exchange rates on the benefits of market integration in the private sector. The Keynesian approach, on the other hand, sees government as a stabilizer of fluctuations in the private sector, equilibrium as a state to be achieved by deliberate policy intervention rather than through the operation of automatic market forces alone, and collective goods as an important component of the social-welfare function. Those who take this view tend to base their concern with explicit balance-of-payments policies in a fixed-rate world and their frequent preference for managed flexibility on the need to insulate the domestic economy from foreign disturbances and to permit national governments to pursue independent macro stabilization policies, in a world of integrated markets. Fundamentally, this view regards exchange-rate policy as one instrument by which governments may preserve some independence in the policy sphere with a minimum of disruption to the benefits of market integration in the private sphere. But full-fledged global monetarism, which tends to regard conventional stabilization policies as both unnecessary and ineffective, is plagued by no such tradeoff and is free to focus on a single criterion for the exchange-rate regime: one that will maximize the efficiency benefits of worldwide integration of commodity and factor markets.

THEORETICAL PROGRESS AND POLICY RELEVANCE: A SCORECARD

Without doubt, the challenges to postwar orthodoxy surveyed in this paper, and the re-

---

[83] Whitman, *Policies for Internal and External Balance,* p. 2.

[84] Meltzer argues that in such models "an essential difference between the multicurrency world that emerged under the Bretton Woods Agreement and the gold standard is overlooked or neglected." See "Monetary Approach to Inflation and the Balance of Payments."

[85] Richard N. Cooper, "Worldwide vs. Regional Integration: Is There an Optimal Size of the Integrated Area?" (paper presented at the Fourth World Congress of the International Economic Association, Budapest, 1974; processed).

[86] For an example, in terms of the tradeoff between inflation and unemployment, see Marina v. N. Whitman, "Place Prosperity and People Prosperity: The Delineation of Optimum Policy Areas," in

Mark Perlman and others, eds., *Spatial, Regional and Population Economics* (New York: Gordon and Breach, 1972), pp. 359–93.

sponses of the modern Keynesians stimulated by them, have engendered rapid progress in the area of theoretical specification and model building. The explicit recognition of the interactions among all markets in a general-equilibrium system; the specification of full equilibrium in the market for money (and other financial assets) in stock as well as flow terms; the recognition that the response of an economy to a devaluation is properly analyzed in a macroeconomic rather than a microeconomic context; and the distinction among impact effects, the dynamic adjustment process, and long-run stationary-state effects of a disturbance—these are only some of the theoretical clarifications and refinements that have emerged from a dynamic process of challenge, response, and synthesis over the past decade.

In terms of policy relevance, it is the monetary approach to the balance of payments—rather than the entire package here termed global monetarism—that has yielded fruitful insights. Its assertion that, under pegged exchange rates, the national money supply should be regarded as an endogenous rather than a policy variable appears to hold almost fully for a few countries in the short-to-medium run, partially for at least a number of others, and not at all for the United States, the major supplier of international reserves in recent years. Even so, the monetary approach has yielded useful implications for the impact of domestic monetary policy in the United States on its own balance of payments, on the internal economies of other countries, and on the viability of the gold-exchange standard that characterized the Bretton Woods system.

Similarly, the flexible-rate analogue of the monetary approach—the asset approach to exchange-rate analysis—has proved extremely valuable for understanding and interpreting the experiences of recent years. It has focused attention on such factors as relative money-market conditions and shifts in portfolio preferences as important determinants of exchange rates in the short and medium run, as opposed to the exclusive focus on purchasing-power-parity conditions and the longer-run structural phenomena usual in Keynesian analysis. This asset-market approach provides a useful framework for consideration of possible problems created by short-run "overshooting" of longer-run equilibria, such as price "ratchets," bankruptcy thresholds created by capital-market imperfections, and related issues.

Most of the more revolutionary policy implications emerge, however, not from the monetary approach or its flexible-rate analogue, but from

the full package of global-monetarist assumptions. And these, by and large, miss the boat for applicability to current problems. In their assumption of perfect substitutability between domestic and foreign goods and financial assets, and of perfect arbitrage across national boundaries in both commodity and capital markets, for example, the global monetarists go too far in correcting an error implicit in much of the earlier Keynesian analysis. Market integration across national boundaries has certainly increased in recent years but, quite apart from the remaining barriers to trade, considerable evidence suggests that, at least for certain classes of commodities and financial assets, domestic and foreign counterparts are not regarded as perfect substitutes, creating substantial deviations from the "law of one price," at least in the short run. More broadly, while the global monetarists perform a service in insisting that the international repercussions of domestic policies must be recognized as more than second-order qualifications to a closed-economy analysis, they tend to dismiss too lightly the fact that the nation-state remains the basic economic entity in the modern world and that policy independence remains an important concern of national governments.

Finally, and most important, by focusing on the long-run general-equilibrium characteristics of the economic system—in particular, by assuming that real output is determined exogenously and that money is neutral vis-à-vis real variables—global monetarism consigns to irrelevance the problems of economic stabilization with which most policymakers are primarily concerned and to ineffectiveness the traditional macroeconomic tools of monetary and fiscal policy. In another context, Okun once concluded that the monetarists "have provided good questions and bad answers."[87] As I see it, the global monetarists have raised some good questions but have buried some even more important ones. Specifically, they insist, correctly, on the importance of recognizing the long-run implications of policies undertaken to achieve short- or medium-term goals, but they are wont, wrongly, to ignore short- and medium-term effects in focusing on the long-term full-equilibrium situation. The questions they thus skip over are important not only because of the short time horizon of policymakers, but also because of differences in social costs associated with different adjustment processes and varying lengths of the transition period. They are important, even more fundamentally, because in

----
[87] Okun, "Fiscal-Monetary Activism," p. 157.

the real world, long-run equilibrium is a state perhaps approached but never reached, and, in a dynamic rather than a stationary economy, the characteristics of the adjustment path, while the economy is out of equilibrium, are bound to affect the characteristics of the long-run equilibrium itself.

As with most challenges to orthodoxy, a winnowing process is now under way, and the most fruitful component of that challenge—the insights of the monetary approach to payments analysis—is rapidly being co-opted into the conventional wisdom itself. Beyond that, global monetarism offers little of policy relevance at this time, and the practical problem remains: "how to marry the monetarist and the Keynesian analysis in a way relevant to the short-run context (albeit a run of several calendar years) with which the policy makers are concerned, and which is characterized both by variations in production and employment as well as in money prices, and by variations in the relations among export, import and non-traded goods prices which are assumed away in the long-run equilibrium analysis of the monetarist approach."[88]

---

[88] Johnson, *Further Essays in Monetary Economics*, p. 14.

---

34. ASSET MARKET EQUILIBRIUM, THE EXCHANGE RATE, AND THE BALANCE OF PAYMENTS*

William H. Branson

Marina Whitman's paper surveys recent developments in the monetary and monetarist approaches to analysis of the balance of payments. The survey is interesting and evenhanded, but as is appropriate for a survey, it offers no new results. Therefore, I have nothing to attack ruthlessly (which would be no fun anyway), and I can offer only differences of approach, emphasis, and interpretation. Whitman's paper begins with global monetarism, and then goes on to discuss other approaches (monetary, Keynesian, elasticities, absorption, any combination of the above) to understanding the balance of payments as extensions of global monetarism. My approach is to treat a generalized *IS-LM* model of short-run equilibrium with several assets as the general case, and then to look at the monetary approach and global monetarism as increasingly special cases of this model. I think this improves understanding, and puts the various approaches in proper perspective. (I am encouraged to wander in the no-man's-land between the "monetarist" and "Keynesian" international schools since I am viewed by some of my professional colleagues as a "die-hard Keynesian" and by others as a "closet monetarist.")

Before getting into a brief discussion of the relationship of the monetary approach and global monetarism to the standard post-Keynesian analysis of the balance of payments, I should point out one aspect of the Whitman paper that I would fault. Toward the end of the paper, Whitman seems to criticize the monetary approach for having nothing to say about the *composition* of the balance of payments. While this observation is true, the monetary approach makes no claim to addressing this matter, so I think that this criticism is misplaced.

Whitman focuses on global monetarism and treats the more general monetary approach to analysis of the balance of payments as an extension of monetarism. She then goes on to relate the monetary approach to the traditional Keynesian elasticities-absorption literature as further extensions. I think that understanding of the roles of the monetary and monetarist approaches would be aided by reversing the order of this discussion, treating the monetary approach as a special case of the traditional post-Keynesian macro framework, and global monetarism as a polar case of the monetary approach. This ordering places global monetarism in proper perspective; Whitman's paper contains many references to scholarly work (published in the journals, rather than in the popular press) on the monetary approach, and few on global monetarism.

Beginning with the standard *IS-LM* model of income determination, I want to introduce, in

---

* From *Brookings Papers on Economic Activity* No. 3, 1975, pp. 537–42. Copyright © 1975 by The Brookings Institution, Washington, D.C. Reprinted by permission of the publisher and the author. William H. Branson is Professor of Economics and International Affairs, Woodrow Wilson School of Public and International Affairs, Princeton University.

the interest rate-income space, a third line that is the locus of points where the balance of payments is zero. Call this the *BP* line; it is positively sloped. If the *IS-LM* equilibrium intersection is above the *BP* line, the economy is experiencing a balance-of-payments surplus; below the *BP* line, a deficit (all of this assuming fixed exchange rates). A change in the exchange rate shifts both the *BP* and *IS* curves in this picture, and the elasticity story is about the direction and extent of these shifts, while the absorption story is about the economy's reactions to them.

The monetary approach simply adds to this story the observation that if the effects of a nonzero balance of payments on the money supply are not sterilized, the momentary *IS-LM* equilibrium point cannot be a full equilibrium, since the money supply is changing. In the absence of sterilization, a necessary (but not sufficient) condition for full stock equilibrium would be an *IS-LM* intersection on the *BP* line, so that the money stock is constant while the money market is in equilibrium. It is worth noting that the role of the balance of payments in changing the money stock in open-economy macroeconomics is almost exactly analogous to the role of the "government-budget constraint" in a closed economy. The Blinder-Solow results in the closed economy (cited by Whitman) are exactly the same as Mundell's famous results with fixed exchange rates.[1]

The key assumption in the monetary approach, which could be a testable hypothesis, is that monetary authorities do not or cannot sterilize (or nullify, in Whitman's term) the balance-of-payments surplus over any significant period. This assumption makes the full stock-equilibrium position the interesting one for the monetary-approach analyst, and his comparisons are usually made between such equilibria. The evidence on whether sterilization is possible is mixed. According to the findings cited by Whitman, some significant persistent sterilization is possible.

The principal inference usually drawn from the monetary approach is that between stock equilibria, changes in exchange rates alter the reserve level by inducing temporary payments

imbalances, but that in equilibrium, the balance is zero. In the monetary approach, exchange-rate policy is reserve policy, not balance-of-payments policy. However, the monetary approach also implies that changes in exchange rates can be effective in eliminating balance-of-payments disequilibria caused by shifts in other variables—a point that is underemphasized in the Whitman paper (and played down by most monetary-approach writers). If the balance of payments is not in equilibrium to begin with, changing the exchange rate could be more effective than waiting for the effects of the disequilibrium on the money stock to work their way through the system. This should be the relevant inference drawn from the monetary approach; after all, changes in exchange rates under the Bretton Woods system were responses to disequilibrium situations.

Global monetarism narrows the monetary approach even further by adding "small country" assumptions—as international economists call them—and wage flexibility to the nonsterilization assumption. According to the small-country assumptions, the economy is a price taker facing a world interest rate and price level, and can buy or sell all it chooses at those prices. These assumptions fix the price level and the interest rate. The assumption of flexible wages fixes output and employment at the full-employment level. With all the determinants of the demand for money fixed, any change in the domestic base has to be offset by a one-for-one change in foreign reserves. In the polar case of global monetarism, the world money stock drives the price level and national monetary policies merely allocate reserves.

The evidence cited above overwhelmingly confirms that movements in foreign-exchange reserves do not offset on a one-for-one basis changes in the domestic base (or vice versa), and it is clear that most countries experience fluctuations in price levels and interest rates relative to world averages, as well as an occasional deviation from full employment. Thus, the polar case of global monetarism may describe some long-run average, but it seems hardly relevant for economic policy.

Whitman discusses asset-market determination of the exchange rate, in the short run, as the flexible-rate dual to the monetary approach with fixed rates. Here the exchange rate is viewed as the relative price of national moneys, and as adjusting in the short run so that the existing stocks are willingly held. In the monetary approach, with fixed rates the balance between demand for and supply of money determines the official-settlements balance; with flexible rates it determines

[1] See Robert A. Mundell, "Capital Mobility and Stabilization Policy under Fixed and Flexible Exchange Rates," in Richard E. Caves and Harry G. Johnson, eds., *Readings in International Economics* (Homewood, Ill.: Irwin, 1968). For the comparison, see also William H. Branson, "Flow and Stock Equilibrium in a Traditional Macro Model," Working Paper G-74-02 (Princeton University, International Finance Section, May 1974).

the exchange rate. In both cases, the basic equilibrium condition is an asset- or stock-market equilibrium.

In the short run, the exchange rate is determined, along with interest rates, in the asset-equilibrium *LM* sector. This is a straightforward extension to the open economy of Tobin's general-equilibrium approach to monetary theory. In a simple case with two countries, each with an imperfectly substitutable bond and a money, asset-market equilibrium conditions determine values for two interest rates and the exchange rate.[2] An immediate implication is that, in the short run, exchange rates should exhibit the variability of stock-market prices. This is an insight of the asset-market approach that was missed by most early advocates of flexible exchange rates.

In the asset-market approach with flexible rates, the exchange rate is determined in the short run by requirements of asset-market equilibrium. The exchange rate then influences the current account with a lag. Since rates are flexible, the capital-account balance is the negative of the current account, so the current-account balance also is the rate of change of net foreign-asset holdings. Thus, the current-account balance feeds holdings of net foreign assets, moving the exchange rate. The system works as follows:

$$\begin{array}{c} \text{Asset} \\ \text{stocks} \end{array} \rightarrow \begin{pmatrix} r \\ e \end{pmatrix} \rightarrow \begin{array}{c} \text{Current} \\ \text{account} \end{array} = - \begin{array}{c} \text{Capital} \\ \text{account} \end{array}$$

Here *r* is the vector of interest rates and *e* is the vector of exchange rates. This system comes into full equilibrium (stationary or growing) when all stocks reach equilibrium values. The important aspect of the current account here is its role as the foreign net-worth account; it gives the rate of net foreign investment.[3] The consistency of this mechanism with long-run purchasing-power parity (PPP), can be illustrated as follows. If from an initial equilibrium, the home government starts running a budget deficit, increasing the rate of growth of supply of home-denominated assets (money *or* debt), the ex-

change rate rises. This stimulates net exports and aggregate demand, pulling up the price level. Eventually, the price increase brings the system back to PPP with a higher exchange rate. The analogy to the Tobin view of the relationship between equity prices and investment should be obvious.

The twist that the monetary-approach analysts such as Kouri and Mussa apply to this asset-equilibrium approach is to drop the securities market, or capital account, from the story. This is done either by making small-country assumptions that fix home interest rates, or by using a two-asset model so that the bond market can be dropped. The balance of payments then becomes a matter of exchange of money for goods, in which the exchange rate is determined *only* by the relative stocks (levels or growth rates) of money. In this special case, the asset-market view of exchange-rate determination collapses to simple consideration of relative money stocks, and money takes on a unique role among assets.

By discussing models without bonds as the initial case, Whitman's paper leaves the impression that the monetary approach and the asset-market approach are the same thing, except for technical details. In fact, the monetary approach is a special case of the asset-market approach, and the gap between the two is as wide as the theoretical distance from Yale to Chicago. The essential simultaneity of interest-rate and exchange-rate determination is clear in the Dornbusch paper on flexible exchange rates cited by Whitman (note 51).

In the flexible-rate case, the current-account balance is the rate of accumulation of net foreign assets by the *private* sector, and is part of the saving decision. This interpretation is clear in the asset-market view of exchange-rate determination. With fixed rates, the current-account balance is the *national* rate of accumulation of net foreign assets, with the intervention policy of the central bank determining, the public-private split. Controlled floating probably should be modeled in this manner.

The important insight here is that the natural separation in the balance-of-payments accounts is between the flow account—the current account—and the two stock accounts—the capital account and the official-settlements balance. The last two are in the *LM* or asset sector of a properly specified model of an open economy, and the first is in the *IS* or flow sector. The interaction over time is that the flows *are* the rates of change of the stocks. Thus, among all the balances, only the current-account balance (give

---

[2] For the analysis, see Lance Girton and Dale W. Henderson, "Central Bank Operations in Foreign and Domestic Assets under Fixed and Flexible Exchange Rates" (Board of Governors of the Federal Reserve System, August 26, 1974; processed).

[3] Charles P. Kindleberger emphasizes this role of the current-account balance in "Measuring Equilibrium in the Balance of Payments," *Journal of Political Economy*, vol. 77 (November/December 1969), pp. 873–91.

or take unilateral transfers and SDR allocations) has an unambiguous interpretation: it is the rate of accumulation of net foreign assets.

The monetary approach makes the official-settlements balance the center of analysis only by lumping together the capital account and current account, or by ignoring the capital account. In doing so, it assumes a uniqueness of money in the spectrum of assets that is convenient for pedagogy and illuminating for analysis, but probably not realistic. (Since private accumulation of foreign money is a capital-account term, the official-settlements balance cannot technically summarize money transactions.) Correct integration of the external accounts into models of domestic economies probably requires separation of the current account, rather than the money account, from the rest.

---

35. THE PRESENTATION OF THE BALANCE OF PAYMENTS*

Robert M. Stern

Thanks to the efforts of the Advisory Committee[1] we now have a revised format for presenting the balance-of-payments statistics of the United States that more closely approximates the realities of managed floating than did the former presentation, which was devised for pegged exchange rates. In the discussion that follows, I shall first summarize what the committee accomplished and then consider some issues of balance-of-payments analysis ·and policy suggested by

---

* Reprinted from Stern et al., *The Presentation of the U.S. Balance of Payments: A Symposium*, Essays in International Finance, No. 123, August 1977. Copyright © 1977. Reprinted by permission of the International Finance Section of Princeton University and the author. Robert M. Stern is Professor of Economics, The University of Michigan.

[1] In response to the recommendations of the Advisory Committee on the Presentation of Balance of Payments Statistics, a revised format for presenting the official U.S. balance-of-payments statistics was adopted in mid-1976. The Advisory Committee, which consisted of nine experts from outside government, was appointed by the president under legislative authority designed to improve official statistical compilation, analysis, and reporting. The Advisory Committee was instructed to recommend to the U.S. Office of Management and Budget changes in balance-of-payments presentation in the light of the change in the international monetary system in early 1973 from pegged exchange rates to managed floating. The full report of the Advisory Committee was published in the *Statistical Reporter* (June 1976) and also in the U.S. Department of Commerce, *Survey of Current Business* (June 1976). Prior to this most recent change, an outside group of experts had last reviewed the U.S. official balance-of-payments presentation in 1965.

This paper was written as part of a symposium designed to evaluate the new balance-of-payments presentation. All page references to the Advisory Committee's report are from the *Statistical Reporter*.

the new presentation. I examine briefly thereafter the problems of international comparability and historical continuity of balance-of-payments statistics.

THE NEW FORMAT

For the benefit of the reader, the main features of the new format are summarized in Table 1 for calendar 1975. The line numbers refer to the more detailed table that was first published in revised form in the June 1976 issue of the *Survey of Current Business*. Comparable line numbers are also given for the old format, which was last published in the *Survey* for March 1976. It is evident that the new format is essentially a tabular listing of credits and debits with respect to goods, services, unilateral transfers, U.S. claims on and liabilities to foreigners, and a statistical discrepancy for unrecorded transactions that is required to equate total credits and debits. The line concordances between the new and old formats are unambiguous except for foreign official and other foreign assets in the United States. In the former case, the new format differentiates foreign official purchases of U.S. Treasury securities from purchases of securities issued by other U.S. government agencies. In the latter case, it differentiates between Treasury securities and other liabilities reported by U.S. banks.

The new presentation makes life easier by recognizing that, in principle, there can be no imbalances of payments under floating exchange rates. Users of the statistics and students will certainly be grateful for the changes, since they no longer need be concerned about the intricacies of defining and interpreting the various overall

Table 1:   Summary of U.S. International Transactions for 1975 ($ billions)

New Format: Line		Old Format: Line	Credits (+)	Debits (−)
1	Exports of goods and services	1	148.4	
2	Merchandise, excluding military	2	107.1	
3–13	Services and other, including military	3–13	41.3	
14	Transfers under U.S. military grant programs	14	1.7	
15	Imports of goods and services	15		−132.1
16	Merchandise, excluding military	16		−98.2
17–27	Services and other, including military	17–27		−33.9
28	Transfers under U.S. military grant programs	28		−1.7
29	Unilateral transfers (excluding military)	29		−4.6
30	U.S. Government grants	30		−2.9
31	U.S. Government pensions and other transfers	31		−0.8
32	Private remittances and other transfers	32		−0.9
33	U.S. assets abroad, net (increase/capital outflow(−))	33,38,58		−31.1
34–38	U.S. official reserve assets, net	58–61		−0.6
39–42	U.S. Government assets, other, net	34–37		−3.5
43	U.S. private assets, net	38		−27.1
44	Direct investment abroad	39		−6.3
45	Foreign securities	40		−6.2
	Nonbank claims			
46	Long-term	44		−0.4
47	Short-term	45,46		−0.9
	Bank claims			
48	Long-term	41		−2.4
49	Short-term	42,43		−10.9
50	Foreign assets in the United States, net (increase/capital inflow (+))	47	14.9	
51–57	Foreign official assets in the United States, net	48,50,55–57	6.3	
58	Other foreign assets in the United States, net		8.5	
59	Direct investments in the United States	49	2.4	
60–61	U.S. Treasury and other U.S. securities	48,50,54	5.4	
	Nonbank liabilities			
62	Long-term	51	0.3	
63	Short-term	52		−0.2
	Bank liabilities			
64	Long-term	53		−0.4
65	Short-term	54	1.0	
66	Allocation of special drawing rights	63		
67	Statistical discrepancy	64	4.6	
	Memoranda:			
68	Balance on merchandise trade (lines 2 and 16)			8.9
69	Balance on goods and services (lines 1 and 15)*			16.3
70	Balance on goods, services, and remittances (lines 69, 31, and 32)			14.6
71	Balance on current account (lines 69 and 29)†			11.7
	Transactions in official reserve assets:			
72	Increase (−) in U.S. official reserve assets (line 34)			−0.6
73	Increase (+) in foreign official assets in U.S. (line 51 less line 55)			4.6

* Conceptually equal to net exports in the U.S. national income and product accounts.
† Conceptually equal to net foreign investment in the U.S. national income and product accounts.
Source: Adapted from "Table 1–U.S. International Transactions," *Survey of Current Business,* 56 (June 1976), pp. 32–33. The old format last appeared in the March 1976 *Survey.*

balances—the current and long-term capital, net liquidity, and official reserve transactions (ORT) —that were formerly published. Gone also is the distinction in the capital account between liquid and nonliquid transactions, and an attempt is now made to provide a more detailed and symmetrical treatment according to the type of transactor instead of the type of asset or liability.

Partial balances are shown as memoranda entries (lines 68–71) rather than being recorded in the table itself. The Advisory Committee actually recommended only the inclusion of the balance on goods and services and the balance on current account, since these balances have been identified traditionally and also are component entries in the national income and product accounts (with adjustments for special military transactions and interest-income payments to foreigners by the U.S. government). In their consideration of the Advisory Committee's recommendation, the Interagency Committee on Balance of Payments Statistics and the Office of Management and Budget decided that there was some merit in including as well the merchandise trade balance (line 68) and the balance on goods, services, and remittances (GSR) (line 70). The justification for including the trade balance was that it was conceptually clear and not seriously subject to misinterpretation by the public. In my view, however, the recording of the trade balance is a needless concession to the past and may quite possibly be misinterpreted. As I point out below, it would be more in keeping with the spirit of the new format to give publicity to exchange-rate changes rather than to any of the partial balances. Recording the balance on GSR was rationalized on the grounds that its use has the effect of including U.S. government grants (line 30) together with all other official and all private capital (lines 33–49) and thus supposedly furnishes a better measure than the balance on current account of the financing element in international transactions, especially for developing countries. Again, this is a rather outmoded conception because it is premised on the need to finance a payments imbalance and thus does not make allowance for the effects of floating.

The Advisory Committee apparently had the most difficulty in agreeing on whether to continue reporting the balance on ORT.[2] Some members felt that it should be continued because it reflected official intervention in the foreign-exchange market, provided an indication of the possible impact on the U.S. monetary base, and met the need for a stable, overall point of reference for the description and analysis of the balance of payments. Those opposed to its continuation argued that the balance on ORT was much less relevant in a system of discretionary

official intervention and was in any case an imperfect measure of such intervention, especially since it included changes in the international financial portfolios of the OPEC countries. Moreover, the balance on ORT was not coincident with a change in the U.S. monetary base to the extent that foreign official institutions dealt in U.S. Treasury obligations and interest-bearing bank deposits.[3] In the final analysis, the drawbacks of presenting the balance on ORT or any other overall balances were judged by the Advisory Committee to outweigh the advantages. However, a compromise was reached by including the changes in U.S. and foreign official reserve assets as memoranda items (lines 72–73) and by quarterly publication in the *Survey of Current Business* of a table recording selected transactions with official agencies.

ANALYZING THE BALANCE OF PAYMENTS

Under conditions of floating, the exchange rate itself becomes the focus in analyzing the balance of payments. Movements in the exchange rate will depend upon demand and supply conditions in the foreign-exchange market. These, in turn, are derived from the underlying changes in incomes, relative prices, rates of interest and profitability, and expectations that manifest themselves in exports and imports of goods and services and international capital movements. Intervention by the authorities in the foreign-exchange market will be reflected in variations in their international reserve assets and liabilities. The question then is how much information on these matters is provided in the revised presentation of balance-of-payments statistics.

Changes in exchange rates for the U.S. dollar are prominently displayed graphically and in tabular form in the official reports on U.S. international transactions published quarterly in the *Survey of Current Business*. The data are given in the form of indexes of the foreign-currency price of the U.S. dollar on a trade-weighted basis against 22 and 10 currencies and against the currencies of 8 major industrialized countries individually. Data on U.S. international trans-

---

[2] The previous committee on balance-of-payments statistics recommended in 1965 that the main balance-of-payments table be organized to focus on the balance on ORT. This balance supposedly reflected the extent of official intervention by other countries in foreign exchange markets for the purpose of keeping their exchange rates pegged within narrow limits according to the rules of the Bretton Woods (IMF) Agreement.

[3] The U.S. monetary base will be directly reduced by an ORT deficit when a foreign central bank acquires dollars through exchange-market intervention and then sells those dollars to the Fed in exchange for international reserve assets, or when the foreign central bank increases its dollar balances with the Fed. When foreign central banks buy U.S. Treasury bills or acquire interest-bearing bank deposits, the U.S. monetary base is unaffected.

actions by geographic area are also published in the *Survey of Current Business,* in the same format as Table 1. It is thus possible, using the regularly published data, to identify in retrospect the changes in exchange rates and the associated changes in international trade and capital movements, both in the aggregate and with respect to the major countries and regions.

Questions do arise concerning the way in which the foregoing information should be released to the media, what the media will report to the public, and what the public may in turn conclude from the media report. The Advisory Committee was clear in its recommendation (p. 231) that the first news release, available six weeks after the close of a quarter, should stress the principal developments that have occurred. It is my impression, however, based on admittedly casual evidence, that the data on U.S. merchandise trade and changes in the trade balance receive undue attention in the press. The public may well conclude that a trade deficit is bad and a surplus is good without really understanding how incomplete and possibly incorrect such a view may be in terms of the impacts on U.S. employment and output. It would be preferable instead to direct public attention to the current- and capital-account changes and especially to the changes that have taken place in the exchange rates for the U.S. dollar vis-à-vis the other major currencies.

Exchange-rate changes in themselves do not reveal everything that has happened, of course, especially insofar as exchange-market intervention may have been important. There is some aggregative information given in the quarterly reports in the *Survey of Current Business* relating to U.S. and foreign official reserve changes and the use of swap arrangements. But it is difficult to determine the extent and impact of intervention from these data. Here the analyst must rely particularly on the periodic reports of Treasury and Federal Reserve foreign-exchange operations published in the *Federal Reserve Bulletin.* But even these reports may be too highly aggregative, and, what is more important, they do not provide information on the intervention that foreign central banks undertake on their own. It is difficult, therefore, to assess the actual extent to which floating has been managed.

Analysts of the official balance-of-payment statistics may also feel hampered by the lack of other supporting detail, particularly with respect to international financial capital movements. The Advisory Committee recommended discontinuance of the distinction between liquid and non-liquid categories of asset claims and of liabilities to foreigners. A distinction is now made with respect to the short-term and long-term characteristics of nonbank and bank claims and liabilities. The Advisory Committee was aware that the classification according to term-to-maturity was rather arbitrary and therefore did not necessarily reflect accurately the economic motivations and behavior of the relevant transactors. Mention was made (pp. 227–28) of the possibility of using bank or bank-reported transactions as a separate classification in the table in order to facilitate analysis of the effects of these transactions on exchange rates. Unfortunately, this classification could not be implemented because of deficiencies in the method of data collection. It is to be hoped that these and other deficiencies can be corrected to permit more effective analysis than is presently possible of the international financial behavior of the important bank, nonbank, and official transactors.

MAINTENANCE OF ANALYTICAL NEUTRALITY

Granting that there will always be deficiencies in data collection, it is of interest to consider broadly the types of supporting data investigators might find useful for analytical purposes. In the United States and elsewhere, for example, there is a significant and growing interest in the monetary approach to the balance of payments and exchange-rate determination. In this connection, some consideration might have been given to including a measure of the effect on the monetary base of changes in U.S. and foreign official reserves. The Advisory Committee was apparently reluctant to make this and similar recommendations because (p. 224) ". . . the maintenance of analytical neutrality was viewed as very important, both for its own sake and for the purpose of maintaining a high degree of credibility for Federal statistics. The statistics should be presented in a way that does not imply unnecessary judgments about economic behavior or support for any particular economic theory."

Later, in discussing the drawbacks of the balance on ORT, the Advisory Committee pointed out (p. 233) that there were now infrequent and limited effects on the U.S. money supply resulting from the acquisition or sale of dollars by foreign central banks in exchange for reserve assets or from changes in official dollar balances held with Federal Reserve banks. Moreover, it stated that even if the U.S. monetary base were affected by these transactions, the Federal Reserve System could sterilize the impact through open-market operations. Whether or not sterilization can be successful is of course a central issue in the monetary approach to the balance of payments. It thus appears that the Advisory Committee was not neutral in this instance and that an empirical judgment was being made that the monetary effects of reserve changes were not of much consequence in the United States.

To gain further insight into this issue, we should note that the effect on the monetary base of changes in the U.S. balance of payments is calculated and reported by the Federal Reserve Bank of St. Louis in its quarterly *U.S. International Transactions and Currency Review*. It is noteworthy that the relevant data are not provided in the *Survey of Current Business* tables, but rather are taken from the *Federal Reserve Bulletin*. Beginning with the figure for "convertible foreign currencies" from the table on U.S. reserve assets (Table 3.12, p. A55 of the January 1977 issue of the *Federal Reserve Bulletin*), the Federal Reserve Bank of St. Louis adds any change in the "Special Drawing Rights certificate account" and deducts "deposits other than member bank reserves with Federal Reserve Banks-foreign" (Table 1.11, p. A4). End-of-period data are taken for each quarter. These data are seasonally adjusted, and the final figures for the categories mentioned above are first differences of the adjusted data.

In an article by Donald S. Kemp ("U.S. International Trade and Financial Developments in 1976," *Review of the Federal Reserve Bank of St. Louis*, December 1976, p. 9), the monetary-base effect for 1975-I to 1976-III was reported as follows (in millions of dollars):

1975		1976	
I	42	I	580
II	−12	II	560
III	141	III	−381
IV	12		

Compared with the overall changes in the monetary base, the effects from III/75 to II/76 were (p. 10) 6.6, 0.6, 34.6, and 21.6 percent of the total increase in the monetary base, while in III/76 there was a negative impact on the base amounting to 19.4 percent of the total change. Without more information regarding the various influences on the monetary base, it is by no means clear how the foregoing calculations should be interpreted. Moreover, we do not know to what extent, if any, the foreign-sector impacts on the monetary base were taken explicitly into account by Federal Reserve officials in the implementation of U.S. monetary policy. The fact remains, however, that the analyst has to go to some length just to perform the necessary calculation. In addition, while the monetary-base effect is perceived to be small and of limited importance in the U.S., this is not necessarily the case in other countries. To the extent that the revised presentation of the U.S. balance-of-payments statistics provides a model for other governments to follow, the official presentation of the monetary-base effect might therefore be worthwhile, as will be noted again below.

The monetary-base effect is only one example of supporting information that some investigators might find useful. Similar remarks could be made about data on prices, interest rates, and other phenomena. If one wishes to probe deeply into the behavior of the foreign sector in the United States and elsewhere, the official balance-of-payments statistics, supporting tables, and textual discussion furnish only the starting point. A variety of other source materials will have to be consulted, and it is by no means clear even to the seasoned investigator where to begin and how reliable and comprehensive the available data may be.

The Advisory Committee may have considered it beyond their mandate to ask how useful the revised presentation of balance-of-payments statistics might be for analytical purposes. In my view, while the revisions in themselves are of great value, serious consideration should be given to the inclusion of even more supporting information. This would not necessarily have to be done in the individual quarterly reports in the *Survey of Current Business*. Rather, it might be possible to expand the annual *Survey* article that covers the entire calendar year. In this regard, some of the series for selected foreign countries currently reported by the Federal Reserve Bank of St. Louis in its *U.S. International Transactions and Currency Review* might be worth including. It would also be useful to include data in current and constant dollars for U.S. trade in total and for the major aggregates, plus some of the relevant information on the stocks of the important components of U.S. claims on and liabilities to foreigners. Judgment would obviously be required on exactly what supporting detail to include. But this should not be an overwhelming task, and it could be accomplished without taking sides on theoretical issues.

THE INTERNATIONAL COMPARABILITY OF THE BALANCE-OF-PAYMENTS PRESENTATION

One result of carrying out the recommendations of the Advisory Committee has been to increase the differences between the ways in which the United States and the rest of the world measure and interpret statistics on the balance of payments. For example, in Table 2, I have summarized the presentations of the U.S. balance of payments for 1975 prepared by the International Monetary Fund (IMF), Organization for Economic Cooperation and Development (OECD), and Bank for International Settlements (BIS).

It should be evident that all three presentations are based on the premise that there is an overall balance-of-payments surplus or deficit that has been financed in some manner. According to the IMF presentation, the United States experienced a deficit of $4.0 billion, which was financed by a net increase in liabilities to foreign official agencies. The OECD recorded a deficit of $2.5 billion for the balance on official settlements, which is more or less equivalent to the balance on ORT and is similar in concept to the IMF formulation. In contrast, the BIS recorded a surplus of $4.6 billion, which is the net difference between the increase in liabilities to foreign official agencies and the increase in the assets of commercial banks.

Even if we disregard the differences in the three presentations, none of them is appropriate for a world in which exchange rates are floating,

Table 2: Summary Presentations by International Organizations of the U.S. Balance of Payments for 1975 ($ billions)

IMF:		
Balance on:		
Trade	$9.0	
Service and private transfers	6.6	
Current account		$15.6
Capital-account balance*		−19.6
Total		− 4.0
Change in liabilities to foreign official agencies†		4.6
Balance financed by transactions in reserve assets (increase(−))		− 0.6
OECD:		
Balance on:		
Trade	9.0	
Services	7.5	
Goods and services		16.5
Private transfers, net	−1.0	
Official transfers, net	−3.6	− 4.6
Current balance		11.9
Long-term capital		−10.5
Basic balance		1.4
Nonmonetary short-term capital	−1.2	
Errors and omissions	4.6	3.4
Balance on nonmonetary transactions		4.8
Private monetary institutions' short-term capital		− 7.2
Balance on official settlements		− 2.5
Total liabilities to foreign national official agencies		3.1
Change in reserves (increase (−))		− 0.6
BIS:		
Current balance		11.9
Capital balance		− 7.1
Overall balance		4.8
Adjustments		− 0.1
Adjusted overall balance (= total external monetary movements)		4.6
Official assets, net		− 3.0
Commercial banks, net		7.6

* Equal to difference between the balance financed by transactions in reserve assets and the sum of the current-account balance and the change in liabilities to foreign official agencies.
† Includes the use of IMF credit and liabilities of the borrowing country that are presumably treated as reserve assets by the creditor country.
Sources: Adapted from IMF, *Annual Report 1976*, Washington, Sept. 19, 1976; OECD, *Economic Surveys: United States*, Paris, July 1976; and BIS, *Forty-Sixth Annual Report*, Basle, June 14, 1976.

albeit in managed form. The same would be true for the balance-of-payments presentations of most other countries, which continue to be premised upon the Bretton Woods concept of obligatory exchange-rate pegging within narrow limits. Thus, the rest of the world, by its continued reliance upon outmoded balance-of-payments concepts, is apparently out of step with the United States. It is difficult to derive any clear interpretation of the overall balances that continue to be recorded and publicized without knowing the actual movement of a country's exchange rate and the volume of official intervention. Perhaps the revised presentation of U.S. international transactions and continuing improvements in supporting data will provide an incentive for international organizations and national governments to institute comparable changes that are more in tune with the realities of present-day foreign-exchange markets.

THE PROBLEM OF HISTORICAL CONTINUITY

Now that changes have been made in the presentation of the U.S. balance-of-payments statistics, one must ask whether and how to maintain continuity with earlier modes of presentation. What must be emphasized here, as the Advisory Committee pointed out (pp. 243–44), is that the presentation of data should be in accord with the institutional arrangements, analytical issues, and policy objectives that are most relevant for the international monetary circumstances at hand. Since the circumstances change over time, it will not be possible to maintain strict continuity in the measurement and interpretation of the data.

In this connection, it is noteworthy that the new presentation that was first reported in the June 1976 *Survey of Current Business* was extended backward on an annual basis to 1960 and on a quarterly basis to 1966. The result has been to expunge the various overall balances and some of the partial balances that were formerly reported. While these balances may have had their limitations, they nevertheless served some function in balance-of-payments analysis and policy in the past. It does not seem appropriate, therefore, to recast the official balance-of-payments statistics prior to 1971. To do so recalls the point made some years ago by Fritz Machlup ("The Mysterious Numbers Game

of Balance-of-Payments Statistics," in *International Payments, Debts, and Gold,* New York, Scribner, 1964, p. 145) that the continued reorganization and reinterpretation of U.S. balance-of-payments statistics in the course of about a decade turned a surplus of over $5.0 billion for calendar year 1951 into a deficit of about $1.0 billion.

To avoid a similar occurrence, it would be desirable to include a footnote in the current presentation of the data in the *Survey of Current Business* to indicate the time period for which this presentation is most relevant and to warn the reader of noncomparabilities with earlier data due to the changes that have occurred in the international monetary system. By the same token, historical statistics of U.S. international transactions should include explanatory footnotes calling attention to the particular international monetary circumstances of the period covered.

CONCLUSION

Now that the Advisory Committee's recommendations on balance-of-payments presentation have been implemented, more attention should be given to the development and periodic publication of additional supporting data that will aid in the analysis of changes in exchange rates and in the components of the current and capital accounts. It would be desirable, furthermore, for the major international organizations and national governments to reorganize their balance-of-payments presentations and analyses to accord more closely with the realities of floating exchange rates.

How long the revised presentation of U.S. balance-of-payments statistics will remain useful depends, of course, on whether and the extent to which floating is continued. Perhaps at some future time, if rates of change in inflation and productivity in the major industrialized countries are brought into closer harmony, it might be possible to reinstitute some type of obligatory exchange-rate pegging. Under such circumstances, something like the balance on ORT could be reviewed as an approximation of the official intervention required to keep exchange rates within specified limits. Thus, if international monetary circumstances change, it will be necessary to revise the format of the balance-of-payments presentation once again.

Chapter

7

COORDINATION OF ECONOMIC POLICY

Various aspects of macroeconomic policy have been dealt with in the last three chapters. Chapter 4 contains a collection of readings relating to fiscal policy, while Chapter 5 provides a corresponding treatment of monetary policy. The readings on the balance of payments and the international monetary system in Chapter 6 contain some references to problems of the conduct of fiscal and monetary policy in an open economy—that is, an economy having trade relations with other economies.

Fiscal policy affects the flow of purchasing power and aggregate demand by altering the relation between government spending and tax collections. Monetary policy also affects aggregate demand by altering the terms on which credit can be obtained to finance certain types of spending and by changing the relationships among the yields available on financial and real assets. Thus aggregate demand can be influenced through the use of either fiscal or monetary policy. Indeed, it may be possible to achieve the same level of aggregate demand with a variety of combinations of fiscal and monetary policy. But these different combinations may have quite different effects on other aspects of the economy's performance—on its rate of long-run growth, on its balance-of-payments position, and so on.

Those responsible for formulating economic policy commonly have a number of goals. In particular, they will usually want to achieve a low level of unemployment, reasonable stability of the general price level, a suitable rate of long-term growth, a viable balance-of-payments position, and an acceptable allocation of resources between the public and private sectors of the economy.

RELATIONS BETWEEN POLICY GOALS AND POLICY INSTRUMENTS

In some cases, if there are several instruments of policy and several goals to be achieved, it may be possible to make a combination of changes in the instruments such that all of the goals are attained. Perhaps the best way to demonstrate this possibility is by means of a relatively simple illustration.

Illustrative Example

Suppose that the economy is described by the following model:

$$C = C_o + cY_d \tag{7.1}$$
$$Y_d = Y - T \tag{7.2}$$
$$T = T^* + xY \tag{7.3}$$
$$I = I_o + iY_d - vr \tag{7.4}$$
$$G = G^* \tag{7.5}$$
$$Y = C + I + G \tag{7.6}$$
$$M_d = M_o + kY - mr \tag{7.7}$$
$$M_s = M^* \tag{7.8}$$
$$M_s = M_d \tag{7.9}$$

Here C is consumption expenditure by households, Y_d is disposable income (i.e., income after taxes), Y is gross national product, T is total tax collections (net of transfer payments, which may be regarded as negative taxes), I is investment expenditure, r is the interest rate, G is government purchases of goods and services, M_d is the quantity of money demanded, and M_s is the money supply. The government is assumed to have three instruments, the values of which it can adjust to regulate the economy: the level of taxes (designated by T^*), the level of government purchases of goods and services (G^*), and the size of the money supply (M^*).

This model is very similar to Model III employed in the introduction to Chapter 1 (pages 7–14). Indeed the only significant difference is that in that model investment was assumed to depend only on the interest rate, whereas in the present model investment depends not only on the interest rate but on disposable income. The coefficients used here are accordingly designated in the same way as in the earlier model, except that we now have one additional coefficient, i, the marginal propensity to invest out of disposable income.

Let us suppose that those responsible for economic policy in this economy have three objectives. First, they want to achieve a level of GNP that is consistent with full employment. Second, they want to achieve a target level of investment that will increase the stock of capital at a rate consistent with the desired long-run growth of productive capacity. Third, they want to achieve a target level of government expenditures that will provide the appropriate allocation of resources between the private and public sectors of the economy. That is, they have three goals which can, for our present purposes, be expressed as target values of Y, I, and G. Let us consider how they might proceed—on the assumption that they had complete knowledge of the structure of the economy—to achieve their three goals.

First, we can solve equations (7.1) through (7.9) for Y as a function of the policy instruments G^*, T^*, and M^*. We begin by substituting (7.2) and (7.3) into (7.1), obtaining

$$C = C_o - cT^* + c(1 - x)Y. \tag{7.10}$$

Substituting (7.2) and (7.3) into (7.4) yields

$$I = I_o - iT^* + i(1 - x)Y - vr. \tag{7.11}$$

Now substituting (7.5), (7.10), and (7.11) into (7.6), we obtain

$$Y = C_o + I_o - (c + i)T^* + (c + i)(1 - x)Y - vr + G^*. \qquad (7.12)$$

This equation, which contains only two variables, Y and r, is the IS curve for this economy.

Next we substitute (7.8) and (7.9) into (7.7) and solve for r, a process which yields the equation

$$r = \frac{1}{m}(M_o - M^*) + \frac{k}{m}Y. \qquad (7.13)$$

This is the equation of the LM curve of the economy. Substituting (7.13) for r in (7.12) and solving for Y, we obtain

$$Y = \frac{1}{1 - (c + i)(1 - x) + \dfrac{vk}{m}}\left[C_o + I_o - \frac{v}{m}M_o - (c + i)T^* + \frac{v}{m}M^* + G^*\right].$$

$$(7.14)$$

The reader will note that this is the same as equation (3.15) in the introduction to Chapter 1, except for the presence of the coefficient i, the marginal propensity to invest out of disposable income.

If C_o, I_o, and M_o are held constant while incremental changes are made in T^*, M^*, and G^*, the change in Y is given by

$$\Delta Y = \frac{1}{1 - (c + i)(1 - x) + \dfrac{vk}{m}}\left[-(c + i)\Delta T^* + \frac{v}{m}\Delta M^* + \Delta G^*\right]. \qquad (7.15)$$

This equation tells us how changes in the level of taxes (ΔT^*), changes in the stock of money (ΔM^*), and changes in government purchases of goods and services (ΔG^*) will affect income.

Next we want to find out how changes in the policy instruments (T^*, M^*, and G^*) will affect investment, since one of the objectives of policy is assumed to be the achievement of a target level of investment. Substituting (7.14) for Y and (7.13) for r in (7.11), we obtain (after considerable algebraic manipulation)

$$\Delta I = \frac{1}{1 - c(1 - x) = \dfrac{vk}{m}}\left[\left(\frac{vkc}{m} - i\right)\Delta T^* + \left(\frac{v}{m}[1 - c(1 - x)]\right)\Delta M^*\right.$$
$$\left. + \left[i(1 - x) - \frac{vk}{m}\right]\Delta G^*\right]. \qquad (7.16)$$

This equation tells us how changes in taxes (ΔT^*), changes in the stock of money (ΔM^*), and changes in government purchases of goods and services (ΔG^*) affect investment.

The third objective of policy, as indicated above, is the achievement of a target level of government purchases of goods and services (G). Since government purchases is itself an exogenous variable, we have the relation derived from (7.5),

$$\Delta G = \Delta G^*. \qquad (7.17)$$

That is, the level of government purchases is not affected by changes in the level of taxes (T^*) or changes in the stock of money (M^*). Thus the relation between government purchases as a target (G) and government purchases as a policy instrument (G^*) is the simple one indicated by (7.17).

At this point it will be useful to summarize our results. The effects of changes in the three instruments, T^*, M^*, and G^*, on the three targets, Y, I, and G, are brought together in Table 1. The entries in this table are taken from equations (7.15), (7.16), and (7.17).

Table 1: Effects of Instruments on the Selected Targets

Targets	Effects Produced by Instruments		
	ΔT^*	ΔM^*	ΔG^*
ΔY	$\dfrac{-(c+i)}{1-(c+i)(1-x)+\frac{vk}{m}}$	$\dfrac{v/m}{1-(c+i)(1-x)+\frac{vk}{m}}$	$\dfrac{1}{1-(c+i)(1-x)+\frac{vk}{m}}$
ΔI	$\dfrac{vkc/m - i}{1-(c+i)(1-x)+\frac{vk}{m}}$	$\dfrac{(v/m)[1-c(1-x)]}{1-(c+i)(1-x)+\frac{vk}{m}}$	$\dfrac{i(1-x)-vk/m}{1-(c+i)(1-x)+\frac{vk}{m}}$
ΔG	0	0	1

The best way to proceed from here is to use a numerical example. Suppose that the equations are as follows:

$$C = 110 + .75Y_d$$
$$Y_d = Y - T$$
$$T = -80 + .20Y$$
$$I = 152 + .10Y_d - 4r$$
$$G = 330$$
$$Y = C + I + G$$
$$M_d = 20 + .25Y - 10r$$
$$M_s = 470$$
$$M_d = M_s$$

This is the model used above with the following parameters: $c = .75$, $x = .20$, $i = .10$, $v = 4$, $k = .25$, $m = 10$, $C_o = 110$, $I_o = 152$, and $M_o = 20$. The values of the policy instruments are $T^* = -80$, $M^* = 470$, and $G^* = 330$. The student can verify that if these values are substituted into equation (7.14), they yield a value of \$2,000 billion for equilibrium income. The corresponding values of all the variables are given in the "Original Equilibrium" column of Table 2.

Suppose now that those responsible for economic policy are not satisfied

Table 2: Numerical Example of Use of Three Instruments to Achieve Three Targets (in \$ billions)

	Original Equilibrium	New Equilibrium	Change
Gross national product (Y)	\$2,000	\$2,100	+100
Consumption (C)	1,370	1,436	+ 66
Investment (I)	300	314	+ 14
Government purchases (G)	330	350	+ 20
Taxes (T)	320	332	+ 12
Disposable income (Y_d)	1,680	1,768	+ 88
Saving $(Y_d - C)$	310	332	+ 22
Government deficit $(G - T)$	10	18	+ 8
Money stock (M)	470	508	+ 38
Tax intercept (T^*)	-80	-88	- 8
Interest rate (r)	5%	3.7%	- 1.3%

with the situation. After careful study, they conclude that GNP should be increased by 100 in order to achieve full employment, investment should be increased by 14 in the interest of achieving the desired rate of long-term growth, and government purchases of goods and services should be increased by 20 in order to arrive at a suitable allocation of resources between the private and public sectors. That is, the policy targets, expressed as increments from present levels, are: $\Delta Y = 100$, $\Delta I = 14$, and $\Delta G = 20$. The problem is to find the combination of incremental adjustments, ΔT^*, ΔM^*, and ΔG^*, in the policy instruments that will achieve the three targets.

As a first step, let us find the values of the expressions given in Table 1. Substituting the numerical values of the parameters into these expressions, we obtain the following results:

	Effects Produced by Instruments		
Targets	ΔT^*	ΔM^*	ΔG^*
ΔY	$-\dfrac{85}{42}$	$\dfrac{20}{21}$	$\dfrac{50}{21}$
ΔI	$-\dfrac{5}{84}$	$\dfrac{8}{21}$	$-\dfrac{1}{21}$
ΔG	0	0	1

Using this table of coefficients, we can write down the following set of equations:

$$\Delta Y = -\frac{85}{42}\,\Delta T^* + \frac{20}{21}\,\Delta M^* + \frac{50}{21}\,\Delta G^*$$

$$\Delta I = -\frac{5}{84}\,\Delta T^* + \frac{8}{21}\,\Delta M^* - \frac{1}{21}\,\Delta G^*$$

$$\Delta G = \Delta G^*$$

We are given the values of the targets—that is, we know that $\Delta Y = 100$, $\Delta I = 14$, and $\Delta G = 20$. We can therefore write:

$$100 = -\frac{85}{42}\,\Delta T^* + \frac{20}{21}\,\Delta M^* + \frac{50}{21}\,\Delta G^*$$

$$14 = -\frac{5}{84}\,\Delta T^* + \frac{8}{21}\,\Delta M^* - \frac{1}{21}\,\Delta G^*$$

$$20 = \Delta G^*$$

Substituting the value $\Delta G^* = 20$ from the third equation into the first two equations, and multiplying the first equation through by 42 and the second equation through by 84 to get rid of the fractions, we obtain the two equations:

$$-85\Delta T^* + 40\Delta M^* = 2{,}200$$
$$-5\Delta T^* + 32\Delta M^* = 1{,}256.$$

Solving these two equations simultaneously, we obtain the values $\Delta T^* = -8$ and $\Delta M^* = 38$. Thus we find that in order to increase GNP (Y) by 100, increase investment (I) by 14, and increase the portion of GNP allocated to the public sector (G) by 20, it is necessary to make the following three adjustments in the policy instruments: increase the stock of money (M^*) by 38, lower the level of the tax function (T^*) by 8, and increase government purchases of goods and services (G^*) by 20. The position of the economy after these adjustments have been made is shown in the "New Equilibrium" column of Table 2. The student should verify the entries in this column by calculating GNP using equation (7.14) with the new values for T^*, M^*, and G^* and then computing the new values of the remaining variables through the use of the other equations.

For the most part, in the discussions of monetary and fiscal policy in the earlier chapters of this book, we have started with the policy instruments and attempted to discuss their impact on income, employment, and other relevant economic variables. That is, the policy instruments were viewed as the independent variables and the various measures of performance of the economy were viewed as the dependent variables whose values were changed as a result of alterations in the policy instruments. It should be noted that in the above exercise this relationship was reversed. We started with the changes in the performance variables (in this case Y, I, and G) that we desired to see take place and calculated the changes in the policy instruments (T^*, M^*, and G^*) that would be required to produce these results. That is, in this exercise the targets (performance variables) were treated as the independent variables and the policy instruments as the dependent variables.

Need for Independence of Instruments

In the above illustration we had three policy instruments, and this enabled us to hit three policy targets at the same time. This suggests the general rule that if we have n policy instruments, we will be able to achieve n policy goals simultaneously. This generalization is, in principle, correct with one major qualification: the policy instruments must be *independent* in their effects on the target variables. The problem that arises if the instruments are not independent may be illustrated by means of a simple example.

Suppose our two instruments are open market operations—i.e., the change (ΔR^*) in the central bank's holdings of government securities—and changes (Δr_d^*) in the central bank's discount rate. Assume that the two targets are a desired change in GNP (ΔY) and a desired change in investment expenditures (ΔI). Finally, assume that the following relationships hold: an open market purchase of $1 billion will increase GNP by $4 billion and will increase investment by $2 billion, while an increase of 1 percentage point in the discount rate will reduce GNP by $2 billion and reduce investment by $1 billion. Thus we may write the following two equations to show the effects on Y and I of making simultaneous adjustments in R^* and r_d^*:

$$\Delta Y = 4\Delta R^* - 2\Delta r_d^*$$
$$\Delta I = 2\Delta R^* - \Delta r_d^*$$

Suppose now that we decide we would like to increase GNP by $10 billion and increase investment by $2 billion. This would require the solution for ΔR^* and Δr_d^* of the two equations:

$$10 = 4\Delta R^* - 2\Delta r_d^*$$
$$2 = 2\Delta R^* - \Delta r_d^*$$

On a moment's reflection, it is apparent that this is an insoluble problem. If we multiply the second equation by 2 we obtain $4 = 4\Delta R^* - 2\Delta r_d^*$; obviously $4\Delta R^* - 2\Delta r_d^*$ cannot simultaneously be equal to 10 and equal to 4. The two equations are inconsistent, and no solution exists. There is an infinite number of combinations of open market operations and discount rate adjustments that will satisfy the first equation. For example, income can be increased by $10 billion by either (*a*) open market purchases of $2 billion combined with a discount rate reduction of 1 percentage point, or (*b*) open market purchases of $4 billion combined with a discount rate increase of 3 percentage points. But by reference to the equation $\Delta I = 2\Delta R^* - \Delta r_d{}^*$, it is apparent that either of these policy adjustments will increase investment by $5 billion. Indeed, any policy adjustment that raises income by $10 billion will also increase investment by $5 billion. In this case the two policy instruments are perfect substitutes for each other, at least insofar as these two goals are concerned. That is, an open market purchase of $1 billion has exactly the same effects as a reduction of 2 percentage points in the discount rate. Thus, the GNP and investment goals referred to about cannot be achieved simultaneously by using these two instruments. Indeed, for all practical purposes, there is only one policy instrument rather than two.

The need for policy instruments to be independent is especially important to bear in mind in connection with monetary policy. It is often said that the Federal Reserve has three instruments of general monetary control: open market operations, changes in the discount rate, and changes in reserve requirements. This might seem to suggest that the Federal Reserve alone could select three goals—for example, full employment, price stability, and a suitable rate of long-term growth—and achieve all three simultaneously by appropriate adjustments in its three instruments. The fact is, however, that the three instruments—at least given the present state of knowledge—are not independent insofar as their effects on the major goals of economic policy are concerned.[1] Their effects are not identical, but we do not yet understand the differences very well, and, in any case, their differential effects on the major goals of policy are probably not great enough to be very significant. By sophisticated adjustments of *both* monetary and fiscal policy instruments, it may be possible to achieve several goals simultaneously; however, such results can hardly be achieved by monetary policy alone.

A special problem relating to the independence of the instruments of monetary and fiscal policy appears to exist with respect to the goals of high employment and price stability. It appears that the causal relationships can be described approximately as follows: (1) The level of aggregate demand in relation to productive capacity determines the level of employment (and unemployment), and (2) the level of unemployment determines the rates of change of wages and prices through a Phillips curve type of relationship, as discussed in the articles by Tobin, Humphrey, and Solow reprinted in Chapter 1. Thus, monetary and fiscal policy, both of which operate on aggregate demand, are not capable of exerting independent effects on the rate of unemployment and the rate of inflation. That is, we cannot achieve the two goals of full employment and price stability by using fiscal and monetary policy instruments only.

It is true, of course, that the chain of causation is not quite as simple as that suggested in the previous paragraph and that monetary and fiscal policy may in fact be able to exert some independent effects on employment and prices. A policy mix involving relatively easy money may stimulate capital accumulation, thereby accelerating the growth of labor productivity. If the faster

---

[1] See W. L. Smith, "The Instruments of General Monetary Control," *National Banking Review*, vol. I (September 1963), pp. 47–76, reprinted in Chapter 3 of this book (reading 12), pp. 190–212 above.

growth of productivity does not cause wages to rise more rapidly, the rate of increase in unit labor costs at a given rate of unemployment may be slowed down, reducing the upward pressure on prices. Offsetting adjustments in monetary and fiscal policy may also, under some conditions, be able to mitigate the effects of changes in the composition of private demand, thereby preventing inflation of the "demand shift" variety.[2] But the possibilities in these respects must realistically be regarded as quite limited. Other kinds of policy measures capable of exerting direct effects on wage and price decisions and on the functioning of labor and product markets are likely to be necessary if the relation between inflation and unemployment is to be changed.

Social Welfare Functions

In the illustrative example given above, we simply assumed that the goals of policy were given—that the authorities wanted to increase Y by 100, G by 20, and I by 14—and calculated the adjustments in the policy instruments that would be required to produce these results. Nothing was said about how the goals themselves were chosen. In principle, the choice of goals requires the use of some explicit or implicit social welfare function by which the authorities balance against each other the benefits that they feel will accrue to the nation from the various alternative outcomes of economic policy.

To illustrate, consider a closed economy (i.e., one without foreign trade), in which the authorities believe that economic welfare depends on the rate of unemployment, the rate of change of the price level, the volume of current private consumption, the amount of resources devoted to capital accumulation, and the amount of resources allocated to government activities. The social welfare function for such an economy might be as follows:

$$W = f\left(u, \frac{\Delta p}{p}, C, I, G\right),$$

where W is welfare, u is the unemployment rate, $\Delta p/p$ is the percentage change in the price level, C is private consumption, I is private investment, and G is government purchases of goods and services. We may suppose that welfare is increased as u is reduced, as $\Delta p/p$ is reduced from a positive number toward zero, as C is increased, as I is increased, and as G is increased.

The social welfare function by itself is of no use in policy formulation. It must be considered in conjunction with some kind of model of the structure of the economy. The scientific procedure would be to maximize welfare subject to the "constraints" imposed by the economic structure. While a formal analysis of this approach is beyond the scope of this book, it is possible to get an idea of its meaning.[3] Suppose that a relation between unemployment and inflation of the Phillips curve type exists. Then an expansion of aggregate demand will yield two types of benefits: it will reduce unemployment (u) directly and it will also increase the total amount of output available to be divided up among

---

[2] For an explanation of "demand shift" inflation, see C. L. Schultze, *Recent Inflation in the United States* (Study Paper No. 1, *Study of Employment, Growth, and Price Levels*, Joint Economic Committee, 86th Cong., 1st sess., 1959).

[3] For relatively simple expositions of this approach to policy making, see C. C. Holt, "Linear Decision Rules for Economic Stabilization and Growth," *Quarterly Journal of Economics*, vol. 76 (February 1962), pp. 20–45; and Henri Theil, "Linear Decision Rules for Macrodynamic Policy Problems," in B. G. Hickman, ed., *Quantitative Planning of Economic Policy* (Washington, D.C.: The Brookings Institution, 1965), pp. 18–37.

the three desiderata, consumption (C), investment (I), and government purchases (G). On the other hand, an expansion of aggregate demand will involve
a cost: the rate of price increase $(\Delta p/p)$ will rise. The mazimization of welfare
will involve expanding aggregate demand to the point at which the marginal
increase in welfare from expanded employment and output will just equal the
marginal loss of welfare from accelerated inflation. Having determined on this
basis how much total demand is appropriate, the relations among government
purchases, tax rates, and monetary expansion should be determined in such
a way as to equate the marginal benefits of the last unit of consumption, the
last unit of investment, and the last unit of government purchases.

While this is an enlightening way to look at the formal process of establishing
economic policy, its practical applicability has, up to now, been very limited.
To solve policy problems in this way the authorities need to have (a) an explicit
form of the welfare function to be maximized and (b) a detailed and accepted
model describing the structure of the economy and its responses to changes
in various policy instruments. Neither of these requirements has been met, with
the result that, while attempts are often made to formulate policy in ways that
are somewhat in the spirit of this approach, its scientific application is not yet
possible.

COMMENTS ON THE READINGS

It is apparent from the above discussion that fiscal, monetary, and other
economic policies must be coordinated and must work in harmony if a satisfactory performance of the economy is to be achieved. The papers in this chapter deal with different aspects of this general point. The readings begin with a
paper by Warren L. Smith (reading 36) in which he discusses ways in which
monetary and fiscal policies can be adjusted both to keep aggregate demand
growing in pace with productive capacity at high employment and to increase
the growth of productive capacity itself. Smith's paper was first published in
1968, and it contains references to a 4 percent unemployment rate as constituting
full employment and forming the basis for calculations of capacity GNP. As is
made clear in the first reading in Chapter 4 (reading 16), as well as in that
chapter's introduction, current estimates of the full-employment unemployment
rate are somewhat higher than 4 percent. However, Smith points out that
selection of any particular percentage, such as 4 percent, is not important for
his purposes. The policies for economic growth which he outlines are just as
relevant today as they were in 1968.

In the next paper (reading 37), Rudiger Dornbusch and Paul Krugman analyze the operation of monetary policy and fiscal policy in a macroeconomic system which includes flexible exchange rates between countries. While they do
not write out an explicit model, much of their discussion is based on a structure
which is similar to the *IS-LM-BP* system outlined in the introduction to Chapter
6. However, the model is extended in a number of important ways by making
further assumptions; for example, exchange-rate expectations are introduced,
results based on the assumption that assets are imperfect substitutes are compared with those obtained assuming that assets are perfect substitutes, and so
forth. The authors examine both the implications of flexible exchange rates for
the choice of an appropriate policy mix for the domestic economy, and the
effects on the rest of the world of monetary and fiscal impulses originating in a
given country.

The concluding paper by Arthur M. Okun (reading 38) reviews and integrates much that has been dealt with earlier in this book with regard to monetary and fiscal policy. He argues that both instruments of stabilization policy are capable of stimulating or restraining demand and reaching the socially acceptable employment-inflation tradeoff. Therefore, it is the side effects of each kind of policy—the impact of monetary restraint on homebuilding and on asset values, the implications of monetary policy decisions for growth, and the effects of budget decisions on the composition of output—which should govern choices between them. Based on these and other considerations, Okun offers a set of working rules for the conduct and coordination of stabilization policy.

36. MONETARY AND FISCAL POLICIES FOR ECONOMIC GROWTH*

Warren L. Smith

INTRODUCTION

In a modern, predominantly free-enterprise nation such as the United States, the central government must accept responsibility for the stability of the economy—that is, for the prevention of excessive unemployment on the one hand and excessive price inflation on the other. There is agreement on this matter not only among political liberals but among most conservatives as well, although, of course, there are still differences of opinion as to the extent of the responsibility, the precise methods to be employed to fulfill it, and, in particular, the selection of the appropriate balance between the goals of price stability and high employment in given circumstances. Still, the area of agreement is far more important than the specific points of disagreement. Indeed, the responsibility of the Federal Government in this regard has been recognized by both major political parties and was formalized in the Employment Act of 1946.[1]

The maintenance of economic stability is primarily a matter of regulating aggregate demand for goods and services. The accepted instruments for controlling demand are primarily the monetary policies of the Federal Reserve System, which exert their influence by altering the supply of money and the cost and availability of credit, and the fiscal policies of the Federal Government, which affect the aggregate flow of purchasing power and spending by altering the relation between Federal tax collections and expenditures.[2]

In the last few years, an additional dimension has been added to the discussion and analysis of economic stabilization. It has come to be recognized that the capacity of the economy to produce goods and services grows month by month and year by year. Full employment and reasonable price stability can be maintained only if aggregate demand grows in pace with productive capacity. We no longer feel, as we used to, that we can indulge in self-congratulation merely because the national income in the current year exceeds that of the previous year, thereby "breaking all records." We now recognize that income and product need to expand each year by as

[1] The intellectual foundation for this view of governmental responsibility was laid in the 1930s by Lord Keynes when he demonstrated that while the free market is an institution of great social utility in organizing production and allocating resources in an efficient manner without detailed central planning, the modern free-enterprise economy does not contain adequate built-in mechanisms for maintaining overall economic stability. See J. M. Keynes, *The General Theory of Employment, Interest, and Money* (New York: Harcourt, Brace and Co., 1936).

[2] Even in the 1920s, of course, the Federal Reserve System, established in 1914 to correct structural defects in the banking system which had let to repeated and sometimes disastrous banking crises in the late 19th and early 20th centuries, came to accept some responsibility for regulating the supply of money and credit in the interest of economic stabilization. Then, in the 1940s and 1950s, a number of economists, following up the work of Lord Keynes, developed the economic theory underlying fiscal policy—that is, the deliberate use of the Federal budget as an instrument of overall economic regulation.

much as the growth of productive capacity if we are to maintain a healthy economy and avoid rising unemployment. On the other hand, if we permit aggregate demand to expand more rapidly than productive capacity, inflationary pressures will result. That is, we must run hard—but not too hard—merely to avoid falling behind.

Thus, recognition that monetary and fiscal policies to maintain full employment and stable prices must be formulated in a framework which makes allowance for the growth of productive capacity is now reasonably well established. Beyond this, it is now accepted by many economists, both in and out of the Federal Government, that by skillful use of monetary and fiscal policies we may be able not only to keep aggregate demand growing in pace with capacity but also to influence the growth of capacity itself.

FULL EMPLOYMENT AND ECONOMIC GROWTH

For purposes of our discussion, the productive capacity of the economy is the output of goods and services that can be produced under conditions of full employment. However, full employment is not an easy concept to define satisfactorily. It can scarcely mean the complete absence of unemployment, since, under almost any conceivable circumstances, there will be a certain amount of so-called "frictional unemployment," resulting from the fact that some workers are always in the process of moving from one job to another.

The best way to arrive at a workable definition of full employment is in terms of the behavior of the price level. Beyond some point, further reduction of unemployment through an expansion of demand will lead to progressively stronger inflationary tendencies for three reasons. First, as production expands, plant capacity bottlenecks are likely to develop in some industries, leading to a rise in the prices of the products of these industries while there is still excess plant capacity available in other parts of the economy. Second, shortages of certain types of labor may be encountered, leading to sharply rising wages which push up prices at a time when the general level of employment is still substantial. Third, as expansion of demand reduces the general level of unemployment and at the same time leads to rising business sales and profits, the strategic position of labor unions in collective bargaining negotiations becomes stronger relative to that of employers, causing wages to rise more rapidly than labor productivity is increasing, thereby raising

labor costs and pushing up prices.[3] Full employment may be defined as the lowest level of unemployment that can be achieved without encountering significant inflationary pressures—or, somewhat more generally, as the level of unemployment beyond which, in the opinion of the responsible public officials (whose decisions presumably reflect the views of the general public), the social benefits of a further reduction in unemployment are not worth the social costs of the inflation associated therewith.

The Kennedy Administration selected a 4 percent unemployment rate as its tentative definition of full employment—its so-called interim unemployment target—in 1961. That is, the Administration presumably believed that it would be possible to reduce unemployment to 4 percent of the labor force without encountering a serious problem of inflation.[4] Although one might quarrel with the selection of this particular percentage as a definition of full employment, the specific definition is not important for our present purposes, and I shall accordingly accept it as a working assumption.

On this basis, we may regard the Gross National Product (GNP) that can be produced when unemployment is 4 percent as a measure of the aggregate productive capacity of the economy. The smooth curve in Figure 1 depicts, at least crudely, the growth of productive capacity in this sense. Capacity GNP, represented by

---

[3] The first two conditions referred to—plant capacity bottlenecks and shortages of certain types of labor—can presumably be corrected by a once-and-for-all adjustment of prices which would adapt patterns of demand and supply to coincide with available resources. Since prices are, in general, more flexible upward than downward, this price adjustment would probably require some rise in the general level of prices. Strictly speaking, such a "one-shot" upward price adjustment does not constitute inflation, since inflation means a *continuing* rise in the price level. In practice, however, the distinction is a difficult one to apply, especially because the "one-shot" adjustment would take some time to work its way through the price structure and while this process was going on would be practically indistinguishable from "genuine" inflation.

[4] During the current expansion, which began in the first quarter of 1961, wholesale prices did not rise appreciably during the first four years while the unemployment rate was falling from 6.8 percent to 4.8 percent. Beginning early in 1965, however, prices began to rise rather sharply; from the first quarter of 1965 to the first quarter of 1966, wholesale prices rose by 4.2 percent as the unemployment rate declined quite rapidly to 3.8 percent. However, during the ensuing year, price pressures moderated considerably while the unemployment rate held steady at just under 4 percent.

Figure 1:   Gross National Product: Actual and Potential

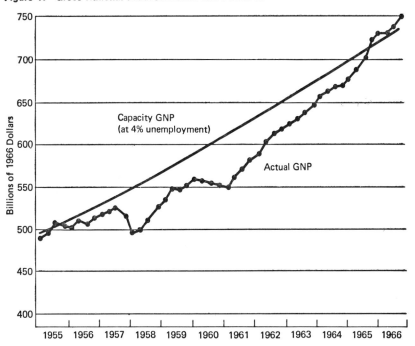

the smooth curve in Figure 1, is valued at 1966 prices, and the assumption is that it was equal to actual GNP in mid-1955 when the unemployment rate was approximately 4 percent. The growth rate of capacity GNP is assumed to be 3.5 percent from mid-1955 to the end of 1962, 3.75 percent from then until the end of 1965, and 4 percent thereafter.[5] The broken line in Figure 1 traces the movement of actual GNP, also valued at 1966 prices.

Capacity GNP cannot be measured or observed directly except when the economy is operating close to the 4 percent target unemployment rate. But there is enough indirect evidence based on levels of GNP achieved when unemployment has been 4 percent in the past, on productivity trends, and so on, to justify the use of the smooth

---

[5] The calculations used here are similar to those made by the Council of Economic Advisers. See the *Annual Reports of the Council of Economic Advisers,* January 1962 (pp. 49–53), January 1965 (p. 81), and January 1967 (p. 44). There are many problems, both conceptual and statistical, in measuring the economy's productive capacity. The intellectual basis for the Council's estimates was provided by Arthur M. Okun in his paper, "Potential GNP: Its Measurement and Significance," 1962 *Proceedings of the Business and Economic Statistics Section of the American Statistical Association, reprinted as Cowles Foundation Paper* No. 190 (Cowles Foundation for Research in Economics, Yale University, 1963).

curve in Figure 1 as a crude working approximation of the recent trend of productive capacity. Moreover, the validity of the estimates for earlier years is borne out to some degree by the fact that when unemployment declined to the neighborhood of 4 percent in late 1965, actual output turned out to be very close to the estimate of productive capacity. The reader is cautioned, however, not to attach much significance to the precise values indicated by the capacity output curve but to regard them as the center of a range of perhaps $5 billion within which the true value lies. Furthermore, the curve cannot safely be projected very far into the future, since the growth of productive capacity may change both because of essentially adventitious factors, such as alterations in the rate of growth of the labor force or in the rate of capital accumulation, and because the choice of economic policies, such as those discussed in this paper, may significantly change the growth of capacity.

What can we say about economic growth and the means of achieving it on the basis of Figure 1? To begin with, it is apparent that, starting from a situation such as existed in early 1961 when unemployment was in the neighborhood of 7 percent of the labor force and the gap between actual GNP and capacity GNP was in excess of $50 billion, a significant amount of growth in actual GNP can be achieved merely by reducing unemployment to 4 percent and bringing actual GNP up to the level of capacity GNP. To illustrate, in order to reduce unemployment to the target level of 4 percent in two years' time beginning in the first quarter of 1961, we would have had to raise GNP from its actual level of $550 billion at that time to its potential level of $652 billion in the first quarter of 1963 (as shown on the smooth curve in Figure 1). This would have been an increase of about 18 percent in two years, or roughly 9 percent per year. Actually, unemployment was not reduced to the 4 percent level until the first quarter of 1966, but even with this relatively slow rate of expansion toward full employment, GNP rose from $550 billion in the first quarter of 1961 to $735 billion in the first quarter of 1966, for an average increase of about 6 percent per year.

Thus, substantial growth is possible in the short run through the elimination of unemployment when the economy is operating substantially below capacity, as was the case in 1961. Under such conditions, if unemployment is to be reduced to 4 percent of the labor force and the associated growth achieved, aggregate demand must expand sufficiently to absorb the quantity of goods and services that will be produced when 96 percent of the labor force is employed—or, to put it another way, aggregate demand must become equal to productive capacity as defined above. As long as demand continues to fall short of this level, producers will not find it profitable to turn out sufficient quantities of goods and services to employ 96 percent of the labor force, and unemployment will remain above 4 percent.

Eliminating transactions in materials and components to be used in further production, the total output of the economy (GNP) must necessarily be absorbed by demands which can be classified into four categories: consumer demand; business demand for new plants and equipment and additions to inventories; net export demand of foreign buyers; and government demand, Federal, state, and local. When aggregate demand is growing less rapidly than capacity, the following measures can be taken to speed up the growth of some or all of these components of demand:

1. Taxes may be reduced, as was done in the Revenue Act of 1964, by cutting the tax rates applicable to various categories of income. The effects will depend to some extent on the exact nature of the tax-reduction measures adopted, but, in general, tax reduction will leave consumers and businesses with larger incomes after tax than previously and thereby lead directly to increases in "consumer demand" and "invest-

ment demand." These increases in demand will generate additional production of consumer goods and capital goods, thereby creating additional jobs. The additional wage incomes and business profits resulting from expanded production and employment will lead to still further consumer spending and generate additional production, employment, and income. Thus, through repeated "rounds" of additional production, income generation, and consumption spending—a process which economists call the "multiplier"—GNP will be raised by an amount in excess of the initial reduction in taxes. The available evidence suggests that a reduction of $1 billion in individual income taxes might lead, in the course of time, to an associated rise in consumption and GNP of roughly $2 billion, thereby giving rise to a "multiplier" of about two. Beyond this, if the expansion of consumption spending produced by the cut in taxes is sufficiently rapid to narrow the gap between actual GNP and productive capacity, it will lead to a more intensive utilization of existing plant capacity and create a stimulus for businessmen to increase their spending on new plants and equipment, thus raising the "investment demand" component of GNP. This will, of course, generate additional income and employment and lead to a further increase in consumption. Although the investment effects are more difficult to estimate than the direct consumption effects referred to above, they may under some circumstances be substantial.

2. Federal expenditures on such projects as highways, dams, and school construction may be increased. Such expenditures will directly raise GNP by adding to the "government demand" component. The added construction activity will put people to work, not only directly on the construction sites but also in factories producing materials needed in construction. As workers receive additional income in wages and salaries, and as businessmen earn additional profits from expanded production, they will increase their spending on goods and services, adding to the "consumer demand" component of GNP and stimulating additional production, employment, and income in industries producing consumer goods. Thus, through repeated "rounds" of additional production, income generation, and consumption spending similar to those set off by tax reduction, GNP will be raised by an amount in excess of the initial increase in government spending. An increase of $1 billion in government spending might lead, in the course of time, to an associated rise in consumption of roughly $1 billion, thereby producing a total rise in GNP of around $2 bil-

lion, taking account of consumption effects only, giving rise to a "multiplier" of approximately two.[6] Moreover, as in the case of tax reduction, the rise in government spending and the associated increase in consumption may, by leading to more intensive utilization of existing productive capacity, induce businessmen to increase their expenditures on additional plant, equipment, and inventories, thus generating a still further rise in GNP.

3. The Federal Reserve authorities may adopt a more expansionary monetary policy by, for example, expanded purchases of U.S. Government securities in the open market. Such purchases increase the cash reserves available to the commercial banks and enable the banks to expand their loans and investments and the amount of money held by the public in the form of bank deposits and currency by an amount equal to several times the additional reserves through the familiar process of bank credit expansion. Thus, bank loans will become easier to obtain, and the interest rates charged will probably be reduced. Furthermore, the expansion of credit will indirectly lower interest rates on bonds issued by private corporations to finance plant expansion as well as on bonds issued by state and local government units to finance highways and schools. Mortgage credit for the financing of new homes and installment loans for the purchase of automobiles and other consumer durable goods will become easier to obtain and less costly. As a result of these developments, some expansion can be expected to take place in those components of demand that are frequently credit-financed, including housing demand, business investment demand, and the demand for consumer durable goods. The increased demand will stimulate production, income, and employment directly, and set off the same "multiplier" effects produced by an increase in government expenditures or a reduction in taxes. While it is generally agreed that measures to increase the supply of money and credit will have a stimulative effect

on the economy, in the present state of knowledge it is difficult to estimate the magnitude of these effects.

Thus, when the economy is operating substantially below full employment, fiscal and monetary measures which expand aggregate demand may, by pushing the economy up to full employment, be able to produce a rather high rate of growth in the short run. Once capacity operations have been achieved, however, the growth of aggregate demand must be slowed down and brought into line with the growth of capacity if an unacceptable degree of inflation is to be avoided. That is, once full employment has been reached, the limit on economic growth is set not by the rate of expansion of aggregate demand but by the rate of growth of capacity. Of course, if full employment is to be sustained on a continuing basis, demand must grow in line with capacity—that is, along the smooth curve in Figure 1. But, under these conditions, if any further increase in the rate of growth is to be achieved without undue inflation, an acceleration in the growth of capacity itself is required.

The achievement of full employment is likely, however, to have a favorable effect on the growth of productive capacity. The productive capacity of the economy at any particular time depends upon the size of the labor force; the skill, experience, and education of the workers; the nature of the technology available and in use; the quantity and quality of social overhead capital, including communication and transportation facilities and facilities for the maintenance of the health of the population; and the size, quality, and age distribution of the stock of private capital. Thus, the rate of growth of capacity depends upon the rate of growth of the labor force; the rate at which its skill, experience, and education are improving; the rate of technological advance; and the rate of accumulation of social overhead and private capital. The achievement of full employment is itself likely to have a favorable effect on some of these forces determining the rate of growth of capacity. In this connection, two factors are likely to be particularly important.

First, the improvement in rates of utilization of existing productive facilities associated with the achievement of full employment is very likely to provide a stimulus to private investment in new plant and equipment, thereby leading to faster growth of the stock of capital. And, since the installation of equipment is often the vehicle by which new technology is introduced into productive processes, the allocation of more resources to investment should also lead to more rapid in-

---

[6] Actually, both a priori reasoning and empirical evidence derived from statistical models of the U.S. economy suggest that the multiplier applicable to an increase in government expenditures on goods and services is a little larger than that applicable to a reduction in taxes. The reason for this is that, in the first instance, the entire increase in government expenditures constitutes, by definition, an increase in demand for goods and services, whereas some portion of a reduction in taxes is likely to be saved so that the resulting direct increase in consumer or business demand will be somewhat smaller than the tax reduction.

troduction of new techniques. Between 1947 and 1955, both years in which unemployment was in the neighborhood of 4 percent of the labor force, real GNP grew at a rate of 4.4 percent per year. This rate is substantially greater than the rate of growth of capacity of about 3.5 percent per annum recorded during the period 1955 to 1962. Probably one of the reasons for the more rapid growth of capacity during the early postwar period is that a substantially greater proportion of the total GNP was allocated to private capital formation in the earlier period. Between 1947 and 1955, business outlays on fixed capital ranged from 10 to 12 percent of GNP, whereas between 1958 and 1963 the ratio was consistently less than 10 percent.[7] No doubt many factors contributed to the decline of the share of national output devoted to capital accumulation, but probably one of the important reasons was that for several years after 1957 markets for goods and services were consistently so weak that most firms were unable to sell at profitable prices the full output that could be produced efficiently with their existing plant capacity. As a consequence, the inducement to invest in further productive facilities was severely weakened. In 1965 and 1966, as markets strengthened, as rates of utilization of existing plant facilities rose, and as the economy moved strongly back toward full employment, investment spending took on renewed vigor, rising to 10.7 percent of GNP in 1965 and 11.2 percent in 1966. At the same time, as noted above, the rate of growth of capacity appears to have moved back up to 4 percent per year.

Second, unemployment and underutilization of productive facilities increase incentives to seek job security and the protection of limited markets through the adoption of restrictive practices which cut down the effective productive capacity of the economy and reduce its rate of growth. Labor unions seek to protect their members by engaging in "featherbedding" and resisting the introduction of improved production techniques

which may eliminate jobs. Businessmen are motivated to adopt pricing policies designed to protect their existing markets and to avoid risky new ventures which might seem attractive in a period of strong and expanding markets.

Undoubtedly, the particular kinds of measures that are used to expand aggregate demand may have some effect on the fraction of national resources devoted to investment during the course of an expansion to full employment. For example, if the expansion is powered by an easy monetary policy which reduces interest rates, expanded investment may play a more important role in the expansion than will be the case if the recovery is caused by a reduction in personal income taxes to stimulate consumption or by an increase in government expenditures. Measures such as the liberalized regulations governing the tax-treatment of depreciation which were put into effect in 1962 and the 7 percent tax credit for investment enacted in the Revenue Act of 1962 may have effects somewhat similar to an easy monetary policy. But when the economy has operated below full employment for a number of years, the most important factor in strengthening the inducement to invest in new plant and equipment is an expansion of aggregate demand which will increase utilization rates of existing facilities. That is, in such circumstances, the generation of additional aggregate demand is much more important than the precise nature of the measures adopted to achieve this objective, even though these specific measures may have a second-order influence on the size of the investment component of the expansion.

POLICIES TO INCREASE PRIVATE INVESTMENT

As indicated above, when the economy is operating below full employment, we may be able to achieve rapid growth in the short run merely by adopting policies to expand aggregate demand, thereby putting existing resources more fully to use. Moreover, the very process of demand expansion which drives the economy to full employment will set up forces conducive to higher rates of investment and more rapid introduction of technological improvements, thus accelerating the growth of productive capacity and creating an atmosphere generally more favorable to long-run growth. Suppose, however, we find that growth is not rapid enough to satisfy our tastes at a time when the economy is already operating at full employment. Under these conditions, mere expansion of aggregate demand will

[7] Actually, the rate of growth of capacity presumably depends (among other things) on the fraction of *capacity* output used for capital formation. In the earlier postwar period unemployment was 4 percent or lower much of the time, so that actual output was more or less equal to productive capacity. From 1958 to 1963, on the other hand, unemployment consistently exceeded 4 percent and output remained well below capacity, as is indicated by the gap between the smooth curve and the broken line in Figure 1. As a result, the ratio of investment to *capacity* output declined even more relative to the earlier period than did the ratio of investment to *actual* output.

not be able to increase the rate of growth without generating inflation. If we are to accelerate growth in these circumstances, we can only do so by reallocating resources from uses that do not contribute to growth of capacity to uses that do so contribute.

One way to increase the rate of growth of capacity under full-employment conditions would be to shift resources from the production of goods and services for current consumption to the production of capital equipment. Two steps would be needed to bring about such a shift of resources from consumption to private investment. First, it would be necessary to increase the overall rate of saving in the economy—to reduce current consumption—in order to release resources for the production of more capital goods. Second, measures would have to be taken to increase expenditures by businesses for plant and equipment in order to absorb the resources released by the increased saving. If we succeeded in accomplishing the first step—the increase in saving—but failed to achieve the second—the increase in spending on plant and equipment—the result would be not an increase in the rate of growth of productive capacity but instead the appearance of unemployment and underutilization of existing productive facilities.

There are a number of methods by which the overall saving rate might be increased, all of which would involve revisions in the tax structure. Private saving might be increased by a shift toward a less progressive tax system—that is, a reduction in taxes on high-income individuals who save a large portion of their incomes, combined with an increase in taxes on low-income persons who ordinarily save relatively little. However, there is evidence that the response of saving to *changes* in income at the margin does not vary greatly among income-size brackets, except perhaps as between the very highest and the very lowest income individuals. Thus, it would probably take a very large redistribution of income to change the aggregate amount of saving significantly. Such a massive redistribution from low-income to high-income individuals would violate accepted principles of equity in the distribution of income.

An alternative means of increasing personal saving would be the enactment of a Federal sales or expenditure tax as a partial substitute for the individual income tax. Since the sales or expenditure tax would not be levied on the portion of income that was saved, it might cause an increase in personal saving. Once again, however, such a substitution of a sales or expenditure tax for

the income tax would be objectionable to many people, because it would reduce the progressivity of the overall Federal tax structure.

Various other tax devices for stimulating personal or business saving could be devised, but in most cases they would probably be found objectionable on the grounds that they would either be inequitable in their effect on the distribution of income after taxes or would distort private decisions concerning the use of resources. Furthermore, in the present state of economic knowledge, it would be difficult to predict the magnitude of the increase in personal or business saving that would be caused by such measures.

Probably the best means of increasing total saving in the economy would be a general increase in taxes or a reduction of the Federal Government's noninvestment expenditures for the purpose of creating a Federal budget surplus. Such a surplus would mean that the Federal Government was contributing to total saving in the economy by withdrawing more dollars from the spending stream through taxation than it was injecting through expenditures.[8] A Federal budget surplus would release resources for private investment in the same way as would an increase in private saving. Whether the surplus should be created by raising taxes or by reducing government non-investment expenditures would depend upon whether it was felt to be socially more desirable to reduce private consumption or public consumption.[9]

If taxes were increased to create a budget surplus, equity could be maintained by distributing the increase in taxation among income brackets in an appropriate way.[10] Since consump-

[8] If the Federal Government was running a budget deficit at the time and reduced the size of its deficit either by increasing taxes or by cutting expenditures, the effect would be the same as would be produced if an equal increase in taxes or reduction in expenditures created a surplus or increased the size of an existing surplus. Reduction of an existing deficit would mean that the Federal Government was absorbing less private saving than before, thereby leaving more available for private investment.

[9] A reduction of Federal investment expenditures—on such activities as education, highways, and so on—would, of course, also increase public saving through the Federal budget. Whether an increase in public saving produced in this way would serve to increase the rate of growth would depend upon whether the productivity of the additional private investment made possible by the increased saving was greater or smaller than the productivity of the Federal Government investment projects which were eliminated.

[10] In a growing economy, it may be possible to achieve the budget surpluses needed for a still further

tion has generally been within the range of 93 to 95 percent of personal disposable income in recent years, a tax increase that was reasonably evenly distributed among income brackets could be expected to reduce personal saving by 5 to 7 percent of the tax increase, thus leading to an overall increase in saving, at the then existing level of income, of about 93 to 95 percent of the increase. A cut in Federal non-investment expenditures on goods and services, on the other hand, would increase the Federal budget surplus dollar for dollar without directly depressing private saving, thereby increasing total saving in the economy by the full amount of the cut. Thus, adjustments in the overall level of taxation or in Federal expenditures would have the advantage over tax devices designed to increase private saving of being both more equitable and more predictable in terms of effects on total saving.

As indicated above, measures designed to increase saving—that is, to release resources from the production of goods and services for current consumption—would need to be accompanied by measures to stimulate an equal amount of additional investment spending. Otherwise, the result would be reduced employment rather than accelerated growth.[11]

One measure that might be taken to stimulate private investment would be to use the budget surplus resulting from the increase in taxes or the reduction in Federal expenditures to retire a portion of the outstanding public debt. By retir-

acceleration of growth without actually raising tax *rates* (or reducing expenditures). Assuming a 4 percent growth of real GNP and a 2 percent annual rise in the average prices of the goods and services included in GNP, capacity GNP at current prices would rise by about 6 percent per year. Thus, under full-employment conditions, starting from present levels, GNP would rise by about $45 billion a year, and with our present tax system, taxes would increase by about 25 percent of this amount, or about $11 billion a year. Unless Federal expenditures were to rise by this amount or unless tax rates were periodically reduced, the budget would show a steadily increasing surplus at full employment. Thus, one possible strategy for accelerating growth would be to limit the secular rise of Federal expenditures while taking monetary or fiscal measures to increase private investment to match the budget surpluses automatically generated by the secular growth of tax revenues.

[11] Paradoxically, if appropriate measures were not taken to stimulate investment, the measures designed to increase saving would reduce income, and this would *depress* saving. When all the adjustments had been completed, therefore, total saving might differ very little from its initial level, but income and employment would be lower.

ing debt, the Federal Government would be putting the funds collected through the budget surplus into the capital market, thereby bringing down interest rates and making the funds available for the financing of private investment.

While the use of surplus funds collected through the Federal budget for debt retirement would be desirable in itself and would help to a limited extent to spur private investment, debt retirement alone would not generate sufficient investment to absorb the full amount of resources released by the initial reduction in consumption spending. That is, one dollar of debt retirement will not generate a full dollar of additional private investment. The reason is that a decline in interest rates will cause individuals and business concerns to increase their holdings of money balances. That is, a portion of the additional dollars injected into the capital market by debt retirement will be "hoarded" in the form of additional money holdings rather than being spent for private investment. In fact, it appears that the demand for money holdings is sufficiently responsive to a decline in interest rates to cancel out a substantial portion of the effect of debt retirement. In other words, an increase in taxes or a reduction in Federal expenditures, combined with the use of the resulting budget surplus to retire an equivalent amount of public debt, would, in all probability, have a net deflationary effect on the economy, thereby causing a reduction in income and employment.

One way to supplement the expansionary effects of using the budget surplus to retire debt would be for the Federal Reserve System to shift simultaneously toward an easier monetary policy. For example, the Federal Reserve could, in effect, retire *additional* publicly held debt through open-market purchases of U.S. Government securities, thereby lowering interest rates directly and also adding to the supply of cash reserves of the commercial banks and permitting them to engage in a further expansion of money and credit.

Under some circumstances, a shift toward an easier monetary policy by the Federal Reserve would be the logical means of supplementing the use of the budget surplus to retire debt as a means of stimulating private investment. However, since the available evidence suggests that private investment is only moderately sensitive to declining interest rates and increased availability of credit, the Federal Reserve System should be prepared to use its full powers to bring about the needed increase in private investment. To the extent that the Federal Reserve failed to act with sufficient vigor, the result would be deflationary, leading to reduced income and employment rather than the desired increase in investment and productive capacity.

Under the conditions that have existed in the last few years—and probably will continue for some time to come—a sharp reduction in interest rates for the purpose of stimulating private investment might seriously increase the U.S. balance-of-payments deficit and lead to a loss of gold. This is because a decline in U.S. interest rates relative to those prevailing in foreign markets would be very likely to cause an outflow of private capital.

What we have described above is what has come to be an almost standard post-Keynesian prescription for increasing the rate of economic growth: a shift toward a tighter fiscal policy to generate a budget surplus through increased taxation or reduced government expenditures, combined with a shift toward an easier monetary policy to spur private investment. However, if monetary policy is constrained by the balance-of-payments situation, as has been the case in the last few years, the second half of the prescription may prove to be impossible to put into effect. If this is the case, a policy of stimulating economic growth will require the use of some measures other than easy money to produce the needed increase in private investment.

If easy money and reduced interest rates should in fact prove to be either inadequate or impossible, there are various tax-incentive devices that might be employed to increase private investment. The most straightforward of these would be a reduction in corporate income tax rates, which would stimulate investment in plant and equipment by leaving corporations with larger after-tax incomes for the internal financing of investment, and also by increasing the prospective after-tax returns on newly installed facilities, and thereby strengthening incentives to invest. An alternative device would be a liberalization of the regulations governing the treatment of depreciation for tax purposes. By allowing faster write-offs of plants, machinery, and equipment, liberalized depreciation would increase the so-called "cash flow" of internal funds for financing investment and would also strengthen investment incentives by increasing the prospective rate of return on new investment. Still a third possibility would be an increase in the investment tax credit enacted in the Revenue Act of 1962 and liberalized in the Revenue Act of 1964. Such a tax credit has somewhat the same effect as would

be produced by a reduction in the initial cost of eligible productive facilities and hence makes investment more attractive to business.[12] In addition, to the extent that it reduces taxes, the credit provides firms with additional internal funds to finance investment. Of the three devices, the last one—an increase in the investment credit—has the advantage of being pinpointed most sharply toward the stimulation of investment, and it therefore seems preferable to the others.

By appropriate adjustments in fiscal policy—and, to the extent that the balance-of-payments situation permits, in monetary policy—it should be possible in the course of time to increase the proportion of national resources employed in private capital formation and thereby to raise to some extent the rate of economic growth. But such a policy adjustment is delicate and risky and should be pursued cautiously. If the fiscal and monetary measures that are designed to increase investment do not have the desired effects, the result will be unemployment and underutilization of existing productive capacity—and probably reduced investment—rather than increased growth of capacity.

The relation of budget deficits and surpluses to economic growth is generally rather poorly understood. It is often said that exponents of the vigorous use of fiscal policy for the maintenance of economic stability believe that continuing budget deficits year after year serve to stimulate growth. This is simply not the position held by the more sophisticated exponents of an active fiscal policy. It is true that when the economy is suffering from unemployment, a reduction in taxes or an increase in Federal expenditures, leading to a budget deficit, may be desirable as a means of increasing aggregate demand and raising economic activity to the full employment level. But, as explained above, if the objective

---

[12] The Revenue Act of 1962 allowed the investor a credit against income tax amounting to 7 percent of investment in eligible assets (including, in general, machinery and equipment but not buildings) having a life of eight years or more (with smaller percentage credits for investments with lives of between four and eight years). Originally, the tax credit had to be deducted from the base on which depreciation was calculated; as a result, the effect on investment was exactly the same as that of a reduction in the price of the asset by the tax-credit percentage. The Revenue Act of 1964 liberalized the credit by eliminating the provision requiring that the credit be deducted from the depreciation base. Thus, at present the tax credit has a stronger stimulating effect on investment than would be produced by an equal percentage reduction in the price of the asset.

being sought is long-run economic growth—that is, growth of productive capacity—budget surpluses, not budget deficits, will, by increasing aggregate national saving, contribute to that end, provided the surpluses are accompanied by monetary or fiscal action which increases private investment sufficiently to employ all the saving, including the surplus, that will be forthcoming at full employment. That is, if effective stimuli to investment can be put into effect, a policy of surplus financing rather than deficit financing is generally recognized by economists as being favorable to long-run economic growth.

OTHER POLICIES FOR GROWTH

In addition to the policy adjustments discussed above to increase private investment, there are other measures involving the use of fiscal policy which might be taken to speed economic growth. Most of these measures would involve either increased spending on government programs which would increase the future productive capacity of the economy or the use of tax incentives to encourage private activities—other than investment in plant and equipment—directed at that end.

Policies to make the labor market work more efficiently should be placed high on the agenda of programs aimed at increasing the effective productive capacity of the economy. Increased appropriations to enable the United States Employment Service to expand its activities in disseminating job information for the benefit of workers seeking employment, the use of Federal subsidies or perhaps credits under the individual income tax to reduce the cost to workers of moving from one locality to another to accept employment, and greatly increased Federal expenditures on programs for the training and retraining of the unemployed would be helpful. Combined with efforts—through such devices as the so-called "wage-price guideposts" of the Council of Economic Advisers—to prevent inflationary excesses in collective bargaining, measures of this kind might permit the unemployment rate to be reduced below 4 percent without creating excessive inflationary pressure. While not necessarily increasing the *percentage rate of growth* of productive capacity, such policies would, if effective, produce a "once-and-for-all" increment to capacity, thereby permitting the growth curve of capacity to be redrawn at a higher level, corresponding perhaps to a 3 percent rather than a 4 percent unemployment rate. Since they would enable the economy to produce larger quantities of goods

and services not only currently but in the future, these measures, should be classified as growth policies. And, since they would reduce the economic distress and disillusionment created by unemployment, they would be valuable measures from the standpoint of social policy as well.

Expenditures on research and development which increase both the size and quality of the available stock of technical knowledge—that is, which expand the scope of the "book of recipes" for combining resources to produce goods and services—are of critical importance for growth. The benefits to society from private expenditures on research and development often cannot be fully captured by those who put up the money to finance the required research activities. This is especially true of basic research of potentially wide applicability, but which may not lead to an immediately marketable product. That is to say, the social benefits of research and development expenditures often exceed the benefits accruing to the private sponsors of such activities. Under these conditions, if the full costs of research and development programs are borne by their private sponsors, the activities of these sponsors will be carried only to the point where private benefits and private costs are brought to equality at the margin, and the resources devoted to research and development will be smaller than would be desirable from the standpoint of society as a whole. This is a classic example of a situation where the free market does not perform its allocative function with optimal efficiency, and some form of government intervention is therefore in order.

The Federal Government's expenditures in support of research and development quadrupled—from $3.1 billion to $12.4 billion—between 1954 and 1964. However, a large portion of its research and development effort is related to the improvement of defense technology and the development of the space program and has limited direct applicability in the private economy.[13] Indeed, Federal support of basic research—the area into which private market incentives are least likely to channel an adequate volume of resources—amounted to only about $1.5 billion in 1964. In view of the probably wide disparity

[13] Knowledge accumulated as a result of defense and space activities does have some private applications. This knowledge is certainly not being disseminated and used to the greatest possible extent at the present time. Expanded efforts by the Federal Government to make available to private users some of the technical knowledge accumulated as a result of defense-and-space-connected research would contribute to economic growth.

between the social benefits of expenditures on research and development and their costs to private sponsors, increased Federal expenditures in support of such activities—especially basic research—would be desirable and would contribute to economic growth.

Another method of increasing expenditures on research and development would be to provide tax incentives to business firms for such expenditures. For example, a tax credit similar to the 7 percent credit for investment in machinery and equipment enacted in the Revenue Act of 1962, could be given for research and development spending.[14] By reducing the effective cost to business of research activities, such a tax credit should be capable of providing a strong stimulus to private research. Any tax credit proposal should disallow credits for such activities as market research and sales promotion, because their contribution to economic growth is likely to be minimal and because, in any case, private market incentives are likely to call them forth in adequate amounts.

Public investment in such fields as health, education, highway construction, the conservation and development of natural resources, and urban planning and development have a vital role to play in spurring economic growth. Accordingly, within limits at least, increased Federal expenditures in these areas—or perhaps grants to state and local government units to permit them to increase such expenditures—should be an important part of any program aimed at increasing the rate of growth. In defining public investment, it is important to avoid emphasizing the accumulation of "bricks and mortar"—public buildings, highways, dams, and so on—and in the process neglect those areas of public investment which do not take this form. Most students of growth believe that outlays for the improvement of human resources are capable of yielding spectacularly high returns. Programs for improving health

and for education and training are of special importance. Investment in the improvement of human resources includes not only outlays for the construction of physical facilities, such as hospitals and schools, but also expenditures required for the current operation of medical and educational institutions, such as the payment of teachers' salaries. The criterion for defining investment should be not the acquisition of physical assets such as buildings and equipment, but rather the existence of a future payoff in terms of increased productivity. Moreover, expenditures for health and education yield benefits in the form of greater happiness and increased personal fulfillment, benefits which are by no means fully reflected in the GNP that is used as a material index of economic growth.

Increased government spending on research and development and on public investment, as well as tax credits which succeed in stimulating private outlays on research and development, will, if introduced at a time when the economy is already at full employment, need to be accompanied by measures designed to depress some other kinds of expenditures if inflation is to be avoided. That is, under conditions of full employment, policies designed to stimulate growth-generating expenditures—whether these expenditures be private or public and whether they be for investment in physical facilities, for research and development to improve technology, or for the improvement of human resources—should be accompanied by measures designed to increase saving (i.e., reduce consumption) in order to release resources to be used for their fulfillment. Thus, the measures designed to increase saving—private or public—discussed earlier in this paper are a necessary accompaniment of policies to stimulate growth-oriented expenditures, whether such expenditures be in the private or in the public sector.

Those who favor an expanded program of public investment aimed at the development of the economy and the improvement of human resources often advocate the adoption of a so-called capital budget by the Federal Government. In a full-fledged capital budget, government expenditures would be classified between capital outlays (which should be defined to include all expenditures yielding future benefits) on the one hand, and expenditures yielding only current benefits on the other. According to the capital-budget principle, taxes should cover expenditures yielding current benefits together with debt interest and amortization, while capital outlays should be financed by borrowing. This procedure is sup-

---

[14] Taxpayers are permitted to deduct outlays for research as current expenses in computing their income tax liabilities. This favorable tax treatment may not, however, be applied to long-lived equipment used for research; the cost of such equipment must be recovered by depreciation allowances spread over its life. As a means of stimulating research and development in the interest of economic growth, the tax reform program proposed by President Kennedy in 1963 contained a provision that would have permitted the taxpayer to deduct the cost of research equipment as an expense for tax purposes in the year in which the equipment was acquired. However, this provision was rejected by the Congress and was not included in the tax reform program as finally enacted in the Revenue Act of 1964.

posed to have the advantage of spreading the cost of financing capital expenditures, in the form of interest and amortization, over the life of the facilities acquired so that the persons who, as a group, benefit from the added productivity of the facilities are required to bear the costs. In addition, a parallel is sometimes drawn between the principles underlying a public capital budget and the tenets often accepted as sound for private finance. The argument runs that just as it is regarded as proper for a business firm or a family to borrow money for the purpose of acquiring long-lasting assets such as an automobile, a house, a store, or a plant, so should it be viewed as appropriate for the government to borrow to finance the construction of a dam, a highway, or outlays for the education of its citizens. Conversely, it would be improper for the government to borrow to finance outlays yielding only current benefits just as it would be improper for a family to borrow to buy food or clothing. Unfortunately, even if this somewhat Puritanical theory of private finance is accepted—note that it is an ethical rather than an economic theory—there is no reason why the same principles should be applied to governments, especially the Federal Government. Indeed, there are two extremely serious objections to the theory as applied to the Federal budget.

First, acceptance of the theory of the capital budget as outlined above might at times interfere seriously with the maintenance of full employment. When the forces of private demand are particularly weak, the needs of economic stabilization may require the Federal Government to reduce taxes or increase expenditure to such an extent that tax revenues would be inadequate to cover even that portion of Federal expenditures yielding only current benefits. On the other hand, at times when private demand is exceptionally buoyant and the economy is therefore threatened by inflation, the maintenance of economic stability may require such a large increase in taxes or reduction in expenditures that tax revenues will be more than sufficient to cover all Federal expenditures including capital outlays. Indeed, it will only happen by accident—if ever—that the Federal budget deficit that would occur when tax revenues were just sufficient to cover expenditures yielding current benefits would be the appropriate budgetary situation from the standpoint of economic stabilization. In other words, the capital budget is almost certain to come into serious conflict with the overriding principles of countercyclical fiscal policy.

Second, the principle underlying the capital budget is not even acceptable in terms of its effects on the allocation of resources, at least to one who, like myself, accepts the idea that the government has an important role to play in influencing the rate of economic growth. If the government wishes to accelerate growth, it may be quite inappropriate to finance public investment by borrowing, since such borrowing may drive up interest rates and reduce private investment which also contributes to growth; rather, from the standpoint of optimal growth policy, it may be desirable to finance government capital outlays by an increase in personal taxes designed to release from private consumption the resources needed for the government's investment program. Indeed, an effective program aimed at the twin objectives of stability and growth requires that the whole complex of monetary and fiscal policies be the subject of flexible adjustments and be kept continuously under review. Dogmatic rules which connect certain kinds of expenditures with certain means of finance are likely to prove unsatisfactory because they prevent appropriate policy adjustments.

Arguments that justify Federal deficits to the extent that they result from borrowing to finance public capital outlays by analogy to so-called sound tenets of private finance are generally fallacious. The soundness of the Federal Government's credit rests not on the value of its assets but on the strength of the economy, its taxable capacity, and, ultimately, on the Government's power to create money. If needed to maintain high employment and optimal resource allocation, borrowing and deficit spending to finance *current* government expenditures are perfectly appropriate—indeed, if the alternative is widespread unemployment, failure to accept the necessary borrowing and deficit financing should be roundly condemned as a failure of the Government to live up to its responsibility for the maintenance of a sound economy. Nor should the capital budget be favored, as it certainly has been by some people and at some times, as a device for justifying deficits that are required to keep the economy operating at full employment. It is better to make the case for deficit financing when needed for economic stabilization on the basis of correct fiscal-policy reasoning rather than to use expedient arguments to justify it by means of false analogies to private finance.[15]

---

[15] Although a capital budget procedure of the kind outlined seems unwise, it is perfectly appropriate—indeed desirable—for the Federal budget to present a breakdown of expenditures between those yielding benefits primarily in the future and those yielding

CONCLUDING REMARKS

I have discussed a number of ways in which changes in the level and structure of taxation, changes in the level and composition of Federal expenditures, and changes in monetary policy might be capable of expediting growth of real output in the United States. Apart from the possibility of accelerating growth in the short run by putting to work resources that are currently idle, nearly all of the measures discussed require significant reallocations of resources—the application of measures to reduce the use of resources for current consumption combined with measures to absorb these released resources into uses that increase the total productive power of the economy, such as private investment in plant and equipment, increased activity in the field of research and development, increased public investment in physical facilities such as highways and development of natural resources, and increased investment in human resources. All of these policies for promoting economic growth require us to make choices: We must decide the extent to which we are willing to give up the current enjoyment of the fruits of the economy in the form of consumption for the purpose of accumulating additional capital of one kind or another which will increase the capacity of the economy to produce goods and services in the future. Moreover, it should be understood that the policy adjustments needed to produce a deliberate speed-up of growth are rather sophisticated, uncertain as to effects, and difficult to put into operation. On the basis of the evidence currently available, it is extremely difficult to predict the magnitude of the effects likely to be produced on the growth of the productive capacity of the economy by any particular measure, such as increased private investment, or by any combination of measures. As a consequence, it is vitally important that we have in our arsenal of fiscal policies instruments that can be employed quickly and flexibly to adjust aggregate demand to whatever the growth rate of capacity turns out to be, if we are to be able to maintain full employment on a continuing basis.

---

benefits primarily in the current year. This breakdown is in fact provided in Special Analysis D of the Federal budget. (See *The Budget of the United States Government for the Fiscal Year Ending June 30, 1967*, pp. 406–25).

It is almost certain that the optimal way to increase economic growth is by the use of some combination of the proposals discussed above: to allocate some additional resources to private investment, some to the expansion of research and development activities, some to increased public investment in physical facilities, and some to the improvement of human resources. The general principle that should underlie selection of the optimal mix of policies for achieving a given growth objective is to carry each of the various growth-generating activities to the point where the marginal social productivities of all of them are equated. Then, having decided the optimal combination of these activities for each given increment to the growth rate, the total amount of resources withdrawn from current consumption for use in promoting growth-oriented activities should be decided on the basis of our willingness as a nation—as reflected in the decisions of our policy makers chosen through democratic political processes—to give up current consumption in exchange for future consumption.

Unfortunately, while it is a relatively simple matter to state, at least crudely, the principles that should underlie the selection of an optimal growth policy, it is, as a practical matter, impossible to make such a rational calculation in the present state of knowledge. Opinions differ substantially concerning the relative magnitudes of the contributions to economic growth that have been made by private investment, technological change, education, and so on; and it is possible to marshal the evidence in such a way as to support a fairly wide range of estimates with respect to these contributions. Of course, further empirical work on the sources of economic growth may in time enable us to make better judgments concerning the contributions of different kinds of growth-promoting activities. For the present, however, about the best that can be said is that a combination of measures aimed at all of the main sources of economic growth simultaneously is probably better than single-minded concentration on one source such as private investment. But, with respect to the relative emphasis to be placed on different kinds of activities, the judgments of qualified students of growth differ, and no clear choice seems possible. In other words, in the present state of knowledge, the choice of an appropriate combination of policies for promoting economic growth is an art rather than a science.

37. THE THEORY OF FLEXIBLE EXCHANGE RATES IN THE SHORT RUN*

Rudiger Dornbusch and Paul Krugman†

Considerable flexibility in exchange rates has marked the seventies. A series of events, starting with the appreciation of the deutsche mark in 1969, and including the realignment in the Smithsonian Agreement in 1971 and a second realignment, have brought the world into a period of controlled flexibility of rates. Flexible rates were the mechanism economists had long advocated for attaining external balance,[1] but the experience in the last few years has led many to reconsider it.

That reconsideration is stimulated by some surprises in the performance of flexible rates. First among these are the recurrent, large cycles in exchange rates. The dollar-mark rate, for example, fluctuated more than 10 percent in less than six months, though there was no comparable discrepancy in the movement of price levels.

Both the fluctuations in rates and their side

* Adapted from "Flexible Exchange Rates in the Short Run," *Brookings Papers on Economic Activity,* no. 3 (1976), pp. 537–75. Copyright © 1976 by The Brookings Institution, Washington, D.C. Reprinted by permission of the publisher and the authors. Rudiger Dornbusch is Associate Professor of Economics, Massachusetts Institute of Technology. Paul Krugman is Assistant Professor of Economics, Yale University.

† We are indebted to Pedro Aspe, Roger Hankin, and Jay Helms for valuable assistance. Helpful comments from Karl Brunner, Jerry A. Hausman, and members of the Brookings panel are gratefully acknowledged. Financial support was provided by a grant from the Ford Foundation.

[1] The literature on flexible rates goes back to Milton Friedman, "The Case for Flexible Exchange Rates," in his *Essays in Positive Economics* (University of Chicago Press, 1953). Subsequent writing includes Egon Sohmen, *Flexible Exchange Rates: Theory and Controversy* (University of Chicago Press, 1961); Richard E. Caves, "Flexible Exchange Rates," *American Economic Review,* vol. 53 (May 1963), pp. 120–29; Harry G. Johnson, "The Case for Flexible Exchange Rates, 1969," Federal Reserve Bank of St. Louis, *Review,* vol. 51 (June 1969), pp. 12–24; Herbert Giersch, "On the Desirable Degree of Flexibility of Exchange Rates," *Weltwirtschaftliches Archiv,* vol. 109, no. 2 (1973), pp. 191–213; Edward Tower and Thomas D. Willett, *The Theory of Optimum Currency Areas and Exchange-Rate Flexibility,* Special Papers in International Economics 11 (Princeton University, International Finance Section, 1976); and Richard N. Cooper, "Monetary Theory and Policy in an Open Economy," *Scandinavian Journal of Economics,* vol. 78, no. 2 (1976), pp. 146–63.

effects soon caused governments to adopt exchange-rate targets and to intervene in the market. Governments realized that exchange-rate movements had real effects: they altered relative prices and real incomes and they caused inflation or could serve to reduce inflationary pressure. Exchange-rate targets were also an attractive alternative to the discipline of external balance imposed by a flexible rate, which was far from appropriate in face of the real disturbances of 1973–74. Confronted with a transitory decline in real income, policymakers much preferred using reserves and borrowing to a free adjustment of exchange rates.

The worldwide recession of 1974–76 demonstrated, with the benefit of hindsight, that even under flexible rates there is scope for coordinated stabilization policy. A coordinated expansion in economic activity would have allowed every country to experience some export-led recovery at stable exchange rates.

Against this background, we propose another look at flexible rates and ask how they fit into conventional macroeconomic thinking. The focus is entirely on the short run. We are concerned with two related questions: How are exchange rates determined, and what role do they play in a short-run macroeconomic context? In this paper we cover theory, from purchasing power parity and the Keynesian model. The theory of purchasing power parity emphasizes the relation between price levels and the exchange rate but is not a theory of exchange-rate determination and has little to say about the macroeconomic role of exchange rates. Keynesian theory, by contrast, places the exchange rate in the center of macroeconomics. The exchange rate is identified with the relative price of goods and thus is a determinant of the allocation of world spending between domestic and foreign goods. Under conditions of capital mobility there is an important link between international interest rates and the exchange rate.

The Keynesian model serves as a starting point for a realistic model but requires several extensions. Hence, we incorporate the implications of exchange-rate expectations, both as part of the adjustment process and as an independent source of macroeconomic disturbances. The model is further extended by a look at the impact of relative prices on the saving rate. It is argued that an exchange-rate movement changes relative prices, or the terms of trade, and therefore changes real income. The change in real income, in turn, may alter saving and spending at an unchanged level of output. The paper ends with a discussion of capital mobility and the suggestion that exchange rates are determined in asset markets. We conclude that asset-market views and balance-of-payments views of exchange-rate determination differ little provided proper emphasis is placed on the capital account in the latter. The model that emerges emphasizes the link between interest rates and exchange rates, identifies the exchange rate with the terms of trade, and assumes that movements in exchange rates will bring about adjustments in the composition of world demand.

THEORY OF FLEXIBLE EXCHANGE RATES

Traditionally, there have been three quite different views of the role and determination of exchange rates. A monetary approach developed in the wake of the experience after World War I holds that domestic monetary upheaval will be reflected in external depreciation. A second strand of analysis, again originating in the twenties, emphasizes relations between relative price levels and the exchange rate—the famous doctrine of purchasing power parity (PPP). Finally, Keynesian macroeconomics of the open economy under flexible rates was developed in the late forties and elaborated in the sixties and stresses the interaction of output and exchange-rate determination.

PRICES AND EXCHANGE RATES

Under the skin of any international economist lies a deep-seated belief in some variant of the PPP theory of the exchange rate.[2] According to the law of one price, a commodity should sell for the same price (freight and duties apart) in various locations. An exchange rate that leaves an international price discrepancy will soon lead to arbitrage and thereby to an adjustment in prices or the exchange rate or both. Given enough time, therefore, the domestic prices of internationally traded goods will correspond to world prices converted at the going exchange rate.

[2] The theory and applications of PPP have been extensively reviewed in Lawrence H. Officer, "The Purchasing-Power-Parity Theory of Exchange Rates: A Review Article," International Monetary Fund, Staff Papers, vol. 23 (March 1976), pp. 1–60.

Even if the arbitrage of traded-goods prices is generally accepted, a number of substantive issues remain. Does spatial arbitrage have any further implications for exchange rates, and, specifically, does it imply that exchange rates are a function of price *levels?* Given domestic and foreign price levels, does the doctrine assert that the exchange rate will attain a particular level?

If all goods were traded with no transport costs or duties and with identical weights in the price index, the law of one price would ensure arbitrage of price levels, as well as of individual commodity prices. Obviously, the departures from these assumptions are sufficiently pronounced that this result should not be expected. One alternative is to consider the *relative* movement of price levels and exchange rates over time. Here it is argued that movements in the exchange rate will offset those in relative prices. This approach will be primarily correct for the case of pure monetary disturbances that leave the relative price structure within a country unaffected, but can be seriously incorrect as a general proposition about actual or equilibrium exchange rates, as Samuelson has emphasized.[3] In an important contribution, Balassa has pointed out that the growth process is likely to change relative price levels systematically.[4] With productivity growth concentrated in the traded-goods sector, the resulting increase in labor cost to the service sector will raise home-goods prices and hence the overall price level in the faster-growing country relative to the rest of the world.

The main points of PPP theory can be formalized by reference to the following equation:[5]

$$\hat{e} = (\hat{W} - \hat{W}^*) + (\hat{w}^* - \hat{w}) + (\hat{\theta} - \hat{\theta}^*). \quad (1)$$

[3] Paul A. Samuelson, "Theoretical Notes on Trade Problems," Review of Economics and Statistics, vol. 46 (May 1964), pp. 145–54.

[4] Bela Balassa, "The Purchasing-Power Parity Doctrine: A Reappraisal," Journal of Political Economy, vol. 72 (December 1964), pp. 584–96.

[5] In equation 1 an asterisk denotes the foreign country, and e is the domestic-currency prices of foreign exchange. Assuming full arbitrage of traded-goods prices, $P_T = eP_T^*$, or $e = P_T/P_T^*$, which corresponds to the absolute version of PPP. Next we assume a relation between traded-goods prices and the price level in each country, $P_T = \theta P$ and $P_T^* = \theta^* P^*$ and use the definition of the real wage $w = W/P$ and $w^* = W^*/P^*$ to form the expression $e = P_T/P_T^* = (\theta/\theta^*)(W/W^*)(w^*/w)$. Equation 1 is the logarithmic derivative of this equation. For further comments see Rudiger Dornbusch, "The Theory of Flexible Exchange Rate Regimes and Macroeconomic Policy," Scandinavian Journal of Economics, vol. 78, no. 2 (1976), pp. 255–75.

Equation 1 summarizes the determinants of exchange rates on the assumption that prices of
traded goods are *fully* arbitraged. Under these
conditions the domestic currency will depreciate
if domestic nominal wages rise faster than foreign
money wages; if foreign real wages rise faster
than domestic real wages; or if the ratio of traded-
goods prices to home-goods prices rises faster
domestically than abroad.

The first term of equation 1 represents the
pure inflation effect or monetary effect. With an
unchanged real structure the country experiencing the higher rate of wage inflation will have
a depreciating exchange rate. The second term
shows the impact of real changes. More rapid increases in real wages (stemming from extraordinary productivity growth) are reflected in an appreciation in the currency. The last term in
equation 1 concentrates on changes in the relative-price structure. An increase in the relative
price of traded goods, given real and money
wages, implies a depreciation of the currency.

Equation 1 is a convenient representation of
the influences on exchange rates. Even so it is
not entirely satisfactory because of two strong
assumptions built into the formulation that are
not supported by empirical evidence for the
short run. First, the only variation in relative
prices is that between home goods and traded
goods; the terms of trade are constant. Second,
the law of one price actually holds.

A more important objection to a formulation
such as equation 1 is that it implies a line of
causation from wages and the real structure to
the exchange rate. Such a view disregards the
interaction between exchange rates and prices.
PPP is at best an equilibrium relation between
exchange rates and prices, not a theory of the
exchange rate.

Nonetheless, one would expect a large part
of exchange-rate movements to be accounted for
by divergent trends in prices $(\hat{W} - \hat{W}^*)$ and in
productivity growth $(\hat{w} - \hat{w}^*)$. To put it differently, the proper approach may be to explain the
discrepancies from equation 1 rather than express
surprise at a tendency for the law of one price to
operate.

KEYNESIAN ANALYSIS
OF FLEXIBLE RATES

Work on flexible rates in a macroeconomic
perspective goes back to Polak, and Laursen and
Metzler, as well as James Meade.[6] The analysis

[6] Jacques J. Polak ,"European Exchange Depreciation in the Early Twenties," *Econometrica,* vol. 11

draws flexible rates into a macroeconomic framework by identifying the exchange rate with the
terms of trade, which in turn affect the composition of domestic spending and are a determinant
of exports. Given the interest rate and the (fixed)
level of domestic prices, a depreciation raises import prices and—assuming appropriate restrictions on elasticities—shifts world demand toward
domestic goods and improves the balance of trade.

In the absence of capital flows the exchange
rate will adjust to maintain the trade balance in
equilibrium. An expansionary domestic policy, for
example, would raise income and import spending. The resulting trade deficit would cause a depreciation and switch demand toward domestic
goods until the deficit was eliminated. For this
simple case, flexible rates make expansionary policies operate exactly as they do in a closed economy. Since the trade balance is maintained in
equilibrium by exchange-rate adjustment, the
economy, in effect, is closed for the purposes of
income determination.

The analysis becomes considerably more interesting when it includes capital mobility and
interaction between countries in the determination of macroeconomic equilibrium, following the
theories of Mundell and Fleming.[7] The notion of
capital mobility is best captured by the extreme
assumption that domestic and foreign securities
are perfect substitutes. Abstracting from exchange-rate expectations, this implies that domestic and foreign interest rates are the same.
That link has very strong implications for monetary and fiscal policy under flexible rates.

The two-country model with perfect capital
mobility is depicted in the diagram below. The
equations are those for monetary equilibrium in
each country (standard *LM* equations) and for
equilibrium conditions in the goods market. In
the goods market, prices are fixed in each country's currency and the supply of output is perfectly elastic. The demand for a country's output
is equal to that country's expenditure plus the
trade surplus or net exports. The trade surplus, in
turn, is a function of the exchange rate—the rela-

(April 1943), pp. 151–62; J. E. Meade, *The Balance
of Payments* (Oxford University Press, 1951); and
Svend Laursen and Lloyd A. Metzler, "Flexible Exchange Rates and the Theory of Employment," *Review of Economics and Statistics,* vol. 32 (November
1950), pp. 281–99.

[7] See Robert A. Mundell, *International Economics*
(Macmillan, 1968), chaps. 11, 17, and 18, and
J. Marcus Fleming, "Domestic Financial Policies
Under Fixed and Under Floating Exchange Rates,"
International Monetary Fund, *Staff Papers,* vol. 9
(November 1962), pp. 369–79.

Figure 1

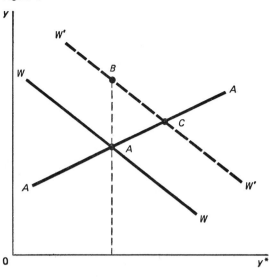

tive price of goods or the terms of trade—as well as of both countries' incomes. The model is completed by the requirement that interest rates be the same in the two countries.

In Figure 1 the AA schedule depicts the combinations of income levels that yield monetary equilibrium *and* equality of interest rates. Given the money supply, an increase in home income will raise equilibrium interest rates. To maintain international equality of interest rates, foreign income would have to rise along with domestic income. The slope of the AA schedule is positive (the essential result) while its magnitude depends on relative income and interest elasticities at home and abroad.[8]

The WW schedule, which expresses equilibrium in the two countries' goods and money markets, is generated by alternative exchange rates, given money supplies and fiscal policy. For

[8] The equations corresponding to the schedules are the following. Solving the money-market (LM) equilibrium for interest rates as functions of income and money: $r = \bar{r}(y,M)$ and $r^* = \bar{r}^*(y^*,M^*)$. Along the AA schedule $\bar{r}(y,M) = \bar{r}^*(y^*,M^*)$, where M and M^* are the domestic and foreign money supplies. The WW schedule represents equilibrium in the goods market: $y = A(\bar{r},y,\gamma) + T(y,y^*,e)$ and $y^* = A^*(\bar{r}^*,y^*,\gamma^*) - eT(y,y^*,e)$, where A and A^* represent domestic and foreign absorption in terms of the respective countries' goods. The terms γ and γ^* represent fiscal policy, and T is the trade surplus. The WW schedule is generated by considering alternative exchange rates and finding the corresponding equilibrium levels of output. In the neighborhood of the initial equilibrium the trade balance is assumed zero. We assume, without much justification, that import spending is not responsive to the rate of interest.

any point on the schedule and an assumed depreciation of the domestic currency, the implied increase in the relative price of foreign goods will shift world demand toward domestic output. To meet the resulting excess demand, domestic output will have to rise while foreign output will decline. The magnitude of the income changes depends on marginal propensities and interest elasticities. The schedule is negatively sloped.

A movement up and to the left along the WW schedule corresponds to a progressive depreciation of the home country's currency, or a progressive worsening of the home country's terms of trade. Accordingly, the movement induces a growing trade surplus that supports the expansion in income. The same point can be made so as to emphasize the absorption approach. A movement to the left along WW implies that domestic income and interest rates rise. With a marginal propensity to spend that is less than unity and with spending further dampened by the higher interest rate, income rises *relative* to spending and thus the home country has an external surplus. Precisely the opposite argument holds for the foreign country.

Initial equilibrium obtains at point A. Given money supplies in each country and fiscal policy at point A, the exchange rate, the interest rate, and income levels are such that goods and money markets clear in each country. At A, interest rates are equalized as required under perfect capital mobility.

Consider now a fiscal expansion at home. At the initial exchange rate the expansion in demand will raise domestic income. Accordingly, the WW schedule shifts up to $W'W'$. In the short run, the fiscal expansion will raise income at home and raise interest rates relative to those prevailing abroad. The differential in interest rates will tend to induce a capital inflow that causes the home currency to appreciate. This appreciation shifts demand toward foreign output, thus dampening the income expansion at home and spurring an expansion abroad. The process continues until point C is reached. At C the fiscal expansion at home will have caused income and interest rates to rise in both countries. Therefore, under perfect capital mobility, fiscal expansion—or any autonomous expansion in aggregate demand—raises equilibrium income everywhere in the world.

A critical link in the transmission of fiscal expansion to the rest of the world is the *appreciation* of the expanding country's currency. This may appear paradoxical: clearly, the initial effect of the expansion must be a worsening of that country's trade balance, which might point toward depreciation, not appreciation. The explanation is that the assumption of *perfect* capital mobility ensures that, with income and interest rates rising, the capital inflow will be potentially infinite and, hence, the capital-account surplus will dominate any trade deficit and force an appreciation of the currency.

What can be said about the new equilibrium at point *C?* The expanding country will have a trade deficit and will experience an actual capital inflow. The argument can be made simply by reference to the absorption approach and consideration of the foreign country. Abroad, income has risen (from *A* to *C*) and has pulled up interest rates. With a foreign propensity to spend that is less than one and with spending further dampened by higher interest rates, foreign income will have risen relative to spending and thus the foreign country will enjoy an improvement in the trade balance and an actual capital outflow. Indeed, the change in the trade balance is the channel through which a fiscal expansion in one country is translated into an income expansion abroad.

One of the very strong predictions of the Mundell-Fleming model concerns a monetary expansion in one country. The model implies that income will rise in the country where the money supply increases and that income will fall abroad. Figure 2 is helpful in understanding that adjustment process. The increase in money would lower domestic interest rates and, therefore, generate a potential capital outflow. The resulting currency depreciation shifts demand toward domestic goods and causes an income expansion. The income expansion boosts interest rates somewhat. Abroad, because demand shifts away from

foreign goods, output declines and so do interest rates. By this process a new equilibrium occurs at point *B*, where interest rates are equalized again at a lower level, domestic income has risen, and foreign income has declined. The home country's currency has depreciated and the trade balance has improved so that there is an actual capital outflow.

Again, the absorption approach helps to explain the trade balance and the direction of actual capital flows. With perfect capital mobility, domestic and foreign securities carry the same yield. Thus capital flows are determined by spending and saving decisions, not by interest rates. At point *B*, interest rates have declined and income has fallen for the foreign country. The declines both of interest rates and of income raise spending *relative* to income, given a spending propensity of less than one. Accordingly, at point *B*, the foreign country has a trade deficit and therefore is borrowing in the world market. The home country is lending or experiencing a capital outflow.

The second diagram showed that a domestic monetary expansion lowers income abroad. The next question concerns appropriate offsetting policies by the foreign country that would leave foreign income unchanged while attaining the domestic target. What policy combination would produce result *C* rather than *B?* Clearly, a monetary expansion by the home country must be supplemented by both monetary and fiscal expansions abroad. The monetary expansion abroad raises the foreign country's income and lowers the home country's. The fiscal expansion raises income in both. A combination of the two will result in a move from *B* to *C*.

Two interesting further results emerge in the context of these offsetting policies. First, perhaps surprisingly, it does *not* matter which country provides the fiscal expansion. If the home country provides it, domestic interest rates will tend to rise, leading to an appreciation of its currency and a shift in demand abroad. The converse will be true if the foreign country provides it. In general, fiscal expansion is shared out to the rest of the world.

Second, and also perhaps surprisingly, the trade-balance effect of the combined policies that expand income in one country while maintaining it in the other involves a shift toward surplus by the expanding country.

From the Mundell-Fleming model we retain the general proposition that foreign monetary or fiscal disturbances are transmitted internationally. Offsetting these disturbances requires active mon-

Figure 2

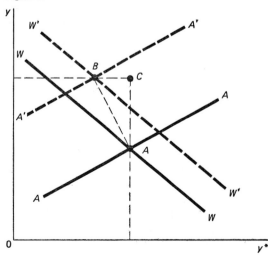

etary or fiscal policy. While a monetary-fiscal policy mix can maintain the *level* of output, it cannot maintain the *composition* between domestic demand and net exports, nor can it maintain the exchange rate and therefore the terms of trade. There is perhaps nothing surprising about the result that foreign real disturbances—including changes in money—have a domestic effect, but these facts certainly stand in sharp contrast to a popular, unqualified belief that flexible rates insulate a country from external shocks.

EXCHANGE-RATE EXPECTATIONS AND CAPITAL FLOWS

The Mundell-Fleming approach to macroeconomics under flexible rates emphasizes interdependence and capital mobility. Capital mobility takes on even more significance when we introduce exchange-rate expectations and their impact on macroeconomic activity.[9] To formalize exchange-rate expectations, assume again a world of perfect capital mobility so that *net* yields on domestic and foreign debt are equalized. Assume, contrary to Mundell-Fleming, that exchange-rate expectations are adaptive, possibly with a disturbance term.

Investors will equate net yields on domestic and foreign assets:

$$r = r^* + \lambda, \qquad (2)$$

where domestic and foreign interest rates are r and r^*, respectively, and the premium or the expected future exchange rate as a fraction of the spot rate is λ. Equation 2 states that investors have to be compensated for an anticipated depreciation of domestic currency ($\lambda > 0$) by a commensurately higher interest rate. If expectations are formed adaptively, the expected premium, λ, is a function of current and past exchange rates (e, e_{-1} . . .) and a disturbance term, u:

$$\lambda = \lambda(e, e_{-1}, \ldots, u). \qquad (3)$$

[9] The role of exchange-rate expectations in a macroeconomic context has been emphasized by Robert A. Mundell, "The Exchange Rate Margins and Economic Policy," in J. Carter Murphy, ed., *Money in the International Order* (Southern Methodist University Press, 1964); Victor Argy and Michael G. Porter, "The Forward Exchange Market and the Effects of Domestic and External Disturbances Under Alternative Exchange Rate Systems," International Monetary Fund, *Staff Papers*, vol. 19 (November 1972), pp. 503–32; and William H. Branson, *Financial Capital Flows in the U.S. Balance of Payments* (Amsterdam: North-Holland, 1968).

Incorporating equations 2 and 3 in the Mundell-Fleming model permits consideration of speculative disturbances and the resulting adjustment process. Assume for some reason—other than current changes in monetary or fiscal policy—that the expectation of a domestic depreciation develops. At unchanged interest rates a capital loss on domestic assets will be expected and, accordingly, at each level of foreign interest rates, domestic interest rates will have to be correspondingly higher. In Figure 3 this is shown by an upward shift of the AA schedule.

A short-run equilibrium is point B, where the expectation of a depreciation has caused the currency actually to depreciate. In response, world demand shifts toward the depreciating country's goods and thus raises output there while lowering it abroad. A speculative disturbance, therefore, exerts a direct impact on equilibrium levels of income. The causation runs from exchange-rate expectations to incipient capital flows to actual exchange-rate movements which affect the composition of world spending and therefore equilibrium output levels. For the depreciating country, where interest rates have risen, the higher level of output is sustained by a trade surplus. Abroad, where interest rates have declined, output is lower as are net sales to other countries. There is a net outflow of capital from the country expected to depreciate and that finances the trade surplus.

What happens when the speculative disturbance subsides? The distribution of output over time will return precisely to the initial equilibrium at point A. A disturbance, therefore, introduces unnecessary variability in the composition of world output and in relative prices.

And how can macroeconomic policies be used to offset the speculative disturbance? A policy

Figure 3

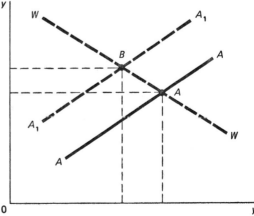

that stabilizes incomes at point *A* requires a monetary contraction in the country expected to depreciate or a monetary and fiscal expansion abroad. Simply pegging the exchange rate in the face of an incipient capital outflow amounts to the correct monetary policy. It implies a decline in the domestic quantity of money and thus brings about the requisite increase in interest rates. With higher interest rates, however, aggregate demand is insufficient to support output and thus a fiscal expansion (or some depreciation) is required. The important point is that pegging exchange rates in the face of reversible speculative movements is an efficient way to stabilize income.

The assumed adaptive character of expectations influences the results. Because adaptive expectations are sticky, they could transmit purely monetary disturbances. Assume an increase in foreign wages, prices, and the quantity of money. If the home country's currency appreciated to offset exactly the higher foreign nominal magnitudes, all real variables—in particular, the terms of trade—would remain unchanged and the home country would feel no impact. But with adaptive expectations this full offset does not occur. Future rates will move only slowly and, as a consequence, purely nominal disturbances will be transmitted internationally.

In the short run, the depreciation of the currency that arises from an increase in money and prices abroad induces the expectation of a future appreciation because expectations are formed adaptively. Therefore, the depreciation falls short of the full price increase and nominal interest rates decline in the country where money and prices have risen. With foreign price increases less than offset by the depreciation, demand shifts toward the home country's goods, thus raising domestic income and interest rates. The short-run equilibrium is therefore the same as in the last diagram. Domestic interest rates and income have risen, foreign real income has fallen, and so have foreign interest rates. The foreign currency is expected to appreciate. Only over time, as expectations adjust, is the price increase translated into an equal depreciation and neutrality restored at point *A*.

Clearly, one way a country can intervene to prevent the transmission of foreign disturbances is to peg the exchange rate and share in the foreign nominal expansion by expanding the domestic money supply. Alternatively, once again a tightening of monetary policy together with a fiscal expansion can maintain the initial equilibrium.

EXCHANGE-RATE EXPECTATIONS, THE TERMS OF TRADE, AND AGGREGATE DEMAND

The Keynesian model, as reviewed in the preceding sections, stresses the identification of the terms of trade with the exchange rate. By raising import prices relative to export and domestic prices, a currency depreciation worsens the terms of trade and in turn shifts demand from the rest of the world toward the depreciating country. A depreciation raises world demand for domestic output and improves the balance of trade.

It has become an accepted fact, however, that in many cases the trade balance worsens over the short term in response to a depreciation, responding favorably only over time. This reversal of direction of the trade effect—which is known as the J-curve and is exemplified by the aftermath of the 1967 U.K. devaluation—is ascribed to a slow adjustment of export prices and physical trade flows in contrast with the rapid increase in import prices.

To understand the operation of the J-curve from a macroeconomic perspective, one must analyze its macroeconomic counterpart. According to the national income identity,

$$Y \equiv C + I + G + T, \qquad (4)$$

where *C* is consumption, *I* is investment, *G* is government spending, and *T* denotes net exports; or, rewriting the identity,

$$T \equiv (S - I) + B, \qquad (4')$$

where *S* is saving and *B* denotes the budget surplus, all measured in terms of domestic output.

The equations point out that a worsening of the trade balance must be reflected in a change in the saving-investment balance or in the budget. The extent to which a worsening of the trade balance, such as arises in the short run from a depreciation, is reflected in the various components depends on (i) the origin of the depreciation, (ii) whether the deterioration of the terms of trade is considered temporary or permanent, and (iii) the speed of adjustment in the substitution of domestic goods for imports and the flexibility in intertemporal substitution.

When substitution possibilities are high even in the short run, a transitory exchange-rate movement exerts the maximum effect on the trade balance. It gives rise to both intertemporal and intercommodity substitution and thus would clearly improve the trade balance. Saving would rise and investment would decline as a reflection of the intertemporal substitution. Such a high degree of substitutability is, however, not characteristic of the average commodity since otherwise patterns such as the J-curve would not occur. Therefore, in what follows, we assume little scope for intertemporal substitution and a slow rate of intercommodity substitution, even for permanent changes in exchange rates.

Consider first the case of a transitory exchange-rate movement and assume, in the extreme, no substitution. As a consequence, physical trade flows and demand for domestic output will be unaffected. The worsening of the trade balance is "financed" by a reduction in saving.[10] Therefore, unanticipated, transitory changes in the exchange rate should have quite similar effects on the saving rate and the trade balance: a depreciation should reduce both, while an appreciation should increase both. The impact on inventory investment also tends to reflect the worsened trade balance. An unanticipated increase in import prices will raise the value of inventory accumulation, thus constituting part of the macroeconomic counterpart of the trade deficit.

In contrast, for a *permanent* deterioration of the terms of trade the response should certainly be an adjustment in the composition and level of spending. As the purchasing power of income, and, therefore, real consumption spending, declines, that reduction will fall on both domestic goods and imports. Furthermore, the substitution effect of a relative-price change will (over time) shift demand away from imports. The demand for domestic goods will rise or fall, and import spending will fall or rise, depending on the elasticity of demand for imports. With the saving rate unchanged, depreciation clearly can exert a deflationary impact unless it is offset by export or investment responses, or by an explicit macroeconomic policy. The impact of the depreciation on investment spending is not predictable. It will depend largely on the behavior of interest rates, aggregate demand, and the relative price of investment goods in terms of output prices and wages. Finally, for exports a quantity adjustment would be expected. A permanent movement in the terms of trade therefore leaves the ambiguity that inelastic import demand may imply a reduction in spending on domestic goods.

To consider the implications of this analysis for short-run macroeconomic policy, assume that in an attempt to expand aggregate demand the domestic quantity of money is increased. At first that policy reduces domestic interest rates and tends to induce a capital outflow and therefore a depreciation. If expectations about the long-run exchange rate are formed adaptively, the fall of the spot rate is viewed as partially temporary; it thus creates expectations of an appreciation and, therefore, allows a decline in domestic interest rates. Nonetheless, the expected long-run exchange rate will fall somewhat, reducing import demand and raising exports. Assuming sufficient elasticity, import spending will decline and net aggregate demand will rise because of the decline in interest rates. Both sources, therefore, contribute to an expansion in demand for domestic output. But with insufficient elasticity, import spending will rise and trade balance will fall. Additional effects stem from the excess of the spot-rate fall over the expected long-run fall. Here it is appropriate to assume that the resulting increase in import prices is not offset by reduced imports or increased exports but rather is financed by a reduction in saving.

Presumably, therefore, an expansionary monetary policy will worsen the trade balance by inducing a fall in the spot rate. Demand for domestic output will rise in response to reduced interest rates and may rise or fall in response to the permanent component of the exchange-rate movement. If the adjustment of trade flows and domestic demand to movements in the permanent rate takes time, a reduction in interest rates may actually reduce demand for domestic output in the short run.[11]

The ambiguity that surrounds the short-run impact of exchange-rate movements on demand for domestic output suggests that when an expansion in aggregate demand is desired, a combination of monetary *and* fiscal policy tools should be applied. Such a policy implies that the exchange rate can remain constant. It avoids the uncertainty (arising from the J-curve) associated with an attempt to expand domestic output through a net increase in exports.

A further advantage of the policy mix is that it avoids the deterioration in the terms of trade associated with a depreciation, which would depress the real income of those already employed.

---

[10] Given unchanged spending on domestic goods and unchanged physical imports at higher prices, total spending must rise, as measured in units of domestic goods or in nominal magnitudes. Measured similarly, saving and the saving rate must decline.

[11] This possibility has been suggested by Jürg Niehans, "Some Doubts About the Efficacy of Monetary Policy Under Flexible Exchange Rates," *Journal of International Economics*, vol. 5 (August 1975), pp. 275–81.

The tradeoff between raising employment and maintaining the real income of those already employed is avoided by a policy that pegs exchange rates in the face of a fiscal expansion.

THE ASSET-MARKET APPROACH TO EXCHANGE-RATE DETERMINATION

Recent discussions of the theory of flexible exchange rates have emphasized the role of asset markets, as opposed to the trade balance or the balance of payments, in determining exchange rates in the short run.[12] But is there, in fact, a significant difference between the stock and flow views?

To start out, the asset-market view relies critically on the assumption of perfect mobility and continuous, instantaneous equilibrium in capital markets. The economy is always in portfolio equilibrium. If domestic and foreign assets are perfect substitutes, the net yields are always and instantaneously equalized. If the assets are imperfect substitutes, a convenient assumption for some purposes, there is nevertheless portfolio equilibrium with respect to the composition of assets at each point in time.[13] The instantaneous achievement of portfolio balance is understood as perfect capital mobility.

Given this definition of perfect capital mobility, imperfect capital mobility is the case in which portfolio substitution in response to international yield differentials occurs only over time. Such a view gives rise to a "capital-flow function."

Either perfect capital mobility with imperfect substitutability or imperfect mobility allows international interest differentials. In both cases, even a small country can affect the interest rate by changing the relative supplies of assets. In sharp contrast, under the benchmark case of perfect capital mobility and perfect substitutability, nominal interest-rate differentials are possible only because of expectational errors, or, in the long run, because of perfectly anticipated differences in inflation rates consistent with equality of real rates.

In its sharpest formulation, the asset-market view focuses on the benchmark case and moreover assumes that income and nominal asset supplies are predetermined at any point in time. With such a set of assumptions, exchange-rate determination comes down to an equation such as 2, in which the equilibrium level of the current exchange rate is determined by nominal asset supplies, and the given level of real income and perhaps nonmonetary assets, and is independent of the current account. By assumption, any current-account imbalance can be financed in the world market at prevailing interest rates. To summarize, in the short run, given wealth and asset supplies, the exchange rate is determined in asset markets, and determines the current account; the current account, through its effects on income, prices, and wealth, affects the rate of change of the exchange rate.[14]

Two extensions of the basic conceptual framework significantly modify its force. With the first, which incorporates rational expectations, the current equilibrium level of exchange rates is a function of the entire subsequent path of the economy, including developments in income, prices, and wealth. Although these variables may be predetermined at a point in time, their subsequent evolution affects the current equilibrium level of the exchange rate and thus restores the general-equilibrium determination of exchange rates that was put in question by some variants of the asset-market view.[15]

---

[12] See, for example, the papers in the *Scandinavian Journal of Economics*, vol. 78, no. 2 (1976), as well as the comments by William Branson and the general discussion on Marina v. N. Whitman, "Global Monetarism and the Monetary Approach to the Balance of Payments," *BPEA, 3:1975*, pp. 537–42, 551–55.

[13] On this point, see Lance Girton and Dale W. Henderson, "Financial Capital Movements and Central Bank Behavior in a Two-Country, Short-run Portfolio Balance Model," *Journal of Monetary Economics*, vol. 2 (January 1976), pp. 33–61, and Rudiger Dornbusch, "Capital Mobility and Portfolio Balance," in Robert Z. Aliber, ed., *The Political Economy of Monetary Reform* (London: Macmillan), forthcoming.

[14] See Pentti J. K. Kouri, "The Exchange Rate and the Balance of Payments in the Short Run and in the Long Run: A Monetary Approach," *Scandinavian Journal of Economics*, vol. 78, no. 2 (1976), pp. 280–304; Stanley W. Black, *International Money Markets and Flexible Exchange Rates*, Studies in International Finance 32 (Princeton University, International Finance Section, 1973); Rudiger Dornbusch, "A Portfolio Balance Model of the Open Economy," *Journal of Monetary Economics*, vol. 1 (January 1975), pp. 1–20; and Rudiger Dornbusch, "Capital Mobility, Flexible Exchange Rates and Macroeconomic Equilibrium," in E. Claassen and P. Salin, eds., *Recent Issues in International Monetary Economics* (Amsterdam: North-Holland, 1976; U.S. distributor, American Elsevier).

[15] Rudiger Dornbusch, "Expectations and Exchange Rate Dynamics," *Journal of Political Economy*, vol. 84 (December 1976), pp. 1161–76, and Pentti Kouri, "Foreign Exchange Market Speculation and Stabilization Policy Under Flexible Exchange

The second extension, imperfect substitutability of assets, provides scope for an independent domestic interest rate on the basis of relative asset supplies rather than exchange-rate expectations. It does not, however, alter the view that exchange-rate determination is independent of the current account. Perhaps the most important corollary of imperfect substitutability is the ability to conduct exchange-rate and interest-rate policies that are independent of one another. With perfect substitutability there is a one-to-one correspondence among interest rates, foreign rates, and the expected premium on foreign exchange. With imperfect substitutability, given the mechanism of, say, adaptive expectations, a central bank can set both an exchange rate and an interest rate.[16]

Models of imperfect substitution remind us that not all exchange-rate movements need be related to monetary disturbances. It is possible to separate an asset-market view from a narrow monetary view of exchange-rate determination. For example, if money demand is independent of wealth and expected yields on foreign assets, shifts in asset preferences between domestic and foreign securities will alter exchanges rates with no effect whatsoever on the monetary sector.

An alternative to imperfect substitutability is slow adjustment in portfolio composition. In such a view, monetary conditions, along with predetermined income, determine interest rates while the balance of payments determines the exchange rate. This view yields, in the short run, the same predictions as a model of imperfect substitution, and shares with the asset-market approach the emphasis on the relation between interest rates and exchange rates. To appreciate this point consider the balance-of-payments equation

$$BOP = T(e,y, \ldots) + K(r,r^* + \lambda); \quad (5)$$
$$\lambda = \lambda(e, e_{-1} \ldots),$$

where K is the net rate of capital inflow. With income predetermined, monetary conditions determine the interest rate. Balance-of-payments adjustment is brought about by the interaction of actual and expected exchange rates. Expected exchange rates serve the important purpose of inducing speculative capital flows.

A decline of domestic interest rates, as would result from a monetary expansion, tends to induce a capital outflow and a balance-of-payments deficit. The resulting fall of the spot exchange rate will proceed until capital outflows just match the trade surplus. The most interesting case is one in which the trade balance responds to the exchange rate either not at all or perversely. Here the interaction between actual and expected exchange rates stands out most sharply. With the trade balance given or deteriorating in response to the depreciation, the capital account will have to improve if balance-of-payments equilibrium is to be restored. The spot rate will have to fall enough to invite a speculative capital inflow even though domestic interest rates have declined. That is achieved by a depreciation of the currency (on the spot rate) sufficiently large to arouse the expectation of an appreciation equal to or larger than the interest differential. The large drop in the spot rate must therefore lead to a speculative capital inflow that covers the depreciation-induced trade deficit.

Such an interpretation seems to accord with the relevant facts about exchange rates and interest rates and, for practical purposes, cannot be distinguished from the asset-market view. Indeed, its focus on speculative capital flows as the chief link between exchange rates and interest rates precisely duplicates that of the asset view.[17] The main issue in an appropriate interpretation of the flow view is realistically defining the importance of the capital account and deemphasizing adjustments in the current account as part of the short-run accommodating movement.

Rates" (paper presented at the Conference on the Political Economy of Inflation and Unemployment in Open Economics, Athens, Greece, 1976; processed).

[16] On this argument, see Henry C. Wallich, "Statement," in *International Monetary Reform and Exchange Rate Management,* Hearings before the Subcommittee on International Trade, Investment and Monetary Policy of the House Committee on Banking, Currency and Housing, and the Subcommittee on International Economics of the Joint Economic Committee, 94:1 (Government Printing Office, 1975), pp. 209–30; and Lance Girton and Dale W. Henderson, "The Effects of Central Bank Intervention in Domestic and Foreign Assets Under Fixed and Flexible Exchange Rates," in D. Logue and others, eds., *The Effects of Exchange Rate Adjustment,* forthcoming.

[17] The flow of capital mobility is emphasized by Peter B. Kenen, "Flexible Exchange Rates and National Autonomy," *Revista Internazionale di Scienze Economiche e Commerciale* [Milan: Bocconi University], vol. 23 (February 1976), pp. 105–27; Polly Allen and Peter B. Kenen, "Portfolio Adjustment in Open Economies: A Comparison of Alternative Specifications," *Weltwirtschaftliches Archiv,* vol. 112, no. 1 (1976), pp. 33–72; Niehans, "Some Doubts"; and John Williamson, "Another Case of Profitable, Destabilising Speculation," *Journal of International Economics,* vol. 3 (February 1973), pp. 77–83, and John Williamson, "Exchange-Rate Flexibility and Reserve Use," *Scandinavian Journal of Economics,* vol. 78, no. 2 (1976), pp. 327–39.

Both views of exchange-rate determination suggest why rates fluctuate a good deal in the short run. These fluctuations simply reflect those in short-term interest rates. A rise in domestic interest rates because of a monetary contraction or an increase in money demand will produce an interest differential that could generate a capital flow. The appreciation of the currency will continue until it is sufficient to cause the anticipation of depreciation at a rate corresponding to the interest differential. The required exchange-rate movement will be larger the higher the elasticity of exchange-rate expectations and the higher the substitutability between domestic and foreign assets. Overshooting of exchange rates thus simply reflects the requirement that expected asset yields be kept in line.

This view is perfectly compatible with a current account that is unresponsive or even responds perversely in the short run. Indeed, the exchange-rate movement will have to be larger the less (or the more perversely) the current-account balance reacts to the exchange rate. The argument that the current account cannot be a determinant of exchange rates because it moves little relative to them misses the point that exchange rates move so much because the current account moves so little.

---

38. RULES AND ROLES FOR FISCAL AND MONETARY POLICY*

Arthur M. Okun†

When economists write text books or teach introductory students or lecture to laymen, they happily extol the virtues of two lovely handmaidens of aggregate economic stabilization—fiscal policy and monetary policy. But when they write for learned journals or assemble for professional meetings, they often insist on staging a beauty contest between the two. And each judge feels somehow obliged to decide that one of the two entries is just an ugly beast. My remarks tonight are in the spirit of bigamous devotion rather than invidious comparison. Fiscal policy and monetary policy are both beautiful; we need them both and we should treat them both lovingly.

THE GENERAL ECLECTIC CASE

In particular, both fiscal and monetary policy are capable of providing some extra push upward or downward on GNP. In fact, if aggregate stimulus or restraint were all that mattered, either one of the two tools could generally do the job, and the second—whichever one chose to be second—would be redundant. The basic general eclectic principle that ought to guide us, as a first approximation, is that either fiscal or monetary policy can administer a required sedative or stimulus to economic activity. As every introductory student knows, however, fiscal and monetary tools operate in very different ways. Monetary policy initially makes people more liquid without adding directly to their incomes or wealth; fiscal policy enhances their incomes and wealth without increasing their liquidity.

In a stimulative monetary action, the people who initially acquire money are not simply given the money; they must part with government securities to get it. But once their portfolios become more liquid, they presumably use the cash proceeds to acquire alternative earning assets, and in so doing they bid up the prices of those assets, or equivalently, reduce the yields. Thus prospective borrowers find it easier and less expensive to issue securities and to get loans; and investors who would otherwise be acquiring securities may be induced instead to purchase real assets such as capital goods. Also, because market values of securities are raised, people become wealthier, if in an indirect way, and may hence increase their purchases of goods and services. Thus many channels run from the easing of financial markets to the quickening of real economic activity.[1]

---

* From James J. Diamond, ed., Issues in *Fiscal and Monetary Policy: The Eclectic Economist Views the Controversy* (Chicago: De Paul University, 1971), pp. 51–74. Reprinted by permission of the publisher and author. Arthur M. Okun is a Senior Fellow, Brookings Institution.

† The views expressed are my own and are not necessarily those of the officers, trustees, or other staff members of the Brookings Institution.

[1] There is general agreement between Keynesians and monetarists regarding the mechanism for trans-

A simulative fiscal action is appropriately undertaken when resources are unemployed; in that situation, an action such as expanded government purchases, whether for good things like hospitals or less good things like military weapons, puts resources to work and rewards them with income. The additional cash received by some people is matched by reduced cash holdings of those who bought government securities to finance the outlay. But the securities buyers have no income loss to make them tighten their belts; they voluntarily traded money for near money. In contrast, the income recipients become willing to spend more, and thus trigger a multiplier process on production and income. So, while fiscal and monetary routes differ, the ultimate destination —the effect on national product—is the same, in principle.

Indeed, the conditions under which either fiscal tools or monetary tools, taken separately, have zero effect on GNP are merely textbook curiosities rather than meaningful possibilities in the modern U.S. economic environment. For stimulative monetary policy to be nothing more than a push on a string, either interest rates would have to be just as low as they could possibly go, or investment and consumption would have to show zero response to any further reduction in interest rates. The former possibility is the famous Keynesian liquidity trap, which made lots of sense in describing 1936, but has no relevance to 1971. With prime corporations paying 8 percent on long-term bonds, interest rates are still higher than at any time in my lifetime prior to 1969.[2] There is plenty of room for them to decline, and, in turn, for states and localities, homebuyers and consumer installment credit users, as well as business investors, to be encouraged to spend more by lower costs of credit.

The opposite extreme, impotent fiscal policy, is equally remote. Fiscal policy must exert some stimulative effect on economic activity (even when the monetary policy makers do not accommodate the fiscal action at all) unless the velocity of money is completely inflexibile so that no economizing on cash balances occurs. Though the money supply does not rise in a pure fiscal action, spending will tend to rise unless people are totally unable or unwilling to speed up the turnover of cash. And money holders do economize on cash to a varying degree—they do so seasonally and cyclically, and they do so dependably in response to changes in the opportunity cost of holding money. The holder of zero-yielding cash is sacrificing the opportunity to receive the going interest rates of earning assets. The higher interest rates are, the more he sacrifices; and hence, economic theory tells us, the more he will economize on his holdings of cash.

And the facts confirm the theory. The negative relationship between the demand for money and the rate of interest is one of the most firmly established empirical propositions in macroeconomics.[3] So a pure fiscal stimulus produces a speedup in the turnover of money and higher interest rates, and more GNP.

The fact that people do economize on cash balances in response to rises in interest rates demonstrates the efficacy of fiscal policy. Anybody who reports that he can't find a trace of fiscal impact in the aggregate data is unreasonably claiming an absolutely inflexible velocity—a vertical liquidity preference function[4]—or else he is revealing the limitations of his research techniques rather than those of fiscal policy.

A few other artful dodges, I submit, make even less sense. Try to defend fiscal impotence on grounds of a horizontal marginal efficiency schedule—that means investment is so sensitive to return that even the slightest interest variation will unleash unlimited changes in investment demand. Or make the case that people subjectively assume the public debt as personal debt and feel commensurately worse off whenever the budget is in deficit. Or contend that businessmen are so frightened by fiscal stimulation that their increased demand for cash and reduced investment spoils its influence.[5] Or use the argument

---

mitting monetary changes. See Milton Friedman and Anna J. Schwartz, "Money and Business Cycles," in Milton Friedman, *The Optimum Quantity of Money and Other Essays* (Aldine, 1969), pp. 229–34. Reprinted from *Review of Economics and Statistics*, Vol. 45 supplement (February 1963), pp. 59–63.

[2] Even when any reasonable allowance is made for inflation, it is hard to view today's *real* rates as low by historical standards.

[3] See Arthur M. Okun, *The Political Economy of Prosperity* (Brookings Institution, 1970), p. 58, and the bibliography on pp. 146–47 for a list of articles reporting empirical results confirming this relationship.

[4] For discussion of a model implying the existence of a vertical liquidity preference function, see Leonall C. Andersen and Jerry L. Jordan, "Monetary and Fiscal Actions: A Test of Their Relative Importance in Economic Stabilization," Federal Reserve Bank of St. Louis, *Monthly Review* (November 1968).

[5] See Roger W. Spencer and William P. Yohe, "The 'Crowding Out' of Private Expenditures by Fiscal Policy Actions," in Federal Reserve Bank of St. Louis, *Monthly Review*, vol. 52, No. 10 (October 1970), pp. 17–24.

that Say's law operates even when the unemployment rate is 6 percent.[6] It's a battle between ingenuity and credulity!

The eclectic principle is terribly important, not because it answers any questions, but because it rules out nonsense questions and points to sensible ones. It warns us not to get bogged down in such metaphysical issues as whether it is really the Fed that creates inflation during wartime. Every wartime period has been marked by enormous fiscal stimulus, and yet that fiscal fuel-injection could have been neutralized by some huge amount of pressure on the monetary brakes. In that sense, the Fed could have been sufficiently restrictive to offset the stimulus of military expenditures. Anyone who chooses to blame the resulting inflation on not slamming on the monetary brakes, rather than on pumping the fiscal accelerator, can feel free to exercise that curious preference. Take another example: Did the expansion following the tax cut in 1964–65 result from monetary policy? Of course it did, the eclectic principle tells us. If the Fed had wished to nullify the expansionary influence of the tax cut, surely some monetary policy would have been sufficiently restrictive to do so. There is no unique way of allocating credit or blame in a world where both tools can do the stabilization job.

SIDE EFFECTS AS THE CENTRAL ISSUE

So long as both tools are capable of speeding up or slowing down demand, the decisions on how to use them and how to combine them must be made on the basis of criteria other than their simple ability to stimulate or restrain. Nor do we typically get any help by considering *how much* work monetary or fiscal tools do, because usually the right answer is, "as much as needed," providing the shift in policy is large enough. In more formal terms, two instruments and one target produce an indeterminate system.

Of course, there are two basic targets of stabilization policy: price stability and maximum production. But the two tools will not serve to implement those two goals simultaneously. A pen and a pencil are one more tool than is needed to write a letter, but the second tool can't be used to mow the lawn. In the same way, fiscal and monetary policy can both push up aggregate demand or push down aggregate demand, but

neither can solve the Phillips curve problem. Subject to minor qualifications,[7] the fiscal route to a given unemployment rate is neither less nor more inflationary than the monetary route to that same unemployment rate.

We can have the GNP path we want equally well with a tight fiscal policy and an easier monetary policy, or the reverse, within fairly broad limits. The real basis for choice lies in the many subsidiary economic targets, beside real GNP and inflation, that are differentially affected by fiscal and monetary policies. Sometimes these are labeled "side effects." I submit that they are the main issue in determining the fiscal-monetary mix, and they belong in the center ring.

Composition of Output

One of the subsidiary targets involves the composition of output among sectors. General monetary policy tools, as they are actually employed, bear down very unevenly on the various sectors of the economy. Homebuilding and state and local capital projects are principal victims of monetary restraint. Although the evidence isn't entirely conclusive, it suggests that monetary restraint discriminates particularly against small business. In the field of taxation, we agonize about incidence and equity. The same intense concern is appropriate in the case of monetary restraint and, in fact, increasing concern is being registered in the political arena. In the 1969–70 period of tight money, many efforts (such as Home Loan Bank and Fannie Mae operations) were made to insulate housing from the brunt of the attack. But the impact on homebuilding was still heavy. Moreover, there is considerable basis for suspicion that these actions defused— as well as diffused—the impact of monetary restraint. A more restrictive monetary policy, as measured in terms of either monetary aggregates or interest rates, is required to accomplish the same dampening effect on GNP if the sectors most vulnerable to credit restraint are shielded from its blows.

The concern about uneven impact may be accentuated because, in 1966 and again in 1969–70, monetary restraint hit sectors that rated particularly high social priorities. But that is not

---

[6] See "Interest Rates and the Demand for Money," Chapter 7 in Milton Friedman, *The Optimum Quantity of Money.* Reprinted from *The Journal of Law and Economics,* vol. 9 (October 1966), pp. 71–85. So far as I can see, Friedman is invoking Say's Law.

[7] An unbalanced composition of demand among regions and industries means more inflationary pressure at a given overall utilization rate. Thus, particularly concentrated excess demands (e.g., for defense goods or for new homes) may harm the cause of price stability. But the degree of balance cannot be uniquely linked to fiscal-monetary choices.

the whole story. Any unusual departure of monetary policy from a "middle-of-the-road" position may lead to allocations that do not accord with the nation's sense of equity and efficiency. For example, in the early sixties, it was feared that a very easy monetary policy might encourage speculative excesses in building because some financial institutions would be pressured to find mortgage loans in order to earn a return on their assets.

In the last few years, some economists—most notably, Franco Modigliani—have argued that monetary policy may have a significant impact on consumption through its influence on the market value of equity securities and bonds[8] in addition to its more direct impact through the cost and availability of installment credit. In my view, the jury is still out on this issue. On the one hand, it's easy to believe that a huge change, say, $100 billion, in the net worth of the American public, such as stock market fluctuations can generate, could alter consumer spending in relation to income by a significant amount like $3 billion, even though that change in wealth is concentrated in a small group at the very top of the income and wealth distribution. On the other hand, previous empirical work on this issue came up with a nearly unanimous negative verdict.[9] In 1966 and 1969, however, the timing

of stock market declines and the sluggishness in consumer demand seemed to fit fairly well with the hypothesis. One would like to believe the wealth hypothesis because it would suggest that monetary policy has broad and sizable effects on consumption, especially on that of high-income consumers; monetary restraint would then be revealed as less uneven and less inequitable. But before embracing that judgment, one should wait for more decisive evidence.

Interest Rates and Asset Values

Another major consideration in monetary policy is its effects on interest rates and balance sheets. Some economists may argue that the only function of interest rates is to clear the market and the only sense in which rates can be too high or too low is in failing to establish that equilibrium. Every Congressman knows better! Interest rates are a social target. That is the revealed preference of the American public, reflected in the letters it writes to Washington and the answers it gives to opinion polls. And this is no optical illusion on the part of the citizenry. They have the same good reasons to dislike rising interest rates that apply to rising prices—the haphazard, redistributive effects. And they are concerned about *nominal* interest rates just as they are concerned about prices. It is not clear that such major groups as businessmen or workers are particularly hurt or particularly helped by tight money (or by inflation), but the impacts are quite haphazard in both cases. The resulting lottery in real incomes strikes most Americans as unjust.

The largest redistributive effect of tight money, like that of inflation, falls on balance sheets rather than income statements. People care about their paper wealth and feel worse off when bond and equity prices nose dive. Even though society is not deprived of real resources when security prices drop, it is hard to find gainers to match the losers. Although Alvin Hansen stressed the social costs of distorted, fluctuating balance sheets in the 1950s,[10] this issue gets little attention from economists. But it never escapes the broader and keener vision of the American public.

Financial Dislocation

A restrictive monetary policy may also have important, dislocating effects on the financial system. The key function of a financial system is

[8] See Franco Modigliani, "Monetary Policy and Consumption—The Linkages Via Interest Rate and Wealth Effects in the Federal Reserve-MIT-Penn Model" (paper prepared for the Federal Reserve Bank of Boston Conference at Nantucket, Massachusetts, June 1971; offset), esp. part I.3. For earlier discussions of the effects of monetary policy as it operates in the Federal Reserve-MIT-Penn Model, see the following: Robert H. Rasche and Harold L. Shapiro, "The FRB-MIT Econometric Model: Its Special Features," in American Economic Association, *Papers and Proceedings of the Eightieth Annual Meeting, 1967* (*American Economic Review,* vol. 58, May 1968), pp. 123–49; Albert Ando and Franco Modigliani, "Econometric Analysis of Stabilization Policies," in American Economic Association, *Papers and Proceednigs of the Eighty-first Annual Meeting, 1968* (*American Economic Review,* vol. 59, May 1969), pp. 296–314; Frank de Leeuw and Edward Gramlich, "The Federal Reserve-MIT Econometric Model," *Federal Reserve Bulletin,* vol. 54 (January 1968), pp. 11–40; de Leeuw and Gramlich, "The Channels of Monetary Policy," *Federal Reserve Bulletin,* vol. 55 (June 1969), pp. 472–91.

[9] See John J. Arena, "The Wealth Effect and Consumption: A Statistical Inquiry," *Yale Economic Essays,* vol. 3 (Fall 1963), esp. pp. 273–84 and "Post-war Stock Market Changes and Consumer Spending," *Review of Economics and Statistics,* vol. 47 (November 1965), pp. 379–91; Saul H. Hymans, "Consumption: New Data and Old Puzzles," *Brookings Papers on Economic Activity* (1:1970), pp. 121–26.

[10] See, for example, *The American Economy* (McGraw-Hill, 1957), pp. 53–55.

to offer people opportunities to invest without saving and to save without investing. If people want risky assets, they can acquire them beyond the extent of their net worth; if they wish to avoid risk, they can earn a moderate return and stay liquid. The trade of funds between lovers of liquidity and lovers of real assets produces gains to all. "Crunch" and "liquidity crisis" are names for a breakdown in the functioning of the financial system. Such a breakdown deprives people of important options and may permanently impair their willingness to take risks and to hold certain types of assets. To the extent that very tight money curbs an inflationary boom by putting boulders in the financial stream, a considerable price is paid. And to the extent that extremely easy money stimulates a weak economy by opening the flood gates of speculation, that too may be costly.

Balance of Payments

The pursuit of a monetary policy focused single-mindedly on stabilization goals would have further "side effects" on the balance of payments, to the extent that it changes international interest rate differentials and hence influences capital flows. There are strong arguments for fundamental reforms of the international monetary system—especially more flexible exchange rates—that would greatly reduce this concern. But those reforms are not on the immediate horizon; nor is the United States prepared to be consistently passive about international payments.[11] Meanwhile, the external deficit casts a shadow that cannot be ignored in the formulation of fiscal-monetary policies.

Growth

A final consideration in the mix of stabilization tools is the long-run influence of monetary policy on the rate of growth of our supply capa-

[11] Editor's note: Since this was written, the fixed-exchange-rate system has been replaced by a flexible-rate system. The events leading up to the change, the nature of the present system, and possible future directions of development are all treated in Chapter 6. The implications of flexible exchange rates for the use of monetary and fiscal policy are discussed by Rudiger Dornbusch and Paul Krugman (reading 37) in Chapter 7.

On the question of a passive stance, see Lawrence B. Krause, "A Passive Balance-of-Payments Strategy for the United States," *Brookings Papers on Economic Activity* (3:1970), pp. 339–60; and Gottfried Haberler and Thomas D. Willett, *A Strategy for U.S. Balance of Payments Policy* (American Enterprise Institute, February 1971).

bilities. An average posture of relatively easy money (and low interest rates) combined with tight fiscal policy (designed especially to put a damper on private consumption) is most likely to produce high investment and rapid growth of potential. That becomes relevant in the short run because the long-run posture of monetary policy is an average of its short-run swings. If, for example, the nation relies most heavily on monetary policy for restraint and on fiscal policy for stimulus, it will unintentionally slip to a lower growth path. The contribution of extra investment to growth and the value of the extra growth to a society that is already affluent in the aggregate are further vital issues. Recently, enthusiasm for growth-oriented policies has been dampened by the concern about the social fallout of rapid growth and by the shame of poverty, which calls for higher current consumption at the low end of the income scale. Nonetheless, the growth implications of decisions about the fiscal-monetary mix should be recognized.

In the light of these considerations, there are good reasons to avoid extreme tightness or extreme ease in monetary policy—even if it produces an ideal path of real output. Tight money can be bad medicine for a boom even if it cures the disease, just as amputation of the hand is a bad remedy for eczema. The experience of 1966 provides an object lesson. Judged by its performance in getting GNP on track, the Federal Reserve in 1966 put on *the* virtuoso performance in the history of stabilization policy. It was the greatest tight-rope walking and balancing act ever performed by either fiscal or monetary policy. Single-handedly the Fed curbed a boom generated by a vastly stimulative fiscal policy that was paralyzed by politics and distorted by war. And, in stopping the boom, it avoided a recession. To be sure, real GNP dipped for a single quarter, but the unemployment rate did not rise significantly above 4 percent; the 1967 pause was as different from the five postwar recessions, including 1970, as a cold is different from pneumonia. Moreover, inflation slowed markedly in the closing months of 1966 and the first half of 1967. What more could anyone want? Yet, you won't find the 1966 Fed team in the hall of fame for stabilization policy. In the view of most Americans, the collapse of homebuilding, the disruption of financial markets, and the escalation of interest rates were evils that outweighed the benefits of the nonrecessionary halting of inflation. The Fed itself reacted by refusing to give an encore in 1967–68, accepting renewed inflation as a lesser evil than renewed tight money.

All of this leads up to my first rule for stabilization policy: *Keep monetary conditions close to the middle of the road.* Let me explain that, no matter how monetary policy affects GNP, the rule must be interpreted in terms of interest rates and credit conditions, and not in terms of monetary aggregates. Suppose, for a moment, that the monetary impact on GNP is so powerful and the growth rate of the money supply is so critical that a growth rate of money only a little bit below normal will offset the aggregate demand impact of a huge fiscal stimulus (just for example, a $25 billion Vietnam expenditure add-on). The results would still be very tight money in terms of credit conditions, interest rates, and the impact on the composition of output. The shift in financial conditions required to "crowd out" $25 billion of private expenditures can hardly be trivial —even if the needed shift in monetary growth were trivial.

The "middle of the road" is deliberately a vague concept, relying on the existence of some general long-run notion of appropriate and normal interest rates and liquidity ratios. To be sure, it is hard to tell when we are in the middle of the road, but it is easy to tell when we are far away from it.

THE IMPLICATIONS FOR FISCAL POLICY

My second rule follows immediately from the first: *Operate fiscal policy to avoid forcing monetary policy off the middle of the road.* If fiscal policy is inappropriately stimulative or restrictive, a conscientious and (at least somewhat) independent monetary authority will be obliged to shoulder most of the burden for stabilizing the economy. In historical perspective, it is important to recognize that this sense of responsibility has not always prevailed. In World War II and again in the initial stages of the Korean War, the Federal Reserve reacted to an inflationary fiscal policy simply by pegging interest rates and creating all the liquidity demanded in an inflationary boom. Through these actions, the Federal Reserve not only passed the buck right back to fiscal policy but became an active accomplice in the inflation, intensifying excess demand by holding nominal interest rates constant as prices accelerated. It was technically feasible for the Federal Reserve to behave similarly during the Vietnam war. The fact that it picked up the ball after the fiscal fumble of 1966 demonstrated a new and greater sense of responsibility by the central bank for overall stabilization. So long as both fiscal and monetary policy makers feel that re-

sponsibility, as they appropriately should, an inappropriate fiscal policy is bound to push monetary policy off the middle of the road. Obviously, fiscal buck passing can also occur in a situation when stimulus is in order. In 1971, a rather neutral fiscal program accompanied by ambitious targets for recovery threatens to overburden the Federal Reserve with the responsibility for stimulus.

FISCAL TOOLS AND COMPOSITION

To avoid pushing monetary policy off the middle of the road, fiscal policy must itself depart from the middle of the road—turning markedly more stimulative or more restrictive than its normal long-run posture—when private demand is especially weak or especially strong. But such swings in fiscal policy must also be made in light of compositional constraints that apply to federal expenditures, and especially to federal purchases of goods and services. Our preferences about the composition of output imply some notion of appropriate levels of civilian public programs. No one would wish to double or halve the size of the Census Bureau or the Forest Service in order to accord with the cyclical position of the economy. Moreover, these limitations based on principle are reinforced by limitations of a practical character. First, federal civilian expenditures on goods and services involve a mere 2½ percent of GNP and thus afford very little leverage for stabilization. Second, most federal programs involving purchases of goods and services have long start-up and shut-off periods that make it extremely difficult to vary timing greatly without impairing efficiency.

Popular discussions of fiscal stabilization tend to stress expenditure variation despite these clear constraints. Why are the lessons ignored? Could any informed person have seriously regarded a curb on civilian public programs during the Vietnam build-up period as a meaningful antidote to the stimulus of increasing military expenditures? Could anybody familiar with the history of the lags in public spending support a public works program as a way to create jobs and strengthen recovery in 1971 or 1972?[12] The evidence suggests that people with strong views on the desirable size of the public sector tend to invoke the cause of stabilization as a ra-

---

[12] For a brief documentation of the disappointing results of the 1962 public works program, see Nancy H. Teeters, "The 1972 Budget: Where It Stands and Where It Might Go," *Brookings Papers on Economic Activity* (1:1971), pp. 232–33.

tionalization for their social preferences. To an advocate of additional government spending, a recession provides a useful additional talking point; to a crusader for cutbacks in government spending, excess demand inflation offers an excellent excuse.

Federal "transfer" programs, such as social security, unemployment compensation, and veterans' benefits, are not subject to serious implementation lags, but their room for maneuver is limited by the principle of intertemporal equity. The aged, the poor, or the unemployed cannot justifiably be treated better in a recession than in prosperity or in a boom. The unfortunate people who are jobless when the unemployment rate is low deserve no less generous benefits than those who are unemployed when the rate is high; indeed, if misery loves company, those unemployed in prosperity may suffer psychically because they have less of it.

Some significant elbow room nevertheless appears for varying such transfer programs. Society's agenda always contains some new initiative or additional step to strengthen transfer programs in a growing economy with growing overall income; and the next step can be timed to come a little sooner or a little later, depending on the economy's cyclical position. In the present context, the administration's family assistance program provides a good example. The proposed initial date for benefits is July 1, 1972, but the program could be made effective six months earlier. Similarly, there is some opportunity for varying the timing of benefit liberalization and of payroll tax increases with respect to the social security program. Congress displayed wisdom early in 1971 by deferring for a year the proposed increase in the maximum earnings base of the payroll tax.

While this pure timing flexibility is important, it may not provide enough leeway for a flexible fiscal policy to respond to the needs of a very slack or very taut economy. Beyond it, the most attractive fiscal tool is variation in personal income tax rates. In principle, significant and indeed frequent changes in these rates are acceptable. Because they affect the huge consumption sector most directly and because their impact is spread over Americans throughout the middle- and upper-income groups, personal taxes are an ideal instrument for flexibility. While the income tax is specifically aimed to redistribute income in a more egalitarian way, the basic function of taxation is simply to restrain demand, given the socially desired level of public expenditures. A prima facie case exists for suspending or repeal-

ing any tax (or tax rate) that is not essential for the purpose of restraining demand sufficiently to avoid both inflation and monetary restraint. Moreover, according to compelling historical evidence, changes in personal tax rates—upward or downward, permanent or temporary—have reasonably reliable effects on consumer spending and hence on GNP.[13]

Political implementation is the one troublesome problem with changes in personal tax rates. Obviously, unlike shifts in monetary policy, any change in tax rates requires legislative action. And the record of congressional response to presidential requests for such changes has left much to be desired. Many constructive proposals have been made to improve that story. In 1961, the Commission on Money and Credit asked Congress to delegate authority for tax changes to the President subject to congressional veto; others have urged Congress to enact rules that would commit it to fast action—favorable or unfavorable—in response to a presidential request. Presidents Kennedy and Johnson made proposals for speeding the legislative process in their Economic Reports of 1962 and 1969, respectively. Herbert Stein presented a constructive proposal along similar lines in 1968. Even the Joint Economic Committee of the Congress expressed its concern in its 1966 report, "Tax Changes for Shortrun Stabilization."[14] But the Congress has generally ignored these proposals, jealously guarding its prerogatives over taxation, and refusing to bind its own hands with respect to procedures.

Under the present rules of the game, the President must ask Congress to do what seems best for the country and must count on presenting the case persuasively. The discussion and debates of recent years have put Congress on its mettle to respond promptly and pragmatically to any

---

[13] See my papers, "Measuring the Impact of the 1964 Tax Reduction," in Walter W. Heller, ed., *Perspectives on Economic Growth* (Random House, 1968); and "The Personal Tax Surcharge and Consumer Demand, 1968–70," *Brookings Papers on Economic Activity* (1:1971), pp. 167–204.

[14] Report of the Commission on Money and Credit, *Money and Credit—Their Influence on Jobs, Prices, and Growth* (Prentice-Hall, 1961), pp. 133–37; *Economic Report of the President together with the Annual Report of the Council of Economic Advisers*, January 1962, pp. 17–19, and *Economic Report*, January 1969, pp. 12–13; Herbert Stein, "Unemployment, Inflation, and Economic Stability," in Kermit Gordon (ed.), *Agenda for the Nation*, (Brookings Institution, 1968), pp. 292–93; *Tax Changes for Shortrun Stabilization*, A Report of the Subcommittee on Fiscal Policy of the Joint Economic Committee, 89 Cong. 2 sess. (1966), p. 16.

presidential request for tax changes designed for short-run stabilization purposes. Moreover, the 1963 and 1967 stalemates reflected special factors that seem obsolete—budget orthodoxy in the earlier case and Vietnam strategy in the later one. Our traditional procedures deserve another try.

These thoughts on the uses of alternative fiscal tools can be summarized as my third rule: *When additional fiscal stimulus or restraint is needed, opportunities for varying the timing of new initiatives in federal spending or tax programs should be the first line of attack: if these are inadequate to achieve the desired swing in fiscal policy, a change in personal tax rates should be sought.* We must keep urging and prodding the Congress to respond more promptly when tax changes are proposed. And we must not give up, for it will heed this message eventually.

FULL EMPLOYMENT SURPLUS

The problems of executive-legislative coordination apply to expenditures as well as taxes. The fractionated process by which appropriations are made on Capitol Hill leads to frightful difficulties in the overall control of federal spending. As I have suggested elsewhere, one path to improvement might involve the following procedures: The President would make explicit the fiscal decision underlying his budget; and the Congress would then focus on that decision, approving or modifying it; and it would then commit itself to undertake an iterative review of appropriations and tax legislation during the course of the year to assure that the budget stayed within the bounds.[15]

I believe that the concept of the full employment surplus can be extremely useful as the focus of the fiscal plan and review. It is a simple enough summary number of the budget's impact on the economy to be understood by the participants, and it is a good enough summary to serve the purpose. It permits the stimulus or restraint in the budget to be compared with that of the previous year and other relevant previous periods.[16] While administration officials cannot hope to provide a scientific demonstration that the budget has the proper amount of stimulus or restraint, they can generate an informed discussion and enlightened decision process by explaining their forecast of the strength of private demand, the proper role for monetary policy, and the likely response of the economy to proposed fiscal changes.

The main function of the full employment surplus in policy discussion is to correct the misleading impression generated by the actual budget surplus or deficit when the economy is off course. In a weak economy, revenues automatically fall far below their full employment level and the budget is hence pushed into deficit. That automatic or passive deficit may be misread as evidence that the budget is strongly stimulating the economy and hence that further expansionary action is inappropriate. By the same token, a boom resulting from a surge in private demand or an easing of monetary policy would automatically swell federal revenues, thereby tending to produce a surplus in the budget. These automatic shifts in federal revenues are important and significant; such built-in stabilizers help to cushion cumulative declines and dampen cumulative upsurges, but they should be properly recognized as shock absorbers rather than either accelerators or brakes.

I believe the focus on the full employment budget by the administration this year has helped to raise the level of fiscal debate. It reveals that the big deficits of fiscal years 1971 and 1972 are symptoms of a weak economy, rather than of a strong budget.

Guide *versus* Rule

The full employment budget shows where the fiscal dials are set; but it cannot say where the dials *ought* to be set. It is an aid to safe driving much like a speedometer, but it cannot prescribe the optimum speed. That depends on road conditions. A maintained target for the full employment surplus represents a decision to drive by the dashboard and to stop watching the road. Road conditions do change significantly from time to time in our dynamic economy. The evidence of the postwar era suggests that zero is too low a full employment surplus for

---

[15] See Okun, *The Political Economy of Prosperity*, pp. 121–22.

Editor's note: With the passage of the Congressional Budget and Impoundment Control Act in July 1974, a new budget process was installed which is designed to provide more unity and focus than the process it replaced, and also better control over spending. Under this process, the "current services budget" is the baseline from which departures are proposed and considered. For a thorough description of the new process, see the paper by Joseph Scherer (reading 21) in Chapter 4.

[16] Arthur M. Okun and Nancy H. Teeters, "The Full Employment Surplus Revisited," *Brookings Papers on Economic Activity* (1:1970), pp. 77–81.

a period of prosperity and too high a full employment surplus for a period of slack and slump. From long-term saving-investment patterns, one might guess that a full employment surplus of one-half of one percent of GNP would be about right on the average to accompany a middle-of-the-road monetary policy. But even that judgment would be highly speculative; and it would not tell us how to identify the rare case of an average year or how to quantify the departure of any particular year from the average. Economists have no right to be presumptuous about their ability to forecast in either the short run or the long run; and it is far more presumptuous to claim that the proper size of the full employment surplus can be determined for the long run than to believe that it can be nudged in the correct direction in any particular year on the basis of the evidence then at hand.

Adoption of a fixed full employment surplus implies a firm determination by fiscal policy makers to counteract any major surprises that arise *within* the federal budget. If Congress rejects the President's proposals for major expenditure programs such as revenue sharing or family assistance, the advocate of a fixed full employment surplus is committed to propose alternatives for those stimulative actions. Similarly, if uncontrollable expenditures spurt, some compensatory action is required to keep the overall full employment budget close to its original position.

At the same time, however, the advocate of the fixed full employment surplus is determined *not* to act in response to surprises in private demand or monetary policy, no matter how large or how definite these may be. The resulting decision rule is illogical and indefensible. Once it is recognized that some surprises within the federal budget are large enough to call for offsetting fiscal action, it must be conceded that some surprises in consumer spending, plant and equipment outlays, or Federal Reserve decisions might also point to shifts in the fiscal course.

In fact, the Nixon administration has not adopted a fixed full employment surplus, but rather a rule that the full employment budget shall be *at least* in balance on the unified basis of budget accounting. The doctrine of balancing the full employment budget has obvious antecedents in the less sophisticated orthodoxy of balancing the actual budget. The new rule is far less harmful than its predecessor, but it is equally arbitrary. Its arbitrariness is perhaps illustrated by the fact that zero on the unified basis for the 1972 fiscal year turns out to be $7 billion on the national income accounts basis, which is

the way Herbert Stein[17] first unveiled the concept and the way every economics student has learned full employment budgeting for a generation.

Statics *versus* Dynamics

The rule really reflects the administration's concern about overdoing fiscal stimulus, and that concern has a valid basis. There is genuine danger that stimulative fiscal action appropriate to today's slack and sluggish economy could commit the nation to stimulative budgets in future years when they would be markedly inappropriate. We might then be obliged to offset that stimulus by relying on monetary restraint or by seeking tax increases or cutbacks in expenditure programs once the economy approached full employment. Reliance on monetary restraint as an antidote to excessive budgetary stimulus violates rules one and two above. And to count on subsequent neutralizing measures of fiscal restraint is to ignore the serious doubts about the political feasibility of such legislative action. Congress is particularly unlikely to raise tax rates for the purpose of bailing out an overly enthusiastic antislump program that added mightily to federal spending. It would see such action as an open invitation to continued upward ratcheting of federal expenditures through time—with major expenditure initiatives in slumps and offsetting tax increases in booms. Whatever one's views on the appropriate size of the public sector, a cyclical ratchet is not a proper tool for decision making in the democratic process.

All of this argues for making stimulative fiscal policy with one eye on preserving our fiscal fitness for the next period of full employment. And that does require a rule, or at least some form of discipline that guards against excessive long-term commitments of revenue or expenditure. Hence, my fourth rule: *Stimulative fiscal programs should be temporary and self-terminating so that they don't jeopardize our future budgetary position.* The rule reminds us that the key issue is not whether full employment balance is maintained when the economy needs fiscal stimulus, but whether the budget remains in a flexible position from which it can be moved back readily into full employment surplus when restraint once

---

[17] Committee for Economic Development, *Taxes and the Budget: A Program for Prosperity in a Free Economy* (CED, November 1947), pp. 22–25; and Herbert Stein, *The Fiscal Revolution in America* (University of Chicago Press, 1969), esp. pp. 220–32.

again becomes appropriate.[18] It cautions against permanent changes in the levels of taxation or expenditure programs for stabilization purposes; it puts a time-dimension on the third rule, which identifies the types of fiscal variation consistent with compositional objectives. Both rules argue against public works as a tool for stabilization. They also cast doubt on the recent liberalization of depreciation allowances as a stabilization device; that measure sacrificed $4 billion of revenue annually on a permanent basis in order to get $2 billion into the economy in 1971.

THE DEPENDENCE ON FORECASTING

The rule for relying on quick-starting and self-terminating fiscal measures is designed to ensure flexibility and thus to limit the time horizon over which the forecasting of aggregate demand is essential to policy decisions. But that time period remains substantial and the success of policy remains dependent on the accuracy of economic forecasting. Tax cuts, for example, add cumulatively to aggregate demand for a considerable period after enactment. Thus, while they deliver some prompt stimulus to aggregate demand, they also involve a package of future add-ons to demand. The only way to lift the economy this quarter is through a tie-in sale that lifts the economy further for several subsequent quarters.

If any fiscal or monetary tool exerted its full impact instantaneously, stabilization policy making would be a different ball game. Indeed, this difference has been highlighted by the Laffer model, which finds that the effects of a shift in the money supply on aggregate demand are concentrated in the very quarter of the policy action.[19] While GNP is determined by the money supply in the Laffer model, the implication for policy strategy is diametrically opposite to that of previous monetarist views. Because of its instantaneous total effects, the Laffer model issues an unequivocal mandate in favor of monetary fine tuning. Monetary policy makers are encouraged to take all the action appropriate to hit their economic targets today; and they should then wait for tomorrow and correct any errors by twisting the dials again. Unlike more tradi-

tional views about the timing impact of economic policies, the Laffer model finds no tie-in sale or longer-term commitment that would caution against large and abrupt changes in policy.

Because Keynesians and most monetarists agree that the time stream of economic impact following a policy action begins virtually at once but continues into the more distant future, they seat the forecaster at the right hand of the policy maker. When policy decisions necessarily affect the future, they must be made in light of uncertain forecasts of the future and not solely on the basis of the facts of the present. To act otherwise is to adopt implicitly the naive forecast that the future is going to be merely a continuation of the present. The historical record of economic forecasting in the past two decades demonstrates that professional forecasting, despite its limitations, is more accurate than such naive models.[20] Moreover, even the naive model that tomorrow will be like today is far more accurate than the super-naive or agnostic model that tomorrow's aggregate demand is just as likely to be below the social target as above it regardless of where today's aggregate demand stands. That agnostic model is the extreme point in the decision analysis set forth by Milton Friedman and William Brainard.[21] If forecasts could not beat the agnostic model, it would be important to do nothing. The stabilization policy maker should simply stay home, for action by him would be just as likely to push the economy in the wrong direction as in the right direction and it could push the economy off the proper course when it would otherwise be there.

In fact, the professional forecaster can beat the agnostic model by a wide margin. I can think of only two years in the past twenty—1955 and

[18] See Frank Schiff's development of this point in "Control of Inflation and Recession" (speech delivered before the Seventy-fifth Annual Meeting of The American Academy of Political and Social Science, Philadelphia, April 1971; processed), pp. 12–16.

[19] Arthur B. Laffer and R. David Ranson, "A Formal Model of the Economy" (paper prepared for the Office of Management and Budget, 1971; offset), pp. 25–27.

[20] See Victor Zarnowitz, *An Appraisal of Short-term Economic Forecasts* (National Bureau of Economic Research, 1967), esp. pp. 6, 14–19, and 83–120; Geoffrey H. Moore, "Forecasting Short-Term Economic Change," *Journal of the American Statistical Association*, Vol. 64 (March 1969), esp. pp. 3–4 and 15; and Victor Zarnowitz, "Forecasting Economic Conditions: The Record and the Prospect" (paper prepared for the National Bureau of Economic Research's Colloquium on Business Cycles, September 24, 1970; offset).

[21] "The Effects of a Full-Employment Policy on Economic Stability: A Formal Analysis," in Milton Friedman, *Essays in Positive Economics* (University of Chicago Press, 1953), pp. 117–132; and William Brainard, "Uncertainty and the Effectiveness of Policy," in American Economic Association, *Papers and Proceedings of the Seventy-ninth Annual Meeting, 1966* (*American Economic Review*, vol. 57, May 1967), pp. 411–25.

1965—when the January consensus prediction of economic forecasters would have led policy makes to administer stimulants when they were inappropriate and no cases when the consensus forecast would have pointed toward sedatives when stimulants were really appropriate.

A PROPENSITY OF OVERREACT?

Nonetheless, the fact that forecasters can guide policy makers to the right choice as between sedatives and stimulants is not necessarily decisive. Even if some sedative medicine would help a patient, he may be better off with nothing than with a massive overdose of sedation. And it is sometimes claimed that policy makers tend to prescribe overdoses.[22] According to this claim, because their medicines operate only with a lag and because neither the time shape of that lag nor the total impact of the policy is readily determined in advance, the policy makers become impatient; hence they continue to take more and more action until they have done too much of a good thing, which may be worse than nothing.

This intuitive argument has a certain appeal as a description of a human foible. We have probably all behaved in much this way in taking a shower. When the water is too cold, we turn up the hot faucet; and, if we are still cold ten seconds later, we may turn up the faucet some more, assuming that the first twist was inadequate. As a result of our first impatience, we may find ourselves scalded. And even after one or two experiences of this sort, we repeat that behavior and indeed find it difficult to discipline ourselves completely. If, indeed, fiscal-monetary policy makers have the same proclivities as the man in the shower, rules or discipline may help them to resist their impulses to overreact. But whether the Federal Reserve Open Market Committee or the Troika overtwist the faucets in their respective showers is an empirical issue, a proposition about their behavior that ought to be supportable or refutable by evidence. And I have yet to see evidence to support the proposition.

In the case of fiscal policy, I believe the record shows that policy makers generally have not behaved like the man in the shower. Below is a list of the major changes in fiscal policy during the past fifteen years, as defined by shifts in the full employment surplus,[23] and a capsule evaluation based on hindsight.

1. During 1958, the full employment surplus was reduced from more than 1 percent of GNP to near zero.
    Stimulative direction proper; inadequate size, and timing delayed.
2. In 1959–69, fiscal policy was sharply reversed toward restraint with the full employment surplus reaching 2½ percent of GNP in 1960.
    Inappropriate restraint.
3. During 1961–62, that surplus was gradually trimmed.
    Stimulative direction proper; inadequate size and timing delayed.
4. After backsliding during 1963, fiscal policy became considerably more stimulative with the enactment of the tax cut at the beginning of 1964.
    Appropriate stimulus.
5. From the second half of 1965 to the end of 1968, the full employment budget was in deficit, reflecting the build-up of Vietnam expenditures.
    Inappropriate stimulus.
6. In 1969, as the result of the tax surcharge and expenditure cutbacks, a full employment surplus of 1 percent of GNP was restored.
    Appropriate restraint; much delayed timing.
7. In 1970 and the first half of 1971, fiscal policy was relaxed a bit with the full employment surplus roughly cut in half.
    Relaxation proper; inadequate size.

Items 1, 3, 6, and 7 all depart from the ideal in the direction of too little and too late rather than too much and too soon. In each of these cases moves that were larger or earlier or both would have produced better stabilization results. Item 5—the inappropriate fiscal stimulus of the Vietnam period—was not the overreaction of the man in the shower. The hot water was turned up, but not because anyone believed that the economy needed warming.

Item 2—the shift to restraint in 1959—can be viewed, in a sense, as a premature and excessive cooling of economic expansion. But that policy simply was not keyed to the general economic diagnosis or forecast, which saw the temperature

---

[22] See "The Role of Monetary Policy," Chapter 5 (esp. p. 109), in Milton Friedman, *The Optimum Quantity of Money*. Reprinted from *American Economic Review*, vol. 58 (March 1968), pp. 1–17.

[23] Okun and Teeters, "The Full-Employment Surplus Revisited," pp. 102–103; Teeters, "Budgetary Outlook at Mid-Year 1970," *Brookings Papers on Economic Activity* (2:1970), p. 304; and Teeters, "The 1972 Budget: Where It Stands and Where It Might Go," p. 228.

as remaining extremely mild, but rather to a non-economic budgetary orthodoxy. The full employment surplus was jacked up enough to balance the actual budget, as an end in itself rather than as a means to curb any present or prospective boom.

By any standard, the preponderant balance of mistakes in fiscal policy is revealed as errors of omission rather than commission—errors of doing too little too late, rather than too much too soon. Our fiscal man in the shower, in fact, tends to wait too long to ascertain that the water is really staying cold before he decides to turn it up. When he finally does turn the faucet he acts timidly and hesitantly. When the water is hot, he also hesitates too long and moves indecisively. To shift metaphors, he is not trigger happy, but, rather, slow on the draw. And so I come to my fifth rule: *Face the fact that policies must be made on the basis of a forecast, and don't be slow on the draw!*

My rules for fiscal discretionary judgment will work well only if stabilization policy is guided by the professional expertise of economists. Obviously, that has not always been the case; and when politics vetoed economics, serious fiscal destabilization resulted. Indeed, in the past generation, the economy has been more severely disrupted by government actions obviously inconsistent with the objective of economic stabilization than by autonomous shifts in private demand. The 1950–51 Korean inflation, the 1953–54 post-Korean recession, the 1960–61 recession, and the Vietnam inflation were all government-induced fluctuations, in which the budget departed from any and all professional prescriptions for stabilization. In three of the four cases, swings in military expenditures created the problem; in the remaining case, it was caused by attachment to a taboo of budgetary balance. In light of these instances, one might well find that a fixed, moderate full employment surplus in peace and war, even years and odd years, would have yielded better overall results than those obtained from the actual fiscal process. But this is no argument for fixed parameters! The proposal to control political officials with a nondiscretionary rule reminds me of the suggestion to catch birds by pouring salt on their tails. Neither the political officials nor the birds will cooperate. If every economist in the nation had sworn (falsely) to Lyndon Johnson and Wilbur Mills that any deviation of the full employment surplus from 0.5 percent of GNP was a mortal sin, that wouldn't have changed fiscal policy in 1965–68. Why not tell our statesmen the truth and try to convince them to heed professional advice on fiscal policy? As unpalatable as that message might be, it has more chance of convincing elected public officials than the rule of maintaining a fixed and rigid full employment surplus for all time. And so I offer my sixth rule: *Presidents should listen to the advice of their economists on fiscal policy and so should the Congress.*

SIGNALS FOR THE MONETARY AUTHORITIES

Under the circumstances I envision, the tasks of the Federal Reserve would depend upon how well the fiscal rules operate. If the budget no longer generates disruptive shifts in aggregate demand and if it offsets, to some degree, any major autonomous shift in private demand, then the monetary policy makers may be able to hold money and credit conditions close to the middle of the road without much difficulty. Under those best of all possible circumstances, economists might begin to wonder what all the shouting was about in the debate on the relative importance of aggregate quantities and interest rates as guides to monetary policy. In 1962–65, a monetary policy that was oriented toward interest rate targets did not produce large or abrupt shifts in the growth of the money stock, simply because the demand for money did not undergo enormous fluctuation. Presumably, if monetary policy had been pursued with respect to quantity rather than rate targets, those quantity guides would have left interest rates reasonably stable. If the demand for goods and the demand for money stay on course, then it makes little difference whether the directives to the trading desk are couched in terms of maintaining a given set of interest rates in the money markets or a given growth of the money supply.

It is not safe, however, to count on the world becoming that tranquil. Surprises will occur, and the policy makers will be forced to decide on the emphasis they wish to give to interest rates and aggregate quantities relative to one another. And it is a matter of degree—of relative emphasis. Anyone interested in diagnosing or influencing financial markets would obviously pay attention to both prices and quantities, just as he would in looking at any other market. Nobody has ever improved on Paul Samuelson's summary that Federal Reserve governors were given two eyes so that they could watch both yields and quantities.[24]

[24] "Money, Interest Rates and Economic Activity: Their Interrelationship in a Market Economy," in

In a more serious vein, James Duesenberry has recently sketched how the monetary authorities might appropriately be guided by both quantities and interest rates.[25] At a theoretical level, William Poole has shown the conditions for preferring rate-oriented, quantity-oriented, or mixed monetary strategies.[26]

Quite apart from the issue of appropriate guides, the chief problem facing the monetary authority is likely to be when and how much to depart from a "normal" or average posture in order to provide additional stimulus or restraint to economic activity. Monetary policy can and should find some elbow room without major deviations from the middle of the road. For one thing, monetary policy is light on its feet; the short implementation lag in Federal Reserve decisions provides an enviable contrast with the long lags in the legislative process for altering fiscal policy. In nudging economic activity to offset modest surprises, the speed of implementation makes monetary policy particularly useful.

Second, there is a case for a belt and suspenders strategy of making fiscal and monetary changes in the same direction when stimulus or restraint is desired. The quantitative effect of specific fiscal and monetary changes on GNP is uncertain. Errors in the estimates of these effects are likely to be negatively related or at worst unrelated—if the economy's response to monetary changes is larger than expected, the response to fiscal swings seems likely to be less than our estimates. How extensive the monetary swings should be and at what point the benefits in aggregate stabilization are outweighed by the costs of the side effects discussed above, are issues that require careful judgment and the best use of discretion.

Any recommendation for discretionary monetary policy runs into the contention that the Federal Reserve also shares a propensity to overreact; I find it more difficult to interpret that contention than the one regarding fiscal policy; but, as I read the evidence, it is also untrue. Whether judged in terms of interest rates or of aggregate quantities, I cannot see that the Federal Reserve has behaved like the man in the shower. It was not overly expansionary during most recessions and early recoveries. If the monetary policies of 1957–58, 1960–62, or 1970 could be replayed with the aid of perfect hindsight, monetary policy would surely be more expansionary than it was in fact. The only example of such a period that might stand on the opposite side is late 1954, when in retrospect the Fed seems to have been excessively generous.

Nor in periods of strong economic advance has the Fed generally applied the brakes too strongly or too soon. It may have done so in the case of 1959, but it clearly stayed off the brakes too long in 1965 and probably in 1955. Most clearly, the Federal Reserve has revealed the propensity to underreact to economic chill in late expansions and early stages of recession: with perfect hindsight, it is clear restriction was maintained too long in 1953 and again in 1957. In my judgment, the error in the 1969 performance should also be interpreted as unduly prolonged restraint—staying on the brakes too long and too hard late in the year—although others might argue that the restraint was applied too vigorously early in the year. There have been other mistakes in monetary policy, like the misdiagnosis of 1968, but they have little to do with either overreaction or underreaction, so far as I can see. Nor does the basic decision of 1967, which gave side effects priority over aggregate stabilization targets, reveal a propensity to overreact.

Thus I come to my final rule: *The makers of monetary policy should be guided by both aggregate quantities and interest rates and by the present and prospective state of aggregate demand; they will serve the nation best by using fully their capability to make small and prompt adjustments in light of the best current evidence and analysis.*

THE LESSONS OF 1969–1971

My rules aren't nearly so elegant nor so definitive nor as capable of making a high school boy a qualified CEA or Federal Reserve Chairman as the rules for maintaining fixed growth of the money supply and fixed full employment surpluses. The only thing in favor of the rules I am offering is that they happen to be better rules. We can do far better by using our intelligence in diagnosing, forecasting, and prescribing than by adopting rigid formulas that ignore the state of economic activity, the outlook for private demand, and the "side effects" of policies.

American Bankers Association, *Proceedings of a Symposium on Money, Interest Rates and Economic Activity* (ABA, 1967), p. 44.

[25] "Tactics and Targets of Monetary Policy," in Federal Reserve Bank of Boston, *Controlling Monetary Aggregates,* Proceedings of the Monetary Conference, Nantucket Island, June 8–10, 1969 (FRB of Boston, 1969).

[26] "Optimal Choice of Monetary Instruments in a Simple Stochastic Macro Model," *Quarterly Journal of Economics,* vol. 84 (May 1970), pp. 197–216.

My kind of rules calls for an activist economic policy. Events since early 1969 strengthen my conviction that the optimum amount of activism is a lot of it. This debate easily degenerates into a semantic game. The opposition scoffs at "fine tuning"; I call it "sensible steering." Some people warn against going overboard; I worry about napping at the wheel. Trying diligently to avoid loaded words, I state as fact that, for better or for worse, the Nixon administration has been much more reluctant than its predecessors to alter fiscal-monetary policies on the basis of discretionary judgment. Apart from the issue of wage-price or "incomes" policy, this has been the biggest difference in economic policy since early 1969. (And the incomes policy difference may also be related to the preference for less activism.)

Along with a messy economic situation, the Nixon administration inherited a reasonably appropriate fiscal policy and an appropriate target of achieving disinflation without recession. The fiscal policy was not altered much within the course of 1969 and it was not controversial. While opinion differed about the extension of the tax surcharge, the repeal of the investment credit, and the desirability of the revenue-losing "tax reforms" of 1969, the controversies reflected primarily preferences for more or less public expenditure rather than for more or less fiscal restraint. Nor did the fiscal 1971 budget program presented in January 1970 seem surprising or unreasonable. What was highly questionable, as I saw it then and see it now, was the emphasis on achieving an *actual* surplus in fiscal 1971 with no explicit contingency for the obvious risk of an economic slump that would make the surplus inappropriate. Although the father of the full employment surplus concept was a member of the Council of Economic Advisers, and one of the most ardent and effective exponents of the concept was the CEA Chairman, the lesson of the full employment surplus was essentially ignored in the initial Nixon budget. Instead, it unveiled a new, very short-lived budget concept known as the "credible surplus."

By May 1970, actual economic developments were clearly far more recessionary than had been predicted by the administration (and by me!) at the beginning of the year. Nonetheless, when the administration re-estimated the budget on May 19, it stuck to a tight fiscal program which called for a $10 billion full employment surplus (on the national accounts basis) in the face of a recession. And it advanced two new proposals to increase tax revenues—a speedup of estate and gift taxes and a tax on leaded gasoline. The economic situation had changed enormously between January and May 1970, but the fiscal posture was not changed. After fifteen months during which fiscal policy had been basically bipartisan, it became strongly controversial at that point.

On July 18, 1970, the President adopted the principle of full employment budgeting, but he did not alter the posture of the fiscal 1971 program. Indeed in August, he vetoed appropriations for education and for housing, endorsing those programs on social grounds but insisting that additional expenditures on them would be excessively stimulative.

After the economy sank far below the target path, the administration set an ambitious goal for rapid economic recovery in 1971, but the fiscal program continued to propose a full employment surplus on a national income accounts basis of about $7 billion, virtually unchanged from the level of 1970. The cautious fiscal program has failed to achieve the bold targets for output and employment growth, but the fiscal program has been reaffirmed. It is hard to understand the midyear decision to stand pat. Does the jack-in-the-box view of private demand linger on? Has the rule of full employment balance on the unified budget paralyzed fiscal policy? Does the rapid monetary growth of the first half of 1971 convince some administration economists that rapid expansion is just around the corner? Perhaps all of these contribute, but I would emphasize still another factor—the propensity to underreact.

Monetary policy in 1969–71 has also differed from the prescriptions that were being offered by outside observers of the Keynesian "new economics" school. Unlike the monetarists, most of us applauded extreme monetary restraint through the spring and summer of 1969 as necessary medicine to halt the investment boom and curb excess demand. In the fall, however, the Keynesians joined the monetarists in calling for less restraint. We heard the economy yelling "Uncle," but the Federal Reserve did not. Thus, extreme monetary restraint was maintained until 1970 began; again the error was in underreacting.

During the first half of 1970, attachment to consistency and a desire for a steady pace of monetary growth inhibited the Federal Reserve from making a full contribution to the end of recession and the start of the recovery. Since the fall of 1970, the Federal Reserve has had a difficult problem of interpreting divergent signals coming from money growth, on the one hand, and interest rates, on the other. From September 1970 to January 1971, credit conditions eased dramatically and interest rates fell sharply, but demands for active cash balances were weak and the money supply grew very slowly despite a high rate of growth of overall bank reserves. For reasons that are not clear, the demand for active balances rose sharply between January and June 1971—more than enough to provide a catch-up for the period of sluggish growth. Meanwhile, interest rates turned up spectacularly. Balance-of-payments problems added further complications. The Federal Reserve has seemed to compromise on these goals: it wishes to strengthen an evidently sluggish recovery, but it wants to avoid a massive outflow of short-term funds and big numbers on money growth. The Federal Reserve official directives focus on money supply targets, while the actions have been much more eclectic and pragmatic. The seeming inconsistency of word and deed had confused the Fed watchers in the financial markets and thereby added to the instability of interest rates and to the demand for liquidity. I strongly suspect that a policy of holding the Treasury bill rate close to some moderate level—like 4 percent—through the first half of 1971 would have produced much lower long-term interest rates *and* slower monetary growth.

At times during the early months of 1971, spokesmen for the administration and the Federal Reserve made no secret of their preference for a more stimulative stabilization policy than was in fact being pursued. The administration's fiscal policy makers emphasized the possibility for additional monetary stimulus while Federal Reserve spokesmen pointed toward additional fiscal stimulus. Anyone familiar with the problems of the bureaucratic division of labor in Washington can understand, sympathize with, and agonize about the tendency to "let George do it." It is only natural that the Federal Reserve would prefer to "let George [Schultz] do it" while the administration would wish the Board to do it. The picture has been disturbing, nonetheless, in raising doubts about the effectiveness of monetary-fiscal coordination between the independent Federal Reserve and the administration. Proper coordination ought to guarantee that the fiscal-monetary mix has approximately the overall degree of stimulus or restraint that seems appropriate to both fiscal and monetary policy makers. Disagreements on the appropriate amount of stimulus may be inevitable, but when both sides agree that more stimulus is necessary, that should be forthcoming. It is much less important how much George does and how much the Board does, than that somebody act with determination to promote the solid recovery the administration wants and the nation needs. The eclectic principle reminds us that both can and should contribute.